3 9077 00980268 0

P9-CBE-284

EUROPEAN WRITERS
The Twentieth Century

EUROPEAN WRITERS
The Twentieth Century

GEORGE STADE

EDITOR IN CHIEF

Volume 9

PÍO BAROJA

TO

FRANZ KAFKA

CHARLES SCRIBNER'S SONS / NEW YORK

Library of Congress Cataloging-in-Publication Data
(Revised for volumes 8–9)

European writers.

Vols. 5–   . Jacques Barzun, editor, George Stade, editor in chief.
Vols. 8–   . George Stade, editor in chief.
Includes bibliographies.
Contents: v. 1–2. The Middle Ages and the Renaissance:
Prudentius to Medieval Drama. Petrarch to Renaissance
Short Fiction—v. 3–4. The Age of Reason and the
Enlightenment: René Descartes to Montesquieu.
Voltaire to André Chénier.—v. 5–7. The Romantic
Century: Goethe to Pushkin. Hugo to Fontane.
Baudelaire to the Well-Made Play—v. 8–9. The
Twentieth Century: Sigmund Freud to Paul Valéry.
Pío Baroja to Franz Kafka.
    1. European literature—History and criticism—
Addresses, essays, lectures.   I. Jackson, W. T. H.
(William Thomas Hobdell), 1915–   . II. Stade,
George.   III. Barzun, Jacques, 1907–   .
PN501.E9   1983   809'.894   83–16333
ISBN 0–684–16594–5 (v. 1–2)
ISBN 0–684–17914–8 (v. 3–4)
ISBN 0–684–17915–6 (v. 5–7)
ISBN 0–684–18923–2 (v. 8)
ISBN 0–684–18924–0 (v. 9)

The following pamphlets in the Columbia University Press Series "Columbia
Essays on Modern Writers" have been reprinted in this volume by special
arrangement with Columbia University Press, the publisher:

Stern, J. P.: *Thomas Mann.* Copyright © 1967 Columbia University Press.
Ziolkowski, Theodore: *Hermann Hesse.* Copyright © 1966 Columbia University Press.
Breunig, LeRoy C.: *Guillaume Apollinaire.* Copyright © 1970 Columbia University Press.
Young, Howard T.: *Juan Ramón Jiménez.* Copyright © 1967 Columbia University Press.
Bien, Peter: *Nikos Kazantzakis.* Copyright © 1972 Columbia University Press.
Sokel, Walter H.: *Franz Kafka.* Copyright © 1966 Columbia University Press.

EDITORIAL STAFF

DANIEL J. CALTO, *MANAGING EDITOR*

JONATHAN ARETAKIS, *Associate Editor*

JOHN F. FITZPATRICK, *Associate Editor*

BRIGITTE M. GOLDSTEIN, *Editorial Assistant*

BETH ANN MCCABE, *Associate Editor*

JOAN ZSELECZKY, *Associate Editor*

EMILY GARLIN, *Proofreader*

GRETCHEN GORDON, *Proofreader*

ERIC HARALSON, *Copyeditor*

CAROL HOLMES, *Proofreader*

TATIANA HOLWAY, *Copyeditor*

W. KIRK REYNOLDS, *Proofreader*

LUCY RINEHART, *Copyeditor*

EMILY WRIGHT, *Copyeditor*

MATTHEW M. KARDOVICH, *Director of Production*

CHARLES E. SMITH, *PUBLISHER*

v

LIST OF SUBJECTS

Volume 8

LIST OF SUBJECTS

CONTRIBUTORS TO VOLUMES 8 AND 9

ALBERT BADES FERNANDEZ
Cornell University
JOSÉ ORTEGA Y GASSET

JARED M. BECKER
Columbia University
ITALO SVEVO

ALBERT BERMEL
*The Graduate School and
University Center of the
City University of New York*
JEAN GIRAUDOUX

PETER BIEN
Dartmouth College
CONSTANTINE CAVAFY
NIKOS KAZANTZAKIS

MARIANNA D. BIRNBAUM
*University of California,
Los Angeles*
ENDRE ADY

LEROY C. BREUNIG
Barnard College
GUILLAUME APOLLINAIRE

MARLENE CIKLAMINI
Rutgers University
SIGRID UNDSET

PELLEGRINO D'ACIERNO
Hofstra University
FILIPPO TOMMASO MARINETTI

HERMAN K. DOSWALD
*Virginia Polytechnic
Institute and
State University*
HUGO VON HOFMANNSTHAL

ULRICH K. GOLDSMITH
University of Colorado
STEFAN GEORGE

ANTHONY HEILBUT
New York City
HEINRICH MANN

F. W. J. HEMMINGS
University of Leicester
MARCEL PROUST

ROBERTA JOHNSON
Scripps College
PÍO BAROJA

CHARLES KLOPP
Ohio State University
GABRIELE D'ANNUNZIO

ROBERT LIMA
*Pennsylvania State
University*
RAMÓN DEL VALLE-INCLÁN

ROBERT E. LOTT
University of Illinois
AZORÍN

PATRICK J. MAHONY
Université de Montréal
SIGMUND FREUD

JAMES R. MCWILLIAMS
University of Oregon
ARTHUR SCHNITZLER

JEREMY T. MEDINA
Hamilton College
VICENTE BLASCO IBÁÑEZ

PHILIP MELLEN
*Virginia Polytechnic
Institute and
State University*
GERHART HAUPTMANN

CIRIACO MORÓN ARROYO
Cornell University
ANTONIO MACHADO

HELEN MUCHNIC
Smith College
ANDREY BELY

HARALD S. NÆSS
*University of Wisconsin,
Madison*
KNUT HAMSUN

MANFREDI PICCOLOMINI
*City University of
New York, Herbert
H. Lehman College*
BENEDETTO CROCE

GERALD PIROG
Rutgers University
ALEXANDER BLOK

ROBERT PYNSENT
University of London
JAROSLAV HAŠEK

OLGA RAGUSA
Columbia University
LUIGI PIRANDELLO

PETER S. ROGERS
Texas A & M University
PAUL CLAUDEL

JAMES ROLLESTON
Duke University
RAINER MARIA RILKE

VINIO ROSSI
Oberlin College
ANDRÉ GIDE

SANFORD R. SCHWARTZ
*Pennsylvania State
University*
HENRI BERGSON

HAROLD B. SEGEL
Columbia University
MAXIM GORKY

MICHAEL SEIDEL
Columbia University
ALFRED JARRY

LEROY R. SHAW
*University of Illinois
at Chicago*
FRANK WEDEKIND

WALTER H. SOKEL
University of Virginia
FRANZ KAFKA

J. P. STERN
*University College
of London*
THOMAS MANN

JOAN HINDE STEWART
*North Carolina
State University*
COLETTE

RICHARD S. STOWE
Lawrence University
MAURICE MAETERLINCK

STEVEN WINSPUR
Columbia University
PAUL VALÉRY

VICTORIA YABLONSKY
Los Angeles, California
ROBERT MUSIL

HOWARD T. YOUNG
Pomona College
JUAN RAMÓN JIMÉNEZ
MIGUEL DE UNAMUNO

THEODORE ZIOLKOWSKI
Princeton University
HERMANN HESSE

PÍO BAROJA

(1872–1956)

LIKE SILVESTRE PARADOX, one of his most enduring novelistic creations, Pío Baroja y Nessi was a man of many contradictions. He was a scientist (a medical doctor), and yet his novels mock science and technology. He revered romantic, idealistic action, and yet he himself lived a sedentary, bourgeois life. He rejected the cultural remnants of the past—church dogma, unfair social hierarchies, and ignorance of scientific knowledge—with a quiet passion, but he never fully assimilated modernity. In many ways Baroja's ambivalence toward modernity is representative of the Spain of his formative years. A conservative Catholic country that had deferred entrance into the modern world, in the late nineteenth century Spain was only just beginning to experience the effects of the industrial revolution. Born in 1872, Baroja witnessed the upheaval caused by this late transition from medieval economic and social forms to modern urban bourgeois life. He experienced Spain's awakening from a long cultural slumber to the artistic and philosophical currents of Europe, from which it had been pretty much excluded since the middle of the seventeenth century. He became an important part of that renaissance.

Significantly, Baroja's birth date coincides with the last Carlist War, which signaled the end of the ultraconservative Carlist movement's attempt to wrest Spain from the jaws of modernization. A bourgeois monarchy triumphed with the restoration of Alfonso XII in 1876. During Baroja's early years Spanish politics were dominated by a peaceful but corrupt "democratic" system that alternated between conservative and liberal monarchists and excluded Republicans and the increasing numbers of socialists and anarchists. Baroja's generation of writers, known as the Generation of '98 (named for the disastrous war with the United States in which Spain lost her last colonies), was defined in part by a desire to find alternatives to the corrupt bourgeois monarchy and the mediocre complacency of the citizens who supported it. His distaste for bourgeois mentality, doubtless developed in his youth, remained with him all his life and is a perennial theme of his novels.

Baroja's family on both his mother's and father's sides were prominent citizens in and around the Basque coastal city of San Sebastián, where he was born on 28 December 1872 and spent his first few years. Members of his father's family were well-known publishers and book dealers of liberal political orientation. Baroja's father, Don Serafín Baroja, a mining engineer, displayed bohemian artistic leanings in the private sphere of his life. He read a great deal, and his extensive library introduced the future writer to Alexandre Dumas *père*, Victor Hugo, Honoré de Balzac, Jules Verne, Frederick Marryat, Xavier de Montepin, and Eugène Sue at a young age. Baroja's early and lifelong reading of romantic adventure novels had a profound impact on his own novelistic production; one of the most interesting aspects of some of Baroja's best novels is his combination of the adventure story with the novel of contemporary social and philosophical concerns.

Baroja's mother, Doña Carmen Nessi y Goñi, was of a more stern, duty-bound nature, and Baroja may have benefited simultaneously from his father's artistic interests and his mother's discipline (he was an extraordinarily disciplined writer, regularly publishing two novels annually in his mature years). Baroja, who never married, was always close to his mother, and he lived with her in Madrid from 1902 until her death in 1935. After 1912 (the year of his father's death), when Baroja purchased a summer home in Vera del Bidasoa in the Basque provinces, their domestic arrangements alternated between winters in Madrid and summers in Vera, punctuated by Baroja's frequent travels about the Spanish countryside with friends and trips abroad to Paris, London, Rome, Germany, Switzerland, and the Scandinavian countries.

Although Baroja's Basque origins form an important part of his novelistic material, especially his very early works and the historical novels written between 1913 and 1935, many of the novels for which he is most remembered are set in Madrid and Castile. The family moved to Madrid in 1879 because of his father's profession, and three years later they moved to Pamplona. They returned to Madrid once again in 1886, one year before Baroja entered medical school at the University of Madrid. He completed his medical training in Valencia in 1891 after another family move. It is important to note that Baroja was brought into direct contact with the capital of Spain shortly after the death of Alfonso XII, who was succeeded by his wife, María Cristina, as regent. María Cristina gave birth to a male heir shortly thereafter, assuring the continuation of the monarchy. The Republicans were disconsolate, and an air of political instability reigned in the turn-of-the-century Spanish

capital. Most of Baroja's novels touch on Spanish politics in one way or another, and no form of government, from monarchy to republic, escapes his ironic treatment.

Baroja had two older brothers: Darío, who died of tuberculosis at a young age, and Ricardo, who wrote, painted, and in general followed in the father's bohemian ways. A younger sister, Carmen, born in 1884, was later an important companion to Baroja. The entire family remained united; they eventually occupied three stories of the same Madrid apartment building: Baroja and his mother on the top floor, Carmen and her husband, Rafael Caro Raggio, who published a number of Baroja's books, on the middle floor, and Ricardo and his wife on the first.

Baroja's years as a medical student colored his outlook on life in an enduring way and provided him material for several novels, the most important of which is *El árbol de la ciencia* (*The Tree of Knowledge,* 1911). But Baroja was a desultory medical student; he had chosen the career more by default than for any true sense of vocation, and medical instruction in Spain was designed more to discourage than to stimulate interest in the profession. Baroja compensated for his lack of interest in medical studies by reading literature, especially nineteenth-century romantic and realist writers. He clearly preferred the former, declaring in a later essay that he held a profound scorn for nineteenth-century realism. Significantly, his favorite authors—Charles Dickens, Stendhal, and Feodor Dostoevsky—are also writers of transitional times in their respective countries. Another diversion from unsatisfactory medical studies was long, rambling walks through Madrid. The visions he retained of the old sections of the city undergoing the pains of modernization and industrialization made their way into his novels of the first decade of the twentieth century.

During his student years Baroja also came into contact with socialist and anarchist ideas, and these, coupled with his firsthand knowledge of the poorer districts of Madrid, stirred his sympathy for those social theories, particularly anarchism. But his political views were eclectic and changed somewhat over time, and his own personal sense of individual freedom made him a poor ideologue. Often in his novels he presents several points of view on political or philosophical matters through the voices of different characters, none of which exactly represents Baroja's own position. These multiple voices rub against each other, creating a kind of kaleidoscopic balance of differences, perhaps indicating Baroja's ultimate desire for a political system that allowed each individual maximum opportunity to develop his or her own point of view. In the 1903–1904 trilogy *La lucha por la vida* (The Struggle for Life) Baroja chronicled the impact of the socialist ideologies on him and his gradual disenchantment with them. But long before the trilogy, Baroja's political preoccupations began to find their way into writing. In the 1890's, he published articles in *El liberal* and began several novels touching on political themes that he never completed.

It was also during his years of medical study that Baroja's interest in philosophy was first aroused, and he began buying and reading cheap editions of Immanuel Kant, Johann Fichte, and Arthur Schopenhauer. Baroja's generation was preeminently philosophical; Miguel de Unamuno, Azorín (José Martínez Ruiz), and Antonio Machado, especially, explored philosophical themes in their literary works. The primary philosophical concerns of the Generation of '98 were the place of the will and the intellect in life, deriving from Friedrich Nietzsche and Schopenhauer; the role of environment in shaping destinies, drawing on Charles Darwin, Hippolyte Taine, and socialist theories; the nature of time and history, fueled by G. W. F. Hegel, Nietzsche, and Henri Bergson; and the relative importance of scientific inquiry and artistic endeavor, informed by Herbert Spencer, John Ruskin, Thomas Carlyle, and Nietzsche. The way to the European secular philosophical tradition, essentially absent in Catholic Spain from René Descartes onward,

had been opened for them by the previous generation of Krausists. Krausism—based on the rational Christian ideas of Kant's heterodox disciple Karl Christian Friedrich Krause—was a major movement in Spain from the 1860's to the end of the century, inspired by the teachings of Julián Sanz del Río. Besides admiring Krause's rationalist faith, Sanz del Río also found a practical side to Krause's philosophy that spoke to his belief that Spain needed not only a philosophical but also a social, political, and cultural regeneration. Krause emphasized the perfectibility of humankind, an idea not incompatible with the entire progressive spirit of nineteenth-century Europe or with several socialist philosophies. Like anarchism, Krausism had a strong utopian flavor.

Rather than a definable doctrine, Baroja's own philosophical position was more of a continuing dialogue on the nature of existence that incorporated Schopenhauer's pessimism about the intellect's weakness in face of the will, Nietzsche's optimism about the will's power, and a belief in scientific materialism. Characters in his novels frequently carry on long conversations about metaphysical and ethical issues that are never fully resolved either in the particular discussions or within the context of the novel's action. One reason for Baroja's achieving no determinate philosophical position is his reluctance to succumb to dogma of any kind, and another is the very real conflicts inherent in his philosophical sources. While the socialist and anarchist ideologies emphasize the importance of environment, specifically the social milieu, on the formation of the individual, the neo-Kantian Schopenhauer and his follower Nietzsche emphasize the power of the human will in determining the direction of an individual human life. This conflict became one of the most interesting Barojian themes and guides the characterization and structures of a number of his novels.

After failing and retaking examinations and changing schools, Baroja finally completed his medical education. Then, in 1893, Baroja spent a year in Madrid working on a doctoral thesis, *El dolor (estudio de psico-física)* (Pain [Psycho-Physical Study], 1896), further indicating his preference for ideas over the practical side of medicine. When he did finally take up medical practice in the small Basque village of Cestona, Baroja's poor medical training, combined with his sensitive temperament, led to his retirement from medical practice after only a few years. However deficient Baroja may have found medical instruction to be in the actual practice of medicine in Spain, he maintained a lifelong reverence for the possibilities of science. And even though his early enthusiasm became tempered with a certain skepticism in later years, he could still claim in his memoirs that Claude Bernard's *Introduction to the Study of Experimental Medicine* (1865) was one of three or four books that had most influenced him in his thinking.

Baroja's return to the Basque provinces for his brief sojourn as village doctor renewed his sense of his Basque heritage and perhaps rekindled the interest in writing that he had abandoned in order to complete his medical degree. Begun while in Cestona, his first published work of imaginative prose, *Vidas sombrías* (Somber Lives, 1900), is a collection of stories with Basque settings. Having left the medical profession behind him, Baroja responded to the summons of an aunt in Madrid to administer her bakery, but he soon discovered that he was no more suited to business than to the medical profession. His return to Madrid, where he found a stimulating cultural and intellectual atmosphere and began to frequent literary café society, encouraged his incipient urge to take up the pen, and he wrote more stories and contributed articles to several journals. Even though the bakery kept Baroja in a constant state of turmoil due to financial struggles and problems with workers, he began *Aventuras, inventos, y mixtificaciones de Silvestre Paradox* (Adventures, Inventions, and Mystifications of Silvestre Paradox, 1901), a novel that reflects one of his favorite diversions of the period—talking to eccentrics who had wild plans for scientific inventions.

In 1898 Baroja visited Paris for the first time, one of many trips abroad that he took during the next forty years. These trips were mostly to northern European countries, the area of the world he preferred for its energy and progressive spirit. Paris, the leading cultural center of the day, was astir with the ideas and writers associated with the modern impetus: Nietzsche's cult of the ego, Gabriele D'Annunzio's aestheticism, Maurice Maeterlinck's spiritualism, and Oscar Wilde's creed of art for art's sake. On the surface Baroja may seem to have been little affected by these new currents; he apparently rejected a self-centered aestheticism. But although his was not a highly elaborated prose style of the art-for-art's-sake kind, as Birute Ciplijauskaite has demonstrated Baroja was highly conscious of certain stylistic matters and was a master of a number of techniques that create an effective distance between the novelist and his material. Furthermore, Baroja was essentially a modernist in his break with nineteenth-century novelistic structures that move the characters through a wealth of detail in narratives designed according to cause and effect sequences.

In Paris Baroja decided to devote himself entirely to writing, and upon returning to Madrid he collected the stories he had written during his rural medical practice in Cestona and published them as *Vidas sombrías,* thus officially launching his career as a serious writer. While the book was not a commercial success, it was very favorably received in literary circles and achieved for Baroja a reputation as a writer with talent and promise. Unamuno, the already well-known elder member of the Generation of '98, and Benito Pérez Galdós, Spain's most revered nineteenth-century "realist" novelist, both mentioned his work publicly. And Azorín, who was Baroja's own age but more precocious in his literary career, sought him out to make his acquaintance, thus initiating a lifelong friendship. In 1901

Baroja and Azorín, along with Ramiro de Maeztu, an essayist and journalist often included in the Generation of '98, briefly formed a group called "Los Tres" (The Three) to foment the social, political, and economic regeneration of Spain. This group, while the only formal, unified effort at reform, exemplifies the spirit of the Generation of '98 in its desire to renew Spanish culture not only in its external political and artistic manifestations but at its philosophical and ideological core. Most of the writers associated with the Generation soon abandoned active public life for the realm of contemplation and solitary writing; thus their greatest importance lies in their literary production rather than in any direct impact on Spanish politics and society. Baroja is the foremost novelist of the Generation, the only one of its members to dedicate himself almost exclusively to fiction; he produced sixty-six novels, and more than thirty other books, including autobiographical works and essays on diverse subjects.

Baroja's first story collection does not give many clues to the direction his mature fiction took, but it does reveal the sensitivity to the complexities of the human situation, rooted in a socio-historical circumstance (in this work the Basque people in the Basque provinces in the late nineteenth century) and influenced by the individual will, that is at the center of his best novels. The element of mysticism and the supernatural (doubtless related to Basque folkloric traditions) that dominates some of the stories disappears altogether in the later work. What does remain is his uncanny ability to set a scene, to capture the ambience of a place, and to focus on the most banal moments of ordinary human existence in a way that turns the mundane into the significant. Although Baroja's literary career was dominated by long fiction, he continued to write short stories occasionally, and these were arranged in several collections, for example *Idilios vascos* (Basque Idylls, 1902), *Idilios y fantasías* (Idylls and Fantasies, 1918), and *Historias lejanas* (Distant Tales, 1939).

THE FIRST PERIOD

In 1900 Baroja also published his first novel, *La casa de Aizgorri* (The House of Aizgorri), though some would deny this generic classification because its dialogue form could ally it with drama. A mixture of Edgar Allan Poe's "The Fall of the House of Usher" (1839) and socialist concerns, the plot centers on the purgation from society of a decadent family whose distillery is destroyed by fire. This work, like the story collection, essentially lies outside the aesthetic and ideological emphases of Baroja's more mature work, but again Baroja's extraordinary ear for lyrical description is evident. The mixture of visual (often painterly) qualities with other sensual properties often surfaces in the later works and for some critics is the best part of Baroja's craft as a novelist.

With *La casa de Aizgorri* Baroja inaugurates the decade in which he wrote the novels that most critics consider his finest work. In fact Baroja himself divided his oeuvre into two parts: "one from 1900 to the World War; another from the War of '14 to now. The first of violence, arrogance, and nostalgia; the second of historicism, of criticism, of irony, and of fluttering about ideas and things." While there is plenty of irony in the first period and no little nostalgia in the second, Baroja correctly designates 1914 as a turning point, although 1912, the year in which *El mundo es ansí* (The Way of the World) was published, is another valid watershed.

Aventuras, inventos, y mixtificaciones de Silvestre Paradox, Baroja's first non-dialogue novel and thus perhaps his first published example of the genre, contains the seeds of many of his enduring aesthetic and thematic concerns. In it appears for the first time one of the hallmarks of Baroja's novelistic aesthetic, an odd pastiche of genres and tones that jar and grate against one another. The underlying motivation and the overt structures of the two most important literary influences on Baroja—nineteenth-century English and Russian novels and the serialized adventure romance—collide in his work to create a hybrid genre with a peculiarly modern flavor.

Baroja's novelistic structures frequently depend on adventure story techniques such as emphasis on action rather than character and a linear plot in which the character moves from place to place getting into and out of scrapes. But through lyrical descriptions and through conversations between characters on ideological and philosophical matters, he simultaneously incorporates a study of the character's milieu in a way that suggests that environment may have influenced the character's particular psychology or predicament. The result is sometimes a violent confrontation between the novel of action and the novel of contemplation or character. Thus many of Baroja's novels seem disjointed and strange, but perhaps they reflect better than traditional forms could Baroja's own conflicts over certain philosophical issues (for example, does environment or individual will prevail in shaping human life in society?) and his ambivalence about the political alternatives available to European nations in the early twentieth century: anarchism, socialism, Communism, democracy, monarchy, and so forth.

Aventuras, inventos, y mixtificaciones de Silvestre Paradox is modeled on Dickens' *Pickwick Papers* (1836–1837). It has an episodic, comic-picaresque format and an eccentric pseudo-intellectual protagonist similar to the indomitable Mr. Pickwick. But the Spanish character is not as financially comfortable as his British counterpart, and thus his adventures also recall the low-life escapades of his Spanish picaresque predecessors. Silvestre is a sometime inventor who, along with several equally eccentric friends, engages in schemes for worthless inventions and publications of dubious merit that gain them little fame and many pecuniary difficulties. Silvestre's life, unlike Pickwick's, never becomes seriously enmeshed in the social or political realities of his time. Turn-of-the-century Madrid hovers in the background but never becomes an overwhelm-

ing threat to the protagonist. Silvestre's paradox is that, as a literary creation, he is developed through two superimposed generic styles—the picaresque, which affirms the importance of socio-political realities, and the adventure tale, which ignores any such influence.

Baroja presents the character Silvestre as a means of mocking the two mainstays of nineteenth-century European life (in which Spain had only latently begun to participate): science and secular philosophy. Baroja's life-long ambivalence toward science makes an early appearance here. His own post-postivist intellectual background and his negative experiences in the medical profession surely contributed to the burlesque attitude he took toward science (or at least technology) in creating "scientists" and inventors of the satirical proportions of Silvestre Paradox and his friend Avelino Diz de la Iglesia. Later novels, especially *The Tree of Knowledge*, question even more seriously the ability of science to illuminate the important moral and metaphysical problems of life. Baroja's ambivalence toward the modern scientific answer to life's mysteries is repeated in his attitude toward philosophy in this early novel. Baroja satirizes the German rationalists he had read during his student years by casting the Kantian categories in a burlesque light. Silvestre writes an incredible treatise in which he explicates his ideas by means of drawings rather than prose. For example, the first page of the treatise, captioned "The I comes from the not-I," displays a series of little circles containing the words "not-I" and one circle with the letter "I."

The tone and intent of Baroja's next novel, *Camino de perfección* (Way to Perfection, 1902), are entirely different from those of *Aventuras, inventos, y mixtificaciones de Silvestre Paradox*. One of Baroja's three or four best works, *Camino de perfección* is a modern quest novel. The protagonist, Fernando Ossorio, is searching not for mystical perfection, as the title ironically suggests (although he has a brush with mysticism), but for a way to integrate the several aspects of his being—the artistic, the sensual, and the spiritual—into a way of life that can be sustained in the modern secular, bourgeois world. Thus Fernando, unlike so many of Baroja's protagonists, does engage with his environment and change through interaction with it. Fernando, rejecting first medical school and then painting (both science and art), undertakes a philosophical and spiritual odyssey in search of a life that can accommodate his peculiar sensitivity. He believes that he has been doomed genetically by a degenerate family and by an environment full of superficial and insensitive souls who are incapable of understanding him.

However, before he sets out on the spiritual journey, which is also a physical journey through the Castilian countryside, Fernando falls into the most abject degeneracy, carrying on a perverted love affair with the aunt in whose home he lives. At the suggestion of a friend, he frees himself from this sordid life by leaving Madrid for rural Castile, where he finds the country folk just as brutal and insensitive as the *madrileños,* only in a less sophisticated way. He finally settles for a time in Toledo, home of the sixteenth-century painter El Greco, whose spiritual renderings of saints and famous *Burial of the Count of Orgaz (ca.* 1584) inspire him to seek spiritual purification. Changes of geographical location are very important to nearly all of Baroja's protagonists, as they are often accompanied by hope that leaving one environment and replacing it with another will alleviate their misfortunes.

In the descriptions of Toledo and Castile as seen through the artist Ossorio's eyes, Baroja displays his painterly descriptive skills. In fact, art, both as a technique and as a theme, is central to *Camino de perfección.* If, as several critics have suggested, the novel is modeled in part on Max Nordau's *Degeneration* (1892–1893), which singles out the artist as one of the greatest perpetrators of degeneration in European civilization, it is more to deny Nordau's assertions than to affirm them. But Baroja does not go so far as Wilde, who

subordinated life to art; rather, art and life ultimately unite in a kind of mutually enhancing equilibrium. At the end of the novel Ossorio marries, normalizing his sensual yearnings, and he returns to his career as a painter.

Baroja's answer to Nordau derives largely from his revised notion of Nietzsche. Under the influence of the Swiss writer Paul Schmitz, Baroja abandoned his early unfavorable impression of Nietzsche's central ideas as being immoral and degenerate, and in 1901 he wrote two articles, both entitled "Nietzsche íntimo" (Intimate Nietzsche), casting Nietzsche's concept of the will in a favorable light. In *Camino de perfección* Fernando meets the German Max Schultze, who, after hearing about the protagonist's futile search for life's way, recommends exercise and reading Nietzsche as solutions to his dilemma. In his visits to Toledo and finally to Yécora, a town totally devoid of art, Ossorio begins to acquire the moral sense that had previously eluded him. But it is by actively reinstating art into his life and by marrying that Ossorio finally achieves a satisfactory solution to his quest for happiness.

Ossorio naively believes that he can assure his child a clearer path to the exercise of his Nietzschean will; he plans to protect him from the alternatively ultra-secular and extremely religious influences that had so perverted his own life. But at the end of the novel the narrator informs us that the child's maternal grandmother secretly placed a religious amulet in the child's crib, perhaps dooming him to an ambivalence similar to his father's. Baroja understood only too well that traditional Spain could not be eradicated in only one generation, Nietzsche's will to power notwithstanding. His prophecy was brutally borne out thirty-four years later, when General Francisco Franco led the reactionary Nationalist movement to overturn the leftist Republic in 1936.

Many critics divide Baroja's numerous protagonists into two groups: the men and women of action who are able to overcome any environmental obstacles and exercise their Nietzschean wills, and those who, following the

Schopenhauerian model, are paralyzed into inaction by excessive contemplation. But in fact many of Baroja's protagonists are more complex and combine or alternate these two attitudes. Even they, however, eventually succumb to one attitude or the other, usually the latter. The novels also generally include a variety of characters who represent a range of possibilities for action and contemplation, few of whom seem to achieve the ideal balance between the two positions.

Like Fernando Ossorio, the protagonist of *El mayorazgo de Labraz* (*The Lord of Labraz*, 1903) wavers between an active and a contemplative life. And also echoing *Camino de perfección*, the novel is ambivalent about whether the character's personal qualities or the environment is ultimately responsible for his frequent lapses into passivity in the face of evil and injustice. But unlike Fernando, Juan de Labraz's defect is not a personal degeneracy but a sort of lofty nobility that impedes his action. He remains silent and impassive in the face of numerous misfortunes. Ramiro, the self-centered, evil stepbrother, marries the woman Juan loves and steals the jewels in the family chapel, which the local people insist that Juan replace at his own expense. But when the townspeople suggest that he abandon Marina, the poor girl who lives with him and who is the only bright spot in his joyless, sightless world (in addition to his many other misfortunes, he has gone blind), he rebels, finds his will, and abandons Labraz, and he and Marina set forth in search of a new life on the Mediterranean coast.

The English romantic novel provides the underlying plot structure of *The Lord of Labraz*. The lugubrious, decadent environment of Labraz and its air of mystery are reminiscent of Emily Brontë's *Wuthering Heights* (1847), as is Ramiro, a gypsy similar to Heathcliff (only more evil), who turns on the family that takes him in, gradually usurping the place of the firstborn. But rather than emphasizing the personal interaction between the "true aristo-crat" (the Lord of Labraz or Hindley Earnshaw, the Lord of Wuthering Heights) and the interloper from the lower classes (Ramiro or Heathcliff) as Brontë does, Baroja makes overt his criticism of the social milieu, especially emphasizing the backwardness and lack of progress in the local system, which scarcely differs from its medieval roots. Thus, as in *Aventuras, inventos, y mixtificaciones de Silvestre Paradox,* Baroja creates another modern hybrid—a cross between the novel of social analysis with its strong moral intent and the romantic formulaic novel of escape.

If *Aventuras, inventos, y mixtificaciones de Silvestre Paradox* echoes the picaresque tale as filtered through eighteenth- and nineteenth-century British romantic novels, Baroja's trilogy *La lucha por la vida* goes back to the original Spanish picaresque format. The linear, episodic plot contains a series of scenes depicting characters and settings from the lower strata of society. The title of the first volume, *La busca* (*The Quest*, 1904), echoes that of Francisco de Quevedo's *Historia de la vida del buscón* (The Quester, 1626), a classic of the genre. *The Quest* has been one of Baroja's most enduring novels, perhaps for the wrong reason: it is often seen as a faithful document of early-twentieth-century Madrid. Biruté Ciplijauskaité and Herbert Ramsden are among the few critics to point out its very considerable artistic merits and highly selective use of contemporary "real" life. In a 1961–1962 poll, a group of forty-nine Spanish novelists, critics, editors, and scholars singled it out as the most highly esteemed twentieth-century novel. And one of the best novels of the post–Civil War generation, Luis Martín Santos' *Tiempo de silencio* (Time of Silence, 1962), draws heavily on Baroja's *La lucha por la vida* trilogy for its character types, milieu, and themes.

Unlike a number of Baroja's other "trilogies," whose novels were originally written as independent works and were later grouped together by theme, *The Quest, Mala hierba*

(*Weeds,* 1904), and *Aurora roja* (*Red Dawn,* 1904) were composed as a unit, with the main characters moving through all three volumes. In fact, the first two were originally published as one work in serial form in 1903. Baroja reworked and expanded the serialized novel to form the first two volumes of the trilogy. The last volume reveals a marked change in style and emphasis from the first two volumes, perhaps due to Baroja's disenchantment with the anarchist ideology that had attracted him earlier. His affiliation with the regenerationist group Los Tres was disintegrating and Baroja, like Azorín and Unamuno, was becoming increasingly skeptical about the possibilities for social change in Spain.

In the first two volumes of the trilogy Baroja portrays a wide range of Madrid's social types, especially workers, thieves, and con men, through the picaresque method of following the fortunes of a waif as he makes his way in the world. But rather than basing these novels on the picaresque assumption that social milieu determines character, Baroja shifts the premises of his trilogy to ask whether environment or individual will prevails in the formation of a person's life trajectory. In the 1904 novels the major addition to this problem, already posed in *Camino de perfección* and *The Lord of Labraz,* is Baroja's linking of this question to political theories, especially to anarchism and socialism. Baroja clearly prefers anarchism's exaltation of individual freedom to socialism, which minimizes the importance of the individual in favor of society; dedicated anarchists are some of the most appealing characters in his novels. But anarchism's ingenuous belief in the fundamental goodness of humankind is belied in the bestiality of many of the secondary characters.

The protagonist, Manuel Alcázar, is one of Baroja's will-less protagonists who drifts in and out of jobs, accepting whatever life seems gratuitously to offer him. At first glance the sordid environment of the Madrid in which he grows up may appear responsible for his lack of will. The novel contains vividly detailed descriptions of beggars, prostitutes, criminals, the homeless, and the hungry in their squalid surroundings, all of which Baroja personally witnessed in his tireless wanderings throughout the city. But on closer scrutiny one notices that something internal to Manuel underlies his malaise, for others, and even he on occasion, can rise above their circumstances. In the first novel of the trilogy, for example, after falling into thievery for a time, he determines to earn an honest subsistence for himself in emulation of a humble junk dealer who has given him employment. But circumstances and his own lack of resolve work against him in the second volume, and he sinks deeper into the criminal world.

Early in *Weeds* Manuel becomes involved in a scam among the marginal upper classes: he hires out to pose as the natural son of a baroness, who extorts money from her ex-lover for their "son." When this "employment" ends he becomes a printer's apprentice. But he meets more vagabonds and falls once again into the low-life activities of gaming, petty crime, and prostitution until his cousin, who had first led him into the underworld, is killed by El Bizco (The Crosseye), one of the most brutal and primitive characters in the novel. The second volume ends with the introduction of the anarchist dreams of salvation for humanity that form the heart of the third volume.

Red Dawn concentrates less on the panoply of Madrid types seen in the first two volumes and instead revolves around discussions of political solutions to the problems exposed earlier. Thus it is a novel more of ideas than of action or locale. Manuel's brother, Juan, the standard-bearer for the anarchist program, who appears for the first time in this volume, is full of idealistic vigor that sharply contrasts with Manuel's indolence. Manuel now lives a much more ordered, "bourgeois" life than heretofore. He attains financial security by purchasing a printing establishment, and he marries Salvadora, whose name ("savior") is both symbolic—she provides the anchor to Manuel's new stability—and ironic. Baroja had a generally negative view of marriage as an institution that harnesses one into the bourgeois yoke and places undue limits on personal freedom. Manuel may be an incarnation of statements Baroja made in journal articles during this period. He ruefully observed in one article that the industrial working class was rapidly becoming a new "perfectly egotistical" bourgeoisie, and in another he denigrated the uniformity and loss of individualism resulting from social mobility.

Thus, the contrast between Manuel and Juan is one of anarchist idealism versus bourgeois complacency. Neither of these solutions is presented in a completely positive light. Juan's extreme idealism and his death, coupled with the shocking brutality of some of the other characters, point to the failure of the anarchist dream. And Baroja clearly rejects the violent aspects of anarchist practice. Toward the end of the novel a bomb is found in Manuel's house, where an anarchist activist is staying. The forthcoming coronation of Alfonso XIII is doubtless the target, but the novel ends with the coronation itself, free of incident. A later anarchist attempt on the life of Alfonso XIII serves as the basis of the plot of Baroja's 1908 novel *La dama errante* (The Wandering Lady).

In each of the three volumes Manuel is poised between characters who represent either the vagabond, even criminal, life or the honorable, willful life. One of the characters constant to the three volumes is the half-English, half-Spanish Roberto Hasting. Baroja's "scientific" interest in racial types (about which much was written in the scientific and popular literature of the time) led him to ascribe qualities of energetic willfulness and decision (perhaps based on Nietzsche's superman) to northern Europeans and animal cunning and opportunism to the Latin and Semitic Mediterranean races. Although he appears to favor the former over the latter, no Barojan character is ever completely positive or negative. The influence of Dickens, so evident in other aspects of Baroja's art, is not to be found in the kind of all-evil or all-good categories into which the English writer placed his characters. Roberto, probably modeled on Vita Sackville-West's father, who went through a lengthy court procedure to settle an inheritance, single-mindedly attempts to prove he is the legitimate heir to a fortune. At intervals he serves as a stark contrast to the will-less Manuel and occasionally helps him find a temporary direction for his life. Roberto's characterization draws on both the opportunism of the Mediterranean type and the diligence and perseverance Baroja normally associates with the northern European type, a combination that makes Roberto's motivations seem rather enigmatic at times.

The historical setting of the trilogy is problematic. Its ending with the coronation in 1902 suggests a period beginning in 1885, but such dating casts many details into anachronism (the Eiffel Tower, certain railways, the phonograph, the automobile). Herbert Ramsden has shown that Baroja simply did not bother to change these details when he revised and expanded the serialized version to form the trilogy. Baroja's purpose was to depict his own time, not to write a historically accurate novel. The wealth of references to technological inventions, even if anachronistic, is fundamental to his portrayal of early-twentieth-century Madrid, the emerging industrial city with its growing bourgeoisie and huge population living on the fringes of the good life—a portrayal very like that of Dickens' London in *Oliver Twist* (1837–1839) or the Manchester of *Hard Times* (1845), but with a notable difference. The evil and corruption that Dickens depicts as a social problem (individual people are evil, but it is the social system that allows them to function) were really more of a philosophical problem for Baroja. While Baroja did not view modern industrial "progress" as the solution to Spain's problems, his primary concern in *La lucha por la vida* does not seem to be an investigation of its evils. Instead, he used the contemporary milieu to pursue his perennial interest in the nature of the individual's relationship to society. Toward the end of *Red Dawn* Manuel muses on how he has arrived at the sedentary bourgeois life he now leads: "So, in life, one often does not know if it is one who initiates events, or if events drag one along."

With *La feria de los discretos* (*The City of the Discreet,* 1905) Baroja initiates a series of novels that take place in more exotic milieus and center on characters in whom a dynamic energy prevails. *The City of the Discreet* is also Baroja's first "historical" novel, one in which he makes a genuine attempt to recapture another era—in this case Cordoba of the 1860's before the end of the reign of Isabel II. The atmosphere is reminiscent of Stendhal's *The Charterhouse of Parma* (1839); in fact, the protagonist laments that he was born too late to serve under Napoleon. It is laden with intrigue, revolution, and romance in the midst of which Baroja exposes an opportunism much more blatant than that of any character in *La lucha por la vida.*

There is very little criticism of the novels of this period, perhaps because Baroja's wedding of his own philosophical and ideological interests to the adventure genre is not as successful here. The fine balance that he maintained between his literary models and the presentation of specific characters in *Aventuras, inventos, y mixtificaciones de Silvestre Paradox, The Lord of Labraz,* and *La lucha por la vida* now tips in favor of the elements of adventure stories—the protagonist's identity, mystery, and intrigue—which overshadow the characters themselves. Mary Lee Bretz demonstrates, however, that Baroja's principal intent in *The City of the Discreet* is to satirize the adventure serial rather than to imitate it.

If, as other critics believe, the protagonist Quintín is modeled on Nietzsche's superman—the quintessential man of action—his actions are mostly of the self-serving and unheroic type, a rather serious modification of Nietzsche's intent. All of Baroja's active protagonists (Quintín, Zalacaín, César Moncada)

lack the kind of specific ideological superstructure found in their romantic models, and in this sense they achieve a Nietzschean "transvaluation of values," but they do not use their modern freedom from a priori ideals to forge a really positive new superior life, and their ultimate fates are decidedly negative. They seek action for itself rather than for any higher idealistic goal, and their activities inevitably lead to destruction, especially of themselves. However, the Baroja protagonists who do have some ideals or moral fiber— Fernando Ossorio, Juan de Labraz, Juan Alcázar, Andrés Hurtado—are certainly not very successful either. But the moral or poetic justice contained in their fates is emotionally satisfying.

The farcical element produced by Baroja's wedding a modern-day moral tale to the adventure novel in *The City of the Discreet* is much more artistically satisfying in *Paradox, rey* (*Paradox, King,* 1906). The successful blend of adventure and farce in *Paradox, King* is partly due to its dialogue format and partly due to its self-conscious acceptance of satirical fantasy as a self-contained artistic form that need not refer directly to a recognizable social milieu. While maintaining adventure as its primary structuring mechanism, it drops the Dickensian comic-picaresque tone of *Aventuras, inventos, y mixtificaciones de Silvestre Paradox* to indulge more fully in exaggerated farce.

At the beginning of the novel Paradox and his sidekick, Avelino Diz, are once again restless and ready for new adventures, so they decide to join a motley group of people from all over Europe who are setting out to establish a Jewish colony in Africa. Through a series of accidents, Paradox becomes a hero. When the captain of the ship dies, he assumes leadership, and his technological prowess, so unappreciated in Spain, serves the travelers well as they set up a colony after a shipwreck, creating a life for themselves in true Robinson Crusoe style. They are captured by a local tribe but manage to free themselves and convince a group of tribesmen to accompany them in establishing another colony. The natives cooperate willingly because their king is despotic and cruel. Eventually the tribesmen remaining in the village revolt, commit regicide, and prevail upon the Europeans to supply them with a new king, who is, of course, Paradox. For a time the Europeans and Africans all live in an ideal socialist state where there is no private property, no money, and no bureaucracy, until French soldiers arrive, declare the place a French colony, and introduce "civilization," which consists of syphilis and dance halls.

The obvious models for much of the plot of this novel are Daniel Defoe's *Robinson Crusoe* (1719–1720) and Joseph Conrad's *Heart of Darkness* (1902), but unlike the English novels, Baroja's version of a European's adventures in an exotic land maintains a pure adventure plot from beginning to end. Not only does the character not change due to his experiences in an alien, exotic milieu, but we hardly know him as a character at all; he is as wooden and hollow as a marionette puppet. And this feature of the book, as well as its dialogue form, calls to mind Alfred Jarry's revolutionary, pre-absurdist play *Ubu roi.* At the time of Baroja's first trip to Paris in 1898, that capital of fin-de-siècle culture was still buzzing about the 1896 premiere of Jarry's iconoclastic play.

Of course, Paradox is a more positive figure than Ubu, the grotesquely gluttonous and cruel king of Jarry's work, who may have been the model for Baroja's African king deposed by his own tribesmen. But it is mostly Jarry's general tone of absurdity and farce that Baroja has recourse to here. The Spanish novel recalls the ridiculous, even impossible, situations that form the basis of Jarry's plot: Ubu is a walking obscenity turned king, Paradox an eccentric inventor elevated to a tribal kingship of heroic proportions. Jarry's Ubu talks to his conscience, which he carries in a suitcase; in Baroja's novel animals and meteorological

phenomena speak, and there are several passages in which the dialogue between the characters gives way to a lyrical voice that praises the accordion, extols the virtues of the merry-go-round, and issues a metaphysical eulogy of destruction that concludes with the dictum, "To destroy is to create."

But even though the adventure-farce tone is more absolute in *Paradox, King* than in any other Baroja novel, the author occasionally throws a tenuous ladder down from the exotic realm in which his hero operates to a world we recognize. The characters sometimes converse on issues of contemporary concern, especially the relative merits of different forms of government. But the topics are couched in such extreme and absurd language that they are not a serious threat to the adventure-farce mood. For example, when the natives approach Paradox's colony to request that the Europeans supply them a king, the Frenchman in the group argues for a native republic. He maintains that his dignity would be sullied if he had to obey a king, but for Paradox the two forms of government are essentially the same:

> "In no country does one obey a king! One obeys a series of laws. It has nothing to do with dignity. In all the countries of Europe we have as the head of State a kind of soldier in uniform, with all the hardware of crosses and plaques on his chest, and you have a kind of notary in tails and top hat with a ribbon in his button hole."
>
> (2:208)[1]

In many ways *Paradox, King* is Baroja's most extreme effort to deny the possibility of an adequate answer to Spain's political and ideological vacuum. The narrative is reduced to a minimum, and the plot and setting dislodge the very real Spanish political questions of the day from their natural environment and place them in the exotic world of a primitive tribe, thus reducing them to an incongruous and ridiculous level. Baroja never again used an absurdist genre that so completely breaks

[1]All quotations are from *Obras completas,* 8 vols. (Madrid, 1946–1951).

with a realistic perspective on the Spain of his time.

His following two novels, *Los últimos románticos* (The Last Romantics, 1906) and *Las tragedias grotescas* (The Grotesque Tragedies, 1907), continue the farcical mode of *Paradox, King* but in a more muted key. Their protagonist, Fausto Gamboa, is a Republican and a romantic who is never able to free himself from his bourgeois bonds to pursue idealistic action. These two novels, along with the two that follow, *La dama errante* and *La ciudad de la niebla* (The City of Fog, 1909), in which the element of farce has disappeared altogether, form a kind of aesthetic and thematic unit. In each set of two volumes, Baroja explores an event in recent European history that marks the end of a certain kind of hope for social regeneration: the Paris Commune in the first two novels, and the anarchist attempt on Alfonso XIII's life in the second two. The communist experiment in Paris fails, and anarchism proves to be more of a threat to social well-being than its salvation. Both sets of novels offer contrasts between Spain and the rest of Europe; Fausto Bengoa, the protagonist of the first two novels, takes up residence in Paris, and María Aracil, protagonist of the second two, lives for most of the second volume in London. Neither Spaniard ultimately succeeds in the foreign milieu. An interesting comparison could be made between Baroja's Spaniards who reside abroad and Henry James's Americans who go to Europe. James's characters are profoundly and permanently marked by their European experiences, while Baroja's protagonists are notably unchanged by their foreign milieus.

In the first set of novels the historical event is the culmination of the action of each work; in the second set it is the catalyst to the novel's action. Once again Baroja explores the way in which environment and the individual interact, this time examining the individual's relation to political history. And he seems to conclude that history and the individual have little to do with one another, at least in the cases of the individuals on whom he focuses. Political events may cause a change of geographical location or may necessitate a character's greater self-reliance for a time, but ultimately the individual has very little effect on the direction history takes, and vice versa.

One of the principal features of *La ciudad de la niebla* is a shift in point of view from first to third person midway through the book, a shift that heightens the problem of the individual's relationship to society. The author makes the shift in a highly self-conscious manner, beginning the second part of the novel with an introduction addressed to the reader that outlines the difficulties of presenting a clear and uncomplicated narrative. Baroja links the problem of narrative to the historical circumstances of the writer; he believed, as did many modern writers, that in modern times nothing is clearly black or white as it was in earlier times. He explains that the modern viewpoint, in consonance with modern moral and metaphysical uncertainty, must necessarily be jaded and respect nothing. And Baroja often employed a shifting narrative voice to underscore the unstable values of his time. In *Camino de perfección* the narrative shifts in a most unsettling way from the perspective of a friend and medical school companion of Fernando Ossorio, in the early chapters, to a third-person omniscient narrative voice that takes over after Fernando leaves medical school to begin his spiritual journey. In *The Lord of Labraz* the narrator is Mr. Samuel Bothwell Crawford, an English painter and eccentric of the Silvestre Paradox sort. It is most incongrous that this burlesque character should recount such a sordid and tragic tale, but this kind of strange incongruity is, of course, typical of much of Baroja's fiction.

Baroja's oft-cited misogyny is belied in his creation of María Aracil, protagonist of *La dama errante* and *La ciudad de la niebla,* who, along with Lula of *The Tree of Knowledge* and Sacha of *El mundo es ansí* is as positive a character as Baroja ever invented. She (as well as Baroja's other positive women and men) ultimately fails to find complete independence, but she does manage to live by and for herself with some success for a time. It seems clear from his memoirs and from his portrayals of women in some of the novels that Baroja did like women, and he attempted to establish a romantic bond with a woman on a number of occasions. But he refused to submit to the institution of marriage, which he believed limited one's freedom. This dilemma became a central subject in Baroja's essays and novels from about 1917 onward.

Zalacaín el aventurero (Zalacaín the Adventurer, 1909) continues Baroja's interest in historical settings, this time fashioned in an adventure tale that takes place during the last Carlist war in his native Basque provinces. For many critics *Zalacaín el aventurero* stands alone outside the mainstream of Baroja's novelistic canon as a more traditional novel in its form and content. Its protagonist is closer to a true hero, and the plot structure is more closed, lacking the usual Barojan digressions on philosophical or ideological issues. But on closer examination we see that, as in many of the works already discussed, Baroja juggles an exotic combination of romantic adventure (here a family-feud love story à la *Romeo and Juliet*) with a description of a concrete physical and historical reality—the decaying ambience of a Basque village. So *Zalacaín, el aventurero*, which has often been considered an anomalous pure adventure story with a more traditional plot, in fact reveals the same generic hybridization that we have examined in *Aventuras, inventos, y mixtificaciones de Silvestre Paradox, Paradox, rey*, and *La dama errante*.

Martín Zalacaín has been seen as an ultimate Nietzschean man of action, and there is much merit in the claim. He has unlimited self-assurance, energy, and (what has been less noted) lack of respect for traditional values of loyalty to one woman or one political cause. Although the story line is based on the classic heroic Renaissance or romantic adventure tale—involving a valiant hero-warrior with the ideal woman waiting at home while he carries out his daring exploits—Zalacaín is the moral reverse of the hero of the chivalric romance or its nineteenth-century counterpart, the adventure romance. Zalacaín does not share either the Carlist conviction that modernization is the ruin of Spain or the Liberals' desire to bring Spain more in line politically and socially with the rest of Europe.

Martín's sole purpose is self-affirmation. He spies, intrigues, and fights for both the Liberals and the Carlists, while his antagonist, the jealous and spiteful brother of his fiancée, Catalina, is a genuine Carlist conservative. Not only are Martín's loyalties politically unstable, but he is also capable of great unkindness to his cherished Catalina, forgetting that she awaits him while he dallies with another woman. And his "heroic" feats, such as the taking of La Guardia, are frequently of dubious merit. In an act of bravado Martín enters occupied La Guardia at night to hoist the liberal government's flag, but the act loses its heroic significance when we learn that the Carlist soldiers had already planned to abandon the city the following day.

Zalacaín el aventurero does not alter Baroja's vision of history and the individual as set forth in his four previous novels, in which the main character, while moving in a recognizable historical milieu, is not at all affected by it. Zalacaín remains unchanged from the beginning to the end of the story. Nor is he limited by the social circumstances into which he was born or by his own biological conditions. However, those who have seen *Zalacaín el aventurero* as a pure adventure novel of escape should not forget the tragedy of Zalacaín's ending. Escapism is curtailed when Zalacaín finally settles down, marries Catalina, and has a child, although the indomitable adventurer is caught out by his wife's brother, who has him treacherously murdered. The reader is ultimately trapped by the mood of ironic fatalism, the seriousness of which is

PÍO BAROJA

underscored by the overtones of legend with which the novel ends. The cycle of revenge that has existed between Zalacaín and Catalina's families is perpetuated (a tale about the ancestor of Zalacaín who was murdered by an ancestor of the same rival family is told early in the novel), and the three women who have loved Zalacaín place roses on his grave as a symbolic ritualistic gesture. The novel begins and ends with all the elements of a medieval or Renaissance romance, but the action itself is propelled by modern values of self-assertion unfettered by traditional loyalties to king or religion.

The protagonist of Baroja's next novel, *César o nada* (*Caesar or Nothing,* 1910), is a much more complex character than Martín Zalacaín. César Moncada, like the earlier Fernando Ossorio, has bouts of energetic action alternating with periods of inertia. In some ways this is Baroja's most political novel, as the central character is a politician in Alfonso XIII's Spain. In 1909 Baroja himself was a candidate for city council, during which time he observed Spain's local politics at close range. But the novel had a dual inspiration: Baroja's personal experiences in Spanish politics merge with the political life of the Italian Renaissance figure Cesare Borgia (1476–1507), whose father, Pope Alexander VI, was of Spanish extraction. Baroja had long been fascinated with Borgia, and he even made a trip to Italy in search of information about Niccolò Machiavelli's perfect prince. But he soon abandoned any idea of writing a historical novel based on Borgia's life. Factual history was ever at odds with Baroja's real interest in philosophical and ideological issues related to his own time.

Baroja's sojourn in Italy provided material for the setting of the first half of the novel. César goes to Rome in search of political backing. But his political ambition seems rather muted and desultory, and he engages in much sightseeing and socializing. During these tourist activities he learns the history of Borgia and engages in a conversation with an English Catholic about Borgia's great energy and his contributions to the church in the political realm (including the consolidation of papal power, the forging of an alliance with the French, and the conquest of city-states), comparing them to Saint Ignatius Loyola's philosophical contribution. They conclude that "today Spain should try to turn this Spanish determination to her own benefit. Its two impulses—material and spiritual—gave our country the Church, an institution that is not only strange but contrary to us. Spain's work should be to organize extrareligious individualism."

In the second half of the novel César returns to Spain, full of energetic plans for his own political career, through which he intends to reform Spain's antiquated political and social system, especially *caciquismo* (a corrupt bossism by which the traditional forces of Spanish society, including the church, controlled local politics). Ironically, César begins his political life in the Conservative Party for reasons of political expediency, and even when he becomes a leader of the local Liberal Party, he ends up becoming a *cacique* of the kind he had planned to eradicate.

There is a second, somewhat latent, theme in *Caesar or Nothing* that reflects a new orientation in Baroja's philosophical position—a radical turning-away from the scientific categories that had earlier penetrated his thinking. Many of Fernando Ossorio's troubles are attributed to his degenerate genetic inheritance and the degeneracy of his milieu, and toward the end of *La ciudad de la niebla*, María Aracil is said to be the product of a tired race. But Baroja now rejects the notion of racial categories: "The individual entity is the only reality in Nature and life. The species, the genera, the race, in the end, do not exist; they are abstractions, means of designating, artifices of science, useful syntheses, but not absolutely exact." In his search for a philosophical paradigm for life, César Moncada rejects mathematics and science because they provide an inexact truth.

It is very likely that Baroja's new position on

scientific abstraction arose from his more and more frequent dialogues with José Ortega y Gasset, the rising young star of Spanish philosophy. Baroja first met Ortega in 1906, when they traveled together from Madrid to Paris, Baroja on his way to London and Ortega on his way to Freiburg, Germany, to study. In about 1908 Ortega and Baroja began to frequent the same literary café circles, and in the second decade of the twentieth century they often traveled together throughout Spain. Between 1908 and 1910 Ortega followed in the neo-Kantian footsteps of his Freiburg teachers, as his first major essay, "Adán en el Paraíso" ("Adam in Paradise," 1910), attests. In that essay he divides the consciousness into three areas: science, ethics, and aesthetics. He proclaims that neither natural science nor moral science (ethics) can adequately explain life because each reduces life to an abstraction. Life, that which is individual, says Ortega, is best captured in art. Baroja, in his contact with the brilliant young philosopher, probably began to sharpen his own vitalist posture, rejecting what he could now see as the abstract quality of the scientific categories.

Baroja states in the prologue to *Caesar or Nothing* that "all that is individual always presents itself mixed, with absurdities in perspective and picturesque contradictions." The observation is borne out in the figure of César Moncada, who is neither the Nietzschean superman nor the passive, indecisive character, but rather combines the two in contradictory and unpredictable ways. But César's attempt to establish himself as a politically dynamic individual finally fails when he is assassinated by the politically conservative forces, just as Zalacaín is. It is not only the opposing reactionary political forces that effect his undoing; his own lapses of will prevent his sustained involvement in politics at the necessary level. "Caesar or nothing," the motto by which Borgia lived and which serves as the ironic title of the novel, does not represent the intermittent energy of César Moncada. He is incapable of the all-or-nothing approach to

life; he is plagued with doubts and periods of passivity that alternate with periods of enterprising action. As in so many of Baroja's novels, the paradigm for the novelistic structure (here Borgia's life, the mystic quest in *Camino de perfección,* or the heroic adventure romance in *Zalacaín el aventurero*) is really an ironic foil for what occurs in Baroja's version. The story of Borgia, like that of Zalacaín's forebear, is repeated in contemporary times to highlight the predecessor's ideological zeal, singularly lacking in the modern man's pursuit of political goals. But the foreshadowing cast by the tragic end of the protagonist's historical counterpart does imbue both *Zalacaín el aventurero* and *Caesar or Nothing* with a certain artistic depth. Rather than having a single vision of a fictional character with a certain set of personal qualities and problems, the reader is constantly aware—in a kind of double vision—of the other figure, the tragic outcome of whose story is already known.

If the time period studied in *Los últimos románticos* is that moment when romantic, idealistic action was becoming impossible because of the crushing weight of materialistic, sedentary bourgeois life, in *Las inquietudes de Shanti Andía* (*The Restlessness of Shanti Andía,* 1911) Baroja sees the adventuresome life as definitely past:

> The conditions in which life today unfolds make most people opaque and uninteresting. Today, practically nothing worthy of being told occurs. Most of us swim in an ocean of vulgarity. Neither our loves, our adventures, or our thoughts are interesting enough to communicate to others unless they are exaggerated and transformed. Society is making life, ideas, and everyone's aspirations uniform.
>
> (2:997)

Baroja dramatizes the contrast between past and present life through the narrative voice; the story of the adventure-filled life of Juan de Aguirre, a sailor who sailed the seas in the days of slave and treasure ships, is told by his nephew Shanti Andía, a modern commercial sailor. Shanti laments that technology has come between man and his environment, making everything predictable: "Today the sea is increasingly industrialized, the sailor, in his iron ship, knows when it will go, when it is going to stop; he has the days and hours calculated . . . ; back then, chance, good luck, a favorable wind carried one along."

The Basque provinces once again serve as the setting for the contrast between early-nineteenth-century life and that of the late nineteenth and early twentieth centuries. Many of the adventures Baroja ascribes to Juan de Aguirre (ship captures, imprisonments, escapes) are tales he heard from friends and relatives in the seaport villages. The sense of a progressive loss of possibilities for action is heightened by the fact that Lope de Aguirre, an actual historical figure who broke away from Francisco Pizarro's conquering legions in Peru to search for riches down the Amazon, is also an ancestor of the narrator Shanti Andía. Thus Shanti's situation is portrayed indirectly as a particularly Spanish dilemma as well as a modern one, but the critique of contemporary Spain is less important in this novel than in *La lucha por la vida* or *Caesar or Nothing,* for example.

The narrative alternates between the tales about Shanti's uncle Juan and Shanti's own life; the result is a counterpoint that constitutes the real interest of the novel, since neither of the two characters or his story maintains the narrative focus. The nostalgia for the past that Baroja ridicules by means of a burlesque bourgeois "romantic" protagonist in novels like *Los últimos romanticos* becomes a genuine sentiment in *The Restlessness of Shanti Andía.* Shanti understands himself and his circumstances too well to fall into the farcical category with Fausto Bengoa: "The desire to reach a goal unsettles all men, even the most tranquil and indolent, and I, for my part, would have liked to live even more in each hour, in each minute, without nostalgia for the past or anxiety for the future."

Here Baroja seems much more ready to ac-cept environment—in this case modern technology—over heredity or personal will as the dominating shaper of human life. His position has clearly shifted since 1908, when in the prologue to *La ciudad de la niebla* he stated his belief that the influence of inherited racial characteristics predominates in the formation of individual characters. Shanti contains the seeds of a man of action, but surrounded as he is by mediocre, complacent people, he never really understands his will and his desire for a different kind of life. Without immediate models or any obvious outlet for his ill-defined "restlessness," he never channels it in any meaningful direction. The roads to action in modern life have been sealed off by mechanization and social leveling.

Baroja was not satisfied with that solution to his favorite question, and he returned to the problem and gave it a more ambiguous treatment in his next and probably most studied and revered novel, *The Tree of Knowledge.* Many critics agree that this is one of his most carefully structured narratives, and it is the least dependent for its plot development on specific genre types such as the adventure tale, farce, the picaresque, or Dickensian ironic realism. The external action follows Andrés Hurtado's life (with many parallels to Baroja's own biography) from his medical school years in Madrid through his short-lived practice as a country doctor to his marriage and retirement from active medical practice. The internal dynamic of the novel centers on the philosophical problem (presented somewhat along the lines of that in *Camino de perfección,* but without the mystical-religious overtones) of life as it is lived in its carnal aspects and as it is contemplated in the intellectual realm. The novel's plot (if its moments or scenes can be called a plot) alternates between Andrés' experiences in life and his periodic withdrawals to read, think, and converse about what it all means. Thus the novel's structure depends on an alternation between raw experience—medical school, observations of human activity, especially in the lower-class *barrios,* family tragedy—and its abstraction in philosophy. The latter is embedded primarily in four conversations between Andrés and his Uncle Iturrioz, also a doctor but of a more pragmatic mind.

Andrés is the prototypical modern man—a man of science, who is searching for an appropriate new moral system and explanation for the forces of the world. In the first part his philosophical quest is awakened during his years in Madrid's antiquated medical school by his professor, Letamendi. (Baroja himself studied with José de Letamendi and may have been similarly stimulated by him to seek philosophical solutions to life's dilemmas.) But the biologist-philosopher's application of mathematics to biology soon disillusions Andrés because of its oversimplification of life's complexities. In part two the first of Andrés' philosophical conversations with his uncle takes place. Andrés has no defined philosophical position, and the uncle's materialistic, positivistic orientation dominates their interchange. Iturrioz responds to Andrés' wish to make sense of all the myriad life forms he has observed, especially the miserable lives of the people in the lower-class areas of Madrid, with a purely biological explanation for life. For Iturriaz there are no universals, such as a universal sense of justice, only pragmatic solutions to suit particular ends.

In the third part of the novel Andrés experiences the most painful event of his life thus far, the death of his younger brother from tuberculosis. After this tragedy he seeks an explanation for life's conundrum in the German idealists Kant and Schopenhauer. Armed with these philosophical weapons, Andrés once again engages in discussion with his uncle in a conversation that comprises the entire fourth and central section of the book. Here positivism and pragmatism confront idealism head on. Iturrioz recommends that Andrés forget the idealists and look to the English philosophers like Thomas Hobbes, who will not remove him to such a distance from

life. But true to his Kantian sources, Andrés stoutly defends the mental categories of causality—time and space. For Andrés the great abstractions of science are the only constructions in which humanity can place its faith. Finally, at the end of this central conversation Andrés and Iturrioz agree that humanity needs a rationalist construction (the lie, according to Iturrioz) in order to live. Andrés says that "the vital instinct needs fiction in order to affirm itself. Thus science, the critical instinct, the instinct to investigate should find a truth, the number of lies necessary for life to survive."

In putting science at the service of life, Andrés presages the conclusion to Ortega's seminal work *Meditaciones del Quijote* (1914), namely, that human life is the radical philosophical category. In fact, the entire novel may be a further working-out of Baroja's dialogue with Ortega on life versus abstraction that begins with Ortega's "Adam in Paradise" and Baroja's challenge in parts of *Caesar or Nothing.* Ortega's Adam is abstract man in the world, groping to make sense of it, and Andrés, whose first name is almost an anagram of the Spanish spelling of Adam (Adán) and whose last name, Hurtado, means stolen (perhaps referring to the apple), ultimately fails to unite the vital and the abstract in his own life, always shying away from sensual and social activities. The title of the book, *The Tree of Knowledge,* echoing that of Ortega's essay, reminds us that the biblical Adam and Baroja's Andrés both choose the Tree of Knowledge rather than the Tree of Life (innocence in Paradise). If in 1910 Ortega still favored conceptual knowledge over raw, lived life, Baroja seems to be a sympathetic critic of his young friend's position. In his own version of the Garden of Eden story, Andrés-Adán ultimately fails to survive.

At the end of the long dialectical interchange between uncle and nephew in the fourth part, Andrés, still carrying his rationalist baggage, undertakes his medical career, first in a backward village (part 5) and then in a Madrid clinic for prostitutes (part 6). According to the uncle's prediction, his metaphysical ideas have not prepared him for life, and he is unsuccessful in both the village and the clinic because he is unable to descend from his abstract idealism to deal with people in practical social terms. He is unwilling to enter into village life in a way that is acceptable to the townspeople, and he finds the prostitutes' passive acceptance of their condition repugnant. However, during this period he achieves a certain equilibrium by avoiding as much as possible the carnal aspects of life; he maintains a vegetarian diet, socializes with almost no one, and does not have relations with women. But life does not leave him alone so easily, and when Andrés is forced to give an opinion in a criminal case, the rival doctor makes his situation in the village so uncomfortable that he resigns his post. On the night before his departure he breaks his sexual abstinence and makes love to his landlady. The experience leaves him so ill and weak that he cannot reach Madrid without stopping to recuperate in Aranjuez.

Upon arriving in Madrid Andrés encounters his uncle, who chides his nephew for believing he could really escape the complications of life through withdrawal to a village: "No man is a star with its independent orbit." Ortega interprets Andrés' problem in a similar way in a 1916 essay, saying that the character lives like a mushroom cleaving to himself, without adherence to his environment, without any exchange of substances with his surroundings. In this conversation with his uncle Andrés accepts for the moment the suggestion that he cannot live outside his circumstances. But he does not really achieve a full integration of the notion into his life. He marries his longtime friend Lulú, retires from active medical practice, and isolates himself in their apartment to translate medical articles. Although Baroja is never very explicit about sexual matters, it is suggested that Andrés also abstains from his matrimonial duties. But once again life imposes itself: Lulú wants

to have children, and Andrés finally succumbs to her tears. Their matrimonial tranquillity is destroyed when the pregnant Lulú becomes jealous and irritable. First Andrés takes morphine to escape the terrors of approaching fatherhood, and when Lulú dies in childbirth, he commits suicide, leaving behind both the Tree of Knowledge and the Tree of Life.

This ending contains Baroja's most complete condemnation of Andrés' extreme rationalist position. Iturrioz's pragmatic counsel at key points in the novel acts as a reminder that science and the rational are only one way to approach life, one branch of the tree that is too thin to support the entire weight of human complexity. Andrés the rationalist and Iturrioz the vitalist remain juxtaposed in a way that denies either position ascendency. Life without reason and reflection is chaotic and ignoble (as with the teeming multitudes of poor in Madrid); reason without carnal life is death. Iturrioz says in the final scene that Andrés was somewhat of a "precursor," the prototypical modern man who has not yet achieved a balance between science and life. The notion of precursor suggests that a successful equilibrium is still possible, that Baroja still held out hope for the future. At the end of *Los últimos románticos* the same note of optimism prevails. A more serious Fausto Bengoa emerges to say: "One forgets everything. Everything becomes erased. You see, I am old, my wife and daughter have abandoned me, and, nevertheless, I have hope. Life . . . never ends. . . . One is always at the beginning . . . and at the end." *The Tree of Knowledge* is in some ways a precursor to the post–World War II novel of existential angst, but Baroja's hopeful pessimism precluded his reaching the radical alienation that Jean-Paul Sartre projects in *La nausée* (1938), for example.

Baroja's enduring achievement in *The Tree of Knowledge,* the one that sets it apart from his other novels, is the felicitous subordination of his many social, political, ideological, and philosophical interests to the story of one man's struggle to find a philosophical solution to life. Baroja's other themes—Nietzschean action versus paralysis, milieu versus will, political ideologies, Mediterranean racial types versus those of northern Europe, the social problems of contemporary Spain—are all present here but are reduced to motifs that artistically support and enhance the overarching concern. Thus Baroja's many interests do not rival one another for attention, as is the case in so many of his other novels.

TRANSITION

Baroja's novelistic production, though vigorous and prolific for many years thereafter, never again achieved the superior edge of *The Tree of Knowledge* or even the freshness and interest that most of the novels written between 1900 and 1911 hold for readers. The reasons for the decline in Baroja's creative vitality from the middle of the second decade onward are doubtless many and complex. One of the usual explanations is that Baroja, now over forty and in what he considered incipient old age, took an introspective turn. And it is true that many of his works after 1912 bear the same personal and autobiographical stamp found in *The Tree of Knowledge* but without that novel's coherent philosophical underpinnings.

It is also interesting to note that in 1915 Baroja resumed writing for the periodical press after a hiatus of some ten years. Many of his journal articles of the second and third decades center on autobiographical matters and on his ideas about novel-writing. One of the important aspects of Baroja's articles of the 1910's and 1920's was a growing debate with Ortega on the nature of the novel, which may hold a further clue to Baroja's artistic decline during this period. We have ample printed evidence of the debate between the novelist and the philosopher, but one suspects that the published material is only the tip of the iceberg, a distillation of many hours of private conversation.

In a 1915 article on Baroja Ortega analyzes the novelist's work in a way that could hardly have pleased the Basque writer. Ortega takes Baroja as a representative national type; he points to the aggressive tone in his novels as a sign of national hysteria and infantilism. Underlying Ortega's dissatisfaction with Baroja's novel-writing is the novelist's mixture of the artistic with recognizable national life. Ortega did not fully formulate his own aesthetics of the separation of life and art until ten years later in *La deshumanización del arte* (*The Dehumanization of Art*, 1925), but it is quite possible that his meditations on Baroja were the catalyst to their genesis and elaboration. The 1925 essay gives Ortega's most complete description of the perfect novel: it should be a hermetically sealed artistic construct without reminders of the world beyond its borders. Baroja answered Ortega's definitive statement on the novel in the "Prólogo casi doctrinal sobre la novela" (A Nearly Doctrinal Prologue on the Novel) that prefaced *La nave de los locos* (The Ship of Fools), also published in 1925. Baroja defends the novel as an open genre, amenable to many styles and to the inclusion of a variety of elements: "The novel today is a multiform, protean genre in formation and fermentation; it takes in everything: the philosophical book, the psychological book, adventure, utopia, the epic; absolutely everything." Novel-writing is not a technique for Baroja but an act of creative imagination always grounded in reality. Baroja's interest in life as it is lived impeded his writing according to the Ortegian formula of a slow, lingering psychological development, a technique whose most extreme cultivator was Marcel Proust. According to Baroja, "The closed novel, without a transcendent element, without pores, without holes through which the air of real life can enter, can undoubtedly and more easily be the most artistic," but for Baroja art could never be an end in itself as Ortega believed it should be.

Baroja had already begun to wrestle with the problem of integrating art and life in his 1912 novel *El mundo es ansí*. He doubtless felt by the second decade and surely by the third that the new aesthetics of "art for art's sake," increasingly evident in the rising avant-garde movements in literature and painting, left him looking rather old-fashioned and passé. (He also ceased frequenting the literary café circles around 1915, since they were becoming dominated by such avant-garde writers as Ramón Gómez de la Serna.) He tried to remain faithful to his own notion of what a novel should be, but surely so much self-examination and reflection on technique blunted his spontaneity and made him a more self-conscious novelist.

In 1918 Baroja stood for election to the legislature in a kind of last attempt to have some impact on public life in Spain, but the election was a disaster for him. This event, coupled with Baroja's profound disgust at the brutality of World War I, signaled the end of his belief in action as a viable remedy to life's dilemma. Also on the wane was his curiosity about what motivates action, the burning question at the center of his finest novels that imparted to them their best quality—an earnest ambiguity both of theme and of form.

Published on the heels of *The Tree of Knowledge, El mundo es ansí* provides an example of Baroja's transition from his first decade of work to that of his second and third decades. It follows the life of Sacha Savarof, a Russian medical student, through two marriages and several countries. At first glance the novel appears to be an autobiographical rehash of Baroja's friend Paul Schmitz's marriage to a Russian woman (Baroja witnessed the wedding in San Sebastián), of Baroja's notions of ethnic typology (one of Sacha's husbands is an opportunistic, materialistic Swiss Jew who displays all the worst traits that Baroja often ascribed to the Mediterranean races, and the other is a self-willed Spaniard, completely devoid of any social morality outside his own wishes and desires), and of his own frustrations and dissatisfactions in love (Sacha is disappointed in love and in turn spurns the attentions of Arcelu, the one character who genuinely cares for her).

But as C. A. Longhurst convincingly demonstrates, the novel represents Baroja's sense of crisis at this point in his career about the integration of life and art. The narrative technique focuses the interest of the novel on the relationship of biography to fictional narrative. As in several other novels, Baroja introduces the protagonist's story through a narrator who is also a character in the book. Then, in the second and third parts, the protagonist herself takes over the narrative function in first-person letters and diaries, with the original narrator apparently acting as editor and publisher of Sacha's own words. This very intricate and complex narrative voice calls up the problem of truth versus fiction and the impossibility of a completely factual representation of anyone's life in writing. A curious postscript to Baroja's continuing involvement with this dilemma is contained in his memoirs, *Desde la última vuelta del camino* (From the Last Bend in the Road), begun in 1941 and completed in 1949, in which he frequently copied whole passages from his novels when relating episodes of his "real" life.

The interesting narrative experiment that Baroja achieves in earlier works and in *El mundo es ansí,* one of the first in a long line of introspective self-assessments, was not repeated. Baroja's novelistic production after 1912 became diffuse, divided among autobiographical fiction, historical novels, and purely escapist adventure fiction, as well as several other types.

THE SECOND PERIOD

The renewed contact with his Basque homeland occasioned by the 1912 purchase of a summer home there brought to Baroja's attention a distant relative, Eugenio de Aviraneta, nephew of his great-great grandfather. He decided to write a series of novels based on Aviraneta's life (1792–1872), which spanned most of the events of Spain's turbulent nineteenth century: the introduction of the ideas of the French Revolution in the late eighteenth century; Napoleon's deposition of the Bourbon monarchy in Spain and installation of his brother Joseph on the Spanish throne in 1808; the Spanish liberal movement that produced a constitution in 1812 and finally expelled the French in 1814, only to find that the restored Ferdinand VII was reactionary and absolutist; and finally, the series of Carlist Wars, beginning in 1833 with the death of Ferdinand, between the liberal forces favoring his daughter Isabel II and the ultra-conservative factions wishing to impose Ferdinand's brother Carlos as king. Aviraneta participated actively in these events, and Baroja carefully researched the history of the times, traveling to many historical sites for background. He had also heard stories about Aviraneta from his relatives since childhood, which he incorporated into the novels.

Baroja devoted more than half of the twenty-two volumes he produced in the years between 1912 and 1935 to the Aviraneta saga, *Memorias de un hombre de acción* (Memoirs of a Man of Action). There have been several explanations for his intense commitment at this point in his career to a historical novel centering on a biographical figure. Perhaps the most convincing is that Baroja, having grown disillusioned with the possibilities for action in modern life, chose to write about a man of action in the past. Aviraneta is a thoroughgoing liberal, and unlike Baroja's invented action-oriented characters, he remains faithful to his ideology and to a course of action intended to further its aims, though these are often unsuccessful. Aviraneta is the quintessential nineteenth-century Spanish romantic, involved first in the War of Independence against France in 1814, then in the subsequent struggles to impose a liberal government on the old-style absolutist monarch Ferdinand VII, and finally in the pro-Isabeline forces against the reactionary Carlists of the middle of the century. But like many of Baroja's protagonists, Aviraneta is not essentially changed by his myriad experiences over a

period of some eighty years; Baroja himself said the character was cut all of one piece.

What is most interesting about the series is the sense it gives of ordinary people's lives during these turbulent times of struggle to change Spain from a medieval to a modern bourgeois society. Rather than a history of great political events, it is history seen from below, from the perspective of common people and of the small-time conspirator working in a small corner of the huge map of the Spanish nineteenth century. Baroja's approach to the historical novel has often been compared to Galdós', especially since the nineteenth-century "realist" writer's long series of *Episodios nacionales* (National Episodes, 1873–1912) deals with much the same historical period as Baroja's *Memorias de un hombre de acción*. The different emphases of the titles hint at the underlying difference of each novelist's approach to fictionalized history. Galdós concentrated on the general movement of Spanish history—its causes, its effects, its progress toward the establishment of a bourgeois hegemony in Spanish life—while Baroja concentrated on the personal experience and especially the personal view of a historical moment. He was highly selective in the events he chose to include in the narration; four of the novels deal with the period 1820–1823, a brief liberal interlude during the reign of the despotic Ferdinand VII, and only two chronicle the long period from 1840–1872, one mostly dominated by the reign of Isabel II. He doubtless found the experience of a liberal living during a brief liberalization of an oppressive regime more dramatic and intense than that of the same man during the more liberal times of the queen's reign.

José López-Marrón has shown that Baroja was more interested in history as narration with a specific point of view than in history as absolute fact. The narrators are frequently distanced in time from the events they recount. For example, an older Aviraneta tells of experiences in the War of Independence from the perspective of a prison cell twenty years later, which thus allows him the wisdom of mature reflection. And Baroja employs a variety of narrators in the series, some of them characters who appear to be introduced only to provide a different perspective from that of Aviraneta on the events of the period. For example, in *La ruta del aventurero* (The Route of the Adventurer, 1916) the end of the liberal triennium (1823) is viewed through the eyes of an Englishman who can display the proper objective horror at the backward, reactionary Spanish political scene. And Alvarito Mendoza, protagonist of the trilogy *Las figuras de cera* (The Wax Figures, 1924), *La nave de los locos*, and *Las mascaradas sangrientas* (The Bloody Masks, 1927), provides the perspective of a progressively disillusioned Carlist in a Spain filled with the most perverse sorts of people—thieves, liars, sexual deviants, and egotistical types of every sort. It is also possible that the experience of World War I, which occurred shortly after Baroja began the series, muted his interest in the bellicose-heroic aspects of Aviraneta's life and caused him to shift the focus of the series away from Aviraneta in these later volumes onto more contemplative and sentimental characters.

During the years that he spent on the Aviraneta series, Baroja continued to write "contemporary" novels, almost invariably following the formulaic pattern in which a sentimental protagonist wanders around Europe engaging in conversations on a variety of Baroja's favorite topics and making unsuccessful attempts to find love. He says in the 1918 prologue to *Las horas solitarias* (The Solitary Hours), "For some time now I have been involved in writing historical novels, but I am not completely comfortable with them, and I have to get away from them, prance about and occupy myself with contemporary things." But with the rise of the totalitarian ideologies—communism and fascism—the world that was evolving after World War I was quite alien to Baroja's amorphous, non-specific political ideas about the human struggle for freedom of action and thought. He really had nothing new to say, nothing pertinent to offer a world that was seeking solutions to human social problems in ways that so sharply restricted human freedom. He looked more and more to himself, to his own personal past and his own private emotional experiences, for his new novelistic material—the dilemma of love, sex, and marriage.

In his autobiographical essays published between 1917 and 1920, Baroja discussed the problem of frustrated sensuality and its roots in the reactionary Spanish system of social mores. In *La sensualidad pervertida* (Perverted Sensuality, 1920) he fictionalized the problem in the story of his protagonist, Luis Murguía, whose life centers on a series of disastrous sentimental and romantic encounters that leave him increasingly withdrawn and solitary. The solution of marriage that "saves" Fernando Ossorio, César Moncada, and Andrés Hurtado (if only temporarily in the cases of the latter two) from the inexorable forces of life is at this point definitely closed for Baroja and for his protagonist, partly by chance and partly by choice. Baroja now appears to have settled on a solution to the question that drives his early novels: does will or environment determine life's path? It is after all a complex interaction of the two, varying according to individual experience, that decides one's vital direction. He states in *Juventud, egolatría* (Youth and Egolatry, 1917): "Life is neither good nor bad; it is, like nature, necessary. Society itself is not good or bad. It is bad for the man who has an excessive sensibility for his times; it is good for him who finds himself in harmony with his environment." Baroja is doubtless closer to the truth in concluding that the forces that shape one's life are less polarized than he had once believed, but arriving at this conclusion robbed his novels' dynamics of their earlier vitality.

The trilogy *Las agonías de nuestro tiempo* (The Agonies of Our Time, 1926–1927), which comprises *El gran corbellino del munda* (The Great Whirlwind of Life), *Las veleidades de la fortuna* (The Caprices of Fortune), and *Los amores tardíos* (Late Loves), continues Baroja's intimate autobiographical turn. He incorporates the settings of northern Europe that he had experienced during his travels to Germany, Holland, and Denmark with Schmitz in 1926 and to France and England in the same year. The protagonist, José Larranga, has many of the traits of Fernando Ossorio and Andrés Hurtado—a reluctance for action, a penchant for reflection—with the new ingredient of a strong desire for sentimental attachment. The novels contain numerous conversations on philosophical, political, and social topics, but the conversations are fragmentary and not well integrated into the works, which have no thematic focus in any case.

Las agonías de nuestro tiempo does maintain some of the momentum of the earlier novels through interesting characterizations of the two most significant women in Larranaga's life: Nelly, a sickly German girl who eventually dies, and his cousin Pepita, who finally returns to her husband. But the autobiographical formula wears thin in Baroja's fiction of the 1930's and 1940's.

During the 1920's and 1930's Baroja also indulged in a series of novels of pure fantasy and adventure that have almost no ideological content. These works entirely miss the complex results of the Paradox novels and of *Zalacaín el aventurero,* where hybridization of the adventure tale and the novel of social or ideological concern results in works of great artistic interest. Baroja also tried his hand at a novel concerning a priest who has lost his faith, perhaps in imitation of Unamuno's highly successful *San Manuel Bueno, martir* of 1924. But the subject did not have the urgency for Baroja that it had for his Basque compatriot.

THE LAST YEARS

In 1931 the ailing Spanish monarchy was weakened to the point that the ever-growing liberal and leftist elements in Spanish politics were able to proclaim a republic. But Baroja did not think that the Republic brought anything new to the Spanish political scene; for him it offered no genuine alternative to the bourgeois vulgarity of the monarchy or to the dictatorship of Miguel Primo de Rivera, who in weak imitation of the rising Fascist dictators of other parts of Europe had dominated the monarchy from 1923 to 1930. Baroja's 1932 trilogy *La selva oscura* (The Dark Forest), which comprises *La familia de Errotuco* (The Family of Errotuco), *El calios de las tormentas* (The Cape of Storms), and *Los Visionarios* (The Visionaries), contains very negative references to the syndicalists and Communists, who increasingly gained power during the 1930's. His comparisons of nineteenth-century liberal romantic heroes to the modern, much less admirable "bourgeois" leaders of the Republic are none too subtle.

In 1934 Baroja was elected to the Royal Spanish Academy for the Language, and thus he officially joined the ranks of the bureaucratic establishment for the preservation of cultural forms. Baroja's life was laden with contradictions of this sort. For example, his virulently anti-bourgeois ideology was contradicted by his own very sedentary, work-oriented, house-bound, comfortable personal life. And Baroja was entirely aware of his contradictions, as is evident in the nostalgia and frustration present in much of his writing, especially in the works after 1910.

When the alternating leftist and rightist governments of the Republic became increasingly polarized and the army finally rebelled against the extreme leftist Popular Front in July of 1936, setting off the bloody three-year Spanish Civil War, Baroja was arrested by extreme rightists at his Basque summer home in Vera. He was promptly released, but having no traces of the love for bellicose involvement that characterized his ancestor Aviraneta and feeling no allegiance to either the Republic or the reactionary Nationalists, he went into self-imposed exile in France for the remainder of the war. He supported himself during this period by writing journal and newspaper articles. The several novels he wrote while in Paris are of scant interest because they lack real engagement with the intense Spanish situation. In 1940, with World War II making France an unsafe haven, Baroja returned to a ravaged and destroyed Spain to establish himself once again in Madrid.

Baroja's last years were spent writing his memoirs; a collection of poetry, *Canciones del suburbio* (Songs of the Suburb, 1944), his only incursion into the genre; and a few more novels that display all the signs of a tired writer no longer capable of fresh and meaningful creation. His real importance during the last sixteen years of his life was as a living legend, a remnant of the glorious Generation of '98, which was seen and continues to be seen as the best that Spanish culture has produced in the twentieth century. Of the principal writers of the Generation, only Baroja and Azorín lived on into the 1940's and 1950's under the Franco regime. Baroja received frequent visits from younger Spanish writers and from foreign novelists. John Dos Passos made several pilgrimages to Baroja's Madrid apartment, and Ernest Hemingway, who claimed that Baroja had a significant influence on his style, saw the ailing writer three weeks before he died on 30 October 1956. Hemingway was asked to be one of Baroja's pallbearers, an honor of which he considered himself unworthy.

A summary assessment of Baroja's achievement is impossible; the work is too vast and too heterogeneous. But aside from the several novels, especially of the early period, that stand out as minor masterpieces, Baroja's appreciable influence on the generation of postwar Spanish novelists should be mentioned. Those writers, including Camilo José Cela, Carmen Laforet, Miguel Delibes, Ana María Matute, Luis Martín Santos, and Juan Goytisolo, whose first vivid memories are of a Spain in conflict and who began their writing careers in the dreary, repressive, reactionary ambience of the Franco regime, found in Baroja's

terse, unrhetorical style a frank treatment of Spanish social problems and an effective incorporation of ideological issues into the narrative fabric. Thus Baroja provided a model for their own attempts to re-create in fiction their frustrations and disillusionment with the unencouraging atmosphere of their historical moment. Although the perspective of the twenty-first century may ultimately determine otherwise, at present Baroja remains Spain's foremost novelist of the twentieth century. His is the largest and most sustained body of fiction to deal in a significant way with the complexities of modern life.

Selected Bibliography

EDITIONS

INDIVIDUAL WORKS

FICTION

Vidas sombrías. Madrid, 1900.
La casa de Aizgorri. Bilbao, 1900.
Aventuras, inventos, y mixtificaciones de Silvestre Paradox. Madrid, 1901.
Idilios vascos. Madrid, 1902.
Camino de perfección. Madrid, 1902.
El mayorazgo de Labraz. Barcelona, 1903.
La busca. Madrid, 1904.
Mala hierba. Madrid, 1904.
Aurora roja. Madrid, 1904.
La feria de los discretos. Madrid, 1905.
Los últimos románticos. Madrid, 1906.
Paradox, rey. Madrid, 1906.
El buscón. Madrid, 1907.
Las tragedias grotescas. Madrid, 1907.
La dama errante. Madrid, 1908.
La ciudad de la niebla. Madrid, 1909.
Zalacaín el aventurero. Barcelona, 1909.
César o nada. Madrid, 1910.
Adiós a la bohemia. Madrid, 1911.
Las inquietudes de Shanti Andía. Madrid, 1911.
El árbol de la ciencia. Madrid, 1911.
El mundo es ansí. Madrid, 1912.
El aprendiz de conspirador. Madrid, 1913.
El escuadrón del Brigante. Madrid, 1913.
Los caminos del mundo. Madrid, 1914.
Con la pluma y con la sable. Madrid, 1915.

Los recursos de la astucia. Madrid, 1915.
La dama de Urtubi. Madrid, 1916.
La ruta del aventurero. Madrid, 1916.
La veleta de Gastizar. Madrid, 1918.
Los caudillos de 1830. Madrid, 1918.
Idilios y fantasías. Madrid, 1918.
Cuentos. Madrid, 1919.
La Isabelina. Madrid, 1919.
Los contrastes de la vida. Madrid, 1920.
La sensualidad pervertida. Madrid, 1920.
El sabor de la venganza. Madrid, 1921.
Las furias. Madrid, 1921.
La leyenda de Juan Alzate. Madrid, 1922.
El amor, el dandismo, y la intriga. Madrid, 1922.
El laberinto de las sirenas. Madrid, 1923.
Las figuras de cera. Madrid, 1924.
La nave de los locos. Madrid, 1925.
El horroroso crimen de Peñaranda del Campo. Madrid, 1926.
La casa del crimen. Madrid, 1926.
El gran torbellino del mundo. Madrid, 1926.
Las veleidades de la fortuna. Madrid, 1926.
Los amores tardíos. Madrid, 1927.
Las mascaradas sangrientas. Madrid, 1927.
Yan-Si-Pao, o la svástica de oro. Madrid, 1928.
Humano enigma. Madrid, 1928.
El capitán Mala Sombra. Madrid, 1928.
La senda dolorosa. Madrid, 1928.
Los pilotos de altura. Madrid, 1929.
El poeta y la princesa o el cabaret de la Cotorra Verde. Madrid, 1929.
El nocturno del hermano Beltrán. Zaragoza, 1929.
La estrella del capitán Chimista. Madrid, 1930.
Los confidentes audaces. Madrid, 1930.
La venta de Mirambel. Madrid, 1931.
La familia de Errotacho. Madrid, 1932.
El cabo de las tormentas. Madrid, 1932.
Los visionarios. Madrid, 1932.
Las noches del Buen Retiro. Madrid, 1934.
Crónica escandalosa. Madrid, 1935.
Desde el principio hasta el fin. Madrid, 1935.
El cura de Monleón. Madrid, 1936.
Locuras de Carnaval. Madrid, 1937.
Susana y los cazadores de moscas. San Sebastián, 1938.
Laura, o la soledad sin remedio. Buenos Aires, 1939.
El tesoro del holandés. Seville, 1939.
Los espectros del castillo. Barcelona, 1939.
Historias lejanas. Santiago, Chile, 1939.
Los impostores joviales. Madrid, 1941.

Anchoca el afilador. Madrid, 1942.
El caballero de Erlaíz. Madrid, 1943.
El estanque verde. Madrid, 1943.
El Puente de las Ánimas. Madrid, 1945.
El Hotel del Cisne. Madrid, 1946.
Los enigmáticos. Madrid, 1948.
El cantor vagabundo. Madrid, 1950.
La obsesión del misterio. Madrid, 1952.
Intermedio sentimental. Madrid, 1953.
Los amores de Antonio y Cristina. Madrid, 1953.
Los contrabandistas vascos. Madrid, 1954.
Paseos de un solitario. Madrid, 1955.

ESSAYS, MEMOIRS, AND AUTOBIOGRAPHY

El tablado de Arlequín. Valencia, 1904.
Nuevo tablado de Arlequín. Madrid, 1917.
Juventud, egolatría. Madrid, 1917.
Las horas solitarias. Madrid, 1918.
Momentum catastrophicum. Madrid, 1919.
La caverna del humorismo. Madrid, 1919.
Divagaciones sobre la cultura. Madrid, 1920.
Divagaciones apasionadas. Madrid, 1924.
Crítica arbitraria. Madrid, 1924.
Entretenimientos. Madrid, 1927.
Intermedios. Madrid, 1931.
Vitrina pintoresca. Madrid, 1935.
La formación psicológica de un escritor. Madrid, 1935.
Rapsodias. Madrid, 1936.
Ayer y hoy. Santiago, Chile, 1939.
El diablo a bajo precio. Barcelona, 1939.
Chopin y Jorge Sand, y otros ensayos. Madrid, 1941.
Pequeños ensayos. Buenos Aires, 1943.
El escritor según él y según los críticos. Madrid, 1944.
Familia, infancia, y juventud. Madrid, 1944.
Final del siglo XIX y principios del XX. Madrid, 1945.
Galería de tipos de la época. Madrid, 1947.
La intuición y el estilo. Madrid, 1948.
Reportajes. Madrid, 1948.
Bagatelas de otoño. Madrid, 1949.
Las veladas del chalet Gris. Madrid, 1952.
Aquí, Paris. Madrid, 1955.
La obra de Pablo Yarza y algunas otras cosas. Madrid, 1956.
La decadencia de la cortesía y otros ensayos. Barcelona, 1956.

PÍO BAROJA

BIOGRAPHIES AND TRAVEL BOOKS
El cura Santa Cruz y su partida. Madrid, 1918.
Aviraneta, o la vida de un conspirador. Madrid, 1931.
Juan Van Halen, el oficial aventurero. Madrid, 1933.
Siluetas románticas y otras historias de pillos y extravagantes. Madrid, 1934.
Ciudades de Italia. Madrid, 1949.
El país vasco. Barcelona, 1953.

POETRY
Canciones del suburbio. Madrid, 1944.

COLLECTED WORKS
Obras completas. 8 vols. Prologue by Azorín. Madrid, 1946–1951; 2d ed., 1978.

TRANSLATIONS

"The Abyss." Translated by W. B. Wells. In *Great Spanish Short Stories,* edited by W. B. Wells. New York, 1932.
"Angelus" and "The Unknown." In *Twentieth-Century Short Stories,* edited by S. C. Bates. New York, 1933.
Caesar or Nothing. Translated by Luis How. Philadelphia, 1983.
The City of the Discreet. Translated by Jacob S. Fassett, Jr. New York, 1917.
The Lord of Labraz. Translated by Aubrey F. G. Bell. New York, 1926.
Paradox, King. Translated by Nevill Barbour. London, 1931.
The Quest. Translated by Isaac Goldberg. New York, 1922.
Red Dawn. Translated by Isaac Goldberg. New York, 1924.
The Restlessness of Shanti Andía and Selected Stories. Translated by Anthony and Elaine Kerrigan. New York, 1962.
The Tree of Knowledge. Translated by Aubrey F. G. Bell. New York, 1974.
Weeds. Translated by Isaac Goldberg. New York, 1923.
Youth and Egolatry. Translated by Jacob F. Fassett and Frances L. Phillips. New York, 1920.

BIOGRAPHICAL AND CRITICAL STUDIES

Alarcos Llorach, Emilio. *Anatomía de "La lucha por la vida."* Madrid, 1973.
Alberich, José. *Los ingleses y otros temas de Pío Baroja.* Madrid, 1966.
Arbó, Sebastián. *Pío Baroja y su tiempo.* Barcelona, 1963.
Baeza, Fernando, ed. *Baroja y su mundo.* 2 vols. Madrid, 1961.
Barja, César. "Pío Baroja." In *Libros y autores contemporáneos.* New York, 1964.
Barrow, Leo. *Negation in Baroja: A Key to His Novelistic Creativity.* Tucson, Ariz., 1971.
Benet, Juan, et al. *Barojiana.* Madrid, 1972.
Bergasa, Francisco. *Baroja, las mujeres, y el sexo.* Madrid, 1973.
Bretz, Mary Lee. *Evolución novelística de Pío Baroja.* Madrid, 1979.
Caro Baroja, Julio. *Los Baroja (Memorias familiares).* Madrid, 1972.
Caro Baroja, Pío. *La soledad de Pío Baroja.* Mexico City, 1953.
Ciplijauskaité, Biruté. *Baroja, un estilo.* Madrid, 1972.
Corrales Egea, José. *Baroja y Francia.* Madrid, 1969.
Criado Miguel, Isabel. *Personalidad de Pío Baroja: Trasfondo psicológico de un mundo literario.* Barcelona, 1974.
Ebanks, Gerardo. *La España de Baroja.* Madrid, 1974.
Flint, Weston, and Norma Flint. *Pío Baroja: "Camino de perfección."* London, 1983.
Flores Arroyuelo, Francisco J. *Las primeras novelas de Pío Baroja.* Murcia, 1967.
——————. *Pío Baroja y la historia.* Madrid, 1972.
García Mercadal, José, ed. *Baroja en el banquillo.* 2 vols. Zaragoza, 1947–1948.
Gómez-Santos, Marino. *Baroja y su máscara.* Barcelona, 1956.
González Arrili, Bernardo. *Pío Baroja, no conformista apacible.* Santa Fe, Argentina, 1959.
González López, Emilio. *El arte narrativo de Pío Baroja: Las trilogías.* New York, 1971.
Granjel, Luis S. *Retrato de Pio Baroja.* Barcelona, 1953.
——————. *Baroja y otras figuras del '98.* Madrid, 1960.
Iglesias, Carmen. *El pensamiento de Pío Baroja.* Mexico City, 1963.
Longhurst, C. A. *Pío Baroja: "El mundo es ansí."* London, 1977.
——————. *Las novelas históricas de Pío Baroja.* Madrid, 1974.

López Estrada, Francisco. *Perspectiva sobre Pío Baroja*. Seville, 1972.

López-Marrón, José M. *Perspectivismo y estructura en Baroja*. Madrid, 1985.

Martínez Palacio, Javier, ed. *Pío Baroja*. Madrid, 1974.

Moral Ruiz, Carmen del. *La sociedad fin de siglo y Baroja*. Madrid, 1974.

Nallim, Carlos Orlando. *El problema de la novela en Pío Baroja*. Mexico City, 1964.

Patt, Beatrice. *Pío Baroja*. New York, 1971.

Pérez Ferrero, Miguel. *Pío Baroja en su rincón*. San Sebastian, 1941.

—————. *Vida de Pío Baroja*. Barcelona, 1960.

Puértolas Villanueva, Soledad. *El Madrid de "La lucha por la vida."* Madrid, 1971.

Quiñonero, Juan Pedro. *Baroja: Surrealismo, terror, y transgresión*. Madrid, 1974.

Ramsden, Herbert. *Pío Baroja: "La busca."* London, 1982.

—————. *Pío Baroja: "La busca" 1903 to "La busca" 1904*. Durham, England, 1982.

Tijeras, Eduardo. *Pío Baroja*. Madrid, 1971.

Uribe Echevarría, Juan. *Pío Baroja: Técnica, estilo, personajes*. Santiago, Chile, 1957.

ROBERTA JOHNSON

COLETTE
(1873–1954)

COLETTE IS ONE of the most prolific literary geniuses of the modern era, the author of a phenomenal number of works: novels, short stories, plays, libretti, dialogues, translations, film scripts, essays, dramatic criticism, fashion articles, book reviews, and a voluminous correspondence. She is a genius who, if we are to believe her, was not so much born as made. Recognized as one of the great stylists of the French language, she liked to insist that she did not have a true writer's vocation and that writing never came easily to her. To the contrary, she says that as a child she neither made excellent grades in composition nor felt any particular impulse to confide her thoughts, hopes, or ambitions to paper; her enchanted adolescence was free from writerly anxiety. She wrote her first book more or less accidentally and the next few practically under duress; necessity, she tells us, one day put a pen in her hand, and the pact was sealed when she received a little money in return for the pages she produced. It was Willy who started it all, just as it was Willy who initially took to calling her by her last name, the name by which posterity knows her.

Willy was her first husband, born Henry Gauthier-Villars, but better known to turn-of-the-century Paris by his pseudonym. He was thirteen years older than Colette, a man-about-town, a music critic, and a ruthless entrepreneur, somewhat sinister and pot-bellied, but unaccountably sexy and genial. He signed his name to dozens of publications produced by a stable of ghostwriters he called his "secretaries." Willy was nothing if not resourceful, spending more time orchestrating the composition of a book to which he would sign his name than he might have spent writing it himself; enamored of publicity of all kinds, he put great quantities of energy into launching his countless publications.

According to Colette, he was also parsimonious and chronically short of money, or he pretended to be. They had been married for a couple of years and she was recovering from a long illness when Willy suggested that she jot down recollections of her school days, specifying that she was not to spare the spicy parts. Perhaps he could make something of her scribblings, for as usual (it was Willy's characteristic lament) there was no money in the house. Obediently, she complied. She bought a supply of exercise books like the ones she had used at school; the ruled pages, the watermark, the red line of the margin, and the black cover with its medallion took her back in spirit to an earlier day and gave her fingers the itch to complete her assignment. Over the next few months she filled the pages with her careful writing (taking care to respect the margins). Then she handed them over to Willy. He took a look, decided they were of no use, and tossed them aside. But one September a few years later, while Willy was cleaning out his monstrous desk, he came across the forgotten notebooks. He understood then that he had been a fool to dismiss them: here was a gold mine. Willy grabbed the notebooks and his flat-brimmed hat and raced to his publisher. In March of 1900 they appeared as *Claudine à l'école* (*Claudine at School*), signed Willy. "And that," explains Colette, "is how I became a writer."

Forty thousand copies were sold in the first couple of months. Naturally, Willy wanted more, so he locked Colette in her room for several hours daily and instructed her to produce a sequel. Thus it was that the next three years saw the appearance of *Claudine à Paris* (*Claudine in Paris,* 1901), *Claudine en ménage* (*Claudine Married,* 1902), and *Claudine s'en va* (Claudine Goes Away, translated as *Claudine and Annie,* 1903), all of them signed by Willy. In 1903, when the last of the series appeared, Colette herself was thirty years old. She separated from Willy a few years later.

This is the story as Colette told it when in her sixties she published *Mes apprentissages* (*My Apprenticeships,* 1936), her account of life in the formidable shadow of Willy. It is without a doubt one of the crucial events of her life, a story that can be interpreted for what it tells us about her first experience of love, a certain kind of victimization, her initial separation from the fruits of her work, and the creation of her first literary persona and alter ego.

But like most of the stories Colette tells, there are problems with this one. She was apparently not nearly so mediocre a student as she would have us believe: according to her teacher, she was in fact always first in composition. And subsequent investigation of Willy's correspondence and those manuscripts of the Claudine series that have been preserved in the Bibliothèque Nationale has revealed evidence that is not completely consistent with Colette's account in *My Apprenticeships:* Willy's role in the creation of Claudine was more extensive than Colette chose to acknowledge. If she was Willy's victim, she was, as has been pointed out, a willing one. She spoke harshly of Willy in her later years, and indeed it is easy

to judge him severely for his unscrupulousness, his questionable values and acts—he sold the Claudine manuscripts, for example, without apparently so much as consulting his former wife—and his exploitation of her talent. But it was nonetheless Willy who intuited and nurtured that talent in the first place and whose brilliant guidance and editing helped give birth to the skilled writer she came to be. It was under his tutelage that she acquired her mastery of the craft, and for this she does not seem to have given him credit. Willy did, in any event, become part of her legend. Colette's third husband, Maurice Goudeket, tells how in 1942 he made a nostalgic visit to the house in Saint-Tropez where he and Colette had once lived. "I am Colette's husband," he told the proprietors. "Come in, Monsieur Willy," they said.

Writing about Colette's life is not easy, precisely because she herself never stopped writing about it, and her own accounts embroider on history. Her characteristic narrative is a subtle, innovative, and virtually unclassifiable mixture of autobiographical fact and fiction. The historical record of her life, then, and the uses to which she put her autobiography stand in fruitful tension. Because Colette herself made constant artistic use of the material of her own life, reviewing its patterns is essential. But it is likewise essential not to allow a profusion of biographical color, excitement, and scandal to eclipse consideration of her work as literature.

She led a life of drama, movement, audacity, intense activity, bizarre symmetries, and stunning contradictions. Mentioning a few of the latter is as good an introduction as any to her work. She dreamed of becoming a dancer and an actress, and as a young adult made good on those dreams. Nevertheless, despite her repudiation of the idea of a literary vocation, she wrote obsessively for over fifty years, while complaining that work was unhealthy for her. Her publications appeared during the entire first half of the twentieth century, the period of dada, surrealism, and existentialism, yet she kept her own literary counsel and affiliated with none of these movements. One of the great writers of what is perhaps the most philosophical of national literatures, she never had more than a rudimentary formal education, and she was fond of pointing out that she herself was no intellectual, that she had no *pensées.* Her books deal with neither politics, philosophy, history, nor religion, and indeed she always seemed uninterested in the Parisian literary and political milieu.

She was vitally attached to home, yet she lived, as one of her secretaries described it, the life of a nomad. If there is an uncanny equilibrium between her first seventeen years spent in the house where she was born and her last sixteen in the apartment where she died, between these extremes she changed Paris apartments and country residences almost as one might change winter coats. In the years of her marriage to Willy she was interested in physical culture and had a gymnasium installed in her flat, complete with parallel bars, ladder, rings, and trapeze; but a decade and a half later, she began to allow herself to become obese. The elderly Colette seems to have impressed visitors both for her genius and, like Léa in *La fin de Chéri* (*The Last of Chéri,* 1926), for her bulk. She died a stout old woman.

Colette had an exuberant love of life, a keen interest in everything human, and enormous curiosity about the vegetable and animal worlds. She loved flowers, food, butterflies, and tapestry, yet as a young woman she nearly died of an illness caused by depression. All her life she was sexually attracted to women, but she married three times for a total of some forty-eight years. With her second marriage, to Henry de Jouvenel, this woman who had danced almost nude on the stage and lived the déclassée life of a bohemian became a baroness. Her greatest attachment was to her mother, Sido, and she wrote compellingly of the maternal bond; but to her only child, Colette de Jouvenel (nicknamed, like Colette herself when she was young, "Bel Gazou"), she

was a mediocre mother. Despite the fact that she adored Sido, she did not attend her funeral, nor that of her brother Léo, nor for that matter her daughter's wedding. In 1932, at the age of nearly sixty, when she was one of France's most renowned writers, already *chevalier* of the Légion d'Honneur and something of a national monument, she scandalized observers by opening a beauty institute, manufacturing perfumes, and applying cosmetics to her clients. After her death she was accorded a state funeral, but on the grounds of her divorces and failure to take the last sacraments the Catholic church refused her a religious burial.

Born Sidonie-Gabrielle Colette, she was called "Bel Gazou" by her father and "Gabri" by other members of the family, while all her life her mother called her "Minet-Chéri." After her first marriage she was known as Colette Willy and after her second as Baroness de Jouvenel (a title that Jouvenel's former wife was also still using); by her third marriage she legally became Madame Maurice Goudeket. But from 1923 on, she signed her publications by a single name, and like many of the most consecrated authors—Molière, Voltaire, Balzac—she is known by that name alone.

LIFE

Colette began life as a robust country girl, born on 28 January 1873 in her mother's house in Saint-Sauveur-en-Puisaye, a village in the countryside of Burgundy—a house and village that her writings immortalized. In two of her autobiographical books, *La maison de Claudine* (*My Mother's House,* 1922) and *Sido* (1929), she speaks at length of her family, her birthplace, and her youth. Her father, Captain Jules Colette, was a one-legged war veteran and her mother Sidonie's second husband; he was passionately jealous of his wife. Sido was irreligious and unconventional; she took her dog to mass, and he barked during the sermon while she read Corneille behind the cover of her missal. There were four children in the household: Achille and Juliette Robineau-Duclos, by Sido's first husband, and two more by the captain, Léopold and Colette, the youngest. She grew up in a house and garden where Sido reigned, and, under her watchful, tender, and disabused eye, learned love and respect for nature. But when she was seventeen, the paradise of her youth vanished. Her elder sister Juliette had married, and her husband, Dr. Roché, demanded their share of the Robineau-Duclos inheritance. The captain, who was not a notably efficient manager, could not comply. There was a break with Juliette, and the Colette family was eventually forced to sell the house at auction and to move in with Achille, who was by then a country doctor in nearby Châtillon-Coligny.

In *My Mother's House* Colette relates Sido's fondness for books and her discriminating taste in literature, and she also tells the bizarre story of her father's literary ambitions. On the top shelf of his study was an impressive display of carefully bound and lettered volumes, bearing titles like "My Military Campaigns" and "From Village to Parliament." After his death in 1905 the family removed them from their shelf and found that only a single page was written upon, the dedication page of the first volume: "To my dearest soul, her faithful husband: Jules-Joseph Colette." The rest of his opus was no more than a hope. Colette recounts the difficulty of disposing of all the paper—sign and legacy of her father's failure; Sido gave it to her granddaughters for drawing and used it to decorate the Sunday leg of lamb. It was up to his daughter to become the writer he never was.

In fact it was her father's literary connections that determined Colette's odd fate. Relegated to the provinces as a tax collector, he had nonetheless kept in touch with a former classmate, Albert Gauthier-Villars, a Parisian publisher of scientific volumes. Gauthier-Villars's son Henry had an illegitimate son of his own, Jacques, who had been put to nurse near Châtillon-Coligny. When Henry came to visit the baby, he visited the Colette family as well—and fell in love with Colette. They married in 1893. She wrote discerningly of her wedding and of the abyss of carnal knowledge that afterward separated her from the simple village girl she had been.

Neither Colette's feelings for Willy nor her relations with him were simple. In *My Apprenticeships* she describes the simultaneous fascination and repulsion she felt for everything he represented: sophistication, experience, celebrity, corruption, Paris. It was to the Paris of the gay nineties that he took her to live, the Paris of André Gide, Marcel Proust, Émile Zola, Henri de Toulouse-Lautrec, Paul Valéry, the music hall, and the café-concert. Willy had entrée into the most important artistic, literary, and musical circles of the era, and Colette soon became intimate with members of his coterie: the actress Marguerite Moreno, who became her dearest friend and with whom she kept up a regular correspondence for decades; the poet Catulle Mendès; the writers Marcel Schwob and Paul Masson. She settled with Willy in his bachelor apartment on the Left Bank, upstairs from the offices of Gauthier-Villars. Kitchenless, gloomy, dank, and drafty, it was painted bottle green and chocolate brown and strewn with old newspapers and Willy's collection of erotic German postcards. A little later, they moved to an apartment on the rue Jacob that was scarcely more reassuring, and it was there that Colette fell ill of resentment and boredom. Sido came and nursed her back to health, and during her convalescence Colette wrote *Claudine at School.*

With its 1900 publication, things changed. Suddenly, Willy's picture was everywhere; the names Willy and Claudine became household words in Paris, and "Claudine" collars, lotions, cigarettes, perfume, and ice cream became everyday items. When a stage version of the Claudine story was created a couple of years later, the title role was given to a wasp-waisted young actress named Polaire. Willy had her and Colette dress alike, and Colette sacrificed her long tresses to match Polaire's short hair. In Paris restaurants, nightclubs, and parks Willy paternally exhibited his two "Claudines," his "twins," one on each arm, encouraging gossip about the provocative trio.

But something else was happening to Colette as well. She had begun to acquire the taste for and, as she later put it in an interview, the honor of writing. If she never had what she called an "irresistible" vocation, she was nonetheless unable to stop once she had begun. She had learned to savor, as her heroine puts it in *La vagabonde* (The Vagabond, 1911), "the voluptuousness of writing, the patient struggle with the sentence as it becomes more supple and coils itself up like a tamed animal, the motionless waiting and stalking of a word which is at last captured." For half a century more she wrote laboriously; she wrote while she danced and acted and sold cosmetics, wrote while her third husband was under arrest by the Nazis, wrote when she was sick, desolate, on vacation, or in love.

In 1904 she signed the book *Dialogues de bêtes* (*Creature Conversations*) with the name Colette Willy. With its appealing cat and dog protagonists—Kiki-la-Doucette and Toby-Chien—the volume was a success, and the following year a second edition (titled *Sept dialogues de bêtes*) was enthusiastically prefaced by the poet Francis Jammes. He called Colette "a true poet" who "sings with the voice of a pure French stream." She was, at last, a writer with a separate identity—or almost. She continued to sign her work Colette Willy until the 1923 publication of her novel *Le blé en herbe* (*The Ripening Seed*), which she signed Colette.

Her domestic life was unhappy. Colette maintains that Willy's miserliness, his infidelities, the whole sordid side of his life, eventually filled her with disgust, and she dreamed of escape. But it was Willy, in the end, who asked her to leave, precipitating their separation in 1906, when Colette moved to a ground-floor apartment on the rue de Villejust. That year marks the beginning of one of the most active periods of her life; its events are refracted in hundreds of letters written to Colette by Sido between 1905 and her death in 1912. (Colette's own letters to her mother were destroyed by Achille shortly after Sido died.)

During the years of marriage to Willy, Colette frequented Parisian lesbian milieus, and Willy himself encouraged her to write about lesbianism in the Claudine series. After the separation she became the lover and occasionally the housemate of the marquise de Belbeuf, née Mathilde de Morny, or "Missy," as she was called. Intelligent, refined, and rich, the marquise was the great-niece of Napoleon III and a transvestite. Photographs show her dressed in contemporary men's clothing—mechanic's overalls or a coat and trousers—or as a Roman emperor, a monk, or an Arab rider. Missy took lessons in mime so that she could appear onstage with Colette, and she even wrote the scenario for a pantomime entitled "Rêve d'Egypte" (Dream of Egypt). When they exchanged a passionate kiss in the 1907 Moulin Rouge production, in which Missy was cast in the male lead, it caused a tumult, and the police closed the show.

But Colette was still not emotionally free of Willy either, and she maintained contact for a while at least. After her departure Willy had set up housekeeping with a young performer who took the stage name Meg Villars (whom he also set to writing). As late as 1907, Willy, Meg, Colette, and Missy vacationed more or less together, occupying adjoining villas. Colette's choice of Missy as a successor to Willy seems to have pleased him, for Willy always liked notoriety. He was reputed to travel in train compartments reserved for "ladies only," and on one occasion when the conductor reprimanded him, he is said to have declared, "But I am the marquise de Belbeuf." Colette stayed with the marquise for almost half a dozen years, and Missy not only nursed her younger friend through hard times but also bought her a house in Brittany, which they called "Rozven." In *Le pur et l'impur* (*The Pure and the Impure*, 1941; originally published in 1932 as *Ces plaisirs* [Those Pleasures]), a long meditation on forms of love and sexuality,

Colette describes Missy as "Le Chevalière," a discreet and unhappy woman whose appearance belied her timid and sensitive nature. Later in life Missy took to calling herself the marquis de Mora; she commited suicide at the age of eighty-one.

Around the time when she moved in with Missy Colette also began her grueling stage career, going on tour throughout France as a dancer and a mime. All the while she continued publishing; and as though her dancing, acting, and novel-writing were not enough, in 1910 she started working as a journalist for a Paris newspaper, *Le matin.* Henry de Jouvenel was its editor, and he and Colette soon fell in love. Three years younger than she, Jouvenel was exceedingly handsome and enjoyed the prestige of an aristocratic heritage and the accomplishments of a talented man. In short order he had turned *Le matin* into one of the most important newspapers in Paris; in later life he became a diplomat, a senator, representative to the League of Nations, and ambassador to Rome. He had already fathered two children by two different mothers, Bertrand in 1903 and Renaud, illegitimately, in 1907. Numerous letters document the upheavals of Colette's relations with Jouvenel, structured by paroxysms of passion, quarrels, and reconciliations. In her correspondence she describes an incident in which Jouvenel's former lover (Renaud's mother, nicknamed "The Panther") in a jealous fury threatened to kill Colette—a menace that Jouvenel took seriously enough to provide protection for her. In 1912 Colette found herself pregnant by him, and they married at the end of the year, not quite three months after the death of Sido. Colette de Jouvenel was born in July 1913, when Colette was thirty-nine years old.

This marriage too was difficult. There were financial problems; Jouvenel was attractive to women and was unfaithful, as Willy had been; and Colette, who was working as a reporter and a film critic, seems to have resisted the considerable demands of her husband's political and journalistic career. Nor was the relation

enhanced by Colette's seducing her husband's shy, intellectual elder son one summer at Rozven when Bertrand was not quite seventeen years old and Colette was forty-seven. The liaison endured for several years—a situation not unlike that of Chéri and Léa in her best-known novel, although the composition of *Chéri* (1920) actually came earlier. Bertrand eventually became a distinguished conservative political theoretician of the right. He has always written and spoken tenderly of Colette (just as Willy's son Jacques has recalled fondly the woman he described as "my very seductive stepmother"), but the recollections of Bertrand's half-brother Renaud are not nearly so flattering: Renaud's interpretations of events during the years she lived with Henry de Jouvenel conflict with Bertrand's on many points. In any event, the marriage to Jouvenel lasted eleven years, a period during which Colette published much of her best work: in addition to *Chéri,* there was *L'Entrave* (*The Shackle,* 1913), *Mitsou, ou comment l'esprit vient aux filles* (*Mitsou, or How Girls Get Wise,* 1919), *The Ripening Seed,* and *My Mother's House,* a collection of exquisite sketches largely focused on Saint-Sauveur.

In 1925 she met the man with whom she spent the last three decades of her life. A businessman who dabbled in literature, he was Maurice Goudeket, born of a French mother and a Dutch father in 1889, sixteen years later than Colette. By Goudeket's account, as well as Colette's letters, they lived an idyll for the next few years, part of which were spent at her house in Saint-Tropez. With Goudeket she embarked in 1932 on her career as owner of a Paris beauty salon. The enterprise lasted long enough for them to inaugurate a branch in Saint-Tropez, but it was nonetheless short-lived; if we are to believe a few of their friends, Colette had more enthusiasm than talent for this sort of thing. She also tried to increase her income by writing subtitles for foreign films. In 1935 she and Goudeket married and sailed to New York on the maiden voyage of the *Normandie,* and a few years later, as reporters for the newspaper

Paris-soir, they traveled to Fez, where they covered the murder trial of a Moroccan prostitute. With the 1944 publication of her last work of fiction, Colette's career had come full circle: *Gigi,* a novella, is the story of an adolescent like Claudine and of her awakening to love.

Colette was elected to the Académie Goncourt in 1945, and 1948 saw the publication of the first volume of her complete works, a project on which she and Goudeket had been collaborating for some time. She was gradually immobilized by arthritis, and starting in 1950 she sought medical treatment annually in Monte Carlo. There she discovered a young British actress who she decided would be perfect in the American adaptation of *Gigi,* and in 1951 Audrey Hepburn created the role on Broadway. In her last years she received national and even worldwide homage, and her mail daily brought letters from admirers and suppliants. She enjoyed the friendship of her Palais-Royal neighbor Jean Cocteau, and in her bedroom she watched actor Jean Marais rehearse for the revival of a stage version of *Chéri.* Meanwhile her best novels, *Chéri* and *The Ripening Seed*, were turned into films. Disabled, insomniac, and in pain, she was confined to her bed, where, in the blue light of a bulb she had fitted with colored paper, she wrote for as long as she could.

On 3 August 1954, in her Palais Royal apartment on the rue de Beaujolais, she died quietly of cardiac arrest, surrounded by her husband Goudeket, Pauline Tissandier, who had been her servant for thirty years, and her daughter Colette de Jouvenel. Her state funeral—she was the first Frenchwoman ever to be honored in this way—attracted thousands to the courtyard of the Palais Royal. It was followed by a private secular burial in Père Lachaise cemetery.

WORKS

Although Colette was reticent about any explicit discussion of her feelings, her friends, or her family, she was, paradoxically, an ex-hibitionist—charming, genial, and often sad, but an extrovert all the same. In an era when the camera was not quite the household article it has become, she was photographed a great number of times, frequently semi-clad or in intimate settings. She loved to show herself on stage, sometimes topless or nearly nude, and to write scarcely disguised stories about her life and loves, sketches in which the names Sido, Willy, Bel Gazou, Achille, and Colette appear routinely. The uses to which she put her persona in her works are the most vital aspect of the discipline she acquired, of the profession she so perfectly understood. She seems to have recorded almost every event of her long life, and she never ran out of material: an encounter with a cat, a few days' residence in a provincial hotel, the recollection of her adolescent appetite for the paraphernalia of writing, a visit with a masseuse or a hat saleswoman, her feelings about passersby, an imperfection in a pane of glass—all these inspired stories. And in life she saw herself as "Colette," the greatest character in her books and one she spent all her adult years creating. Goudeket has written about his first meeting with her: she was over fifty years old, stretched out like a big cat on a sofa, lustily eating a piece of fruit. At first, he thought she was playing the part of Colette. She was an uncommonly seductive woman.

Throughout her opus traditional genres tend to metamorphose into each other so that many of her works, varied and ambiguous, fall between recognizable literary categories. Just as her autobiography takes considerable license in dealing with historical fact, so it is almost impossible to draw the line between her essays and short fiction. Colette herself is both the narrator of and a character in "Le képi" ("The Kepi," 1943), the melancholy "La dame du photographe" ("The Photographer's Missus," 1944), and the strangely haunting "La lune de pluie" ("The Rainy Moon," 1940). The anchoring of stories like these to periods of Colette's own life and the confusion of the authorial and narrative voices that distinguishes them seem to suggest that they are more autobiographical than they in fact are. At the same time works like the Claudine series and *La naissance du jour* (*Break of Day,* 1928) shade into autobiography, and *The Vagabond* and *Julie de Carneilhan* (1941), her last full-length novel, are also coded versions of her own experiences. But the relation between fiction and life was not unidirectional: just as *Chéri* anticipates Colette's affair with Bertrand de Jouvenel, *Claudine and Annie,* in which the author eliminates Claudine's "daddy-husband" Renaud, preceded by three years Colette's 1906 separation from Willy. And Claudine cut her hair before Colette. "Everything one writes happens," Colette said.

Since it is impossible to discuss her vast and varied oeuvre at length here, or even to deal properly with all her important pieces, it seems reasonable to concentrate on a few of the major novels. The best of them can be read in one or two sittings, their length typically falling somewhere between that of a novella and that of a short novel.

It all began, of course, with *Claudine at School,* a fictionalized account of some of Colette's experiences as a schoolgirl in Saint-Sauveur. The volume takes the form of the journal that Claudine, the fifteen-year-old narrator, keeps during her last year in a village school. With its eroticism, lesbianism, and cuteness it capitalized on the vogue for stories of nubile schoolgirls and schoolish pranks, although Claudine's diary is distinguished by the fact that the heroine is simultaneously sexually alert and clinically innocent, a curious combination of sensuousness, irreverence, and analytical power. In a way the originality of all of Colette's work can be found in this combination. After the first novel her books began to appear in rapid succession. The next four novels—including *La retraite sentimentale* (*The Retreat from Love,* 1907), which, despite the absence of the name from the title, continues Claudine's story—take Claudine from the village school to Paris, marriage, sophistication, disillusionment, and widowhood. In their use of Colette's and Willy's contemporaries as models of dissolution, jealousy, and homosexuality, these novels are sometimes very indiscreet, although they are doubtless less titillating now than they were in the first decade of the twentieth century. All her life, moreover, she remained faithful to the loosely autobiographical conception of literature that worked so well with *Claudine at School:* she continually exploited her own sensual experience in ways that are unusually direct, and she tirelessly memorialized the landscapes she loved.

Colette's next important work of fiction is *The Vagabond,* a transposition of the career she began in 1906 as a music-hall dancer. It examines, also in journal form, female work and independence, and, speaking more urgently than her later works to concerns of women of the late twentieth century, it anticipates what has come to be considered the feminist novel. This is a lucid portrayal of a woman alone—"une dame seule," as the heroine labels herself with bemused sarcasm, borrowing the phase that the proprietors of her apartment house use to describe the building's clientele—and the novel gives just measure to questions of female loneliness, health, money, friendship, and aging.

It is based loosely on Colette's affair with Auguste Hériot, the department store magnate who vigorously courted her, encouraged by Missy after the separation from Willy. The main characters are only barely camouflaged. Like Colette, the heroine, Renée Néré, is an ex-writer who has been divorced for several years from a man whom she initially adored, a man older than she, the portraitist Adolphe Taillandy, a "seductive and unscrupulous ruffian" and inveterate Don Juan like Willy. The recollections in Renée's journal of her marriage to Taillandy are never sustained descriptions, but the choice of details is piquant and suggestive. In conversation with her friend she attempts to explain what marriage meant to her:

No, it's not a question of betrayals, you're mistaken. It's a question of conjugal domesticity, which turns so many wives into a kind of wet nurse for adults. To be married means—how shall I put it?—to tremble for fear that Monsieur's cutlet is overdone, his mineral water insufficiently chilled, his shirt badly starched, his detachable collar limp, or his bath too hot.

(4:150)[1]

Renée nurses the wounds inflicted during eight years of marriage while earning a meager living as a music-hall dancer and mime, working in partnership with her teacher, Brague (Colette herself took lessons from and performed with the celebrated mime Georges Wague). She is disillusioned about love, which has a tendency, she says, to throw itself unexpectedly across one's path, either obstructing the way or leaving the path in ruins. She confides regularly in her old friend Hamond (in the early 1900's Léon Hamel, a kind and wise dilettante, became Colette's confidential friend) and occasionally in Margot, her former sister-in-law, who resembles the marquise de Belbeuf in her generosity and who, like Missy, has divorced and sworn off men. Maurice Chevalier recognized himself in the portrait of a singer named Cavaillon.

This volume, along with *Mitsou*, another work about a dancer's love affair, and *L'Envers du music-hall* (*Music-Hall Sidelights*, 1913), a series of vignettes that unfold against a theatrical backdrop, is a behind-the-scenes portrait of the cabaret and the life of the artiste in all its shabby splendor. Renée's journal conveys the texture, the peculiarities, and the satisfactions of that existence. Poor, tubercular, or suffering from enteritis, her colleagues are an uncomplaining lot, nimble, resourceful, thrifty, and seclusive despite their apparent promiscuity. She feels a wistful pride in her association with them.

A man erupts into Renée's life and disturbs the fragile balance of edifying hard work and weekend lunches with Hamond. Maxime Dufferein-Chautel is rich and leisured and is as

[1]All quotations are from *Oeuvres complètes de Colette*, 15 vols. (Paris, 1948–1950).

tender and direct as Taillandy was shameless. He has fallen in love while watching her night after night onstage. Renée is at first exasperated by his persistent attentions, then bored, then aroused and even jealous, but she inevitably compares him to her first husband and is continually reminded of that disastrous experience. Max's admiration makes her understand that she would relish a friend, a lover, a spectator of her life and person, but that she is afraid of once more acquiring a master. Does a new love, she asks Hamond rhetorically, destroy the memory of a first love or revive it? Gradually she gives herself over to the pleasure of loving again, but she must soon leave Max to go on a forty-day tour of music halls in the south of France. She decides that they will not become lovers until her return, and she writes to him daily. Her letters describe the theaters, hotels, and trains that punctuate her exhausting and exhilarating trip, as well as the enchanted countryside and cities through which she passes; but they gradually become letters of dissimulation, for absence, meditation, and the very act of writing modify her perspective. When Max writes that on her return she will no longer be Renée Néré but "Madame ma femme," Renée senses the threat of entrapment and alienation implied in the suppression of her name, and in the end she decides to forsake the lover who trustfully waits and whom her body craves. To a settled life in the shadow of a man, even a man as devoted as Dufferein-Chautel, she prefers the solitary life of a professional and a vagabond.

The novel describes the manifestations of masculine lust and the contours and contradictions of feminine desire. Colette excels at conveying everything undefinable, inevitable, and inexplicable about love: the surface feelings, the almost invisible reflexes, the subtlety and force of unexpected arousal. Renée understands from the moment that Max first enters her dressing room what he ultimately wants. Of her attempts to rebuff him in a lighthearted way, she notes: "He does not laugh because he desires me. He does not want what is best for me, that man, he simply wants me. . . . The ardent desire he feels for me gets in his way like a clumsy weapon. He has no interest in jokes, even dirty jokes." As she grows to like him, she still cannot forget his desire for her, which is palpable and menacing: "My admirer's slightest glance, his most proper handshake, remind me of why he is there, and what it is he hopes for." Her astute sense of detail translates her hesitation, the incompatibility of her sensual needs and intellectual doubts, her simultaneous attraction and repulsion:

> I cannot touch the fabric of his vest without a nervous little shudder, and when he speaks I instinctively turn away from his breath, even though it is healthy. I would never consent to tie his tie, and I would rather drink from Hamond's glass than from his. Why? Because . . . this fellow is *a man*. In spite of myself, I keep remembering that he is *a man*.
>
> (4:84)

But even as Renée disdains his conversation and avoids his breath and touch, she is sufficiently flattered to allow him to court her with flowers and fruit and automobile excursions and his adoring gaze, all the while feeling uncomfortably that his presence in her home is "as out of place as a piano in a kitchen."

Colette frequently uses animal imagery to convey the beast in humanity, to throw into relief qualities at once beautiful and threatening. Renée speaks of her feline feelings, while in Max's uncomplicated, obstinate adoration she identifies a canine quality. He watches her from the first row of the orchestra "like my dog Fossette when I am dressing to go out" and then follows her with "a dog's obstinacy" or turns to her with "the cumbersome friendliness of a big dog" or again looks at her with the eyes of a sheepdog. One of his first gifts is, appropriately enough, a collar for her dog, a gesture whose symbolism Renée is subtle enough to grasp. When a doe crosses their path on a walk through the woods, Renée asks whether Max, a hunter, would ever kill such a beautiful creature. One might as well kill a woman, he responds.

During the weeks when she tries to resist him, she understands the nature of her response to him: "He makes me remember, too often, that desire exists, imperious demigod, unbridled faun who cavorts around love and does not obey love; and that I am alone, healthy, still young, and rejuvenated after my long moral convalescence." With desire and all it represents, she contrasts her laboriously won peace of mind and body; but when she closes her door behind her with a sigh, she wonders whether it is "a sigh of fatigue, of relaxation, of solace, or the anguish of solitude."

Margot, Renée's former sister-in-law, is cynical like Taillandy, but benevolent, and the pension she gives Renée helps her to survive. Scornful of the institution of marriage, which she labels monstrous, Margot warns Renée away from men even as she dismally predicts the unlikelihood of her advice being followed. She raises dogs, on whom she bestows all her severe affection, and she preaches the importance of good health in animals and humans. She has taught Renée to take scrupulous care of her throat, her skin, her intestines:

> Margot and I know the price of health and the anguish of losing it. A woman can get by living alone, we get used to it; but to languish alone and feverish, to cough all through the endless night, to struggle on tottering legs as far as the rain-beaten windowpane, only to return to a crumpled, rumpled bed—alone, alone, alone!
>
> (4:63–64)

Colette writes pressingly of the nature of desire and of questions that she understands to be equally female: not just health but also money (Renée speaks of her "very female appetite for money") and aging, work, and writing. She is thirty-three-and-a-half years old—counting not just the years but also the months. At every opportunity she instinctively looks to her mirror for reassurance of her beauty, and as she becomes progressively more attached to Max, her glances toward the mirror become almost compulsive. How fast everything changes, she laments—especially women. She is frightened at the thought of growing older and losing her looks, and is fearful of the effect this would have on her handsome lover: he is, after all, "only a man." And if she declines to take him with her on her tour, it is because, despite her physical and emotional craving for him, she is persuaded that it would be folly to expose herself, over-worked, tired, traveling, unkempt, and bad-humored, to his gaze.

When she refuses him in the end, it is partly because of her fear of ultimate rejection but partly too for a more positive cause: Renée realizes the value of having her own work and a life of her own; from the start she has written almost lyrically of her pride in earning her living. (Combining marriage and a career is not an option that occurs to the heroine of a 1911 novel.) She is vaguely scandalized each time she recollects that Max has no occupa-tion, no function, but lives a life of idle com-fort, enjoying the revenues of his family's hold-ings in forestland. She decides that she must act, after all, "as if there were nothing more urgent in the world than my desire to possess with my own eyes the marvels of the earth"; she must see the world for herself, not through the reducing lens of a man's eyes. In her "poor woman's pride" she must remain as she was, "frightfully alone and free."

In 1913 there appeared a sequel to *The Vagabond* entitled *The Shackle*. By the time of its publication Colette had married Jouvenel and had given birth to their daughter. In fact, she commented humorously on the race be-tween the manuscript and the baby trying to be born. She was about to begin a more sta-tionary, more bourgeois existence, and in the novel, too, the heroine has given up her career for a life of travel and relative ease, made possible by an inheritance from Margot. When she meets a man who desires and arouses her, after some hesitation and an anguished affair Renée chooses to settle down with him, com-promising her sense of identity and indepen-dence and turning from a life of wandering to one of bondage, firmly moored to a man who is himself something of a roamer. This work is less compelling, less tightly woven, than *The Vagabond,* and the ending is more conven-tional and disappointing. Colette tried to re-write it but could not.

Like much of Colette's fiction, *Chéri,* her next major novel and the one for which she is best known, appeared in serial form before its publication as a book. It was published in 1920 but is set around 1912 against a back-ground of luxury and moral laxity, in a decor of silks, laces, pearls, and fabulous beds, where middle-aged courtesans try to preserve elu-sive charms and console themselves for amo-rous contretemps by drinking creamy hot choc-olate and eating amber grapes in bed. In this atmosphere the protagonists have little to do but make love.

At forty-nine Léonie Vallon—known as Léa de Lonval—is sumptuously beautiful—blue-eyed and long-legged—and leads a life of ordered elegance. She dresses, with the help of a maid named Rose, in tender shades of pink and judges her fruits and wines with the eye of a connoisseur and the palate of an epicure. She manages her servants with benevolent firm-ness and is quick to point out to her *maître d'hôtel* any spot of dust or sign of negligence. After a long (and, dare we say, distinguished) career as a kept woman, Léa is keeping a lover of her own. Half her age, Chéri (a character inspired, like Max in *The Vagabond,* by Au-guste Hériot) is gorgeous and is as vain and spoiled as Léa is gracious and giving. Only his wife will call him by his real name, Fred Peloux, while his nickname, Chéri, suggests the sexual ambiguity surrounding this slightly too handsome young man. His mother, another ex-courtesan named Charlotte Peloux, is Léa's friendly enemy, and they engage periodically in verbal sparring matches. Charlotte has ar-ranged his marriage of convenience to nine-teen-year-old Edmée, rich and timid daughter of still another courtesan, and neither Chéri nor Léa imagines the event as having much consequence. In the novel's opening pages the lovers discuss wedding arrangements with detachment and mockery. At the end of the first chapter Chéri leaves Léa's bedroom to meet Edmée, and Léa watches from the window as shopgirls in the street pay homage to his good looks. His departure from Paris for an extended honeymoon involves a revelation for both.

After his wedding Léa is beset by vague anxiety and chills and realizes at last the folly of having kept the same lover for six years—an "adoption," she sarcastically labels it. Practical-minded and decisive, she resolves to take a trip of her own; six months in the south, she hopes, will cure her of Chéri. When he returns to Paris to find her gone, Chéri in turn slumps into lassitude, forsaking the bedroom of his young wife and moving into a hotel with Desmond, a down-and-out friend, and frequenting bars and opium dens. He stalks Léa's street for signs of her return. When at last he sees the "electric globe of the courtyard shining like a mauve-colored moon above the lawn," the service door wide open, and light filtering through the blinds on the second floor, he is overwhelmed: " 'Ah!' he said very low, 'Is this happiness? . . . I didn't know. . . .' " It is not so much that he needs to see her right away as that he needs to know that she is there. "Exorcised," he can return to his wife.

Léa has come home, fifty years old and full of good resolutions about creating a new life without Chéri, but she is a little thinner, under stress, and a trifle fretful about what the future holds. "How good you smell!" Charlotte tells her, cattily adding, "Have you noticed that as skin becomes flabbier, perfume goes on better?" The lovers' ultimate reunion one night after a separation of more than six months is spectacular. Chéri arrives unannounced, and, hearing his footsteps on the stairs, Léa runs to powder her nose in an instinctive gesture of self-preservation. He bursts into her bedroom and throws himself at her with a kind of brutality: "I've come home!" At first she tries

to keep a cool distance, but when she realizes how much he wants her, she can hardly suppress a burst of laughter, which warns her that her rational self is about to be submerged and "that she is about to give herself up to the most terrifying joy of her life."

But the passion reborn that midnight is undone in the light of day. Léa has aged not altogether imperceptibly in the previous half year, and Chéri, with a young and beautiful wife at home, has grown up a little. In the small morning hours, after making love, he looks with a new eye at a thoroughly infatuated Léa, contemplating her "with the frightening force and fixity of a confused child or an incredulous dog. An illegible thought was being born in the depths of his eyes." But he falls asleep in her arms, and she rises early, elated, planning an elopement and in her mind drafting a letter of explanation to Edmée, calculated to cause the least pain possible. Chéri watches her surreptitiously from the bed, dissembling his wakefulness as he has never before done. Inattentive for once to her appearance, she has imprudently stood in the light of the window, and her sagging chin and wrinkled neck are clear to his critical gaze. But Léa is still blissfully unaware of this. "You came back," she tells him. "It was our destiny." And then:

> "Ah!" she added in a lower voice, "when I think of all I haven't given you, of all I haven't told you. . . . When I think that I took you for a passerby like the others, only a little more precious than the others. . . . How stupid I was, not to understand that you were my love, love itself, the love that comes only once."
>
> (4:145–146)

Half numbed and incapable of making any response, Chéri returns a dazed stare. In the devastating conversation that follows, Léa finally understands that the young man's vision of his old lover has inevitably changed: describing her role in his life, Chéri instinctively uses the past tense. Distraught, she reproaches herself for allowing "perverted mother love" to dominate her, but even in her disarray she finds the strength to comfort him and to send him back to Edmée. He leaves at the very end, and Léa's eyes move from the reflection in her long bedroom mirror—where "a panting old woman" repeats her gestures—to the window: "Chéri lifted his head toward the spring sky and the flowering chestnut trees, and . . . as he walked, filled his lungs with air, like an escapee."

Chéri covers just under a year, from June 1912 to April 1913. The main action occurs entirely in Paris and its suburbs, although the novel includes several flashbacks that allow us to grasp the characters' past: the childhood of Chéri, alternately neglected and pampered as the son of an egotistical and frivolous ex-dancer; and the beginnings of his liaison with Léa in Normandy, where she puts weight and muscle on her "naughty nursling" of nineteen, feeding him farm-grown chicken and strawberries and cream and arranging boxing lessons with an ex-lover of hers. There are also allusions to several trips, especially Chéri's honeymoon and Léa's escape to the Pyrenees. The ending returns the action to its point of departure, and the cyclical and symmetrical structure is reflected in the multiple symbolic details that expand the implications of the drama.

The most important of these include Léa's bed, mirrors, and pearls, symbols of luxury with lustrous surfaces and dreamy depths in which the play of reflections fascinates and menaces. The enormous wrought-iron and ornamental brass bed, shining "like a suit of armor," dominates Léa's bedroom; in and around it occur the novel's first and last scenes. Arena of Léa's triumphs, it is also the setting of her final defeat. Strategically located mirrors decorate the house: not only the mirror in the bedroom where she catches the glimpse of a mad old woman at the novel's end, but even a large dining-room mirror in which she can complacently watch her reflection at table. Chéri looks at mirrors, at home and in the street, at least as frequently as Léa. They si-

lently emphasize invisible change, distortion, vanity, futility, and the fragility of beauty.

Léa's pearl necklace appears in the first sentence of the novel, its forty-nine pearls representing the forty-nine years of her life. She no longer sleeps with it because the exquisite pearls fascinate Chéri, whose morning gaze she prefers not to fix on a neck that is less white and firm than it once was. "You're straining the thread," she explains as Chéri, garbed in silk pajamas and doeskin slippers, fondles the necklace. "The pearls are heavy." Léa's magnificent necklace of pearls contrasts with those of other characters: Edmée wears a "milk-white" necklace of "little pearls, very beautiful, very round, all equal," suggesting her youthful, innocent, bland, and tentative beauty. La Copine, on the other hand, an aged, opium-smoking ex-courtesan with whom Chéri attempts to forget for a while his misery during Léa's absence, wears a necklace of "big, hollow, light pearls" on which Chéri fixates. As a wedding gift, Léa proposes to buy Chéri a pearl to wear on his shirt. "A rosy one," he exclaims, but Léa retorts: "Not on your life, a white one, something masculine, if you please!"

Homes are symbolically important throughout Colette's fiction, reflecting and explaining the characters. According to Renée Néré of *The Vagabond,* her tiny apartment, which appears cosy and intimate to her admirer and in which she is almost seduced by him, in fact reeks of indifference, abandonment, impending departure, and a sense of uselessness: casually fitted with the cast-off furnishings of her marriage to Taillandy, the flat is the very image of her vagabond existence. And later, on tour, she realizes that she feels more at home and freer in a shabby hotel room than among her haunted furniture. In another paired set of novels, *Duo* (1934) and *Le toutounier* (1939), virtually all the action occurs either in and around the country residence of the heroine, Alice, in the first of the two novels, or in her sisters' Paris flat in the second; the uses the author makes of these intensely concentrated spaces, dilapidated or claustrophobic, elucidate the jealousy, antagonism, eroticism, and violence on which the stories turn.

In *Chéri* the interior scenes are set chiefly in two homes, Léa's and Charlotte's. While Léa's is a place of luxury and refinement, good taste and good cooking (she prides herself on her recipes for lobsters and dessert creams), where visual and auditory sensations, such as rose-colored curtains and clothes, the blue of her eyes, and the silky sound of her voice, all suggest comfort and warmth, Charlotte's is a house of turbulence and false economy. "Peloux's Palace," Chéri calls it sarcastically, and Léa labels it a "bazaar." It is painted hospital green and is filled with the "successive errors of [Charlotte's] preposterous taste and greed." "The house of a mad ant," one of her friends calls it. Throughout it reverberate the piercing, "trumpeting" accents of undersized Charlotte Peloux and the cackling, obsequious tones of the desiccated cronies who live off her. When Léa visits Charlotte after the wedding, the sight, sound, and touch of these "mummies" precipitate a terrible crisis for her, both moral and physical: is her attachment to Chéri as absurd as the liaison between seventy-year-old Lili, who looks like a "corseted eunuch" in sailor dress, and her mute, adolescent Italian lover? Léa stares aghast as Lili's pearl necklace plays a grotesque game of hide-and-seek, now visible, now buried in the "deep ravine" of her neck. Is all this a cruel caricature of Léa and Chéri in a few more years? Léa races home and takes to her bed shivering; she rises to pack and leave for the south, determined to give up her lover gracefully.

The novel demonstrates that despite its links with money, one-upmanship, and infidelities—the dubious values governing the marginal class to which Chéri and Léa belong—love is finally a question of something more than all of these. *Chéri* is a story that might have been vulgar but that is redeemed by the power of Colette's art, for the intelligence of her writing rivals its sensuousness. There is dignity in her portrayal of Léa, whose complicated love for her protégé, part mater-

nal, part romantic, seems neither sordid nor indecent. Colette shows us the depths of Léa's wit, humor, and loss, just as she shows us the opaqueness of Chéri's character, alternately comparing him to a hunting dog, a ram, or a jungle dweller.

La fin de Chéri (*The Last of Chéri*) was published in 1926 and modulates the sense of the conclusion of the earlier novel. If Chéri left Léa's house that spring morning surrounded by signs of renaissance while his lover interrogated the mirror image of an aged fool, in the sequel we find Léa happily installed in comfortable old age whereas Chéri founders in despair. Colette said of the two novels that they show that a love affair between a young man and an older woman is potentially more dangerous for him than for her.

Some six years separate the plots of the two novels (the chronology is imprecise), and Chéri has returned from the war. From the frightened innocent she appeared to be in *Chéri*, Edmée has turned into a self-assured woman, a little impudent and rather plebeian but with a certain poise and even a bit of social conscience. She efficiently manages their stocks, works as a hospital administrator, and has taken an American doctor as a lover. Even Charlotte Peloux has found a useful niche for herself in postwar society, and Chéri, mirthless and mopish, drifts aimlessly in a world whose values he does not recognize. In the central scene he pays a visit to his old lover, who appears in the novel only this once, and as he crosses from the dark hall into the daylight of her apartment, he expects this apparent dawn to signal the rebirth of his world. Once inside, however, he discovers not the slim and seductive being he left years earlier but an immensely stout woman in nondescript dress with cushions of flesh below her armpits, whose very bulk is the visual sign of her repudiation of sexuality. She is asexual in her size and shape, masculine in her tone of voice, and virile in her gestures, but intensely human; her startling blue eyes and rich womanly laughter link her to his former mistress.

She calls him "child" and lectures him benevolently about the "disease of his generation," the pitfalls for soldiers like him returning from war; he must resist nostalgia, disillusion, and lethargy. He finally kisses the puffy hand she extends and dizzily retreats. After the visit Chéri becomes progressively more despondent and haunts the smoky flat of La Copine, who reminisces about Léa's exploits as a beautiful young woman and entertains him in a room papered with pictures of the earlier Léa. One day he stretches himself out on the couch in La Copine's absence and, staring at all the Léas on the wall, whose downward gaze returns his own, he thinks about the war and about Léa, how, together, they have dispossessed him, expelled him from the very times in which he lives. Murmuring over and over "Nounoune," his pet name for her, he puts a revolver to his head and pulls the trigger.

The acceleration of the aging process that afflicts Léa during the war years adds to the novel's symbolic and mythical weight. This is an allegory of love and aging, a demonstration of melancholy truths. The sequel is slower, wordier than the original novel, and almost oppressive in its atmosphere of sullen despair—a volume for aficionados of Colette. But as with the first novel, this scrutiny of a single character and the tawdry trappings of his mind and existence is paradoxically a work of impressive scope, a review of the ambiguity of masculinity and femininity. Together the two novels comprise a classic study of the irresistible enticements of an old love, an astute analysis of an affair between a young man and an older woman, and a sensitive portrait of torturous middle age and cheerful old age.

Before its 1923 appearance in book form, *The Ripening Seed* was serialized in *Le matin,* but its publication in the newspaper was abruptly suspended when readers expressed outrage at the plot. Like *Chéri* it portrays a love affair between a woman and a young man half her age, but it is also a story about the sexual awakening of two adolescents, set against the sun-drenched coast of Brittany in late summer. Colette knew the area well, for she had spent the summers of 1921 and 1922 there with the three Jouvenel children. In her observations and interactions with them (including the beginning of her liaison with Bertrand) she found some of her inspiration.

The novel evokes the peculiar mingling of the carnal and the sentimental that characterizes adolescent love. The young heroine and hero, Vinca Ferret and Philippe Audebert, symbolize the purity and intransigence of youth, the joys of summer, and the mysteries of desire. They have known each other since birth, having shared each summer the villa their families rent. At sixteen and a half and fifteen and a half, respectively, "an invisible thread joins them"; their love is tender and anguished, full of awkwardness, impatience, and contradictions. But this summer a more mature lodger, a woman of about thirty named Camille Dalleray, arrives on the coast and rents a neighboring villa. Sophisticated, beautiful, acerbic, and even virile, "the lady in white," as he calls her, seduces the boy in a setting of fire and ice. On a sultry late-summer day, she invites him into the unnatural coolness of her villa, with its red and black living room full of the odor of burning incense, and startles him as she plunges her diamond-studded hand into his drink to remove the ice cube. Overwhelmed and overwrought after their first tentative encounter, he tosses her a bouquet of sea thistle—and bloodies her cheek with it. When they make love shortly thereafter, he feels as though she speaks to him "from depths where life is a terrible convulsion," and his sexual initiation seems to him a seismic event. In the hours and days that follow he trembles, faints, and cries, for the world appears a harsher place and less comprehensible. Strolling with Vinca on the day after he has first made love with Camille, he nervously winces when she nonchalantly steps on a little crab, making it crack like a hazelnut, and he becomes weak and pale when she stabs a conger eel:

He tried his best to hide a pain he did not understand. What then had he conquered the night before, in the perfumed shadows, in arms intent on making of him a victorious man? The right to suffer? The right to swoon with weakness before a child both innocent and hard? The right to tremble inexplicably, before the delicate life of the animals?

(7:316)

But his adolescent pride is strong enough for him sullenly to refuse Camille Dalleray the homage she wants: that he should act as a suppliant, grateful for her favors and eager to articulate his attachment to her. It is sex he has shared with her and not love, for Philippe remains aware that the woman who has revealed to him some perplexing truth and in whose arms he has tasted the thrills of pleasure is in fact only a stranger, a passerby. How to reconcile this with his love for Vinca? For her part, the girl intuitively grasps what has happened and simply wants to know why Philippe did not ask *her* rather than Madame Dalleray. After the latter's departure, in the last few days of summer, she gently forces Philippe to initiate her just as Madame Dalleray initiated him.

Vinca, whose name means periwinkle, has eyes whose blue rivals the sea, the sky, and spring rain: her purity imitates nature too, as do likewise her strength and endurance. On the morning after they make uneasy love for the first time, Philippe waits outside her window, trembling for the girl whom, despite all the evidence to the contrary, he persists in regarding as delicate. He imagines her inconsolable, tearful, convulsive as he was a few days earlier, and he plans to reassure her, to explain that love is of course more than a botched encounter in the grass. But when she appears at her balcony window, she has roses in her cheeks; her first act is to remove a twig from her lovely, unkempt hair, her second to water the fuchsia. And then she begins to sing. Philippe is stunned, almost devastated. Is it possible that she reacts so casually, as though nothing had happened, as though today were just like yesterday? His bitter meditation is the novel's last line: "Neither a hero nor an executioner. A little pain, a little pleasure. That's all I will have given her, that's all."

The Ripening Seed (which Colette originally intended to be a play entitled *La seuil* [*The Threshold*]) is a trenchant study of adolescence as the threshold to adulthood and of the agonizing conflicts between adolescent sexual awareness and emotional immaturity. It is also a stunning description of the sand coves, the sea, the shore wind, the thistle, the eels, the shrimp, and the peaches and melons of late August, all of which are portrayed with a conviction that makes Colette's melodic prose vibrate in primary hues of white, red, and blue. Philippe and Vinca are individualized, memorable in their beauty, their love, and their suffering, yet Colette takes pains to emphasize that they are not really special. The narrator pokes gentle fun at the predictability of their ambitions and the likely future of these thoroughly enculturated members of the bourgeoisie, who have assimilated not just the gestures but also the values of their class. Vinca's mother, well-intentioned and boring like the other adult members of the family (the narrator calls them "phantoms"), has decreed that her daughter will help out at home until her inevitable marriage. No career for her. Vinca acquiesces, obediently dresses as instructed for dinner, and dutifully mends hand-me-downs for her little sister, a carbon copy of Vinca herself. If her docility in this regard annoys Philippe, he is in fact no more original than she, for he is destined to do his military service and to go to law school or into business with his father. In fact, neither Vinca nor Philippe inspires in the reader the desire to know them ten years hence, and this is precisely how Colette must have wanted it. But that fact in no way renders the story of their adolescence less engaging or their youthful experience less affecting.

The novel demonstrates as well as any the peculiar mixtures that characterize Colette's craft: susceptibility to the sensual as well as the sentimental and an understanding of the perverse connections between them. There is a simultaneous disdain for both these areas, the conviction that they should never be allowed to interfere with a good meal or a night's sleep. Typically in Colette's fiction, the female characters understand these things far better than the silly males.

Twenty years later, in 1943, Colette published a short story called "The Kepi," which returns to the subject of the love affair between a middle-aged woman and a young man. Here Marco, a mild and mousy woman of forty-five who earns her living as a ghostwriter, answers an ad in the personals and becomes the mistress of a handsome young lieutenant of twenty-five. The experience transforms her, and in her "belated puberty" she discovers the range of sensual pleasures. She discovers too the intensely feminine concerns of dress and make-up, which she discusses with the narrator (named Colette), and she grows plump on sex. But in her gratification she forgets, like Léa, that an aging woman must always think of her appearance. One rainy day, gamboling with her lover on the divan bed, unkempt and in a crumpled chemise, she jauntily slaps the young officer's cap on her head and begins to hum a military tune for his and her own amusement. He is not amused. The playful gesture exaggerates the evidence of Marco's age, and her lieutenant stares at her with a look that she cannot understand and that she finds almost "hideous." It is, for all intents and purposes, the end of the affair.

In fact, a favorite theme of Colette is the irreconcilability, the incompatibility of men and women, the vague and persistent hostility that animates them even in moments of union—just as Philippe and Madame Dalleray or he and Vinca are worlds apart as they make love, just as Léa still wonders until the end what makes Chéri tick, and just as Marco never quite grasps the meaning of the lieutenant's "incomprehensible" look. Colette describes love and friendship between the sexes,

and yet, beneath the surface, there is a nagging lack of understanding, a strange and subtle enmity: even her good friend Hamond does not really understand Renée Néré's qualms about marriage. A collection of very short stories called *La femme cachée* (*The Other Woman*) appeared in 1924, the year of Colette's separation from Jouvenel. In the title story a young wife goes to a fancy dress ball at the Paris Opéra without telling her husband, who winds up there in disguise himself. He recognizes her in her Pierrot costume and follows her obsessively throughout the evening, determined to learn whom she has come to meet. He finds out, contrary to his expectation that her pleasure is both more innocent and more guilty. She is meeting no one; she has simply given in to the temptation of enjoying for a time "the monstrous pleasure of being alone, free, honest in her natural brutality, of being the unknown woman, forever solitary and shameless." Her disguise has paradoxically liberated her for a few hours from the necessity of role-playing.

Colette excels at showing woman's "irremediable" solitude and healthy knack for dissembling, often in stories of female rivalry. *La seconde* (*The Other One*, 1929) is the account of a wife's discovery that her playwright husband has been having an affair with his live-in secretary, Jane. That the brash and dashing Farou is unfaithful comes as no surprise to Fanny, who has tolerated with good grace his previous affairs. But this time his lover is Fanny's friend, and she is devastated at Jane's betrayal. When the wife insists that the secretary leave, Jane explains that Farou really means nothing to her; her deepest attachment to the household has always been to Fanny. The two women acknowledge then that although Farou is indispensable, the essential bond for both is the female bond. In a sobering and bittersweet conclusion they admit that men are as fundamentally contemptible as they are necessary, and they recognize the need for alliance between women. Jane will stay. How could Fanny do without her?

In other volumes Colette has written in a similar vein about the ravages of jealousy and about the resolution of rivalries. In the last pages of *The Pure and the Impure* she gives a wonderful account of the former jealousy between the narrator and a "Madame X." They hated each other, but as long as they expended an equal amount of energy on it, everything was kept in equilibrium and no harm done. Once, though, Colette got caught up in her writing and forgot her maledictions. Her antagonist, meanwhile, devoted all her leisure to wishing Colette ill, and this imbalance resulted in Colette's bronchitis, the loss of a manuscript of which she had not kept a copy, and the death of three angora cats. But in the end they became friends and regaled each other with stories of how each had once wished the other dead, or worse. This story recalls an experience Colette recounts in *My Apprenticeships,* her first discovery of Willy's infidelity a few months after her wedding. On the basis of information contained in an anonymous letter, she rushed off to the flat of a dwarflike woman named Charlotte Kinceler, and there the young wife did indeed find her husband—not in Charlotte's bed but bent with her over an account book: how like that calculating scoundrel to mix his love affairs and his business! But Colette became friends with Charlotte and visited her in her herbalist's shop until Charlotte committed suicide a few years later.

In another triangular story that appeared in 1933, the rival is a cat. The short novel called *La chatte* (*The Cat*) is one of Colette's most elegant and original. Twenty-four-year-old Alain and nineteen-year-old Camille marry. He comes from an old family whose fortune was made in the silk trade; hers, more prosperous but with shorter roots, owes its wealth to the washing-machine business. They are young, leisured, and gorgeous. Never was a couple so well matched and so ill suited to each other. Alain characteristically retreats from life, while Camille meets it head on. Red-blooded, high-spirited, and good-humored (if initially flat-chested until, like Marco in "The Kepi," sex puts a little weight on her), she is a fitting scion of a family whose money comes from the manufacture of electrical appliances, for she loves everything new and modern, and she drives their roadster fast and well. Alain, on the contrary, is dreamily attached to his past, represented by his white-haired mother, their elderly servants, and their stately old house and ample garden in Neuilly, outside of Paris. His home is one focus of Camille's mental energies. She wants eventually to rearrange the kitchen and the servants' quarters: what a lot of wasted space in the old place! Already the building is in renovation and lodgings are being prepared for the young couple. Meanwhile they set up housekeeping in a small borrowed flat in the city, located on the ninth floor of a triangular edifice of glass and chrome. If Alain feels alienated and insecure there, Camille is at ease, and within weeks it is clear to Alain that he must at all costs prevent this modern young woman from violating his ancestral home.

The symbols surrounding Alain are his bedroom, his bed, his dreams, and the sleepiness to which he continually abandons himself. Camille, on the other hand, like Léa and Vinca and so many Colette heroines, astonishes by her eyes—exorbitant, constantly alert eyes that Alain finds by turns menacing and ugly. Before the wedding he takes a pencil to his fiancée's photograph and tries to make them look smaller. Camille's sensuality follows the course of the season: it is sleepy in May, blossoms in June, grows intense in July, and becomes fatal in August. "You are like the smell of roses," her new husband rebukes her, "You take away one's appetite." Her nonchalant nudity as she walks about the bedroom on the morning after their marriage stuns and offends him, and, like Chéri after his last night of love with Léa, he watches her secretly and disapprovingly from the bed.

Between the two protagonists is Alain's beautiful and intelligent cat, Saha; while Alain is fair and Camille dark, the cat is gray. As the difficulties between the honeymooners become accentuated, Alain turns more and more to his cat. On hot July nights he leaves the nuptial bed to sleep with Saha on a sofa. One afternoon Camille and the cat are alone on the terrace of the ninth-floor apartment. The young wife succumbs to an impulse for revenge on her rival, for a chance at survival in her marriage. After a tense encounter in which she silently pursues the cat from one end of the narrow terrace to the other, she pushes her off the parapet. The cat survives, and Alain is almost glad for this excuse to divest himself of the young woman whose uninhibited appetite for food, drink, sex, and laughter intimidates him. He packs his suitcase and Saha's basket and retreats to his mother and garden.

The story is told with such subtlety that it is credible; Alain's love for his cat, his apprehensions, his anger at Camille, and the choice he makes between his two females do not really surprise. Colette cannily analyses the animal side of human nature and the quasi-humanness of animals—areas that, from *Creature Conversations* through her last writings, interested her deeply. Her women are, like Camille, healthy and practical, strong and sensual. Her men are, like Alain, a little indolent and unreasoning, a little caught up in their chimeras, a little out of tune with reality; or, like Chéri, they are weak and opaque, flaccid and indecisive, lacking the vigor, the sureness of women. Even after her attempt to get rid of the cat, Camille is eager to try to save the marriage. She comments to Alain that she should not have admitted what she did. He is shocked: "That idea does you honor," he says ironically. And Camille responds: "Oh, honor, honor. . . . It wouldn't be the first time the happiness of a couple depended on something shameful or unconfessed."

CONCLUSION

Like Camille in *The Cat*, Colette understood the uneasy alliances that exist among shame, dissimulation, and happiness; she knew that honor is a relative term, like everything else. Like Renée Néré, she understood the grace, the inconvenience, and the "clumsiness" of desire. She was not unusually pessimistic, but she was no fervent romanticist either. Her writing interests us precisely because it shades the differences between traditional opposites: the pure and the impure, heterosexuality and homosexuality, maternal and romantic love, friendship and infatuation, femininity and masculinity, sensuality and intellect. Just as she blurred literary distinctions, she refused to abide by easy classifications such as "natural" and "unnatural" and recognized instead the complexity of the human animal, which she studied with as much curiosity as respect. Hers is a sensuous, rhythmic style, rich or austere, variegated or blanched, with carefully constructed and balanced sentences and selective details. For her, preoccupations with dress, cooking, sewing, and gardening go hand in hand. Nothing human seemed to her discordant. Her endings tend to be neither happy nor unhappy.

In her essays the subject may initially seem imprecise, elusive, or nonexistent; and in her fiction neither narrator nor characters announce their concerns in clear speeches. They avoid directly addressing the larger moral or philosophic issue at hand and concentrate instead on its manifestations at the level of the quotidian. Even though they leave many things unsaid, their conversations about plants, cats, brassieres, or remedies for various ills reveal their compassion and even their identity. Their gestures, offhand remarks, questions— all these translate the depths of their feelings as well as the humanness and impurity of their motives. We discover that Colette's exquisite adolescents and middle-aged women may well be hedonistic, fierce in the determination to survive, and sagacious in their view of human nature, all at the same time. In memoirs like *L'Étoile vesper* (*The Evening Star*, 1946) and *Le fanal bleu* (*The Blue Lantern*, 1949), rich and digressive meditations that she wrote in her last years, the subject, in all its apparent diffuseness, turns out to be life itself, an effort to elucidate her own existence and her life's work.

Colette was especially interested in women's experience of love, the female element in life, and the feminine in writing. She wrote not only of love and sex but also of home and cooking, of flowers and sewing—subjects with strong feminine associations—and of words and writing. And she wrote about the female nature itself. In *The Vagabond,* Renée Néré warns:

> "She is dying of grief. . . . She died of grief. . . ." When you hear these words, shake your head with more skepticism than pity: a woman hardly ever dies of grief. She's such a solid animal, so hard to kill! You think grief gnaws at her? Not at all. Far more often, even though she was born weak and sickly, in grief she acquires hard-wearing nerves, an unbending pride, the ability to wait, to dissimulate, which makes her greater, and the disdain for those who are happy. In sufferance and dissimulation, she exercises herself and grows supple, as though from a daily routine of risky gymnastics.
>
> (4:34–35)

Colette's opus is in some ways a gloss on these lines. In the gymnastics of life her women are heroic, even if their heroism is confined, as in the case of "The Photographer's Missus," to facing the daily routine of cooking her husband's supper: "I did breast of veal with peas just last Saturday," she says; "One must not overdo it." It is the heroism of tolerance and unarticulated loyalty to some all-embracing notion of creation that distinguishes women from men, who tend to be of a frailer nature, fixated on a single idea, or incapable of functioning outside a specific sphere. The women demonstrate the capacity for healthy adjustment to life's changes, whereas Alain (*The Cat*), Chéri (*The Last of Chéri*) and Michel (*Duo*) cannot quite disentangle themselves from their past. While Philippe struggles to reconcile sex with family and nature, Vinca spontaneously perceives the links among emo-

tional and sensual needs, family loyalties, bourgeois values, and the world of crabs and shrimps—and she assimilates them all.

Colette's favorite writers were Honoré de Balzac, whom she admired all her life, and her contemporary Marcel Proust, born two years before she was. Her books have affinities with both. Like Proust she was an assiduous worker who grappled doggedly through revision after revision to find *le mot juste.* Her correspondence alludes continually to the effort writing cost her, even to the trouble she had in creating protagonists who were not herself. Like Balzac's her characters can be forcefully allegorical and larger than life, and like Balzac she used reappearing characters; not only do we meet the same protagonists in pairs of novels like *The Vagabond* and *The Shackle* or *Duo* and *Le toutounier* and in series like the Claudine books, but Sido, Willy, the narrator Colette, and other characters—Valentine, Clouk, Chéri—recur in a variety of fictional and essay forms. Like Balzac's *La comédie humaine* (*The Human Comedy,* 1842–1848) Colette's work investigates, almost as though it were a kind of natural history, representatives of a certain class, a certain time, and a certain mentality.

Her books are concerned, in the last analysis, with vision; nothing was too trivial, too dubious, or too unpleasant to merit her patient gaze. Sido, she recounts, used to whisper in almost religious accents: "Regarde!" (Look!) And Goudeket reports that this was Colette's own dying imperative. It is no accident that eyes play a central role in her writing, that they are the most visible signs of humanity and of erotic interest. Colette herself seems to have seen and known just about everything. Her astonishing accumulated wisdom characterizes her multi-volume work, including details on everything from how to dress (pink flatters aging skin), how to wear makeup, and how to choose jewels, to how to catch shrimp and eat lobsters. She understands how the acacia sheds its leaves, how dogs and cats communicate, and that raw beans make the breath smell bad. In short, she knows recipes for truffles and for life. She inventories not only flowers and vegetables but also forms of love-making, and she sharpens the focus on sizes and shapes of women's breasts.

Her work is firmly anchored in a time and place—a provincial school of the late nineteenth century, the Parisian demimonde of 1912, the music hall, café-concert, or boudoir at the turn of the century—yet it is in some senses universal in scope. Its effect may be compared to a play of mirrors—one of her chief literary metaphors—with their smooth, shiny, meretricious surfaces, their apparent distortions, and their alluring depths. The milieus she expended the energy of a lifetime describing may appear trivial and vulgar, and it is true that her characters may be either marginals or middle-class bunglers. But she forcefully associates her gigolos, courtesans, young wives, or adolescents with the spaces in which they live, and at the same time her portrayal of them transcends the conditions of their immediate existence. As restricted as individual pieces on, say, a corset maker or a playboy or a sick child may appear, they are in fact perceptive psychological studies. *L'Ingénue libertine* (*The Innocent Libertine*, 1909), an early novel that has dismayed critics who find little to redeem its explicit preoccupation with sexual fulfillment, nevertheless contains a stunning description of female orgasm, as graphic as it could possibly be without becoming pornographic, and ending with the designation "miracle" for this carnal encounter—which reconciles a sensual young woman and her pimply-faced husband. Colette knew, as Cocteau said, how to make soap bubbles out of mud. She was alive to the ephemeral, the unexpected, the intuitive—in vegetables, animals, and humans alike—and she worked miracles on men, women, and words. She was fascinated by shifting sexual differences, which unite and estrange, liberate and shackle her fictional couples, and in portraits of Claudine and Renaud, Chéri and Léa, Phil and Vinca, Farou and Fanny, Michel and Alice, or Alain and Camille, these kaleido-scopic allegiances and couplings create a dazzling play of meaning. She understood eroticism and jealousy, the anxieties of youth, the melancholy pleasures of love, and the repose and vexations of old age, and she conveyed these subtle truths in a style alternately lush and pungent.

Bibliography

EDITIONS

INDIVIDUAL WORKS

Claudine à l'école. Paris, 1900.

Claudine à Paris. Paris, 1901.

Claudine en ménage. Paris, 1902.

Claudine s'en va. Paris, 1903.

Sept dialogues de bêtes. Preface by Francis James. Paris, 1905.

La retraite sentimentale. Paris, 1907.

L'Ingénue libertine. Paris, 1909.

La vagabonde. Paris, 1911.

L'Envers du music-hall. Paris, 1913.

L'Entrave. Paris, 1913.

Mitsou, ou comment l'esprit vient aux filles. Paris, 1919.

Chéri. Paris, 1920.

La maison du Claudine. Paris, 1922.

Le blé en herbe. Paris, 1923.

La femme cachée. Paris, 1924.

La fin de Chéri. Paris, 1926.

La naissance du jour. Paris, 1928.

La seconde. Paris, 1929.

Sido. Paris, 1929.

Ces plaisirs. Paris, 1932. Reissued in 1941 as *Le pur et l'impur.*

La chatte. Paris, 1933.

Duo. Paris, 1934.

Mes apprentissages. Paris, 1936.

Le toutounier. Paris, 1939.

Chambre d'hôtel. Paris, 1940. Includes "La lune de pluie."

Julie de Carneilhan. Paris, 1941.

Le képi. Paris, 1943. Includes "Le képi."

Gigi et autres nouvelles. Lausanne, 1944. Includes "La dame du photographe."

L'Étoile vesper. Geneva, 1946.
Le fanal bleu. Paris, 1949.

COLLECTED WORKS
Oeuvres complètes de Colette. 15 vols. Paris, 1948–1950. Reissued in 16 illustrated vols., including some posthumous pieces, 1973–1976.

TRANSLATIONS

The Blue Lantern. Translated by Roger Senhouse. New York, 1963.
Break of Day. Translated by Enid McLeod. New York, 1979.
The Cat. Translated by Antonia White. In *Seven by Colette.* New York, 1955.
Chéri and The Last of Chéri. Translated by Roger Senhouse. Baltimore, 1974.
The Complete Claudine. Translated by Antonia White. New York, 1976. Includes *Claudine at School, Claudine in Paris, Claudine Married,* and *Claudine and Annie.*
Creatures Great and Small: Creature Conversations, Other Conversations, Creature Comforts. Translated by Enid McLeod. New York, 1978.
Duo and Le Toutounier. Translated by Margaret Crosland. New York, 1974.
The Evening Star. Translated by David Le Vay. London, 1973.
The Innocent Libertine. Translated by Antonia White. New York, 1978.
Julie de Carneilhan and Chance Acquaintances. Translated by Patrick Leigh Fermor. London, 1952.
Letters from Colette. Translated by Robert Phelps. New York, 1980.
Mitsou and Music-Hall Sidelights. Translated by Anne-Marie Callimachi. New York, 1957.
My Apprenticeships. Translated by Helen Beauclerk. New York, 1978.
My Mother's House and Sido. Translated by Una Vicenzo Troubridge and Enid McLeod. New York, 1979.
The Other One. Translated by Elizabeth Tait and Roger Senhouse. New York, 1960.
The Other Woman. Translated by Margaret Crosland. New York, 1975.
The Pure and the Impure. Translated by Herma Briffault. New York, 1979.
The Retreat from Love. Translated by Margaret Crosland. New York, 1980.
The Ripening Seed. Translated by Roger Senhouse and Herma Briffault. New York, 1978.
The Shackle. Translated by Antonia White. New York, 1976.
The Tender Shoot and Other Stories. Translated by Antonia White. New York, 1958. Includes "The Kepi," "The Photographer's Missus," and "The Rainy Moon."
The Vagabond. Translated by Enid McLeod. New York, 1955.

BIOGRAPHICAL AND CRITICAL STUDIES

Cottrell, Robert D. *Colette.* New York, 1974.
Crosland, Margaret. *Colette: The Difficulty of Loving.* New York, 1973.
Dormann, Geneviéve. *Amoureuse Colette.* Paris, 1984. Translated as *Colette: A Passion for Life* by David Macey and Jane Brenton. New York and London, 1985.
Eisinger, Erica, and Mari McCarty, eds. "Charting Colette." Special issue of *Women's Studies.* Vol. 8, no. 3 (1981).
———. *Colette: The Woman, the Writer.* University Park, Pa., and London, 1981.
Goudeket, Maurice. *Près de Colette.* Paris, 1956. Translated as *Close to Colette* by Enid McLeod. London, 1957.
Marks, Elaine. *Colette.* New Brunswick, N.J., 1960.
Phelps, Robert. *Belles saisons: A Colette Scrapbook.* New York, 1978.
———, ed. *Earthly Paradise: An Autobiography of Colette Drawn from Her Lifetime Writings.* New York, 1966.
Richardson, Joanna. *Colette.* New York, 1984.
Rosasco, Joan Teresa, "*Chéri,* ou le collier de Léa." *Teaching Language Through Literature* 19: 3–21 (1979).
Sarde, Michèle. *Colette, libre et entravée.* Paris, 1978. Translated by Richard Miller as *Colette Free and Fettered.* New York, 1980.
Stewart, Joan Hinde. *Colette.* Boston, 1982.

JOAN HINDE STEWART

AZORÍN
(1873–1967)

J OSÉ MARTÍNEZ RUIZ, who adopted the pseudonym Azorín in 1905, was born on 8 June 1873 in Monóvar (Alicante) Spain and died on 2 March 1967 in Madrid. His long life extended from the Bourbon restoration through the Miguel Primo de Rivera dictatorship, the Second Republic, the Spanish Civil War, and the first twenty-eight years of the Franco regime. Thus he was a witness to and often a participant in the anarchist and socialist movements of the turn of the century and, later, the conservative reaction to them. He also lived through Spain's defeat in the Spanish-American War (in which Spain lost her last overseas colonies) and through the activities of the Generation of '98—not to mention World Wars I and II, although these two great conflicts were relatively unimportant to his work. He went through several very diverse stages. Initially he was an aggressive, angry young radical, struggling mightily to establish himself as an important writer both in his copious journalistic output and in his creative writing (primarily prose fiction but also the essay and drama). He later adopted two new roles. First, as a peculiarly personalistic and often ironically skeptical commentator on Spanish society, literature, authors, regions, and towns, he wrote in a mode of subdued lyricism from 1905 on. Second, he participated in the general artistic experimentation that occurred after World War I. In literature, then, he was involved in the reaction against nine-teenth-century realism and naturalism and was deeply affected by impressionism and symbolism before becoming interested in surrealism, expressionism, and magic realism, as he understood these movements. We will see these currents in his literary production, particularly his novels, but before examining his novels closely, it is first necessary to trace the essential events of his life and to describe the major aspects of his works in general and of his journalism and drama in particular.

THE AUTHOR AND HIS WORKS

The author's father, Isidro Martínez Soriano, was a conservative and fairly well-to-do landowner in Monóvar and was the mayor of the small city. His mother was María Luisa Ruiz Maestre. His father and his brothers contributed to local newspapers and his grandfather, José Soriano García, wrote two books. Young José was first educated in Monóvar and then sent in 1881 to study for seven years as a boarding student at the Colegio de los Padres Escolapios in Yecla, which, though not distant in kilometers, was emotionally and psychologically far away from his home life in Monóvar. The harsher parts of this experience are reflected in *Las confesiones de un pequeño filósofo* (Confessions of a Little Philosopher, 1904), which describes the rigid and austere daily routine of these years, although the intellectually beneficial aspects of the experience are revealed through the fictional characters Yuste, Fray Carlos Lasalde, and others.

In 1888 his parents sent the youth to study law at the University of Valencia, and for over a decade he did everything but fulfill the requirements for a law degree (which he never obtained). He participated in all sorts of literary, political, and intellectual activities, and at various times he transferred to the universities of Granada, Salamanca, and Madrid. Taking up residence in Madrid from November 1896 on, he began his apprenticeship as a creative writer with *Bohemia: Cuentos* (Bohemian Stories, 1897). Among several interesting pieces in this collection is "Fragmentos de un diario" ("Fragments of a Diary"), a fictionalized account of the author's hunger and exhaustion and his fainting on the street (his poverty was quickly alleviated by aid from his family). This minuscule work also anticipates the more sustained piece of fiction *Diario de un enfermo* (The Diary of a Sick Man, 1901). In it the ill writer is in a state of anguish, illness, and prostration. Eventually he meets an attractive and mysterious young woman, but shortly after their marriage she dies of tuberculosis. This work, though short and sporadic, is considered the author's first novel, and for that reason it has attracted considerable critical attention. Many themes and technical features later associated with the author are seen in these two works: the emphasis on landscape and the use of impressionism to describe it, the short, highly nominal (often verbless) sentences that produce a sense of fragmentariness, the brief, elliptical dialogue, the diary technique, the use of ellipsis and associationism, and the preoccupation with time.

Even as he tried his hand at fiction, he continued his journalistic endeavors. In his heart he wanted to be a writer and an acerbic critic like his early idol "Clarín," pseudonym for Leopoldo Alas, the then highly influential novelist and critic who wrote for the prestigious Madrid newspaper *El imparcial*, which also had a renowned Monday literary supplement. Finally, after a ten-year struggle, in 1904

and 1905 he achieved his goal of becoming a contributor to major Madrid newspapers—*España, El imparcial*, and *ABC*. As he noted many times later in life, especially in chapter 4 of *Madrid* (1941), three newspapermen helped him to establish himself as a prominent journalist: Manuel Troyano of *España* and later of *ABC*, José Ortega Munilla of *El imparcial*, and Torcuato Luca de Tena, the founder of *ABC*. The association with *El imparcial* fulfilled a lifelong dream but was soon cut short, probably because of his somewhat indecorous attack on the prime minister, Francisco Romero Robledo, followed by publication of the latter's false denial of the charges of venality made by Azorín. The two articles devoted to the visit with Romero follow the five important articles commissioned by *El imparcial* in April of 1905, which were later published under the title *La Andalucía trágica* (Tragic Andalusia) in *Los pueblos, La Andalucia tragica, y otros artículos (1904–1905)* (1973). They constitute a sensitively written and conscience-shaking indictment of the shameful treatment of Andalusian farm workers, whose problems included chronic unemployment and underemployment, extremely low wages, malnutrition, tuberculosis, a very high mortality rate, total lack of communication with the landowners, and perennial governmental neglect. From 1914 on these articles have regularly been published with *Los pueblos* (Towns, 1905), a work called "one of the best books written in Spanish" by José María Valverde, who also says that it was a great success for Azorín to have combined in the same book the emotionally charged style of the Andalusian pieces with the sparse, terse, and emotionless style of *Los pueblos,* a work that lyrically evokes Castilian towns and their pasts. He adds that from this time on, when Azorín had also completed the important novel *La voluntad* (Will, 1902), Azorín as a writer was "basically complete and formed."

Azorín's growing conservatism was marked by his affiliation with *ABC* and was confirmed by his 1907 election to parliament, where he served five terms in the Conservative Party, first under Antonio Maura and later under Juan de La Cierva. There were several concurrent changes in his personal life: he became less poor; in 1908 he married Julia Guinda Urzanqui, who exerted a decisive influence on his life; and he had the leisure to travel and to record his impressions in his writings. There was hardly a topic that did not interest him, but once he recognized the finite limits of the human being's creative abilities, he became more selective and concentrated on descriptions of places, landscapes, and types as well as on sensation and memory and how they affect time and human experience. Of his marriage Kathleen M. Glenn says:

> In 1908 . . . the former critic of the institution of marriage and advocate of free love married. Julia . . . , in many ways like Azorín's mother, was the ideal companion for him. Her optimism and warmth provided a counterbalance to his pessimism and aloofness. On several occasions Azorín paid tribute to his wife's spontaneity and eternal youthfulness.
>
> (*Azorín,* pp. 19–20)

In addition to his five terms as a representative, Azorín was also undersecretary of education in 1917–1918 and in 1919.

A decade of Azorín's literary maturation was celebrated at a banquet held in his honor in Aranjuez on 23 November 1913; it was presided over by José Ortega y Gasset. The years leading to his appointment in 1924 to the Royal Spanish Academy of the Language are of special interest because his work *Un pueblecito* (A Small Town, 1916) was so successful that it inspired Ortega's essay "Azorín, o los primores de lo vulgar," by which phrase Ortega meant that "the delights of the commonplace," or the highly detailed treatment of intimate details, constituted not necessarily a defect but rather an advantage. He also established the generally held view that Azorín's art consists of retrospectively reviving man's sensitivity from ages past through the present and of showing all things as inevitably subject to death.

In addition to his Spanish journalism, Azorín began to contribute various types of articles to the Buenos Aires newspaper *La prensa;* among his topics were France and its importance during World War I and its aftermath; politics, on which he expressed some conservative and some moderate-to-liberal views; and literature. Other books written during this period include *Rivas y Larra* (1916); *Los dos Luises y otros ensayos* (The Two Luises and Other Essays, 1921)—about Fray Luis de Granada and Fray Luis de León, two renowned prose artists of the sixteenth century; and *Una hora de España entre 1560 y 1590* (*An Hour of Spain Between 1560 and 1590,* 1924), part of which he read as the acceptance speech after his unanimous election to the Royal Spanish Academy.

During this time Azorín resumed fiction-writing with the understated treatment of the Don Juan legend in *Don Juan* (1922) and with what many consider to be his fictional masterpiece, *Doña Inés* (1925). In regard to the Primo de Rivera dictatorship (1923–1930) Azorín, generally supportive of it, did take certain stands. For example, in an article published in *La prensa* in 1924, he vehemently protested the government's exiling of Miguel de Unamuno. Beginning in 1926, he took an active interest in the theater and wrote several plays that, though of limited commercial success, have attracted considerable critical attention. Finding inspiration in Maurice Maeterlinck and other symbolist playwrights, he produced three or four plays that successfully treat the age-old problems of illusion, dream, and fantasy as they conflict with reality. The first of these was *Lo invisible (Trilogía)* (The Invisible: Trilogy, 1927–1928), which Azorín said was inspired by Rainer Maria Rilke's *Die Aufzeichnung des Malte Laurids Brigge* (*The Journal of My Other Self,* 1910), though it owes much more to one-act plays by Maeterlinck such as *Les aveugles* (*The Blind,* 1896).

Three of these plays treat the invisible omnipresence of death, as is typical of literary symbolism, which often includes personifications of death, the use of ominous symbols, and the creation of an eerie atmosphere. *Angelita* (1930), Azorín's best play, shows how illusion and delusion infringe not only upon reality but also upon sanity. In this respect it is an important early example of the general *evasionista* (semi-fantastic and sentimental) theater of the time, as seen in the plays of Alejandro Casona and Miguel de Mihura. Since it also emphasizes the themes of disillusionment and renunciation, Azorín was justified in referring to it as an *auto sacramental,* a religious, allegorical play. The plot is simple. A personification of time called El Desconocido (The Stranger), who is aware of Angelita's fears and who desires to satisfy her illusions, gives her a magic ring each turn of which causes a year to elapse. She turns it twice and finds herself in a strange house, married to someone she does not know. In act 2, now living in a country house, she follows her husband's laughing suggestion that she turn the ring five times. She does so and finds herself five years later in the same place, which is now an insane asylum. One of the attendants, Brother Pablo, advises her to resolve her anguish through renunciation, charity, and the love of God. This is the path that she follows in act 3 rather than accept El Desconocido's offer of alternate lives: either to go to New York or to live as a scientist's wife and co-worker.

Another play, *Cervantes, o la casa encantada* (Cervantes, or the Haunted House, 1931), comes closest to Azorín's stated goal of surrealism because it successfully blends real and oneiric experiences. A poet named Víctor Brenes, who is ill and is obsessed with the idea of completing a work to be called "The Haunted House," visits such a house and, when given a magic potion, is led back to the time of Miguel de Cervantes. Eventually he is able to send Cervantes a fragment of his uncompleted work. The overlapping of time zones, the fusion of the real and unreal, and the inclusion of a sort of "play within a play" exemplify Azorín's artistic use of "interior du-plication," or what current theory calls "meta-theater."

During the Second Spanish Republic, Azorín's liberalism was partially rejuvenated. From 1930 to 1941 he stopped publishing in *ABC* and wrote for other papers, among them *El sol, Crisol,* and especially *Ahora,* producing several important articles on political issues, as has been documented by Valverde. Azorín continued to write for *Ahora* until the beginning of the Spanish Civil War. During the war years he went into exile in Paris, where he supported himself and his wife by means of his contributions to *La prensa,* many of them poignant stories and pieces about Spain later published in the books *Españoles en París* (Spaniards in Paris, 1939) and *Pensando en España* (Thinking of Spain, 1940). While in Paris he often saw his old friend Pío Baroja. After the war he resumed his life in Madrid and wrote six new novels and hundreds of articles, most of them for *ABC.* He received many awards and two literary prizes; these included honorary membership in several academies, the Alfonso el Sabio Gran Cruz (1955–1958), and the March Foundation 500,000 peseta Prize for Literature (1958). On 2 March 1967 he died at the age of 93; Julia died in 1974.

The centennial of his birth in 1973 led to the publication of many articles and monographs on Azorín and his works, and recent years have seen a renewal of interest, especially among foreign Hispanists but also among Spaniards interested in his early works and his important role in the history of ideas and the development of modern journalism in Spain. In addition to the earlier editions of his books and of his *Obras completas* (Complete Works, 1947–1954), there are now available many volumes of his formerly uncollected articles, although much remains to be done in editing his works and in evaluating his place in the history of Spanish letters.

To many, the key to understanding Azorín's importance in Spanish literature lies in the early years of his literary life, although of course the works that came afterward have genuine merit of their own and must be included in any study of the author that seeks to be fully comprehensive. In his struggle to express his worldview and gain recognition, the youthful Martínez Ruiz underwent several painful but predictable phases. Among his pseudonyms were "Ahriman," the name for the Persian god of evil, and "Cándido," after Voltaire's character; these and other pseudonyms and initials he designed tended to place him at one or more removes from the reality he treated. The early works reflect his interest in various related topics: anarchism as a philosophy of total independence, criminal sociology, and repeated praise of Peter Kropotkin and other reformers—see especially *La sociología criminal* (Criminal Sociology, 1899).

His interest in "the soul of Castile" is prominent in *El alma castellana (1600–1800)* (The Soul of Castile [1600–1800], 1900), a work in which he brings to fruition many of his ideas on Spain, its places, and its people—ideas to which he repeatedly returned. Primary among these topics are the following: the causes of Spain's decadence in the seventeenth century as manifested in its wars, the Inquisition, the expulsion of the Jews and Moors, and so on; the lack of a Spanish industrial revolution; the view of history as a giant web of small and apparently insignificant details (his notion of *microhistoria*); and the persons who were especially influential in the evolution of the Spanish sensibility.

Critics usually think of the cycle of novels with Antonio Azorín as their protagonist as a trilogy. These novels are *La voluntad, Antonio Azorín* (1903), and *Las confesiones.* But E. Inman Fox, unlike Valverde and most other critics, believes that the trilogy actually starts with *Diario de un enfermo* and includes *La voluntad* and *Antonio Azorín,* the last of which Fox considers to be an earlier version of *La voluntad,* although the latter was published the year before *Antonio Azorín.* Hence, from his trilogy Fox excludes *Las confesiones,* which describes the childhood schooling and adolescence of Azorín, and he includes instead *Diario de un enfermo.* The reasons adduced by Fox in support of his theory that *Antonio Azorín* was written prior to *La voluntad* are both extrinsic—the author referred to having abandoned the manuscript of *Antonio Azorín* for a long time while living on Carmen Street, where he composed *Diario de un enfermo*—and intrinsic, since situations, character types, stylistic features, and other elements in *La voluntad* are duplicated less successfully in *Antonio Azorín.* The vital struggle of the poor artist in *Diario de un enfermo* is more akin to that of the protagonist in *La voluntad* than to that of the protagonist in *Antonio Azorín.* I would add that the whimsicality and playful irony seen in *Antonio Azorín* and *Las confesiones,* absent in the earlier novels, became increasingly prominent from about 1904 on, especially after the 1905 adoption of the pseudonym Azorín, and this is his alter ego's corresponding ironic-sentimental tone in *Los pueblos, La ruta de don Quijote* (Don Quixote's Way, 1905), and other works. Still, it could be argued that *La voluntad* is a work unique to itself and that the subdued lyricism and impressionistic subjectivism that characterize the other three novels became recurrent features of the author's subsequent work.

La voluntad places a heavy charge of personal conscience and criticism on Spanish society, making it one of the most overtly rebellious of the Generation of '98 novels. Psychologically, *La voluntad* enabled the author to undergo a cathartic process that finally allowed the *hombre-reflexión* (contemplative man) to overcome the *hombre-voluntad* (strong-willed man of action). Hence it is unfair to blame him, as Carlos Blanco Aguinaga has done, for having modified his attitudes and behavior or to suggest that he committed a self-serving betrayal of the radical ideals expressed in this work. It would appear, rather, that the change from radicalism to conservatism was the result of a long, ongoing process. Certainly, after his journalistic success and marriage, a conservative and skeptical outlook process. Certainly, after his journalistic success and marriage, a conservative and skeptical outlook became a permanent part of his literary persona and enabled him to assume the role he preferred, that of the sensitive, contemplative observer, occasionally moved to initiate new and, for him, "experimental" trends in his plays, stories, and novels of the late 1920's and the 1930's, as well as in his six post–Civil War novels, written from 1942 to 1944.

The topic of Azorín as a literary critic has been the subject of several books—notably one by Fox and one by Manuel María Pérez López—and has also been treated in biographies and general studies on him, for in Azorín literature, history, towns, types, landscapes, ideas, and feelings are constantly shuffled, amalgamated, contrasted, repeated, and evoked in ever-changing but recognizable patterns. Hence, reading about Azorín involves going over a great deal of familiar terrain—the critics who treat one topic inevitably are forced to treat many related ones.

Some of the author's basic ideas on literature were set out as early as 1899 in *La evolución de la crítica* (The Evolution of Criticism). Here he more or less rejected formalist (grammatical), utilitarian, and scientific (analytical) criticism; accepted, with modifications, the major tenets of sociological criticism and of psychological criticism (especially the ideas of Hippolyte Taine); and embraced the skeptical ideas of his leading source of inspiration during these years, the French critic Marie-Jean Guyau. His only "rule" at this stage was constantly to reinterpret great writers and works in the light of contemporary views and feelings of reality; he believed that a classic should always be made relevant to us. Needless to say, these notions were later reviewed, added to, and modified greatly because of the author's extensive readings, and the influence of his peers. He was also always conscious of the need for innovation and renewal; he often said that no major writer could count on a reading public for more than ten or fifteen years because in our times the succession of literary

schools and tastes has become greatly accelerated. Thus while he was in his fifties and sixties (during the 1920's and 1930's), Azorín made rather astonishing attempts to drastically revise his own mode of creative writing, especially in the theater and in fiction. His essay style, however, remained constant.

Although several of the very early works of criticism are still worth mentioning—especially *Moratín* (1893) and *Buscapiés* (1894)—most critics concentrate on the works done from the late 1890's on, especially the "great critical tetralogy," as Pérez López has called the four collections of articles published close together: *Lecturas españolas* (Spanish Readings, 1912), *Clásicos y modernos* (Classics and Moderns, 1913), *Los valores literarios* (Literary Values, 1914) and *Al margen de los clásicos* (Marginalia on the Classics, 1915). In these works there is quite naturally a great emphasis on Spanish writers Azorín always approved of: the prose writers Juan Luis Vives, Antonio de Guevara, Diego de Saavedra Fajardo, and Cervantes; the poets Garcilaso de la Vega and Luis de Góngora; and moderns such as Mariano José de Larra. Larra was constantly praised; no other writer since Cervantes was so deeply appreciated by Azorín, not even Pérez Galdós or Alas. Among the "modern classics" only Baroja and, to a lesser degree, Unamuno (Valverde traces Azorín's ambivalent attitudes toward Unamuno) are equal to the great figure of Larra and the more remote medieval writers (Berceo and the Arcipreste de Hita mainly) and those of the Golden Age. In these works he also provides a significant treatment of the writers of the Generation of '98 and of the concept of generations. These ideas have been so influential that they have been incorporated into virtually every work on this group of writers.

In *Los valores literarios* he is especially concerned about the changes in concepts of literary groups and movements as they are opposed to new generations of readers and critics. There is emphasis also on works like Fernando de Rojas' tragicomedy *La Celestina* off this impressive assortment of essays with brilliant assessments of the "primitive poets" of the early Middle Ages, of the *Romancero* poets, and of Fray Luis de León and the mystics. Later he returned to Luis de León and Santa Teresa de Jesús; he also devoted more attention to the playwrights Lope de Vega and Calderón de la Barca, Francisco Gomez de Quevedo y Villegas and other satirists, moralists like Baltasar Gracián, and various writers of the eighteenth and nineteenth centuries. Among foreign writers he always had a predilection for the skeptic Michel Montaigne, early pessimists like Giacomo Leopardi (who was often associated with Arthur Schopenhauer), refined prose stylists like Gustave Flaubert and the Goncourt brothers, and philosophers like Friedrich Nietzsche and Guyau. The French were especially well known to him, the Italians less so, whereas his knowledge of other modern European masters seems to have come to him through the French. He did not appear to know much about German or Anglo-American literature, nor about Spanish-American literature, except for the work of Rubén Darío and a few others.

In short, though not well prepared to be a professional critic of world literature, he did make a very important contribution to the development of literary criticism in Spain, especially in his evaluation of works and their authors in relation to their physical and historical environment. He also formulated criteria—sensitivity, relativity, and understanding—that fostered a revaluation of Spanish literature in his time. This was a source of some pride, for he felt that critics of his time had views that were far too narrow and wrote in a form inaccessible to the general Spanish reading public. Thus, like Alas and a few others before him, like Ramón Pérez de Ayala and Ortega during his lifetime, and like many later followers, he helped modernize literary criticism in Spain. What he says about writers of the late nineteenth century—Galdós (generally favorable), Pardo Bazán (negative), Alas (usually favorable but with some strong reser-

vations, as Valverde has shown)—and about contemporaries such as Baroja and Gabriel Miró is also of great interest, as are his ideas on more recent trends, like the development of surrealism and of the cinema.

AZORÍN'S NOVELS AND HIS EXPERIMENTS IN THE NOVEL FORM

From his first novel, *Diario de un enfermo*, to his last, *Salvadora de Olbena* (1944), Azorín was intensely involved in experiments with the novel form. *Diario de un enfermo* itself, a study in the "aesthetic of repose" and a significant foreshadowing of future Azorínian themes, exploits a format, that of the diary, little utilized in earlier Spanish literature and not used subsequently until the appearance of Camilo José Cela's *Pabellón de reposo* (Rest Home) in 1943. *La voluntad* and *Antonio Azorín,* despite their emphasis on the themes and aims of the Generation of '98, constitute a strong reaction against the nineteenth-century novel, which was traditionally concerned with imitationalism or mimesis—that is to say, the relatively objective and true-to-life representing of events and circumstances, usually given in chronological order and providing the information needed to follow the development of the characters and to understand fully their psychological, moral, and social attitudes and preoccupations. Azorín's reaction consists first of a deliberate anti-realism, a breaking-up of that essentially explanatory-biographical method. Situations and events are presented in isolated fragments, with a great deal left unsaid about the connections among them. The method, of course, is that of impressionism. Azorín presents a series of landscapes, settings, situations, and events, which initially seem to be very insignificant, and slowly, by accretion, through the process of association, contrast, and symphonic structuring (leitmotifs and echoes), he achieves the desired effects.

Diario de un enfermo is a good example of this general procedure and of the author's

Diario de un enfermo is a good example of this general procedure and of the author's intimate mode of writing. The work consists primarily of the thoughts and feelings of the protagonist, which are interspersed with brief, evocative descriptions and a skeletonlike plot—he suffers as he writes in poverty; he marries; his wife dies; life appears to be futile. Everything is filtered through the main character's highly refined, overwrought sensibility. A case in point is the 5 March entry:

> It's snowing, snowing. . . . Thick and silent snowflakes, whirling slowly, intermittently, softly, are falling. The whole orchard is white. The white silhouette of the mountain cuts off the horizon. . . . She wanted to get up to see the landscape. She cannot stand. At the balcony, anxiously, she put her arms around my neck and I felt her thin body tremble against mine. The snowfall continued endlessly; the big flakes whirled silently. . . . She could resist no more; she was exhausted. Her eyes shone with supreme sadness. I convulsively clawed my fingernails in the wood of the chair in order not to feel her ecstatic look lose itself in the infinite whiteness.
>
> (*Obras completas*, 1:730–731)

Two weeks later his wife dies, and the last entries in the diary reflect his profound lassitude and sorrow.

The opening pages of *La voluntad* include a superb impressionistic description of Yecla at sunrise and a masterful characterization of the town and its inhabitants. The townspeople are imbued with a sense of skeptical indifference to life and with acceptance of death's inevitability. The Christian virtue of resignation is carried to perverse and destructive extremes in the case of Justina, who, influenced by her uncle, the priest Puche, will both figuratively and literally lose her life to a falsely conceived and executed plan of pious living. Antonio Azorín, her former sweetheart, is angered by her sacrifice when she enters a convent. His bitterness is intensified in long conversations with his professor and mentor, Yuste, about life versus will (the latter a destructive force in the Schopenhauerian sense) and about the relativity of all values. The general mood of passivity and pessimism is augmented by the deaths of Yuste and Justina. At the end of part 1 Antonio watches the sunset and twilight from a country farmhouse and meditates on the meaninglessness of life and reality. In part 2, after a ten-year gap, we reencounter the disillusioned iconoclast in Madrid. Part 2 begins:

> Azorín, as a result of Justina's death, abandoned the town and came to Madrid. In Madrid, his instinctive pessimism has been reinforced; his will has ended up being dispersed in this spectacle of vanities and wretchedness. He has been a revolutionary journalist and he has seen the revolutionaries in secret and profitable agreement with the exploiters. . . . Azorín . . . does not believe in anything.
>
> (*Obras completas*, 1:913)

The opening scene shows him walking along Alcalá Street near the Ventas bullring, on the road to the cemetery. He sees the futility of life as if it were a dance of death. As the people eat and dance, black and white funeral cars pass by, carrying their black and white coffins to the cemetery until at one frenzied moment pieces of meat hanging from the stalls are fused in a gruesome montage with the funeral cars and coffins:

> A black funeral coach goes by; a white funeral coach goes by. . . . The people empty glasses, devour chops, and the coffins almost rub against the tables. . . . Azorín continues. On a corner olive oil bubbles in huge frying pans and pieces of meat are sizzling. . . . In front, at the level of the enormous skinned beeves and hogs hanging from hooks on the wall, the funeral coaches pass by. And, at one moment, the black spots of the coffins stand out amid the smoke of the pans, against the bloody spots of raw meat.
>
> (*Obras completas*, 1:914)

The sense of the finality of everything is reiterated during the protagonist's visit to Toledo, especially in the scene in which a white coffin is delivered, after several wrong stops, to the home of a young girl who has died. The pessimistic worldview of the novel is seen in the protagonist's musings about life as a dance of death as he thinks of Honoré Daumier's lithograph and of the theories of Schopenhauer and Nietzsche:

"Atoms are inexorable! They carry things in incomprehensible combinations toward Nothingness; and they cause this mysterious force, called Will by Schopenhauer . . . , to be resolved in the artistic work of a genius or in a futile crime. . . . One of Daumier's famous lithographs represents the final Galop in a dance at the Opera in Paris; it is a picturesque, delirious, frenetic chaos of heads covered by unreal masks, running legs, arms in violent postures, of masks that dance in a final orgiastic spasm. . . . This dance will . . . be eternal. The Eternal Return is only the indefinite, repeated combination of the human dance."

(*Obras completas,* 1:933)

Again in the Rastro (Madrid's flea market), Antonio Azorín thinks of the dance of death analogy: "'Everything passes brutally, inexorably! . . . And all this instinctive surging forth fills me with an almost nostalgic longing! And I think of an immense Dance of Death, blind and frenetic, which toys with us and carries us to Nothingness. . . . Men die, things die. And things remind me of men.'" Additional cases of disillusionment finally compel Antonio to return to Yecla. There he encounters the energetic Iluminada, whom he later marries after returning to the Catholic Church and who assumes total control of his will, a fact that later surprises the author when he pays a visit to Antonio Azorín in Yecla and writes about the latter's abulia and general decline in letters to their mutual friend, the novelist Enrique Olaiz (who is based on Baroja).

The narrative method employed in *La voluntad* is mainly third-person narrative but also includes the use of a dramatic method (characters, dialogue, stage directions), the presentation of the third part in the fragmentary

form of Antonio Azorín's notebook (in the first-person singular), and, as epilogue, the inclusion of three fictional letters from the author to his real-life friend Baroja. In *Antonio Azorín,* as the author had promised at the end of *La voluntad,* he returns to an earlier stage in Antonio Azorín's life and treats it as if it had not ended in the quagmire of abulia and apathy seen at the conclusion of *La voluntad.* In it the narrative is also primarily third person, with the protagonist almost always as the center of consciousness but with some interspersing of the epistolary method in the third part.

The style, too, represents an open break with the traditional nineteenth-century prose style, which still had broad resemblances to the style of Cervantes and other Golden Age writers. The style, as the author himself described it later, is highly paratactic—"Poner una cosa después de otra y no mirar a los lados" (Place one thing after another and do not look aside); direct and bare—"No entretenerse; no amplificar" (Do not tarry; do not amplify); rapidly moving—"El mayor enemigo del estilo es la lentitud" (Slowness is style's worst enemy); and elliptical, involving judicious use of the associative and evocative values of words. And yet despite these rules there is an indefinable element that depends on the genius and talent of the writer—an element Azorín referred to as *movimiento,* by which he meant the essential vitalizing element, that which energizes and casts the various particles in a personal and unique form. At the same time the style partakes of symbolist qualities, especially in the use of associative techniques and leitmotifs, and of impressionistic qualities, especially in the depiction of landscapes (though one must bear in mind that these are settings seen and "painted" under a brilliant southern sun and are thus at variance with the fog, mist, and blurring of contours found among northern European impressionists).

There is a shift from the anguish and the socially critical involvement of the abulic protagonist of *La voluntad* toward a more whimsical attitude in *Antonio Azorín,* though the protagonist is still an angry young man concerned about the constant demands made upon him by his now-successful career as a journalist. Like *La voluntad,* this novel begins with a minutely detailed, impressionistic description of the landscape and then of the protagonist's house, a technique Azorín used often, as in *Doña Inés* and *Salvadora de Olbena.* The character's life is described as if *La voluntad* had never existed. First he gets rather elaborately involved in the lives of some very entertaining insects and arachnids, Ron, King, and Pic; this emphasis on the character as observant naturalist attests to the influence of works by Maeterlinck, such as *La vie des abeilles* (*The Life of the Bee,* 1901). The protagonist engages in an important correspondence with his mentor in Petrel, Pascual Verdú, whom he visits in part 2. The ascetic Verdú is contrasted with Antonio's epicurean friend Sarrió. There is an amenable interchange of rather conflicting ideals among the three friends. Eventually Antonio, though strongly attracted to Sarrió's daughter Pepita, feels compelled to go to live and work in Madrid. Part 3 comes to a rapid close as Antonio Azorín, in Madrid, has to say goodbye to Sarrió, his only link with the past.

As a novel *Antonio Azorín,* though inferior to *La voluntad,* is interesting in the modernity of its details, including the interest in the multifarious lives of insects by comparison with which our own lives become insignificant, an interest stimulated by entomology, an infant science at the time. The more serious parts again constitute a version of the novel of the intellectual hero, since they successfully recapitulate the young provincial's trials and errors, so to speak. However, the tone is much more conciliatory; this Antonio Azorín is very different from his counterpart in *La voluntad.*

In *Las confesiones de un pequeño filósofo* the ineffable and nostalgic memories of Antoñito Azorín's upbringing and harsh schooling are presented by means of an intimate first-person-singular narrative, very frequently interspersed with passages in the first-person plural and the intimate form of the second-person plural (*vosotros*), the latter indicating the readers. Here, the static and fragmentary nature of the novel becomes more pronounced than in the immediately preceding novels, as do the qualities of suggestive incompleteness and of seeking the essential in delicate nuances. Thus the overwhelming oppressiveness of death and stultification in the previous two novels is here toned down to a still-dominant but more enigmatically expressed puzzling over omnipresent death and the relentless passing of time. *Confesiones* is a series of impressionistic vignettes that treat three main blocks of the protagonist's life: (1) the early childhood years of Antoñito in Monóvar, including the experience of receiving the "special" attention of the brusque schoolmaster because he was the mayor's son as well as the perennial anxiety of being sent away to the boarding school in Yecla; (2) his harshly ascetic life in the school and the experiences among the students and the priests, including his descriptions of being wrenched from delightful pursuits like secret readings about the outer world as well as of the teacher's violence; and (3) the whimsical treatment of Antonio Azorín as an awkward and quite eccentric *señorito.* A fine example of the evocative method is chapter 9, which is both a generic and unique treatment of the school routine: early rising, mass, breakfast, study hall, classes, dinner, study hall, classes, recess, study hall, supper accompanied by edifying readings, and evening prayers. Other interesting chapters treat the idiosyncrasies of several of the priests and of fellow students and, later, of his relatives.

The short novel's qualities of suggestiveness and impressionism are enhanced by the author's adoption of a child's point of view. Witness to this fact is the simple sentence structure, with its heavy reliance on vocatives, appositives, a great variety of repetitive figures—repetition, polysyndeton, anaphora, and anadiplosis—and the abnormally frequent use of the pronoun *yo* (I). At the same time the style is sufficiently complex in the interweaving of associative and contrasting themes ("pathetic" contrast, the harsh breaking of childhood illusions, is one of the key features of the novel) and in the blending of unique and generic scenes, an effect that is achieved in part by the peculiar use of the demonstrative "this" and the adverb "now" and in part by the skillful switches from the imperfect indicative to the present and present perfect to avoid monotony and infantilism.

During approximately the next twenty years Ruiz, under the pseudonym Azorín, devoted himself primarily to word-painting of the landscapes, towns, and types of Castile in his search for the essence of Spain's former greatness. He used mainly the essay form, which nevertheless often greatly resembled the short story, especially in the evocative reconstructions of famous Spanish literary characters, whom he liked to consider in circumstances other than those given in the original: he often looked through the interstices, so to speak, seeking the essence of the character in the daily and seemingly insignificant and describing these characters after the passage of several years after the original ending or with a changed ending. The best and most fictional of these treatments are found in *Castilla* (Castile, 1912). In pieces like "Una ciudad y un balcón" (A City and a Balcony), "Las nubes" (The Clouds), "Lo fatal" (Fatality), and "Una flauta en la noche" (A Flute in the Night), which are often structured in a tripartite form, the passing of time is shown to have many effects, but not that of freeing man from his essential feature, suffering, nor that of releasing him from a gigantic and inexorable slow return or repeating of the past in the present and of the present in the future (an adaptation of Nietzsche's notion of eternal return). The progression toward more ellipsis and intimacy in the method continues, but there is also a new use of supernatural narrative devices such as a magic telescope that skips several decades of time, as well as the use of a frequently diachronic point of view, most prominently in "La catedral" (The Cathedral).

Azorín wrote two longer fictional works during this period, *Tomás Rueda* (1915) and *Don Juan*. *Tomás Rueda* was first published with the title *El licenciado Vidriera* (Vidriera the Licentiate), named after its distant model, Cervantes' exemplary tale by the same name. A very free adaptation of the earlier work, it is an evocation of what Azorín considers Cervantes to have left unsaid about his character. Thus a full third of the book treats the boy's early childhood, before the point at which Cervantes begins his story. Two students take an eleven-year-old boy whom they find by the wayside with them to the University of Salamanca. Azorín uses a self-consciously infantile narrative tone to show elliptically and suggestively the events of the story: the death of the boy's mother; the death of his father after financial difficulties; the disappearance not only of his mother's prized belongings and furnishings but also of the beloved servant Mari-Juana; and the boy's subsequent upbringing by Lorenzo, a steward of his father's farm, and by a former soldier who teaches him and inspires him with an enthusiastic interest in Flanders and Italy. But Azorín also shows the boy's profound love of silence and stillness, thus revealing the essential ambiguity that continually motivates him: the dichotomy between a life of action and one of contemplation.

Azorín's Tomás is not afflicted by the monomaniacal delusion that he is made of glass and is thus fragile, as Cervantes' Tomás is; instead he is a writer whose creative efforts are hindered by another kind of fragility, neurasthenia. The action-withdrawal theme, the struggle between activism (vital participation, as in the lives of Santa Teresa, Cervantes, and Lope) and Franciscanism (withdrawal, as in St. Francis of Assisi) that modifies the earlier paradoxical duality of Antonio Azorín as an *hombre-voluntad* and *hombre-reflexión*, is sketched out in regard to Tomás's creative efforts, his departure from Spain, and his marriage to Gabriela. The ending is left open, though it is suggested that they will go back to Spain.

Don Juan uses the theme of a reformed Don Juan to enlarge upon the activism-Franciscanism contrast found in *Tomás Rueda.* The work treats not only action versus withdrawal but also cruelty and indifference versus compassion and charity as well as rich elegance versus simple poverty. The method employed is deceptively simple: straight third-person narrative by an omniscient author who experiments only in the continued use of delicacy, ellipsis, and a kind of narrative question used to suggest, not state. Especially effective is the skillful use of carefully graded contrasts. For example, Don Juan himself, recovered from a nearly fatal illness through the intervention of the indulgent Virgin Mary, reacts against his former activism and selfishness to form a new and more precious appreciation of charity, understanding, and simplicity that leads him to total renunciation of the world and, as we see in the epilogue, to become a monk. The other characters also represent one side or the other, usually individually. Thus the characters and chapters are often grouped in contrasting pairs, a procedure that became increasingly common in Azorín's writing. One bishop, one governor, and some prominent officials and residents are severe, follow the letter of the law, and lack tolerance and compassion. But their counterparts and some other residents are blessed with the virtues of charity and understanding and thus are willing to bend the law to aid suffering human beings, especially children. Finally, Don Juan is tempted by two very different women; the coquettish and vivacious Jeannette and the discreetly sensual Sor Natividad. Acts of charity help him overcome both temptations.

There are other fundamental contrasts, too. The Castilian city reflects an essential duality from its earliest history, as in the rigid Bishop García de Illán's earlier suppression, after a long struggle, of the freedom-loving nuns. Another basic contrast is that between France and Spain, a dichotomy personified in Jeannette, who lives half the year in Paris and half in Spain. This contrast is reflected in many details chosen to emphasize the basic differences in the way of life in the two countries.

In *Doña Inés* the contrastive techniques of *Don Juan* are refined, perfected, and balanced by the use of associative techniques such as correspondences and analogical parallelism (chapters and events set in pairs). These balances and contrasts contribute to a form of stasis that is in deliberate opposition to the dynamism of the former lives of Doña Inés and Don Juan. Doña Inés, like Don Juan before her, overcomes her natural inclinations, gives up the prospect of the love of a younger person, and devotes herself to a life of renunciation (partial in her case since she does not enter a convent) and good works. Approaching the decline of her youthful beauty, she is rejected by her latest lover, Don Juan (no doubt Azorín had in mind the names of José Zorrilla's protagonists in *Don Juan Tenorio* [1844]), returns to her home in Segovia, and in a strange case of what Leon Livingstone calls "interior duplication" enacted in the form of cyclic repetition, finds herself inexorably drawn to identify herself with an ill-fated ancestress, Doña Beatriz, and with a young poet, Diego, Doña Beatriz's medieval troubadour-lover. The story of Beatriz is a colorful episode in the family history, which within the novel is being written by Inés's aged uncle Don Pablo.

Set in 1840, *Doña Inés* is in a sense an historical novel because the change from the older civilization based on Roman law, Christian ethics, and a Renaissance-derived code of behavior to the new, *Encyclopédie*-inspired and bourgeois-oriented society of the post-Enlightenment era is taking place. This historical perspective is especially important for understanding the characters and the action: if the novel were based in more recent times the climactic, sensual kiss of Inés and Diego in the cathedral would have aroused less of a scandal—a scandal that, along with her realization that Diego would inevitably tire of her, leads Inés to depart for Buenos Aires, where

AZORÍN

she establishes an orphanage. In Argentina the cyclic recurrence appears ready to begin again, this time in the person of a sensitive boy who will be a poet and will fall in love with an unattainable woman.

Contrast is seen between Inés and Plácida, a servant who is in love with Diego, and between other characters as well, especially the energetic, active, and disorderly Tía Pompilia and her lethargic and routine-enslaved husband, Tío Pablo. Pablo's character is itself based on an anguished inner dichotomy or contrast, as revealed in his creative efforts, which oscillate painfully between fertility (*plenitud*) and sterility (*sequedad*), and in the suffering he endures because his hypersensitivity and intelligence are not supported by sufficient strength. But he rejects a lobotomy like exchange of part of his intelligence for part of a simple shepherd's strength. God proposes this solution to him in a dream, saying that life in our universe is a set of contrastive equivalences and also explaining that man's world, unlike God's, and man's understanding of himself in that world are inevitably bound up in a set of polar opposites, such as matter and empty space, movement and inertia, light and shadow, life and death, unity and diversity. A great deal of Azorín's subsequent literary output is desperately preoccupied with probing into, testing, and trying somehow to go beyond the terrible restrictions of this antithetical duality. Of primary and most vital urgency is the struggle against the fatal time-death continuum in which man lives. Alleviation, escape, suspension—something must be tried.

In this novel Azorín attempts to overcome these oppositional limitations by means of a divine, relatively atemporal point of view. As Miguel Enguídanos shows, the city, its inhabitants, and their history are seen from a supraterrestrial vantage point that utilizes the accelerated passing of generations and centuries to show essential formative factors and significant changes, such as the disappearance of a formerly thriving weaving industry, depicted in chapter 9. By contrast, time is sometimes decelerated to the point that it seems to stop, as in the description of a rainy day in chapter 46. This total, multi-generational view of time is also applied to the main characters, and not only in the aforementioned cyclic recurrence but also in the so-called "Hoffmann's malady" (referring to the German writer, composer, and illustrator E. T. A. Hoffmann), which is seen slightly in Inés and especially in Tío Pablo, whose "mitigated psychosis" (neurasthenia bordering on the schizoid) is motivated primarily by his ability to see the future in the present (see Francisco Marco Merenciano's psychoanalytic study of Pablo and other Azorínian characters for an explanation of these terms). This causes him pain and relates him clearly to those who suffer the *dolorido sentir* (sorrowful feeling) in earlier works. To a lesser degree Inés also approaches abnormality in her simultaneous nearness and remoteness, an ambiguous self-offering and withdrawal that reflects her childhood and life experience and her inability to love completely. As usual, Azorín pays a great deal of attention to the nuances of feeling that are evident in these "twilight" or "in-between" states, using third-person narrative but in an indirect, symbolist manner that obliges us to re-create the characters by means of our empathic sensitivity. Thus he achieves aesthetically pleasing unity and cohesiveness in thematic, psychological, technical, and stylistic aspects.

Finally, it is noteworthy that *Doña Inés* is at once a synthesis of previous novels and a precursor of those that follow it. Azorín, drawing from his own experience as a writer, focuses our attention on the psychology and creative struggle of Tío Pablo, who needs monastic seclusion, order, and simplicity in order to write, and whose creative efforts are often painful, for he obsessively fears the menacing emptiness (*vacío*) of sterility and senility. All of these matters are emphasized in subsequent novels.

During the late 1920's and early 1930's Azorín was vitally concerned with avant-garde movements, as is apparent in his critical writings, in his plays, in which he made startling innovations in dramatic technique, and in his short stories. The most radically experimental of all his works, however, are three novels in which he suggests surrealism (without actually achieving it) by carrying his former associative, contrastive, and elliptical techniques and stylistic devices (all essentially rooted in impressionism-symbolism) to their logical extremes. He accomplishes this by adopting an infinitive- and noun-dominated "telegraphic" prose style, and by using images and themes to suggest the flow of the unconscious. In each major technique, for aesthetic reasons of his own, Azorín draws back from full-fledged surrealism. For instance, rather than free association he prefers guided associationism, which often involves symbolic correspondences or pathetic contrasts (the cosmic versus the minute, the rich and lofty versus the poor and humble); he prefers a controlled use of the unconscious and of fantastic or marvelous elements to the surrealist merging of the oneiric (the unconscious and the fantastic) and the real; and he prefers a mysterious or magical, half-whimsical, half-fateful chain of events that reveals a discernible pattern and intention to the eerie, objective chance and fantasy found in surrealism, where objects are seen as real but are incongruously associated. At the same time he uses other experimental techniques such as montage, which is not limited to surrealism, and the expressionistic technique of drawing a psychic correlation between the emotional attitude or state of the character and the represented reality, most usually manifested in distorted and fluctuating dimensions or in whirling, gyratory movement. An example of Azorín's experimental style is the narration of his character's awakening in a strange hotel room:

No se oye nada. Sopor dulce. ¿Se nota ya un hilito de luz allá enfrente? La conciencia de Félix va a la deriva. Despertar tras la penumbra entre el sueño y la vigilia. En pie. El cuadrado lumi-

noso de la ventana. Un trazo vertical de tiza blanca—el faro—y abajo un inmenso papel azul, de intenso azul, que por el borde cercano se mueve agitado por el aire: el mar.

One hears nothing. Sweet lassitude. Is a thin thread of light now noticeable out front? Félix's consciousness is drifting. To awaken after the semi-darkness between sleep and wakefulness. Standing. The luminous square of the window. A vertical streak of white chalk—the lighthouse—an immense blue paper, deeply blue, which on the nearby edge moves agitated by the air: the sea.

(*Obras completas,* 5:60)

In *El caballero inactual* (The Timeless Gentleman, 1928), originally published under the title *Félix Vargas,* the poet-protagonist immerses himself in a theme in order to make an evocative recreation of it, a dangerous creative method that threatens him with self-annihilation. His creative process so absorbs him that he loses contact with the exterior world, roaming freely in his mind from place to place and time to time, although terrible periods of sterility alternate with these moments of plenitude. If it can be said that in the works prior to *Doña Inés* history and external reality outweigh art, the contrary occurs here. Art, based on illusion and imagination, at times replaces the external world; the ordinary norms of time and place are inoperative. But the escape from time into timelessness is only temporary and partial. Félix, an extremely sensitive poet—modeled, according to Valverde and other critics, on the poet Jorge Guillén—is summering in fashionable San Sebastián. As he completes the final draft of his evocative study on the political writer and novelist Benjamin Constant and the French society wit Mme Récamier, he is upset by an urgent request to compose a portrait of Santa Teresa, a project that he eventually carries out, partly because of the fortuitous presence of an elegant, refined young married friend, Andrea. Through her he establishes the link between his two separate topics and thus is able to write the drained of the feelings necessary for creativity and prepares for his return trip to Madrid. He knows that just as Santa Teresa, the subject he is writing on, crowded out the images of Constant and eighteenth-century France, so will new themes, images, and sensations crowd out the present ones. The only hope is for new themes to keep his vital creative powers working and for the unconscious to work its associative magic.

El libro de Levante (The Book of the Levant, 1929), originally published with the title *Superrealismo* (Surrealism), is a "pre-novel," a shadowy sequential series of contrasts and associations between a simple elegance and a more refined, abstracted elegance, highlighted first by a Pirandellian confrontation (actually a self-confrontation) between the author and the protagonist and later by the meeting between the protagonist and his angel. The work proceeds conditionally with each step, as amorphous colors, lines, shapes, and concepts partially coalesce into the setting, the character, the theme, etc. The author often uses *regate,* or total erasure and backtracking. The prevailing theme is that an angel reveals to the protagonist glimpses of the "surreal" in the sense of the superhuman, that which is beyond the limits of time and space. These glimpses are seen in the cell of a monk who is writing on infallibility. This final scene follows a train trip from Madrid to the Mediterranean province of Alicante, a voyage described in detail but always in the prevailing sketchy style that, with its high proportion of infinitive phrases and enunciative, suggestive noun clauses and its tendency to omit active verbs, lends a curiously intimate, self-imperative tone to the whole novel, as if the author were addressing himself, not the reader. The brief supernatural vision granted the protagonist allows him to witness an intimate but dramatic scene in which the color white wins out over black, a symbol of good conquering evil within the monk's mind as he struggles to create and is able to create. The monk had previously been terrified by manifestations of the supernatural, but now, as he writes his book about the illuminating role of reason in even the most obscure human experiences, he finds himself forced to appeal to God (represented by the color white) to win out in his struggle against the forces of evil (represented by the color black). At dawn, light and the good prevail, indicating that instead of the surreal *beyond* the real), this work has presented the "supra-real" (*above* the real), placed in a spiritual context.

Pueblo (The People, 1930) retreats still further from the traditional novel. In it the undefined writer-observer—who uses the first-person plural to involve the reader—proceeds from a cosmic view of suffering humanity to an absolutely self-rejecting immersion in the *pueblo* (common people), whose lot in life is irrevocably to suffer. Gigantic, even cosmic, pathetic contrasts are used to drive home this point. The subtitle, "Novel of Those Who Work and Suffer," clearly indicates the main thrust of the novel as far as the content is concerned. Just as Azorín had returned to the *pueblo* in *La voluntad* after a brilliant but relatively short career in Madrid, so in this work the amorphous mass of the *pueblo* comes to dominate the unnamed protagonist, who had uselessly sought to rise above this group but now has to submerge himself in their prosaic, poverty-stricken state. As readers, we are brought to the most obscure and self-effacing level and made to share in the recognition of the people's deep spiritual values (love, humility, and resignation) and of their simple, humble ways of life. After several curious interludes that highlight the social criticism latent in this work, a dream-epilogue reveals that the *pueblo* in its blind will to live is to be consumed by the exhaustive force of intelligence. Intelligence feeds on will; self-analysis paralyzes instinct. Hence, what is left is the exhaustion of will and, ultimately, the demise of the human race.

Pueblo marked the end of a trajectory; after writing it Azorín changed perspective, emphasis, style, and method, but not the basic themes, which continue to be the same though treated with different nuances. This change is revealed in the series of novels initiated by *El escritor* (The Writer, 1942), completed after an interval in which Azorín wrote mainly articles and short stories.

El escritor begins ex nihilo, as if the author-narrator were only conditionally writing a novel, as is the case in *El libro de Levante.* The narrator's initial preoccupation is whether to write about a novelist who is young and virile or one who is old, contemplative, and uncertain. This decision quickly resolves itself in a form of *desdoblamiento,* or splitting of the self, in which the "I" of the novel is converted into the latter type of character and is given the name Antonio Quiroga, and in which Quiroga chooses to write about a young writer, Carlos Dávila, despite Quiroga's initial mistrust of and antipathy toward Dávila. Azorín's topic, in turn, is the writer as embodied in these two figures. The situation is further complicated by the fact that Quiroga is modeled on Azorín himself, being of his same age and a member of the Generation of '98. The first two-thirds of the novel treat the delicately described problem of sincerity, so difficult to attain; Quiroga's inability or unwillingness to understand the younger generation; and his indifference and envy, which yield to an initially begrudging and later genuine admiration for the young novelist and his fiancée, Magdalena. The last thing written by Quiroga in the main narrative is a description of Magdalena's house as he imagines it, which he prefers to her description of it as it really is. Quiroga's earlier trend toward daydreaming (*ensoñación*) and withdrawal from physical reality (*desasimiento de las cosas*) is continued. Imagination, illusion, and art prevail over reality, except in two closely related, anguished aspects: Quiroga's fear of sterility and his obsession with inexorable time.

Then there is a sudden break in the narrative, and Carlos Dávila assumes the narrator's role in order to complete these annals left unfinished by Quiroga. At this point three years, the Civil War years, have passed, during which Quiroga has lived in self-imposed exile in Paris and Dávila has led a very active life as an officer of the Spanish army. Dávila is at the peak of his powers and popularity whereas Quiroga is out of favor and very poor. Even Dávila, who rather indifferently befriends Quiroga, considers him a relic of the past who suffers from the strange malady of having lost the sense of value relationships among things and of spending his time dreaming but without believing in his dreams, that is, using illusion-art as a consolation, not a refutation of the time-death continuum.

This situation is enigmatic to Dávila until he undergoes a conversion to another kind of heroism, saintly activity, and repents of his self-centeredness. With the aid of his wife he uses his fortune to build a hospital and give poor people needed medical service, though not before having had an experience with a younger novelist that is similar to the earlier one between Quiroga and himself in that it causes him to feel unsure of his creative powers, to feel distrustful, and so on. Again we see the "eternal return" and the action-withdrawal theme but this time with an ending like that of Azorín's play *Angelita,* in which service to others is the solution.

This novel is presented in a nuanced and enigmatic way that, however, is somewhat more traditional and more reminiscent of *Doña Inés* than of the intervening novels. The basic technique is again that of contrast. The style employs adjectives to greater advantage; nominal phrases and main infinitive clauses are very seldom used; and the active verbs are sometimes placed in the future and conditional tenses (especially at the beginning) in order to suggest the conjectural and the hypothetical—chapter 2, for example, is called "Pudiera ser" (It Might Be). Azorín used this last style feature even more in later novels.

Like *El escritor, El enfermo* (The Sick Man, 1943) has as its protagonist an elderly, autobiographically derived writer concerned about his capacity to create in the face of sterility and senility, but here the psychological treatment is much more detailed and more profound. Víctor Albert, who is seventy and has been writing for fifty years, has become accustomed to a rigorous routine that allows him to work six hours daily, from two A.M. to eight A.M., in the strictest seclusion and silence (such were Azorín's work habits during his later years). Only as a result of two conditions, tenuousness (*tenuidad*) and muffling (*amortiguamiento*) can he keep out distractive elements and capture and express the finest shades of meaning and feeling. It is in the dawn and the similar twilight hours that he feels most authentically himself; he finds the rest of the day almost intolerably crude and abrasive, and during this period his sense of identity weakens. Sleep both restores him and allows his unconscious to make its indispensable preparations for his creative writing, in which there is always a semi-autonomous, superhuman element. The twin qualities of tenuousness and muffling also reflect, in a larger sense, his attitude toward life: fixed habits and conditions, a devoted wife and select friends, and even the sedatives he takes keep the harsh and swiftly impending realities—sterility, senility, and death—at bay.

As a writer Víctor is vitally concerned with his creative process and with the basic problems of "dosage" or proportioning (of the spiritual and the concrete), distancing, and elimination or selection. He is a compulsive writer who finds that the satisfaction that comes from having written is the best alleviation of the real or imaginary pains that he feels while writing. The work in progress during the course of this novel is Víctor's novel about a sick man, another case of interior duplication. This topic involves Víctor in background readings by famous pathologists such as Richard Bright, the founder of modern theories on nephritis, or Bright's disease, and G. M. Beard, who invented the term "neurasthenia" to describe neurotic depression. He feels symptoms described by them, talks about them to his doctors, and allows them to dominate his

everyday reality. Simultaneously his own illness progresses from a kind of mitigated psychosis involving elements of hypochondria, neurasthenia, and depersonalization to brief amnesiac periods, the unreal fusing of the three local doctors (who attend him successively) into one, and a final state of partial ataxia (the inability to coordinate bodily movements), which he had so greatly feared. And yet these symptoms are kept sufficiently muted and under control for Víctor to continue functioning as a writer until near the end, when the novelistic-psychological theme is united to the illness theme and Víctor is overcome by lethargy and prostration. The next and concluding chapter presents Víctor and his wife taking leave of El Sirerer (The Cherry Orchard), an old family estate and country house that they must now give up forever. Why, we are not told, but most likely they must leave for reasons of money, health, and old age. The tone is elegiac, and the atmosphere is one of preparation for death.

El enfermo is one of Azorín's most tightly written novels. The main character is almost constantly present, and everything moves swiftly and dramatically to the ending. The secondary characters and events serve to highlight the main action and to show the mysterious uniqueness of each man and his destiny, whether he be sick or well. The style is perhaps the purest and most precise in Azorín's novels, with an absolute minimum of description of the Alicante setting and with much more dialogue than usual. The nuances and "in-between" states are remarkably well captured. Instants of time that would go unnoticed by many take on great importance, as in the "threshold scene" in which Víctor is on the verge of beginning creation anew as night draws to a close.

Just as *El escritor* and *El enfermo* are closely related stylistically and thematically in their treatment of the problems of creative writing, psychology, and macrobiotics—first seen in Tío Pablo and thus representing a link between *Doña Inés* and *Salvadora de Olbena*—so are the next two novels, *Capricho* (Caprice, 1943) and *La isla sin aurora* (The Island Without Dawn, 1944), related. They share a marked conditionality or potentiality, *Capricho* in its narrative method, which utilizes provisional or tentative thematic material (as in *El libro de Levante*) viewed from multiple perspectives, and *La isla sin aurora* in both method and style.

Azorín's prologue states that *Capricho* intends to be what its title indicates: a capricious, whimsical playing with plot, characters, and, occasionally, certain words. He explains that in this venture the authorial narrator will play the role of Cervantes in *Don Quijote,* that of the omniscient, God-like author, free to intervene at any moment to add his semi-corrective but seldom serious comments to what is said about or by the characters. The frame and subject of the novel are as follows. A story, "El problema" (The Problem), initiates the novel. In the story a millionaire drawn toward a life of simplicity and abnegation leaves a million pesetas in a small country house whose poor inhabitants are temporarily absent. The rich man leaves, and here the story ends. Its author, employed by a newspaper, narrates in the first person how he wished to leave the tale with an open, suggestive ending, but his editor rejected it because it lacked real, concrete details. The editor decided to appeal to various writers and employees of the paper for a satisfactory ending. (Thus we are already involved in a "caprice," a highly unlikely sort of situation fertile in possibilities for whimsy.) The author-narrator is then submerged within Azorín's omniscient third-person narration, which serves to present the problem and to characterize, chapter by chapter, each man whose opinion will be requested. Each is portrayed as living in illusion, no matter how pragmatic and realistic he thinks he is. The author-narrator's comments and reservations are given at the end of most of the chapters, and he is allowed to reappear after the editor suggests the writing of a novel in which his employees will be the characters and will propose a solution to the original

"problem" or story. (The characteristics of interior duplication or metafiction become increasingly complex here, causing the whole work to take on the quality of a kind of "riddle-novel." Then the author-narrator dedicates the following self-portraits of four beautiful women to the poet, who he had earlier confessed was himself.

The above constitutes part 1. In part 2 the author-narrator exhorts his characters, in a Pirandellian tone, to visit the house in which the millionaire left the money, telling each one to state his truth. God-like, he offers them space and time (future, present, or past) to enable them to arrive at a solution. There follow the characters' various solutions, without authorial commentary, each presented chapter by chapter in what José Carlos Mainer aptly calls a "chapter-interview" technique, and each revealing the personality of the character in question. Finally, Azorín addresses his author-character and tells him that nothing happened, that the millionaire changed his mind, gathered his money, and left, not realizing his caprice, and that the author must now take leave of his characters and of his habit of writing at early dawn.

In the third part, called "Addition," the fictional author contradicts Azorín. Mentioning that he has been reading Lucian of Samosata, the second-century Greek satirist, he says that the problem of literary influences is extremely complex and that literary characters do have an existence beyond the work for which they were created. To prove his point he calls forth (as Lucian had done in such festive, bantering works as "Dialogues of the Gods" and "Dialogues of the Dead") famous literary characters—the impoverished squire of *Lazarillo de Tormes,* the dreamer Alonso Quijano (who became Don Quijote), Quevedo's Pablo the rogue, and others—each of whom refuses the money, which would have provided no solution to their problems. This is followed by the author's (and here there seems to be a perfect fusion of the internal author and Azorín) "definitive ending" to the novel: a plea for tolerance because of the mutability and fragility of our being, a protest against nothingness as the end of his characters, and a statement regarding the inevitable mystery of our lives, being or nonbeing, reality or nonreality.

The above interpretive outline of *Capricho* scarcely does justice to the half-serious, half-playful nature of the thematic material of the novel, undoubtedly Azorín's most complex and most Cervantine in its narrative method. The author's autobiographical *desdoblamiento*—his splitting-up among various characters of qualities known to be typical of himself—at once enhances the novel's complexity or "density" and refutes the superficial charge that he was unable to create literary characters. In short, the novel is a masterful utilization of favorite Azorínian motifs—especially time, Franciscanism, and the superiority of illusion over reality—cast in a technically virtuosic and highly original narrative form.

As was his habit, Azorín tipped his hand, though a little whimsically, by mentioning Lucian in *Capricho*, because *La isla sin aurora* is similar to Lucian's parodistic novel *Vera historia* (*True Story*) in several respects. Like Lucian's novel, *La isla sin aurora* is a voyage into the "marvelous" on a ship that sails for a time through the air, and there are several mystery-filled adventures and encounters with mythological and supernatural or strange beings. Azorín's novel especially recalls the episode of book 2, chapter 3 of *True Story*, in which the voyagers are on the Island of the Blessed among creatures of the afterlife, who are bodiless and impalpable but who seem real and who live in a land of flowers where everything is eternally the same, without bright day or night, where one is always in the grayness of early dawn. While the riotously fanciful elements of the *True Story* do not appear in *La isla sin aurora*, there are similarities.

There is also similarity between the characters of *La isla sin aurora* and those of *Capricho*. The most important character, the poet, is like the poet of *Capricho*, and the playwright

has ideas like those of the drama critic in *Capricho*—both visualize and arrange all human experience into theatrical scenes and acts. The third member of this group, the novelist, is of secondary importance. Thus we again see different facets of Azorín's personality as a writer embodied in different characters.

The first chapter represents a voyage taken by the poet, the novelist, and the playwright to a tropical island in the Pacific. There is no dawn and thus, symbolically, no mystery to foster the illusion of ideal beauty or the creative capacity. Therefore the poet takes the first boat home, the novelist the second, and the playwright remains.

But what is represented in chapter 1 turns out to be only the reading of the poet, who has dreamed that he was dreaming and who actually had only blank paper in his hand and made up the story. This initial "dream frame" is never terminated; several rather arbitrary and casual references indicate that in a dream anything can happen or not happen. This condition is what imparts to the entire novel a fanciful air of unreality that could better be classified as magic realism than surrealism because the dream frame is used to study vital Azorínian preoccupations revolving around illusion and disillusionment (in the context of a potential voyage) and not primarily to blend the real and the oneiric in contexts of the unconscious. Such a distinction seems valid even though it is hard to draw the line between the surrealist "marvelous" element and "objective chance" and the unreality of this magic realism and the employment of an ambivalent narrative method to explore the art of potentiality. Here there is a *trasmundo*, a world of inner, mysterious reality behind the world of external reality, just as there is an authentic self hidden within the apparent self. The voyage and the experiences on the island permit a fanciful and playful treatment of "Robinsonianism," rather like Jean Giraudoux's in *Suzanne et le Pacifique* (Suzanne and the Pacific, 1921). Here the Robinson Crusoe experience is employed as a kind of exploratory wish-ful-fillment involving an incongruent or ironic contrast between the classical tradition and European civilization on the one hand and the myths involving natural man living in a para-disiacal state on the other.

The atmosphere of magic realism creates conditions in which the main characters, who are creative artists, can simultaneously act in and observe the so-called real and unreal worlds. The playwright, the artist among them who is most bound to reality, expresses Azo-rín's problem. For his art the playwright needs real characters and real events and facts (*hechos*), but he also needs the mysterious and ineffable. He thinks that on this island he may find the desired synthesis. Because of the at-mosphere and the narrative method there is a maximum degree of potentiality or arbitrary conditionality, which at first seems far more important than the literarily represented "ac-tuality." Such extreme potentiality or condi-tionality destroys, refutes, or at worst post-pones the effects of time, which are change, loss, and destruction. With the help of illusion and imagination it eliminates time's effects: experiences can become open and suggestive, with multiple perspectives. But an *hecho* is an *hecho* and precludes the possibility that any-thing else could occur in its place. Thus the author eventually leaves the reader's curiosity and desire to penetrate into the mysterious un-satisfied, as in the scenes on the Bosporus, on the way to the island, where the illusory is destroyed. The author even sketches a false, unreal arrival and then intervenes to explain that he will backtrack, using a *regate* or *rehurte* (a "dodge"), and rewrite the arrival, since all is licit in dreams, which are illogical.

The concluding third of the novel deepens our interest in these serious underlying themes amid fanciful elements: the "sifting-out" of the island's true atmosphere; the poet's incred-ible encounter with Hada Nemorosa, the sylvan fairy; the apprehension of the old man who has stolen the dawn in order to become a philan-thropist of light and color; his mock trial, in which the testimony of his dog, Trik, is heard and the squirrel and badger perform official duties; the letter from Silvano Arbóreo to a dryad praising natural life and life in nature; and the double disillusionment of a Spanish Crusoe, Pedro Serrano. These encounters illus-trate the three stages in the acquisition of wis-dom: to limit oneself in order to be strong and to know, to measure and use one's strength cautiously, and to know one's authentic self. In chapter 33 these concerns, mixed with the po-et's probings into the unavoidable disillusion-ment of life on the island, lead him to a state of anxiety with which he imbues his companions. The anxiety is caused by the lack of hope, which is the lack of a future and therefore of the possibility, however remote, of some sort of palingenesis, some way out of the restriction imposed by the time-death continuum in which man lives, even when he dreams. In order to avoid total disillusionment, it is better not to penetrate into mystery and ideal beauty. At this point Azorín makes the last of his authorial interventions and anticipates the epilogue.

Prior to the epilogue there are four "in-terview-chapters" underscoring the theme of *desengaño* (metaphysical disillusionment). They consist of an old faun's expression of nos-talgia for Europe and his diatribe against Rob-insonian and Rousseauian ideas and the gos-siping frivolity of a young undine and an older siren who can no longer sing. In the epilogue, cast in a Pirandellian dialogue, the characters remark that the author has freed them to do as they please and that they need a denouement, but not a false, sensational one. As if by magic one presents itself in the form of a ship called *Sin Retorno*, which goes away but never returns anywhere, a symbol of life because one cannot return to youth, illusion, or fervor. With this ending the novel stops. We are still within the poet's dream, to be sure, but the theme is nev-ertheless the same one: the exploration of po-tentiality leads to disillusionment. Time and death do exist and will conquer all.

The conditionality of the events is reflected in the use of the conditional mood and in the arbitrarily alternative nature of the style. Thus the novelist makes tentative descriptions, as in the seascape imagined in chapter 2. Conditional sentences and phrases indicating conditionality are used significantly, as in chapter 13. Dreamlike potentials are common, as in these sentences from chapter 23: "El bergantín, si es que no era goleta, si es que no era bricbarca, si no es que era quechemarín, navegaba con lentitud" (The brigatine, unless it was a schooner, unless it was a three-master, unless it was a ketch, sailed slowly); "Traía una larga y negra barba; la traía y no la traía; era barbudo y al mismo tiempo lampiño" (He wore a long, black beard; he wore it and he didn't; he was bearded and at the same time clean-shaven).

In keeping with the dreamlike atmosphere there are occasional incongruities in the sequence of statements, unexpected time lapses, and shifts to different places. Also there is some Giraudouxian ironical and elegant incongruity in the playful contrasts between the modern and the primitive or natural, as in the whole idea of packaging and selling the dawn or of gathering shadows for Europe or of drinking the sky and sea upon raising one's head to drink coconut milk. Also frequent is the use of precision-seeking and self-correcting anadiplosis, which also contributes to the air of conditionality: "All these blues could give the exact impression of the sea. Exact up to a point"; "The cloud passes and the tree remains; the cloud sees its image for an instant in the water, and the tree sees its always; always or almost always, the poet thinks, because this depends on the light."

Azorín's Pacific island, then, is an idealized environment that permits the interplay of the young poet's illusion (used in the broad sense of the word to include *ensoñación* or daydreaming as well as having connotations of art and literature as evasions of reality) and reality, especially his underlying psychological and philosophical concerns regarding senility, sterility, and death. These preoccupations are made apparent in part by motif associationism

and by the contrapuntal interview technique, which allows several points of view to be associated and contrasted. This kind of perspectivism, along with the same vital problems, is also prominent in *Salvadora de Olbena.*

But between these two novels there is an intervening *novela rosa,* or sentimental novel, *María Fontán* (1944). Written in a traditional form and manner, it presents the story of Edit Maqueda, born into a Spanish Jewish family but sent by her Whitmanesque uncle to live and study in England and France under the names of Mary Fontan and Marie Fontan. In Spain she becomes known as María Fontán. A platonic relationship develops into an unconsummated marriage to a very wealthy and aged Parisian who leaves her his entire fortune. After benefitting several worthy young friends she returns to Madrid, where she meets and marries a struggling painter and goes to live with him in the Bosphorus.

The main interest of this novel is not technical or stylistic but psychological. María Fontán's enigmatic and whimsical playing with situations of poverty and wealth reflects the deep-seated emotional attitudes that she had developed during her childhood as the daughter of a Toledan tanner—an ambivalent mixture of carefree joy and an inexplicable, millenial sadness.

Salvadora de Olbena begins with a cross-sectional listing of the facts and persons associated with timepieces and lights seen at two A.M. in the town of Olbena. Salvadora, after a long absence, is in her house; Dr. Casal is ready to retire; and a recently arrived traveler is in his hotel room. Then in chapter 3, which constitutes a kind of prologue or key to the novel's method and tone, Azorín says that the opening chapters were history—simple, objective facts—and that what follows will be a novel. That is to say, it will be an imaginative, partially subjective interpretation of the mere facts, with strangeness in the plot-making and in the language. This "prologue" also treats what becomes the novel's basic characteristic: its "romantic" nature, which justifies the subtitle "Novela romántica" and hints at a relationship between this work and both *María Fontán* and *Doña Inés*. But this novel is romantic only in that it imparts a sense of a gentle *desengaño* resulting from a farewell to youth and a sacrificing of illusion as depicted in an older person's abandoning the prospect of marrying a younger person. Rather paradoxically, the model is in part Nicolás Fernández de Moratín's classical *El sí de las niñas,* a work that like *Salvadora de Olbena* is also concerned with old age.

The next two chapters resume the cross-sectional technique in order to render, now with emotional overtones, the night sounds of Olbena as the train arrives and departs, dogs bark, clocks strike, and the rain falls. All sounds are muffled by intervals of profound silence and a sense of remoteness, which is precisely the feeling Azorín wishes to instill in us. Remote and secluded, Olbena is a place that is half unreal, despite the objective and highly detailed and technical vocabulary used to describe it. It is a kind of limbo or suspended state in which one is simultaneously and ambiguously in closer contact with things and also removed from them. This muffling atmosphere makes communication with other persons unnecessary and seems to bring out the characters' self-centeredness, thus causing a total impression of perspectivism and ambiguity that is heightened by Azorín's using the interview technique again in this novel. Because of this atmosphere and the diverse points of view, the major characters are seen from multiple and partial perspectives, as if reflected in mirrors from a distance.

The story revolves around a beautiful and rich widow in the last bloom of youth whose hand is sought by three very different men: the young and passionate local poet, Paco Ardales; the elegant and witty middle-aged Count of Valdecebro, who has pursued Salvadora to Olbena; and Don Juan Pimentel, a seventy-five-year-old aristocrat to whom Salvadora is strongly attracted. Dr. Casals is an interested observer, as indeed are all the towns-people, many of whose ideas are given in stylized monologues resulting from the chapter-interview technique. All the characters are well drawn, and the reader's interest is directed at once to them and to their conflicting attitudes toward Salvadora and one another. The monologues follow several episodes that depict the major characters somewhat directly and that terminate in varying concepts of Salvadora's relations with Don Juan Pimentel. Mystery and ambiguity prevail, and with the "fanning-out" of attitudes and points of view the truth becomes increasingly complex. But instead of resolving the mystery and providing a definite outcome, in the final two chapters Azorín has the houses of Olbena and the ancient garden speak their minds. Who could know Salvadora better? At the end she is depicted in the garden at three stages of her life: as a happy child, as a pensive young woman, and as a sad, mature woman who has lost a loved one. Although this ending is open, we are nevertheless given the impression that Salvadora will follow the path of renunciation and thus avoid the disillusionment that a new marriage might bring.

This, Azorín's last novel, shows no decline in his inventive powers. In fact, it is one of his best novels. The language and style are precise and pure, the psychology is true, the associative and contrastive techniques are masterfully employed, and the narrative method is perfectly appropriate for the perspectivistic view of reality underlying the novel. The time-death continuum seems to be mitigated, even suspended, since time (mainly the past and the present) is arrested within the minds of the various characters and since the message appears to be one of self-control and renunciation. And yet Salvadora's choice can only reflect her awareness of the finality of love, of her beauty, and of herself.

Azorín's novels reveal a constant experimenting with the novel form. The key to this self-renewing process is Azorín's self-realizing *intimismo* or "intimism," which can be interpreted as a profound self-knowledge that made him conscious not only of a certain timidity and fear of sterility that had to be overcome but also of the related problems of limitation, dosage, and distancing. In each case the problem within the work is presented as a constantly adapting inner reflection of the author's own problem, which he solved by limiting himself to his basic preoccupations as a human being and creative writer at each stage of his literary output. (This, in the broadest sense, is Livingstone's interior duplication.) His creative process was simultaneously self-conscious, self-realizing, and even, since for him to live was to create, self-preserving.

The creative flow necessary for this process to work was derived from partial withdrawal and escape from reality and the restrictions of time and space. For Azorín, achieving a form of timelessness and a sense, at least, of eternity through contemplation, creative plenitude (the supernatural ability to create when under the influence of a beneficent *azar* or mysteriously patterned chance), and the cultivation of illusion is the strongly positive force that conquers the negative threats of anguish, sterility, and the time-death continuum.

In order to summarize Azorín as a writer, one would have to address not only the author's worth as an important creative artist but also his considerable achievements as an essayist, as a landscape artist, as a literary critic, and as the creator of highly effective sketches—his twentieth-century-style *cuadros de costumbres* (vignettes). It would also be necessary to study his general role as a commentator on the Spanish scene and as an important voice in expressing the common concerns of the members of the Generation of '98 as well as his participation in many innovative artistic movements and experiments in style and literary techniques. Another of his most lasting contributions was his general renovation of Spanish prose style. Valverde is especially eloquent on this topic, and more technical studies have been provided by others. From a broader view Azorín was a major

innovator in the novel form, as Livingstone has so convincingly shown, not only among Spanish novelists of his time but also within the mainstream of European literature. Antonio Risco has also shown how close he was to the *nouveau roman* before the fact. Thus, despite a temporary drop in Azorín's literary stock during his declining years and after his death, he left a great legacy, one that can only be enhanced with the passing of time. It is especially gratifying to see in recent years a renewed interest in Azorín among his compatriots, a trend that justifies foreign Hispanists' continued dedication to the close study of the author and his works.

Selected Bibliography

EDITIONS

INDIVIDUAL WORKS

Works written before 1905 were published under the name José Martínez Ruiz. Works written in 1905 and after were published under the pseudonym Azorín.

NOVELS
Diario de un enfermo. Madrid, 1901.
La voluntad. Barcelona, 1902.
Antonio Azorín. Madrid, 1903.
Las confesiones de un pequeño filósofo. Madrid, 1904.
El licenciado Vidriera, visto por Azorín. Madrid, 1915. Now published under the title *Tomás Rueda.*
Rivas y Larra. Madrid, 1916.
Los dos Luises y otros ensayos. Madrid, 1921.
Don Juan. Madrid, 1922.
Una hora de España entre 1560 y 1590. Madrid, 1924.
Doña Inés. Madrid, 1925.
Félix Vargas. Madrid, 1928. Now published under the title *El caballero inactual.*
Pueblo. Madrid, 1930.
El escritor. Madrid, 1942.
El enfermo. Madrid, 1943.
Capricho. Madrid, 1943.
La isla sin aurora. Barcelona, 1944.

AZORÍN

María Fontán. Madrid, 1944.
Salvadora de Olbena. Zaragoza, 1944.

PLAYS
Lo invisible. Madrid, 1928.
Angelita. Madrid, 1930.
Cervantes, o la casa encantada. Madrid, 1931.

SHORT STORY COLLECTIONS
Bohemia: Cuentos. Madrid, 1897.

OTHER WRITINGS
The following works are collections of essays and/
or vignettes, sketches, and other writings. Many
of the author's short pieces are ageneric and mix
elements of the story, the essay, the sketch, and
other forms.

Moratín. Madrid, 1893.
Buscapiés. Madrid, 1894.
La evolución de la crítica. Madrid, 1899.
La sociología criminal. Madrid, 1899.
El alma castellana (1600–1800). Madrid, 1900.
Los pueblos. Madrid, 1905.
La ruta de Don Quijote. Madrid, 1905.
Lecturas españolas. Madrid, 1912.
Castilla. Madrid, 1912.
Clásicos y modernos. Madrid, 1913.
Los valores literarios. Madrid, 1914.
Al margen de los clásicos. Madrid, 1915.
Un pueblecito. Madrid, 1916.
Superrealismo. Madrid, 1929. Now published under
the title *El libro de Levante.*
Españoles en Paris. Buenos Aires, 1939.
Pensando en España. Madrid, 1940.
Madrid. Madrid, 1941.

COLLECTED WORKS
Obras completas. Edited by Angel Cruz Rueda.
9 vols. Madrid, 1947–1954; 2d ed., 1959–1963.
Obras selectas. Edited by Angel Cruz Rueda. 3d ed.
Madrid, 1962.

MODERN EDITIONS
Antonio Azorín. Edited by E. Inman Fox. Barcelona,
1970.
Artículos olvidados de José Martínez Ruiz. Edited by
José María Valverde. Madrid, 1972.
Castilla. Edited by Juan Manuel Rozas. Barcelona,
1973.

Cuentos. Edited by José García Mercadal. Madrid,
1956.
De Valera a Miró. Edited by José García Mercadal.
Madrid, 1956.
Doña Inés. Edited by Elena Catena. 2d ed. Madrid,
1975.
———. Edited by Leon Livingstone. New York,
1969.
*Los pueblos, La Andalucía trágica, y otros artículos
(1904–1905).* Edited by José María Valverde.
Madrid, 1973.
La ruta de Don Quijote. Edited by H. Ramsden.
Manchester, 1966.
La voluntad. Edited by Joaquín Entrambasaguas. In
Las mejores novelas contemporáneas, vol. 2. Bar-
celona, 1958. Includes complete bibliography.
La voluntad. Edited by E. Inman Fox. Madrid, 1969.
Includes complete bibliography.

TRANSLATIONS
Don Juan. Translated by Catherine A. Phillips.
London, 1923; New York, 1924.
An Hour of Spain Between 1560 and 1590. Trans-
lated by Alice Raleigh. London, 1930.
The Sirens and Other Stories. Translated by Warre
B. Wells. London, 1931.

BIOGRAPHICAL AND CRITICAL STUDIES
Abbott, James H. *Azorín y Francia.* Madrid, 1973.
Alfonso, José. *Azorín, íntimo.* Madrid, 1950.
———. *Azorín: En torno a su vida y a su obra.*
Barcelona, 1958.
Biervliet d'Overbroeck, Malcolm D. van. "Azorín's
Comedia del arte and *Angelita: Auto sacramen-
tal*—Two Misunderstood Titles, Two Misunder-
stood Plays." *Journal of Spanish Studies* 5:47–55
(1977).
Blanco Aguinaga, Carlos. *Juventud del '98.* Madrid,
1970.
Catsoris, John A. *Azorín and the Eighteenth Cen-
tury.* New York, 1972.
Enguídanos, Miguel. "Azorín en busca del tiempo
divinal." *Papeles de Son Armadans* 4:13–32
(1959).
Espadas, Elizabeth. "Azorín's Prose Style: Theory
and Practice." *Hispanófila* 20:49–73 (1977).
Fox, E. Inman. *Azorín as a Literary Critic.* New York,
1962.
———. "José Martínez Ruiz: Sobre el anarquismo

del futuro Azorín." *Revista de Occidente* 12: 157–174 (February 1966).

————. "Lectura y literatura: En torno a la inspiración libresca de Azorín." *Cuadernos hispanoamericanos* 75:5–27 (1967).

————. "La campaña teatral de Azorín." *Cuadernos hispanoamericanos* 76:375–389 (1968).

————. *La crisis intelectual del '98.* Madrid, 1976.

García Mercadal, José. *Azorín: Biografía ilustrada.* Barcelona, 1967.

Glenn, Kathleen M. *Azorín (José Martínez Ruiz).* Boston, 1981.

Granell Muñiz, Manuel. *Estética de "Azorín."* Madrid, 1949.

Krause, Anna. "Azorín, the Little Philosopher: Inquiry into the Birth of a Literary Personality." University of California Publications in Modern Philology 28:159–280 (1948).

————. *Azorín, el pequeño filósofo.* Translated by Luis Rico Navarro. Madrid, 1955.

LaJohn, Lawrence A. *Azorín and the Spanish Stage.* New York, 1961.

Livingstone, Leon. "Interior Duplication and the Problem of Form in the Modern Spanish Novel." *PMLA* 73:393–406 (1958).

————. "The Pursuit of Form in the Novels of Azorín." *PMLA* 77:116–133 (1962).

————. "The 'Esthetic of Repose' in Azorín's *Diario de un enfermo.*" *Symposium* 20:241–253 (1966).

————. "The Theme of Intelligence and Will in the Novels of Azorín." *The Romantic Review* 58:83–94 (1967).

————. *Tema y forma en las novelas de Azorín.* Madrid, 1970.

————. "Novel and Mirror, the Eye and the I." In *Homenaje a Azorín.* Edited by Carlos Mellizo. Laramie, Wyo., 1973.

————. "Self-Creation and Alienation in the Novels of Azorín." *Journal of Spanish Studies: Twentieth Century* 1:5–43 (1973).

Lott, Robert E. *The Structure and Style of Azorín's "El caballero inactual."* Athens, Ga., 1963.

————. "Azorín's Experimental Period and Surrealism." *PMLA* 79:305–320 (1964).

————. "Sobre el método narrativo y el estilo en las novelas de Azorín." *Cuadernos hispanoamericanos* 76:192–219 (1968).

————. "Considerations on Azorín's Literary Techniques and the Other Arts." *Kentucky Romance Quarterly* 19:423–434 (1971).

Mainer, José Carlos. "Para un análisis formal de *Capricho* y *La isla sin aurora.*" *Insula* 23:5, 11 (1968).

Maravall, José Antonio. "Azorín: Idea y sentido de la microhistoria." *Cuadernos hispanoamericanos* 76:28–77 (1968).

Marco Merenciano, Francisco. *Fronteras de la locura: Tres personajes de Azorín vistos por un psiquiatra.* Valencia, 1947.

Martínez Cachero, José María. *Las novelas de Azorín.* Madrid, 1960.

Ortega y Gasset, José. "Azorín, o primores de lo vulgar." In *Obras completas,* vol. 2. Madrid, 1946.

Pérez López, Manuel María. *Azorín y la literatura española.* Salamanca, 1974.

Pérez Minik, Domingo. "Azorín, o la evasión pura." In *Debates sobre el teatro contemporáneo.* Santa Cruz de Tenerife, Spain, 1953.

Pérez-Rioja, José Antonio. "El estilo de Azorín y su proyección en la literatura contemporánea." In *Azorín: Homenaje al maestro en su nonagésimo aniversario,* edited by José Antonio Pérez-Rioja. Madrid, 1964.

Rand, Marguerite C. *Castilla en Azorín.* Madrid, 1956.

Riopérez y Milá, Santiago. *Azorín íntegro.* Madrid, 1979.

Risco, Antonio. *Azorín y la ruptura con la novela tradicional.* Madrid, 1980.

Servodidio, Mirella d'Ambrosio. *Azorín, escritor de cuentos.* New York, 1971.

Valverde, José María. *Azorín.* Barcelona, 1971.

BIBLIOGRAPHIES

Gamallo Fierros, Dionisio. *Hacia una bibliografía cronológica en torno a la letra y el espíritu de Azorín.* Madrid, 1956.

ROBERT E. LOTT

ALFRED JARRY
(1873–1907)

IN THE COURSE of three scandalous hours on a wintry Parisian evening in 1896, Alfred Jarry, for better or worse, made himself famous. His bizarre play *Ubu Roi,* about a farcical usurpation of the Polish throne, had the audience literally rioting in the aisles of Aurélien-Marie Lugné-Poe's avant-garde Théâtre de l'Oeuvre. *Ubu Roi* was published in June 1896, before its production in December, and many in the opening-night audience came prepared to exhibit hostility even before the action of the play commenced. They sensed what Jarry had in store for them, and they in turn had something in store for Jarry when he appeared onstage to introduce the piece.

JARRY AND THE PARISIAN AVANT-GARDE

The evening of *Ubu*'s premier galvanized the controversy surrounding the still-recent emergence of revolutionary avant-garde art in France at the end of the nineteenth century. Jarry and his *Ubu* clearly stood in, after a fashion, for a young generation of radical writers and artists. Not only had some of Paris' outstanding artists collaborated in designing the play's sets—Henri de Toulouse-Lautrec, Pierre Bonnard, and Édouard Vuillard all helped—but the outrageous action and language of the production were the subject of caustic exchanges in leading contemporary journals and periodicals. By the night of *Ubu Roi*'s single, uproarious, disastrous performance, the play had already been primed for a public happening. It was one of those works whose reputation was fated to extend far beyond any pedestrian notion of its merits.

No sooner had the curtain risen on the sparse, schematic set (depicting by prop and backdrop all the meteorological zones of the earth), and no sooner had the leading actor, borrowed for the occasion from the Comédie Française, appeared in his sordid and awkwardly draped costume, looking like a giant puppet, than the rumbling in the audience began. And with the play's first word—uttered by Ubu in a sharply pitched and clipped intonation: "merdre"—the audience proceeded to hoot and howl in earnest. The extra rolled "r" in Ubu's "merdre"—the equivalent in English to the superfluous "y" in "shyit"—served as the final insult added to expected injury. Bodies rose; fists flew.

The screaming, stomping, and brawling continued for fifteen minutes, the general tumult abating only when the management raised the houselights, thereby hinting at an earlier end to the evening than even Jarry's enemies might have wished. With the audience temporarily, but only temporarily, resettled, the play resumed. But so did the tumult at the very next "merdre." The chaotic action onstage—usurpation and revolution—was more than rivaled by the chaotic action off. Each scatological utterance, each repeated obscene gesture, each wave of the usurping Ubu's kingly scepter, his "shitterstick," produced roars of outrage or glee from Jarry's abusers and supporters.

The battle waged between factions of the audience mirrored the battle fought after the publication of the play and the one that would continue after its production for months, even years, beginning with the colorful post-mortems in the next morning's journals and periodicals. The debate arising from the *Ubu* crisis extended finally to the host of major manifestos for avant-garde art proclaimed in subsequent years against the conventional, realist, predictable values of nineteenth-century drama, literature, painting, music, and sculpture. In and of itself Jarry's play ranged between the amusing and the execrable; in terms of what it represented as an event, it was the one *fin-de-siècle* spectacle above all others that inaugurated in its primitive and vulgar way movements as significant and diverse as surrealism, dadaism, expressionism, and the theater of the absurd.

The great poets and dramatists of the period—Guillaume Apollinaire, Stéphane Mallarmé, August Strindberg, Oscar Wilde—did not so much turn to Jarry for inspiration as celebrate the occasion of *Ubu Roi* as a public spectacle of principles implicit in their own works. Mallarmé was in the opening-night audience and argued on the play's behalf as part of his ongoing attack on the hidebound quality of bourgeois drama and poetry. Also among the witnesses to the evening's fiasco was a thirty-year-old Irish poet and playwright, William Butler Yeats, whose curious notes about the performance were more memorable than anything actually in it. Yeats was appalled by the rawness of Jarry's play and the emotions attending it, and he considered it a dubious privilege to have been there. Yet he recorded in his *Autobiography* (1926) a haunting, enigmatic, and troubling assessment of radical modernism in Europe conjured by Jarry's play: "After us the Savage God." To understand why Yeats would say such a thing,

and why he would include himself in the pronoun "us," is to come to grips with the contexts of modernism in Europe just before the turn of the century.

It could be argued, indeed Yeats hinted at it, that both in his work and in his person Jarry represents the most militant version of modernist literature during the period roughly between the Franco-Prussian War of 1870–1871 and the outbreak of World War I in 1914. To imagine Jarry as an avant-garde symbol of the *belle époque* is also to identify him as a younger or older contemporary of Sigmund Freud, Friedrich Nietzsche, Paul Cézanne, Pablo Picasso, Franz Kafka, James Joyce, Virginia Woolf, Henrik Ibsen, Marcel Proust, Albert Einstein, Thomas Edison, and the Wright brothers. In the longer view Jarry is but a mote in the eye of philosophical, artistic, political, and, to some extent, scientific revolutions that went under such names as aestheticism, impressionism, symbolism, surrealism, and relativity theory. It is precisely Jarry's auxiliary service at the fringes of all this newness, however, that makes him such a powerful symptom of modernity.

During the heyday of the *belle époque* (the two decades surrounding the turn of the century), Jarry worked very hard to cultivate himself as the avant-garde's strangest human embodiment. His flamboyant appearances at the publishing offices, theaters, salons, and cafés of Paris made him a notorious public display piece. Very short and odd-looking, he wore lipstick, absurd hats, flowing capes, and women's blouses, and always brandished a pistol loaded with blanks. He spoke in exaggerated, clipped, and uniquely accented phrases— André Gide said he sounded like a talking nutcracker. He threw wild parties; he rented restaurants for banquets; he drank himself into oblivion. Jarry remarked of his Parisian street life, "N'est-ce pas beau comme la littérature?" (Isn't it lovely as literature?)

When Gide re-created the turn-of-the-century world of the Parisian avant-garde in his famous novel *Les faux-monnayeurs* (*The*

Counterfeiters, 1926), the only figure he felt compelled to name directly was Alfred Jarry. Gide has "Ubu" Jarry, as everyone had begun to call him, show up drunk and drugged at a publisher's banquet, where he discharges his pistol near the ear of the wife of the president of the Republic. She faints in shock. Gide's novel places Jarry in the role of the avant-garde's agent provocateur; his antics are enough to make the most prominent and influential drop in their tracks.

As a term, "avant-garde" has a Gallic cast to it. It gained wide currency in reference to Parisian culture and aesthetics during the 1880's and 1890's, but its origins are political and revolutionary. At first the term referred to the political cadres opposed to the monarchies and bourgeois republics of Europe. The avant-garde stood squarely, violently against the economic, conventional, aggrandizing attitudes entrenched in Victorian England, Second Empire and Third Republic France, the kaiser's Prussia, the emperor's Austria-Hungary, Victor Immanuel's Italy, and the tsar's Russia. The great imperial-bourgeois cultures of Europe had reached the height of their power and complacency during the later nineteenth century. They enacted their industrial and material historical pageant as the great March of Progress, facilitated in Europe (and in Gilded Age America) by capitalist energies exercised on machine-age societies. Only the wars and revolutions of the early twentieth century sounded this epoch's death knell, and ironically the very industrial expansion that characterizes the age produced as part of its program the devastating modern weapons that were to help end the real and illusory splendor of *belle époque* Europe.

In the 1870's the anarchist Mikhail Bakunin founded a radical journal in Switzerland called *L'Avant-garde,* and by the 1880's his followers had welcomed an alliance with the more progressive members of the cultural and aesthetic avant-garde. It became clear from Bakunin's famous dictum—"The desire for destruction is at the same time a creative desire"— that anarchy could serve both politics and art. And that is precisely the way it served for Alfred Jarry. Indeed, some of Jarry's radical artist friends struck the more sinister chords of anarchism by participating directly in terrorist incidents in *fin-de-siècle* Paris. Later, after World War I, the more actively revolutionary tendencies of the avant-garde were channeled into the aesthetic militancy of one of Jarry's avowed followers, Antonin Artaud, and his theater of cruelty. Artaud had the idea of firing live machine-gun ammunition at his audiences, although the Parisian authorities, who had a say in these matters, held different notions of legitimate theatrical fare.

No uniform manifesto defined the avant-garde, but a unified sensibility did: a proclaimed and often-enacted resistance to established aesthetic, social, and political traditions, resources, values, and audiences. Jarry's shorthand for the modern order is "the accursed Bourgeois," which he identifies in an early periodical essay, "Visions actuelles et futures" (Visions of Present and Future, 1894). He begins his essay for the avant-garde *La revue blanche* by citing the anarchist Émile Henry, addressing the entrenched authorities in France: "You're out to get every last anarchist. I'm out to get every last bourgeois." At issue in the relation of avant-garde aesthetics to anarchist politics is the assumption that social and political forms are by their nature corrupt and corrupting. Human activity as an expression of will is bound to be freer once separated and released from all cultural restraints. Insofar as anarchism is an idea rather than a purely terrorist program, its ethos was applicable to literary and artistic activity. To put it another way, the aesthetic avant-garde adopted terrorist principles when it could do so publicly and in regard to ideas of violent action rather than to violence itself. When Alfred Jarry fired a gun in public places, he made sure that he had loaded his pistol with blanks.

Avant-garde artists do not thrive in secret. They work best when they enjoy the liberties and licenses of the culture they attack openly and outwardly. It is almost as if the very

ALFRED JARRY

institutions—the courts, the universities, the theaters, the newspapers—that avant-gardists try to outrage end up publicizing and even patronizing their activity. This may have something to do with the presumably dangerous nature of the activity for which the military term "avant-garde" stands. The advance cadre or advance line is allowed the privilege of shooting because it takes upon itself the risk of being shot at first. Despite the abuse directed at the avant-garde for the positions it takes, society also tends to value those of its members who extend themselves furthest critically and aesthetically. This is surely the case with Jarry. He made the society that suffered him feel liberal.

It might even be arguable that free societies become so by recognizing, indeed by institutionalizing, lines of countercultural expression. Older "avant-garde" phenomena like the Greek satyr play, the Roman saturnalia, or the medieval carnival perpetuate the notion that the deeply subversive can become by force of expression a kind of allowable frenzy. Many who would call themselves avant-garde take as much pleasure in the fact that their outrages are permitted as they do in the substance of those outrages. Furthermore, at least in the Paris of the 1890's, avant-gardists took an extra-special, if secret, pleasure in the very bourgeois conventions and values they attacked. Jarry's radical tirades against his bourgeois world, for example, were effective to the extent that he also indulged in what he savaged. Jarry was fascinated with the paraphernalia of the *belle époque,* an age that produced innovations not only affecting but also facilitating some of the more significant forms of aesthetic representation on the stage and in exhibition halls: the refinement of photography, the installation of electric lighting, the invention of the telephone, the automobile, the airplane, the motion picture camera, the radio, and the phonograph. All these make appearances as part of the focus and the bourgeois "stuff" of Jarry's avant-garde art and his radical essays or *spéculations* in *La revue blanche.*

If avant-garde expression in Europe seems to draw its own subversive energy from the vitality and excitement of the culture it challenges, nowhere is this better displayed than in that urban jewel of the civilized world, Jarry's Paris of the 1890's. Paris was already transformed in the 1870's, when Baron Georges Eugène Haussmann redesigned its streets, giving the city a new breadth and a modern airiness. The Eiffel Tower later rose to commemorate the shape and strength of steel in a world whose social and aesthetic life lost little in gaiety despite the grim presence of the proletariat underclass whose labor made Paris monumental. The city's literary, social, and cultural life engaged the Parisian radical as fully as it did the conservative bourgeois, titillated the artiste and the boulevardier in the haunts of the demimonde, fêted them in new cafés, hotels, and restaurants on the elegant Right Bank, stimulated them in the artist colonies of the Latin Quarter and Montmartre. Jarry reveled in a Paris that attracted modernity just as he reveled in the grander modernism of which he was a smaller part. No one enjoyed being French, being Parisian, being a literati in the brightest city of the Western world more than Jarry.

During the glory years of the *belle époque,* Paris marked the center of a world of exquisite fashion and style, a world that made Proust, in one of the few purely social joys of his *A la recherche du temps perdu* (1913–1928), pine in 1920 for the sunny years of the 1890's in which men in elegant morning suits and women in superb dresses strolled the Champs-Élysées and the paths of the great parks and gardens of Paris. And one squat little vital midget in a stovepipe hat would have been on constant parade in that scene: "Ubu" Jarry. In his most expansive and best-known narrative satire, *Gestes et opinions du docteur Faustroll, 'pataphysicien: Roman neo-scientifique (The Exploits and Opinions of Doctor Faustroll, 'Pataphysician: A Neo-Scientific Novel),* published posthumously in 1911, Jarry presents an enthralling travelogue through the districts of his city, in which he associates various suburbs of Paris with the creative, innovative, and revolutionary art of his friends and contemporaries. It seems from this detailed tribute to Paris that the avant-garde radical is very much at home in the city he so outrages and that so outrages him.

LAVAL, RENNES, PARIS

Joyce always thought it one of the particular strokes of his own genius in *Ulysses* that he picked 8 September, the feast of the Nativity of the Holy Virgin, for Molly Bloom's birthday. Alfred-Henri Jarry had an even greater reason to take pleasure in that date since, by the whimsy of nature's time clock, he was born into the world on it in 1873. Alfred-Henri was the son of a struggling entrepreneurial father, Anselme, and a relentlessly eccentric mother, Caroline. The Jarry name was well known in the town of Alfred-Henri's birth, Laval, near the region of Brittany. For hundreds of years the male line of the family was among the town's prominent masons, craftsmen, and carpenters. Jarry's father, trained as a mason, was the first of his family to move up and out to the world of bourgeois trade and production. He represented and later managed a factory for woolen manufactures.

As part of the natural ambition that compelled Anselme Jarry to cross the gulf between the world of craft and the world of the trade, he planned, and indeed managed, to marry differently than had any of his ancestors. He chose—and oddly enough was chosen by—a remarkable woman, Caroline Quernest, the daughter of a prominent Breton magistrate. Of solid bourgeois and boasted aristocratic background, Caroline had a pedigree perhaps better than Anselme ought to have expected, but her behavior in his eyes surely was not. Her habits were wilder than her husband or the town of Laval could bear. Her dress, her tastes, her opinions, her artistic temperament, led the local townsfolk to believe that she suffered

from the congenital insanity known to run rampant in her family.

While Anselme was on the road selling his woolen goods, Caroline and her children lived with her retired father in nearby Saint-Brieuc on the Brittany coast. It was obvious that the separation suited Caroline; her psychic center had little to do with her husband and everything to do with her children, who in their grandfather's house could live in ease and leisure while taking advantage of the books in a well-stocked library. Whatever her eccentricities, Caroline provided intense intellectual encouragement for her children, Alfred-Henri and his older sister, Charlotte. That she did so as a kind of protest against everything the male Jarry heritage represented may have been the case, but the effect on the youngsters, especially the pampered Alfred-Henri, was enormous.

Alfred was something of a prodigy, producing at an early age long imitations of romantic poetry in the style of Victor Hugo. He was also capable of brilliant satiric vignettes mimicking and parodying the local citizenry. Caroline smothered the child with attention, prodded his talents, nurtured his curiosity, and was not in the least shy about any of her efforts. Jarry's own childhood memory is of a whimsical and prepossessing mother who allowed him his opinions on anything provided he agreed with her beforehand about everything. It was Caroline who insisted on steering her boy through the French educational system if possible right up to the highly competitive École Normale in Paris. Such a course would be the first for any male offspring of the Jarry line.

In 1888 Madame Jarry moved with her children to Rennes, a day's journey from Laval. Already a precocious twelve-year-old poet and schoolboy playwright, Alfred attended the lycée at Rennes, where he performed sporadically but brilliantly in all fields, from ancient Greek to modern physics. His behavior at school as well in the streets and shops of Rennes was another matter. Jarry and his friends were notorious as pranksters: brash, rude, unpredictable, indefatigable, and exciting. For the schoolboy Jarry, all of Rennes was his stage and his friends and schoolmates the resident troupe of local farceurs. Jarry's antics were a form of provocative street theater, with such props as explosives from the school laboratory, oddball costumes, sabers, knives, and firearms, and an ever-present bicycle, a real and imaginative prop that entered his psyche at about the same time it began to figure prominently as one of the visible symbols and pleasures of the *belle époque.* The street performances that marked Jarry's adolescence in Rennes became the model for the even more bizarre performances that would mark his life in Paris—performances made visually and aurally interesting by his squealing nasal tones, jerky puppet gestures, heavy-browed face, and bandy-legged body capable of surprising athletic feats.

Jarry's artistic exploits at this early point in his career in Rennes were stimulated by a legendary physics teacher, Professor Hébert, who was the ongoing subject of a burlesque myth passed from generation to generation of students at the lycée. Hébert, or Heb as he was known to the students, was a wonderful character, absent-minded, chaotic, bourgeois to the core—in short, the stuff of parody, ridicule, and, in a way, mock adulation. Jarry's participation in the Heb cycle consisted of collaboration with friends and other students on an almost endless series of sophomorically inventive dramatic fragments, with Père Heb as the inspiration for an absurd system of physics—'Pataphysics—vaguely mimicking the actual physics he taught. Heb's nature, like that of François Rabelais's academicians, whom he resembles, takes in all the satiric wonders of the world. His series of adventures mushroom to include global political and scientific fantasies.

Jarry and his friends arranged or performed bits and pieces of the Heb chronicles as attic puppet plays, and it is easy to see how the Père Heb material from Jarry's youth set the stage for the cycle of *Ubu* plays and the legends of

Doctor Faustroll, which have sustained Jarry's literary reputation, such as it is, ever since. Jarry began the Père Heb shenanigans with two friends, Henri and Charles Molin. It was actually the Molin brothers who hit on the idea of making the bumbling Heb a usurper of the Polish throne, the partitioned realm becoming a kind of Nowhere Land, an amalgam of all European absurdities. They called their puppet play "Les Polanais" (The Poles). This was the ur-text for Jarry's *Ubu Roi.* Later, in Paris, Jarry used the primitively written texts that he and the Molin brothers produced as the basis for other marionette adaptations of the *Ubu* cycle (Père Heb and Père Ubu were interchangeable characters) performed in his cluttered apartment at the dead end of an alley off the boulevard du Port-Royal.

Jarry had moved to Paris with his mother's blessing in 1891 at seventeen. There he continued his education at the Lycée Henry IV in preparation for attendance at the École Normale. The advanced lycée was a revelation to the boy. He studied eclectically, and barely any field of knowledge proved unfruitful for him. Jarry took special interest in the philosophy lectures given by the renowned Henri Bergson. When old enough to do so, Jarry applied to the École Normale, but he was passed over for reasons that may or may not have had to do strictly with the nature of the very stiff competition. He reapplied on other occasions, but when the École was finally ready for him in 1893, he was no longer ready for it, having established himself by then as a rising literary star in the avant-garde circles of Paris.

While in Paris Jarry first made contact with influenial patrons and with impressionist painters and symbolist writers, poets, and musicians at the weekly reception held in the offices of the *Mercure de France;* there, along with Jarry, the young Gide, Maurice Ravel, Paul Valéry, and the anarchist Félix Fénéon circulated among the city's aesthetic elite. With the assistance of well-placed friends, Jarry began publishing in journals; his first effort was a dialogue called "Guignol," in the magazine *L'Écho de Paris* (April 1893), a dialogue that recycled older material from Rennes with the character Père Ubu as a practitioner of 'Pataphysics, the science of supplements and exceptions.

It was at this time early in his burgeoning career that Jarry's mother died during an influenza epidemic. She had just returned home to Laval after traveling to Paris to take care of her son, who had a lesser case of influenza. Jarry was badly shaken by his mother's death, feeling that he had in a sense killed her. Alone in Paris at twenty, Jarry continued to count on connections at the *Mercure de France* for the publication in 1894 of his first long work, *Les minutes de sable mémorial* (Minutes of Memorial Sand). Here, too, he rehashes older Heb and Ubu material, but this time he includes many new symbolist poems, prose fragments, and even a few of his own primitive drawings. Whatever the ultimate range of his talents, Jarry's visual imagination contributed to his verbal one—his words and expressions have the dimensional quality of objects seen, felt, touched, pushed, squeezed. And as is the case with much in symbolist literature, Jarry's *Les minutes de sable mémorial* depends for its effects on the immediacy and suggestiveness of its images and moods, since little of it makes any sustained or argumentative sense apart from these.

Having come of age aesthetically among his friends and supporters at the *Mercure,* Jarry relied on the same circle to provide him with opportunities for his first sexual liaisons, which, like those of Gide and Proust, who orbited in similar circles, seem to have been indiscriminate in regard to gender. Jarry's one recorded and disastrous affair was with the aging mistress of one of his collaborators and fellow writers, Rémy de Gourmont. The unhappy revelation of the affair shaped Jarry's subsequent views on sexuality. Unlike others in the avant-garde of French life and letters, Jarry's views on sexual liberation are more strained and difficult than his views on aesthetic liberation. He associates sexuality with

a quest for power, a destructive power at that, as when a rampant puppet-phallus in one of his early poetic dramas destroys the temple at Halderablou, or when a sex-registering voltage machine conspires with a sexual insatiate to blow the premises (and each other) to smithereens in the marvelous narrative *Le surmâle* (*The Supermale,* 1902). In any case, Jarry's literary works express such general disgust with human sexuality that one can guess his energies were never happily sustained with either sex. Rather, Jarry was more interested in the abstracted notion of love, as in *L'Amour absolu* (Absolute Love, 1899), where the loved "other" serves as a narcissistic symbol for one's other self: what one formerly was or what one will be in time.

No doubt even more traumatic than Jarry's sexual adventures in the early 1890's, and much better documented, was his brief military career. Drafted in 1894, Jarry lasted only a few months at his hometown barracks near Laval before driving nearly everyone who had anything to do with him to despair. He was never overtly rebellious—in fact, he was obsessively polite to the military hierarchy—but his studied incompetence in the routines of military life and his many visits to the infirmary for maladies of mysterious origin gained him a much-welcomed, though trumped-up, medical discharge. Rumor had it that his discharge papers carried the phrase "precocious imbecility."

Back in Paris in 1895, Jarry resumed his literary adventures. When his father died in August, he was able to put together enough cash from a small inheritance to found two art magazines, *L'Ymagier* and *Perhinderion,* both of which published his own rough drawings, cartoons, and woodcuts in addition to fine reproductions of famous works, including a sequence of extraordinary Albrecht Dürer woodcuts. These magazines failed within the year after only a few issues, and Jarry lost most of the little money he had.

It was at this time that he channeled his energies into the famous 1896 production of

Ubu Roi with the help of his producer-director friend, Lugné-Poe. As noted, the preparations for the play were closely followed by the Parisian avant-garde. Jarry worked on all the play's facets, from its set designs to its costuming, from its casting to its publicity. He even contributed the program notes for the premiere; after the performance he entered as a combatant into the paper wars set off by the evening's riot. He wrote an essay for *La revue blanche* in January 1897 called "Questions de théâtre" (Questions of the Theater). Jarry's critical arguments here centered on his severe scorn for anything on the modern stage resembling the stale dramatic plots, the stuffy decor and costuming, and the predictable characterization of the bourgeois theater. His bias was of an anarchist cast:

> In that art and comprehension are so incompatible we might have made a mistake in launching a direct attack on the public in *Ubu Roi;* but perhaps, whether they admitted it or not, the members of the public resented the play because they understood it full well. . . . It is because the public is an inert, obtuse, and listless glob that it needs to be shaken on occasion so that we can assume from its bearlike grunts where it is and what it thinks.

As for his play, Jarry writes in the same essay:

> It would have been simple to revise *Ubu* to conform to the taste of the Parisian public by making the following minor alterations: the opening word would have been "Shoot" (or "Shoottr") [in French, "Zut" or "Zutre"], the unspeakable brush [shitterstick] would have metamorphosed into a pretty girl in bed, the uniforms of the army would have been in the fashion of the First Empire, Ubu would have knighted the tsar, and numerous husbands would have been cuckolded—but in that case the play would have been viler.

After *Ubu* Jarry truly began to work at making himself into a kind of anarchic figure on the Parisian scene. His essential objective was to sustain the effect created by the *Ubu* premiere: he wished to become a public outrage, a walking anti-type. Just as in his youthful days at Rennes, he was dedicated to the theatrical gesture: stalking the streets of Paris armed with swords, knives, rifles, and snubnosed pistols; carousing in cafés and restaurants to all hours of the night and early morning; partying with savage indignation; squandering what little funds he had on renting restaurants for lavish dinner parties with courses disguised as parts of the human body; drinking absinthe and cheap liquid ether.

Jarry lived off a back alley on the rue Cassette in a sordid little hovel jammed with paraphernalia, live owls, and religious icons. The apartment had actually been quartered by its landlord, all of its living space reduced by a factor of four. In one of the other quadrants lived Jarry's friend, the painter Henri Rousseau. Apollinaire charitably described Jarry's living space as half a room, containing half a bed, half a writing desk, a mutilated portrait of Jarry by Rousseau, a small, cheap library, and a phallus on the mantelpiece covered with a velvet skullcap. Jarry claimed that the phallus was a "reduction" of his own, although it was far larger than any organ one might have thought could comfortably grace the body of such a miniaturized example of the species *Homo sapiens.*

Although much of his time was taken up in and by public spectacles, Jarry never stopped writing in the years after *Ubu Roi.* With his fresh fame as a calling card, his best years were those just before and after the turn of the century. He produced a series of satiric narratives ranging from the picaresque hallucinatory adventures of a soporific soldier named Sengle in *Les jours et les nuits* (Days and Nights, 1897), to the exploits and opinions of the famous *Doctor Faustroll* (completed in 1898, although not published until 1911), to the sexual acrobatics of the empress Messalina in his 1901 novella *Messaline: Roman de l'ancienne Rome* (Messaline: A Novel of Ancient Rome, translated as *The Garden of Priapus* [*Messaline*], 1901), to the wild antics of André the Superman in *Le surmâle.* Jarry also continued to capitalize on his *Ubu* material even if he could get no one to put on another full-scale live dramatic production. His wonderful *Almanach illustré du Père Ubu* (Pa Ubu's Illustrated Almanac, 1901) is a potpourri assault on the state of Parisian culture at the birth of the new century. The Pierre Bonnard cartoons of Ubu in this parodic almanac are among the best and wittiest ever, the pear-shaped King of Base Nature revealing himself in a variety of roles, poses, and unseemly activities.

In order to supplement his earnings as a writer, Jarry wrote hundreds of reviews, translations, and hack-work pieces commissioned by the dozens of Parisian periodicals with which he had connections. As the years passed, he engaged in a sustained effort to heighten what he thought of as his special brand of hallucinatory perception by drinking huge quantities of absinthe when he could afford it and ether when he could not. Jarry's debilitating vices were so obvious to his contemporaries and so prominent in the legends handed down about him that it almost comes as a breath of relief to realize that he also enjoyed pursuits of a lazy-Sunday-afternoon variety common to the most ordinary of the Parisian bourgeois. With his closest friends, the editor of the *Mercure de France,* Alfred Vallette, and his wife, Rachilde, Jarry loved to fish, canoe, and above all to cycle, having put a down payment (and forgotten the installments) on one of the most expensive two-wheelers in France, a Clément luxe. There was a wholesome, endearing, and human side to Jarry, almost as if his fondest private pleasures stood in direct opposition to his destructive public ones.

To approach Jarry as a human being is to encounter not only the freak of the radical avant-garde but also a sweet and sympathetic figure. His closest friends admired his good nature as much as they did his capacious intellect. Beyond or beneath Jarry's affected weirdness was a deep and astonishing intelligence; and in spite of his brash public rudeness, he possessed a consistently open and generous heart. When one of the characters in Gide's *The Counterfeiters* claims that Jarry looks absolutely ferocious, another, who knows him well, responds: "Oh, that's just his way. In reality he is the kindest of creatures."

During the last years of his life, Jarry worked intermittently on a long, visionary, and virtually incomprehensible narrative, *La dragonne* (The Dragon), published posthumously in 1943. The last chapter of his work, "Descendit ad infernos" (Descent into Hell), stands as a biographical metaphor for the progress of Jarry's last years. He was in a sense willing to trade his life for hellish illusion. Gravely ill—weakened in mind and spirit, undernourished, tubercular, and ravaged by his intake of alcohol and ether—Jarry had made his pact with the lord of his underworld to live in a different state, whatever it be, before the next different state that would kill him. As much as we can adduce reasons for such pronounced annihilative behavior, Jarry wanted, as Roger Shattuck puts it, to commit suicide by hallucination. His body could bear up only so long under such a systematic assault. Alfred-Henri Jarry died at thirty-four years of age on All Saints' Day, 1 November 1907. One of his friends discovered him partially paralyzed in his tiny room on the rue Cassette. He clung to life only a brief while after being taken to the hospital, and in a final absurdity worthy of King Ubu he made a last, semi-comatose request for a toothpick.

WRITER AS 'PATAPHYSICIAN

The power of Jarry's writing derives essentially from the burlesque and mock-epic elements he constantly employs in realigning cultural myths to his own particular vision in his own particular idiom. His literary tactics are Rabelaisian, as he himself would have readily admitted—he even dramatized Rabelais in a libretto called *Pantagruel* (posthumously published in 1910), and he went to Gargantuan lengths for his shocking comic effects. In an updated brief parody of the Christian myth, similar to the opening scene of *Gargantua et Pantagruel* (1534) but even cruder, Jarry considers the advisability of facilitating all future Virgin Births with suppositories.

Although parody and burlesque (invariably scatological) account for a large part of Jarry's writings, the literary principle that sustains almost all his work is satirical in a more universal sense. Jarry's satire is of a subversive sort, one that has little recourse to notions of correction or even notions of normalcy. He rarely retreats to the comforting, assured position of satire—the position that there is after all a sane way to conduct one's life and a sane way to impose order on the lives of others. Rather, Jarry's satire wishes anarchy upon all order. He entertains few illusions about any human institution or practice. In his representation of tyranny, say, in *Ubu Roi,* Jarry assumes that the elimination of tyrannical abuses would merely reveal less obvious abuses. The normal, for Jarry, is disguised tyranny, and he takes as much pleasure in ridiculing normalcy as he does in castigating venality, hypocrisy, or oppression. It is not the fact that all things are going awry that beckons the call of Jarry the satirist, but the complacency inherent in the position that anyone could believe otherwise.

In all his works—dramatic, poetic, or fictional—Jarry is never far from the voice of satiric assault, from insult, opprobrium, tirade, foul apostrophe, absurd violence. He presents human institutions by debasing the humanity within them. Hence the nature of figurative language in his work tends to make values, laws, systems, and theories into complicated and rude bodily jokes. Everything in its way is given absurd and appetitive life: objects, machines, governments, economies. Things that are alive tend to do unpleasant things—not so much by will as by bodily reflex. A satirist such as Jonathan Swift, from whom Jarry learned much, operates on much the same principles in his *A Tale of a Tub*

(1704) or his *Discourse Concerning the Mechanical Operation of the Spirit* (1704). So does Jarry's revered Rabelais, in whose works all ideas and all utterances take shape as a kind of bodily activity: sexual, digestive, and expulsive.

What is innovative and riotous in Jarry's satire is the way he adapts human gesture, human action, human speech to a phenomenal range of modern intellectual and scientific pursuits, from interstellar physics to biochemistry. Jarry had the ear of a mimic and the mind of a polymath. He makes best use of his capacious, eclectic learning in his short occasional prose pieces or *spéculations* published in various issues of *La revue blanche.* These are madly wonderful mixtures of contemporary affairs, science, and scientific chop-logic on all conceivable schemes and projects from modern armaments to medicinal cures to time-space flight. As bizarre or unorthodox as are the subjects of Jarry's *spéculations,* the human, absurd dimension in them is never lost. Jarry's efforts anticipate his friend Apollinaire's later capsule definition of surrealism as the reinvention of the wheel as if the inventor were trying to imitate a man walking.

The plots of Jarry's works often consist in acting out a scientific, mechanical, or metaphysical metaphor. For Jarry both science and art test what metaphor is: a comparative possibility in another realm. He assumes that metaphors exist precisely to be acted out—their very function constitutes *meaning* in the literary experience. Jarry's pseudoscientific and parodic style insists on the concentration of potential meaning in the poetic figure, in the symbol. Symbolism was the dominant avant-garde experimental trend of Jarry's time, practiced in poetry and literature by Verlaine, Rimbaud, Mallarmé, Valéry, and Apollinaire. Jarry warms to the amalgam of formalism and freedom in symbolism, a style that could concentrate on the resonance of words with little regard for their possible deleterious effects—their effrontery, eroticism, or, in Jarry's case, scatology—on the audiences who read them or

ALFRED JARRY

hear them. Since right and wrong were not part of Jarry's critical vocabulary, only the vividness of expression and its phenomenal fallout provided matter for meaning. The unlikely, the impossible, the outlandish, are made significant merely by being capable of articulation and representation.

These assumptions govern Jarry's first full-length book, the heavily symbolist *Les minutes de sable mémorial,* which contains everything from lyric passages on the pleasures of opium to prose descriptions of the phonograph. The title suggests the written record, which is the time or "minutes" of memorial sand, but a translation of "sand" misses the coloration of the French *sable,* the kind of crossover or mixture of noun and image that occurs in symbolist poetry when words take on a life of their own. The title also reflects the symbolic doubling that is a prominent feature of Jarry's language: the written minutes record time just as the sand in the hourglass does. The piece, in a sense, is time and time again. Prose and poetic bits of time make up the volume and make up the metaphor of the volume. Jarry even makes his work a memorial by including in it fragments of his own writings already published. This is a technique of redundant composition he continued to employ. Many of his works are not only self-referential but also self-repeating.

For the first five years of his literary career, Jarry sustained himself largely by patching up and rewriting his earlier material, including the *Ubu* marionette plays. His first important full-length original work after *Ubu Roi* was a semi-novel published in 1897, an extended prose-poetic mélange, *Les jours et les nuits.* This narrative reverie fictionalizes Jarry's notion that the keenest of mental and bodily experience is an isthmus between waking and sleeping, a state in which reality takes on the guise of hallucination. Jarry readies his hero, Sengle, a military recruit, to live by an assertion of imaginative dominance in the face of a regimented army life. Days and nights constitute not only a division of time in relation to who possesses power when, but also a more

subtle play of imaginative projection in which days give way to nights, in which reverie is an augmentation of reality and a reworking of it into different forms and different shapes. Jarry realizes in his simple title the essential rhythm of opposition that at once merges and distinguishes experiences. Days and nights are both the dull repetitiveness of the soldier's life and the variations in his life that make it worth living or imagining. When nights are different from days, the nature of that difference results in a powerful shadow or ghost experience. Jarry's narrative depicts the way hallucinations reflect and distort commonplace experience into something far richer and more mysterious, something like an opium dream. It is no coincidence that among Jarry's journeyman pieces are translations of the opium-inspired poems and passages of the English romantic Samuel Taylor Coleridge, one of Jarry's poetic heroes. The most profound hallucination for Sengle, as for Jarry, is the most profound altered state: being out of one's body, being alive in death.

> Sengle free is condemned to death, and he knows the date. Now his white iron bed floats along in the shape of a gondola. Sengle, like an Eastern king, is encased to his waist in a black marble sheath that bit by bit envelops him. He recalls a walk in the woods with his brother, feeling as though he had imbibed quantities of hashish. His body walked underneath the trees, material and well-articulated; and he sensed a strange vapored essence above like a cloud made of ice— it must have been his astral body. Something else, more tenuous, moved a thousand feet above—perhaps his soul—and a visible thread linked the kitelike forms.
>
> (book 1, chap. 3)

The hallucinations that take place in *Les jours et les nuits* annihilate the living self to free the imagining one. Just as for Sengle, the supreme creative moment for Jarry in his own life was the imagination of a state beyond bodily constraints. Jarry's living world is nominally a separation of life and death, day and night, but aesthetically it is a merging of day into night, waking into sleeping, life into death. The dream state represents what Jarry's best critic, Roger Shattuck, calls "neither day nor night," but the state of the continuous nature of living and perceiving (and hence writing): "life as sustained hallucination." Shattuck's recurrent point about Jarry is that he tried intensely to live what he tried to write, and that his almost complete disintegration in the last years of his life was the result of his efforts to sustain the hallucinatory condition that he first wrote about in *Les jours et les nuits.*

In a passage from *Les jours et les nuits,* called "'Pataphysics," Jarry explains the process by which Sengle tries to trigger his hallucinations into his writing:

> Sengle constructed his literary efforts, curiously and precisely equilibrated, by sleeping a good fifteen hours, after eating and drinking, and then ejaculating the result in a wayward half hour's writing. This could be anatomized and atomized indefinitely, each molecule crystallized, according to the laws of matter, in a vital hierarchy, like the cells of the body. Some philosophy professors declare that the resemblance here to natural processes constitutes a Masterpiece.
>
> (book 4, chap. 2)

That Jarry offers imagination as a dream-induced "Masterpiece" in a section of his work called "'Pataphysics" requires some further explanation. Jarry's universe consists of a parodic anti-world, a world delineated by what from his boyhood days he defined as the science of 'Pataphysics, a system designed to treat not predictable laws but surprising exceptions. 'Pataphysics is a hallucinatory version of day reality—a simulacrum with a space of its own and operating under laws that exist *because* they are imagined.

Jarry's "original" science of 'Pataphysics, devised for Père Heb and Père Ubu, is fully revealed in the Rabelaisian adventures of *Doctor Faustroll.* 'Pataphysics is, very simply, imaginative potential, and Jarry stipulated that the word should always be preceded by an apostrophe, so that, like poetry personified

by the Muses, it can invoke itself as prelude to its very existence. He writes of 'Pataphysics in the second book of *Doctor Faustroll* as "the science of imaginary solutions, which symbolically attributes the properties of objects, described by their virtuality, to their lineaments." This makes 'Pataphysics the science of linguistic supplement, the world as actual derived from the word as possible ("l'univers supplémentaire").

'Pataphysics is not only a science and metaphysics for art, it is also a theological formula for the existence of God. The calculus in *Doctor Faustroll* holds that "the shortest distance between 0 and 00, in either direction," or "the tangential point between zero and infinity" is God. This makes God one of 'Pataphysics' imaginary solutions. Jarry tends to think of all experience as the line of movement or connection that unifies potentially opposite points. His notions carry some of the ancient and medieval baggage of hermetical or gnostic philosophy, in which the universe exists at all times in two versions that are at once opposite and identical. It is the radical nature of opposition that produces for Jarry an exhilarating or hallucinatory image of truth. His is not a formal or physical theory of opposition, one that would produce, say, the balance of the arch; nor is Jarry working toward a dialectical form of opposition where counterforces result in historical synthesis or progress. Rather, he sees in opposition that fusion of idea and image that augurs both destruction and escape. The idea that can be imagined is most powerful when the image that can be imagined is radically annihilating.

Since Jarry's notions of 'Pataphysical opposites are at once abstract and parodic, some specific examples might clarify what he means, although they may not fully explain the significance of what he means. In one of his short essays on modern progress, Jarry considers the image of two giant railway engines making their way in opposite directions on separate tracks, and then, in a 'Pataphysical gesture, he re-imagines them hurtling at each other from opposite directions on the same track. That, Jarry concludes, would produce the result he desires, a moment of transitory difference before a moment of devastating fusion: two machine-age dinosaurs in full splendor impacting and annihilating.

Jarry is not entirely solemn about his images of fused opposites. In *Doctor Faustroll* he speaks of Père Ubu having discovered in one of Jarry's earlier plays about the collapse of divinity, *César-Antéchrist* (1895), the identity of opposites ("l'identité des contraires") by means of his "physics stick." After an elaborate geometrical and dimensional description, the "physics stick" turns out to be a detached phallus. Jarry's discovery of the principle of 'Pataphysical opposition is therefore never very far from mocking, in one form or another, the energetic displays of sexual union, the fused opposition, that perpetuate the race.

Love is a recurrent theme in Jarry and a recurrent joke. The supposed "otherness" of sexual relations is primarily a projection of the self. Sengle has this to say about the joy of love in *Les jours et les nuits*: "It is not the communion of two beings in one, like the two halves of a man's heart, which, in the fetus, is double and separate; but the enjoyment of anachronism and of chatting with one's past." The self is in love with the projections of past and future time; that is, love is another form of imagination:

> The present, possessing in the heart of another its past, lives at the same time in its Self and its Self plus something more. If a moment of the present or a moment of the past existed separately at one point in time, it would not perceive this "plus something," which is simply the Act of Perception. This act for the thinking being is the most joyful one imaginable, very different from the sexual act.
>
> (book 2, chap. 1)

Jarry continues writing along these lines in *L'Amour absolu*, where his hero takes on the name of God, Emmanuel Dieu, and contemplates the nature of love as a series of relations possible when an individual has the multiple identities of a god. The female lead here, so to speak, is the Virgin Mary, whom Jarry compares with Jocasta, providing both a Christian and Greek cast for the family romance. Right around the time of Freud but with no knowledge of him, Jarry worked out a notion of ego-centered and conflicting love relations that exist for the individual when roles and desires prove unstable.

The subject of love and its discontents continues to occupy Jarry in his next two works, in many ways his finest narratives, the novellas *Messaline* and *The Supermale*. These are companion pieces, the first of which is set in the decadent Rome of the emperors and the second in the vaguely futuristic present.

Jarry derives the story of Messalina, the wife of Emperor Claudius, from the historical writings of Tacitus and Suetonius. In his version the account becomes a surreal and occasionally pornographic parody of the French neoclassical literary *bienséances* or proprieties. Jarry's empress/whore is as grand and bombastic and perhaps even as insatiate as a Racinian heroine, but much less willing to repress her desires. The narrative, deeply erotic, contains moments that are among the most brilliant of Jarry's writing. There is, for example, an almost poignant chapter (and chapter title), "Dansait quelquefois la nuit" ("He Danced Sometimes at Night"), in which the actor Mnester is compelled to perform at the birthday celebration of the emperor Claudius. At first he stands silent in front of the raucous and degenerate guests, complaining that people listen badly when they do not understand ("Le peuple attend mal quand il ne comprend pas"). Jarry must have remembered the time he stood before the curtain with the audience murmuring at his own *Ubu Roi*. Mnester next excuses himself by claiming that he has "just slept with Orestes," and only the intelligent Claudius understands that Mnester means he has just read the role from the Greek tragedy—everyone else assumes Orestes is his local homosexual lover. Messalina impatiently waves aside Mnester's excuse, claiming, as well she might, that she has just slept with dozens of Oresteses. The actor finally performs, reluctantly, deliberatively, and cunningly, after he realizes that Messalina intends to punish him by making love to him and then having him poisoned.

Jarry's penultimate chapter, on the death of Messalina, "Atropos dans les jardins de Lucullus" ("Atropos in the Gardens of Lucullus"), provides another extraordinary moment in the narrative. It is a tour de force on sexual dying in which ecstasy takes shape as agony. (Jarry returns to this theme with a comic difference in *The Supermale.*) In the ancient version Messalina is about to be brutally stabbed by a tribune, but throughout the episode she confuses the fate that is to befall her with the desire that has defined her. Readiness is all—for love or death. She prepares to take the sword in the same way she would like to take the swordsman. Everyone knows what is about to happen, even Messalina, but she summons in her memory all her lovers to stymie the final moment or, in another sense, prolong it. The ecstasy is such that even the malformed Claudius, her husband emperor, is called up. That he appeals to her sexually is more a final appeal to *him* before her violent end. Her reverie seems to count on the cadences of the biblical Song of Songs, presumably a 'Pataphysical or imaginative potential since she would not know it otherwise:

> Claudius, my love, stay so that I this evening can undress you! You are beautiful because you are old, old, and bald, so bald that nothing can be more naked! nor uglier, oh, my love! Where man's ugliness stops, at his paroxysm, there only does the beauty of the flower begin. Come, lily of the gardens! come, my emperor!
>
> (chap. 7)

Messalina confuses her ruling passion with her ruling husband. What comes to her instead is the naked blade of the tribune's sword. Messalina dies only when the blade is with-

drawn from her body, not when it enters. As the sword falls on the bed of flowers at her feet, the perpetrator who provided her with her last ecstasy mutters, "Whore."

The sexual companion piece to *Messaline, The Supermale,* is Jarry's funniest and most original short novel. Jarry begins with his hero Marceuil's claim that the sexual act is capable of indefinite duration, a proposition that obviously goes beyond the erotic finale of *Messaline.* But before he works out the sexual plot of his narrative, a scheme based on the metaphor of perpetual motion, Jarry takes up the same subject in a more overtly absurd and mechanistic guise. He depicts an amazing ten-thousand-mile bicycle race from Europe to Russia and back, in which a five-man cycle is pitted against a locomotive engine. Jarry had a fascination with bicycles. In one of his most outlandish short essays, he announces the Stations of the Cross and the Passion of Christ as if he were doing the commentary on a bicycle race. In *The Supermale* he simply makes the bicycle the symbol of all that is scaled to human potential and to human absurdity.

The five pedalers, whose feet are interconnected with straps and an aluminum rod, are fed on "Perpetual-Motion-Food," something concocted by an American Gilded Age chemist. The race begins and the riders pedal for three days at a tremendous rate without stopping, until something horrifying goes wrong. Jarry has one of the cyclists, Ted Oxborrow, later describe the event in a news article. He remembers noticing the figure in front of him jerking strangely to the rhythm of the pedaling. Soon after, his nose catches wafts of "the *cadaverous* stench of an incomprehensibly accelerated decomposition." Here Jarry's marionette-inspired imagination takes over. The dead rider, a stiff in modern idiom, is still animated by the pedaling motion of the connecting rod but in a recalcitrant and irregular way. To win the race, the cadaver must be gotten back in sync:

> It was an onerous task, one that I hope never to experience again in any race. The man kicked,

counterpedaled, *seized up.* It was extraordinary how this term, which applied to the friction of machines, also applied to the cadaver, which continued to do what it did right under my nose. Ten times we were tempted to disconnect the rods that secured our five pairs of legs together—counting the dead man's. But he was bound up, locked in, weighted, wrapped, and sealed into his seat—and then . . . he would have been a *dead* weight (I needn't search for the phrase), and a dead weight was surely not essential in order to win this trying race.

(chap. 5)

The four live riders fed on Perpetual-Motion-Food and the flailing corpse killed by it finally reset the cadence: "'Let's get going, uh?, you pig.' Little by little he got into the swing of it, his legs following ours, his *ankle play* [italicized in English by Jarry] sequencing in, and, finally, he began pedaling in mad fury." Paced by the newly coordinated energy of the corpse, the five-man team speeds past the finish line ahead of the train, which had disintegrated near the end of the course, when its owner in desperation began dumping Perpetual-Motion-Food into its steam engine. But another curious bike racer joins in for the last few minutes, a racer merely using the occasion to warm up for the contest to follow: this is Jarry's super-hero, André Marcueil.

The idea in *The Supermale* is to make modern performance extend at once beyond the historical performance represented in *Messaline* and the machine-age performance represented in the bicycle-train race. There is a further issue involved in Jarry's companion novels: Messalina represents the female sexual instinct, and now André is on hand to represent the males. In his two narratives Jarry tries re-answering the riddle put to the mythical Tiresias, who at various times in his life was a man and woman, about who experienced greater sexual response. Tiresias answered woman; Jarry answers man. But his real answer is that sex finally kills. In every sense Messalina takes the sword; Marcueil, later disguised as an Indian complete with tomahawk (Jarry has translated the notion of empire westward), engages in an epic lovemaking contest with an American girl, while seven Parisian doxies, stimulated to the brink of a participatory orgy, look on. At the end of the exhibition, Marcueil, "like any ordinary Jove," proves indefatigable. In a final test of his perpetual manhood or motion, he is hooked to a voltage-generating machine to see if he can inspire it to superhuman (or machine-like) feats of love. He does so, actually making the machine respond to him by infusing it with his current, exciting it. But he gets the contraption so revved up that it shoots its voltage back through him and fries him to a crisp. This is one of the most absurd moments in all of Jarry's writings, but it also fulfills one of the primary principles of 'Pataphysical fiction: we witness an exceptional performance, one whose final effect is annihilative.

Jarry's *Supermale* is the closest he came to sustaining a narrative action with a semblance of a plot. In his most famous non-dramatic work, *Exploits and Opinions of Doctor Faustroll, 'Pataphysician: A Neo-Scientific Novel,* published posthumously, plot is a secondary matter. *Faustroll* is Jarry's hodgepodge of narrative bits and pieces ranging from the imaginary voyage, to legalistic parody, to scientific double-talk, to mock biography, to sheer nonsense. The narrative is what is known in the literary tradition as menippea, a form named after the Greek satirist Menippus, whose particular skill was mimicking dozens of literary styles in the same work. Lucian's *True History,* Rabelais's *Gargantua and Pantagruel,* Cyrano de Bergerac's *Comical History of the States and Empires of the Sun and Moon,* Swift's *Gulliver's Travels,* and Lewis Carroll's *Alice in Wonderland* are other famous examples of menippea. Jarry surely knew the form, since in the catalogue of Faustroll's library, itself a standard feature of menippea, he cites both Rabelais and Cyrano as precursors. He also cites his *Ubu* cycle, a dramatic version of menippea. Therefore Jarry is his own precursor, which may be inescapably true for all artists whether or not they admit it.

Doctor Faustroll presents a sequence of adventures, none of them possible and all of them outlandish. Jarry's parodic odyssey is adapted to the medieval legend of Faust, the pursuer of forbidden knowledge. Faustroll's forbidden knowledge is the familiar 'Pataphysics. Like Faust, Faustroll is reborn in old age: "Doctor Faustroll was born in Circassia in 1898 (the 20th century was [-2] years old) at the age of sixty-three years." He is constantly on the move with creditors at his heels, having incurred most of the bad debts of Western bourgeois civilization. Covered with hair below the groin and hairless above, he is something of a *belle époque* satyr. As with all Jarry's creations, Faustroll knows little modesty. Having been created by Jarry, he then becomes all-powerful. When some locals ask him if he's a Christian, he responds, "I am God." If so, he is a prankster god. Similar to the medieval Faust *geste* book, the *gestes* in Jarry's title means both "exploits" and what it has come to mean, "joke" or "jest." Jarry's Faustian impulse here recalls his constant theme: the imagination as a hallucinatory summoning or invocation, and the price exacted for the opportunity to experience what the imagination has to offer. Death is still the end of imagination, its goal and its finality.

The narrative begins with Faustroll's arrest warrant, which appears in his text as an elaborately printed document complete with its official seal. Faustroll is arrested, of course, less because of his ostensible failure to pay arrears on his rent than because, like the avant-garde he represents, he is unconventional. In literary terms, he is not only unconventional but represented or portrayed as illegal. Like the *Grand Testament* of the famous fifteenth-century poet and outlaw François Villon, Faustroll's testament is the apology of the outcast, the scapegrace, the bourgeois radical. Faustroll even judges himself as others would judge him—he hangs himself almost daily with an order-of-merit ribbon, which is a kind of ritual and sexual death known to the world of sadomasochism, and also a telling comment on the relation of the avant-garde to the bourgeois. Faustroll employs the archetypal French insignia, the order of merit, for violent and by implication debasing ends. Of course, if he can be born at the age of sixty-three, he can also hang himself without dying.

Faustroll's journey consists of a voyage in a bed, transformed, as is the case with Sengle's gondola in *Les jours at les nuits*, into a boat capable of traveling on air, land, or water. Accompanying Faustroll on his travels to strange lands—more or less the districts and suburbs of Paris—is a bailiff named Pamphule and a deformed lackey named Bosse-de-Nage, who follows everyone else's expostulations with a short laugh: "Ha!" The "Ha!," which Jarry calls the adventure's natural punctuation, is both the narrative's larger joke and the potential reaction of Jarry's readers to him and he to them.

Like Jarry in his writings, during his travels Faustroll navigates in another dimension, between the lines of the books and artists who make up his avant-garde dreams. Each of Faustroll's realms is dedicated to one of Jarry's literary or artistic friends or acquaintances (Aubrey Beardsley, Paul Gauguin, Mallarmé), and each seems in some central way related to its dedicatee. Beardsley's place is the Land of Lace, and a mere glance at a Beardsley illustration makes sense of this description of his territory. Gauguin inhabits the exotic Land of Fragrance. Mallarmé is depicted on the Isle of Ptyx, whose physical surface is much like the expressive verbal surface of Mallarmé's symbolist poetry. It is as if the features of Faustroll's travels formed a composite allegory of *belle époque* literary and visual art. That is precisely why *Doctor Faustroll* holds so prominent a place, along with the *Ubu* cycle, in the collective mythology that surrounds Jarry as the incarnation of the radical avant-garde sensibility.

THE UBU CYCLE

To review the *Ubu* cycle is to review Jarry at his best and worst, at his most liberated and sophomoric. Even if Jarry's best is in a sense his worst, there can be no doubt that Ubu is a memorable figure on the modern theatrical landscape. If nothing else, Jarry with his *Ubu Roi* can, as the theater historian Martin Esslin argues, lay primary claim to being the father of the theater of the absurd. The remarkable advent of Jarry's notorious play in 1896 framed the attack on bourgeois literary, social, and political forms and aesthetic values that would be sustained in the surrealist movement of the pre–World War I decade. After the war Jarry's *Ubu* plays contributed in no small part to Artaud's theater of cruelty and to Bertolt Brecht's epic theater. And the innovative devices in the *Ubu* cycle—including the undermining of realistic stage action, the stark, almost assaultive rendering of stage scenery, the disjointed, hostile, and shocking dialogue, the radical nature of characterization—would reappear in markedly similar ways in the post–World War II work of Jean Genet, Eugène Ionesco, and Samuel Beckett, whose plays contain the same kinds of modulations between convention and iconoclasm that characterize *Ubu Roi.*

Moreover, there is a political element in the *Ubu* cycle that touches modernism in ways Jarry could not have known in the 1890's but that he might have predicted. Ubu is base man, the scourge of power without restraint, of ambition without law, and of violence without mercy. The twentieth century has seen tyrants like him, and ex post facto, we can mark in *Ubu Roi* the contours of a bleak and vicious vision of fascist man. For Jarry a world subject to supreme tyranny falls into a violent state of hypocrisy. Just how this state of hypocrisy turns into Nazi Germany or even Vichy France is a phenomenon that would have fascinated Jarry, though not surprised him.

There are four plays in the *Ubu* cycle: *Ubu Roi* (*Ubu the King*, 1896), *Ubu cocu* (*Ubu Cuckolded*, published posthumously in 1944), *Ubu enchaîné* (*Ubu Enchained*, 1900), *Ubu sur la butte* (*Ubu on the Mound*, 1906). Only the first play was fully performed by actors during

Jarry's lifetime, although the last two of the cycle were performed in marionette versions at the Parisian Théâtre des Pantins and the Théâtre Guignol des Gueles de Bois. The least significant of the cycle, *Ubu sur la butte,* is like the interlude of a more substantial dramatic trilogy and as such seems minimal as part of the sequence—it is also thematically backsliding in that Ubu appears much more as a marketable part of the social order than as its antagonist.

The phases of the cycle represented by the three major plays all point to aspects of Ubu as a human contrary. He is born in the anti-system of 'Pataphysics, and he sustains the mark of his birth. Ubu as ruler, as pervert, and as slave evolve from Jarry's madcap formulations for the marionette theater at Rennes. The subtitle of *Ubu Roi* for its Parisian publication alludes to its provincial origins: "Drama in five acts in prose restored and performed as it was performed by the marionettes of the Théâtre des Phynances in 1888."

Of course recycled juvenilia is not the whole story of the *Ubu* cycle. Jarry kept refashioning his work in accord with his voracious reading at the Parisian lycée and in accord with his exposure to the work of his avant-garde colleagues. Most of all the *Ubu* cycle thrives on a body of allusion to landmark works in the Western dramatic and narrative tradition. From its titles to its actions—usurpation, rebellion, enslavement, betrayal—we see and hear the ghosts of Oedipus, Prometheus, Macbeth, Don Quixote, El Cid, Don Juan, and Faust.

When Mallarmé wrote his review of the opening-night performance of *Ubu Roi,* he could not help thinking of what Jarry had done with his play in terms of the repertoire of the classical tragic theater, or at least the perpetuation of that repertoire as ideal literary fare: "He enters into the repertoire of high taste and haunts me." It is as if Jarry loomed above even Pierre Corneille. In the dedication of the published version of the play to his friend Marcel Schwob, Jarry writes in the pseudo–Old French

ALFRED JARRY

he employs in the play that Ubu is the conti-
nental manifestation of the great Shakespeare,
that Ubu was "subsequently ordained Shakespeare by the English" ("dont fut depuis
nommé par les Anglois Shakespeare"). His
pear-shaped head, like Shakespeare's, proves
that he, Ubu, is the author of many tragedies.
What Jarry means is that many tragedies have
authored *Ubu.*

Tragedy is not the only haunt of Ubu as
king. Perhaps looming even more prominently
"behind" him is Shakespeare's Falstaff, the
sine qua non of comic vulgarization. Like
Falstaff, Ubu is one of those great comic
demiurges of literature, the clever, dissimulat-
ing buffoon playing the role of materialist
subversive. He is the mind that eats in
conjunction with the belly that thinks. Ubu is
appetite without scruple—Rabelais's Stomach
God. Jarry said that what he depicted onstage
he wished the public to see as an exaggeration
of its own nature, an ignoble, gluttonous,
crafty, self-serving, tyrannical nature wearing
the mask of a comic scapegrace.

Another way to think of the *Ubu* cycle is to
imagine Jarry as both an amateur puppeteer
and a practicing cartoonist, as indeed he was
throughout his career. His cartoon of Ubu in
the 1896 edition looks much like a caricature
of Jarry himself, in a bowler with a funny little
mustache and goatee. All Jarry's drawings and
woodcuts for his specialized periodicals have
the outline of Ubu in them; that is, when Jarry
came to help design the costumes and settings
for the play's production in 1896, he adapted
the raw and primitive cartoon shapes of his
earlier drawings to the stage. He even arranged
to hang drawings on cardboard signs around
the characters' necks to make them seem hastily and brusquely conceived rather than realistically represented. Jarry's onstage speech to
the opening-night audience referred to Ubu as
a spherical form possessing the greatest number of facets—a caricature, a puppet, a grotesque sketch.

The love of puppets and the love of caricature is the love of the irregular outline, the

mechanically crafted, and the oddly disposed.
Jarry's drawings, figures, and characters look
odd; those of his characters that move, move
awkwardly; those that make noise, make noise
strangely. Jarry insisted to his producer,
Lugné-Poe, that he find an actor capable of the
special movements and accents he intended
for Ubu. He wanted live figures pretending to
do inanimate imitations of animate people.
Jarry told the audience that he would have
used giant marionettes if he could, and that he
had even considered attaching strings from
the rafters to each of his actors. His masked
and starkly costumed characters resembled
the heavily stylized figures in a Greek satyr
play, probably the original—as Jarry conceived it—of the life-size puppets of the stage.

Had Jarry lived long enough to experience
the commercial animated cartoons made possible by the invention of the motion picture
camera, he would have seen in the spirit of
animation what he attempted in the physical
action of the *Ubu* cycle. In fact, if it is possible
to capture the feeling of Jarry's work by analogy, a Popeye cartoon might do the trick nicely.
It boasts of the same recuperative mayhem,
rapid changes of fame and fortune, and violent
absurdities. In *Ubu Cuckolded,* for example,
one of Jarry's characters gets impaled and
then, as an afterthought, disimpaled, not
much worse for wear in either case. Ubu plans
to beat another character, twisting his nose
and ears, pulling out his tongue, extracting
his teeth, lacerating his ass, hacking at his
spinal cord, shredding the fibers of his brain,
beheading, drawing, and quartering him. After
all this Ubu promises clemency so the character can be ceremonially hanged in order that
no more harm can come to him.

The plots of the Ubu plays usually make as
little sense as the nature of the action represented in them. *Ubu Roi* consists of the violent
usurpation of the Polish throne, a long-standing European joke, in that the throne of Poland
was not only contested as an elected principal-
ity but also perpetually divided among the
imperial powers of Europe. Poland is a symbol

of misappropriated territory, and the theme of the play is the instability of the appropriating "state" of mind, the same theme Shakespeare employs to such effect in *Macbeth.* Usurpation is nightmarish possession.

The curtain opens on a painted backdrop indicating a wide range of climate: a blossoming apple tree, a bare tree with snow, and tropical trees. A door opens into a painted sky; a skeleton dangles near the door. Ubu appears robed center stage and prepares to utter the infamous "Merdre," whose extra "r" reappears in other of Jarry's works as a floating signifier. Ubu is preparing to usurp Poland at the beginning of the action. Metaphorically, the play commences where the anarchist avant-garde always wishes to be—in the supposed ethical, social, political vacuum created by the bourgeois orders of Europe. Of the king of Poland's masses of children, Madame Ubu asks the significant question "Why not massacre the lot of them and take their place?" In the meanwhile Ubu, a violent rival, presents the Polish king he plans to assassinate with the gift of a reed pipe. The gesture is sinister and Oedipal in that the Polish king says he is too old to learn to play his instrument; the weak king gives way to the phallic Ubu, who will then take the crown, the scepter, and the name of the father: Pa Ubu.

Ubu has no plans; his rule is predicated on the tactics of the immediate. He governs at the bench of negligent justice, where sentences are rendered before witnesses are called. In his world tyranny is anarchy, greed is equity. He begins by distributing the wealth of the bankers and industrialists to the people, but only so that he can bribe his way to complete power. His first real pleasure as king comes not from the distribution of gold but from witnessing his subjects bashing in each other's heads in the courtyard to gain the booty. Policy as spectacle makes Ubu's rule akin to that of the degenerate emperors of Rome, where bread was interchangeable with circuses. Ubu is fated to have a short-lived reign. He represents power, but power without the spirit of conservation.

"Who is this Ubu?" someone asks. Bougrelas, the Polish king's son, whose name takes on a more unseemly connotation in French than in English, replies, "An adventurer from no one knows where, an abject derelict, a groveling tramp" ("Un aventurier sorti on ne sait d'ou, vile crapule, vagabond honteux"). Ubu claims he has come to change everything, but the anarchist's creed is a mere reflex or self-reflex in Ubu's case. He makes this remark after he has rid himself of the Polish nobility and judiciary and is ready to face down the financiers. Naturally the financiers argue conservatively that there is nothing that needs changing. Their ideological position is tinged with irony, since after Ubu there *is* nothing left to change.

The power play in *Ubu Roi* turns out to be mercurial: in short order Ubu loses what he has just taken. Jarry introduces an even bigger European bully, the tsar's army, to assist the Polish military officers in wresting the Polish throne back from Ubu. At the end of the play, Ubu is in flight on the Baltic Sea heading toward Hamlet's Elsinore. The fate of the deposed king is very close to the scatological parody that Jarry announced from the play's first word. Jarry puns on the tragic denouement (unknotting) and on the wind let out, so to speak, of Ubu's royal sails: "We're doing a million knots an hour, and once tied these knots can't be untied again. We have the wind in our poop" ("nous avons vent arrière").

In *Ubu Cuckolded* (which found neither a producer nor a publisher in Jarry's lifetime) Ubu the deposed king has "beetl'd o'er his base" back into bourgeois France. Actually he never really left, since the material in this play is drawn from the domestic myth of the old Père Heb chronicle, not the international one. This play, parts of which appeared in Jarry's first publication, *Guignol,* was virtually complete before Jarry patched *Ubu Roi* together. If *Ubu Roi* is absurd epic drama, *Ubu Cuckolded* is violent French farce. In this play Ubu is a mere professor of 'Pataphysics cuckolded by Ma Ubu and an Egyptian named Memnon

ALFRED JARRY

(after the musical statue). Memnon, a garbage truck driver, spends the play disguised as a clock. The action proper (or, more accurately, improper) begins when Ubu takes over the house of a loser named Achras, a professor of Polyhedra. Contested territory is reduced from Poland to a cluttered domicile. Ubu debates with his Conscience (a separate character) whether or not he ought to kill his host immediately and be done with it. Conscience says no because Achras is defenseless, but Ubu responds, with a logic perfectly appropriate to him, that Achras' defenselessness is all the more reason to kill him.

In the fashion of French farces, a good deal of action takes place in a single room, although the performance would be easier for puppets or for cartoon characters than for actors. Ubu, for example, impales Achras, but the professor, revived by Ubu's conscience, prepares a trapdoor descent for Ubu, who then gets stuck in the opening. Immobile, he has to watch the action go on around him—the cuckold plot on the one hand and the guest-host plot on the other. Achras, with Ubu as captive audience, threatens to read his guest to death by reciting his sixty-years-in-the-making treatise on the characteristics of Polyhedra. This is a ridiculous play from beginning to end, and when Jarry offered either *Ubu Cuckolded* or *Ubu Roi* to Lugné-Poe for production in 1896, Lugné-Poe selected *Ubu Roi* for obvious reasons.

The third play of the cycle, *Ubu Enchained* (bound), is named after Aeschylus' *Prometheus Bound*. *Ubu Enchained* is the natural sequel to *Ubu Roi*. In it Ubu remembers the Polish experience and acts to counter its effect. The play begins with Ubu in France sometime after his Baltic escape from Poland. He comes forward onstage silently as Ma Ubu hectors him about the scandalous opening word—"Merdre"—of the first Ubu play: "You surely haven't forgotten the word?" Ubu responds that the word got him in so much trouble the first time around that he would just as soon skip mentioning it. Jarry has made the

action in *Ubu Roi,* onstage and off, a metaphor for his own artistic history. It is as if the first play were Jarry's "Polish" usurpation, and this one his French slavery. Ubu first wished to possess a throne, now he merely wished to preserve his freedom. Slaves, he figures, are all-powerful in enlightened European nations. In the France of liberty, law, and equality ("l'égalité" puns in French on "légalité"), Ubu can hold little power until he gives it all away.

Playing on Jarry's doctrine of the identity of opposites, *Ubu Enchained* turns *Ubu Roi* around. All that is desirable there is anathema here. Asked by Ma Ubu about his scepter from *Ubu Roi,* his "shitterstick," Ubu says he does not use it anymore—it amuses children but frightens grownups. This is not only a capsule history of the course of Jarry's puppet theatrical career from Rennes to Paris, but also a capsule description of the nature and reception of avant-garde art generally. What the unrestrained imagination can assimilate appalls the conventional mind.

Ubu Enchained inverts and parodies French ideas about bourgeois citizenship. Throughout the play, Ubu tries to be the perfect slave in search of the perfect conventional master. As the charmingly named Pissedoux (Sweetpiss) puts it: "There are those then who can't bear the idea of being free?" ("Il y a donc des gens que cela embête d'être libres?") Those who refuse to enslave Ubu, he robs or threatens with violence. It finally occurs to the renegade king that what he requires as the ideal French habitat is prison. There he can be truly at home. Prison replaces the palace as the object of anti-bourgeois desire. The persistent joke in the play is that the free in France are hostage to the French system—risk, poverty, crime—whereas the slave or prisoner lives like a king.

Because the freedom to be absolutely free is a kind of will to slavery in France, the occupation of choice in the land is the military. And the free French take most pleasure in the strictest of military drill, where every motion is monitored and commanded. Since those who are soldiers by their own free will enjoy

684

the right not to obey the rules, they tend to do the exact opposite and obey them to the letter just to prove they are free to do so. The play, of course, enacts the paradox of bourgeois life: individuality is hapless conformity. At the end, Ubu worries that he will be crowned king again because he so much does not want to be. He would rather serve in the sultan's navy as a galley slave.

But Ubu cannot escape his fate. He actually becomes king of the slaves and re-enacts his circle of tyranny with the ex-prisoners in his retinue until his French masters disappoint him by rebelling against the conditions of their freedom. They too wish to be slaves, and demand of Ubu that he relinquish his ball and chain. Ubu struggles valiantly to retain his status as prisoner, refusing to give orders to his fellow slaves. They obey anyway because in the midst of anarchy they are free *not to.* The only solution is to ship out of France by finding a convenient Turkish galley fleet, which in the geopolitical fantasy of the *Ubu* cycle is as available as any other imaginary solution. Ubu storms aboard the flagship of the galley fleet, claiming that the French have stolen his accoutrements, his ball and chain, and routed him out of prison. He rants, raves, and creates general havoc aboard ship until the Turks promise to enslave him. The last scene reveals an ecstatic Ubu chained to a bench at the head of a bank of oars as the galley moves further and further from France. If *Ubu Roi,* the first of the cycle, concludes with Ubu on the high seas, a failed tyrant moving toward France, *Ubu Enchained* concludes with Ubu on the high seas, a failed slave moving away from France. Jarry circles around the myth of Ubu he has created by rendering its 'Pataphysical opposites as inverse actions.

POSTHUMOUS JARRY

Although much of the story of Jarry will forever focus on one event—the premiere evening in 1896 of *Ubu Roi*—his reputation has undergone a spirited revival in the post–World War II avant-garde world of Europe. Even after World War I, Jarry enjoyed something of a cult status, and those of his works unpublished during his life were printed for the first time. By the 1940's and after, not only were Jarry's already-published works reprinted in prestigious new complete editions, but revivals of his plays also caused excitement and controversy wherever they were staged. An early 1960's revival of *Ubu Roi* in Los Angeles, for example, resulted in the local West Hollywood police issuing an arrest warrant for a certain Alfred Jarry, playwright, on charges of public obscenity.

In Europe after World War II, a kind of absurd honor society was formed around Jarry's memory under the auspices of a supposed College of 'Pataphysics. Established in France in December 1948, this pseudo-college, with its own series of publications, was the brainchild of a number of Europe's most prominent literary and artistic figures, including the dramatist Eugene Ionesco, the writer Raymond Queneau, the filmmaker René Clair, and the artists Marcel Duchamp, Jean Miró, and Jean Dubuffet.

The large and elaborate effort of the College of 'Pataphysics was much in keeping with the spirit of Jarry's life and works: it was a serious hoax. Officers of the college took upon themselves highblown titles and lowborn functions, such as the "Regent of the Dialectics of Useless Sciences," the "Regent of Erotics and Pornosophy," and the "Regent of Blablabla and Mateology." A series of commissions, such as the "Commission of Ellipses, Eclipses, and Anaesthetics" or the "Commission of Unpredictabilities," undertook the work of the college and designated material to appear in its various publications. In May 1960, twelve years after the founding of the college, the American avant-garde journal *The Evergreen Review* devoted an entire issue to the origin, history, and ancillary publications of the College of 'Pataphysics. The college's branches were now spread worldwide. Roger Shattuck, located then in Austin, Texas, was the "General Proveditor Propagator for the Islands and Americas," while the same function for Jarry was taken up on the other side of the world's ideological iron curtain by one Nicolaj Nicolaievitch Kamenev, "Proveditor Propagator for the Scythian, Slaveonic, and Lower Tartar Regions." In a bizarre way, not incommensurate with his own 'Pataphysics as the science of imaginary solutions, Ubu Jarry still lives on all over the globe.

Selected Bibliography

EDITIONS

INDIVIDUAL WORKS
Works published after 1907 are posthumously published.

Les minutes de sable mémorial. Paris, 1894.
César-Antéchrist. Paris, 1895.
Ubu Roi. Paris, 1896.
Les jours et les nuits. Paris, 1897.
L'Amour absolu. Paris, 1899.
Ubu enchaîné. Paris, 1900.
L'Almanach illustré du Père Ubu. Paris, 1901.
Messaline: Roman de l' ancienne Rome. Paris, 1901.
Le surmâle. Paris, 1902.
Ubu sur la butte. Paris, 1906.
Pantagruel. Paris, 1910.
Gestes et opinions du docteur Faustroll, 'pataphysicien: Roman néo-scientifique. Paris, 1911; new ed., 1923.
Ubu Roi: Drama en cinque actes, d'après les éditions publiées du vivant de l'auteur et les documents icono-bibliographiques qui s'y rapportent. Preface by Jean Saltas. Paris, 1921.
Les minutes des sable mémorial, suivies de César-Antéchrist. Foreword by Jean Saltas. Paris, 1932.
La dragonne. Paris, 1943.
Ubu cocu. Geneva, 1944.

COLLECTED WORKS
Oeuvres poétiques complètes. Edited by Henri Parison. Introduction by André Frédérique. Paris, 1945.
Oeuvres complètes. Monte Carlo and Lausanne, 1948.
Tout Ubu. Edited by Maurice Saillet. Paris, 1962.

Oeuvres complètes. Edited by Michel Arrivé. Paris, 1972. Pléiade edition.

TRANSLATIONS

The Garden of Priapus (Messaline). Translated by Louis Coleman. New York, 1932.
Selected Works. Edited by Roger Shattuck and Simon Watson Taylor. New York, 1965. Includes *Exploits and Opinions of Doctor Faustroll, 'Pataphysician: A Neo-Scientific Novel,* translated by Simon Watson Taylor.
The Supermale. Translated by Barbara Wright. New York, 1977.
The Ubu Plays (Ubu Rex, Ubu Cuckolded, Ubu Enchained). Translated by Cyril Connolly and Simon Watson Taylor. London, 1968.
Ubu Roi: Drama in Five Acts. Translated by Barbara Wright. New York, 1951.

BIOGRAPHICAL AND CRITICAL STUDIES

Arnaud, Noël. *Alfred Jarry, d'Ubu Roi au Docteur Faustroll.* Paris, 1974.
Arrivé, Michel. *Les langages de Jarry: Essai de sémiotique littéraire.* Paris, 1972.
————. *Lire Jarry.* Paris, 1976.
Barrault, Jean-Louis. *Jarry sur la butte; spectacle d'après les oeuvres complètes d'Alfred Jarry.* Paris, 1970.
Behar, Henri. *Jarry: Le monstre et la marionette.* Paris, 1973.
————. *Jarry dramaturge.* Paris, 1979.
Cahiers du College de 'Pataphysique, nos. 2–28 (1950–1958), and *Dossiers du College de 'Pataphysique,* nos. 2, 5, 8, 13, 18–20, 22–24, 26–27 (1958–1965).
Caradec, François. *À la recherche d'Alfred Jarry.* Paris, 1974.
Church, Dan M. "Pere Ubu: The Creation of a Literary Type." *Drama Survey* 4:233–244 (1965).
Cooper, Judith. *"Ubu Roi": An Analytical Study.* New Orleans, 1974.
Esslin, Martin. *The Theatre of the Absurd.* New York, 1961.
Evergreen Review 4, no. 13 (1960).
Grossman, Manuel. "Alfred Jarry and the Theater of the Absurd." *Educational Theater Journal* 19: 473–477 (1967).
————. "Alfred Jarry and the Theater of His Time." *Modern Drama* 13:10–21 (1970).

Humphries, John Jefferson. "The Machine as Metaphor: Jarry's *Pompe à merdre.*" *Romantic Review* 73:346–354 (1982).

Knapp, Bettina. "A Spiritual Heir: Antonin Artaud and the Théâtre Alfred Jarry." *Dada/Surrealism* 4:10–16 (1974).

Poggioli, Renato. *The Theory of the Avant-Garde.* Translated by Gerald Fitzgerald. Cambridge, Mass., 1968.

Rachilde, Madame de. *Alfred Jarry, ou Le surmâle des lettres.* Paris, 1928.

Shattuck, Roger. *The Banquet Years: The Arts in France 1885–1918.* New York, 1955.

Springer, Michael. "From Actor to Ubu: Jarry's Theater of the Double." *Modern Drama* 16:1–11 (1973).

Stillman, Linda Krieger. *Alfred Jarry.* Boston, 1983.

Wallarth, G. E. "Alfred Jarry: The Seed of the Avant-Garde Drama." *Criticism* 4:108–119 (1962).

MICHAEL SEIDEL

HUGO VON HOFMANNSTHAL

(1874–1929)

HUGO VON HOFMANNSTHAL's appearance on the literary scene in Vienna in the early 1890's was an unprecedented phenomenon. Stefan Zweig, an Austrian contemporary, called him "one of the wonders of early perfection" and claimed that he had made an eternal name for himself in literature by the age of seventeen with unforgettable verse and unsurpassed prose. Hermann Bahr, another contemporary, was equally enthusiastic about the young Hofmannsthal and welcomed him as a writer who could foster for a new age the modernity Bahr called for, and thus help to rejuvenate Austrian writing. The world of letters in the 1890's was open to the young poet who stood at the head of his Austrian contemporaries; indeed, he was soon approached from Germany by Stefan George, who asked Hofmannsthal to join him and his circle in leading a so-called literary dictatorship of taste.

Hofmannsthal was born on 1 February 1874 in Vienna, Austria, where he was brought up in the world of the Viennese aristocracy. His family heritage was cosmopolitan; his grandparents were of Austrian, Italian, and Swabian blood. As a reward for service to the people, Ferdinand I of Austria had raised his great-grandfather, Isaac Löw Hofmann, a Jewish industrialist, to the nobility in 1835 with the title "Edler von Hofmannsthal." Hofmannsthal's father, Hugo August Peter von Hofmannsthal, had studied law and then be-

come the director of a leading bank in Vienna. In 1873 he married Anna Maria Josefa Fohleutner, the daughter of a judge and imperial notary, and their son, Hugo, was born a year later.

An extremely intelligent youth, Hofmannsthal was educated by private tutors at home until he entered Vienna's famous high school, the Akademisches Gymnasium, which he attended from 1884 to 1892. By the age of twelve he is said to have read Wolfgang von Goethe, Friedrich von Schiller, Heinrich von Kleist, and Franz Grillparzer. By the age of fifteen he knew Homer, Dante, Shakespeare, Voltaire, Robert Browning, and Lord Byron. And by the age of eighteen he was acquainted with the works of Plato, the major Russian and Scandinavian writers, the French philosophers, Friedrich Nietzsche, and the works of most of his own contemporary Europeans. He wrote in five languages and read eight fluently. Before he graduated from the Akademisches Gymnasium, he had published poems and essays under the pseudonyms Theophil Morren and Loris Melikow because high school students were not allowed to publish under their own names at that time in Vienna. Before he was twenty he had produced a masterful piece, the lyrical play *Der Tor und der Tod* (*Death and the Fool*, 1900). In 1892 he entered the University of Vienna to study law. Six years later, having changed disciplines in the meantime, he completed his doctorate in Romance languages and literatures with a thesis on Victor Hugo, but soon gave up plans to become a university professor in favor of devoting all his energies to writing.

Hofmannsthal's activities as a writer took many directions and reached extraordinary levels of achievement. As a writer of verse in his early years he produced a small but highly significant corpus of lyric poetry comparable to the works of Goethe in depth and style. His essays, beautifully constructed and perceptive, deal with a remarkably wide range of topics from literature, art, music, and theater to politics and history. Not a few of them are devoted to descriptions of travel. All are marked by a lucidity of style that complements their intention to persuade and inform, and their language matches that of his poetry and plays in elegance and grace, richness and beauty. From the publication of his first essay in 1901 as a youth of seventeen publishing under the pseudonym Loris until his death in 1929, he wrote over two hundred essays. But it was as a playwright and as a librettist for Richard Strauss that Hofmannsthal finally became most successful and famous.

In June 1901 Hofmannsthal married Gertrud Schlesinger and moved to a house in Rodaun near Vienna. There, with their three children—Christiane, a daughter, born in May 1902, and two sons, Franz, born in October 1903, and Raimund, born in May 1906—they lived for the remainder of Hofmannsthal's life. During these years Hofmannsthal traveled widely and worked constantly to develop his gifts as a writer.

World War I brought an end to the Austrian monarchy and Viennese society he had known since birth, and from that time on he worked to restore his world in a larger, European context. Two years before the war began he edited a collection of older narrative writers, published in 1912 under the title *Deutsche Erzähler* (German Storytellers). It includes twenty prose classics from Goethe and Schiller to Jeremias Gotthelf, Gottfried Keller, Grillparzer, and Adalbert Stifter, and was intended to remind the German-speaking world of its cultural heritage. In 1915 he began to edit the *Österreichische Bibliothek* (Austrian Library, 1915–1917), a series of twenty-six small volumes on the culture and history of the Austrian monarchy. During the war years he also gave lectures and published essays on subjects intended to promote unity and raise the national consciousness of his Austrian and European contemporaries.

Through the experience of World War I, which brought about the dissolution of the Austrian monarchy and a disintegration of European society, Hofmannsthal developed a political and cultural view with Europe as its center, and this view continued to find expression after the war. In 1920, for example, he helped to found the Salzburg Festival in an effort to restore European culture. In 1927, in one of his most famous speeches, "Das Schrifttum als geistiger Raum der Nation" (Literature as the Spiritual Realm of the Nation), given at the University of Munich, he offered his view of a European unity and called for a "conservative revolution" designed to bring about a new German reality in which the entire nation could participate.

On 15 July 1929, two days after the suicide of his son Franz, Hofmannsthal died of a cerebral hemorrhage at his home in Rodaun.

Throughout his life, Hofmannsthal enjoyed a wide circle of friends, both men and women, who influenced and enriched his thought and development. These friendships resulted in an enormous amount of correspondence that offers useful insights into the poet, his correspondents, and the cultural and political history of their time. His early Austrian friends include the writers Arthur Schnitzler, Richard Beer-Hofmann, Felix Salten, Bahr, and Leopold von Andrian; he met many of these friends in the famous literary coffeehouse known as the Café Griensteidl in Vienna. In 1891 he met the German poet George in Vienna and began a stormy relationship that ended with bitterness in 1906. In 1900 Hofmannsthal met Richard Strauss in Paris and six years later began a lifelong successful collaboration with the composer. Other important friends of Hofmannsthal's include, to name but a few, the German diplomat and industrialist Eberhard von Bodenhausen, the German writers and critics Rudolf Borchardt and Rudolf Alexander Schröder, the Swiss historian and diplomat Carl J. Burckhardt, and the famous director Max Reinhardt, who produced many of Hofmannsthal's plays in Germany and Austria.

Hofmannsthal's relationship with George, which began with their meeting in Vienna in 1891, was doomed from the start by their radically different temperaments and artistic goals. Hofmannsthal simply could not share George's view that literature should exist for a chosen few. For a time, Hofmannsthal contributed to George's new, elite journal, *Die Blätter für die Kunst,* but by 1893 he no longer wished to be associated with George's circle. Despite their differing views on the role of the poet in society, however, and Hofmannsthal's unwillingness to be subservient to the master, Hofmannsthal continued to admire the greatness of the German poet's work.

Although they were few in number, it was Hofmannsthal's poems that first attracted George's attention to the young Viennese poet and helped establish his early reputation as a literary genius. Zweig compared him to John Keats and Arthur Rimbaud. Others recognized in his verse a mastery of the German language and a skill not seen since Goethe.

These early years of lyrical productivity were marked by a state of mind that Hofmannsthal later called "pre-existence" in his collection of autobiographical notes and meditations titled "Ad me ipsum" (About Myself, 1930). Pre-existence was a "glorious but dangerous condition" in which the poet had a magical perception of life and experience without being bound up with them. Glorious as the condition may have been, Hofmannsthal recognized its dangerous aspect of isolation from human beings and knew that it was a state of youth that could not be carried over into manhood. Nevertheless, it enabled him to produce a collection of unusually mature verse.

In view of Hofmannsthal's remarkable appearance on the literary scene in Vienna, his break from lyric poetry and turn to the dramatic form, which concluded his first creative period around 1900, was startling. Since the break from lyric poetry was matched by a period of unproductivity, critics wrote of a premature development and claimed to recognize the drying up of Hofmannsthal's inspiration. Far from marking the end of his literary production, however, the end of Hofmannsthal's early period was a decisive phase in his artistic development that led to the bulk of his important work—the dramatic works that won for him a major place in the history of German literature and in the theater.

One of the major forces contributing to Hofmannsthal's turn to drama and to the theater was the language crisis reflected in his most famous essay, "Ein Brief" ("The Letter of Lord Chandos," 1902). In this essay Hofmannsthal deals with the question of the adequacy of words and expresses doubt about the power of language and thereby about his chosen vocation of writing. This was a turning point in the poet's career and the beginning of his need for dramatic form and for the theater.

There were two problems connected with this early crisis: the question of the adequacy of words and "der Weg ins Leben" (the path to life). In Hofmannsthal's prose writings the question of words appears again and again. As early as 1895, in a monograph on the famous actor Friedrich Mitterwurzer, he wrote:

> People are tired of listening to talk. They have a deep aversion to words: for words have taken the place of things. Hearsay has engulfed the world. . . . Thus a desperate love has awakened for all arts that are practiced in silence: music, dance, and all the tricks of the acrobats and jugglers.
>
> (*Prosa* 1, p. 228)

As late as 1928, in an essay on his own opera *Die ägyptische Helena* (*The Egyptian Helen*), Hofmannsthal claimed: "I shy away from words; they deprive us of the best things." The turn to drama was an effort to solve the language problem by replacing the printed word with the spoken word of plays and by supplementing the spoken word with the action of plays and all of the traditional non-verbal means of expression available to the dramatist and the theater, from as simple a device as the gestures of actors to pantomime, dance, and the elaborate music dramas Hofmannsthal wrote in collaboration with Strauss.

That is why gesture and pantomime are important features in all of Hofmannsthal's plays and why in 1911 he wrote the essay "Über die Pantomime" (On Pantomime), in which he emphasized the extreme expressiveness of the human body. The collaboration with Strauss is a further example of Hofmannsthal's need and search for more than words to express himself. It was also a means of reaching and winning a larger audience.

Coupled with the crisis of language reflected in "The Letter of Lord Chandos" was the problem Hofmannsthal faced in finding the path to life. Although often misunderstood as an aesthete removed from the joys and sorrows of life, Hofmannsthal rejected aestheticism early in his career and sought ways of forming solid personal relationships. He found one important way to pursue this goal in his turn to drama and the theater: it is reflected both in the content of his plays, in which finding the path to a full life of commitment and establishing ties with other human beings became a central theme, and in his own participation in the theater as a social institution that, Hofmannsthal claimed, has bound man to man for centuries and has had an exceedingly rich tradition in Austria and especially in Vienna.

Thus, despite enormous production in other genres (including over a dozen volumes of correspondence, four volumes of essays, and three volumes of stories, poetry, and miscellaneous writings), Hofmannsthal came to think of himself as a dramatist above all and occupied himself with the theater from the turn of the century until his death in 1929. His early efforts were devoted to mastering his craft, establishing his reputation as a dramatist, and creating a poetic theater where works like his own and others he believed in could be performed with success. After World War I he began to concentrate more and more on using the theater to unify European society and to reawaken humanity to its better qualities.

A second force active in Hofmannsthal's turn to drama and to the theater was his ever-increasing awareness of the Austrian theater tradition. Hofmannsthal himself cited its influence on his development as a dramatist in a letter from 1921 to Max Pirker, who was working on a study of the poet as a dramatist:

> For preliminary work on "Hofmannsthal as a poet of the theater" the following: the basic theme approximately thus: an individual with poetic talent appears, occupies himself subjectively, individually, with dramatic-lyrical forms. But he is a Viennese, and gradually the forces of his origin have their effect, attract him to traditional forms.
>
> (*Aufzeichnungen*, p. 369)

Numerous diary entries such as "The Austrian quality. A natural bond with the theater" also give evidence of his ties to the stage.

From an early age Hofmannsthal was exposed to Viennese theater, to the Kasperle-Theater in the Prater and to the great traditional Burgtheater. This exposure became a part of his aesthetic and dramatic education. He also knew of the historical significance of Viennese theater. In the first of the so-called "Vienna Letters," for example, which he wrote for readers of the American magazine *The Dial*, he gives a brief résumé of the tradition of the theater in Vienna: "Since the end of the eighteenth century—indeed, if one cares to, one can go back another eighty years— not only has Vienna been the theatrical center of Germany and practically of Italy because of dynastic connections, but it has had as a theater city only one rival: Paris."

But as glorious as the tradition of the Austrian theater was and as strong a force as "the forces of his origin" exerted on Hofmannsthal's turn to the theater and development as a dramatic artist, the contemporary theater scene in Vienna at the time of his appearance as a dramatist was no longer as rich as it once had been nor as friendly as it could have been. During his lifetime only eleven of Hofmannsthal's plays were performed in Vienna, and only four of the eleven at the Burgtheater. Five of his plays had their premiere in Vienna; for all the others, except *Das Salzburger grosse Welttheater* (*The Salzburg Great Theater of the World,* 1922), which was first performed in Salzburg, Hofmannsthal had to turn to Germany—mainly to Otto Brahm and Max Reinhardt in Berlin. Even so "Austrian" a comedy as *Der Schwierige* (*The Difficult Man,* 1921) had its premiere in Munich in 1921, three years after it was completed, and it was not performed in the author's native city until 1924, when Reinhardt produced it at the Theater in der Josefstadt.

During the first part of the century Hofmannsthal seemed resigned to the situation of the theater in Vienna, which made it necessary for him, a deeply Austrian writer, to turn to the north German stage for performances of his plays. But by 1918, when institutions were collapsing all around him following the war, he took an active interest in the leading theater of his homeland and wrote two essays, "Zum Direktionswechsel im Burgtheater" (On the Change of Directors in the Burgtheater) and "Zur Krisis des Burgtheaters" (On the Crisis of the Burgtheater), intended to stimulate a renewal of the old Burgtheater tradition. He also tried to engage Reinhardt as a director through an exchange between the Burgtheater and the Deutsches Theater in Berlin. Reinhardt was to have the opportunity to direct major productions in the Burgtheater with some of his best players and also use some of the Burgtheater's best players for productions in Berlin. For reasons best known to the conservative management of the Burgtheater, however, negotiations broke down. Reinhardt was invited to produce some pieces at the Redoutensaal in Vienna, and eventually he returned to Vienna in 1923 as director of the Theater in der Josefstadt. There he delighted its small audiences with some of the best theater performances in Vienna of the present century, including the production of Hofmannsthal's *The Difficult Man* in 1924 and *Cristinas Heimreise* (Cristina's Journey Home, 1910) in 1926.

Unsuccessful in his efforts to revitalize the Burgtheater and bring Reinhardt to Vienna as its director, Hofmannsthal turned his energies to the concept of the Salzburg Festival, which was founded in 1920 with Reinhardt's production of Hofmannsthal's *Jedermann* (*The Salzburg Everyman,* 1911). The Salzburg Festival, an expression of the Austrian theater tradition that was so much a part of Hofmannsthal's background, served as festival theater that could revive the spirit of European humanism and regenerate the soul of mankind after the collapse of values during World War I. In addition, it was a vehicle for the production of some of Hofmannsthal's own dramatic works.

It is difficult to determine a single originator of the festival idea, but there is no doubt that Hofmannsthal was the guiding force behind it. In numerous essays he wrote between 1919 and 1928, he called the festival into being, established its format, and imbued it with the spiritual mission of regenerating Western civilization.

The important place of the mystery play in the Austro-Bavarian theater tradition of the Salzburg Festival offered fertile ground for performances of Hofmannsthal's own plays—*Everyman,* based on the medieval morality play of the same name, and *The Salzburg Great Theater of the World,* inspired by Pedro Calderón de la Barca's *El gran teatro del mundo* (*The Great Theater of the World,* 1675). It also enabled the poet's ideals for a Salzburg Festival, expressed in theory, to be realized in practice. In the case of *Everyman,* for example, although it was not written for Salzburg and had had successful performances in Berlin and Vienna prior to its Salzburg Festival premiere, only in Salzburg did the work seem to come to life for Hofmannsthal and at the same time breathe life into the festival itself.

As a morality play, *Everyman* was ideally suited to the traditional aspect of the Salzburg Festival. This revival of a centuries-old tradition of theater and of its place in the heart of the people was of particular value to Hofmannsthal, who wrote: "All this seemed natural to the peasants who came in droves, first from the suburbs, then from the neighboring villages, then from farther and farther away. They said, 'Plays are being performed again. That is good.'"

Everyman had had its festival premiere in a brilliant production by Reinhardt before Salzburg Cathedral in August of 1920. Inspired by its warm reception by festival audiences, Hofmannsthal completed *The Salzburg Great Theater of the World* during the following year, and the play had its Salzburg Festival premiere in August 1922. Reinhardt, who was also responsible for this production, obtained permission from the archbishop to stage the play in the Kollegienkirche, an event that had not taken place in a Catholic church in Salzburg since the sixteenth century and that gave a new dimension to the festival. The response to the production by public and critics alike was enthusiastic. Hofmannsthal himself, who had been writing articles of general cultural interest for *The Dial,* devoted one letter to the 1922 festival in general and to *The Salzburg Great Theater of the World* in particular. Here, in keeping with his concept of the mission of the Salzburg Festival, he emphasized once more the ability of such a universal morality play and such a festival to bring together a truly international audience of all classes and thus build a spiritual bridge between nations.

During the few years left to Hofmannsthal between the founding of the festival in 1920 and his death in 1929 at the age of fifty-five, there were annual performances in Salzburg of *Everyman* (except for the years 1922–1925) and two productions of *The Salzburg Great Theater of the World.* Salzburg also provided the opportunity for the production of two of Hofmannsthal's operas, *Ariadne auf Naxos* (*Ariadne on Naxos,* 1912) and *Der Rosenkavalier,* 1911), which were performed between the years 1920 and 1929 as the festival appropriately expanded from the single production of *Everyman* in the inaugural festival year to include a large repertoire of stage plays of international authorship as well as operas and concerts. After his death *Everyman* became a cornerstone and major attraction of the festival and has been performed annually except for the war years from 1938 to 1945, when Hofmannsthal's works, because he was part Jewish, were denied performance at the festival he helped to create. Two of his other major plays, *The Difficult Man* and *Der Turm* (*The Tower,* 1925), have also been performed at the Salzburg Festival in recent years.

Hofmannsthal's early plays were written between 1891 and 1898. They belong to the period that he labeled in the letter to Max Pirker his "first, predominantly lyrical-subjective epoch," and while they possess "dramatic and even theatrical elements," the early plays are marked mainly by intense lyrical qualities and few dramatic ones. They are rich in ideas and mood but poor in dramatic conflict and action. Hofmannsthal himself was aware of the dramatic shortcomings of his early plays and made a conscious effort to master dramatic form by studying Otto Ludwig's works and theoretical writings and by distancing himself from lyric form.

Although Hofmannsthal recognized the importance of his first play, *Gestern* (Yesterday, 1891), within the whole of his literary production and personal development, the work never gave him personal satisfaction. Subtitled "A Dramatic Study in One Act in Verse" and completed in 1891, the play is not dramatic in the conventional sense. Its verse is beautiful, and the young Hofmannsthal showed a remarkable ability to create a mood and reproduce the period of the late Renaissance through careful attention to detail of scene, costume, and characterization. But his main concern with the moral idea leads to lengthy speeches and reflection not suited to the stage, while dramatic action remains secondary. The formula for the play was a favorite of Hofmannsthal's: the verse proverb with a moral (that is, the hero postulates a thesis at the beginning of the play, then a trifle occurs that forces him to reverse his thesis). In *Gestern* Andrea is the young hero who at the beginning of the play lives only for the moment and believes only in today. Then he discovers that his mistress Arlette has deceived him the day before, and he is forced to face the reality of yesterday and to learn that yesterday cannot be forgotten as long as he knows it existed.

Hofmannsthal's second dramatic effort, *Der Tod des Tizian* (Titian's Death, 1901), followed in 1892 but was a fragment. In 1893 he completed the minor masterpiece *Death and the Fool*. Like *Gestern, Death and the Fool* is primarily a lyric play, rich in mood and moral content. For that reason, perhaps, critics long misunderstood it as an example of Hofmannsthal's aestheticism and decadence, while Hofmannsthal himself considered *Death and the Fool,* like *Gestern,* to be an example of his efforts to find higher personal relationships and "the path to life" and a rejection of artistic isolation and aestheticism. The problem of the aesthete is expressed through the play's hero, Claudio, the fool who, isolated in his world of art from the cares and joys of man, learns too late the meaning of fidelity when confronted with his own imminent death and promises too late to seek meaningful relationships and to give as well as to take. Faced with the sudden appearance of death and characters from his misspent life, Claudio recognizes the emptiness and loneliness of his aesthetic existence. As the figures from his life—his mother, a girl, and a friend—appear and bear witness that he was unable to establish any meaningful contact with his fellow creatures

because of his own limitations, Claudio embraces death as the first real thing he has encountered and undergoes a transformation, recognizing that the true life consists not only of receiving from others but also of giving of oneself.

The year 1897 was particularly productive for Hofmannsthal. He completed four plays— *Die Frau im Fenster* (Madonna Dianora, 1899), *Der weisse Fächer* (*The White Fan,* 1907), *Das kleine Welttheater oder Die Glücklichen* (*The Little Theater of the World,* 1903), and *Der Kaiser und die Hexe* (*The Emperor and the Witch,* 1900). The first three of these he wrote during a two-month bicycle trip to Italy in August and September.

Inspired perhaps by a visit he made to the burial plot of the Colleoni family in Bergamo, Italy, a few days before he started work on *Die Frau im Fenster,* Hofmannsthal wrote the play in three days. It is based on a story by the Italian writer Gabriele D'Annunzio and tells of a Renaissance woman of noble birth who enters a good marriage but finds the satisfaction of fulfilled love only with a lover. One evening while she waits for her lover, her husband discovers her and strangles her with the rope ladder intended to carry her lover to her arms. The horror of her punishment constitutes an early study of the violence to be found later in Hofmannsthal's Greek plays. The figure of Dianora is a preview of the unfulfilled woman, the "woman without a shadow," and of the large role women play in later works. While close to its immediate predecessors, *Gestern* and *Death and the Fool,* in its emphasis on mood and atmosphere, *Die Frau im Fenster* employs more dialogue and uses gestures effectively.

The White Fan was the last of the three plays Hofmannsthal completed during his productive trip to Italy in 1897. Characterized by the author as an interlude, the play is a delightful, beautiful work, but undramatic. It is an important work, however, for the poet's development as a dramatist because of its use of prose combined with poetry, which softens the lyric overtones of the early works, and the motif of the importance of children to the fulfillment of life, which recurs often, most notably in the opera (and prose tale) *Die Frau ohne Schatten* (*The Woman Without a Shadow*, 1916). The setting for the play is the entrance to a cemetery near the capital city of an island in the West Indies. Fortunio and Miranda, each of whom has recently lost a wife and husband respectively and has rejected life in favor of an unseemly and unbounded state of mourning, must learn to appreciate life and find happiness in a new union with each other. Here Hofmannsthal treats the motif of fidelity ironically, for it is an exaggerated fidelity toward the dead that keeps these young people from the living.

Die Hochzeit der Sobeide (*The Marriage of Zobeide*, 1899) and *Der Abenteurer und die Sängerin* (The Adventurer and the Singer, 1899) were both completed for the stage at the end of 1898 and offer a dramatic conclusion to the lyric-dramatic efforts of the young Hofmannsthal. Although both plays show a greater command of dramatic technique than any of the other works of the early period, *The Marriage of Zobeide*, subtitled "A Dramatic Poem," reflects his dramatic development less. Yet even here Hofmannsthal had progressed beyond the preponderant lyricism and monologue form of the majority of the early plays. For the first time the action of objectified characters is more important than mood or atmosphere, and for the first time the problem of the play is presented and advanced by well-drawn and carefully posed characters rather than by monologues. The story of Sobeide is a simple one: Having married a wealthy and elderly merchant for her parents' sake, Sobeide cherishes a secret love for another man, Ganem. On her wedding night, after the guests have departed, she confesses her love for Ganem to her husband, who sets her free to go to her lover. Sobeide goes to Ganem only to discover that he does not share her love. Knowing no other course but to flee from life itself, she returns to her husband's garden and plunges to her death from a tower.

The problem of the play, Sobeide's inability to establish a relationship with life, is the result of her false interpretation of her fate in her own unreal dreamworld. Couched in a heart that was never securely bound to the real world, her belief that her destiny lies with Ganem is refuted by his inability to enter into any but a purely sensual, one-sided relationship (the fate of the Don Juan or adventurer figure who appears in later works). Instead, what Hofmannsthal called "the mystery of marriage and procreation" is offered as the possible means to fulfillment in life. Having been rejected by Ganem and dishonored, Sobeide recognizes this just before her death when she accepts the merchant as her husband and suggests with her last words, "We should have lived a long life together and had children."

Shortly after the completion of *The Marriage of Zobeide*, Hofmannsthal purchased a copy of Giovanni Casanova's memoirs in the hope of finding in the archetypal adventurer's life a suitable subject for a play. Within a day he had found just what he wanted and began work on *Der Abenteurer und die Sängerin*. As the last and only major work prepared for the stage during the period when Hofmannsthal was striving to establish contact with the theater and develop his dramatic technique, *Der Abenteurer und die Sängerin* is the most successful of the early plays. There is more development of major and minor characters, more use of dialogue, more dramatic action, and livelier movement of characters on the stage.

The use of the "proverb" introduced in *Gestern* recurs in this work, and here it is the adventurer type, Baron Weidenstamm, whose style of life is put into question by a past that suddenly confronts him. The play begins fifteen years after the singer's encounter with the adventurer, and Vittoria's story is revealed in retrospect when she meets the adventurer again by chance. As a woman embodying fidelity and permanence, Vittoria cherishes her memory of the adventurer and owes to him the two most important things in her life—her art and Cesarino, her son. The sudden appearance of the adventurer poses a threat to the fragile harmony she has established by marrying a devoted husband and presenting her illegitimate son as her brother. But when the adventurer confuses her with another woman and another place, she realizes he has forgotten her. In contrast to Vittoria, the adventurer embodies infidelity and constant change; he therefore loses himself in passion but never in the woman he temporarily "loves." In the course of the play the adventurer's love of the moment and of erotic extremes are questioned, and he is finally viewed as a tragic figure unable to establish a real relationship with life. He lives life fully on the surface but never enjoys the happiness of a true, lasting relationship. It is both ironic and characteristic of his tragic nature that he does not know what to do upon meeting his son, the one true product of an otherwise false life. As the play concludes, the adventurer goes off to a rendezvous with another woman without even a last glance at the house in which his son remains. In so doing he forfeits his opportunity to continue in time through his offspring.

Following the lyric-dramatic plays of the early period and their failure to capture a theater public, Hofmannsthal turned to earlier, classical models in his second period in an effort to master traditional dramatic form and conquer the stage. The period extends from 1900 to about 1907 and includes four tragedies—*Elektra* (*Electra*, 1904), *Das gerettete Venedig* (*Venice Preserved*, 1905), *Ödipus und die Sphinx* (*Oedipus and the Sphinx*, 1906), and *König Ödipus* (*Oedipus Rex*, 1910), a translation of Sophocles' play. The period is filled with plans for dramatic works and is marked by Hofmannsthal's interest in all aspects of the living theater—not only the writing of effective stage plays but the problems of staging, casting, and directing as well.

The transition from Hofmannsthal's youthful writing to that of his manhood, which accompanied the change from lyric-dramatic to purely dramatic form, was not an easy one, and for the first two years of the new century he wrote practically nothing. This was the time of the crisis in his career represented by the "The Letter of Lord Chandos." Gradually, however, he began to view drama as the appropriate form for his view of the world, and he focused nearly all his work in the second period on the stage. From the beginning of the period he made frequent references in his letters to the numerous plans he had for dramatic works. The majority of these plans were never developed beyond scenarios, if that far, but they represent an emphasis on drama—from translations and adaptations of plays to ballet, pantomime, and prologues—that reveals the involvement with theater that determined the future course of his creative output.

Hofmannsthal's work on *Electra* in 1903, the first play of the second period, was stimulated by Reinhardt, who at that time directed the Neues Theater in Berlin, and by Gertrud Eysoldt, a leading actress of the day. This ideal situation for a dramatist—the specific need for a classical (Greek) play by a noted theater and a prominent actress for whom to create a leading role—made it possible for Hofmannsthal to complete *Electra* in a few months, and the play had its highly successful premiere in Berlin on 30 October 1903.

Work on *Electra* gave Hofmannsthal little pleasure, and its dark, negative theme of murder and revenge was palatable to him only when he thought of its lighter counterpart, "Orest auf Delphi" (Orestes in Delphi), a companion piece that was never completed. But in spite of his dissatisfaction with *Electra*, the play indicates a remarkable awareness of the requirements of the stage and an improvement in dramatic technique, and Hofmannsthal succeeded in turning what he once labeled "a free, very free adaptation of Sophocles' *Electra*" into a powerful, if desolate, work for the modern stage. Its immediate success in Berlin was followed by stage successes elsewhere until the opera version with music by Richard

Strauss came to replace the stage play after the opera's premiere in the Royal Opera House in Dresden in 1909.

As with no earlier play, Hofmannsthal was greatly concerned with the stage presentation of *Electra*. In 1903 he published an essay, "Szenische Vorschriften zu *Elektra*" (Scenic Directions for *Electra*), in which he gave explicit instructions for the set, lighting, and costumes. They are an essential and effective complement to the play and are aimed at establishing a harmony of content and form throughout a performance.

Electra, one of the most powerful characters Hofmannsthal ever created, dominates the play from beginning to end. Her opening monologue, in which she envisions the revenge for her father Agamemnon's murder, begins the frenzied action that does not end until her brother, Orestes, returns and through her urgings executes their mother, Clytemnestra, and her lover, Aegisthus; with order restored by the act of revenge, Electra collapses in ecstasy on the stage.

Fidelity, the predominant theme of *Electra*, appears in earlier works and recurs in later ones, but here it is the driving force that motivates Electra and also consumes her. Unlike her sister, Chrysothemis, who is eager to forget the horrible past and fulfill her role as a woman by marrying and having children, Electra can think only of revenge and her duty to remain true to the memory of her father. She devotes herself entirely to restoring the order disrupted by her mother when the latter murdered her husband and broke the sacred configuration of the family—father, mother, and children. In seeking revenge for Agamemnon's murder, Electra's innermost being and personal identity are consumed by her fidelity to her father and by the act of revenge. And yet, basically the dreamer type, Electra is incapable of performing the act of revenge herself and even fails to give the ax to Orestes when he sets out on his task.

Das gerettete Venedig, the second play of Hofmannsthal's second period, is based on the Englishman Thomas Otway's tragedy *Venice Preserved, or A Plot Discovered* (1682). Like its forerunner, *Electra, Das gerettete Venedig* is a free adaptation of the original source, with which Hofmannsthal had become acquainted several years earlier in 1896 while on military duty in Tlumacz in East Galicia. Otway's play about revolutionaries in Venice in 1618 made a great impression on Hofmannsthal, and upon reading it again in 1901, he thought of using the material for a novella, of which only a brief description he gave in a diary note remains. In 1902 he developed a scenario, followed by the completion of the five-act play in 1903. Readings to various friends, however, revealed the need for revisions that were postponed until the completion of *Electra,* and *Das gerettete Venedig* did not have its stage premiere until 1905, at the Lessingtheater in Berlin.

Although the premiere was a failure, partly because of a heavy-handed production under Brahm's direction, Hofmannsthal much preferred *Das gerettete Venedig* to *Electra* and considered the play to be an important step forward in his development as a dramatist. Ironically, considering that George did not care for the play and did not share Hofmannsthal's interest in the stage, *Das gerettete Venedig* was dedicated to the poet. What marked a turn to the theater for Hofmannsthal also marked the end of the unsteady relationship between him and George, for Hofmannsthal felt at that time more than ever before that his role as a poet lay in the theater, in joining the masses rather than turning from them as George urged him to do.

Das gerettete Venedig reveals new strengths in creating exciting situations and contrasts. There is a great deal of action on the stage and a wealth of conflicts and contrasts—between father and daughter, husband and wife, revolutionaries and the republic, and good and evil and weak and strong characters. The weakness of the play is the problematic relationship between Jaffier and Pierre, for it is difficult to believe that the strong Pierre would befriend and trust the weakling Jaffier, who ultimately betrays him. Hofmannsthal, however, was interested in the main theme underlying Jaffier's character—that Jaffier believes he belongs to the revolutionaries, to the strong, while he really belongs to the lackeys, the weak.

In spite of the stage failure of *Das gerettete Venedig,* Hofmannsthal did not lose courage in his struggle to become a successful dramatist and worked with enthusiasm on a new play, *Ödipus und die Sphinx.* As was the case with *Electra, Ödipus und die Sphinx* was first conceived as part of a larger work, in this case a trilogy, of which he completed only the first and second part, *Ödipus und die Sphinx* and *Oedipus Rex,* a translation of Sophocles' tragedy. Hofmannsthal was fortunate to have Reinhardt interested again in staging a new play, and the premiere of *Ödipus und die Sphinx* in 1906 at the Deutsches Theater in Berlin was a success.

In Sophocles' *Oedipus Rex* the Theban tragedy reaches its climax when Oedipus realizes that the prophecy of the oracle at Delphi that he would murder his father and commit incest with his mother has been fulfilled. As a prologue to Sophocles' play, Hofmannsthal's *Ödipus und die Sphinx* deals with Oedipus' visit to Delphi, when he decides to flee from all human contacts in an effort to ward off and escape the fate prophesied for him, and the eventual fulfillment of that fate, unknown to him, when he kills Laius and wins the throne of Thebes and Jocasta as his queen. By definition the prologue should be shorter than the main play, but in fact *Ödipus und die Sphinx* is twice as long as the central play of the projected trilogy.

Kreon and Oedipus are the two main characters. Kreon plays a major role both as an example of the dreamer type, like Electra, who is unable to act, and as a foil to Oedipus. Like Claudio in *Death and the Fool,* Kreon is blind to the world around him, filled with self-doubt, and unable to fulfill his destiny because he cannot give of himself. Oedipus, on the other hand, is filled with strength and belief in himself and is anxious to fulfill his destiny and perform deeds. When at the end of the play Oedipus realizes that all of his actions have been predetermined, he offers his life to Kreon in a gesture of self-sacrifice that shows his conquest over himself.

Following his turn to old theater masterpieces in an effort to master traditional dramatic form during the second period of his work as a playwright, the demands of traditional theater were of primary importance during Hofmannsthal's third and final period, from about 1907 to his death in 1929. During these last twenty years of his life he produced a number of successful comedies for the stage and as operatic texts, two mystery plays, and a major tragedy. These works represent the mature plays upon which his reputation today rests. In themes and style they also reflect Hofmannsthal's natural connection with the theater as an Austrian, and especially as a Viennese.

The beginning of Hofmannsthal's third period was filled with excitement about a wealth of dramatic ideas, anticipation of success, and satisfaction with his development as a playwright. It was also marked by a turn to comedy as the form Hofmannsthal considered most compatible with his nature. In 1909 he had plans for at least five comedies—*Silvia im "Stern"* (Silvia in the "Star," 1959), *Cristinas Heimreise, The Difficult Man, Der Rosenkavalier,* and *Lucidor: Figuren zu einer ungeschriebenen Komödie* (*Lucidor,* 1910). Only two of these, *Cristinas Heimreise* and *The Difficult Man,* were ever completed as stage plays. *Silvia im "Stern"* remained uncompleted, although Hofmannsthal returned to it time and again with affection. *Der Rosenkavalier* and *Lucidor* (first published as a "prose sketch" and entitled *Arabella* in its final form [1933]) were completed as libretti for Richard Strauss.

Cristinas Heimreise, the first comedy Hofmannsthal completed for the stage during his third period, had its premiere in Berlin in

February 1910, immediately after it was written. It was based on Casanova's memoirs, and although it was intended originally as an opera text for Strauss, Hofmannsthal felt it was more important to produce another stage play for Reinhardt first; when Strauss balked at the idea of the stage play preempting the premiere of the opera, the opera text was never written.

The adventurer type, introduced through Baron Weidenstamm in *Der Abenteurer und die Sängerin,* is fully developed and thoroughly negated in the character of Florindo in *Cristinas Heimreise.* In this play, Florindo meets Cristina in Venice in act 1 just as she is about to return home to her mountain village after an unsuccessful attempt to find a husband in the city. Captivated by her grace and simplicity, Florindo pursues and seduces her in act 2, but he cannot bring himself to marry her. Instead, he leaves her in the company of Tomaso, a retired sea captain who is looking for a wife and an opportunity to settle down. In act 3 Tomaso, as might be expected, woos and wins Christina, who recognizes in him a man of substance, in contrast to Florindo, who charmed her but had to move on to other mistresses. When Florindo reappears briefly at the end of act 3 in the company of another woman, Cristina has the opportunity to compare him with Tomaso and turns to Tomaso without regret as her companion for life. Ironically Florindo, who appeared to have everything in the beginning, goes off to yet another empty encounter, while Cristina and Tomaso, who had nothing in the beginning, now have each other and the opportunity to share the richness of their relationship.

Following the unsuccessful premiere of *Cristinas Heimreise* in the complete version, Reinhardt decided to shorten the play by removing the slow-moving third act in subsequent performances. Over the years theater critics have debated which of the two versions is more successful on the stage, and most have favored the complete play. Certainly the third act is important to the substance of the play,

for in it the erotic and ethical elements of life find balance in the basic social institution of marriage.

Carl J. Burckhardt, Hofmannsthal's close friend, recalled an occasion when Hofmannsthal asked him if he knew the quotation from Novalis "After lost wars, one must write comedies." *The Difficult Man* was the first comedy Hofmannsthal turned to after World War I. It was probably completed for the stage in 1918, although it was not published until 1920, when it appeared in installments in Vienna's leading newspaper, the *Neue freie Presse.* It was not performed until 1921, at the Residenz-Theater in Munich. In the meantime it has taken its place as one of the two or three greatest comedies in German literature.

Hofmannsthal's earlier conception for a play on the subject of "a difficult man" dates from 1908. At that time three elements may have been present: the idea for Count Kari Bühl, the Chandos-like hero of the play who doubts the efficacy of verbal communication; the theme of marriage; and the autobiographical element of the "difficult person," a type Hofmannsthal sometimes considered himself to be. The overall background for the play, however, would seem to be the period from 1908 to 1918, which heralded the decline of the society depicted in the play.

The action of the play, as should be the case in any good comedy, is extremely simple. Count Kari Bühl, "the difficult man," is called upon by his sister, Crescence, to win the hand of Helene Altenwyl for his young nephew Stani. Instead, thanks to Helene's initiative, Kari's deep affection for her is brought out, and he wins her hand for himself.

Kari illustrates two themes of utmost importance to Hofmannsthal, which are at the heart of many of his most important works: the problem of communication and the importance of marriage. Almost two decades after the statement of the language problem in "The Letter of Lord Chandos," the problem continued to be of concern to Hofmannsthal and was presented in a comic fashion in *The Difficult*

Man. Kari's difficulties lie in his unwillingness to express his deepest thoughts and feelings because of his belief that "it is impossible to open one's mouth without causing the most hopeless confusion." Much of the comedy of the play is indeed caused by confusion resulting from the speeches of others and from the subject of marriage—which he calls "the institution . . . that transforms chance and impurity into necessity, permanence, and something of value." This is reminiscent of a statement Hofmannsthal made in a letter to Burckhardt to the effect that he could not imagine life without marriage, for marriage is truly the most important sacrament.

Although *The Difficult Man* offers an honest depiction of the weaknesses of a social class and society on the verge of decline, Kari and his intended, Helene, are examples of the quality of inner strength also present in that society; Kari and others belie its weaknesses when Neuhoff, the North German who pits his strength against the weakness of the Austrians by trying to dominate them, is defeated by them at his every attempt to exert the force of his will.

Five years later, Hofmannsthal completed a second, less accomplished comedy than *The Difficult Man;* it was called *Der Unbestechliche* (The Uncorruptible Man, 1950). For the first time since 1905, when he created the role of Electra for the actress Gertrud Eysoldt, he had the chance to write a role for a specific actor, in this case the role of "the uncorruptible man" for the brilliant comic actor Max Pallenberg, whom he had seen play Jourdain in 1918 in an opera he had written for Strauss, *Der Bürger als Edelmann* (The Bourgeois as Nobleman, 1918), based on the play by Molière. In 1922, shortly after his first mention of work on a new comedy, Hofmannsthal met with Pallenberg to discuss plans for the play and the part for the actor. The play was completed and enjoyed a successful premiere in Vienna in March 1923.

Der Unbestechliche is another example of Hofmannsthal's turn to traditional theater in his last period, and he once called the play "a comedy directly descended from Terence by way of Gil Blas and Figaro." Theodor, "the uncorruptible man," is the servant, à la Beaumarchais's Figaro, who lords it over his master, Jaromir, and keeps the master in check.

As the play begins the household is in chaos because of the expected arrival of houseguests and the sudden resignation of Theodor. Theodor has given notice because Jaromir has invited two former girlfriends to spend the weekend with him and his wife and children. Incensed by the immorality of this situation, which he views as an affront to his own person, Theodor agrees to stay only when the baroness, Jaromir's mother, agrees to give him a free hand in dispatching the two women shortly after their arrival. With a masterful command of the situation Theodor succeeds in his mission, and not only sends the two women off but also instills in Jaromir, an adventurer type, a sense of duty as husband and father. Although *Der Unbestechliche* does not have the greatness of *The Difficult Man,* it is a lively comedy and continues to delight theater audiences.

Contemporaneous with his work with comedies in his final period, Hofmannsthal worked in the genre of the morality or mystery play, first in *Everyman* in 1911 and later in *The Salzburg Great Theater of the World* in 1922. Perhaps nowhere more than in the medium of these mystery plays and through their performance within the framework of the Salzburg Festival did Hofmannsthal achieve his goal of mastering traditional theater.

Hofmannsthal's interest in the Everyman theme stemmed from his reading of the anonymous English morality play *Everyman* early in 1902, and it became one of several ideas for plays that he entertained at the beginning of his second period. He did not finish *Everyman,* however, until 1911 because other works took precedence. Hofmannsthal considered his play a "renewal" of the English source, in which he found universal truths that were as important to the twentieth century as they were to the fifteenth-century audiences who first saw the original play. In reworking it for a modern audience, he hoped to restore a tradition that had lost its vitality over the centuries and return it to its proper place in European civilization.

The message of *Everyman* is that this transitory life is part of a greater, more meaningful life; the whole world is a stage, and for a man's actions on it he will be called to account on Judgment Day. Unlike his source, in which Everyman confronts death at the beginning and then seeks assistance, Hofmannsthal provides psychological background and develops Everyman's character before Death appears on the stage. Through various encounters Everyman's lofty position in society, his relationships with friends, family, and mistress, and his wealth and power are vividly portrayed. Everyman, however, has lost sight of the law that stands above the individual and must be reminded of it by the sudden appearance of Death. He tries to arrange to be accompanied by his friends, family, mistress, and money as he goes to face judgment. These efforts fail, and he must learn that his only help in finding salvation will come from his good deeds, which are meager, and his faith, which is weak. The tragedy of Everyman ends after his friends, family, and mistress forsake him one by one and his last hope, his money chest, opens to reveal the demon Mammon, who, it turns out, is Everyman's master, not his servant. The morality begins when Everyman accepts Good Deeds and Faith as his only means to finding salvation, and they keep the devil at bay as Everyman descends into the grave to leave this life and face his maker.

Although *Everyman* had its premiere in 1911 in a Berlin circus shortly after it was written, it was the play's success in an open-air production in front of Salzburg Cathedral in 1921 that inspired Hofmannsthal to undertake a second mystery play, *The Salzburg Great Theater of the World.* Recognizing the effectiveness of the production of *Everyman* in a natural setting, Hofmannsthal planned from the beginning to have *The Salzburg Great Theater of the World* staged in the Kollegienkirche, a magnificent Catholic church in Salzburg.

In a prefatory note to the text edition of *The Salzburg Great Theater of the World,* Hofmannsthal establishes the relationship of his work to its source, Calderón's *The Great Theater of the World,* and, further, to the treasure of myth and allegory that had its beginning in the Middle Ages:

> The whole world knows that there is a religious play by Calderón called *The Great Theater of the World.* From it is borrowed here the metaphor that supports the whole: that the world builds a stage upon which people present the play of life in the roles given them by God; borrowed further are the title of this play and the names of the six figures by whom mankind is represented—otherwise nothing. These elements, however, do not belong to the great Catholic poet as his invention, but belong to the treasure of myths and allegories that was formed by the Middle Ages and bequeathed to the centuries that followed.
>
> (*Dramen,* 3, p. 259)

Here and elsewhere Hofmannsthal felt the need to explain his relationship to his sources, partly in defense against the many voices that for years had accused him of lacking poetic imagination, partly by way of explaining his method of working as a poet. Important in *The Salzburg Great Theater of the World,* as in his other works that are based on a source from another time, is the question of what Hofmannsthal was able to do with the material, and there is no doubt that he created a drama that combined the best of two possible worlds—the traditions of the past and the poet's own contemporary genius.

In *Everyman,* through the vehicle of the medieval allegory or morality play, Hofmannsthal presents the familiar concept of the whole world as a stage and conveys the message that this life is but a small part of a greater life for which life on earth is a preparation. In *The Salzburg Great Theater of the World* the same concept of the world as a stage reappears, and here a world stage is constructed upon which man must play his various roles before God and be judged and rewarded (or punished) at the end for his performances. So much the poet had from Calderón. To this Hofmannsthal adds the figure of the Beggar and the social problem he represents, with its roots in the poet's own time.

As the play opens on a two-level stage representing the universe with its upper level (the eternal) and its lower level (the temporal), God, the Master, announces that he wants to see a play about man's actions on earth. There will be six allegorical roles played by unborn souls: King, Beauty, Wisdom, Rich Man, Peasant, and Beggar. The way the souls play their roles is important, not the roles themselves, but the soul who is to play the Beggar refuses his part until he is persuaded that the players will have a God-given freedom of action. For Hofmannsthal the Beggar is the central figure, and in place of the passive Beggar of the old mystery plays, he creates an active Beggar who questions the world order and demands his share of what others have. In the action that follows, in the play within the play, the Beggar rebels vigorously against the order of the "haves" and the "have-nots." He demands a new order and is about to raise an ax to strike down the old when Wisdom prays for his soul and a religious transformation takes place in which the Beggar recognizes a true order above all others—God's eternal order. By failing to commit the negative act that would strike down the old order and bring chaos, the Beggar performs the positive act of his life in the exercise of his free will. As he turns from the world to take up solitude in the forest until it is time to enter into eternity, he expresses the modern moral of the play with the admonition that there must indeed be a new order on earth, too.

Hofmannsthal's final masterpiece, his tragedy *The Tower*, is the capstone of his work. Here the poet realized his desire to master the theater and contributed a monumental play to the German language and stage. The progress made from his first lyric dramas is striking;

the conception of *The Tower* and its execution are totally dramatic. The tragedy revolves around Sigismund and his destiny, but the relationships and fates of others are carefully interwoven: King Basilius, his father, and Ignatius, a monk; Julian, his keeper and mentor, and the revolution he inspires; Olivier, the firebrand, and the ochlocratic revolution. In a succession of actions and counteractions filled with dramatic suspense, the tragedy strides inexorably forward against a rich and varied backdrop that perfectly complements the play and the players. There are effective mass scenes with color and ceremony, and there are delicate dialogues demanding all of the actors' skills. Pantomime had never played a more important role in Hofmannsthal's plays nor been used with more skill and dramatic effect.

From the turn of the century, when the Spanish poet Calderón's work first enlivened his imagination, Hofmannsthal struggled greatly with the material for *The Tower* and its fragmentary forerunner, *Das Leben ein Traum* (Life Is a Dream, 1957), which he patterned after Calderón's *La vida es sueño* (*Life Is a Dream*, 1635). From Calderón Hofmannsthal borrowed the basic story of the hero, Sigismund, who has been banished from the court by his father, King Basilius, because of a prophecy at Sigismund's birth that he would one day rebel against his father and usurp the throne and its power. Ultimately, the work reflects Hofmannsthal's own need to come to grips with the fundamental problems of his era, especially after the events of World War I and the new direction European society had taken.

He first worked with the Calderón material began in 1901. At that time he planned a free adaptation in trochaic verse of Calderón's play, but this work was not completed, and he did not return to the subject again until after World War I. This second attempt to weave the Calderón material into a work of his own lasted from 1920 to 1925 and resulted in a first version that was published in 1925. Since his first preoccupation with the material at the turn of the century, Hofmannsthal had witnessed the collapse of his own world in the fall of the Austro-Hungarian monarchy. This historical experience serves as the background of the tragedy, in which he tries to reconcile the role of spirit in a world dominated by force, in the relentless dynamics of history in the making.

In his efforts to complete the 1925 version of *The Tower,* Hofmannsthal struggled over the last and fifth act for almost four years. The problems he faced were fundamental to the play: how to find a place for the role of spirit and how to offer in the final act a ray of hope in contrast to the dark events the play depicts.

Since birth, because of the prophecy that he would one day seize the throne, Sigismund has been kept prisoner in a tower under the care of Julian, in a dreamlike state of innocence and ignorance of the real, outside world. Upon the death of his nephew, King Basilius hopes to find in his banished son an heir to the throne and has Julian return with Sigismund to court. Sigismund, as prophesied, reacts violently to his father, strikes him down, and is returned to the tower. A year later Julian has masterminded a revolt against the king but is unsuccessful in his efforts to enlist Sigismund's support because Julian has convinced Sigismund that the outside world he encountered was only a dream. After Olivier, a rebellious soldier, betrays Julian, he too is unsuccessful in his attempt to use Sigismund as the spiritual representative of his ochlocratic revolution. Only a group of good people who approach Sigismund as their messiah succeed in winning him to the cause of putting down the revolt and establishing a new order. To do this Sigismund must leave the dreamworld of his tower of inwardness and enter the real world. In the final act of the play he has done this and is depicted as a thinker and tactician—as the synthesis of spirit and power. This final step, however, is not complete. He succumbs, momentarily but tragically, to the magic world of a gypsy woman, Olivier's mistress, who has come to avenge her lover's death and who cuts

him with a poisoned knife. Before he dies, however, his place is taken by a new savior, the Children's King, who is a kindred spirit and who holds forth the renewed promise of a new order.

Hofmannsthal found an answer to the dark events of the play (and his time) in the synthesis of spirit and power incorporated in Sigismund and in the promise of its continuance after Sigismund's death with the establishment of a new utopian order by the Children's King. He found this answer unsatisfactory, however, and two years later, in 1927, he published a second version of *The Tower* in which he directly confronted the dark forces of history. Here, instead of a solution in which spirit overcomes the mercilessness of the age, the forces of the age prevail. In the midst of this terrible world, no bright future shines forth; the only hope lies in a transcendental world beyond the present one.

Hofmannsthal rewrote the last part of *The Tower* on the basis of a deeper insight into the forces of history and the courageous honesty to confront them; but the second version of the play is also a stage version with major changes in acts 4 and 5. The changes he made were prompted in part by Reinhardt and by Hofmannsthal's own realization that the appearance of the Children's King with its utopian implications for a resolution of the tragedy was not valid.

The first three acts of the second or stage version of *The Tower* are essentially the same as the first. The acts are shorter, some speeches show minor changes, and minor incidents are omitted. The major change, made in preparation for a completely new ending to the play, occurs at the end of act 3 after Sigismund has been subdued and the king restored to power. Now Basilius is drawn as the true despot, his terrible power and nature are depicted vividly, and the act ends on a note of despair.

Instead of the time lapse of one year between acts 3 and 4, only a few days elapse in the new version, and the play concludes at the court. Basilius has sentenced Sigismund and

Julian to death, but before the execution can be carried out a palace revolt topples the king, and Sigismund is placed on the throne. Julian hopes again to win him for the revolt he has inspired but fails and is destroyed by Olivier, who now represents raw power and brute force. Olivier considers himself to be the instrument of history and, finding Sigismund of no use to him, has him shot. On this note the second version ends. Sigismund, the embodiment of spirit in a world out of joint, falls victim to the new reign of terror and force. There is no Children's King to set things right and carry on his work, only his fatal exhortation: "Bear witness, I was there, even though no one recognized me."

In addition to his plays for the spoken theater, Hofmannsthal wrote the texts for six major operas with music composed by Richard Strauss, which are still performed today throughout the world to enthusiastic audiences. The Hofmannsthal–Strauss collaboration, documented in over six hundred pages of correspondence between the poet and composer dating from 1900 to 1929, is a brilliant chapter in both literary and music history, for rarely have librettist and composer been so talented, and rarely have opera texts shown such artistic merit and depth of meaning. Fortunately for English-speaking readers, the correspondence, collected in *Richard Strauss—Hugo von Hofmannsthal: Briefwechsel* (1970) is available in a good English translation under the title *A Working Friendship*. The title is apt, for although the two artists were able to work together productively for over twenty years, their friendship was indeed a working one, and they never developed any other kind of relationship. From time to time Hofmannsthal expressed exasperation over Strauss's failure to grasp a deeper meaning or intention in his texts, but he always recognized the composer's theatrical sense and found in their collaboration the opportunity to achieve the higher goal of festival theater. Early in their collaboration Strauss called Hofmannsthal

"the born librettist," and later, on the occasion of Hofmannsthal's fiftieth birthday in 1924, Strauss wrote to Hofmannsthal that it was the poet's words that drew from him the best music he could offer.

Shortly after meeting Strauss for the first time in Paris in 1900, Hofmannsthal wrote to the composer to remind him of his possible interest in composing the music for a ballet, *Der Triumph der Zeit* (The Triumph of Time, 1901), which Hofmannsthal planned to write. He enclosed a detailed scenario of the ballet, and Strauss liked the poet's ideas but declined politely to take up the composition because of other plans he had at the time. Thus their collaboration did not begin until 1906, when Strauss started to work on the music for Hofmannsthal's stage play *Electra*. By late 1908 Strauss had completed the music, and *Electra*'s premiere as an opera in Dresden in January 1909 was as successful as its stage premiere in Berlin.

Having recently composed *Salomé* (1905) and then *Electra* (1909), two similarly dark works, Strauss wanted next to write the music for a comic opera. When their intention to write an opera based on Casanova's memoirs failed because Hofmannsthal preferred first to write the stage play *Cristinas Heimreise*, in 1909 Hofmannsthal offered the initial idea for another operatic text, *Der Rosenkavalier*. With their joint work on this project, which became one of their most famous operas, the collaboration, tenuously begun with *Electra* in 1906, continued in earnest and lasted until the poet's death. By the end of 1910, after working closely with Strauss on *Der Rosenkavalier* for two years, Hofmannsthal completed the opera, and on 26 January 1911 it had its premiere in Dresden.

Like *Cristinas Heimreise, Der Rosenkavalier* is a product of the second period in Hofmannsthal's work as a playwright, when he was trying to master dramatic form. Like *Cristinas Heimreise*, it is a comedy dealing with love and marriage in a serious manner. The form is a marvelous example of comedy in the old Viennese tradition—including cloak-and-dagger, mistaken identity, and farce—and shows Hofmannsthal's debt to the Austrian theater tradition, in particular to the plays of Ferdinand Raimund and Johann Nepomuk Nestroy. The setting for *Der Rosenkavalier* is eighteenth-century Vienna during the first decade of Maria Theresa's reign, around 1740. Hofmannsthal greatly admired the empress and her era and gave a faithful portrayal of one phase of the social history of that time.

The opera, a "comedy for music," as Hofmannsthal subtitled the libretto, opens on a scene in the boudoir of Princess Werdenberg, a mature woman in her thirties, who is also known as the Marschallin because her husband is a field marshal. While her husband is on a hunting trip, the Marschallin has spent the night with her young lover, Octavian, who she knows will one day leave her for a younger woman. As Octavian prepares to depart, a relative, Baron Ochs von Lerchenau, makes a sudden appearance to request that a cavalier present a silver rose to his fiancée in the traditional custom, and Octavian disguises himself as a maid to avoid discovery. Ochs, a bald, blustering adventurer type who is to marry for her dowry a young girl, Sophie von Faninal, the daughter of a member of the new nobility, flirts with the maid and suggests they dine together. After Octavian, Ochs, and others leave, the act ends on a note of melancholy as the wise Marschallin views herself in a mirror, perceives the passage of time, and reconciles herself to the wisdom of letting go.

In act 2, at the residence of Sophie's father, Octavian arrives to present the silver rose, and he and Sophie fall in love at first sight. Ochs then arrives to sign a marriage contract. His coarse behavior toward Sophie repulses her and offends Octavian, who draws his sword on the baron and wounds him slightly. The act ends after Ochs receives a message from the "maid" he met in the Marschallin's chamber and prepares to dictate a note to her to arrange a rendezvous.

In act 3 Octavian has made arrangements at a small inn for a tryst with Ochs and appears in disguise as the maid he pretended to be in the first act. Now everything comes to a comic conclusion as Ochs behaves in characteristically coarse fashion and is shown up for the rogue he is in the presence of Sophie and her father, who have been summoned by Octavian. The Marschallin arrives at the end to set things right. In her selfless though bittersweet act of renunciation, the Marschallin lives up to the greatness of her namesake, Maria Theresa, and corrects the misalliance of her own relationship with the young Octavian and of Ochs's relationship with the young Sophie by accepting the union of Octavian and Sophie.

Shortly after the premiere of *Der Rosenkavalier* in Dresden in 1911, Hofmannsthal approached Strauss with the idea for an opera based on Molière's *Le bourgeois gentilhomme* (*The Self-Made Gentleman,* 1670) with a concluding divertissement, the classical text *Ariadne auf Naxos (Ariadne on Naxos)* by Hofmannsthal. In this version, *Ariadne on Naxos* was intended to be a special entertainment given by Monsieur Jourdain in Molière's comedy. Completed in 1911 and performed in Stuttgart in October 1912 under Reinhardt's direction, the combination of the two works, drama and opera, proved to be unwieldy and in the end unsuccessful. Hofmannsthal therefore prepared a new version of the opera, the work that is performed today, which had its premiere in Vienna in October 1916.

Set in Vienna in the eighteenth century in the house of a wealthy Viennese bourgeois gentleman, the prologue now replaces the Molière text, introduces all of the players and singers, and announces the basic theme of the opera to follow. The gentleman, who never appears in the work, is planning an entertainment for his guests, but there is trouble among the artists. The music teacher objects to the idea that a comedy will follow his protégé's serious opera, while the commedia dell'arte performers, led by the coquettish Zerbinetta and including the stock figures Harlequin, Scaramuccio, Truffaldino, and Brighella, complain that they will never get the audience to laugh after it has been bored to death by the prima donna in her classical role of Ariadne, the symbol of human loneliness who longs for death after Theseus has abandoned her on Naxos. The problem is resolved when the wealthy gentleman changes his mind and decides that both the comedy and tragic opera will be performed simultaneously.

The opera following the prologue is based on the non-Homeric version of the Ariadne legend, in which Theseus, having slain the Minotaur on Crete and escaped from the Labyrinth with the help of Ariadne, the princess of Crete, deserts her on Naxos, an island in the Aegean Sea. There Bacchus, who has just escaped from the enchantress Circe, finds Ariadne and makes her his wife.

As the opera begins, Zerbinetta and her friends try to relieve Ariadne of her pain. When songs and dances fail to distract her, Zerbinetta tries to teach her her own philosophy of love and life, which is to live for the moment, forget, and go from man to man in a never-ending series of romantic encounters. Combining the opera buffa with the opera seria in this fashion was a tour de force that enabled Hofmannsthal to contrast the lower, adventurous world of Zerbinetta and her followers with the higher, serious world of Ariadne and the gods. As in *Electra,* the work's underlying theme is fidelity. Zerbinetta is happy only when she goes from one man to another; Ariadne can love only one man, and when Theseus deserts her she is ready for death. That is why she welcomes Bacchus, whom she believes to be the messenger of death. But both Ariadne and Bacchus are ready for a true and lasting love. Ariadne is transformed by Bacchus and reborn; Bacchus is transformed by Ariadne and recognizes himself as the god he is. For Zerbinetta, who will never understand the meaning of fidelity and permanence, Bacchus is just the next man in Ariadne's life.

As early as March 1911 Hofmannsthal mentioned an idea for a magic fairy tale analogous to Wolfgang Amadeus Mozart's *Die Zauber-*

flöte (*The Magic Flute,* 1791). This work occupied Hofmannsthal for the next eight years and finally appeared in 1919 both as his longest completed prose narrative and as the opera text *Die Frau ohne Schatten.* On 10 October 1919 the opera had its premiere in Vienna, but it was not as successful as their earlier joint works had been because Hofmannsthal's symbol-laden text was difficult for audiences to understand.

The basic theme of the work is the need for deep human ties and the possibility of salvation through sacrifice and self-conquest. A beautiful fairy princess has recently wed the emperor of the Southeastern Islands after he captured her on a hunt. The empress has lost her magic gift of changing into various kinds of animals, but after twelve moons she does not yet possess a shadow. She therefore stands between two worlds—neither released from the world of the spirits nor a part of the world of humans. Through motherhood she could obtain a shadow, but the emperor's love for her is selfish, and he does not want a child. If within three days she does not have a shadow, the emperor will be turned to stone, and she must return to the world of the spirits. With the help of her nurse, a Mephistopheles-like representative from the spirit world who knows and detests the human world, the empress tries to obtain a shadow. The nurse knows how to get a human shadow and seeks out a young, haughty woman, the wife of a lowly dyer, who cares little for her husband and is childless. In return for riches and other enticements, the dyer's wife agrees to sacrifice her shadow and, along with it, fertility. But when the empress hears the cries of the dyer's unborn children and feels the dyer's human misery, she refuses the shadow. Through the act of sacrifice and self-conquest in refusing the shadow, the empress is saved, and her action also saves the emperor and the dyer and his wife. All are reunited, both pairs are purified, and the opera ends with the joyous voices of the unborn children.

Following the premiere of *Die Frau ohne*

Schatten in Vienna in 1919, nine years passed before their next opera, *Die ägyptische Helena*, was completed and had its premiere in Dresden in June 1928. In the meantime Hofmannsthal and Strauss worked on a festive spectacle with dances and choruses called *Die Ruinen von Athen* (The Ruins of Athens, 1924), which was based in part on Ludwig van Beethoven's ballet *Die Geschöpfe des Prometheus* (The Creatures of Prometheus). This work had its premiere in Vienna in September 1914. Hofmannsthal was also involved in a film production of *Der Rosenkavalier,* for which he wrote the film script using a novelistic approach to the subject. Although Hofmannsthal tried to convince Strauss that the film version would not compete with the stage work—in fact he suggested that it would be good advertising and whet the public's appetite for the opera— Strauss took little interest in the project and had to be persuaded by Hofmannsthal to conduct the work for its film premiere in Dresden in January 1926, fifteen years after the work had its stage debut in that city.

Like its predecessor, *Die Frau ohne Schatten, Die ägyptische Helena* has a beautifully poetic but extremely difficult and complicated text and therefore did not become the success that Hofmannsthal and Strauss had hoped it would be. Just before its premiere, Hofmannsthal published a rather long essay, "Die ägyptische Helena," intended to inform the public about the subject of the opera and his treatment of it. Of interest to Hofmannsthal was the theme of marriage as demonstrated in the relationship of Helen and Menelaus on their return home after the Trojan War. He incorporated into the work Euripides' idea of a phantom Helen; that is, the Helen Menelaus retrieved from Troy was a phantom, and the real Helen had been taken to Egypt for safety. In Hofmannsthal's libretto Menelaus is tricked by a sorceress into thinking he has killed the phantom Helen in an act of revenge and now has the real Helen at his side. Rejecting the notion that the Trojan War could have been fought for ten years for a phantom, however,

Menelaus believes that he must have killed the real Helen and that the Egyptian Helen has been offered by the sorceress as a mere consolation. Helen decides to let him know the truth through a magic potion and expects him to kill her, but Menelaus now sees her as no man has ever seen his mortal wife before, and he forgives the past. The opera ends with the appearance of their young daughter, Hermione, and the restoration of the family unit.

Arabella, Hofmannsthal's last opera for Strauss, appeared in 1933, four years after the poet's death, and had its premiere in that same year in Dresden. Pressed by Strauss for a new comic libretto in 1927, Hofmannsthal turned to two sources: earlier notes for a play about a fiacre driver as a count and the prose sketch *Lucidor: Figuren zu einer ungeschriebenen Komödie,* which included "figures for an unwritten comedy." He completed *Arabella* just before his death in 1929.

Like *The Difficult Man* and *Der Rosenkavalier, Arabella* is a Viennese play. It takes place in the year 1860 and portrays the society of that time. The plot is relatively simple and light; in fact, Strauss was concerned about its being too close to the genre of operetta. Count Waldner, a retired and impoverished cavalry officer, is ensconced with his wife and two daughters in a hotel in Vienna. He hopes to marry off Arabella and acquire some funds in the bargain. Because of the cost of offering two daughters at once, Zdenka, Arabella's younger sister, poses as a boy. Arabella has several suitors, none of whom she cares for. The most ardent of the lot is Matteo. Although Zdenka is in love with Matteo herself, she encourages him on Arabella's behalf because she fears that he will kill himself if Arabella rejects him. In the meantime Waldner has written to an old comrade whom he does not realize is now dead, and his comrade's nephew, Mandryka, has opened the letter, fallen in love with Arabella from the picture of her Waldner has enclosed, and come to Vienna to woo her. When Arabella and Mandryka meet, it is love at first sight, but several comic events must occur before they (and Zdenka and Matteo) are finally joined.

The ideas in *Arabella* do not have the depth of those in *Der Rosenkavalier,* but Hofmannsthal created a number of delightful characters, from the blustery Count Waldner, who is addicted to gambling, and his superstitious wife, Adelaide, to the coquettish Fiakermilli. The two sisters, too, are charming and show the strength of character Hofmannsthal's women often possess. Like Helene in *The Difficult Man,* each in her own way takes the initiative to win the man of her choice, and Arabella even teaches her man a lesson about truth and trust. The young Zdenka also teaches Arabella a lesson: that one should only give and should always go on loving.

Although Hofmannsthal's major interest was in the theater, his few prose narratives and essays were major accomplishments and served no less than his verse, plays, and libretti to establish his reputation as a European writer of the first rank.

Hofmannsthal's prose narratives span a period of twenty-four years, from 1895 to 1919. They include three masterful stories, a major novel that remained uncompleted, and the prose version of *The Woman Without a Shadow,* which is best known in the opera version by Richard Strauss. Several other short stories also exist, but only as fragments.

Das Märchen der 672. Nacht (best rendered into English from its subtitle as The Tale of the Merchant's Son and His Four Servants, 1905) has little if anything to do with the fairy tale of the 672d Arabian Night. Completed in 1895, it was Hofmannsthal's first attempt at a prose narrative and is closely related, in both content and style, to the poetic and lyric-dramatic attempts of the young author. The story recounts the dreamlike tale of a young man who, having never cared for his friends nor met a woman so beautiful that he must have her at his side, has withdrawn from life and society at the age of twenty-five to live among his possessions and a few faithful servants. In his isolation his possessions grow ever more important and begin to represent life for him. At the same time, however, he perceives their ultimate uselessness as well as their beauty and is haunted by the thought of death that this void suggests. Although his four servants surround him, their relationship lacks human feeling, and he regards them as possessions, too. Faced with the possibility of losing them when a mysterious letter accuses his manservant of wrongdoing, he goes into the city to defend his possessions. There, in an ugly labyrinth, he gets lost and meets his death. He dies hating his life because it has led him to a premature death. And he dies not because he loved his servants but because he viewed them as possessions he could not bear to lose. Like *Death and the Fool,* the tale of the merchant's son exposes the negative side of human isolation. Unlike Claudio, however, who learns just before his death to reject his egoistic aesthetic life and embrace his fellow man, the merchant's son never learns this lesson and meets an ugly death that markedly contrasts with the beauty he has prized in life. He fails life and perishes because he was an observer of life and not a participant.

The ugly side of life depicted at the end of *Das Märchen der 672. Nacht,* and experienced personally by Hofmannsthal during his period of compulsory military duty, recurs in his second novella, *Reitergeschichte (A Tale of the Cavalry,* 1905), completed in 1898. Here, the ugly village through which the story's hero rides is a foreshadowing of the death his unwarranted dreams of undeserved rewards and glory will bring. The story of the cavalryman Anton Lerch, a sergeant under Baron Rofrano's command on the Austrians' side in their 1848 war against the Italian liberation army, begins early one morning as the unit begins a march on Milan. After a series of minor and successful skirmishes and events, the troops march in triumph through the city. Attracted by the face of a woman he believes he recognizes, Lerch breaks away from his unit, is tempted by thoughts about the woman

HUGO VON HOFMANNSTHAL

and her luxurious quarters, and vows to return and take up residence with her. At this moment he falls victim to his desires and dreams for the pleasures of the civilian life and undeserved gains. Even a subsequent ride through the ugly village and the appearance of his double cannot distract him from the pleasures and rewards he desires. When he rejoins his unit and engages in another battle, now bloody and brutal, he captures the first of the prizes he longs for, a beautiful iron-gray horse. Having lost his sense of duty through his dreams of the beautiful, undisciplined life, Lerch refuses the order from Baron Rofrano to release his booty. This act of insubordination demands its punishment, and Lerch is summarily executed, a victim of his own fall from a life of order and discipline.

In 1900 Hofmannsthal completed the last of his three short tales, *Das Erlebnis des Marschalls von Bassompierre* (*An Episode in the Life of Marshal de Bassompierre,* 1905). Based on a translation by Goethe of the memoirs of Marshal Bassompierre, published in Cologne in 1665, Hofmannsthal's tale is a considerable amplification of the original and of Goethe's translation, to both of which it adds color, atmosphere, and depth. The incident Marshal Bassompierre recorded in his memoirs recalls a brief love encounter between him and a young shopkeeper he has seen from time to time when crossing a bridge on business in Paris. On one such occasion the woman indicates that she is at his service, and they spend a beautiful night together. Enchanted by her frank attraction to him and inflamed with unexpected passion for her, he arranges to meet her again three nights later in her lodgings rather than in the disreputable setting of their first encounter. When he arrives at her lodgings, however, filled with longing and anticipation, he discovers the dead bodies of the woman and her husband, who have fallen victim to the plague raging through the city.

An Episode in the Life of Marshal de Bassompierre shares with *Das Märchen der*

672. Nacht and *A Tale of the Cavalry* the theme of the beautiful life, or dreams of it, ended abruptly and unexpectedly by an ugly death. The shopkeeper, who would betray her worthy husband only for a lover like the marshal, forsakes her ordered life in doing so and meets an ugly fate that contrasts with both the ordered life she has had and the pleasure of her brief encounter with a lover of high station.

Begun in Venice in 1907 and resumed in 1912 and 1913, Hofmannsthal's uncompleted novel *Andreas, oder die Vereinigten* (*Andreas, or the United,* 1932) bears the mark of a masterpiece even in its unfinished form. Intended as a *Bildungsroman* (novel of education) in the great tradition of Goethe's *Wilhelm Meister* (1796), the novel was to follow "the development of a young Viennese to manhood," as Hofmannsthal wrote to Strauss in 1914. For Andreas von Ferschengelder, the hero of the story, that represents his growth and development from a naive and insecure young man to a whole person worthy of the ideal love of Romana, a young farmer's daughter of noble spirit whom he meets at the outset of his journey to Venice. In the process Andreas must learn first to become capable of love and then that body and spirit are one.

The novel begins in Venice, a city to which Andreas has been sent by his parents to broaden his education. Soon after he settles into lodgings with the impoverished Count Prampero, who, together with his wife, works in a theater across the street, a flashback recounts Andreas' humiliating experience on the way from Vienna to Venice. His evil servant, Gotthilff, who had forced his services on Andreas, had assaulted a maid at a farm in the mountains of Carinthia where they had stopped and then made off with his master's horse and half of his money. Andreas, who had fallen in love with the farmer's lovely daughter, Romana, had to leave in disgrace, unworthy of Romana's love. As he left, however, Andreas realized that just as an eagle he sees soaring above him can unite all below in his gaze, so he too can unite the parted and have

Romana with him wherever he is. This insight points to the possibility of his union with Romana once he has become a complete man.

The remainder of the unfinished novel continues in Venice and introduces some of the characters and kinds of experiences that shape Andreas' growth and development into manhood. These include the count's younger daughter, Zustina, who, to raise funds for her family, has established a lottery whose first prize will be her virginity; Nina, the count's older daughter, who is a coquette; the Maltese knight Sacramozo, who will serve as Andreas' spiritual mentor; and Maria, a shy and pious schizoid Spanish lady under Sacramozo's protection, whose other personality is Mariquita, a bold and foward coquette. The fragment ends with Andreas' discovery of the dual personality—the lady Maria and the coquette Mariquita—but he does not know that they are one and the same person.

The remainder of Hoffmansthal's work on *Andreas or the United* consists of sketches for the continuation of thc novel. Here he provides more details about the fascinating split personality Maria/Mariquita, for which Hofmannsthal received inspiration and a model from the Boston psychiatrist Morton Prince's book *The Dissociation of a Personality*, published in 1906. It is obvious that the duality of this character symbolizes the initial split in Andreas' character and points the way to the integration of personality, of body and spirit, that Andreas must achieve by the end of the novel.

One of Hofmannsthal's favorite sayings, "The whole man must move at once," from Joseph Addison, was an ideal by which he lived and wrote throughout his life. From his earliest years Hofmannsthal perceived the unity of the world and sought to show that its contrasting parts constitute a whole. To this end, in his private life and in his works he sought relationships and fulfillment in the social world. Fidelity, commitment to others, sacrifice, self-conquest, transformation of one-self and others, marriage, childbearing—these are the major themes that inform his works and give them an ethical foundation. In spite of the fame of his early works, however, they were widely misunderstood as the products of an aesthete, as art for art's sake. Critics failed to see the moral issues and to understand that from the beginning of his career Hofmannsthal sought the ideal of the whole person. Today, the moral value and greatness of Hofmannsthal's works are clear. No writer in the twentieth century achieved so much in so many genres—lyric, essay, drama, libretto, prose narrative—and the deep interest of the public and critics in his works since World War II is richly deserved. Hofmannsthal was both one of the first truly modern writers in German and the last classical writer in the tradition of Goethe.

Selected Bibliography

EDITIONS

INDIVIDUAL WORKS

POETRY AND VERSE PLAYS

Gestern. Vienna, 1891. Published under the pseudonym Theophil Morren.

Die Hochzeit der Sobeide. Berlin, 1899.

Theater in Versen. Berlin, 1899. Includes *Die Frau im Fenster, Die Hochzeit der Sobeide,* and *Der Abenteurer und die Sängerin.*

Der Kaiser und die Hexe. Berlin, 1900.

Der Tor und der Tod. Berlin, 1900.

Der Tod des Tizian. Berlin, 1901.

Ausgewählte Gedichte. Berlin, 1903.

Das kleine Welttheater oder Die Glücklichen. Leipzig, 1903.

Kleine Dramen. 2 vols. Leipzig, 1907. Includes *Gestern, Der Tor und der Tod,* and *Der weisse Fächer* in vol. 1; *Das Bergwerk zu Falun, Der Kaiser und die Hexe,* and *Das kleine Welttheater* in vol. 2.

Die gesammelten Gedichte. Leipzig, 1907.

Der weisse Fächer. Leipzig, 1907.

Der Abenteurer und die Sängerin, oder die Geschenke des Lebens. Berlin, 1909.

Die Frau im Fenster. Berlin, 1909.

HUGO VON HOFMANNSTHAL

Die Gedichte und kleinen Dramen. Leipzig, 1911.
Gedichte. Leipzig, 1922.
Nachlese der Gedichte. Berlin, 1934. Includes poems not in previous editions.
Die Gedichte und lyrische Dramen. Leipzig, 1955.

BALLET
Der Triumph der Zeit. Berlin and Leipzig, 1901.

PLAYS AND LIBRETTI
Elektra. Berlin, 1904.
Das gerettete Venedig. Berlin, 1905.
Ödipus und die Sphinx. Berlin, 1906.
Cristinas Heimreise. Berlin, 1910. A second version also appeared in Berlin in 1910.
König Ödipus. Berlin, 1910.
Alkestis. Leipzig, 1911.
Jedermann. Berlin, 1911.
Der Rosenkavalier. Berlin, 1911.
Ariadne auf Naxos. Berlin and Paris, 1912. A new version, subtitled *Oper in einem Aufzuge nebst einem Vorspiel,* appeared in Berlin in 1916.
Josephslegende. Berlin, 1914.
Die Frau ohne Schatten. Berlin, 1916.
Der Bürger als Edelmann. Berlin, 1918.
Dame Kobold. Berlin, 1920.
Der Schwierige. Berlin, 1921.
Das Salzburger grosse Welttheater. Leipzig, 1922.
Florindo. Vienna, 1923.
Der Turm. Munich, 1925. A new stage version appeared in Berlin in 1927.
Szenischer Prolog zur Neueröffnung des Josefstädter Theaters. Vienna, 1926.
Die ägyptische Helena. Leipzig, 1928.
Arabella. Berlin, 1933.
Das Bergwerk zu Falun. Vienna, 1933.
Semiramis: Die beiden Götter. Munich, 1933.
Dramatische Entwürfe aus dem Nachlass. Vienna, 1936.
Der Unbestechliche. Frankfurt, 1950. This is the first edition to publish the play in its complete form.
Danae oder die Vernunftheirat. Frankfurt, 1952.
Silvia im "Stern." Bern and Stuttgart, 1959.

PROSE NARRATIVES
Das Erlebnis des Marschalls von Bassompierre. Vienna, 1905.
Das Märchen der 672. Nacht und andere Erzählungen. Vienna and Leipzig, 1905.

Reitergeschichte. Vienna, 1905.
Lucidor: Figuren zu einer ungeschriebenen Komödie. Leipzig, 1910. This sketch was later reworked by Hofmannsthal into the libretto *Arabella.*
Die Frau ohne Schatten. Berlin, 1919.
Andreas oder die Vereinigten. Berlin, 1932.

ESSAYS
Studie über die Entwickelung des Dichters Victor Hugo. Vienna, 1901.
Ein Brief. Berlin, 1902.
Unterhaltungen über literarische Gegenstände. Berlin, 1904. Includes "Über Gedichte: Ein Dialog" and "Über Charaktere im Roman und Drama."
Die Wege und die Begegnungen. Bremen, 1913.
Prinz Eugen der edle Ritter: Sein Leben in Bildern. Vienna, 1915.
Die prosaischen Schriften gesammelt. 3 vols. Berlin, 1907–1917.
Augenblicke in Griechenland. Regensburg and Leipzig, 1924.
Früheste Prosastücke. Leipzig, 1926. Includes "Das Dorf im Gebirge" and "Das Glück am Weg."
"Das Schrifttum als geistiger Raum der Nation." Munich, 1927. A speech presented in the Auditorium Maximum of the University of Munich on 10 January 1927.
Loris: Die Prosa des jungen Hugo von Hofmannsthal. Berlin, 1930.
Die Berührung der Sphären. Berlin, 1931. A collection of prose pieces published for the most part in periodicals between 1896 and 1929.
"Beethoven." Vienna, 1937. A speech presented in Zurich on 10 December 1920.
Österreichische Aufsätze und Reden. Vienna, 1956.

AUTOBIOGRAPHICAL WORKS
"Ad me ipsum." In *Jahrbuch des freien deutschen Hochstiftes.* Frankfurt, 1930.

COLLECTED WORKS
Gesammelte Werke in Einzelausgaben. 15 vols. Edited by Herbert Steiner. Stockholm and Frankfurt, 1945–1959. This is the collection most widely used; it comprises the following:
Die Erzählungen (1945). Includes *Andreas oder die Vereinigten, Das Erlebnis des Marschalls von Bassompierre, Lucidor, Das Märchen der 672. Nacht,* and *Reitergeschichte.*
Gedichte und lyrische Dramen (1946). Includes

HUGO VON HOFMANNSTHAL

Gestern, Der Kaiser und die Hexe, Das kleine Welttheater, Der Tod des Tizian, Der Tor und der Tod, and *Der weisse Fächer.*

Lustspiele 1 (1947). Includes *Cristinas Heimreise* and *Der Rosenkavalier.*

Lustspiele 2 (1948). Includes *Der Schwierige* and *Silvia im "Stern."*

Lustspiele 3 (1956). Includes *Ariadne auf Naxos.*

Lustspiele 4 (1956). Includes *Arabella* and *Der Unbestechliche.*

Prosa 1 (1950). Includes "Eine Monographie," an essay on Mitterwurzer.

Prosa 2 (1951). Includes "Ein Brief."

Prosa 3 (1952). Includes "Über die Pantomime," "Zum Direktionswechsel im Burgtheater," and "Zur Krisis des Burgtheaters."

Prosa 4 (1955). Includes the essay "Die ägyptische Helena" and the speech "Das Schrifttum als geistiger Raum der Nation."

Dramen 1 (1953). Includes *Der Abenteurer und die Sängerin, Die Frau im Fenster, Die Hochzeit der Sobeide,* and *Der Triumph der Zeit.*

Dramen 2 (1954). Includes *Elektra, Das gerettete Venedig, König Ödipus,* and *Ödipus und die Sphinx.*

Dramen 3 (1957). Includes *Die Frau ohne Schatten, Jedermann, Das Leben ein Traum,* and *Das Salzburger grosse Welttheater.*

Dramen 4 (1958). Includes *Die ägyptische Helena, Die Ruinen von Athen,* and *Der Turm.*

Aufzeichnungen (1959). Includes "Ad me ipsum" and "Brief an Max Pirker."

Gesammelte Werke. In zehn Einzelbänden. Edited by Bernd Schoeller. Frankfurt, 1979–1980. An expanded and reorganized version of the 15-volume *Gesammelte Werke in Einzelausgaben.*

CORRESPONDENCE

Hofmannsthal had an exceptionally large number and wide range of correspondents. The collections of letters cited here are the most important ones that have appeared in book form.

Briefe 1890–1901. Berlin, 1935.

Briefe 1900–1909. Vienna, 1937.

Briefwechsel zwischen George und Hofmannsthal. Edited by Robert Boehringer. Düsseldorf and Munich, 1953.

Hugo von Hofmannsthal—Arthur Schnitzler: Briefwechsel. Edited by Therese Nickl and Heinrich Schnitzler. Frankfurt, 1964.

Hugo von Hofmannsthal—Carl J. Burckhardt: Briefwechsel. Edited by Carl J. Burckhardt. Frankfurt, 1956.

Hugo von Hofmannsthal—Eberhard von Bodenhausen: Briefe der Freundschaft. Edited by Dora Freifrau von Bodenhausen. Düsseldorf, 1953.

Hugo von Hofmannsthal—Edgar Karg von Bebenburg: Briefwechsel. Edited by Mary E. Gilbert. Frankfurt, 1966.

Hugo von Hofmannsthal—Harry Graf Kessler: Briefwechsel 1898–1929. Edited by Hilde Burger. Frankfurt, 1968.

Hugo von Hofmannsthal—Leopold von Andrian: Briefwechsel. Edited by Walter H. Perl. Frankfurt, 1968.

Hugo von Hofmannsthal—Rainer Maria Rilke: Briefwechsel 1899–1925. Edited by Rudolf Hirsch and Ingeborg Schnack. Frankfurt, 1978.

Hugo von Hofmannsthal—Richard Beer-Hofmann: Briefwechsel. Edited by Eugene Weber. Frankfurt, 1972.

Hugo von Hofmannsthal—Rudolf Borchardt: Briefwechsel. Edited by Marie Luise Borchardt. Frankfurt, 1954.

Hugo von Hofmannsthal—Willy Haas: Ein Briefwechsel. Edited by Rolf Italiaander. Berlin, 1968.

Richard Strauss—Hugo von Hofmannsthal: Briefwechsel. Edited by Willi Schuh. Zurich, 1970.

WORKS EDITED BY HOFMANNSTHAL

Hesperus. Leipzig, 1909.

Deutsche Erzähler. 4 vols. Leipzig, 1912.

Österreichischer Almanach auf das Jahr 1916. Leipzig, 1915.

Österreichische Bibliothek. 26 vols. Leipzig, 1915–1917.

Neue deutsche Beiträge. Munich, 1922–1927. First series, vols. 1–3; second series, vols. 1–3.

Deutsche Epigramme. Munich, 1923.

Deutsches Lesebuch. 2 vols. Munich, 1922–1923.

Grillparzers politisches Vermächtnis. Leipzig, 1926.

Schillers Selbstcharakteristik aus seinen Schriften. Munich, 1926.

Wert und Ehre deutscher Sprache. Bremen, 1927.

TRANSLATIONS

Andreas, or The United. Being fragments of a novel by Hugo von Hofmannsthal. Translated with an introduction by Marie D. Hottinger. London, 1936.

Ariadne on Naxos. Translated by Miles Malleson. Boston, 1969.

Death and the Fool. Translated by Elizabeth Walter. Boston, 1914.

The Egyptian Helen. Translated by Hilde D. Cohn. Cleveland, 1956.

The Fool and Death. A metrical translation of Hugo von Hofmannsthal's poetic drama *Der Tor und der Tod* by Herbert Edward Mierow. Colorado Springs, Colo., 1930.

Hugo von Hofmannsthal: Three Plays. Translated with an introduction by Alfred Schwarz. Detroit, 1966. Includes *Death and the Fool, Electra,* and *The Tower.*

The Lyrical Poems of Hugo von Hofmannsthal. New Haven, Conn., and London, 1918.

Poems and Verse Plays. Edited by Michael Hamburger. New York, 1961. Includes *Death and the Fool, The Emperor and the Witch, The Little Theatre of the World,* and *The Marriage of Zobeide.*

Richard Strauss: "Der Rosenkavalier." Comedy for music in three acts. Libretto by Hugo von Hofmannsthal. Story adaptation by Anthony Burgess. Boston, 1982.

The Salzburg Everyman. Translated by M. E. Tafler. Salzburg, 1929.

Selected Plays and Libretti. Edited by Michael Hamburger. Various translators. New York, 1963. Includes *Arabella, The Cavalier of the Rose, The Difficult Man, The Salzburg Great Theatre of the World,* and *The Tower.*

Selected Prose. Translated by Mary Hottinger and Tania and James Stern. Introduction by Hermann Broch. New York and London, 1952. Includes *Andreas, A Tale of the Cavalry, An Episode in the Life of Marshal de Bassompierre,* "The Letter of Lord Chandos," *Lucidor,* and *The Woman Without a Shadow.*

The White Fan. Translated by Maurice Magnus. Florence, 1909.

A Working Friendship: The Correspondence Between Richard Strauss and Hugo von Hofmannsthal. Translated by Hanns Hammelmann and Ewald Osers. London and New York, 1961.

BIOGRAPHICAL AND CRITICAL STUDIES

Alewyn, Richard. *Über Hugo von Hofmannsthal.* Göttingen, 1958.

Bangerter, Lowell A. *Hugo von Hofmannsthal.* New York, 1977.

Bauer, Sibylle, ed. *Hugo von Hofmannsthal.* Darmstadt, 1968. A collection of outstanding essays on Hofmannsthal and his works.

Broch, Hermann. *Hofmannsthal und seine Zeit: Eine Studie.* Munich, 1964.

Fiechtner, Helmut Albert. *Hugo von Hofmannsthal: Der Dichter im Spiegel der Freunde.* Vienna, 1949.

Haas, Willy. *Hugo von Hofmannsthal.* Berlin, 1964.

Hammelmann, Hanns. *Hugo von Hofmannsthal.* New Haven, Conn., 1957.

Hederer, Edgar. *Hugo von Hofmannsthal.* Frankfurt, 1960.

Heuschele, Otto. *Hugo von Hofmannsthal: Bildnis des Dichters.* Mühlacker, 1965.

Naef, Karl J. *Hugo von Hofmannsthals Wesen und Werk.* Zurich and Leipzig, 1938.

Schäeder, Grete. *Die Gestalten.* Berlin, 1933.

Sulger-Gebing, Emil. *Hugo von Hofmannsthal: Eine literarische Studie.* Leipzig, 1905.

Volke, Werner. *Hugo von Hofmannsthal in Selbstzeugnissen und Bilddokumenten.* Hamburg, 1967.

Wunberg, Gotthart, ed. *Hofmannsthal im Urteil seiner Kritiker: Dokumente zur Wirkungsgeschichte Hugo von Hofmannsthals in Deutschland.* Frankfurt, 1972.

Yuill, W. E., and Patricia Howe, eds. *Hugo von Hofmannsthal: Commemorative Essays.* London, 1981.

CATALOGS, INDEXES, AND BIBLIOGRAPHIES

Exner, Richard. *Index Nominum zu Hugo von Hofmannsthals Gesammelten Werken.* Heidelberg, 1976.

The Hofmannsthal Collection in the Houghton Library. A descriptive catalog of printed books. Edited by James E. Walsh. Heidelberg, 1974.

Jacoby, Karl. *Hugo von Hofmannsthal Bibliographie.* Berlin, 1936.

Weber, Horst. *Hugo von Hofmannsthal Bibliographie: Werke—Briefe—Gespräche—Übersetzungen—Vertonungen.* New York and Berlin, 1962.

Weber, Horst. *Hugo von Hofmannsthal: Bibliographie des Schrifttums 1892–1963.* Berlin, 1966.

HERMAN K. DOSWALD

THOMAS MANN
(1875–1955)

IN THE YEARS that have passed since Thomas Mann's death, his literary reputation has not had an easy time. The ideas that inform his novels and novellas are dismissed as being irrelevant to our present concerns, the subtle ironies of his narrative and discursive styles and the intricacies of his narrators' perspectives are said to founder in an excess of literary self-consciousness, demanding elaborate study rather than giving spontaneous pleasure. One recent critic has called him "irresponsible" and "an insidious . . . force for evil," and others, less extravagantly, have questioned the genuineness of the values intimated in his writings. Vladimir Nabokov (like Mann, a master parodist of academic prose) saw Mann as a purveyor of "the Literature of Ideas," which he identified with "topical trash coming in huge blocks of plaster." Excessive or outdated intellectualism on one hand, esoteric formalism or shapelessness on the other—these, broadly speaking, are the present charges against him.

The charges are both plausible and misleading. Plausible because Mann's concern with "ideas" is indeed more marked than that of any other modern European novelist, so that on occasion he does not scruple to present living characters as determined by the intellectual convictions they more or less clearly profess or by the current of ideas to which they more or less consciously react; and the dialectician's enthusiasm in demonstrating every thrust and parry of verbal combat does occa-

sionally lead him to write at inordinate length. But the charges turn out to be misleading as soon as we realize that there is nothing inadvertent or "abstract" about the patterns of Mann's stories, that the interplay of "ideas" and life is an integral part of his fiction: he saw life in the form of this interplay, and here above all lies the distinctness of his art. That the "ideas" are present in a way in which they are not in the work of Henry James is obvious enough; certainly, T. S. Eliot's tribute to James—"a mind so fine that no idea could violate it"—does not apply to Mann. The violation of a mind by an idea, on the other hand, may well serve to define one of Mann's central themes; and intellectualism, not as the novelist's failing but as a motif of his narrative, as a thing hostile to life, is another.

Like the work of every great artist, Mann's writings challenge established critical preconceptions. The distinction between creativeness and criticism loses much of its force in a body of work that is itself (in Matthew Arnold's phrase) quite manifestly "a criticism of life." He is one of the few novelists of our age—André Gide is another—whose major works were written with the full and explicit cooperation of his critical intelligence. For him, creation is itself partly a critical act, a scrutinizing of the values by which the world—which is no longer quite our world—lives, a questioning of what is valuable in experience and true to its facts. Consequently the heroes of his tales are often men and women who, from their stations in life and their limited points of view, contribute to the criticism and scrutiny of values that is his own preoccupation. One may on occasion wish he would be more self-effacing, but given that modern men are as often intellectuals as they are gamekeepers or bullfighters, Mann's preoccupation is, after all, hardly very esoteric.

When Mann's *Buddenbrooks: Verfall einer Famile* (*Buddenbrooks*, 1901) appeared, he was twenty-six years old; not even the blandest of weekly reviewers could have called the two-volume work merely "a first novel of promise," for the simple reason that here all, or almost all, is achievement. (Forty-three years later, after emigrating to California, Mann was moved to hear his friend Franz Werfel describe the work as "an immortal masterpiece." "I wonder," Mann then wrote, "whether it is not this book which, among all my works, is destined to last.") Its subtitle is "The Decline of a Family"; its setting, not named, is the patrician world of the free city of Lübeck, into which Mann himself was born and in which he grew up. Like several other stories, the novel reflects Mann's own mixed parentage (his father, a senator, came from Hanseatic stock, while his mother was born in Brazil of a part German, part Creole family); and the family whose life he describes over three-and-a-half generations closely resembles his own. This unsparing or embarrassing (it depends on one's point of view) use of autobiographical elements is characteristic of much of his fiction, and so is his use of historical and scientific data and philosophical theories; to the traditional realism of social circumstance he adds the realism of knowledge.

The Buddenbrooks begin as rich shippers and corn brokers. The story opens in 1835, takes us through the abortive Revolution of 1848, and ends some thirty years later. In the course of it the fortunes of "the Firm" rise to their highest peak of prosperity and then catastrophically decline. Several disastrous marriages, a physical exhaustion in the family strain, one or two imprudent business transactions—these are the "effective causes" of the decline, causes such as we know them from the tradition of the realistic *romanciers.* And the exquisite, leisurely details in which Mann describes them—a piece of precise physical characterization here, an affectionately and ironically evoked episode there, an occasional scene of ribald humor aimed at a piece of ineptitude, or again the melancholy resignation of disappointed hopes, set out against a background of fine old silver and china and sumptuous dinner parties—all this makes the "effective causes" of that decline into a rich and varied spectacle of life, so much so that instead of asking *why,* we delight in the contemplation *that* it should be so. The young novelist's achievement is all the more remarkable if we bear in mind that Mann had little by way of an indigenous tradition to draw on; except from the Berlin novelist Theodor Fontane (to whom in the early 1920's Mann paid generous tribute), German literature has nothing to compare with the social realism of the English, French, or Russian novelists of the nineteenth century. What it does have is *Heimatdichtung,* the literature of local color, and it is part of Mann's sure touch as a European realistic novelist that he can draw on this homely tradition without succumbing to the provincialism and sentimentality that are apt to limit its interest outside its own time and country.

We proceed through the novel in an orderly way: from Johann Buddenbrook the elder, the shrewd businessman and driver of hard bargains, to Jean, the first consul; to Thomas, the novel's central character, so much less firm in his decisions and his health than his predecessors, frequently in need of comfort from heavy Russian cigarettes and of revivification from eau de cologne, with his beautiful but distant wife, Gerda, and his disarmingly silly sister Toni; and finally to Thomas' son Hanno, who, after a muddled life of unending infections, awful school reports, questionable friendships, and ecstatic improvisations on the senatorial grand piano, dies in a typhoid epidemic at the age of fifteen. But as we proceed along this plane of action we become aware that not everything we witness belongs to the theme of decline. We notice, for instance, that there is in Jean a feeling of compassion and disinterested sympathy, which is stronger in him than it was in Johann. We notice that in Thomas (Jean's son) compassion is joined by a strange and eventually unnerving capacity to think and feel himself into the minds of people, contact with whom is apt to impair his business sense. And we come to understand why Thomas is able to assert the old virtues of prudence, self-control, and hard work only vis-à-vis his brother Christian, a melancholy hypochondriac obsessed by an incontinent "artistic" passion for miming slightly off-color stories—a passion that Thomas understands only too well and that the older Buddenbrooks would have found most peculiar and objectionable. By now we are hardly surprised when Thomas happens upon a book of pessimistic philosophy (it is Arthur Schopenhauer's) that speaks enticingly of death and of the anonymous, timeless future waiting for "us" beyond the prison of individuation, on the other shore; and we find it no less convincing that in a moment of feverish insight, on the very margins of his ordinary existence, Thomas should fall under the spell of this philosophy and on the morrow, the spell having done its work, forget it all again. We notice that to his wife, Gerda, Hanno Buddenbrook's beautiful mother, neither "the Firm" nor even the family means very much; the only thing that makes life tolerable for her is the violin. Here, then, there is something like a second theme, which stands in ironical (that is, hidden) contrast to the theme of decline and finds its completion in Hanno's musical precocity, in his sad little life that is draining away to the sound of erotically charged ingenious arpeggios and cleverly contrived modulations into minor keys. (No reader unacquainted with the novel's genealogy could guess that its composition began at the end, with the idea of a novella written around the figure of Hanno.)

The "effective causes" of the decline, we can now see, are not its "sufficient causes." The theme of decline is counterpointed by the growth of a strange, problematic spirituality. Some characters are shown to acquire an understanding and an empathy that eventually exceed their vital resources; others possess artistic talents or aspirations that turn out to exceed their experience of life. Is it, then, this defective spirituality, this *Geist* (spirit) unsustained by the will to life, that we are to take as the sufficient cause of the decline of family and firm? Mann doesn't say so. The realistic novelist leaves his reader to draw his own conclusion—which is, that the full final cause is neither one (the commercial, social, and biological decline) nor the other (the growth of intellectuality and art in excess of a family's vital resources), but this very particular and living combination and conflict of both. And the abundant presentation of forces that in their isolation are hostile to each other makes for the novel's criticism of life and of the civilization that came to an end in August 1914, which is no less profound for being transmuted into pure story. (Fontane, had he lived, would have been its best reader.) The mercantile ethos (lacking in compassion, self-knowledge, and a sense of values beyond its vital and business interests) pitted against spirituality and aestheticism (lacking in and ultimately contemptuous of life itself)—these are the story's protagonists. Were they also among the major causes of the European decline? Perhaps. What is certain is that a whole class of articulate intellectuals and their public believed that they were.

Mann's métier appears to absorb his every interest. Even his private letters slip easily into the tone of public utterances, and these in turn are couched in his semi-private tone of irony. In an undramatic, conscientious, almost pedantic way his was a life wholly devoted to art, while his art was at all times deeply involved in the life of his native country. Thus it was the art itself rather than any political ambition that drew him into the vortex of public events and ideological battles. When World War I broke out he was living in Munich, the artistic center of Germany since the 1850's. He was happily married to the daughter of a well-known German-Jewish family of financiers (in one generation) and scientists and intellectuals (in the next), with a growing family of highly gifted children. He was the renowned author of two novels, several exquisite novellas, among the finest examples of the genre in any language, a number of critical essays, and a melodramatic and overcharged play about Fra Girolamo Savonarola.

The war years put a temporary halt to Mann's fictional work. Like other German and Austrian writers, he allowed himself to be absorbed by the national emergency; he too was affected by the national hysteria that seized most of his fellow writers. The long essays written during the war, which include a remarkable study of Frederick the Great, were published in 1918 in a collection entitled *Betrachtungen eines Unpolitischen* (*Reflections of a Nonpolitical Man*). His partisanship—such as it was—of the German cause has often been severely criticized, though any condemnation of the book as war propaganda is as paradoxical as the book itself, if only because much of it was published after the cause he "served with his pen" was lost. The book is written in search of a definition of Germany. The quality that gives it such doubtful value as war propaganda—the scrupulousness and unnerving truthfulness of the search—also gives it its lasting, indeed its literary, interest. We know that many of its views were already out of date by the time they were put down: the book speaks for a whole generation of German artists and intellectuals who, in asserting a self-consciously "nonpolitical" attitude, tried to salvage and validate the politics and ideology of the kaiser's *Reich* in terms of an unworldly and spiritual conservatism. But then, the imagination of most novelists is "out of date" in the sense of being engrossed by a more or less distant past. The progressive, left-wing attitude of Mann's brother and fellow

writer Heinrich, the antagonist in the dialectical arguments of the *Reflections,* may well be a good deal more congenial to us, and Heinrich's opinions are certainly a good deal less ambiguous; yet in their commitment to, and advocacy of, a single, progressive point of view, his opinions are a good deal less searching and therefore, in some ways, less interesting.

Great writers (as the East Germans found while Bertolt Brecht lived in their midst) make uneasy political bedfellows. Certainly Mann understands this, and some of his argument is designed to secure for the "nonpolitical" writer the freedom from political commitment necessary for his work. Where Mann is less clear (and this unclarity he shares with many of Germany's greatest literary men) is in the recognition that this freedom, and indeed the "nonpolitical" attitude generally, is itself also a factor in a political situation. A valid criticism of *Reflections* is that in a sense the book does not take the analysis of the situation far enough, that its basic contradiction remains unresolved. It is concerned, in much of its argument, with the role of artists, writers, and intellectuals in German public life. Their views, and intellectual ideas generally, have been taken a good deal more seriously in German public life than comparable views have been taken elsewhere; it is notorious that German political parties have invariably felt the need to call upon the support of all kinds of "philosophers" and "theoreticians" (even the thugs who formed the early National Socialist Party had to have their ideologists and literary henchmen). Thus the situation in which Mann's essays were written and that they analyze was such that their eventual publication was bound to make a political impact—and the more telling the analysis, the more lasting this impact would be. Yet (and this is the other side of the contradiction), *Reflections* is anything but a political manifesto. It is the characteristic product of a writer who at all times (except in the period 1933–1945, the years of the Third Reich), refused to commit himself to a cut-and-dried political

THOMAS MANN

message. The book is concerned with questions of the German national ethos; with Germany's foreign policy; with its conduct of the war with Russia, France, and eventually Italy; with the problems of art and culture in the modern world; with the "German" alternative to the ideas of the French Revolution; with German literature and philosophy and the Lutheran religion; and, again and again, with German music and its function in the life of the nation. And on all these questions Mann brings to bear the same complex and truthfully inconclusive and ironical attitude that in *Buddenbrooks* yields such remarkable illuminations of both characters and history. Yet for all that, *Reflections* necessarily raised, and was made to fulfill, the expectation of a political message—after its complex and subtle antitheses had been blunted in the way that practical politics always blunts the subtle ideas of those who are more concerned with insight than with action.

This dilemma held an endless fascination for Mann. At the height of the Cold War (1955), introducing a collection of letters and last wills written by men and women condemned to death during World War II, he comments on the hopes for a new humanity expressed in these documents:

> Was it all in vain? Their dream and their death—all wasted? It cannot be so. No idea for which men of pure hearts have fought has ever perished from the face of the earth. Each one has attained reality—and, though in the process it takes on all the blemishes of reality, yet it gains life for itself.
>
> (*Politische Schriften und Reden*, 3.361)[1]

No author can help having his thoughts corrupted. The difficulty in *Reflections* is that Mann's insight stopped short of a clear recognition that the meditations of the nonpolitical

man, however ironical and ambivalent, were in themselves liable to become an unequivocal political factor. The conservatism that the book ironically advocates is a high-minded and spiritual thing; it aims at preserving the *bürgerlich* attitude of mind from which had arisen some of the finest products of German culture. But practical politics is the sphere of association in which the best are often placed under one common label with the worst. It is therefore not surprising that in spite of his many addresses in support of the new social-democratic regime Mann found himself quoted, well into the 1930's, as one of the advocates of the "conservative revolution" that aimed to destroy the Weimar Republic, hoped to avail itself of the fruits of Adolf Hitler's revolution of 1933, and finally sealed its own fate in the failure of the officers' plot of July 1944.

One way *and* the other, most of Mann's political utterances are unfortunate. To say this is not to discount the great, heartfelt effort he put into them, the "commitment" they express. But what is he committed to? A generation earlier, and in an altogether simpler situation, Fontane confessed to a friend that "my preoccupation with politics was, after all, only a literary affair." And this, when we have sifted the dialectics and heart-searchings of *Reflections*, is true of Mann also. In his responsibility to his art lies the glory of the artist and the travail of the man. The *Reflections*, as well as the many subsequent pronouncements on behalf of Weimar parliamentarian and social democracy, are, "after all, only" a trial ground for the arguments that inform Mann's works of fiction, most obviously and immediately *Der Zauberberg* (*The Magic Mountain*, 1924). With that in mind we may understand why his political arguments are often so very personal in tone and why the substance of his novels is so often couched in public, historical terms.

One other aspect of *Reflections of a Nonpolitical Man* needs emphasizing. It is the first but by no means the last of Mann's books in which he claims to be representative of the

[1] All translations, with the exception of this one, made directly from the German text, are based upon H. T. Lowe-Porter's English translations of Mann's works. Page citations are omitted from extracts, because of the many different editions of Lowe-Porter translations published. See the bibliography.

culture and of the intellectual development of his country. All forms of representativeness involve a fictional element, and fiction is, after all, more properly the mode of the novel than of politics; the nonpolitical man's position is perhaps best expressed in an equation: "politics + fiction = 'engagement' − responsibility." This position is made evident in Mann's insistence on the special value and significance that are to be ascribed to his role as narrator and commentator. Again and again in *Reflections* he takes pride in comparing the effort their composition cost him with the effort of his countrymen at war; again and again the strenuousness of both undertakings is commended as the supremely "German" virtue. Given that the author sets up his literary emporium at a safe distance from the battle—a *vivandière's* enterprise seems more honorable—his effort can hardly be regarded as a heroic value. In any event, this elevation of the difficulties of composition to existential heights is part of a value scheme that hasn't worn very well. There was too much strenuousness, most of it "beyond good and evil," in the decades that followed for us to believe in it as uncritically as Mann does.

The Magic Mountain, like *Buddenbrooks,* depicts the immediate past, yet by projecting that past and its dominant ideas into the present it gives an impression of contemporaneity. The novel spans seven years in the life of Hans Castorp, a "very ordinary young man" from the North German plain, and it ends in 1914, when its hero disappears into the muddy inferno of a battlefield in Flanders. The seven years, described with many ingenious variations of tempi, are Hans's years in a tuberculosis sanatorium above Davos, where he arrives, "just for a short visit," to stay with his cousin, Lieutenant Joachim Ziemssen, who is one of the patients there.

The location is characteristic, and so are the experiences recounted; the story is placed, all of it and quite explicitly, on the margins of ordinary human life, in a "hermetic" situation:

the host who presides over this prolonged house party is death itself. Since his arrival Hans Castorp has been in a febrile state, perhaps of mind and certainly of body. After a few days' stay he has a thorough check-up and is found to be suffering from a slight tubercular lesion. What could be more natural than that, having assured himself that his financial affairs in the "flatlands" will easily bear the strain, he should decide to stay on for the cure? But we are compelled to ask: is that the real reason why he stays? Hans, with his mixture of inertia and far from aimless curiosity, stays on even after it has become doubtful whether he is really ill—but then, even when "the little moist spot" on his lungs was first discovered, he was told that most young men are at one time or another liable to the disease, at least in its latent form; and more doubt-provoking still, after a short time on the Magic Mountain Hans has read enough medical information to know that high-altitude conditions are likely anyway to bring the latent disease to a head.

And this is what the Berghof sanatorium does: it brings that disease and many others to a crisis; it shows a whole range of emotions, mental attitudes, and ideological conflicts in their most acute, most "critical" form.

Of Hans Castorp's past in the "flatlands" we know two things: that he was a bright young naval engineer of good family, about to begin his professional career, and that several bereavements in his immediate family have left him with a more than "normal" awareness of the shadow that lies on all life. He is neither a bouncy extrovert nor a morbid melancholic. He is an attractive young man with an abundant but ultimately not undiscriminating appetite—an appetite not for action but for knowledge-and-experience. He is intelligent but far from intellectual—indeed, one of the lessons he learns on the Magic Mountain is that intellectualism is as defective a way of life as mindless, irrational emotionalism. He *learns:* for his is a story of initiation, somewhat in the hallowed manner of the bildungsroman. But with such moribund company and

THOMAS MANN

in such a febrile, overcharged atmosphere, is it not more likely to be a parody of those leisurely and circumspect tales of initiation in which nineteenth-century German novelists had described their heroes' journey into the good life? Here again Mann recasts the boundary line of genres: creation and critical act merge, for parody is to him not so much a humorous inversion of the original as a critique of it. Take this fragment from a conversation between Hans and Clavdia Chauchat, the Russian femme fatale with Kirghiz eyes to whom Hans is bound by a sympathy stronger than the tie of a single night of love; it begins with a request for a cigarette:

> She stretched out her hand. "With those, at least, you are provided." She took a cigarette, negligently, without thanks, from the silver case he held out to her. . . . Then he said: "Yes, I always have some. I am always provided, one must be. How should one get on without them? It's what is known as a passion, isn't it, when one is reduced to that. To tell the truth I am not at all a passionate person. But I have my passions, phlegmatic ones." "I am extraordinarily relieved," she said, breathing out as she spoke the smoke she had inhaled, "to hear that you are not a passionate person. But how should you be? You would have to be different from the rest. Passionate—that means to live for the sake of living. But one knows that you all live for the sake of experience. Passion, that is self-forgetfulness. But what you all want is self-enrichment. *C'est ça.* You don't realize what revolting egoism it is, and that one day it will make you the enemies of the human race."

As the passage shifts from the personal and particular to the historical and general (from the formal *Sie* for "you" to the plural familiar *Ihr* and *Euch*), a good deal more than a critique of the bildungsroman and its solipsistic preoccupation with *Erlebnis* is accomplished. (Whether or not Mann was aware of it, *Erlebnis*, denoting a vivid, lived experience, is a latecomer in the abundant German vocabulary of psychic events. It is much more dramatic than *Erfahrung*, implying experience with some claim to objective validity; the term became one of the hallmarks of the cult of authenticity in the transition from the disturbed 1920's to the violent 1930's.) The shifts into the critique of history are subtle: the concrete narration is not disrupted. These people may not be "us," but they are of our flesh and blood. Only occasionally, when looking up from the book, are we apt to wonder (as after a prolonged reading of Sigmund Freud) whether anything will ever again be just its innocent self—can a mere cigarette or a mere pencil ever again be simply a smoke or a writing utensil, mercifully free of symbolic meanings?

The Magic Mountain is a story of initiation, but into what? Into life? But we are always *in* life, and so is Hans Castorp, so how can he expect to be initiated into it? Here again the location—Hans's experiences on the margins of life—is splendidly vindicated by the peculiarly experimental character of his seven years, which in turn is contrasted with a sense of the absolute passing of time, irretrievable and anything but experimental.

What exactly does Hans do in those seven long-and-short years? He makes a number of friends, he enters into a great many disputes, and, when he has had enough of them, he withdraws; he becomes the cause of a duel; he falls in love with Clavdia Chauchat, sees her leave, and somewhat fitfully awaits her return; he reads a good many medical books and dabbles in Freudian psychology and in various natural and occult sciences; he learns to ski and almost freezes to death in a snowstorm; he discovers in himself a love of music; he accompanies his cousin Lieutenant Joachim Ziemssen and a good many other people, not all of them very dignified, to death's door and sees them off. *The Magic Mountain* is, above all, a conversational novel, a work in which action is mostly replaced by talk about action; since most of the inhabitants of the Berghof are about to die, it is hard to see how things could be otherwise. Worse than that, the time that is not devoted to talk is taken up by vast meals, macabre promiscuity, a tragicomic duel and two suicides (as if the "normal" rate of demise weren't high enough), and by the kind of entertainments that sick people devise for themselves with the help of those who make a living from their sickness—a sickness unto death for most, and salvation there is none. For, worst of all, the question of what the lesson of all those years is meant to yield is answered as ambiguously as is the question of exactly why Hans remains in this hothouse amidst the snowy peaks in the first place. Of course, the long conversations and the "morbid" action are all part of the marginal situation in which the novel is placed and that it is designed to illuminate, but why place it in that situation? What is the author's end that he should make it so difficult to attain?

As a matter of fact, the impression the novel leaves us with is the opposite of morbidity and boredom. The sense of irony and humor that enlivens the story almost everywhere (it does have its sluggish parts, too) isn't exactly of the homely kind, and some of it is pretty black. Yet it is not a sick humor but rather humor about sickness, and thus a liberation; about chaos and decay, and thus a harbinger of order and life; about the indignities of death, and thus a brave rebuttal of all the existential blather about death's majesty. The style of the novel, elaborate and finicky and curiously pedantic even while it describes physical decay and the corruption of souls, is in firm and deliberate contrast with its subject matter. And the humor arises where style and one's expectations about the subject matter clash. Thus men and women who are mortally ill claim to have more wisdom than "the stupid, healthy people down below," yet are made silly by accidie and the terror of death; a mixture of spirituality and national Bolshevism is preached by an inquisitorial maniac (many of whose views were Mann's own in the *Reflections*); accurate insights into human motives are vouchsafed to people who haven't enough life left to act on them yet claim a special nobility for their disability; and love itself, the most life-giving of the passions, is now heightened, now dispossessed, by the proximity of death.

Whatever Hans Castorp is meant to learn from his protracted sojourn, it is unlikely to be a maxim. The initiation into life is itself a piece of life; it will not yield an unambiguous precept: do this—avoid that. And the lesson that death, Hans's grim host, teaches him? What Hans learns in a dream during a snowstorm on that skiing expedition from which he almost doesn't return is that the untrammeled dominion of death over men is as corrupting to their minds and hearts as is the frivolous avoidance of all thought of death. To allow life to be informed but not paralyzed by the apprehension of disease and the expectation of death—to strive for a refinement of life through an intelligent knowledge-and-experience of life's enemies: that is the vision that (again, only briefly and unsteadily and on the margins of life) opens up before Hans. Whether he can live up to it is another story.

The Marxist critic György Lukács (who himself makes a far from flattering fictional appearance in the novel as an inquisitorial "Jewish Jesuit," accurately anticipating the subsequent terroristic theories of Herbert Marcuse, whom Mann was to encounter in California) has pointed to the historical symbolism that lurks behind many figures and arguments in the novel. In a lecture at Princeton in May 1939 Mann himself underlined its critical and European dimension, pointing out (surely an act of supererogation) that its characters embody a great many of the political, social, and philosophical ideas that came to a head in the fateful summer of 1914. Moreover, the intellectual plot of the novel is full of deliberate anachronisms; the most interesting of these is the intricate treatment of various kinds of time, which corresponds closely to the concept of relative time as presented in Albert Einstein's "special theory of relativity," first advanced in 1905 but available to a nonspecialist public only in Einstein's own popularization of it in 1916.

THOMAS MANN

When Mann began writing *The Magic Mountain* in 1912 it was to be a short novella, built around the visit of an impressionable young man to a sanatorium. When he finished it twelve years later, it had grown into a panorama of modern Europe. And it speaks for his art even if it does not speak for human nature that no opinion expressed in the novel is so absurd that it was not in fact seriously defended in the Europe of that age by some intellectual aesthete or caveman. Yet the young hero is never lost sight of. It is as much for his sake as for the sake of the critique that "the ideological fighting-cocks and pedagogic prattlers" around him (shades of Lukács/ Marcuse but also of Mann and his brother Heinrich) conduct their disputations; for, as Hans says in his dream, "Man is master over the opposites" of life and death, and not only over these. And here lies one of the meanings of the novel's "message," in the recognition that ideology and isms and dialectics are not enough, that the *Gegensätze* (contradictions) on which European intellectuals and politicians and humbler people, too, had been reared and for the sake of which they had gone to war were a lethal chimera. A maxim after all? To those who have never experienced or even contemplated the spell of ideological commitment, it may look as though the Magic Mountain has given birth to nothing more than a commonplace mouse. "The subject is exhausted not in its conclusion but in the working out of it; nor is the result attained the real whole, but it and the process of arriving at it," says the gnomic G. W. F. Hegel. Mann's characteristic truthfulness, as well as the real value of his insight, lies not in a detachable message but in the weight of the odds against which the insight is achieved, in the imaged and full presentation of the case for the other side. And here, too, in the worded resistance of the represented world to the impact of ideas and ideals, lies the novel's realistic vein; to the variety of existing fictional modes it adds the realism of knowledge.

Hans Castorp, with all his engaging modesty, occasional exasperation, and consistent good humor, is an enormously important person. He is the heir apparent of the European cock-pit; it is he who will have to live in it. Or will he? At the end of the novel the two planes, the personal and the historical, intersect. The penultimate chapter, in which the national and ideological antagonisms among the inmates gather momentum, is called "The Great Irritation." Then follows "The Roll of Thunder." General mobilization is declared in Germany, Hans abruptly leaves, and the last glimpse we have of him is through a barrage of shells and heavy machine-gun fire, ducking in the mud and, Franz Schubert's "Der Lindenbaum" (The Linden Tree) on his lips, advancing on the enemy.

Is that the lesson he has learned—the end to which he undertook that strenuous journey of initiation? It is. Certainly Hans's was a special case, special in Aristotle's sense of "eminently good of its kind," and therefore representative, which is why his story was eminently worth telling. But he was not so special that he should be exempt from the logic of events—events, too, let loose by some of the ideas he had contemplated on the Magic Mountain. We might well prefer him to conclude his "initiation" and "cure" of his own free will rather than by following the trumpet call of the Fatherland, but realism triumphs. The call was sounded, and it ill behooves us, by confusing 1914 with 1939, to doubt that Hans could obey it with a good conscience and a noble hope in his heart. It is possible though not very likely, the author tells us as he bids us farewell, that Hans may survive the slaughter and then put into practice that knowledge-and-experience, that critical and intelligent love of life, he acquired in his seven years on the mountain. But come what may, it is his story, an experiment yet a thing irretrievable, an initiation and a life. The rest is in the lap of the gods.

"The artist and society"—one scans the phrase with a sinking feeling: it has suffered such overexposure by the critics. Long before

Buddenbrooks, Mann's literary work began, in the 1890's, with short stories that center on the relationship between the sensitive or artistic man and "the world" around him that shows no understanding of his gifts and very little sympathy for the deprivations that go with those gifts. Many of Mann's greatest novellas refer quite explicitly to this theme: *Tristan* (1903), from which grew *The Magic Mountain;* and *Tonio Kröger* (1903) and *Der Tod in Venedig* (*Death in Venice,* 1912), his two most famous stories. Indeed, there is no major work, hardly an essay or sketch, hardly even a letter, in which the topic does not receive his ever-renewed attention. Many a reader has been put off by what he or she has felt to be a self-conscious and esoteric preoccupation, and some critics have not made things easier by insisting that Mann should be seen above all as "an artist's artist," that "the mediation of art" is his paramount concern. It may well be true (a discouraged reader will argue) that the claims of art are at odds with the claims of ordinary morality; that (as Friedrich Nietzsche was not the first to remark) poets are liars; that the "putting on ice" of personal feelings is, as Tonio Kröger says, the precondition of artistic success; that some of the greatest achievements of modern art are the offspring of decadence; that the discipline that informs an artist's style is more properly the place to seek for an intimation of his or her moral worth than are the opinions expressed in the work; and that the intricacies, even the most technical, of the craft of letters are of consuming interest. But are these matters that ought to go into a fictional story? What authentic concern are they to those of us who are not artists? Is not this indulgence in "artistic" themes, this aesthetic circle, itself a sign of a regressive, self-regarding imagination?

There is little doubt that these artist stories owe their great success and fame in the first instance to a public that felt flattered at being in the know, at being taken (sometimes quite literally) behind the scenes. But their more permanent value emerges wherever the aesthetic circle is breached, wherever "art" or "literature"

is used also as a symbol for the creative activity of the human spirit in its more varied aspects. Art, then, is seen as a mission and a fate. It is achieved at the cost of a personal or emotional sacrifice. Its ends are illumination and delight, but it is a profoundly uneconomical activity—the means are apt to seem vastly in excess of the ends. Often, when exploring this theme, Mann tends to stress the gulf between means and ends, art and life, thus making it difficult for art to function as a symbol. But in doing so he is not acquiescing in the separation of life from the things of the spirit, but criticizing that separation and pointing to the impoverishment it entails. In *Tonio Kröger* those who have no inkling of art are idealized as blue-eyed, fair-haired, enviable innocents, and the gulf between them and the knowing artist is not really bridged. (Curiously enough, the earlier *Buddenbrooks* is wholly free from this sort of sentimentality.) In *Tristan* the hypersensitive hero, author of a few arty sketches, is reduced to a sterility only a little less ridiculous (because more vulnerable) than the brutish cheerfulness and bewildered jealousy of his antagonist, the owner (alas) of a sausage factory. In *Death in Venice,* on the other hand, the theme of the separation and ensuing decadence is taken so far and treated so singlemindedly that the living story it yields carries us beyond the esoteric restriction.

In the context of these artist stories Mann's passion for leitmotifs and symbolical correspondences enables him to breach the aesthetic circle; happily it works in the direction not of literariness but life. Where "A pencil is never just a pencil" on occasion results in a narrowingly literary effect, "Art is more than just art" results in a liberation. *Death in Venice* is the story of an aging literary master who has spent a lifetime in the increasingly exacting service of his craft. When the story opens, Gustav von Aschenbach is at the height of his fame. In a moment of spiritual and physical exhaustion he is exposed to the seductions of Eros and the blandishments of death. It seems poetically right that his agony should be consummated in Venice, that city of supreme artistry and artifice where Richard Wagner too had died, at the height of his fame and in surprising solitude. For just as Venice, so very obviously, "stands for" art, it is also a rich and ornate piece of life. Again Mann chooses a marginal situation—the passion of the erstwhile moralist for a beautiful boy—and uses this "scandalous" though unrequited relationship to clinch the corruption of the entire being of a man whose achievements, literary and existential, have risen from the ashes of self-denial. Aschenbach succumbs because, in a lifetime of "service to the spirit," he stifled within himself those "early precious tribulations of the heart" which are at war with morality and order. His knowledge of man (of himself) and hence his literary achievement have been bought at less than the highest price. Now come corruption and collapse—but they are indistinguishable from the moment of delight and the last tremors of creativity. And beyond all this, enveloping almost the whole story, is Mann's ironical, elaborately circumstantial, yet enigmatic style, embodying the story's highly organized structure with its suggestive episodes, contrasting moods, and telling (occasionally too telling) images. Once again the material, intimating chaos, is conquered by the creative mind, and an ambiguous victory results.

This victory too is a part of the story: "The magisterial pose of our style is lies and foolishness, our fame and high repute a farce"—so Aschenbach in his mind addresses the boy Tadzio, to whom he has never actually spoken. But his story gives the lie to the lie. As the poet's psyche capitulates before Eros and Thanatos (the forces he had denied), the veil of irony drops and the full price of knowledge-and-experience is exacted: the climax of the story illuminates no longer merely "an aesthetic problem" but the human condition. The reader is left not merely with the picture of an aging potential homoerotic killed by a stroke on the Lido of a plague-ridden Venice but with a parable on the text "Man cannot live by his will alone."

In all these prewar stories, then, the negative, disabling aspect of the artistic activity predominates. *Death in Venice* contains the fullest statement of the predicament. Form, the hallmark of the artist's achievement (we read there), is Janus-faced, "moral and immoral at the same time: moral, insofar as it is the result and expression of rigorous discipline, immoral—yes, even hostile to morality—in that its very nature is indifferent to good and evil." But is even that true? Is "the result and expression of rigorous discipline" in and of itself moral? Is passionate intensity enough, regardless of its object?

Mario und der Zauberer (*Mario and the Magician*, 1930) is among the finest novellas Thomas Mann ever wrote. It obeys the rules of the genre by being centered around "a single extraordinary event" (as Johann Wolfgang von Goethe observed about the form) and by exploring to the full the circumstances of that event. The story is set in a fashionable Italian seaside resort in the era of Benito Mussolini. It is told in the first person by a cultured, sophisticated German intellectual who continues his holiday with his wife and family at Torre di Venere after the foreign visitors' season is over. It all begins with the weather:

> The heat was excessive . . . It was African: the power of the sun that shone down on us was frightful, relentless. . . . Do you like that sort of thing? For weeks on end? Of course, it is the South, it is classical weather, the climate wherein the culture of mankind first came to flower, the sun of Homer, and all that. But after a while, you know, one can't help feeling a sort of leaden inertia come over one.

This torpid atmosphere is made more uncomfortable still by spiky hints and occasional rudeness from a few chauvinistic Italians. Clearly, the thing to do is to pack one's bags and go home.

Into this mood comes Cavaliere Cipolla, a traveling magician and hypnotist whose gala performance is attended by all Torre, including visitors and the native population. The narrator takes his family to the show for the same reasons, or lack of reasons, that made him stay on: listlessness, a curious fascination, an aimless, detached desire to see what will come next. The whole thing turns out to be something of a scandal. In a very few minutes it becomes clear that the show is a piece of cheap sensationalism, quite unsuitable for the children. But first, here is Cipolla himself:

> He came on to the stage with a rapid step that expressed his eagerness to serve his audience and gave rise to the illusion that he had come a long way at the same pace to appear before them, whereas of course he had only been standing in the wings. His apparel supported this fiction of a sudden arrival. A man whose age it was hard to determine but by no means young, with a sharp, ravaged face, piercing eyes and a compressed mouth, a small black waxed mustache and a so-called imperial in the hollow between lip and chin, he was dressed in street clothes of a sort of complicated evening elegance. He wore a wide black sleeveless cloak with a velvet collar and a satin-lined shoulder cape which, since his arms were hampered [by a riding whip hidden under the cloak], he held together in front with his white-gloved hands. He had a white scarf around his neck, and a top hat with a curved brim sat at a rakish angle well down on his forehead. . . . Cipolla had in his whole appearance much of the historic type of mountebank and charlatan; his very clothes emphasized it, pretentious as they were, for in places they were pulled tight and in others fell in absurdly loose folds. Something was wrong with his figure, both fore and aft, which was to become plain later on. But I must emphasize that there was not a trace of personal jocularity, let alone clownishness, in his pose, his expression, or his behavior.

The evening begins with a few card tricks, feats of arithmetical memory, and thought reading. Gradually the Italian public is drawn into the performance—first the simple fishermen of the place, a waiter or two, then some visitors, and a solemn young gentleman from Rome. From thought reading Cipolla moves on to hypnotism, his real art, and now the macabre fun begins in earnest. The audience is only too ready to provide volunteers, people egg each other on to join the battle of wills, and Cipolla triumphs over them all. One is made to dance, another to perform complicated calculations on the blackboard, a third to tell his most private thoughts, a fourth to impersonate his girlfriend and implant a kiss on Cipolla's sweaty gray cheek. The pandemonium reaches its climax when the entire stage is filled with will-less performing marionettes, dancing, contorted, stuttering, all firmly held on the magician's leading strings. An endless barrage of comments and explanations ("Parla benissimo," say the Italians admiringly), cracks of the whip, dirty, gray torrents of smoke issuing from behind defective teeth, frequent recourse to a bottle on the table behind him—the artiste Cipolla is giving his all. And as the hold of his will on victims and audience increases (they are all under his spell now, including our skeptical, bemused narrator), so the tone of Cipolla's comments gradually changes from flattery and mockery and cajoling to veiled insults, ridicule, contempt, searing hostility, all the way to open derision and malevolent triumph. The triumph of the ugly, misshapen, and sinister charlatan is a triumph of the ravaging will over an audience composed of "normal," trusting, nonwilling people. For this is what their ravished wills are reduced to: all they can do is to will *not* to do what Cipolla wills them to do, and from "willing not to" (the narrator claims) it is but a short step to not willing at all.

There is perhaps no single work in which the predicament of the European liberal mind in the grip of the demagogue's will is so dramatically and effectively portrayed as in this novella. The whole complex relationship between the demagogue and the masses is here. They are linked in a strange nexus of mutual fear and mutual need, for not only are the masses presented as the mindless, will-less victims of the magician's will, but his defective being is also in bondage to their subjection and obedience; the moment his will gives out, they will destroy him. And the relationship that is here depicted embraces also the intellectuals and aesthetes, who (to begin with, at any rate) are too bemused, too fascinated, by the lurid spectacle to protest against it.

Comparisons with the fascist situation and with the Germany of Hitler's mass meetings of the 1920's are left implied; the macabre cabaret is left to tell its own story, which is completed by an ending almost as convincing as it is horrifying. Yet the political parallel is defective; there is something wrong with the motivation. An actual hypnosis cannot lead to heterogeneous action; the Schopenhauerian sophism doesn't really work, for sane people cannot even under hypnosis be made to perform actions that are wholly at odds with their ordinary morality. In the actual political event it was neither the Duce's nor the Führer's hypnotic (or demonic or whatever) personality that made the people into willing followers, but rather the knuckle-dusters and lead-filled truncheons of the faithful along with a whole range of perfectly rational though partly evil promises. What in fictional terms is a dramatically satisfying motivation is, in political terms, mystification, which is more or less the opposite of Mann's conscious political intention.

Mann is not that languid narrator, that tacitly approving intellectual. Far from it. In many articles and open letters written before 1933 and after, he urged on his countrymen and the world at large a firm stand against the dictators, at least those of the right. But his literary achievement—the delight and illumination he was able to create by exploring one of the most characteristic situations of our age—has less to do with political partisanship than with imaginative insight. The problem of the artist—Mann's favorite theme—is again addressed here, but what it expresses is no longer a private, aesthetic concern. While describing a personal fate, the story extends into a political meaning. Where Gustav von Aschenbach's "rigorous discipline" of the will is

presented as a positive value, Cipolla's no less intense devotion to his métier is shown to be a source of evil. Yet there is no facile condemnation. As in all great literature, the full meaning of the implied moral judgment is inseparable from an intimate understanding of, and sympathy with, the thing condemned. It is a fellow feeling that enables Mann the artist to enter into that figure of deprivation eked out by the "creative" will, the figure of the artiste Cavaliere Cipolla.

On 30 January 1933 Hitler accepted President Paul von Hindenburg's offer of the chancellorship. Ten days later Mann left for Holland on a lecture tour; he did not set foot on his native soil again until July 1949. (His diaries show how long it took him, and how reluctant he was, to make an open and public break with Hitler's regime.) Throughout the twelve years of the Third Reich, which Mann spent in Switzerland, southern France, and the United States, he was tireless in his condemnation of national socialism and in his propaganda on behalf of "democracy of both kinds," Western and Eastern. Deprived of his German nationality, he became for a short time a Czechoslovak citizen, then American, and finally Swiss. During his American sojourn he found himself the unofficial spokesman of the German emigrants in the West, a benevolent father figure to many less successful writers and intellectuals, and a representative of what was called "the other Germany" during World War II; yet he was realistic enough to discourage any attempt to form a government-in-exile, recognizing that any future settlement would have to be based upon the unconditional defeat of Germany.

He did not live "the dark night of exile" (the phrase is Karl Marx's)—certainly not in the sense of material hardship. He traveled widely and found himself the recipient of many honors (he was awarded the Nobel Prize in 1929); he held a teaching post at Princeton; and in the house he built near Los Angeles he assembled around him his large family and circle of friends. (Among those who didn't belong to this circle—now amusingly dramatized in Christopher Hampton's *Tales from Hollywood* [1983]—was Brecht, whose dislike of Mann's person and politics went hand in hand with his distaste for Mann's style.) Yet an anxious concern for the state of Germany and Europe never left him. It is voiced in his letters, diaries, and public lectures (the violent denunciations contained in his wartime BBC broadcasts were—and still are—resented in Germany), it delayed the completion of the *Joseph* tetralogy, and it is imprinted on *Doktor Faustus* (*Doctor Faustus*, 1947), his last great work. Nor did the end of the war in 1945 bring release. In 1949 his oldest son, the writer Klaus Mann, committed suicide. When in June 1952 Mann left America for good, the country was in the throes of the McCarthy era, and he felt as though he were reliving the situation of Germany in 1933. His sympathetic references to the East German regime were met by some Western critics with bitter hostility and personal invective. There is a sense in which his active political stand after 1933 may be seen as the paying of an old debt—the debt of the erstwhile "nonpolitical man"; and he paid dearly indeed. He died in Zurich on 12 August 1955, at the height of his fame, the last survivor of a generation of writers who, rooted in the Germany of the nineteenth century, belong to the Europe of our own, less securely accommodated age.

Joseph und seine Brüder (*Joseph and His Brothers*), begun in 1926 and completed in 1943, is implicitly related to the exigencies of that period in being Mann's tribute to the national life and religious spirit of the Jews in their darkest hour. The massive four-volume work is encompassed by the Old Testament's most laconic and most attractive story—the story of Jacob, his brother Esau, and his wives Leah and Rachel in volume 1; of Joseph and his brethren in volume 2; of Joseph's life in Egypt in volume 3; and of their great family reunion in volume 4—"I am Joseph; doth my father yet live?" (Genesis 45:3). Not the least but the greatest tribute one can pay the work is to say that it exquisitely and movingly fills in the interstices of the biblical story—that no reader of the novel can ever return to Genesis, indeed to the Old Testament, without feeling how enriched the human substance of it has become. Of the immense and painstaking labor of reconstruction, buttressed by extensive study of biblical and archaeological scholarship, no pertinent judgment can here be given beyond saying that its diverse learned sources are wholly integrated in the work; the story itself, at all events, is told with a narrative ease that forms the volumes into a seamless garment. The elaborate theological, or rather cosmological, speculations, on the other hand, though necessary to the story, are more problematic.

Literary works based on historical facts or accepted myth invite—they certainly cannot avoid—comparison with the patterns from which they were taken. (Referring from the new version to the old is comparable with—in Mann's fictions it is indistinguishable from—the referentiality of realistic prose to the world.) Such a comparison raises an essential question: in this vast panoramic retelling of the fortunes of Jacob/Israel's family, what constitutes an enrichment of the familiar story? First, and most successfully, the traditional task of the storyteller is accomplished: Mann connects the discrete biblical episodes by motivating them in "human, all too human," terms. (In his correspondence with Károly Kerényi, he speaks of connecting ancient myth with modern psychology and religion with Freud.) Among the countless examples of such felicitous connections are, particularly, the affairs of Potiphar's sumptuous household, which include Joseph's quick rise to the position of highest trust, Potiphar's high intelligence, gentle wisdom, and impotence, his wife's passionate infatuation with the young and handsome Hebrew servant and her hysterical denunciation of him—all culminating in the grand scene in the courtyard where, before the assembled household, Potiphar tries Joseph and, secretly aware of the falsehood of the accusation, with a show of great severity passes a most lenient sentence. But then, almost any of the human relationships so affectionately described could be used as examples: Jacob's relationship with the crafty and dour Laban; Reuben's with his brethren, after they have thrown Joseph into the well and Reuben has returned to find out whether their father's favorite is "quite dead"; or Joseph's with the young pharaoh, "the dreamer" Amenhotep IV, who is more interested in the problems of monotheism, on which his chancellor can converse with such perfection, than he is in the chancellor's equally accomplished knowledge of agriculture and economics. Any of the numerous relationships on which the Bible touches only briefly (and others that it doesn't mention) offer the delight of a humanly motivated and richly imaged narrative. And the early scenes—Jacob's first meeting with Rachel at the well, his love for his tender and brave young bride, and his sorrow when she dies in childbirth—these form perhaps the most moving parts of the whole story.

On this simple narrative plane the tetralogy has a richness of life and a Tolstoyan abundance of characters, episodes, and concrete circumstance that are unique in Mann's entire work. But beyond this, Mann is intent on informing the biblical story with a modern concern. A double theme holds this narrative profusion together, and with that double theme he returns to the preoccupation of a lifetime. He asks the age-old questions: What is it in the characters of the members of this family, in the lives of their forebears, that made them chosen by God? What is the sign of their election? Why did God speak to Jacob on that fateful night at Bethel? Why did he never speak to Esau or Laban? And to these questions, which the Bible also asks, Mann gives two closely connected answers, which arise from the biblical argument but lead into a sphere that is alien to its spirit.

The family sign of the election (so runs the first part of the answer) is a supreme quality of *Sorge* (care)—a deep, unsettling, unappeasable caring for spirituality and for a God; a worrying, "neurotic" concern for the right and godly way of life; a turning away from the enticements of the tangible world; and a contempt for those who put their trust in a settled existence and its monuments of stone, the pyramids. Abraham had received this spiritual sign when he pondered on his God—when he all but created that God in the image of his own caring—and Jacob, too, with his limp, had received this sign when, in spite of his great prosperity and "miraculous" success as a sheepherder, he packed up all his possessions and left Laban, his incensed father-in-law.

Nor is Mann's depiction of this existential care for God to be equated with ordinary morality. Take the scene in which young Jacob, having by a fraud extracted the blessing from Isaac, his gullible and half-knowing blind father, runs away from home and on his inglorious flight is overtaken by his revengeful cousin, young Eliphas. What ensues is a scene of sheer humiliation. Jacob simply grovels before the handsome, strong boy. He talks and talks in order to placate him. He cringes in the desert dust, kissing Eliphas' feet, until Eliphas turns away in disgust from the undignified spectacle. Jacob will do anything—deny the fraud, put the blame on his mother, even belittle the significance of the blessing; he is prepared to part with every single one of his possessions (except, incidentally, a ring that he has carefully hidden in his belt). And he comes away from the encounter having lost all that men prize most dearly: his honor and good name, his courage and manliness, every shred of human dignity. Yet it is not just his bare life that he buys so dearly. For his is a special kind of life, which he knows to be worth more than all the decent sentiments and possessions that he cast down before the foolish warrior-boy: a life that he, Jacob, knows to be blessed, now and forever. He has stolen the blessing, but it is *his*. Hungry, weary, the tears of fear and shame hardly dry on his cheeks, he

THOMAS MANN

walks by the side of his lame camel through the desert. He is on the very margins of life; his sense of humiliation will not allow him to seek out the company of men. He finds a circle of boulders and there lies down to sleep. And what he dreams is the dream of his life, which he will never forget. The dream discloses to him, for a brief night only, the knowledge of his God, on whom he will meditate and whom he will serve in sorrow and care throughout his life, a knowledge of good and evil not as the world knows it.

Or take again the story of the brethren's ghastly slaughter of the circumcised Shechem and his Canaanites, their revenge for the defilement of Dinah, the daughter of Leah. These events are presented as part of an essentially spiritual concern to which the barbaric, "pagan" morality of the Canaanites or the Egyptians is irrelevant; the events are justified and become meaningful as part of God's design with his chosen people. And at the reconciliation and reunion of the family in Egypt, their new home, the election for grace once again falls not on him who rose to highest office and greatest glory among the foreigners but on him who was ever the most troubled by his sins of the flesh, on him who, among them all, most deeply cared: it is Judah and not Joseph who receives the dying Jacob's last and most solemn blessing. This is why Joseph, although he dominates all but the first part of the story, is by no means its sole hero. He is certainly the most attractive and charming hero Mann ever created. The lucky and adventurous course of his life shapes much of the novel; the narrator's richest imagination is lavished on his character, the places in which he dwells, and the countless men he so easily befriends. And it may be said that in presenting Joseph as an artist in the medium of life Mann sees in him the concrete fulfillment of those aspirations toward a unity of art or spirit and world that the heroes of his artist stories strive for in vain. But it is precisely because Joseph is so lucky and handsome and successful, because his concern with the religion of his father and forebears is informed by a worldly interest and not an anxious care—because, in brief, he is "the provider of bread"—that he is not the novel's hero in the fullest sense, that he is not chosen.

While this mode of election through care has its origin in the biblical story, the characters who display it have a family likeness with the earlier heroes of Mann's novels (as well as with his Doctor Faustus). Thomas Buddenbrook, Gustav von Aschenbach, and Hans Castorp are not the elect of the God of the Israelites, yet in their different circumstances and ways they too are searching for the most strenuous, the most exacting, deliverance. And the suggestion is present in those earlier works—as it is present here—that the strenuousness of the search itself is the only intimation we can have of its validity. This is why, in the *Joseph* novels, the question of the truth of faith is never directly raised: the strenuous commitment to the spiritual is meant to intimate a positive answer. But at this point, where the high existential price of belief is made to stand as proof of the validity of belief, where (in Rainer Maria Rilke's phrase) "the strenuous labor of the heart" is made to do service as an ontological proof, we leave biblical ground and enter on an existential preoccupation characteristic not only of Mann but also of German literature in the first half of the twentieth century.

In a work that ranges as freely and as playfully over eons of time as do these volumes, it would be absurd to complain of anachronism. Mann playfully invites the charge only to rebut it. In order to contain the episodic profusion, he constructs an ingenious scaffolding of symbolical cross-references, typological correspondences, and sea changes of time, to and fro across the books of the Old Testament and into the New. Biblical exegesis from medieval times onward has always insisted on the essential continuity of the Judaic and Christian traditions and has seen Christ and the Virgin Mary prefigured in certain characters of the Old Testament. So here

730

too the narrative mode of the novel appears to be anchored in traditional exegetic practice: taking its origin from the biblical text, the novel appears to be fulfilling its expectations. But now the second half of the answer to the novel's central question begins to emerge, taking us far away from the Bible and into a literary maze.

To the storyteller's traditional task of connecting and motivating his episodes Mann adds a further device: he allows his characters to share in his task. Jacob, Joseph, Judah, Potiphar, and the young pharaoh are all treated as historical personages who lived at a certain time, but there are also moments when their lives blend with those of their forefathers. (Eliezer, for instance, who is Jacob's oldest servant, talks to the young Joseph as though he had been Abraham's servant, too.) Moreover, they all experience moments of consciousness that allow them to see themselves, and occasionally one another, as parts of a cosmic plan, a preordained whole. But the peculiar effect of this kind of knowledge is to deprive the novel of some of its dramatic quality; a man's exposure to a final and irrevocable decision and its consequences is avoided. The disillusioning thing is not that there is a plan but that the actors occasionally know the plan, that they see themselves as only God could see them—God or the novelist. God *or* the novelist? The oneness in which the two merge is no mystical union but a literary knowingness, a consciousness in excess of story.

Jacob's loss of Rachel is moving precisely because it is unaccompanied by any literary theodicy; his sorrow is left unassuaged by any knowledge of what happens next. Here at all events the hands that cover the weeping eyes are firmly clenched. To be sure, the results of this Pirandellian device (whereby fictional characters are made to share their author's knowledge of what lies in store for them) are by no means always barren. Even the scene when Joseph is thrown into the well by his exasperated brothers, his terror duly diminished by his curiosity about what will happen next, is not without its charm. But then Joseph need not experience the fullest rigor of despair, for he will not ultimately be the one chosen from among them. But what of the others? Who is there to carry the theme of existential and spiritual care, the sign of the election, to the end, undistracted by a sense of déjà vu? Who is there to take the leap into faith, unknowing? Who will say with Job, "He is of one mind, and who can turn him: And what his soul desireth, even that he doeth"? Even Mann's Abraham, ready to sacrifice Isaac, knows in his heart of hearts that all will be well. What God, who is not a novelist, do they all believe in? It is not the narrator's omniscience that gives the novel its disillusioning literariness, but the characters' share in that omniscience. It is not only the novelist's mode of presentation that is ironical, but the consciousnesses of those presented. In this way the use of irony ceases to be discriminating, and there are scenes where it becomes a mannerism.

There is a close connection between the two encompassing themes, the existential and the literary. Leitmotif, irony, anticipation, Freudian analysis, and Jungian typology are all designed to take the sting of finality out of experience, to make it repeatable. But in this habitual avoidance of the shocks of immediate and final experience Mann is apt to jeopardize the ultimate motivation of the whole, and to replace religious faith by a literary faith, a sort of "pan-literariness." The existential is here a spiritual effort that receives its validation not from a goal, not from something it strives for, but from its own intensity, from within itself: a means comes to figure as an end. But since (shades of Nietzsche's idea of eternal recurrence) there is no further goal, the effort, which is a conscious one, can only contemplate itself. And so it happens that the lives of the main characters appear, both to us and to themselves, as parts of a fully determined plan, that is, as an aesthetic spectacle. Early on in *The Birth of Tragedy* (1872), Nietzsche's first book and the inspiration of almost every major work of modern German literature, the creative artist is likened to one who "amid the perils and terrors of dream finds reassurance in calling out to himself, 'It is a dream: I want it to go on!'" Mann takes Nietzsche's thought one step further: not only is the dreamer aware of his own dreamlike state, his awareness is shared by the figures in his dream.

Reflecting on the effect of high artifice in excess of its purpose, Rilke likens it to "the many-digited calculation that solves into zero." But Mann doesn't see it in this way. He doesn't appear to heed the disillusioning literariness of his idea of God. To call this device "disillusioning" is not to put forward any theory of the ineffable; there is no question here of "language straining to the limits of the sayable." There are ages when poets have written without embarrassment about God and his design with men, and ours is not one of them. But there are also situations that, though not beyond the power of language to describe, are beyond the scope of that literary self-consciousness to which Mann so readily resorts. And one need be no theologian to conclude that, whatever it is in this work that constitutes an enrichment of the laconic story of Genesis, it is not Mann's idea of God, the encompassing motivation of his novel.

The late Ernest Newman called *Doctor Faustus* "the greatest achievement of the greatest living man of letters"; it is certainly Mann's strangest and most powerful novel. If *Joseph and His Brothers* marks the farthest point away from "the German question" at which his imagination can operate (and we have seen that even there the motivation hinges on twentieth-century concerns), with this "Leben des deutschen Tonsetzer Adrian Leverkühn, erzählt von einem Freunde" (Life of the Composer Adrian Leverkühn, as Told by a Friend), as the novel is subtitled, Mann returns to the fountainhead of his inspiration and travail. How emphatically German a work this fictional biography is may be gauged from the hostility of its first German critics, who found it offensive to their patriotic sense. In their polemics in the wake of the defeat of 1945 they turned against the symbolical intention of the work, condemning the fundamental disproportion (as they saw it) between the life depicted and the criticism of Germany intimated through that life. The fate of a single man, the drama of a solitary, desolate soul, they argued, cannot be made to "stand for" the fate of a whole nation—not without overstraining the resources of narrative art and doing scant justice to history. This criticism is not unfounded; the signs of strain are certainly there. In the autobiographical *Die Entstehung des "Doktor Faustus": Roman eines Romans* (*The Story of a Novel: The Genesis of "Doctor Faustus,"* 1949), Mann tells us that the writing of the novel undermined his health and almost broke his spirit—the Saint Sebastian posture all over again. The discursiveness of some chapters (occasionally curbed by his daughter Erika's editing), the variety of narrative devices, disguised quotations, and levels of action, the indulgence in all sorts of technicalities, the profusion of anecdotes and occasional looseness of structure—all these suggest a work written at the point of utmost spiritual and imaginative exertion, and occasionally beyond it. And the equation of man and history—Leverkühn and Germany in the first forty years of this century—*is* in some ways lopsided. The novel does belong among those "baggy monsters" of German literature for which the special plea is entered that to practice narrative economy would be to betray biographical and historical truth. (Hermann Hesse's *Magister Ludi* [1943] is another case in point.) Mann's intention to draw an explicit parallel between the life and times of Adrian Leverkühn cannot be ignored. Yet a reader of Mann will at all times do well to moderate his or her appetite for "symbolical" parallels; first attention should be to the personal story the work offers.

Its foregrounded subject matter is the life and times of a major modern composer (the subtitle uses the archaic *Tonsetzer*), for which

THOMAS MANN

a number of details are taken from the biography of Nietzsche, the philosopher who was at all times the chief inspiration of Mann's work. In this as in several other respects Mann takes up a characteristic German topos theorized by Schopenhauer—the kinship of philosophy and music.

To list the most obvious parallels: Nietzsche and Adrian Leverkühn are both men of the late nineteenth century; both grew up in small, old-fashioned towns in central Germany, in strict Protestant settings with strong roots in the Reformation and in the spirituality of the German Middle Ages. Both are precocious boys and highly gifted students fascinated by theology who change their subjects and follow their teachers to Leipzig. (Nietzsche and Mann share the quaint belief that faith and theology exclude each other.) Both contract syphilis under precisely the same circumstances (Mann here enlarges on an episode from the life of Hugo Wolf and on a memoir written many years after the event by a friend of Nietzsche's, the authenticity of which is not in doubt). Both the philosopher and the musician live a life of solitude that is the condition of their creativeness, and the friendships that breach it are intermittent and ultimately of little account. Both experience moments of deep despair in which they appear to be possessed by demonic powers: "I think of myself as the scrawl that an unknown power scribbles across a sheet of paper, to try out a new pen," writes Nietzsche; and Leverkühn, threatened by artistic sterility, purchases fresh musical inspiration by concluding a pact with the devil. Both propose marriage by using a friend as a go-between, and both are rejected. In Leverkühn's case the infection he contracts is followed by a period of intense creativeness; Nietzsche reflects on the pathology of genius. Mann follows these reflections and relates his hero's artistic achievement causally to the disease, and both Nietzsche and Leverkühn find the connection confirmed in the works of Feodor Dostoevsky. In both Nietzsche and Leverkühn the disease leads to a general paralysis and total mental darkness lasting ten years. Nietzsche's last demented notes of December 1888 and January 1889 contain pathetic identifications with Christ, and Leverkühn hopes for salvation by performing a heartrending act of attrition. Both die on 25 August (1900 and 1940).

The story is told by one Serenus Zeitblom, doctor of philosophy, Leverkühn's lifelong friend and companion. Through the urbane, circumstantial, and pedantic pen of *Studienrat* Zeitblom—a classical philologist and amateur musician—Mann once again does his strenuous best to impart meaningful form to vast and potentially inchoate subject matter. The sources on which he draws for the background and various episodes of Leverkühn's life include the writings of Martin Luther and the German Reformation, an early Faust chapbook, and Goethe's drama; they range from Nikolai Gogol's diaries and Ivan Karamazov's conversation with the devil in Dostoevsky's *The Brothers Karamazov* (1880) to Nietzsche's letters, as well as studies of Ludwig van Beethoven, Peter Ilyich Tchaikovsky, Wolf, and (mediated by Theodor W. Adorno) Arnold Schoenberg. There are motifs from Newman's Wagner biography, Richard Strauss, Gustav Mahler, and Søren Kierkegaard's *Either/Or* (1843); Wilhelminian nationalists, Spenglerians, and the racialists of the 1920's appear on the scene; salient points in the history of Germany, from the early years of the century to the Allied bombing of "Festung Europa" (Fortress Europe) in the 1940's, are retraced in terms of individual lives; and botany, organic chemistry, and alchemy, as well as musical theory and philosophical speculation, provide much of the symbolism. The instrumentation of this biography in the grand manner is indeed complex and abundant.

The central experience of Leverkühn's life is his solitude. Is it caused by his musical precocity and genius, or are these the consolations of a proud and aloof mind? Is the disease he knowingly contracts the price of his musical gift, the cause of his lonely distinction?

Is the pact he signs with an icy hyperborean devil (who speaks the language of Luther's visitor at the Wartburg) the means that secure him further creative inspiration? Yet they but confirm the underlying conviction that Leverkühn's election for tragic solitude is inseparable from his election for greatness.

A rich panorama of life, most of it seen through the eyes of Zeitblom, is evoked around Adrian. The friendships he attempts, the love affair that comes to nothing, the several circles and cliques that form around him, the family ties that are interposed between him and his fate—all the ingredients of the realistic novel are here. But (and this is one of the novel's triumphs) the social realism is there not in order to round out and give substance to Adrian's life but, on the contrary, to set off the core of the novel—which is the single, solitary man, infinitely moving in his proud, chilly isolation, the bearer of a gift that destroys him. It is not the purchase of the gift from the devil (at a time when his "natural" inspiration is about to peter out) that is Adrian's ultimate impiety. The guilt of hubris, which is inseparable from his creativeness, is not a moral guilt but a disposition of mind, the sign not of riches but of deprivation—a deprivation so radical as to be destructive of life in Adrian and around him. That, certainly, is a theme in the grand manner. Mann's excessive readiness to cushion the shocks of experience no longer applies here. The crowning achievement of the novel is the strange charm—a charm that belongs to every tragic hero in literature— that lies like an aura around the solitary Leverkühn, heightening the poignancy of his fate.

Solitude is not a theme commonly found in European fiction, but it is emphatically a German theme. Furthermore, it is significant that Adrian is a composer, that he writes a work intended to "take back" Beethoven's Ninth Symphony (as his life "takes back" the life of Goethe's Faust). Thus there is a sense in which it is not fanciful to see solitude itself as something like a musical theme—one thinks

of the isolation of the human voice from the orchestration in Schoenberg's *Pierrot lunaire* and of Alban Berg's *Wozzeck.* Mann's task, we can now see, is complex: not only must he transpose a musician's work and thinking about his work into words, but Leverkühn's whole mode of life as a musician and as a solitary requires this kind of transposing. Adrian's desolation of soul is as absolute as a novel involved in social circumstances can make it. Indeed, *Doctor Faustus* stands as the measure of the theme in world literature.

The penultimate chapter of the novel takes place on a farm not far from Munich where Leverkühn, about to succumb to paralysis and insanity, has been living in retirement. In a moment of euphoria he has invited a large number of acquaintances, musical critics, writers, singers, and cultural busybodies to tell them of his latest composition, *Doctor Fausti Lament,* and to play to them piano excerpts from it. The invitation, the anxious Zeitblom tells us, is wholly uncharacteristic. The scene that ensues in the large hall of the ancient Bavarian farmhouse is carefully set in several contrasting moods. Humorous, even ribald effects are derived from the contrast between the withdrawn unworldliness and inward concentration of the host, Leverkühn, and the various visitors: some blasé and sophisticated, others hoping for a sensation and indulging in the scandalous nature of the occasion; some affectionate and fearful of the outcome, others pompously conscious of "the historic moment." But there is no danger that these humorous openings will impair the tragic climax. Only the last sentence that Leverkühn addresses to his worldly audience is concerned with the choral-symphonic work that he has just completed. The long, all but incoherent, yet meaningful speech that he delivers, to their growing embarrassment, is his life's confession. In that strange German full of Lutheran archaisms and idiosyncratic turns that he affects in his illness, he tells them of the impious origin of his inspiration and work, his transactions with the devil, his cold pride, and his terror of the damnation of his soul. He is demented. Clearly, all the visitors think him so; even the solicitous Zeitblom, it appears, whose heart bleeds for his friend, believes that Adrian's confession and searing self-accusations are insane.

Is Christopher Marlowe's Faustus insane? Is that last great speech of his no more than a monstrous psychotic delusion? Certainly Mann has provided the grounds for a detailed psychosomatic explanation; accordingly, the story of the conversation with the devil and many similar episodes of a supernatural kind may be seen as mere devices to dramatize a pathological delusion. Yet the tragedy of the modern Doctor Faustus retains a spiritual and religious meaning. If we accept Leverkühn's own account of his deliberate contracting of the disease that eventually leads to his insanity as objectively true, then his sin of spiritual pride and its punishment must be given the same status. This account also, it is true, is viewed by some of the characters in the light of psychological explanation, as a delusion. And so we trace the disease farther back still, to Adrian's boyhood and the congenital migraine from which he suffered. But however far back we go in the history of the man, there always remains an element of spiritual-religious motivation that eludes the causal accounts of psychology or medicine. If Mann can present the religious element in no other way than as an asymptotic line that comes ever closer to a psychological explanation yet is never quite coincident with it, then that, once again, is a sign of his dialectical truthfulness. Spirituality is acknowledged against the greatest odds that his imagination can devise.

Yet (to return to our earlier argument) *Doctor Faustus* cannot be read exclusively in terms of a personal history. Germany is *in* the novel —it is in Adrian's blood and in Zeitblom's. Germany's otherworldliness and bellicosity, its metaphysics and paroxysms of hysteria, its provincialism and grand airs, its humanity and inhumanities, its solitude and music—all these are present as both background to and aspects of Adrian's own life. This complex reciprocity between life and times is found throughout the novel, and a telling example of it occurs in Mann's account of Leverkühn's last and greatest musical composition. The state of mind in which he purchases his inspiration from the devil is one of exhaustion. What is exhausted is not only Adrian's creative vein but also (as he sees it) the musical tradition in which he was reared; it is as though all possible, possibly valid changes have been rung, and "natural" inspiration can invent no new ones. Before him lies anarchy, the license to do anything, anything at all, in order to avoid the banal and derivative—a false freedom that settles "like mildew" upon the soul. (This is how the conservative revolutionaries experienced Weimar.) The inspiration Leverkühn buys in this predicament vouchsafes him an escape from both compositional sterility and personal isolation, an escape into "polyphonic objectivity," that is, a music (a state of mind, an ideology, the revolution of 1933) that replaces "the mildew freedom" of the individual with "the choral discipline of the collective." In this vicarious way Adrian's solitary soul attempts to grapple itself to humanity: by exchanging an unmanageable personal freedom for the assurance of discipline and regimentation, by escaping from a desolate subjectivity into conformity with "the objective forces of history." And the readiness for just such a diabolical exchange (as Erich Heller has pointed out) was among the major causes of the undoing of Germany in our time.

But there is another aspect to this parallel that does not seem to be under the control of Mann's critical intelligence. Will this modern Doctor Faustus be saved? The hope he expresses at the end of the novel is for a salvation made at least possible through that arduousness which has dominated his life:

Perchance, too, God will this descry, that I sought out the hard things and labored with might and main [*dass ich das Schwere gesucht und mirs habe sauer werden lassen*], perchance,

perchance it will be counted unto my credit and benefit that I diligently applied myself and strenuously wrought all to completion.

But when applied to the analogy the novelist and the narrator set up between the life of the hero and the history of Germany in his time, this idea of "salvation" yields shocking implications. Are we meant to conclude that the recent course of German history, too, being supremely arduous and "authenticated" by an unsparing commitment to "the hard things," was a way—the "historically necessary" way—to salvation? Are we to conclude that the Hitler regime pursued its course in accordance with the Manichaean injunction to seek salvation through "bold sinning"? Indeed, the narrator, Zeitblom himself, speaks on more than one occasion of "the spiritual advantage" Germany had gained over the victorious West through its suffering and defeat in World War I, and again of "Germany's way to the Cross and readiness for death" (*Opfergang und Todesbereitschaft*), suggesting a train of thought encountered in *Reflections of a Nonpolitical Man*. More than that: this language of sacrifice, which speaks of the exactions of fate and of the "saving" value of authenticity seen as a commitment to the supremely hard task—this very language was part of the propagandist vocabulary of the Third Reich, and probably its most effective part as far as the German intellectuals were concerned.

Certainly, this horrifying implication is at odds with the author's general intention in the novel, with his own political views and pronouncements while he wrote it (between February 1943 and January 1947), and with the narrator's indignant protests against what the regime was doing to Germany and to Europe. Yet the implication is there, alongside the protests, and once again it is the overstraining of the notion of "representativeness" that imperils the logic of the narrative. We have to take it as best we may. It is a part of the continuous re-creating of the temper of an age and of that balance—delicate and easily up-

set—between the solitary man and his time and country of desolation. Reading *Doctor Faustus* almost half a century after it was written, we can see that it is not its ideology that transcends its time, but the work in which that ideology is encompassed. By making of the connection between art (Leverkühn's music) and society (the Germany of his day) an authentic fictional theme, the novel yields the illumination and delight that only the greatest historical novels can give.

The genealogy of *Bekenntnisse des Hochstaplers Felix Krull* (*Confessions of Felix Krull*, 1954), Mann's last—unfinished—novel, is indicative of the remarkable coherence of his inspiration. Begun in 1909, the first five chapters of these "Memoirs of a Confidence Man," as the novel is titled, were published as a fragment in 1922; the novel's first and only volume was completed in 1954, without any alterations from and in the same tone as the early fragment. The voluble first-person tale of this amiable sharper in the Edwardian Europe of luxurious grand hotels, grand titles, and grand passions, full of ribald episodes and stylistic spoofs, is above all an act of liberation, for its creator as much as for his readers—indeed for everybody except its hero. The literary parody harks back to the picaresque novels of the seventeenth century, yet the narrator's disclosures, at once outrageous and urbane, seedy and comic, belong to the world of the great con men of the twentieth—the Romanian Georges Manolescu (also known as the duke of Otranto), whose memoirs Mann read in 1906; the famous swindler Serge Stavisky, whose corrupt dealings shook the French political scene in the 1930's; and the actor-dramatist Sacha Guitry, whose would-be autobiography *If I Remember Right* (1935) undoubtedly helped Mann to resume work on his spoof autobiography.

Krull is a virtuoso in the medium of life and a servant of Hermes, god of thieves. His story demythologizes Joseph's life in Egypt and parodies his immense successes among its high society. The mode is occasionally satirical, as in the superb scene when the young Felix avoids conscription into the German Imperial Army by feigning an attack of epilepsy, his convulsions rendered the more convincing by his protestations of eagerness to do his patriotic duty. (Incidentally, this part of the novel was written ten years before Jaroslav Hašek in *The Good Soldier Schweik* [1920–1923] and fifty years before Joseph Heller in *Catch-22* [1961] used the same ploy—the ploy of showing a hero battling against a hostile military bureaucracy and winning the battle by displaying a public-spiritedness so vigorous as to qualify him for the madhouse.) But Mann's satire is mild; the comic muse prevails. In many of his earlier novels he gives free rein to his love of descriptive detail, the realism of bric-a-brac. Here a glittering parade of exquisite pieces of jewelry and of magnificent shop windows and hotel interiors, lavish displays of delicatessen and haberdashery, all faithful to their age of luxury and precarious stability, pass before our eyes. An old man's peroration on the riches that furnished the world of his youth? Yet the gaiety and humor are untainted by any nostalgia except the hero's; and *he* has good reason for being nostalgic, seeing that he composes his memoirs in prison.

Once again the use to which Mann puts an elaborate social realism is characteristically his own: whereas in *Doctor Faustus* it serves to set off the central fiigure in his tragic solitude, here the very solidity of the world of material things and social classes, the rotund phraseology and fine manners, are evoked to show how easily this world may be conquered and exploited by a young man with good looks, a quick intelligence, and an almost infinite adaptability, which is tested when he assumes the name and role of his friend the marquis de Venosta. A charming ease in manner and thought, in speech and amorous intercourse, in learning to play tennis or listening to a learned discourse on the origin of the species—such a charming ease is Felix Krull's device in life. In another world it might amount to a grace. But here, once again, it is a parody, a guying of Mann's own lifelong concern with the strenuous deliverance of man; and on that validation too Krull's easy conscience offers a last ironical comment. An act of liberation penned by a jailbird? The novel remains unfinished; we don't know which of Krull's adventures landed him behind bars. But Mann would not be ineluctably German were he not to believe, with his dubious hero, that "to love in true freedom is to live symbolically," that is, in the spirit. But the spirit in which and through which Felix Krull has his being is no grand philosophical abstraction, it is "der Geist der Erzählung" (the spirit of storytelling); and Krull's confessions of a lifetime "lived figuratively but not literally, in short . . . lived in the symbol" are Mann's last tribute to his art and *its* life—a life lived "figuratively," in the metaphors of fiction.

In concentrating on the more difficult of Mann's works, many other amiable divertissements must be omitted. Chief among these is *Königliche Hoheit* (*Royal Highness,* 1909), a story of princely initiation told in the easy style of an ironic fairy tale for grown-ups. The young ruling prince of an imaginary kingdom on the verge of bankruptcy, his exotic and extravagantly rich bride, and her American millionaire father form a parade of characters that might belong to a gay *Golden Bowl* (Henry James's 1904 novel) without any of its moral problems; Prince Klaus Heinrich's tutor, on the other hand, the passionate intellectual Dr. Raoul Überbein, anticipates the fanatical Naphta of *The Magic Mountain* before Lukács and Marcuse, his real-life prototypes, had ever crossed Mann's path.

The list of omissions is embarrassingly long. It includes Mann's numerous literary essays, among the finest of them his studies of Freud (1936), Wagner (1937), Dostoevsky (1946), Nietzsche (1947), Anton Chekhov (1954), and Friedrich von Schiller (1955); it also includes *Lotte in Weimar* (*Lotte in Weimar* [*The Beloved Returns*], 1940), written in 1939, between the third and fourth volumes of the *Joseph* novel, and a tour de force of literary and biographical reconstruction of a few days in Goethe's life in 1816, truthful to the ironic aspect of "the sage of Weimar" and to Goethe's critical attitude toward the Germany of his time. The interest of these works, too, is complex. They certainly illuminate their respective subject matter, and in doing so they also contain sketches for a portrait of the artist and intellectual in our time. Finally, some slighter works have also been left out, mainly of Mann's last decade, in which the dialectics of knowingness serve to illustrate his lifelong belief that modern fiction may hide but should not deny its intellectual origins. To have omitted a closer look at Mann's diaries (four huge volumes in German so far) may not require an apology, for their publication has done little to endear their author to the common reader. Where the trivia of a literary man's daily routine are ransacked for representative meaning, the charge of self-importance is hard to refute. The diaries provide yet another slant on episodes, encounters, and ideas already worked over in the completed fictions, emphasizing the author's husbandry of his resources in accordance with a sound Protestant work ethic.

The difficulty on which this study has concentrated is in the first instance a matter of Mann's literary styles. Hardly ever simple and direct, informed by a variety of allusions and parodistic devices, they have a fatal tendency to be reduced in English translations to a single, regrettable level of archness. This is a misleading impression, which only a new generation of translators can rectify. The syntactic finesses, stylistic impersonations, and quotational devices serve not a single point of view but a complex mode of indirection. The high points of Mann's narratives are almost always placed on the margins of human experience, but the kinds of language he chooses come from the center of *bürgerlich* intellectual discourse. "Intertextuality" is carried to the point where the same referential status is accorded to events prefigured in books as to events taken from life: spontaneity, in a literature conceived as "criticism of life," is apt to be rare. The aim is rational insight issuing in high intellectual delight; and through its chinks we glimpse an impenetrable solitude. Impenetrable because no longer subject to any dialectic, this solitude constitutes, for Mann, the ground of the being of modern man.

And yet "the Magician" was the name the Mann children gave to their father when he told them stories at bedtime. The impression we, too, are left with is one of immense narrative ease behind the complex syntactic devices—an ease that now intimates, now conceals that idea of the strenuous deliverance and validation of man to which the author returns throughout the six decades of faithful devotion to his métier. Of this idea and mode of life *Doctor Faustus* is the final and greatest embodiment. As we have seen, the religious dimension of Leverkühn's life is acknowledged against the greatest odds the novelist's imagination and truthfulness can devise. Beyond that, "I cannot say and have no courage to hope," as Leverkühn says at the end of his last speech, for, as the poet says, "Hope would be hope for the wrong thing." Beyond this cloud of unknowing Mann cannot go. Whenever he tries to penetrate it, a disillusioning knowingness takes over. But here, beneath the cloud, speaks one of the authentic voices of an age whose inheritors we are. And in his commitment to that age, not despite it, lies his claim upon the attention of posterity. In *Death in Venice* he defines the grounds on which fame—his fame, at all events—is likely to rest:

A significant creation of the mind can only then yield an immediate influence that shall also be deep and lasting if it is founded in a secret affinity and consonance between the personal destiny of its author and the destiny of his contemporaries in general. Men do not know why they bestow fame on a work of art. . . . The true ground of their commendation is an imponderable: it is sympathy.

THOMAS MANN

Selected Bibliography

EDITIONS

INDIVIDUAL WORKS

NOVELS
Buddenbrooks: Verfall einer Famile. 2 vols. Berlin, 1901.
Königliche Hoheit. Berlin, 1909.
Der Zauberberg. 2 vols. Berlin, 1924.
Lotte in Weimar. Stockholm, 1940.
Doktor Faustus: Leben des deutschen Tonsetzers Adrian Leverkühn, erzählt von einem Freunde. Stockholm, 1947.
Joseph und seine Brüder. 3 vols. *Die Geschichten Jaakobs* and *Der junge Joseph,* vol. 1; *Joseph in Ägypten,* vol. 2; *Joseph der Ernährer,* vol. 3. Stockholm, 1943–1948.
Bekenntnisse des Hochstaplers Felix Krull: Die Memoiren Erster Teil. Frankfurt, 1954.

NOVELLAS AND STORIES
Der kleine Herr Friedemann. Berlin, 1898.
Tristan. Berlin, 1903. Includes *Tonio Kröger.*
Der Tod in Venedig. Berlin, 1912.
Novellen. 2 vols. Berlin, 1921. Includes *Fiorenza.*
Unordnung und frühes Leid. Berlin, 1925.
Mario und der Zauberer. Berlin, 1930.
Die vertauschten Köpfe. Stockholm, 1940.
Das Gesetz. Stockholm, 1944.
Ausgewählte Erzählungen. Stockholm, 1945.
Der Erwählte. Frankfurt, 1951.
Die Betrogene. Frankfurt, 1953.

ESSAYS
Friedrich und die grosse Koalition. Berlin, 1914.
Betrachtungen eines Unpolitischen. Berlin, 1918.
Rede und Antwort. Berlin, 1922.
Bemühungen. Berlin, 1925.
Die Forderungen des Tages. Berlin, 1930.
Goethe und Tolstoi. Berlin, 1930.
Leiden und Grösse der Meister. Berlin, 1933.
Freud und die Zukunft. Vienna, 1936.
Achtung, Europa! Stockholm, 1938.
Deutsche Hörer! 55 Radiosendungen nach Deutschland. Stockholm, 1945.
Adel des Geistes: Sechsehn Versuche zum Problem der Humanität. Stockholm, 1945. Includes essays on Wagner.

Neue Studien. Stockholm, 1948. Includes essays on Dostoevsky and Nietzsche.
Die Entstehung des "Doktor Faustus": Roman eines Romans. Amsterdam, 1949.
Ansprache im Goethejahr. Frankfurt, 1949.
Meine Zeit. Amsterdam, 1950.
Der Künstler und die Gesellschaft. Frankfurt, 1953.
Altes und Neues. Frankfurt, 1953.
Versuch über Tschechow. Frankfurt, 1954.
Versuch über Schiller. Berlin, 1955.

COLLECTED WORKS
Politische Schriften und Reden. 3 vols. Frankfurt, 1968.
Gesammelte Werke. 13 vols. Edited by E. Loewy. Frankfurt, 1960–1974.

CORRESPONDENCE AND DIARIES

Briefe, 1889–1936; 1937–1947; 1948–1955. 3 vols. Edited by Erika Mann. Frankfurt, 1961–1965.
Briefe an Paul Amann, 1915–1952. Edited by H. Wegener. Lübeck, 1959.
Briefwechsel: Hermann Hesse—Thomas Mann. Edited by A. Carlsson and V. Michels. Frankfurt, 1968.
Tagebücher, 1918–1921; 1933–1934; 1935–1936; 1937–1939. 4 vols. Edited by P. de Mendelssohn. Frankfurt, 1977–1980.
Thomas Mann—Heinrich Mann: Briefwechsel. Edited by H. Wysling. Frankfurt, 1968.
Thomas Mann—Karl Kerényi: Gespräch in Briefen. Edited by K. Kerényi. Zurich, 1960.
Thomas Manns Briefwechsel: Bibliographie gedruckter Briefer Thomas Manns aus den Jahren 1889–1955. Edited by G. Wenzel. Berlin, 1969.

TRANSLATIONS

The Black Swan. Translated by W. R. Trask. London, 1954.
Buddenbrooks: The Decline of a Family. Translated by H. T. Lowe-Porter. New York and London, 1924.
Children and Fools. Translated by H. G. Scheffauer. New York, 1928. Includes the 1898 story *Little Herr Friedemann.*
Confessions of Felix Krull, Confidence Man: The Early Years. Translated by D. Lindley. London, 1955.

Death in Venice. Translated by K. Burke. New York and London, 1925; rev. ed., translated by H. T. Lowe-Porter, London, 1928. Includes the title story, *Tristan,* and *Tonio Kröger.*

Diaries, 1918–1921, 1933–1955. 2 vols. Translated by R. and C. Winston. New York, 1970.

Diaries, 1918–1939. Selection and foreword by H. Kesten. Translated by R. and C. Winston. London, 1983.

Doctor Faustus: The Life of the German Composer Adrian Leverkühn, as Told by a Friend. Translated by H. T. Lowe-Porter. New York, 1948.

Early Sorrow. Translated by H. T. Lowe-Porter. London, 1929.

Essays of Three Decades. Translated by H. T. Lowe-Porter. New York and London, 1947.

Freud, Goethe, Wagner. Translated by H. T. Lowe-Porter and R. Matthias-Reil. New York, 1937.

The Holy Sinner. Translated by H. T. Lowe-Porter. New York, 1951.

Joseph and His Brothers, The Tales of Jacob; Young Joseph; Joseph in Egypt; Joseph the Provider. 4 vols. Translated by H. T. Lowe-Porter. New York and London, 1934–1944.

Last Essays. Translated by R. and C. Winston and T. and J. Stern. New York and London, 1959.

The Letters of Thomas Mann, 1889–1955. 2 vols. Translated by R. and C. Winston. London and New York, 1970.

Letters to Paul Amann, 1915–1952. Edited by H. G. Wegener. Translated by R. and C. Winston. Middletown, Conn., 1960.

Listen, Germany! Twenty-Five Radio Messages to the German People over BBC, 1940–42. New York, 1943.

Lotte in Weimar (The Beloved Returns). Translated by H. T. Lowe-Porter. New York and London, 1940; rev. ed., translated by C. McNab, Harmondsworth, England, 1979.

The Magic Mountain. Translated by H. T. Lowe-Porter. New York and London, 1927.

Mario and the Magician. Translated by H. T. Lowe-Porter. London, 1930.

Mythology and Humanism: The Correspondence of Thomas Mann and Karl Kerényi. Edited by K. Kerényi. Translated by A. Gelley. Ithaca, N.Y., and London, 1975.

Order of the Day: Political Essays and Speeches of Two Decades. Translated by H. T. Lowe-Porter, A. E. Meyer, and E. Sutton. New York, 1942.

Past Masters and Other Papers. Translated by H. T. Lowe-Porter. New York and London, 1933.

Pro and Contra Wagner. Translated by A. Blunden. Introduction by E. Heller. London, 1985.

Reflections of a Nonpolitical Man. Translated by W. D. Morris. New York, 1983.

Royal Highness. Translated by A. C. Curtis. London, 1916; rev. ed., with a new preface, translated by H. T. Lowe-Porter, New York, 1939; 2d rev. ed., translated by C. McNab, London, 1962.

A Sketch of My Life. Translated by H. T. Lowe-Porter. Paris, 1930.

Stories of Three Decades. Translated by H. T. Lowe-Porter. New York and London, 1936.

Stories and Episodes. Selected by E. F. Bozman. Translated by H. T. Lowe-Porter et al. Introduction by E. Heller. London, 1940.

The Story of a Novel: The Genesis of "Doctor Faustus." Translated by R. and C. Winston. London, 1961.

The Tables of the Law. Translated by H. T. Lowe-Porter. New York, 1945.

Three Essays. Translated by H. T. Lowe-Porter. New York, 1929. Includes *Goethe and Tolstoy* and *Frederick the Great and the Grand Coalition.*

The Transposed Heads: A Legend of India. Translated by H. T. Lowe-Porter. New York and London, 1941.

BIOGRAPHICAL AND CRITICAL STUDIES

Adorno, T. W. "Standort des Erzählers im zeitgenössischen Roman." In *Noten zur Literatur,* 1. Frankfurt, 1955.

Apter, T. *Thomas Mann: The Devil's Advocate.* London, 1978.

Bauer, A. *Thomas Mann und die Krise der bürgerlichen Kultur in Deutschland.* Berlin, 1946.

Beddow, M. "Fiction and Meaning in Thomas Mann's *Felix Krull." Journal of European Ideas* 10 (1980).

————. "Der Zauberberg." In *The Fiction of Humanity.* Cambridge, England, 1982.

————. "Analogies of Salvation in Thomas Mann's *Doktor Faustus." London German Studies* 3 (1986).

Bergsten, G. *Thomas Manns "Doktor Faustus": Untersuchungen zu den Quellen und zur Struktur des Romans.* Stockholm, 1963.

Bertram, E. "Thomas Manns *Betrachtungen eines Unpolitischen.*" *Mitteilungen der literarhistorischen Gesellschaft in Bonn* 20 (1917).

Blackmur, R. P. "Hans Castorp, Small Lord of the Counterpositions." *Hudson Review* 1 (1948).

Blume, B. *Thomas Mann und Goethe.* Berne, 1949.

Brennan, J. G. *Three Philosophical Novelists: James Joyce, André Gide, Thomas Mann.* New York, 1964.

Burgin, H., and H.-O. Mayer. *Thomas Mann: Eine Chronik seines Lebens.* Frankfurt, 1965.

Carnegy, P. *Faust as Musician.* London, 1975.

Cassirer, E. "Thomas Manns Goethe-Bild: Eine Studie über *Lotte in Weimar.*" *Germanic Review* 20 (1945).

Corngold, Stanley, et al. *Thomas Mann 1875–1975.* Princeton, N.J., 1975. Critical essays.

de Mendelssohn, Peter, et al. *Thomas Mann 1875–1975.* Munich, 1975. Critical essays and international bibliography.

————. *Der Zauberer: Das Leben des deutschen Schriftstellers Thomas Mann.* Frankfurt, 1975.

Diersen, I. *Thomas Mann: Episches Werk und Weltanschauung.* East Berlin, 1979.

Eichner, H. *Thomas Mann: Eine Einführung in sein Werk.* Berne, 1953.

Eloesser, A. *Thomas Mann.* Berlin, 1925.

Faesi, R. *Thomas Mann, ein Meister der Erzählkunst.* Zurich, 1955.

Fest, Joachim. *Die unwissenden Magier: Über Thomas und Heinrich Mann.* Berlin, 1985.

Flinker, M. *Thomas Manns politische Betrachtungen im Lichte der heutigen Zeit.* The Hague, 1959.

Fougere, J. *Thomas Mann, ou la séduction de la mort.* Paris, 1947.

Fourrier, G. *Thomas Mann: Le message d'un artiste-bourgeois, 1896–1924.* Paris, 1960.

Gray, R. D. *The German Tradition in Literature, 1871–1945.* Cambridge, England, 1965.

Hamburger, K. *Thomas Mann und die Romantik.* Berlin, 1932.

————. *Thomas Manns Roman "Joseph und seine Brüder."* Stockholm, 1945.

Hamburger, M. *From Prophecy to Exorcism.* London, 1965.

Hamilton, N. *The Brothers Mann: The Lives of Thomas and Heinrich Mann.* London, 1978.

Hatfield, H. *Thomas Mann: An Introduction to His Fiction.* London, 1952.

————. *From the Magic Mountain: Mann's Later Masterpieces.* Ithaca, N.Y., and London, 1979.

————, ed. *Thomas Mann: A Collection of Critical Essays.* Englewood Cliffs, N.J., 1964.

Heller, E. *The Ironic German: A Study of Thomas Mann.* New York, 1979.

Heller, P. *Dialectics and Nihilism.* Amherst, Mass., 1966.

————. *Probleme der Zivilisation: Versuche über Goethe, Thomas Mann, Nietzsche, und Freud.* Bonn, 1978.

Herzfelde, C. *"La montagne magique" de T. Mann: Facettes et fissures.* Paris, 1979.

Hirschbach, F. D. *The Arrow and the Lyre: A Study of the Role of Love in the Works of Thomas Mann.* The Hague, 1955.

Hofmiller, J. "Thomas Manns neue Erzählung (*Der Tod in Venedig*)." *Süddeutsche Monatshefte* 10 (1913).

Hollingdale, R. J. *Thomas Mann: A Critical Study.* London, 1971.

Holthusen, H.-E. *Die Welt ohne Transzendenz.* Hamburg, 1949.

Kaufmann, F. L. *Thomas Mann: The World as Will and Representation.* Boston, 1957; New York, 1973.

Keller, E. *Der unpolitische Deutsche: Eine Studie zu den "Betrachtungen eines Unpolitischen."* Berne, 1965.

Klussmann, P. G., and U. Fechner, eds. *Thomas-Mann-Symposion, Bochum, 1975.* Kaustellaun, West Germany, 1978.

Koopmann, H. *Die Entwicklung des "intellektuellen Romans" bei Thomas Mann.* Bonn, 1980.

————. *Der klassisch-moderne Roman im Deutschland: Thomas Mann, Alfred Döblin, Hermann Broch.* Stuttgart, 1983.

Lammert, E. "Thomas Manns *Buddenbrooks.*" In *Der deutsche Roman,* vol. 1, edited by B. von Wiese. Düsseldorf, 1963.

Lehnert, H. *Thomas Mann: Fiktion, Mythos, Religion.* Stuttgart, 1956.

Lesser, J. *Thomas Mann in der Epoche seiner Vollendung.* Munich, 1952.

Lindsay, J. M. *Thomas Mann.* Oxford, 1955.

Lukács, G. *Die Theorie des Romans.* Berlin, 1920; rev. ed., 1963.

————. *Thomas Mann.* Berlin, 1949; rev. ed., 1957.

741

————. *Wider den missverstandenen Realismus.* Berlin, 1958.

Lublinski, S. *Essays on Thomas Mann.* London, 1964.

————. *Die Bilanz der Moderne: Geistige Struktur um 1900.* Tübingen, 1974.

McWilliams, J. R. *Brother Artist: A Psychological Study of Thomas Mann's Fiction.* Lanham, Md., 1983.

Mádl, A. *Thomas Manns Humanismus: Werden und Wandel einer Welt- und Menschenauffassung.* Berlin, 1980.

Mann, E. *Das letzte Jahr.* Frankfurt, 1956. A memoir by Mann's eldest daughter.

Mann, K. *Unwritten Memories.* Edited by E. Plessen and M. Mann. Translated by H. and H. Hannum. New York, 1975. A biographical study by Mann's wife.

Mann, V. *Wir waren fünf.* Konstanz, West Germany, 1949.

Mayer, H. *Thomas Mann: Werk und Entwicklung.* Berlin, 1950; 2d ed., Frankfurt, 1980.

Michielson, G. *The Preparation of the Future: Techniques of Anticipation in the Novels of T. Fontane and T. Mann.* Berne, 1978.

Muschg, W. *Tragische Literaturgeschichte.* Berne, 1948.

Neider, C., ed. *The Stature of Thomas Mann.* New York, 1947.

Pascal, R. *The German Novel.* Manchester, 1956.

Peacock, R. *Das Leitmotiv bei Thomas Mann.* Berne, 1970.

Reed, D. K. *Doktor Faustus: The Novel and the Nazi Past.* New York, 1985.

Reid, T. J. *Thomas Mann: The Uses of Tradition.* Oxford, 1974.

Ridley, H. *Buddenbrooks.* Landmarks of World Literature series. Cambridge, England, 1987.

Samuel, R. H. "Thomas Mann und Hans Grimm." *German Life and Letters* (January 1937).

Schaukal, R. "*Der kleine Herr Friedemann.*" *Die Gesellschaft* 14 (1895).

Schroter, K. *Thomas Mann.* Hamburg, 1964.

Seidlin, O. *Von Goethe zu Thomas Mann.* Göttingen, 1963.

Sontheimer, K. *Thomas Mann und die Deutschen.* Munich, 1961.

Staiger, E. "Thomas Manns *Doktor Faustus.*" *Neue Schweitzer Rundschau* (November 1947).

Stern, J. P. *History and Allegory in Thomas Mann's "Doktor Faustus": An Inaugural Lecture Delivered at University College.* London, 1973.

————. "The Theme of Consciousness in Thomas Mann." In *Modernism 1890–1930.* Harmondsworth, England, 1976.

————. "Living in the Metaphor of Fiction: On Thomas Mann's *Felix Krull.*" In *Comparative Criticism,* vol. 1. Cambridge, England, 1979.

————. "Relativity in and Around the Magic Mountain." In *The Novelist as Philosopher: Modern Fiction and the History of Ideas,* edited by P. Horden. Oxford, 1982.

————. "*Deutschtum*: On Mann's *Reflections.*" *London Review of Books* (3 April 1986).

Swales, M. *Thomas Mann: Students' Guide to European Literature.* London, 1980.

Thomas, R. H. *Thomas Mann: The Mediation of Art.* Oxford, 1956.

Walser, M. *Besichtigungen des Zauberbergs.* Biberach, West Germany, 1974.

Weigand, H. J. *Thomas Mann's Novel "Der Zauberberg."* New York, 1933; repr., Chapel Hill, N.C., 1964.

Wenzel, G., ed. *Vollendung und Grösse Thomas Manns: Beiträge zu Werk und Persönlichkeit des Dichters.* Halle, East Germany, 1962.

White, A. *Thomas Mann.* Edinburgh, 1965.

Wilkinson, E. M. "*Tonio Kröger.*" Oxford, 1946. Introduction to edition of *Tonio Kröger.*

Wiston, R. *Thomas Mann: The Making of an Artist, 1875–1911.* London, 1982.

BIBLIOGRAPHIES

Burgin, H. *Das Werk Thomas Manns: Eine Bibliographie.* Frankfurt, 1959.

Jonas, K. W. *Fifty Years of Thomas Mann Studies: A Bibliography of Criticism.* Minneapolis, 1955.

Matter, H. *Die Literatur über Thomas Mann: Eine Bibliographie 1896–1969.* Berlin and Weimar, 1972.

J. P. STERN

ANTONIO MACHADO

(1875–1939)

ANTONIO MACHADO WAS born in Seville in 1875, the year of the Restoration, as Spanish historians commonly call it. Since 1713 and the Treaty of Utrecht, the Bourbon dynasty had occupied the throne of Spain, but in 1868 a revolution led by some generals sent Queen Isabel II into exile. A period of political unrest ensued in which the country witnessed several forms of government: regency, the reign of an Italian prince, the First Republic (which lasted only eleven months, from 1873 to 1874), another military regency, and finally the return of the Bourbons in the person of King Alfonso XII (1875–1885), son of Isabel II.

The Revolution of 1868 brought about the recognition of some new civil liberties in Spain. Whereas the majority of the country—and certainly the most conservative sectors—saw the restoration of the monarchy as the only hope for political stability, democrats, liberals, and Republicans—almost synonymous terms in that period—retained an enduring nostalgia for the Republican experience, however short-lived it had been. Thus the Constitution drafted and promulgated in 1876, which remained in force until 1931, respected the new rights gained by the citizens during the revolutionary period. These included the possibility of universal suffrage, freedom of worship, and a certain measure of freedom of the press and of teaching.

LIFE

Antonio Machado's family belonged to the liberal, Republican camp. His grandfather, a professor of medicine, was a champion of Darwinism in Spain. The poet's father, Antonio Machado y Álvarez, pioneered in the scholarly study of Spanish folklore, authored several books on the subject, and maintained a scholarly exchange with the famous German philologist Hugo Schuchardt.

In 1883 Machado y Álvarez moved with his family to Madrid. Two years later the Institución Libre de Enseñanza (Free Institution of Teaching) established a course in folklore and offered it to him. He did not take it, probably because it offered an insufficient salary and threatened to limit his movement. Financial difficulties forced Machado y Álvarez to seek employment in Puerto Rico, then a Spanish colony. He went to the island in 1892, but a few months later he returned to Spain seriously ill and died in Seville before he could reach Madrid. He left behind his wife and five sons, the oldest of whom, Manuel, an illustrious poet himself, was nineteen years old, a student of history at the University of Seville.

Antonio was the second son. His elementary education took place at the Free Institution of Teaching from 1883 to 1889. The Institution was an elementary and secondary school founded in 1876 by the prestigious intellectual Francisco Giner de los Ríos and other colleagues dismissed from the official university for political reasons. It was called "free" because it was independent from state and church, the powers that at the time controlled the schools in Spain. It was also "free" in the sense that it promoted a strictly secular mode of reasoning. The basic assumption of the school was the native goodness of the child, and the Institution stressed respect for the student, student involvement in the learning process, opposition to memorization, emphasis on the education of women, contemplation and enjoyment of nature, and respect for all religious beliefs. The *institucionista* (individual educated at the Institution) came to be known as a person of high ethical standards, though not necessarily attached to any particular religion.

Machado was an *institucionista,* and he remained grateful to the Institution and its teachers throughout his life. In 1915 the founder, Giner de los Ríos, died, and Machado wrote a poem in which he extolled Giner as the initiator of a new creative ferment in Spanish life and culture.

Little is known about the poet between 1889 and 1899, the year of his first trip to Paris. His schooling was irregular, and he did not obtain a high school diploma until 1900. His first literary works were prose articles published in 1893 in the literary journal *La caricatura* under the pen name Cabellera. These articles, written when the poet was only eighteen, already reveal great maturity. They are humorous vignettes of popular types and customs, including some caricatures. Machado seems to have frequented *tertulias* (literary circles), and for a while he aspired to be an actor. In the midst of this activity he seems to have read intensely the classics of Spanish literature, for in 1913 he wrote: "For twenty years I have been almost daily in the National Library."

In 1899 Machado went to Paris, at that time the cultural capital of the world. For Spanish writers it was the ideal place to become informed about the newest literary trends and to

be reassured as to the value of their own writings. Paris was also the city of "the banquet years." The defeat of France in the Franco-Prussian War (1870–1871) was far behind, and international political activity created the illusion that war might be eliminated forever. Progress and scientific optimism made those years the epitome of "the good old times," the *belle époque* par excellence. Machado describes the cultural milieu of Paris in these words: "Paris was then the city of symbolism in poetry, impressionism in painting, and skepticism in critical theory. I met Oscar Wilde and Jean Moréas. The great literary figure, the consecrated writer, was Anatole France."

In October of the same year the poet, who had earned his living by translating for the publisher Garnier, returned to Madrid. Machado went back to Paris for a few months in 1902 and found employment in the consulate of Guatemala. The consul was Enrique Gómez Carrillo, a prolific writer and admirer of French literature who was instrumental in the spread of French symbolism in Spain.

The intellectual life of Madrid, in which Machado took part in the early years of the twentieth century, can be defined with three terms: modernism, symbolism, and the so-called Generation of '98. Modernism refers to the new generation's attitude of rebellion against the conservative tendencies of Spanish life in all its aspects: politics, culture, customs, and values. Under the names liberalism, Krausism (referring to the German philosopher Karl Christian Friedrich Krause), and anarchism, or under the banner of Arthur Schopenhauer and Friedrich Nietzsche, the young writers bitterly criticized present-day Spain and the preceding three centuries of Spanish history.

Symbolism is the predominant manifestation of modernism in literature. Symbolism was originally the search for the sensorial—musical and pictorial—values of words in preference to their representational capability, as vehicles of ideas. Paul Verlaine's verse "Before all else, music" became for the symbolists a fundamental principle of poetry and aesthetics.

Some intellectuals and poets, such as Miguel de Unamuno, were not satisfied with what they considered a mere aesthetic game. They called for a poetry with human and social content but did not reject the basic principles of symbolism. On the contrary, they believed that individual and social experiences could be expressed in words that would convey ideas and at the same time radiate in their sensorial and emotional capabilities. This effort to use words to their fullest intellectual, sensorial, emotional, and structural capacities of expression can be seen in the following verse by Unamuno: "Let us, then, sculpt the mist." Here the clear idea is the concept of sculpture, and the musical, pictorial, and emotional values of the poem inhere in the notion of mist.

In contrast to this broader idea of symbolism, the French writers of the period remained more on the sensorial level. One of those writers, Gustave Kahn, spoke of "the landscapes of the soul," a term later used by Unamuno, but those landscapes were in general mere stimulants for sensation, not for reflection on the nature of man. In symbolism nature becomes fused with the poet and the poet becomes fused with nature. Machado later wrote poems on "the galleries of the soul," clearly in the context of the intimate landscapes of the symbolists, but with an intellectual message as well.

For Spain 1898 was a watershed year. Cuba, Puerto Rico, and the Philippines, remnants of the old Spanish empire, were lost in the Spanish-American War. Especially in opposition circles this defeat was seen as the logical result of the distorted course of Spanish history in the preceding three centuries. The most original *modernista* writers engaged in an interpretation of "the Spanish soul," which inspired essays such as Unamuno's *En torno al casticismo* (In Search of the National Identity, 1895), Azorín's *El alma castellana* (The Castilian Soul, 1900), and many others. The vague concept of an ethnic, collective "soul"

became the key concept for their investigations of Spanish society and history.

Machado was a modernist, a symbolist, and a member of the Generation of '98. He considered himself a disciple of Unamuno, maintained friendly relations with Ramón del Valle-Inclán, Pío Baroja, and Azorín (the members of that generation), and shared in their ideals and aesthetic principles. Their friendly relations and common ideals did not prevent these writers from disagreeing on many points, which explains the polemical tone of many of their texts. Machado, for example, had a sincere respect for Rubén Darío, the most prestigious modernist poet, but he had a different conception of poetry. Unamuno derided modernist aesthetics while sharing some of its basic principles. In general terms, all of these writers coincided in their criticism of conservative Spain and in the theory of symbolism, but they disagreed on the application of the theory, specifically on whether art should be a predominantly formal or a primarily human psychological and sociological exploration.

In 1903 Machado published his first book, *Soledades* (Solitudes). With it he was recognized as a leading figure in the literary world of Madrid. Two years later, without a university degree, he applied to the government for a position as professor of French in a public high school, and in 1907 he was awarded the chair of French language in the high school of Soria, a city of seven thousand people in Old Castile, some two hundred miles northeast of Madrid. Soria became "the landscape of the soul" for Machado, who said, "You have reached deep into my soul." In this city he wrote the book *Campos de Castilla* (Fields of Castile, 1912) and married Leonor, then fifteen years old. While the city of Soria will always remain associated with Machado's interpretation of "the soul" of Castile, in fact he applied for a transfer on several occasions. The rural setting and mentality of the small town squared neither with the liberal views nor with the intellectual aspirations of the poet.

In 1910 he received a one-year fellowship to

study philology in Paris from the Junta para Ampliación de Estudios e Investigaciones Cientificas, a sort of national council of research founded in 1907 to foster the scientific recovery of Spain. In January 1911 he went to Paris for the third time, accompanied by his young wife. At the Collège de France he attended lectures given by the famous philologist Joseph Bédier and by the philosopher Henri Bergson.

The stay in Paris was cut short due to a serious illness of Leonor's. The couple returned to Soria, and she died on 1 August 1912. In deep sorrow the poet left the city and applied for a teaching position at another high school, Baeza, some two hundred miles south of Madrid on the Andalusian border with Castile. The poet had returned to his native region, but far from showing him as feeling more at home, his poetry and letters between 1912 and 1917 exhibit both personal frustration and growing pessimism about the political situation of the country.

In 1919 Machado obtained a transfer to Segovia, which had the attraction of being closer to Madrid. Madrid offered a better intellectual climate than the provinces, and he spent most weekends and vacations there. Two years earlier he had published two collections of poetry: *Páginas escogidas* (Selected Pages) and *Poesías completas* (Complete Poems). In 1923 the political instability of the country, exacerbated since 1917, ended in a coup by General Miguel Primo de Rivera, who governed Spain as a dictator for seven years, from 1923 to 1930. During those years Machado and his older brother Manuel engaged in playwriting. Together they revised classical Spanish texts of the seventeenth century and wrote seven original plays, presented to the public with varying degrees of success between 1925 and 1932. The plays have been published in *Obras completas de Manuel y Antonio Machado* (Complete Works of Manuel and Antonio Machado, 1947).

All the plays were in verse, in the best tradition of the Spanish classical theater, and were intended to be popular. The brother poets aspired to create lasting works of art by taking local legends and elaborating on the universal features of human behavior they exhibited. The plays were written in verse with the intention of accomplishing in the twentieth century something similar to what Lope de Vega had accomplished in his time: delving into universal human experience on the basis of national history and legend, and finding roots in popular poetry. Their idea of art, combining local color, universal features common to popular poetry of different cultures, and a modernization of traditional Spanish theater, especially Lope de Vega's, coincides with the ideal of the young poets of the "Generation of 1927," Federico García Lorca and Rafael Alberti. Machado was to some extent their precursor, although he disagreed with them on other aspects of poetics.

Machado had been a widower since 1912. In 1928 the poet met Pilar de Valderrama, a woman who had a profound and enduring impact on his life and writings. A young poet and author of several books, she was married and, according to all reliable testimonies, was loyal to her husband and family. Her love for Machado was apparently a matter of profound admiration, maternal tenderness for the hapless older man, and joy in the sensation of confidence that his company projected. The poet loved her so deeply that he called her "my goddess" or, if the word "goddess" became too repetitious, "my queen."

Machado's love experience was kept secret, even from his brothers; in the love poems he calls her Guiomar. In 1950 fragments of Machado's letters to Guiomar were published with no attempt to reveal her identity, which eventually became known in literary circles. In 1981 Pilar de Valderrama published her memoirs under the title *Si, soy Guiomar* (Yes, I Am Guiomar) and put all doubts about her identity to rest.

The dictator Primo de Rivera became the target of attacks from different sectors of Spanish society. Unamuno opposed the dictatorship from the beginning and was exiled to the Canary Islands in 1924. The Republicans and some monarchists also left and maintained a propaganda war. Two attempted coups by other generals also took place. The king, who in 1923 had accepted the dictatorship as the best means to restore law and order, perceived that the prestige of the monarchy was eroding along with the prestige of the dictator. In January 1930 General Primo de Rivera, sensing the adverse mood of the army and the country, gave up the government and went into exile in Paris. The king attempted a return to the old parliamentary system, but, as Ortega y Gasset pointed out at the time, after seven years in which the constitution of 1876 had not been respected even by the king, the return to the old constitutional system was an illusion. Two short-lived cabinets in 1930 and 1931 failed to gain acceptance from the populace. On 12 April 1931 an election for town councils gave a majority of votes to the Republican candidates in the most important cities, and as a result the election was seen as a rejection of the monarchy on the part of the people. The king left Spain, and the country was declared a republic on 14 April 1931.

The government of the Republic opened three new high schools in Madrid in 1932. Machado became a teacher of French in one of them, and between 1932 and 1936 he lived and taught in the capital. In July 1936 the army, under the command of General Francisco Franco, rebelled against the government in the Spanish possession of Morocco, and the Spanish Civil War began. The poet sided with the legitimate government, and during the war he put his pen into the service of the popular armies.

In November 1936 Madrid, encircled by the insurgent troops, became dangerous, and the poet was transferred to Valencia by the government of the Republic. There he lived for a year and a half until April 1938, when he was moved to Barcelona. Finally, in January 1939, when the victorious armies of Franco were entering the city, he, his mother, and other members of his family were taken to France. After a harsh journey through the Pyrenees, in which he shared the plight of many thousands who were escaping the prospect of death or long imprisonment, he arrived in the small French village of Collioure. He was sixty-three; his mother was eighty-five. He had suffered for years from heart illness, and his condition worsened in the middle of February. He died on 22 February 1939. Three days later his mother followed him to the grave.

Ironically, a few days before the Civil War had started, Machado's beloved brother Manuel had gone to Burgos, where Franco established his headquarters. Manuel remained in that city and became a loyal adherent to the Franco regime. The war did not destroy the love of the brothers, but it ruptured the bond established by many years of companionship and collaboration. Manuel died in 1947.

POETRY

According to reliable witnesses, Machado was a dedicated writer but was very demanding and therefore discarded a great deal of his writing. For this reason his literary legacy is not voluminous; it consists of four books of poetry, one of philosophical and literary aphorisms in prose, another one of prose and verse related to the Spanish Civil War, and various poems, speeches, articles, and letters published in journals during his lifetime and collected in volumes after his death.

The books of poetry went through several revisions during the poet's lifetime and the last edition to be supervised by Machado was the fourth of his *Poesías completas,* published in 1936 and often reprinted by the Madrid publisher Espasa-Calpe. This edition lists 184 poems numbered in Roman numerals, divisions within each poem being indicated by small Roman numerals. The edition includes four books: *Soledades* (now dated 1898–1907), *Campos de Castilla* (now dated 1907–1917), *Nuevas canciones* (New Songs, 1924 [now dated

1917–1930]), and *De un cancionero apócrifo* (From an Apochryphal Songbook), the latter never published as an independent book.

Although this arrangement reflects the structure preferred by the poet for his poems, a scholarly study cannot be based on this edition. The years appended to the books do not correspond to the actual years in which they were published. *Campos de Castilla,* for example, now dated 1907–1917, was first published in 1912. In the edition of 1917 Machado introduced new poems related to the same topics of the book and to the memory of his wife. A study of the original content and context of the book must take this material into account, but must be conscious of a change in the poet's attitude precisely between 1912 and 1917, a change that is visible in the poems included in the second edition. For this reason we will base our study on the original versions of Machado's books, which are also available in modern editions and which contain several poems that were excluded from the 1936 collection. The poems found in the Espasa-Calpe edition will be quoted with the Roman numeral, those not included in it with the name of the editor indicated in the bibliography.

The first book, *Soledades,* appeared in 1903. It consists of forty-one short poems grouped in four sections: "Desolaciones y monotonias" (Desolations and Monotonies), "Del camino" (Of the Road), "Canciones" (Songs), and "Humorismos, fantasías, y apuntos" (Humorisms, Fantasies, and Sketches). The themes of the first part are the afternoon, songs of children, winter, the sad sea, and autumn. Machado contrasts radiant colors with sober emotions; even the bright summer afternoons bring memories of "old pains." The poem "Cenit" (Zenith), which in its title promises of spring, is no exception; in it the poet contrasts the joy and vitality of the water with the labyrinthine nature of man's existence:

The clear water that smiled under the sun
above the marble of the fountain, told me:

if the riddle of the present disturbs you,
learn the sound of my psalm.

(Ferreres)

The psalm of the fountain is a prophecy: the water's destiny is to smile, while the poet will spend his life as a wayfarer in search of himself.

All the poems of the book evoke a sentiment of nostalgia. They usually begin with the description of a past experience with which the poet deeply identifies. The evocation of the experience recalls the natural surroundings in which it took place, and the evoked landscape is fused with the present, with the moment of the writing. The verbs are for the most part in past tense; thus the recollection brings about the lyrical emotions of nostalgia and yearning. The adjectives emphasize the quietude of nature and the calm of the soul.

Ultimately the identification of the poet with nature results in nature becoming a "landscape of the soul." It would be wrong, however, to suggest that Machado writes a pantheistic poetry, one in which the poet would disappear through immersion in nature. The ego, the voice of the poet, never disappears, even when he inhales the fragrance of the flowers or appears embedded in the radiant sunset, and even when nature is contemplated in the present. In addition, the present evokes past memories and thus enhances the historical character of the experience. A few examples taken almost at random will substantiate and clarify these observations.

The first poem of the book is titled "Tarde" (Afternoon). It recalls a dialogue of the poet with a fountain:

It was a clear afternoon, sad and somnolent afternoon of the calm summer. The ivy showed up over the wall of the park, black, dusty . . . far away a smiling fountain sounded.

(VI)

This is the original version of the poem, which in Spanish includes two alliterative patterns: *soñolienta del lento verano* (somnolent afternoon of the calm summer), and *fuente riente* (smiling fountain). These stylistic devices, very dear to French symbolists, were discarded in the definitive version, in which the alliteration is eliminated. The poet enters the park and approaches the fountain:

> The fountain was singing:
> brother, does my present song
> remind you of an old dream?
> It was a calm afternoon
> of the calm summer.
>
> (VI)

Here the adjective *lento* (calm) was kept. This and similar adjectives describe not an objective quality of the afternoon or the summer, but rather the feelings aroused in the poet by the sedative atmosphere. At the same time, he is not content with the present sensation and evokes two levels of the past. First, the poem itself is already a past experience: "It was a clear afternoon." Second, on that afternoon the fountain reminded the poet of old dreams that had taken place in a more remote past.

The fountain is the main motif in the poems of this first section, and water is the element of nature preferred by the poet. In "La fuente" (The Fountain), he writes:

> There are strange loves in the history
> of my long journey without love;
> the greatest one is the fountain
> whose pain mutes my pains,
> whose listless smiling mirror
> diffuses my clouds and my grudges.
>
> (Ferreres)

The fountain and the water mirror the poet in an attitude of alienation. Only rarely is the smiling water a sign of joy and hope; rather, it is seen in its undefined vagueness and its repetitious monotony. Even when the poem associates water with the song of children, it represents not optimistic projection and expectation, but rather anxiety before the unknown:

> In the lips of children
> the songs bear
> a confused story,
> yet a clear pain,
> like the clear water
> carries the story
> of loves in the past
> that never return.
>
> (VIII)

The season of this book is summer with its long, slow, calm afternoons and with sunsets that fill the poet with color, perfume, and yearning. The evening is golden, red, and green, and through the fragrance of the flowers nature becomes a landscape of the soul. Perfume was a basic motif of the French symbolists. Through smell nature enters the very body of the poet, effecting even a physical identification.

Given the nostalgic mood of Machado in these poems one might expect the autumn to be his preferred season, but his penchant for color makes that choice impossible. The season does not inspire him, as he says in "Otoño" (Autumn):

> The purple autumn
> has no legends
> for me. I have never listened
> to the psalms of dead leaves
> carried by the wing.
> I do not know the psalms
> of the dry leaves,
> but the green dream
> of the bitter earth.
>
> (Ferreres)

Sometimes the search for sensations of color and fragrance leads to the use of words that are not genuinely Spanish, as in "Crepúsculo" (Twilight): "Donde ígneos astros, como nubes, flotan / informes en un cielo lactescente" ("Where igneous stars, like clouds, float / vague in a milky sky"). But this happens very rarely; "Crepúsculo" was not collected in subsequent editions. In other cases, when the poem was revised the words in question were suppressed. In general, the poet mastered the art of simplicity as he became free from the influence of French symbolism; here, the adjective *lactescente* (milky) was probably inspired by Jean Moréas, Paul Adam, and especially Arthur Rimbaud, in his "Le bateau ivre" ("The Drunken Boat"): "Et de lors, je me suis baigné dans le Poème de la Mer, infusé d'astres, et lactescent, dévorant les azurs verts" ("And from then on, I have swum in the poem of the sea, infused of stars and white like milk, devouring the green blues"). The second section, "Del camino" (Of the Way, From the Journey, or Of the Road), is the best in the book. It consists of sixteen poems without titles preceded by a prelude that gives the entire section the coherence of a single poem. The three translations proposed for the Spanish title "Del camino" express the complexity of the expression, its symbolic meaning. *Camino* refers not only to the physical road but also to the human journey as a metaphor for human existence and to the "way," an ambiguous term with various nuances.

The poems in this section already exhibit Machado's unique interpretation of symbolism. In contrast to the French symbolists, whose influence upon the Spanish modernists has frequently been mentioned, Machado produces a fusion of color, emotion, and idea. Mere sensation aroused by nature gives way to a reflection on some essential aspect of the human being: a Senecan meditation on death, a remembrance of a lost love that the poet tries to retrieve, or a dialogue with himself. External nature is not forgotten, but it is linked to the soul through invisible galleries.

The phrase "galleries of the soul" raises several questions: What do these galleries consist of? What grows in them? What is their landscape? One poem conveys the sense of this section better than abstract descriptions:

Upon the bitter earth
dream has labyrinth-like roads,

winding paths,
gardens in bloom, in shadow and in silence;
deep crypts, ladders above the stars;
a polyptych of hopes and memories.
Little shapes that go by and smile
—an old man's wistful toys—
friendly shapes
at the flourishing turning of the path,
and rosy fantasies
that open their ways . . . far off.

(XXII)

This poem shows how Machado interpreted "galleries of the soul": as the identification with nature enriched with a poetical reflection on human existence. Here, the earth is called "bitter." In this case the adjective reflects not the attitude of the poet but rather the clumsy nature of earth, which at the same time bears and shelters all the powers of death (fall) and resurrection (spring). On this earth the human dream finds itself at a crossroads that unites the infernal and the heavenly, the past and the future, love and hatred or indifference. The dreamer is never limited to and by his environment or circumstances: beyond all the coordinates that seem to determine the course of our existence, there is freedom and creativity, there are the poet's "rosy fantasies / that open their ways . . . far off" into the unknown. At the same time the unknown, because it is unfamiliar and uncanny, arouses a feeling of insecurity and anxiety. The poet penetrates into the galleries from which the basic questions about human life spring.

The way, intimate as a gallery of the soul or external as a road in the fields of Castile, continued to be a key term or sign in Machado's poetry, where it means life, search, crossroads. In 1913 he wrote lines explaining that the way is opened by the very walking of it and that there are not ready-made roads:

Wayfarer, the road
is your footsteps, nothing else.
Wayfarer, there is no road
you open it as you walk it.
The walking opens the road

and when you turn your eyes back
you see the path you'll never
walk again.
Wayfarer, there is no road,
but wakes on the sea.

(CXXXVI, xxix)

Compared to the poems of the first book, this one is more intellectual, almost a philosophical aphorism. The dramatic images of the wayfarer, the road, and the sea guarantee the poetic quality of the message, but the idea about human existence is here conveyed in a direct manner. In this case the symbol has become an allegory: authentic life does not follow ready-made roads; rather it is a search that opens its own way. Life is life at the crossroads; we may always make the wrong choices in our most critical decisions. And when something has been attained, it has to be permanently tended, conquered, or else it vanishes: our conquests are wakes on the sea. This attitude is opposed to any kind of dogmatism. The seeming contradiction implied in conquering what has already been attained reflects the old wisdom revealed in Pindar's injunction to "become what you are."

These three signs—water, way, search—are so deeply associated with each other and so deeply ingrained in the imagination of the poet that some years later he applied them in a clearly allegorical sense, in "La saeta" (The Dart):

O, the *saeta*, the song
to the Christ of the gypsies
always with blood in his hands,
always stifled by the nails.
O, you are not my song,
I cannot and I do not want to sing
to that Jesus of the log,
but to the one who walked on the sea.

(CXXX)

The *saeta* is a popular song, sung especially in Seville in the processions of Holy Week. It is a "dart" launched by the pious soul to the suffering redeemer. Machado, a native of Seville, renounces that song because the "Je-sus of the log," that is, Christ nailed to the cross, represents quietude, conservatism, and dogmatism, while the Jesus of the sea is the symbol of life as search.

The two remaining sections of the book, "Canciones" and "Humorismos, fantasías, y apuntos," are similar to the ones already described. What is important about them is their popular tone; in these sections the poet reveals the influence of the latest trends from Paris as well as the poetic values, actually the symbolist values, of Spanish popular poetry. Eventually this popular vein became the ideal poetry for Machado.

The second book, *Soledades, galerías, y otros poemas* (Solitudes, Galleries, and Other Poems), was published in 1907. It incorporates many of the poems of *Soledades,* some of them with changes, and adds new ones. The three parts of the title correspond to the three sections of the book. In it the poet exhibits the results of strenuous work on both the praxis and the theory of poetry. He has acquired a personal voice.

The book opens with a poem not included in the 1903 edition: "El viajero" (The Traveler). This poem epitomizes Machado's unique type of symbolism, combining momentary sensations with the revelation of universal structures of human behavior. The traveler leaves the family home, and his family feels the vacuum created by his absence. In the course of time both the traveler and the family rebuild their respective worlds without each other. When they meet again, there is an uncomfortable silence. This thoughtful poem at the beginning of the book casts a new light on those that still emphasize music and color over ideas.

The section "Galerías" consists of thirty short poems preceded by an introduction in which Machado expresses his understanding of poetry at that time:

Reading one bright day
my beloved verses
I have seen in the deep mirror of my dreams

that a divine truth
is trembling out of fear
and is a flower that wants to throw
its fragrance to the wind.
The soul of the poet
reaches into the mystery. Only the poet can
look into what is far away
inside the soul,
wrapped in a murky and magical sun.

(LXI)

Poetry is a search, the disclosure of the intimate memories and desires of the human being. The intimate is nothing private, idiosyncratic; the poet reaches into structures that are common to all human beings.

In addition to considering the nature of poetry, in this book Machado emphasizes the painful aspects of life. If we did not know that he was not even married in 1907, we might read some of the poems as inspired by his wife's death. Expressions of hope are not totally absent (see "Renacimiento" [Renaissance]), but they are the exception.

His ideas about the nature of poetry led Machado to select his favorite models from the classics. We know that he was a persevering reader in the Madrid National Library for twenty years, and this reading resulted in an original assimilation of the classics. Machado praised the medieval poet Jorge Manrique for a poem in which he refers to personal experiences and life. Manrique is a model of Machado's poetic ideal in that period, when he viewed poetry as the expression of an intuition, a sincere feeling. Insofar as it expresses sincere feeling poetry is *palabra en el tiempo* (word in time), not the expression of abstract thoughts with personal emotion and beautiful language. Motifs of other Spanish classic authors such as Garcilaso de la Vega and Francisco de Quevedo are also perceptible in this book. But the presence of certain motifs or the simple resonance of other poets does not diminish Machado's originality; indeed, he chose his own influences on the basis of an original poetics.

Love appears in this book as a radiant horizon of hope and joy and as a drama brought about by the difficulty of dialogue between human beings: "Are you the thirst or the water in my journey? / Tell me, shy virgin, my companion." The descriptive elements in all these poems are the spatial support for a dialogue that takes place between an I and a Thou, sometimes within the poet himself. The last poem of the section, "Del camino," is a quest for the authentic voice of the poet. It can serve as an example of Machado's style at this juncture in his development:

O, tell me, friendly night, so long
beloved, you who bring me the picture of
my dreams ever deserted and desolate,
and only with my phantom in it,
my poor, sad shadow on the barren land
and under the scorching sun,
or dreaming of sad things
in the voices of all mysteries.

Tell me if you know it, my old beloved,
tell me if the tears I shed are mine!
The night answered me:
You never revealed your secret to me.
I never knew, beloved,
if that phantom of your dream
is truly you.

I never ascertained whether its voice
was yours or the voice of a grotesque clown.
I told the night: faithless mistress,
You know my secret,
you have seen the deep cavern
where my dream fabricates its crystal,
and you know that my tears are mine
and you know my pain, my old pain.

(XXXVII)

The poet dramatizes his doubts as to whether he speaks sincerely (is a voice) or only echoes (is an actor). Machado felt so intensely the need for sincere, intuitive expression that he feared words might betray that aspiration.

The section "Canciones y coplas" (Songs and Verses) contains a re-elaboration of Andalusian popular songs. Machado's father had collected Andalusian folklore, and one aspect of the modernist theory was a penchant for simplicity, which coincided with the aesthetic theory of pre-Raphaelitism. In addition to this European trend, the Spanish writers of the Generation of '98 tended to value the Middle Ages as an epoch of freedom and viewed the ascendance of the Austrian dynasty in 1517 as a deviation from "true" Spanish history. Study of "the national soul" led to appreciation of popular poetry as the most genuine expression of that soul. Unamuno, who profoundly influenced Machado, sought the identity of a nation in its "intrahistory," the life of the common people, and not in "history," the activities of the public figures. Popular poetry was viewed as the expression of collective aspirations, and Machado's popular style found the appropriate echo in a group of writers, readers and literary scholars well prepared for its reception.

The fusion of French symbolism with the popular tradition may have been inspired by yet another source. *Soledades,* the title of Machado's book, is also the title of a poem by the baroque poet Luis de Góngora. Góngora, who was in fact revaluated by the modernists as a precursor, was also the author of many *letrillas* (popular verses). Machado, like Góngora, sought a poetry that could authentically search for new modes of expression in terms of literary experimentation and fashions, and at the same time express unchanging human feelings.

The section of the book "Humorismos, fantasías, y apuntos" contains poems of the type suggested by its title. They use popular rhythm and anticipate the sententious aphorisms found in Machado's later works. A representative example of this section is "Las moscas" (The Flies):

> You, all too familiar
> inevitable gluttons
> you, flies from everyday
> evoke all things to me.
>
> Oh, old voracious flies
> like bees in April,
> old, bothering flies
> over my infant scalp.

> Flies of the first tedium
> in the parlor of the family,
> in the bright afternoons of summer
> when I began to dream . . . !
>
> Inevitable gluttons,
> you neither work like bees
> nor glitter like butterflies.
> Tiny, restless,
> you, old friends,
> evoke all things to me.
>
> (XLVIII)

The flies are familiar objects; they are part of everyday life, and old friends. Many things may be preserved from childhood and many change as we travel the roads of life, but the flies are ever-present and unchanging, a sort of unifying force in man's existence, and an example of the continuity of the simple and common.

Other writers have used the flies as symbols, too. Jean-Paul Sartre in his drama *The Flies* makes them a symbol of the forces that impede prompt and clear decisions; the flies are the codified values, the remorse that has to be dissipated. For Machado they do not have negative connotations; they are "familiar," a symbol of something permanent in the changing stages of human existence.

In summary, *Soledades, galerías, y otros poemas* displays a variety of aesthetic principles, themes and styles. Some poems written within the principles of French symbolism reveal a still-insecure voice. Other poems are masterpieces of poetry written in an original voice that combines sincere personal emotion with intellectual exploration of universal structures of human existence. In the book we find a definitive synthesis of brilliant sensations (in the face of a bright day or a radiant sunset) on the one hand, and the revelation and analysis of internal experiences—landscapes of the soul—on the other. The human experiences to which the poet returns throughout the work are personal identity (reality/dreams, voice/echo), time (past/future, memory/hope, nostalgia/yearning), man and the earth (with the sun, the fields, and the springs), love, solitude, loneliness, and boredom as the experience of nothingness. Finally, some aphoristic poems are also contained in the book, a style that later attracted the poet more and more. In this first book are the basic directions of the entire poetic corpus of Machado, and most of his best poems.

In its first edition *Campos de Castilla* contained the poems written by Machado between 1907 and 1912, the year of its publication, with a few written before 1907. The title refers to the city of Soria, where the poet had lived since 1907. The title implies a change in the focus of the poet's attention: he opens the internal galleries of his soul (with their dreams, labyrinths, and ample plains of boredom) to the air of the Castilian plain. Critics generally see in this book a departure from symbolism toward a poetry of social and epic tone in that Machado relates the Castilian man to his landscape, associates Castile with its heroic past history, and attempts to revive the romance—the expression of Spanish popular epic since the fifteenth century. At the same time, however, critics recognize the presence of symbolist motifs in the poems. The identification of the landscape with the feelings of the poet is no less visible in this book than in the preceding ones; the only significant difference is that the landscape has been expanded. In *Soledades* nature was the object of a momentary impression that stimulated the poet to make a universal statement about human existence. In *Campos de Castilla* the feelings of the poet include a vision of Castilian history as part of his own. The horizon is larger in both space and time; the poet sees the landscape as inhabited, no longer as the point of departure for a personal reaction.

Of the seventeen poems included in the original version of the book, only four can be called "epic" in the broad sense of the term, that is, as referring to a collective way of life: "A orillas del Duero" (Along the River Duero), "Por tierras de España" (Through the Land of Spain), "Un Criminal" (A Criminal), and "La tierra de Alvar González" (Alvar González's Land). A poem to "Don Miguel de Unamuno" in which Machado chides the Spaniards as "a people of mule carriers and gamblers" and speaks of "the soulless soul of the race" dates from 1905, when Unamuno published his *Vida de Don Quijote y Sancho* (*Life of Don Quixote and Sancho*). Although the poem to Unamuno was motivated by the latter's book, it contains sociological statements and was written in what is considered Machado's "modernist" period. In fact, the transition to a more objective poetry may be due to Unamuno's influence. In the prologue to *The Life of Don Quixote and Sancho,* he mercilessly criticizes poets who are concerned only with personal feelings and with the music of their verses. He advocates a poetry with precise ideas, social commitment, and popular roots. Machado heeded the bidding and exited from the interior galleries into the social realm.

In the poem "A orillas del Duero" the poet describes himself walking on a summer afternoon through the barren, rocky hills that surround the city of Soria:

It was mid-July. It was a beautiful day.
I, alone, through the clefts
of the rocky hill was climbing
slowly, seeking the corners in shade. . . .
The river Duero crosses
the oaken heart of Iberia and Castile.
Oh sad and noble land, of high plains and barren
fields and rocks. . . .

(XCVIII)

According to Machado, this beautiful land with a glorious history is at present populated by a decadent people whose only concern in life is to migrate from their homes into the wide sea in search of a living. This need to migrate contrasts with the journeys of adventure in past centuries, when Castilian captains won fame with their feats in both Europe and America. The poem continues with a contrast between the glories of the past and the stagnation of the present.

ANTONIO MACHADO

Since the social and historical allusions are framed in the narrative of a walk along the river Duero, the final verses describe the poet's return at sunset:

The sun is far down the sky. Through the quiet air
the music of distant bells reaches my ear,
time for old women in black to go to prayer.
Two pretty weasels slip out of rocky lairs. . . .

(XCVIII)

The epic motifs—the contrast of past and present in the history of Castile—are framed in the lyrical contemplation of nature. If in the previous book the poet looked at the colors of the "temporal landscape"—the sunrise, the sunset, and the seasons—here he dwells on physical objects as well—the river, the rocks and the flowers. The mere mention of their names instills in the reader the sense of their beauty. In his description of the movement of time and the different shadows cast by the sun, Machado attains an impressionistic portrait of the landscape. In this sense, the epic poem that criticizes the Castilian present is also a lyrical poem that incorporates an important element of symbolism. Machado enriches his world and his personal form of symbolism without making a drastic evolution.

His evolution toward a critical view of Spain is more evident between 1912 and 1917, the year of the first edition of Machado's *Poesías completas*. In this collection some poems of the preceding books are suppressed or corrected, and some new ones are included under old titles, with no indication that they were written after the first editions of the books.

Both personal and social events explain a growing bitterness in Machado since 1912: his wife's death, his experience of the stagnant Andalusian city, the assassination of Prime Minister Canalejas in 1912, and the ongoing struggle between the liberals and the church for the control of education. Each of these events informs the poem "El mañana efímero" (The Ephemeral Tomorrow), the most representative of Machado's attitude in those years:

The Spain of fanfare and noise
bullfight and sacristy,
devoted to Frascuelo and to Mary,
of disrespectful spirit and stagnant soul,
shall also have its marble and its day,
its infallible tomorrow and its poet.
The empty yesterday will engender a tomorrow
equally empty and happily ephemeral.
That inferior Spain that prays and yawns,
old, gambler, devious, sad,
That inferior Spain that prays and charges,
when deigns to use its head.

(CXXXV)

Conservative Spain is associated with the church and with the bullfight, which most liberal thinkers detested. When the traditionalist uses his head it is only to pray—with a wrong idea of God and religion—and to charge like a bull. This Spain is the outcome of an "empty yesterday," three centuries of which the present is the result, and it can give birth only to something ephemeral, devoid of lasting value.

The only ray of light that Machado saw in this bleak atmosphere was the action of certain generous groups, such as the one associated with Giner de los Ríos at the Free Institution of Teaching, and the inexhaustible energy of the common people. Machado believed that the common people, well led, possessed the potential for reviving the old virtues. In 1915, at the death of Giner, Machado wrote "A Don Francisco Giner de los Ríos" (To Don Francisco Giner de los Ríos), in which Giner's message is contrasted to the message of the conservatives, once again identified with the Spanish church:

As the master had gone away
the morning's light
said to me: it is three days
since my brother Francisco has not worked.
Did he die? We only know
that he left us along a bright path
and told us: mourn me with effort and hope.
Be good and nothing else,
be what I have been among you: a soul.

Live, life goes on,
the dead die and the phantoms vanish.
Only he who leaves something behind
takes something along.
Only he who has lived goes on living.
Anvils, resound; keep silent, bells.

(CXXXIX)

The contrast between the anvils and the bells is the contrast between two Spains: the one symbolized by the church and the new one symbolized by Giner's message. Light, work, and hope are the symbols of his legacy. This legacy is lasting and will prevail over the ephemeral past and future of the other Spain.

The ephemeral as a synonym of emptiness appears also in "Llanto de las virtudes y coplas por la muerte de Don Guido" (Lament of the Virtues, and Songs for Don Guido's Death), a satire on the "Andalusian gentleman," the embodiment of everything that the poet finds disgusting:

Good Don Guido
now you are gone
and for ever and ever.
Some may say, what did you leave?
I ask you, what did you take along
to the world where you now are?

(CXXXIII)

What is here formulated in the form of a question is an assertion in the poem to Giner: "He who leaves something behind is the one who takes something along."

These poems, in which a social commitment is evident, are still poems, not political pamphlets. The images of light, the call to effort and hope in the case of Giner, and the satiric stylization of the critical poems conform to the idea of poetry as a use of the language in its fullest capacity of expression. If a simple political essay could still reflect the deep emotions of the poet, in this case the images and the rhythm guarantee the poetic character of the verses. They do not have the poetic qualities of those that identify the land-scape with the soul, but Machado tried to be faithful to that principle.

The sociological concerns of this period culminated in Machado's effort to write a new kind of epic poetry that would reflect the new situation of Spain. In the wake of a romantic conception of epic poetry as popular poetry, Machado intended to write in that style, reviving the old Spanish romance, a composition in lines of eight syllables alternating an a-b assonant rhyme. Around 1910 the most authoritative interpreter of the romance in Spain was the philologist Ramón Menéndez Pidal, who insisted on the popular nature of this epic. Machado followed in the steps of Pidal. At the same time he recaptured the popular vein already visible in his first book, and by expressing the feelings of the people he purported to express universal feelings; if the epic expresses collective sentiment or beliefs, nothing is more universal than popular poetry.

This is the context of "La tierra de Alvar González," the most innovative poem in *Campos de Castilla*. It consists of 710 lines of eight syllables, and tells the somber story of three brothers, one of whom migrates to America while the other two remain in the village and, unable to develop in a creative way, kill their father in order to inherit his land. A curse reigns over the fields from the moment of the crime. The immigrant brother returns and brings new life to the house until the brothers kill him too. Since then the shadow of Cain hovers over these sinister fields. The Castilian man of 1912 has degenerated from an old adventurous *conquistador* to a potential parricide.

The poem is based on a legend of Soria that Machado turned into a version of the myth of Cain and Abel. He makes the local anecdote poetic and universal by inserting it into the atemporal story of the Bible. The poem was dedicated to Juan Ramón Jiménez, a poet who spent his life in search of more and ever greater lyrical beauty. Jiménez was very displeased with Machado's experiment, and Machado abandoned the project of resurrecting the old romances. His would have been the anti-epic of "invertebrate Spain," the expression used by Ortega in 1921 to describe the situation of the country.

Campos de Castilla, in its original version of 1912, contains basically the same themes as the preceding books, though with some differences. The internal landscapes of the soul give way to the external land of Castile, contemplated with love. The inhabitant of the new landscape is no longer the individual poet, but the people. In 1917 Machado published two collections of his poetry: *Poesías completas* and *Páginas escogidas.* In *Poesías completas* the book *Campos de Castilla* includes the verses with a political tone that have been mentioned, but it also includes a few poems to the death of his wife and to her memory. The latter are the expression of a sincere pain and evoke a profound empathy in the reader:

> I dreamt you were taking me
> along a white path,
> amid the green field,
> towards the blue of the mountain ridges,
> towards the blue mountains
> one bright morning.
> I felt your hand in mine,
> your hand of faithful companion,
> your voice of a child in my ear,
> like a new bell,
> like a virgin bell
> of a morning dawn in spring.
> Your voice and your hand
> were so true in the dream!
> Live on, hope, who knows
> what the earth has swallowed!
>
> (CXXII)

The poem exhibits the style and motifs of the preceding books: dreams, the past, mountains, and paths. But here we discover two new themes: the absent love and the absent God. The walks in *Soledades, galerías, y otros poemas* are those of solitude and monotony; here a walk with the beloved wife is remembered. The second new element is the unknown God. Machado, baptized in the Catholic church, did

not practice the public rites of Catholicism— in fact he wrote harsh words against the Spanish church—but at the moment of intense sorrow he probes the sense of life and yearns for the immortality of the soul envisioned by Catholics. He neither asserts nor denies the immortality of the soul; rather, he yearns for it, for nothing makes sense if the human being dies completely and forever. In the twilight of doubt and yearning Machado wrote: "Live on, hope, who knows what the earth has swallowed."

In 1912 Unamuno published his most famous philosophical essay, *Del sentimiento trágico de la vida en los hombres y en los pueblos (The Tragic Sense of Life in Men and Nations).* The tragic sense is for Unamuno the struggle between Esau and Jacob, between reason and the human spirit's will to believe. Reason and science make it difficult to believe in the immortality of the soul, while the heart needs to believe in order to find meaning for the human being. In 1912 Machado, a faithful admirer of Unamuno, went through the experience revealed and explored in the latter's book. In a simple prayer Machado writes:

> O Lord, you took from me what I loved most,
> Hear again, my God, my heart cry out.
> Your will has been done, O Lord, against mine,
> O Lord, now we were alone: my heart and the sea.
>
> (CXIX)

With the loss of his wife Machado cries out to God and sees himself lonely, confronted by the sea. The sea possesses three different meanings in Machado's poetry: death, life, and insecurity.

Death is the boundless, mysterious vacuum into which the river of life flows, an image Machado appropriated from the medieval poet Manrique: "Our lives are like rivers that flow into the sea." Life is a river or life is a journey; both end in the sea, which is death. But the sea also means life; in the poem "La Saeta" Machado opposes the "Jesus of the log" to the one who walked on the sea. This opposition, which

757

corresponds to the distinction between intu-ition and concept in Machado's poetics, is intended to emphasize the poverty of intellec-tual schemes as opposed to life's richness. The sea is the inexhaustible treasure of all possible experiences, which can never be en-compassed by intellectual constructs. Thus, the sea is also life's insecurity. We may dream of finding ready-made paths for our journey, but they are all walks on the sea. With the death of his wife, the poet's references to his world have broken down, and if love for the other person had helped him find a direction to follow, the road has now become a path in the woods, a sea. The tragic sense of life lies in man's anxiety about his destiny after death.

The political poems and the ones to the death of his wife were written by Machado in Baeza, after he left Soria. Not surprisingly, the distance purified his vision of the Castilian city. The cemetery of Soria that holds the remains of his beloved wife becomes a holy place. In this attitude, Machado wrote one of his most beautiful poems, "A José María Pala-cio" (To José María Palacio):

> Palacio, good friend,
>   is Spring
> already dressing the branches of the poplars
> along the river and the roads? . . .
> With the first lilies
> and the first roses of the gardens,
> on a blue afternoon, go up to the *Espino,*
> the high *Espino* where her earth is found.
>
>   (CXXVI)

(*Espino* is the name of the cemetery where Machado's wife is buried.)

Section CXXXVI of *Campos de Castilla* con-tains fifty-four poetico-philosophical apho-risms titled "Proverbios y cantares" (Proverbs and Songs). The emotional participation of the poet through interrogation or exclamation or a brief reference to nature guarantees their poetic character. At the same time each one expresses in an ingenious style an idea or a riddle about human life. No thematic or struc-tural pattern is visible in the ordering of the aphorisms; they simply reiterate the poet's dearest ideas and concerns: "Why call paths / the furrows of chance? / All travelers walk / like Jesus, on the sea"; "Yesterday I dreamt that I saw / God, and that I spoke to God, / and I dreamt that God heard me. . . . / Then I dreamt that I was dreaming."

The 1917 edition of *Campos de Castilla* also includes a number of occasional poems in praise of friends. The one quoted in honor of Giner is a good example of their content and poetic character. Machado displays great per-spicacity in capturing the personal gesture or intellectual and literary style of the individual referred to.

Critics differ in their evaluation of *Campos de Castilla* in the context of Machado's work. Those inclined to moral and sociological lit-erature prefer it to the others and see in it the climax of the poet's inspiration. Others, in-cluding Juan Ramón Jiménez, saw in this book a deviation from what they considered the right path. Machado himself considered it transitional and indicated that his greatest poetry was still ahead. Presumably he in-tended to give a sample of that poetry in *Nuevas canciones.*

In the 1936 edition of *Poesías completas* this book comprises fourteen titles, most of them subdivided into sections. The first com-position, "Olivo del camino" (Olive Tree on the Road), contrasts the Andalusian olive tree to the Castilian oak. This is similar to poems in *Campos de Castilla,* and at times one has the impression that Machado was writing in *Nuevas canciones* a sort of "Fields of Andalu-sia." Unlike Soria—mountainous, rocky, and barren—Andalusia is a garden of wheat, oil trees, carnations, and roses. Castile reminds Machado of medieval prowess, of "a people who envisioned God beyond the war," of the *romancero* and the reconquest of Spain from the Muslims. Andalusia, on the other hand, evokes memories of pagan life and myths under Roman influence, as well as Islamic memories.

The subject of "Olivo del camino" is the myth of Demeter, the goddess of fertility. It must be noted that while the popular poetry of Castile was "romantic" as opposed to the classical, "learned" poetry, the popular poetry or mythology of Andalusia was precisely classical. This poem shows that true poetry is not limited to any particular style and that the contrast between popular and learned (romantic and classic) poetry may prove useless. In turning to classicism Machado embraces whatever is genuine without attachment to any particular style. The following verse associates classicism with popular simplicity; it was part of poem CLIV in its original version, but was not included in the 1936 edition of Machado's poetry:

> Once again the ancient world
> without original sin:
> the bright world of Homer.
> Nausicaa again washes
> her clothes.
>
> (*Obras*, p. 750)

Classical poetry can be called popular because in it the gods, the princes, and the princesses perform humble chores as common people do. If in *Campos de Castilla* the romance was used as a means to capture some permanent features of Castilian poetry in contrast to the ephemeral present, in *Nuevas canciones,* as the title suggests, the same is intended with regard to Andalusia, only this time through the popular poetry of this region.

The Andalusian songs are short, sometimes *soleá* (three-line poems). In such short structures the following elements must be present: an ingenuous idea and an expression of deep feeling—for example, "Hour of my heart / the hour of a hope / and the hour of a despair"—or a beautiful visual image—for example, "From my window / the field of Baeza / under the bright moon."

The Moorish past, which constitutes a permanent feature of Andalusia, is referred to in the third poem, "Hacia la tierra baja" (Towards the Low Land, another contrast to "the high land" of Soria). Here, the Andalusian girl is trapped behind the Moorish grate of her window. She may dream of gypsies and heroic brigands, but legendary Spain is gone; only prosaic employees move through the streets of the town. Yet life's mediocrity is framed within nature's inebriating beauty. Nature remains unchanged, and its beauty justifies all legends.

The fourth poem of the book, "Galerías" (Galleries), is similar to the poems with the same title published in 1907; the same fusion of man with unchanging, beautiful nature is apparent. The galleries, however, are the sky, the water, and the earth with its trees and its *retamas de oro* (golden broomflowers). Nature's galleries offer greater beauty and interest than the internal galleries of the soul. The symbolist identification of the poet with his landscape is preserved, but this time he emphasizes the landscape. Admiration for nature, popular poetry, songs to Andalusia, and nostalgic memories of Soria constitute the basic principles of poems CLIII–CLX.

Poem CLXI, subdivided into ninety-nine short compositions, contains sententious, aphoristic poetry of philosophical content. The large number of aphorisms in *Nuevas canciones,* roughly one-third of the book, indicates that Machado is leaning in the direction of an intellectual poetry. As mentioned above, the poet obtained a master's degree in philosophy in 1918 and was always interested in the basic questions of human existence. Thus it is not surprising that many of these new "Proverbios y cantares," dedicated to the famous philosopher Ortega y Gasset, refer to philosophical questions.

The aphorisms are not organized according to a particular thematic or structural pattern, but can be classified with a certain measure of accuracy into the following themes: affirmation of the other; allegorical messages involving natural elements such as the road, light, and the river; ideas on poetry; and the contrast between the inherent heterogeneity of the real and the unifying tendencies of human reason.

A few examples will give an impression of the content of these aphorisms: "In order to have a dialogue / first ask, / then . . . listen"; "Today is always still." In just one line the poet manages to reveal the complexity of the human "here and now"; when we say "now" we seem to refer to a momentary experience that we can fully embrace and master, but in fact we refer to many layers of past and future— to heritage, situation, and ideals. What looks like a point in time is in fact a continuum. A final example is the following aphorism on poetics: "Wake up, singers / let the echoes stop / and the voices begin." In his obsessive search for a true poetic voice Machado warns himself and others against the falseness of mere words without a message.

Poem CLXII is titled "Parergon," which means something not directly intended, an addition. In this poem Machado tries to evoke the memory of his dead wife and expresses the experience of forgetfulness. With the death of a loved one our world crumbles, but life goes on, and eventually we rebuild our world without the dead person. Forgetting is the rebuilding of a new world, and once this has happened, the pain of the loss becomes a mere feeling of compassion or nostalgia. The experience described here resembles that in "El viajero."

Legend, popular song, and the search for a lasting voice led Machado to a new appreciation of the classic writers as the truly popular poets—not only the "popular" Homer but all the classic writers, including the "learned" ones, such as Dante, Lope de Vega, and Shakespeare. This explains his turning to the sonnet, the most prestigious form of lyric poetry in Europe in the sixteenth and seventeenth centuries. In *Nuevas canciones* a section of sonnets is titled "Glosando a Ronsard y otras rimas" (Glosses on Ronsard and Other Rhymes). The sixteenth-century poet Pierre de Ronsard was revived by the symbolists for the brilliance and freedom of his work, and Machado professed his admiration for him in

1907: "I adore beauty and in modern aesthetics / I cut the old roses from Ronsard's garden" (XCVII). With the imitation of Ronsard's sonnets Machado completes his poetic world by achieving a synthesis of the popular and learned traditions after the example of Lope de Vega, whom Machado considered the great classic writer of Spanish literature. *Nuevas canciones* closes, like *Campos de Castilla,* with some occasional poems dedicated to friends.

Nuevas canciones is the last book of poetry Machado wrote. In 1924 he initiated a collaboration in playwriting with his brother Manuel. In the same year André Breton's *Manifeste du surréalisme* (*Surrealist Manifesto*) constituted a sort of climax to the many theoretical manifestos on the nature of art and poetry that had given rise to as many schools of literary theory during the previous two decades. In Spain the European ferment was assimilated by a group of excellent young poets who brought about a second "Golden Age." Jorge Guillén, Lorca, Vicente Aleixandre, who won the Nobel Prize in 1977, and Alberti are probably the best known of these. Machado had been a self-conscious poet from the beginning of his career, but at this time the cultural situation and his interest in philosophical aesthetics further stimulated his theoretical reflections. From 1924 until his death prose predominates over verse in his writings; yet during this time he wrote some of his finest poetry, including "Canciones a Guiomar" (Songs to Guiomar), some of the poems in *De un cancionero apócrifo,* and "El crimen fue en Granada" (The Crime Was in Granada, 1936).

Guiomar was the poet Pilar de Valderrama, with whom Machado had been in love since 1928. The relationship as it is described in the poems was pure, courtly; Guiomar is called "my goddess," "Madonna," and, since her name was Pilar, "The Virgin of the Pilar." Pilar is a famous sanctuary in Zaragoza, Spain, and at one point she is referred to as "Madonna del Pilar." This love cannot be consummated in marriage or sexual intimacy; instead it thrives on distance, which breeds intellectual probing into the nature of love and also generates a measure of irony when the poet considers his age: he cannot believe that a beautiful young woman could be attracted to him.

The poems contain elements of deep emotion. Guiomar is his Dulcinea, the emblem of all the poet's aspirations:

Everything in this light of April is transparent;
Everything in the today of yesterday, the still
that in its mature hours
time sings and counts,
becomes fused in only one melody,
which is a choir of evenings and dawns.
For you, Guiomar, this nostalgia of mine.

(CLXXIII)

Nature in its pure beauty and transparency and the flow of time repressed in an instant of unchanging love and enthusiasm bring about the poet's experience of eternity, of the "essential."

Other poems in *De un cancionero apócrifo* are like the kernels of philosophical reflection in verse, without losing their value as poems. The most famous of these is the sonnet "El gran cero" (The Great Zero):

When the being that is created nothingness
and rested, for he well deserved it
then the day had night, and man had company
in the absence of his lover.

(CLXVII)

The being that created nothingness is not God but organic life, which eventually evolved into human reason. Human reason projects all its specific notions on the idea of being, which is not concrete and which acts as a blackboard on which all ideas are inscribed. Thus, nothingness gave origin to philosophy and to intellectual life in general, and since then man has not needed a companion; he speaks to himself in his loneliness. The poet's task, however, is to return from the cold, universal blackboard to the human experience of life as love, death, and forgetfulness. The combina-

tion of prose and poetry of which *De un cancionero apócrifo* consists presents the metaphysical and aesthetic ideas of a fictional Professor Abel Martin and twelve other "apocryphal" poets.

In 1936 the Spanish Civil War brought anarchy to Spain, and hideous crimes took place on both sides. The poet Lorca, conspicuous for his cultural contributions during the period of the Republic, fell victim to Fascist hatred in August of that year. Machado wrote a poem to his memory, condemning the crime as madness, and pointing the finger at Lorca's native city as a curse: "The crime was in Granada, in his Granada." During the war the poet wrote a few more compositions, generally related to the contemporary situation, and many articles. Some of these writings were published in 1937 under the title *La guerra* (The War).

From his first book in 1903 to the last verses written during the Civil War, Machado persevered in a search for a richer poetry while adhering to the same theoretical idea and ideal of poetry. The basic idea and its variations constitute Machado's poetics.

WRITINGS ON POETICS

Not only was Machado conscious of the assumptions of his own poetry; he was also a reader of the classics and held a master's degree in philosophy. As a philosopher he was a more than occasional reader of Gottfried Leibniz, Immanuel Kant, Schopenhauer, Bergson, and Max Scheler. In 1927, when Martin Heidegger became famous in Europe for his book *Sein und Zeit* (*Being and Time*), Machado found in existential philosophy reinforcement for his idea that poetry was "word in time." Machado's reflections on the nature of poetry reach such a level of rigor and originality that even today they must be considered a valid contribution to aesthetics and critical theory. The poet expressed his theoretical ideas in short prologues to new editions of his books, beginning with the prologue to *Páginas es-*

cogidas; in several of his poems and poetic aphorisms; in a book of notes written from 1914 through 1925 known as *Los complementarios* (The Complementaries, 1957); in *De un cancionero apócrifo*; and in *Juan de Mairena: Sentencias, donaires, apuntes, y recuerdos de un profesor apócrifo* (Juan de Mairena: Epigrams, Maxims, Memoranda, and Memoirs of an Apocryphal Professor, 1936).

Four notions summarize Machado's idea of poetry: intuition, concept, the word in time, and essence. His criticisms of styles that displeased him refer to his ideas about these four notions. The two main targets of his criticism were the baroque and the contemporary avant-garde movements. According to Machado, the baroque poets generally produced "rhymed logic," not true poetry. Pedro Calderón de la Barca in particular makes ingenious plays with words, but true sentiment is not visible in his poems. The young poets of the 1920's are liable to the same objection. They searched for audacious, novel images, but according to Machado the image is secondary in poetry; the image is external, while poetry must express a sentiment that is at once lucid and true, not just a superficial feeling. Machado believed that the young poets, following the trend of what Ortega y Gasset called in 1925 "the dehumanization of art," wrote a poetry of concepts, not of intuition.

The distinction Machado makes at the beginning of his career between intuition and concept must be related to the same distinction in Benedetto Croce's *Estetica come scienza dell'espresione e linguistica generale* (*Aesthetic as Science of Expression and General Linguistic,* 1898). For Croce poetry—indeed literature—originates in intuition. Intuition is not a sort of instantaneous hunch; it means that the word is not a mere vehicle of ideas but is rather an expression that conveys an intellectual message, establishes emotional communication between writer and reader, and shows its musical and pictorial content, that is, its sensory and structural capabilities. Ideas can also be present in a poem, but they should be dramatized within a dialogue or in the actions of the characters (in their emotional communication). In poetry the word radiates in its full musical and pictorial value. As Heidegger put it years later, the world (the poem) causes the earth (the word) to be itself, to reverberate as word. In everyday communication the word becomes mere vehicle; in poetry, on the other hand, it becomes truly the word.

This conviction seems to inform the following statement of Machado's about the reading of his own poetry: "A poet, when he writes his verses, is always in agreement with himself, even if the verses are a failure; but, after a few years, the man who judges his own work is very far from the man who produced it" (Prologue to *Páginas escogidas*). The poet writes in unity with his intuition, but the poet as reader uses only his intellect and can no longer reproduce the whole of the intuition.

The distinction between the simple idea and the totality of the poet's participation (intuition) led Machado to define his own poetry and poetry in general as "word in time." In 1917 he recalled his poetics of 1902 by distinguishing himself from Rubén Darío, specifying the difference in the following words:

> For me the poetic element was neither the word for its musical value, nor color, line or a bunch of sensations, but a profound palpitation of the spirit; what the soul puts if it puts anything, or what it says if it says anything, with its own voice, in contact with the world.
>
> (Prologue to *Soledades*)

Intuition, time, a true voice in contrast to a mere echo—that was poetry for Machado. The opposition between intuition and concept and its correlative, the opposition between time and the atemporal, could also be formulated in the terms of the Bergson's basic ideas about intuition and the intellect, time and space. Machado assimilated Bergson's ideas, but his notion of time encompasses the intimate and the external, the personal and the social, and the instant in the trajectory of human existence. For this reason Machado saw himself more as a precursor of Heidegger than as a follower of Bergson.

Machado expressed the application of his poetics to the actual writing of poetry in the following words written on 15 June 1914:

> The adjective and the noun,
> eddies of the limpid water,
> are accidents of the verb
> in the lyrical grammar,
> the today that will be tomorrow,
> of the yesterday that is still.
>
> (CLXIV, vii)

This was my aesthetics in 1902. It has nothing to do with Verlaine's poetics. My aim was simply to put lyric poetry within time, and as far removed as possible from space. "From the imperfect tense / Romance originated in Castile."

(*Los complementarios*, p. 35)

The "genuine" Castilian epic, the romance, was a narrative poem in which the past of the verb was commonly expressed with the imperfect. This poetic theory explains Machado's preference for the past tense, especially for the imperfect. It also explains his attempt to revive the romance and his criticism of the baroque as a poetry of space and of the intellect.

Juan de Mairena is a book of philosophical reflections that Machado began to publish in newspapers in 1934. Mairena is a professor of gymnastics who also teaches rhetoric. The rhetoric class allows him to engage in discussion of the basic questions of life: metaphysics, religion, politics, and poetics. One day the humorous teacher gives his students the assignment to write a poem on boiling an egg. The students waste their energy describing the shiny pots and other external circumstances, using nouns and adjectives. The professor comments: "We forgot the egg because we never truly saw it, were unable to live inside the whole process of its cooking and make it our own." Some student should have written:

"and the egg was boiling." Word in time means identification, the word revealing reality.

Simplicity of description put Machado at odds with the avant-garde schools of poetry. He criticized their obsession with metaphors and images and the abstract, atemporal character of their poetry. Machado wrote a summary of his poetics for *Poesía española* (Spanish Poetry, 1932), an anthology of contemporary poets prepared by Gerardo Diego, another representative of the new generation. In it we read:

> I think . . . that poetry is the essential word in time. Modern poetry, which in my opinion begins, at least in part, with Edgardo Poe, has been until our own days the history of the great problem that the poet faces in view of two imperatives that are to a certain extent contradictory: essentiality and temporality.
>
> (p. 149)

Logic is the discipline of "the essential," of the atemporal, while poetry tries to capture temporality. In order to make his thoughts clear, he uses Santa Teresa's phrase: to immerse oneself "in the very waters of life."

Temporality does not exclude "the essence"; on the contrary, temporality means the penetration into the core of nature or of experience: hence the fusion with landscape in *Soledades*, the fusion of Castile and Andalusia with the life and history of their people. Nature is not merely described; it is an ingredient of the individual's or of the people's existence.

The new synthesis of the temporal and the essential leads Machado to abandon the traditional romance in the imperfect tense in order to assimilate popular poetry, which, in an atemporal present, is no less temporal and intuitive. Temporal becomes synonymous with sincere, something seen from inside, something embraced. Hence the connection between the popular songs and classicism. Machado wrote: "Poet, rather than old romance, songs of little girls."

The fusion of temporality and "essentiality"

explains the double effort he made as his poetry evolved: toward an ever-greater simplicity and toward ever-greater authenticity. As Machado opened himself to the multiple possibilities of true poetry, he added the social element to the search for intimate truth, associating popular poetry with children's songs and with the beautiful traditional songs of Andalusia. But since 1917 political and social problems progressively attracted the attention of intellectuals, and Machado ended his career by envisioning a poetry that remains truly poetic and at the same time socially constructive. The poetic element is outside the individual: Jorge Meneses, one of his apocryphal poets, devises a *máquina de trovar,* a sort of computer that writes poems. The poet of the "desolations and monotonies" in *Soledades* has gone full circle from "I sing" to "language sings."

Machado's poetics was, like his poetry, an enthusiastic search for sense. Machado, like his fictional double Juan de Mairena, had some clear ideas and was to a certain extent dogmatic. But his clearest idea was awareness of his limitation: he espoused a sound and exemplary skepticism. His fictional aliases display a marvelous art of irony that is the most remarkable characteristic of their creator. Irony is the lucid perception of our own limitations and the limitations of our objects, and Machado's prose is an excellent example of ironical writing. The only characters Machado treated with disdain are the fanatic and the hypocrite.

Selected Bibliography

EDITIONS

INDIVIDUAL WORKS

POETRY
Soledades. Madrid, 1903.
Soledades, galerías, y otros poemas. Madrid, 1907.
Campos de Castilla. Madrid, 1912.
Páginas escogidas. Madrid, 1917.

Poesías completas. Madrid, 1917; 2d ed., 1928; 4th, last authorized ed., 1936.
Nuevas canciones. Madrid, 1924.
Poesía española. (Prepared by Gerardo Diego.) Madrid, 1932. This anthology of contemporary Spanish poetry includes Machado's summary of his poetics.

PROSE
Juan de Mairena: Sentencias, donaires, apuntes, y recuerdos de un profesor apócrifo. Madrid, 1936.
La guerra. Madrid, 1937.
Los complementarios. Buenos Aires, 1957; Madrid, 1971.
"Carras á Guiomar." In Pilar de Valderrama, *Si, soy Guiomar.* Madrid, 1981.

COLLECTED WORKS
Obras completas de Manuel y Antonio Machado. 4 vols. Madrid, 1947.
Poesie di Antonio Machado: Studi introdduttivi, testo criticamente riveduto. Milano, 1959. An excellent bilingual edition.
Antonio Machado: Prosas y poesías olvidadas. Paris, 1964.
Obras: Poesia y prosa. Edited by Guillermo de Torre. Buenos Aires, 1964.

MODERN EDITIONS

Campos de Castilla. Edited by Rafael Ferreres. Madrid, 1970.
Juan de Mairena. Edited by José María Valverde. Madrid, 1972.
Nuevas canciones y De un cancionero apócrifo. Edited by José María Valverde. Madrid, 1971.
Soledades. Edited by Rafael Ferreres. Madrid, 1968.
Soledades, galerias, y otros poemas. Edited by Geoffrey Ribbans. Madrid, 1983.

TRANSLATIONS

Antonio Machado: Selected Poems. Translated by Alan S. Trueblood. Cambridge, Mass., 1982.
Juan de Mairena. Translated by Ben Belitt. Berkeley and Los Angeles, 1963.
Selected Poems by Antonio Machado. Translated by Betty Jean Craige. Baton Rouge, La., 1978.

BIOGRAPHICAL AND CRITICAL STUDIES

Aguirre, J. M. *Antonio Machado, poeta simbolista.* Madrid, 1973.

ANTONIO MACHADO

Alonso, Dámaso. Several studies in *Obras completas,* vol. 4. Madrid, 1975.

Caravaggi, Giovanni. *I paesaggi emotivi di Antonio Machado: Appunti sulla genesi dell'intimismo.* Bologna, 1969.

Cerezo Galán, Pedro. *Palabra en el tiempo: Poesía y filosofía en Antonio Machado.* Madrid, 1975.

Chaves, Julio César. *Itinerario de don Antonio Machado.* Madrid, 1968.

Cobos, Pablo de A. *El pensamiento de Antonio Machado en "Juan de Mairena."* Madrid, 1971.

Espina, Concha. *De Antonio Machado a su grande y secreto amor.* Madrid, 1950.

Guillén, Claudio. "Stylistics of Silence." In *Literature as System.* Princeton, N.J., 1971.

Gullón, Ricardo. *Una poética para Antonio Machado.* Madrid, 1970.

Hutman, Norma L. *Machado: A Dialogue with Time.* Albuquerque, N.M., 1969.

López Morillas, Juan. "Antonio Machado's Temporal Interpretation of Poetry." *Journal of Aesthetics and Art Criticism* 6:161–171 (1947).

Machado, Antonio. *Expediente académico y personal.* Madrid, 1975.

Machado, José. *Últimas soledades del poeta Antonio Machado.* Madrid, 1977.

McVan, Alice J. *Antonio Machado.* New York, 1959.

Pérez Ferrero, Miguel. *Vida de Antonio Machado y Manuel.* Madrid, 1973.

Pradal Rodríguez, Gabriel. "Antonio Machado: Vida y obra." *Revista Hispánica Moderna* 15:1–80 (1949).

Ribbans, Geoffrey. "Antonio Machado's *Soledades:* A Critical Study." *Hispanic Review* 30:194–215 (1962).

Ruiz de Conde, Justina. *Antonio Machado y Guiomar.* Madrid, 1964.

Sánchez Barbudo, Antonio. *Los poemas de Antonio Machado: Los temas, el sentimiento, y las expresión.* Barcelona, 1967.

Serrano Poncela, Segundo. *Antonio Machado (1875–1939): El hombre, el poeta, el pensador.* Madrid, 1980.

Socrate, Mario. *Il linguaggio filosofico della poesia di Antonio Machado.* Padua, 1972.

Tuñón de Lara, Manuel. *Antonio Machado, poeta del pueblo.* Barcelona, 1967.

Valverde, José María. *Antonio Machado.* Madrid, 1975.

Young, Howard T. *The Victorious Expression: A Study of Four Contemporary Spanish Poets.* Madison, Wis., 1964.

Zubiría, Ramón de. *La poesía de Antonio Machado.* Madrid, 1969.

CIRIACO MORÓN ARROYO

RAINER MARIA RILKE

(1875–1926)

IN 1927 THE Austrian novelist Robert Musil said of Rainer Maria Rilke, who had died at the age of fifty-one on 29 December 1926: "This great lyric poet did nothing other than to make the German poem perfect." For all the debate Rilke's work has generated since then, Musil's judgment retains its suggestiveness. Rilke's "perfection" can, in fact, be understood in at least three ways. First, there is the extraordinary logic of his biography: Rilke saw his vocation as that of a poet and simply refused to compromise for any reason, not for human relationships and certainly not for an ordinary job to support his writing. As a result he can sometimes seem rather precious and aloof in his huge correspondence: he makes emotionally committed statements only to withdraw subsequently, through stylization and careful modification of his own words, into a self-absorbed and self-justifying artistic isolation. Some of his letters to wealthy (usually female) admirers are actually thinly disguised requests for money; but when one thinks of today's research scientists and their open dependence on public grants, one has to concede that Rilke was simply assuming a comparable public significance for poetry, and indeed his decorous letters can be read as quite businesslike grant proposals. There is in fact something daring about Rilke's determination to live exclusively as a poet, for at the moments in his life when he felt most tempted to make a full commitment to a woman, he made it very clear that he was not an ascetic, that his renunciations were genuine and painful. Rilke had no preconceived model of a poetic vocation. What he did know was that poetry, in order to be great, must speak of the entire historical experience of an age— and that the poetry of his time, with its inherited hostility to middle-class civilization, was gradually ceasing to be effectively rebellious and becoming merely decorative, a voluntary exile from history. Poetic language either registered every nuance of feeling and perception, or fell silent, paralyzed by the fear that poetic subjectivity had become detached not only from the norm of experience in industrial society, but from the very objects words sought to designate. This so-called language crisis (*Sprachkrise*) was articulated by many turn-of-the-century writers, notably Hugo von Hofmannsthal in his "Chandos Letter" of 1902.

In order to "perfect" his poetic vocation, then, Rilke had to forge a language that would embody precisely the historical experience of language's failure. His success in doing so is what Musil most clearly refers to when he says that Rilke made "the German poem perfect." For Rilke achieved an astounding linguistic virtuosity, an ability to make the German language burst through the limits of what had been expressible in the nineteenth century. This achievement is comparable only to that of Johann Wolfgang von Goethe and Friedrich

Hölderlin at the end of the eighteenth century. These poets had emancipated the language from a provincialism of stylized feeling and tasteful word-painting. A century later German poetry seemed mired in a new provincialism, a self-conscious intimacy dissolving all clarity into gestures of dream; and to a large extent it was Rilke who, by opening words simultaneously to the "hardness" of external objects and to the perceptual fragmentation threatening human subjectivity, propelled German poetry into a full-fledged international modernism. Only the very greatest modernist poets—Stéphane Mallarmé, Paul Valéry, T. S. Eliot, Ezra Pound, Wallace Stevens, Boris Pasternak, Federico García Lorca—can be considered Rilke's equals. And the remarkable fact is that Rilke's early writings are marked by the worst provincialism of the 1890's. Although with hindsight one can see the origins of the poet's mature preoccupations and motifs, Rilke's early collections (in his ambitiousness he published too much too soon, as he himself rapidly realized) are emotionally decadent and linguistically diffuse. But this very weakness is intimately linked to the miracle of Rilke's "perfected" style. For very early on he realized that he could take nothing for granted, that it was not just a matter of learning how to express himself: his expressive goals were completely inseparable from his technical needs, his poet's vocation. His personal history thus coincided with the history of the poetically possible in his time; clearly perceiving the weakness of his earliest publications, Rilke took the crucial second step of treating language as raw material, words as entities to be isolated, molded, polished. Rilke's linguistic virtuosity is thus rarely an end in itself. It is born of historical necessity, the necessity that linked poetry decisively to the visual arts (the works of Auguste Rodin, Paul Cézanne, Pablo Picasso), the necessity we have come to know as modernism. For the way out of the language crisis of the 1890's did indeed prove to be the epochal shift from an aural and suggestive to a visual and sculptural model of language, or, in other words, from impressionism to expressionism.

If Musil is right, then Rilke's bringing the German poem to perfection has a third kind of significance, as an ongoing provocation of the question: what is poetry and what is its function in the twentieth century? This question involves more than just the traditional assertion of premier rank for that which is perfect. Raphael is often called a perfect painter and is in no danger of losing his high rank; but there are epochs and schools of painting for which Raphael is without interest. With Rilke indifference seems impossible. In 1910 the violent expressionist Georg Heym termed Rilke's poetry effeminate; and the years immediately after Rilke's death are dominated by assertions, like that of Bertolt Brecht in 1927, that "all great poems have documentary value." In other words, Rilke's uncompromising insistence on the autonomous function of art is confronted in our century by equally uncompromising points of view that subordinate art to social claims, whether humanistic or frankly political, and regard the idea of artistic autonomy as meaningless. The very notion of artistic perfection is viewed as a mask for conservative politics. This conflict is in a sense perennial. What is new is the emancipation of both sides from overtly religious programs. Rilke's aesthetic absolutism uses religious motifs but refuses all gestures of belief; conversely, when his detractors attack Rilke's emphasis on individual isolation and social stability as inherently conservative and elitist, a gesture of belief is implicit in the attack, namely the belief in the need for social change.

Interestingly, although Rilke would hardly reject the labels of conservatism and elitism, his poetic achievement is such that young, "political" writers, like W. H. Auden in the 1930's, repeatedly drew nourishment from its integrity and linguistic radicalism—in short, from its perfection. In a time when the prestige of literature is becoming a dim memory, we only have to open Rilke's texts to be challenged again to think and feel on a large scale.

For although the theory of aesthetic autonomy was central to Rilke's own productivity, it is in no sense a prerequisite to reading him. And the essential reason is that Rilke repeatedly staged, in his poems, the very crisis of value and language for which the texts themselves are to embody momentary solutions. Rilke has been linked to every kind of politics and philosophy, not because he was an original political or philosophical thinker, but because his writing is so intimately attuned to the new century's intellectual currents that the agendas of all the various disciplines enter his work by historical osmosis. For Rilke the poem makes its claim to irrefutable value only through emotional, perceptual, and linguistic struggle; without such struggle there is no viable poem. A poem neither records nor expresses; rather, it uses a moment of intense awareness to invoke the entire set of questions as to what feeling and observing, expressing and recording, involve exactly and how they are intertwined.

René Maria Rilke (he began calling himself Rainer in 1897) was born in Prague on 4 December 1875. His childhood was characterized by strong contradictions that haunted his later life and led to a deeply ambivalent attitude toward childhood (as inaccessible innocence and well-remembered horror) in his poetry. On the one hand his overprotective mother dressed him in girls' clothes for even longer than was the custom at the time; and on the other hand his father insisted that he be sent to a military academy, from 1886–1891, where mindless discipline and spiritual desolation permanently affected the poet. Moreover his parents separated in 1885. One can see that he internalized these clashing experiences as poetic sources: he idealized women, particularly their capacity for love, while transforming his wholly negative experience at the military school into a quest for supposedly noble ancestors—and into an allegorical celebration of the hero figure. The latter interest resulted in Rilke's biggest "best-seller," a prose poem entitled *De Weise von Liebe und Tod des Cornets Christoph Rilke* (*The Lay of the Love and Death of the Cornet Christoph Rilke*, written in 1899, first published in 1906).

Rilke's biographer Wolfgang Leppmann terms his education "fragmentary": he spent a year at business school in Linz (1891–1892), then studied privately—and successfully—back in Prague from 1892–1895 to achieve his diploma. The most important event of these years, however, was the growing realization that his vocation was literature (his first published book, *Leben und Lieder* [Life and Songs], came in 1894). In 1896 he moved to a genuine metropolis, Munich, where in May 1897 there occurred the decisive encounter of Rilke's life, the meeting with Lou Andreas-Salomé, a married woman of Russian descent who, already a prominent intellectual, had been in Friedrich Nietzsche's circle and was to become a leading student of Sigmund Freud. Rilke and Lou were lovers for three years and remained close friends and correspondents throughout the poet's life. They made two trips to Russia together (in 1899 and 1900), visiting eminences such as Leo Tolstoy as well as the sites of Lou's girlhood. Most important about these trips was the impact of Russian religious services on Rilke: while not inducing belief in him, these ardent ceremonies can be linked to an enduring theme in his poetry, the sense that there exists an ancient, vital, communal way of life no longer imaginable in Western European cities. The Russian experience is fundamental to Rilke's first important poems, contained in *Das Stundenbuch* (*The Book of Hours*), written in three parts in 1899, 1901, and 1903, and published in 1905. Essential to these lyrics is the notion of "building God": the imagery for such building is drawn from the literal building of cathedrals as well as from figurative structuring of an ascetic life (the first part of the work is entitled *Das Buch vom mönchischen Leben* [*The Book of Monastic Life*]). But the central impulse of these poems, in the context of Rilke's mature achievement, is the metaphysical claim they implicitly make for language as such. The texts' religiosity can quickly be decoded as aesthetic ambition: poetic language is to fuse silence and ceremony, individual and community, daily living and ritualized dying.

In 1900 Rilke joined an artists' colony in Worpswede, near Bremen. There he met two young women, Clara Westhoff (whom he married in 1901) and Paula Becker, who married another member of the colony, Otto Modersohn, and whose death in 1907 (from childbirth complications) resulted in one of Rilke's most moving long poems, "Requiem für eine Freundin" ("Requiem for a Friend," 1908). Although they never divorced, Rilke and Clara did not live together long: their daughter, Ruth, was born in December 1901, but in August 1902 Rilke moved to Paris alone. He and Clara maintained friendly relations and were together from time to time throughout his life; some see Rilke's marriage as "liberated" while others view it as typifying his emotional limitations. In any case the move to Paris crystallized two enduring themes of his life and work: on the one hand the horror and anonymity of mass existence in a metropolis (in vivid contrast to the communal vision of Russian religion); and on the other hand the ideal of the artist's existence as a ceaseless and solitary working relationship with the human and natural environment. This ideal was embodied for Rilke in the sculpture of Rodin, whom he met in 1902 and whose secretary he became for a time in 1905–1906. These two themes dominate in counterpoint the great achievements of Rilke's Paris years: the dark, obsessive prose work, often called a decisive influence on the modern novel, entitled *Die Aufzeichnungen des Malte Laurids Brigge* (*The Notebooks of Malte Laurids Brigge*), completed and published in 1910; and the sculpturally conceived, linguistically taut *Neue Gedichte* (*New Poems*), published in two parts in 1907 and 1908.

The contrast between the fluid softness of *The Book of Hours* and the rigorous flexibility of *New Poems* is striking; an intermediate collection, however, *Das Buch der Bilder* (*The Book of Pictures,* first edition 1902, second edition 1906), illuminates the continuity of Rilke's maturing process. It is tempting yet slightly misleading to adopt the poet's own excited perspective on his goals, emphasizing the production of poems as linguistic objects, as self-contained, as hard and existent as ordinary "things." As we shall see, the problem of how and whether language expresses the external world, as well as Rilke's increasing insistence on a text's social-didactic function, were ceaselessly being worked through, as much in the "thinglike" poems as in their rhapsodic predecessors.

Already in the Paris years Rilke became a restless wanderer, setting a pattern for his poet's existence, which assigned a representative quality to the sites he visited and the countries he lived in. Rilke came to discern in this geographical network a Europe that had once existed and must urgently be reimagined. An entire book by Eudo Mason has been devoted to the intricate nature of Rilke's Europe. As his fame grew, the poet himself became conscious that his evident rootlessness opened the possibility of a symbolic rescue of European values, that the countries most important to him (Russia, Spain, the Scandinavian countries) were, despite or perhaps because of their location on Europe's periphery, spiritually central to the European idea, as Rilke saw it. Rilke's attachment to Italy was not as strong as that of many writers; and his attitude toward both Germany and his native Austria ranged from ambivalence to hostility. He disliked both militaristic nationalism and the bureaucratized soullessness he saw in the final decrepitude of the Habsburg Empire. He seems to have sought a valuation of national roots (such as he perceived in Russian religion) fused with a cosmopolitan culture. Indeed he thought he discerned such a fusion, near the end of his life, in the program of Benito Mussolini, whom he praised in a controversial 1925 letter. For Rilke himself, however, "roots" were out of the question; the poet's vocation necessitated both travel and tranquil isolation. The most important of the aristocratic ladies willing to help him achieve these goals was Princess Marie von Thurn und Taxis, whose invitation in 1912 to her castle at Duino, near Trieste, proved decisive. There he wrote the first poems in the *Duineser Elegien* (*Duino Elegies,* 1923), which he could not complete as a set until 1922; immediately, however, he realized that they were to be his life's crowning task.

In retrospect Rilke's wanderings through Europe during the decade 1910–1920 can be seen as the basis of his final "perfect" achievement. The experience itself was a prolonged crisis for the poet, a tormented awareness that he and the civilization he cherished had lost their way, perhaps definitively. Rilke himself felt that he had identified the poetic enterprise too closely with the visual arts; both in his essays on Rodin (1903 and 1907) and in his rhapsodic reception of a Cézanne exhibition (documented in letters to Clara, October 1907), he had developed an intensely spatial vision of art as a kind of colonization of the physical environment, an absorption into itself of wind, gravity, atmosphere. He began to think, in the crisis years, that his concentration on the visual had somehow atrophied his capacity to tap the traditional sources of poetry, particularly his capacity to love. Thus he wrote in a famous admonition to himself in the poem "Wendung" ("Turning-Point," 1914):

> *Werk des Gesichts ist getan,*
> *tue nun Herz-werk.*

> The work of the eyes is done,
> do now the work of the heart.
> (2. 83)[1]

In literary terms we can identify a powerful new influence: Friedrich Hölderlin, whose po-

etry was being rediscovered and reissued in a modern edition by Norbert von Hellingrath in these years before 1914. The impact of Hölderlin's hymnic, syntactically complex, and open-ended style can be seen everywhere in Rilke's work at this time, notably in the first two Duino Elegies. But the demands of a hymnic, cosmological poetry were particularly difficult for Rilke to fulfill after his close identification with Rodin's craftsman ideal. Moreover he was becoming aware of emotional limitations in himself, habits of withdrawal that seemed to condemn him to a sterile rather than productive isolation. Did the artist's vocation *have* to mean a deliberate stunting of life feelings, as Rilke's near contemporaries Thomas Mann and Franz Kafka thought? In the early months of 1914 Rilke made his greatest attempt at "breaking out" of his self-imposed emotional solitude, in an intense involvement with the pianist Magda von Hattingberg ("Benvenuta"). But his rigorous poetic vocation was by then too clearly established: the more Rilke imagined spending his life with her, the more Benvenuta became frightened at the demands such a role would place on her, and so she gently disengaged herself.

And then there was World War I. Rilke joined in the general enthusiasm for the war in August 1914, writing the "Fünf Gesänge" ("Five Songs") in the hymnic mode of Hölderlin, for whom the national idea had been important at the time of the Napoleonic Wars. But his disillusionment was immediate, and Rilke became an explicit pacifist. Drafted into the Austrian army in late 1915, he was spared active service at the front thanks to the efforts of friends such as his publisher, Anton Kippenberg, and his wife, Katharina, and influential writers such as Hofmannsthal and Karl Kraus. Instead he was assigned duties deemed appropriate to a writer at the Imperial Archives, where he was to engage in "hero-trimming"— rewriting news dispatches so that the Austrian cause would appear just and flourishing. But there was clearly no basis for accommodation

---

[1]All references in the text are made to the authoritative six-volume critical edition edited by Ernst Zinn (1955–1966).

between Rilke and the Austrian army. Released from service in June 1916, Rilke returned to Munich, his base during most of the war years.

Since leaving Paris in 1910, he had been traveling more and more; his growing fame (and the generosity of Kippenberg) made such travel financially possible. But his increasing mobility and his creative difficulties were intertwined. As the war dragged on, Rilke became ever less able to write, ever more aware that this horrific transformation of the world, far from being a release from stagnation (as it continued to appear to the younger, expressionist generation), threatened everything he valued. The inner link between his poetic language and the historical moment, which had so nourished his achievement, now became a heavy destiny: Rilke simply could not work amid the destruction; indeed, Leppmann says he spent the year 1916–1917 "in a state of suspended animation." Like others at this time, Rilke became interested in occult matters as a temporary escape from the relentless rhythm of impersonal, technological death. There was a brief creative spell in November 1915, when Rilke completed the Fourth Duino Elegy; and the posthumous publication of the poems and sketches he worked on in these years reveals continuous experimentation, a quest for the new language he had glimpsed in 1912 (I shall be analyzing this process in some detail). But Rilke came to see the war years as a necessary vocational torment, a time of negation and sterility both in himself and in the world; if he could fully internalize this negativity, then, he felt, he might find his way forward to a historically adequate language. Always he resisted suggestions from his friends that he undergo psychoanalysis (although he met Freud on several occasions, for the last time in December 1915). As Rilke put it, if they drove out his devils, they would drive out his angels also. This might be acceptable if he were to give up writing. But writing was his very essence; he had no other existence.

After the end of the war Rilke remained for nine months in Munich, still unproductive, and ambivalent about the workers' revolution erupting around him. On the one hand he was impressed by the new ability of ordinary people to view social structures with clarity and by their willingness to cooperate and utilize talent purposefully, all of which suggested to him the return of the communal idea, of a large social vision. But on the other hand he was appalled by the violence, the ruthlessness, the dominance of an opportunistic minority; without gentleness, without spiritual change, there could be no "revolution" as Rilke understood the term. And how could these qualities be expected after the years of senseless killing? In 1919 Rilke and his friends became preoccupied with the need to find him an appropriate place to live, a place where the "double rescue" could be achieved: the personal rescue of everything Rilke felt unfinished and open about his past, particularly the past embodied in the unfinished Duino Elegies; and the reclaiming in language of certain stabilities of prewar Europe, particularly the high valuation of art and nature as key sources of human inspiration. The country of destiny turned out to be Switzerland, where Rilke was invited to give a series of lectures in the fall of 1919. After extensive travels and a return visit to Paris it seemed Rilke had found, in November 1920, the right place to live—Castle Berg am Irchel, near Zurich. The continuity with the past and the quietness of the present seemed ideal, yet Rilke still could not settle down fully. He began translating Valéry's poems into German, an important exercise that culminated not only in a friendship with Valéry but also in his own series of poems in French, written in his last years. He left Castle Berg in May 1921 and, with his last significant lover, Baladine Klossowska ("Merline"), began to look for a replacement home. Near Sierre in the Valais region they stumbled upon what turned out to be the ideal place, a small thirteenth-century castle named Muzot, lacking water or electricity. Rilke's friends did everything possible in terms of money and creature comforts to make this new "relationship" work, and gradually, as 1921 wore on, Rilke and Muzot developed a complete symbiosis.

Then, in the single month of February 1922, fulfillment came: Rilke completed the ten Duino Elegies in a sustained burst of inspiration. To the public at the time the miracle must have seemed even greater than it does now, since Rilke had published virtually nothing since the *New Poems* in 1907–1908 and the novel *Malte* in 1910. Although he had written important individual poems, he was dominated by the idea of the completed cycle. (Musil's notion of perfectibility certainly applies to Rilke's view of himself.)

Of the Elegies themselves, the first two had been written at Duino in 1912, the Third in Paris in 1913, the Fourth in Munich in 1915; preliminary versions of the Sixth and Tenth also existed. But some of the most astonishing were both conceived and completed in these weeks: the Fifth, with its harrowing evocation of the inauthentic lives of circus people (Rilke had been profoundly moved by the famous Picasso painting *Les saltimbanques*); and the Seventh and Ninth, with their grandiose development of the themes of "rescuing" past values and experience and of fulfilling the world's secret, innermost longings by reproducing things as "invisible" poetic language. And what Rilke had not anticipated was the simultaneous production, in the three weeks between 2 and 23 February, of fifty-five *Sonette an Orpheus* (*Sonnets to Orpheus,* 1923). Many regard these poems as even greater than the Elegies because they are pure "achievement" (*Leistung,* a favorite Rilkean term), containing the high aspirations of the Elegies and the immediacy of a localized event within the disciplined parameters of the sonnet form. To be sure, these sonnets are not rhetorically symmetrical in the manner of Shakespeare's sonnets. Often the outpouring of images is so overwhelming that the reader, as it were, "forgets" the sonnet form. But looking back from the fourteenth line, one sees the balancing procedures, the structure that sustains the flow.

Rilke saw the sonnets as a "gift," while the Elegies were the completion of his life's central task. In his last years he engaged several times in explication of the Elegies, particularly of the controversial figure of the Angel, who is to be understood as an image of perfection always already achieved, in no sense as a mediating figure in the Christian tradition; the essential text in this respect is the long letter from Rilke to his Polish translator, Witold Hulewicz (13 November 1925). Opinions will always differ about a work making such uncompromisingly cosmic claims as the Elegies; but there can be no doubt that Rilke's life and work culminate in them and that a viable Rilke interpretation cannot sidestep their less accessible passages. In his last years Rilke concentrated on short poems, not often sonnets but clearly developing the concise style of the *Sonnets to Orpheus.* Intellectually the late poems are even more compressed, while the experience celebrated (*Rühmen* [to celebrate; to praise] is another key word for Rilke) often has a new, delightful simplicity, an absorption in the seasonal processes around Muzot. Rilke also wrote a large number of poems in French (over two hundred pages in the critical edition, edited by Ernst Zinn); these can be readily linked to his growing "Europeanness," his awareness of his own representative role as bearer of civilized values in a world threatened by political turbulence and ill-understood technology. ("All past achievements are threatened by the machine" is the opening line of one of the *Sonnets to Orpheus.*)

Rilke's biographer, Leppmann, argues that the exhaustion felt by the poet at the completion of the Elegies lasted in a sense the rest of his life. He continued to sleep unusually long hours after February 1922, and his health became increasingly problematic. At the end of 1923 he experienced a real collapse, probably the first impact of the leukemia that killed him three years later. Thereafter, periods of energy and productivity alternated with spells of depression and visits to the sanatorium at Val-Mont, where Rilke died in December 1926. For a poet whose texts continuously invoke the need to integrate the processes of living and dying within consciousness, the preparation for his death was typically complex. Thus he wrote a famous epitaph for himself, a masterly drawing of dying into the infinite life-symbol of the rose as

> reiner Widerspruch, Lust,
> Niemandes Schlaf zu sein. . . .
>
> pure contradiction, delight
> in being no one's sleep. . . .
>
> (2.185)

But a text also survives from the month of his death, his very last poem, which concludes thus:

Bin ich es noch, der da unkenntlich brennt?
  Erinnerungen
reiss ich nicht herein.
O Leben, Leben: Draussensein.
Und ich in Lohe. Niemand der mich kennt.

Am I still the one burning there unrecognizably?
I cannot grasp memories into myself.
O life, life: to be outside.
And I being consumed by fire. No one there who
  knows me.

(2.511)

Rilke experienced an intense fear of death, and he felt the urge to avoid facing it that is common to us all. But he was not untrue to the life goals projected by his poetic production, and at the same time his despair neither cancels nor is cancelled by the aesthetic perfection of the rose epitaph. The only way Rilke could reach such perfection was through enduring the long seasons of sterility as well as drawing out the sweetness of the creative moment.

The fact that Rilke withheld from publication so many complete and fragmentary poems written between 1906 and 1926 gives the reader a special opening into his world and his cosmology. For the more Rilke came to define his goals in terms of the completed cycle of the Elegies, the more clearly we can discern, in the poems that in his judgment did *not* achieve those goals, the perceptual, ethical, and linguistic problems with which he continually struggled. Two versions of Rilke's career are thus available to us: the documented achievement of the poetry authorized for publication (in which the stylistic differences between early, middle, and late periods become somewhat exaggerated through the omission of "in-between" texts); and the probing, often completely unprotected articulations of the problems confronted by a poet as soon as he attempts to circumscribe an experience and situate it in language. We will begin with the latter series, the "workshop" poems, juxtaposing poems that illuminate the developing relationship between specific motifs and the problem of writing itself. Even though years may separate these texts, they can readily be understood as stages in a single, exceptionally complex creative struggle.

A section of a poem entitled "Improvisationen aus dem Capreser Winter" ("Improvisations from Winter on Capri"), written in December 1906, reads as follows:

Gesicht, mein Gesicht:
wessen bist du? für was für Dinge
bist du Gesicht?
Wie kannst du Gesicht sein für so ein Innen, drin
  sich
immerfort das Beginnen
mit dem Zerfliessen zu etwas ballt.
Hat der Wald ein Gesicht?
Steht der Berge Basalt
gesichtlos nicht da?
Hebt sich das Meer
nicht ohne Gesicht
aus dem Meergrund her?
Spiegelt sich nicht der Himmel drin,
ohne Stirn, ohne Mund, ohne Kinn?

Face, my face:
whose face are you? for what kind of things

are you the face?
How can you be the face for such an interior,
  where
beginnings perpetually join
with dissolvings to produce a transient fixity.
Does the forest have a face?
Does not the mountains' basalt
stand faceless?
Does not the sea
crest without face
as it rises from its depths?
And is not the sky mirrored therein,
without forehead, without mouth, without chin?

(2.12)

The human face is an essential symbol for
human destiny: it insists on unity, form, symmetry. And the paradox is that, on the one
hand, nothing in nature seems to insist on a
complete unity—phenomena are comfortably
ensconced in fluidity and multiplicity—and,
on the other hand, if we look within ourselves
we find a virtual chaos, a perpetual motion of
thoughts and instinctive reactions that seems
to contradict utterly the persistent, symmetrical, and logical unity of our face, as others see
it and as we may contemplate it in a mirror.
What unity then is our face expressing?
Clearly it is the unity that our perceptions and
our language impose on the world. The great
human achievement is to describe that unity,
to integrate natural phenomena, first at the
minimal level of language and then, dynami-
cally as civilization unfolds in time, in the
intuitive and majestic gestures of art. But is
the unity expressed in our face then a unity
that exists only *outside* our individual being?
Is that not an impossible paradox? It is certainly one that fuels Rilke's entire metaphysics
of art; and virtually all his poems are metaphysical in that sense, posing the question of
their own status in the very process of their
unfolding. Two months after this first text,
while still on Capri, Rilke wrote, on 15 February 1907, "Ein Frühlingswind" ("A Springtime
Wind"):

Mit diesem Wind kommt Schicksal; lass, o lass
es kommen, all das Drängende und Blinde,

von dem wir glühen werden—: alles das.
(Sei still und rühr dich nicht, dass es uns finde.)
O unser Schicksal kommt mit diesem Wind.

Von irgendwo bringt dieser neue Wind,
schwankend vom Tragen namenloser Dinge, über
  das
Meer her was wir sind.

. . . Wären wirs doch. So wären wir zuhaus.
(Die Himmel stiegen in uns auf und nieder.)
Aber mit diesem Wind geht immer wieder
das Schicksal riesig über uns hinaus.

With this wind comes fate; let, o let
it come, all the thrusting, blind urges,
which will cause us to glow: all that.
(Be still, don't move, that it may discover us.)
O our fate comes with this wind.

From somewhere far this new wind brings,
  unsteady
from bearing so many nameless things,
across the sea to us—our very being.

. . . If only that's what we were. We'd be at home.
(The heavens would rise and fall within us.)
But with this wind fate rushes perpetually
through and beyond us, immense, remote.

(2.16)

The shift from imagery of face to imagery of
wind is the crucial shift from space to time. The
paradox of the face can, in one sense, be resolved by this shift: the unity of a person's face
is the unity of experienced time, the order imposed by an individual on that experience. But
in another sense the paradox is merely displaced. For what *is* experience? Once again,
what seems to be inside us is essentially outside, a series of disorderly events that exercise
an impact on our sensorium: our minds impose
an order on these events and declare them to be
our own, indeed our personal fate.

In this poem we encounter Rilke's curious
use of the word "fate," which receives its best-
known explication at the start of the Ninth
Elegy. Essentially he inverts Aristotle. Fate is
precisely not something deep within us working itself out through a series of predestined,
dramatically sequenced events. On the con-

trary, fate is the pure externality of events, the things that happen to us without any necessity whatever, simply because we conduct (and mentally unify) our lives in time. We wish this apparently meaningful sequence were really meaningful; as Rilke puts it in the Ninth Elegy, echoing the word's traditional usage, we "long for fate."

But Rilke is not simply demystifying our self-importance; the double movement of the poems shows very clearly that he is determined to master the situation, to reformulate the question of our being, of our ontology. We should welcome fate as it pours in on us, the random gusts of a windy spring; but we must also, somehow, internalize its otherness, center our experience in the irreducible fact that events do not belong to us or to anyone. For even as nature imperiously ignores us, something non-random is happening; human history and civilization are realities as actual and enduring as nature's indifference. Again and again, over the centuries, human beings have had the courage to confront that indifference and to assert the value of their being nevertheless. Very often such assertions have had a religious basis, but this has not diminished their validity. For Rilke religious answers are not available in themselves, but their cultural expression is very much available; it constitutes the history of human achievement that lives in the world, not only in books and museums but also in the natural world as it has been subtly modified by civilization. The forces that impel nature, which we would so like to transfer by analogy to our own lives, are utterly alien from us; but the traces of human resistance to those forces are everywhere to be seen, forever yielding in defeat yet never eliminated. Their perpetually precarious survival constitutes what we call civilization. Thus Rilke is able to sustain his original paradox, the paradox of the face: it *does* make sense to say that our face is the face of the world outside us, for in the spots and moments of that world the essence of our inner being is after all to be found.

Rilke sees himself as very much the inheritor of the fragmented story of civilization. Those whose courage and energy produced that civilization were generally nourished by religious or comparable illusions. Rilke is resolved to jettison all illusions; for him the only way forward is through grasping and actualizing the civilizing drive itself. He is not a detached anthropologist, working without commitment. On the contrary, the productions of art and civilization that Rilke invokes in his poetry are all creations of the past that have entered his experience. (His many travels, particularly to Russia, Spain, and Egypt, were indispensable to his artistic program.) Rilke was especially interested in letters of women long dead, letters that express, through the gradual purification and transcendance of a hopeless love, the essence of an entire human existence; in such letters he saw the potency of civilization, which is not confined to the production of artworks but rather extends, through the power of the transforming impulse, into every detail of an ordinary life— when it is consciously lived as such. We have reached the word "transformation" (*Verwandlung*), a notion indispensable to Rilke's metaphysics, indeed to the metaphysics of anyone whose project is to justify the world without God. For it is only through transformation that the double movement of the poem we are studying makes sense: we are to absorb fate as it rushes in upon us and release it again as it transcends us. If there is to be meaning in this sequence it can only be through the idea of the transforming consciousness: *something* of what hurtles through us is retained and *something* of the wind's destination is glimpsed through a flash of recognition, a momentary glimpse of a fragment of civilization as it is battered once again by nature's indifferent power.

If we broaden the perspective on this metaphysical enterprise beyond Rilke himself, we immediately think of Nietzsche; Erich Heller early pointed out the parallels between Rilke's and Nietzsche's thought. But the differences are almost as significant as the parallels, and the fundamental one is that whereas Nietzsche wills the end of the metaphysical tradition (his "transvaluation of all values"), Rilke embraces it, wills its rescue: "transformation" is but a means to that end. Thus for Nietzsche art is an instrument of radical change, a way of galvanizing the redirected will; humanity is deemed a transitional stage, a bridge leading to intensified Being; and our very understanding of time is to be revolutionized by the thinking of the Eternal Return. It is not necessary to explore Nietzsche's thinking any further to discern Rilke's wholly different points of emphasis. For Rilke the goal of art is not to change the world but to enter it, to participate in the processes of transformation always already going on—and to fulfill the function preordained for art in the invisible order of things. Rilke saw it as his life's work to articulate that function, and in doing so to actualize it, to make it exist. Human beings, in Rilke's eyes, are in a remote exile from the spirituality of their essential existence, which is both communal and solitary, sensuous and ascetic. One thinks of the imaginary monastic ideal of the *Book of Hours,* or of the Russian religion, which was seminal for Rilke; or indeed of the idea of continuous, dedicated work embodied in the sculptor Rodin, whose slogan, adopted by Rilke, was "Toujours travailler!" (Always work!). Certainly this is a conservative ideal. In contrast to Nietzsche, Rilke dreamed of reactivating human possibilities that have *always been there;* his goal is not transvaluation of value but gradual, patient, ascetic recovery of values that have already been fully imagined.

Andras Sandor has pointed to a kinship between his thought and that of Walter Benjamin, rooted in the concept of "rescue"; certainly their ideas of time, crucial to the structure of poetry, are closely linked. Like Benjamin, Rilke focuses intently on the past in quest of that moment of intersection, of electric flow from present to past and back; in such moments the past ceases to be past and the present is emancipated from its continuous defeat both by natural forces and (more ominously) by the indifference of technological time. Whereas Nietzsche imagines a transformation of time as such, Rilke (and Benjamin in his very different way) seek only to reactivate and guarantee the immense images of human time that civilization has generated in profusion but that have become enigmatic, inaccessible to the "progressive" uniformity of commodified, complacent modern time.

Transforming the raw material of experience, rescuing the achieved moments of civilization, these are key ingredients in Rilke's conception of the poem as the "face" of what is outside as well as what is inside the self. Another idea crystallizing during the fruitful winter on Capri is that of accepting, indeed celebrating, limits; the poem "Sonnen-Untergang" ("Sunset") was written in Paris in August 1907:

Wie Blicke blendend, wie eine warme Arene,
vom Tage bevölkert, umgab dich das Land;
bis endlich strahlend, als goldene Pallas-Athene
auf dem Vorgebirg der Untergang stand,
*   verstreut von dem gross ihn vergeudenden Meer.*
Da wurde Raum in den langsam sich leerenden
*   Räumen;*
über den Bergen wurde es leer.

Und dein Leben, von dem man die lichten
*   Gewichte gehoben,*
stieg, soweit Raum war, über das Alles nach
*   oben,*
füllend die rasch sich verkühlende Leere der Welt.
Bis es, im Steigen, in kaum zu erfühlender Ferne
sanft an die Nacht stiess. Da wurden ihm einige
*   Sterne,*
als nächste Wirklichkeit, wehrend
*   entgegengestellt.*

As if gazing with blinding force, like a warm
    arena,
inhabited by the day, the land surrounded you;
until, radiant at last, a golden Pallas Athena,
the sunset stood poised on the outer rock,
    dispersed, squandered by the extravagant sea.
Then the surrounding spaces began to be emptied
    out;

above you, above the houses and trees,
above the mountains the void grew.

And your life, all its light attachments loosened,
rose above everything, as far as the space opened,
filling the world's rapidly cooling emptiness.
Until, rising, at a scarcely imaginable distance,
it encountered the night. Then certain stars,
now its closest reality, were placed in resistance
   to it.

(2.28–29)

The image of the soul soaring off into the sky on its own is highly traditional (see, for example, Joseph von Eichendorff's famous "Mondnacht" [Moonlit Night]), and tradition is indeed crucial to Rilke's purpose here. For the rescue of the tradition is to be accomplished by a double reactivation of imagery. On the one hand powerful symbols of motion and strength are frankly invoked and given new life as abstractions: thus the springtime wind of the previous poem becomes impersonal fate, while the dissolution of visual forms at sunset becomes, in the present text, explicitly a void, a vast opening for imaginative flight. Meanings that are merely implicit in the traditional images are spelled out by Rilke. How then does he avoid the dryness of purely abstract language? The answer lies in his counterstrategy, what I have called his celebration of limits. This complementary use of traditional motifs involves the use of those cosmic realms that are nominally outside experience—and presenting them in highly concrete, even intimate language. In our previous text we read, in a confidential parenthesis: "(The heavens would rise and fall within us)." Rilke is speaking, of course, of what in actual experience does *not* happen; but in linguistic terms it *does* happen, the conscious naïveté of the fantasy draws us close to the self as it is swept aside by its tempestuous, impersonal fate.

This imagining of limits, of otherness, of what lies outside human potential enables Rilke to give new life to the entirety of the tradition, not just to its last phase, that moment of his youth when striving was becoming a mem-

ory, dissolving into dreamlike passivity. What he does is to re-stage the rising, striving motion as an open fiction: the opening word of this poem, *Wie* (as if), launches a typical Rilkean sequence. But the suddenly intimate tone at the very limit of the rising sequence converts the fiction into a new kind of reality, situating it in an almost primitively concrete universe. In "Sunset" we encounter "certain stars" at the limit of the self's ascent; indeed they are explicitly "placed in resistance to it." The stars are absolutely other, as they have always been to the primitive imagination; and Rilke here converts the fictive rise to "a scarcely imaginable distance" into an awed closeness to the alien cosmos. The effect is actually not playful, since the whole momentum of the poem is thrust against this limit. "Stars" and "angels" are of course well-known Rilkean symbols of otherness. My concern here is to show how they actually work for him, how such ancient symbolism lives again inside a technological universe. Primitive imaginations fear stars; they loom without distance. For Rilke, a constellation is a "known figure" (*gewusste Figur*); the imagery of tradition is never employed with false innocence. But the knowing does not alter the fact of otherness. In accelerating the metaphysical rush to the limits and then pausing there, hovering with only the support of language, Rilke makes us share his longing not to transcend limits, but to populate the emptiness with words from the everyday. The historical and physical distances that always surround human experience are simultaneously opened up, through drastic abstraction, and drawn back down again, through the intimate imagining of limiting zones.

It should be clear that for Rilke there is no distinction between metaphysics and poetic craft: the poem *is* the realization of his speculative moves. While that could perhaps be said of most philosophical poets, what is specific to Rilke is the third element, which is in equally complete interdependence with the other two: namely the project of rescuing, reactivating the entire Western tradition of myths and forms. The self who addresses us in Rilke's texts is no stranger to us; he knows our everyday anxieties. But at the same time he has a mission both to enlarge the possibilities of experience and to persuade the reader, often quite didactically, to join him on that mission. We have only to recall the erratic and provincial quality of Rilke's own education to see why his autodidactic enthusiasm is so infectious.

His quest for a language adequate to his project of rescue is paradoxically a rather humble enterprise. Rilke continuously discovered and absorbed, as the key to his ever more self-conscious poet's life, the excitements of the tradition for himself. At the same time, as the vast scope of his poetic goals became clearer to him, he developed a language more in harmony with those goals, indeed one of astounding flexibility. The developing dynamics of his language—the new virtuosity with which his poetry valorizes that zone between the soaring aspirations of human experience and the silence, the otherness that limits it—is evident in "An die Musik" ("To Music"), the only poem Rilke completed in 1918:

Musik: Atem der Statuen. Vielleicht:
Stille der Bilder. Du Sprache wo Sprachen
enden. Du Zeit,
die senkrecht steht auf der Richtung vergehender
Herzen.

Gefühle zu wem? O du der Gefühle
Wandlung in was?—: in hörbare Landschaft.
Du Fremde: Musik. Du uns entwachsener
Herzraum. Innigstes unser,
das, uns übersteigend, hinausdrängt,—
heiliger Abschied:
da uns das Innre umsteht
als geübteste Ferne, als andre
Seite der Luft:
rein,
riesig,
nicht mehr bewohnbar.

Music: breath of statues. Perhaps:
stillness of pictures. O language where languages
end. O time,

standing vertically against the flow of mortal emotions.

Feelings for whom? O transformation
of feelings into what? Into audible landscape.
O strangeness: music. Zone of the heart
grown away from us. Our most intimate being
thrusting beyond us, transcending us,
sacred farewell:
when our inner world surrounds us
as distance shaped through practice, as other
face of the air:
pure,
immense,
no longer habitable.

(2.111)

A paradox of Rilke's poetry is that it resists as far as possible the atmosphere of paradox, of contradictory realities. Rilke's goal is to expand his reader's mental landscape to the point where contradictions dissolve, where the irreconcilable is reconciled, either at the spatial limits of the cosmos or in the overlapping time zones of history or memory. As Beda Allemann has pointed out, this reconciling movement in Rilke distinguishes him sharply from Mallarmé, with the latter's invocation of "the flower absent from all bouquets." One can call Mallarmé's insistence on absence either uncompromising aestheticism or rigorous neo-Platonism; it is certainly very different from the absence that pervades our present text. Rilke's absence remains a longing for and intimation of possible presence; it is never at rest like Mallarmé's white purity. As critics noted early on, Rilke's perpetual motion is akin to the imagery of another great modernist, Eliot. In section two of "Burnt Norton" (1935), the first of the *Four Quartets*, Eliot imagines the simultaneity of ordinary, repetitive reality with a rhythmic affirmation of that same reality:

Below, the boarhound and the boar
Pursue their pattern as before
But reconciled among the stars
. . . And do not call it fixity,
Where past and future are gathered. Neither
    movement from nor towards,

Neither ascent nor decline. Except for the point,
   the still point.
There would be no dance, and there is only the
   dance.

Even more than Eliot, Rilke refuses to transcend the everyday. The more seemingly remote his images, the more they throw tendrils back toward the familiar earth. The phrase "Zone of the heart / grown away from us" illustrates this process in "To Music." Music is expressive in ways of which ordinary feeling hearts no longer seem capable. But this means that music is *not* "other" than ourselves; through a historical process our powers have atrophied, but musical achievements recall those powers and challenge us to embark on a mission of recovery. "Grown away" (*entwachsen*): this typically Rilkean participle loosens the web of paradox that the poem itself has constructed ("O language where languages / end"), redefining the text as inside rather than outside history, a narrative both of loss and of movement toward recovery. Music is a central version of the "face" outside ourselves: not only does it activate our most elemental rhythmic responses, it requires equally our most highly developed formal understanding in order to impose itself on human time. Thus even as it transcends us, it must carry us with it, impelling us to contemplate what has become of the inwardness with which we have lost contact in ordinary existence. As Rilke celebrates this particular limit, the limit of sublimely organized music, he opens the poem back toward the possibilities of memory and the actualities of momentary exhilaration. It is the very formality of music that forces the buried connectedness of our experience into consciousness. And thus the final phrase, "no longer habitable," has an impact diametrically opposed to Mallarmé's remoteness; what is no longer habitable is in fact a dwelling rising again into "invisible" existence, built out of new word structures for music's movement, for the "language where languages / end."

Rilke consummated this "ultimate" language in the miraculous month of February 1922. It seems appropriate, then, that our last look into his "workshop" should focus on an untitled poem written on the first day of that month:

. . . *Wann wird, wann wird, wann wird es genügen*
das Klagen und Sagen? Waren nicht Meister im
   Fügen
menschlicher Worte gekommen? Warum die
   neuen Versuche?

Sind nicht, sind nicht, sind nicht vom Buche
die Menschen geschlagen wie von fortwährender
   Glocke?
Wenn dir, zwischen zwei Buchern, schweigender
   Himmel erscheint: frohlocke . . . ,
oder ein Ausschnitt einfacher Erde im Abend.

Mehr als die Stürme, mehr als die Meere haben
die Menschen geschrieen . . . Welche
   Übergewichte von Stille
müssen im Weltraum wohnen, da uns die Grille
hörbar blieb, uns schreienden Menschen. Da uns
   die Sterne
schweigende scheinen, im angeschrieenen Äther!

Redeten uns die fernsten, die alten und ältesten
   Vater!
Und wir: Hörende endlich! Die ersten hörenden
   Menschen.

When will, when will, when will it suffice
The lamenting and telling? Have there not
   already been
masters in the weaving of the human words?
   Why the
new attempts?

Are not, are not, are not human lives
battered by the book as by a ceaselessly ringing
   bell?
When between two books the silent sky looms up:
   rejoice . . . ,
or a sector of simple earth at evening.

Above the storms, above the seas have human
   cries
resounded . . . What extra dimensions of quiet
must dwell in the universe, that the cricket
   remained audible
to us, us clamoring humans. That the stars
seem silent, in the ether bombarded with our
   cries!

O that the most distant, most ancient ancestors
    could speak to us!
And that we would finally hear! Would be the
    first hearing humans.

                    (2.134–135)

The immensities of time and space traversed by this poem are matched by its visionary summation of the history of language. The exhaustion of language arises from the repetitive ordinariness of fear and grief. Yet this ordinariness has already been distilled by the great poets of the past. We can see what might be termed Rilke's sliding use of paradox at work: the poem asserts simultaneously the pointless repetition of the language of pain and the pointlessness of trying to match the masters of that language. Clearly the two kinds of pointlessness do *not* reinforce each other; the image of an already fulfilled poetry actually subverts the notion of repetitious complaining. Certain unique "complaints" endure. And so the paradoxical style "slides" to a new negative vista, the idea (already promulgated by Feodor Dostoevsky in *Notes from Underground* [1864]) that human feeling is inauthentic, the mere product of books.

This sliding from authentic-but-repetitive to feeling as mere reproduction is highly instructive in terms of the metaphysical movement we have noted throughout the "workshop" poems. As before, the language is abstract but passionate, and it thrusts toward a limit, this time a downward limit, a minimizing of human potential. And at this limit the language changes from abstract to concrete: the bell rings, glimpses of evening silence are vouchsafed. And the possibility of utter silence, freedom from words, is imagined. But how could such imagining be articulated? Of course in language, the language of "rejoicing." In our previous text music is praised as the "language where languages end"; Rilke's poetry can only aspire to that status. The evocation of wordlessness at the center of this poem can only be verbal.

But to stop there, to take refuge in "moments," would be to betray the opening rhetoric. This poem asks questions about the entirety of human speaking, the ongoing history of noise as well as the silence that defines it by contrast. And so the abstract language resumes, with another slide in the paradox. Human history is now inscribed in a spatial image, the image of the universe filled with human outcries. The paradox, as it now appears, is that the concept of silence has survived at all, given the senseless accumulation of pain that crowds out all the more gentle modes of feelings. Rilke has thrust against another limit. And as is typical with him, the intense bleakness of the vision instantly softens at the edges, the sliding of the paradox continues. For everything about this "hopeless" vision suggests grandeur: the accusing human cry (which opens the First Elegy, written ten years earlier and answered here); the glimpses of simplicity (the cricket) and serenity (the stars) that persist through the racket; indeed the very act of imagining the entirety of history as a single spatialized event.

For even though Rilke has insisted on the unmeaning, the repetitious darkness, of this history, the actual movement of his poem continually points in other directions, opening the dimension of the possible. Thus far in the poem, that dimension has been confined to the extrahuman, the little silences outside history. But we have noted how the very processes of linguistic evocation undermine such limiting, and thus, as the inferno of human history is gathered up into a single moment, the poem seems to drive beyond that moment, to insist on release. And Rilke's conclusion is adequate to the challenge; suddenly this compression of history is not a confused babble but a lucid conversation between the beginning and the end of the time humanity has so far traversed. The man of today is released from speaking; he becomes the pure receiver of meaning. The mood is subjunctive, to be sure—the world of the last lines cannot yet be. But Rilke has achieved a marvelous image of how his mission as a poet might be fulfilled. His "hearing" is of course poetic "speaking"; anti-language remains language. But such speaking would be a genuine rescue of history as a whole, neither adding more laments to the babble nor escaping into the magic moments of twilight: the translation of the most ancient human experiences into a language that distills both the darkness and the light from their history— this is the goal Rilke finally articulated for poetry, and that he achieved in the remaining days of February 1922. In that month he completed both the *Duino Elegies* and the *Sonnets to Orpheus.*

The purpose of this traversal of Rilke's "workshop" (my usage of this term does not imply ranking: some of his greatest poems belong here, including "Es winkt zu Fühlung" [A Summons to Feeling], in which the famous term *Weltinnenraum* ["world-inner-space"] is coined) has been to establish continuities. We have seen how an extremely fragile and vulnerable poetic self is both challenged and fulfilled by the vision of the Western tradition as a whole. On the one hand the myriad voices of the past crowd in on the individual sensibility, threatening to drown out all personal language. But on the other hand the poet becomes ever more adept at shaping poetic structures out of the very process of being "drowned"; the initial paradox of the face "outside" the self becomes less and less paradoxical and more the simple reality of poetic existence. And matching this metaphysical continuity is a continuity of method: traditional images (stars, sunsets) are invoked in an abstract mode, one that includes their traditional roles and probes their structure; conversely the extreme enigmas, the limiting zones of human existence, are explored as if it were in fact possible to explore them, through the spare, minimal imagery of irreducible, "meaningless" concreteness. A much-discussed 1914 poem, "Ausgesetzt auf den Bergen des Herzens" ("Exposed on the Mountains of the Heart"), provides a virtual map of this poetic landscape. As the poet ascends the mountain of feeling, passing above the zone of

language into ever more forbidding regions, he notices that the "void" is in fact populated:

*Hier blüht wohl
einiges auf; aus stummen Absturz
blüht ein unwissendes Kraut singend hervor.*

Here something
blooms; from out of a silent crevice
an unknowing weed emerges singing into
  existence.

(2.94)

Understanding these continuities of style and metaphysical project helps us read all of Rilke's published poems, particularly the early ones. But it is important not to limit ourselves to the study of how poetic texts unfold through reflection on their own reason for being. Such a procedure might be justified in the case of Mallarmé (to pursue once again Allemann's comparison of Rilke with another master modernist), for Mallarmé's language wills its own otherness from all everyday concerns. But Rilke is quite different: both his intention and his historical impact are emotionally intimate as well as urgently didactic. He wants his poems to have an effect on the world; and this they have certainly achieved. He would welcome the questions: Well, so you've summed up, "rescued" the Western tradition—but why? What good is it to us? And what do you yourself have to tell us? It is important to shift our focus from structural to thematic concerns, and one good reason is that Rilke's two great themes are ultimately inseparable from his metaphysics of poetry. That is, his themes are "life-ideas," to be used by ordinary people in everyday existence, but their impact is guaranteed by their poetic shaping (*Gestalt*) precisely because Rilke's own response to his life challenges was to live the poet's life as an endless task and inescapable responsibility. The special quality of his writing is to force us to modify our traditional usage of the word "aesthetic." To Rilke the very existence of aesthetic objects, of art as such, represents an inescapable imperative: human beings *must* live their daily lives in some sort of harmony with the great achievements of the past. It is the responsibility of the poet to match those achievements directly; it is the responsibility of the rest of us not to live trivial lives, not to be mocked by art.

Rilke's perennial themes can be summarized as willing change and making objects or, more abstractly, as intervening in time and intervening in space. Clearly they fit the poet's own activity very well: the poem, a compression of experienced time, is to be inserted into the spatial flux as an independent object laying claim to permanence. But in Rilke's eyes the twin themes fuse the two poles of human action in the world, a polarity well understood by the Greeks and other ancient civilizations yet forgotten by a technological age in which human and natural time are sundered while the distinction between object and image disappears in the commodity, in the texture of illusion and consumption. Time is the element in which human beings must live, but it is inert and sterile, unless they concentrate their energies on it, drawing the time of the organic world, the time of the human past, and the fragile time of the individual present into some kind of productive unity. And to think such a unity is already in some sense to think spatially. As the romantic thinker Novalis put it: "Space is the precipitate of time." In the world around him Rilke saw a space almost infinitely contaminated by the inauthentic: cities of identical houses forcing the organic qualities of humanity into an industrial world designed to kill them and replace them with a "life" of prepackaged commodities, and images dominated by advertising and politics, pictures aiming always to substitute an imaginary life for reality, utterly alien to the traditional function of physical images as fulfilling and celebrating the real. Rilke's countermove, his insistence on "intervention," on marshaling all the powers that are dormant within us, is thus essentially anti-political, at least as politics is normally understood. But it is not

opposed to the "politics of community" that, at a deep level of idealism, nourishes socialist and conservative thought alike. To engage the organic realm, as in the following early text, "Eingang" ("Entering," 1900), is to be involved by definition in an urgent human dialogue:

Wer du auch seist: am Abend tritt hinaus
aus deiner Stube, drin du alles weisst;
als letzes vor der Ferne liegt dein Haus:
wer du auch seist.
Mit deinen Augen, welche müde kaum
von der verbrauchten Schwelle sich befrein,
hebst du ganz langsam einen schwarzen Baum
und stellst ihn vor den Himmel: schlank, allein.
Und hast die Welt gemacht. Und sie ist gross
Und wie dein Wille ihren Sinn begreift,
lassen sie deine Augen zärtlich los . . .

Whoever you are: step out in the evening
from your room where all is known to you;
your house is just this side of great distances:
whoever you are.
With your eyes which, exhausted,
barely free themselves from the worn threshold,
you raise up, slowly, a black tree
and place it against the sky: slender, alone.
And you've made the world. And it is vast
and like a word which ripens still in silence.
And as your will begins to grasp its meaning,
your eyes release it gently . . .

(1.371)

Written in February 1900 in Berlin-Schmargendorf, this is the first poem, the "entrance," to the *Book of Pictures.* And immediately a subtle Rilkean tension is established with the opening gesture. For the "entering" is actually a leaving, a moving out of the known into the forever "unknown" fullness of the natural world. The contrast between internal and external, human and natural, might seem oversimple except that Rilke immediately causes all opposites to slide, almost to rotate around the creative principle as it is gently activated, both in life and in the book of poems. For the self or reader being addressed does not "find" anything outside his home. He simply intervenes in life, draws together the powers dissipated by the familiarity of things; and this creative move is open to anyone—*all* houses are "just this side of great distances." In comparison with later texts already discussed, this poem is soft-edged: the negative image of the familiar ceases to be necessary for the later Rilke, and the notion of "releasing" the world that eyes have constituted in the tree seems rather precious, excessively ritualistic in the manner of much early Rilke. But if the contrast is made with even earlier (as opposed to later) poems, the significance of this "entering" is more clearly perceptible. Just a few months before, in October 1899, Rilke had completed the first part of *The Book of Hours—The Book of Monastic Life.* There the ritual apparatus is much more elaborate: in its monk's persona, the self insists on ascetic regularity ("I live my life in growing rings"), and the outcome of the various intensities is nothing less than the "rebuilding" of God. In other words Rilke's poetic beginnings are encumbered both with an excess of subjective pomposity and with elaborate "objective" goals, images of purified new/old divinities.

The present text, then, endeavors to focus the act of intervention, which is synonymous with creation, in a way that Käte Hamburger has termed "phenomenological." To concentrate one's powers on a tree is to "create" that tree, to isolate and realize its being, which cannot meaningfully exist without human intervention. The only requirement of the self is that it delve inward and release its powers; and the tree refers to nothing but its own existence. Neither purified subjectivity nor a larger project are necessary. But what certifies Rilke's text as poetry rather than phenomenological thought is the way in which the tensions involved in the concentration on the tree ripple into the open toward the end of the text. The tree's isolation is stressed, but "you've made the world." The very informality of the phrase points in opposite directions: Rilke is being playful about his own imagery but is simultaneously "embracing the limit," acknowledging the human impetus toward ulti-

mates. In the very creation of the tree, questions about both the meaning of the natural order and the status of the questioning consciousness continue to reverberate. They point to the aspiration of the poem itself, the paradoxical urge of language, the quintessential man-made system, to "ripen" like an organism with a guaranteed place in the world. (Jacob Steiner has shown the frequency and thematic importance of Rilke's references to "the word"; here, even in the prevailing soft image-making, the simile has a slightly disruptive effect, as if the poem's organic ambitions were being prevented by a consciously strained analogy.) And the questions readmit the human agent: "tired" at the outset of the poem, his "will" is now engaging the "meaning" of what is essentially his own performance. The term "will" reminds us also of the continuing quest of the self, its need to interpret and criticize its own productive moment. None of these tensions are stressed: what Rilke does is to imagine the perfection of an aesthetic act, an obvious analogue to his own poem, *and* to open the moment of achievement into the continuity and dissatisfaction of living. The title thus gains an extra dimension: this text really is an "entrance" into both the integrity and the perpetual struggle of Rilke's poetic maturity. The creative gaze at its center becomes, in the poem "Archaïscher Torso Apollos" ("Archaic Torso of Apollo," 1908), almost infinitely dynamic and nuanced:

Wir kannten nicht sein unerhörtes Haupt,
darin die Augenäpfel reiften. Aber
sein Torso glüht noch wie ein Kandelaber
in dem sein Schauen, nur zurückgeschraubt,

sich hält und glänzt. Sonst könnte nicht der Bug
der Brust dich blenden, und im leisen Drehen
der Lenden könnte nicht ein Lächeln gehen
zu jener Mitte, die die Zeugung trug.

Sonst stünde dieser Stein enstellt und kurz
unter der Schultern durchsichtigem Sturz
und flimmerte nicht so wie Raubtierfelle;

und bräche nicht aus allen seinen Rändern
aus wie ein Stern: denn da ist keine Stelle,
die dich nicht sieht. Du musst dein Leben ändern.

RAINER MARIA RILKE

We never knew his unimaginable head,
wherein the eyeballs ripened. But
his torso glows still like a chandelier
in which his gaze, but forced back inwards,

maintains itself and shines. The thrusting rib
   cage
could otherwise not blind you, and in the gentle
   turning
of the hips a smile could not go
to the body's procreative center.

This stone were otherwise disfigured, cut short
under the shoulder's transparent plunge
and would not shimmer like a predator's mane;

and would not burst from all its confines, like
a shooting star: for there is no spot there
which does not see you. You must change your
   life.

(1.557)

Another "opening" poem, this one was written in the early summer of 1908 and placed at the head of the second part of the *New Poems,* where it faces the volume's dedicatory note: "A mon grand ami Auguste Rodin." It is one of Rilke's great achievements, showing how easily the idea of the "thing-poem" (*Dinggedicht*) can be misunderstood. Certainly the texture and monumental presence of Rodin's sculpture were revelations to the poet; certainly, too, one of Rilke's great themes is the need to intervene in space. But this need is never separable from the explicitly poetic intervention in time; Rilke's experiences of painting and sculpture in his Paris years enable him to transform the metaphysical, self-conscious space of the poem written in 1900 into a concreteness that blends the multiple textures of earth, air, light, and stone. But he is also emancipated from the need to "include" the theme of poetry in his meditation; this poem *knows* that it is language, that language is the vehicle of time, and that its relationship to sculpture can never be one of mere transcription or evocation.

The text weaves four distinct temporal dimensions together, not in smoothly artificial harmony but in a series of linguistic tension points, "interventions" through which the sculpture is reborn into a complexity of time zones. There is first the time of the absent head, the lost past of the original statue, the art-historical dimension that might logically open backward into the conditions of the archaic past. However, Rilke instantly reverses direction: in its absence the statue's gaze is all the more "present"; the god Apollo himself lives with increasing, not diminishing intensity as time passes and, as it were, adheres to the torso, compressing ever more history into the same space. The third dimension is the movement of the observer's eye down and around the torso: in contradiction to the traditional aesthetic tenet (Gotthold Lessing's) that a visual work of art is perceived as a whole in a single instant, what we witness is a dramatic, conflict-ridden passage over the torso's surface, a movement in time equivalent to the time of the poem itself. Finally there is the time of the observer's own life: this life is "absent" in an exactly complementary sense to the absence of the statue's head. As that absent gaze insists on its presence in every detail of the surface, so the private life of the spectator, hiding initially in the anonymous "we" of the first line, is drawn into an ever more intense involvement with the gaze—until the "we" of the opening becomes the "you" of the conclusion.

In the poem "Entering" the notion of "ripening" is strategically assigned to the (poetic) world, but here the ripening is withdrawn entirely from the known world; it names the entrance of the god himself into the absent, indeed unimaginable eyes of the statue. But the very flexibility with which Rilke uses this organic term underlines its importance to him. It connotes the poem's ambition to become a "thing," to intervene and take root in space. And whereas in 1900 Rilke still favored a soft-edged, gradual movement in his lines— that is, an "imitation" of ripening—here the text moves immediately to a rhythm of growth that imitates nothing and belongs entirely to the movement of language itself. The poem is a sonnet and exploits all the conventions of the sonnet to convey both the charged weaving of time dimensions and the torso's powerful presence in space. Enjambment, the spilling-over from one line to the next, is central to its rhythm. Thus the "growing" of the god's gaze in the first quatrain is embodied in the way lines turn in on themselves, expanding yet not released. Release comes in the transition from the first to the second quatrain: one has to "see" the sonnet structure in order to feel the powerful self-assertion of the verbs that open line five. This instant establishment of the god's gaze is in turn essential to the strong image of "to blind." Given the detached, narrative tone of the poem's opening, there is an almost shocking impact in the arrival of this verb in line six: it is a spurt of "growth" in which the observer is suddenly enmeshed. Skillfully Rilke immediately mitigates the shock, shifting the verbs to the more controlled subjunctive mood and, as the poem nears its center, stressing the statue's gentleness. The god's gaze becomes a smile; and a balance between god and observer is struck as the lines use a smooth enjambment to achieve a "turning" motion, a graceful arabesque both in the torso's texture and in the observer's move around it.

The opening of the tercets seems to maintain the balance, as the observer meditates on the aesthetic necessity of god's gaze: without it the torso would be incomplete, shapeless. But as the observer enters into the realm of the gaze, the momentum of growth resumes, the relation of enjambment between the lines begins to express acceleration. The image of the predator suggests the observer's loss of freedom. And at the opening of the final tercet the enjambment literally evokes the "bursting" of the statue's power out into the observer's life: the god's gaze has always been expressed as light; now it is a shooting star, invoking absolute otherness and strangeness (Rilke's constant attributes for stars), that nevertheless overwhelms the observer with its immediacy. The balance at the poem's center has shifted drastically: the spectator may have "produced" the gaze initially, by unlocking

the history compressed within the torso, but by the end of the poem he is wholly within its power. The time zones of both archaic history and aesthetic contemplation have culminated in radical "un-freedom," which is what makes the final phrase so remarkable. The poem's "growth" has proceeded through drastic shifts and decelerations to this most extreme of all shifts. From "un-freedom" the command issues forth: regain control, act in freedom. These words are spoken in all four time zones at once: the archaic world of authentic gods addresses the modernity of alienated lives; the god's gaze, compressed within the torso, is finally interpreted by the observer—the oracle speaks, and the visual culminates in the verbal; the act of contemplating the torso and simultaneously producing the poem has resulted not in harmony but in the intervention of the statue/poem in life itself; and finally, the words can be heard as accusatory, a charge from god to observer that instantly translates to the reader. As the god's gaze has overwhelmed the observer, so the simultaneously emerging poem overwhelms the reader. But this overwhelming sets all merely aesthetic force relations radically into reverse: the transparency of the stone (line ten) is a historical and social transparency, a linkage of eras rendering museums and even statues irrelevant to the ethical imperatives that produced oracular language—and hence poetry. These last words express the single "truth" that oracles of all times and places have spoken. The aesthetic is the only "godlike" authority we have left: without the ethical charge, which is both premise and purpose of all creation, we will have nothing. And in Rilke's later poems, he repeatedly explores this moment of fusion between the interrogative and the imperative, the aesthetic and the ethical, the temporal and the spatial. This exploration is particularly characteristic of the *Sonnets to Orpheus,* for example of sonnet 18 of part two:

Tänzerin: O du Verlegung
alles Vergehens in Gang: wie brachtest du's dar.

*Und der Wirbel am Schluss, dieser Baum aus
Bewegung,
nahm er nicht ganz in Besitz das erschwungene
Jahr?*

*Blühte nicht, dass ihn dein Schwingen von vorhin
umschwärme,
plötzlich sein Wipfel von Stille? Und über ihr,
war sie nicht Sonne, war sie nicht Sommer, die
Wärme,
diese unzählige Wärme aus dir?*

*Aber er trug auch, er trug, dein Baum der Ekstase.
Sind sie nicht seine ruhigen Früchte: der Krug,
reifend gestreift, und die gereiftere Vase?*

*Und in den Bildern: ist nicht die Zeichnung
geblieben,
die deiner Braue dunkler Zug
rasch an die Wandung der eigenen Wendung
geschrieben?*

Dancer: you transmutation
of all fading into motion: how you shaped that
role.
And the whirl at the end, this tree of movement,
did it not wholly contain the year's vibrating
essence?

Did not its tip blossom, responding to the
embrace of your emotion,
suddenly into stillness? And above that,
was it not sun, was it not summer, the warmth,
this infinite warmth from in you?

But it sustained also, it sustained, your tree of
ecstasy.
Are they not its peaceful fruits: the jug,
ripened by a passing touch, and the more fully
ripened vase?

And in the pictures: has not the drawing
remained,
which the dark movement of your brow
quickly sketched on the screen of your own
turning?

(1.763)

Written between 17 and 19 February 1922, this
sonnet distills, in the figure of the dancer, the
essence of Rilke's great interlocking themes of
"intervention" in time and in space. In certain
respects Rilke draws closer to Mallarmé's procedures in his final period (perhaps his contact with Mallarmé's disciple Valéry had an
effect); the elaboration of internal verbal relationships, particularly assonances, makes the
movement of certain lines almost impossible to
translate; and there is an increasing exploration of what is superficially absent from empirical reality, such as the dancer's "tree of
movement." Yet to notice the proximity to Mallarmé is again to notice the gulf that divides the
two poets. There is never a significant shift, in
Rilke, toward a hermetic poetics, a sealing of
language into its own realm of pure play. Rilke
never breaks faith with the ethical imperative of
Apollo's torso. The evocations in this sonnet of
the dance's traces, the residues of time in
space, are designed not to draw us into an esoteric realm but, on the contrary, to expand our
understanding of all those realities that we
limit by abstract description: movement, time,
action, feeling. The Apollo poem transforms
our very definition of the word "statue" by em-
bedding the torso in the dynamic "absence" of
the god's eyes; an object in space becomes shot
through with multiple tracks of time. In the
Orpheus sonnet the poetic movement is in a
sense the reverse: the poem is willed to "become" its theme, the dance. Far from being
structured as a magisterial continuity from archaic past to the opening into a possible future,
the present text whirls in self-limiting circles,
stopping, restarting, adding new images instead of drawing out the old, compressing time
into space. A comparison of the uses of enjambment is instructive: in the Apollo sonnet
almost every one is structurally important, accelerating or decelerating the virtuosic forward
movement; here, by contrast, no enjambment is
stressed—each line seems to be relished in its
self-containment as emblem of the dancer's
quicksilver turns.

With Apollo a statue becomes movement;
with Orpheus movement becomes a statue.
The equation is oversimple, but it points to the
unity of Rilke's concerns. The imperative to
"change your life" resounds in the Orpheus
sonnets also; but instead of a response to

history's infinitely deep surface, the injunction here is to insist on the movement, to imagine the myriad changes in the world activated by the dance's fulfilled movement. Here it is pertinent to quote again Eliot's lines: "Except for the point, the still point, / There would be no dance, and there is only the dance." We cited this previously in relation to music; here, of course, the relevance is explicit: Rilke's sonnet revolves around a "still point," an invisible rhythmic center that represents a "limit" embraced as intensely as the transcending structures of music. The center is the generative power of the dance itself, a fruitfulness inaccessible to the dancer's personality. But Rilke did have a specific dancer in mind, the dedicatee of the sonnets, Wera Ouckama Knoop, who had died three years before at the age of nineteen. Thus even as he moves toward the limit at her center, that ancient rhythm that she cannot "know," his goal is to re-invent very specific, simple things in the room around her, to give back to her in homage what her movement has brought into existence. Here Rilke diverges from Eliot (as, in a different sense, we have seen him diverge from Mallarmé): unlike Eliot, Rilke never ultimately celebrates abstraction; his embrace of limits is always part of a rhythm of return— return to concreteness, to individuality that, however focused and refined, can and must live in multiple relationships.

The poem begins by naming the center, qualifying it only with the abstractions that give dance its possibility of meaning. In a sense we are immediately at the Rilkean "limit"; in his late poetry Rilke is impatient to launch the return. The word "fading" is an inadequate rendering of *Vergehen,* which links aimless motion to the process of mortality itself: the dancer does not resist mortality, but she intervenes in the process, accelerating it into a single dance. As we have noted in relation to motifs like stars and angels, Rilke's imagining of the dance is deeply and affirmatively traditional. Into these brief abstractions he compresses all the meanings elaborated in past dance images—and begins his quest for a language of specificity. It is no accident that he begins at the end of the girl's performance. He seeks to locate the secret of the dance after it has ended, to add another time dimension (that of memory), and to strive for precision in defining exactly how the dancer alters space. Thus the imagery at the end of the first quatrain, the "tree" of movement that distills the essence of the year just past, is still much too general for Rilke. His poem merely describes the pattern of the dance it wishes to consummate.

The second quatrain is made of two very differently phrased questions. The first is elaborate, circling around the dancer's final pirouette, focusing on the "tip" of the tree, presumably her upstretched hands. Perhaps it is there, at the point of symbolic aspiration and conclusion, that the medium of language can find legitimacy, can respond to some need expressed within the perfection of the dance. The second question is probing, still general but less closed than the question in line four, as if sensing the possibility of precision in the energy given off by the dancer's hands. The repetition of "was it not" is tentative; the repetition of "sustained" is suddenly confident. At the center of the poem occurs the shift from question to answer. Rilke finds his answer within the traditional imagery of the dancer as living tree. The dancer's arms are "branches"; they give off energy flows during the dance as well as at the conclusion, imparting to the jug and vase the "organic" legitimacy that a casual eye can see in them but cannot explain. We are here at the center of Rilke's mature concerns: at stake in this dance is the poetic argument of the Ninth Elegy, the notion that the essence of human language is to speak the meaning already compressed into the simplicity of domestic objects, as well as the accumulated cultural meaning ready to be unlocked in Apollo's torso. This sonnet is thus acting out, or rather dancing, the metaphysic of the Elegies: the wholeness and the rightness of simple objects derives from the graceful movements that have occurred and, in their repetition, accumulated in the space around such objects.

Rilke's "answers" continue, of course, to be phrased as questions. One is reminded of the use of the subjunctive mood in the Apollo sonnet: the more intensely concrete the imagery, the more important it is to the poet to retain links to the reader's world, to co-opt the reader's doubts. Here the shift to the present perfect tense at the start of the last tercet has a double effect: the question, with the key thematic term "remained," becomes more assertive, but simultaneously the dance itself, which until now seems to have just finished, moves a little further into the past. This is explicitly a remembered moment, and it is through memory that Rilke reaches most boldly into the specificity of the dancer's intervention in space. To express his meaning he has to impel the language toward a new kind of abstraction, one whose assonances ("Wandung . . . Wendung") cannot be translated. This is non-generalizable abstraction, however, language of a given moment coined to re-imagine that moment only—and its residue in space. The dancer's movements generate energy and simultaneously harness that energy into enduring "drawings," sketches bound to a particular place (like frescoes in that respect) but living in the observer's mind (where art must always live). The poem remains a sequence of questions.

Unlike Eliot, Rilke never stabilized his aesthetic "theory." Theorizing is a continuous element of his poetry, but it is always only a moment, an embrace of limits from which a return must follow. Rilke's truth is always that of the Apollo sonnet: "You must change your life"—in the direction of fuller life. In the sonnet to Orpheus that fuller life is in the dance—which is thus far too important to be passively admired. Awareness of fullness means new responsibility, responsibility to remember it and to draw it back into daily usefulness. For Rilke, the man of words, the responsibility is to enlarge continuously the scope of what poetry can do along these lines. And as his words reach their readers, they become equipment for the task of focused life-change that is everyone's.

This double journey through Rilke's development (through the "workshop" and then through the landmark collections) has, I hope, demonstrated the extraordinary unity between his work on perfecting poetic language and the work of living itself. His "ideas" leap from the text to the reader's mind precisely because they are not exactly ideas at all, but intuitions of meaning produced by a particular moment and guaranteed by the integrity with which that moment has been transformed. Their flexible, even chameleonlike quality derives from their rootedness in the language of experience. They may sound abstract, but often the abstraction (like the famous "world-inner-space") is simultaneous with the event of thinking and hence itself a kind of temporal object. And far from confining Rilke's impact, this essentially experimental quality renders it inescapable. For he so expanded the expressivity of the German language that his verbal nuances, even his personal agenda, reverberate through it whenever ordinary people try to say what they feel. His influence on poets is clear: it is obviously at work in the linguistic inventiveness of, say, Paul Celan and Karl Krolow, two major German poets of the years immediately following World War II; and one can equally say that the sober, militant style of such conscious opponents of Rilke as Brecht, Hans Magnus Enzensberger, and Erich Fried is dialectically involved with what it opposes. (Dominant figures of the 1960's, Enzensberger and Fried frequently defined political poetry through polemics against Rilkean "aestheticism.") But the "perfection" of Rilke's achievement implies even more than that. His is a language forged in a crisis of historical change, both reflecting and resisting that change. And the continued convulsions of German history since his death seem to have reinforced the staying power of his language.

RAINER MARIA RILKE

Some of his formulations may seem over-aesthetic, even precious (an analogy with Virginia Woolf suggests itself); but when people struggle to express their sense of crisis, of alienation, or of secret continuities, Rilke's words are simply *there,* a repertoire to be shaken out, adapted, perhaps angrily rejected, but never discarded.

The objection is sometimes heard that Rilke hasn't really earned this status, that his linguistic virtuosity masks an excessive self-absorption, even an insincerity. If the goal of Rilke's quest is always ultimately poetic language, so the argument runs, then he has trapped his readers in a vicious circle: they cannot challenge the quality of his expressed "meaning" since that meaning is ultimately inseparable from its linguistic vehicle, the poem. In my survey of Rilke's development I hope to have shown how profoundly the poet was aware of this problem, how his mature achievement is conditioned by ruthless self-criticism, indeed for much of the decade 1912–1922 by a sense of almost certain failure. In fact I think the "vicious" circle can be restated as a "hermeneutic" circle: Rilke's achievement is certified by the fact that his texts continually demand interpretation, provoking readers spontaneously to make his language their own. The works' authenticity is demonstrated by the public's continued involvement with them: there are many poetic virtuosi (one thinks of Rilke's near contemporary Stefan George) whose texts do not reverberate in this manner.

But there is one further argument to be made. During Rilke's Paris years, when his poetic project found its fulfillment in the *New Poems* (which include the magisterial "Archaic Torso of Apollo"), he produced simultaneously an extraordinary prose text, *The Notebooks of Malte Laurids Brigge,* completed in January 1910. This book is the dark shadow against which the sunlit *New Poems* are to be read. Rilke always saw it as autobiographical, therapeutic, to be read "against the grain" (it includes portions of his letters virtually unchanged). Although it is not "formless"—

much recent criticism has been devoted to its eccentric structural symmetries—it is an extremely loose text, seemingly always threatened by disintegration and silence. Since the *New Poems'* chief characteristics are integration and eloquence, a comprehensive "rescue" of images both immediate and inherited, it is easy to see why *Malte* needed to be written. Its language is very like that of the poems, but it speaks of impossibilities, the impossibility of holding the intensity of experience in language, the impossibility of asserting any value against the indifferent weight of time. Above all it speaks of horror: the disease and decay lurking just beneath the surfaces so lovingly celebrated in the *New Poems.*

Although *Malte* is usually called a novel, it challenges the very notion of the traditional novel: a central theme is that it is no longer possible to "tell stories." And in challenging formal conventions the book has played a significant role in this century's fictional developments, linking Rilke to the contemporary innovations of Hofmannsthal, Musil, and James Joyce. The prose of *Malte* is stylistically homogeneous, but the forms inhabited by its voice include the extremes of intimate reflection, documentary impression, theological speculation, and a romanticized yet esoteric historical fable.

Malte is a young Dane living in Paris. Obsessed by a childhood he feels he has not digested, he is equally vulnerable to the repressed horror of ordinary lives in the metropolis, the ways in which death, now the modern world's only obscenity, erupts onto the surface of a life becoming ever more deathly as it strives to refuse death's truth. Malte's "notes" oscillate between exploration of the negativities, which seem to consume his own existence, and memories, ostensibly from childhood, where definable values existed. A key figure here is his grandfather, who died a "great death," a ritual performance from which no one in the community could escape. In his grandfather's time, too, stories could be told,

790

sequences of authentic experience. And in a memory from his childhood, his Aunt Abelone crystallizes some of these stories—stories of women, of medieval nuns, and also of Goethe's friend Bettina von Arnim, whose love transcended its object and hence could fill the world with its intensity instead of being consumed. But these fullnesses of death, love, and storytelling are not simply played off nostalgically against present decay. The shifting, skeptical quality of Malte's writing is such that the closer he comes to a stabilized truth, the more it seems to dissolve into doubt and into a new quest into the penumbra of the past.

Judith Ryan has called the narrative mode "hypothetical," based on the refusal of even the smallest certainty. And it is in this dissolving of its own true-false antithesis that the text gains its authenticity. Malte's quest for his own life must remain unfulfilled: the novel ends with a version of the story of the prodigal son that refuses an ending, refuses the pretence of love and community. But precisely in Malte's lack of "own-ness" lies the strength of his perceptions: Malte's experience is vicarious; he tells stories that he *cannot* know to be true, stories of his fellow-sufferers within the inauthentic. His project turns out to be a rescue operation complementary to that of the *New Poems.* Where the poems rescue the achieved moments of civilization as well as the quiet simplicities that are being lost to technology, Malte rescues all that has failed in the past and the present, the "living" that hardly deserves the name.

To give a sense of the text I quote excerpts from a fairly long early section set in Paris:

> It is good to say it out loud: "Nothing has happened." Again: "Nothing has happened." Does it help? . . .
>
> I have always been on the move. God knows in how many cities, sections of cities, cemeteries, bridges, and alleyways. Somewhere I saw a man pushing a vegetable cart. He cried, "Chou-fleur, Chou-fleur," the "fleur" with a strangely opaque "eu" sound. Beside him walked an angular, ugly woman, who jabbed him from time to time. And whenever she jabbed him, he cried out. Sometimes he cried out of his own accord, but then it turned out to have been pointless, and right away he had to cry out again, because a house that might buy had been reached. Have I already said that he was blind? No? Well, he was blind. He was blind and cried out. I'm falsifying when I say that, I'm leaving out the cart he was pushing, I'm acting as if I hadn't noticed that his cry was about vegetables. But is that essential? And even if it were essential, isn't it a question of what the whole thing meant to me? I saw an old man who was blind and cried out. I saw that. Saw it.
>
> . . . You could see the inside [of demolished houses]. On the various stories you could see internal walls to which the hangings still clung, here and there a fragment of wall or ceiling. Next to these walls there persisted, along the whole outside wall, a dirty-white space, and through this there crawled, in revolting, serpentlike, softly absorbing patterns, the open, rusted duct of the toilet pipe. . . . The resistant life of these rooms refused to be stamped out. It was still there, hanging on to the remaining nails, standing on the remains of the floors, barely a hand's width, creeping into the attachments of the corners, where one could still speak of an interior. You could see that it inhabited the color which it had slowly, year in, year out, transformed: blue into moldy green, green into grey, and yellow into an old, worn out, decaying white. . . .
>
> For a while yet I can note all that down and tell of it. But there will come a day when my hand will be far from me, and when I order it to write, it will write words which I don't mean. The day of a different interpretation will dawn, and no word will stay attached to the next, and all meaning will dissolve like clouds and pour down like water.
>
> (4.748, 749–750, 756)

Just as Rilke's project of rescue is discernible in *Malte,* so too we can speak of the structure of limits. But instead of the limits that control the human imagination, toward which the poetry thrusts and which it strives to inhabit, Malte explores the limit at the very beginning of consciousness, the ability to connect one thing with another, on which poetry depends. Beneath that limit lies the threat to all language, hence to consciousness itself—a world where all old connections are corroded, to be replaced by a kind of prehistorical, inhuman causality. This is Malte's world. In all the quoted descriptive passages we see his drive to record and connect the sequences of this quasi-life ignored by everyone. But the very process of translating the inarticulate into language forces him to look at what he's doing, to ask why and to realize that he has no answer. Anticipating Beckett he can only reiterate: "Saw it." Significantly, the most elegant, coherent imagery—that of clouds and rain—is generated by the moment when all connections are to be lost forever.

For Malte one absence leads to another: from the vestigial life of the blind man he can only move to the disgusting, meaningless traces of past human living in the demolished, gaping interiors. In this world the very thought of presence and fullness is suspect, with its apparent ignoring of time's absolute corrosive power. And this desolate world is the ultimate ground of Rilke's poetic achievement. His celebration of moments of joy, of the wonders of imagining long past, of the incredible toughness of the human spirit (the same spirit that won't let go of rusty nails)—all this celebration is conditioned by the fear, indeed the certainty of loss. And in the world of Malte, our world, such loss knows no possibility of rescue: the movement from half-life into death is without ritual, barely noticeable. To have produced a language of celebration that never denies the radical darkness of this knowledge: this is Rilke's lifework and usable legacy.

Selected Bibliography

EDITIONS

INDIVIDUAL WORKS

Leben und Lieder: Bilder und Tagebuchblätter. Strassburg and Leipzig, 1894.

Larenopfer. Prague, 1896.

Wegwarten: Lieder, dem Volke geschenkt. Prague, 1896.

Traumgekrönt. Leipzig, 1897.

Advent. Leipzig, 1898.

Am Leben hin: Novellen und Skizzen. Stuttgart, 1898.

Ohne Gegenwart: Drama in zwei Akten. Berlin, 1898.

Mir zur Feier: Gedichte. Berlin, 1899.

Zwei Prager Geschichten. Stuttgart, 1899.

Vom lieben Gott und Anderes: An Grosse für Kinder erzählt. Berlin and Leipzig, 1900. Second (1904) and subsequent editions are entitled *Geschichten vom lieben Gott.*

Das tägliche Leben: Drama in zwei Akten. Munich, 1902.

Die Letzten. Geschichten. Berlin, 1902.

Das Buch der Bilder. Berlin, 1902; 2d, much-expanded edition, 1906.

Worspswede: Fritz Mackensen, Otto Modersohn, Fritz Overbeck, Hans am Ende, Heinrich Vogeler. Bielfeld and Leipzig, 1903.

Auguste Rodin. Berlin, 1903.

Das Stundenbuch, enthaltend die drei Bücher: Vom mönchischen Leben, Von der Pilgerschaft, Von der Armuth und vom Tode. Leipzig, 1905.

Die Weise von Liebe und Tod des Cornets Christoph Rilke. Berlin, 1906.

Neue Gedichte. Leipzig, 1907–1908. Published in two parts.

Requiem. Leipzig, 1909.

Die Aufzeichnungen des Malte Laurids Brigge. Leipzig, 1910.

Das Marien-Leben. Leipzig, 1913.

Erste Gedichte. Leipzig, 1913.

Die weisse Fürstin: Eine Szene am Meer. Berlin and Steglitz, 1920.

Puppen: Mit Zeichnungen von Lotte Pritzel. Munich, 1921.

Duineser Elegien. Leipzig, 1923.

Die Sonette an Orpheus: Geschrieben als ein Grabmal für Wera Ouckama Knoop. Leipzig, 1923.

Vergers suivi des Quatrains Valaisans. Paris, 1926.

Ewald Tragy: Erzählung. Munich, 1929.

Späte Gedichte. Leipzig, 1934.

Aus dem Nachlass des Grafen C. W.: Ein Gedichtkreis. Wiesbaden, 1950.

COLLECTED WORKS

Gesammelte Werke. 6 vols. Leipzig, 1927. Volume 6 contains Rilke's translations ("Übertragungen"), of which the following are the most important: *Elizabeth Barrett-Brownings Sonette aus dem Portugiesischen* (1908), *Maurice de Guérin: Der Kentauer* (1911), *Portugiesische Briefe: Die Briefe der Marianna Alcoforado* (1913), *André Gide: Die Rückkehr des verlorenen Sohnes* (1914), *Die vierundzwanzig Sonette der Louise Labé, Lyoneserin, 1555* (1918), *Michelangelo-Übertragungen* (1913–1921), *Paul Valéry: Gedichte* (1925).

Sämtliche Werke. 6 vols. Edited by Ernst Zinn. Wiesbaden, 1955–1966. The standard critical edition, fully annotated.

Übertragungen. Edited by Ernst Zinn and Karin Weis. Frankfurt, 1975.

CORRESPONDENCE AND DIARIES

Briefe. Edited by Karl Altheim in cooperation with Ruth Sieber-Rilke. 2 vols. Leipzig, 1950. This selection has remained standard, being reissued in a single volume in 1980. However, many complete correspondences have appeared subsequently.

Briefe an Auguste Rodin. Leipzig, 1928.

Briefe an eine Freundin [Claire Goll-Studer], *1918–1924.* Edited by Richard von Mises. Aurora, N.Y., 1944.

Briefe an eine junge Frau [Lisa Heise]. Leipzig, 1930.

Briefe an einen jungen Dichter [Franz Xaver Kappus]. Leipzig, 1929.

Briefe an Nanny Wunderly-Volkart. 2 vols. Edited by Niklaus Bigler and Rätus Luck. Frankfurt, 1977.

Briefe an seinen Verleger [Anton Kippenberg], *1906–1926.* 2 vols. Wiesbaden, 1949.

Briefe und Tagebücher aus der Frühzeit, 1899–1902. Leipzig, 1933.

Briefwechsel [Hugo von Hofmannsthal]. Edited by Rudolf Hirsch and Ingeborg Schnack. Frankfurt, 1978.

Briefwechsel in Gedichten mit Erika Mitterer. Wiesbaden, 1950.

Briefwechsel mit Helene von Nostitz. Edited by Oswalt von Nostitz. Frankfurt, 1976.

Briefwechsel mit Inga Junghanns. Edited by Wolfgang Herwig. Wiesbaden, 1959.

Briefwechsel mit Katharina Kippenberg. Edited by Bettina von Bouchard. Wiesbaden, 1954.

Briefwechsel mit Lou Andreas-Salomé. Edited by Ernst Pfeiffer. Zurich, 1952.

Briefwechsel mit Marie von Thurn und Taxis. Edited by Ernst Zinn. Zurich, 1951.

Die Briefe an Gräfin Margot Sizzo, 1921–1926. Wiesbaden, 1950.

Gesammelte Briefe. 6 vols. Edited by Ruth Sieber-Rilke and Carl Sieber. Leipzig, 1936–1939.

Lettres à Merline [Baladine Klossowska], *1919–1922.* Paris, 1950.

Lettres à une amie vénétienne [Mimi Romanelli]. Verona, 1941.

R. M. Rilke—André Gide Correspondance, 1909–1926. Edited by Renée Lang. Paris, 1952.

So lass ich mich zu träumen geben: Briefe an Magda von Hattingberg. Gmunden, Bad Ischl, 1949.

Über Gott: Zwei Briefe. Leipzig, 1933.

TRANSLATIONS

Since the question of Rilke's reception in the English-speaking world is inherently interesting, the listing of early and current translations is extensive, and is given in chronological order. Many early translations, particularly those by Leishman, MacIntyre, and Norton, are still widely available in paperback editions.

Poems. Translated by Jessie Lemont. New York, 1918.

Auguste Rodin, Part I. Translated by Jessie Lemont and Hans Trausil. New York, 1919.

The Life of the Virgin Mary. Translated by R. G. L. Barrett. Würzburg, 1921.

Ten Poems. Translated by B. J. Morse. Trieste, 1926.

Two Duino Elegies. Translated by B. J. Morse. Trieste, 1926.

The Story of the Love and Death of Cornet Christopher Rilke. Translated by B. J. Morse. Osnabrück, 1927.

The Notebook of Malte Laurids Brigge. Translated by John Linton. London, 1930.

The Journal of My Other Self. New York, 1930.

Elegies from the Castle of Duino. Translated by Victoria and Edward Sackville-West. London, 1931.

Stories of God. Translated by Nora Purtscher-Wydenbruck and M. D. Herter Norton. London and New York, 1932.

Letters to a Young Poet. Translated by M. D. Herter Norton. New York, 1934.

Poems. Translated by J. B. Leishman. London, 1935.

Sonnets to Orpheus. Translated by J. B. Leishman. London, 1936.

Later Poems. Translated by J. B. Leishman. London, 1938.

Translations from the Poetry of Rainer Maria Rilke. Translated by M. D. Herter Norton. New York, 1938.

Duino Elegies. Translated by J. B. Leishman and Stephen Spender. London, 1939.

Fifty Selected Poems. Translated by C. F. MacIntyre. Berkeley, Calif., 1940.

Poems from the Book of Hours: Das Stundenbuch. Translated by Babette Deutsch. Norfolk, Conn., 1941.

Primal Sound and Other Prose Pieces. Translated by C. A. Niemeyer. Cummington, Mass., 1943.

Sonnets to Orpheus and Duino Elegies. Translated by Jessie Lemont. New York, 1945.

Letters of Rainer Maria Rilke 1892–1910. Translated by Jane Bannard Greene and M. D. Herter Norton. New York, 1945.

Letters of Rainer Maria Rilke 1911–1926. Translated by Jane Greene and M. D. Herter Norton. New York, 1948.

The Notebooks of Malte Laurids Brigge. Translated by M. D. Herter Norton. New York, 1949.

From the Remains of Count C. W. Translated by J. B. Leishman. London, 1952.

Letters of Rainer Maria Rilke and Princess Marie von Thurn und Taxis. Translated by Nora Wydenbruck. Norfolk, Conn., 1958.

New Poems. Translated by J. B. Leishman. New York, 1964.

Duinesian Elegies. Translated by Elaine E. Boney. Chapel Hill, N.C., 1975.

Rilke on Love and Other Difficulties. Translated by John Mood. New York, 1975.

Duino Elegies and Sonnets to Orpheus. Translated by A. Poulin. Boston, 1977.

The Roses and the Windows. French poems, translated by A. Poulin. Port Townsend, Wash., 1978.

Nine Plays. Translated by Klaus Phillips and John Locke. New York, 1979.

Selected Poems. Translated by Robert Bly. New York, 1981.

Poems 1912–1926. Translated by Michael Hamburger. Redding Ridge, Conn., 1981.

Selected Poetry of Rainer Maria Rilke. Translated by Stephen Mitchell. New York, 1982.

The Lay of the Love and Death of Cornet Christoph Rilke. Translated by Stephen Mitchell. San Francisco, 1983.

Sonnets to Orpheus. Translated by Kenneth Pitchford. Harrison, N.Y., 1983.

The Notebooks of Malte Laurids Brigge. Translated by Stephen Mitchell. New York, 1983.

Prose and Poetry. Edited by Egon Schwartz. New York, 1984.

The Book of Pictures. Translated by Stephen Mitchell. New York, 1984.

Rilke: Between Roots. Translated by Rika Lesser. Princeton, N.J., 1986.

New Poems. 2 vols. Translated by Edward Snow. Berkeley, Calif., 1984, 1987.

Sonnets to Orpheus. Translated by David Young. Middletown, Conn., 1987.

BIOGRAPHICAL AND CRITICAL STUDIES

Allemann, Beda. *Zeit und Figur beim späten Rilke.* Pfullingen, West Germany, 1961.

————. "Rilke und Mallarmé: Entwicklung einer Grundfrage der symbolistischen Poetik." In *Rilke in neuer Sicht,* edited by Käte Hamburger. Stuttgart, 1971.

Andreas-Salomé, Lou. *Rainer Maria Rilke.* Translated by A. Von der Lippe. Redding Ridge, Conn., 1984. (German original published 1929.)

Baron, Frank, Ernst S. Dick, and Warren R. Maurer, eds. *Rilke: The Alchemy of Alienation.* Lawrence, Kans., 1980. An important recent collection of articles in English. Contributors include Hans Egon Holthusen, Stephen Spender, Lev Kopelev, Walter H. Sokel, Andras Sandor, and Erich Simenauer.

Butler, Eliza M. *Rilke.* Cambridge, England, 1941.

Demetz, Peter. *René Rilkes Prager Jahre.* Düsseldorf, 1953.

Guardini, Romano. *Rilke's "Duino Elegies": An Interpretation.* Chicago, 1961.

Hamburger, Käte, ed. *Rilke in neuer Sicht.* Stuttgart, 1971. This important collection includes articles by Eudo C. Mason, Beda Allemann, and Jacob Steiner, and Käte Hamburger's own seminal study, "Die phänomenologische Struktur der Dichtung Rilkes."

Heller, Erich. "Rilke and Nietzsche." In *The Disinherited Mind.* Cambridge, England, 1952.

Hendry, J. F. *The Sacred Threshold: A Life of Rainer Maria Rilke.* Manchester, England, 1983.

RAINER MARIA RILKE

Holthusen, Hans Egon. *Rainer Marie Rilke: A Study of His Later Poetry.* New Haven, Conn., 1952.

Jayne, Richard. *The Symbolism of Space and Motion in the Works of Rainer Maria Rilke.* Frankfurt, 1972.

Leppmann, Wolfgang. *Rilke: A Life.* New York, 1984.

Liebnitz, Jennifer, and John E. Holmes. *Rilke and the Visual Arts.* Lawrence, Kans., 1982.

Mason, Eudo C. *Rilke, Europe, and the English-Speaking World.* Cambridge, England, 1961.

Musil, Robert. *Rede zur Rilke-Feier in Berlin am 16. Januar 1927.* Berlin, 1927.

Ritzer, Walter. *Rainer Maria Rilke Bibliographie.* Vienna, 1951.

Rolleston, James. *Rilke in Transition: An Exploration of His Earliest Poetry.* New Haven, Conn., 1970.

Ryan, Judith. *Umschlag und Verwandlung: Poetische Struktur und Dichtungstheorie in Rainer Maria Rilkes Lyrik der mittleren Periode (1907–1914).* Munich, 1972.

Salis, J. R. von. *Rilke: The Years in Switzerland.* Berkeley, Calif., 1964.

Sandor, Andras. "Rilke's and Walter Benjamin's Conceptions of Rescue and Liberation." In Baron et al. (see above).

Schnack, Ingeborg. *Rilke Leben und Werk im Bild.* Frankfurt, 1966.

Steiner, Jacob. *Rilkes Duineser Elegien.* 2d ed. Berne, 1969.

Webb, Karl E. *Rilke and Jugendstil.* Chapel Hill, N.C., 1978.

Wood, Frank. *Rilke: The Ring of Forms.* Minneapolis, 1958.

JAMES ROLLESTON

FILIPPO TOMMASO MARINETTI
(1876–1944)

MARINETTI AND MODERNITY

Creare vivendo. [To create by living.]
—Marinetti, *Marinetti e il futurismo*

FILIPPO TOMMASO MARINETTI—poet-revolutionary and the creator of Italian futurism, the artistic and political movement he founded in 1909 and whose intricate parallel lives as an international avant-garde movement and a culture-bound Italian phenomenon he choreographed until his death in 1944—was one of this century's foremost and most flagrant exponents of aesthetic and cultural modernism. Under the banner of futurism or, what amounted almost to the same thing, the modernist avant-garde, Marinetti and his group waged a cultural revolution that, based on the extension of avant-garde artistic and ideological practices into a way of life, aimed at "futurizing" all spheres of human life, from art to politics. It should be stressed from the very start that the distinction between artistic and cultural (and even political) revolution, although crucial to the delineation of the specific terrains upon which the Marinettian revolution operated, was the very distinction Marinetti sought to collapse. Marinetti's most extreme, and therefore most dangerous, contribution to "the project of modernity" was, in fact, the elaboration of a strategy of total and permanent revolution that sought nothing less than a global seizure of the real in the name of art, that is, a transfiguration of "life" (culture, the surrounding environment, the human subject) into a total work of futurist art.

Marinetti's futurism, rather than being a strictly defined ideology, was an attitude toward life, a way of understanding existence radically as ardor, adventure, and revolt, as the perpetual struggle against inertia and repetition, especially the most virulent form of repetition: *passatismo* (passéism or worship of the past). Futurism, notwithstanding its status as a way of life, was deeply ideological and political in intent, for it conceived the way to avant-garde art ("formal revolution") as leading to a social revolution. Consequently, the global and militant project of aestheticization Marinetti undertook in the name of futurism was a means of catalyzing a more fundamental moral and social upheaval. Crucial to this project was the elaboration of a radically new conception of the functions of art and the artist. Resorting to the slogan texts that were his trademark, Marinetti encapsulated his program in the two rallying cries Art = Life and Art = Action. What was intended, however, was a rather complex operation by which the boundaries between art and life, art and action, text and world, were destroyed or at least put into crisis. Art as a form of action was to pass violently into life; life (the shocks, speed, and "synthetic violence" of the new technological universe) was to pass violently into art.

Such a project contested the traditional status of the artwork: "Futurism wishes to introduce life into art brutally; it combats the old ideal of the aesthetes, static, decorative, effeminate, precious, fastidious, which hates action." Marinetti's radicalization of the bourgeois work of art took the form of a profound instrumentalization by which art, desublimated and stripped of the illusion of its autonomy from society, was deployed as a model *of* and *for* action and ultimately as a medium of action whose function was to change life: to produce revolutionary events or, as a surrogate form of revolution, to produce itself as a revolutionary event.

Marinetti wrote in 1912 that "a *formal* revolution prepares for and assists a *fundamental* revolution . . . [because] no one knows where inspiration ends and will begins." However tangential the link between formal and fundamental revolution may be, it is clear that behind this statement lies the belief that revolution can emerge from the theorization and practice of avant-garde writing and that futurist art and literature heralded a new age in which form itself would become central. From this point of view, there is no explosion except the text; that is, the futurist text "contained" the revolution in the sense that its desacralization of art and its iconoclastic shattering of syntactic connections were, for the futurists, homologous to the shattering of those cultural institutions blocking the paths to modernization.

Marinetti's practice of textual politics, however, went even further than this "virtual" politicization of the textual site, than this shattering of language and the institutional status of the traditional work of art. He programmed his works, above all his manifestos—and as I shall need to demonstrate, all of Marinetti's works (poems, plays, novels, performance pieces, "happenings") are manifestos of sorts—to be translated into action. In short, textual violence, whether produced by the disruption of social forms openly called for in Marinetti's writings or by the disruption of form and language, was to be converted into extra-textual and immediately political violence. Such violence could take the "ethical" form of the love of danger and the daily heroism of a futurist life: "Every man will live his best possible novel. The most gifted spirits will live their best possible poems." In other words, every man ought to be an avant-gardist. This textual violence could also take the form of explicit political action, culminating in an audacious, futurist death. After all, the ultimate futurist textual performance was war; "futurism intensified," war was the most beautiful of futurist poems. And the pleasure of this text was, as Marinetti put it, the joy of playing billiards with death.

The notion of the text as performance, of futurism as action, as life-style/death-style, brings us to the most "totalitarian" aspect of the futurist project: the transposition of the life-world (*Lebenswelt*) into a work of art, the so-called "Futurist Reconstruction of the Universe." Marinetti and his futurist cohorts regarded culture neither in the coercive terms of economy (as did Karl Marx) or repression (as did Sigmund Freud) nor even as an aesthetic phenomenon in which tragedy figured (as did Friedrich Wilhelm Nietzsche), but rather as a formal or semiotic system, as a phenomenon to be aestheticized (revolutionized) by linguistic and textual means. Cultural warfare was thus regarded as a form of textual warfare—a battle of languages—in which futurism had to seize and destroy the passéist text imposed by the dominant late-nineteenth-century culture. Futurism, in fact, began as a "technical" revolution in poetic language concerned with extending the revolution announced by the French symbolists and carried forward, at the turn of the century, by the *vers-libre* (free-verse) practitioners. Marinetti soon recognized that free-verse experimentation was an inadequate basis for the absolute and totalitarian claims of avant-garde revolution. Therefore, he undertook, under the sign of *parole in libertà* (words in freedom), a more radical destruction of poetic language, one that assaulted the canonic structures of language itself—syntax, the sentence, the page as a unit of writing. It was this revolutionary shattering of syntax and sense that Marinetti and the other futurists attempted to extend into the other artistic areas, from painting to theater, dance, sculpture, cinema, and even to daily behavior.

Marinetti's aesthetic "totalitarianism" can be regarded as a twentieth-century ("geared-up" and mass-cultural) version of the late-nineteenth-century elitist aestheticisms practiced, on one hand, by the symbolists, and, on the other, by Nietzsche. It was based on two sets of militant imperatives:

1. *To destroy the past* at all costs and categorically (the future must be established as the privileged ontological dimension of human existence, for, as Marinetti put it, "the past is necessarily inferior to the future"); to destroy once and for all the nineteenth century, with its sentimentality and its historicist sensibility; to destroy, in particular, the petit-bourgeois and philistine elements of late-nineteenth-century culture that, having made the turn into the new century, threatened to block the rapid march toward universal mechanization; to destroy the traditional work of art as part of a more comprehensive desacralization of values; to destroy repetition and its grip on the technologically backward and static Italy of Giovanni Giolitti and the liberal reform (1900–1911); to destroy "history" in order to build a new history and to break the hold of those fossilized traditions which colonized Italy's present and future in the name of *passatismo* and its pernicious mental forms: archaeology, academism, senility, quietism, cowardice, pacifism, pessimism, nostalgia, sentimentalism, tourism, erotomania, and other forms of necrophilia.

2. *To make it new* at all costs, that is, to create a radically modern and anti-traditional art that incorporated, in its language and structure, the values of the technological universe—speed, mechanical splendor and beauty, intuition and instinct—and that embodied the revolt of action against contemplation and pacified existence; to kill the master-piece by creating a form of art that was permanently provisional, ephemeral, and strategic to the point of setting itself into permanent crisis; to erase art as repetition by creating avant-garde "manifestations," as opposed to "works" of art, that perpetually transgressed the limits of art (in Marinetti's words, futurism is "a continual effort to transcend the laws of art, and art itself, into something unexpected that could be called *life-art-ephemera*"); to change the rules of the game of bourgeois art in such a way that the new game does not degenerate into the game of breaking the rules and, as a guarantee of this, to break the ultimate rule that stipulates that the realms of art and politics should not be confused; to reconstruct the world as a futurist work of art, thereby rendering the modern world, already partially aestheticized by its machinic and electrical flows, into a totally realized futurist aesthetic phenomenon.

It is this compelling—albeit extreme—cultural vision in which art, as opposed to religion or politics, was to serve as the dominant means of structuring reality that is Marinetti's ultimate contribution to the ideology of modernism. This revolutionary program, informed by what Marinetti called "artificial optimism" and his opponents called "dilettantish revolutionism," took the historical form of aggressive cultural battle, punctuated by the forays into the arena of real politics that Marinetti and the futurists waged for over thirty years, including the futurist campaign for Italian intervention in World War I. During this period, futurism passed through three stages: a pre–World War I phase, its so-called heroic phase (1909–1915, sometimes extended to 1920), in which Marinetti, by defining the program of Italian futurism, set the artistic and ideological agenda of the European avant-garde in general; a proto-Fascist phase (1916–1922) in which the movement became more and more entrenched in Italian politics, founding its own party in 1918 and helping to create the Fasci di Combattimento (combat groups) in 1919; and a para-Fascist phase (1923–1944) in which futurism, despite Marinetti's various disagreements with the regime, was annexed by Fascism, becoming its official art and executing a long good-bye to the avant-garde. In other words, the futurist revolution became futurism in service of revolution and finally futurism in the service of the Fascist counterrevolution. Paradoxically, the more futurism became overtly "political," the more it lost its original political efficacy, which was of a countercultural sort.

It goes without saying that Marinetti's value as a thinker of the modern condition lies in the extremity of his positions and in the exorbitance of the language in which he couched them. Futurist discourse is a language of battle in which no distinction is made between war and politics, between art and war. Like Nietzsche, Marinetti is a "prophet of extremity." And like Nietzsche, whose myth of the superman he rewrote in futurist terms (love of danger, instinct, force, courage, sport), Marinetti was fascinated by power: the power of machines, the power of a racing motorcar, the power of speed and flight, the power of the human body in motion, the power of youth, the power of imagination, especially its "amorous" power to forge analogies that connect "distant, seemingly dissimilar, and hostile things."

MARINETTI'S "AUTHOR-FUNCTION"

Born in 1876, Marinetti belongs, along with such modernist masters as James Joyce, Franz Kafka, Ezra Pound, Igor Stravinsky, and Pablo Picasso, to the generation of 1905, which, according to Robert Wohl's genealogy (*The Generation of 1914 and Modernism,* 1986), constitutes the third generation of the modernist movement. This generation launched the avant-garde movements in the period between 1905 and 1914 and installed, as part of its "revolution of the word," the languages of transgression upon which the canonic works of high modernism would be based. Unlike

the other masters, who would realize their major work in the 1920's, Marinetti executed his most significant—ideological as well as literary—work in the period extending from 1909 to 1920, and his impact was greatest during the pre–World War I period, the "futurist moment," so called because the artists and poets of this period in their longing for a revolution that seemed imminent automatically assumed futurist stances.

With the publication of the incendiary "Fondazione e manifesto del futurismo" ("The Founding and Manifesto of Futurism"; henceforth "The Futurist Manifesto") on 20 February 1909 in the Paris newspaper *Le figaro,* Marinetti and futurism exploded onto the European stage in a blaze of publicity and controversy. Calling for a new futurist poetry that would embody the realities of modern life and for the destruction of traditional structures and institutions, the manifesto had the effect of a shot heard round the world of the first machine age. Couched in violent and subversive language, the manifesto was one of the first great "shocks of the new" as well as one of the first codifications of a twentieth-century art based on the shock-practice. It catapulted Marinetti into the role of a major player in that dramatic shift by which the "culture of time and space," as Stephen Kern has called it, attempted to come to grips with the artistic and ideological implications of the various manifestations of rapid technological progress—motor cars, airplanes, electric lighting, wirelesses, machine guns— all of which would become part of futurist iconography. Indeed, Marinetti made the mastering of time and space by human energy the very pivot of his aesthetics of speed: "Time and space died yesterday. We already live in the absolute, because we have created eternal, omnipresent speed."

Marinetti, assuming the tone of a Karl Marx gone P. T. Barnum, announced, for all intents and purposes, that the specter of futurist revolution was haunting Italy and all of Europe and that the destruction of the traditional work of art and the academic museum culture enshrining it was under way. He declared that "no work without an aggressive character can be a masterpiece" and that "art, in fact, can be nothing but violence, cruelty, and injustice." In other words, "the death of art" as heretofore known and, in its way, the "Futurist Manifesto" had a purport similar to that of Nietzsche's more momentous declaration regarding the death of God. Modern man must learn to do without the beautiful illusion and the peace treaty imposed by the immortal masterwork; the various sublimes of the European ideal of art—Truth, Goodness, Beauty, Happiness, Salvation—must be violently replaced by the futurist sublime—the new space of danger, action, and revolt opened by art's transgression of its traditional status as "pensive immobility, ecstasy, and sleep."

Often cited as an illustration of Marinetti's genius as a showman, the publication of the manifesto on the front page of Le figaro, a leading Paris newspaper rented for the apocalyptic launching of futurism, is more correctly regarded as both a calculated attempt to command a mass audience by appropriating the new means of cultural production—the media—and a demonstration of art's new desublimated status as propaganda and commodity form. The manifesto, by the way, elicited well over 10,000 letters of response, most of which were in protest. Long before Marshall McLuhan, Marinetti had grasped that the medium was the message, and he would go on to stage the remainder of his work and the scenario of the futurist movement as a media event.

The "Futurist Manifesto" is Marinetti's single most important and most compelling work. It was the first of over fifty manifestos, on every aspect of art and life, from painting to theater to lust and politics, with which Marinetti and the futurists blitzed the regime of passéist culture between 1909 and 1916. That the futurists appropriated the manifesto—the political form of expression par excellence—as their fundamental polemical instrument indicates that they recognized that artistic and cultural power must be won under the same conditions as political power. Although we shall examine in a moment the specific ways in which the Marinettian manifesto functions as a disturbing hybrid that enacts a perpetual exchange between literary and political registers, it is important to recognize that the manifesto is the discursive form that dominates Marinetti's work in general. It is not so much a question of Marinetti's having converted the manifesto into a work of art but rather of his having converted his literary works into manifestos by programming them to illustrate and disseminate futurist aesthetics and to function as instruments of futurist revolution.

Unlike the other masters, Marinetti's claim to a place in the modernist canon does not rest on the merits of a single immortal masterpiece or even on the cumulative effect of a conventionally executed oeuvre. On the contrary, Marinetti's anti- or counter-oeuvre is informed by an attempt to destroy the masterpiece: "To the conception of the imperishable, the immortal, we oppose, in art, that of becoming, the perishable, the transitory, the ephemeral." At one point, he even called for an art that—in dadaist fashion—systematically "prostituted" classical art: play a Beethoven symphony backward, boil all of Shakespeare down to a single act, perform Parsifal in forty minutes. How then are we to approach Marinetti's work, given that it seeks to subvert its own status as art and to disestablish the notion of the author? What has fashionably come to be called "the death of the author" was already prefigured by Marinetti, who expressed his authorship through the collective apparatus of the avant-garde movement and regarded the function of the artist to be as much the production of events as the creation of works. Furthermore, he dispersed his authorship in what might be called avant-garde laboratory work on language and in a series of seemingly disposable "works": manifestos, pamphlets, agitprop, unrepeatable futurist performances and "happenings."

Therefore before we may proceed, two questions must be raised, the first regarding the instrumental or operative status of his literary work, the second regarding his function as an author. Starting out as a free-verse poet trying to go beyond the "crisis in symbolist values," he went on to produce, in the various and often superimposed guises of poet, playwright, novelist, polemicist, political theorist, performance artist, and joker in the futurist pack, a large body of experimental writing, including pieces for futurist theater and performance. He was, however, primarily a poet. His attempt to create a linguistic apparatus capable of registering and reproducing the shocks of twentieth-century reality was conducted in terms of poetic language and involved a move from free verse to the futurist words-in-freedom, his revolutionary attempt to break up classical writing by liberating words from their syntactic and semantic constraints. His greatest poetic achievement, "Zang Tumb Tumb" (1914), a description of the siege of Adrianople, was written in free-word style, and he would deploy versions of it in writing novels, autobiographical texts, and other hybrid texts that can be thought of as prose poems. In addition to his form-shattering poetry, Marinetti's counter-oeuvre comprises the following ultraconvulsive avant-garde texts: genre-breaking ("polyphonic") novels written in free-word style, the most important being *Marfaka le futuriste* (Marfaka the Futurist, 1910) and *Gli indomabili* (*The Untamables*, 1922), both of which are futurist fantasy narratives employing an allegorical mode of writing; other surcharged "prose poems" that extend and modify *paroliberismo* (free-wordism) in various directions, such as the "explosive novel" *8 anime in una bomba* (8 Souls in a Bomb, 1919), the surrealistic *Spagna veloce e toro futurista* (Speedy Spain and Futurist Bull, 1931), and his autobiographical texts *La grande Milano tradizionale e futurista* (The Great Traditional and Futurist Milan; translated selections appear in Flint's *Marinetti: Selected Writings*) and *Una sensibilità italiana nata in Egitto* (An Italian Sensibility Born in Egypt; selections in Flint's *Marinetti*),

both published posthumously in 1969; provocative theatrical spectacles, the most significant of which are extremely short pieces called *sintesi* (syntheses), that commit a kind of assault and battery on the public in their attempt to abolish the distance between spectacle and spectator; inflammatory manifestos and other polemical writings, volatile mixtures of aesthetic and political discourse, which, in Marinetti's hands, are elevated into works of art; galvanizing slogan-texts, blasts, rallying cries, titles and subtitles, and other telegraphic pronouncements, which often assume a life of their own and which are symptomatic of Marinetti's rhetoric of speed in general ("Quick, give me the whole thing in two words!"); and a series of disruptive futurist gestures, "happenings," and events, the chief of which was Marinetti's life, programmed to unfold—to explode—as a dynamic and aggressive futurist work of art.

As a whole, these works are perhaps best described as "manifestations," the category that contemporary critics have adopted to describe the avant-garde "work" in general and the way in which it builds into its own structure an attack against the traditional artwork. As will become apparent, the covering term "manifestation" is particularly well suited to describe the Marinettian text, because it bears within it the figure of the "manifesto." Although critics have traditionally recognized that Marinetti is at his best in what he himself called the "art of writing manifestos," they have failed to realize that the manifesto is the discursive form he always employs, however implicitly. All of his works function as manifestos in the sense that they are polemical declarations of futurist principles and demonstrations of futurist aesthetic procedures—and therefore immediately political. Like the futurist manifestos themselves, they are violent provocations designed to coerce their readership or theatrical audience into a reciprocally violent gesture of response. They seek to put the public into a linguistic and ideological crisis that can be resolved only by a response of futurist election or rejection. For this reason and because they seek to introduce heterogeneous elements (violence, excess, shock, danger) into the reader's homogeneous and normal world, they are aggressively subversive texts. Furthermore, by foregrounding their stylistic practices and their verbal fireworks, they function as allegories of futurist creation. For example, Marinetti's free-word compositions are technical demonstrations of futurist poetics, theorems in the form of poetry; his futurist plays have no other theme or purpose than the provocation of the audience; his novels are stagings in narrative form of the various scenes of futurist revolution, the very scenes that are staged more explicitly in the theatrical segments of the manifestos themselves. It is precisely this unsettling slippage between manifestation and manifesto that has troubled readers and critics, especially those who have tried to read Marinetti's anti-aesthetic works in terms of traditional categories.

The negation of the traditional work of art and its replacement by the "manifestation-manifesto" leads us to the larger problem of Marinetti's "author-function," to use Michel Foucault's fruitful category. (Foucault states that a writer can be the author of more than simply a book, and can "author" a theory or tradition within which new books and authors can proliferate.) Marinetti's function as an author far exceeds the limits of his literary production and must be extended to include his "authorship" of the futurist movement, arguably his most fully accomplished and influential "artistic" production, for through it he created the prototype for the other historical avant-garde movements, from the other futurisms (Russian cubo-futurism, British vorticism, and the like) to dada and surrealism. Furthermore, Marinetti's author-function must also be reckoned in terms of the artistic and cultural revolution he effected and the overall strategy by which he attempted to escalate an artistic revolution into a full-blown cultural revolution and eventually a political revolution. The Marinettian artistic revolution is

both a "technical" linguistic revolution focused on the creation of words-in-freedom and a more comprehensive textual and media revolution in which certain futurist forms of textuality (the collage, the manifesto, the performance, the sound poem, the artbook, and so forth) were defined and set into circulation. The most authoritative account of this revolution and its importance for modernism can be found in Marjorie Perloff's *The Futurist Moment* (1986).

For our immediate purposes, it is important to stress his overlooked role as a practitioner of a communications revolution in which he attempted to "heat up" the media, as McLuhan would say. This "heating-up" involved not only the dramaturgies of futurist performance—the lecture-declamation, the cabaret evenings, the theater, the cinema, the dance, the concert, the radio—but the graphic media of writing and print, especially the manifesto and visual poetry.

This question of "heating up" the media must be linked to the historical problem confronting Marinetti of how to dominate the revolt of the machines. It was not enough to practice an ideology of the machine, even to the point of absorbing its amorality or, conversely, to give the machine anthropomorphic traits. As Manfredo Tafuri has pointed out:

> What was needed was to see the plain fact that the new social relations instituted in the monster city dominated by technological anonymity would not develop without a violent break with the old means of communication. It was the machine that was now determining the modes of communication, and its messages were compounded of pure energy that had no need for syntactical nexuses. The technological language was based on something new: shock, pure signs assaulting the interlocuter all at once.
> (*Modern Architecture* [New York, 1980], p. 121)

And Marinetti succeeded in reproducing the new technological language by shattering syntactical connections and bombarding his reader with words liberated of sense and syntax.

From this point of view, Marinetti's author-function becomes extremely important to the experience of modernity as it unfolds throughout the twentieth century, for futurist discourse establishes a way of speaking not only about temporality (the "revolt of the future") but about the technological imagination itself (the revolt of the machines). Indeed, the mechanism of our electrical culture, the society of the spectacle or the image, in which Marinetti's "multiplied man," multiplied by machines and the media, is constantly bombarded with messages and with aesthetic experiences of all kinds, is simply the end result of the revolution already grasped and theorized by Marinetti. However, the textual and cultural revolution that can be attributed to Marinetti is extremely contradictory, for its implications go far beyond the iconoclastic shattering of syntax and the desacralization of the work of art itself.

THE DANGEROUS ADVENTURES OF A FUTURIST LIFE

Ritti sulla cima del mondo, noi scagliamo, una volta ancora, la nostra sfida alle stelle!
[Erect on the summit of the world, once again, we hurl defiance to the stars!]

> Marinetti, "Fondazione e
> manifesto del futurismo"

In all things exorbitant, Marinetti managed to be born at least twice: his natural birth to wealthy Milanese parents in Alexandria in Egypt (in 1876) and his mechanical birth "at the hands" of a speeding automobile in Milan (in 1908). At the beginning of the "Futurist Manifesto," Marinetti rehearses the scene of his rebirth as a futurist, which occurred when, during the now legendary joyride that culminated in the invention of futurism, he capsized his swerving car into a factory ditch:

> Oh! Maternal ditch, almost full of muddy water! Fair factory drain! I gulped down your nourishing sludge; and I remembered the blessed black breast of my Sudanese nurse. . . . When I came up—torn, filthy, and stinking—from under the capsized car, I felt the white-hot iron of joy deliciously pass through my heart!

> (Flint trans., 1971, pp. 40–41)

Rosalind Krauss is quite right in reading this passage as "a parable of absolute self-creation," finding in it a model of the avant-gardist's claim to originality: to re-create the self from ground zero, to be born without the taint of ancestors. Marinetti, however, is also acting out, in the form of a rite of passage, a cultural parable: his passage from a "natural" state into the reality of the new technological world, which confers upon him a second or mechanical nature. The centaur's birth announced earlier in the manifesto has been realized; man is now a metalized four-wheeled creature. And futurist man so multiplied by the machine can escape the old myths and mental categories and explode into the future. Horsepower aside, there are other forces at work in this passage of what Stephen Bayley has called "sado-masochistic kitsch." For one, Marinetti's mechanical birth, his initiation into the mental and symbolic universe of the machine, is the provision for his creation of futurism. For another, there takes place a less-than-clandestine eroticization of the automobile, the "beautiful shark," which, through his caresses, becomes Marinetti's mechanical bride. In other words, there is a complete subtext of desire—an agenda to some degree hidden even from the poet—underlying Marinetti's cult of the machine and his representation of the technological imagination, one that leads directly to the royal road of the unconscious of the first machine age.

What is of immediate importance, as we begin our account of Marinetti's dangerous (and sometimes dangerously banal) adventures as a futurist, is that, at the very moment in which he consummates his own metalization, he recalls his Sudanese wet-nurse, the emblem of his fabulous childhood and adolescence in Egypt. This counterpointing of the new and the old, the contrast between the technological place (industrial Milan and elsewhere modern Paris) and the archaeological place (Egypt and elsewhere Italy, both realms of "mummies and museums"), remains a constant of Marinetti's imaginary universe. Throughout his writing and especially in his African novels, there occurs a grotesque hybridization of the technological and the Oriental, a grafting of futuristic elements onto a mythical and at times comic-book version of Africa that, contrary to critical opinion, has very little in common with Gustave Flaubert's *Salammbô* (1863). Therefore, Marinetti's African roots were crucial to the formation of his sensibility, a sensibility whose contradictions are best epitomized by the title of his autobiographical text, *Una sensibilità italiana nata in Egitto.*

Marinetti's extraterritorial childhood was determinative in other respects; it assured that he grew up bilingual. French, in fact, was the language of the first stage of his literary career, and his repatriation to Italy took place through the detour of the bohemian Paris of the "Banquet Years." It also engendered in him a fierce sense of "Italianism"; he defined himself as "a futurist sensibility dominated by an urgent sense of being Italian." Once again, we find the genesis of a contradiction that would inform his adult life: his identity as a cosmopolitan intellectual linked to the avant-garde milieu of Paris versus his radical Italianism, which, for all its masculine patriotism and good-soldier protocols—in the style of Ernest Hemingway—would remain little more than a provincial nationalism. Egypt was important for another and purely pragmatic reason. Marinetti's father, a prominent commercial lawyer, amassed a considerable fortune there. Once Marinetti inherited this money, he was able to underwrite the futurist movement and to undertake various tours to disseminate futurism, such as those to London in 1910 and to Moscow and Saint Petersburg in 1914.

After he had been expelled from his French Jesuit high school in Alexandria (for introducing, as the story goes, Émile Zola's novels to his classmates), Marinetti went to Paris in 1893, earning his *baccalauréat* in literature there and spending "rowdy and triumphant months" at the Sorbonne. But then, at the behest of his father, who had in the meantime returned the family to Milan and who was little disposed toward his son's poetic fancies, he took up the study of law, graduating from the University of Genoa in 1899 with a thesis on parliamentary government. His first literary triumph was "Les vieux marins" (The Old Sailors), a short poem in free verse published in *Anthologie-revue* in 1898. Subsequently it won the first prize in a poetry contest that was part of the "samedis populaires" given by the famous actress Sarah Bernhardt, who when declaiming it, according to Marinetti, made his free verse sound a bit monotonous. One of the judges, Gustave Kahn, the creator of free verse and ideologist of the new "street aesthetics," became Marinetti's "affectionate patron."

Following this auspicious beginning—"all agreed I am a poet of genius"—he dedicated himself strictly to the pursuit of a literary career. Inserting himself within the avant-garde circles of Paris, he entered the debate on poetic form provoked by free verse and by the attempt to go beyond symbolism, which, for all its technical innovations, had not really encountered the experience of modernity. Although he always worked within the symbolist context and much of his program for words-in-freedom was foreshadowed by the French poetical tradition, his passage to futurism ultimately involved an outright rejection of his symbolist masters (Edgar Allan Poe, Charles Baudelaire, Stéphane Mallarmé, and Paul Verlaine) and their old poetry of "nostalgic memory," of "distance and wild solitudes." In their place, he would establish this genealogy of futurist precursors: Émile Zola, Walt Whitman, rosny aîné, Paul Adam, Gustave Kahn, and Émile Verhaeren, whom Marinetti called a "glorifier of machines and tentacular cities." This rejection of symbolism was, in part, a consequence of his attempt to adapt free-verse poetics with its destruction of metrical order to the task of representing the new technological nature, especially the new urban reality. And he would extend free verse into the first futurist style by exploiting its "polyphonic dimension" and "its orchestration of images and sounds in emotion" to express "our contemporary life, intensified by the speeds made possible by steam and electricity, on land, on the seas, and in the air."

Marinetti's proto-futurist literary production, in fact, took place under the sign of free-verse experimentation. He published *La conquête des étoiles: Poème épique* (The Conquest of the Stars: An Epic Poem, 1902), *Destruction: Poèmes lyriques* (Destruction: Lyric Poems, 1904), and a play in prose, *Le roi bombance: Tragédie satirique* (King Riot: A Satirical Tragedy, 1905), a pessimistic political allegorical (anti-passéist, anti-Bolshevik) in the form of a Rabelaisian gastronomic farce. Despite its political pretensions, the play, produced in 1909 at Lugné-Poë's Théâtre de l'Oeuvre, amounts to little more than a recycling of Alfred Jarry's *Ubu Roi* (1896) replete with scatological metaphors: "King Riot, Sacred Bowel of the World, Intestine of Intestines, Grand Stomach of the Kingdom of Blunder." All of these early works display the technique of fragmented allegory, a fireworks style characterized by a baroque squandering of imagery, and, despite the presence of Parnassian and decadent attitudes, an aggressive anti-intellectualism in pursuit of modern thematics.

During the year 1905, he founded, together with Sem Benelli and Vitaliano Ponti, the Milan-based international review *Poesia*, which was to serve as a platform for free-verse poetry. The journal marks Marinetti's attempt to become a cultural broker actively dedicated to the renewal of Italian poetry. Marinetti's experience with *Poesia* and his subsequent collaboration on the Florentine experimental newspaper *Lacerba* (1913–1915) were necessary chapters in the formulation of a theory of formal and cultural revolution. The avant-garde journal would serve both as an instrument for spreading futurist ideas and as a vehicle with which to forge an ideological and political identity for futurism.

In 1905 he published in *Poesia* the pre-futurist poem "A l'automobile" (To the Car, later called "A mon Pegase" and "A l'automobile de course"), in which he identified for the first time the automobile as his new muse, even though his enthusiastic celebration of speed was still couched in symbolist language. That the automobile was a symbol whose time had come is evidenced by the work of Mario Morasso, whose *La nuova arma* (The New Weapon, 1905) and *Il nuovo aspetto meccanico del mondo* (The New Mechanical Aspect of the World, 1907) celebrated "the man of speed" (the "Wattman") and prefigured Marinetti's new "aesthetic of speed."

In 1910 he published his first futurist novel, *Marfaka le futuriste,* which he described as "polyphonic": "It's a lyrical song, an epic, an adventure, and a drama all at the same time." Set in a mythical Africa, the novel recounts the exploits of the warrior Marfaka, a Marinettian version of Nietzsche's superman and a prototype of the futurist leader. The novel, called by James Joll "a tedious rhetorical tale of rape and battle," culminates in Marfaka's creation—a technological parthenogenesis—of a son named Gazouramah, a mechanical winged "over-man." Gazouramah kills his father as he ascends, Icaruslike, forever upward to challenge successfully the sun, thereby realizing "the great dream of total music." The creation and ascent of the futurist technological man, "the happy Oedipus" who liberates himself from the family myth and all earthly bonds, reveals the Icarian or mystical elements of futurism. In the novel Marinetti stages the scene of futurist revolution for the first time and under its most utopian aspect.

Marfaka was the subject of three trials for obscenity, which Marinetti in typical fashion exploited for all the publicity they were worth. Some of the reasons for the censorship are suggested by John Golding's wicked response:

> Marfaka, a supermacho if there ever was one, is one of the most objectionable creations in all fiction. Apart from his general awfulness, Mar-

faka's most notable and presumably most notice-able characteristic was his eleven-meter-long penis which he wrapped around himself while asleep; I picture him in this condition as a sort of recumbent Michelin man—but of course less benign.

For an acute diagnosis of the phallocentrism and misogyny at work in this "fascist fantasy narrative," see the brilliant reading under-taken by Alice Kaplan in *Reproductions of Banality* (1986). With all its deliberate offen-siveness (Marinetti prefaces it with the claim: "I announce to you that the spirit of man is an untrained ovary: we [the futurists] are the ones who fertilize him for the first time"), *Marfaka* stands as an example of Marinettian provocation and of the way in which the manifesto effect molests both the story line and the reader. Its "demonstration" of the futurist's celebration of technology as a supe-rior transcendent value provokes affective re-actions of great intensity because it is linked in a disconcerting way to a series of heteroge-neous elements (the leader, masculine vio-lence, masculine procreation).

THE MANIFESTO AS A TEXT: THE CULTURAL AND TEXTUAL POLITICS OF FUTURISM, 1909–1915

20 February 1909: The launching of the "Futurist Manifesto" marks Marinetti's first appearance in his role as militant theorist of futurism's down-with-the-past ideologies and as high priest qua technician of its "new religion-morality of speed." It is almost impos-sible to disentangle the ideological threads—anarchism, libertarian socialism, Sorelism (the exaltation of violence), Nietzscheanism (the destruction of values), nationalism, and so forth—that were at work in his negation of the past. On the other hand, the "positive" elements of his program can be linked to a need to celebrate the new ethos of the techno-logical world and to dominate the revolt of the

machines. The first manifesto is particularly significant both as a document of cultural modernism in which Marinetti sets out his major ideological positions (*anti-passatismo,* dynamism/activism, *modernolatria* or the cult of the modern, automobilism, and the futurist sensibility) and as a revolutionary text, a text that produces a scenario for revolt that in-volves the reader—however vicariously—in the production of violence. Although traditionally regarded as the appropriate polemical instru-ment and media package for the expression of his down-with-the-past ideologies, the Mari-nettian manifesto has not been adequately treated as a textual site, as a cultural text that both calls for a violent break with the old modes of communication and sets forth in its own syntactic, lexical, and "rhetorical" prac-tices a new ideology of communication.

First of all, what is the status of the mani-festo and its discourse? By treating the mani-festo as a "text," one circumvents all too easily the problem of whether the manifesto should be regarded as belonging primarily either to the literary register or to the extraliterary register, in which the rhetoric of its prose would tend to emphasize emotion and the appeal to action. To establish the boundaries of the manifesto as a genre—a particularly modern genre, even though the Ten Commandments, the oracle, the Jeremiad, the Philippic, the Bull, the *ars poe-tica,* and the like would constitute the "arch texts" of the manifesto—we might place, on one side, Marx and Engel's *Communist Manifesto* (1848) as the decisively extra-artistic, political, and pragmatic deployment of the form and, on the other side, Anna Livia Plurabelle's "mam-mafesta" in James Joyce's *Finnegans Wake* (1939) as the purely literary use of the form. Obviously, Marinetti's deployment of the man-ifesto falls somewhere in between these two extremes, and, in fact, it is appropriate to read Marinetti's manifestos as disturbing hybrids that enact a perpetual exchange between the literary and political registers.

They are "literary" in a most complex way, because they mix textual procedures in a vio-

---

FILIPPO TOMMASO MARINETTI

lent and unforeseen fashion, and because insofar as they are programs, they exploit their own metatextual aspects. This textual contamination has usually been assimilated by using the interpretative figure of the prose poem, but in fact the Marinettian manifesto unfolds as an unsettling alternation between narrative and programmatic elements. The structure of the "Futurist Manifesto" is a perfect example of this: an opening narrative section or prologue, setting forth the genesis of the manifesto, the manifesto itself with its notorious eleven points, and a final narrative scene projected into the future and forecasting the ultimate reception of futurism and the impending obsolescence of the futurists. Within these two narrative sections are inscribed certain (allegorical) scenes: the scene of writing, the scene of mechanical birth, the scene of instruction, the scene of murder or violence, and so forth. For example, the first section of the manifesto represents a scene of writing or, to be exact, a scene of blocked writing. Marinetti and his cohorts have stayed up all night trampling their "atavistic ennui into rich Oriental rugs, arguing up to the last confines of logic, and blackening many reams of paper with frenzied scribbling." Having reached an impasse, the futurists are summoned by the call of the wild, in this case, "the famished roar" of automobiles and the din of metropolis at dawn. Marinetti and company hit the road to play "Mad Max" with their automobiles. What has transpired is the exchange of the scene of writing for the scene of action: it is speed, peremptory action, the scenario of danger, that produces the manifesto.

Such scenes frame the programmatic elements, which, in turn, alternate between metalanguage and language, between criticism as project and writing as the demonstrative realization of that project. In other words, the programmatic assertions about the futurist work of art are, in fact, put into practice by the signifying procedures of the manifesto itself. Consider, for example, the eleventh point of the manifesto:

We will sing of great crowds excited by work, by pleasure, and by revolt; we will sing of the multicolored, polyphonic tides of revolution in the modern capitals; we will sing of the vibrant nightly fervor of arsenals and shipyards blazing with violent electric moons; greedy railway stations that devour smoke-plumed serpents; factories hung on clouds by the crooked lines of their smoke; bridges that leap the rivers like giant gymnasts, flashing in the sun with a glitter of knives; adventurous steamers that sniff the horizon; deep-chested locomotives pawing the tracks like enormous steel horses bridled by tubing; and the sleek flight of planes whose propellers chatter in the wind like banners and seem to cheer like an enthusiastic crowd.

(*Futurism and Futurisms*,
Asterisco trans., pp. 514–516)

To confront the sentences of Marinetti is to be assaulted by a principle of immense mechanical energy. In this sentence, we find the futurist performative impulse at work: "We will sing." Repeated three times, it is then followed by a cosmic enumeration of the new objects to be used as material for the futurist work: the crowd, the metropolis, and finally the catalog of the "new nature" composed of artificial and technological things. Beyond the recognition of the muse value of the new nature of technological reality, the text also performs a negation and demystification of nature as a source of sense and permanent values. This operation occurs, on the one hand, by means of metaphoric substitution: train as serpent, bridge as giant gymnast, locomotive as horse, propeller as banner, and so forth. Here in preliminary form is the "strict net of analogies," the poetics of the "wireless imagination," that will be elaborated in the "Manifesto tecnico della letteratura futurista" ("The Technical Manifesto of Futurist Literature," 1912). Highly significant is the fact that the metaphors (similes, to be exact) are not used for the purpose of anthropomorphic projection—rather nature is displaced or translated into the new technological nature, as part of what might be called a "machine naturalism."

Moreover, another linguistic operation is also taking place through the deployment of adjectives, what classical rhetoric designates as hypallage: *greedy* railway stations, *adventurous* steamers, *deep-chested* locomotives, and so forth. Through such metonymic contamination, the properties of nature are dislodged and attached to the machine nature. Furthermore, at the level of the macrosentence (the passage consists of eight sentences joined by semicolons), there is produced an extraordinary assemblage of objects all floating on the same syntactic and semantic plane, with the same specific gravity, in the constant movement of the assembly line of Marinetti's paratactic machine. Thus, in this sentence we see how the manifesto both projects and demonstrates its own writing practices.

First Exhibit of Futurist Violence: "War, the World's Only Hygiene"

When we confront the extraliterary (or political) aspects of the manifesto, we find at work a militant and strategic rhetoric that seeks to move the reader to action. It is this rhetoric of action that simultaneously constructs a rallying point (the new aesthetics of speed and the cult of the modern) and destroys a point of attack (*passatismo* and pacified existence), thereby effecting a shift away from "literature" toward what Northrop Frye calls "direct verbal and kinetic emotion." Consider the main body of the "Futurist Manifesto." Having been provided with an object lesson in "the love of danger" by the scene of action in the prologue, the reader is then assaulted by eleven blasts that constitute, in the form of a chain reaction, the eleven commandments of the futurist way of life/art. The manifesto appears on a cursory reading—the one engendered by the "violence and precision" that Marinetti claimed were essential to the "art of writing manifestos"—to be an appeal to activism and other strong and noble values:

1. We intend to sing the love of danger, the habit of energy and fearlessness.

2. Courage, audacity, and revolt will be essential elements of our poetry.

3. Up to now literature has exalted a pensive immobility, ecstasy, and sleep. We intend to exalt aggressive action, a feverish insomnia, the racer's stride, the somersault, the punch, and the slap.

(p. 514)

Notice, first of all, that Marinetti uses the royal (futurist) "we," thereby immediately forcing the reader into a position of inclusion or exclusion, and that the sentences are emphatically cast as speech acts or performatives: they are declarations and directives whose very utterence *seems* to bring about the state of affairs they refer to. For example, by uttering "we intend to sing the love of danger," Marinetti, in effect, performs or produces a version of that danger. From this point of view, the manifesto-as-a-speech-act, in calling for a futurist poetry of aggressive action, that is, a poetry not concerned with what it means but with what it does and incites to do, is already an operative demonstration of that poetry of action.

Furthermore, at the level of content, the first three propositions effect a transformation of "ethical" values (courage, struggle, and the other strong and noble values of futurism) into aesthetic values. Notice that their enumeration goes from the general to the more specific, from "love of danger" to "the punch" and "the slap." In short, Marinetti posits a poetry exalting a thematics of aggressive action and revolt that is itself a form of action. Hence the boundaries between art and life, art and action, art and ethics have been erased. Poetry is no longer regarded as a protective barrier before the danger of life but as a release of the very forces that are devoted to the destruction of its traditional and ideal status: its "pensive immobility, ecstasy, and sleep." In the third declaration, Marinetti initiates his attack on *passatismo*, confined, for the time being, to the institution of poetry, to *l'art pour l'art*. Implicit in this attack is the futurist imperative:

FILIPPO TOMMASO MARINETTI

to destroy in order to create. This theme of creative destruction becomes explicit in the seventh proposition ("Except in struggle, there is no more beauty. No work without an aggressive character can be a masterpiece") and will be given an extraliterary form in the last three propositions and the epilogue, where real social targets are designated.

It is, however, only in the fourth declaration that the major aesthetic program of futurism is rendered specific:

> 4. We say that the world's magnificence has been enriched by a new beauty; the beauty of speed. A racing car whose hood is adorned with great pipes, like serpents of explosive breath—a roaring car that seems to ride on grapeshot—is more beautiful than the *Victory of Samothrace*.
>
> (p. 514)

Here the great shift of paradigm is enacted: the displacement of the static icon of classical art and the ideal of passéist beauty by the noisy and turbulent poetry in motion of a racing car. The transvaluation of values continues, as speed in this and succeeding propositions is raised to an aesthetic-ethical principle. But it is only in the ninth and tenth propositions that a concrete program of "political" action is spelled out, thereby introducing the meaning that was absent from the preceding laconic phrases:

> 9. We will glorify war—the world's only hygiene—militarism, patriotism, the destructive gesture of freedom-bringers, beautiful ideas worth dying for, and scorn for women.
>
> 10. We will destroy the museums, libraries, academies of every kind, will fight moralism, feminism, every opportunistic or utilitarian cowardice.
>
> (p. 514)

These two propositions, camouflaged as supplements to the aesthetics of speed, are in fact the grids by which the whole manifesto can be read. The dangerous slippage between ethical and aesthetic categories culminates in these calls for political agitation and cultural destruction. Futurist poetry must be a political *act*—the ultimate political act being war. And the *act* of political revolution is *poetic*.

There is no gloss that can extenuate the implications of these statements: the aesthetics of the machine leads ineluctably to the rendering aesthetic of politics and war. To point out that "the hygiene of war" is not a figure of general extermination but rather a therapeutic measure against the "normal" disease of *passatismo,* an athletic regimen that brings out the best in the individual and the nation, is insufficient. Nor does it suffice to offer an historical gloss that explains the hygiene as a cure for Italian history, as "the cleansing of a society from the adiposities of an unadventurous *borghese* peace" (to use Reyner Banham's phrase) that kept unresolved the problem of *Italia Irredenta* ("Unredeemed Italy," that is, Italian-speaking areas subject to other countries). The ultimate gloss is the one recently provided by the historian Renzo DeFelice as part of his fundamentally revisionary analysis of Marinetti:

> War was seen by him as fullness of life and even as rejoicing, essentially as an individual and artistic fact, which became collective for the Italians in 1911 and more particularly in 1915–18 (as it did for the other nationalities, please note) because it took on the value of a "revelation" of the "true Italian powers," that is, of the triumph of, "futurism" over "passéism." The word "hygiene" used by Marinetti when speaking of war is significant in this context.
>
> (*Futurism and Futurisms*, p. 492)

The trouble with such "hygienic" glosses, regardless of how corrective they may be, is that they cut the dangerous productivity of the Marinettian text: its effect as force or shock, its distressing capacity to displace the exciting value of one element (technological speed) onto an adjacent element (political and historical speed: revolution). The Marinettian text, like the amoral machine it mimes, seeks to place itself beyond good and evil.

FILIPPO TOMMASO MARINETTI

The question of "scorn for woman," on the other hand, was extenuated to a minor degree by Marinetti himself, who went on to build into futurism a highly problematic "feminist" component. He sought the demystification of woman as bourgeois erotic ideal, the divine reservoir of *Amore,* and romantic voluptuary obsession of the poets: "There is nothing natural and important except coitus, whose purpose is the Futurism of the species." Linking this demystification with both an endorsement of women's suffrage and an attack on parliamentarism, whose demise he hoped would be precipitated by the entry of women into the political process, he wrote in "Contro l'amore e il parlamentarismo" ("Against *Amore* and Parliamentarism," 1911–1915): "In this campaign of ours for liberation, our best allies are the suffragettes, because the more rights and power they win for woman, the more will she be deprived of *Amore,* and by so much will she cease to be a magnet for sentimental passion or lust" (Flint trans.). Marinetti's "virilization" of the feminine is continued by Valentine de Saint-Point, the house "feminist," who in her "Manifesto futurista della lussuria" ("Futurist Manifesto of Lust," 1913) unflinchingly declares: "After a battle in which men have died, *it is natural for the victors, proven in war, to turn to rape in the conquered land, so that life may be re-created.*"

Returning to the tenth proposition, one finds that the passéist targets have been sighted: the academic culture ("museums-cemeteries"), the ethical values of the status quo, and the "opportunistic or utilitarian cowardice" of the parliamentary regime. Exercising their will to power/will to art, the futurists assume their roles as guides of that total revolt of things and mobs released by the revolt of machines: "the multicolored, polyphonic tides of revolution in the modern capitals."

Finally, in the epilogue, Marinetti enacts the murder of the past, framing it with the rhetoric of liberation: "We want to free [Italy] from its smelly gangrene of professors, archaeologists, Ciceroni, and antiquarians." The scene of the crime is projected by means of linguistic performatives (exortations and imperatives) and presented as if the destruction were taking place in the world of objects and not only in the judgment of the reader:

> So let them come, the gay incendiaries with charred fingers! Here they are! Here they are! . . . Come on! Set fire to the library shelves! Turn aside the canals to flood the museums! . . . Oh, the joy of seeing the glorious old canvases bobbing adrift on those waters, discolored and shredded! . . . Take up your pickaxes, your axes and hammer, and wreck, wreck the venerable cities, pitilessly!
>
> (Asterisco trans., p. 516)

Art risks itself; Marinetti establishes the fiction of escaping from fiction, from art, by means of action. Action alone transforms the world, in other words, transforms the world into a futurist fiction. The reader has been futurized, caught in the "double bind" set by Marinetti: action in the service of fiction or fiction in the service of action.

It is exactly this transgression of the limits of both literary and political discourse and the corresponding productive violence of the Marinettian text—its graphic, grammatical, and lexical aggressiveness—that should prevent the reader from regarding the manifesto as a work of art to be processed or consumed according to aesthetic protocols. Such a reconsecration of the manifesto as a work of art has dominated Marinetti scholarship, which has come to regard the manifestos as the most artistically realized elements of Marinetti's oeuvre and, in fact, as a mode of compensation for his failure to produce the great futurist opus. Such an emphasis on the sheerly aesthetic function of the manifesto is particularly deforming, for it suppresses the avowed anti-aesthetic operations of the manifesto: "Each day we spit on the altar of art," to cite an instance of Marinetti's ideal "spleen." In fact, the overall negative intention of the manifestos is to attack the autonomous status of the bourgeois work of art, to destroy its traditional

811

organic quality, and to produce a new contestatory form of textuality—of which the manifesto itself is a paradigm.

Second Exhibit of Futurist Violence: The Murder of the Moonshine

Marinetti's manifestos, which at times he compares to revolvers, always commit explicit murders. These are some of his exquisite cadavers: Giovanni Bellini altarpieces; the tango and tango-tea; Wagner's *Parsifal*; such passéist cities as Venice and Rome; the mechanical snobbery of the English; the mechanical awkwardness of the Germans; the French symbolist masters and their lesser brother, Gabriele D'Annunzio; and even pasta, on the grounds that "it is heavy, brutalizing, and gross. . . . It induces skepticism and pessimism. Spaghetti is no food for fighters." All these little murders culminate in the cosmic murder of the past, which is epitomized in the murder of the moonshine. For Marinetti, "moonshine" serves as a kind of negative "floating signifier" that chiefly signifies the old nature and the passéist mentality still anchored to the principle of mimesis, as opposed to the new nature of technological reality and the futurist mentality anchored to the principle of mechanical reproduction. Consequently, the moonshine represents the virulent source of all nostalgias: *Amore,* that double bind of lust and sentiment, that romantic voluptuary obsession chaining man to the carnal antimachine that according to Marinetti is woman; the entire nineteenth century with its ideal organicity and its historicist sensibility; the entire poetics of the French symbolists, who deploy the moon as a "soft-machine," as an ambiguous object that finds its correspondence in linguistic ambiguity. Thus, the textual equivalent of "moonshine" is what Walter Benjamin calls the "aura" of the traditional and organic work of art. It is precisely this aura of the traditional work of art that Marinetti seeks to destroy, and along with it the traditional status of the artistic object as a thing whose

historical value is a function of its ability to resist rapid consumption and whose immortality as opposed to its obsolescence is what is planned.

The Marinettian manifesto should be read as a site of ostensive murder in which no attempt is made to get rid of the traces. Consider, for example, the murder of the moonshine as set out in "Uccidiamo il chiaro di luna!" ("Let's Murder the Moonshine!," 1909):

> A cry went up in the airy solitude of the high plains: "Let's murder the moonshine!"
>
> Some ran to nearby cascades; gigantic wheels were raised, and turbines transformed the rushing waters into magnetic pulses that rushed up wires, up high poles, up to shining, humming globes.
>
> So it was that three hundred electric moons canceled with their rays of blinding mineral whiteness the ancient green queen of loves.
>
> And the military Railroad was built. An extravagant Railroad, following the chain of the highest mountains on which our vehement locomotives soon set out, plumed with loud cries, down one peak and up another, casting themselves into every gulf and climbing everywhere in search of hungry abysses, ridiculous turns, and impossible zigzags.
>
> (Flint trans., 1971, p. 51)

Here the futurist reconstruction of the universe is achieved at the level of the imaginary and by the underhanded means of performative utterances and utopian or mythical discourse raised to the pitch of hysterical representation. Marinetti resorts to an exasperated allegorical machinery in this manifesto: the binary oppositions constituted by the *Podagrossi* and *Paralitici* (the throngs of Gout and Paralysis, the tribes of passéism) and by the futurists, by the madmen and beasts and by the virgins, and the like. The narration is an "allegory-in-freedom" more or less along the lines of Walter Benjamin's modernistic notion of allegory as a mode of fragmentation and interruption. It is a purely utopian representation insofar as it neutralizes the historical or real oppositions in early-twentieth-century society. For Marinetti, what is important in the text is not what it means, but what it does and incites to do: not the displacement or eclipse of the moon it enacts, but the displacement it effects in the reader, the charge of affect it contains and transmits. For Marinetti, the text is beyond good and evil, like the amoral machine it celebrates. Consequently, what we have here is not merely the scenario of the murder of the moonlight by the 300 electric lights, the allegory of the virile technological civilization that displaces the natural world. Nor should we read the scenario as a benign exercise of Marinetti's technological imagination in which "the furious technophile" strikes the Faustian bargain with the technological universe. Indeed, the methodical or moderate man is tempted to cry out that the bargain has too easily been struck, that the replacement of the mana of the moon by the mana of electricity constitutes a violation, that Marinetti has got it the wrong way round: the victory of man over nature, in fact, is the victory of the machine over man. The moderate man would tell Marinetti to read Sophocles' "Ode in Praise of Man" in *Antigone*. But this is to be reactive in the Nietzschean sense, and the role of reactive forces is to cancel action. And here we approach the productive power of the Marinettian text: to force the futurist man, the master, the active, to act his reaction. As Nietzsche puts it, "The true reaction is that of action."

In this manifesto, a typology of forces (futurist versus passéist) is represented through the allegorical machinery. But this typology of forces and the new image of thought it provokes are rotated into a topology, symbolized by the trajectory of the futurist railway breaching its way to the heights of Gorinsanker. The futurist thinker, then, must be forced to go to the place where those forces that make thought active and affirmative reside. This is the significance of the futurist railway: it leads to those extreme places, to those extreme circumstances, which produce action: the aerial dance of the machine gun, the joys of playing billiards with death and of the furious coitus of war.

Third Exhibit of Futurist Violence: The Burning of the Gondolas.

On 8 July 1910, the futurists released 800,000 leaflets containing the manifesto "Contro Venezia passatista" ("Against Past-Loving Venice," 27 April 1910) from the top of the clock tower in Saint Mark's Square. Therewith began the campaign that the futurists would wage for three years against Venice, "the cloaca maxima [great sewer] of passéism." As part of this agitation, Marinetti improvised a speech to the Venetians that provoked a terrible battle in the piazza. The orchestration of such riots would become one of the major instruments of Marinetti's cultural battle against passéist Italy and would be escalated into political demonstrations at three junctures: in 1911, in favor of the war against Libya; during the pre–World War I period, urging Italy to join the war against Austria and Germany; and after 1918, in conjunction with the Fascist uprisings. Regarding these tactics, Benedetto Croce wrote in *La Stampa* on 15 May 1924:

> For anyone who has a sense of historical connections, the ideological origins of Fascism can be found in futurism, in the determination to go down into the streets, to impose their own opinion, to stop the mouths of those who disagree, not to fear risks or fights, in this eagerness to break with all traditions, in this exaltation of youth which was characteristic of futurism.

Whatever the long-term implications of futurist agitprop may have been, the specific thrust of the Venetian campaign and the futurist "happening" in general was the destruction of the stereotype as a means of rejuvenating Italian culture. Venice, according to Marinetti, had been reduced by foreigners and by "caravans of lovers" to a cosmopolitan boudoir for the consummation of erotic adventures infused by "venal moonlight." Consequently, Marinetti

FILIPPO TOMMASO MARINETTI

called for the burning of the gondolas: "We
want to prepare the birth of an industrial and
military Venice that can dominate the Adriatic
Sea, the great Italian lake. . . . Let the reign of
holy Electric Light finally come, to liberate
Venice from its venal moonlight of furnished
rooms."

The preceding three exhibits of futurist violence force the reader to come to grips with the
cultural and textual politics of futurist revolt:
its "creating" action of destruction. For our immediate purposes, I cannot undertake an extended contextual analysis of the Marinettian
manifesto and its evolution from 1909 to its
ultimate political deployment in *Futurismo e
fascismo* (Futurism and Fascism, 1924). Let me
simply indicate that the Marinettian manifesto
should be regarded as a strategy of domination,
as an instance of what might be called textual
micro-fascism. As such, it should be read "politically" and in a manner that calls into question, on one hand, its status as a manipulative
form of self-advertisement for Marinetti and
the futurist movement that employs coercive
rhetorical strategies and shock effects, and, on
the other hand, its role as a liberating avant-
garde textual practice leading the reader to anarchic revolt and ultimately to emancipation
from the discipline of bourgeois culture. Such
a political reading would emphasize the ideological nature of the manifestos as hysterical
representations and their function as libidinal
devices that elicit the reader's will to power in
order to trap it. Such a reading would concentrate on the following features of the manifesto:
the language of the manifesto as speech acts
that cast the reader into an illogic of performative declarations, the overall rhetorical situation of the manifesto that involves the reader
in a "virile" process of masculine election and
an assassination of the "feminine" reading position, the Marinettian sentence as a syntactic
machine in which the words of "natural language" are made technological, and, finally,
the previously described scenes of murder and
the tracing of the textual operations through
which the murders are perpetrated.

WHAT THE WHIRLING PROPELLER TOLD MARINETTI: WORDS-IN-FREEDOM, 1912–1914

Whereas the motor car provided the model
for Marinetti's first installment of the aesthetic
of speed, the airplane and the multiplied perceptual field it opened up provided the specific
impetus for his attempt to create a linguistic
apparatus that would register and reproduce
the shocks of the new technological environment. He frames his attempt to create a free
writing, one that would shatter the syntactic
and semantic restraints and the linearity governing traditional literary representation, with
the following anecdote:

> Sitting on the gas tank of an airplane, my stom-
> ach warmed by the pilot's head, I sensed the
> ridiculous inanity of the old syntax inherited
> from Homer. A pressing need to liberate words,
> to drag them out of their prison in the Latin
> period . . . ! This is what the propeller told me,
> when I flew two hundred meters above the
> mighty chimney pots of Milan.
>
> ("Technical Manifesto of Futurist
> Literature," Flint trans., 1971, p. 84)

And so at the behest of the whirling propeller, Marinetti initiated a radical deconstruc-
tion of traditional poetry that sought not only
to deregulate and decodify "literary" language
but to shatter language itself. This dismantling
of language took place under the banner of *parole in libertà* (words-in-freedom) and involved
the creation of a set of complementary technical procedures: the destruction of syntax; *immaginazione senza fili* (imagination without
strings, or wireless imagination); the effect of
simultaneity, the magic word of the futurism of
this period; essential and synthetic lyricism;
the use of various typographic formats; and the
introduction of onomatopoeia as part of a new
"art of noise." The purpose of this new "technology" of poetry was to bring poetry and life
closer to being a simultaneous experience.

Marinetti elaborated his concept of words-
in-freedom both in practice and in theory,
composing such free-word texts as "Battaglia

peso + odore" (Battle Weight + Smell, 1912), "Zang Tumb Tumb," his greatest achievement in this style, and "Dune" (Dunes, 1914)—all written in close conjunction with the theorizing set out in three "technical" manifestos: "Technical Manifesto of Futurist Literature," with its appendix, "Risposte alle abiezioni" (Answer to Objections, 11 August 1912); "Distruzione della sintassi—Immaginazione senza fili—Parole in libertà" ("Destruction of Syntax—Imagination Without Strings—Words-in-freedom," 11 May 1913), and "Lo splendore geometrico e meccanico e la sensibilità numerica" ("Geometric and Mechanical Splendor and the Numerical Sensibility," 18 March 1914). As previously mentioned, practice and theory, language and metalanguage (language that reflects on its own operations), constantly overlap in Marinetti's writing. The metalinguistic aspect—the manifestation-manifesto effect—is particularly prominent in his free-word compositions because their discontinuity is "illustrated" by explosive typographical arrangements approximating what is now called concrete or visual poetry. In other words, Marinetti's attack on the canonic structures of language—syntax, above all—extends itself to the printed page, exploding it, dispersing it as a plurality of fragments. This "blowing up" (in both the sense of an explosion and an enlargment—for Marinetti used typefaces of various sizes to emphasize the relative importance of each fragment) renders the text as a form that simultaneously *says* and *shows,* thereby calling into question the very status of literary representation. This spatialization of form and the poetics of juxtaposition or montage upon which it rests owe, in fact, a great deal to the collateral experiments in futurist painting. Particularly influential were those conducted by Umberto Boccioni (1882–1916), who attempted to resolve the problem of simultaneity by representing the human figure in terms of its "universal vibration," its dynamic multiplicity. Similarly, the three technical manifestos, which graft excerpts from the free-word compositions into their own writing in order to im-

mobilize them and to subject them to a process of axiomization, are composed in a synthetic and telegraphic style: they also *do* what they *say*. Such a style released "axioms-in-freedom," through which the new program could be easily disseminated. From this perspective, Marjorie Perloff is absolutely correct in maintaining that Marinetti's manifestos provide an elaborate program of "collage" aesthetics (a term Marinetti does not use) while standing themselves as "collage works of a new kind."

Marinetti's theory of words-in-freedom represents a complete break with free verse on the grounds that the latter, although a necessary stage in the freeing of "the lyric power of the human race from shackles and rules," keeps intact "the syntactic order of the word," "the logical channels of syntax." The recognition that free verse was at most a half-measure is symptomatic of the gap between experimentalism and avant-gardism in general. The preparatory work of free-verse experimentalism focused on the revamping of existing codes and was so condemned to remain within the general text of symbolism. Marinetti, in keeping with the totalitarian and absolute demands of the avant-garde, realized that an extreme rupture of linguistic and ideological codes was called for, one that had to be couched in the mythic terms of an avant-garde breakthrough. Therefore he packaged words-in-freedom as a boundary-break: "Words-in-freedom split the history of thought and poetry neatly in two, from Homer to the last lyric outburst on earth." Before the legitimacy of such a claim can be assessed, it is necessary to examine in some detail the specifics of the propeller-dictated program for words-in-freedom and the manner in which it is perfected in "Zang Tumb Tumb," a free-word composition that "reports" the Bulgarian siege of the Turkish city of Adrianople in 1912, which Marinetti had witnessed as a war correspondent for *Gil Blas*.

Words-in-freedom is a violent contestation of the sentence as a grammatical, syntactic, graphic, and semantic entity, a subversion that belongs to a larger negative project that seeks to deny the linear quality of literary signification. It attempts to create a new space of writing, a configuration of words on the page functioning as a high-energy construct capable of reproducing the force lines and the omnipresent and simultaneous field of the new mechanical and electric "free-scape." It involves, on one hand, a set of deconstructive operations aimed at liberating the word from "traditional and intellective syntax" and, as a corollary, liberating the poetic utterance from the lyrical interference of the author, from those linguistic signs that refer back to the writer, the sign "I." On the other hand, it involves a series of constructive operations that employ analogy and juxtaposition as elementary units in the construction of a larger spatial form, kept in perpetual motion by the energy flow created by "strict nets of images or analogies" and by an innovative typography that impresses on "words (already free, dynamic, and torpedo-like) every velocity of stars, the clouds, airplanes, trains, waves, explosives, globules of seaform, molecules, and atoms."

The deconstructive operations by which language is dissociated into constitutive parts are the following:

1. To destroy syntax so as to liberate all nouns from fixed connections, thereby endowing them with an infinite freedom to align themselves in innumerable unexpected combinations;

2. To use infinitive verbs "because they adopt themselves elastically to nouns and don't subordinate them to the writer's 'I' that observes or imagines";

3. To abolish adjectives and adverbs, because they are static and compromise the pure energy of the noun and verb [Subsequently, Marinetti reintroduced the use of adjectives that were set apart and made to function as absolute nouns, what he called semaphoric adjectives and lighthouse—or atmosphere—adjectives.];

4. To abolish all conjunctions, since words such as "like," "as," "similar to" make the grammar of analogy too explicit and are superfluous to modern man, whose accelerated sensibility permits him to grasp immediately the telegrammatically established analogy;

5. To abolish punctuation and to introduce in its place the musical symbols and mathematical symbols (: + − × =), which are capable of accentuating certain movements and indicating their direction;

6. To eliminate all stereotyped images and faded metaphors, for "poetry should be an uninterrupted sequence of new images";

7. To bravely use the "ugly" in literature, even to the point of introducing "noise";

8. To create a maximum amount of disorder in the arrangement of images;

9. To destroy the "I" in literature, that is, human psychology, and to replace it with a "lyrical obsession" toward matter.

These deconstructive operations clear the path for a writing based on analogy, a kind of telecommunication generated by assembling analogies or images into chains or "strict nets" designed "to catch and gather whatever is most fugitive and ungraspable in matter." This telecommunication Marinetti calls appropriately the wireless imagination, or imagination without strings: "the absolute freedom of images or analogies expressed with unhampered words and with no connecting strings of syntax and with no punctuation." This writing practice required a new grammar of analogy based on radical juxtaposition or montage and a new conception of "forced" analogy, even though the symbolists' "demon of analogy" and, further back, the farfetched metaphors of baroque conceits can be regarded as precedents. Marinetti distinguished between the "immediate analogies" of traditional poetry that make comparisons in terms of photographic resemblance and his technique, in which "there is an *ever-vaster gradation of analogies,* there are ever-deeper and more solid affinities, however remote." Consider the examples he gives: fox terrier = very small thoroughbred (an immediate or traditional analogy); fox terrier = a little Morse code machine (a more daring and advanced analogy); fox terrier = gurgling water (the Marinettian analogy). In other words, Marinetti replaces the traditional concept of analogy based on immediate resemblances between objects with a more daring one that joins dissimilar things at their points of resemblance and, even more daringly, at their points of difference. "Analogy," he wrote, "is nothing more than the deep love that links distant, seemingly dissimilar and hostile things."

The most explicit form of this linking is the doubling of the noun: "man-torpedo boat," "woman-gulf," "crowd-surf," "piazza-funnel," "door-faucet." Such doubling creates a dynamic vibration not unlike the dynamism of futurist paintings. Analogy, moreover, can also be established by completely suppressing the first term or referent, that is, by an implicit linking in which the analogue or metaphor-word displaces the first term, which the reader must then divine by intuition. These analogies, whether explicit or implicit, are then assembled or mounted into syntagmatic chains that communicate a movement—a tremor, a shock, a vibration—that traverses the entire chain and ultimately the entire space of the text.

Words-in-freedom and imagination without strings are not merely stylistic or formal gestures. They are rather the means of appropriating (of mastering by means of representation) "the multiform and mysterious life of matter." Syntax, "the born-dead Latin period," had to be demolished, for as a category of old thought it served as a barrier preventing literature from entering "directly into the universe and becoming one body with it." Instead, the divine intuition at work in the analogical imagination grasped the analogical foundation of life—the view from the airplane confirmed the "montage-collage" structure of reality—and opened the way to an intuitive psychology of matter. The essence of matter, however, could be registered by poetry only if the "I" and the interference of human psychology were eliminated. Once this occured, the free play of intuition—the lyric obsession with matter—could "capture the breath, the sensibility, and the instincts of metals, stones, wood, and so on, through the medium of free objects and whimsical motors." In sum, words-in-freedom should be regarded as a new theory of mimesis by which the analogical and technological imaginations (the two were one for Marinetti: "Through intuition we will conquer the seemingly unconquerable hostility that separates our human flesh from the metal of motors") could represent the geometrical and mechanical splendors of the new technological universe. This new poetry of mimesis would even reach the point of representing the "infinitely small and the vibration of matter, e.g., lightening movement of molecules in the hole made by a howitzer," as in "Zang Tumb Tumb." As such, it is a new form of communication that, by stressing the materiality of words, became capable of registering the materiality and non-semantic movement of the mechanical universe—the shocks, the tremors, the displacements of force at work in the new perceptual field. For example, Marinetti sought to reproduce the following aspects of objects (I quote him directly): "1. Sound (manifestation of the dynamism of objects); 2. Weight (objects' faculty of flight); 3. Smell (objects' faculty of dispersing themselves)." Notice that the dynamism of objects is reproduced by a permanent synesthesia. Such a molecular representation of things (the landscape of smells perceived by a dog, the conversations produced by motors) leads to a new conception of the page as a field upon which matter can impress itself. The page becomes a picture, the imitation of its content. For example, Marinetti employs "designed analogies" or *calligrammes*—such as the famous "capture balloon" in "Zang Tumb Tumb"—synoptic tables of lyrical values, and free expressive orthography and typography. All of these techniques amount to a revolution of the page by which it is made to function as a dynamic and convulsive spatial form, that is, as a transgression of the static page of the traditional book.

The typographic format of the first page of "Zang Tumb Tumb" immediately brings home to the reader Marinetti's peremptory claim to have revolutionized the word:

Correzione
di bozze + desideri
in velocità

Nessuna poesia prima di noi
colla nostra immaginazione senza fili parole
in libertà vivaaaaAAA il FUTURISMO finalmente finalmente finalmente finalmente
finalmente

FINALMENTE

pOESIA NAScERE

treno   treno   treno   treno   **tren**   **tron**
tron   **tron**   (ponte   di   ferro: **tatatluuun-**
tlin)   **sssssssiii**   **ssiissii**   **ssiisssssiiii**
treno   treno   febbre   del   mio

Correction
of proofs + desires
in speed

No poetry before us
with our imagination with out strings words
in freedom FUTURISM livessssSSS finally finally finally finally
finally

FINALLY

pOETRY TO BE **BORN**

train   train   train   train   **chug**   **chug**
chug   **chug**   (iron   bridge: **claackitty-**
clack)   hiisssssss   hisshiss   hisshiissssss
train   train   fever   of   my

(*Teoria e invenzione futurista*, p. 563)

This graphic arrangement forces the reader's "eye-ear" into a simultaneous operation of "seeing-hearing": seeing sounds and hearing sights. Marinetti regarded "Zang Tumb Tumb" as "a score for recitation" and often made its declamation the centerpiece of his futurist *serate* (evenings). Of course, recitation dis-

solves the warfare between sound poetry and visual poetry that is the very principle of the printed text—of Marinetti's "writing aloud." The expressive typography represents the explosive birth of poetry; thus the text states: "finally/poetry to be born." Here we find at work the operation of simultaneous form; the text shows what it states. Furthermore the use of the infinitive *nascere* (to be born) demonstrates how the futurist antigrammar attempts to dynamize the nexus between noun and verb. By eliminating tense and voice, Marinetti can erase the sign "I," thus establishing himself as a "subject-in-freedom," that is, as an extroverted subject who can project himself onto external objects so completely as to obliterate the I. The "lyrical obsession" with matter is induced by the motion of the speeding train, in which the poet sits correcting the proofs of his poem. The trajectory of the train (treno treno treno **tren tron tron tron**) becomes the train of thought, the track of writing. Growing evermore insistent, the fever train merges with his consciousness and leads to a complete dissolution of the boundaries between the poet and the external world. On the next page Marinetti-in-speed, fixed in his compartment and "stung by the sea salt," registers his synesthetic impressions by means of words-in-freedom:

(**GLUTTONOUS SALTED PURPLE STRANGE INEVITABLE INCLINED IMPONDERABLE FRAGILE DANCING MAGNETIC**) i will explain these words i want to say that sky sea mountains are gluttonous salted purple etc. and I am gluttonous salted purple etc. everything outside of me is **also in me** totality simultaneity absolute synthesis ══ superiority of my poetry over all of the others stop

(p. 564)

Here Marinetti sets into play the various devices of his program: lack of punctuation, lighthouse adjectives set off by parentheses, the disruption of syntax, the chain of analogies created by the adjectives, and so on. This particular segment, of course, remains quite readable and culminates in a programmatic statement of his intentions. More significant, however, is the way in which the images and sensations keep moving and keep the reader moving. Marinetti does succeed in transferring to the reader the energy imparted to him by the speeding train and by the perceptual field, accelerated and energized, by the "train-shark." In free-word composition the position of the poet is no longer a fixed point exterior both to reality and to language. Rather, the poet is a kind of transistor who relays the energy imparted to him from the outside into the high-energy construct of the poem, which, in turn, relays it to the reader. The "I" is a shunt to be avoided except, as is the case here, to declare the superiority of one's poetry.

A second example from "Zang Tumb Tumb" will prove useful in illustrating Marinetti's technology of language, which is, in fact, a technology for eliminating the poetic self as it imposes itself between reality and writing. The passage reproduces the sound and fury of battle and thus takes us into the kinetic, and at times tragic, madness of battle that is the central subject of "Zang Tumb Tumb":

PULVERIZED RED RED STRIATED TREMBLING ETERNAL
urrrrraaaah urrrrraaaah
to win to win joy joy vendetta to massacre to continue
tatatatatatatatatatatata
END DESPERATION LOST NOTHING-TO-BE-DONE USELESS
to plunge freshness to expand to expand to open to soften to expand
plum plamplam pluff pluff pluff frrrrr
horse-dung urine bidet ammonia typographic-odor

(p. 664)

Placed vertically on the page, these eight lines are an example of what Marinetti calls "multilinear lyricism": "On several parallel lines, the poet will throw out several strings of colour, sound, noise, weight, thickness, analogy." Often criticized as an example of his impoverishment of poetic means or of the madness of his method, the passage, despite its apparent madness, produces an extraordinary amount of information. First of all, the noise of the second, fourth, and seventh lines does not consume information but becomes information. Second, the strings of images in the third and fifth lines represent simultaneously the contrasting psychological states of the two contesting sides. The drawing-up of the battle lines (Bulgarian versus Turkish space) and the resulting doubling of perspective is the dominant strategy of the poem and its means of presenting the contest-structure of war. And third, each of the eight lines produces a particular dominant sensation— visual, acoustic, tactile, and olfactory—resulting in a kind of vertigo. This vertiginous effect is underlined by the alternation of six different typefaces and culminates in the shocking olfactory sensation of the last line, the reader being made to see-smell the "typographic-odor."

It is important to note that the hygiene of language effected by words-in-freedom is inextricably linked to the hygiene of war. As Marinetti pointed out: "Words-in-freedom were born on two battlefields, Tripoli and Adrianople." However absurd the comparison may first appear, "Zang Tumb Tumb" can be read as a modernistic and fragmented version of the first great poem of force, *The Iliad*. It is, of course, devoid of any heros except for language itself and recorded in the spasmodic jargons of the electrical culture, resembling at times an epic press release, a Homeric telegram. It becomes most powerful in its molecular description of war, for war, "a zone of intense life," is an ultimate version of mechanical speed and splendor. Marinetti does not make an outright apology for war; rather, he makes war into the apology for his text. War is regarded as a text-generating process, and the constant destruction and reinvention of war become a structural analogue for the linguistic destruction and reinvention at work in the poem. Here we approach the dangerous ground of Marinetti's aestheticization of war and the political and ethical implications of an artistic revolution that makes the poem into a form of violence, a surrogate of war.

To say, as did Roman Jakobsen in an essay of 1919, that words-in-freedom was "a reform in the field of reportage, not in the field of poetry," is to miss the point. Such a critique, along with Ezra Pound's, which accuses futurism of being a "sort of accelerated Impressionism," fails to recognize the subversive-thrust of Marinetti's destructive poetics and the way in which it effects a violent break with the old modes of communication. The theory of words-in-freedom is perhaps best understood as a significant chapter in what Donald Lowe, in *History of Bourgeois Perception* (1982), has called the perceptual revolution of 1905–1915. This revolution involved the displacement of linearity by multiperspectivity (what the futurist called "simultaneity") and the creation of a new perceptual field, constituted by an electronic culture superimposed over a typographic culture. The revolutionary typography (Marinetti's "writing aloud"), the introduction into poetry of nonliterary modes of communication such as the telegram, the wireless, the newspaper, and the creation of a spatial form set into vibration by analogies can all be seen as part and parcel of this larger perceptual revolution. There is no better description of what occurs in "Zang Tumb Tumb" than the superimposition of an electronic culture over a typographic culture. Like all formal revolutions, Marinetti's was "political" in the sense that it shattered linguistic, and therefore ideological, norms, infiltrating the bourgeois culture of the sentence with the madness of writing.

Marinetti's theory of words-in-freedom immediately became the "lingua franca" (to use John Golding's term) of futurism, and the futurists extended its iconoclastic shattering of syntactic nexuses to other domains, from painting to theater, cinema, architecture, dance, and so forth. Its impact upon the-historical avant-garde was equally great. As Marjorie Perloff puts it: "Marinetti's program stands behind or anticipated almost every *ism* of the early war years, from Russian Cubo-Futurism and *zaum* to Anglo-American Vorticism to Dada."

THE THEATER OF SURPRISE AND THE PLEASURE OF BEING BOOED

TUTTO È TEATRALE QUANDO HA VALORE. [EVERYTHING OF ANY VALUE IS THEATRICAL.]
—Marinetti, "Il teatro futurista sintetico"

Marinetti made posturing—the most blatant form of his elaborate stagings of the self—into a discipline based on the shocking gesture and the calculated overstatement. By his own account, he was the most modern man in all of Italy. According to the French press, he was "the caffeine of Europe," the agent provocateur of the bourgeoisie and the technique for troubling its most sacred institutions. All of Marinetti's manifestations, including his performed self, were confrontational gestures in the guise of spectacles. Although his outrageous performances can be read as exercises in self-promotion, they are more properly regarded as installments in the heroization of the artist begun in the romantic period. With Marinetti, however, the heroism of the artist comes to be translated into its commodity form: the artist who packages himself and his work as a disruptive media-event designed to shock and to captivate the newly established mass audience of the first machine age.

Marinetti's performance of the self was part and parcel of the larger dramaturgy he staged in the name of futurism. Futurism was theater, living theater by virtue of its forays into the piazza, its *serate* that culminated in fisticuffs with the audience, and its making of revolution, ridiculous theater by virtue of its carnivalization of all norms, total theater by virtue of its appropriation of all possible stages (the lecture hall, the cabaret, the legitimate theater, the media, and even the battlefield) as its performance spaces. Marinetti was a man of the theater even before he became a man of the theater in the strict sense. He was celebrated for his galvanizing appearances as lecturer, orator, and performer. In fact, the process by which the microperformance of the lecture-declamation was expanded into the cabaret evening and ultimately into the futurist variety theater and its subsequent transformations, constitute the central and most authentic expression of futurism, for it is through the futurist spectacle that cultural battle could be most efficaciously waged. Indeed, through the futurist "theater of surprise," Marinetti could present to the bourgeois public his lecture on modern times. The dramaturgy of futurist performance can be read as the mise-en-scène of the informational society, as the staging of the new urban reality of the metropolis—as M. Tafuri points out—as a sort of machine emitting incessant and non-syntactic messages that bombarded metropolitan man, subjecting him to a series of shocks and stimuli. In other words, the futurist theater involved a staging, in denuded form, of the daily life of modern experience and, to use Marinetti's language, its "fragmentary dynamic symphonies of gestures, words, lights, and sounds."

Within Marinetti's general theatricalization of the futurist activity and his staging of futurist revolution as a spectacle, there occurs a specific attempt to create a futurist theater. Futurist theater sought simultaneously to assault the public and to elicit its collaboration, especially that most perverse form of collaboration: the pleasure of being booed. Marinetti's theater is above all a shock-practice, a theater of surprise in which repetition is rendered impossible and the subversion of the conventions of traditional theater, especially the performance-audience line, become the

dominant thematic. Although Marinetti wrote a series of full-length plays, his most significant theatrical innovations can be found in his short plays. These *sintesi* (syntheses), as he called them, reduced the well-made play of passéist theater into a series of micro-scenes that "compress into a few minutes, into a few words or gestures, innumerable situations, sensibilities, ideas, sensations, facts, and symbols."

Marinetti's numerous manifestos on futurist performances amount to a seismography of the theater, a catalog of the devices by which the futurist "marvelous" and its shocks can be produced. The most important of these are: "Il teatro di varietà" ("The Variety Theater," 1913), "Il teatro futurista sintetico" ("The Futurist Synthetic Theater," 1914–1915), "Il teatro della sorpresa" ("The Theater of Surprise," 1921), and "Il teatro tattile" ("The Tactile Theater," 1924). His other manifestos on dance, music, cinema, and radio should also be considered as part of his attempt to develop a theory and practice of futurist performance. (See Michael Kirby's *Futurist Performance*, 1971.)

Marinetti begins the "Variety Theater" manifesto by attacking the contemporary theater for its stupid vacillation between the historical reconstruction and the photographic reproduction of daily life. He proposes the variety theater—music hall, cabaret, night club, and circus—as the appropriate model for futurist theater because, as a product of the electrical culture, it has no traditions and no masters, no dogmas, and is permeated by current reality. Furthermore, it is strictly "show business": its purpose is to distract and amuse. Therefore it is in permanent revolution, for it must incessantly invent new elements of astonishment with which to captivate the public. The variety theater as such was a kind of laboratory that spontaneously developed the techniques of "the futurist marvelous," "the crucible in which the elements of an emergent new sensibility are seething." In other words, Marinetti intended to expropriate the theatrical "text" produced by popular culture, locating in it a proto-theater of the absurd and ridiculous and then submitting it to a "highbrow" avant-garde operation by which its subversive energy was programmatized into a radical protest against bourgeois theater.

The futurist variety theater sought to push to the limits the alogical and absurd elements, the multi-media experiments, and the dissolution of the barrier between spectator and spectacle already at work in the variety theater. What resulted was a theater of surprise and ridicule, one that sought to destroy the "Solemn, the Sacred, the Serious, and the Sublime." Its surprises were to take place at the expense of the immortal masterworks (a Beethoven symphony played backward, actors reciting Victor Hugo's *Hernani* [1830] while tied up to their necks in sacks, all of Shakespeare boiled down to a single act), at the expense of the audience (seats covered with glue, the same ticket sold to ten people), and even at the expense of the actors, who would slip on the deliberately soaped floorboards. Behind this dramaturgy of shocks lay the idea of theater as the manufacture of "negative experience" (to use Erving Goffman's phrase [*Frame Analysis,* 1974]), that is, a theater introducing disorganization, frame breaks, breaches in the performance-audience line, illogical chains of surprises and gestures hurled at the audience without psychological anchoring in a story or character. It was a theater dedicated to destroying logic and making "the absurd and unlifelike triumph on the stage." For example, the chanteuse would paint her hair green, arms violet, décolletage blue, and so on, so as to produce a transgressive version of the female erotic spectacle. Furthermore, once made-up in "punk" style, she would interrupt a song with a revolutionary speech or "spew out a *romanza* of insults and profanity."

To psychology and the representation of inner life, Marinetti opposed *fisocofollia* (body-madness), by which he meant a genuine physical language of things and bodies whose movements were no longer controlled by the

logic of a role-character formula or of a fixed script. The movements of the theater and of the performance itself—the theater was to be a school of heroism, daredevilism, record setting much like the circus or athletic event—were those of direct and "unstaged" action. Such a theater of spellbinding movement exalted "action, heroism, life in the open air, dexterity, the authority of instinct and intuition."

The futurist variety theater, although it served as groundwork for subsequent theatrical productions and can be linked to those practices employed in the *serate* that the futurists began performing in 1910, remained primarily a theoretical construct. The publication in 1915 of the "Futurist Synthetic Theater" manifesto lead to an intense period of theatrical activity which saw the staging of programs of *sintesi* in Milan, Rome, and Paris (1914–1919). This manifesto established the *sintesi*—the synthesizing of "fact and idea in the smallest number of words and gestures"—as the module of futurist performance. The passwords for this entirely new theater were, in addition to "synthetic," the following: atechnical, dynamic, simultaneous, autonomous, alogical, unreal. Here we can see the protest against the exhausted forms of bourgeois theater coming into a clearer focus. Marinetti calls for the abolition of the farce, the vaudeville, the sketch, the comedy, the serious drama, and the tragedy and proposes to replace them with newly created futurist forms: "lines written in free words, simultaneity, compenetration, the short, acted-out poem, the dramatized sensation, comic dialogue, the negative act, the re-echoing line, 'extralogical' discussion, synthetic deformation, the scientific outburst that clears the air." This new repertory of forms, coupled with various strategies for symphonizing "the audience's sensibility by exploring it, stirring up its laziest layers with every means possible" and for forcing the stage action to invade the audience's space, endow the futurist theater with a deconditioning power and represent a valid interrogation of the very materiality of the theater. Of course other and darker readings of Marinetti's theater can be made, ones that, for instance, explore his claim "*We think that the only way to inspire Italy with the warlike spirit today is through theater*" [italics in original].

CITIZEN MARINETTI: FROM MASCULINE PATRIOTISM TO THE FUTURIST AS FASCIST, 1915–1944

Marciare non marcire! [To march and not to rot!]
—Marinettian slogan

Marinetti, for instance. You may have heard of him! It was he who put Mussolini up to Fascism. Mussolini admits it. They ran neck and neck for a bit, but Mussolini was the better politician.
—Wyndham Lewis, *Blasting and Bombardiering*

"Avant-garde" means the artist shows the way. But to what and to whom? To the first part of the question, Marinetti's patent response would be the future, and in a certain sense such a claim would have to be taken quite seriously, for a more or less futurist program along Marinettian lines has realized itself in the spectacular and electrical mechanisms of our post-modern (and perhaps post–avant-garde) culture. As already indicated, it was Marinetti who, as a strategist of cultural revolution, was among the first to divine the aesthetic economy of the informational society and to attempt a global seizure of the means—the media—of cultural production. Whether Marinetti truly grasped the grammar of the future as "Napoleon grasped the grammar of gunpowder"; whether he merely perpetuated, as Tafuri maintains, the figure of the "artist-magician [who] gets close to the new world of industrial production but then withdraws immediately because of the use he makes of it" or whether he succeeded in elaborating a complex attitude toward technological reality that permitted him to go beyond the mere idolatry of the machine remains open to debate. It is certain, however, that he did (im)pose in epochal fashion the question of the relationship between

technology and literature and did anticipate as well as contribute to the aestheticizing of culture that would take place throughout the twentieth century. These questions regarding Marinetti's legacy are all posed from a historical perspective, and the cruel speed of history has exposed rather pitilessly the reactionary core of the futurist movement, especially its points of ideological and practical collusion with Fascism—that consummate exercise in summoning up anachronistic phantoms. And this brings us to our second question: To whom did the futurist avant-garde show the way? Whose avant-garde was it? This question remains highly problematic because, despite futurism's initial success as a cultural avant-garde performing a demolition job, the most determinate aspects of Marinetti's program—the mysticism of action, the rehabilitation of violence as the dominant question, and the advent of youth to power—especially when conflated with Marinetti's exaggerated cult of nationalism, were so easily appropriated by Fascism. Furthermore, Marinetti's heating up of the media, his methods of disseminating propaganda, and his development of revolutionary signifying practices by which the futurist text was situated outside the domain of art, *through art*, were so easily instrumentalized by Fascism, becoming part and parcel of the regime's vast arsenal of "new techniques of inspiration." (For a detailed account of Marinetti's contribution to the "activist revolt" that helped to form the mentality of Fascism, see Adrian Lyttelton's *The Seizure of Power*, 1973.)

On the other hand, Antonio Gramsci, writing in 1921 from the position of a Marxist revolutionary in search of instruments with which to produce a proletarian culture, praised Marinetti and the futurists as cultural revolutionaries:

The Futurists have carried out this task in the field of bourgeois culture. They have destroyed, destroyed, destroyed, without worrying if the new creations produced by their activity were on the whole superior to those destroyed. They have had confidence in themselves, in the impetuosity of their youthful energies. *They have grasped sharply and clearly that our age, the age of big industry, of the large proletarian city and intense tumultuous life, was in need of new forms of art, philosophy, behavior and language.* This sharply revolutionary and absolutely *Marxist* idea came to them when the Socialists certainly did not have as precise an idea in politics and economics, when the Socialists would have been frightened (as is evident from the current fear of many of them) by the thought that it was necessary to shatter the machine of bourgeois power in the state and in the factory. In their field, the field of culture, *the Futurists are revolutionaries* [italics in original].

(*Selections from Cultural Writings,* p. 51)

Written one year before the march on Rome by which the Fascists came to power and in which the futurists participated, Gramsci's assessment underscores the contradictory nature of Marinetti's political identity, an identity whose radical Italianism translated itself into a masculine and warriorlike nationalism and into a series of polemical stances: anticlerical (calling for the "de-Vaticanization of Italy"), antipacifist, anti-parliamentarian, anti-monarchist, anti-Socialist. However, his anti-Socialism, as Renzo DeFelice has pointed out, was also contradictory, for while condemning Communism as a bureaucratic cancer, he was in general sympathy with the demands of the subversive movements of the left. Furthermore, the anarchic and libertarian elements at work in the futurist program and Marinetti's commitment to permanent revolution would remain incompatible with the totalitarian regime. Therefore, Marinetti's paradoxical political identity can perhaps best be focused, but by no means exhausted, by the formula: the futurist (read: avant-gardist, modernist, anarchic individualist, elitist) as Fascist. The story of Marinetti's life—his initial appearance as international hero of the avant-garde, his ever-increasing commitment to a futurist Italy that led him from irredentism (advocating the recovery of Italian-speaking areas subject to Austria) and revolutionary interventionism (supporting Italy's entry into World War I) to an active role in Fascism as a movement (the Fascism that predated the march on Rome and seemed to promise a genuine revolution) to his perverse acceptance of "Fascism as regime," despite serious reservations, and his self-identification with Mussolini to the very end—all of this has come to be historicized, often in ideological form and to the detriment of Marinetti's reputation, as a cautionary tale illustrating the dangers of mixing revolutionary poetry with revolutionary politics. The previously cited quote by Wyndham Lewis represents the most flippant version of Marinetti's political legend, whereas Walter Benjamin's critique of Marinetti's "introduction of aesthetics into political life" that culminates in the rendering aesthetic of war itself is the most damning version of it. However, if we are to understand Marinetti's exemplarity as a cultural radical, we must account for, on one hand, the mythical politics he elaborated at the discursive and imaginary level, a kind of fictional and libidinal politics that can be read, as Robert Dombroski has done, as "a utopian figure of Fascism" and, on the other, Marinetti's participation in the practical politics of pre-Fascist and Fascist Italy. In both cases, it is important to avoid the simplistic historiographic shorthand according to which futurism and Fascism are substantially the same. Since it is beyond the scope of this piece to examine in detail the problematic convergence of the two movements, the reader is relayed, somewhat cautiously, to the standard treatment in English of Marinetti's relationship to Fascism, James Joll's *Three Intellectuals in Politics* (1960), and advised to check Joll's reading of futurism as "one of the paths that led to Fascism" by consulting the Italian historian Renzo Defelice's more recent entry on "Ideology" in *Futurism and Futurisms* (1986). DeFelice locates the beginnings of both futurism and Fascism in "a common existential condition," "the traumatic crisis of modernization and massification of traditional civilization," and then proceeds to describe Marinetti's failed attempt to preserve an autonomy for futurism vis-à-vis the regime.

In their attempt to exalt and glorify Italy, the futurists alternated artistic with political propaganda. Marinetti's first intervention into real politics took the form of Irredentist speeches and anti-Austrian demonstrations. The first political manifesto, calling for pride, energy, and national expansion, was launched by the futurists at the time of the general elections of 1909. A second political manifesto (October 1911) supported the colonial war against Libya and set into circulation one of Marinetti's most serviceable political slogans: "The word *Italy* must prevail over the word *Freedom*." This initial agitation paved the way for the more extensive campaign of 1914–1915, which saw the futurists urging Italy to enter the war against Austria and Germany. Upon the declaration of war, Marinetti and his futurist followers immediately enlisted in the Italian army, determined to put their warrior code to the test. Marinetti, who was wounded, acquitted himself extremely well as a man of action, being decorated twice for valor. World War I, however, took its toll on futurism, depleting from its ranks such key figures as the painter Umberto Boccioni and the architect Antonio Sant'Elia. Accordingly, historians have tended to regard the war as marking the end of futurism as a "coherent movement." Marinetti, nevertheless, would adhere to his warrior ethos throughout his life, regarding war as the ultimate aesthetic phenomenon of the technological universe: "War is beautiful because it establishes man's dominion over the subjugated machinery by means of gas masks, terrifying megaphones, flame throwers, and small tanks. War is beautiful because it initiates the dreamt-of metalization of the human body." In the "lived novel" *L'alcova d'acciaio* (The Steel Alcove, 1921), a diary of his wartime experiences and an ecstatic hymn to the armored car (the steel alcove: his new mechanical bride), he elaborated an Italian art of war, what he called "heroism without a warrior training," "the maximum flexibility in

passing from useful violence to absolute kindness towards the defeated and disarmed."

Having placed futurism into the service of action, Marinetti's next step was the adoption of the political party as a medium of revolutionary action, and he founded, even before the war had ended, the Partito Politico Futurista. (The program was set out in a manifesto published in *L'Italia futurista* in February 1918.) In the immediate postwar period, he joined forces with Mussolini in various attempts at political agitation, and in March 1919 he helped to found the Fasci di Combattimento, the fighting squads that were to constitute the original Fascist Party. In April of the same year, he participated along with Mussolini in the infamous Battle of Piazza Mercanti, which culminated in the destruction of the offices of the Socialist newspaper *Avanti!*, of which Mussolini was the former editor. Also in 1919, the year of his greatest political prominence, Marinetti ran unsuccessfully for parliament on the slate of the Fascist Party, second only to Mussolini. Subsequently, both he and Mussolini were briefly imprisoned for sedition. Marinetti's friendship and alliance with Il Duce would prove decisive and more or less constant, despite Marinetti's temporary withdrawal, in 1920, from the Fascist Party in angry response to Mussolini's refusal to carry out the futurists' anti-monarchist and anticlerical demands and, in 1938, his public condemnation of the regime's adoption of an anti-Semitic policy. The intricate and at times exploitative relationship between these two strong personalities is perhaps best described as a mimetic rivalry, with Mussolini frequently speaking in futurist language and Marinetti, as in his portrait of Mussolini, *Marinetti e il futurismo*, projecting onto Mussolini the lineaments of a "marvelous futurist temperament." Whatever the considerations—pragmatic as well as psychological—may have been that ultimately led Marinetti to an accommodation with the regime, it is clear that he understood, as early as 1924, that Fascism would not create the new consciousness and the new national spirit the futurists hoped for: "The victory of Vittorio Veneto and the coming to power of Fascism constitute the realization of the minimum futurist program. . . . Futurism is a movement that is strictly artistic and ideological. It intervenes in political struggles only in hours of grave danger for the nation."

Marinetti's participation in active politics led him to produce, in the early 1920's, a series of political writings that reflect a definite disenchantment with politics and culminate in the blast: "Destroy, annihilate politics, which opaques everybody. It is a tremendously tenacious leprosy-cholera-syphilis!" Among the most significant are *Al di là del comunismo (Beyond Communism,* 1920) and the free-word novel *The Untamables.* In *Beyond Communism* he attacks Soviet Communism on the grounds that it is a passéist, bureaucratic, and mediocritist formula unsuitable to the revolutionary aspirations of an Italian people that "dreams of individualist anarchy." Instead, he calls for a futurist revolution that will bring art and artists to power, creating a government by "the vast proletariat of gifted men" that will extend the "intellectual art-alcohol" to everyone, thereby producing "a race almost entirely composed of artists." Here, once again, Marinetti proposes an imaginary or utopian solution to the social problem. *The Untamables,* on the other hand, because it inserts the scene of futurist revolution within a cyclical vision of history remains pessimistic to the point of being dystopian. Like *Marfaka,* set in Africa, this genre-breaking narrative (adventure novel, symbolic poem, science fiction à la H. G. Wells, philosophical-social vision) can be described as a futurist version of Plato's myth of the cave, in which the imprisoned Untamables (embodiments of instinctive and unconscious forces) attempt to raise themselves up to the level of the ruling Paper People (symbols of ideas) and, once having acquired revolutionary consciousness, to liberate the River People (the crowd as brute force) from their servitude. The revolution fails and will have to

be waged again and perhaps repeatedly, although with an ever-increasing heightening of consciousness. Two elements of the work are particularly noteworthy: it is, in part, a roman à clef with the all-too-cautious Mah, one of the Paper Revolutionaries who guide the insurrection against their own class, representing Mussolini and with other elements of the Italian historical situation coded into the text; and, as part of its elaborate allegory, there is a stunning scene of "futurist skywriting" in which the Paper People, who are born from books and are in fact just texts, are transformed into projectors that print "blinding, diamond words-in-freedom on the sky." Mirmofim, the leader of the Untamables, upon reading the words "THE FUTURIST MANIFESTOS / MARINETTI," makes the following recognition: "The great book of Futurism teaches us to make up everything, even God! We've got to make up a leader for the crowd. And the leader is me! Come on, let's go!"

At the level of literary production, the second period of futurism (1921–1944) represented a period of consolidation and even of regression with respect to the boldness of Marinetti's technical experiments. Although he continued to produce interesting exercises in free-word composition, above all the surrealistic travel book *Spagna veloce e toro futurista,* perhaps his most innovative work during the 1920's involved sensory experiments in tactilism, or the art of touch, in which he assembled disparate materials such as sandpaper, silk, and small feathers to form "tactile plates." He even extended his tactilist concerns into culinary form, issuing a wickedly frivolous manifesto dedicated to futurist cookery in which he attacked the Italian diet of pasta and orchestrated the menus for elaborate futurist banquets designed to provoke the palate by antithetical combinations of food.

In all things exorbitant, Marinetti managed to die at least twice: his death as a futurist poet and avant-gardist as symbolized by his appointment by Mussolini to the Accademia d'Italia in 1929 and his actual death in Bella-

FILIPPO TOMMASO MARINETTI

gio in 1944, during the time of the Republic of
Salò. Even a staunch advocate such as Luciano
DeMaria, remarking the "fraility" of Marinetti's
later work, has written: "The triumph of Fascism reduced futurism from an all-encompassing movement which was necessarily also political, to a stale 'school,' whose official poetic
technique was *paroliberismo*." During the
1930's, he did attempt, however, to break new
ground by formulating the technique of *aereopoesia*, which sought to exalt the airplane and
the "immense visual and sensory drama of
flight." As theorized in *Il manifesto dell'aereopoesia* (The Manifesto of Aero-Poetry, 1931)
and as realized in *L'aereopoema del golfo dell
Spezia* (The Aero-Poem on the Gulf of La Spezia, 1935), *aereopoesia*, in its emphasis on simultaneity and its attempt to overcome all the
"literary laws of gravity" so as to have words-
in-freedom quite literally "take flight," constitutes, at the formal level, little more than an
extension of *paroliberismo*. Marx's maxim stating that originary events upon being repeated
turn into farce also holds, it seems, for avant-
garde breakthroughs, for *aereopoesia*, notwithstanding its appropriation of the airplane as a
new futurist signifier and its fairly innocuous
linking of the poetics of flight to the emerging
aeronautics industry, would degenerate into an
instrument of Fascist propaganda, as for example in the pictorial essay entitled "Il Duce
aviatore," published in the "Aereovita" section
of *Futurismo* on 1 February 1934. Furthermore,
Marinetti, realizing that *aereopoesia* would
find its natural vehicle in the radio, broad-
casted his aero-poems to celebrate the exploits
of Fascist aviators such as the triumphant return from America of Balbo's Atlantic Air
Squadron in August 1933.

Notwithstanding the ever-increasing institutionalization of futurism and the use value
of *aereopoesia* for the regime, the founder of
futurism would find himself, in the second
half of the 1930's, having to defend the avant-
garde mandate against the attacks made by
the reactionary wing of Fascism as part of its
campaign against "degenerate art." Always the

good soldier, Marinetti, despite being well
over sixty, went as a soldier to fight in the
Ethiopian campaign in 1935–1936 and served
on the Russian front for a twenty-three-month
period in 1942–1943. His last literary compositions were composed in the style of *aereopoesia* qua *paroliberismo*, whether under the
private sign of peace, such as the love poems
to his wife, the aero-poet Benedetta (*Poesie a
Beny*, published posthumously in 1971)—"If
these words-in-freedom endure it is because
they resemble you"—or under the public sign
of war, such as his last poem, "Quarto d'ora di
poesia della X Mas" (Fifteen Minutes of Poetry
on the X Mas, 1945), written shortly before his
death and dedicated to the soldiers of the
Italian Republic. Here the oratorio of battle
receives its ultimate consecration as a mystical and quasi-religious event, the orisons of
the machine-gun blasts rewriting in futurist
form the kiss of death:

> The voluptuous first line of battle vibrates
> like stretched cords strummed by projectiles. A
> thundering cathedral prostrate to call on Jesus
> with the ache of lacerated breasts
> We will be we are the kneeling machine guns
> whose barrels throb with prayer
> I kiss I kiss again the weapons nailed down
> by a thousand thousand thousand hearts all
> pierced by vehement everlasting forgetfulness
> (Flint trans., 1971, p. 36)

As part of the institutionalization of the
historical avant-garde and the canonization of
its founding figures that has taken place over
the last twenty years, Marinetti has been accorded his rightful place—however problematic—in the pantheon of modernists. Ever
since the publication in 1968 and 1969 of the
first volumes of the Mondadori edition of his
selected works, Marinetti has been the subject
of an ongoing process of revision conducted
both by cultural historians of modernism
and by neo–avant-gardists, who have turned
to his experiments for inspiration. That the
most extensive exhibition of futurism ever

to be mounted was held (3 May to 12 October 1986) at the Palazzo Grassi in Venice—of all places!—is further proof of the movement back to futurism. In the same year, *Caffe in d'Europa,* a biography of Marinetti in comic-book form containing fifty-three panels drawn in futurist visual style, was published in the magazine *Linus.* Such signs of a new penetration into mass culture would have greatly delighted Marinetti, who was equally pleased when, in the heyday of futurism, he had roused the popular imagination to such an extent that Italian children played futurists instead of cowboys and Indians. Whatever revisionary ratios may ultimately be employed in reinterpreting Marinetti, it is imperative to remember that his life and work remain exemplary because they raise the question of the relationship between revolutionary politics and poetry, that is, the question of the freedom of poetry. Because his revolutionary project so insistently and so militantly confuses the realms of poetry and politics, his work demands what might be called "a dangerous reading." Furthermore, his work positively calls for such a reading by virtue of its foregrounding of politics and war, its distressing sexual politics, and its fetishizing of the machine, which, even though it confers upon the machine the status the hero held in traditional culture, amounts to an erotics, a Kama-sutra, of the machine, and its stylistic and formal experiments, which, as codified in the technical manifestos, constitute a death kit for the sentence and the traditional work of art. Such a dangerous reading must come to grips above all with Marinetti's role as a technician of violence: artistic and linguistic violence directed, on one hand, at the bourgeois public and, on the other, at its hallowed institution of art and its formal languages; ethical violence stemming from the iconoclasm of the futurist life-style and the Marinettian imperative to make one's life into a futurist work of art; and political violence, the means by which artistic and cultural revolution can be escalated into social revolution and the price the past exacts for the revolt of the future.

Selected Bibliography

EDITIONS

THEORETICAL, CRITICAL, AND POLITICAL WRITINGS, INCLUDING THE PRINCIPAL MANIFESTOS

For present purposes, it is impossible to list all of the manifestos and to describe in detail their intricate publication histories. The manifestos, many of which were launched as leaflets, were as a rule first published formally in avant-garde journals, often in both French and Italian versions, and then republished in collective anthologies of futurist manifestos, edited either by Marinetti or under his auspices. The three major collections published during the movement's "heroic period" (1909–1920) are: *I manifesti del futurismo* (The Futurist Manifestos, 1914), *Noi futuristi* (We Futurists, 1917), and *I manifesti del futurismo* (1919). See annotated entries below. Marinetti also repeatedly recycled the manifestos and other previously-published texts in retrospective collections of his own writings. Such volumes of futurist history as *Guerra, sola igiene del mondo* (War, the World's Only Hygiene, 1915) and *Marinetti e il futurismo* (Marinetti and Futurism, 1929) are cases in point. In order to provide the reader with a chronology of the manifesto activity, the principal manifestos have been listed below according to the date of composition and with the place of first formal publication indicated. For a definitive version of the manifestos together with variants and details of their publication, see *Teoria e invenzione futurista* (Futurist Theory and Invention, 1968), listed below.

Gabriele D'Annunzio intime. Milan, 1903.
Les dieux s'en vont, D'Annunzio reste. Paris, 1908.
"Fondazione e manifesto del futurismo." Published for the first time in French in *Le figaro* (20 February 1909) and in Italian in *Poesia* 5, nos. 1–2 (February–March 1909).
"Uccidiamo il chiaro di luna!" (April 1909). First published in French in *Poesia* 5, nos. 7–9 (August–October, 1909), and subsequently in Italian as a volume. Milan, 1911.
Enquête internationale sur le vers libre et manifeste du futurisme. Milan, 1909.

FILIPPO TOMMASO MARINETTI

"Primo manifesto politico" (1909). In *Guerra, sola igiene del mondo*. Milan, 1915. First launched as a leaflet during the general elections of 1909.

"Contro Venezia passatista" (27 April 1910). In *Manifesti del futurismo*. Florence, 1914. Originally printed on leaflets that were thrown from the clock tower in Venice on 8 July 1910.

Le futurisme. Paris, 1911.

"Secondo manifesto politico" (11 October 1911). In *Guerra, sola igiene del mondo*. Milan, 1915.

"Manifesto tecnico della letteratura futurista" (11 May 1912). First published as the introduction to *I poeti futuristi*. Milan, 1912.

"Distruzione della sintassi—Immaginazione senza fili—Parole in libertà" (11 May 1913). Published in two parts. *Lacerba* 1, no. 12 (15 June 1913), no. 22 (15 November 1913).

"Il teatro di varietà" (29 September 1913). *Lacerba* 1, no. 19 (1 October 1913).

"Lo splendore geometrico e meccanico e la sensibilità numerica" (18 March 1914). Published in two parts. *Lacerba* 2, no. 6 (15 March 1914), no. 7 (1 April 1914).

I manifesti del futurismo. Florence, 1914. This collection published by the journal *Lacerba* contains the principal manifestos written by Marinetti and the other futurists from 1909 to 1913.

Guerra, sola igiene del mondo. Milan, 1915. Contains a complete translation of *Le futurisme* (1911) with various supplements, including "Contro l'amore e il parlamentarismo."

"Il teatro futurista sintetico" (11 January 1914–18 February 1915). In *Teatro futurista sintetico*. Milan, 1915.

Noi futuristi. Milan, 1917. A miscellaneous collection of manifestos organized according to field: literature, politics, painting, and so forth.

"Manifesto del partito futurista italiana" (1915–1918). *L'Italia futurista* 3, no. 39 (11 February 1918).

Democrazia futurista—dinamismo politico. Milan, 1919.

I manifesti del futurismo. 4 vols. Milan, 1919. Containing fifty-nine manifestos, this edition published by the Istituto Editoriale Italiano is the most comprehensive collection of manifestos edited by the futurists.

Al di là del comunismo. Milan, 1920.

"Il tattilismo." First published in *Comoedia* (11 January 1921).

Futurismo e fascismo. Foligno, 1924.

Marinetti e il futurismo. Rome and Milan, 1929.

Primo dizionario aereo italiano. In collaboration with F. Azari. Milan, 1929.

La cucina futurista. In collaboration with Fillia. Milan, 1932.

"Il Duce aviatore." *Futurismo* (1 February 1934).

CREATIVE TEXTS

The hybrid nature of Marinetti's literary texts and the fact that he wrote novels as well as poems in free-word style make any attempt to organize his work according to genre highly problematic. For example, *8 anime in una bomba* is best described as a "novel-poem," *Patriottismo insetticida* as a "drama-story," and *Spagna veloce e toro futurista* as a "poem-story-travel book." Given this caveat, the reader will find below a provisional listing by genre.

POETRY: FREE-VERSE, WORDS-IN-FREEDOM, AERO-POETRY

La conquête des étoiles: Poème épique. Paris, 1902.

La momie sanglante. Milan, 1903.

Destruction: Poèmes lyriques. Paris, 1904.

La ville charnale. Paris, 1908.

La bataille de Tripoli (26 octobre 1911) vécue et chantée par F.T. Marinetti. Milan, 1912.

Zang Tumb Tumb, Adrianopoli, ottobre 1912, parole in libertà. Milan, 1914.

Scelte di poesie e parole in libertà. Milan, 1918.

Poemi simultanei futuristi. La Spezia, 1933.

L'aereopoema del golfo della Spezia. Milan, 1935.

Il poema del vestito di latte: Parole in libertà futuriste. Milan, 1937.

Il poema africano della Divisione "28 Ottobre." Milan, 1937.

Gli aeropoeti futuristi dedicano al Duce il poema di Torre Viscosa: Parole in libertà futuriste di F. T. Marinetti accademico d'Italia. Milan, 1938.

Il poema non umano dei tecnicismi. Milan, 1940.

Canto eroi e macchine della guerra mussoliniana. Milan, 1942.

NOVELS AND PROSE COMPOSITIONS

Marfaka le futuriste: Roman africain. Paris, 1910.

Le monoplan du Pape: Roman politique en vers libres. Paris, 1912.

Come si seducono le donne. Florence, 1916.

L'isola dei baci: Romanzo erotico-sociale. In collaboration with Bruno Corra. Milan, 1918.

Un ventre di donna: Romanzo chirurgico. In collaboration with Enif Robert. Milan, 1919.

8 anime in una bomba: Romanzo esplosivo. Milan, 1919.

L'alcova d'acciaio: Romanzo vissuto. Milan, 1921; repr. 1985.

Gli amori futuristi: Programmi di vita con varianti a scelta. Cremona, 1922.

Gli indomabili. Piacenza, 1922.

Scatole d'amore in conserva. Rome, 1927.

Novelle colle labbra tinte, simultaneità, e programmi di vita a scelta. Milan and Verona, 1930.

Spagna veloce e toro futurista. Milan, 1931.

Il fascino dell'Egitto. Milan, 1933.

PLAYS

Le roi bombance: Tragédie satirique en quatre actes en prose. Paris, 1905.

Poupées électriques: Drame en trois actes, avec une préface sur le futurisme. Paris, 1910.

Teatro sintetico futurista. 2 vols. Milan, 1915–1916.

Elettricità sessuale: Sintesi futurista. Milan, 1920.

Tamburo di fuoco: Dramma africano. Milan, 1922.

Prigionieri e vulcani. Milan, 1927.

Il suggeritore nudo: Simultaneità teatrale in 11 sintesi. Milan, 1929.

Patriottismo insetticida. Milan, 1939.

POSTHUMOUS EDITIONS

Quarto d'ora di poesia della X Mas (Musica di sentimenti). Milan, 1945.

Teatro. 3 vols. Edited by G. Calendoli. Rome, 1960.

Teatro della sorpresa. Edited by F. Cangiullo. Livorno, 1968.

Poesie a Beny. Turin, 1971.

An edition of Marinetti's letters has not yet appeared. The Beinecke Rare Book and Manuscript Library, Yale University, contains a rich archive of various correspondences and other Marinettiana.

COLLECTED WORKS

Opere di F. T. Marinetti. Edited by Luciano DeMaria. Milan, 1968– . The contents are as follows: Vol. 1: *Scritti francesi.* Edited by Pasquale Janini. Milan, 1983. Part 1 includes works from 1902 to 1908. Part 2, including works from 1909 to 1912, is forthcoming. Vol. 2: *Teoria e invenzione futu-rista: Manifesti, scritti politici, romanzi, parle in liberta.* Edited by Luciano DeMaria. Milan, 1968. Vols. 3 and 4: *La grande Milano tradizionale e futurista* and *Una sensibilità italiana nata in Egitto.* Edited by Luciano DeMaria. Milan, 1969. The Mondadori Edition is the closest we come to having a definitive edition of Marinetti's complete works. The second volume, containing a collection of Marinetti's major works written from 1909 to 1945, is not without lacunae. It remains, however, a ground-breaking attempt to establish a canon of Marinetti's writings.

TRANSLATIONS

Futurism and Futurisms. Exhibition catalog. See entry under Biographical and Critical Studies, below.

Futurist Manifestos. Edited by Umbro Apollonio. Translated by R. Brain, R. W. Flint, J. C. Higgit, and C. Tisdall. New York, 1973.

Marinetti: Selected Writings. Edited with an introduction by R. W. Flint. Translated by R. W. Flint and A. Coppotelli. New York, 1971. The definitive English translation of Marinetti.

"Marinetti's Short Plays." Translated by Victoria Ness Kirby. In *Tulane Drama Review* 17 (1973). (The appendix to Michael Kirby's *Futurist Performance* contains thirteen manifestos and forty-eight playscripts also translated by Victoria Ness Kirby; see entry below.)

BIOGRAPHICAL AND CRITICAL STUDIES

Apollinaire, Guillaume. *Apollinaire on Art.* Edited by Leroy C. Breunig. Translated by Susan Suleiman. New York and London, 1972.

Banham, Reyner. *Theory and Design in the First Machine Age.* New York and London, 1960.

Bayley, Stephen. *Sex, Drink, and Fast Cars.* New York, 1986.

Benjamin, Walter. "The Work of Art in the Age of Mechanical Reproduction." In *Illuminations,* translated by Harry Zohes. New York, 1968.

Bergman, Pär. *"Modernolatria" et "Simultaneità": Recherches sur deux tendances dans l'avant-garde littéraire en Italie et en France à la veille de la première guerre mondiale.* Uppsala, 1962.

Briosi, Sandro. *F. T. Marinetti.* Florence, 1969.

Calvesi, Maurizio. *Le due avanguardie.* Milan, 1966.

————. *Il futurismo.* 3 vols. Milan, 1967.

Cangiullo, F. *Le serate futuriste*. Naples, 1930.

Clearfield, Andrew. *These Fragments I Have Shored: Collage and Montage in Early Modernist Poetry*. Ann Arbor, Mich., 1984.

Clough, Rosa Trillo. *Futurism: The Story of a Modern Art Movement—A New Appraisal*. New York, 1961.

Crispolti, Enrico. *Il mito della machina e altri temi del futurismo*. Trapani, 1969.

————, *Storia e critica del futurismo*. Rome, 1986.

DeFelice, Renzo. *Mussolini il rivoluzionario, 1883–1920*. Turin, 1965.

DeMaria, Luciano. "Introduzione" to *F. T. Marinetti: Teoria e invenzione futurista*. Milan, 1968.

————, ed. *Per conoscere Marinetti e il futurismo*. Milan, 1973.

Dombroski, Robert. *L'esistenza ubbidiente: Letterati italiani sotto il fascismo*. Naples, 1984.

"E.S.," ed. *Marinetti futurista*. Naples, 1977.

Folojewski, F. *Futurism and Its Place in the Development of Modern Poetry*. Ottawa, 1980.

Futurism and Futurisms. Catalog of an exhibition at the Palazzo Grassi, Venice, 3 May to 12 October 1986, organized by Pontus Hulten. New York and Milan, 1986. Includes selected writings by Marinetti, criticism and other supplementary material, and contains translations of several important manifestos not included in other translations. The following entries in the supplemental "Dictionary of Futurism" are of particular importance: "Ideology" by R. DeFelice, "F. T. Marinetti" and "Words-in-Freedom" by L. DeMaria, "Reconstruction of the Universe" by E. Crispolti, and "Theater" by M. Verdone. Translations of Marinetti's writings into English for the exhibition were done collectively by "Asterisco."

Golding, John. "The Futurist Past." *New York Review of Books,* 14 August 1986.

Gramsci, Antonio. *Selections from Cultural Writings*. Edited by David Forgacs and Geoffrey Nowell-Smith. Translated by William Boelhower. Cambridge, Mass., 1985.

Joll, James. *Three Intellectuals in Politics: Blum, Rathenau, Marinetti*. New York, 1960.

Kaplan, Alice Yaeger. *Reproductions of Banality: Fascism, Literature, and French Intellectual Life*. Minneapolis, 1986.

Kern, Stephen. *The Culture of Time and Space 1880–1918*. London, 1983.

Kirby, E. T., ed. *Total Theatre*. New York, 1969.

Kirby, Michael. *Futurist Performance*. With Manifestos and playscripts translated from the Italian by Victoria Ness Kirby. New York, 1971.

Krauss, Rosalind. *The Originality of the Avant-Garde and Other Modernist Myths*. Cambridge, Mass., 1985.

Lista, Giovanni. *Arte e politica: Il futurismo di sinistra in Italia*. Milan, 1980.

————. *Futurism*. New York, 1986.

————. *Marinetti*. Paris, 1976.

————, ed. *Marinetti et le futurisme*. Lausanne, 1980.

Lyttelton, Adrian. *The Seizure of Power: Fascism in Italy 1919–1929*. New York, 1973.

Martin, Marianne. *Futurist Art and Theory*. Oxford, 1968.

Pagli, Luigi. *Invito alla lettura di Marinetti*. Milan, 1977.

Papini, Giovanni. *Esperienza futurista*. Florence, 1919.

Perloff, Marjorie. *The Futurist Moment: Avant-Garde, Avant Guerre, and the Language of Rupture*. Chicago and London, 1986.

Poggioli, Renato. *The Theory of the Avant-Garde*. Cambridge, Mass., 1968.

Rawson, Judy. "Italian Futurism." In *Modernism*, edited by M. Bradbury and J. McFarlane. New York and Harmondsworth, England, 1976.

Raye, Jane. *Futurism*. New York, 1972.

Russell, Charles. *Poets, Prophets, and Revolutionaries: The Literary Avant-Garde from Rimbaud Through Postmodernism*. New York and Oxford, 1985.

Saccone, A. *Marinetti e il futurismo*. Naples, 1984.

Sanguinetti, E. "La guerra futurista." In *Ideologia e linguaggio*. Milan, 1975.

Taylor, Christiana. *Futurism: Politics, Painting, Performance*. Ann Arbor, Mich., 1974.

Taylor, Joshua C. *Futurism*. New York, 1961.

Tisdall, Caroline, and Angelo Bozzolla. *Futurism*. New York, 1978.

Vaccari, W. *Vita e tumulti di F. T. Marinetti*. Milan, 1959.

Verdone, Mario. *Cinema e letteratura del futurismo*. Rome, 1967.

BIBLIOGRAPHIES

Contributo a una bibliografia del futurismo letterario italiano. Rome, 1977.

FILIPPO TOMMASO MARINETTI

DeMaria, Luciano, and Mauro Pedroni. "Aggiornamenti bibliografici sul futurismo." *Il verri* 33–34 (1970).

Drudi Gambillo, Maria, and Teresa Fiori. *Archivi del futurismo*. 2 vols. Rome, 1959–1962.

Eruli, Brunella. "Bibliografia delle opere di F. T. Marinetti (1898–1909)." *La rassegna della letteratura italiana* 2–3 (May–December 1968).

Falqui, Enrico. *Bibliografia e iconografia del futurismo*. Florence, 1959.

PELLEGRINO D'ACIERNO

HERMANN HESSE
(1877–1962)

HERMANN HESSE'S FAVORITE pastimes were painting and gardening. We should bear this in mind. Better still, we should visualize the writer in his overalls, contentedly burning weeds on a terraced slope or, palette in hand, gazing from beneath a broad-brimmed hat at the radiant vistas of southern Switzerland. Since intellectually and linguistically Hesse is an heir of the chronic dualism that has afflicted German writers at least since Friedrich von Schiller, he tends quite casually to use such ear-filling generalities as Spirit and Nature, Intellect and Sense, Ideal and Reality, Art and Life, Yin and Yang. But if we remember the poet with his paintbrush and spade, we can put the dialectical polarities into a more human perspective and lend substance to the heady abstractions.

Almost all Hesse's heroes are riven by these conflicts. They are artists alienated from life, intellectuals who eye the senses warily; or, conversely, they are sober citizens unsettled by a vague longing for freedom, men disenchanted with reality who yearn for an ideal. The dialectical rhythm takes many forms. Hesse's earliest works affect a haughty aestheticism characteristic of the *fin de siècle,* but his first major novel, *Peter Camenzind* (1904), represents a complete about-face to a Rousseau-like return to nature. In such later works as *Demian* (1919) or *Der Steppenwolf* (*Steppenwolf,* 1927) the conflict is acted out within the soul of a single individual, while in *Narziss und Goldmund* (*Narcissus and Goldmund,* 1930) the dual roles are assigned to two representative heroes. *Siddhartha* (1922) lays out the realms of sense and intellect geographically in a symbolic landscape through which the hero passes, whereas the protagonist of *Das Glasperlenspiel* (*The Glass Bead Game,* 1943) is confronted with a choice between a *vita activa* and a *vita contemplativa.* But no matter how the dualism is expressed and no matter which way the pendulum seems to swing in individual works, everything goes back to the recluse in his garden, who is equally content pruning his bushes or trying to capture their beauty in pastels.

When we take a close look at Hesse's aquarelles, many of which were painted to illustrate autograph manuscripts of his poems and stories, two basic types strike our eye. First, the more realistic ones depict the semitropical landscape of the Ticino in bold, bright colors: planes are emphasized almost cubistically, silhouettes are marked with strong lines, and the entire scene is reduced to its salient motifs. The setting is instantly recognizable, but it has been intensified, sharpened, and enhanced by the painter. This heightened realism characterizes Hesse's prose as well. In his fiction as in his paintings the details that create a naturalistic effect are effaced. The dialogue is not differentiated, and the episodes stand out in high relief without the transitions that make for verisimilitude but add nothing to the essential meaning of the picture or plot. It is a realism that at its best borders on symbolism, and at its worst flattens out into pretentious allegory.

In the second category all concessions to realism are absent: human bodies sprout out of fantastic trees, flowers unfold faces, animals display blossoms instead of heads, lovely but indecipherable designs captivate the eye. This fantasy style distinguishes the many fairy tales that Hesse wrote during and after World War I. But it also dominates the grand visions of *Demian,* the Magic Theater of *Steppenwolf,* the self-portrait of the painter Klingsor in *Klingsors letzter Sommer* (*Klingsor's Last Summer,* 1920), and many scenes of *Die Morgenlandfahrt* (*The Journey to the East,* 1932). Through such bold images that link disparate facets of life, Hesse expresses, in his painting as well as in his prose, the unity of all being that he envisages as the ultimate resolution of the conflict between nature and spirit, reality and ideal, and the other polarities.

We must not imagine that this resolution was solely an artistic prerogative for Hesse. In the idyll *Stunden im Garten* (*Hours in the Garden,* 1936) Hesse describes with affectionate detail his daily routine, whose high point arrived when he heaped up the day's accumulation of rubbish, leaves, and dry twigs to burn. "For me, fire signifies an alchemistic-symbolic cult in the service of the divinity: the retransformation of multiplicity into the One." The language is ponderous, but the meaning is clear. Fire (as well as water—another medium of the gardener) enters his works frequently as a symbol for the leveling unification of opposites. Nature, spirit, unity—thesis, antithesis, synthesis: this is the rhythm of Hesse's works, but it is a rhythm that emerged first in his own life and for which his works provide the subsequent metaphors. It is easy to lose sight of this sequence and to forget that his own existential experience inevitably underlies the romantic abstractions of which Hesse was so fond. However tempting it may seem to establish neat theoretical schemes in order to explain Hesse's works, it is a danger to be avoided. For there is a constant and delicate interaction between Hesse's life and his writings. The abstractions have no inherent validity, only the significance that they receive from Hesse's own experiences. His scope as a writer was narrow because he was constantly obsessed with his own personality and its pendulation between spirit and nature, between painter and gardener. But his works display a grand imaginative sweep by virtue of Hesse's poetic ability to find ever new images, symbols, and structures through which to express what he conceived to be man's basic dilemma.

Hesse was fond of saying that he decided to become a writer at the age of twelve or thirteen. Born on 2 July 1877 into a family of Protestant missionaries, he was destined to follow the academic path that led from his South German birthplace of Calw through the University of Tübingen to a life of spiritual service. Spirit and service ultimately came—they are central themes in his later works—but not exactly as his family had planned. From the start Hesse rebelled so vehemently against restraints at home that his parents toyed with the idea of sending him away to school. For twelve years they were able to cope with the headstrong boy—first in Calw, then from 1881 to 1886 in Basel, and then again in Calw, where his father had taken over the Calw Missionary Press. (In many of his works it is this absurdly picturesque Black Forest town that provides the background for the narrative.)

By the time he was twelve, Hesse could no longer be handled at home. His family, as his father had written as early as November 1883, was "too nervous, too weak," to contend with his energies. So he was packed off to preparatory school in nearby Göppingen, where stern discipline went hand in hand with academic excellence in preparation for the dreaded regional board examinations that provided entry and tuition to one of the famous "seminaries" of Württemberg. During the year and a half at Göppingen, portrayed in the novel *Unterm Rad*

(*Beneath the Wheel*, 1906), he applied himself so diligently that he was among the privileged few who passed the examinations in the summer of 1891, thereby winning a place in the educational system that had produced a dynasty of Swabian intellectuals, including Johannes Kepler, Friedrich Hölderlin, and G. W. F. Hegel. Hesse entered the theological secondary school at Maulbronn, a beautifully preserved Cistercian monastery that later provided the medieval setting for his novel *Narcissus and Goldmund*. At first he responded enthusiastically to new friends and to the outstanding classical education offered to the aspiring young theologians and academicians. But within a few months Hesse's old restlessness showed itself again. In March 1892 he ran away and had to be brought back, after a night spent in a haystack, by the forest patrol. This episode was the prelude to such a severe fit of depression that his parents withdrew him from school.

For the next few months the future Nobel Prize winner was sent from one institution to another. First his parents turned him over to a fashionable exorciser in Bad Boll who tried to pray him back to health, with the perhaps not surprising result that the troubled youth tried to commit suicide. Next he was sent to a home for weak-minded children in Stetten where, as part of his rehabilitation, he worked in the garden and tutored less gifted classmates. After a third abortive attempt at a school in Basel, Hesse attended the *Gymnasium* at Bad Cannstatt for a year, where he spent most of his time frequenting bars and piling up debts—a period of despondency and profligacy recounted in the fourth chapter of *Demian*. By this time Hesse's parents realized as clearly as he that formal education was not for him. (Paradoxically, Hesse's catastrophic experiences with the school system of Wilhelmine Germany caused him in his later writings to return almost obsessively to the school as setting and to education as a theme.) In October 1893 he contracted as a bookdealer's apprentice in Esslingen but after three days

ran away again and returned to Calw, where for half a year he did little but embarrass his family by his presence. From June 1894 to September 1895 Hesse settled down to the rather dull job of filing gears as a mechanic's apprentice in the Calw Tower Clock Factory, an experience that paid off in his early stories by giving him a sympathetic insight into the mentality of small-town workers and apprentices.

Finally Hesse seemed to find himself. Again he signed on as an apprentice bookdealer—this time at Heckenhauer's bookstore in the university town of Tübingen—and actually managed to remain in the position for the four years necessary to receive his apprentice's letter. At last his dream of becoming a writer began to materialize in more than his unorthodox behavior. His poems were accepted from time to time by journals and newspapers. He found a coterie of compatible friends who styled themselves *le petit cénacle* (the little literary circle) and posed for group photographs lying, in Wildean lassitude, before *Jugendstil* backgrounds. During these same years he began the broad reading that eventually produced, besides the impressive monograph *Eine Bibliothek der Weltliteratur* (A Little Library of World Literature, 1929), scores of essays on writers and books. But though his reading was often sturdy—Johann Wolfgang von Goethe was a favorite—his own efforts remained rather precious. The poems published in his first volume, *Romantische Lieder* (Romantic Songs, 1899), feature languishing poets who loll in the fragrant night listening to lovely ladies playing Frédéric Chopin's nocturnes on grand pianos.

A second product of the Tübingen years was the series of misty prose poems entitled *Eine Stunde hinter Mitternacht* (An Hour Beyond Midnight, 1899), which is clearly indebted to Maurice Maeterlinck. By this title Hesse hoped, as he indicated in the 1941 introduction to a new edition, to adumbrate "the dreamland of my creative hours and days, which lay mysteriously somewhere between time and space." In these prose poems Hesse sought to create "an artist's dreamworld, an isle of beauty; its poetic character was a retreat from the storms and depressions of the everyday world into night, dream, and lovely solitude." Although his Pietist parents were probably gratified that the *enfant perdu* was beginning to support himself and to attain a certain success as a writer, they could not have been much comforted by such letters as the one in which he wrote, in 1897: "For a long time I have had the firm conviction that morality is replaced, for artists, by aesthetics." His spiritual mentor, of course, was Friedrich Nietzsche, who peered down at the young poet from two pictures on the walls of his sparsely furnished room. His aesthetic idol was Chopin, whom Hesse found "noble in every respect, though often degenerate."

The dialectical rhythm asserted itself when Hesse left Tübingen in 1899 to work in a bookshop in Basel—the home of Nietzsche, the cultural historian Jacob Burckhardt, and the painter Arnold Böcklin. Hesse's principal undertaking at that time—to write a history of German romanticism—soon led him to conclude that the period of romanticism was over and that young writers in the new century needed to find a new mode for their expression. His work-in-progress at the time, *Hinterlassene Schriften und Gedichte von Hermann Lauscher* (The Posthumous Writings and Poems of Hermann Lauscher, 1901), was, he later explained, a conscious attempt "to conquer for myself a piece of world and reality." Written under the impact of the most realistic of German romantics—E. T. A. Hoffmann—it sought to look objectively, even ironically, at the years of his literary bohemianism. The work was impressive enough to interest S. Fischer, the enterprising publisher who was building up one of Germany's most exciting presses. Hesse sent Fischer the manuscript of his next novel, which exchanged the perfumed hazes of his early poems and prose for the invigorating *plein-air* of the Swiss Alps, which Hesse had discovered since his arrival in Basel. *Peter Camenzind* was an immediate success

that brought Hesse international recognition, prizes, and—not least—his first financial independence. Peter Camenzind, in many respects a literary descendant of Gottfried Keller's Green Henry of *Der grüne Heinrich* (1854–1855, 1879–1880), is a Swiss peasant boy who attains fame as a writer and succumbs for a time to the glamour of the city with its salons and intellectual attractions. But ultimately he renounces the empty freedom of aestheticism and returns to his village in the Alps for a life of modest responsibility.

In Hesse's biography life reveals a pronounced tendency to imitate art. After the success of *Peter Camenzind* he married Marie Bernoulli, who might easily have stepped out of one of his early poems. A daughter of a distinguished family of Basel mathematicians and nine years older than Hesse, she played Schumann and Chopin beautifully and loved nothing better than melancholy solitude. The couple rented a peasant house on the German shore of Lake Constance and settled down to a life of what Hesse envisaged as rustic familial bliss. On the surface things went well; the eight years in Gaienhofen were immensely productive in a number of ways. Following the pattern of vaguely melancholy realism established in *Peter Camenzind,* he turned out a stream of stories set in a fictional town called Gerbersau and dealing with little people—shopkeepers, apprentices, tramps—that were incorporated into commercially successful volumes with such titles as *Diesseits* (In This World, 1907), *Nachbarn* (Neighbors, 1908), and *Umwege* (Byways, 1912). These works are a far cry from the romantic poems and timeless-spaceless dimensions of his first efforts. In *Beneath the Wheel*—a school novel of the type being produced in those years by Rainer Maria Rilke, Robert Musil, and others—he reassessed the anguish of the uncertain years surrounding his education at Maulbronn, showing how easily he himself, like his hero Hans Giebenrath, might have ended in suicide. The novel *Gertrud* (Gertrude, 1910) reflects the company he kept in Gaienhofen;

although he received occasional visits from fellow writers, Hesse preferred to associate with musicians and painters. The hero of *Gertrude,* which bears a strong resemblance to *Tonio Kröger* (1903) and other early works by Thomas Mann, is a crippled musician whose art prevents him from achieving happiness in life, a spiritual affliction symbolized by his physical disability.

Stimulated by trips to Italy, Hesse wrote biographical studies of Giovanni Boccaccio (*Boccaccio,* 1904) and Saint Francis of Assisi (*Franz von Assissi,* 1904). He prepared popular editions of lyric poetry and romantic authors and reviewed scores of books. He was a frequent contributor to the satirical weekly *Simplicissimus* as well as one of the founding editors of the liberal-oppositional journal *März* (March). And three sons were born, who played about him happily as he worked in his garden. Fortune smiled brightly on the bespectacled young man who, only a few years earlier, had been standing behind the counter of a bookstore in Basel.

But external circumstances are deceptive in this case. While he was leading the life glorified in his books, Hesse was chafing inwardly. He felt that he was rapidly vegetating in the land of the philistines, which he heartily detested. Squatting in his garden, he asked himself uneasily if he was not really more of a nomad than a planter. This tension between security and *Wanderlust* betrayed itself in the ever more frequent lecture tours that took him away from Gaienhofen for weeks at a time. When the trips to Italy and the lectures in Germany, Austria, and Switzerland no longer satisfied this nomadic urge, Hesse embarked in 1911 on a two-month voyage to Sumatra and Ceylon with his friend, the painter Hans Sturzenegger. (Hesse never set foot on the subcontinent of India itself.)

The Orient had long represented an ideal in Hesse's mind. His grandfather Hermann Gundert had spent over two decades as a missionary in India and was the author of many scholarly works on the East, including the standard dictionary of the Malayalam language. His father, Johannes Hesse, had worked in Mangalore for four years before poor health necessitated his return to Europe. The Pietist Mission House in Calw, where Hesse spent the most impressionable years of his childhood, entertained a constant stream of visitors heading for India or coming from there. "From the time I was a child," Hesse wrote in the important essay "Mein Glaube" ("My Belief," 1931), "I breathed in and absorbed the spiritual side of India just as deeply as Christianity." It was inevitable that the nomadic impulse that lured him in ever-widening gyres away from the bourgeois security of Gaienhofen should ultimately lead him to India. "We come to the South and East full of longing, driven by a dark and grateful premonition of home, and we find here a paradise," he reported in the travel account *Aus Indien* (Out of India, 1913). "We find the pure, simple, childlike people of paradise." But Hesse had failed to reckon with the problematics of his own nature, which could not be cast off so easily as his European overcoat: "We ourselves are different; we are alien here and without any rights of citizenship. We lost our paradise long ago, and the new one that we wish to build is not to be found along the equator and on the warm seas of the East. It lies within us and in our own northern future." Although the trip to India bore fruit ten years later in the "Indic poem" *Siddhartha,* it was initially a disappointment. Hesse still did not realize that his flights into the world were not flights from Gaienhofen, but evasions of himself.

Shortly after his return to Europe he attempted to alleviate his restlessness by moving from the isolation of Gaienhofen to the more urban atmosphere of Bern. In *Rosshalde* (1914), the last major work of these prewar years, Hesse posed the question that he had not yet dared to ask in reality: Is a happy marriage conceivable for an artist, for a man "who not only lives by his instincts, but who—above all—wishes to observe and depict as objectively as possible?" In the novel the answer is no. The painter Veraguth is so wholly committed to his art that the only tenuous bond still linking him to his wife is their son Pierre. They have a brief moment of closeness when their son falls ill with cerebral meningitis, that symbolic disease which plays a role in so many novels about artists—for example, Mann's *Doktor Faustus* (1947) and Aldous Huxley's *Point Counter Point* (1928)—because it afflicts precisely those senses of sight and sound so important to the artist. When Pierre dies, their marriage has no further justification: "All that he had left was his art, of which he had never been so assured as now. All that he had left was the solace of the outsider, to whom it is not given to seize life and drink it to the dregs." It was two more years before Hesse, still imitating his own art, was forced to a similar conclusion.

His most popular work in the years before his crisis was a series of three stories revolving around the character Knulp (*Knulp,* 1915). Here, in a lighthearted form with undertones of tragedy, Hesse approaches the problem of planter versus nomad, bourgeois versus artist, from another point of view. Knulp is a lovable vagabond who wanders from town to town, staying with friends who regard it as a privilege to feed and shelter the happy ne'er-do-well, and consistently refusing to tie himself down to any one of the many trades for which he has an instinctive facility. At the end of his life, as he lies dying in a snowstorm, Knulp has an interview with God in which he reproaches himself for his wasted life. God explains that it had been the whole purpose of Knulp's life to bring "a little nostalgia for freedom" into the lives of ordinary men. So Knulp dies with a contented smile. But hidden beneath the light surface of the three stories is the guilty conscience of the artist who suspects that his life and freedom are worthless, even immoral. This is the quandary of Hesse's early heroes: Veraguth longs for freedom and feels restricted by his marriage and family responsibilities, while Knulp's enjoyment of his freedom is tempered by his feeling that he should do something worthwhile for society.

World War I shattered the last vestiges of the happy idyll that Hesse had tried to build in the years following *Peter Camenzind.* Unlike most Europeans, he did not share the now almost incomprehensible elation at the birth of a new era that characterized the public reaction to the outbreak of the war. In a series of essays subsequently collected under the title *Krieg und Frieden* (*If the War Goes On,* 1946), he exhorted his countrymen and foreigners alike to pacifism, to a spirit of transcendent internationalism, to a grand humanism; and he reaped mainly scorn and vituperation for his efforts. The best-selling author was now branded publicly as "a viper nourished at the breast" of an unsuspecting audience, as he recalled these years in his "conjectural autobiography," "Kurzgefasster Lebenslauf" ("Life Story Briefly Told," 1925). Until the end of the war Hesse worked selflessly for Swiss-based relief organizations, edited books and a biweekly literary supplement for German prisoners of war, and contributed regularly to a newspaper for German internees in Switzerland. But during these same years Hesse was struck by a series of personal blows: his son Martin became seriously ill; in 1916 his father died; and his wife suffered such a severe nervous disorder that she soon had to be put into a sanitorium. Hesse's marriage and family had disintegrated. Life was catching up with art. But unlike his hero Veraguth, who has at least the consolation of his art, Hesse had lost faith even in his writing. When he was asked, a few years later, to prepare an edition of his selected works, he refused. As he explains in "Vorrede eines Dichters zu seinen ausgewählten Werken" (A Writer's Preface to His Selected Works, 1921): "There was nothing there to select. . . . There was no doubt in my mind that of all my stories not a single one was good enough as a work of art to be worth mentioning."

Hesse was saved as a man and restored as a writer by the intensive self-scrutiny precipitated by psychoanalysis. As the result of a nervous breakdown, he undertook in 1916 and 1917 a series of consultations with Josef B.

Lang, a disciple of Carl G. Jung, in a sanitorium near Lucerne. Lang, who became a close friend and who crops up in Hesse's letters and narratives under the pseudonyms Longus and Pistorius, introduced Hesse to the writings of Sigmund Freud and Jung and helped him with the systematic analysis of his problematic mentality—an exercise that found its literary precipitation in the various fantasies and fairy tales that Hesse wrote during this period. Lang's own notebooks indicate that he received much in turn from Hesse, who greeted psychoanalysis not as a radically new invention but rather as the systematization of instinctive knowledge long present in the works of his favorite writers, as Freud himself did to some extent. In any case, Hesse perceived that his ever more frantic flights, in the years 1904 to 1914, had been flights from himself, projections into the outer world of his own torments. And his writing had been correspondingly subjective, as he noted in the 1921 "Vorrede": "All these stories dealt with me, reflected my own path, my own secret dreams and wishes, my own bitter anguish." Renouncing his mandarin pose of detachment, he proclaimed his own complicity in the events of a world gone insane.

The immediate product of this rebirth was the novel *Demian*, written in a few hectic weeks of 1917. *Demian* is the probing account of a young man's search for personal values, his quest for identity, and thus it is a supratemporal, almost mythic tale. At the same time it is dated to the extent that it is a response to the specific needs of the youth of World War I, a generation that Hesse—now forty years old—viewed with an objectivity lacking in his earlier works. Hesse himself was a bitter opponent of the war, yet through the figure of his hero he attempted to explain the mystical fervor with which the youth of 1914 greeted the outbreak of the war as the beginning of a new era. Hesse was always an outsider, but in the novel he presents the appeal of community and the solace of solidarity. Inasmuch as Hesse exploits these and other factors—the

rebellion against the father, the messianic belief in a new humanity, the evangelical rhetoric of language—it can be argued that the novel is a response to and an interpretation of the generation of German expressionism. These qualities explain the immense appeal of the novel, which rapidly captured an entirely new group of readers for its author.

At the same time it is a deeply personal book, tracing symbolically in the life of a much younger man Hesse's own development during the period of his psychoanalysis. The hero of the first-person narrative, Emil Sinclair, recounts certain crucial episodes from his life between the ages of ten and twenty. Sinclair's boyhood revolves around his friendship with the mysterious Max Demian. When he goes off to boarding school, he slumps at first into profligacy. But the ethereal love he conceives for a girl he glimpses in the park and the mystical pronouncements of a new friend, the renegade theologian Pistorius, gradually steady his uncertainties. At the university he meets Demian again and enters into an ambiguous relationship with his friend's mother, Frau Eva. This year of happiness is ended by the war, which soon claims Demian as a victim but leads Sinclair to the final stage of spiritual independence, in which he no longer has need of external mentors.

Hesse's own vacillation between the two imagined poles of being is introduced in the first chapter as the "Two Worlds" of which Sinclair becomes aware. At home, in the harmonious security of his father's house, Sinclair has grown up in a "light" world of order and Christian ethics. But when he goes down to the servants' quarters or sees drunks on the streets being hauled off to jail, he perceives the existence of a "dark" world—a world of sex, violence, and lust—that is wholly denied by his parents and toward which the boy Sinclair feels himself ineluctably attracted. For he senses with the first stirrings of puberty that this "dark" world, rejected so disdainfully by his family, is no less a natural part of life than their own artificially rationalized "light" world. At first Sinclair wavers back and forth between the two worlds of his experience, finding satisfaction in neither. With the aid of Demian, he discovers that he longs inchoately for a new deity, an ideal embracing both worlds: "a god who also encompasses within himself the devil, and before whom one wouldn't need to close one's eyes in shame when the most natural things in the world go on." The novel is the story of this search for a new deity, a search that leads Sinclair from one teacher to another until, transcending them all, he discovers a new source of values within himself.

Even this brief sketch of the novel's theme reveals something about the strengths and weaknesses of Hesse's mature prose and helps to explain the mixed feelings it arouses in his readers. The rejection of established values, the search for personal identity, the need for moral commitment—these are essentially modern themes that anticipate the mood of our own time. But in Hesse's works these themes are radically internalized, producing an essentially lyrical fiction in which the customary attributes of the realistic novel as we have grown to know it are missing.

In *Demian* the themes are reflected in a form and language largely determined by religious symbols. The episodes of Sinclair's life are patterned explicitly on Christian motifs and metaphors. His expeditions into the "dark" world are related to the parable of the prodigal son, and he looks back longingly at the security of his parents' world as at "a lost paradise." Sinclair, Demian, and the others who rebel against the world of their fathers bear "the mark of Cain," and they feel more sympathy for the unrepentant thief at Christ's crucifixion than for the third man on the cross, who "celebrates lugubrious festivals of betterment and remorse." Sinclair is first thrust out of the paradise of his childhood because he claims to have stolen forbidden apples; his acceptance of the new deity is related in a chapter entitled "The Struggle with the Angel"; and his search for new values is likened to Parzival's quest for the Grail.

The two central symbols of the book are likewise religious. The bird breaking its way out of an egg—an image of spiritual rebirth that recurs constantly from the first page to the last—is borrowed, by way of Johann Jakob Bachofen's writings, from late Roman cultism. Here, of course, the symbol has been redefined to correspond to the theme of the novel. The egg represents a dualistic world that insists on arbitrary distinctions between good and evil, a world that must be shattered if a new reality is to be formed. And Abraxas, the god of good and evil to whom Sinclair is introduced by Demian and Pistorius, is a central Gnostic deity. Mother Eva, finally, is a Christian archetype colored by the Jungian conception of *anima* (i.e., the feminine aspect of a man's unconscious). With her son Demian she anticipates the hermaphroditic goal of unification in which the tensions of the novel are ultimately resolved.

This play with religious forms, which shapes both the language and the structure of the novel, not only reflects the path of Sinclair's development; it also provides the background for the key figure, Demian himself. For only within such an ironically religious framework do we realize that Demian is a Christ figure. The brightness of his forehead, his "miracles" of control over his fellow students, his teaching by parables, his belief in a new kingdom, his band of disciples—all these traits, taken singly as they are scattered through the novel, might easily be overlooked. But within the symbolic framework they coalesce to constitute the image of a modern Christ—but with an ironic twist since his teaching is anything but Christian.

At this point we begin to comprehend the unity of the novel. A first-person narrative about a Christ written by a devoted disciple is known as a gospel, and *Demian* has all the characteristics of a gospel—the travesty of a gospel! Just as the novel represents structurally a reshaping of common Christian myths, it constitutes thematically a revaluation of Christian ideas. The theme of *Demian* is essentially Nietzschean. But as Hesse repeatedly stated, for him Christ and Nietzsche are not contradictory but complementary: they are both outstanding examples in the history of mankind of the individual search for personal values. In this search they are allied, though the way their systems are formalized may cause them to seem far apart.

Demian was published in 1919 under the pseudonym Emil Sinclair. Hesse was striving for the effect of authenticity with this pseudonym, but above all he did not wish to be identified with what he now called his "sentimental-bourgeois" works, whose validity he had begun to question and whose appeal to the generation of *Demian* he rightfully doubted. The deception was so nearly complete that the book was awarded the Fontane Prize for first novels. It was almost a year before Hesse was unmasked by an enterprising journalist and returned the prize. But he had succeeded in freeing himself from the stigma of his earlier reputation and in capturing a new audience, including such contemporaries as Jung, by whom Hesse was analyzed in 1921. Although his subsequent works were published under his own name, he continued, around the end of World War I, to use the pseudonym Sinclair for a series of essays addressed to the younger generation. In the most characteristic of these, "Eigensinn" ("Self-Reliance," 1919) he justifies the theme of personal values that he had treated fictionally in *Demian*: "There is one virtue that I particularly love: Self-Reliance. All the other popular and praised virtues represent obedience to laws handed down by men. Only self-reliance does not ask about these laws. He who is self-reliant obeys another law, a single and absolutely sacred law: the law within himself, his own law."

Another of these essays, "Zarathustras Wiederkehr" ("Zarathustra's Return," 1919), is written in conscious, and skillful, imitation of Nietzsche's hymnic style. As the crowds of young admirers swarm around him, disappointed that he offers them no facile solutions to the problems of life, Zarathustra smiles: "Behold, Zarathustra is not a teacher. . . . Zarathustra has seen much, he has suffered much. But only one thing has he learned, only one thing constitutes his wisdom, only one thing is his pride. He has learned to be Zarathustra. You should learn to be yourselves, just as I have learned to be Zarathustra." This is a refrain that Hesse echoed in hundreds of letters to readers who approached him for advice on conduct. His works, he insists, do not present examples to be followed specifically, only models of lives that question reality in an attempt to find the private solution. The questions may be the same for every man, but the answers vary from individual to individual. "Loneliness is the way," Zarathustra continues, "by which destiny leads man to himself."

Loneliness was the course that Hesse now chose. In the isolated village of Montagnola, above the valley of Lugano, he found the surroundings in which he spent the remainder of his life. During the summer of 1919, in a great surge of activity, he wrote several major essays as well as two of his finest novellas, and he discovered the avocation that brought him rich hours of contentment in the following years: painting. The external restlessness that had marked his life until 1914 was sublimated. From this time on his problematic quest was wholly internalized. Instead of being wasted on fruitless expeditions through the world outside, it was concentrated into works of a new quality that differ, by their intensity and control, from the older works as much as the Hesse of Montagnola differed from the young householder of Gaienhofen. In a certain sense it might be said that at this point Hesse ceased to be merely contemporary and became modern. Although his early writings anticipate his later ones in many individual points, the early books rarely transcend the level of considerable talent, whereas the works after 1917 often place him in the company of the finest writers of the twentieth century.

Despite all superficial differences between them, *Klein und Wagner* (*Klein and Wagner*, 1919) and *Klingsor's Last Summer* are complementary works. They are Hesse's two longest—and finest—novellas. In both, the action is compressed geographically and temporally into a brief period and into a southern landscape that reflect Hesse's own life in the summer of 1919. Both of the title figures are forty-two (Hesse's age at the time of composition) and thus are notably older than the heroes of his earlier tales. And in both the protagonist's death is preceded by a grand vision of unity in which the polarities of life are resolved.

Friedrich Klein is more than an autobiographical mask. He exemplifies the guilty conscience of many literati of the twentieth century who regard their way of life as somewhat illicit, if not downright criminal. (This symbolic consciousness raises Hesse's mature work above the merely private and relates it to the thematics of contemporaries like Mann, Hermann Broch, or André Gide, in whose writings the equation "artist = criminal" also plays a central role.) Klein is an embezzler. After a lifetime of sobriety as a reliable clerk, a steady husband, and a devoted father, he has absconded with a huge sum, deserted wife and children, and fled to the south under the assumed name Wagner. But Klein finds no immediate pleasure in his new, illicit freedom. To be sure, he is convinced that his previous life was a false one, modeled more after the expectations and demands of his wife than after his own wishes; for her sake he had subdued the "criminal," adventurous side of his nature. Yet certain bourgeois traits are so firmly ingrained in his character that he is disconcerted by the provocative glance of a pretty blond wearing bright lipstick and shoes with stiletto heels.

It was Hesse who penned the title *Klein and Wagner;* in his own mind Klein poses the question as Klein *or* Wagner. Klein (which means "small" in German) represents the bourgeois side of his personality; the artistic, "criminal" part he calls Wagner. This refers not only to Richard Wagner as an exemplum of overriding artistry but also to a *cause célèbre* of the years just before the war: the case of the psychopathic schoolteacher Ernst Wagner, who murdered his wife and four children. Klein, as a child, had always hated his name, which seemed to epitomize the pettiness of his life: "Wagner was the murderer and the fugitive within him; but Wagner was also the composer, the artist, the genius, the seducer, the inclination to *joie de vivre,* sensual pleasure, luxury." Klein-Wagner's malaise stems from his inability to reconcile what he regards as the two contradictory poles of his personality. Thus, in the main episode of the novella he is both attracted and repelled by the dancer Teresina, who personifies the sensuality that he had always longed for and yet feared.

By the end of the week he manages to overcome his inhibitions and rise to the heights of the illicit passion of his imagination. Yet when he awakes that night from bad dreams and peers down at Teresina's nude beauty, he reverts to his bourgeois abhorrence of sensuality and seizes a knife in order to kill her. Coming to his senses at the last moment and horrified by what he has almost done, he flees from the house and rows out to the middle of the lake. As he sits there, his legs dangling in the water, he reflects on the implications of the philosophical imperative to let oneself go. Translating Arthur Schopenhauer's thought into action, he sinks into the dark waters and, in a great concluding vision, sees the poles of his being not as contradictory, but as parts of a greater whole: "The whole secret was: to let oneself go! If he had done that a single time, if he had succumbed, surrendered, yielded himself; if he had renounced all supports and all firm ground underneath. If he listened only to the guide in his own heart, then everything was won, everything was all right: no longer any fear, no longer any danger." At this point of awareness, of course, his suicide becomes meaningless. But since life and death are also one and the same, further life becomes irrelevant as well. So

Klein-Wagner dies in total surrender to the water that so often serves the symbolic function of unification in Hesse's works.

Klein and Wagner is a tightly constructed novella that bears detailed comparison with such masterpieces of the genre as Mann's *Der Tod in Venedig (Death in Venice,* 1912). *Klingsor's Last Summer,* in contrast, is a loose series of sketches tied together only by their painter-hero. Thematically the two works are close: the final vision of an all-encompassing unity revealed to the drowning Klein is paralleled here in the Marc Chagall–like self-portrait that Klingsor paints just before his own death:

> He saw many, many faces behind his own face in the large mirror framed by stupid rose vines, and he painted them into his picture: the sweet and astonished faces of children, the foreheads of young men filled with dreams and fire, scornful drunkard's eyes, thirsting lips. . . . And not his face alone, or his thousand faces were painted into this portrait, not merely his own eyes and lips. He also painted hordes of naked women, driven past like birds in a storm, sacrificial offerings to the idol Klingsor, and a youth with the face of suicide, distant temples and forests.
>
> (*Gesammelte Werke,* 5: 348–350)

But whereas the scenes in *Klein and Wagner* are tempered gloomily by the uneasy conscience of Klein, whose feelings of guilt cast a pall upon the very landscape, the atmosphere in *Klingsor's Last Summer* is radiant with the beauty that Hesse, wandering around the Ticino with his camp stool and palette, had begun to discover in the world. These stories provide a perfect example of what Ralph Freedman has called the lyrical quality of Hesse's fiction; the external reality—which is identical in both works—is so disposed as to reflect the different inner moods of the two heroes. Both works together constitute the entirety of Hesse's own vision: the schizophrenic rapture and depression of Klein along with the euphoric intoxication of Klingsor.

The theoretical background for the visions of unity in which the two novellas culminate is supplied by two important essays on Feodor Dostoevsky that Hesse wrote in 1919 and that, peripherally at least, entered English literature through T. S. Eliot's notes to *The Waste Land* (1922). (Eliot was so deeply impressed by *Blick ins Chaos* [*In Sight of Chaos,* 1920] —the collective title of the essays—that he made a trip to Montagnola to visit Hesse.) In "Die Brüder Karamasoff, oder Der Untergang Europas" ("The Brothers Karamozov, or The Decline of Europe") Hesse projects onto the scale of cultural history the conflict between "two worlds" that is still largely private in *Demian.* The pure, "light" world, clinging desperately to a system of order that depends on the categorical rejection of certain attitudes defined arbitrarily as "bad," is represented by European Man. Opposed to this position, which is no longer tenable in the face of the relativism emerging in every area of modern science and philosophy, is Russian Man, personified by Dostoevsky's Karamazovs. Their ideal is "the departure from all established ethics and morality in favor of an attempt to understand everything, to accept everything." Unwilling to make absolute distinctions between good and evil, right and wrong, Russian Man worships a god who is at the same time Satan. (Here we see clearly an extension of Abraxas in *Demian.*) As this new spirit gradually permeates the West, the decline of traditional Graeco-Roman, Judaeo-Christian Europe becomes imminent.

From the standpoint of European Man this "Russian" attitude seems criminal, a view that accounts for the criminal symbolism of *Klein and Wagner.* But simple awareness of the "criminal" impulses within us, the "chaos" of our souls, suffices; it is not necessary to proceed to the criminal act. Hesse demands merely that the New Man, confronted with—or abandoned by—a deity who will not prescribe our decisions by handing down convenient tables of law, should take upon himself the burden of this freedom and the responsibility of choice in a pluralistic world. "The decline of Europe" will be no violent upheaval, but an inner revolution: "the re-interpretation of worn-out symbols, the transvaluation of spiritual values." Hesse advocates a new morality linked closely to the attitudes advanced in the essay on self reliance. Instead of cringing in despair or, like Klein, being driven to suicide by the apparent discrepancies between vision and reality, we should greet the breakdown of values as an occasion to assert ourselves in freedom as individuals. (If such thoughts sound familiar, it is because they anticipate in many respects the humanistic existentialism identified with such midcentury philosopher-novelists as Albert Camus and Jean-Paul Sartre.)

Hesse's "Gedanken zu Dostojewsky's *Idiot*" ("Thoughts on Dostoevsky's *Idiot*") offers a solution to the dilemma outlined in the first essay. Prince Myshkin, the "idiot" of the 1868 novel, is misunderstood and feared by his friends because his manner of seeing reality differs so radically from theirs. Whereas they are European Men, clinging to the values of a defunct system, he accepts all of life as it thrusts itself upon him. Especially during certain visionary moments (his epileptic seizures) he has stood at the magical boundary where all opposites are canceled out. As long as we remain within the framework of traditional reality, Hesse argues, we see life in terms of clashing opposites. If we can step outside the system, only for a moment, it becomes evident that these apparent opposites actually constitute complementary parts of a greater whole. "Magisches Denken" (Magical Thinking) is Hesse's rather romantic term for the act of mental projection that permits us to escape the sphere of polarities: it is a spiritual revaluation of life that proceeds from an uncompromising examination of the chaos in our own souls. The very opposite of anarchy, Magical Thinking implies the acknowledgment of a meaningful totality beyond chaos, for chaos is "chaotic" in a pejorative sense only from the standpoint of traditional concepts of order.

Such thoughts as these, outlined here and in other essays, explain why such symbols of unity as fire and water and grand culminating visions play a central role in Hesse's works. In the fairy tales (*Märchen*, 1919) that he wrote during these years he renders imagistically the various processes of transformation through which unity and totality can be expressed. In "Piktors Verwandlungen" ("Piktor's Metamorphoses," 1922), for instance, the hero is transformed into a stone, a tree, a bird—images for the identity of all being. But even in his less fanciful fiction, unity is expressed in similar symbols and visions. *Demian* translates the Gnostic god Abraxas into a modern symbol of synthesis; *Klingsor's Last Summer* renders the unification of all extremes in the artist's self-portraits. Like *Klein and Wagner*, Hesse's next novel, *Siddhartha*, culminates in an epiphany of unity when the hero peers into the river and sees mirrored there thousands of images that inundate his own reflection.

Siddhartha is a novel of classical symmetry—a perfection achieved, it might be added, at the cost of naturalness. Instead of style, it approaches stylization; instead of symbolism, allegory; instead of characterization, typology. Like Emil Sinclair, Siddhartha experiences the duality of nature and spirit before he finds the synthesis in a higher unity. But instead of vacillating between the impulses of his own personality, he finds the realms of spirit and nature spread out geographically on a symbolic landscape in the India of Buddha.

The son of a Brahman, Siddhartha discovers at eighteen that the religion of his father does not offer him the peace he seeks. So he sets out with his friend Govinda in search of the divine Atman, the universal soul from which, according to Hindu belief, all individual souls arise. His first venture leads him away from the river of his birth to the ascetic Samanas, who cultivate the mind to the total exclusion of the senses. Gradually it becomes clear to Siddhartha that spirit alone cannot fulfill his expectations. Leaving Govinda among the followers of Buddha, he returns to the river and crosses into the land of the senses, where he tarries for twenty years in the company of the courtesan Kamala, becoming a fat and prosperous businessman. At forty, however, Siddhartha realizes that sensual gratification has brought him no closer to happiness than did pure intellect and spirit. He goes back to the river, which flows between the two symbolic worlds and joins them in its fluidity, and becomes the humble helper of the ferryman Vasudeva. For twenty more years he remains with Vasudeva the sage, learning not so much from his teaching as by his example that the true road to happiness is complete affirmation of all being, of *both* realms. As Hesse later explained in the essay "My Belief," "*Siddhartha* glorifies not cognition, but love; it rejects dogma and revolves around the experience of unity."

In this novel Hesse's experience of Indonesia in 1911 reaches fruition. The book should not be read as a glorification of Buddhism. In a diary note from 1920 Hesse stated categorically that he opposed Buddhism to the extent that it attempted to establish a fixed pattern of development—the Eightfold Path—just as he opposed any rigid religious dogma. Rather, it is a glorification of the man Buddha, who went his way just as doggedly as Christ and Nietzsche and whose life provides still another example of the qualities that Hesse admired above all others: self-reliance and rugged independence.

Here more than in any of Hesse's other works the inner vision shapes external reality. The abstract concepts of spirit and nature wholly determine the Indian landscape of the book: the land of the Samanas is arid, while the land of Kamala is lush and verdant. The representatives of each geographical sphere are rigidly predetermined by their symbolic function in the novel: the Samanas never cross into the realm of the senses, and Kamala can go no further toward the realm of spirit than to the bank of the river. The language in the novel is equally stylized. Lacking the mystical rhetoric of *Demian* or the expressionistically fervent exuberance of *Klingsor*, it flows along with a paratactic smoothness that reflects the

symmetry of the total structure. Siddhartha spends twenty years (his youth) in the realm of spirit, twenty more years among the "child-people" of the senses, and then twenty years on the synthesizing river before he finds his inner sense of unity. A taut discipline holds the novel together, just as Siddhartha's face—in the final vision—contains within it the seething masses of all humanity as beneath a thin film.

Siddhartha is a literary tour de force, and its virtuosity stems from a concentrated effort to offset certain difficulties inherent in the theme. "My Indic poem got along splendidly as long as I was writing what I myself had experienced," Hesse explains in a 1920 diary note. "When I had finished with Siddhartha the Sufferer and wished to portray Siddhartha as a Victor, an Affirmer, a Subjugator—I couldn't go on." Again we sense the dialectical tension that underlies all of Hesse's works. Attempting to depict an ultimate synthesis that he himself had not attained, Hesse was forced to compensate for experience with an aesthetic structure that strains the potentialities of the genre. The resulting lyrical novel has undeniable shortcomings as fiction.

The year that followed the liberating euphoria of 1919 was "probably the most unproductive of my life, and thus the saddest," Hesse noted in his 1920 diary, and this is borne out by the difficulties he experienced in composing *Siddhartha*. After the completion of the novellas and the major essays, he killed time with other activities. From 1919 to 1922 he edited *Vivos Voco,* a journal devoted to the moral reconstruction of Europe. He wrote a number of minor essays, translated medieval Latin tales into German, and edited works of his favorite writers: Jean Paul, Novalis, Hölderlin, and others. Cut off from his family and former friends, he saw few people during these years except his future biographer, the Dadaist poet Hugo Ball, and Ruth Wenger, to whom he was married for a few months in 1924. Depressed by postwar developments in Germany, he became a Swiss citizen in 1923. For several grim years Hesse sat on his mountain in Switzerland, trying to come to terms with himself. Again, his life had not caught up with his art. It was 1924 before Hesse, like the Zarathustra of his own essay, persuaded himself to descend to the marketplace.

Forced to take a cure for rheumatic pains, in 1923 Hesse began visiting the spa of Baden outside Zurich, where for years he stayed regularly at the Hotel Verenahof. For the first time since his voluntary exile he found himself thrust into the midst of a society not of his own choosing. The unexpected result was the emergence of a sense of humor. Although some of his early stories are imbued with a certain melancholy humor, Hesse's works after 1917 are grimly serious. *Demian, Siddhartha, In Sight of Chaos*—these are the products of a mind obsessed with grave problems and wholly unrelieved by the airiness of humor. They present ideal visions that are not open to question or doubt. Hesse's flight into solitude in 1919 was in part a flight from the necessity of confronting this ideal with the reality of the world around him. By 1924, however, the confrontation had become inevitable, and Hesse was forced to concede that reality bore little resemblance to the visions so sincerely outlined in his novels and essays. If he was to survive outside the hermetic isolation of Montagnola, he had to find a means of mediating between real and ideal. This is essentially the subject of two long autobiographical essays: *Kurgast* (*At the Spa*, 1925) and *Die Nürnberger Reise* (*The Journey to Nuremberg*, 1927).

At the Spa, published originally under the title *Psychologia Balnearia* (1924), is inspired formally, as are many of Hesse's works, by the writings of the German romantics: in this case by Jean Paul, the great humorist of romanticism. (There is another conspicuous parallel: Mann's *The Magic Mountain*, which appeared that same year. Although there are vast formal differences between the essay and the lengthy *Bildungsroman*, they share the abstracted setting of a health resort, the pervasive humor,

and the symbolic parallel between art and disease.) Here for the first time Hesse sensed the humorous possibilities of his dialectical sense of life: "We patients at Baden are especially in need of that knowledge of the antinomies: the stiffer our bones become, all the more urgently we require an elastic, two-sided, bipolar way of thinking."

During his psychoanalysis Hesse had come to acknowledge the relativism of all concepts. But it had not yet occurred to him to draw the final conclusion that this very relativism was in itself relative, that his view of life was meaningless to such ebullient types as the Dutch burgher in the adjoining room, who disturbed Hesse constantly with the earthy sounds of his living (another startling parallel to *The Magic Mountain* and its Mijnheer Peeperkorn). Hesse's paean expressing incredulous distaste for the Dutchman is a humorous effervescence worthy of Thomas Wolfe, a writer Hesse later admired. But the meaning of the episodes is deeper, for the noisy neighbor becomes for Hesse a personification of the reality that he had to accept with love and humor: "My task was quite clear: I had to do away with my worthless hatred, I had to love the Dutchman. Then let him spit and bellow; I was superior to him, I was safe. If I succeeded in loving him, then all his healthiness, all his vitality could no longer help him. Then he would be mine, then his image could no longer resist the idea of unity." This was not easy, and—in anticipation of the hero of his next novel—he often longed for his "home in the steppes." But by the time he was well enough to leave the spa, he had realized that humor is the only way to survive the otherwise tragic clash between reality and ideal. (When Hesse uses the word "humor," it always connotes irony, as it does in German romanticism.)

By this time Hesse's attitude had shifted and grown more complex. He no longer reacted with apocalyptic rage or indignation to discordant aspects of life but sought to incorporate them with ironic understanding into his vision of unity. (This is especially true of *Steppen-*

HERMANN HESSE

wolf, which has as its milieu the cocktail lounges and jazz bars of the 1920's, which Hesse abhorred.) And he envisaged a more sophisticated style in which the "two worlds" of *Demian* and the two realms of *Siddhartha* would no longer be separated in an artificial dichotomy but would be delicately intermingled as they are in reality. In the conclusion of *At the Spa* he wishes that he had the counterpoint of the musician at his disposal: "Then without difficulty I could write a two-voiced melody consisting of two lines, two series of tones and notes that correspond to and complement each other, but that simultaneously are antagonistic and circumscribe each other." This stylistic predicament preoccupied Hesse incessantly during the next years. "This is my dilemma and my problem," the work ends. "I shall never succeed in bending the two poles of life together, in writing down the double voice of life's melody."

The Journey to Nuremberg, which records the author's impressions during a lecture tour, marks another step forward in the development of the fine sense of irony that Mann and Gide admired in Hesse's later works. "If, under the increasing pressure of my life, I retreat into humor and view so-called reality from the fool's point of view," this is, he explains, nothing but "an attempt to bridge the gap between Ideal and Experience." The lecture tour brought him into constant contact with other people, "realists" who regarded the writer as little more than a spectacle to be stared at and who had little or no understanding of the meaning of his works. Hesse concluded that if this breakdown of communication was inevitable, then it was no longer necessary to restrict himself to the relatively simple forms that he had usually employed in his works. This experience explains the cavalier playfulness of form that characterizes most of his subsequent works.

After 1925 Hesse began to spend his winters in Zurich. He repeatedly documented his complete lack of sympathy with technological civilization in all its manifestations. "I don't believe in our science," he observes in a letter of 1930, "nor in our politics, nor in our way of thinking, believing, amusing ourselves. I don't share a single one of the ideals of our age." This is more than the grumbling of a crabby reactionary. By "the ideals of our age" Hesse implies the blind materialistic faith in technology that Rilke and D. H. Lawrence decried. At the same time, with his customary frankness in self-evaluation, Hesse was quick to admit that his disavowal was largely the result of his own instinctive insecurity in the world of reality. In the afterword to the volume of poems *Krisis* (Crisis, 1928) he reasons:

> A great part, yes, the greatest part of the darker, perhaps deeper half of life was unconsciously passed over or prettified in my earlier writings. The reason for this lay, I believe, not in a naive repression of the sensual, but in a feeling of inferiority in that area. I was much more at home in the Spirit, in its broadest sense, than in the Senses.

This is the situation that Hesse portrays in his next novel. *Steppenwolf* is the ultimate novel of intellect in despair. Its hero is an intellectual who loses faith in the ideals of the spirit and regains it, ironically, by learning to affirm the senses and the world of the trivial and everyday that he had previously feared and rejected.

Structurally, *Steppenwolf* is the most daring of Hesse's works—as bold, Mann felt, as James Joyce's *Ulysses* (1922) and Gide's *Les faux-monnayeurs* (*The Counterfeiters*, 1926). However, for Hesse experimentation meant only the reshaping of traditional forms, not the contrivance of totally new structures. In its form the novel is closer to the realistic fairy tales of Hoffmann than to most modern novels. It was Hoffmann who transplanted the fairy tale from the gloomy Teutonic forests to the cities of his own time. They are "fairy tales" (*Märchen*) because they reproduce inner visions on the same level of authenticity as everyday occurrences. And that is the structural principle of Hesse's novel, which attempts to render the "double-voiced melody" of which he speaks in the essay *At the Spa*. All the action is recorded with the same degree of realism. The phantasmagoric effect is produced, as in Franz Kafka's works, by the fact that many of these events are actually imaginary. The escalation from reality to imagination is so subtle that the line between real and ideal is effaced; the reader must interpret every event on two levels; the double-voiced melody is achieved.

Harry Haller is a forty-eight-year-old intellectual who is able to bear his despair only because he has promised himself the luxury of suicide on his fiftieth birthday. Hesse motivates his hero with intimately personal details: separated from his wife, alienated from his friends for ideological reasons, suffering from poor eyesight and sciatica, and grievously alarmed by the glaring discrepancy between the ideals of his library and the reality of daily life, Haller is a photocopy of Hesse, with one great exception—he has no sense of humor.

This fictitious autobiography, which begins at the nadir of Haller's despair, records the events of a crucial month in his life. Haller has devoted himself wholly to the Spirit, to the "Immortals" (Goethe, Novalis, Wolfgang Amadeus Mozart), to the "golden trace" that gives life its meaning. We meet him just at a time when certain incidents have raised grave doubts in his mind: "Were those things that we called 'Culture,' that we called 'Spirit,' that we called 'Soul' and 'beautiful' and 'sacred'—were those things merely a spectre, already long dead and still considered genuine and alive only by a few fools like me?" Around this time he obtains a mysterious document entitled the "Tract of the Steppenwolf," which throws a new light on his dilemma. Haller has prided himself on being an outsider, a wolf from the steppes, cut off from bourgeois inhibitions. But from the "Tract" he learns that, far from being an objective and serene outsider, like the true Immortals, he is wholly bourgeois in his instinctive fear of prostitutes and in his antipathy toward the jazz culture of his times.

The Immortals that he worships were by no means men who rejected reality: their vision incorporated and transcended it, and Goethe and Mozart were not only sublime geniuses but also very much men of their times. Ordinary mortals like Haller, who are incapable of sustaining the icy isolation of the Immortals, can contend with everyday reality by learning to laugh at it and by striving to recognize the "golden trace" even in the most trivial events of everyday life.

Quite by chance Haller is thrown into contact with this demimonde that he has previously avoided. To his amazement he discovers that he is able to enjoy the dancing, idle chatter, and love-making of the prostitute Hermine, the musician Pablo, and their friends. In their conversations he gradually begins to hear echoed the voices and thoughts of the Immortals. But the line between reality and the ideal becomes tenuous. It is by no means clear—to Haller or to the reader—whether this wisdom actually comes from Hermine and Pablo or whether Haller himself is projecting these thoughts into otherwise trivial conversations and occurrences. In any case, the result is the same: Haller begins to recapture, during the month of his sensual apprenticeship, a new sense for the values of life.

His spiritual re-education culminates in the scenes of the Magic Theater, a narcotic fantasy induced by Pablo's drugs after a masquerade ball that Haller attends with Hermine. Here he visualizes himself in dozens of situations that he had previously rejected indignantly. He perceives, with the vividness of reality, that his rigid categories have completely collapsed, for he is theoretically capable of committing—and enjoying!—every human act, from the basest to the noblest. This total acceptance of being characterizes the Immortals, but it involves a dreadful freedom that Haller is unable to sustain without the stimulation of drugs. Growing sober in the early hours of the morning, he slips back into his old dualistic patterns and displays a fit of murderous jealousy when he finds Hermine in Pablo's arms.

In his final vision Harry is confronted by a jury of the Immortals to whom he had aspired. For his failure, for his confusion of the Magic Theater with mundane reality, he is condemned to remain in the world until he learns to laugh at the discordant aspects of life, until he perceives—in other words—the symbolic identity of Mozart and Pablo.

Steppenwolf is less symmetrically structured than the classicistic *Siddhartha,* but its organization, which bears detailed comparison to that of the sonata, is just as tight. (The musical analogy is not gratuitous. In this novel, which on both levels of reality—Mozart and Pablo—deals with music and musicians, Hesse consciously exploits a musical form.) Rather than force the book to a balanced conclusion, Hesse leaves Haller suspended at the end: "Pablo was waiting for me, Mozart was waiting for me." He is still very much enmeshed in the world of reality, but he faces it now with the consolation of humor and without the pathos of rigid intellectualism. The novel reflects the triadic rhythm of humanization that Hesse outlines in the important essay "Ein Stückchen Theologie" ("A Bit of Theology," 1932). From an initial state of childlike innocence, thinking men graduate to a second level: knowledge of good and evil. Confronted there with the disparity between the real and the ideal, either they are crushed by despair or they struggle through to a third stage: a higher innocence beyond good and evil—faith. This *principium individuationis* underlies almost all of Hesse's fiction. Here, however, he describes not an ideal process of individuation, as he does in *Siddhartha,* but a more realistic one. Most mortals, Hesse concludes, never attain the third level permanently; having glimpsed it, they continue like Haller to teeter precariously on the boundary between the world of men and the realm of the Immortals.

Steppenwolf repelled many readers, who failed to see that the book is not a glorification of sex, jazz, and drug addiction but a search for the eternal in the transitory, the divine in the mundane, the Immortals in the Jazz Era. (In an ironic parable entitled "Vom Steppenwolf" ["Harry the Steppenwolf," 1928] Hesse characterized the varied responses to his novel, ranging from moral outrage to the adulation of radical chic.) His next novel was a more popular success. As early as 1908 Hesse had written several chapters of a novel entitled *Bertold* (translated as the short story "Berthold" in *Tales of Student Life*), the story of a renegade seminarian in seventeenth-century Cologne who breaks his vows, murders, and flees into the world of sensual adventure. Although the work remained a fragment, for many years the figure of the hero kept running through his mind—the renegade monk as another exemplification of the obsessive dualism between spirit and nature. When he started work in 1927 on the novel *Narcissus and Goldmund,* he took up the old plan again, moving it to the fifteenth century and somewhat shifting the original emphasis. Instead of allowing the conflict to take place within the soul of a single hero, as in *Demian* and *Steppenwolf,* he conceived a *Doppelroman* (double novel) after the fashion of such romantic writers as Jean Paul and Hoffmann, in which the two attitudes are embodied symbolically in two different heroes: Narcissus the priest, who rises to the position of abbot, personifies pure spirit sealed off from the world by the walls of his monastery; and Goldmund—Golden Mouth in English, Chrysostomus in Greek—the renegade monk who runs away from the monastery to seek life, women, and, ultimately, art, embodies the world of nature and the senses.

As in *Siddhartha* the two worlds are separated spatially: the monastery is the preserve of spirit, and the wide world outside is the realm of nature. The book itself falls into other over-obvious structural divisions that occur when Hesse tries too hard to objectify his feelings. The first six chapters, during which Narcissus helps Goldmund to discover that he is not cut out for the life of a celibate, take place in Mariabronn (where Hesse has described his own school at Maulbronn). During the ten central chapters, in which Goldmund brawls his way through the world—making love to countless women, witnessing war, murder, pillage, and rape, and becoming a gifted woodcarver—Narcissus entirely disappears from the scene. In the last four chapters, reappearing like a deus ex machina to rescue Goldmund from prison and execution, the priest leads him back to the monastery, where the restless artist soon dies.

The original picaresque narrative of the ten middle chapters is a lively adventure story, and its erotic titillations account at least in part for its popularity. But the book bogs down in ponderous, almost embarrassing symbolism. Narcissus tells his friend:

> "Your home is the earth and ours is the idea. Your danger is to drown in the world of the senses, and ours it is to suffocate in airless space. You are an artist; I am a thinker: You sleep at the mother's breast while I lie awake in the desert. The sun shines for me, for you the moon and the stars. Your dreams are of girls, mine of boys. . . ."
>
> (*Gesammelte Dichtungen* 6:51)

We might excuse one such passage, but similar ones recur throughout the novel. At the end Goldmund has become a physical wreck, his features etched by the trials of the world, whereas Narcissus, hermetically sealed off in his monastery, has remained unravaged by time. Goldmund emerges triumphant since as an artist he has found the means to overcome time. His art, he tells Narcissus, represents "the overcoming of transitoriness. I saw that something remained and outlived the fool's game and the death-dance of men: the works of art." The very security of his existence has cut Narcissus off from those things that give life its meaning. Goldmund has been worn out by the world, but he has achieved a contentedness denied to his friend. For life is epitomized not by the spiritual father-image of the monastery but by the elusive figure of the Mother that Goldmund pursues—a symbol reminiscent of Mother Eva in *Demian*. Goldmund

realizes that this archetypal Mother represents not only love and life: "one could also call her a grave and decay. . . . She was the source of bliss and the source of death; . . . in her, love and cruelty were one." In pursuit of life Goldmund ends up realizing that this ultimate symbol encompasses all reality—knowledge, he implies rather smugly, that has been denied Narcissus in his monomaniacal preoccupation with the "paternal" spirit: "How will you die, Narcissus, if you have no mother? Without a mother one cannot love. Without a mother one cannot die." Since Goldmund himself dies before he can complete his final masterpiece—the carving of "the great Eve-Mother"—he cannot transmit his vision to the world. Hesse suggests by this conclusion that the artist gains an intuitive cognition denied to the intellectual but is prevented from revealing it in its ultimate form.

Narcissus and Goldmund, which was published in 1930, appeased those readers who prefer philosophy served up in spicy packages to the agonizing honesty and incisive analysis of books like *Steppenwolf.* But the novel has almost an anachronistic effect. With its heavy-handed symbolism, its Jungian mother figure, its labored dichotomy of "two worlds," and its total lack of humor, *Narcissus and Goldmund* seems to be a regression to the period of *Demian;* it has little in common with the more sophisticated Hesse of *Steppenwolf* and later works.

In 1931 Hesse married for a third time and moved with his wife into a new house in Montagnola. His happiness is reflected in *The Journey to the East,* a private symbolic autobiography. In contrast to the studied earnestness of *Narcissus and Goldmund,* the tone of *The Journey to the East* is ironic from the title on—an irony that Gide emphasizes in his preface to the French translation. The title is ironic because the narrator, H. H., never succeeds in telling us about his journey. Ten years earlier, in the period "after the Great War," H. H. had joined the League of Eastern Wayfarers in order to participate in a great pilgrimage to the East. But early in the journey the servant Leo disappeared, and this seemingly trivial occurrence created such dissension in the ranks that all members deserted one by one. When H. H. tries to write the history of the League, he discovers that he remembers nothing but superficial details: its spirit has escaped him completely. He wonders: What if the Order had not distintegrated around him? What if he himself had unwittingly deserted the League? He succeeds in finding Leo, whose harmonious existence contrasts sharply with H. H.'s own wretchedness. Leo assures H. H. that the Order is still intact and leads him to its archives so that H. H. can complete his history of the journey. In the archives H. H. learns that the humble servant Leo is in fact the Superior of the Order, that he embodies its ideal of humble service. H. H. himself has been so much obsessed with his own individuality that he has neglected the first rule of the Order—service—and thus has become apostate to the Order. Once he realizes his error he is punished by being smiled at by the assembled members and is then reaccepted into their ranks on the third level of Hesse's *principium individuationis,* where individuality, being assured, gives way to the higher ideal of service.

Apart from the ideal of service, another central theme of the story is the idea that those who implicitly believe in an eternal realm of the spirit understand it intuitively but that its secret can never be communicated to those who do not believe in it. As a result, from the moment when H. H. deserts the League, he is no longer able to comprehend its journey. And at the end, when he is absorbed once more into the spiritual order, he is no longer able to communicate his experience to the non-initiate reader. The "journey" of the title takes place before and after the narration. The act of narration itself is actually a gesture of the narrator's despair, since any true member of the League realizes the futility of trying to communicate the essential secret of the Order. Because Hesse succeeds in expressing all of

this through the words of his narrator, who only gradually becomes aware of his own position, the tone of the narrative assumes a delightful irony that offsets the underlying mood of despair.

To lend form to a story that by its very theme might easily collapse into a formless jumble, Hesse employs a conventional framework— again ironically, as is the case with the biblical prefiguration in *Demian.* Down to the most astonishing details of plot and description, his League and its leader Leo have characteristics borrowed from the Gothic romance of the late eighteenth century. The physical apparatus of the League's castle, the appearance of the "genius" of the League, the apprenticeship of the novice (H. H.)—all these features can be easily identified.

At the same time the whole narrative is a cunningly contrived symbolic autobiography. All the places mentioned, many of the incidents, and most of the characters (who are introduced under sobriquets) represent stages and events in Hesse's own life. Thus the Chinese Temple refers to the home of a friend in Winterthur; "Ninon, known as 'the foreigner,'" is a grammatical play on the maiden name of his own wife, Ninon Ausländer (*Ausländer* means "foreigner" in German); the rubric *Chattorum r. gest.* in the archives refers to the name that Hesse bore as a Latin student at Göppingen (Chattus) and to his subsequent deeds (*res gestae*). It is the most private book that Hesse wrote; every line contains allusions accessible only to the initiate. Yet the general meaning is obvious even to those who have never read another work by Hesse.

The "East" of the title is not, of course, a geographical specification; as early as 1911 Hesse had learned that the Orient can no longer be a paradise for modern man. Rather, the title indicates a realm of spirit variously defined, in the course of the story, as a "psychocracy," a "unification of all times," and a "melee of life and poetry." In this Eastern kingdom one is "free to exchange inner and outer reality playfully" and "to shift time and space like stage sets." What we have is a symbolic representation of the Magical Thinking of *In Sight of Chaos.* But the tone, rather than being apocalyptically severe as it is there, is serenely playful here. In the magical atmosphere of the story it is perfectly possible for H. H. to visit a celebration attended by figures from his own works (Pablo, Lauscher), by writers and musicians of the historical past (Hugo Wolf, Clemens Brentano), and by living friends of Hesse's (Hans C., Max and Tilli, Ninon). And all these characters are presented on the same level of fictional reality; there is absolutely no difference, here, between real and ideal.

But in the real world of the 1930's, there was a glaring discrepancy between reality and ideal. Hesse's home in Montagnola provided an initial point of orientation for many refugees from Hitler's Germany, and he displayed toward this new generation of political victims the same resourcefulness and understanding that had motivated his actions during World War I. Hesse's thoughts on politics, which are essentially ethical rather than political, had remained relatively constant ever since he lost his political innocence during World War I. His experiences at that time taught him to distrust all forms of nationalism and ideology. As he writes in the poem "Absage" (Letter of Decline, 1933), he would rather be killed by the Fascists or the Communists than commit himself to either party—an attitude perfectly consistent with the stubborn individuality that marked all his thought. As a result, Hesse almost always refused to sign manifestos or to make public proclamations, arguing that they usually did no good and frequently caused a good deal of harm. He had already learned during World War I that anyone who attempts to remain politically independent in times of turmoil becomes the enemy of all parties, and this bitter lesson was repeated in the 1930's. Since Hesse was a Swiss citizen, he did not share all the sentiments and emotions of the various exile groups. The émigré press attacked him rancorously because he continued to publish reviews and articles in German

periodicals for several years after 1933; and the Nazis reviled him because in those very reviews he attempted to direct the attention of Germans and foreigners alike to the important Jewish and non-Nazi writers who were condemned by the cultural guardians of the party. Yet despite—or, more precisely, because of—growing tensions in the real world, Hesse continued increasingly to cultivate the ideal in his thought and works.

The idyll *Hours in the Garden* describes how Hesse, working among his flowers, liked to let his thoughts wander far afield, pulling together in the most startling combinations ideas or figures from the cultural tradition of the world. In *The Journey to the East* he gives a charming fictional form to this pastime, but by 1936 he had found a new name for this "*unio mystica* of all disparate elements of the *Universitas Litterarum*." He now called it the Glass Bead Game.

Hesse's last novel had a longer and more complicated genesis than his other books. Composed over a period of some eleven years, it was originally intended to be the story of "a man who, in several reincarnations, experiences the great epochs in the history of mankind"—a man who lives a series of parallel lives beginning in prehistoric times, running through the Golden Age of India, the patristic period of early Christianity, and eighteenth-century Pietism in Germany, and ending in a pedagogical province in the future. But gradually Hesse's intentions shifted. By 1938 he had decided to focus his main attention on the final stage—Joseph Knecht in the Castalia of 2400. The other episodes were retained but were incorporated into the novel as school exercises written by young Knecht.

The pedagogical province of Castalia was originally envisaged as another variation on the Journey to the East—the representation of an ideal kingdom of the spirit, here centered on the Glass Bead Game, which is defined in the Introduction as "a refined, symbolic form of the search for perfection, a sublime alchemy, an approach to the spirit that is unified in itself beyond all images." But by 1938 two great influences had altered Hesse's thinking. First, his study of the historical writings of Jacob Burckhardt—the Pater Jacobus of his novel—made him aware of the relativism of all historical organisms, including even such an idealized society as Castalia. He was no longer able to posit Castalia as an absolute ideal, valid for all times and under all circumstances. Second, the horrors of Nazism in Germany had opened his eyes to the futility of purely aesthetic ideals in the world of reality: like many of his contemporaries he became convinced of the necessity for the existential engagement of the individual. Thus *The Glass Bead Game,* which was begun in 1931 as a hymn to the aesthetic kingdom of the spirit, became by the time of its publication in 1943 a repudiation of disengagement in favor of personal commitment. In this sense Hesse's novel, like Broch's *The Death of Vergil* (1945), is a compelling document of the transition from the aestheticism of the early twentieth century to the *littérature engagée* of our own times.

Structurally the novel falls into three parts. The long Introduction sketches the history of the Glass Bead Game up to the time of Joseph Knecht and outlines the organization of the pedagogical province. The poems and fictitious lives written by Knecht while he was a student are reproduced in a bulky appendix. The twelve central chapters, which follow the pattern of the traditional German *Bildungsroman,* trace the story of Knecht's development from his boyhood in the preparatory schools of Castalia through his rise to the top of the order and, finally, his abdication. The world of *The Glass Bead Game,* in radical contradistinction to Hesse's other novels, is not polar—is not divided between Nature and Spirit—but is divided into three "powers" suggested to Hesse by his reading of Burckhardt: church, state, and culture. Young Knecht grows up in the province of culture. It is only when he is sent as a representative of Castalia to the monastery of Mariafels, where he spends two

years in the company of Pater Jacobus, that he begins for the first time to question the validity of an order devoted exclusively to the cultivation of the spirit. Aroused by his debates with Pater Jacobus, Knecht rapidly recognizes the dangers inherent in the pedagogical province. In his best friend, the musician Tegularius, he witnesses the ravages visited on a brilliant mind that broods narcissistically. During his eight years as Magister Ludi, the supreme title in the hierarchy of Castalia, Knecht preserves the sense of historicism acquired from Pater Jacobus, which affords him a certain ironic distance from the games he performs with an unmatched virtuosity.

Knecht realizes that Castalia is heading toward collapse, that an art wholly divorced from life and moral commitment is suicidal. In order to make a gesture of his alarm, Knecht decides to defect and go into the world, where he intends to devote himself to the service of mankind. (*Knecht* means "servant" in German.) Discarding disengagement, he takes upon himself the responsibility of action and volunteers to tutor the son of his worldly friend Plinio Designori. Just as art must perish without life, life becomes brutish without culture. Since the official realms of state and culture have lost virtually all contact with each other, existing side by side in a state of mutual contempt, only responsible individuals like Knecht can mediate between them. On the third morning of his defection, however, Knecht's sense of personal commitment causes his death. His young pupil Tito plunges into the icy waters of a mountain lake for a swim, and Knecht, reluctant at such an early point in their relationship to betray any lack of solidarity, follows him into the water and drowns. A great deal has been written about the symbolic overtones of Knecht's death, but Hesse has made the basic meaning quite explicit. He wrote in a letter of November 1947:

> Knecht could have refrained, finely and intelligently, from leaping into the mountain water despite his illness. Yet he does it all the same

because there is in him something stronger than intelligence, because he cannot disappoint this boy who is so difficult to win over. And he leaves behind a Tito for whom this sacrificial death of a man vastly superior to him will remain forever an admonition and an example.

(*Gesammelte Briefe* 3:453–454)

Yet the true beneficiary of Knecht's death is not Tito or anyone else living at the time of Knecht, but rather the generation represented by the anonymous narrator, who writes some years after Knecht's death. This narrator describes the Castalia of the past, the pedagogical province devoted exclusively to the cultivation of spirit in the abstract, with the irony that has by this time become customary for Hesse. The later Castalia in which the narrator lives is one that has profited from Knecht's criticism and example; it is a Castalia far removed from pure aestheticism, a realm of culture that exists in a healthy tension and interaction with state and religion.

Hesse has moved away from the position of pure contemplation that seemed to constitute his ideal in the 1920's and early 1930's. In the terms of the novel he strives for a synthesis of the *vita activa* and the *vita contemplativa.* In Castalia the ideal is symbolized by music, which requires a constant compromise between practice and theory, the abstract and the concrete, the spiritual and the sensual. For this reason the old Magister Musicae, more than any of the brilliant constellation of mandarins in Castalia, anticipates Knecht's final resolution and decision. Hesse's last novel is in no way a depiction of the charms of disengagement but rather a plea for human commitment and for an art nourished by life, for a life enriched by art.

The Glass Bead Game was Hesse's last novel. Plagued by increasingly poor eyesight, by the leukemia that precipitated his death in 1962, by the entreaties of hundreds of correspondents, and by the other demands made upon literary figures of world renown, he barricaded himself in Montagnola behind a sign

reading "No Visitors Please." Yet during these last twenty years his literary production continued at an astonishing pace. It is easy to forget—particularly in light of the remarkable cult that arose in the United States around his name and novels in the decade following his death—that Hesse was never an otherworldly guru but was a professional writer who produced, in the course of an active literary career spanning some sixty years, a quantity of work so vast that it has yet to be thoroughly cataloged. As a young writer with a wife and three children to support, he could hardly afford the pose of the aesthete. And twice during his career—notably during World War I and again during the 1930's—he lost his audiences, and his means of support, for political reasons. Accordingly, from 1900 to 1962 he wrote some twenty-five hundred reviews for many of the better newspapers and journals in Germany, Austria, and Switzerland. He edited and introduced almost sixty editions of German literary classics as well as an astonishing variety of works from world literature, many in his own translation. He wrote dozens of essays on topics ranging from the literary and the political to the confessional. Yet despite the enormous productivity, not a single piece can be characterized as literary hackwork. Indeed, his reviews served an essential political purpose during the 1910's and 1930's, and his essays amount to important credos on issues ranging from ethics to politics. In addition, he painted scores of watercolors, many of them as illustrations for holograph editions of poems and fairy tales that he produced to supplement the often uncertain income from his books. Finally, he wrote over twenty-five thousand letters to friends and admirers, many of which constitute minor essays in themselves.

All this activity continued virtually unabated during his last years, when, apart from hundreds of private letters, Hesse wrote a number of stories, autobiographical reflections, circular letters to his friends, and poems that fill several volumes. In these last works Hesse's attitude is distilled into what might be called the classicism of revolt. Under the deceptively simple surfaces of landscape descriptions, childhood reminiscences, or episodes from the daily life of a septuagenarian, we find a preoccupation with the same themes that characterize his works from 1917 on. "All my works," he suggested to a German student in a letter of March 1954, "can be interpreted as a defense (sometimes also an anguished cry) of the individual." In this later prose it is not the attitude that has changed, but the tone. German scholars are fond of speaking of the *Altersstil*—the style of old age—of their writers: the brittle, symbolic, classically reduced, and often ironic style that is pronounced in, for instance, the late works of Goethe or Mann. There is no better example of this *Altersstil* than Hesse's late prose, which has shed the pathos of individualism to immerse itself wholly in its object.

Hesse's growth as a writer parallels the development of literature in the twentieth century from aestheticism to engagement. But he was always an amused observer, never a member of movements or a frantic participant in the contest to keep abreast of the times. He was drawn to themes that are perhaps more urgent today than in ages with accepted patterns of belief, but that are still universal: the quest for identity, the search for personal values, the impulse to moral commitment. Just as he was reluctant to concern himself with issues that are merely timely, he also refused to engage in pure innovation and stylistic experimentation. Even in the least conventional of his novels he simply reshapes existing forms. His achievement is to have shown to what extent modernity is traditional in its thought and in its form; his works bridge the gap, so to speak, between romanticism and existentialism. His range was narrow and his expression essentially lyrical, for he rarely went beyond himself. At most, after 1917, he transposed his themes from the minor key of the private to the major key of the symbolic. For this reason Hesse does not rank, as a novelist, with Marcel Proust, Joyce, or Mann; and in his poetry he never approached Rilke, Eliot, or Paul Valéry. But in the realm of poetic fiction—a province marked out by his favorite romantic authors and explored by Rilke, Broch, Virginia Woolf, Gide, and others—his best works are unsurpassed. Sometimes, in this difficult terrain, he stumbled through a landscape cluttered with thickets of allegory. But with *Steppenwolf, The Journey to the East,* and *The Glass Bead Game* he added lasting names to the map of our poetic imagination.

Selected Bibliography

EDITIONS

INDIVIDUAL WORKS

NOVELS, NOVELLAS, AND STORIES
Hinterlassene Schriften und Gedichte von Harmann Lauscher. Basel, 1901.
Peter Camenzind. Berlin, 1904.
Unterm Rad. Berlin, 1906.
Diesseits. Berlin, 1907.
Nachbarn. Berlin, 1908.
Gertrud. Munich, 1910.
Umwege. Berlin, 1912.
Rosshalde. Berlin, 1914.
Knulp: Drei Geschichten aus dem Leben Knulps. Berlin, 1915.
Demian: Die Geschichte einer Jugend von Emil Sinclair. Berlin, 1919.
Märchen. Berlin, 1919.
Klingsors letzter Sommer. Berlin, 1920. Includes *Klein und Wagner.*
Siddhartha: Eine indische Dichtung. Berlin, 1922.
Der Steppenwolf. Berlin, 1927.
Narziss und Goldmund. Berlin, 1930.
Die Morgenlandfahrt. Berlin, 1932.
Das Glasperlenspiel: Versuch einer Lebensbeschreibung des Magister Ludi Josef Knecht samt Knechts hinterlassenen Schriften. 2 vols. Zurich, 1943.
Berthold: Ein Romanfragment. Zurich, 1945.

PROSE POEMS AND POETRY
Romantische Lieder. Dresden, 1899.
Eine Stunde hinter Mitternacht. Leipzig, 1899; 2d ed., Zurich, 1941.

HERMANN HESSE

Krisis: Ein Stück Tagebuch. Berlin, 1928.
Gedichte. Zurich, 1942.

ESSAYS

Boccaccio. Berlin, 1904.
Franz von Assissi. Berlin, 1904.
Blick ins Chaos: Drei Aufsätze. Bern, 1920.
Kurgast. Berlin, 1925.
Die Nürnberger Reise. Berlin, 1927.
Betrachtungen. Berlin, 1928.
Eine Bibliothek der Weltliteratur. Leipzig, 1929.
Krieg und Frieden: Betrachtungen zu Krieg und Politik seit dem Jahr 1914. Zurich, 1946.

MISCELLANEOUS

Aus Indien. Berlin, 1913.
Stunden im Garten: Eine Idylle. Vienna, 1936.
Späte Prosa. Berlin, 1951.
Prosa aus dem Nachlass. Edited by Ninon Hesse. Frankfurt, 1965.

COLLECTED WORKS

Neue deutsche Bücher: Literaturberichte für "Bonniers Litterära Magasin," 1935–1936. Edited by Bernhard Zeller. Marbach, 1965.
Prosa aus dem Nachlass. Edited by Ninon Hesse. Frankfurt, 1965.
Gesammelte Werke. 12 vols. Frankfurt, 1970. This edition, now the most complete one, is an augmented version of the seven-volume *Gesammelte Schriften* (Frankfurt, 1957), which is an augmented version of the six-volume *Gesammelte Dichtungen* (Frankfurt, 1952).
Die Erzählungen. Edited by Volker Michels. 2 vols. Frankfurt, 1973.
Die Kunst des Müssiggangs: Kurze Prosa aus dem Nachlass. Edited by Volker Michels. Frankfurt, 1973.
Die Gedichte. Edited by Volker Michels. 2 vols. Frankfurt, 1977.
Kleine Freuden: Kurze Prosa aus dem Nachlass. Edited by Volker Michels. Frankfurt, 1977.
Politik des Gewissens: Die politischen Schriften. 2 vols. Edited by Volker Michels. Frankfurt, 1977.

CORRESPONDENCE

Briefe: Hermann Hesse—Romain Rolland. Zurich, 1954. Revised edition entitled *D'une rive a l'autre,* edited by Pierre Grappin. Paris, 1972.
Kindheit und Jugend vor Neunzehnhundert: Hermann Hesse in Briefen und Lebenszeugnissen.
2 vols. Edited by Ninon Hesse. Frankfurt, 1966, 1978.
Briefwechsel: Hermann Hesse—Thomas Mann. Edited by Anni Carlsson. Frankfurt, 1968; rev. ed., 1975.
Briefwechsel: Peter Suhrkamp—Hermann Hesse. Edited by Siegfried Unseld. Frankfurt, 1969.
Briefwechsel aus der Nähe: Hermann Hesse—Karl Kerényi. Edited by Magda Kerényi. Munich and Vienna, 1972.
Briefwechsel: Hermann Hesse—R. J. Humm. Edited by Ursula and Volker Michels. Frankfurt, 1977.
Briefwechsel mit Heinrich Wiegand. Edited by Klaus Pezold. Berlin and Weimar, 1978.
Briefwechsel: Hermann Hesse—Hans Sturzenegger, 1905–1943. Edited by Kurt Bachtold. Schaffhausen, 1978.
Gesammelte Briefe. 4 vols. Edited by Ursula and Volker Michels. Frankfurt, 1973–1986.

TRANSLATIONS

Autobiographical Writings. Translated by Denver Lindley. New York, 1972. Includes "Life Story Briefly Told," *At the Spa,* and *The Journey to Nuremberg.*
Beneath the Wheel. Translated by Michael Roloff. New York, 1968. First translated as *The Prodigy* by W. J. Strachan (London, 1957).
Correspondence: Hesse–Rolland. Translated by M. B. Hesse. London, 1978.
Crisis: Pages from a Diary by Hermann Hesse. Translated by Ralph Manheim. New York, 1975. Bilingual edition.
Demian. Translated by Michael Roloff and Michael Lebeck. New York, 1965. Also translated under the same title by N. H. Priday (New York, 1923) and by W. J. Strachan (London, 1958).
Gertrude. Translated by Hilda Rosner. London, 1955.
The Glass Bead Game. Translated by Richard and Clara Winston. New York, 1969. First translated under the title *Magister Ludi* by Mervyn Savill (London, 1949).
The Hesse–Mann Letters: The Correspondence of Hermann Hesse and Thomas Mann, 1910–1955. Translated by Ralph Manheim. New York, 1975.
Hours in the Garden and Other Poems. Translated by Rika Lesser. New York, 1979. Bilingual edition.
If the War Goes on: Reflections on War and Politics. Translated by Ralph Manheim. New York, 1971.

In Sight of Chaos. Translated by Stephen Hudson. Zurich, 1923.

The Journey to the East. Translated by Hilda Rosner. London, 1956.

Klingsor's Last Summer. Translated by Richard and Clara Winston. New York, 1970. Includes *Klein and Wagner.*

Knulp. Three Tales from the Life of Knulp. Translated by Ralph Manheim. New York, 1971.

My Belief: Essays on Life and Art. Translated by Denver Lindley and Ralph Manheim. New York, 1974.

Narcissus and Goldmund. Translated by Ursule Molinaro. New York, 1968. First translated under the title *Death and the Lover* by Geoffrey Dunlop (London, 1932); reprinted under the title *Goldmund* (London, 1959).

Peter Camenzind. Translated by Michael Roloff. New York, 1969.

Pictor's Metamorphoses and Other Fantasies. Translated by Rika Lesser. New York, 1982.

Poems. Translated by James Wright. New York, 1970.

Reflections. Translated by Ralph Manheim. New York, 1974.

Rosshalde. Translated by Ralph Manheim. New York, 1970.

Siddhartha. Translated by Hilda Rosner. New York, 1951.

Steppenwolf. Translated by Basil Creighton. London, 1929. Rev. ed. translated by Joseph Mileck and Horst Frenz (New York, 1963); rev. ed. translated by Walter Sorell. (London, 1963).

Stories of Five Decades. Translated by Ralph Manheim and Denver Lindley. New York, 1972.

Strange News from Another Star and Other Tales. Translated by Denver Lindley. New York, 1972.

Tales of Student Life. Translated by Ralph Manheim. New York, 1976.

Wandering: Notes and Sketches. Translated by James Wright. New York, 1972.

BIOGRAPHICAL AND CRITICAL STUDIES

Ball, Hugo. *Hermann Hesse: Sein Leben und sein Werk.* Berlin, 1927. Augmented edition edited by Anni Carlsson and Otto Basler. Zurich, 1947.

Böttger, Fritz. *Hermann Hesse: Leben, Werk, Zeit.* Berlin, 1974.

Boulby, Mark. *Hermann Hesse: His Mind and Art.* Ithaca, N.Y., 1967.

Field, George Wallis. *Hermann Hesse.* New York, 1970.

Freedman, Ralph. *The Lyrical Novel: Studies in Hermann Hesse, André Gide, and Virginia Woolf.* Princeton, N.J., 1963.

————. *Hermann Hesse: Pilgrim of Crisis.* New York, 1978. The most readable and sophisticated biography.

Greiner, Siegfried. *Hermann Hesse: Jugend in Calw.* Sigmaringen, 1981.

Hermann Hesse als Maler. 44 watercolors selected by Bruno Hesse and Sándor Kuthy. Frankfurt, 1977.

Hsia, Adrian. *Hermann Hesse und China: Darstellung, Materialien, und Interpretation.* Frankfurt, 1974.

Kleine, Gisela. *Ninon und Hermann Hesse: Leben als Dialog.* Sigmaringen, 1982.

Liebmann, Judith, ed. *Hermann Hesse: A Collection of Criticism.* New York, 1977.

Marrer-Tising, Carlee. *The Reception of Hermann Hesse by the Youth in the United States.* Bern and Frankfurt, 1982.

Matzig, Richard B. *Hermann Hesse in Montagnola: Studien zu Werk und Innenwelt des Dichters.* Basel, 1947.

Michels, Volker. *Materialien zu Hermann Hesses "Der Steppenwolf."* Frankfurt, 1972.

————. *Materialien zu Hermann Hesses "Das Glasperlenspiel."* 2 vols. Frankfurt, 1973–1974.

————. *Materialien zu Hermann Hesses "Siddhartha."* 2 vols. Frankfurt, 1975–1976.

————, ed. *Hermann Hesse: A Pictorial Biography.* Translated by Theodore and Yetta Ziolkowski. New York, 1975.

————, ed. *Über Hermann Hesse.* 2 vols. Frankfurt, 1976–1977.

————, ed. *Hermann Hesse: Sein Leben in Bildern und Texten.* Frankfurt, 1979.

Mileck, Joseph. *Hermann Hesse: Life and Art.* Berkeley, Calif., 1978.

Pfeifer, Martin, ed. *Hermann Hesse's weltweite Wirkung.* Frankfurt, 1977.

Rose, Ernst. *Faith from the Abyss: Hermann Hesse's Way from Romanticism to Modernity.* New York, 1965.

Schwarz, Egon, ed. *Hermann Hesses Steppenwolf.* Königstein, 1980.

Zeller, Bernhard. *Hermann Hesse in Selbstzeugnissen und Bilddokumenten.* Reinbek bei Hamburg, 1963.

———, ed. *Hermann Hesse: Eine Chronik in Bildern.* Frankfurt, 1960. Expanded edition, 1977.

Ziolkowski, Theodore. *The Novels of Hermann Hesse: A Study in Theme and Structure.* Princeton, N.J., 1965.

———. *Der Schriftsteller Hermann Hesse: Wertung und Neubewertung.* Frankfurt, 1979.

———, ed. *Hesse: A Collection of Critical Essays.* Englewood Cliffs, N.J., 1973.

BIBLIOGRAPHIES

Bareiss, Otto. *Eine Bibliographie der Werke über Hermann Hesse.* 2 vols. Basel, 1962–1964.

Koester, Rudolf. *Hermann Hesse.* Stuttgart, 1975.

Mileck, Joseph. *Hermann Hesse and His Critics: The Criticism and Bibliography of Half a Century.* Chapel Hill, N.C., 1958.

———. *Hermann Hesse: Biography and Bibliography.* 2 vols. Berkeley and Los Angeles, 1977.

Unseld, Siegfried. *Hermann Hesse: Werk und Wirkungsgeschichte.* Frankfurt, 1973; expanded edition, 1985.

Waibler, Helmut. *Hermann Hesse: Eine Bibliographie.* Bern and Munich, 1962.

THEODORE ZIOLKOWSKI

ENDRE ADY

(1877–1919)

ENDRE ADY, the elder son of a Calvinist family of lesser nobles, was born in Érmindszent, a village in southeastern Hungary, on 22 November 1877. His father, like many of the impoverished gentry, cultivated his small estate and shared the concerns of his peasant neighbors. Ady's maternal grandfather represented the learned segment of the family. He was a Protestant pastor who later, however, worked as a farm manager and road surveyor. Ady's younger brother, Lajos (1881–1940), became an educator who published on topics of literature and pedagogy. Ady completed elementary school in his native village and attended high school in two nearby towns, first in Nagykároly and then in Zilah, where he began writing. His earliest poems were published in the school's newspaper, *Ifjúság* (Youth), which he also edited.

Ady first visited Budapest in 1896 in the company of fellow students who toured the nation's capital on the occasion of the Millennium, the thousandth anniversary of the appearance of the Magyars in the Carpathian Basin. During the same year Ady completed his high school education and enrolled at the University of Debrecen in order to study law. His interest, however, was more literary than legal. He began contributing to the local papers and soon, against the wishes of his family, abandoned his legal studies to become a journalist, first in Debrecen, later in Nagyvárad. During this period his poetry and prose expressed the liberal patriotic ideas of the Hungarian middle class. In his articles he attacked the backwardness of the gentry, the hypocrisy of the clergy, and the blind nationalism of the conservatives. During his stay in Nagyvárad he briefly contemplated joining the Freemasons, whose political goals he later frequently criticized. Very little of his early poetry exhibits the unique linguistic qualities that characterize his later verse.

His meeting with Adél Diósi, a married woman who became his most important love, in 1903 and his first trip to Paris in 1904 brought revolutionary changes in his life, yielding his first collection of poems, *Új versek* (New Poems), in 1906.

While his poetry was influenced by the symbolists (primarily by Charles Baudelaire and Paul Verlaine), it also contains the arbitrary distortions and accents found in contemporary expressionist verse. Yet his cosmic images and his ideas of the poet's prophetic role in society prove that the romantic vision dominated his work most consistently.

Ady was a contemporary of Sigmund Freud, Franz Kafka, Marcel Proust, Aleksandr Blok, Rainer Maria Rilke, and Robert Musil. Yet in outlook and style Ady, while sharing several concerns of the new century, belongs to the previous one. His poetic language displays the features of post-romanticism, and his lyrical "I" is in the style of Friedrich Nietzsche. Neville Masterman's assessment is correct: "Ady, like Byron, Pushkin, Hugo and many other poets, can only be firmly appreciated if his writings are seen against the role he played in history." What should be added, however, is that the poets in whose company Ady appears in this quotation were romantics who preceded him by many decades. He is rightly counted among them because, all his modernist features notwithstanding, he was a late romantic whose commitments were different from those of Baudelaire or Verlaine. He was a political poet as well.

Ady was engaged and alienated at the same time, the fate of many Hungarian artists and intellectuals of the *fin de siècle*. A dependent part of the Austro-Hungarian Empire, Hungary suffered from a decadent, suffocating atmosphere created by a powerful feudal class and a gigantic bureaucracy, both of which were busily trying to patch over the ever-widening gap between the megalomaniac dreams of the empire and a glum reality that pointed to unavoidable catastrophe. The outbreak of World War I was a devastating and terrifying awakening for the middle class, but not for those who, like Ady or Musil, had long been aware of what was in store. Ady, a prophetic witness of the fateful decades before the war, responded to the crisis with the thunderous voice of the great romantics of Hungary, such as Sándor Petőfi, Mihály Vörösmarty, and János Arany.

Ady felt repelled by the cultural wasteland of Hungary and hated the "barbarian gentry" with its institutionalized provincialism. "My existence here is empty and without soul," he wrote to friends. "I shall perish in Budapest." Most Hungarian nationals were chauvinistic, and Ady, who called for the nations of the region to unite for the sake of a better future, as in the poem "Magyar jakobinus dala" (Song of a Hungarian Jacobine, 1908),[1] stood alone among the narrow-minded nationalists who sought a superior position for Hungary. Ady

consistently rejected any manifestation of nationalism, which he believed to be the most powerful weapon of the conservative ruling classes. As a line from "Song of a Hungarian Jacobine" proclaims, "The sounds of the River Danube and River Olt are the same": he was one of the few Hungarians who had no prejudice against his Romanian neighbors.

Since Ady came from an old Calvinist family, his work is rich in biblical allusion and imagery and employs archaic biblical vocabulary. Yet it also abounds in pagan images evoking Hungary's pre-Christian history: the poet identifies with the rebellious pagan leaders who fought against the church and were put to death by it.

Ady was not a true believer but a quasi-agnostic with a private and "intimate" relationship with God, often represented as a dialogue between two equals. In his "special kinship with God," he depicts God in human and zoomorphic shapes. He criticized the organized church and its role in Hungary's feudal history, and he longed for a loving, understanding God in whom he could find solace.

Although Marxist critics such as György Lukács, József Révai, and István Király cannot resolve the conflict between Ady's revolutionary and God-seeking attitudes, they are but two sides of the same desire to belong and of the same impulse to provoke rejection. His desire to belong remained unfulfilled in both politics and religion because he could never relinquish his doubts and his insistence on protest.

In one of Ady's great poems about fear, love, and doubt, God appears as a horrendous whale. In "A nagy cethalhoz" (To the Giant Whale, 1908) the poet implores him, "On your awesome back we dance. / Don't move, your skin is slippery!" In "Uram, ostorozz meg" (God, Flog Me, 1908), God is depicted as a village squire enraged at his farmhand for stealing his women and songs and for drinking his wine. Among the wealth of images of divinity in Ady's poetry, God also appears as a

---

[1]For ease of reference, poems in this essay are referred to upon subsequent mention by their English titles. These poems have not necessarily been translated into English.

mysterious woman who spends nights with the poet but disappears in the morning in order to remain distant and unfamiliar, as in "Éjszakai Isten" (The Night-God, 1908).

His desire for acceptance by God frequently causes him to overcome this cynical abuse. In "Álmom: Az Isten" (My Dream-God, 1908) the poet admits that his fear of death drives him back to believing. While in some poems God listens to and embraces him, in others God simply does not hear him or understand his needs, as in "Hare a Nagyúrral" (Battle with the Swine-Headed Lord, 1906), "Az Úr érkezése" (The Lord's Arrival, 1908), and "A Sion-Megy alatt" (Below Mount Zion, 1908). In the latter the poet wipes tears from the cheeks of an old, distraught God.

In one of Ady's most powerful poems, "Battle with the Swine-Headed Lord," God and the poet collide with equal force. Frequently, as in "Sötét vizek partján" (On the Shore of Dark Waters, 1907), "Ádám hol vagy?" (Adam, Where Art Thou?, 1908), "Az Úr érkezése," "Az Isten balján" (On God's Left, 1908), and "Szeress engem Istenem" (God, Love Me, 1908), God unexpectedly appears in order either to stand by the poet's side or to compete with him. In the last poem, Ady suggests that the two stop tormenting each other. While in some poems God is the compassionate Last Judge, in others, such as "Isten a vigasztalan" (The Cheerless God, 1908), Ady depicts a cruel and whimsical despot who is bored by and indifferent to his own creation: "He is all, and without cheer / This only and horrible God."

The God of the Old Testament appears in "Adam, Where Art Thou?" to conquer and destroy the poet's enemies. The poet concedes that his occasional victories are attributable to God, who clears his path with a "flaming sword." "Below Mount Zion" summarizes Ady's feelings: his struggle against God is replaced by "nonrecognition." God, a frail old man, cannot help the poet because the poet cannot recall the old man's name.

Stress on human vice and life's darkest side may have been impressed upon Ady's poetry by

Baudelaire, but it was his own society's obvious defects that were placarded in it. He was familiar with the poetry of Baudelaire, Verlaine, Arthur Rimbaud, and Stéphane Mallarmé, having been introduced to their work by his friend and Parisian cicerone, György Bölöni. Dezsö Baróti has shown that Rimbaud's famous "drunken boat" metaphor influenced some of Ady's fantastic poems. But in Ady's work there is no distance between the poet and his subject. Both his adherence to the principles of romantic composition and his personality made it necessary for him to throw his entire being into his poetic message. In addition to following the modernists, Ady was influenced by the French naturalists, such as Émile Zola, and by a genre then fashionable in the Parisian cafés, the chanson. He wrote several chanson-like poems that were set to music and performed in the cabarets of Budapest, among them "A nagy pénztárnok" (The Grand Cashier, 1907), "Elfogyni az ölelésben" (To Be Consumed by Embraces, 1909), and "Orizem a szemedet" (I Shall Guard Your Eyes, 1918). Béla Reinitz set 180 Ady poems to music.

Any subject that Ady took up was mythologized or magically transformed in his poems. A typical example is "Battle with the Swine-Headed Lord," in which the poet asks the Swine-Headed Lord for gold in order to visit his loved one. The bargaining for a loan turns into a vision of a mortal combat that shakes heaven and earth.

His synecdochic use of "gold" for money, capitalism, power, and callousness was not confined to literature in this period. During the post-romantic era, literary expressions penetrated even the language of newspapers, and this use of "gold" can be found in the articles of Socialist and Social Democratic papers. All dipped into the same pool of metaphors, and it was not unusual for the poets to be the authors of such articles.

Ady incorporated material from his reading into his poetry, especially of those poets who had influenced his early style. For example, his "A Halál rokona" (The Kinsman of Death,

1907) is influenced by the atmosphere of Baudelaire's *Les fleurs du mal* (*The Flowers of Evil*, 1857). Ady, too, declared that he was drawn to hopeless loves, dying roses, fading women, hours of sadness, and people who leave one's life. He professed his longing for death, for his deserted, hoary fields, for tearless crying, and for a kind of peace that only sages, poets, and the very ill can reach. Ady translated three of Baudelaire's sonnets and excerpts from Jehan Rictus' poetry into Hungarian. Both Baudelaire and Rictus influenced Ady's tropes.

Király has called attention to Ady's indebtedness to the German poet Heinrich Heine. Ady identified with the self-tormenting, critical love Heine felt for his own nation and with the rebel who longed for his country while in exile. He also identified with the "faun" in Heine, the devilish, sarcastic man who mistrusted order and social norms. Ady visited Heine's grave in Paris in 1904 and wrote a poem about his experience, "Heine úr lovagol" (Master Heinrich Goes for a Ride, 1904).

Ady's anti-capitalist poems, in which money assumes mythological proportions, also contain elements of late romanticism. They reflect neither a steadfast and consistent political credo nor a particular ideology, even if his Marxist critics claim they do. His stand did not lead him into the socialist camp; instead he guarded jealously his "loneliness" and his role as poet and prophet, which predisposed him to aloofness from any mass movement. Although it refers to contemporary bourgeois values, his rejection of money has a quality of the medieval mystery plays in which love of riches is excoriated as one of the deadly sins.

Money and treachery grow into a topos in his poetry. His volume *Vér és arany* (Blood and Gold, 1907) ties the two together in an eternal causal relationship. This relationship finds a characteristic expression in the title poem: blood and gold are the two substances that move the world. This twin imagery places Ady on the side of the romantics of nineteenth-century Western Europe. He displays his contempt for money from the vantage point of an aristocrat who despises his own need for gold—i.e., payment for his poems. In "Futás a Gond elöl" (Flight from Worries, 1907) the romantic Asian past and the memory of a proud nomadic people are evoked through depiction of the early Magyars, who were free and indifferent to gold. These "brave pagans" were corrupted by the West. The superiority of the early Magyars is a recurring motif in Ady's poetry and is juxtaposed with the backward Hungarians of his own time.

In "Pénz és karnevál" (Money and Carnival, 1907) the poet prays to money as if it were a deity. He ends his supplication with: "Vicious, vile god: Money, Money, / Take pity on us, Amen."

Mammon is Ady's favorite metaphor for money. In "Mammom szerzetes zsoltára" (The Psalm of the Monk of Mammon, 1907) the poet prays to his leader, Mammon, to permit him to stay chaste, untouched by worldly treasures. In another poem, "The Grand Cashier," God is the great bank teller, who exchanges dreams, character, and youth for money (there is a special assessment for those who bear the curse of having been born Hungarian). In some of these poems it is only the language that redeems the repetitiveness and sentimentality of the thoughts.

The main topic of *Vér és arany*, contained in the title itself, seems to mark the poet's move away from concentration on himself. However, in the end it turns out that Ady, as always, sees the world as a reflection of his own soul and his own changing moods. He insisted on his uniqueness and turned everything that touched him into a magical and special experience. For example, in the poem "Az anyám és én" (My Mother and I, 1907) the mother's dark hair throws out sparks, her hazel eyes dart flames, and a curse sits on her "bizarre chignon." She was born for one purpose only—to give birth to "the most bizarre, the saddest son."

Ady attacked hypocrisy and found pleasure in scandalizing society with poems such as "A fekete zongora" (The Black Piano, 1907). In it he compares the world to a bordello in which God, the blind piano player of the establishment, entertains the customers.

Ady's primary goal was originality, and he needed to assume the role of the alien in order to emphasize his uniqueness. In the first few years of the twentieth century, in his cultural revolutionary period, he was interested in allying himself, albeit temporarily, with any group in search of change. Ultimately, however, he chose the role of a loner who viewed the historical process with "lordly haughtiness" and "arrogance"—terms he used positively when referring to these traits in himself. The notion of the poet in exile, made into a topos by Ovid, had gained great popularity in Central Europe, where the educated elite had felt alienated from their provincial compatriots throughout history.

In the nineteenth century, especially after the "discovery" of the Ossianic songs, the literatures of many European countries showed great interest in the Orient. The Hungarian romantics, influenced by Johann Wolfgang von Goethe, further developed the topics of the mysterious East. Around the turn of the century the images and impulses of the symbolist movement reached Hungary. Ady's poetry provides a fascinating dichotomy, displaying both "Oriental longings" and a sense of Western Europe's superiority compared to the backwardness of Hungary.

The motif of an exotic bird or plant pining away in a hostile environment is a popular one in world literature. In Hungary Baudelaire's famous *L'Albatros* (*The Albatross*, 1857), first translated into Hungarian in 1887, was preceded four hundred years earlier by Janus Pannonius' "De amygdalo in Pannonia nata" (An Almond Tree in Pannonia, late 1460's). Closer to Ady's time, Gyula Reviczky's "Pálma a Hortobágyon" (Palm Tree on the Hungarian Plains, 1884) also employs the motif. Thus Ady's "Lótusz" (Lotus, 1903), in which the poet speaks about his "foreign soul," and its companion poem, "A Tisza-parton" (On the Tisza River, 1906), follow a long-established tradi-

tion. The poems are true mirrors of his own feelings, and at the same time they are imitations of feelings.

In "On the Tisza River" he asks, "I came from the banks of the Ganges. . . . What am I doing at the banks of the Tisza?" As opposed to the Danube, which flows through a large part of Europe, the Tisza is a Hungarian river only. The poem contains two quatrains. The elegant images of India in the first stanza are replaced by a robust Hungarian landscape in the second, and an appropriately terse vocabulary in the second stanza accentuates the difference between the two experiences.

In addition to his frequent allusions to his "Hungarian exile" and to his yearning for Paris, there is one poem in which Ady gives these feelings a romantic, fictitiously "historical" context, "Mátyás bolond diákja" (Matthias' Demented Scholar, 1907). Possibly an allusion to the Neo-Latin poet Pannonius, the poem's hero was unable to compose in the Hungarian vernacular because when he began to write, "a Petrarch sang within his heart."

Ady's contradictory desires and different assumed roles are acted out in his poems about Hungary, in which he either rejects his homeland or professes to be her faithful son. Among his messianic roles, the most significant is presented in "A magyar Messiások" (The Hungarian Messiahs, 1907). In it he weeps for the Hungarian messiahs who are precluded even from sacrificing themselves, for their country is doomed. Here the romantic notion of Hungary's special sufferings finds expression in a Christian metaphor in which the messiahs stand for the country's liberal intellectuals.

Among Ady's favorite targets were the representatives of conservative Hungary. His antifeudal and anti-capitalist sentiments appear as recurrent themes in his poetry. In addition, he attacked narrow-minded provincialism and nationalism as the greatest foes of progress. As Király points out, Ady's short story "Borz báró esete" (The Case of Baron Borz, 1904) is one of the first pieces to debunk the "heroism" of some "noble" participants in the 1848–1849 War of

Independence against Austria. However, Ady was also capable of using nationalistic slogans—including the ill-conceived racist ideology of Turanism—against his enemies in order to prove that he belonged to the most "ancient stratum" of Hungarians. Later he alternately idealized his "Scythian" origins and arrogantly dismissed his compatriots by stating, "I hate my base Oriental race."

The young Ady went through a Sturm-und-Drang period, a revolution in feelings that soon became connected with a revolution in language and style. While his style crystallized and became inalienably his own, his revolutionary ideas never settled into a consistent attitude. He remained impulsive and patronizing and made contradictory statements and commitments. He was a revolutionary without a party and did not attach himself to any leftist intellectual groups.

While he embraced democratic demands for land reform and for the abolition of urban poverty in his poems "A grófi szérűn" (On the Count's Land, 1908), "Csák Máté földjén" (On Máté Csák's Estate, 1908), and "Proletár fiú verse" (Poem of a Young Proletarian Boy, 1909), Ady abhorred the thought of bloody revolution. He referred to the Paris Commune as "the horrible hundred days." In "Vörös szekér a tengeren" (Red Chariot on the Sea, 1906) he poses the question in anguish, "Is it the glow of a new daybreak / Or is it just blood, just blood again?"

Even in Ady's political poetry, the rich language of the post-romantics obfuscates the message and generalizes its goal and target. In József Reményi's words:

> The ideological and emotional components of his poetry show the constraint between the need for salvation and nihilistic indifference, sensuality and restraint, faith and lack of faith, vitality and aridity, a spiritual nostalgia for Catholicism and an adherence to Calvinistic dignity, a childlike need for God and a pagan separation from Christianity, a baffling simplicity and a phraseological artificiality.
>
> (*Hungarian Writers and Literature,* p. 202)

One may claim that Ady was a left-wing democrat who was a revolutionary only as a poet, but precisely those poems in which he openly and directly demands social change are his weakest.

The contradiction between his hopes and fears surfaces in his poetry especially after 1905, the year of the first Russian Revolution, and again during World War I.

Király aptly calls Ady "a democrat without the masses." Indeed, Ady always stayed away from and remained above the common people, whose cause he championed in his poems. He detested what Horace called *profanum vulgus* (vulgar masses) and contrasted his own individuality with any mass ideology. As late as 1908 Ady referred to himself as a liberal anarchist, a pose that, as it turned out, was more literary than political. (A connection between anarchist movements and literary modernism can be identified in most literatures of the *fin de siècle* and in the first decade of the twentieth century.)

Ady's view of history can be culled from those poems in which events of the Hungarian past are evoked. Ady came from the lesser nobility and regarded himself as the embodiment of Hungary's thousand-year history, in which his class carried the burden of defending the country. He identified with György Dózsa, also a lesser noble and a leader of the ill-fated peasant uprising in 1514, as he shows in "Dózsa György lakomáján" (Feasting on György Dózsa, 1908) and "Dózsa György unokája" (Grandson of György Dózsa, 1908). Poems about Dózsa, heroes of the Rákóczi uprising against Austria (1703–1711), and Sándor Petőfi, the revolutionary poet who died in the War of Independence against the Habsburgs in 1848, prove his commitment to the popular, progressive causes in the country's history.

Yet Ady had no intention of becoming the poet of a certain group or class. He wanted to be the prophet, the spokesman, for his entire nation. "I came not as a magician but as everything," he wrote loftily. With this attitude he joined the ranks of the nineteenth-century Hungarian poets, such as Arany, Vörösmarty, and József Bajza, who felt it their mission to save their country. His position was closest to Petőfi's radicalism, a radicalism that bordered on anarchism. As opposed to earlier poets, however, Ady also saw the problems presented by the multinational character of Hungary. His poetry draws parallels between Hungary's position in the monarchy and his own position in his homeland. He resolved the contradictions in his life by identifying them with perceived national issues, as in "Régi énekek ekhója" (Echoes of Old Songs, 1913), where he sees Hungary on the edge of a precipice and himself embodying his country's fate.

He charged Hungary with having suicidal tendencies and with running toward its own destruction. In "A Halál-tó fölött" (Above Death Lake, 1908), he likens Hungary to a "death-lake" from which emanates a putrid smell that kills everything—love, ambition, and patriotism. Yet in another poem, "Nekünk Mohács kell" (We Need Mohács, 1908), which refers to the fateful battle against the Turks in 1526, he implores God for a new threat of destruction because only such a catastrophe can awaken the country.

His main political target was István Tisza, Hungary's prime minister, the incarnation of all that was feudal and reactionary in Hungarian politics. Ady attacked him both directly and in a plethora of easily decoded metaphors. In Ady's eyes Hungary was a wasteland, a "fallow" on which nothing, neither wealth nor ideas, could grow, as in "A kürtösök szava" (Bugle Calls, 1908) and in "A magyar ugaron" (The Hungarian Fallow, 1906). In "A Hortobágy poétája" (The Poet of the Hortobágy, 1906) Ady is the poet of this wasteland—spent, unappreciated, and misunderstood:

He was a large-eyed youth of Cuman stock,
Tormented by wistful hopes and dreams,
He herded cattle, and set out for
The famous Hungarian Plains.

Pale mirages and soft sunsets
Seized his soul a thousand times.
But the cattle came to graze upon
Each song that grew out of his heart.

In his mind a thousand thoughts:
He thought of women, death and wine,
In the midst of other nations
He would have been a revered bard.

But whenever he had to take a look
At his filthy mates and at the herd,
He buried the song between his lips,
And whistled or spat out a curse.

Here the alienation of the poet is further emphasized by his rejection of both the masses and his fellow intellectuals. Király points out that "csordanépek" (cattle folk) was Ady's translation of Nietzsche's *Herdenvolk* (herd) concept. "The Hungarian Fallow," Ady's coinage for the country's social and cultural backwardness, became the political slogan of later generations.

The bard without a worthy audience and the messiah with the message that no one wants to hear were Ady's favorite pessimistic self-images. Yet another part of his personality cherished these roles. He was a leader who, in fact, rejected his followers. His ego is always present; the first-person singular is his dominant mode of communication. He relished his separatism. It has been pointed out that conjunctions such as "still," "nonetheless," "yet," "all the same"—each used by Ady as a gesture of rebellion and antagonism—pervade his work. This separatist stance is akin to Rimbaud's in France. Rimbaud's *Les illuminations* (published by Verlaine in 1944 and containing his "Sonnet des Voyelles" ["Sonnet of the Vowels"]) reflects a similar self-image: the poet is mysterious, arcane, and rebellious at the same time.

Ady fought his war against his political foes, but he attacked just as vehemently those whom he identified as his enemies in Hungarian cultural life; these were primarily the conservative critics Jenö Rákosi and Gyula Szekfü. He led an outspoken campaign against conservativism, calling his critics cowardly, un-Hungarian, and primitive. In the poem "A harcunkat megharcoltuk" (We Fought Our Fight, 1909), he referred to his literary and political foes as "bloodhounds," "toads," and "cowardly roosters" fighting on top of a garbage heap.

Ady was an easy target for the conservatives in their battle against modernism. His style and message were denounced with great fervor. Against such attacks Ady's true haven was the periodical *Nyugat* (Occident). Founded in 1908, *Nyugat* was the most important literary journal published in Hungary until 1941, when its license was not renewed. The journal was liberal but had contributors voicing radical and populist opinions as well, and it represented the tastes and aspirations of an urban and urbane section of society. Almost every issue of *Nyugat* brought to the public at least a couple of poems by Ady. Some contained his vicious attacks against the conservative camp.

Ady's political poetry, explosive and thunderous, became an easy prey for later political parties and has been exploited by all, from the far left to the far right; each has emphasized a different aspect of his work. Ady was not formally affiliated with any party. He stood for land reform and social justice, and his stance is amply exemplified in the poems that treat the Hungarian countryside; but he did not represent a consistent political program in either his poetry or his prose. The color red, which frequently figures in his verse, as in "A vörös nap" (Scarlet Sun, 1908), "Vörös jelek a Hadak Utjan" (Crimson Signals in the Milky Way, 1908), and in "Röpülj piros sárkányom" (Fly My Scarlet Kite, 1913), was the color of the Social Democrats. His revolt was intellectual and moral, based on personal convictions rather than on any systematic philosophy. Often the Bible or the daily press provided the topics for his engaged poems. He might call for a revolution in one poem and entertain the idea of escaping to his village in another. Although he took the side of the oppressed against the exploiters, Ady spent most of his time in pubs and cafés, living the life of a bohemian, to the further detriment of his already precarious health (he was ravaged by syphilis). His cronies were anything but social revolutionaries.

Ady's openness about his loneliness and doubts bordered on exhibitionism. It is displayed in "Szeretném, ha szeretnének" (I Desire to Feel Loved, 1909):

> Neither offspring, nor forefather,
> Neither kin nor friend nor lover,
> Am I to anyone.
> Am I to anyone.
>
> I am, like all men, lonely majesty,
> North Pole, strangeness, mystery,
> Faraway Light of the marshes,
> Faraway Light of the marshes.
>
> Alas, I cannot thus remain.
> I want to show myself,
> I want to be understood,
> I want to be understood.
>
> Therefore, all: self-torture and song.
> I desire to feel loved
> And to belong to someone:
> To belong.

Yet he was inconsistent in his relationships and, to use his own metaphor, hardly had a friend whom he had not "bitten" at one time or another.

Similarly, he was demanding and immature in his love affairs. The great love of Ady's life, who led him to an emotional and poetical revolution, was Adél Diósi, a married Jewish woman whom he called "Leda" (her name spelled backwards).

At their first encounter, just after her return from Paris in 1903, Ady, a provincial journalist and poet, was mesmerized and awed by the sophisticated socialite on the arm of her prosperous husband. Leda was different from the women Ady had known. She embodied the *belle époque* in her looks, clothing, and most of all her interest in the arts. He writes in "Hiába hideg a hold" (In Vain Is the Moon Cold, 1909):

> This was the woman I always loved.
> I lived in her heart and between her lips.

ENDRE ADY

She was my heart, she was my lips.
A drunkard and forlorn
I wandered in the Varad nights,
Having buried my throne, and when
Fate flattened me poor and turned
Me into less than the lowliest on earth.

In the beginning of their tempestuous relationship, which lasted from 1903 to 1912, Ady conceived of her as a female twin who became not only a mirror-image of the poet's soul but also "wore" his facial features ("large, sad eyes") and duplicated his moods ("she is sad"). In this poem, "A vár fehér asszonya" (The White Woman of the Fort, 1906), Ady's eyes, used as a synecdoche for his entire being, appear as "two large, dark windows" looking at the world. Ady's eyes were indeed the most striking of his features and, for this reason perhaps, were frequently chosen as the main elements of self-description.

Leda's eyes, as dark as his own, reaffirmed the "sameness" of the poet and his lover as well as their belonging to one another. Even on the verge of one of his final breaks with her, Ady writes in "Nem adom vissza" (I Shall Not Give Back to You, 1910):

I shall return all that you gave me
. . . .
but I shall never
. . . .
return your eyes.

In "Hunyhat a máglya" (Let the Fires Die Out, 1906) "these mournful, ancient eyes" promise never to look at any woman but Leda. His beloved's eyes had to become the mirrors of his own. "Your eyes reflect / Blessed wonders," he tells her in the poem "Mert engem szeretsz" (Because You Love Me, 1906).

Eyes also appear in some of his early death poems, such as "Ha holtan találkozunk" (When Dead, We Meet, 1908):

Our open dead eyes
Will light up the night and ask:
Why weren't we kind to each other
While still alive?

While in his political poetry he addresses his readers from majestic heights, the magisterial personality temporarily disappears from the love poems written to Leda. He is worried and, at the same time, proud to transfer his own sufferings and bad reputation to his lover. In "A könnyek asszonya" (The Lady of Tears, 1906) he reveals to her his "bloodstained heart." Her saddened face looks down upon her lover, and from her eyes the tears pour onto his tortured heart. In "Hiába kisértesz hófehéren" (In Vain You Haunt Me Whitely, Like Snow, 1906) he begins by declaring:

I cannot but soil you,
. . . .
with blood, with pus, with gall, with tears.

"I am an aching, hurting, burning wound," writes Ady in "Tüzes seb vagyok" (I am a Burning Wound, 1906); but here the wound is caused by Leda. She had power over her lover and tormented him: "My skin was torn by desire / I was bloodied by your kiss." The same vocabulary is used alternately for Leda and for himself; they are each other's amorous victims. Ady viewed their love, as he viewed everything to do with himself, as unique and superior to emotions experienced by others. During the brief time of total bliss, they were "royalty" who rarely mingled with the "crowds." "I the king and you my queen" is Ady's image of the twosome in "Egy ócska konflisban" (In an Old Hansom, 1906).

By changing her name to Leda, the earthly love of Zeus, Ady confirmed his own "divine" self-image and defined their respective roles in their relationship. Only the love of Ady, the divine being who visits her in disguise, permitted Leda to become part of the world of the gods. Her being was therefore dependent on her partner, who might or might not continue to visit her.

The poet's coming to visit as a god in disguise is only one of the ways in which Ady mythologized himself in that relationship. In "A vén faun üzenete" (Message of an Aged Faun, 1906) he describes himself as Apollo wearing the garb of a faun. His pure beauty is hidden inside him; a lecherous mask covers his face in order to protect him from the world. The Apollonian self-image returns in "A krisztusok martirja" (Martyr of Many Christs, 1906):

> I was born as a peasant Apollo
> Strong, a singer of pagan songs,
> Who on the sunset of his life
> Will fall singing, in love's embrace.

As Király observes, in addition to using the pure masculine beauty of Apollo, Ady liked to apply the word *gyermek* (child) to himself in order to point to his uncomplicated innocence. The child as a literary topos, so popular at the turn of the century, appears in his poetry, and, as can be expected, it refers to the child *he* once was ("Egy ismerös kisfiú" [A Little Boy I Know, 1907]). He also equated the innocence of the child with the eternal "child-genius," especially in phrases referring to himself.

Ady and Leda's was an open, passionate affair of two unusual people who flaunted convention by loving each other. The nakedness of his desire for her and Leda's eager response fill Ady's love poems with an erotic charge entirely new in Hungarian letters.

In the first years of their affair, Leda was the most important person in Ady's life; her love was the essence of his poetry. In "Absolon boldog szégyene" (Absolom's Happy Disgrace, 1906) the biblical hero, another of Ady's alter egos, turns a deaf ear to the calls for battle and remains in the "snow-white arms" of his beloved.

The *perdita* cult (cult of the fallen woman) of the late nineteenth century is also mirrored in Ady's early verse. But Leda, the "fallen woman" and the wife of another man, is called "sacred" in his poems.

Determined to make Leda a part of himself instead of an equal, Ady had a constant need to diminish and conquer her. "A hundred times I kill you in my heart," he confesses in "Örök harc és nász" (Eternal War and Nuptial, 1907). Yet in "Valamikor lyányom voltál" (Long Ago, You Were My Daughter, 1907) he reaffirms: "We are

the same, the two of us! . . . Who else could give me your unique warmth?" In fact, the two dare the world together, as he declares in "Bihar vezér földjén" (On the Land of the Tribal Leader Bihar, 1907).

Soon she was not permitted to have her own fate; instead it was designed by her lover. She is sentenced to death in many of Ady's poems, and each time her death is related to him, as in "Csónak a Holt Tengeren" (Boat on the Dead Sea, 1907): "I know that you'll descend into my soul, / And there you'll find your death, my love!"

Leda *had* to be sad; Ady desired his lover to be sad because she was the mate of "the saddest man." In the role he assigned her, she had to become the woman of tears, a sphinx-like woman, a mystery, or a holy woman whose tears fall on the poet's heart ("The Woman of Tears"). He depicts the two of them as fallen angels in "Lédával a Tavaszban" (With Leda in the Spring, 1908). And there are instances when Leda appears in the poems larger than life—a goddess between whose lips the poet wants to hide ("Léda ajkai között" [Between Leda's Lips, 1908]).

He frequently describes their relationship as that of two uniquely morbid and moribund lovers who must destroy each other. "Lédával a bálban" (With Leda at the Ball, 1907) and "Jöjj, Léda, megölellek" (Come, Leda, Let Me Embrace You, 1907) are typical examples. In "Léda a kertben" (Leda in the Garden, 1907) Leda sits in a "sad garden" in which dying flowers hold tears in their petals. In "Szent Junius hivása" (Saint June Is Calling, 1907) she has "autumnal eyes" in which the image of death is reflected. The similarity of Leda's eyes to the poet's is expressed in an imagined total exchange of vision ("Add nekem a szemeidet" [Give Me Your Eyes, 1907]) in which Ady implores Leda:

> Give me your eyes
> That find me beautiful
> . . . .
> Loving you, I love myself
> It is your eyes for which I envy you.

Later he insolently states that he loves only himself through every woman.

Some of Ady's poems about Leda contain topics common to the writings of his Hungarian contemporaries. His "Fekete hold éjszakája" (The Night of the Black Moon, 1908), a pseudo-classical poem written in the third person, has its parallel in Géza Csáth's short story *A varászlo halála* ("The Magician Dies") published in the same year. In the poem the poet's heart is possessed by a "bad and haughty woman"—Ady's furious response to the power of Leda's love over him. His periodic revolt against Leda is also shown in "Maradhatsz és szerethetsz" (You May Remain and Love Me, 1907), which is addressed to an imaginary young virgin whom he "permits" to stay and to love him.

Still, Leda governed all the early love poems. She ruled supreme in the heart of the poet. She was the model for all the female types Ady could conjure up in his verse—types that run the gamut from the Virgin Mary to Veronica. She embodied the dichotomy to which modern psychiatry refers as the Madonna-whore complex. In "Mária és Veronika" (Mary and Veronica, 1907), which could be a textbook example of this complex, Ady begs:

> Lull me to sleep, Leda
> Let me dream that you are
> My mother.

Indeed, Leda was the only competition to Ady's mother. Even though the two women had little affection for one another, in Ady's poem "Az én két asszonyom" (My Two Women, 1907) they appear together as in a diptych: the mother who gave him life and the woman who will order him to die. But in another poem, "Várom a másikat" (I am Waiting for the Other, 1908), Ady refers to Leda as the one who forces him to live.

Despite their exultant love, or perhaps precisely because of it, Ady continued to torment Leda with poems in which he denies his feelings. In "Csukott szemű csókok" (Kisses Kissed with Closed Eyes, 1908), he "dreams" about an unknown woman to whom he belongs and whose love he forever seeks while substituting for it the kisses of others. He alludes to Leda by mentioning her dark hair, but it is the "fuzzy blond curls of others" that bring her memory into his room.

Ady's total, and frequently brutal, frankness was nurtured by his exhibitionism. He was eager to disclose everything about himself. This intensity of passion often embarrassed his contemporaries, who had been reared on more refined and tentative expressions. Images of violent, destructive, and self-destructive love permeate the Leda poems. The sado-masochistic language of some poems, such as "I curse you," "I shall tear into your body," "I violently bite into your flesh," and "Trample on me, kick me in scornful laughter," were shocking even for those who had read *Le jardin des supplices* (The Garden of Torments, 1898) by Octave Mirbeau, the short stories of Csáth, or even *Psychopathia Sexualis* (1886) by Richard von Krafft-Ebing. But in some poems a more honest self-image, or rather a self-pity that replaces the inflated image of the self, can be found. In "Megcsókolom Csók-kisasszonyt" (I Shall Kiss the Girl of Kisses, 1907) he writes: "I have paid for every woman. / I have paid for every moment." But he flaunts his contempt for women in "Elindult egy leány" (A Girl Set Out, 1909), where he claims:

> I shall love somebody soon.
> Tell her to come, to rush to me;
> Tomorrow, another grateful woman
> Will, like a dog, lick my hand.

Ady had a recurring desire to escape from the "sizzling burden" of his love for Leda. He wanted to die and to dissolve in her embrace, as in "Elfogyni az ölelésben" (To Be Consumed by an Embrace, 1909). In this piece, however, the misogynistic influence of the period can also be felt. In a number of Leda poems, especially the weaker ones, the heroine is destructive: she tortures and annihilates her lover in

"Come, Leda, Let Me Embrace You" and in "Nem mehetek Hozzád" (I Cannot Go to You, 1907).

Their love could never promise harmony, but harmony was not Ady's goal. He strove for the opposite—for rebellion and discord—and his affair with a married woman guaranteed both. Leda became both "sacred" and "demonic" in Ady's poetry, and this dual character lends a special tension and a unique inner force to the poems devoted to her. In order to match her the poet also split his persona in two. Thus, in "Message of an Aged Faun" he became Apollo disguised in the garb of a faun:

> I need you in this spring
> That you take me in your arms
> And say, with a kiss, what only you know,
> "My ugly faun, for me you were Apollo."

Love and death as well as unfulfilled desire and the poet's escape from fulfillment are recurring themes in the Leda poems. The scene of their lovemaking is often depicted as a battlefield where "kissing combats" take place in which the partners deeply wound each other. There is nothing soft or redeeming in their love affair, and there is nothing soft or generous in Ady's poems about it.

The last two years of their relationship (1911–1912) were even more deeply marred than the rest by violent and often public quarrels. However, for each poem in which Ady declares his desire to leave her, there are several in which he reaffirms his commitment to Leda. Yet images of young, unattainable girls, and Ady's poems yearning for "virginal bodies," "fresh fragrances," and "the women of the day after tomorrow" also began to appear at the same time as his poems "of kisses and blood."

Leda had to share the poems with scores of other women. In the fall of 1911 Ady received a letter from Berta Boncza, a young student recovering from consumption in Switzerland. The correspondence became frequent and intimate, and Ady became increasingly inter-ested in the young girl who seemed to have read all his poems and admired him so much. By 1912 Ady had ended his affair with Leda. In addition to his "Elbocsátó szép üzenet" (A Kind Message of Dismissal, 1913), his "A magunk szerelme" (Love of Ourselves, 1913) put the final touch to the relationship.

The ultimate rejection of the great love came in "A Kind Message of Dismissal"—the most cruel message a man could send a woman. This poem not only carries references to other women but, more importantly, reveals Ady's hostility to a relationship in which both partners desire to rule and neither is willing to abdicate. He "dismisses" Leda as if she were an old servant no longer useful to her master. He insists on their inequality and declares he no longer feels anything but pity for her. All his love poems to her are withdrawn in this last missive, and he claims that the "kisses" described in the poems were "kissed with others." He thanks her, however, for all her "pseudo-images" with as much feeling as a man is able to produce when "he steps over a boring, old embrace."

During this last "meeting" with Leda, Ady insists on telling her that he has never loved her but has only loved himself as seen through her. She was merely a figment of the poet's imagination—a small question mark that became answered only through him. She did not exist before the poet first saw her, and she ceased to exist when the poet discontinued seeing her. It is a cruel, humiliating farewell, yet it is one of the most brilliantly alive poems in Hungarian literature. After seventy years it still reverberates with the same passion and hatred it had when first committed to paper.

Of all the feelings displayed in the Leda poems, gentleness and selfless grace are conspicuously missing. Although he claimed that "only small loves kill," Ady was out to kill the love in himself in his farewell poem and to humiliate the woman whom he owed too much to be able to feel his own genius.

On 27 March 1915 Ady married Berta Boncza against the wishes of her family. Their first personal contact was preceded by several years of correspondence. After they met, Ady declared:

> I am all that you have been hoping for,
> I am all that you can't even guess,
> I am all that I could become.
>
> . . . .
>
> You are all that is possible to be,
> You can be all that I am longing for;
> Perhaps nothing, perhaps all.

The poem reveals a great deal of self-confidence, yet it was written in a confused state. Ady thought he had made a poor impression on the young girl and her family. Accordingly, the title of the poem is "Vajjon milyennek láttál?" (How Did You See Me?, 1923).

Berta was a genuine "princess of the castle." Her family owned a lordly manor house in Csucsa in which the pair spent their honeymoon. By his marriage to her Ady believed he had arrived at "the harbor of youthful arms." His mortal illness notwithstanding, the experience of his new life lent Ady a feeling of rejuvenation that became the leitmotif of his first poems to his young wife

Ady found in Csinszka, his nickname for Berta, what he always had dreamed of and viciously held up to Leda in many poems—a clean, young virgin, a pure Christian girl of the gentry. "We share a race," he writes in "O fajtám vére" (Blood of My Race, 1918):

> Our shared race
> Of old tempests
> Made your two young arms
> Wait for me.

Ady's love poetry to Csinszka is markedly different from the cycles he devoted to Leda. In the poems written to his wife, an aging, sick man is thankful for the last happy hours he receives from a young woman. While some of his Marxist critics consider these pieces to be his greatest lyrical achievement, others—including myself—believe that Ady was at the height of his creativity during the years he shared with Leda.

The poems written to Csinszka seem to display simpler, clearer language and imagery than the ones dedicated to other women, especially to Leda. In the context of other poems written during the same period, however, a general quieting of Ady's language and a striving for a new richness of simplicity are evident. This is particularly true of his last great pacifist poems, published in *A halottak élén* (Leading the Dead, 1918).

In addition to the feelings Leda evoked in Ady, she also introduced him to his other great love, Paris. Initially, he had wanted to go there in order to follow Leda and her husband, but later he found in Paris a second beloved home that soon became a topic of his dreams and poems. Between 1904 and 1910 Ady made several trips to Paris, never staying longer than a few months.

As Király points out, Paris provided for Ady a "counter-Hungary." It became a social and political haven that Ady shared with other tourists and temporary emigrants.

> I am your son, Paris
> Banished, exiled,
> But still your son,

he declares when Leda leaves him to return to Paris ("Léda Párisba készül" [Leda Is Leaving for Paris, 1906]). The magnet of Paris, where in the words of Gertrude Stein "the twentieth century was," became irresistible to many young artists and scholars.

Not only for Ady but for his entire generation, as well as for the next generation of Hungarian intellectuals, Paris was the symbol of freedom. It became a new Arcadia where they could gather to think and talk about Hungary. "Egy párisi hajnalon" (A Parisian Dawn, 1905) is a highly expressive example. The city serves merely as a frame for the message Ady wants to deliver about himself and his "Asian" self-image. Similarly, in one of his most haunting poems, "Este a Bois-ban" (An Evening in the Bois, 1906), the carriage in which the poet is riding could be rolling in any park because it is not the park but the past that the poet is visiting. The lively and glittering city is persistently pitted against the "Hungarian graveyard," as in "A Gare de L'Est-en" (At the Gare de L'Est, 1905). In it the son of the "sunless Orient" dies as he enters the train and is forced to return to his homeland.

Ady saw himself living a double existence in his new role: one side of him lived on the banks of the Danube, while the other lived along the Seine. "Two lives in two shapes / Lived by a single corpse," he writes in "A Szajna partján" (Along the Seine, 1906).

In yet another of the Paris poems, "Párisba beszökött az ősz" (Autumn Slipped into Paris, 1906), the poet and his thoughts are at the center. He contemplates his own death on the boulevard Saint Michel. His mood, evoked by the sudden swirling of fallen leaves, could have hit him with the same unexpected force on any of the streets of Budapest. Paris had a strictly literary function as a metaphor for freedom in Ady's verse, illuminating his yearning for "something other" than his own country.

The "otherness" gained importance only to the extent that Ady wanted to use it as a vehicle for his lyrical message or for a momentary thought. Although he translated a few French poems and sent back occasional reports to Hungary about events in the French capital, he remained uninvolved in the pulsating literary and artistic life of Paris. He barely spoke French, knew none of the representatives of the many flowering movements in the arts, and had very little contact with anyone outside the Hungarian colony that camped on the terrace of the Café Dôme.

Ady could read in a number of foreign languages, among them German, French, and Romanian, and was an especially devoted reader of foreign newspapers, but he never learned to speak any foreign language properly. As Margit Vészi, a writer and an intimate friend of Ady, noted in her diary about Ady's 1904 Paris stay, "We always teased him because he would never learn to find his way home from the city, even

after so many months there; and he could not speak a decent French." Still, like a sponge, Ady soaked up information from a large variety of sources—journals, personal observations, and conversations with his friends, colleagues, and drinking pals. He had little patience for systematic investigation of any subject, which was one reason why he never perfected his knowledge of any foreign tongue.

His friend Artur Elek wrote that it was Hungarian acquaintances who made Paris attractive and intimate for Ady: "Paris never meant more for him than a Budapest that fit his taste." In *Nyugat* Elek made a similar comment about Ady's trip to Italy and especially about his stay in Rome, where the two spent several days together. "For him Rome became a part of Hungary, and perhaps therefore he was so delighted with it."

There are a few street names in his poems to create local color, just as the reference to the Gare de L'Est does. But with few exceptions, Ady's Paris poems could have referred to any city. He adopted Paris as his other home city, not in addition to Budapest but instead of it. In Paris he was a genuine alien, without any responsibility. In *Margita élni akar* (Margita Wants to Live, 1921), he writes:

> Paris became our adopted country,
> Magyar-baiting our painful joy.
> We avoided Asia on the Danube,
> While talking about her all the time.

Yet even his interest in Paris was more rhapsodic than substantial, and he rapidly shed the symbolist, decadent role acquired in Paris once he returned home.

Ady hated all feudal manifestations of Hungary. Yet at the same time he never learned to love Budapest, where the urban influence of the West was overwhelming by Ady's time. As in everything, in this matter too Ady's attitude was self-contradictory. On the one hand, he considered the Hungarian capital an intellectual desert, especially when compared with Paris. On the other hand, he longed for the "simple honesty" of the village of his birth, Érmindszent.

Budapest became a topic in Hungarian literature only relatively late. The village and the Hungarian provincial town long remained the subjects of choice in poetry and fiction. During the first decade of the twentieth century, only a few authors wrote intimately about Budapest. The city appeared mostly in the writings of those who found it intimidating and who were accustomed to the smaller proportions of the regions from which they had come. These emigrants, including Ady, viewed Budapest as the spoiler of natural feelings and as a city of sin, while the provinces remained the *locus amoenus,* the place of the lost idyll. Not even the authors of *Nyugat* displayed a consistently urban attitude. The image of the "wicked city" also appeared in the pages of this first modernist periodical. It is therefore not surprising that Ady, at once the most modern and the most archaic poet, never became a poet of the Hungarian capital. In "Miért is tettem?" (Why Have I Done It?, 1908) he curses Budapest for "ruining those who do not belong." The poem—published in *Nyugat,* where it appeared along with his "Kis falusi ház" (A Small House in the Village, 1908)—is a romantic, nostalgic piece about his home. In his "A Duna vallomása" (The Confession of the River Danube, 1908) the old river looks contemptuously at the capital on its banks. Similarly, in his "Zúg-Zeng a jég-cimbalom" (The Ice-Cimbalon Rings and Clangs, 1909) the dirty gray waves of the river are metaphors of the city's decay:

> Outside in the streets
> Big boys are brawling.
> Brazen and orphaned,
> Like dirty ice floes drifting
> On the Danube's face.

For Ady even these allusions were unimportant; his natural habitat everywhere remained his own soul.

The two capitals appear together in the only long piece among Ady's works, *Margita élni akar,* a verse novel. At the age of thirty-five Ady turned to this nineteenth-century genre, practiced among others by Aleksandr Pushkin in *Yevgeny Onegin (Eugene Onegin,* 1832) and Petőfi in *Az apostol (The Apostle,* 1848). Ady's work is the story of the Calvinist poet and his Jewish love, modeled on Vészi and several other women. *Fin-de-siècle* Budapest and Paris provide a fascinating gossip column–like background to the work. It is, however, of no lasting artistic value nor does it display any of the dominant features of Ady's other poems. Its language is the lingo of the streets and is therefore obsolete for today's reader. Some of the characters of this roman à clef are depicted with a venomous hostility that is even less attractive in such a genre than in Ady's passionate lyrical works.

The most unique quality of Ady's poetry, and at the same time the most elusive for translation, is its language. He created a new vocabulary, gave arbitrary new meanings to words, and used archaic Hungarian innovatively. The most important aesthetic effect in Ady's poetic language is that his highly conscious choice of words can still be felt. He always selected carefully a word other than the one that would readily come to mind. Thus the effectiveness of Ady's use of archaic Hungarian is enhanced by the *absence* of the expected modern word, which is clearly felt in the *presence* of the one replacing it. Ady's insertion of archaic words, phrases, or mini-structures creates a radiation in his entire poetic text and rearranges it comprehensively in form and meaning.

Ady frequently used words and phrases from early editions of the Bible. Since this archaic vocabulary has a particular socio-cultural function, transposing it into a different type of text makes it momentarily the most essential part of its new semantic content because use of biblical vocabulary in a modern work contributes to an elevated atmosphere and, in the case of poetry, to a heightened "lyrical state."

In Hungary the long-lasting ideas of the romantic revival, a nineteenth-century Central

European movement engaged in reviving the old glories and virtues of each nation, included a taste for medieval words, and Ady's own penchant for a romantic self-image spurred his desire to use archaic vocabulary. It underscored his messianism, which was a function equally rooted in the ideology of romanticism.

Furthermore, Ady realized that tension builds when revolutionary thoughts are expressed in the terms of an older mode of consciousness. He used the vocabulary found in the earliest Hungarian linguistic monuments, some of which go back to the twelfth century, and infused his language with a "pagan" message that frequently attacked the remnants of the very feudal system they were meant to mythologize.

Often his obsolete vocabulary, archaic predication, or use of dialect in a sophisticated modern message creates the contrast. Frequently, phonetic variants alone reduce a word to a regional usage, and their presence adds a special connotation to many of Ady's texts. But the real achievement in Ady's innovative use of archaisms lies in his creation of archaic-sounding neologisms.

Ady also used inversion (the reversal of normal word order), the most frequent vehicle of literary archaization in Western poetry. In his case, inversion emphasizes the mythologized self-image of the poet and also enhances the messianic aura of the message, as in "A megszépítő fátuma" (The Fate of the Embellisher, 1913):

> Evenings, when in them I roam,
> I decorate with wonders sweet,
> And those arriving after me
> By my sweet dreams shall fall asleep.

Repetition of words, lines, and at times entire stanzas imparts an incantatory supernatural and magical quality to many of his poems.

He used refrains in order to illuminate his ideas from several angles and moods. The Hungarian folk-song stanza provided the skeleton of a familiar genre on which to hang his outrageous message.

In Ady's poetry innovative archaisms extend from the sound to the word, from the word to the phrase, and from there to the entire line or stanza. Intertwined, they create the inimitable texture of his poetry. Because of this singular language, Ady had no genuine followers; he had only epigones whose weakness lies precisely in the fact that their studied combinations could never reproduce the same highly artistic and unique amalgam.

Tension characterizes most of Ady's poems. Therefore, it is not surprising that many are phrased in the imperative. They have been compared to those poems of Petőfi and Vladimir Mayakovski which achieve their dramatic quality by the same method, although different in content.

In Ady's poetry the Western (quantitative) and the Hungarian (stressed) meter intermix, and the loosening of the iambic beat is particularly discernible. This was pointed out by his earliest critics.

Sensuous imagery, sensitive use of colors, and frequent expressions of anxiety are also characteristic features of *fin-de-siècle* art. All three are recognizable in different combinations in Ady's verse. Disharmony within a poem, a typical property of avant-garde poetry, appears mostly in Ady's idiosyncratic employment of refrains within and at the end of the stanzas.

The tension between language and experience, so typical of avant-garde literature, is also manifest in Ady's verse. Instead of more tranquil nominal constructions Ady frequently uses verbal constructions. A case in point is the first stanza of "A sárga láng" (The Yellow Flame, 1906):

> It set fire to my dreams,
> The yellow flame.
> Dip me into a golden stream,
> Give me, give me, asylum.

His employment of *epanalepsis* (the repetition of words after the intervention of a word or several words) often adds stress and dynamism to his message even in poems such as "Sirni, sirni, sirni" (To Weep, to Weep, to Weep, 1907), in which the verbs appear in the infinitive.

Although his poetry was his most significant contribution to Hungarian letters, Ady was also a prominent journalist and published close to four hundred articles in *Napló* and in *Magyar közélet* before he left for Paris in 1906. He was also a free-lance contributor to *Budapesti napló,* the most prestigious paper of the time. These journals represented the aspirations of the liberal middle class and its genuine and deep interest in Western culture. Ady's poetry and prose were mainly published in *Nyugat,* the most distinguished literary publication of Hungary between 1908 and 1941, and in its immediate predecessors, *Szerda* and *Figyelő.*

Ady shared the ideas that moved the editors of *Nyugat,* but only to a degree. In his own mind the conflict between art for its own sake—the platform of *Nyugat*—and engaged art—the mass-oriented platform of the Socialist papers—was never resolved.

Ady's short stories are a less significant part of his prose work. They are written in the popular late-naturalistic style of the period, and their language is strikingly old-fashioned and provincial compared to that of his poetry. His most interesting piece is "Mihályi Rozália csókja" (The Kiss of Rosalie Mihalyi, 1908), in which Ady recapitulates his encounter with the woman who infected him with syphilis. The story is not simply autobiographical. Its heroine is transformed into the symbol of death. (It is noteworthy that many decades later Thomas Mann treated the same subject in the same manner in his *Doktor Faustus* [1947].) The memories of a sinful past appear with ever-increasing frequency in Ady's later work. He flagellates himself for his earlier wicked life until, in the last poems, he humbly accepts his fate.

Baróti has pointed out Ady's predilection for metaphorical ships in his poems. In addition to the obvious and immediate French influence, Ady used the ship in a traditional way as one of the oldest metaphors for travel and adventure, but also as a blind object navigated by death. Based on these concepts, his poems contain journeys to unattainable women, some of whom are dead. There is an additional sphere, however: the grand, erotic metaphor of the ship, the vessel, as it appears in "Ifjú karok kikötőjében" (In the Harbor of Young Arms, 1913):

> From the harbor of sweet love
> Of wonder, beauty and ecstasy,
> There is no God, Kiss, Miracle, or Death
> That could remove my pirate ship and me.

In "Az elhagyott kalóz-hajók" (Abandoned Pirate Ships, 1914) he returns to the same metonymy as he confesses his love for Csinszka:

> Now I am me, proudly taking
> Into sacred, young and crazy storms
> The one and only to be kissed:
> And my life's most fateful ship.

One of his first self-images was that of a sailor daring the unmapped, "new" seas, and one of his last poems also employs this self-image. In "Az utolsó hajók" (The Last Ships, 1918), later used as the title for his posthumous volume of 1923, he writes about himself:

> My soul was a free and faithful sea,
> . . . .
> My sea always found its rightful shore.
> . . . .
> Don't cause me more pain—
> This faithful sea is dead.
> It yawns. Its eyes are salty, cold, and bored.

It is a final, proud message.

Death images occur in Ady's poetry from the very beginning. As early as 1907 he writes about a drunken midnight vision in which death comes to fetch him, and he gallops away on his "coffin-stallion" holding bloody bridles in his left hand and a swishing whip in his right ("Az én koporsó paripám" [My Coffin-

Stallion, 1907]). This is still the romantic image of the nineteenth century; death visits the poet à la Edgar Allan Poe.

Similar romantic images of lust and murder appear in "Megöltem egy pillangot" (I Killed a Butterfly, 1906):

> All gold should turn into fire;
> Into poison each happy kiss.
> You have wings, flutter and fly;
> I therefore kill you now
> And shall be happy, for I have killed.

Ady always saw himself as death personified, carrying destruction to those he loved: "Those whom I kiss will pale away / My own mother I turn away . . ." ("Akit én csókolok" [Those Whom I Kiss, 1908]). Visualizing oneself as dead is another frequent feature of the romantics that was adopted by the artists of the *fin de siècle*. The romantic death images conjure up self-pity in the poet. "What a beautiful corpse I'll be," Ady writes in "Az utolsó mosoly" (The Last Smile, 1906), in which the poet depicts himself on his bier.

Self-pity emanates from the poems in which he, "the poor poet," watches the orgies of the idle rich. He sees himself as Lazarus ("Lázár a palota elött" [Lazarus in Front of the Palace, 1907]). On the other hand, self-pity is frequently accompanied by rebellion, ending in his death. The hopelessness of the messianic side of his poetic ego also gives cause for self-pity, as in "The Hungarian Messiahs."

In his mask of the "eternal alien," he pitied himself for having to die in Budapest. He writes in "Költözés Átok-városból" (Moving Away from Curse-City, 1906): "My sparkling man—that's how you'll end / Ugly Budapest becoming your bier?"

Ady's death poems first echoed the Western models of the *fin de siècle*, but soon his own tragedy provided their content. The poems became a genuine response to his life-threatening syphilis, which he had contracted from a provincial actress. The disease, which brought recurring inflammation, boils all over his body, and tremendous pain, caused death to be a close companion to love in his poetry.

Among Ady's many other self-images is that of the rebel. It gave rise to his *kuruc* poems (imitating Hungarian folk songs of the eighteenth century sung by Hungarian soldiers), in which the struggle against Austria is put in a historical continuum extending through the centuries of oppression to his own days. Similarly, in "Páris az én Bakonyom" (Paris Is My Bakony Mountain, 1907) Ady refers to the outlaws of old who used the mountain range for hiding from their pursuers. He styles himself as such an outlaw hiding in Paris and being chased by the "Scythian hordes" smelling of the Orient. He appears as Apollo in "Az Ős Kaján" (The Ancient Demon, 1907). As a "carousing Apollo" he meets his "Oriental relative," the pagan demon Kaján. During a brawl, which ends in a drinking bout, he asks his pagan ancestor, "What is it worth to be Hungarian?" In this poem the East wins over the West; the strong Asian ancestor conquers the West and will go on doing so, while the poet, his tired descendant, remains behind virtually in rigor mortis with the cross clutched in his hands.

The morbid, decadent poet was a familiar image to readers of the period. Ady particularly enjoyed such a self-portrait and declares in "A Halál rokona" (A Kinsman of Death, 1907):

> I am a kinsman of Death.
> My loves are fleeting and fading:
> I desire the kisses of those
> Who depart.

Even if Ady had not contracted syphilis, his early poetry would probably still have had a death-awaiting character; it corresponded to a current Western European fashion.

That Ady also saw himself as the last of the pagan songsters rebelling against the straitjacket of Christianity can be seen in "Góg és Magóg" (Son of Gog and Magog, 1906). The pagan Magyar was only one of Ady's favorite self-images. He soon chose the opposite of a pagan by fashioning himself into a Christlike figure tempted by Satan in "Rózsaliget a pusztán" (Rose Garden in the Desert, 1906), while the prophet's pose is taken in "Korán jöttem ide" (I Arrived Too Early, 1906), in which he complains, "This desert destroys me / Where I call out in vain."

Ady was a showman, but that particular mask was also his real self. His prophet's voice, assumed for the sake of self-aggrandizement, turned out to be truly prophetic. He was often hysterical and neurotic in his responses to Hungary's realities, but his dedication was real and lasted throughout his life.

His self-image as prophet is underscored by the title of his 1908 volume, *Az Illés szekerén* (In Elijah's Chariot). The tragedy of the prophet who is not listened to by the people he wants to save is depicted in the figure of Elijah, Ady's alter ego, a victim who is forever doomed to ride the chariot between heaven and earth. In another poem, "Judás és Jézus" (Judas and Jesus, 1907), he embraces the role of Judas, "the twin of Jesus," who betrayed him:

> I sold you out, my Prince
> Because Life is my love
> I, too, have grand dreams;
> I am a poet.

However, after the confession of "professional competition," the following stanzas reveal that it was money and a demanding woman that brought the disciple to treachery. At the end of the poem, the lyrical "I" splits into two as Ady, referring to himself, makes Judas say, "Future, sad and sinful eyes / will understand."

In his role as the lonely prophet Ady later saw himself as "the Lost Horseman" in heavy mist and fog and separated from the rest of the world ("Az eltévedt lovas," 1918). In 1912, however, his self-image was much less noble; in "A vén csavargó" (The Old Tramp) Ady depicts himself as an old tramp walking alone in the rain in the chilly streets of Budapest.

Beyond voicing criticism of the social conditions in Hungary, Ady stressed his alienation, his "not-belonging." His rejection of his homeland and his pose of royal solitude, which again vitiated his socially committed side, did not permit him to share the concerns of the common people but caused him to address the issues from above.

This is the Nietzschean self-image translated into the realities of the Hungarian provinces. The image of the *vates* (prophet, sage) towering over his people is crucial in Ady's poetry, which therefore cannot be conceived of as the credo of a democrat. Ady never thought of himself as one of the people whose cause he championed. He placed himself above everyone as a self-elected member of "royalty" who was patronizing to and contemptuous of those he represented. He writes about the "prophets" in the title poem of *Az Illés szekerén:*

> Their hearts aflame, their minds of ice,
> The earth's laughter from below
> Pitying, the sun strews diamond dust
> To cover their cold, icy road.

The fiery chariots juxtaposed with icy peaks and the earth and sun assuming human attributes emphasize the preeminence of poets. In this magnificent, boldly painted vision, the poets rise up to the Lord, who has afflicted them with his unique love.

Ady's relationship to God and to people obviously reflects the influence of Nietzsche. Ady is the hero who refuses to be the poet of the gray masses in "Uj vizeken járok" (Departing for New Waters, 1906). He is God's competitor; "rebellious god . . . worm . . . fallen titan" are the images chosen for himself in "Ima Baál Istenhez" (Praying to God Baal, 1906). In "A Parisian Dawn," he writes:

> Who am I? The Sun-god's priest
> . . . .
> I am a priest, but a pagan one
> I am the martyr of the Sacred Orient
> . . . .
> A vagrant hero of the pagan past.

He sees himself as the issue of King Midas, whom only the future would learn to cherish, in "Midász király sarja" (The Descendant of King Midas, 1906). At the same time, he appears as "the king of a gray country" in "Ne lássatok meg!" (Do Not See Me!, 1906).

In another poem, "Ülök az asztal-trónon" (I Sit on the Tabletop Throne, 1906), he writes, "I sit on the tabletop throne / I, Prince of Ecstasy. . . ." In 1906 he appears as the "Poet of the Hortobágy," the Great Hungarian Plain, a region unfit for tilling. He uses the area as a synecdoche for the whole of Hungary, where no ideas are permitted to grow. In the same poem he calls himself "a sacred songster," and the elegance of the self-image is accentuated by the lowliness of the rest of his comrades, to whom he refers as "his filthy, feeble-minded friends."

The lyrical "I" is often the carrier of the main message of the poem. Ady is "the forlorn spirit of a gaudy town" in "El a faluból" (Away from the Village, 1906), "a born patron" in "Bucsú Siker-asszonytól" (Farewell to Dame Success, 1906), and Zarathustra in "Ének a porban" (Song in the Sand, 1906). In "On the Tisza River" he fashions himself a Hindu guru.

He did not want to become "domesticated" and even depicts himself as a wild horse that cannot be tamed in "Lelkek a pányván" (Tethered Souls, 1906). This was the period when he particularly strove for images of contrast and for qualities that cancel each other out, as in "Vizió a lápon" (Vision on the Marsh, 1906):

> I am shining light, hidden in fog.
> I am power, petrified.
> I am the miracle of the marshlands,
> Born for light, yet here remaining.

The romantic self-image is expressed in phrases such as "my heart is the sacred mount of songs" in "Bugnak a tárnák" (The Caves Are Roaring, 1906) or in his depiction of himself as Bacchus at his last feast in the vineyard of *"les temps perdu"* in "Elillant évek szőlő-hegyén" (In the Vineyard of Bygone Years, 1907).

"I don't need the dreams that have been dreamed before," declares Ady in "Új vizeken jarok" (Departing for New Waters, 1906), in which the poetic self-image is that of an explorer in search of unmapped continents.

> Don't fret, my ship, tomorrow's hero steers you!
> Let them tease the drunken rower at the oars!
> Fly, fly my ship,
> Don't fret, my ship, tomorrow's hero steers you!

Ady's androgynous self-image has metaphysical sources only. As a messianic poet, he had to place himself above both sexes. He was also an "ancient deity," incorporating in himself all mankind and watching it from above. In "Ha fejem lehajtom" (When My Head I Rest, 1906) he writes:

> Whenever my large satyr's head
> In a woman's lap I allow to rest,
> I recall—
>
> In ancient times, a giant female,
> I wandered in exotic regions,
> Dreamily.
>
> Far away in ancient times I was
> A woman of opulent size,
> In love.
>
> Sickly, young men followed me,
> Smoothly and desirously,
> I recall—

In another poem, "Akiknek dajkája vagyok" (Those Whose Wet Nurse I Am, 1907), Ady fashions himself as the wet nurse of Hungarian poetry and the feeder of frail infants—his fellow poets—who would grow only after having sucked him dry. He firmly believed in his own genius and swore that no frontiers would stop his poetry from reaching European fame, as in "Az értől az oceanig" (From the Brook Ér to the Ocean, 1907). Using the brook at his birthplace, the Ér, as a metaphor (it means "artery" in English), Ady boldly proclaims his rightful place in the center of European culture:

I want it, with a somber daring
To make it the wonder of the world
To set out from the tiny Ér
And reach the sacred giant seas of earth.

This variety of self-images was not unique to Ady. The poet/*vates*, the poet/pagan god, and the poet/eternal alien had been exploited by many European artists during the preceding decades and even centuries. However, Ady's sustained penchant for them, the frequency with which he needed to appear in his verses in roles other than his everyday self, is unique.

Ady was proud of his old Calvinist background and frequently identified it as the true national faith of Hungary. His own God was often closer to the awesome Jehovah of the Old Testament than to the soft and loving Lord of the New Testament. Whenever he comes to the poet's aid, he arrives in order to destroy his enemies.

Although Ady's poetry seems full of contradictions because he frequently disavowed logic, it is better to think of his work as an enigma. The mystery of the universe and an equally exciting mystery, that of his own feelings, remain alive in his entire work. Ady remained a puzzle to himself, as he does in "A békés eltávozás" (Peaceful Departure, 1912):

Not even a whisper should give away
What was the secret of my soul.

. . . .

Unanswered, a question long forgotten,
Let me plunge into silence supreme.
If I was not, I should not be,
And if a secret,
Let me so remain.

Ady's personal decline coincided with the end of World War I, in which Hungary was on the side of the losers. His last poem was a message to the victors ("Üdvözlet a győzőnek" [Hail to the Conqueror, 1918]), imploring them to spare his country, "the poor Hungarians," who had been "misused" by others.

Ady was deeply disturbed by the tragedy and by the prospects of his country's future.

He also felt entirely isolated. Three volumes of poetry were kept in the drawers of his desk until 1918, when his *A halottak élén* finally appeared. By then he was mortally ill. He first suffered a stroke, then succumbed to pneumonia. He died on 27 January 1919 in Budapest.

Selected Bibliography

EDITIONS

INDIVIDUAL WORKS

POETRY

Új versek. Budapest, 1906.
Vér és arany. Budapest, 1907.
Az Illés szekerén. Budapest, 1908.
Szeretném, ha szeretnének. Budapest, 1909.
A minden-titkok versei. Budapest, 1910.
A menekülő élet. Budapest, 1912.
A magunk szerelme. Budapest, 1913.
Ki látott engem? Budapest, 1914.
A halottak élén. Budapest, 1918.
Margita élni akar. Budapest, 1921.
Az utolsó hajók. Budapest, 1923.

PROSE

Sápadt emberek és történetek. Budapest, 1907.
Új csapáson. Budapest, 1909.
A tizmilliós Kleopátra és egyéb történetek. Budapest, 1910.
Igy is történhetik. Budapest, 1910.
Muskétás tanár úr. Budapest, 1913.

ESSAYS

Jóslások Magyarországról. Edited by Géza Féja. Budapest, 1936.
Vallomások és tanulmányok. Edited by Gyula Földessy. Budapest, 1944.
Életem nyitott könyve. Edited by Miklós Kovalovszky. Budapest, 1977.

COLLECTED WORKS

Összes versei. Budapest, 1930; rev. ed., 2 vols., 1955.
Összes novellák. Budapest, 1961.
Összes versek. Budapest, 1961.
Összes versei. Budapest, 1977.
Összes prózai művei. 11 vols. Budapest, 1955–1982. Critical edition.

ENDRE ADY

CORRESPONDENCE

Ady Endre válogatott levelei. Edited by György Bélia. Budapest, 1956.

TRANSLATIONS

The Explosive Country: A Selection of Articles and Studies 1898–1916. Translated by George F. Cushing. Budapest, 1977.

Poems. Translated by René Bonnerjea. Budapest, 1941.

Poems of Endre Ady. Translated by Anton N. Nyerges. Buffalo, N.Y., 1969.

BIOGRAPHICAL AND CRITICAL STUDIES

Ady, Lajos. *Ady Endre.* Budapest, 1923.

Ady, Lajosné. *Az ismeretlen Ady.* Budapest, 1943.

Baróti, Dezsö. *Az elhagyott kalózhajók.* Budapest, 1977.

Bölöni, György. *Az igazi Ady.* Paris, 1934.

Congdon, Lee. "Beyond the 'Hungarian Wasteland': A Study in the Ideology of National Regeneration, 1900–1919." Ph.D. dissertation, University of Michigan, 1975.

Földessy, Gyula. *Ady-tanulmányok.* Budapest, 1921.

Gulyás, Pál. *Ady Endre élete és munkái.* Budapest, 1925.

Halász, Elöd. *Nietzsche és Ady.* Budapest, 1942.

Hatvany, Lajos. *Ady: Cikkek, emlékezések, levelek.* Budapest, 1959; rev. ed., 1974.

Horváth, János. *Ady és a legújabb magyar lyra.* Budapest, 1910.

Király, István. *Ady Endre.* 2 vols. Budapest, 1972.

Klaniczay, Tibor, ed. *History of Hungarian Literature.* Budapest, 1983. Pp. 339–349.

Lukács, György. *Ady.* Budapest, 1948.

Masterman, Neville. "Ady as Political Thinker." *New Hungarian Quarterly* 19:162 (1978).

Reményi, József. *Hungarian Writers and Literature.* New Brunswick, N.J., 1964.

Révai, József. *Ady.* Budapest, 1945; rev. ed., 1965.

Révész, Béla. *Ady Endre trilógiája.* 3 vols. Budapest, 1935–1938.

Schöpflin, Aladár. *Ady Endre.* Budapest, 1934.

Szekfü, Gyula. *Három nemzedék.* Budapest, 1934.

BIBLIOGRAPHIES

Vitályos, Lászó, and László Orosz. *Ady-bibliográfia 1896–1970: Ady Endre önállóan megjelent művei és az Ady-i-rodalom.* Budapest, 1972.

MARIANNA D. BIRNBAUM

GUILLAUME APOLLINAIRE
(1880–1918)

"THERE ARE THREE Polish writers known today, and none of them writes in Polish: Conrad in England (he has talent), Przybyszewsky in Germany, and myself in France." Guillaume Apollinaire thus described himself in a letter to Madeleine Pagès in 1915. His real name was Kostrowitzky, which his fellow soldiers at the front quickly transformed into "Cointreau-whiskey." If it is true, as seems most likely, that Apollinaire's father was an Italian army officer, this would make him only half-Polish. Some biographers claim, although with little proof, that through the duke of Reichstadt, known as "the Eaglet," he was the great-grandson of Napoleon. Pablo Picasso among others hinted that his father was a high dignitary of the Catholic church, possibly the pope. And if Apollinaire never denied such rumors it was simply because he loved nothing more than to let legends proliferate about him.

The facts are that Apollinaire was born in Rome in 1880, the illegitimate son of a Polish woman, Angelica de Kostrowitzky, whose father was a minor official in the Vatican, and that he was baptized Guillelmus Apollinaris de Kostrowitzky. From his birth to his death in Paris on the eve of the Armistice (9 November 1918), when, again according to Picasso, the last words he heard from his bed were "Down with Guillaume!" (it was the crowd on the boulevard Saint-Germain shouting against Kaiser Wilhelm), Apollinaire's life has long made a fascinating subject for biography. He resembles such French poets as Gérard de Nerval, Arthur Rimbaud, Paul Verlaine, and Alfred Jarry, in whose lives biographers find a mystery more enticing than the poetry itself. His unconventional childhood on the French Riviera; the terror that he and his younger brother Albert felt for their baccarat-playing mother, whom the poet Max Jacob has described as a demoniacal coquette with a barking, raucous voice, swinging a dog whip and wearing jewels that looked like snails returning from a pawnshop; the sojourn in Belgium at Stavelot, with the two boys posing as Russian princes while Angelica lost all her money in the gambling houses of nearby Spa; the year as a tutor in the Rhineland, spent singing German folk songs, visiting Munich, Prague, and Vienna, and courting Annie Playden, a puritanical governess from Clapham, near London; the all-important meeting in 1904 with Picasso, whose poetic counterpart he became for a decade, leading the avant-garde experimentation in poetry and defending the cubist painters in the Parisian press; his imprisonment on charges (proved to be false) of complicity in the theft of statuettes from the Louvre, which earned him the reputation of being connected as a "Russian anarchist" with the 1911 theft of the Mona Lisa; the series of clandestine erotica he published in order to earn a few francs; his life as a soldier, spent feverishly writing epistolary poems from the front-line trenches until a German shell fragment pierced his skull and made him a Left Bank hero with bandaged head, idolized by the dadaists and future surrealists as he sat on the terrace of the Café de Flore; his stormy love affairs with a painter, Marie Laurencin, whom he graciously called a "cubist," with a *grande dame* (Louise de Coligny-Châtillon), with a schoolteacher (Madeleine Pagès), and with a "pretty redhead" (Jacqueline Kolb), whom he married just a few months before his death—all this makes tempting fare for a scintillating biography of a most engaging figure, like Yorick, "a fellow of infinite jest, of most excellent fancy," and one of the few writers— Jean-Jacques Rousseau was another—whom readers affectionately address by his first name. But the charm of Apollinaire does not entirely explain the originality of his poetry.

His being half Polish is in itself less important than that he was a hybrid. In a land whose major writers rarely doubted their pure Frenchness even in their revolt against it, as with Stendhal and Rimbaud, the case of Apollinaire is something of an oddity. It was by chance that the French language became his instrument. Instead of dragging her two boys to Monte Carlo, Mme de Kostrowitzky might have taken them to San Remo, Wiesbaden, Marienbad, Corfu, or any other resort well stocked with casinos. The education Guillaume received in Monaco was very solid, and the chauvinistic critics who have attributed the linguistic liberties in *Alcools* (1913) and *Calligrammes* (1918) to Apollinaire's ignorance of French are most disingenuous. Unlike that other foreigner in Paris, Picasso, who after a decade was still massacring his adopted tongue, writing "tableux" for *tableaux,* "vien" for *bien,* and "esculptures" for *sculptures,* Apollinaire had a thorough mastery of the language—its grammar, its orthography, and its punctuation. True, when his masterpiece, *Alcools*, appeared in 1913, the main reason for the scandal it caused was the total absence of punctuation marks. Actually, however, the commas, semicolons, and periods had all

been there up to the moment when he corrected the final proofs, and then, in one of those cavalier gestures so typical of his manner, he peppered the margins with the delta sign for "delete" alongside every mark. That most of the French poets since Apollinaire have followed suit would seem to vindicate his judgment.

It was precisely because of his assurance in French that Apollinaire felt free to throw in occasional foreign words and expressions (Hebrew, Italian, German, English) without that hint of self-conscious effort perceptible in T. S. Eliot's and even Ezra Pound's borrowings. Apollinaire loved the French language. Few poets—one thinks of François Villon and Verlaine—have composed such beautifully limpid lines in the rigorous octosyllabic mold. But his love did not amount to idolatry; he had little of the sense of the immutable correctness of the language that even the most revolutionary French poets share. To a journalist who once asked him if it didn't annoy him to see his name constantly misspelled as "Appolinaire," he replied, "Je m'en fous" (I don't give a damn). This foreigner who could twist its language at will was just what France needed at the turn of the century to recover from what Pound termed the effete "talcum powder style" of the minor symbolists.

The peculiar circumstances of Apollinaire's birth had an even deeper effect, however, since they color the very substance and structure of his poetry. For "Kostro," as his friends called him, not only was a foreigner; he was a bastard. And if he knew the name of his father, he never divulged it. The mystery of his parentage haunted him. In "Cortège" he writes:

Un jour
Un jour je m'attendais moi-même
Je me disais Guillaume il est temps que tu
  viennes
Pour que je sache enfin celui-là que je suis. . . .

One day
One day I was waiting for myself

GUILLAUME APOLLINAIRE

And I said to myself Guillaume it's time for you
   to come
So that at last I can know just who I am

Apollinaire was above all a lyric poet, and the bulk of his verse is in the first person. The elusiveness of the self and the emotions it excites constitute a dominant theme in his poetry. Indeed, he was one of the first and the most lucid among the hordes of twentieth-century writers—and readers—engaged in the search for their undefinable identities.

His rootlessness generated an exhilarating sense of freedom. He felt bound by no traditions, no taboos. Whether or not he inspired the character of Lafcadio in André Gide's *Les caves du Vatican* (*The Vatican Swindle*, 1914), as has been claimed, Apollinaire was a fine example of Gidean *disponibilité*, the total willingness to experience new sensations and beliefs. But non-involvement also weighed heavily on him at times, and so he often reveals a desire for more binding ties. What made the so-called Mona Lisa affair so traumatic was his fear of being deported from France, and perhaps the main reason for his volunteering to join the army in 1914 was the prospect of automatically becoming a French citizen.

Such oscillation in turn reveals a deeper trait in Apollinaire, his congenital indecisiveness. Coming from no particular direction, he knew not what direction to take. A recurrent image in his poetry is the compass pointing in all four directions at once. In one of his little quatrains of *Le bestiaire, ou cortège d'Orphée* (*Bestiary, or the Parade of Orpheus*, 1911), entitled "L'Ecrevisse" ("The Crayfish"), he apostrophizes incertitude, calling it his delight and adding that "you and I" go along like the crayfish, "backwards." Aimlessness explains the workings of his mind as well, which was apparently unable to follow a neatly developed chain of reasoning. His thought proceeded by free association, hopping at random from one notion or image to another. The prose suffers a bit from this. From such works as the rollicking, mock-heroic novel *Le poète assassiné* (*The Poet Assassinated*, 1916) and the short stories that follow it, there emerges a patchwork effect that disconcerts many readers. And the prose of his art criticism (*Méditations esthétiques: Les peintres cubistes* [*The Cubist Painters: Aesthetic Meditations*, 1913] and the posthumous *Chroniques d'art* [*Apollinaire on Art*, 1960]), for all its brilliant insights and rich, metaphorical style, lacks the cogency of another poet-critic, Charles Baudelaire, whose writings on art were collected in *Curiosités esthétiques* (Aesthetic Curiosities, 1868).

Apollinaire might well have disintegrated into an inert mass of neutralizing contradictions but for his vigor and his lucidity. From someone (Napoleon?) he had inherited such intense energy that his indecisiveness, far from leading to Hamletism or apathy, produced a gargantuan desire to embrace everything: "Je suis ivre d'avoir bu tout l'univers" (I am drunk from imbibing the whole universe). Thanks to his lucidity he came to realize that in the very weakness of his undirected thought processes lay his strength and originality as a modern poet. He had only to transform "primitive disorder" (if we may adapt the terms of Kenneth Rexroth) into "sophisticated disorder."

It is obvious, of course, that during that fruitful prewar decade in Paris Apollinaire did make a choice—in favor of modernism. As spokesman for the new trends in painting and poetry in both the daily press and the little magazines, he regularly defended whatever was the newest. This took a lot of legerdemain, since Paris had never been so heady with "isms." They were sprouting on both banks: fauvism, neo-symbolism, unanimism, cubism, futurism, dramatism, orphism, simultanism, paroxysm, and the like. Apollinaire got involved in many internecine struggles, and it took all his charm to placate friends of one school who felt he had betrayed them for another.

Take for example cubism, undoubtedly the

most important of these movements, which for certain literary historians encompasses a school of poetry as well as painting. Apollinaire was its most ardent champion in the press from 1910 to 1912, but between the completion of his manuscript for *The Cubist Painters* and the correction of the proofs he became fascinated by the canvases of one of the earliest abstract painters, Robert Delaunay. Sensing the importance of this new "pure painting," he decided then and there to call it "orphic cubism" and added the new category to the proofs. Then, only ten days after the book appeared, he announced that cubism had given way to "orphism" pure and simple: "The reign of Orpheus has begun." This of course incensed the cubists, and a year later, when Apollinaire lauded the "futurism" of Delaunay, he brought down upon him the wrath of Delaunay and futurists alike and came near provoking a duel.

What Apollinaire really espoused was avant-gardism. He was less concerned with the contents of this or that manifesto than with championing what was new. His most earnest desire was to form a common front in the fight against traditionalism, and his acrobatics with labels represent successive efforts to designate the overall trends of the moment by stretching the meaning of this or that "ism". The last label he sought to impose, without much success in spite of its greater accuracy, was simply *"l'esprit nouveau"* (the new spirit).

The cult of newness can be not only superficial but downright dangerous as a way of life. For the poet, however, it can generate the enthusiasm, the sheer joy, of singing what has never been sung before. In his 1917 lecture, "L'Esprit nouveau et les poètes" ("The New Spirit and the Poets"), Apollinaire asked rhetorically:

There's nothing new under the sun? I don't believe it.

What! I had my head X-rayed. I've peered while alive into my own skull, and there's nothing new about that?

Solomon was probably thinking of the Queen of Sheba, and he loved the new so much that his concubines were innumerable. . . . Perhaps for the sun there's nothing new . . . but for man . . . !

In "Zone" the Eiffel Tower, which the symbolists had ignored as a hideous new monstrosity, is described by Apollinaire as a gracious shepherdess guarding her bleating flocks, the bridges over the Seine. He presents the actual shape of the tower typographically in some of his "calligrams," those picture poems that are the forerunners of today's "concrete poetry." In "Lettre-océan" letters representing street sounds and objects are arranged in circles and radiating lines; it is only upon noting in the center the figure "300 meters high" that the reader suddenly realizes he is looking down upon the tower as from an airplane. (Delaunay presents the same view in several of his paintings.) The airplane fills Apollinaire with the amazement of a child: it can actually land without folding its wings! All the latest discoveries of science find their way into his imagery. The real poets today, he claims, are the scientists; one of the first in France to pronounce the name of Sigmund Freud, he prophesied vast discoveries in the "abysses" of the human mind.

Unfortunately the new has the bad habit of never staying that way. The calligram of an automobile in "La petite auto" (The Little Car") definitely betrays its 1914 lines, and Apollinaire's modernism, when only that, is paradoxically the element of his poetry that has aged most quickly, sounding at times like an infelicitous mixture of Walt Whitman and Filippo Tommaso Marinetti. The spurts of old-fashioned optimism and the hopes for a bright future, when the union of the spiritual and the technological will ensure the felicity of mankind, seem woefully passé, and Apollinaire would be forgotten today were he merely the voice of the "counter-decadence" of the first decade-and-a-half of the century.

His very rootlessness saved him, however, for among the contradictions it inspired was a fascination with the past just as intense as his anticipation of the future. A simple pirouette, and the Eiffel Tower becomes the Tower of Pisa. It is customary to divide Apollinaire's poetry into two neat categories, poems of "Order" and of "Adventure," the terms he himself used in "La jolie rousse" ("The Pretty Redhead"), his final "testament," in which he acts as moderator in the struggle between "tradition" and "invention." The poems of "Order," his biographers say, are those carefully composed lyric pieces, usually in regular meter, love poems, and *Lieder* (songs) for the most part, in the tradition of Verlaine, Villon, or Pierre Ronsard. "Le pont Mirabeau" ("The Mirabeau Bridge") is the classic example, and most of them date from the *Alcools* period (1898–1912). The poems of "Adventure" comprise all the experimental pieces, usually in free verse and stripped of a discursive framework. The most famous example is "Zone," the prefatory poem of *Alcools.* The last poem of this volume to be composed (1912), it announces all the new ventures of the *Calligrammes* period (1912–1918).

This classification, while by no means false, especially as a very general chronological division, represents an oversimplification that can be misleading. Apollinaire began experimenting much earlier than 1912, and his experiments include the use of modernist imagery—the Eiffel Tower pops up as early as 1902—whereas *Vitam impendere amori,* a booklet containing some of the purest octosyllabic lines and traditionally tender, nostalgic sentiments, was published in 1917, the year of the lecture on the "new spirit." As a matter of fact, it is hardly accurate to speak of oscillation between Order and Adventure, for the individual poems seldom fall exclusively into one category or the other but contain a mixture of both.

In any case, mere dualities fail to explain the complexities of Apollinaire's inspiration. His spiritual ubiquity, his claim to be at once "au zénith au nadir aux 4 points cardinaux" (at the zenith of the nadir at the 4 compass points), as he phrases it in "Merveille de la guerre" ("Marvels of War") made him feel a deep affinity with the "fourth dimension" as he defines it in *The Cubist Painters:* "It figures the immensity of space eternalizing itself in all directions at a given moment." That this is hardly a scientific definition is beside the point; for Apollinaire it reflects in his poetry the constant effort to perfect a multi-directional style so as to express the intense radiation of his compass-boxing emotions. The stages of this effort make up the chapters of Apollinaire's biography as a poet.

His first two known pieces, written at seventeen, are signed "Guillaume Macabre," and indeed much of the early verse has the morbid tone of the *fin de siècle* that we associate with the symbolist movement. In symbolism Apollinaire also found nourishment for his love of out-of-the-way myths and fairy tales, which he had felt since childhood. Greek, Hebrew, and Celtic myths lodge side by side in these youthful efforts as they do in his first prose work, *L'Enchanteur pourrissant* (The Rotting Magician, 1909). The death of Pan, the metamorphosis of Lilith into an osprey, the imprisonment of Merlin the magician under a crystal bell by the fairy Vivian—these are some of the rather decadent themes of this period.

Apollinaire excluded most of his teenage works from *Alcools,* and we know them only through their posthumous publication in *Il y a* (There Is, or There Are, 1925), *Le guetteur mélancolique* (The Melancholy Watchman, 1952), and "Poèmes retrouvés" (Rediscovered Poems) in the Pléiade edition of the *Oeuvres poétiques* (1959). Three fairly long poems that date from around 1900 are included in *Alcools:* "Merlin et la vieille femme" ("Merlin and the Old Lady"), "Le larron" ("The Thief"), and "L'Ermite" ("The Hermit"). The alexandrine quatrains and the narrative or (in the case of "The Thief") dramatic form give them a deceptively neat, traditional appearance. Actually they are among the most enigmatic poems Apollinaire wrote. Their obscurity comes in part from the strangeness of the three legendary characters (Merlin is the only one named): a hermit, a thief, and a magician, all of whom represent the Poet. They are isolated figures who seem to exist out of time and place. The lack of localization recalls the symbolist manner, which creates "landscapes of the soul" through the filtering process of the poet's memory.

Yet these pieces differ from the typical symbolist poem that seeks through a "medley of metaphors" (in Edmund Wilson's phrase) to communicate a certain mood, an *état d'âme* that no matter how ineffable is nonetheless coherent and consistent. What is striking here is the incongruity of the juxtapositions and the disconcerting shifts of tone. The recluse of "The Hermit," who has been praying and fasting, apostrophizes a skull in the best *fin-de-siècle* style—Hamlet's Yorick speech was a great favorite in Paris at the time—when suddenly in his hunger he sees the orbits in the head as holes of a piece of Swiss cheese and notes that *gruyère* rhymes with *prière* (prayer). Apollinaire was much too earthy to remain disembodied for long.

"The Thief" seeks to evoke a mythical pagan land, a composite of ancient civilizations and peoples to whose shores the Christian outsider, the "thief," comes as an intruder. Unlike the vague never-never lands of Maurice Maeterlinck's *Pelléas et Mélisande* (1892) and Villiers de l'Isle Adam's *Axel* (1890), the mystery here derives from a mass of very precise but recondite allusions based on an incredible amount of erudition for a twenty-year-old: the Pythagorean peacock, the Tanagra rooster, the stuttering leader, etc. (The glossary in Scott Bates's *Guillaume Apollinaire* is recommended for readers who wish explanations.) To these are added oracular statements that may or may not make sense: for example, "Le tact est relatif mais la vue est oblongue" (Touch is relative but sight is oblong).

After all, "touch *is* relative," as Francis Steegmuller points out, "and sight *is* oblong when you come to think of it: it is the why of

the double statement's being made here that is hermetic." Unlike a poet such as Stéphane Mallarmé, Apollinaire often dissipates the mystery with little explosions of humor, puns, and obscenities, examples of what the French call the *insolite*. The word literally means "unusual," but from Baudelaire down through Eugène Ionesco and Samuel Beckett it has taken on the connotation of "bizarre" or "weirdly unexpected." Apollinaire was a master of black humor.

Other, shorter poems of this period show the influence of Verlaine: delicate, melodious pieces filled with moonbeams, anemones, columbines, and faded gardens, all imbued with gentle melancholy. "Clair de lune" ("Moonlight") is typical—or would be were it not for one little touch that makes it read like a parody of itself. After using one of the most hackneyed examples of synesthesia—"mellifluous" or "honey-flowing moon"—Apollinaire adds that the stars can stand "fairly well" for the bees and with this bit of mockery destroys the mood of the metaphor on which the poem is based.

Beginning in 1897 the Dreyfus case split France into two camps on the issue of national security versus individual rights, and by bringing many poets down from the ivory tower into the market place it contributed heavily to the reaction against symbolism. In 1898 Apollinaire not only declared himself a "Dreyfusard" but also expressed his sympathies for the strong anarchist movement then in vogue. One result was a little poem entitled "Au prolétaire" ("To the Proletariat"), which its author himself quite understandably never published. It is frankly bad (unless it is a deliberate pastiche), largely because of the clash between the subject matter and a highly precious vocabulary: the smoke from the ugly factories is blown by the *aquilon,* and the proletarian seamen who have drowned are lulled by *nenias,* or Greek funeral dirges. Yet for all its awkwardness the poem reveals that Apollinaire was becoming attuned to a new source of inspiration, the modern industrial city, and like the Belgian poet Émile Verhaeren was trying to combine the urban themes of naturalism with the techniques of symbolism. His visits to Cologne, Düsseldorf, Berlin, and other large cities of Germany and Middle Europe in 1901–1902 gave a more authentic tone to this inspiration.

The German period is one of the richest in Apollinaire's career. He had a truly remarkable gift for immediate assimilation. In Stavelot, where he spent the summer of 1899, he had picked up the Walloon dialect and the local legends of the Ardennes in the space of three months. One of his best short stories, "Que vlo-ve?" (What Do You Want?) in *L'Hérésiarque et cie* (*The Heresiarch and Co.,* 1910), comes from this period. In the Rhineland, where he served as tutor for a year at Neu-Glück, the family manor of the vicomtesse de Milhau in the Siebengebirge region, and also at Honnef on the Rhine, he discovered a new language and new landscapes, customs, and legends that he made his own. Although he concealed the importance of this sojourn by grouping only nine poems in the "Rhénanes" series in *Alcools,* this single year produced almost a third of the works in the collection.

The wide range of subjects and styles suggests that he was intentionally experimenting in new forms and putting the French language to new uses. "La Loreley" is a conscious adaptation of the Clemens Brentano and Heinrich Heine versions of the Lorelei theme. "Nuit rhénane" ("Rhenish Night") and "Automne" ("Autumn") incorporate elements of German folk songs, and "Les cloches" ("The Bells"), although completely original, has the lilt of a *Lied.* A number of poems are directly inspired by the landscape: the pine forests ("Les sapins" ["The Pines"], "Le vent nocturne" ["Night Wind"]); the orchards in autumn ("Automne malade" ["Sick Autumn"]); and a herd of cows grazing among the meadow saffron ("Les colchiques" ["Crocuses"]). Others record little incidents or snapshots caught by the poet: two orthodox Jews arguing on their way to the synagogue in Unkel ("La synagogue" ["The Synagogue"]); children playing in the cemetery of Honnef on All Saints' Day ("Rhénane d'automne" ["Autumn Rhinesong"]); a prostitute on the Hochstrasse of Cologne ("Marizibill"); housewives chatting in the home of a Honnef winegrower ("Les femmes" ["The Women"]); a boat trip down the Rhine ("Mai" ["May"]); and a visit to a mortuary in Munich ("La maison des morts" ["The House of the Dead"]). Only one, "La tzigane" ("The Gypsy"), is directly inspired by a personal, intimate experience, a visit made by the poet and his beloved, presumably Annie Playden, the English governess in the household, to a gypsy fortune-teller.

In these pieces Apollinaire was seeking to combine a form of lyricism anchored in reality, whether urban or rural, with the symbolist notion of the poem as an enigma. This involved turning some of the techniques he had tried during his apprenticeship in a new direction and exercising them with more subtlety than is found in the purely mechanical juxtapositions of "To the Proletariat." The imagery becomes more direct. Clearly stated similes replace tenuous metaphors based on synesthesia and other *correspondances,* so that the enigmatic quality derives less from the images in themselves than from the arrangement of the lines in which they lie. Two closely related devices predominate: structural ellipsis, inherited from the symbolists, and free association, more peculiar to Apollinaire.

The ellipsis is most obviously indicated by double spacing, an invitation to the reader to fill in the blank. The final line of "Rhenish Night," for instance—"Mon verre s'est brisé comme un éclat de rire" (My glass broke like a burst of laughter)—is set off from the rest of the poem. There is no explanation for why the wineglass breaks; it is up to us to feel the shatter of glass and laughter alike as a sudden catharsis after the intense grief caused by the boatman's song. "May" is composed of four stanzas like four separate blocks, the connection among them remaining unexplained because it is one of mood rather than of logical sequence. Within each block as well there are

GUILLAUME APOLLINAIRE

missing links. If the reader tries to fill in the ellipses, he is bound to destroy the effect. Let us examine for instance the opening stanza of "May," putting English words in brackets to indicate the omissions:

> Le mai le joli mai [I was] en barque sur le
>   Rhin
> Des dames regardaient du haut de la
>   montagne
> [And I said to them] Vous êtes si jolies
>   mais la barque s'eloigne
> [And they made me wonder] Qui donc a fait
>   pleurer les saules riverains

> May pretty May in a boat on the Rhine
> Some ladies were looking down from the
>   mountain
> You are so pretty but the boat moves on
> Who made the river willows weep

We are not really certain which links to supply, and this ambiguity heightens the tenuous relationship between the rapid glimpse of the ladies and the sorrow of the willows. The *tempus fugit* theme is a commonplace, and no image could be more trite than the weeping willow, but the elliptical expression rejuvenates these elements by creating a fleeting effect in the form, which harmonizes with the fleeting impressions from the boat moving rapidly down the Rhine.

Free association is an extreme form of structural ellipsis in which the link may be hidden or may not be there at all. In such cases it is not clear whether a line is mysterious or simply mystifying. In "Crocuses" the poisonous flowers resemble mothers, "daughters of their daughters." Is there a cryptic connection between an imaginary cyclical process uniting generations and the circle around the eyes with which the flower has already been compared? And does this "eternal return" suggest the fatality of the poet's poisoned love? Or is Apollinaire simply enjoying the repetition of the word *filles* for its own sake? His fantasy can often be quite gratuitous, and it would be a mistake to attempt to explicate him as

though he were the author of the hermetic lines of Mallarmé or Valéry.

In "The Gypsy," on the other hand, there is some free association that effectively intensifies the dominant mood, the poet's feeling that his love is damned. No obvious connection exists between love dancing like a bear, the bluebird losing its feathers, and the beggars losing the Aves of their prayers. For some readers the sequence may seem as nonsensical as a Mother Goose rhyme, but for others the deep sense of heaviness and loss is as magically and as effortlessly conveyed as by a Mother Goose rhyme. The same kind of nonsense lines provide a weird conclusion to the mad dance in the later poem "Salomé," which is worth contrasting with the Salomé of Mallarmé's *Hérodiade* (1869) in order to appreciate the difference between the master of symbolism and the forerunner of surrealism.

The year in Germany was much more than a training period for the twenty-one-year-old poet. It produced several of those little one-page masterpieces that are among the most loved poems of *Alcools* ("Crocuses," "The Gypsy," "Sick Autumn," and others), and from it emerged the ingredients of the multi-directional style that in new arrangements and fusions form the substance of the major works.

In fact, it was only one year later, 1903 (according to his own account), that Apollinaire composed "La chanson du mal-aimé" ("The Song of the Unloved Lover"), which many consider his greatest poem and one of the masterpieces of French lyric poetry. Inspired by Annie's rejection of his love in London, where he pursued her after the return from Neu-Glück, it contains all the shades of the poet's ambivalent feelings, from deep desire and despair to the most virulent hostility. Much of its power comes from the tension between the opposing principles of continuity and discontinuity in the structure. The octosyllabic five-line stanzas with their *a b a b a* rhyme scheme flow along smoothly, carrying the song of the poet's lost love through the subtly shifting moods—at least *within* each section. The sections themselves, however, stand out like separate, distinct blocks that by their juxtaposition produce a series of unexpected breaks in the flow, as though Igor Stravinsky were driving wedges into Claude Debussy.

The poem opens in the prosaic manner of a short story—"One foggy evening in London . . ."—but it takes off almost immediately because of the resemblance between the street urchin that the solitary narrator meets and his love. The ambiguity of the word *amour* (is it the person or the sentiment or both?) gives a strange, unwholesome quality to the poet's attachment. An obvious analogy, partly visual, partly verbal, between the street lined with red bricks and the passage through the Red Sea allows the poet to become the Pharaoh as he pursues the hoodlum. The king of Egypt is the first of a series of legendary monarchs with whom he identifies himself throughout the poem. We know that in London Apollinaire saw the famous Shakespearean actor Beerbohm Tree playing Richard II. Did the "sad stories of the death of kings" spark the poem, not to mention "Thus play I, in one person, many people . . ."? In any case the device of changing personae is a particularly effective example of what one critic has called the "plasticity of the self," the constant metamorphoses that Apollinaire undergoes, like a new Proteus.

After protesting candidly to his absent mistress that he really is the king of Egypt *if* she is not his only love (thus developing and destroying the association simultaneously), the poet apparently loses sight of the urchin, who is replaced by the fleeting vision of a drunken woman with a scar on her neck coming out of a pub into the "bleeding fog" at the moment when "I recognized the falseness of love itself."

These first five stanzas transform the modern city into a phantasmagoria more eerie than sordid in which the narrator becomes the suffering hero of some strange legend, unknown because it is new. With these several lines Apollinaire brings us much closer to the

streets of André Breton's *Nadja* (1928) and Louis Aragon's *Paysan de Paris* (*Nightwalker*, 1926) than to the castles of *Axel* and *Pelléas et Mélisande.*

Beginning with the sixth stanza a sharp break in the narration evokes the happy return of the mythical kings, Ulysses and Dushyanta, to their faithful wives. These two vignettes create a change in tone that serves to intensify by contrast the poet's grief at the faithlessness of his own beloved. The ensuing stanzas flow smoothly on the "beautiful ship" of the poet's memory backward in time to the dawn of his love affair, leading to an *aubade* (dawn song), the first of three interludes set apart typographically within the poem.

Rarely has a writer borrowed from himself so much as Apollinaire. The majority of the poems in *Alcools* and many in *Calligrammes* contain individual lines, stanzas, or whole sections removed from their original position and placed in different surroundings. If this is "collage," as it is often called, Apollinaire was practicing it long before Georges Braque and Picasso. In "The Song of the Unloved Lover" we know from their manuscripts that the reply of the Zaporozhye Cossacks and the section on Shakuntala, the wife of Dushyanta, were composed earlier as separate pieces. The same may well be true of "Aubade," and even for the readers ignorant of such bits of scholarly evidence the interludes and the other equally autonomous groups of stanzas make for a quiltlike pattern in the poem as a whole.

The jubilant neoclassical tone of "Aubade" gives way immediately to a mood of despondency. The poet knows that the pagan gods have died, as have indeed the Christian God and love itself; the only idols he can adore are the memories of his love. He thus remains faithful to something defunct, like the wife of King Mausolus. The thought that he is unable to free himself from this empty adoration exasperates him so intensely that some kind of an explosion is bound to follow, and it is delivered in the reply of the Zaporozhye Cossacks to the sultan of Constantinople, certainly one of the most unexpected (*insolite*) fragments in any love poem. The Cossacks, who have just received an ultimatum to surrender to the Muhammadan monarch, compose with a burst of mirthless laughter their foul-mouthed reply. For them the laugh is an act of defiance, but for the poet-lover it is a purge for his grief and his mortification at finding himself the victim of a passionate, impossible attachment. And indirectly, through a kind of poetic logic, the impassive young puritan girl who inspires the poem is splattered by the most ungallant ribaldry.

Apollinaire revels in contrasts. In his fiction sadistic orgies give way to pastoral scenes. Similarly, the beautifully mysterious stanza that comes after the Cossacks' reply and that constitutes a refrain by its repetition elsewhere in the poem—"Voie lactée ô soeur lumineuse . . ." (Milky Way oh luminous sister)—evokes the quiescence of the poet's grief after the catharsis. There follows a long section of fourteen stanzas setting forth the subtle modulations of the emotions of "The Song of the Unloved Lover"—resignation, nostalgia, self-pity, morbid longing—and leading to the third interlude, "Les sept epées" ("The Seven Swords"), of the poet's melancholy. Adapting to his own purposes the symbolism of the Madonna of the Seven Sorrows and of the Seven Swords of the tarot cards, Apollinaire creates a highly original and hermetic projection of the facets and phases of his love. Numerous exegeses, astrological, philological, and erotological, have sought to pierce the mysteries of these lines. Perhaps the most satisfying approach is simply to imagine that the seven stanzas were penned by some anonymous medieval bard who happened to have lived in the twentieth century under the name Guillaume Apollinaire.

For all its hermeticism "The Seven Swords" serves to objectify the sorrow of the poet-lover and thus to prepare the resolution of "The Song." Before reaching the conclusion, however, we pass through a block of stanzas that, because of its position just prior to the conclu-

sion, parallels and pathetically contrasts the section near the beginning on the happy monarchs, Ulysses and Dushyanta. It presents the ill-starred brothers Ludwig and Otto of Bavaria, both mad, and particularly the lovelorn Ludwig, who drowned himself in a lake "Près d'un château sans châtelaine" (Near a château with no châtelaine). This final paroxysm of grief is perhaps the most intense in the entire poem, with its suggestion in "The Song" that suicide is the only solution.

The parallelism is even neater between the concluding five-stanza section and its counterpart of equal length at the beginning. In this tale of two cities the June sun, the noisy street, and the cafés of Paris offset the fog and the weird, unwholesome silence of London. The poet no longer has the heart to die. In the frank, authentic atmosphere of his own city he recognizes beyond a doubt that his love has no future, no ambiguous hopes. The sun, which becomes a flaming lyre burning his aching fingers, symbolizes the poet's need, his decision (as with the symbolists and Marcel Proust among others) to convert the heartrending experience through which he has passed, and which we have witnessed all along the way, into a work of art, the very one that he has just written and that we have just read. The final lines repeat emphatically an earlier stanza declaring the hero's knowledge of the secrets of song: "I who know . . . songs for the sirens." Later on Apollinaire wrote that "those who are reasonable, that is to say the poets, profit from their sufferings in love by singing them." However, this does not necessarily imply, as the symbolists would imagine, an absolute victory of "Art" over "Life." "Song" is a more modest word; the grief is still there, and the most we dare say is simply that Kostrowitzky has become Apollinaire.

We need only recall the single, fixed décor of the most celebrated French love poem of the nineteenth century, Alphonse de Lamartine's "Le lac," to appreciate the tremendous diversity of material in "The Song of the Unloved Lover." Disparate blocks of imagination jostle

GUILLAUME APOLLINAIRE

each other between the two terminal points that locate the poem in reality. Discontinuity, of course, is a risky technique that can easily become the enemy of coherence. The problem for Apollinaire was to create an effect of disorder reflecting the turbulence of the poet-lover's distraught soul while imposing enough order to make the poem aesthetically valid. Hence the necessity for a compromise with the devices of continuity: the regular verse form, the more or less symmetrical architecture (avoiding at all costs the coldly mathematical), the transitional stanzas uniting certain but by no means all of the sections. Thanks to these compromises the lyric sentiment is at once multifaceted and unified. Projected into the vastness of history and legend, it retains at the same time all the intimacy of the subjective self. Much of the power of "The Song of the Unloved Lover" derives from the delicate balance it achieves between Order and Adventure, the Apollonian and the Dionysian.

"L'Emigrant de Landor Road," which dates from the same period (1904–1905), commemorates—with a transposition of the sexes—Annie Playden's departure from her home on Landor Road for the United States in order to escape the importunities of "Kostro." Its rich patchwork structure foreshadows the 1907–1908 period, when structural ellipses and free association based on the principle of discontinuity are most fully developed and incorporated into a new aesthetic.

Meanwhile Apollinaire passed through a period of deep discouragement and sterility. Was it a kind of "Season in Hell" à la Rimbaud? We have little information on his state of mind at this time. The year 1906 is almost a complete blank. In reply to an interview in September, he said, "I have no significant work, and I regret it." (The manuscript of "The Song of the Unloved Lover" was lying in the desk drawer of the editor of *Le mercure de France,* waiting to be discovered three years later.) "Cortège," which seems to date at least in part from this time, reveals the poet's an-

guished search for his identity, the relationship of his "I" to the rest of the universe, and concludes with a eulogy of the past as opposed to the "colorless" future.

In 1908 Apollinaire emerged with the publication of a surrealist text, "Onirocritique" ("Dreamcritique"), and two major poems, "Le Brasier" ("The Brazier") and "Fiançailles" ("The Betrothal"), that announce the discovery of a new poetic language. The rough draft of "The Betrothal" in particular and of course the text itself constitute our main source of knowledge of the crisis he had just gone through. During the war he wrote that he considered this poem, along with "The Brazier," his best work. Posterity has not confirmed this judgment, but "The Betrothal" is probably the most important work for his development, his *Demoiselles d'Avignon* (1907), as it were. In fact, it is dedicated to Picasso and was conceived at roughly the same time as the painting. For those who like to call Apollinaire a "cubist poet" it is tempting to imagine the two men working out their new aesthetic together.

A more verifiable influence is that of the neo-symbolist *Phalange* group, with which Apollinaire began collaborating in 1907 and which was engaged in a revaluation of Mallarmé's poetics, with its concept of the poem as an autonomous object subject to a multiplicity of interpretations. Rimbaud too must have played a formative role—"Onirocritique" could hardly have been written without *Illuminations* (1886)—but external evidence is lacking. Apollinaire was always strangely silent about Rimbaud.

In any case, if neo-symbolism and nascent cubism were the midwives of "The Betrothal," the birth pangs were Apollinaire's own. It is the first poem in which he confides so openly about his ecstasies and sufferings as a poet. He tells of his grandiose projects as a youth, and in fact the first two of the nine sections are fragments from two long 1902 poems, one pastoral, one urban, like exhibits on display exemplifying two distinct styles that the poet intends to fuse. He tells how he sought for absolute purity but realizes now that perfection lies in the moment, that poetry is a state of mind rather than a work. He confesses the "torments" of silence that he has just suffered. At times he sees himself as a divine stellar force: it is toward *his* eyes that Icarus rises. Then again he glimpses only his mortal self with death rushing upon him "like a hurricane." He proclaims his omniscience—only to ask forgiveness for his ignorance. The single constant in these fluctuations seems to be his love, a love so all-inclusive that it must embrace the totality of life.

"The Betrothal" ends triumphantly with a phoenixlike regeneration of the poet's spirit. More specifically—and here perhaps lies the key to understanding this very obscure poem— it is his "incertitude" that is reborn out of its own ashes. In this one word Apollinaire sums up all the oscillations and indecisions of his mercurial character, which were constantly threatening to make a jumble of inconsistencies of his rootless existence. "The Betrothal" is thus the dramatization of a decision, not the decision to choose from among the conflicting forces within him, since this would mean suppressing others—and on what basis could the choice be made?—but rather the decision to embrace them all by fully recognizing their simultaneous existence. Of "incertitude" itself he would make a principle and a source of plenitude, bringing his life and his poetry into focus as through a single lens.

Rereading the poem with this in mind, we discover that its very style illustrates this sense of totality. Whether it is called "cubism" or more accurately "simultanism" (with a broader connotation than that of the 1912 school Apollinaire attempted to incorporate into his term "orphism"), the poem's style consists of the interlocking of opposites in new syntheses through the use of words and images with multiple meanings placed in discontinuous lines and sections in an effort to nullify the flow of time and thus achieve an effect of ambivalent immediacy.

The trouble with "The Betrothal" is its very excess of riches. Intoxicated by his revelation, the author packs the poem with a bewildering profusion of ambiguities, fused dichotomies, shifting images with shifting meanings, collages that only he can recognize, and secret allusions to which he holds the keys. Although "The Brazier" grew out of the same drafts, it is more coherent because, as the title indicates, it centers on the single element of fire. One of the main traits of Apollinaire's imagery in general is its volatility. Objects visually perceived and simple in themselves constantly melt into one another, a bit like the underlying phallic motif on the amphorae and frescoes of ancient Knossos, which appears alternately as a fleur-de-lis, a torso with arms akimbo, a neck with two bosoms, an octopus head, a butterfly. Whole chains can be established in Apollinaire: leaf to hand to flame to heart; shadow to snake to flame to sun to neck. Like Michelangelo, who believed that moving figures should be given the form of flames, he apparently realized around 1908 that the image of fire is paramount because it connects and contains the others. Although its presence in "The Betrothal" is more diffuse than in "The Brazier," it becomes in both poems the all-embracing symbol of poetic inspiration in general, of the poetic rebirth of 1908 in particular, and of the multiplicity-into-unity principle upon which it is based. Later on, in *The Cubist Painters,* Apollinaire sums up the genius of Picasso in two words: "enormous flame."

The note of hope and affirmation at the end of "The Betrothal" persists in the 1909 poems: "Poème lu au mariage d'André Salmon" (Poem Read at the Marriage of André Salmon), "1909," and especially "Vendémiaire" (*vendémiaire* is the first month in the French Republican calendar). The uninterrupted ebulliency of the last work makes it perhaps the most Dionysian piece that Apollinaire wrote. Few French writers—perhaps Rabelais, Victor Hugo, Paul Claudel—have reached such sustained dithyrambic intensity. Apollinaire turns his visionary power outwards upon the modern cities, transfiguring those of France, of Europe, of the entire world into great vats of intoxicating wine. And it is the poet himself who drinks it all, for he is "the throat of Paris," the supreme city.

"Le voyageur" ("The Traveler"), another offshoot of the 1908 discoveries, turns the techniques of simultaneity inward upon the poet's deep solitude, relating his sense of isolation to his sense of the instability, the constant flux of existence. The two opening alexandrine lines, separated like two monostichs, announce the dual theme:

Ouvrez-moi cette porte où je frappe en pleurant
La vie est variable aussi bien que l'Euripe

Open up this door where I knock weeping
Life is as changeable as the Euripos

The first line has all the dramatic urgency of an anguished cry emerging from nowhere. The second, which alludes to a strait in Greece famous for its surging currents and countercurrents, reads like an aphorism, a detached observation. The two together fuse the subjective and the objective views of the poet-traveler's condition. They also announce the form of the poem, which consists of a montage of isolated and uncertain recollections and free associations surging forth helter-skelter from the memory of the poet, who may be addressing either an unnamed interlocutor or, more probably, himself. The reader who tries to find a sequence in the fragments of the poem would do well to remember of T. S. Eliot's observation in *The Use of Poetry and the Use of Criticism* (1933):

Why, for all of us, out of all that we have heard, seen, felt, in a lifetime, do certain images recur, charged with emotion, rather than others? The song of one bird, the leap of one fish, at a particular place and time, the scent of one flower, an old woman on a German mountain path, six ruffians seen through an open window playing cards at night at a small French railway junction where there was a watermill; such

memories may have symbolic value, but of what we cannot tell, for they come to represent the depths of feeling into which we cannot peer.

(p. 148)

In "The Traveler" fragments of remembered reality fall in alongside strange dreamlike scenes, such as the recurrent picture of the two sailors. There seems to be no rigorous necessity in the selection and arrangement of the "old photos" the narrator examines. Apollinaire might have chosen others, but these were simply the ones that tumbled out. The one section that seems least automatic, consisting as it does of four highly polished alexandrine quatrains, is actually a kind of recollection in itself, an old manuscript of Apollinaire's that he inserts as a private piece of collage. It is far from gratuitous, however. The silent, bearded shadows passing across a mountain, holding their lances before them, seem to emerge from the dim, mythical past of a Jungian memory. Like the allusions to the monarchs in "The Song of the Unloved Lover" these lines cause the poem to open out into a mysterious new perspective in time.

The poem ends as it begins. Nothing is resolved, but the two lines of the opening, enriched now by all the evocations within, restate with greater intensity the same sense of solitude and instability and even suggest as well the absurdity of this condition. The effect of incoherence in the form reflects the meaningless incoherence, the "deadendedness," of life. Less ambitious—it is tempting to say less pretentious—than the other major poems of the period, "The Traveler" is undoubtedly one of the most authentic and deeply moving poems in *Alcools*. It might not be an exaggeration to call the emotion it conveys a mixture of pity and terror.

The high-reaching revelations of "The Betrothal" did not preclude the composing of little poems and songs. From 1908 to 1912 Apollinaire wrote quite a few that it would be a great mistake to consider as mere divertissements. The original version of *Bestiary* first appeared in *La phalange* in 1908 between the publication dates of "The Brazier" and "The Betrothal." (It was published in book form with woodcuts by Raoul Dufy in 1911.) The sprightly humor of these well-chiseled four- and five-line pieces often veils some very complex sentiments. The "incertitude" of the crayfish, for example, is the same as that of the bird in "The Betrothal."

Two of the best short poems in *Alcools* were inspired by the unhappy end of the liaison with Marie Laurencin in 1912: "The Mirabeau Bridge," the famous anthology selection, and "Cors de chasse" ("Hunting Horn"). The second illustrates more richly the 1908 aesthetic. The opening line, "Notre histoire est noble et tragique" (Our history is noble and tragic), is ambiguous enough to refer either to an entire people (it inspired Archibald MacLeish's "Men," beginning, "Our history is grave noble and tragic") or to a private love affair. The themes of tragic ineluctability evoked in this first stanza and of the poisonous effects of Thomas De Quincey's opium in the second (as set forth in his *Confessions of an English Opium Eater* [1821]) recall a similar relationship between love and poison in "Crocuses." The difference, however, is that in the Rhineland poem the mothers, "daughters of their daughters," are compared to the poisonous flower in an explicit simile joined by *comme* ("like" or "as"), whereas in "Hunting Horn" the structural ellipsis between the two stanzas obliges us to make the associative leap. For De Quincey, dreaming of his Anne, there is a sense of fatality in love that makes it tragic. We thus experience more immediately the sense of the poisonous inevitability of love, its predestined permanence. The very moment, however, that we grasp this feeling, we read that all is ephemeral: "Passons passons puisque tout passe" (Let us pass on let us pass on since all passes by). And we are told that even memories die:

> *Les souvenirs sont cors de chasse*
> *Dont meurt le bruit parmi le vent*

> Memories are hunting horns
> Whose sound dies away in the wind

Thanks to the omission of "buts" and "yets" and "howevers" the reader shares with the poet the full impact of the very Heraclitean dialectic of permanence and flow. "The Mirabeau Bridge" presents essentially the same theme, but through the use of ellipsis "Hunting Horn" develops it more subtly. And as Marie-Jeanne Durry points out in her study of *Alcools,* the concluding couplet, isolated from the rest, becomes the quintessential expression after Alfred de Vigny, Baudelaire, Verlaine, and Jules Laforgue of the hunting horn–memory motif in French poetry.

The loss of Marie Laurencin is only one factor contributing to the inspiration underlying "Zone." This work was long considered most important as Apollinaire's manifesto of modernism. Although "Zone" was the last poem to be composed for *Alcools,* its position at the beginning of the volume and the categorical statement of its opening line—"A la fin tu es las de ce monde ancien" (In the end you're tired of this ancient world)—seems to announce an abrupt change of direction in 1913, the decision, like that of Marinetti's futurists, to sing of the dynamism of the twentieth-century world. The first twenty-four lines, which evoke the beauty of the industrial age, confirm this impression, as do a number of the poems composed thereafter, most of which appeared in Apollinaire's avant-garde magazine, *Les soirées de Paris.* Today most of us would be inclined to agree with Hart Crane, who wrote bluntly in a letter: "All this talk from Matty [Matthew Josephson, the American biographer] on Apollinaire about being gay and *so* distressingly and painfully delighted about the telegraph, the locomotive, the automat, the wireless, the street cars and electric lamp posts, annoys me." Actually, as we have seen, Apollinaire had already developed a more profoundly modern sensibility and style long before the composition of "Zone," and if the poem still has a strong appeal more than a

GUILLAUME APOLLINAIRE

half-century later as one of the major poems of *Alcools,* the reasons are completely different.

It is perhaps the masterpiece of what might be called Apollinaire's peripatetic poetry. He loved to walk. To a collection of essays on Paris he gave the title *Le flâneur des deux rives* (The Left- and Right-Bank Stroller, 1918), and the action of his short stories often grows out of a strange encounter on a city street, as in "Le passant de Prague" ("The Wanderer of Prague"). Whether on the open road or the open street it is as a wanderer, usually alone, that the poet or a persona he creates sets the scene in such diverse poems of *Alcools* as "The House of the Dead," "Marizibill," "Autumn Rhinesong," "May," "The Song of the Unloved Lover," "L'Emigrant de Landor Road," "Annie," "Rosemonde," "Cortège," "The Betrothal" (parts 2, 7, and 8), "The Traveler," "Marie," and "Vendémiaire." And the practice is continued in *Calligrammes* with such "*poèmes-promenades*" as "Le musicien de Saint-Merry" and "Un fantôme de nuées" ("Phantom of Clouds").

Apollinaire's penchant for this type of poem comes primarily from his *disponibilité,* the feeling of openness to whatever encounter the moving landscape might provide. Like the surrealists after him he depended upon fortuitous occurrences to trigger his imagination. In "Lettre-océan" ("Letter-Ocean") he writes:

Je traverse la ville (I cross the city)

nez en avant (nose first)

et je la coupe en (and I cut it in)

2

It is the immediate contact between the external scene and the poet's "nose" as an antenna that sets the poem going.

"Zone" is particularly successful as a *poème-promenade* because the peripatetic motion governs the form throughout. The title suggests both the Parisian term for the suburbs surrounding the city and, etymologically, the somewhat beltlike or circular direction of the walk, which continues from one morning to the next, interrupted by several stops (the Gare Saint-Lazare, a bar, a restaurant, a brothel) before the poet returns at sunrise to his apartment in the suburb of Auteuil. The correlation between the ever-increasing fatigue of the walk and the despondency of the poet is implied throughout.

Within this framework, which shows the real city unfolding before him, the poet introduces a series of memories from the various stages of his past life, and it soon becomes apparent that he is endeavoring to reconcile present and past time on a single plane, or, more precisely, to reconcile his conflicting feelings toward two sets of opposites in time. The opening lines seek to proclaim enthusiastically the rejection of the past in its obvious connotation of "old" in favor of the present as "new." But the ratio is not so simple. "Voilà la jeune rue et tu n'es encore qu'un petit enfant" (That's the young street and you're just a small lad) introduces a sudden switch, as in a chiasmus. Newness becomes associated with the past, the poet's childhood, as he recalls his religious fervor at the Collège Saint-Charles; and the naive image of Jesus as an aviator, along with the imaginary parade of the birds that welcome the "flying machine," simply manifests a desperate effort to impose the enchantment of his boyhood faith upon the modern world of today. The attempt fails, and the sections beginning with the line "Maintenant tu marches dans Paris tout seul parmi la foule" (Now you are walking in Paris all alone in the crowd) suggest the other pair of the reversed ratio: the present has become old, the past, new. The present about him has lost all its freshness, and the poet finds himself overwhelmed by his despondency. As he continues his walk, he desperately attempts once more to resuscitate his past in a series of rapid flashbacks in the present tense beginning with "Maintenant tu es au bord de la Méditerranée"

895

(Now you are on the shore of the Mediterranean). Gradually, however, the magic of the memories pales, and nothing is left at the end but the pitiful sordidness of the actual city with its emigrants and prostitutes: "Tu regardes les yeux pleins de larmes ces pauvres émigrants" (With eyes full of tears you stare at these poor emigrants). The poet gradually makes his way home to sleep among the only remnants of his lost faith, the "fetishes from Oceania and Guinea . . . the inferior Christs of dark hopes." Daybreak—the hour for guillotinings in France—calls up through free association the final sinister image of the rising sun as a severed neck: "Soleil cou coupé" (Sun clean-cut neck). (The terse dissonance of this line made it famous among the surrealists, and the black revolutionary poet Aimé Césaire has used it as the title of one of his principal volumes.)

As an attempt to deal with the contradictions implicit in the concept of time, "Zone" is the poetic counterpart in miniature of a novel that began to appear the same year: Proust's *A la recherche du temps perdu* (*Remembrance of Things Past,* 1913–1927). Both seek to surpass the division between past and present in a new synthesis that, through memory, would resurrect *le temps perdu* ("lost time") in all its resplendence. Unlike Proust, Apollinaire sought the palingenesis through religious faith, which makes the confession of his failure all the more poignant. His compassion for the outcasts toward the end of the poem is certainly a Christian virtue, but faith and hope have gone. Only charity remains.

Its stark ending did not prevent "Zone" from becoming the great avant-garde banner of "counter-decadence" (another term for *l'esprit nouveau*), and it is usually cited as the "cubist" poem par excellence. No doubt it produces a fragmented, multi-dimensional effect through such devices as the telescoping of syntax, the almost exclusive use of the present tense, the rapid shifting of personal pronouns, the abrupt changes of locale, and the suppression of connectives and, of course, of punctuation. However, its basic structure remains sequential rather than simultaneous. If cubism is indeed a "sum of destructions," as Picasso claimed, in the sense that the fragmented elements of reality are rearranged so as to create a state of tension between the opposing forces of unity and multiplicity, then both the structure and the greater degree of polyvalence in "The Betrothal" and "The Traveler" make them more truly "cubist" than "Zone," which for all its zigzags flows along in time like "The Song of the Unloved Lover."

The reputation of "Zone" as a cubist poem stems in part from its first appearance in the newly founded *Soirées de Paris.* Right up to the outbreak of World War I this magazine was one of the principal mouthpieces for the new type of painting, with which Apollinaire found himself more feverishly involved than at any other time. Almost half the entire output of his art criticism dates from this two-and-a-half-year period. He visited scores of galleries, lectured at the important cubist "Section d'or" exhibit, visited England with Francis Picabia, went to Berlin with Delaunay to lecture on modern painting, published *The Cubist Painters,* issued a manifesto on futurism, wrote about the New York Armory Show, and introduced Marc Chagall, Giorgio de Chirico, Alexander Archipenko, and numerous other unknown artists to the Parisian public.

A mere glance at the first section of *Calligrammes* shows how the poems of this period were affected by Apollinaire's involvement with art. Lyricism gives way to experimentation, and most of the experiments are designed to bring poetry closer to painting. "Les fenêtres" ("The Windows"), composed for the catalog of a Delaunay exhibit, and "A travers l'Europe" ("Across Europe"), inspired by a visit to Chagall's studio, seek to evoke with words the spirit or style of a painter; and in the posthumous works are pieces on Picasso, Henri Rousseau, Picabia, Leopold/Survage, Irène Lagut, et al. The first calligrams or picture poems, also called *idéogrammes lyriques,* appeared in *Soirées de Paris,* accompanied by the critic Gabriel Arbouin's explanation that they oblige our mind to understand "synthetico-ideographically" instead of "analytico-discursively." The outbreak of the war prevented Apollinaire from carrying out his plan to publish them separately under the title "Moi aussi je suis peintre" (I too am a painter).

In general the 1912–1914 poems push the cubist principle of fragmentation to the extreme. The "blocks" are shorter, the images and statements more heterogeneous. Notations replace complete sentences. Free, blank verse is the rule. Like the futurist-coined *parole in libertà* (words-in-freedom) the lines, if not always the actual words, have declared their independence. Has coherence become taboo? Has the reader who earnestly seeks some elusive "objective correlative" become a fool? That depends upon the poem. In some, no doubt, chance plays the dominant role. The *poèmes-conversations* such as "Lundi rue Christine" ("Monday rue Christine") record the haphazard flow of real scraps of conversation around the pivotal point of the poet. In "Liens" ("Bonds"), on the other hand, the diverse images all relate to the theme of bonds or ties announced by the title, and the poem's coherence derives from the harmonious fusion of the techniques of simultanism in the form and the ambivalent feelings toward interdependence that they express. With "Arbre" (Tree) we can't be sure. Is the statement toward the end—"L'univers se plaint par ta voix" (The universe moans through your voice)—the thematic magnet that attracts all the disparate lines, or do they remain scattered? The poem seems to hover between the cubist principle of composition and the destructive anarchy of dada. Its 1916 publication in the dadaists' first magazine, *Le cabaret Voltaire*, confirms that they claimed the poem as their own.

Their selection of a prewar poem by Apollinaire further suggests that by August 1914 he had in effect reached the limits of his experimentation. The war poetry, which constitutes about three-fourths of *Calligrammes*, intro-duces a completely new décor, but the techniques, for all their regroupings, are familiar. The peacetime imagery is replaced by trenches, barbed wire, cannon, and hand grenades, but the analogies are as volatile as before; for example, a German shell becomes in turn a woman's breast, a rose, a heart, a star.

If the same techniques persist it is simply that Apollinaire himself did not change. "Incertitude ô mes délices" (Uncertainty oh my delight). True to himself Apollinaire sensed that every attitude generates its own contradiction and that in the horror of war lies its very fascination. In his poetry from 1914 to 1918 ambivalence continued to wear the garb of simultanism.

Critics often accuse him of prettifying war, of watching a battle as jubilantly as a fireworks display on Bastille Day; and they quote the famous line from "L'Adieu du cavalier" ("The Horseman's Good-bye"), "Ah Dieu! que la guerre est jolie" (Oh God, how lovely is war). Only out of context, however, can the line be taken literally, for the soldier who utters it is immediately killed.

Apollinaire's experiences at the front intensified his black humor. From his youth he had felt the influence of Jarry, but it was not until 1915 that he made a direct reference to Ubu, calling the war, in a rather bad pun, "Obus-Roi" ("Shell-King," referring to artillery shells). Like Jarry he mingles farce and fury, turning the tragic inside out, and by making death a subject for laughter, he more freshly conveys all its horror. Faced with death, he can affect the most insensitive cheerfulness, a kind of amused detachment, or a puckish smile. He can make the most abrupt leaps from the anguished, heavyhearted self within him, who feels deeply the tragedy of man's condition, to himself as persona, detached, inhuman, an "image d'Epinal" soldier, "Guy au galop," a stranger as mysterious and alarming as the stylized characters of a Guignol theater. Breton has recalled the sound of Apollinaire's laughter as he heard it shortly before the poet's death: "It made the same noise as a

first burst of hailstones on a windowpane."
The implication is that this laugh had nothing
contagious about it; it caused no merriment
but a shudder, a feeling of malaise. Was it not
a sudden outburst of the more unfeeling, destructive side of the poet's nature? The only
difference between Apollinaire and his *hypocrite lecteur* (hypocritical reader) was that he
fully recognized this aspect of himself and
expressed it freely.

The war also sharpened his perception of
the mysterious links between death and Eros.
"The terrible, warlike god of love," he writes.
Through the hundred-odd poems addressed
from the front to "Lou" and to Madeleine,
published posthumously in *Ombre de mon
amour* (Shadow of My Love, 1947) and *Tendre
comme le souvenir* (Tender as a Memory,
1952), there runs a current of violent sensuality that the occasionally modified versions
selected for *Calligrammes* only partially reveal. The privations of trench life and the
constant presence of death exacerbate the poet's desires to a point where he often fuses in
richly ambiguous imagery the instruments of
devastation and those of propagation, turning
no-man's-land into a vast erogenous zone. The
analogies work both ways. A white trench
(Apollinaire fought on the chalky soil of Champagne) becomes a deathly-pale nymphoma-
niac enticing her soldier-lovers ("La tranchée"
["The Trench"] in *Tendre comme le souvenir*,
abridged in "Chant d'honneur" ["Song of
Honor"], *Calligrammes*). In "Chef de section,"
as the soldier stands poised, watch in hand,
waiting to give the signal for an attack, his
beloved becomes the enemy and his mouth a
Gehenna full of flames. Because of its restraint
and concision, "Fête" ("Festival") in *Calligrammes* is perhaps the masterpiece of this
genre. It consists of a subtly iridescent play
between the triple analogy of bursting shell,
rose, and bosom, and the twofold sentiment
uniting fear of death with erotic desire.

On 17 March 1916, as Apollinaire was sitting in the trench reading the *Mercure de
France*, a shell fragment pierced his helmet
and entered the right temple. Convalescence
after the trepanation was slow, and it was not
until August that he began to frequent the
cafés of Montparnasse and the Café de Flore
close by his apartment on the boulevard Saint-
Germain. In a final letter to Madeleine in
November he confessed his lassitude and admitted he had changed. Actually the same old
incertitude is there, but for the next two years
it oscillates mainly along the axis between
avant-gardism and conservatism, two poles
that Apollinaire does not always manage to
synthesize.

In his appearance at least he succeeded, as
he sat chatting with Left Bank dadaists in his
horizon-blue uniform and the *croix de guerre*,
which appears in both the Picasso and Ame-
deo Modigliani portraits. (It was this same
uniform that saved the authors from the fists of
a scandalized audience at the premiere of the
Cocteau-Satie-Picasso-Massine ballet *Parade*
in 1917, or so Cocteau claims.) Apollinaire's
patriotism instilled in him the obligation to
preach the good old virtues of French classicism: honor, duty, and above all order. The
man who only four years earlier had issued
his revolutionary manifesto, *L'Antitradition
futuriste* (The Futurist Antitradition), now
claimed prudently in his lecture on the new
spirit that "as a rule you will not find in France
those *parole in libertà* of the Italian and Russian futurists who have pushed the new spirit
too far; for France abhors disorder." Shortly
before his death Apollinaire confided to Picasso that he was writing verse "more in line
with your own preoccupations of the moment.
I am trying to renew my poetic tone but within
the classical rhythm." (Picasso was in fact
embarking on what has been called his
"classico-expressionist" style.) And in the
same letter he adds: "What could be newer
today, more modern, more unadorned and
richer than Pascal? You enjoy him too, I believe, and rightly so." Beneath all the farcical
chaos of *Les mamelles de Tirésias* (*The
Breasts of Teresias*, 1918) lies a comic plot in

the best seventeenth-century manner. Like Monsieur Jourdain in Molière's *Le bourgeois gentilhomme* (*The Bourgeois Gentleman*, 1620) Thérèse wants to become what she is not, in her case a feminist. However, after she changes into Tirésias it doesn't take her long to realize that she is better off as a woman, and the metamorphosis back to Thérèse makes her a good housewife ready to produce progeniture for the *patrie*. *Castigo ridendo mores* (One corrects manners by laughing at them).

"Kostro," it seems, had finally taken root—in the age of Louis XIV! Yet his biographers inevitably entitle the 1916–1918 period "*L'Esprit nouveau*," and there is ample evidence to show that he was still out in front of the avant-garde. He states, for example, that *l'esprit nouveau* seeks to "explore every field that can provide literary material for the exaltation of life in whatever form it occurs." His thirst for spiritual ubiquity remains as strong as ever, but he is less concerned with the techniques of simultanism in poetry alone than with the discovery of new media and sources in all the arts. The bars are down. So long as it extends the range of expression, any means is acceptable. "We want new sounds new sounds new sounds," he exclaims in "La victoire" ("The Victory"), and he proposes consonants without vowels, prolonged nasals, tongue-clicking, finger-snapping, drumlike beats on the cheek, imitations of a spinning top. In 1917, in the gallery of the art dealer Paul Guillaume, he announces the birth of a new art, the "tactile art" based on surprising combinations of stickiness, elasticity, softness, the oily, the silky, the velvety. More serious are his hopes for the phonograph and the cinema, "vaster than the plain art of words," and he predicts the day when they will replace printing, giving poets a freedom hitherto unknown.

Meanwhile he chides the poet of his day for his "crawling imagination," long since outdistanced by the scientists, and exhorts him to dig into his unconscious for new riches and to focus his imagination on the everyday event:

"The dropping of a handkerchief can be the lever with which he will lift up a whole universe." This notion of the infinite sources of inspiration is most beautifully expressed in "The Pretty Redhead," where Apollinaire addresses the traditionalists in the name of the avant-garde:

Nous voulons vous donner de vastes et d'étranges
  domaines
Où le mystère en fleurs s'offre à qui veut le
  cueillir
Mille phantasmes impondérables
Auxquels il faut donner de la réalité

We want to give you vast and strange lands
Where mystery in bloom is free for the picking
A thousand imponderable phantasms
That must be given reality

Above all Apollinaire campaigns for works that would orchestrate the various arts on a vaster, more modern plane than the Wagnerian *Gesamtkunstwerk* (total art) that had influenced the symbolists. *Parade* delighted him for this very reason, since Jean Cocteau's script, Eric Satie's music, Picasso's sets and costumes, and Léonide Massine's choreography fused the elements of contemporary reality—music-hall motifs, skyscrapers, typewriters, American ragtime—in one "total" scenic poem. To characterize this amalgam, in his program notes for the premiere Apollinaire coined a word: surrealism. A month later (June 1917) the same concept of total theater is implicit in his second use of the word as the subtitle (*Drame surréaliste*) of *The Breasts of Teresias,* for the prologue stresses that the collaboration of the arts ("sounds gestures movements masses color") produces not the imitation of "a slice of life" but life itself in its totality.

When the surrealists appropriated the word seven years later, with the publication of Breton's *Manifeste de surréalisme* (*Surrealist Manifesto*) in 1924, they stripped it of both its theatrical and its aesthetic connotations, substituting (but without giving credit) Apollinaire's notion of "the automatic life," as Roger Shattuck has called it. This term describes the belief that one should act "in total response to one's deepest nature without rejecting the contradictions or paradoxes inherent in that nature."

Apollinaire was so feverishly involved in other fields during his last two years that his poetry suffers. *Calligrammes* includes only four pieces written after the convalescence. *Vitam impendere amori* and a handful of other pieces published posthumously complete the entire output. Yet these few works give a truer picture of the poet's complex *état d'âme* (state of soul) than the fictional, dramatic, and critical writing. If he had neatly trimmed his thought to the simple dualities of Order and Adventure how can we explain the dejected conclusion of "The Pretty Redhead" ("Ayez pitié de moi" [Have pity on me])? What is the "secret misfortune" in "Tristesse d'une étoile" ("A Star's Sadness"), the "heavy secret" of *Vitam impendere amori,* the recurrent theme of suffering in "Les collines" ("The Hills"), which was in all probability composed at this same time? These poems retain the rich polyvalence Apollinaire discovered a decade earlier with "The Betrothal." The flame returns as the all-inclusive image; in fact in the "New Spirit" lecture he explicitly uses it as the symbol of polyvalence in speaking of "the immense unknown where the joyous fires of multiple meanings blaze forth."

In "The Pretty Redhead" the flame not only succeeds in fusing Order and Adventure in a single entity—"La raison ardente" (The Ardent Reason; *ardente* retains from its old French root, *ardre,* the original meaning of "burning")—but further associates this entity with the red hair of the beloved (Jacqueline), the hot summer (the poet's maturity), the sun (the force that generates ardor), and a lightning flash that endures (the continuity of his inspiration). At this point, however, a dissonant note is introduced through the image of flames in withering roses, which suggests the

connection between fire and death. This is the final image that leads directly to the dejected conclusion of the poem. In "A Star's Sadness" the same adjective, *ardente,* modifies the secret "suffering" that the poet carries within him, like the flaming body of the glowworm, like France within the heart of the soldier, like pollen within the heart of the lily. Here we go a step further, since the similes make it clear that the suffering is simultaneously destructive and regenerative, but its exact nature remains a mystery. Perhaps "The Hills" can give a clue to this enigma.

This poem has much the same visionary tone as "The Betrothal" and "The Brazier," with the poet not only seeing himself as an omniscient celestial force endowed with the gift of prophecy but also predicting the divinization of mankind. Yet this messianic optimism is offset by the insistence that the future will be a time of deep suffering and indeed that suffering, like the unconscious, will become a subject for scientific study. This theme is so emphatic that it strikes one less as a prediction than as a vast projection of the poet's own obsessive "secret," and it introduces a disquieting contradiction to the ebullient hopes. The flame image is particularly effective in underlining this ambivalence. At the beginning of the poem two airplanes are fighting. One is the poet's youth, the other the future. When we read "Où donc est tombée ma jeunesse?" (Where has my youth fallen?), we understand which plane has won the battle, but how then do we interpret the line "Tu vois que flambe l'avenir" (You see the future in flames) except as an expression of the poet's contradictory feelings toward the future, which is flaming gloriously and tragically at the same time? Similarly, in the concluding stanza the secret of life itself is summed up in the line "Tout n'est qu'une flamme rapide" (All is but a rapid flame), which in the context must be read with the contradictory meanings of "flame" fused.

"The Pretty Redhead," like "The Brazier," derives its coherence from the element of fire, but in "The Hills," as in "The Betrothal," this element remains more diffuse, mingling with numerous other images in one of the most volatile poems Apollinaire wrote. The rapidity of the metamorphoses that the poet presents or undergoes builds up to such a frenetic, desperate pitch that it may at last give us a clue to the nature of his secret torment. "The Hills" is a fine example of surrealism insofar as it is composed of a vertiginous sequence of images, each one of which, to apply a remark of Aragon's, "obliges you at each moment to change your view of the entire Universe." Like Apollinaire, surrealism sought to convey to modern man a feeling of transcendency outside the perimeter of religion, but as Yves Bonnefoy has pointed out, surrealism lived on a paradox that it refused to admit—a contradiction between its desire for participation in the sacred and "its secret love of nothingness."

Did Apollinaire admit such a contradiction? Not in so many words. Yet the nihilistic undertone that occurs in "The Traveler" and "Zone" recurs in "The Hills," particularly in an arresting image that describes the act of going back so completely into oneself that only an abyss remains. In this context the famous "statue of nothing" in *The Poet Assassinated,* the void a half-meter wide and two meters deep that the dead poet's artist friend creates as a memorial (and Picasso, who realized that he was the friend referred to, actually intended to make such a statue in Paris after Apollinaire's death), is more than a mere *sic transit gloria mundi* reflection; it becomes a terrifying glimpse into the void of the poet's own self. His rootlessness, the elusiveness of his identity, must have made him sense that the thirst for total presence presupposes the state of total absence.

In a study on Apollinaire Margaret Davies suggests that his "secret" was his feeling of inadequacy as a poet, his fear of poetic impotence; but if this were true how could the suffering become regenerative, as both "A Star's Sadness" and "The Hills" imply? Is the "secret" not rather the dread of the "abyss," the

lucid awareness of which converts that dread into hope? Only if the poet accepts the reality, the palpability, of nothingness can the *nihil* become the fuel that feeds poetic ardor—and in a 1917 short story, "Mon cher Ludovic" ("My Dear Ludovic"), Apollinaire does in fact speak of the solidity of the void. One of the stanzas from "The Hills" inscribed on his tomb in the Père Lachaise cemetery contains the following lines (italics mine):

> *Et j'ai scruté tout ce que nul*
> *Ne peut en* rien *imaginer*
> *Et j'ai soupesé maintes fois*
> *Même la vie impondérable*
> *Je peux mourir en souriant*

> And I have studied the *nothing*
> That no one else can even imagine
> And countless times have I tried the weight
> Of life the imponderable
> I can die with a smile

Like the *statue en rien* of *The Poet Assassinated,* does not the *rien* of this passage suggest a solid substance?

Apollinaire never attempted to elaborate as a concept the dialectical thinking that lies beneath the simultanism and the polyvalence of his poetry. Nothing indicates that he had read G. W. F. Hegel; he knew Blaise Pascal and Friedrich Nietzsche, but how extensively we cannot be sure. The influence of Mallarmé's poetics and the theories of cubism made him formulate in his prose writings such paradoxes as "truth within the lie," "clarity within obscurity," "humanity within inhumanity." Above all, however, it was through the very intimate and painful exploration of his own ambiguous nature that he intuitively evolved his multi-directional style. "One must have chaos in one," writes Nietzsche, "to give birth to a dancing star"; and Apollinaire's victory as a poet sprang from the maze of contradictions within him as a man. Poets have understood at least since Heraclitus that "of everything that is true, the converse also is true," and time and again they have sought to pronounce *odi et* amo (hate and love) in one breath. Yet the fact that the word "ambivalence" was not coined until 1916 is sufficient indication that the general acceptance of this concept is predominantly a twentieth-century acquisition. It is in this sense and not simply because he sang of the Eiffel Tower that Apollinaire is profoundly modern.

He once claimed that he would be happy with only seven readers: a black American boxer, an empress of China, a German journalist, a Spanish painter, a young woman of good French blood, an Italian peasant girl, and an English officer in India. He thus seems modestly to offer a prism that is only heptagonal, but as readers on the lookout for a single facet come across more and more, they suddenly discover that the immediacy of these poems lies in the simultaneity of all their facets—and in their universality as well, for Apollinaire assures us that we are as complex as he when in "The Hills" he promises us secrets

> Qui se dévoileront bientôt
> Et feront de vous cent morceaux
> A la pensée toujours unique.

Which will soon unveil themselves
Making of you a hundred fragments
Around a single common thought.

Selected Bibliography

EDITIONS

INDIVIDUAL WORKS
L'Enchanteur pourrissant. Paris, 1909.
L'Hérésiarque et cie. Paris, 1910.
Le bestiaire, ou cortège d'Orphée. Paris, 1911.
Alcools: Poèmes, 1898–1913. Paris, 1913.
Méditations esthétiques: Les peintres cubistes. Paris, 1913.
Le poète assassiné. Paris, 1916.
Vitam impendere amori. Paris, 1917.
Calligrammes: Poèmes de la paix et de la guerre, 1913–1916. Paris, 1918.
Le flâneur des deux rives. Paris, 1918.
Les mamelles de Tirésias. Paris, 1918.

La femme assise. Paris, 1920.
Il y a. Paris, 1925.
Anecdotiques. Paris, 1926.
Ombre de mon amour. Geneva, 1947.
Tendre comme le souvenir. Paris, 1952.
Le guetteur mélancolique. Paris, 1952.
Poèmes à Lou. Geneva, 1955.
Chroniques d'art. Paris, 1960.
Les diables amoureux. Paris, 1964.

COLLECTED WORKS
Oeuvres poétiques. Edited by Marcel Adéma and Michel Décaudin. Paris, 1956; rev. ed., 1965. Includes Alcools, Le bestiaire, and Vitam impendere amori.
Oeuvres complètes. 4 vols. Edited by André Balland and Jacques Lecat. Paris, 1965–1966.
Oeuvres en prose. Texts annotated and presented by Michel Décaudin. Paris, 1977.

MODERN EDITIONS

INDIVIDUAL WORKS
Alcools: Choix de poèmes. Edited by Roger Lefèvre. Paris, 1971.
Calligrammes: Poèmes de la paix et de la guerre, 1913–1916. Preface by Michel Butor. Paris, 1966.
Chroniques d'art 1902–1918. Edited by L. C. Breunig. Paris, 1981.
L'Enchanteur pourrissant. Edited by Jean Burgos. Paris, 1972.
Lettres à Lou. Edited with a preface by Michel Décaudin. Paris, 1969.
Méditations esthétiques: Les peintres cubistes. Edited by L. C. Breunig and J.-C. Chevalier. Paris, 1980.
Le poète assassiné. Edited by Michel Décaudin. Paris, 1979.

TRANSLATIONS

Alcools. Translated by William Meredith. Introduction and notes by Francis Steegmuller. New York, 1964.
Alcools. Translated with notes by Anne Hyde Greet. Foreword by Warren Ramsey. Berkeley and Los Angeles, 1965.
Apollinaire on Art. Translated by Susan Suleiman. New York, 1972.
Bestiary, or the Parade of Orpheus. Translated by Pepe Karmel. Boston, 1980.

The Breasts of Teresias. Translated by Louis Simpson. *Odyssey* 1:125–163 (1961).

Calligrammes. Translated by Anne Hyde Greet. Introduction by S. I. Lockerbie. Commentary by Anne Hyde Greet and S. I. Lockerbie. Berkeley and Los Angeles, 1980.

The Cubist Painters: Aesthetic Meditations. Translated by Lionel Abel. New York, 1949.

The Heresiarch and Co. Translated by Rémy Inglis Hall. New York, 1965.

"The New Spirit and the Poets." Translated by Francis Steegmuller. In his *Apollinaire: Poet Among the Painters.* New York, 1963.

The Poet Assassinated and Other Stories. Translated by Ron Padgett. San Francisco, 1984.

Zone [from *Alcools*]. Translated by Samuel Beckett. Dublin, 1972.

BIOGRAPHICAL AND CRITICAL STUDIES

Adéma, Marcel. *Guillaume Apollinaire, le mal-aimé.* Paris, 1968.

Auster, Paul, ed. *The Random House Book of Twentieth-Century French Poetry.* New York, 1982.

Bates, Scott. *Guillaume Apollinaire.* New York, 1967.

Bohn, Willard. *Apollinaire et l'homme sans visage.* Rome, 1984.

Bowra, C. M. *The Creative Experiment.* London, 1949.

Breunig, L. C. "Le roman du mal-aimé." *La table ronde* no. 57 (1952).

Chevalier, Jean-Claude. *"Alcools" d'Apollinaire: Essai d'analyse des formes poétiques.* Paris, 1970.

Davies, Margaret. *Apollinaire.* London, 1964.

Debon, Claude. *Guillaume Apollinaire après "Alcools."* Paris, 1981.

Décaudin, Michel. *Le dossier d'"Alcools."* Paris, 1960.

Durry, Marie-Jeanne. *Guillaume Apollinaire: "Alcools."* 3 vols. Paris, 1956–1964.

Fabry, Anne de, and Marie-France Hilgar, eds., *Études autour d'"Alcools."* Birmingham, Ala., 1985.

Greet, Anne Hyde. *Apollinaire et le livre de peintre.* Paris, 1977.

Lawler, James. "Apollinaire et 'La chanson du mal-aimé.'" *Australian Journal of French Studies.* 1 (1964).

Lockerbie, S. I. "*Alcools* et le symbolisme." *Revue des lettres modernes* 85–89 (1963).

Morhange-Bégué, Claude. *"La chanson du mal-aimé" d'Apollinaire.* Paris, 1970.

Pia, Pascal. *Apollinaire par lui-même.* Paris, 1954.

Raymond, Marcel. *De Baudelaire au surréalisme.* Paris, 1947.

Rees, Garnet, ed. *Guillaume Apollinaire: "Alcools."* London, 1975.

Renaud, Philippe. *Lecture d'Apollinaire.* Lausanne, 1969.

Samaltanos, Katia. *Apollinaire: Catalyst for Primitivism, Picabia, and Duchamp.* Ann Arbor, Mich., 1984.

Shattuck, Roger. *The Banquet Years.* New York, 1955.

Shattuck, Roger. "Apollinaire's Great Wheel." In *The Innocent Eye.* New York, 1984.

Steegmuller, Francis. *Apollinaire: Poet Among the Painters.* New York, 1963.

Teurnadre, Claude, ed. *Les critiques de notre temps et Apollinaire.* Paris, 1971.

LeROY C. BREUNIG

ANDREY BELY
(1880–1934)

IN ONE OF his autobiographical novels, *Zapiski Chudaka* (Notes of an Eccentric, 1922), Leonid Ledianoi, Andrey Bely's alter ego, reflects on two kinds of biography. One is an official biography, the record of "ephemeral dates" such as "the year and day" of a man's "entrance into the world," his subsequent comings and goings, and the events of his day-to-day existence. (Bely's "official" biography would note that he was born Boris Bugaev in Moscow on 26 October 1880, and died there on 8 January 1934.) Yet to Bely, this is no more than an accumulation of trivia, a spotty covering thrown over the real human being that serves only to conceal him: "We can say of any one: there now, he's young; there, his beard is sprouting; there, it has already turned gray; there, he has died." Such observations have nothing to do with the essence of a life, which can be revealed only by the one who has lived it, in his true biography, an individual's intimate knowledge of himself. Over the years Bely, who was always interested in "the essence" of things, in "the real human being," gave us this true biography of himself, sometimes explicitly, in memoirs, in overtly autobiographical novels, and in the self-transformations of his fictions, and sometimes implicitly, even in his technical, "scientific" studies. We can read the story of his spiritual biography in all his writings, for he never stopped examining and explaining himself. His special theory of symbolism, his unique literary style, his critical experiments and innovations, are the images and echoes of an intense, elaborate, and unremitting introspection. His mind was avid. In addition to literatures and languages, it explored the natural sciences, mathematics, religions, history, and metaphysics; but the outside world was nonetheless shadowy to him. It impinged on his vivid inner life, and his novels dramatize how the data of the "unreal" outside world are transformed by the imagination into the stuff of art, while his memoirs and other writings demonstrate the method of his mind in organizing and synthesizing the raw material it studies into a systematic theory of the nature of art.

Bely's story begins with the autobiographical novel *Kotik Letaev* (1922). "Kotik," that is, "kitten," is the pet name of little Nikolai Letaev, who is actually Boris (or Boren'ka, in its affectionate diminutive) Bugaev, or Bely. For an epigraph to this novel, which takes the boy up to his fifth year, Bely chose the following bit from *War and Peace* (1863–1869): "'You know, I think,'" said Natasha in a whisper, 'when you remember, remember, remember everything, you remember how things were even before you came on earth.' " To Bely this charming notion of Leo Tolstoy's young heroine was no mere fancy but an article of faith dictated by anthroposophy, of which he was an ardent devotee at the time of this novel's writing. According to this doctrine memory is innate, prenatal, and independent of the body, since an individual's life itself is the memory of a preceding one, and, in consequence, anything remembered consciously is "memory of memory." Thus, Kotik's first recollections are of his existence before birth, when, in the immeasurable abyss of the "Mothers," before consciousness has entered his puny body, he undergoes an experience of overwhelming fear, such that had he been able to speak and understand, he would have cried out for help. But "he could not speak, could not understand," and "was not understood." Only metaphors, myths, and grandiose images of nature can suggest the horror of his subliminal experience: "Myths are ancient existences, myths once appeared to me as continents, as seas." Worlds of seas, of cosmic storms raged within him in "frenzied red swarms of delirium"; he was in the Titan's grasp, hissing snakes surrounded him, and a tree, his developing awareness, branched out and sprouted leaves inside him. Whatever philosophic or scientific meaning may be read into this memory of precorporeal existence, there is no denying that it conveys very powerfully a sense of utter helplessness and isolation, of terror, anxiety, and pain.

Once Kotik is born the rest of his story traces the gradual development of his awareness in a world that is only a bit less terrifying than the chaos from which he has emerged. From total confusion and a despairing sense of inadequacy, he gradually progresses to a measure of understanding, a degree of clarity about himself in relation to his surroundings, even to something like self-assertion; he learns to observe, appreciate, and disapprove—he begins, that is, to discover preferences and to establish values.

This is not easy. He must learn to distinguish not only between himself and others but also between himself and the very space around him, between his body and all that is outside his body. Here is how the first moment of the break between inward experience and the outside world is recorded in Kotik's awakening consciousness:

Darkness slipped away from me (the way skin slips off a young snake); sensations separated from skin, slipped under the skin . . . the skin seemed like a vault to me: as space appears to us; my first perception of it is that it is a corridor. Subsequently our corridor appears to me as a memory of the time when it served me as my skin.

(*Kotik Letaev*, 1922, p. 26)

The vague, "imageless," prenatal, and infantile experiences gradually cluster around perceptions of the world in a wonderful tangle of associated impressions: there is his nursery, and behind it there is a hole that passes into another hole, an oven's mouth, and between the two holes there is a confusion of mingling, interfusing, changing images, "a current of driving images." Among these there is "an extremely long reptile, Uncle Vanya, who crawls out from behind . . . bewhiskered, serpent-legged" and who is later split in two: one part of him comes to dinner and the other appears on the cover "of an extremely useful book, *Extinct Monsters*," where it is called "dinosaur." Then, out of the jumble, human beings begin to appear and take form: members of the family—grandma, Aunty Dottie, a cousin—and servants—Afrosinia the cook, Dunyasha the maid, and so on. Next appear friends, colleagues, and acquaintances. And all of these—the apartment on the Arbat with its rooms and furnishings, the view of Moscow from its windows, the people who live in it or visit it—all are the setting for a drama that is the focal point of the story: the rift between the child's parents and its traumatic effect on him.

Stroke by stroke, portraits of the Letaevs emerge: the father, kindly and absentminded, a brilliant, world-renowned mathematician, a respected and beloved professor, eccentric in manner, uncouth in dress, and quite phenomenally ugly of face; and the mother, a capricious beauty who loves luxury, is bored and unhappy at home, dislikes her husband, and resents his influence on their son. (As we learn from other sources, these are largely accurate representations of Professor Nikolay Vasilevich Bugaev, Bely's father, dean of the Faculty of Science at the University of Moscow, and of his wife, Alexandra Dmitrievna.) To Kotik the father is at first a formidable presence. In enormous galoshes he flings out the front door, and on the wings of his unbuttoned raccoon coat he sails through the sky like a huge comet toward that distant star called "University," which is somehow related to the universe for Kotik. Later he sees his father as a quick-eyed, stocky, bespectacled man who bursts into the dining room from a passage that leads into another world "to talk awhile, to live with us awhile"; he is a man who says, "Mathematics is the harmony of a sphere. The chasuble of the world oscillates according to the form of inflexible laws: along it roll the stars," and who sometimes recites poetry and improvises doggerel verses of his own. But, Kotik explains, "we do not listen to Papa. We live our own life, Grandma, Mummy, and I." And Mummy does not find Papa's verses amusing: "I see Mummy's glance turned on Papa, Grandma straightens her kerchief, Mummy straightens her dress; my Mummy is like a picture. . . . I am not happy when I see Mummy's glance turned on Papa."

The child loves his parents equally but differently. He loves his father when, "pushing up the sparkle of his glasses onto his wrinkled, rounded forehead" and bending down his "gigantic face," he takes the boy's small hand into his big palms and "from his mustache-bearded mouth" blows warmth into his sleeve and murmurs "something about the sky: it is a sphere, the harmony of an incomparable cosmos is in it, stars roll on it in accordance with laws of a heavenly mechanism." Kotik also loves him when he reads from a thick little book "about Adam and Eden, about Eve and the tree, about earth, and of good and of evil," and when, before flying off to the university, he whispers: "Kotinka, repeat after me, my dear, Our Father, which art in heaven. . . ." The boy repeats this, hoping Mummy will not wake up to hear him: "I love my Papa very much, but he teaches me, and

it's a sin for me to learn—(this I know from Mummy)."

But Mummy is still asleep. When she wakes up she will summon him, will lift him onto her bed and rumple his hair, and he, in delight, will turn somersaults like Almochka, her puppy, pretending that he too is a puppy, slyly wagging his tail with a hand at his back. She will laugh and call him "Baby" and pat him as she pats her little dog. He loves these games with her and loves to turn somersaults to amuse her. But he also loves to think, and thinking is not allowed. Mummy complains that Papa is ruining their child, "developing him prematurely. Imagine: showing the alphabet to a five-year-old! A big-headed boy. He'll grow up to be another mathematician!" Sometimes she kisses him, then suddenly starts crying and pushes him away. "He is not like me, he is like his father," she says, and there is talk about "the Letaev foreheads, noses, chins, and slanting eyes." The boy is in disgrace because of his "Letaev forehead."

And is it his fault that he knows that the earth is a sphere and that thunder is "an accumulation of electricity"; that he can point out "prehensile-tailed monkeys, marsupials, sloths in the zoological atlas"; that he has heard from Papa about "differentials and integrals"; and that he knows that Papa corresponds with Jean-Gaston Darboux and that Henri Poincaré is fond of him? "I am not allowed to talk with Papa; if I do, Mummy will say, 'Well, he is prematurely developed,' " and premature development is something monstrous and abnormal. He is afraid that Papa is developing him *prematurely,* that this may have happened already, and that he is turning into "a second mathematician." He has become "a mathematical dot" at the point of intersection between Papa's and Mummy's ideas on the upbringing of children, and he sees this as his fault: "I sin with Mummy against Papa, I sin with Papa against Mummy. What can I do not to sin!" "You are not Papa's, not Mummy's," he decides, "you are your own, and you are alone." Therefore he decides he will not talk at all with anyone or will "invent what to say." And so, he explains, "I concealed my thoughts until a very late age, and in school passed for a fool: but at home I was 'Kotik,' a pretty little boy in a frock who stood on all fours to wag his tail for everybody."

Luckily, there is Raissa Ivanovna, the governess who has replaced his nanny. "Dearest Raissa Ivanovna!" She understands him, allays his nightmare terrors, brings into his life moments of blissful peace. The chapter devoted to her is the only one of simple happiness in the entire book. But Aunty Dottie and a gossipy neighbor mumble darkly about "people taking the child away from the mother," about "unnatural caresses," about a stranger "worming her way into the house." And Raissa Ivanovna is dismissed. The boy is disconsolate. The days that used to be all "radiant holidays" are ordinary weekdays now. He searches for Raissa Ivanovna "under the pillow, under the couch, under her armchair," and on walks in the city he thinks he sees her on the street, at the counter of a store, walking on the boulevard, sitting down on a bench. He rushes to her, but none of these ladies is Raissa Ivanovna.

Kotik Letaev was written in 1915–1916 in Dornach, Switzerland, where Bely was working on the construction of Rudolf Steiner's "Johannesbau" (John's Temple). *Kreshchenyi Kitaets* (The Baptized Chinaman, 1927), its sequel, was written in Soviet Russia in 1920–1921. In this novel the character Kotik is at a later stage of his development. He has passed through the slow and painful process of emergence from the crepuscular, confused, and terrifying condition of an indefinite being without consciousness or identity and has become a distinct, recognizable entity in a world that is still puzzling and hostile but not wholly inchoate and impenetrable. There are now discernible shapes in its vastness and glimpses of light in its darkness. The objects he now discerns are in focus, and the persons he meets are real. "The novel," Bely said, "is half biographical, half historical" with "ac-

tual, existing persons" mentioned in it by name and drawn from life. However, the historical part—a sketch of Moscow, particularly of its intelligentsia at the end of the nineteenth century—provides the setting but is hardly the theme of the novel. The theme is the growth of Kotik's mind.

His life is now less terrifying, but it is still very strange and in some ways more difficult. For now that he sees his parents more clearly and appreciates each of them more deeply, it is harder than ever for him to choose between them, to know how to behave, and to decide which of their conflicting values and ideas to adopt for himself. Their disagreements have become more pronounced and intense. The child understandably feels sorry for himself, but his story is as much about his parents as about himself and is a tribute to them both. The essence of Bely's future work is here: the roots of his beliefs and tastes, the characteristic modes of reasoning that he later develops, the intellectual presuppositions on which his writings are based before and after the creation of Kotik Letaev.

When speaking of his mother Kotik makes lavish use of diminutives (in which the Russian tongue is wonderfully rich) to evoke a feeling of protective tenderness inspired by her exquisite beauty. He speaks of her delicate, chiseled *little* nose, her *small* mouth, the *barely perceptible* dimple on her skittish chin, and so on:

If she laughs, dimples will show. A plump little lip will be lifted and little teeth will appear. Little eyes, screwed up, will peep through the flapping bridal veil of lashes and emit two small sparks; the little head, bent to one side, will be covered in thickets of luxuriant chestnut hair.
(*Kreshchenyi kitaets*, p. 87)

When his mother plays the piano, the boy is transported into another realm: "She has become so little, so darling. . . . Shyly she walks over sounds, on tiptoe, a little girl . . . gracefully, in vivid gradations, in gestures of musi-

ANDREY BELY

cal scales: from the singing of birds, to a scream, to a tiger. . . . I enter this life." Beneath her small fingers, across the piano's "little black bones," roulades of bright crystals drop to the floor, are gathered and strung on the thread of a scale; a delicate starlike note is driven forth from a windfall of peals ringing out in a forest; another star "stars" out of the first, and the stars are fragmented in trills, treble showers of brilliance; they hammer once more on a rocky base, and joyously clanging, they bathe stony chords in bubbling foam; then the clear contours of the roulade are dimmed in the haze of the pedal.

As he tries to convey his experience of music Kotik's prose becomes rhythmic, lyrical, occasionally rhymed, and profuse in images of nature: water, sky, and land. This, Bely would have us know, is the most that words can do with the flowing harmony of sounds; the world of music, never to be made explicit in words, can only be hinted at in the pictorial symbols that it suggests, or faintly echoed in rhythmic gestures and cadenced speech. "Passing is time, but heavy is time, it mumbles of days that were given; and resounds for us in our ears, in our hearts." This sentence, repeated like a refrain, is as close as one can come to defining the province of music, its major theme or concealed "meaning," which, if it exists at all, is sensed only in the depths of consciousness.

Something resembling a lesson does emerge from the mother's playing: "Between the treble and the bass, a suffering, human voice is stifled" and "perishes without a trace—I cry." He watches his mother as her eyes turn emerald (in Bely's idiom they "emeraldize") and skip from the bottom of the page to the top of the next: "I stand, I look: I fall in love! This is poison; this is sweet Renaissance poison, where one comes forth in action, observes decisively, loves and destroys not by rules but in sounds; a life that is not at all moral—but musical." Such is the Mummy whom Kotik loves, the enchanting young beauty, the playmate with whom he laughs, romps, and rolls on the floor. "All the bright light I live by is Mummy in me."

His father is "father-grandfather . . . father-friend," a large-headed gnome with a Scythian profile, "a most absurdly constructed head . . . a head with a very, very big, protruding forehead and deep-set, small, very slanting, Tartar-like eyes, piercing as arrows." Kotik loves his very ugliness, his awkwardness and eccentricity, his absentmindedness, self-forgetfulness, and unassuming simplicity; he loves him for the way that, on the street, in his shabby overcoat, he looks more like a ragged hoodlum than a celebrated scholar, for the helpless way with which he meets his wife's indifference and hostility, and for his beliefs, his principles and rules. In sum Kotik loves him for everything that contradicts, point by point, all that, as the child can see, irritates and infuriates his mother—all that, in his eyes, she lives by and stands for.

Papa reasons, explains, and expounds, and Mummy is so bored with his talk that when he steps out of his study with a volume of French philosophy in his hand, she sits down at the piano, and Papa, to whom music is noise and harmony is revealed not in sounds but in numbers, retreats to his room with the thick tome in which "the light of reason is explained." "The vague, the immeasurable, he pushes away from him," and for hours on end he contemplates the minute. A tiny fly delights him: "You know," he says, "a fly is like a small bird, a splendid little machine." He also loves to argue and is known as "a great squabbler" among his colleagues. This is how Kotik describes him after a violent argument:

He leans back, become wholly kind, brightens up, and sits peacefully—in great tenderness—just like this, for no rhyme or reason; large-headed, bespectacled, with a fallen lock of hair across his forehead, leaning to the right, sideways, one shoulder lowered, slanting somehow; his hands, quite becalmed, thrust under the cuff; he has shouted his fill, and now sits quietly—in great tenderness—just like this, for no rhyme or reasons, smiles brightly, most gently—to himself and to everything that is.

(*Kreshchenyi kitaets*, p. 21)

With this affectionate portrait Bely begins the chapter on his father in *Na rubezhe dvukh stoletii* (On the Border of Two Centuries, 1930), the first volume of his nonfictional autobiography, thereby erasing any possible doubts as to the identity of the fictional Professor Letaev and the real Professor Bugaev.

Kotik watches a casual encounter between father and mother and reflects, "Oh, no—never will they truly understand each other, but I—I do understand." The conflict between them intensifies. The mother grows hysterical, has tantrums, and makes life difficult for everybody. Professor Letaev apologizes for her: "Mummy is ill," he says. But finally even his forbearance gives way. One day after she has refused, despite many quiet requests, to let him work in peace, Professor Letaev drives her out of the room with a threat and a terrible banging of metal on metal that he knows she cannot tolerate. Kotik falls ill, has frightful nightmares, and screams in his delirium.

How is he to cope, how is he to choose between these beloved, antagonistic persons? He cannot choose, and, an innocent young Hegelian, he intuitively finds another solution: not choice but fusion, a reconciliation of opposites. Despite all their differences, his parents, he perceives, are similar, almost identical, in one fundamental respect. He sees his mother as the beautiful, hunted fox in a picture he knows, who, with bared teeth, has turned on a pack of baying hounds—she is an exotic, gifted, wild creature, trapped among the mean-minded conformity of dull professors' wives who dislike her, who in "wry-mouthed malice" reduce her at times to tears, and who frighten Kotik as well. His Mummy is at bay, fighting for her life. Papa alone, that wise old Chinaman, is able to transform the deadly women on the Arbat into Fates and their pompous meanness into the lofty quietude of Lao-tzu. But this philosophical transformation is not one that the brilliant, wild creature can accept.

But Papa too is an "innocent victim" enmeshed in the pettiness of daily life; solitary, he is ridiculed for his eccentric simplicity, for his "complete atrophy of professorial grandeur," for his nonconformist treatment of all human beings as equals. Simple people adore him—the floor polisher, the cook, the cab-driver—but to most academics this simplicity seems debasing. "You know," they sneer, "Professor Letaev must be already affected by softening of the brain." What the boy implies is that however irreconcilable their disagreements, his father and mother are united in a greater incompatibility, their conflict with the world they live in. And even more significant in the light of Bely's development is his perception that their very different kinds of knowledge are, in their deepest implications, the same—that both mathematics and music reach out far beyond the circumscribed, immediate experiences of life to the illimitable possibilities of some transcendent reality and ineffable truth. Bely's mind was engrossed in such truths and realities throughout his life. From first to last, his spiritual history appears as a series of infatuations with whatever or whomever seemed capable of showing him the way to the supernal truth, the universal harmony, in the existence of which he believed passionately and which he hoped to discover through a succession of ever-widening syntheses: of science and art, of art and philosophy, of philosophy and religion.

In *Na rubezhe dvukh stoletii* Boris Bugaev's life is continued, but this time as his own story, not as Kotik Letaev's. And at the start the story is intensified with added particulars to an almost Dostoevskian drama of fear, cruelty, and humiliation. Fearing to provoke his mother's fury by a show of learning, he answers his father's questions nonsensically (a stratagem his father does not understand); he plays the fool, and as pretense turns into habit, he becomes convincingly a fool—frightened, speechless, tongue-tied, unable to answer the simplest questions, provoking the general opinion that "Bugaev's son is a little idiot." Only in the last years of school, when he is sixteen and seventeen, does he manage with considerable difficulty to tear off this mask of idiocy. When he is seven his mother decides to take her son's education upon herself and sets out to give him grammar and piano lessons. Predictably, they are a disaster. Angry and impatient, she brings the boy to a state of helpless terror, hits him, drives him away in tears, and then obliges him to beg for another lesson. Each day he longs for night to come and falls asleep dreading the next day. He believes himself to be an utter failure; there is no one in whom he can confide, so he becomes inured to silence. "From five to eight," Bely writes, "is a period of such profound pessimism that, later, Schopenhauer's philosophy seems but an echo of the past."

Then, when he is eight years old, the "quarantine" from his father is partially relaxed, and he is allowed to teach the boy once more, though still under threat of his wife's displeasure, so that the boy prepares his lessons timorously, afraid of bringing on another harrowing confrontation. Next, in the spring of 1889, a worthy successor to Raissa Ivanovna makes her appearance: Mlle Bella Ruden, an ideal governess under whose tutelage the boy regains confidence in himself. In school he is inspired by a teacher of genius, Lev Ivanovich Polivanov, and he also finds "a second home" with a family whose influence on his life is next only to that of his father and Polivanov. These are the Solovyovs: Mikhail Sergeevich, brother of Vladimir Solovyov, the most renowned of Russia's religious philosophers and a poet; his wife, Olga Mikhailovna, a person well versed in the arts, sympathetic to new trends, and herself an artist; and their son Sergey, five years younger than Boris. "From 1895 to 1903," Boris visited the family and sat at their "round tea table opposite Olga Mikhailovna, Serezha opposite Mikhail Sergeevich," talking and arguing about art and literature, philosophy and religion. Bely's enthusiastic portraits of the persons he admires are detailed, appreciative, splendidly vivid. His memoirs are full of them, but they are counterbalanced by the equally entertaining portraits

in another vein, the brilliant satires of those he dislikes.

At home, meanwhile, his mother discovers that her Borya understands music. She takes him to symphony concerts and the opera. They share "a wild passion for Wagner," he introduces her to Edvard Grieg and other modern artists, and they read Anton Chekhov, Henrik Ibsen, Gerhart Hauptman, and Maurice Maeterlinck together and attend performances of the Moscow Art Theater. She wonders at his taste and supposes that the Solovyovs have had much to do with it. This makes Professor Bugaev uneasy: he distrusts the artistic interests of the Solovyovs and fears that they will turn his son away from science. "They are sick people, Boren'ka," he says, "and the philosopher Vladimir Solovyov, although unquestionably gifted, is also sick. Yes, you know, he has hallucinations." In Grieg and Richard Wagner Professor Bugaev "hears only noise, in the Moscow Art Theater he detects a cult of 'neurosis.' " He considers that art can be understood only by one "who devotes himself to the study of art history and of 'scientific' aesthetics" and is distressed by the very thing that makes his wife rejoice, that Boren'ka is not likely to become another mathematician after all.

But when his father reminds him that he must soon decide on his course of study at the university, Boris, prepared for the question, replies, "I've already thought of this, I'd like to take up the natural sciences." (What he does not tell his father is that he has decided on an eight-year program, four in the Faculty of the Natural Sciences, then four in the Faculty of Philology.) His father is radiant. He is pleased with his son, his conversations with him on scientific matters are redoubled, and he slips him books to read: "Thus, at home, a new covenant is inaugurated with my parents: talk about science with my father and about 'new trends' with my mother."

Now he embarks on a period of frenetic study. "In the summer of 1899, preparing for the university, I surround myself with piles of books, textbooks, and very serious works" and

ANDREY BELY

am "already entranced by . . . the philosophy of
the exact sciences." He has a purpose in mind:
"With all my interest in the sciences and facts,
I set myself the goal of mastering a method for
interpreting facts in the spirit of a world outlook, built on two columns: one, aesthetics,
the other, natural sciences; the problem of the
world outlook—the coordination of two lines."
This creates what Bely calls "the problem of
the scissors." At home his "covenant" is a
bridge over the gap between science and art,
with a diplomatically attained safe-conduct
that gives him freedom of passage from the one
to the other. But now he is determined to
achieve something more: he wishes to unite
science and art in the synthesis of a transcendent metaphysics.

This ambitious project was in keeping with
the extravagantly hopeful mood of young intellectuals at the turn of the century, a drastic
change from gloom to high expectancy, as Bely
describes it in *Vospominaniia o A. A. Bloke*
(Reminiscences of A. A. Blok):

In 1898 and 1899 one listened to the shift of
winds in the psychic atmosphere: before 1898 a
north wind blew under a grayish sky. *Under the
Northern Sky* is the title of [Constantine] Balmont's book; it reflects the closing nineteenth
century; in 1898 a different wind blew; one
sensed the collision of winds from the north and
the south, and as the winds mingled, fogs appeared, fogs of consciousness.

In 1900–1901 the atmosphere cleared; under
the caressing sky of the twentieth century's beginnings we saw all things differently; Balmont
sang, "We shall be like the sun." And [Alexan-
der] Blok, subsequently recalling these years in
the line "And dawns, dawns, dawns," characterized the mood that had seized us.

(*Epopeia*, 1:31 [1922])

Pessimism, fatalism, and dogmatism were giving way to hope, will, and free inquiry. For Bely
the philosophies, the concepts, and the artists
he had but recently found most attractive—
Buddhism, Nirvana, Arthur Schopenhauer, Edward Burne-Jones, Dante Gabriel Rossetti—

were fading away, to be replaced by others who
diffused an optimistic sense of infinite possibilities and high idealism, of strength, activity,
and aspirations instead of lassitude and despair. There was, of course, Vladimir Solovyov,
and then suddenly there was "the one great
book" that at this juncture "resounded like
thunder," Friedrich Nietzsche's *The Birth of
Tragedy* (1872). "The period from the fall of
1899 to 1901 is primarily adorned for me by
Nietzsche," Bely explained. He read and reread
his works, *Thus Spoke Zarathustra* (1883–
1891) was always at his side, "and the old was
separated from the new; and with different eyes
we looked on the world in 1900–1901; pessimism became tragedy; and our conscience experienced a catharsis, perceiving a cross in the
intersection of lines." "The border of two centuries" was an epoch like that at the beginning
of Christianity: "Antiquity, sunk in the night,
was illumined by the light of a new consciousness; nights mingled with light; and beneath
'northern skies' souls were irradiated in the
colors of dawn." The highly colored idiom of
this passage is also in keeping with the taste
of the times and is especially characteristic
of Bely.

Historically, then, 1901 marked a distinct
break with the past. All the themes that before
1901 were muted or furtively voiced now rang
out in the open, and those that at the end of the
century sounded loud and clear were now uttered on the sly. And for Boris Bugaev, a sharp
turn in his personal biography coincided with
that of history. In 1901 he came of age; at the
Solovyovs he was transformed from the little
boy Borya to a member on equal terms with the
adults at their "round tea table." Finally, 1901
was the year when "Andrey Bely" appeared.

That spring Borya Bugaev read to the Solovyovs parts of a long work he had been composing. "You are a writer!" said Mikhail Sergeevich
in his habitually quiet way, and he undertook
to have the work published. But now, so that
Professor Bugaev might be saved embarrassment, a pseudonym was essential. Borya suggested "Boris Burevoy," that is, "Boris the

Stormy," but Mikhail Sergeevich laughed, pointing out that "Burevoy" would be read "Boriy Voy" ("Borya's Howl"), and he suggested "Andrey Bely," which means "Andrew the White." Thus, wrote Andrey Bely, "the Solovyov apartment bound me to authorship. In 1901 I hesitated. What am I? Composer, philosopher, biologist, poet, literary critic? I believed in the 'critic,' even in the 'philosopher,' more than in the 'writer.'" The Solovyovs decided for him.

The work that impressed them was *Simfoniia* (Symphony, now referred to as The Second Symphony, 1902), subtitled *Vtoraia, dramaticheskaia* (The Second or Dramatic). *Severnaia simfoniia* (Northern Symphony), subtitled *Pervaia, geroicheskaia* (The First or Heroic), was written earlier but published later, in 1904. *Vozvrat: Tret'ia simfoniia* (The Return: Third Symphony) was published in 1905, followed by *Kubok metelei: Chetvertaia simfoniia* (The Goblet of Blizzards: Fourth Symphony) in 1908. The Symphonies are curious compositions, neither poetry nor prose, written in lines of strongly marked rhythm that periodically break into rhyme. In the first two Symphonies the lines, varying in length from one word to twenty and more, are numbered and grouped in sections, also of different lengths; and the whole composition is divided into parts, the Third Symphony into three and the others into four, of which those of the Fourth Symphony have titles, like the chapters of a novel. The themes of all four are abstruse, the characters visionary, the settings dreamlike; events take place in infinity and eternity, and the lines, with their marked, rhythmic beat, have a hypnotic effect. The First Symphony, for example, begins:

1. A large moon swam along torn clouds.
2. Now here, now there, heights arose overgrown with young birches.
3. Bald hills were visible, covered with stumps.

What are the Symphonies about? Composed of moods, dreams, and fragments of experience, they are fantasies that do not lend themselves to summary descriptions. The recognizable places, people, and things glimpsed now and then in the background are permeated with a sense of hidden meanings as much as the visionary settings and personages are. But if the Symphonies are conundrums that admit of various solutions, they may be seen as a whole, perhaps, as images of the great antinomies that the young Bely had set out to reconcile. On this assumption, the First Symphony, with its medieval, pre-Raphaelite, fairy-tale setting, could be seen as a dramatization of good and evil; the Second—a complex tissue of mundane and supernatural events, of abstruse speculations, of satire and vision—could be interpreted as a discourse on religious and intellectual error, on the failure, indeed, of most attempts to understand reality; the Third—in which myth and reality are blended—might be viewed as a representation, in a conflict between soul and mind, of the inadequacy of reason to answer basic questions about life; and the Fourth, the most intricate of all, would appear to be a tangled metaphor of elemental nature in its most turbulent contrasts of rage and peace—an image of passion and a characterization of profane and sacred love.

In his first year at the university Bely was performing a wonderful balancing act on the blades of his wide-spreading scissors. With his right hand he wrote the Third Symphony, in which his hero, a young scientist, is presented as being driven mad by his work in a laboratory, while with his left hand he performed experiments in the very laboratory that he was describing as a madhouse. And his performance was even more remarkable than this, for Bely was also developing his theory of symbolism in a series of articles that were published in journals between 1902 and 1909 and then in three collections, *Lug zelenyi* (The Green Meadow) and *Simvolizm* (Symbolism) in 1910 and *Arabeski* (Arabesques) in 1911. They are a presentation in expository form of the world view that the Symphonies express in the form of art and of the kernel of

ANDREY BELY

the philosophy that Bely continued to elaborate and expound.

These articles do not make easy reading, partly because their theme is innately difficult, partly because they were written in too great a hurry, and possibly also because their author loved obscurity. Their dazzling display of erudition is not always convincing or necessary. But in the opinion of Steven Cassedy, who has translated and analyzed several of these essays (including some of the most difficult ones), their difficulty does not arise "from Bely's lack of clarity concerning his terms and arguments," as is generally supposed, but rather "from poor writing and organization." Ironing out the confusions and convolutions of Bely's style, Cassedy has shown, notably in his analysis of the central essay, the tortuously argued "Emblematika smysla" ("Emblematics of Meaning"), how Bely reaches his desired goal, the all-embracing synthesis that he was always seeking, the kind of knowledge, beyond the capacity of science to provide, that will "console us and explain the puzzles of our existence to us." This was knowledge of what Bely called the "Symbol Embodied," which he placed at the apex of a diagram designed to illustrate how the antinomies of science and art, cognition and creation, are resolved in a supreme unity in which "*all* ages and *all* nations" are as one. This is "the universal generative force," according to Cassedy's summary, "on which symbolism both as an aesthetic movement and as a worldview is based, the force that in the future will overcome all time and permit men to experience past, present, and future all at once."

Whatever one may think of Bely's theory in itself, in his intellectual history it is an important chapter, for it represents a resolution of the art versus science discord that burdened and obsessed him. He had found a way of coping with the "scissors," could now shut and open them at will. In 1909 "The Emblematics of Meaning" was first published, and this is also the year in which Bely argued that aesthetics could be "an exact science" and in

which, in a number of essays devoted to a study of the meter and rhythm of Russian poetry, he laid the foundations of the new science of poetics. The year 1909 was also when his first novel, *Serebrianyi golub'* (*The Silver Dove*), appeared in serial form.

But to understand this novel, we must turn back to the period that followed 1901–1902. The happiness of that "year of dawns" was short-lived. In the winter of 1903 Mikhail Sergeevich Solovyov succumbed to a lingering illness, and Olga Mikhailovna killed herself on the very night he died. In the spring there was another death, Professor Bugaev's. Boris had just completed his university course in the Faculty of Science and was planning to go with his father on a trip to the Caucasus. After the funeral he and his mother went down for the summer to their country place, "Silver Well." Bely brooded, took solitary walks, wrote many lyrics, and read philosophy, principally Immanuel Kant, in whose "tangle of ideas" he was caught like a fly in a spider's web. Struggling to work free of Kant's "iron tracery," he got more and more embroiled in it and did not manage to extricate himself until years later. Meanwhile he endured a kind of double life consisting of "the ecstasy of lyric foam and the fiber of spidery ideas." New "scissors" kept materializing: on the one hand a sense of his own "suffocating wisdom" and on the other an "ironic sneer" at himself as "a mere poet." The scissors that had been closed in 1901 spread apart again in 1903, and he suffered the rationalist conviction that a poet was "no sage."

He also wrote letters to Alexander Blok, continuing a correspondence that had started in January of that year, when, in what seemed to Bely a symbolic act of fate, their first letters crossed in the mail. They had heard about each other through the Solovyovs and knew each other's writing before they met. Olga Mikhailovna and Alexandra Andreevna, Blok's mother, were cousins and friends. They kept each other informed about their gifted sons, and Sergey Solovyov, who worshiped his cousin Sasha, would bring to the round tea table the still unpublished poems that he received from Blok. Bely was startled when he heard them: here was another symbolist poet who felt as he did and held the same interests and beliefs. Their correspondence opened with expressions of admiration. Blok had just read Bely's "Formy iskusta" (The Forms of Art), the first of his theoretical essays. "Your article is brilliant," he wrote. "It is frank. It is a 'song to system' for which I have long been waiting." And Bely wrote:

> In your poems one sees a positively unbroken continuity. It is as if [Mikhail] Lermontov, [Afanasy] Fet, Solovyov had laid their hands on you in blessing. You are continuing their work, you illuminate, reveal their thought. . . . I will tell you frankly, for me your poetry pushes into the background nearly all contemporary Russian poetry.
>
> (*Perepiska*, p. 7)

Some remarkable letters followed. By no means confined to panegyrics, they contained poems, discussions of ideas, criticism of each other's work, and—especially on the part of Bely—revelations of recondite experience.

They were "soul-brothers." Both were devoted to Vladimir Solovyov's idealism, his cult of the Divine Sophia as the soul of the universe and embodiment of divine wisdom. Just as Blok's poetry came to Bely as a "shock of recognition," so Solovyov's philosophy and poetry came to Blok as a confirmation of his own beliefs. Spiritual affinity was not, in these cases, a matter of influence but rather the corroboration of independent, individual perception and experience. In the history of Russian literature their names are always linked as major figures in the symbolist movement. But they were very different, as both men and artists. Their friendship turned out to be tempestuous, with violent breaks and reconciliations, protestations of devotion, and challenges to duels. And their quarrels had as much to do with ideology as with emotional involvements. Temperamentally, Blok was more realistic, more restrained, more independent. Although they were the same age—Blok was just one month younger than Bely—Bely looked up to him as to an older brother. Intellectually Blok could not tolerate abstract theorizing; Bely lived in it. Blok's visions were firmly grounded in his experience, Bely's were escapes from it or transformations.

They met in 1904, and their friendship, with all its convolutions, continued to the end— that is, until Blok's death in 1921 and the superb memoir that Bely wrote of him immediately afterward. His *Vospominaniia o A. A. Bloke* (Reminiscences of Alexander Blok, 1922–1923) is one of his best works. And the five years following their meeting were exceptionally important for Bely. As he wrote many years later in *Nachalo veka* (The Beginning of the Century, 1933):

> At a distance . . . the year 1904 seems very dark; it stands for me as the antithesis of the year 1901. . . . From 1904 to 1908 I felt that the ground was slipping away from under my feet. I did little creative work; contacts with people took up all my time, hour-long conversations, the reading of theoretical works.
>
> (pp. 410–411)

In the autumn of 1904 he became a student in the Faculty of Philology at the University of Moscow, where he was required to take courses in modern and ancient philosophy, Greek, Latin, and Russian history. Books, stuffed with slips of paper marking pages needed as reference for seminar reports, were heaped high on his desk, gathering dust. He had no time for them. Every evening there was a meeting to attend, a review or article to write. He wanted, "no matter what," to write a "Theory of Symbolism," all the while feeling with annoyance that he was not prepared to do so: "The youthful swoop of the year 1901 into all realms of culture ended in the terrible groan and moan of a fallen aviator, who only in 1909 began slowly to recover from the ideological mutilations he had inflicted on himself in 1904."

These, of course, were the years of the Russo-Japanese War and the Revolution of 1905. They were also the years of Bely's infatuation with Blok's wife, Lyubov' Dmitrievna Mendeleeva, the "Lady Beautiful" of her husband's celebrated poems. On 9 January 1905, known in Russian history as "Bloody Sunday," Bely happened to be in St. Petersburg, visiting the Bloks. His memoirs contain graphic accounts of this day and of later days that year when he "rushed through the streets of Moscow in 'revolutionary' fashion" without clearly understanding, until sometime later, what "the year was all about." His quarrel with Blok, he wrote in *Mezhdu dvukh revoliutsii* (Between Two Revolutions, 1934), the last volume of his memoirs, was "linked with the theme of revolution, with thoughts about all kinds of terrorist acts. . . . The revolution and Blok in my fancies are in inverse proportion to each other; the farther I departed from Blok the more was I filled with social protest." The painful involvement with Lyubov' Dmitrievna led him to flee abroad at the end of 1906. (He and the Bloks had agreed not to meet for a year.) Returning to Moscow the following March, Bely plunged into a life of frenzied activity: writing, lecturing, engaging in bitter literary polemics. That summer he finished his Fourth Symphony, "The Goblet of Blizzards," which he had started before his departure and worked on while he was abroad. It was published in the spring of 1908, and Bely sent a copy to Blok, who wrote him, in acknowledgment, that he found it "blasphemous," "incomprehensible," and "profoundly alien" to him in spirit. "You write," he said, "that this Symphony is the sincerest of all: in that case I don't understand you at all, shall never understand, and no one will understand." To this Bely replied that since they could not understand each other, he was "liquidating" the complexity of their relations by "breaking them off" altogether.

"The six years from 1905 to the end of 1910," Bely wrote in explanation of the title "Omut" (The Slough) for the first part of *Mezhdu dvukh revoliutsii,* "is the passage through a slough of a man sucked into it, a passage through years of reaction, through the most bitter experiences of his personal life, through disappointment in people. . . ." In these gloomy years of national defeat, broken hopes, and apprehension about the future, Bely's depression was part of a general unhappiness. The state of Russia was a prime topic of debate among intellectuals—Russia's history, Russia's fate, Russia's position between East and West. Some talked of "Eastern occultists who were working through the subconscious of Russians to unleash 'wild passions beneath the yoke of a waning moon,'" as Bely put it. His second book of poems, *Pepel* (Ashes, 1909) was filled with realistic sketches of a poverty-stricken countryside and dismal city streets. But it had a bad press, and Bely was seized by "something like persecution mania." Furthermore, he wrote of this time, "it seemed to me that we were all of us mixed up, that we lacked real experience of life, that some kind of hostile forces were consciously destroying us; I lived with a sense of an approaching occult peril." This was a feeling characteristic of the period, and it was propelling numbers of Bely's friends toward occultism and theosophy, a doctrine of religious mysticism based on a belief in the power of direct psychic participation in the Divine Essence. He too began to read Annie Besant and Helena Blavatsky's *The Secret Doctrine* (1888) and to attend meetings of a theosophical circle, attracted to it by its atmosphere of peace.

In 1909 Bely was on the verge of a nervous collapse. At one lecture session he lost control of himself, shouted insults at a speaker, was persuaded to apologize, and was then taken away to a friend's estate, Bobrovka, where, waited on by an old deaf-mute servant, he stayed in a large, ancient house with a well-stocked library of occult literature. There he began writing the novel *The Silver Dove.*

This novel became the first volume of a trilogy on the theme of East and West. One may read the book in this light, as an allegory of Russian society, provided that East and West are understood in terms of cultural trends, the West standing for cultural progress and the East for regression. The theme crops up in discussions that take place in the novel and even in its geographical design (most of the action occurs in a village situated between a regressive town to the east of it and a progressive though flawed estate to the west). But although such an allegorical reading is possible and although all that was distressing in the atmosphere of the day is present—the general mood of depression, the sense of loss, the presentiment of insidious, occult dangers and of peril from the East—the novel is not so much a comment on society as a fairy-tale version of "The Goblet of Blizzards," that tangled chronicle of passion and deadly entrapment which according to Bely himself objectified the haunting sense of persecution from which he suffered. Current ideas, tendencies, and perceptions were stamped on Bely's mind as on a sensitive plate, but his art is not a record but a transformation of them in terms of his own private experience. So in *The Silver Dove* the prevalent notions of Russian intellectuals in the first decade of the twentieth century are concentrated in the person of the hero, Pyotr Daryalsky, who, with a few traits borrowed from Sergey Solovyov, is one of Bely's unmistakable self-portraits, while the heroine, Katya, is also modeled on a real person, Asya Turgeneva, who "appeared on Bely's horizon" in the spring of 1909 and a year later became his "life's companion."

A poet and university student, Daryalsky has spent the past two summers with a friend in a rented cottage in the village of Tselebeyevo so as to be near Katya, whom he loves, but also to become better acquainted with Russian peasants, for he believes that the salvation of Russia lies with them. He makes a point of talking with the villagers, dresses in peasant costume, and attends their church services. But to them—that is, to the more sensible and mature among them—he is a puzzle. The girls find him attractive, but the men think him pretentious and affected, and some of them wonder if he might be a student agitator trying to stir up trouble. As for himself, Daryalsky is both drawn to the villagers and afraid of them. "In the forest thickets of the people" he senses something glorious and something sinister. In his third year in the neighborhood he and Katya are engaged, and he stays with her at Gugolevo (west of Tselebeyevo), the estate of her grandmother, the Baroness Todrabe-Graaben.

The story opens as he walks to Tselebeyevo to go to church. It is a warm, sunny Trinity Sunday, and all is well with him, but for some unfathomable reason he feels anxious and depressed. On the way he stops by a pond to look at the sky. It is noon, and the sky is a pale blue, but when he looks at it closely it turns completely black. (This is an observation taken directly from an experience of 1904, when for the first time Bely spent several summer days with the Bloks at Shakhmatovo, their family estate. It was a memorable visit, and on one occasion Blok pointed out to Bely this disquieting heavenly phenomenon.) Daryalsky trembles: some mysterious danger seems to be threatening him from the sky, as it had threatened him before more than once; it is as if some terrible mystery, kept in the sky for ages, secretly beckons to him. He says to himself, "Hey, don't be scared, you're not up in the air; watch how mournfully the water is lapping the planks." Then, as he lowers his eyes from heaven to earth, he sees on the planks a pair of sturdy legs beneath a tucked-up red skirt and a pair of hands doing some washing. The holiday bell is ringing, and the water is so blue that it's indistinguishable from the sky, but Daryalsky is overcome by a feeling of immeasurable sadness like the sadness, he thinks, that unaccountably comes over you in childhood and drags and carries you away while everybody calls you odd, and you, unaware of anything, talk nonsense, and they smile at your talk and shake their heads.

He wonders what is the matter with him, why even the thought of the pleasant day he has just spent in Gugolevo does not cheer him. Doesn't he have everything he wants? "Darling

Katya," he thinks, "my bright one," and as he enters the church, ready to listen to the sacristan and bow down to pray to the Queen of Heaven, he notices in the corner of the church a peasant woman staring at him. She wears a red and white kerchief over a red dress, and her face is pockmarked and browless. He is mesmerized by her hideous stare, "scorched by a wave of inexplicable terror." He grows pale, can hardly stand, and does not hear the service; when he comes to, the mass is almost over. As he goes up to kiss the cross held out to him by the priest, he notices the woman smiling at him. In vain does he invoke Katya, repeating to himself, "My good bride, my kind bride." The incantation does not work. The pockmarked woman awakens in him primordial feelings he has never experienced before, but her face is familiar: it has come to him in childhood, in nightmares.

That day he does not return to Gugolevo, although he knows he is expected there. Instead he goes to the village tavern, gets drunk, and in his drunkenness remembers the past. (What he remembers is very like what Bely remembered about himself, and recorded in *Na rubezhe dvukh stoletii*: his school days, his feeling about his father, and especially his sense of loneliness, of being misunderstood by everyone.) When he emerges at sunset, he catches a glimpse of the red blouse and the red and white kerchief by the cottage of Kudeyarov, the village carpenter and chief of "The Silver Dove," a mystic, murderous cult (according to Bely, a prevision of Rasputin), and he sees the woman once again by the pond, where, in a state of drowsy intoxication, he has sat down for a while and has heard, he thinks, the cradlesong his nurse once sang to him. Their eyes meet as he goes away.

Following this, an extraordinary chapter traces his way through the night to Gugolevo, a chapter that is a kind of lyric poem in which he struggles through the woods, now in darkness, now in the light of a faint lunar mist, jumps over an evil-smelling ditch of putrid water, and weaves his way among menacing pine trees and damp, unfriendly ferns that press around him, his every motion echoed by a memory or a resolution it has evoked. This chapter consists of a continuous stream of thought that, in concert with his actions at the moment, re-creates the terrors of his life up to the day when Katya enters it to rescue him:

> Don't confuse me, my agelong, cursed thoughts! (At his back a green eye glared at him unblinking: it was a glowworm.) Never again will I go to the village . . . never again to the temple of God . . . never again look into the eyes of peasant women. . . . You alone, Katya, are my life. . . . Drive away the demon. . . . In the very first moments of my life, there was fear. . . . I waited, and out of the darkness people appeared. . . . A terrible call summoned me from a distance. . . . I waited, I called, but no one came. When I spoke of what I heard in the rustle of trees, no one understood.
>
> (*Serebrianyi golub'*, vol. 1, 1922, pp. 127–129)

But all his protestations, and his love, are powerless against the witchery of the demonic group into whose clutches he has fallen through the expert help of the pockmarked woman, their instrument, the evil witch of this horrendous fairy tale. He is eventually destroyed by the very people whom he admires in theory, and it will not do to explain his fate as the price he must pay for having made the wrong choice among them. For the point of the story is that he cannot and does not choose, that he is manipulated by some brutal, supernatural, inexorable power that even worshipful prayers will not appease.

Stylistically the book derives from Nikolay Gogol. Indeed, anyone familiar with Gogol's prose might be excused for thinking that he is reading some newly discovered tale of Gogol's when he first comes upon the introductory description of Tselebeyevo: "A fine village is Tselebeyevo, not far from town; amid hillocks it is, and meadows; its little cottages are scattered about here and there, richly adorned in patterned carving like the curly-headed face of a regular lady of fashion." Or such a reader might think that he has encountered another one of Gogol's hymns in praise of Russia when he reads the meditation on the Russian soul provoked by Daryalsky's mysterious experience:

> Where has Pyotr gone? What has happened to him? Never, nowhere, nothing like this has ever happened to him before. Nowhere, never, nothing like this is ever dreamed of anywhere except Russia. But here among these simple, unsophisticated folk, all this is dreamt. Russian fields know secrets as Russian forests know secrets; in those fields, in those forests bearded peasants live and multitudes of peasant women. They have few words, but instead they have a surplus of silence; come to them and they will share this surplus with you; come to them and you will learn to be silent; you will drink in those dawns that are precious wines; you will nourish yourself on the scent of pine tar. Russian souls are dawns; strong, resined are Russian words; if you are Russian, you have a beautiful secret in your soul and like sticky resin will be your soul-flung word; it is not showy but it will stick, and its spirit is beneficent and pleasant.
>
> (*Serebrianyi golub'*, vol. 2, p. 93)

Over the years Bely had assimilated Gogol; the inmost sounds of Gogol's prose had become his own. But while the music of the prose is Gogolian, the story, as a whole, is not; its plot, "meaning," and psychology are more intricate and obscure, more sophisticated, and less amusing than Gogol's. This is not a drama of Russia in the dismal years that obscured the radiant dawns of 1901 but a drama of Bely's pilgrimage through his own "slough of despond" between 1905 and 1910. *The Silver Dove* appeared serially in *Vesy* (The Balance) in 1909 and in book form the following spring. Blok, in a lecture of 8 April 1910 on "The Present State of Symbolism in Russia," called it a "work of genius." Bely, delighted and touched, wrote a warm letter. Blok answered in kind, and after two years a reconciliation took place.

In looking back over these years, Bely saw his stay at Bobrovka as "the watershed" be-

tween two periods of his life: 1901 to 1909, a time of transition from pessimism to "the problems of Vladimir Solovyov" and symbolism; and 1909 to 1916, which led from "symbolism as a method of describing experience in images to the symbolism of secret knowledge, the path of self-knowledge." The first of these was the period of the Symphonies and of attempts to "establish the grounds" of symbolism; the second was the period of the novels, and of anthroposophy, a doctrine derived by Rudolf Steiner from theosophy and like theosophy a conglomerate of diverse mystic teachings from ancient to modern times: Greek, Indian, Jewish, and Christian. The chief difference between them was that theosophy emphasized Indian mysticism, anthroposophy Christian gnosticism and a mystic interpretation of natural science. It was also the time of Asya Turgeneva, the prototype of Daryalsky's Katya and a major influence in the next stage of Bely's spiritual development.

For several years, as fascination with the occult, especially in the aspect of theosophy, continued to intensify among his close friends, Bely too was increasingly drawn into it. At Christmastime in 1908 he had a vision: two old men came toward him in a boat and he heard, "We are on the threshold of a tremendous spiritual upheaval." A friend to whom he described this event was so shaken that the two of them resolved thenceforth "to harken to the *premonitions* arising from the coming brotherhood of Spirit." About this time also Bely read a book by Steiner, about whom his friends were talking. "What a boring man!" he thought. But a few years later, at a meeting of theosophists, a lecture was read that set his head spinning as from "a kind of revelation," "a storm" of light. The author, he was told, was Steiner, and Bely decided in amazement that "the boring man" could write things that even Vladimir Solovyov had not so much as dreamed of! He managed to acquire other Steiner lectures, those composed not for the general public but for small esoteric groups, and by the beginning of 1909 Bely "turned to him in profound reverence."

919

Now it appeared that Turgeneva and her sisters were also impressed by anthroposophy. In 1910 Bely spent July and August with her in Bogolyuby, "in the loveliest little house separated by a shady grove of oaks from the house where the Turgenevs settled (that is, Campioni, the forester of the region, Asya's stepfather, her mother, and sisters Tanya and Natasha)." Turgeneva, dainty and delicate in appearance but very strong in spirit, resolute and independent, might have served as model for Ivan Turgenev, to whom she was distantly related. (There is an engaging portrait of her in Marina Tsvetayeva's memoir of Bely.) That summer, perched in the branches of a splendid oak, she and Bely talked for hours about Russia, about the soul, and about spiritual knowledge, and they decided to join forces in building a good life. At the end of the year they left Russia on a trip to Italy, Sicily, Tunis, and Turkey—a journey recorded in Bely's *Putevye zametki* (Travel Notes, 1921). They returned in 1911.

That summer, again in Bogolyuby, "strange things" began to happen. There were sounds that could not be accounted for: rumblings of invisible wagons, knocks, sparks, whispers, the tramping of bare feet when no one was around, and so on. Subsequently, Bely referred to it as "the summer of thundering silence." In 1912 he and Turgeneva went to Brussels, where the marvels increased. He described them to Blok in a long letter that recounted the "epic" experience they had lived through; its hero was Rudolf Steiner, and its outcome was a devoted consecration to him and his cause. They became his disciples, "students, first grade, of a strict, esoteric professor," working on his assignments and following him wherever his lectures took him. For a whole month, Bely wrote, they lived "in complete isolation in a little village in the mountains." Time passed in learning German, preparing reports, studying the "doctor's" lectures, meditating, and writing. Had they found what they were seeking? "Yes, yes, and yes! . . . Limitless horizons opened out . . . clarity about oneself terribly increased. . . . Everything transformed . . . everything in a new light."

At this time Bely was at work on the novel that in his 1910 preface to *The Silver Dove* he had promised his readers. He had said that most of its characters would appear again in the sequel and that the theme of East and West would be further developed. But as the writing progressed *The Silver Dove* faded away. The new novel asserted its independence and evolved its own set of characters. In 1911 almost half of it was written, but its first complete version appeared in the journal *Sirin* in 1913–1914, as a book in 1916, and in revised form in 1922. This novel was *Peterburg* (*Petersburg*), Bely's best-known creation and, as is generally acknowledged, one of the most remarkable works of modern prose fiction. (Ivanov-Razumnik's *"Peterburg" Belogo*, 1923 [reprinted as *Belyjs "Peterburg,"* 1972], is a detailed history and comparative analysis of its several versions.)

The historic time of the novel is specifically indicated, its events taking place between 30 September and 9 October 1905. It is not, however, as one might reasonably expect, a chronicle or an analysis or a dramatic enactment of this year of revolution, nor even a meditation on it, although some of its aspects are noted in a general, almost abstract, way: there is mention of peasants dropping their harrows and wooden ploughs and setting their landlords' colonnaded houses on fire; of a strike in the outskirts of the city; and in the city, of a talkative, generic kind of personage with a Browning pistol in his pocket and a shaggy cap pulled down over his eyes, thrusting leaflets into people's hands. But the focus of the story is an individual crime, a potential parricide; and everything that happens is involved, in one way or another, with the preparation for this crime and the aftermath of the attempt.

What of the theme of East and West? It is present here, but in a more complicated and less schematic form than in *The Silver Dove.* It protrudes in all kinds of ways: in the Oriental origin of the central characters, the Ableu-

ANDREY BELY

khovs, father and son, with their slanting eyes and Tatar name, and in the symbolism of their coat of arms; in the yellow color that reappears constantly with an implicit cultural or racial significance and is associated with the frightening Mongol face of a madman's hallucinations; and, on a more superficial level, in the taste of fashionable society for Oriental dress and furnishings. But the signals are mixed; the Ableukhovs, for example, despite their Tatar origin, represent both East and West. And most important is Bely's specific definition of "Mongolism." For him and also for Blok, he explained in his memoirs, "Mongolism" had a special meaning, not political but cultural, moral, and religious. Its threat was apocalyptic; it symbolized the dragon of the Book of Revelations. By "Mongolism" in *Petersburg* he had in mind "the substitution" of a dark, mechanical, soulless, statistical, reactionary conservatism for "a revolution of spirit and creativity." Revolution was the injection of new energy into mankind, which energy, however, without a "spiritual shift of consciousness" unleashed "wild passions" in the individual and, in society, "a riot of retrogression."

If renewed, beneficent energy is the meaning of "revolution," then the terrorist act that is the core of the plot is not revolutionary but its opposite. Nikolay Ableukhov, son of the powerful, reactionary Senator Apollon Apollonovich Ableukhov, is suddenly called upon to fulfill the promise that thoughtlessly, not to say frivolously, he made years ago and has by now quite forgotten: he had pledged to commit whatever act the group with which he has allied himself demands of him when they are ready for it. What they demand of him now is that he murder his father. Now, although relations between father and son are not exactly cordial, although the father thinks his son a scoundrel and the son has a like opinion of his father, beneath their antagonism there is a deeply concealed but genuine, profound, mutual affection. Nikolay Apollonovich does not desire his father's death. But the time bomb has been delivered, he himself has inadvertently set it in motion, and the novel takes its frantic course as the infernal mechanism ticks away the moments toward a dreadful and unwanted doom. It is a waking nightmare that encloses other, actual nightmares, like those of the pathetic, mad conspirator, Alexander Ivanovich Dudkin, the pitiful tool of the terrorist group, who delivers the bomb to Nikolay Ableukhov and who, ill, feverish, and delirious, is subject to frightful visions. The most chilling of these, a phantom of Nemesis, is that of Peter the Great, who, having descended from the bronze monument that dominates all Petersburg, comes lumbering up the rickety stairs to his miserable attic room.

Just as the theme of *The Silver Dove* is passion rather than the state of Russia, so the theme of *Petersburg* is terror, not revolution. This is what the novel is about: terror as terrorism, terror as emotion, terror as prophecy. The poet Vyacheslav Ivanov has said that it was moved by "a genuine inspiration of horror"; Osip Mandelshtam excluded *Petersburg* from his denunciations of Bely: the Symphonies and *Zapiski chudaka*, he said, might be false and affected, but *Petersburg* was unmatched by any other Russian writer in its evocation of pre-revolutionary turmoil and anxiety. And Konstantin Mochulsky described it as "a rendition of delirium unprecedented in literature . . . a world—unbelievable, fantastic, monstrous, a world of nightmare and horror, a world of distorted perspectives, of disembodied people and living corpses."

It is indeed a fantasy, but an elaborate one, poetic and philosophic. Its shadowy people "circulating" through the streets of a visionary city are something other than fairy-tale ghosts; they are projections of a metaphysical idea. At the end of the first chapter we read:

We have seen in this chapter Senator Ableukhov; we have also seen the senator's idle thoughts in the shape of the senator's house, in the shape of the senator's son, with his own idle thoughts in his head; we have seen finally another idle shadow—that of the stranger.

921

> This shadow came into existence by chance in the consciousness of Senator Ableukhov, received there its ephemeral being, but the consciousness of Apollon Apollonovich is a shadowy consciousness, because he too is the possessor of an ephemeral existence and the result of the author's fantasy—an unnecessary, idle, cerebral game.
>
> (*Peterburg,* vol. 1, 1922, p. 74)

Bely has created these illusions, has hung them up and ought to take them down, but he will do no such thing; he has every right not to remove them. For Apollon Apollonovich, even though only a figment of the author's brain, still has the power to terrify "with another, staggering existence that attacks in the night," and as long as he is alive, with his thoughts about the stranger, "the stranger will not vanish from the avenues of Petersburg" because "thought itself has a life of its own." And so, as the stranger pursues the senator and is himself trailed by a pair of black shadows, so too, says Bely, addressing the reader, will the aging senator stalk you at your heels: "He will, he will . . . and you will never ever forget him."

What is this? Is Bely amusing himself with a bit of innocent fun? Yes and no. The fun is there, but it is not innocent. He is, of course, boasting about the power of art: he has hung up frightening illusions and will not take them down; you will never forget them, and they will terrify you for the rest of your life. But if art is illusion, so is everything that usually passes for reality. The senator's house, the senator's son, the stranger who appears at the window of his carriage—all these exist by virtue of the senator's mind, are creations of his idle thoughts; and yet his consciousness itself is invented. Reality is in the mind, and what seems to be reality is but the shadow of ideas. This is why "the streets of Petersburg possess one indubitable quality: they change people to shadows"; and this is why Bely's city is an eerie phantasmagoria through which shadows, not people, "circulate." A few, like the Ableukhovs and Dudkin, are singled out and fleshed out sufficiently to become representations, caricatures, or dreams. And Bely's semi-humorous exposition of philosophical idealism—Vladimir Solovyov's, the symbolists', and Steiner's—is as uncanny and disturbing as anything that happens in the story.

But in the background, and permeating the whole, is the unshadowy reality of Russian literature. Every chapter bears as epigraph a quotation from Alexander Pushkin, and *The Bronze Horseman* (1833) dominates the whole. But Gogol's *Nevsky Prospect* and the "misty," "unreal" Petersburg of Feodor Dostoevsky's *Crime and Punishment* (1866) are also there in hints and echoes. And there is one page of grandiose rhetoric in which Pushkin and Gogol are united.

In *The Bronze Horseman* Pushkin identifies the steed of the monument with Russia, ruled by the iron curb of its rider Peter the Great, the builder of Petersburg, and made to rear on the brink of the abyss. "Where," he addresses it, "dost thou gallop, haughty steed? And where wilt thou plant thy hoof?" In this tragic poem Petersburg, Peter's magnificent creation, has been devastated by a flood. It remains, however, and will be rebuilt, but in the confrontation between man (Peter) and nature at their mightiest, the ordinary, unassuming individual, Pushkin's hapless little clerk, Yevgeny, is crushed. The question Pushkin poses is a question of victims and heroes, of power and justice, of values and the price of grandeur. Gogol asks Russia a similar but different question in the celebrated "galloping troika" pages that bring to a close the first part of *Dead Souls* (1942): "Russia, where art thou flying? Answer! She gives no answer. In wonderful ringing the little bell exults; the air, torn to shreds, thunders and becomes wind; everything flies past, everything on earth, and looking askance, other nations and governments stand aside and make way for her."

And now Bely, addressing Pushkin's Horseman but in the rhythms and style of Gogol, fuses their invocations in exalted rhetoric:

Thou, Russia, art like the steed! Into darkness, into the void, thy forehooves have plunged, and firmly planted in granite soil are thy rear hooves. Dost thou wish to break loose from the rock that holds thee as some of thy witless sons have broken away from the soil? Dost thou too wish to break loose from the rock that holds thee and hang in the air, unbridled, and then plunge down into the watery chaos? Or, perhaps, thou wouldst fling thyself, cleaving the mists, through the air, to vanish in the clouds along with thy sons? Or, having reared up, art thou sunk in meditation for long years, oh, Russia, on the stern fate that has thrown thee here into this gloomy north where the sunset itself is many-houred, where time itself lurches now into frosty night, now into radiant day? Or, frightened by thy leap, shalt thou once more set down thy hooves and carry, snorting, thy great Horseman into the depths of spacious plains, away from illusory lands?

May this not be!

Once he has reared and measured the air with his eyes, the bronze steed will not set down his hooves. There will be a leap over history; great shall be the tumult, the earth shall be cloven; the very mountains shall fall in the mighty tremor; but our native plains will rise in humps from the tremor; on the humps will appear Nizhny, Vladimir, and Uglich.

But Petersburg will sink.

All the peoples of earth, in those days, will rush forth from their places; there will be mighty warfare, unheard of on earth. Yellow hordes of Asia, moving from their age-long places will redden the fields of Europe in oceans of blood. This will be, this will be! There will be Tsushima! There will be a new Kalka!

Kulikovo Field, I await you!

And on that day the final Sun will glow over my native land. If, oh Sun, thou shalt not rise, then oh Sun, beneath the heavy Mongolian heel the shores of Europe will sink and foam, will twirl over these shores; earthborn creatures will sink once more to the floor of oceans, into primordial, long forgotten chaos.

Arise, oh, Sun!

(*Peterburg*, vol. 1, 1922, pp. 130–131)

The differences in these three eloquent addresses are interesting. Pushkin's is the most rational, specific, and humane, concerned with the fate of "the little man" in a world of power, and it is characteristically undogmatic in its unresolved, discordant sympathies: admiration of grandeur and pity for its victims. Gogol's is a patriotic song of unqualified pride and exultation in a people's strength, recklessness, and exuberance. Bely's is a warning and a prophecy, and in its historic references to victories and defeats there might seem to be an echo of his day's racial prejudices. For Pushkin Russia is a government, for Gogol a nation, for Bely—if his definition of "Mongolism" is accepted and the historic references interpreted in its light—an idea. Thus we pass from the specific and concrete to the general but still earthy to the purely cerebral—which is emblematic of some striking changes in intellectual attitudes from the early nineteenth century to the early twentieth.

In February 1914 Bely and Turgeneva moved to Dornach, in Switzerland, to work together with other devoted anthroposophists under Steiner's supervision on his "Johannesbau," which they themselves designed and built by hand. Years later in *Zapiski chudaka,* the third of his autobiographical novels, Bely described their life there in glowing terms as a period of love, friendship, exaltation, and intellectual excitement. But in his letters at the time, notably in one to Blok in June 1916, the picture is very different: it describes states of profound depression and exhaustion; bone-chilling cold in winter, both at home and at work; and the equally destructive spiritual chill of suspicion, enmity, and malice on the part of co-workers. His posthumously published *Vospominaniia o Shteinere* (Reminiscences of Steiner, 1929) provides a very good idea of the man himself and of the nature of his influence. For Bely he seems to have been a combination of teacher, father, religious guide, and psychiatrist. His emphasis on self-knowledge must certainly have encouraged Bely to indulge his gift of introspection; it was in Dornach that *Kotik Letaev,* the first of his autobiographical works, was written. War shattered the peace of Dornach; the sound of cannons booming in Alsace could be heard there. And in 1916 Bely was ordered back to Russia for military service. Turgeneva did not go with him.

For the next six or seven years Bely's life was very difficult. He was not taken into the army, but the reason is not entirely clear; he had declared himself a pacifist, and then the revolution doubtless interfered. Like Blok Bely "accepted" the revolution, but unlike Blok he refused to be disillusioned and was for this reason accused by many former friends of accommodating himself to the regime at the price of his ideals—which is unfair because his ideals were so ethereal and abstract that, given a few provisos, anything in the matter of human affairs could be harmonized with them in perfect honesty. As always, he worked furiously, probably overworking himself: he had a hand in various cultural enterprises, lectured constantly at the Anthroposophical Society in Moscow and at the Free Philosophical Association, of which he was a founder, contributed to the last symbolist publications, *Alkonost* and *Zapiski mechtatelei* (Notes of Dreamers), continued the study of prosody on which he had been engaged since 1910, and wrote three long essays in cultural history: *Krizis mysli* (The Crisis of Thought, 1918), *Krizis zhizni* (The Crisis of Life, 1918), and *Krizis kul'tury* (The Crisis of Culture, 1920). In 1920 he wrote a long narrative poem, *Pervoe svidanie* (*The First Encounter,* 1921), a lively, witty reminiscence of his student days; it is the best of all his poems, an outstanding work by any standard and, in Russian literature, often ranked among the highest.

But living conditions were becoming ever more unbearable. In the terrible winter of 1920–1921 he sustained a back injury and spent ten miserable weeks in a lice-ridden hospital. Permission to leave the country was denied several times but was finally granted in the fall of 1921, soon after the death of Blok in

August. Bely went to Germany and stayed there two years, mostly in Berlin, where there were many Russian émigrés, whose accounts of Bely at this time picture a man on the verge of madness. Nevertheless, he managed to write a prodigious amount—among other things *Vospominaniia o A. A. Bloke* and *Zapiski chudaka,* which he had started in 1918 and put aside.

Zapiski chudaka is meant to be a story of insanity, like Gogol's *Notes of a Madman* (1935). It is a mixture of involved, turgid, wearisomely cadenced prose, the diary of the writer Leonid Ledianoi (Leonid the Icy), who, like Bely himself in 1916, is traveling in wartime from Dornach to Moscow by way of England and Scandinavia. His thoughts are a jumble of reminiscences, laments, impressions, and elaborate pseudo-philosophic meditations. He calls up the image of "Nelly," whom he loves and who is not with him, thinks he is constantly spied upon, and broods over the nature of his own identity. He thinks of himself simultaneously as a great martyr and a pitiful victim, a Christlike figure. But alternating with the bombast and confusion there are pages of genuine humor, fine description, and excellent satire. In a 1923 review that must be one of the most cruel ever written, Mandelshtam denounced the book as tasteless and fraudulent. He did not know that at the time of writing Bely was almost literally "beside himself." (Parts of the work were published as a separate book called *Vozvrashchenie na rodinu* [Returning Home] in 1922.)

Friends in Moscow, learning of his state, elected one among themselves to go to his rescue. This was Klavdiya Vasileyeva, a good friend whom he had often met at the Anthroposophical Society, of which she was an active member. For the rest of his life she stayed with him, marrying him when it became clear that Turgeneva would not return and when Vasileyeva's husband agreed to a divorce. What we know about his last years comes almost entirely from her. Her reminiscences have been published in the original Russian (*Vospomi-*

naniia o Belom, 1981) with an introduction and notes in English by John E. Malmstad, who pays her a heartfelt tribute as a devoted, understanding person. She surrounded Bely with "the harmony and comfort that he had so much missed his whole life long." (These words belong to the poet and critic Vladislav Khodasevich.) Her unassuming, truthful, self-effacing book throws an equable and gentle light on this gifted, complicated man; in it he appears as something other than a wild eccentric.

They lived primarily in Kuchino, a place in the country not far from Moscow. Bely's writing continued to be as prolific as ever and his plans as ambitious. He wrote novels, memoirs, criticism, literary theory, and travel sketches, and although his imposing plans were not all completed, some of his best works belong to this period, the most important among them being his three volumes of memoirs, which conclude with his departure with Turgeneva for Italy; two volumes of a projected four-volume historical novel; and *Masterstvo Gogolia* (The Art of Gogol, 1934). He died on 8 January 1934.

The long novel was to be a history of the Communist revolution. The completed volumes were *Moskva* (Moscow, 1926), consisting of two parts, *Moskovskii chudak* (The Moscow Eccentric) and *Moskva pod udarom* (Moscow Under Siege), and *Maski* (Masks, 1932). In a preface to *Moskva,* written in 1925, Bely proffers "a few explanatory remarks": the novel, he said, described the "demoralization" of prerevolutionary life in the form of "satiric caricatures," and "in the person of Professor Korobkin, a scholar of worldwide importance," it depicts the "helplessness of science in the bourgeois regime." Five years later Bely described *Maski* as a picture of corrupt Russian society in the fall and winter of 1916 as it had impressed him after a four-year absence abroad. The third volume, he explained, would be about the revolution and part of the period of "military Communism"; the fourth would portray "the end of the NEP [Lenin's "New Eco-

nomic Policy"] and the beginning of the period of reconstruction." This was his intention, he said, but "intention is not execution." "He who intends thinks mechanically, cerebrally, quantitatively," but in the process of writing, this abstract "quantitative" way of thinking becomes "qualitative"; a cerebral "abstract construction" is, "so to speak, boiled down" to a "qualitative" expression in images. He could not therefore make definite predictions about the outcome, but in general, in the third and fourth volumes "the author hopes to show his heroes in the synthesis of the dialectical process, which takes place in each of them in his own way." The second volume is "antithesis," in which "Hamlet's question of 'to be or not to be,' . . . of how to live in such a rotten world, . . . is brought to a head by the author." The first volume is thesis, the second antithesis; synthesis must follow.

Obviously Bely was acquiring a new Marxist vocabulary to describe his own creative experience, in which, as in *The Silver Dove* and *Petersburg,* the finished work turned out to be a "boiled-down," "qualitative" version of the original, abstract intention. What these last two novels are is not entirely clear. Their characters are not allegorical figures or metaphysical shadows like those of *The Silver Dove* and *Petersburg.* Still less can they be called "realistic." "Grotesque caricatures" would perhaps be the best label. The plots, in twists that create suspense, suggest detective stories and contain episodes of hideous sadism, like the torture of Professor Korobkin in *Moskva.* When Bely was asked why he wrote such scenes, he replied that they express his own suffering. It would seem that he was feeling his way in a new society that he admired, or persuaded himself that he admired, one in which he hoped one day to feel at home. The society appeared to him to be idealistic, its communal spirit friendly and democratic, and he was studying its attitudes, language, and behavior. But life in it was very difficult and he suffered.

About the merits of the book on Gogol there can be no question. It is a brilliant piece of literary criticism of which Konstantin Mo-chulsky wrote appreciatively:

> There is something profoundly symbolic in the fact that during the last years of his life, Bely turned to Gogol, his faithful guide, teacher, and inspiration. The author as the writer of *The Silver Dove* and *Petersburg* is indebted to Gogol for everything. And his best book before his death is the gift of reverent and grateful love.
>
> (*Andrey Bely,* p. 269)

This gift is an exhaustive study of Gogol's technique, a definition of his unique quality. It is a kind of funnel-shaped study that begins with a broad classification of Gogol's work into three phases that correspond to three stages of his life; continues with a close comparison of major works representative of these three phases; proceeds to specific studies of Gogol's use of color, sound, gesture, rhythm, and perspective; then analyzes verbal effects such as retardation, repetition, parallelism, hyperbole, and comparisons; moves on to the role of verbs, adjectives, and nouns in the sound and structure of his sentences; and finally discusses the sounds of letters and of syllables. At every stage the analysis is explicit and minute. But Bely introduced this book as no more than a gathering together of raw materials that, he hoped, might be useful as "an introduction" to the elements of "Gogol's poetic grammar." This modest claim is a measure of his devotion to Gogol. Not a word of his escapes him. He seems to know Gogol by heart. It is almost as if he had transformed himself into Gogol.

Unavoidably, then, one learns from his analysis almost as much about himself as about his subject. The work is a summation of Bely's views on art, a demonstration of how his theories can be applied, and an expression of his beliefs and tastes. He admires Gogol because of his originality, which is organic because his creative process is like "the circulation of the blood"; because his works, nourished by this creative process, are like fingernails that may be snipped but continue to grow and "can never be completed"; because his prose is "volcanic,"

his sentences "explosive"; because his stories are music, "story-songs"; because "Gogol is not only a writer, but a composer of melodies"; and because "a word for Gogol is like a raisin or a pebble thrown into water; it draws from the water a musical sound, and forms rings—ring after ring." The "scissors blades" of Bely's university days are here sharper than ever and are brought together most expertly: exact science is here an instrument of minute, accurate observation used to reveal the deeply concealed inward essence of art, the *music* of words, images, and colors.

"Organic originality"—this is the key to Bely's thought and writing. "Originality," provided it is not just external, artificial, or merely novel, but "organic," is the essence of art for Bely; it has to be an expression of the individually true, which cannot be a copy or an imitation. Bely demanded "organic originality" of himself, looked for it in others, and was its champion and defender against traditionalists who opposed all new trends and also, in his own case, against nontraditionalists who tagged him with the labels of new schools to which he did not belong: "decadence" at first, "formalism" at the end.

He was a symbolist, and symbolism did not espouse pessimism and decay, nor did it prize the external, formal aspects of art above all others. Symbolism, he explained time and again, was not a school of art but a way of life. He himself never "became" a symbolist but was born one, he said in a booklet composed in 1928 and posthumously published in 1982, *Pochemu ia stal simvolistom* (Why I Became a Symbolist). If a work of symbolism seemed incomprehensible, it would become familiar as soon as the right approach to it was pointed out. "The impressionists," he argued in his preface to *Maski,* "were not understood until someone whispered: this is the way one must look at them; from that moment, *suddenly* they became comprehensible." And hinting at the right approach to his own work, he whispered some suggestions about it: he wrote not for the eye but for the ear; his prose was really not prose but poetry and was printed in prose only to save space. *Maski* was "a big epic" written in anapests.

Years before Bely had insisted that the whole of *Petersburg* was built on sound, on one ominous, humming sound—"OOOO-OOOO-OOO"—that is heard all through the novel, and on other sounds with specific meanings: "l-k-l-pp-pp-ll, where k is the sound of stuffiness, pp-pp—stiflingness, the pressure of the walls of the Ableukhovs' yellow house . . . ," and so on.

> "No, you're inventing!" "But if you please, was it *I* or not *I* who wrote *Petersburg*?" "You—but you yourself are making an abstraction of it." "In that case I did not write *Petersburg*; there is no *Petersburg*; for I won't let you take my child away from me; I know it to a degree you've never even dreamt of."
>
> (*Literaturnoe nasledstvo*,
> vols. 27–28, *Simvolizm*, p. 453)

It would be wrong to dismiss these claims as sheer fantasy and exaggeration. They are in accord with Bely's metaphysics, which, like his prescriptions for art, was not just a system of ideas but the very structure of his perceptions and emotions. He seems not only to have believed but also to have lived on the assumption that the world is an idea (most often his own idea). Of this we can find ample evidence in his interpretations (or misinterpretations) of art, of people, of events. Nevertheless, in all his opinions, criticisms, and mistakes there is a wonderful consistency. Creatures of earth are interesting to him only in their significance as measured against an ideal of supreme excellence, wisdom, and beauty, and are judged in their relation to ultimate truth—which is ineffable. There is praise for unspoken, intuitive wisdom—the "surplus of silence" of Russian peasant folk, the "secrets" of Russian fields and forests; for music, which is the greatest of the arts because it is farthest removed from the circumscribed, the definable and material;

and for the *how,* whether in living or in art, rather than the *what.*

In these presuppositions Bely is very far removed from the Russian realists of the nineteenth century, whose realism depends on attitudes to life so foreign to him that he can misunderstand them completely, as he misunderstood Anton Chekhov, for example. Russian realism depends on respect for the individual person, the individual instance, and the concrete material object as they are in themselves without ascription of "meanings," without abstract conceptual frames being necessary to make them interesting. This was a pluralistic view of life that Bely could not understand at all. In his ardent praise of Chekhov it is not Chekhov he praises but his own ideas that he reads into Chekhov, twisting characters and events to his own purposes in order to appropriate him for symbolism. The realists identified themselves with the characters they created. Bely distanced himself from his creations and looked on them from the long perspective of some ethereal being not of this earth. He wrote not about human beings but about human attributes and feelings, and he created arrangements and images of life: not characters but caricatures; not representations but outlines of living; not life at specific moments of history but life in the light of infinity and eternity. And in this respect his contribution to literature is in keeping with a dehumanizing tendency in much of twentieth-century art, which is characterized by a shift of emphasis from mimesis to fantasy, abstraction, analysis, and pure design.

Selected Bibliography

EDITIONS

INDIVIDUAL WORKS

POETRY
Zoloto v lazuri. Moscow, 1904.
Pepel. St. Petersburg, 1909.
Urna. Moscow, 1909.

ANDREY BELY

Khristos voskrese. Petrograd, 1918.
Pervoe svidanie. Petrograd, 1921.
Posle razluki. Berlin, 1922.
Zvezda. Petrograd, 1922.

FICTION

Simfoniia: Vtoraia, dramaticheskaia. Moscow, 1902.
Severnaia simfoniia: Pervaia, geroicheskaia. Moscow, 1904.
Vozvrat: Tret'ia simfoniia. Moscow, 1905.
Kubok metelei: Chetvertaia simfoniia. Moscow, 1908.
Serebrianyi golub'. Moscow, 1910. Reprinted as 2 vols. in Berlin, 1922.
Peterburg. Moscow, 1916; rev. ed. in 2 vols., Berlin, 1922. First published serially in the journal *Sirin,* 1913–1914.
Kotik Letaev. Petrograd, 1922.
Zapiski chudaka. Berlin, 1922.
Vozvrashchenie na rodinu. Moscow, 1922. Includes parts of *Zapiski chudaka.*
Moskva. Moscow, 1926.
Kreshchenyi kitaets. Moscow, 1927.
Maski. Moscow, 1932.

LITERARY CRITICISM AND PHILOSOPHY

Lug zelenyi. Moscow, 1910.
Simvolizm. Moscow, 1910.
Arabeski. Moscow, 1911.
Rudolf Shteiner i Gete. Moscow, 1917.
Na perevale I: Krizis zhizni. Petrograd, 1918.
Na perevale II: Krizis mysli. Petrograd, 1918.
Na perevale III: Krizis kul'tury. Petrograd, 1920.
Glossolaliia: Poema o zvuke. Berlin, 1922.
O smysle poznaniia. Petrograd, 1922.
Poeziia slova. Petrograd, 1922.
Ritm kak dialektika i "Mednyi Vsadnik" Pushkina. Moscow, 1929.
Masterstvo Gogolia. Moscow, 1934.

AUTOBIOGRAPHICAL WORKS

Ofeyra: Putevye zametki. Moscow, 1921.
Vospominaniia o A. A. Bloke. Published in four issues of the journal *Epopeia.* Berlin, 1922–1923.
Veter s Kavkaza. Moscow, 1928.
Na rubezhe dvukh stoletii. Moscow, 1930.
Nachalo veka. Moscow, 1933.
Mezhdu dvukh revoliutsii. Leningrad, 1934.

Pochemu ia stal simvolistom. Ann Arbor, Mich., 1982.
Vospominaniia o Shteinere. Paris, 1982.

CORRESPONDENCE

A. A. Blok—Andrey Bely: Perepiska. Moscow, 1940.

TRANSLATIONS

Complete Short Stories. Translated by Ronald Peterson. Ann Arbor, Mich., 1979. Includes "We Await His Return" (1906), "The Bush" (1906), "The Mountain Princess" (1907), "Adam" (1908), "The Yogi" (1918), and "A Man" (1918).
The First Encounter. Translated and introduced by Gerald Janecek. Notes and comments by Nina Berberova. Princeton, N.J., 1979.
Kotik Letaev. Translated by Gerald Janecek. Ann Arbor, Mich., 1971.
Petersburg. Translated, annotated, and introduced by Robert A. Maguire and John E. Malmstad. Bloomington, Ind., 1978.
Selected Essays. Translated and edited by Steven Cassedy. Berkeley and Los Angeles, 1985. Includes "The Emblematics of Meaning."
The Silver Dove. Translated by George Reavey. New York, 1974.

BIOGRAPHICAL AND CRITICAL STUDIES

Alexandrov, Vladimir E. *Andrei Bely: The Major Symbolist Fiction.* Cambridge, Mass., 1985.
Bugaeva, K. N. *Vospominaniia o Belom.* Edited, annotated, and introduced by John E. Malmstad. Berkeley, Calif., 1981.
Christa, Boris. *The Poetic World of Andrey Bely.* Amsterdam, 1977.
Cioran, Samuel D. *The Apocalyptic Symbolism of Andrej Belyj.* The Hague, 1973.
Elsworth, J. D. *Andrey Bely.* Letchworth, England, 1972.
————. *Andrey Bely: A Critical Study of the Novels.* Cambridge, England, 1983.
Ivanov-Razumnik, V. R. *"Peterburg" Belogo.* Petrograd, 1923. Reprinted as *Belyjs "Peterburg."* Munich, 1972.
Janacek, Gerald, ed. *Andrey Bely: A Critical Review.* Lexington, Ky., 1978.
Khodasevich, V. F. "Andrey Bely." In *Nekropol.* Paris, 1976.

ANDREY BELY

———. "Ableukhovy–Letaevy–Korobkiny." In *Izbrannaia proza*. New York, 1982.

Kovac, Anton. *Andrej Belyi: The "Symphonies" (1899–1908)*. Bern, 1976.

Kozlik, F. C. *L'Influence de l'anthroposophie sur l'oeuvre d'Andrei Bielyi*. 3 vols. Frankfurt, 1981.

Literaturnoe nasledstvo. Vols. 27–28, *Symvolizm*. Moscow, 1937. Pp. 371–456 and 575–638.

Mandelshtam, Osip. "Andrey Bely: *Zapiski chudaka*." In *Collected Works*, vol. 2. New York, 1966.

Maslenikov, Oleg. *The Frenzied Poets: Andrey Biely and the Russian Symbolists*. Berkeley and Los Angeles, 1952.

Mirsky, D. S. *A History of Russian Literature*. New York, 1949.

Mochulsky, Konstantin. *Andrey Bely*. Translated by Nora Szalavitz. Ann Arbor, Mich., 1977.

Nivat, Georges. "Éléments pour une biographie d'Andrej Belyj." *Cahiers du monde russe et soviétique* 15:17–21 (1974).

Steinberg, Ada. *Word and Music in the Novels of Andrey Bely*. Cambridge, England, 1982.

Tsvetayeva, Marina. "Plennyi dukh." In *Izbrannaia proza*, vol. 2. New York, 1979.

Valentinov, N. *Dva goda s simvolistami*. Stanford, Calif., 1969.

Woronzoff, Alexander. *Andrej Belyj's "Petersburg," James Joyce's "Ulysses," and the Symbolist Movement*. Berne, 1982.

HELEN MUCHNIC

ROBERT MUSIL

(1880–1942)

EVEN TODAY, Robert Musil's *Der Mann ohne Eigenschaften* (*The Man Without Qualities*, 1930–1943) may be said to be a unique novel in that its hero is usually engaged in the stationary act, so hard to portray in novelistic form, of thinking. Musil, by way of the narrator's commentary, remarked as much and used vast portions of the novel, his major literary achievement, to satirize what he believed were the many "wrong forms" that thinking could take. By contrast, the remainder of the novel is devoted to following his protagonist's attempts to discover what a "real" structure of thinking might resemble, an endeavor heavily fraught with irony, euphoria, and despair. Musil's preoccupation with characterizing the various forms of thought and the intensely original poetic means he used to render these stationary, purely interior states within a fictional narrative constitute, in large measure, his contribution to and extension of the novel form into the modern period.

Musil was born on 6 November 1880 in Klagenfurt, Carinthia, Austria, the son of Alfred Musil and Hermine, née Bergauer. Alfred, an engineer of Austrian descent from a bourgeois family of military officers, civil servants, and professionals, held a variety of academic and administrative posts as a civil engineer, eventually winning the chair of mechanical engineering at Brno. Biographers have characterized him as a rather remote, pedantic, and timorous man from whom Musil

inherited the habit of scientific precision in the observation of technical processes and a tireless drive in researching, writing, and publishing. Hermine, whose family was of Bohemian descent, has been characterized as hysterical, temperamental, and overtly sensuous and is said to have given Musil a poetic sense of fantasy and possibility. In a sustained and explicit triangle unusual for the day, Hermine appears to have taken a lover, Heinrich Reiter, who moved in with the Musil family in 1880 and stayed for the next forty years. Alfred bore this stoically throughout their marriage.

Robert was an only child; a sister, Elsa, died four years before his birth. The theme of the mourned and rediscovered sister plays a major role in *The Man Without Qualities* in the story of the separated and then rediscovered sister Agathe. As an adult, Musil recalled his childhood as one filled with moody, melancholy states of brooding and inactivity.

Musil attended military boarding schools, including the Mährisch-Weisskirchen Academy in Moravia (now Czechoslovakia), which Rainer Maria Rilke had attended several years earlier. Both Rilke and Musil wrote about the brutality and humiliations they suffered at the hands of older boys at the school. Weisskirchen, commonly thought to be the model for the boarding school at which the fictional Törless' adolescent homosexual experiences take place, was in reality a much more savage environment than that depicted in Musil's early novel, *Die Verwirrungen des Zöglings Torless* (*Young Törless*, 1906). Biographers have characterized the place in a manner not unlike George Orwell's description of boarding school in "Such, Such Were the Joys" (1952); they have described it as a spartanly uncomfortable and disciplinarian institution whose filthy conditions filled the adult Musil with a lasting revulsion and perhaps accounted for his lifelong obsessive personal cleanliness and fastidious attention to dress.

At seventeen, after one year at the Military Academy of Technology in Vienna in 1897, Musil changed his course of study from military training to civil engineering and returned to Brno to study. In Brno he began attending lectures on literature, went to the theater and the opera, and began to record his thoughts and literary impressions in the diaries he maintained throughout his life. Offered an assistantship in mechanical engineering at the Technical Institute in Stuttgart, he accepted, but, having published two papers on engineering topics and having patented an improved design for a color wheel (a device used in visual psychology testing), Musil again became dissatisfied and turned to the study of philosophy. He spent mornings in the study of philosophy, and, tired and unreceptive by afternoon, he took up writing out of boredom. Out of the residue of his philosophical studies he began *Young Törless*. It was published in 1906 to critical, though not popular, acclaim.

Between 1903 and 1908 Musil undertook a program of philosophy and experimental psychology, at that time a single course of study, at the University of Berlin; this provided the intellectual basis for his later writings. He studied with Carl Stumpf, who conducted research in perception and to whom Edmund Husserl later dedicated his *Logische Untersuchungen* (*Logical Investigations*, 1900–1901). Among Stumpf's students were Wolfgang Köhler and Kurt Koffka, who later became proponents of Gestalt psychology, and Johannes von Allesch, who became Musil's closest friend. Allesch later pursued an academic

career in psychology. He also knew the writer and editor Franz Blei and others from the artistic and literary world of Berlin.

While in Berlin Musil met Martha Marcovaldi, née Heimann, a Berlin-born Jewish woman seven years his elder. She had been married twice previously, once to a cousin who died within the year, and then to an Italian businessman, Enrico Marcovaldi, from whom she later separated. She and Musil married in 1911. She was a trained visual artist and studied at a school founded by Lovis Corinth. Biographers have characterized her as a passionate, undisciplined, free-thinking intellectual on the margins of the artistic avant-garde of Berlin society.

In 1908 Musil was offered an academic post in Graz after writing a doctoral dissertation on the physicist, psychologist, and philosopher Ernst Mach, but he refused the position in order to pursue writing. His refusal was remarkable in that, although he was by this time almost thirty, he was still entirely financially dependent upon his parents. Throughout his life, spent alternately in Vienna and Berlin, he supported himself only precariously, first through a post in the library of the Technical University in Vienna obtained for him by his anxious father, then as a reviewer and cultural critic for a succession of journals. His break from an academic career, however, marks his decision to withdraw from all other career possibilities and devote himself to writing. *Vereinigungen* (Unions), a collection of two novellas entitled *Die Vollendung der Liebe* (*The Perfecting of a Love*) and *Die Versudung der stillen Veronika* (*The Temptation of Quiet Veronica*), appeared in 1911 to essentially negative reviews, and *Drei Frauen* (Three Women), three additional stories about women ("Grigia" ["Grigia"], "Die Portugiesin" ["The Lady from Portugal"], and "Tonka" ["Tonka"]), appeared in 1924. (All five stories have been published in English translation in *Five Women*.) But *The Man Without Qualities*, begun in 1924, took up the remainder of his energies and was to remain unfinished at his death.

ROBERT MUSIL

In his memoirs Elias Canetti depicts Musil as an uncomfortable, proud, and intensely private man. He could pass considerable amounts of time in company at cafés without uttering a single word and required ritually propitious attitudes of respect from others before embarking on conversation. He avoided shaking hands and other physical gestures of contact, and hated to touch money; he never carried it, and as an adult he was accompanied everywhere by his wife, who procured tram fares and paid café bills. As a writer Musil was intensely competitive. He praised few contemporary writers other than Rilke, whom he revered. He disparaged Thomas Mann and Hermann Broch, although both of these men admired his work and although each at various times provided Musil with financial assistance.

Throughout the writing of *The Man Without Qualities* Musil struggled against bouts of depression and a severe writing block. Some of this depression was no doubt brought about by an almost total critical neglect, which worsened during his financially straitened, anxiety-ridden last years. Impoverished by inflation and opposed to Nazism, in 1933 he returned from Berlin to Vienna for the last time and, with his wife, emigrated to Switzerland, his final home, in August 1938, six months after the *Anschluss* (the Nazi annexation of Austria). Until 1932, he had received advances from his publisher, Rowohlt, in anticipation of the publication of new sections of *The Man Without Qualities.* However, Rowohlt's fortunes declined with the advent of Nazism. From 1934 until his death he depended for financial support on the Musil-Gesellschaft, a voluntary monthly subscription program supported by a handful of wealthy patrons, and on other charitable organizations. These, however, were hardly sufficient for his needs. In April 1942 he died of a stroke at his home in Geneva, Switzerland.

Young Törless, a remarkable first novel, establishes many of the major themes that reappear in *The Man Without Qualities.* It is a *Bildungsroman,* a novel of the education of both the senses and the moral intellect; but in this work these two modes of apprehension remain firmly at odds with each other, and as a result Törless emerges from his academic year with an insistently double vision. In his mind aspects of the irrational, such as the mathematical phenomenon of imaginary numbers, vie with and undermine the school chaplain's unproblematic moral precepts. Likewise he contrasts the "respectable" married love between his parents with the attractions of Bozena, the local peasant prostitute, and with the sadistic homosexual acts of his schoolmates, Beineberg and Reiting, toward their catamite, Basini. In the novel's climactic speech Törless speaks of having developed a "second sight," presumed necessary for dealing with these contradictory manifestations of the same sexual impulse; thus he indicates the impossibility of ever combining these contradictory experiences into a single program of moral education.

Of the five stories constituting the two prose fiction collections, *Vereinigungen* and *Drei Frauen,* "Tonka" is undoubtedly the most successful. Like "Grigia" and "The Lady from Portugal," it creates situations whose experiential truth defies factual reality. But whereas these two stories are rather abstract parables narrated in a flat, neutral tone distanced from the narrated events, "Tonka" is a successful experiment in what Musil later does so expertly in *The Man Without Qualities:* create an active, disembodied narrative voice that serially and discontinuously merges with and separates from the protagonist's point of view. In this way texture and story are interwoven to create a heightened poetic effect.

"Tonka" is the story of a humble shopgirl seduced and eventually brought to the city by a young scientist of means. Despite her lower social origins, her simplicity and unaffected emotion attract him. Throughout, he perceives her as dumb, undissimulating Nature struggling to grasp Mind; he is the complex and ambivalent one, she transparent and willing. But her pregnancy, beginning during a period when he was on a journey, and her subsequent infection with a venereal disease that he does not have force him to conclude that she has been unfaithful. At Tonka's death the rationality and logic of the biological evidence are pitted against his perception of her as faithful and good. This double vision creates for the student an irresolvable conflict between scientific reason and quasi-mystical states of faith.

Tonka "was not stupid, but something appeared to prevent her from being intelligent"; she embodies a recurrent theme of Musil's, a state of mind he names "autism" in the notebooks. It appears as a trait of both Ulrich and Agathe in *The Man Without Qualities,* as well as of other minor characters whose emotions and sensations are depicted as being helpless in the face of language and rationality. In a philosophical sense such characters have an immediate, nonverbal access to experience rather than reflecting on experience in synthesized categories of thought. Tonka's unmediated relation to experience is thus, as the narrator explains, "the language of the totality of things." The texture of the narrative implicitly underscores this heightened form of perception by representing her speech by means of a highly poetic range of metaphors.

THE MAN WITHOUT QUALITIES

Musil worked continuously from 1924 until his death in 1942 on his major work—the novel that, after many changes, was in 1930 entitled *The Man Without Qualities.* Aside from the early short stories, the two novellas, a few lyric poems, two plays—*Die Schwärmer* (The Visionaries, 1921) and *Vinzenz und die Treundin bedeutender Männer* (Vincent and the Mistress of Important Men, 1923)—and the early novel, *Young Törless,* the long novel was his central artistic endeavor, ranging in length from 1600 to 2100 pages, depending on the edition. It is accompanied by over 500 published pages of personal and literary journals, Musil's *Tagebücher* (Notebooks), as well as by

a vast number of essays on literature and culture, speeches, and journalistic criticism.

The novel remained unfinished at his death in 1942, with roughly one-third to one-half of the existing material unedited and unpublished at that time. The intended plan involved four parts. Book 1, published in 1930, consists of part 1, "A Kind of Introduction," and part 2, "A Like(-ness) of It Happens," which sketches in parodied form the social world of Vienna in 1913 from the perspective of the distanced and ironic protagonist, Ulrich, the titular "man without qualities." Book 2, published in 1933, contains only the first thirty-eight chapters of a projected part 3, "Into the Millennium (The Criminals)," the story of Ulrich's retreat from this society with his newly restored sister, Agathe. This retreat of sister and brother into an experiment in the possibilities of a "pure" spiritual union was clearly intended to balance the banal, *kitschig,* tendentious portrait of the age painted in book 1, part 2. "A Kind of Conclusion," balancing "A Kind of Introduction," was to have constituted the final part 4. Musil's death at age sixty-two has made the central critical debate surrounding *The Man Without Qualities* still more difficult than it would otherwise be. This debate is about whether Ulrich and Agathe's union, symmetrically posed against the degraded values of the age, represents a purified *alternative* to the banal spiritual life available to the secondary characters of the novel, or whether their union constitutes a similarly parodied and misguided *repetition* of it. A related question concerns not only the degree of Musil's irony toward the attempt at a total union but also the degree to which he creates protagonists, Ulrich and Agathe, who can share this ironic attitude toward the experience of spiritual union even while attempting it.

Musil's final intention about the material that remained unpublished at his death was made even more uncertain by his method of composition, which was to constantly rework his material, with the result that some chapters exist in as many as twenty substantially different drafts. The widely accepted 1952 edition attempts to order the material chronologically and to select from among these fragments and drafts.

The Man Without Qualities deals with the theme of withdrawal from public life. Ulrich, anticipating the Christological age of thirty-two, decides that his present role in public life as a mathematician and experimental scientist is unsatisfactory; he yearns for a life of greater meaning, intellectual certainty, and spiritual intensity. He decides to withdraw from the public sphere for a one-year "experiment in living" in order to revaluate the moral, spiritual, and emotional values that ought to underlie action of any kind. The intention that guides his search for *das rechte Leben* (the correct life) is to discover the original, inner springs of action, to try to live "at one with himself and the world" and to live wholly in each moment. His is above all a spiritual quest for a way to achieve moments of mystical intensity. Much irony results from the combination in Ulrich of the qualities of mathematical rigor and exactitude on the one hand and his desire to find mystical states of union on the other.

In the course of his search, which extends throughout the novel, he perceives the difficulty of achieving union sometimes as an epistemological and scientific problem, sometimes as a sociological and ideological problem, and sometimes as a moral and spiritual problem; in the course of his reflections he adduces arguments and perspectives from each of these warring intellectual systems. These different areas of intellectual authority can, in general, be assimilated to the conflict between religion and science and can be summarized in the questions: Is there clearly a unity behind all the diverse appearances of phenomena? Is there an ultimate meaning? Is there a God? Or does the world instead move along and proliferate in a vast, unorganized manner without any central unity? These various intellectual systems clearly challenge each other's assumptions, methodologies, and

areas of authority, and the conflict among them turns Ulrich's reflections into an arena for intellectual debate.

By depicting a reflective, intellectual protagonist, the novel announces a shift away from the type of subject traditionally represented, and from the novel's traditional narrative domain—a depiction of the dramatic interaction of characters, or action per se—and toward a repeated depiction of the isolated, stationary act of thinking. Because Ulrich is an intellectual and reflects on the bases of thinking and on the ways in which our thinking and our ideologies determine action, he appears to reflect as a fictional character on the questions that ordinarily concern the authorial consciousness and that function beyond the scope of the consciousness of fictional characters. The enlarged scope of Ulrich's thinking process suggests that there exists a partial or occasional continuum of consciousness between narrator and fictional protagonist.

Because of the intermittently shared voice of narrator and protagonist, Ulrich's interior reflections function ambiguously within the novel. As traditional internal monologues his reflections function dramatically to reveal his character. But his reflections also have an independent status; that is, they function essayistically, laying out areas of conflict between the respective authorities of science and of religion. This is not a fictional (dramatic) conflict between characters, but rather a conflict between the status of warring truths of different intellectual disciplines. Indeed, some critics have complained that such problems are not a suitable topic for fiction. Ulrich therefore occupies a paradoxical status as, on one hand, a fictional character who acts and thinks in accordance with the novel's larger narrative plan, and, on the other, as a "transparent" de-fictionalized voice whose ruminations turn the novel into a philosophical essay. Whether to see the content of Ulrich's reflections as subsumed and "claimed" by the fictional contexts in which they appear or to see them as independent and perhaps themselves "authorizing" the future course of the novel is a question insistently left open throughout the novel.

Ulrich is hampered in his search for the key to *das rechte Leben* by two limiting requirements that he imposes on his own thinking and that the narrator endorses. He adheres to two notions that are central to the novel—to the peculiar notion of being "without qualities" and to its complement, having a *Möglichkeitssinn* (sense of possibility). In conceiving of a self "without qualities," Ulrich attempts to cast off the concepts that conventionally mediate our view of ourselves and to see the external world in its varieties of flux and contradiction. In a world without qualities objects would lack defining properties and fixed identities. Concepts like "personality," "ego," and "the soul" mediate other characters' views of their experience and block their access to the "wild untamedness of things," as Ulrich puts it, things lacking a socializing nomenclature and fixed identity. "Exactness, correctness kills; that which is definable, or concept, is dead, turned to stone, a skeleton," Musil writes in his essays, echoing this belief.

Ulrich's mind works by tolerating complication and contradiction, by teasing out the ambiguities in concrete truths that give the lie to apparent absolutes. Does the statement "The grass is green," he asks, tell us anything about the color of lawns? Is it "grass-green" or only "green as grass," and is that the shade of green that occurs before a rain or not? "Green" is not a concept abstractly available to us but has contextually "shaded" meanings. By pressing on such contradictions, Ulrich undermines the truth of linguistic categories. The consistent inability of language to refer to precise conditions in the physical world, as in the problematic meaning of "green," has an important correlation in the realm of ethical behavior. Ulrich declares early in the novel that there are no axiomatic principles of ethical behavior. Musil, in agreement, claims in his essays, "There is no ethical behavior, only an ethical condition."

"The sense of possibility," a complementary principle to being without qualities, creates the mental framework of a protagonist who is disposed to "new" concrete moments of consciousness. The novel offers as a purely logical proposition the idea that if there are *Wirklichkeitsmenschen* (realists) there must also be *Möglichkeitsmenschen* (or possibilitarians, to use the word Wilkins and Kaiser use in their translation, *The Man Without Qualities* [1968]). By postulating simply that the world could always be *anders* (other), the name given to Ulrich in an earlier version of the novel, the "sense of possibility" presumes an absence of historical or psychological causality determining the world as it is.

The mental space created by the "sense of possibility" provides Ulrich with a mental arbitrariness and an abstract freedom that are radically discontinuous with the conceptual order of the existing culture; moments can be "new," not impinged on by the forces of one's history or biography. The narrator tells us that this "new" terrain that Ulrich sets out to explore can lead either, in a gifted individual, into a realm of "extraordinary" ideas or else simply into deviant, "disordered" unintelligibility vis-à-vis the standards of meaning of the existing culture. The risk in this new direction is that it can lead to madness, and madness, which afflicts two secondary characters, Moosbrugger and Clarisse, is one of the explicit themes of the novel.

Musil opposes the notion of the extraordinary individual capable of new ideas that deviate from cultural norms with the notion of the conventional *Durchschnittsmensch* (mediocre person), who relies on conventional wisdom and lives comfortably within the culture's conceptual norms. The capacity to be an extraordinary intellectual, or genius, is closely related to the freedom of the "sense of possibility"; the question of whether Ulrich is achieving new forms of thought through reflection or whether his mental meanderings are nothing more than self-indulgent trivia provides the basis for the drama and aporia of

Ulrich's reflections. The traceable pattern is that Ulrich's excitement turns to doubt, and out of doubt yet a third change in consciousness occurs.

This third movement, this "turn," is the phenomenon that reveals the striking originality and poetic beauty of the novel. During Ulrich's moments of reflections, his consciousness is abruptly transformed, made "different" (*anders*) according to the principle of "possibility." Series of associated thoughts ensue, partly related to the moment preceding them, and partly, as suggested by *Möglichkeitssinn,* freed from their contextual, fictional confines. Sometimes Ulrich conceives of these moments as the occurrence of *Einfälle* (intuitions); at other times these abrupt changes of mental texture appear to be simply characteristic of the way thinking gets done. These moments generally give rise, in Maurice Blanchot's words, to "an illuminating image," epiphanic but preserving its mystery and opacity. During some of these reflections Ulrich perceives his intuitions as heralding an impersonal vision of the world, one different and possibly true in a scientific sense and, importantly, one likely to be detached from self-interest; these moments have an ethical as well as an aesthetic function in that they represent the opportunity to go beyond the confines of egoistic individual perspective and self-limiting ideology. At other times these moments are linked with the pathos of Ulrich's self-doubt, his despair that his intellectual quest is the mere eccentricity of an invalid "going off course." Ulrich is then attacked by the despair of the hopeless desire that there be significant order to life; he feels the delusion in his search for significance. As the novel progresses Ulrich comes to name these mental states, which grow in intensity, duration, and complication, *der andere Zustand* (the other condition). At these times the world is transformed into a state of flux through a poetic and metaphoric language that appears paradoxically to have both a personal/hallucinatory and an objective/naturalistic range of meanings.

Yet it must not be thought that the novel deals only with Ulrich's inner states of reflection. The place is Vienna, the time August 1913, and much of the novel is given over to depicting all of the conventional, fixed perspectives—the ideologies—that we are likely to find in a sophisticated society. The repeated effort of the novel is to undermine the reality of this panoply of figures, to ensure that this static configuration of characters and their comic mythologies and intellectual errors—the concerns of a traditional novel—are not mistaken for the true subject of this one. These are characters without a plot embedded in a narrative that, as the first chapter proclaims, "does not get anybody anywhere." We meet character upon character here but can derive no sense that a plot is being built upon their interactions. The basis of Musil's satire of conventional characters, and their hallmark, is the single, fixed perspective that each one inflates into a totalizing system. From this set of terms we can begin to see the large contours of the polarity between Ulrich's experience and those of all the secondary characters.

The satire of the public world is extensive and leaves no possible ideological position in the "real" world safe from satire. Musil includes in this epic presentation many varieties of political ideology, both centrist liberalism and conservatism, both of which shade off into extreme forms of, respectively, Marxism and Fascism. The conservatives include the bureaucrat Tuzzi and his superior Graf Leinsdorf, between whom there are vivid and subtle differences in ideology. Arnheim, a figure based upon the liberal industrialist Walther Rathenau but also containing some satire leveled against the *grosse Schriftsteller* (great artist) and *bedeutender Mann* (intellectual superstar)—pretensions that Musil identified with Mann—is the liberal of the novel, and the contradictions inherent in his ideology and "charismatic" personality are particularly adeptly handled. Musil also presents Walter, the failed artist who has retreated from the city to the "simple life" of a rural cottage and who plays

Wagner operas in four-hand reductions with his wife, Clarisse, all day. He claims to have retreated from the fallen values and false sophistication of his age, but it is also hinted that he has done so because his bid to become an artist recognized by artists and the intelligentsia has failed. His moral outlook is steeped in a transparent *ressentiment.* In all these portraits Musil shows himself to be a skillful social psychologist who has learned much from Friedrich Nietzsche about the relationship between world view and self-interest.

Other views represented are those of Fischel, the cynical but trepidant Jewish banker, of the Fascist Meingast, who advocates a bloodbath purification ritual to restore Europe's moral well-being, and of the vulgar Marxist Schmeisser, Ulrich's gardener, who discounts the function of consciousness in social change and insists that the proletarian revolution will occur without any human agency. In these portraits one finds a great deal to regret in Musil's eschewing of all class and political affiliations. The vulgarity of Schmeisser's position, for instance, makes him an unremarkable and easy target for satire. Then there is the criminal Moosbrugger, the murderer of prostitutes, who displays an irrationality that is very close to Ulrich's "other" form of consciousness. Early parts of the novel that describe his murder trial debate definitions of lunacy and legal responsibility in a satire of the legal mind's reliance on firm definitions of rationality. Hagauer and Lindner are the two educators, each of whom has a mechanistic formulation of Ulrich's central query about how moral precepts are "applied" to life in order to determine action.

The centrists of this party as well as a number of the women, who are generally articulated through their attitudes to culture and to sex rather than to politics, are involved in a curious cultural and political scheme called the *Parallelaktion* (parallel action). This is the name for a grand polemical plan to celebrate for an entire year the seventieth year of the reign of the Austrian emperor Franz Joseph. The plan is chosen in a spirit of nationalistic

competitiveness because it represents the theft of a Prussian plan to celebrate the thirtieth year of Emperor Wilhelm II's reign. Hence it is a parallel action, scheduled to take place in the year 1918. Much satire results from the intention of the planners to choose a theme "representative" of the empire's cultural identity as a whole. As an ironic counterpoint to this search for a single, simple symbol of reality, Musil dwells humorously on the loose agglomerate of *Kakania*'s (*kaiserlich und königlich* [kaiserly and kingly], abbreviated as *k.u.k.,* a scatological pun on the slang word *kacken* [to excrete], ironically equating excrement with the trappings of the kaiser) diverse political entities, reminding us of the uneasy hegemony of the German-speaking Austrians within the Austro-Hungarian Empire, and he places the search for a symbolic expression of political unity in the ironic perspective of the impending catastrophe of 1914.

Ulrich is appointed secretary of the *Parallelaktion,* and the task of choosing the campaign's central theme falls to him. Of course the theme is the disarray of reality and the vain attempt to impose a simplifying narrative thread and a suitable emblem. Choosing the theme involves endless discussions of the "true" meaning of themes like "the true and the beautiful." In a *reductio* of the quest for an adequate symbol for the age, Ulrich examines the results of a write-in campaign in which citizens propose as emblematic their special field or monomania; for example, one proposes stamp-collecting, and another a certain system of shorthand as the metaphor for wholeness. Each one would like to come up with the ultimate symbol with which to summarize or structure reality, a symbol that would in effect replace reality or substitute for it. But through Ulrich's eyes we see that this quest for metaphor, for the symbolic replacement and reduction of reality, is unsuccessful. The list of themes—sign-painting, shorthand, the Buddha, Jesus Christ, Nietzsche—creates a chaotic, expansionary effect, inclusive or coextensive with reality and thus metonymic rather than metaphoric. Each item extends the boundaries of reality a bit farther, rather than heightening or structuring it through the choice of a crystallizing symbol. This is an instance of Musil's oft-repeated strategy of satirizing the search for significance, that is, for a single structure "behind" sequential manifestations.

In a variety of ways Musil declared his intention to clear a "negative" space in which to write his novel, one from which a traditional narrative that renders the daily lives and fates of individuals is absent. In book 1, part 2, the events of the social world are introduced as "Seinesgleichen geschiet" ("A Like[-ness] of It Happens"), and the first chapter of the novel, entitled "Woraus bemerkeuswerter weise nichts hervorgeht" ("In Which, Remarkably, Nothing Happens"), announces the determined plotlessness of the novel. His plan for the novel calls for "portraying at least one hundred characters . . . the principal contemporary types" and for letting them interact, giving them conventional psychological characteristics "so that they don't get confused in the reader's memory." He summarizes as useful to his own program of portraying profession-bound types Friedrich Hölderlin's dictum in *Hyperion* (1797–1799), "In Germany there are no people, only professions," and he writes in the journals: "The real explanation for real events does not interest me. . . . What interests me is what's typical of the spirit of the age, I'd almost say, the *ghostly inhering in real events*" (my emphasis). The "ghostly" quality of the novel's ironic presentation of reality reinforces the validity of Ulrich's "sense of possibility." The narrator subscribes to the notion that the world could be "other" and that its method of organization, far from conforming to the principles of conventional order upheld by secondary characters, is instead "the well-known contextlessness of ideas [*Einfälle*] and their way of proliferating without a central point, which is characteristic of the present age and constitutes its peculiar arithmetic, which multiplies

from the hundreds into the thousands with no basic unit-y [*Einheit*]."

Musil's rejection of all metaphors for wholeness and, most important for his artistic practice, his particular rejection of the unity of character stem in part from his reading of two authors who are major influences on his work, Mach and Nietzsche. Mach, the radical empiricist philosopher and psychologist, made the argument in *Beiträge zur Analyze der Empfindungen* (*Contributions to the Analysis of the Sensations*, 1885) that the world is constituted out of irreducible, discrete "elements" or sensations, which combine and recombine to become the objects and the other egos that our perceptions are then capable of registering. The thing and the "I" do not exist as such; rather, they are "provisional fictions," practical, not real, unities, made up of many smaller components. The variety of recombinations of the same set of elements gives objects and other egos their apparent unqiue "individuality." Our experience of another ego and of things is based in each case on a particular complex of sensations that we somewhat contingently associate with them. Our practical knowledge of others is based on the context in which we experience them; their identities, or rather identity-constellations, are thus relative and contextual, not essential and unchanging.

Since identities and meanings depend on context, it is impossible to isolate a thing or an ego, to identify its particular essence, uniqueness, or unity. Mach's program is thus a direct attack on all metaphysical notions of the ego, the personality, and the soul, and, further, of identity or totality as such. Musil takes up this critique of the metaphysical notions of the ego, of essences and totalities, in his satiric presentation of character in *The Man Without Qualities*. His adoption of Mach's radical and revolutionary scientific outlook thus signals the incorporation of the "new" scientific sensibility into the methodology of the novel, a significant alignment of narrative sensibility with that of the protagonist, Ulrich. This radical relativism also enables Musil to claim that all ethics are situational and to reject conventional morality. Further, the notion that there are not unique "essences" defining differences between egos (that in fact "subjective" and "objective" are not meaningful distinctions, but merely represent the recombinations of elements that account for differences in perception) is important in analyzing the novel. We should note the pun now revealed in the passage quoted above; metaphysically we conjure with, or calculate with, building blocks, or mathematical *units* (*Einheiten*) whose discreteness belies any metaphysical *unity* (*Einheit*).

TOTALIZING SYSTEMS

Es muss also das "Ganze" ein anderes Gesicht bekommen.
["Wholeness" must assume a new face.]
—from Musil's diaries

Musil uses the characters of the social world of the novel to criticize the metaphysical notion of *das Ganze* (wholeness), both as it relates to the notions of unity, meaning, or order that these characters rely on in their own internal "narratives" and as it relates to the notion of "character," here perceived as being itself an artificial unity. Let us look briefly at an extended interior monologue of the reigning government bureaucrat of *The Man Without Qualities,* the originator of the *Parallelaktion,* Graf Leinsdorf. In a chapter entitled "Die wahre Erfindung der Parallelaktion durch Graf Leinsdorf" ("The True Invention of the Parallel Action by Count Leinsdorf"), he is introduced sitting at his desk contemplating his scheme. "Erfindung," suggesting an invention or figment of the imagination, creates an oxymoron when linked with "wahre" (true) and is reminiscent of the novel's overall program—the ghostly undermining of the real in its guise as the true.

As he meditates on the political unity to be achieved through the *Parallelaktion,* he is con-

vinced that "the true, deeply understood world of the bourgeoisie was exactly what he himself believed in." Leinsdorf's ideology, that of the naive aristocrat, rests on the assumption that political unity already exists within the empire, his job as government functionary being merely to express that unity. This task, however, involves collapsing real political distinctions between aristocrat and burgher and between right and left in order to achieve a harmonious "totality." As he continues to reflect on this—to him—profoundly exciting promise of unity through the "great idea" of the *Parallelaktion,* he is "convinced that *true* socialism was in accord with his own world view," and it remains a personal ambition "which he partially hid even from himself" to build a bridge "over which the socialists might march into his camp." In a series of homilies Leinsdorf rehearses to himself his convictions that "the people" are "good," that he himself is "merely a patriot," that political conflict comes from "the subversive element," and that in "the natural order of things" the "true" aristocrat is as necessary as the "true" artisan.

Hardly a word of Leinsdorf's extended interior monologue reports his speech directly, and even though many of the words are of the vocabulary Leinsdorf might use, they are satirized through emphasis and repetition. His monologue is cast in free indirect speech, a narrative device of the novel in which narrator and character blend in a "dual" voice, typically to allow the narrator a means of reporting the character's internal, perhaps only semiconscious, thoughts and associations. This device is often used to enter intimately into a character's own inner voice, to convey the free rhythms and loose associativeness of the ordinary thought process. But such is not the case here. Rather, the use of the technique here results in what can be called an "oxymoron of form"; the subject's supposedly intimate thoughts are here fully controlled by the narrator for purposes of satire. We expect to penetrate to the possibly intriguing core of Leinsdorf's personal, even irrational, system of metaphors so as to *discover* his ideology, as Broch allows us to do so successfully in *Die Schlafwandler* (*The Sleepwalkers,* 1931–1932), in which his protagonist's unexpected metaphor of the ledger book of rights and wrongs indicates his view of justice. But here Leinsdorf's ideology is served up to us directly, without its being dramatized through metaphors or through Leinsdorf's dwelling on an impressionistic moment. The narrator's proximity to Leinsdorf in his extended monologue produces only generalization. Instead of an intimate glimpse, we are given an already synthesized and synoptic view of the count's political philosophy, and moreover, this is a view with no surprises, one telling a predictable and banal story, and, strangest of all, a view apparently being shared, if not told, by Leinsdorf himself.

This "failure" to dramatize has irritated some English-speaking readers accustomed to a greater degree of realism. However, Musil in no sense seeks to create realistic characters with unique or personal cores. For him the ironic disjunction between form and narrative content is the interesting poetic action of a text, the one capable of conveying, as it does here, "the ghostly aspect in reality." The drama of the novel occurs not within the fiction, that is, not between one character and another, but rather between the fictional world and that of the reader, between text and reader.

A German critic, Götz Müller, has added to our understanding of the narrator's synoptic treatment of secondary characters by analyzing in detail the synthetic construction of character. He explores an important compositional technique of Musil's, a *Prinzip des Zitats* (principle of pastiche) in which, for purposes of parody, Musil builds his characters from a pastiche of quotations from late-nineteenth-century adherents of *Lebensphilosophie* (a popular strain of German philosophy that celebrated the intuitive, irrational, and subjective elements in the individual's response to the external world). Thus Leinsdorf's notion of the state as organism, as a "natural" totality, is modeled on the romantic political theories of Adam Müller and Alois Prinz Liechtenstein; Leinsdorf's semiconscious convictions are the well-worn commonplaces of an earlier day. Müller's analysis reveals that several secondary characters in *The Man Without Qualities* are fully synthesized, constructed from the "preformed" material of historical sources and readily recognizable intellectual products and created to illustrate intellectual errors. The penetration to Leinsdorf's "inner" consciousness, then, reveals a "ghostly" reality. Musil's literary practice is to replace any notion of characters being drawn spontaneously from nature with a rigorously stylized character exposition.

The exposition of Leinsdorf, however, involves a further complication in this notion of a ghostly, stylized reality. If Musil seems to replace the loose, metaphoric, impressionistic texture of a naturalistic interior voice with an overly systematized synoptic overview of character, this is not in fact fully true. As Leinsdorf's monologue continues the narrator does allow him to dwell on a special metaphor that has cosmic meaning for him, and through this image seems to attempt to give the reader a sense of the preverbal, preconscious foundation of Leinsdorf's political philosophy, Leinsdorf's preconscious—authentic—thought process. Beyond love of country, beyond desire to see Austria lead the world, beyond even his articulated philosophy of statecraft, Leinsdorf senses the powerful image (*Vorstellung*) of the eighty-eight-year-old emperor. This image had stirred him to the creation of the *Parallelaktion* as a *Gleichnis* (metaphor) for the expression of his patriotic devotion. The "enriching power" of this metaphor now raises in him "great and painful hopes." "A great idea" has seized him, although much of "this thought still lay in darkness." This idea "flowed with glowing clarity immediately into such exalted and radiant images as that of the sovereign, the fatherland, and world happiness."

To justify the obscurity of this metaphor, Leinsdorf then seeks an analogy in the theological doctrine of the *contemplatio in cali-*

gine divina (the contemplation in divine darkness), endlessly clear in itself, he knows, but paradoxically for man a *Blendung und Finsternis* (dazzling darkness). The patriarchal associations of his philosophizing continue with a homily from Oliver Cromwell about the ever-obscure appearance of a man's actions to himself. Leinsdorf gives himself up happily to the enjoyment of his metaphor, acknowledging that its "uncertainty moved him more strongly than any certainties."

The suspicion of satire is confirmed as the commonplace metaphor of brightness and darkness for clarity and obscurity of understanding suddenly escalates into a full-scale theological symbolism, with the elaborate oxymoron of "dazzling darkness" expressing the paradox of divine law as understood from man's imperfect perspective. Götz Müller has isolated a general satiric technique in *The Man Without Qualities,* the inappropriate analogy. Here the inflation of the metaphor into a full-scale theological trope reinforces an authoritarian connection between the divinity and the emperor, a connection naturally in keeping with the aristocratic and authoritarian bent of Leinsdorf's articulated political philosophy. The banality of the preconscious or preverbal image of the emperor, as well as its virtual identity with Leinsdorf's explicit ideology, leads us to the conclusion that the "unreal" consciousness of this character is balanced by an "unreal" unconscious. There are no layers to penetrate here; character is oversystematized, and both the conscious and the unconscious "poles" are immediately available through an analysis of explicit ideology. Metaphors, which typically work in novels to express the complications and unconscious impulses of characters, are here reductive and tautological. The relation between the explicit conscious pole of character and the unconscious pole, glimpsed through metaphor, is not naturalistically incongruous or mysterious, but is rather one of identity.

We have a notion from Musil's journals about how to evaluate the real revelatory power

that a metaphor possesses: "Wesen der Metaphorik. Der Vergleich eines Mundes mit einer Koralle . . . wäre eine Heruntersetzung, wenn nicht durch das hineingetragene Unklare die Wirkung entstünde." (The essence of metaphor. The comparison of a mouth with coral . . . would be *reductionistic* if the effect did not arise out of the *lack of clarity* thereby introduced [my emphasis].) Full clarity is, he feels, reductionistic; it produces tautology, or identity between the tenor and the vehicle of the metaphor. *Unklare* (lack of clarity), on the other hand, the "lack of correspondence" between things, suggests either indeterminate or overdetermined correspondences. An essential part of Musil's poetic program, which is to elaborate the dual notions of being without qualities and of having a sense of possibility, is condemnation of the systematic, that is, the oversystematized, and commitment to its opposite—the irrational, complex, and unique situation of an idea—and to the notion of *Unklare,* which produces partial correspondences (rather than identities) whose principles of correspondence provide the novel's seductive power. The chapter treating Leinsdorf ends on a metaphor suggestive of such *Unklare* and provides us with an affirmative image that, through its contrasting *Unklare,* further undermines this "character-constellation."

The narrator leaves Leinsdorf "sitting motionless at his desk" unaware that he is smiling to himself, slowly pans to an aerial view of his house, and then discusses the historical significance of the collision of architectural styles reflected in his townhouse; the wide rococo facade that is grafted onto the narrow townhouse dimensions symbolizes, we are told, the transition from the feudal to the bourgeois era. This discussion of the collision of styles, of course, contains a reference to Leinsdorf's arch-conservative political philosophy. Framed beneath one of the arches stands Leinsdorf's doorkeeper, accoutred in a gold-braid coat and gold-knobbed staff, motionless in "die helle Flüssigkeit des Tags" (the bright fluidity of the day) while "die Fussgänger schwammen vorbei wie in einem Goldfisch-glas" (pedestrians swam by as in a goldfish bowl). The sudden freedom of this imagery and its suspended, dreamlike quality—the absence of gravity and perspective in this fluid scene, and the attribution of interesting sensations to the anonymous doorkeeper—detach us from the perspective of Leinsdorf and attach us to this surrogate symbol of his rank.

Indeed, we are told that the doorkeeper is a metonym for the higher office. Anyone who did not know the count saw only the doorkeeper, the gold of his braid and staff:

> In good weather this doorkeeper stepped in front of the entrance; then he stood there like a gaily colored jewel visible from afar, inserted in a row of houses that never entered anyone's conscious mind. . . . A great number of the "people" linked [Leinsdorf's] name with nothing but the recollection of this doorkeeper.
>
> (1:91)[1]

This bright jewel stimulates as no reductive metaphor would, by its sudden and unanticipated beauty, unexpectedly far-flashing in a row of houses paradoxically unavailable to any consciousness in the novel. In this image there is much resonance and visual stimulation and also some uneasiness about its role within the action of the novel. This image is produced by the narrator for the benefit of the reader only; it is sealed off from the perspectives of characters within the novel. Its detachment from any fictional sensibilities serves as a contrasting appearance of the irrational and of *Unklare;* it serves to set off the constructed reality, the "true invention" of Count Leinsdorf that preceded it.

The transference of our interest from Leinsdorf to the anonymous doorkeeper creates both a feeling of loss and melancholy and a feeling of heightened fascination with the curious poetic effect so achieved. It is clear that this transfer of interest is meant to undermine further Leinsdorf's independent existence and

to satirize him. But in the process an affirmative image is created that contrasts with the loss of Leinsdorf as a fully real character. It is rather like the characteristic gesture of Louis-Ferdinand Céline, at the close of several chapters in *Voyage an bout de la nuit* (*Voyage to the End of Night,* 1932), when, moving up beyond the squalid, claustrophobic streets of criminal Paris, he re-creates the horizon as a place of sheer, illimitable, unpeopled freedom. Here, the release from the oppressive satiric exposition of character into a "free" metaphor unattributable to ideology, through a transaction taking place only between narrator and reader, is both eerie and exhilarating. Structurally, this interruption of the narrative by such a metaphor creates non-mimetic narrative possibilities very closely akin to Ulrich's own "sense of possibility," the sense of proliferating out in many directions. Here we can see the beginning of an exploration of a new sort of authorial freedom parallel to the freedom given to the novel's protagonist.

ULRICH AND THE "SENSE OF POSSIBILITY"

A single capacity of Ulrich's, his *Möglichkeitssinn,* or "sense of possibility," replaces the notion of character and the values that are built on it. It sets him apart from all other characters. The function of his "sense of possibility" is a purely formal one; it has no content and advances no single affirmative value. It claims only that for every set of conditions that we accept as being the case, another set of conditions might also be the case. The "sense of possibility" performs a purely negative act upon existing relationships or values; by putting every assertion in the perspective that "things might just as easily be completely different," it challenges all hierarchies of value or interpretation and undermines notions of causal or relational thinking; it resists concept and generalization, and imposes a perpetual flux upon the act of thinking. In the narrator's words it is the enabling

[1] All extracts are translated from *Gesammelte Werke in Einzelausgaben,* 3 vols., 1952–1957.

structure for "the imagination, fantasies, and the subjunctive mood."

Vis-à-vis the *Wirklichkeitsmensch* (realist), to use the narrator's term, the "sense of possibility" functions critically much as did Nietzsche's attack on metaphysical values. Nietzsche, whom Musil read extensively, warns in *Die fröhliche Wissenschaft* (*The Gay Science*, 1887):

> The total character of the world . . . is in all eternity chaos . . . in the sense of a lack of order, arrangement, form, beauty, wisdom and whatever other names there are for our aesthetic anthropomorphisms. . . . Let us beware of thinking that the world is a living being. . . . We have some notion of the nature of the organic; and we should not reinterpret the exceedingly derivative, late, rare, accidental that we perceive only on the crust of the earth and make of it something essential, universal and eternal.
>
> (Walter Kaufmann, trans.
> [New York, 1974], pp. 167–168)

Elsewhere Nietzsche characterizes as part of the striving for survival the need to "invent signs and formulas, with the help of which we may reduce the swirling complexity to a purposeful, useful scheme."

Nietzsche's critique of imposing order upon a chaotic world can be usefully compared to Ulrich's description of a random moment of sensation:

> One could also be sitting on a fallen tree trunk or on a bench in the mountains, watching a herd of cows grazing and just then feel oneself all at once transported into a different life! . . . And suddenly . . . you cannot even form the words "graze" or "pasture" because a lot of intentional, useful concepts belong to them which you've suddenly lost. What remains on the picture plane is something perhaps best called a throng of sensations.
>
> (1:761–762)

The "sense of possibility" leads Ulrich to regard concepts as simplifying, abstract constructs, and therefore he rejects them for the emotional and physiological plane of sensation; the generalizing, abstracting, and organizing procedures of "concepts" are rejected for the ambiguity and complexity of "the throng of sensations." This opposition prepares the ground for the rejection of ideologies in narratives containing so little "individual" character development and unfolding with such intellectual predictability that they are clearly immediately reducible to ideology, as is the case with the Leinsdorf example.

It is important that the "sense of possibility" be understood as an operation of consciousness, as an essentially non-narrative impulse that paves the way for complex, associative, nonlinear mental processes detached from any fictional character's judgments or values. It is a formal or logical possibility that operates as a mathematical function does. It enables Musil to set aside, as another metaphysical construct, the traditional novelistic tool of the individual ego or fictional character, here presented as the static product of ideology, in favor of a consciousness more various, opaque to analysis of "motivation," and contradictory in impulse. In the journals Musil formulated as a goal of his writing the depiction of an "entire life" coextensive with the disarray and complexity of our experiential life. This would suggest an essentially metonymic treatment of the details of that life rather than their transformation and symbolization into a metaphoric "whole." This opposition, formulated by Roman Jakobson in *The Fundamentals of Language* (1956) and in his essay "Linguistics and Poetics" (included in *Style in Language,* 1960), contrasts texts that are extensive and inclusive, which he calls metonymic, with those that create symbols and patterns through the substitution or replacement of one term by another, which he calls metaphoric. The metonymic and the metaphoric, which he claims constitute the two poles of language, characterize novels and poetry respectively.

As a corollary to its treatment of narrative and character exposition, the "sense of possibility" sets itself against historical explanation and causality, which in the realistic novel acts upon and helps shape individual response. Thus Musil wishes to create in Ulrich a character both without the *Eigenschaften* (social determinants or properties) that form the ego and without the connection to self-interest or ideology that mars the imagination and limits its moral breadth. The term *Eigenschaften* contains the root *eigen,* meaning "one's own," "intrinsic," or "unique," and has strong references to the individual ego. This reference is reinforced by the strong connection to the world *eigentlich,* meaning "authentic" or "essential," a reference to mystical cults of the self and to a naive individuality espoused prominently by secondary characters in *The Man Without Qualities.* However, *Eigenschaften* is also the chemical term for the "properties" that combine in various ways to form chemical compounds, and this connection to scientific thinking contains the germ of Musil's anti-metaphysical thinking. The "sense of possibility" holds in ironic equilibrium opposite notions of the self, on one hand the constellation of properties grouping and regrouping into egos as described by Mach, and on the other the essentialist view of the self represented by *Lebensphilosophie.* The journals express the utopian urge to turn singular properties into common property ("Eigenschaften werden zu Allerschaften!"), suggesting as a utopian basis a radical exchange of characteristics as opposed to a proprietary ego.

Before examining an example of the "sense of possibility," it is first important to note the way in which the concept is introduced. It appears first in book 1, chapter 4, and we learn that it can create a man without qualities. In chapter 5 we learn that Ulrich is such a man. Thus the condition of being without properties exists *in potentia;* it preexists individuals who embody it. And the paucity of biographical data that the novel offers about Ulrich gives no clue as to how *Möglichkeitssinn* was formed in him. Both in its origin and in its functioning *Möglichkeitssinn* is an acausal, ahistorical principle.

When we meet Ulrich, a mathematician by profession, he has decided to take a year's leave from his research. He has also begun to appear to himself both as a *Möglichkeitssmensch* (possibilitarian) and as a man without qualities. Having decided to buy and renovate a house, Ulrich has trouble deciding how to choose among the many available architectural styles. He is confronted with an array of styles ranging from "the Assyrian to cubism" and with renovative principles ranging from the notion of a "stylistically pure restoration to that of complete recklessness." However, just as he has no fixed essence of personality, he is drawn to no particular style. Unlike Leinsdorf, who is linked to feudalism through his townhouse and his ideology, Ulrich has no ideological identity and thus no basis for aligning himself with any historical moment. Styles, which in *The Man Without Qualities* are immediately linked to historical periods and ideological perspectives, have for Ulrich become emptied of their historical meanings. They thus appear to him as an arbitrary array of merely aesthetic choices. It follows that the present artistic moment can have no revolutionary or avant-garde importance for him; all historical moments are synchronically and equally available to him. Furthermore, since Ulrich perceives history as a perpetual "going off course," he can see that "a new time is beginning all the time." Any attempt at arbitrary periodization bestows on an epoch, as on character, a constructed and artificial identity. The synchronous pressure and competing claims of all preceding historical moments, which have the effect of defeating choices, actions, or ideological alignments, are suggested in Ulrich's tumbledown château, a stylistic construct that "already possessed three styles superimposed upon each other."

At this point Ulrich, paralyzed in his attempt at furnishing his abode, considers the claim of the art journals: "Tell me what your house is like and I'll tell you who you are." He decides to design his own architectural personality, but here he encounters the problem connected with attempting to throw off the determinants of history and to keep open the spirit of possibility: the inability to translate thought into action, or, to put it another way, to weave a single narrative thread:

> But whenever he had thought out a shape that was solid and impressive, it occurred to him that one could just as easily put a tensile, technically functional form in its place; and when he had come up with a reinforced concrete form consumed by its own strength, he would recall the springlike, slender outlines of a thirteen-year-old girl and begin to dream instead of making up his mind.
>
> (1:20)

Ulrich's train of thought runs from one design possibility to its opposite, then to yet a third option, and finally to the abandonment of direction altogether in favor of a reverie induced by the association between an element in the design and a young girl's body.

The turn from one ideological choice to another and thence to the contemplation of a metaphor exemplifies the characteristic turn in *The Man Without Qualities* away from a linear sequence toward a heightened, poetic, non-narrative, metaphoric moment that is held and sustained. Musil claims that this heightening process is a structural prototype of the mind, one that confounds and refutes narrative, by which he means (and perhaps even wrongly conflates) all that we mean by the linear, the chronological, and the causal. In his journals he notes: "It has been a central idea—or central illusion—of my life that the *mind has its own history* and *elevates* itself in *a stepwise progression,* regardless of everything that happens in the practical world" (my emphasis). The mind follows its own history and diverges, through its own complicating, heightening, and metaphoric practice, from the familiar sequence of events typically narrated in traditional novels.

This narrative liberty justified by the "sense of possibility" has consequences for our expectations of character and of the form the novel will take. Linear narrative is stymied; narrative "ends up" in metaphor instead of concerning itself about motivation or character. The inclusion of solitary reverie as a part of consciousness defies psychological or sociological analysis. Elsewhere Musil describes this sort of indeterminate reflection as the expression of "unorganized dynamic forces of the mind," "free association," and "the loosening of the control of the conscious mind, something that was undeniably very stimulating." Thus the benefit of the freedom of the *Möglichkeitssinn* is the uncovering of new, stimulating associations between terms, the possibility for a new metaphoric principle. Musil's counterpoise to the determinism of the ego is not a model giving wider scope for psychological development, but rather a receptivity to randomness. The "overdetermined" ego is opposed by the indeterminacy of the *Möglichkeitssinn.*

This sort of free association, rather than being a window on the unconscious, in fact weakens our picture of the fictional character Ulrich. The association used here breaks through the fictional situation to create a purely evocative and immediate consideration of the resemblance between two terms. The association between an architectural shape and the lines of a young girl's body sheds no particular light on either conscious or unconscious aspects of Ulrich's personality; this is neither a particularly typical nor a highly revealing metaphor for him to choose. Nor does it lead back into Ulrich's past experiences, as such a device might for, say, Marcel Proust. Nor is it part of a symbolic network of images that accrete meaning by repetition or resonance, as in Joseph Conrad's work. Rather, this image is characteristic of those found in *The Man Without Qualities;* it is part of the ordinary world and depends on a basic and accessible similarity that stimulates the senses—here the visual sense. The point is not that the image is banal, the sort of grandiose, "poetic," or clichéd image Musil saves for the degraded consciousnesses of his secondary figures. Rather, like many of Musil's images, it is a domestic one, not the rare or strange one

946

we might expect from Ulrich's rather eccentric mind. Nor will those who would see in Ulrich an expression of the aesthetic decadent sensibility find here exquisite or exotic images of beauty such as are found in Joris-Karl Huysmans's *A rebours* (*Against the Grain* or *Against Nature,* 1884). Rather, the image is of the material of the commonplace, and its power lies in a direct accessibility that simply temporarily abandons the fictional picture plane.

The association "defictionalizes" the moment, dissolving the marks of Ulrich's personality and making the moment available to us as an immediate perception of a new relationship in the external world, perceived without an ego. Ulrich himself notes the phenomenon of "the ego's disappearance in moments of intense activity," in reflection. These transparent moments of perception lie "equidistant" between reader and protagonist. In these moments of immediacy the reader does not read by making analogies between the protagonist's experience and his own; he does not filter what he reads through the protagonist. Rather, the palpable association of objects, the evocativeness of the images themselves, becomes the involving stimulus for him. The effect of passages of reverie and reflection like this one is centrifugal, throwing the reader out of the narrative into a more speculative and sensual train of associations of his own.

The narrator reinforces the validity of *Möglichkeitssinn.* Rather than commenting ironically on Ulrich's reflections or stepping outside their range with distancing metaphors as he does with Leinsdorf, he underscores the general validity of the non-narrative outward "proliferating" structure of the mind by offering it up as a general "characteristic of the age."

Möglichkeitssinn, then, is a vague expression for a precise narrative structure, that is, a turning away from plot and dramatic action toward poetry. This turn as a narrative device finds a parallel in the novel's major explicit theme, Ulrich's turning away from the world of social interaction toward a life in which thinking and reflection constitute its main activities. We may then expect that Ulrich's thinking process will not be the closely argued exposition of character laid out in accordance with a familiar ideology for satiric effect; rather, it will be closely bound up with the philosophical question of the mind's possibility of having "freely occurring, undetermined" thoughts, with the related problem of the autonomous function and independent value of the ideas thus created as opposed to the social and psychological forces that shape the character who thinks, and with the authority of such processes when conducted as "scientific" investigations. Musil notably contrasted his novelistic concern with that of James Joyce by distinguishing his own attempt to catch the idiosyncrasies of "the *thought* process" from Joyce's interest in "the shortened forms of orthodox verbal formulas . . . the *speech* process."

This is Musil's notion of the autonomous role of thinking, and Ulrich's solitary states of contemplation become an increasingly greater part of the main "action" of *The Man Without Qualities.* Examining some of Ulrich's extended meditations throughout the novel will reveal some of the implications of Musil's view of the novel, of his attempt to portray the solitary and stationary act of thinking within the traditionally interpersonal drama of the novel. Here the human drama of interpersonal relationships is replaced by the clash between different types or structures of thought.

Early in the novel, in "Ein Kapitel das jeder überschlagen kann der von der Beschäftigung mit Gedanken keine besondere Meinung hat" ("A Chapter That Can Be Skipped by Anybody Who Has No Very High Opinion of Thinking as an Occupation"), Ulrich sits down at his desk and sets himself the topic of "water" as a subject for thought, with the narrator wryly noting that nothing is so difficult to represent by literary means as a man thinking. Pulling his study curtains shut, Ulrich begins with a mathematical equation on "the state of water"; we are told that the precision and sureness of this kind of thinking, with "no parallel anywhere in life," fill him with a kind of melancholy. Surely also the rarified intellectual task, conducted at the boundary of the "new" with the world shut out, contributes to this melancholy sensation of abandonment by the world. Soon Ulrich strays from his mathematical calculations to a rehearsal of the mythic conceptions that have been associated with water. What follows is an abbreviation of a much longer passage that nevertheless gives the character and progression of this meditation:

> [Water] was long believed to be related to air. The great Newton believed this, and nevertheless most of his other ideas are still up to date. According to the Greeks, the world and life evolved out of water. It was a god, Okeanos. Later, water spirits, elves, mermaids and nymphs were invented. . . . And wasn't water still used for baptisms? And naturally the man without qualities had modern knowledge somewhere in his consciousness, whether he was thinking about it or not. And then water became a colorless—blue only in thick layers—odorless, and tasteless liquid . . . and this prototype of all liquids was, physically, in essence not a liquid at all but, depending on the circumstance, a solid body, a liquid, or a gas. Ultimately this totality dissolved into a system of formulas, which somehow were connected with each other, and in the whole world there were only a dozen people who agreed on as simple a thing as water; all the others talked about it in vocabularies that were at home somewhere between the present and several thousand years ago. . . .
>
> He felt annoyed. . . . He thought of that stupid-intense, exciting impression touching immediately upon the self that one has when one sniffs one's own skin. He stood up and pulled the curtain away from the window.
>
> The bark of the trees was still moist from the morning. Outside on the street lay a violet-blue haze of gasoline. The sun shone into it, and people moved briskly. It was an asphalt-spring, a spring day in autumn removed from the seasonal round such as only cities can conjure forth. . . .
> (1:112–114)

In effect Ulrich performs a semiotic analysis of water, showing how the various linguistic

codes that have historically surrounded it are related to its life-giving, creative powers. On the subject of water, however, Ulrich's thinking is paradoxically "arid." The original power of water derived from a myth of creation. Now palpable life no longer emerges from water; rather, the palpable substance water itself has "dissolved" from a mythic totality, *Okeanos,* into a system of cultural formulas, concerning which the only task now left is their codification by an intelligence sufficiently historicizing and scientifically exact. The reverse has occurred from the previous example of the image of the young girl; rather than being seized by an image that frees his associative powers and stimulates a sensuous reverie, Ulrich has merely stirred up the historical-cultural "sediment" on which the sign "water" floats. "Modern knowledge," the synchronic pressure of the history of the sign, vitiates the impulse of the self to assert itself in subjective opposition, to claim the image for a personal field of associations, to metaphorize. Ulrich's "immersion" in thought here produces not a state of pure consciousness in which the outlines of the self dissolve but the altogether shallower rill of a synthesizing historical analysis of the theme of creativity.

In one of the very few passages in the novel in which Ulrich is explicitly named as "the man without qualities," he is also linked, through the scientific analysis of the substance "water," to "modern" or scientific knowledge. Water, "the prototype of all liquids," here represents the scientific paradigm. It allotropically migrates from state to state, discontinuously, without identifiable essence or original state; in Jakobson's terms, it operates metonymically rather than metaphorically. It is accessible to empirical observation only in its successive forms: a solid body, a liquid, or a gas. "Family resemblances" in successive states may be traced through a descriptive principle of behavior and may be linked under the concept of water, but "correspondence" and "identity" are metaphors that have no place here. No metaphysical concept of wholeness, no organizing metaphor, "underlies" its successive empirical embodiments. This conflict between a metaphysical and an empirical paradigm—between religious myths and the modern scientific structure of successivity or sequence—is a basic and repeated one and is Musil's primary means of setting off Ulrich's consciousness against those of the secondary characters in the social world of the novel. Ulrich's reflections represent not the empirical paradigm alone, but rather the conflict between paradigms.

This conflict between a scientific and a metaphysical paradigm seems itself to constitute a kind of paradigm and thus to simplify and order a good deal of the novel. However, it should be kept in mind that Ulrich's relation to notions of wholeness, certainty, and belief is much more complex and ambivalent than any neat conflict of paradigms would suggest. A closer look at the "turn" in this passage will demonstrate this, for it, too, resembles, although in different form, the turn previously noted toward the "heightening in stepwise fashion" from the accretion of linear details (the metonymic collection of codes connected with water) to their transformation into a "structured" association, that is, one with metaphoric power.

Here a metaphoric paradigm is being created on the very basis of a linear structure demonstrating the impossibility of paradigms. In the above passage we learn that Ulrich's arid and unsatisfying reflections, the mere rehearsal of historical codes, are "annoying" to him. Rising from his desk, he pulls the curtain back from the window. The life going on outside is described in a passage striking for its elegiac and timeless quality. The "prototype of all liquids" reappears here, now in all its variety of forms. The "violet-blue haze" of gasoline vapor and the "moist" morning dew are reminiscent of two of the states in which water appears. The haze permeates the scene, hanging over and blanketing the street. The sun shining into the "haze" seems to increase its shiny, hazy denseness and to give the impression of a hovering diffuseness and formless ubiquity.

Temporally, it is a moment out of history and sequence, a springlike autumn day out of season. The verbs used are notably verbs of existence and the nouns ("people," "sun," and "trees") suggest a universalizing and abstracting portrait rather than an anecdotal moment. We can find here a theme developed by Nietzsche in "Vom Nutzen und Nachteil der Historie für das Leben" ("The Use and Abuse of History," 1910), the restoration of a sensuous present wrested from oppressive memory and from consciousness of historical determinants. Here we witness a momentary freedom from the synchronic pressure of competing paradigms, which weighed so heavily on Ulrich during his reflection and stifled his subjective impulses. Ulrich's impulse to "sniff his own skin" announces the attempt to restore a sensuous, unmediated present through contact with the "next" moment beyond his fruitless reflections.

One could go farther and suggest that Ulrich's fixed gaze out the window represents, through the action of the water, which takes the form of a ubiquitous haze, an allegory of lost and restored unity between himself and the present moment, an interpretation suggested by the previous identification between himself and water. His longing for wholeness is allegorized through the action of water diffusing itself over the street in a formless, undifferentiated presence, a diffusion that is intensified by the generalized nouns and static verbs, which indicate the desire to prolong the merging. The watery element actually accomplishes this merging, its formless plenitude and dissolution strongly contrasting with the structured alternatives of Ulrich's previous reflections.

Because the unifying action and ubiquitous presence of water binds Ulrich's field of vision into an undifferentiated, foggy whole, Ulrich accomplishes a projection of himself onto the world of the present and away from his historical tracings in an attempt to reestablish a unity between self and world that he had forgone in his scientific investigation, the theme of which was precisely all metaphysical notions of unity.

Yet this contrasting "present" is of a complex sort. As Bernd-Rüdiger Hüppauf has pointed out, the movement from inner to outer in German novels, typically signaled by the gaze out of windows, conventionally raises the reader's expectations for a shift from an imaginary and subjective state to a real and objective one. Here something like the reverse occurs. The inner "vision" is an experience of the "impersonal," while the "turn" to the scene outside represents an allegory of the supremacy of the subjective vision. It could even be claimed that "inner" and "outer" in *The Man Without Qualities* are merely two facets of a single theme that in fact originates in Ulrich's inner reflections. The narrative voice contributes to the ambiguous relation between inner and outer worlds by intermittently merging with the character's voice so that it is impossible to determine the degree to which a character's inner experience is validated and objectified by its convergence with the narrative voice. The result, as here, is that the external world, which appears to counterbalance Ulrich's internal processes, is "dematerialized" and so serves not as a contrasting pole but rather as only one aspect of an interior phenomenon. The notion that the external world is a construct and that Ulrich's process of constituting and recombining the elements of the external world, in the fashion described by Mach, out of themes taken from his own prior, inner reflections (an example of the "stepwise heightening of the mind"), is sanctioned by the narrator, and this makes problematic any simple pairing of the opposed terms "subjective" and "objective." That Ulrich can be said in some sense to "author" the world outside himself suggests the momentary collapse of the distinction between the objective consciousness of the narrator and the subjective world of his characters.

This ironization of the structural terms of the novel through both an ambiguity in point of view and the occasional erasure of the boundaries between character and narrator is central to the realization of Musil's ethical views of art. He considered the traditional relation between omniscient narrator and characters with limited perspectives to be an authoritarian relation. As an experiment in the parallel activities of living and writing, it was too safe, too controlled. This notion of the riskless nature of omniscient narration is explicitly taken up in the novel. Musil emphasized the radical irony attached to the ultimate reality of *The Man Without Qualities* when he distinguished his project of "constructing and synthesizing" from that of other modernists like Proust and Joyce, which he characterized somewhat uncharitably as "simply rendering dissolution through the method of an associative style with blurred boundaries."

THE "SENSE OF POSSIBILITY" AND IRONY

The ambiguity surrounding Ulrich's experiences of perception demonstrates the necessity for a highly ironic reading of *The Man Without Qualities.* The simultaneous construction and perception of "reality" that is demonstrated at the crucial moment of intellectual investigation, at the height of the desire to "know," signals the irreducible irony attached to this desire. And since Ulrich as a scientific investigator is posited as a protagonist desirous of precise, objective, and "true" knowledge, this paradigm of desire and its frustration due to the impossibility of unproblematic knowledge constitute a central irony of the novel.

At this point one could conclude that the passage containing Ulrich's reflections on "water" functions uniquely as a central and privileged index demonstrating such irony for the novel as a whole. But it would be wrong to claim either that this passage functions in such an emblematic way or that it is unique in breaking through an otherwise undisturbed fiction to a more allegorical level. This would be incorrect for two reasons. First, the entire fabric of the novel is designed to suggest the "ghostly" quality inhering in reality: the dissolution between inner and outer, the ambiguity of perception, and the irony consequently attached to all perceptions. This, then, is not a privileged moment; rather, it is only one example of many similar passages in which an arid reflection leads to an epiphany and in which, in turn, the epiphanic image is confounded when we reflect on its ironic context.

Second, Musil sought to dramatize the irony of perception as such, to indicate the ironic and paradoxical implications of such passages for the reading process as a whole. While Ulrich is working through the various codes of water, engaged in the process of assembling and ordering its historical appearances, the reader should be experiencing a similarly complex train of thought. For example, the reader should be conscious here not only of the conflict of paradigms arising out of Ulrich's reflections but also of parallels between this and other passages where a similar conflict of paradigms arises through the use of wholly different material. Moreover, there are thematic resemblances between this and other passages. Water is a favorite image of Musil's and turns up in different forms in many other passages. Additionally, the reader can import culturally available associations not explicitly mentioned in the novel itself. The most obvious association the reader might bring to bear on this passage is the significance of the connection between water as a physical substance and myths of creation and creativity. There is a paradox in this association, never alluded to explicitly: Ulrich's infertile intellectual exercise works itself out on the very emblem of creativity—which is also an emblem for Ulrich himself. That "water" turns up repeatedly as a component (and sometimes even as the "transparent" medium) of perception must exert considerable fascination for the reader. The reader might also contemplate some associations that Ulrich mentions—baptism, the emergence of life out of water, hedonistic or Dionysiac

rites—and some that he omits—the "depths" of the unconscious, the romantic notion of a "deep" hermeneutic knowledge falsified by "surface" rationality. (*Young Törless* begins with an epigraph taken from Maurice Maeterlinck describing how fabulously beautiful underwater pearls are transformed to cheap colored glass when brought to the surface.) Images of fog, mist, waves, rain—water in some form—find their way into a great number of metaphors throughout the novel. These cannot be systematically glossed to arrive at an unambiguous statement of the symbolic role of "water" in the novel, yet their repeated use suggests that patterning is a device for producing signification. Similar patterns, too complex to demonstrate here, are built upon other tropes. Thus this passage stimulates a proliferation of converging themes with ironic associations leading in many directions.

The novel encourages this fascination, this network of associations and unexpected convergences, by presenting parallel but nonidentical situations. We are teased along with the mystery of emerging paradigms, but the minute effect of our train of associations, parallel to Ulrich's own sense of converging and contradictory patterns, is to slow down the reading process, to make it "dense" (or *dicht,* for Musil a component of *Dichtung* [poetry]). We may note that this is a "parallel action" of a different sort from that concerning the empire's centennial celebration; this one establishes a parallel between the reader's quest for a pattern of meaning and Ulrich's. Both Ulrich's and the reader's involve similar thought processes and parallel "turns" into creative reveries. The reader, too, must slow his pace in order to ponder the identities and differences among the associations that arise throughout the reading process. We can again recall Musil's notion of the heart of metaphor, that the comparison would be merely reductive if not for the "denseness" created by the lack of correspondence between associated terms. In this sense the reader must always read the novel "ironically," in relativizing fashion, with

951

one eye on all the other similar yet non-identical paradigms. In this way the reader will not make the mistake of privileging any moment as a heightening process once and for all "achieved." Each "turn" perceived by the reader, each "illuminating image," is only a part of a metonymic "series" of similar epiphanies.

Such an ironic reading makes of the present moment a "recombination" of the past for the reader. The resonances of past upon present have the effect of throwing the reader centrifugally out of the forward motion of the plot into a meditative, distanced mode. We can recall a similar though much less complex "turn" toward the meditative or speculative when Ulrich gives up his reflections on design in order to contemplate the female form as a particularly pleasing architectural shape. The present moment is thus constructed by, not merely "seen through," a temperament, to quote Émile Zola's phrase. The larger differences implied in this philosophically complex issue of perception distinguish literary modernism from the earlier moments of naturalism and realism.

The density and resonant power of the moment depend on how many resemblances from the past the reader can bring to bear. The quality of the present poetic moment is a function of the particular mind at work. The novel requires a precise reader who, like Ulrich, values scientific precision. Indeed, our model for an intelligence of this kind—one that analyzes the variety and sequences of a phenomenon for resemblances and differences—is Ulrich himself. The question of levels of intellectual competence is explicitly taken up in the novel through the exploration of the question "What is genius?" (This question is posed satirically in passages that describe, for instance, "the racehorse of genius," a popular debasement of the concept of genius, and it is also posed seriously in the cluster of chapters surrounding the "Gienialität als Frage" ["Question of Genius"] in the posthumously published sections of the novel, the *Nachlass*.) The new and as yet unborn reader demanded by Musil must be someone competent to undertake this plethora of finely discriminated combinations. This state of contemplation, of attunement to convergences and divergences between past and present—both the reader's and Ulrich's project—is what the novel names *der andere Zustand* (the other condition); it is a realization of the "sense of possibility" that tolerates contradiction and paradox.

Notwithstanding the narrative nondevelopment of *The Man Without Qualities,* its moments of "the other condition" deepen and become more remarkable after Ulrich becomes reunited with his long-forgotten sister Agathe at the beginning of part 3, almost 700 pages into the novel. Their reunion, brought about by the death of their father, provides Ulrich with a companion with whom he can begin to explore and sustain "the other condition." In this portion of the novel Agathe often provides the occasion for further discussion of topics that are by now familiar through Ulrich's reflections in previous sections of the novel: living completely in accord with oneself, a project difficult for a radical ironist such as he; perceiving moral values as functional and circumstantial rather than as absolute and unchanging; the intermittent ebbing and swelling of our perceptions of reality and the dissolution of these perceptions when no longer fully felt; and the resulting incommunicability of these quasi-mystical states, which cannot be induced at will but lived only momentarily and involuntarily. The extended conversations between brother and sister are termed *heilige Gespräche* (holy conversations) in keeping with the deepening mystical strain of the novel.

THE NOVEL AS THOUGHT EXPERIMENT

Musil wrote in his essay "Analyse und Synthese" (Analysis and Synthesis, 1913): "Let one be mistrustful of nothing so much as of all desires for the decomplication of literature and life, for a Homeric or religious frame of mind, for consolidation and completeness."

We have looked at some of Musil's strategies for foiling all attempts at "decomplication" on his protagonist's part and for ironizing and complicating the parallel endeavor on the reader's part: the ironic use of "the wrong form," the internal monologue, to convey a synoptic overview of character; the invention by each secondary character of a totalizing metaphor of *das Ganze* and the narrator's sly method of "scrambling" these metaphors for the absolute by juxtaposing them; and the employment of heightening and epiphanic metaphors that signal the onset of "the other condition" and their ultimate indeterminateness for a single consistent reading of the novel as a whole. A few larger structural ironies should also be noted.

The author's sleight-of-hand in relation to the satire of the social world of the novel is also significant. The use of satire in depicting the minor characters causes the reader to expect a standard or normative certainty against which to judge these characters' errors. The task of providing such a norm should fall to Ulrich. But although he occupies a wider mental horizon than these characters, he cannot be said to provide certainties of any kind. Indeed, the novel's description of his much more difficult project, his attempt to recapture an unmediated present and to reject all fixed concepts, raises much greater interpretive problems than those raised by the minor characters. To oppose satire with a deeper ironic ambiguity rather than a normative standard is yet another of the novel's paradoxes that ensure that no "decomplication" can occur.

One might try to establish a norm from another perspective, namely, the perspective of history. It is at times suggested in the novel that the mythologies of minor characters are produced by contemporary developments in the history of ideas, in particular by the fact that for the first time the enlarged authority of modern science has begun to threaten the hitherto inviolable region of myth and religious belief. The suggestion that the ghostly quality of reality results from peculiarly modern conflicts, however, is foiled by the novel's definition of history as a continual process of "going off course." No prior epoch in which greater spiritual harmony was enjoyed can be adduced from such a discontinuous view of history; the elimination of cause and effect from history refutes such a historical retracing. The implication for the novel is that the conflict between science and religion is both a modern problem and an eternal, structural conflict of the mind. The real and the ideal, the historical and the absolute, are paired in an intentional disequilibrium. In fact, the novel as a whole is located in a strange equipoise, both within and outside of history. The novel seems to represent history as it is depicted in realist novels, but it does not. Thus we can see why Musil insists upon the polemical point, perhaps the novel's least convincing, that there is no such thing as history. This point is necessary to maintain the weird equipoise between the real and the possible; and this intellectual framework allowed Musil to represent in the narrative the free responsiveness to Ulrich's states of reflection, to allow the exploration of "the other condition" and of impersonal states of mind.

Virginia Woolf also felt the formal constraints of the traditional notion of the ego. In her essay "The Narrow Bridge of Art" in *Granite and Rainbow* (New York, 1975) she complains of the tired predictability of the "psychological novelist" and of the "poeticization" of the new "impersonal" novel of the future:

> The psychological novelist has been too prone to limit psychology to the psychology of personal intercourse. . . . We long for some more impersonal relationship. We long for ideas, for dreams, for imaginations, for poetry. . . . [The new novel] will be written in prose, but in prose which has many of the characteristics of poetry. . . . It will stand further back from life. . . . It will resemble poetry in this, that it will give not only or mainly people's relations to each other and their activities together, as the novel has hitherto done, but it will give the relation of the mind to general ideas and its soliloquy in solitude.
>
> (pp. 18–19)

953

Like Musil, Woolf is more interested in consciousness, in the mind's "soliloquy in solitude," than in character. She advocates a novel that can accommodate the flux and ambiguity of experience. For both Musil and Woolf the impersonal self is a means to the enlargement of experience, and the new novel must be able to express this enlargement of consciousness. The dissolution of the ego makes possible "the unknown and uncircumscribed spirit" of life. In Woolf's celebrated formulation, the self experiences the world as a "luminous halo, a semi-transparent envelope surrounding us from the beginning of consciousness to the end"; the freedom to experience the "uncircumscribed" realm of "ideas, dreams, imagination, and poetry" (Musil's equivalent phrase conceives of the novel as *Gedankenexperiment* ["thought experiment"]) is indicated by the "transparency" of the self in moments of experience, or, to put it another way, the occasional disappearance of the fictional self due to the supremacy of states of consciousness. At these moments the distinction between inner and outer, between self and world, dissolves. At the same time the fictional voice becomes fused with the narrative voice, and an ambiguity of voice results. This suppression of the fictional personality and fusion with the narrative voice is a tendency Musil and Woolf share, but with substantially different results.

The novel as *Gedankenexperiment* deals with the repeated emergence from the narrative of the *idea* as an objective and autonomous event that serves to structure, heighten, and universalize the narrated moment. The heightening and universalizing add an aura of apparent significance and symbolic meaning to the empirical details being narrated; yet conversely they embed the universal within concrete determinants. As Musil said of the method of *The Man Without Qualities:* "Style, for me, is the exact working out of an idea. I mean an idea which is also in the most beautiful form that I can achieve."

The autonomy of the idea in this novel is closely connected to the infinite variety of thought and to the insurmountable irony that is attached to the status of thought. The experience of thinking is not the rehearsal of reified concepts but rather an aspect, as the narrator describes it, of "the sliding logic of the soul." Thinking is protean; it can assume a variety of forms and even create new forms. Style is the embodiment of an idea in a particular, engaged form, in a complex of combinations and recombinations. Out of the creation of fictional characters depicted in the experience of thinking, a collection of such engaged forms can be gathered together. This procedure, repeated many times throughout the novel, suggests the emergence of an objective structure to the thought process, a transcendence of the realist narrative toward the depiction of an objective and universal, ahistorical and structural, thought process. As Ulrich formulates it himself during one of his meditations, one branch of his life had always been dedicated to trying to "live the history of ideas instead of the history of the world," to live, as Musil rather slyly puts it, "as a figure in a book with all the inessential elements left out, the essential residue of it undergoing a magical integration." Musil's book, of course, questions the hierarchy of the essential/inessential. Ulrich realizes that these tendencies are "anti-realistic in their abnormal, epigrammatic intensity" but that nevertheless they "brought an unmistakably ruthless passion to bear upon reality."

Despite this longing for significance Ulrich, and the novel, repeatedly repudiates even those moments in which he appears to have "derived" an unassailable paradigm or absolute principle out of the plethora of empirical sensations and events. In one instance Ulrich provides a corrective for his own longings for absolute form, which is to focus on the egotism and infantile rebellion involved in the impulse to discover an entelechy for modern life. Thus Ulrich's own example demonstrates to the reader that the question of what to make of the structure of the thinking process, of how to regard the many "objectifications" of the idea out of the fictional narrative, is fraught with difficulty. The allegories or "illuminating images" that tempt one to take them as moments of epiphanic truth are unstable at best or, in many cases, so subtle and ambiguous as to seem almost hallucinatory. In the allegorical moment following Ulrich's ruminations upon "water," for instance, the final passage could be read as nothing more than a contiguous, neutrally narrated, and inconclusive final sequence in which a vista meets Ulrich's eyes as he lifts his head from his work, turns his gaze to the outside world, and passively allows a cityscape to impinge upon his consciousness. The cityscape exists both in the naturalistic sense, as the "inessential," untransformed quotidian, and as the poetic occasion for a subjective, projective allegory born of the desire for the absolute.

The twofold, indeterminate nature of "the other condition" is therefore not an epiphany of transcendence, as some critics maintain, but an epiphany of irony. Its dual vision registers both the human desire to transform and heighten reality and the neutrality of reality, its resistance to symbolic forms. The formal patterning of chapters is designed to raise the possibility of a symbolic, structuring, or transforming process capable of subduing reality, but not to confirm the existence of such a process. Thus the intuition that another heightened, utopian reality exists where thought takes precedence over the resistant medium of reality functions simultaneously in a utopian and ironic manner.

Thus, rather than viewing the heightening process as achieving a new stable reality as in Woolf's view of the universalizing function of art, we see in *The Man Without Qualities* only the recurrence of the aestheticizing activity, the patterning and reconstituting of reality without the emergence of an ultimate form or stabilizing vision. This disembodied activity points to the narrator's "production of significance" through the creation of allegories; this activity is both a utopian and desiring activity and an ironic and intellectual one. The oscillation of the narrative voice between imper-

sonal heights and sudden fusings with Ulrich's and Agathe's inner experiences enables it to accommodate two thoroughly disjunctive perspectives: first, knowledge of the radically nonhuman, impersonal "other condition" of the universe, and second, the human desire for self-extension, for incorporation and symbolic transformation of otherness into self.

This irony reflects Musil's suspicion of form as such, of its arbitrary claim to authority through its ability to impose the power of structure. Musil is clearly fascinated by the unreality of forms. Once invented in the imagination, they have an ontological force; forms can create "new" realms of being and can extract a false sense of closure and completeness out of the bits and pieces of the empirical world. Form as the receptacle of being is oxymoronic; form is the *wahre Erfindung,* the "true invention," of the novel, and the life forms depicted in the novel represent a ghostly "action" "parallel" to what reality? Ulrich declares at one point, "God intends the world in no way literally; it is an image, an analogy, a figure of speech . . . and naturally is always insufficient."

This is where Musil parts company with Woolf's notions about the challenges that the modern novel must undertake. Musil is committed to the dissolution of the ego and to the defictionalization and depersonalization of character as Woolf expresses it in "The Narrow Bridge of Art." He does not, however, accept her dictum that the "new" novel will bring to bear a "generalizing and simplifying power" upon "tumultuous and contradictory emotions" and that "everything in a work of art should be mastered and ordered." "Generalization" and "simplification" are suspicious activities for Musil. His sensitivity to form as artifice and as evidence of the reification of experience leads him to tolerate only those forms that lead to the perception of paradox and irony. He would reject Woolf's frank aestheticization of experience and her conviction that the function of art is to order, depersonalize, and universalize experience. He would also disagree with her conclusion that the achievement of art is the transcendental order of which the work, the novel, is the concrete artifact. Woolf resolves her portrayals of the complex flux of human life with an approving portrayal of the figure of the artist, who glimpses and tends the transcendental order. For example, Lily Briscoe's painterly vision of aesthetic order provides the apotheosis of *To the Lighthouse* (1927). Musil would look beyond such a vision to the ultimate uninterpretability of the world.

To return for a moment to the "sense of possibility," this most indeterminate and inclusive form-giving principle of the novel, we can see not only that it has a very wide range of implications but that it ultimately bridges a paradox. Initially it appears to refer to Ulrich's notion of imagination and potentiality, of living *anders*, which distinguishes him from the *Wirklichkeitsmenschen*, the one-dimensional realists of the social world of the novel. When we begin to inquire into the manifestations of the "sense of possibility," however, this "half" of the logical opposition between "realists" and "possibilitarians" seems itself to incorporate an opposition. The "sense of possibility" appears to mean, on one hand, the heightened, symbolic attainment of form and the drive toward greater meaning and integration of self and world, and, on the other, the basically random and chaotic movement of the universe, proliferating in all directions "without any central unity." This notion, that of the world's impersonal, unmanageable, and irrational activity, widens the sense of possibility as a category of meaning to such an extent that it metonymically includes all possible instances of experience, upon which no structuring principles can be superimposed. Looked at this way, the "sense of possibility" is no longer an organizing category but simply a way of indicating the phenomenal universe. It is no longer a heightening principle but rather a principle of extension, identical to the random flow of impersonal nature.

The "sense of possibility" thus mediates

between Ulrich's longing for fusion and transparency, for the "oceanic" dissolution of the ego into a named and understood universe, and the opposed recognition that the world will always be resistant to what Nietzsche calls "aesthetic anthropomorphisms" and symbolic forms. It can mean the emergence of the allegorizing idea, the superimposition of "structure upon sequence," in Jakobson's formulation, that occasionally gives the reader a particularly mystical sense of the fusion of the particular and the universal. On the other hand it can refer to the unartified mere reproduction of the sequential moments of "an entire life," as Musil described his goal for *The Man Without Qualities.*

With this paradoxical perspective in mind we can appreciate a larger structural irony of the novel that never found expression because the novel remained uncompleted. It will be recalled that the series of "holy conversations" between Ulrich and Agathe occupying the main action of the latter part of the novel was intended to balance the political scheme of the *Parallelaktion*. Of course the *Parallelaktion* is a burlesque series of attempts to "heighten" and unify the Austrian national identity by proclaiming a national "theme." It is clear that there are as many different metaphors for unity as there are citizens in the land. To see the "sense of possibility" stretch out in this way is an obvious but good joke. To see the implications of this for a "parallel" movement, Urlich's exploration of a new morality with Agathe, throws an undeniably ironic light on their search.

This is not to suggest that the novel be read by "inserting a few pages between glass plates" and changing them from time to time, a method Musil proposed for the densely poetic pair of novellas entitled *Vereinigungen*, the only one of his works he claimed to take pleasure in rereading. Yet a centrifugal motion out of the linear narrative and into a reverie is suggested in Musil's proposed way of reading the novellas. The paradox of "neutral immanence" that accompanies each "turn" from narrative to reflexive heightening seems to invite a similarly centrifugal movement in the reader that "completes" or extends a series originating in the fictional narrative. There are many instances in the novel in which Ulrich worries an idea until he creates a logical contradiction, then characteristically "turns" from his logical thoughts to the outside world to make reassuring contact with a nature beyond his thoughts. It seems clear that at the end of each chapter the reader, confronted with a multitude of peculiar, contradictory, and stimulating associations, is invited to do the same, to lift his head from the confines of this concatenation of expressions of desire for wholeness and from the constraints of irony and seek in his own visual environment an extension of such neutral immanence. The victory of a novel that ultimately aims at extension and inclusion rather than at symbol and structure would be to incorporate the "next" moment of consciousness: the one beyond its own possible boundaries. Musil's notion of boundaries as hermetic lines to be crossed when "the dream state reaches over into day" can be extended in this direction to refer to the world beyond the book, to the reader's own present, and to endow it with this wholly unpolemical, even hallucinatory, intermittent immanence of structure behind neutrality.

Despite the obvious commonality between Musil's artistic methods and those of the other major literary modernists such as Proust, Joyce, Mann, and Woolf, he has been sadly ignored by the English-speaking world since his death in 1942. Marginal in his personal relations both with the European literary giants of his day and with "the common reader," he looked to an audience of the future for fuller appreciation. Indeed, traces of Musil's influence can be found in the metaphysical ironies of the work of a younger generation of German-speaking writers. One thinks of the Musilian paradoxes hovering under the surface and, indeed, traceable in the title of Peter Handke's short novel *Die Stunde der wahren Empfindung* (*A Moment of True Feeling*, 1975). The

"true" of the title is itself a gentle oxymoron. Because of the social and psychological analysis of the sort performed in *The Man Without Qualities,* there are now many such words that cannot survive without brackets. Despite its inconclusiveness, *The Man Without Qualities* contains Musil's fullest analysis of the social and psychological determinants of the reader's situation that necessitate such ironies.

Selected Bibliography

EDITIONS

INDIVIDUAL WORKS
Die Verwirrungen des Zöglings Törless. Vienna, 1906.
Vereinigungen. Munich, 1911.
Die Schwärmer. Dresden, 1921.
Vinzenz und die Freundin bedeutender Männer. Berlin, 1923.
Drei Frauen. Berlin, 1924.
Der Mann ohne Eigenschaften. Book 1, parts 1 and 2. Berlin, 1930. Book 2, part 3 (the first 38 chapters). Berlin, 1933. Book 3, part 3 (conclusion) and part 4 (edited material from the *Nachlass* [unpublished papers]). Edited by Martha Musil. Lausanne, 1943.

COLLECTED WORKS
Gesammelte Werke in Einzelausgaben. 3 vols. Edited by Adolf Frisé. Hamburg, 1952–1957. Vol. 1: *Der Mann ohne Eigenschaften,* 1952. Vol. 2: *Tagebücher, Aphorismen, Essays und Reden,* 1955. Vol. 3: *Prosa, Dramen, Späte Briefe,* 1957.
Gesammelte Werke. 9 vols. Edited by Adolf Frisé. Hamburg, 1978. Paperback edition. Vols. 1–5: *Der Mann ohne Eigenschaften.* Vol. 6: *Prosa und Stücke.* Vol. 7: *Kleine Prosa, Aphorismen, Autobiographisches.* Vol. 8: *Essays und Reden.* Vol. 9: *Kritik.*

TRANSLATIONS
Five Women. Translated by Eithne Wilkins and Ernst Kaiser. New York, 1966.
The Man Without Qualities. 3 vols. Translated by Eithne Wilkins and Ernst Kaiser. London, 1968.

Young Törless. Translated by Eithne Wilkins and Ernst Kaiser. New York, 1964.

BIOGRAPHICAL AND CRITICAL STUDIES

Arntzen, Helmut. *Satirischer Stil.* Bonn, 1960.

Baur, Uwe, and Dietmar Goltschnigg, eds. *Vom "Törless" zum "Mann ohne Eigenschaften."* Munich, 1973.

Berghahn, Wilfried. *Robert Musil in Selbstzeugnissen und Bilddokumenten.* Hamburg, 1963.

Blanchot, Maurice. *Le livre à venir.* Paris, 1959.

Canetti, Elias. *The Play of the Eyes.* Translated by Ralph Manheim. New York, 1986.

Cohn, Dorritt. *Transparent Minds.* Princeton, N.J., 1978.

Gradischnig, Hertwig. *Das Bild des Dichters bei Robert Musil.* Munich, 1976.

Heydebrand, Renate von. *Die Reflexionen Ulrichs in Robert Musils Roman "Der Mann ohne Eigenschaften."* Münster, 1966.

Hickman, Hannah. *Robert Musil and the Culture of Vienna.* London and Sydney, 1984.

Huber, Lothar, and John J. White, eds. *Musil in Focus.* London, 1982.

Hüppauf, Bernd-Rüdiger. *Von sozialer Utopie zur Mystik.* Munich, 1971.

Kermode, Frank. "A Short View of Musil." *Encounter* 15:64–75 (1960).

Kühn, Dieter. *Analogie und Variation.* Bonn, 1965.

Laermann, Klaus. *Eigenschaftlosigkeit.* Stuttgart, 1970.

Luft, David S. *Robert Musil and the Crisis of European Culture, 1880–1942.* Berkeley, Calif., 1980.

Müller, Götz. *Ideologiekritik und Metasprache.* Munich, 1972.

Peters, Frederick G. *Robert Musil, Master of the Hovering Life.* New York, 1978.

Pike, Burton. *Robert Musil: An Introduction to His Work.* Ithaca, N.Y., 1961.

Rasch, Wolfdietrich. *Über Robert Musils Roman "Der Mann ohne Eigenschaften."* Göttingen, 1967.

Roth, Marie-Louise. *Robert Musil: Ethik und Ästhetik.* Munich, 1972.

Ryan, Judith. "The Vanishing Subject: Empirical Psychology and the Modern Novel." *PMLA* 95: 857–869 (1980).

Schaffnit, Hans Wolfgang. *Mimesis als Problem.* Berlin, 1971.

Strutz, Josef, and Johann Strutz, eds. *Robert Musil: Literatur, Philosophie, und Psychologie.* Munich, 1984.

VICTORIA YABLONSKY

ALEXANDER BLOK
(1880–1921)

THREE YEARS BEFORE his death, Alexander Blok wrote:

Catullus' personal passion, like the passion of every poet, was permeated with the spirit of his epoch. Its fate, its rhythms, and its meters, like the rhythms and the meters of the poet's verses, were inspired by the time in which he lived. For in the poetic perception of the world, there is no break between the personal and the general: the more sensitive the poet is, the more inseparable he feels what is "his" and what is "not his" to be. Thus in times of storm and turmoil even the most gentle and intimate aspirations of the poet's soul become filled with storm and turmoil.

(6:83)[1]

There surely was no time in Russian history more stormy and tumultuous than the years during which Blok lived. And no one of his generation was more sensitive to its sounds or spoke more eloquently of its terrors and strange beauty than did Blok himself. Indeed, Blok was the preeminent spokesman for his age, the last poet of a long line of great poets of the nineteenth century and the first unquestionably great Russian poet of the twentieth. For many people of his time he was *the* poet, who expressed the complex aspirations and alienation of the Russian intelligentsia in the anxious, early years of this century. As Anna Akhmatova wrote of him in her poem "On prav—opiat' fonar', apteka" ("He's right—once again the lamp, the drugstore," 1946),[2] he stands "like a monument to the beginning of the century." In a sense, he was their greatest poet of what they had irretrievably lost.

Nurtured on the tradition of nineteenth-century Russian lyric poetry, Blok controlled its thematics and forms with consummate skill and authority and used them to create a lyrical persona wholly of his own epoch. It is perhaps thanks to the particular nature of this tradition, in which the personal life of the poet is so inextricably linked to the history of his nation, that his uncanny sense of the historical moment and his prophetic vision of the catastrophes that were to befall his times could be expressed in the personal and intimate language of lyric poetry. This is particularly clear in "Golos iz khora" ("A Voice from the Chorus," 6 June 1910–27 February 1914[3]):

How often do we weep, you and I, over our pitiful life! O, if you only knew, my friends, the cold and darkness of the days ahead!

Today you press your beloved's hand, you playfully toy with it, only to weep when you discover

---

[1] All quotations from Blok's writings are from the standard collected works: *Sobranie sochinenii v vos'mi tomakh*, 8 vols., edited by V. N. Orlov et al. (Moscow and Leningrad, 1960–1963).

[2] For ease of reference, poems in this essay are referred to upon subsequent mention by their English titles. These poems have not necessarily been translated into English.

[3] Blok meticulously dated his poems by their dates of composition throughout his life. These dates, and not dates of publication, appear in the citations in this essay.

treachery or a dagger in that dear hand, you child, poor child!

There is no end to the deceit and falsehood, and death is far ahead. This terrible world will grow darker still, and the whirlwind of the planets will become all the more insane, for centuries, centuries to come!

And we shall see, you and I, the last age, worse than all the rest. Oppressive sin will eclipse the sky, laughter will freeze on everyone's lips, and there will be a painful longing for death. . . .

You will await the spring, my child—spring will deceive you. You will exhort the sun to rise in the sky—the sun will not rise. And your cry, when you begin to shout, will sink into oblivion, like a stone. . . .

So be content with your life, be quieter than water, and lower than grass! O, children, if you only knew the cold and darkness of the days ahead![4]

(3:62)

Blok's poems are profoundly autobiographical. Yet, while they record in the minutest detail his emotional response to the world from day to day—each poem is dated as in a journal—deciphering the often obscure allusions to the "real" biographical facts behind the poems does not usually help to understand them better. This is not merely a matter of critical methodology. From the earliest days of his poetic career Blok hoped to fashion a coherent narrative out of his separate verses and to create a "life drama" that would expose the internal links that held together disparate events. He strove to penetrate the chaos of the contingent world of appearances and to reveal at least a trace of a radiant world beyond his own. Blok was purely a poet. He sublimated his entire life—in its every aspect, it seems—into his writing, especially his poetry, and it is this lyrical image that gave a face to his time. In his poem *Vozmezdie* (*Retribution*, 1922) he clearly expresses his ambivalent feelings:

[4]Blok's poems are translated in prose throughout this essay.

The twentieth century . . . more homeless, more terrifying, is the gloom of life (and blacker yet, and vaster, is the shadow cast by Lucifer's wing). The smoky conflagrations of the sunset (prophecies of our day), and in the skies, the ominous phantom of the awesome, tailed comet; Messina's merciless end (the elemental powers cannot be controlled), and the inexhaustible roar of machines, that day and night forge destruction. The dread awareness that all our former petty thoughts and creeds were but illusion; and the first airplane's flight into a void of unknown spheres. . . . Both repulsion from life, and yet an insane love for it; and for our country, both passion and great hate. . . . And the black and earthly blood, swelling our veins, destroying all bounds, portends unheard of changes, and unexampled rebellions.

(3:305–306)

Blok's poetry possesses an extraordinary ability to evoke in the concrete details of everyday life a reality beyond the personal and immediate. His sense of the immanence of the infinite and miraculous shaped his life and poetry. The events of his inner life were the only ones that were truly important and genuinely real for him, and these took place against the background of another, mystical reality. In "I nam ne dolgo liubovat'sia" ("We are not long given to admire," January 1902) he writes:

We are not long given to admire these earthly feasts: secrets are revealed to us and distant worlds glitter before us.

(1:162)

At the same time, however, there is a strain of ironic skepticism that grows throughout his poetry and distorts this vision, giving rise to doubts about his ability to grasp this mystical reality and fix it in the language of his art. These hopes and fears are expressed in the poem "Predchuvstvuiu Tebia" ("I sense Your coming," 4 June 1901):

I sense Your coming. The years go by—always in the same form do I sense Your coming.

The whole horizon is in flames—and intolerably clear, and I await silently—"grieving and loving."

The whole horizon is in flames and the apparition is near, but I am terrified: You will change Your form.

And You will awaken insolent suspicion, once You have at last changed your familiar features.

O, how I will fall bitterly and low, unable to conquer my mortal dreams!

How clear the horizon! And Radiance is near. But I am terrified: You will change Your form.

(1:94)

For Blok there is always the unresolved problem of the relation between art and life and the ability of language to mediate between them and bring wholeness and continuity to the troubling ambiguities of immediate experience. His poetry records the constant conflict between the claims of a prophetic knowledge of the terrors of history on the one hand and the claims, pleasures, and pains of the moment on the other, as in the poem "Milyi drug, i v etom tikhom dome" ("Dearest friend, even in this quiet house," October 1913):

Dearest friend, even in this quiet house the fever strikes me. I cannot find a place in this quiet house next to the peaceful hearth!

Voices sing, the blizzard beckons, and I fear this coziness. . . . Even behind your shoulders, my dear one, someone's eyes stand watch!

Behind your quiet shoulders, I hear the rustle of wings. . . . And with burning eyes, boring into me, the Angel of storms—Azrael.

(3:286)

Great Russian poets, their lives passionate and filled with intense spiritual longings, often die young, as did Blok. In the tradition of so many Russian writers, Blok was a "maximalist." His world was a world of absolutes, and his poems aim at provoking our strongest feelings. Like the other symbolists, Blok strug-

gled against positivism and attempted to create a form, a style, an expression that strove to elude reason and reach the reader through other channels. However much his poems are grounded in real facts or historical events, at their best they are capable of evoking an experience that can only be called musical. This "music" depends on several characteristics of his poetic style, all of which almost completely escape English translation.

Their base in the tradition of classical nineteenth-century Russian poetry, for example, tends to sound bombastic, archaic, and rhetorically outdated in English. Moreover, as his modern translators Jon Stallworthy and Peter France point out, Blok's use of traditional meters, often the dactyl, does not correspond to English poetic tradition, and Blok's frequent recourse to symmetry, repetition, and strong rhymes is extremely difficult to render effectively in English.

These are difficulties that all translators face when dealing with Russian poetry, but they are particularly resistant to solution in Blok because as a symbolist he developed methods that increase the semantic load of any given word by multiple associations with other words in a poem and with all his other poems. Words are used with deliberate vagueness in order to increase their associative potential. The result is often, as F. D. Reeve puts it, the ambiguity of an inadequately defined but melodically intoned emotion. This is particularly true of Blok's early poems, which try to express some metaphysical intuition without having the intellectual organization to make the intuition clear. They are most often poems of mood and vague feelings. Always laconic, Blok invests every word with such resilience of meaning, sound, and associative significance that one cannot hope to reproduce very much of its effect in translation.

Another difficulty for the English reader of Blok is his frequent use of traditional figures, some of which border on clichés or stereotypes, that resonate within the larger experience of Russian literature as a whole, a use that can be associated with Blok's fascination with the language and situations of such "low" genres as the melodrama and the most banal Gypsy romances. The *chastushka,* an improvised quatrain popular among factory workers and semi-industrialized peasants, actually forms the basis of *Dvenadtsat'* (*The Twelve,* 1918), Blok's greatest poem. Many of Blok's poems hover near the boundaries of kitsch or bad taste, and yet, as with Feodor Dostoevsky's greatest moments, they rarely if ever succumb to their lowly generic origins.

Of singular importance to a real appreciation of Blok's poetic achievement is the ability to read all his poems as he had always conceived them to be read and reread: as parts of a continuous whole, whose interweaving of complex emotions reflects Blok's own experience of the interpenetration of the mystical and quotidian worlds. All his life Blok obsessively arranged and rearranged his poems. From the start, he conceived his poetry as forming a continuous narrative in which every poem, regardless of its individual quality or value, was a necessary part of a cycle, the sum of which cycles formed a book. The three volumes of his poems eventually formed a "novel in verse," a lyrical trilogy of "incarnation." No doubt there is mystical significance in the number three, as well as a correspondence with his division of symbolism into three phases. In practical terms this continuously emerging structure afforded Blok an enormous range of associative possibilities. His collected poems in three volumes deliberately provide a self-contained gloss for any one of the poems. Except, perhaps, in the case of his *Stikhi o Prekrasnoi Dame* (Poems About the Most Beautiful Lady, 1905), chronological order is never the single determining factor in their organization, although it frequently coincides with the order of cycles in a book and provides a structure for all three volumes. The cycles are more often developed on a quasi-narrative base that generates a meaning beyond that of an individual poem and even the manifest narrative content itself. It may not be too far off the mark to say that Blok brought the romantic song cycle to its ultimate and most highly developed level. (Many of Blok's poems have, in fact, been set to music, including an excellent song cycle by Dmitry Shostakovich based on some of his early poems.)

BLOK AND SYMBOLISM

Although the range of his poetry as well as its importance and quality are not contained within the neat rubrics of a literary school, nevertheless Blok cannot be understood outside of the symbolist movement in Europe and Russia. Complex, highly factionalized, and divided geographically between St. Petersburg and Moscow, Russian symbolism contained within its fold writers who struggled against the weight of their own literary heritage by asserting the primacy and inviolability of art for art's sake, as well as writers with theurgic claims, who strove to transcend the limits of art and touch realities that had always been the special preserve of religious experience. All were poets and all were drawn together by a common *fin-de-siècle* sense of foreboding and expectation that had roots in the real political turmoil and increasing social unrest they witnessed each day. Sometimes their anxiety was expressed in their poetry in macabre images of the modern cityscape with its rumbling echoes of the urban masses. Its leading journals—Sergey Diaghilev's *Mir iskusstva* (World of Art), Valery Bryusov's *Vesy* (The Scales), and Dmitry Merezhkovsky's *Novyi put'* (New Way)—and Bryusov's Skorpion, its main publishing house, were models of publicist acumen and had the patronage of some of the wealthiest merchant families of Moscow and St. Petersburg and the collaboration of some of Russia's finest artists and designers. In a short time they skillfully cultivated a public who avidly followed the new literature and who bought subscriptions to their beautifully designed journals and volumes of poetry.

ALEXANDER BLOK

The Russian symbolists were deeply cultured people who were often as familiar with the world of classical antiquity in its most esoteric aspects as they were with European modernism, particularly French and Belgian symbolism. The range of their interests and reading was enormous and many of them had seriously studied European philosophy, particularly Plato, Immanuel Kant, Friedrich Schelling, Arthur Schopenhauer, Friedrich Nietzsche, and the contemporary neo-Kantian philosophers.

What united all of them was a strong revulsion against bourgeois materialism and philistinism. They also rejected positivist philosophy with its faith in the exclusive power of science, mathematics, and reason for gaining ultimate knowledge of the world. To these, they opposed a kind of pan-aestheticism that proclaimed beauty to be the essence of all reality and the single greatest power capable of transforming the world. They were especially attracted to cultures and epochs they perceived as having a similar aesthetic orientation—classical antiquity, the Renaissance, the romantic age—and to figures such as Richard Wagner, Nietzsche, and, to a lesser extent, John Ruskin. Beauty as a philosophical category took precedence over all others, such as ethics and logic, and it usurped the redemptive power of religion. This last idea is particularly well expressed in one of Blok's early poems "Ishchu spaseniia" ("I seek salvation," 25 November 1900):

I seek salvation. My bonfires burn on the summits of mountains—they light up the whole realm of night. But brighter than all of them is the spiritual eye within me. And You are far off. . . . But is it You? I seek salvation.

Solemnly, the astral choir intones in the heavens. Generations of men curse me. For You alone I have lit a fire in the mountains. But You are a vision. I seek salvation.

The astral choir grows weary and falls silent. Night departs, and doubt flees. There You descend from the far, bright summits. I awaited

You. My spirit is prostrate before You. In You is salvation!

(1:68)

In their efforts to reveal the true essence of all reality beneath its crude material shell, they aestheticized the historical world, forming its every aspect into their art. Indeed, art's paramount importance in this scheme of things derived from the very fact that in it the aesthetic was most clearly expressed. Symbolism went beyond romanticism in that it replaced nature with art as the source of all knowledge.

What was generally true for all the Russian symbolists was particularly true for the so-called younger generation, whose leaders, Vyacheslav Ivanov, Andrey Bely, and Blok, attempted to systematize all these ideas into a coherent aesthetic and cognitive theory. At the base of all their writing is a kind of Platonic dualism, whose particular interpretation they inherited from Vladimir Sergeevich Solov'ev. Into the traditional Platonic opposition of the real, eternal, and ideal world of ideas to its illusory, secondhand, and ultimately false reflection in the material world, Solov'ev, drawing upon gnosticism, interpolated a divine feminine principle, Sophia, who served as a mediatrix between God and man. Solov'ev did not entirely reject the physical reality of human sexuality. Instead, he elaborated a complex system of gradations, from the reproductive urge without love or sexuality in the lowest organisms to sexual love that has no necessary link with reproduction and is manifested in its purest form in divine love.

In a characteristic reaction to theory and philosophical writing that continued throughout his life, the young poet Blok was bored by Solov'ev's prose (as he might well have been). Still, he did find in the philosopher's poetic recasting of his ideas, with its mystical eroticism and self-irony, a voice that spoke directly to the experiences of his own life.

This highly personal recasting of the philosophical and aesthetic movements of his day is perhaps the key to the popularity and accessibility on some level of even Blok's most esoteric verse and to his stature as Russia's greatest symbolist poet and perhaps the only Russian poet of his age who is still read by lovers of poetry. In an age of self-consciously stylized art, when high artifice often turned to mere gimmickry, and pretentious rhetoric sometimes stood for poetry, Blok's lyric voice remained authentic and uniquely his own. He came to the new Russian poetry as a poet already well developed and cultivated in the traditions of the classical poetry of his own country and European romanticism, and a fully formed image of these literary traditions resonates clearly in his early poetry. And if he always wrote from within his own experiences, it was his fate to have had a life that was a paradigm for the poetic sensibilities of his time. Blok *lived* the life that others were merely writing about. He absorbed the literary movements of his day organically, testing their techniques and theories against the music of time, to which he was so keenly attuned. He always maintained a stubborn artistic independence, and yet the development of his poetry reflects on some deep level the changing currents within symbolism and its eventual crisis in 1910.

EARLY LIFE

Blok was born on 16 November 1880 on the grounds of St. Petersburg University, where his maternal grandfather, Andrei Nikolaevich Beketov, a distinguished botanist, was rector. Blok's father, Alexander L'vovich, was an extraordinarily gifted man with an extremely unbalanced mind. In 1879, at the age of twenty-six, he moved to Warsaw with his young bride, Alexandra Andreevna, in order to take up the chair of state law at Warsaw University (Poland at that time was still partitioned and was thus the westernmost province of the Russian Empire). The couple returned to St. Petersburg two years later on the occasion of Alexander

L'vovich's dissertation defense. Alexandra Andreevna, pregnant and drastically transformed by her husband's cruel treatment, was persuaded to remain in St. Petersburg by her father, who was concerned about her health and that of her unborn child (she had already given birth to a stillborn child in Warsaw). Eventually, after the birth of her son and after many stormy scenes with her husband, Alexandra Andreevna heeded her parents' advice and did not follow Alexander L'vovich back to Warsaw. Instead, she began separation and divorce proceedings that dragged on for almost eight turbulent years because of the intransigence of Alexander L'vovich, who refused to grant her a divorce until he had found someone to take her place.

Blok hardly knew his father and met him reluctantly and sullenly during the latter's infrequent visits to St. Petersburg. His letters to him are dry, formal, and scant, in marked contrast to the effusive, intimate, almost daily correspondence he maintained with his mother throughout his life.

Blok's relations with his stepfather were not particularly close either. In 1889 Alexandra Andreevna finally obtained a divorce and one month later married her brother-in-law's brother, an officer in the Imperial Grenadier Guards, Franz Feliksovich Kublitsky-Piottukh. Franz Feliksovich was a kind, honorable, rather self-effacing man whose only interest was the affairs of his regiment. He did not intrude into the intimate world of his wife and stepson.

Theirs was a world steeped in the liberal traditions of mid-nineteenth-century realist literature and humanist culture and visited by its most outstanding representatives. It was a world in which music, literature, and art occupied a central place. And it was a world dominated by women. Like her mother and sisters, Alexandra Andreevna translated French poetry, including that of Charles Baudelaire, and she was the first in her family to be interested in European decadence.

Blok always viewed his position in society as a highly privileged one. Although they were not wealthy, the Beketovs lived a comfortable if frugal life in St. Petersburg. In spite of their rather high standing in society, by the end of the nineteenth century they had long since lost their family wealth, which had not survived the emancipation of the serfs in 1861. Their one piece of property was the very modest Shakhmatovo estate outside Moscow, which grandfather Beketov had acquired along with the heavy burden of a long-term mortgage in 1875. Shakhmatovo was the beloved retreat to which the entire Beketov family traveled as early as possible each summer. Here, in the idyllic setting of the Russian countryside, Blok spent some of his happiest days and developed the profound love of nature that is so fundamental to much of his early poetry.

The boy's winter home was a stark contrast to his summer haunts. The Grenadier barracks, where he lived with his mother and stepfather, were located on the far side of the island that faces the grand imperial center of St. Petersburg. From his home there Blok could see the industrial region of dark factories and smokestacks, workers' quarters and the urban poor. It was from these islands opposite the barracks that the workers marched out in 1905, while Franz Feliksovich led a detachment of Grenadiers to hold the bridges against them. The many winters Blok spent there gave him intimate, firsthand knowledge of the social divisions that soon ripped his beloved city apart.

In order to spare his having to face the bone-chilling winds and inclement weather of the wintry northern capital, Alexandra Andreevna decided to send her eleven-year-old son to a local school for boys close to his stepfather's barracks rather than to a better school for more gifted and privileged boys across town. From the cultured gentility of his grandparents' circle Blok entered a world of ugliness, coarseness, and intellectual mediocrity, where, in his words, "the boys quickly became debauched." Except for his excellence in Latin and Greek, a passion that he maintained throughout his life, Blok was an undis-

tinguished student and had the lowest opinion of his school, which he and his family regarded as a necessary evil. His real education, "the sentimental education of a Russian gentleman," as he called it, went on within the family circle at home in St. Petersburg or at Shakhmatovo.

Throughout her life Blok's mother periodically fell into profound depression and anxiety that at times brought her to the brink of suicide. Blok shared his mother's acute sensitivity and depressive tendencies, and his closest friends at school were no more emotionally stable than he. One of them, Nikolai Gunn, eventually committed suicide in 1902 for "romantic reasons" and may well have been an inspiration for Blok, who threatened his own suicide in the same year and for similar reasons.

In 1897 Alexandra Andreevna's mental condition worsened, and after she was diagnosed as also having serious heart disease, a trip to the German health resort of Bad Nauheim was prescribed. The sixteen-year-old Blok accompanied his mother, aunt, and grandmother, and soon he was involved in an affair with Kseniia Mikhailovna Sadovskaia, a beautiful, dark-haired woman of approximately the same age as his mother. It is uncertain how far their affair really went, but it did serve to inspire his first serious poetry, which was written during the next few years. Its memory, evoked during a third visit to Bad Nauheim, where he stopped with his wife for a short rest on his way home from Italy in 1909, inspired a nostalgic cycle of poems entitled "Cherez dvenadtsat' let" ("After Twelve Years," 1916). It was at this later date that Blok made the following telling recollection in his notebook: "My first infatuation, if I am not mistaken, was accompanied by a secret feeling of repulsion for the sexual act. (It is impossible to unite oneself with a very beautiful woman; for that one should choose only ugly ones.) Perhaps, though, this was the way it was before."

It was in the year following his affair with Sadovskaia, and thus under the spell of his "first infatuation," that he fell in love with

ALEXANDER BLOK

Lyubov' Dmitrievna Mendeleeva, his future wife and the inspiration for most of his poetry between 1898 and 1904. The daughter of the great scientist Dmitry Ivanovich Mendeleev—the discoverer of the periodicity of chemical elements, one of Professor Beketov's oldest friends, and the owner of the Boblovo estate, not far from the Beketovs' retreat—Lyubov' Dmitrievna shared Blok's passion for the theater and played Ophelia to his Hamlet in their amateur summer productions. The first years of their relationship were marked by separation and intermittent indifference on Lyubov' Dmitrievna's part. Part of the reason for Blok's infrequent visits to Boblovo in the summer of 1899 was that he was still undergoing another difficult and painful course of treatment for syphilis, which he had contracted in Petersburg brothels, and was too ill to arrive in a grand manner riding his own white horse. Lyubov' interpreted his absence as a loss of interest and responded with coldness and indifference. They continued to meet occasionally at social gatherings but the emotion of their first attraction seemed to have passed.

In the winter of 1900 Blok met Lyubov' Dmitrievna by chance at the theater. She had recently returned from Paris and was strikingly beautiful in her newly acquired Parisian clothes. In a short time they both knew that they were more in love than ever before. The next "mystical summer" of 1901 was spent in long walks through the countryside talking about poetry. Much later in her memoirs, Lyubov' Dmitrievna described their summer relationship as something resembling love, but in fact consisting of only literary conversations. She noticed that the very phrases Blok spoke to her during their conversations often appeared later in the poetry he wrote about her. But the excitement and romance of being the subject of his poems gave way to her desire to be other than an object of his distant adoration, and she regretted that they "never once lost their way among the flowering shrubs." The poems written during the summer and autumn of this year eventually formed the

nucleus of Blok's first published book of poetry, *Stikhi o Prekrasnoi Dame.*

Blok considered 1901 to be a decisive year. At Easter his mother gave him a volume of the poetry of the philosopher, mystic, and religious thinker Solov'ev, whose poems and writings about the eternal feminine, platonic idealism, and human sexual love provided the young poet with the generic form and philosophical base to transform his summer and autumn experiences with Lyubov' Dmitrievna into the subject of his poetry.

Shortly after his return to St. Petersburg, Blok changed his course of study at the university from law to the five-year program in Slavic and Russian philology. In addition to his regular assigned readings of the classics, Blok immersed himself in contemporary Russian literature and attempted to analyze the new literary scene in his notebooks. He continued to meet Lyubov' Dmitrievna alone in the capital, and in the autumn of that year she introduced him to the great baroque spaces of the St. Petersburg cathedrals, which she would visit when there were few people and no service in progress. Here, often in Blok's presence, she would conduct the rites of her own private cult of the Holy Virgin.

As time wore on, however, Lyubov' Dmitrievna became increasingly impatient with Blok's lack of physical ardor and at the same time bewildered by what she took to be expressions of his love. His poems during this time express the difficulty Blok had preserving his chaste religious concentration in the face of his ever more complicated relationship with Lyubov'. It is during this period that in his poetry his own powerfully repressed sexuality first erupts from beneath the forms of an aestheticized religion and asceticism in the guise of his ironic double, as seen in his "Dvoiniku" ("To My Double," 27 December 1901):

> I completed a difficult task over her, but O, my poor friend! Did you notice her dress—so festive and wonderful, and the strange spring flowers?

I waited for you. And your shadow flickered in the distance, in the fields that I also crossed, where she once rested, where you sighed over the secrets of existence.

And did you know that I would triumph? That you would disappear, accomplished but unloving? That I would find your crazy, young fantasy without you in the bloodstained flowers?

I need neither you nor your deeds. You are ridiculous, pitiful, old man! Your heroic deed is mine as well as its reward: wild laughter and an insane cry!

(1:152)

By January 1902 Lyubov' Dmitrievna was ready to end their relationship through a letter in which she complained that Blok had made of her some sort of abstract idea, a fantastic fiction only of his imagination, and had consequently failed to see the real woman with her desires and needs: "From life, you have removed me to a place where I am cold, afraid, and . . . bored." The letter remained unsent, as did the several letters Blok wrote in his own attempt to break with her. Thoughts of suicide enter his diary, and finally on 7 November 1902 he went to meet Lyubov' Dmitrievna with a suicide note in his pocket. A long conversation led to an understanding, and, in part because she was impressed by his threat to take his own life and in part out of her own desire, Lyubov' Dmitrievna accepted Blok's proposal of marriage.

Their relationship remained as chaste as ever, however, and even after their marriage in August 1903 in Shakhmatovo, they maintained a "white marriage" for the first year. In 1904 they finally began what Lyubov' Dmitrievna in her memoirs reports to have been a highly unsatisfying sexual life, which, however, came to an end in 1906.

During the years 1901–1902 Blok made his first steps into the literary society of the time and published his first poems in the leading journals of the "decadent" press. These events in Blok's personal and creative life coincided with the newly emerged Russian symbolist

movement's rise to hegemony over the world of letters in Russia.

Blok personally entered the heady society of Russian symbolism in 1902, when he met the doyen of the St. Petersburg symbolists, Dmitry Merezhkovsky, and his sharp-tongued wife, the poet Zinaida Gippius. Through them he became acquainted with the writings of the brilliant poet, novelist, and theoretician Bely, a man of Blok's own age, whose friendship influenced Blok during the next five years more radically and deeply than any other. Soon they began an extraordinary correspondence, questioning each other's understanding of the esoteric issues that occupied their minds and exchanging poetry and views on the literary scene.

Blok finally met Bely personally during the winter of 1904, when he and his wife traveled to Moscow. Bely was at the center of all the symbolist activities in the ancient capital, and he introduced Blok to all its leading figures. Arrangements for the publication of Blok's first collection of poems were made at the publishing house Grif, and Blok was acclaimed as "the first poet in Russia" by Bely and his young cohorts, who called themselves the Argonauts.

From the beginning, Bely had invested his friendship with Blok with a mystical significance and by extension saw in Lyubov' Dmitrievna the incarnation of Solov'ev's divine Sophia (lyubov' is also the Russian word for "love"). By 1905 this semi-religious cult of Lyubov' Dmitrievna turned into a grotesque masquerade, exacerbated by Bely's boisterous immaturity and the painful complexities of the Bloks' actual conjugal life. Finally, Bely's attempt to seduce Lyubov' Dmitrievna and her own indecision over whether she would leave Blok for Bely nearly resulted in a duel between the two friends and led to a serious break in their relationship.

Ultimately, the fashionable mysticism and intellectual extravagance of the Moscow symbolists were alien and repellent to Blok and were later echoed by the strange cardboard characters of his play *Balaganchik* (*The Puppet Show,* 1908). During this period of enormous success among the literary elite, Blok was, in fact, inwardly growing away from their world of spiritualism and religion toward one whose "outward form is now that of cries, madness, and—often—of painful dissonances."

LOVE POETRY

Blok is more than anything else a love poet and one, furthermore, who seeks in the experience of love knowledge about the world and the ineffable. And it is perhaps in his love poetry that the autobiographical "facts" of Blok's life serve not so much to explain the meaning of his individual love poems as to disclose the hidden motives for their creation in the first place. The duality between the fallen material world and the world of spiritual purity that dominates Blok's poetry finds its reflection in his own tortured sexual life. Blok struggled against what he felt to be the defilement of beauty in physical sexuality in order to find real freedom and purification in poetry. Blok wrote in order to transform a passionate emotion evoked by the merely physical into a spiritual quality so pure that it could outlive its cause. This is the theme of his poem "Devushka iz Spoleto" ("The Girl from Spoleto," 3 June 1909):

> Your figure is shapely, like a church candle, your gaze is like stabbing swords. Girl, I do not await a blinding meeting—grant, as to the monk, to ascend the pyre!
>
> I do not demand happiness. Caresses are not needed. Shall I offend you with clumsy caresses? Like an artist, I only watch beyond the fence, where you pick flowers—and I am in love!
>
> Past, all the while past—you are driven away by the wind, burned by the sun—Maria! Allow my gaze to begin to see clearly the cherubim above you, allow my heart—to come to know the sweetest pain!

Silently into your dark curls I weave a precious diamond of secret verses. Greedily I cast my loving heart into the dark source of your glowing eyes.

(3:101)

In the mystical and erotically charged climate of Russian symbolism, Blok's relationship to his wife was immediately cast by his symbolist friends and by Blok himself into the forms of religious worship already given in some of Blok's earliest poetry. In the poem "Vkhozhu ia v temnye khramy" ("I enter dark churches," 25 October 1902) the poet experiences the presence of his beloved in liturgical, mystical forms:

> I enter dark churches and perform a humble rite. There I await the Beautiful Lady in the glimmer of the icon's red light.
>
> In the shadows near a pillar I tremble at the creak of the doors. But there peers into my face, all illuminated, only an image, only a dream of Her.
>
> O, I know well the veil of the Majestic Eternal Feminine! High along the cornices there flit smiles, fantasies, and dreams.
>
> O Holy One, like caressing candles, how comforting is Your form! I hear neither sighs nor speech, yet I believe: You are my Beloved.

(1:232)

Although these external rites eventually became a source of great annoyance to his wife and were soon rejected by the young couple, they nevertheless reflected a deeper wish on Blok's part to keep his love for his wife ideal and thus remote from any carnal gratification. As much as this remoteness inflamed the imagination of the poet, it was, in the life of the man, the cause of his greatest anguish. In fact, in the near-perfect match of the poet's biography with the man's, this sexual complex is the principle driving force, Blok's source of inspiration, the way he called upon his muse.

By making the tangible cause of his carnal emotion inaccessible, the poet exalts it, claiming to give an earthly form to the divine. And like many other love poets, from Dante Alighieri to Baudelaire, Blok chose to use religious language to speak of his experience. This is as true of Blok's early poetry as it is of his first letters to his fiancée. The poet sees the soul reflected in the body's physical beauty, and what he asks of the flesh is spirit. The source of this idea is Neoplatonism, whose treatises on love have as their central image the celestial ladder that leads from earthly human beauty and love to divine love. Blok is thus involved in a mystical tradition of love poetry that sees in earthly feminine beauty a mirror in which the divine archetype may be glimpsed. As in Dante, to whom Blok felt very close, love poetry records the lover's intuition of the divine in the human lover. Love itself becomes a kind of gnosis, and poetry its verbal expression. This may be seen in "Sbylos' prorochostvo moe" ("My prophecy has come to pass," 7 March 1901):

> My prophecy has come to pass: before the approaching grave Your sanctuary has yet again become inflamed by a secret force.

> And filled with solemnity, I am drunk with a great secret and I firmly know—that it was not by chance that the prophetic words have come to pass.

> (1:82)

But if the spiritual essence manifests itself only in a body, the poet always runs the risk of falling into the seduction of the merely physical. He writes in "O, net! Ia ne khochu, chtob pali my s toboi" (O, no! I do not wish for us to fall," February 1912):

> O, no! I do not wish for us to fall into passionate embraces. That the torture last a long time, when neither unraveling our intertwined arms, nor separating our lips—is possible in the murk of night!

> I do not wish to be blinded by the storm's lightning, nor hear the wail of violins (those frenzied sounds!), nor experience the breaking waves of ineffable boredom, buried in the ashes of your burning head!

> Like the first man, consumed by divine flames, I want to return you forever to the blue shores of Eden, murdering all lies and destroying venom. . . .

> But you beckon me! Your venomous glance foretells a different paradise! I succumb, knowing that your serpent's heaven is a hell of bottomless ennui.

> (3:55)

In the original Russian this poem is a sonnet, thus making a clear reference to both Francesco Petrarch and Baudelaire and to the poetry of ideal love.

For Blok to have the body would be a profanation and a sacrilege. By offering him something he can easily get somewhere else, his muse denies him something he can only get from her. In his earlier poetry he relies on her persistent "No," which transfigures her in his eyes into a vision of unbreachable chastity. In "Khranila ia sredi mladkh sozvuchii" ("I have preserved among the young harmonies," 17 October 1901) the speaker is a woman who maintains her lofty purity as she spurns the earthly desires of the poet:

> I have preserved among the young harmonies a pensive and tender image of the day. Suddenly a whirlwind blows, and a cloud of dust arises in flight, and the sun is no more, and I am surrounded by twilight.

> But in my cell it is May, and I live, unseen, alone, in flowers, and I await a different spring. Be gone—I sense the coming seraphim, your earthbound dreams are foreign to me.

> Be gone, wanderers, children, gods! I will blossom yet on the last day. My dreams are holy mansions, my love casts no shadow.

> (1:132)

His later poetry expresses his fear of a great loss should she say "Yes." In "Vnov' u sebia . . . Unizhen, zol i rad" ("Once again I am in my room," 29 January 1914) the speaker is the poet himself, faced with the corruption and loss of his ideal:

Once again I am in my room . . . humiliated, angry, and glad. Is it night or day there in my window? It's the moon, like a clown, above the roofs, who grimaces to me. . . .

Diurnal sun—be gone! Repentance—be gone! Who dares to help me? Into my devastated brain, only the night bursts in, only the night bursts in! Into my empty breast, only your gaze penetrates, only your greedy stare claws at me. All will be lost forever, "never" will begin when you cry out: "Yes!"

(3:56)

A great part of Blok's poetry, then, may be read as a theodicy through the labyrinths of his own sexuality. From the pure, monkish devotion of his early cycle "Ante Lucem" ("Before the Light," 1916) and *Stikhi o Prekrasnoi Dame,* through the stormy eroticism of *Snezhnaia maska* (The Snow Mask, 1907), "Faina" (1916), the "Chernaia krov'" cycle ("Black Blood," 1914), and the "Carmen" cycle (1914), even up to *The Twelve,* Blok needed to maintain his longing for the constancy of his feminine ideal. The contrast, the sensuality, and the sexual passion of his later verse are always guilty against this standard and created the necessary tension to give his creative energy material form: This is demonstrated in "K Muze" ("To My Muse," 29 December 1912):

There is in your secret refrains a fateful announcement of perdition. There is a cursing of all the sacred commandments and a profanation of joy.

And such an attractive force, that I am ready to affirm the rumor that it was you who brought down the angels, seducing them with your beauty.

And when you mock faith, suddenly there glows above you that indistinct, purple-gray aureole that I have once seen.

Are you evil or good?—You are a stranger here. And wisely it is said of you: for some you are a Muse and a miracle. For me you are a torment and a hell.

I do not know, why at dawn, at the hour when I no longer had the strength, I did not perish, but I espied your visage and begged for your comfort.

I wanted us to be enemies, so why did you grant me a meadow with flowers and a universe of stars—the whole curse of your beauty?

More treacherous than the Northern Lights, more intoxicating than golden champagne, and more fleeting than a gypsy's love, were your terrible embraces. . . .

And there was a fateful exultation in the desecration of cherished, sacred things, and this bitter passion, like wormwood, was an insane delight to my heart!

(3:7–8)

Blok's passionate involvement with two other women resulted in three excellent cycles of poetry. During Vsevolod Meyerhold's highly successful, avant-garde production of Blok's play *The Puppet Show* at the New Dramatic Theater in the winter of 1906–1907, Blok became involved with the beautiful actress Natal'ya Nikolaevna Volokhova. For the first time he exposed his passion to full public view, and Volokhova was instantly cast in the role of Blok's Stranger, the antithesis of his Most Beautiful Lady. The poems of *Snezhnaia maska,* which this affair inspired, were written during a brief period of intense inspiration and are imbued with all the sinful passion and voluptuousness that were apparently absent from the actual affair. The theatrical setting in which this liaison was played out supplied the rhetorical context and props, while the city provided the elemental forces of the deadly blizzards that wed this passion to death in the poems' imagery.

Late in 1913 Blok fell in love with an artist of the Conservatory Theater, Lyubov' Alexandrovna Andreeva-Del'mas, whose star role was Carmen in Georges Bizet's opera. The actress' fiery beauty matched the passionate Gypsy's fatal attractiveness, and Blok was carried off again on another wave of intense inspiration that produced the "Carmen" cycle. Bizet's opera had all the elements that Blok

ALEXANDER BLOK

needed to inspire his imagination. It had its famous Gypsy femme fatale and love triangle as well as a pure feminine figure who struggles to save the soul of Don José. This dramatic structure paralleled in many ways the torturous sexual triangle the Bloks were once involved in with Bely. To make the symmetry complete, Del'mas' name combines the names of both Blok's wife and his mother.

Blok had admired Del'mas from afar since October 1913, and six of the poems were written just before he had actually arranged to meet her in March 1914 at a performance of Wagner's *Parsifal.* The remaining four were written a few days after their first meeting and all but two were published that same year in Meyerhold's journal *Liubov' k trem apel'sinam* (A Love for Three Oranges). As he did in his other grand passion, for Volokhova, Blok thrived on the public spectacle of this equally theatrical affair.

At the same time that Blok was stalking Del'mas, he wrote most of the poems of the cycle "Black Blood." Unlike the Carmen poems, where the Gypsy's name appears in nearly every poem, this dark cycle is addressed to a woman whose "very name is contemptible." She is the nameless whore, whose passionate sensuality overpowers the poet and draws him into an orgy of vampirism and sadism. Compared to these guilty, demonic, misogynistic poems, the Carmen cycle, with its liberal quotation from Bizet's melodrama, is a comic opera. Yet both cycles are about poetic inspiration and share some common images that link death with sexual passion.

In "Ia ee pobedil, nakonets" ("I have conquered her at last," October 1909) from the "Black Blood" cycle it is the poet's hatred of the woman that inspires him. The poet wavers from being a man repulsed by her overt sensuality to one who finally triumphs over her and, like the vampire, draws sustenance from her blood:

The candles, the eyes, the words are all extinguished—You are dead, finally dead!

I know, I have drunk your blood. I place you in a coffin and sing—

On a gloomy night, your blood will sing in me of the voluptuous spring!

(3:58)

After he has beaten her and driven her away, ("Nad luchshim sozdaniem bozh'im" ("Above God's best creation," 13 March 1910) he stands alone and listens to the music of violins that

sing wild songs about how I've become free! About how I've exchanged a low passion for a better lot!

(3:59)

The Carmen poems are marked in part by a nostalgia for the time of the Most Beautiful Lady ("Serdityi vzor bestsvetnykh glaz" ["The angry gaze of your colorless eyes," 25 March 1914]):

And the song of your gentle shoulders, which I know to the point of horror, and my heart is fated to preserve your image, forever dear, like the memory of another country. . . .

And there, the doomed man shouts: "Let us leave, leave life, let us leave this melancholy life!"

(3:233–234)

The poet, not unlike the humble monk of his early poems, stands silently apart from Carmen's other admirers ("Sredi poklonnikov Karmen" ["Among the admirers of Carmen," 26 March 1914])

and remembers the spring days amidst raging harmonies. He looks at her melodious figure and sees dreams of art.

(3:232)

Poetry arises out of his love, as seen in "O da, liubov' vol'na, kak ptitsa" ("O yes, love is free like a bird," 28 March 1914):

You will rise like a stormy wave in the river of my verses, and from my hand, Carmen, I shall not wash the smell of your perfume.

(3:237)

971

But the poet of these verses is no longer the innocent youth of his early poetry. In "Bushuet snezhnaia vesna" ("A snowy spring is raging," 13 March 1914), he has long since passed through a second baptism of sexual passion and has learned that with this sensuality comes death if poetry is to arise from it:

> And I forgot all the days, all the nights, and my blood beat down upon my heart, washing away the memory of my homeland. . . . And a voice sang: "The price you'll pay to me for love shall be your life."

> (3:231)

Not unlike the last poems of "Black Blood," however, in which the sated man triumphs violently over the woman, the last poem of the Carmen cycle, "Net, nikogda moei i ty nich' ei ne budesh' ("No, never mine, nor anyone's will you ever be," 31 March 1914), echoes Don José before he murders Carmen: "No, never mine, nor anyone's will you ever be!"

The theme of poetry and death appears again in a poem, "Khudozhnik" ("The Artist," 12 December 1913), which Blok wrote during this same period:

> In the heat of the summer and the blizzards of winter, on the day of your weddings, solemn occasions and funerals, I wait, so that a light ringing, which has never been heard before, might frighten away my mortal boredom.

> There—it emerges. And with cold concentration I wait to understand, to seize, and to kill it. And ahead of my vigilant expectation, it stretches its barely discernible thread.

> Is it a wind from the sea? Or are heavenly sirens singing in the leaves? Or has time stood still? Or have May apple-trees sprinkled their snowy blossoms? Or has an angel flown by?

> The hours drag on, carrying all that is worldly. The sounds grow broader, as do motion and light. The past stares madly into the future. There is no present. There is no regret.

> And finally, at the threshold of the conception of a new soul, of some unknown forces,—as if by lightning, my soul is struck down: artifice gathers strength and kills inspiration.

> Then in a cold cage I lock up the light, gentle, free bird, the one which wants to take death away, the one which wants to save the soaring soul.

> Here is my cage—metallic and heavy, glowing like gold in the sunset. Here is my bird: once happy, it now swings in a ring and sings at my window.

> Its wings are clipped and its song is memorized. Do you like standing under my window? Do you like the songs you hear? But tortured, I wait for something new, and am bored again.

> (3:145–146)

Here the poet writes of the moment when mystical inspiration is replaced by creativity. It is reminiscent of his important essay "O sovremennom sostoianii russkogo simvolizma" ("On the Present State of Russian Symbolism," 1910), which deals with the moment when the vision of a higher reality is embodied in the coarse, impoverished medium of human words. Like the image of the dead doll in his essay, death in this poem is at the center of the imprisoning form of art. The true mystic's vision is incommunicable. What the poet says must be a lie in comparison to what the prophet sees. For the seer this is a profound tragedy: instead of a religious experience, there is merely a poem. In the love poetry the love that promises a glimpse of the ideal world is instead entangled in the carnal embrace of the earthly lover. The visionary finds himself trapped in the poisonous hell of art—hell because for the modern, art is chained to the corrupt, historical world and unable to perform the function of a liturgy.

BLOK AS CIVIC POET AND THE CRISIS IN SYMBOLISM

The events of Blok's personal and artistic life took place against the background of several disastrous events in Russia. The Russo-Japanese War began in January 1904, raged for more than a year and a half, and resulted in enormous losses in life and prestige for Russia.

From early 1905 a series of industrial strikes intensified and culminated in armed rebellion in Moscow in December. Blok witnessed the day-by-day unfolding of the first Russian Revolution from his home in the Guards' barracks and watched as troops went into formation to put down the demonstrators in the infamous Bloody Sunday massacre. Even so apolitical a person as Blok could not help being swept up in the events of the time, and when he found himself in the middle of a general strike, he joined a demonstration and carried a red flag at the head of a procession. Characteristically, he always viewed the revolution as but a sign of events taking place in "other worlds, but which we have witnessed in our own souls." The landscape in which these events took on historical form was the city—Russian literature's favorite protagonist, St. Petersburg.

By the end of the nineteenth century Russian intellectuals were deeply troubled by the fragmentation of modern urban, industrial life. Artists felt both commercially dependent on and aesthetically and morally repelled by an anonymous audience whose values they no longer shared. In Russia the first generation of genuinely urban painters, poets, and musicians reached maturity during the 1890's. The city replaced nature as the subject of their art. They responded to a completely different rhythm of life and speech and expressed their new vision in sometimes shocking images, patterns of color, and sounds. They saw more clearly than others, perhaps, the signs of profound social fragmentation and felt that their own traditional alienation from the uneducated masses had reached a terrible crisis.

During this period of upheaval, Blok wrote his last, quiet poems dedicated to the Most Beautiful Lady and struggled to find a new voice that could express his own experience of inner rebellion. Many of the poems he showed Bely in 1905 met with the latter's strong disapproval. Their political engagement as well as their blasphemous playfulness in using folk imagery were alien to Bely's views on what poetry should be. Instead of the grand ecclesiastical spaces of St. Petersburg or the radiant heavens of the Russian countryside, Blok's poetry now concerned what were already his favorite haunts: the winding, ugly back streets of the icy capital with their overburdened workers, exhausted prostitutes and drunks, and cheap restaurants and taverns. The "terrible world" of the capitalist city emerged as a major theme in his new poetry, and Blok stands with Nikolay Gogol and Dostoevsky as one of the greatest writers of the modern urban scene in its phantasmagoric Russian variant. The nocturnal, snow-swept city provided the proper space in which the dark, demonic side of his character—inherited, he said, from his father—could emerge. These poems were collected in the cycle "Gorod" ("The City," 1904–1908), which contains "Neznakomka" ("The Stranger," 24 April 1906), one of his greatest and most popular poems before *The Twelve*.

Blok also wrote most of his works for the theater during this period. In addition to *The Puppet Show*, Blok wrote *Korol' na ploshchadi* (*The King in the Square*, 1908) and a third play, *Neznakomka* (*The Unknown Lady*, 1908), which were banned by the censor on political and religious grounds. A fourth play, *Pesnia sud'by* (*The Song of Fate*, 1919), written under the influence of his affair with Volokhova, betrays some of its tormented and masochistic aspects.

Blok's tremendous burst of creative activity was not exhausted by the "decadent" eroticism of his many Volokhova poems. The wild, ecstatic rhythms of "The Snow Mask" and "Faina" are followed by the direct, sober blank verse of a group of superb poems called "Vol'nye mysli" ("Free Thoughts," 1907). The transformation of his lyrical persona in these poems is remarkable. Inspired by his solitary wanderings throughout St. Petersburg during June and July 1907, these poems' confident objectivity and simple realism complement a side of Blok that was emerging during this period and that continued to alienate his symbolist colleagues, especially Bely.

Blok the "civic" writer came forth during

this period of terrible political reaction and expressed his views on political and social issues in lectures and articles. Like his contemporary Maxim Gorky, to whom Blok had always felt a spiritual affinity, Blok wrote of the responsibility of the intelligentsia to the great impoverished masses of peasants, who represented the real Russia, and whose threatening power would someday erupt in the elemental "cleansing fire" of revolution.

Because of the virtual absence of public political life in Russia, writers there had always been cast in the role of social critics. For this reason Russian writers always regarded their cultural mission with an intensity unknown in the West. A variety of factors affecting the political scene in Russia during the end of the nineteenth century and the beginning of the twentieth created a political vacuum that caused the intelligentsia to experience confusion and anxiety. This situation encouraged creative artists vigorously to reassert their claim to be the spokesmen for new values and the leaders of cultural and social reformation. In the Russian context this search for a synthesis of art and ideology led to some of the greatest achievements of modernism at the beginning of this century. The artist was transformed into a prophet and revolutionary whose task, Blok said, was "to remake everything. To build things in such a way that everything be new; so that our false, filthy, boring, monstrous life may become just, clean, merry and exquisitely beautiful."

Like almost all Russian writers who sought to understand and define their national essence, the symbolists were avid readers of folklore collections and ethnographic literature. They were attracted to the idea that the most ancient myths of Slavic culture were preserved in the still-living traditions of oral poetry and that it thus contained the keys to the secret language of a sacred tradition about the origins of things. The symbolists sought answers to the mysteries of human history not by rationally investigating documentary evidence but by trying to re-create an intimate and profound religious experience. They posited an edenic state of innocence and unmediated presence of the transcendent, a state of preliterate—but not pre-poetic—society, in which words themselves were not separate from the world. It was a state in which man could still read in the world the language of creation itself. The word in symbolism harks back to that idealized time of plenitude when poetry, cognition, music, and speech were one. Poetry, they thought, calls into being another discourse that is more fundamental, more primal—a discourse that ultimately grounds its truth in a reality that transcends language itself.

Blok yearned for this idyllic state of harmony, and it is this yearning that fuels his critique of Russia's Westernized intelligentsia, which divided the world into civilization and culture. His work on the interrelated themes of Russia and the responsibility of the artist culminated in 1908 in two articles, "Narod i intelligentsiia" ("The People and the Intelligentsia") and "Stikhiia i kul'tura" (The Elements and Culture, translated as "Nature and Culture"), in which he proclaimed that the true bearers of culture were the people who lived in harmony with the rhythm of nature. Related to these essays is the cycle of majestic poems "Na pole kulekovom" ("On the Battlefield of Kulekovo," 1909), which draws its inspiration from the medieval epic poem by the priest Sofoniia of Riazan, the "Zadonshchina" (Beyond the Don), a celebration in verse of the victory of Prince Dmitry Donskoi over the Tatar Golden Horde in 1380. This victory marked the beginning of the end of the Russian princes' submission to a foreign power.

Blok continued to be active in the literary world and in April 1910 he delivered a paper, "On the Present State of Russian Symbolism," in which he formulated his poetic credo. Written in richly metaphorical, lyrical, and allusive language, it is one of the most important documents for an understanding of Russian symbolism and Blok's place in it.

From the very start, Blok asserts that it is about language that he speaks. He divides the history of Russian symbolism into thesis and antithesis phases. The first is characterized by an agreement that there exists another reality separate from that of the historical world. This is a period characterized by intuition and vision but not, significantly, by language. It is a period whose poetry evokes the musical sounds emanating from beyond this world but does not and, indeed, cannot name them. Blok refers to his *Stikhi o Prekrasnoi Dame* as prime examples of this phase.

It is precisely at the moment when the ineffable is given form in language that it is lost. He writes:

> If I were painting a picture, I would depict the experience of this moment like this: in the lilac dusk of an unencompassable world, there hovers a huge white catafalque, and on it there lies a dead doll with a face sadly reminiscent of the one which appeared among heavenly roses. . . . And so it came to pass: my own enchanted world became the arena for my personal actions, my "anatomical theater" or puppet show, where I myself play a role alongside my marvelous dolls. . . . In other words, I had already made my own life art. . . . Life became art. I pronounced the incantation and before me arose at last what I myself have called "The Stranger": a beautiful doll, a blue phantom, an earthly wonder.
>
> (5:429–430)

Blok explains the reasons for this transformation in the following pithy statement: "This is what happened: they were prophets and they wanted to be poets."

What is given in the thesis phase is the silent intuition of being itself. Lost in the deafening sound of human language is the elusive means to effect the union of different orders of reality, which results in the hopeless dilemma of the modern poet who would make of his art more than the merely aesthetic, more than a matter of profane sensual pleasure, more than a sensual adornment of profane life. The chain of communication between the poet and the ideal world is broken by the very signs that at first led

him to this unity of being. The poet's language has lost its power to conjure this higher reality and fix it. It is precisely at the moment when the "radiant maiden" is given a name, when she is fixed or encoded in human language, that she vanishes. In her place remains a lifeless mannequin, which lacks the essence that was intuited at a time before words. Through fixation in the word, the intuition is limited, and by this limitation it is falsified. For Blok a beautiful woman is indeed a sign, but for him the act of signification is a broken rite.

Blok's silence, his skepticism, and his disinclination to verbalize the precise meaning of Sophia or the Most Beautiful Lady have their source in a great mystic stream that runs through his life and works and on some profound level determines their course. Like many poets, whose experience of life can only be called mystical, Blok's experience of this dimension does not so much obliterate personal psychology as fuse with it, giving desire a voice and a language, both of which strain to exceed ordinary human experience.

Blok's relationship with his wife, for example, for all the psychoanalytic insight we might bring to bear on it, remains fundamentally incomprehensible without this mystical dimension. On the brink of despair and suicide over a possible break with her in 1912, Blok wrote: "She is my link with the world, the affirmation of the world's inexpressible content. If this inexpressible exists, then I will bear much, everything that is required of me. If not, if it breaks off, deceives, is forgotton—no, that I cannot accept."

Blok's poetry is a record of this agony within the very specific historical context of a disintegrating culture, one that no longer provided a set of beliefs capable of grounding the poet's vision in a communal experience akin to religion. Instead of being an instrument to gather the faithful into a celebration of mystery, the language he had to use could not escape the falseness, fragmentation, and corruption of the modern urban setting. Addressing the faithless audience in "O, kak smeialis' vy nad nami" ("O, how you laughed at us," January 1911), Blok proclaims:

> O, how you laughed at us, how you despised us for loudly denouncing you with our quiet verses! But we are still the same. We are poets. For your sake do we long for you, preserving the sacred love, repeating the ancient vows. And just as simple is our quiet temple, we read the writing on its walls. . . . So laugh, do not believe us, don't read our lines about the streams which sing below the ground, about the wandering lights. . . .
>
> But remember Tiutchev's testament: "Be silent, keep low, and hide your feelings and your dreams. . . ."
>
> (3:90)

Insisting on the religious basis of all true Russian literature, Blok admitted to himself in his diary that he might not be able fully to carry on in this tradition: "Who am I as yet? It is only that I have seen something in dreams and awake that others have not yet seen." Nevertheless, this vision had to be understood and shared with others, and he calls upon the poet to take up this important task in the prologue to *Retribution*:

> Life has no beginning and no end. Chance stalks us all. Above us hangs either an everlasting twilight or the radiance of the divine visage. But you, artist, steadfastly believe in endings and beginnings. Know where heaven awaits us or where hell. It is your lot to measure everything you see with a dispassionate ruler. Let your eye be firm and clear. Erase all fortuitous strokes of chance—and you will see: the world is beautiful. Learn to find the light and you will grasp the darkness. Let everything pass slowly through the heat of your soul and the cold of your mind: what is holy in the world, and what is sinful.
>
> (3:301)

The "civic poet" and the symbolist visionary merge in Blok's mature poetry, and for this reason his thoughts on poetry in "On the Present State of Russian Symbolism" must be seen within the context of his thoughts on history. Within two months of his essay on symbolism, Blok wrote the first draft of his historical poem *Retribution*. His excoriation of the nineteenth century was exceeded in this poem only by his bitter repudiation of his own century. With World War I on the horizon and revolution inevitable at home, Blok began his poem convinced of the decadence of his own moribund culture. As he reflected on his own vices, he became aware of the enormous corruption of his society, and he saw in autobiography a way to write about his time.

The great "high priest" of Russian symbolism, Ivanov, reacted to Blok's *Retribution* in a way that is indicative of the crisis in symbolism already signaled in Blok's personal and creative life. Ivanov viewed its stark realism and worldly theme as a betrayal of the theurgic principle he felt to be fundamental to symbolism. Blok did not disagree with the symbolists' claim to prophetic vision. However, with his flawless intuition of the truth of Russia and its historical moment, he understood that the poet of his time no longer had the means to give this vision form. The crisis of Russian symbolism comes with its failure to comprehend history through art invested with religious pretensions.

LATER LIFE AND DARK POETRY

The apocalyptic sense of doom that Blok expresses in his civic writings found its parallel in his sense of despair over the growing complication and misery of his private life. His wife's decision in January 1908 to join Meyerhold's troupe on a long tour in the south and his mother's move to Revel (Tallinn, Estonia) to join her transferred husband left Blok bereft of the two most important people in his life. More and more he sought relief in drinking and dissipation.

In August 1908 Lyubov' Dmitrievna, already several months pregnant, finally returned to St. Petersburg. Blok received the news with apparent joy and accepted the child as his own. The boy's death in February 1909, only eight days after his birth, greatly saddened him and inspired a bitter poem, "Na smert' mladentsa" ("On the Death of a Child," February 1909), in which he rejects the consolation of the Orthodox liturgy of the dead. For the next few months his poetry continued the mood of his winter verse: tragic, depressed, and despairing of everything except "the people," whose time of ripening had finally come. Soon after the child's death, the Bloks made arrangements to travel abroad together and make a long-desired tour of Italy.

Blok's "Ital'ianskie stikhi" ("Italian Poems," 1911–1912), a small, exquisitely crafted cycle of poems, represents a poetic synthesis of all that he had achieved thus far. Confronted by the works of art that arose out of the very philosophical idealism that was so close to the symbolists' own worldview, Blok saw, as he had never seen so clearly before, the predicament of the modern who tries through his art to bridge the abyss that separates the real from the ideal. All of the themes central to his poetry—the problematic relationship of art to life, the modern capitalist city, history and nationalism, the idealization of women and its misogynistic opposite in her denigration and violation—crystallize in a highly complex and interwoven system of images. The city, the Madonna, and the real women he encountered become associated through a kind of metaphoric inference that had been working its way through much of his poetry up to this time.

When Blok returned to Russia, he spent the rest of the summer reading books on Italian history and art, including some of Ruskin's writings. Soon he was caught up again in the literary circles he hated and made arrangements to have some of his "Italian Poems" published in the new journal *Apollon.*

In October 1909 Blok wrote "Pesn' Ada" ("The Song of Hell"), a long poem in terza rima in which the poet, bereft of his Beatrice, meets his double, who is condemned to eternal punishment for his dissolute life on earth. The double theme appears again in another

remarkable October poem, "Dvoinik" ("The Double"):

Once, I wandered in the October mist trying to recall a refrain. (O, moment of unbartered kisses! O, embraces of unbought girls!) And there—in the blind fog—there arose the forgotten refrain.

And I began to dream of my youth, and of you. . . . And the fantasy began to carry me away from the wind, from the rain, from the darkness. . . . (Thus does early youth return in dreams. But you, will you ever come back?)

Suddenly I see, reeling out of the foggy night toward me, an aging youth. (Strange, haven't I seen him before in a dream?) He walks out of the foggy night and comes right up to me.

"I am tired of roaming," he whispers, "and of breathing this dank fog; of being reflected in other men's mirrors, and of kissing other men's women. . . ." And it began to seem strange to me, that I would meet him once again. . . .

He smiled insolently—and suddenly there was no one near me. . . . This lugubrious image was familiar, I had seen it somewhere. . . . Or was it perhaps myself that I had just met on the smooth plane of a mirror?

(3:13–14)

At the end of November Blok received news that his father was dying of tuberculosis and a heart condition. Afraid that his sudden arrival would betray to his father the seriousness of his illness, Blok delayed his trip. When he finally did arrive in Warsaw on 1 December 1909, his father had already died in the presence of his estranged second wife and seventeen-year-old daughter, Blok's half-sister, Angelina. His father's death filled him with conflicting emotions, which he attempted to sort out during the next few years in his long historical poem *Retribution.* In this unfinished poem, which Blok worked on until the day he himself died, he attempted to locate his own family within the larger scene of Russian history. Its third part deals with his father's death and its centrality in his own experience of coming to know and, for a moment, love his father. As F. D. Reeve comments, it is a somber meditation on the horrors of history and progress and the story of generation and sterility; it tells of the failure of love between fathers and sons.

Alone in a foreign city, Blok wandered its streets, beginning a new period of debauch, which continued throughout that winter.

In February 1910 Blok persuaded his mother to return to St. Petersburg for treatment of her depression and heart condition. Blok and Lyubov' Dmitrievna took a new flat, which they connected to his mother's adjacent apartment. The bitterness that Lyubov' Dmitrievna had always felt over her husband's excessive attachment to his very neurotic mother reached intolerable proportions. The impossibility of their married life and Lyubov' Dmitrievna's frequent angry words with Alexandra Andreevna drove Blok to direct his pathological outbursts of anger against his wife. Blok explained his continuing attachment to Lyubov' Dmitrievna by referring to the "mystical" years 1898–1902, which "have made things so that I love her and cannot leave her." In the ensuing years they shared the same apartments and at times found comfort in each other, but they continued to live separate lives.

The year 1911 left a gaping hole in Blok's books of poetry. Always careful to date his poems, Blok wrote very few for this year. Indeed, it was a terrible year for him, and a poem he wrote in December, "Unizhenie" ("Humiliation"), tells of his masochistic degradation in a brothel. It ends with this notorious last stanza:

> You are bold! So be yet more fearless! I am neither your husband, nor bridegroom, nor friend! So drive your sharp French heel into my heart—O Angel of yesterday!

> (3:32)

Another poem of the same year, "Da, tak diktuet vdokhnovenie" ("Yes, thus does inspiration dictate," September 1911–February 1914), deals with poetic inspiration and links the civic theme with the general humiliation of the world around him:

Yes, thus does inspiration dictate: my free dreams have always had a weakness for places where there is humiliation, where there is filth, and darkness, and poverty. Go there, there, more humbly and lowly—from there the other world can better be seen. . . . "Have you seen the children of Paris, or the beggars by the bridge in winter?" Open your eyes to the impenetrable horror of life, open them quickly before the great storm sweeps away everything in your native land. Let righteous anger ripen. Prepare your hands for work. . . . And if you cannot, then let melancholy and boredom gather and burn in you. . . . But only wipe off the greasepaint of this false life and, like the timid mole, burrow away from the light into the earth, and there lie prone, cruelly hating all of life and despising this world. And though you cannot see the future, you tell the present days: "No!"

> (3:930)

Blok continued to work on *Retribution* and made arrangements for the publication of the second and third volumes of his collected poems, *Sobranie stikhotvorenii v trekh knigakh* (Collected Verses in Three Volumes, 1911–1912). In Shakhmatovo he discovered August Strindberg and recognized in the Swedish playwright's misogyny something akin to his own attitude toward his wife. He dedicated the poem "Zhenshchina" ("A Woman," 1914) to Strindberg.

While Blok was in the country, Lyubov' Dmitrievna was traveling in Germany and France. Blok joined her in Brittany in July and was inspired by the old Breton customs and legends to write what eventually became *Roza i krest* (*The Rose and the Cross,* 1916). Originally commissioned as a libretto for a ballet, the work evolved into a play that was completed in 1913.

Blok returned from Europe exhausted and depressed and again sank into dissipation, after which he eventually succumbed to a rather serious case of syphilis. Lyubov' Dmitrievna continued to work in the theater and was soon involved with a young actor, an affair that drove Blok to agonizing jealousy. They agreed to separate so that Lyubov' Dmitrievna could follow her lover to the provinces. The separation was more than Blok could bear, however, and when she received a letter in which he intimated suicide, Lyubov' Dmitrievna returned to him for a short time.

Blok's poetry of 1912, written almost exclusively during November and December, is as excellent as it is pessimistic. During this time he wrote the cycle "Pliaski smerti" ("The Dances of Death," 1912), which contains the powerfully direct poem "Noch', ulitsa, fonar', apteka" ("Night, a street, a lamp, a drugstore," 1912):

> Night, a street, a lamp, a drugstore, a senseless and dim light. Live another quarter-century and all will be the same. There's no way out.
>
> You'll die—and you'll start again from the beginning. And everything will repeat itself, as before: night, the canal's icy ripple, a drugstore, a street, a lamp.
>
> (3:37)

He also wrote the important poem "Osennii vecher byl. Pod zvuk dozhdia stekliannyi" ("It was an autumn night. Beneath the vitreous sound of the rain," 1912) with its subtexts from Johann Wolfgang von Goethe and Edgar Allan Poe, and "O no, I do not wish for us to fall." During the last days of this year he wrote the poem "To My Muse," whose importance he marked by later choosing it to begin the third volume of his second edition of collected poems (1916).

WAR AND REVOLUTION

On 1 August 1914, Germany declared war on Russia. Blok and his wife immediately set out to assist in any way they could. Lyubov' Dmitrievna spent nine months working as a nurse in military hospitals, and Blok worked in government volunteer organizations helping the families of enlisted men. If he at first welcomed the war, seeing it as yet another cataclysmic event that could reveal the elemental music of another world, in time he came to share the disillusionment of his countrymen.

By the beginning of 1916 Russia's casualties in the war were being counted in the millions, and there was chaos and demoralization both at home and at the front. In order to avoid being conscripted as a combatant, Blok signed on as a member of a semi-civilian force that was sent near the front to supervise the work of building fortifications and digging trenches. Blok was a good comrade, and, contrary to his initial fears, he actually enjoyed his first experiences of communal life. As had always been the case, as his bodily fitness increased through hard, physical labor, his nervous disorders diminished, and he proved himself to be a very competent and hardworking administrator.

By the end of 1914 Blok's fame had reached new heights. His poems were being published in the most popular newspapers, and *The Puppet Show* and *The Unknown Lady* were staged by Meyerhold. In the spring of 1915 he prepared another three-volume edition of his poems, which sold out instantly when it was published in the following year, and he made significant progress on *Retribution*, completing the meditation on the twentieth century.

During this war period Blok began to establish himself as a great patriotic poet. A group of previously published poems was collected under the title "Na voinu" ("To War") and published in the liberal newspaper *Russkoe slovo* (on 21 September 1914). Among them is the well-known poem "Greshit' besstydno, neprobudno" ("Shamelessly, endlessly sinning," 26 August 1914):

> Shamelessly, endlessly sinning, losing count of the nights and days, and with a head made heavy by liquor, you creep into God's church.
>
> Bowing down three times, signing yourself seven times with the cross, you secretly touch your feverish forehead to the bespattered floor.
>
> Putting a copper penny into the basket, three, nay, seven times you kiss the poor, centuries old icon border, already worn with kisses.
>
> And returning home, shortchanging someone by that same penny, hiccupping, you kick a starving dog away from the gate.

And under the icon lamp, you drink your tea while clicking away at an abacus, then drool over bonds in a fat-bellied chest of drawers,

And collapsing onto a deep feather bed you fall into a heavy sleep. . . . Yes, even as you are, my Russia, I love no country more.

(3:274)

In 1916 Blok's *Stikhi o Rossii* (Poems About Russia) appeared. Contrary to Blok's usual practice, the poems were published without dates, so that by an editorial sleight of hand poem cycles such as "On the Battlefield of Kulikovo," which had been published earlier, were read as if for the first time, within a totally new historical context of war and heroic patriotism. In the public's view Blok was now a national poet, beyond any single critical "school." He himself was glad to be dissociated from European "decadence" and welcomed his public recognition as a patriotic writer.

Blok was still near the front in February when he learned of the rioting in Petrograd, of the forced abdication of the tsar, and of the establishment of the Provisional Government. Desertion from the front was widespread, and Blok himself left his post to return to the euphoric capital in March 1917, where he immediately offered his services to the new state. Eventually, he was assigned to the Extraordinary Commission of Inquiry established to investigate the newly imprisoned members of the tsar's government and was appointed editor in charge of preparing stenographic reports of the interrogations for publication. So close to what had been the center of power in Russia, Blok saw and heard "something that almost no one hears or sees, that only very few have the opportunity to observe once in a hundred years." In a letter to his mother, he describes his historical prose narrative, *Poslednie dni imperatorskoi vlasti* (The Last Days of the Imperial Regime, 1921), as "an absorbing novel in the spirit of Dostoevsky."

From the beginning and in the spirit of his earlier political essays Blok firmly believed that "power should go to the proletariat, because only children can make anything new and interesting out of that old toy." As he wrote in his essay "The People and the Intelligentsia," he now saw the coming cataclysm as a violent clash between the people of Russia and the Europeanized professional class. For Blok, tired of the compromises, growing reaction, and general inconclusiveness of the Provisional Government, Bolshevism seemed to be the "cleansing fire" that would clear away the vulgar philistinism that surrounded him. In his view, expressed in *Dnevniki* (Diaries, 7 August 1917), the intelligentsia had an important role to play:

But that is the task of Russian culture—to direct this flame onto what must be burnt; . . . to set such limits to the destruction as will not weaken the force of the fire but will organize its force; to organize ungovernable freedom; to direct the slothful putrefaction, which also hides the possibility of outbursts of violence, into the Rasputin-dominated corners of the soul, and there to fan it into a sky-high conflagration, so that our cunning, slothful, servile sensuality may be consumed in the flames.

(7:297)

In November 1917, soon after the Bolsheviks had taken power under Lenin's leadership, the local peasantry overran Shakhmatovo and sacked it. His reaction to this act of violence fit his highly developed sense of sin, guilt, and retribution. Shortly afterward, as if in response, he wrote in "Intelligentsiia i revoliutsiia" ("The Intelligentsia and the Revolution," 1918): "We are answering for the past. We are links in a single chain. Or do the sins of the fathers not lie on us?"

During the terrible winter of 1918, when Petrograd was covered in snow, when all public transportation had stopped, in the darkness of a general power failure, in the depths of profound famine and starvation, and with enemy planes droning overhead, Blok concentrated his visionary powers on the task of understanding all that was happening around him. Early in January, he began to hear a roaring sound like the beginning of an earthquake. Soon he began to discern a musical order in this rumble and wrote two lines that eventually became a couplet in section 8 of *The Twelve*. Later that month, he was seized by an irresistible poetic force, and in two more days he had written his greatest work, *The Twelve*. Significantly, its dramatic core is a love story.

Between that first moment of inspiration and its culmination in the writing of the entire poem, Blok returned to the theme of his 1908 political writings in the essay "The Intelligentsia and the Revolution." He reasserts his belief in the profound gap that separates the great mass of uneducated Russians from the educated few and speaks once again of the elemental force of revolutionary violence:

> Don't be afraid. Surely you don't think that so much as one grain of what is truly valuable can be lost? We have loved but little if we are so afraid for that which we love. "Perfect love driveth out fear." Do not fear the destruction of fortresses, palaces, pictures, books. They should be preserved for the people; but having lost these, the people have not lost everything. A palace destroyed is no palace. A fortress wiped off the face of the earth is no fortress. A tsar who tumbles off his throne of his own volition is no tsar. Fortresses are in our hearts, tsars in our heads. Eternal forms, that have been revealed to us, are taken from us only with our hearts and with our heads.

(6:16)

For Blok the depth of corruption and evil of the old world, its "anti-musicality," justified the violence and destruction of the revolutionary storm. Within the roaring violence all around, Blok heard a new music that came forth from "the collapse of the old world":

> We loved those dissonances, those roars, those pealing sounds and unexpected transitions . . . in the orchestra [of the February Revolution]. But, if we really loved them and were not merely soothing our nerves after dinner in a fashionable theater, we must listen to and love those very sounds that are now flying forth from the world orchestra, and while listening, we must understand that they are about the same thing, the very same thing.

(6:11)

He proclaimed that it is the duty of writers to hear "this great music of the future," and he ends his essay with an ecstatic exhortation: "With your whole body, with all your heart and consciousness—listen to the Revolution."

In the October Revolution Blok saw the triumphant uprising of the primordial force of the Russian people, "the final destruction," "a worldwide conflagration" and the end of "new history." It was the culmination of the eschatological visions that had troubled him from his early youth. Blok's obsessive theme of inherited guilt and retribution took on global, even cosmic, proportions.

The Twelve records the sound of those days. Its roughhewn rhythms and stanzas lurch forward with ineluctable force and violence. Its cacophony and constantly changing meters are orchestrated with an immediacy and truthfulness that go beyond anything he had ever written before. From within the whirlwind of a constant musical obligato, scraps of dialogue, dialectal expressions, obscenities, quotations from liturgical texts, and political slogans break out like voices in a raging storm. The poet is possessed by the terrible elemental forces of the uneducated mob and speaks in their language. The landscape is again snowswept Petersburg, and in the dark night of the uprising we hear the voices of the urban poor, factory workers, prostitutes, the nameless dregs of the great urban center's back streets, come at last to wreak revenge on the complacent, cowering world of the bourgeoisie. During his years of wandering and dissipation in these back streets, Blok stored the sounds of the taverns, slums, and whorehouses in his memory. He learned the rhythms of the drunken Gypsy melodies and the vulgar love songs of the organ grinder. Like Dostoevsky, Blok heard in the vulgar banality of the urban streets the fantastic song of some elemental force. In capturing the exact cadences and dialectal forms of the language of the people in revolt, Blok embodied a mystical vision of primordial power and destructive freedom. The poem is not about an extraordinary historical event but about the same forces that Blok had earlier likened to the earthquake and volcanic eruptions that destroyed Messina. His assertion that "the Bolsheviks are right to beware of *The Twelve*" is amplified in his late essay *Katilina,* where he presents the idea of permanent revolution. In his understanding of history the Bolshevik Revolution was but another phase that would also be swept away when the real revolution came.

Blok's use of dialogue and the common language of the street gives the poem a theatrical quality. In a very real sense it is Blok's most successful dramatic poem and the culmination of his lifelong attraction to the theater. At its center is the love story of Kat'ka-Petrukha-Van'ka, an inspired reformulation of the old Columbine-Pierrot-Harlequin triangle, which had served him so well so many times before. In his notes to the poem Blok clearly links *The Twelve* to his two great erotic cycles, "The Snow Mask" and "Carmen," which are also closely associated with the theater: "For the last time, in January 1918, I surrendered myself to elemental forces no less blindly than I had in January 1907 or March 1914. For that reason, I do not disavow that what I had written then was also written in accord with the elements." As he does earlier, Blok weds the forces of sexual passion to destructive power and death. The love story in *The Twelve* is a continuation of Blok's major theme and points to a meaning beyond any straightforward interpretation that might be forced out of this highly enigmatic poem. Blok himself rejected any overt political interpretation. His notes make this explicit:

> For a few days during and after the completion of *The Twelve*, I physically heard a great noise all around me—a continuous sound (most likely the noise of the collapse of the old world). Therefore, those who see political verses in *The Twelve*, whether they be friend or foe of my poem, are either very blind to art, or they stand ear-deep in the mire of politics, or they are gripped by enormous spite.
>
> (3:474)

Like some of the great mystics, Blok's contact with the other world, with its "music," was experienced erotically. The low-life romance of the poem takes on tragic proportions because it is played out within this mystical storm and draws its destructive power from it.

Blok had already joined this mystical love with brutal violence at the end of his essay "Nature and Culture," in which he juxtaposes two poems, one an ecstatic prayer about holy love, the other a vulgar street song about a knife-wielding gang of thugs. For Blok the profoundly religious character of the Russian people does not contradict its equally violent, volcanic potential:

> In these days of the approaching storm, both these songs are merging: it is clear to the point of horror that those who sing about "forged steel knives" and those who sing about "sacred love" will not sell each other because an elemental power is with them, they are children of a single storm.
>
> (5:359)

The confluence of these two great forces results in the apocalyptic power that carries out from its depths the barely visible figure of Christ leading the twelve Red Guardsmen. As Blok writes in his diaries, it too is erotically evocative: "If one looks into the columns of the snowstorm, on this path one sees Jesus Christ. But I myself sometimes deeply hate this feminine phantom." This androgynous Christ, wreathed in a garland of roses, recalls Blok's essay on symbolism with its image of the face that appears amidst the heavenly roses. In this highly evocative and elusive last scene Blok succeeds in creating his most perfectly symbolist poem. It is not Christ's religious meaning in the ordinary sense that gives this moment of revelation its power. It is rather the haunting silence with which we must encounter it: its elusive yet palpable significance, its resistance to explication, is what makes it so disturbing and effective. It is one of the most perplexing, at times infuriating, and unforgettable moments in all Russian literature.

Riding on what remained of this tremendous wave of inspiration, Blok wrote his last significant poem, *Skify* (*The Scythians,* 1918), within two days of *The Twelve.* This poem is a direct response to Germany's continued advance on Russia despite the Soviets' attempt to cease hostilities in a unilateral declaration of peace. It draws its central image of an advancing barbaric Asiatic horde from Solov'ev's writings about Russia's buffering position between degenerate Europe and the forces of "pan-Mongolism" threatening from the East. In Blok's own writing, the "yellow peril" figures prominently as early as 1911. In Russian literature it finds its most perfect expression in Bely's novel *Peterburg* (*Petersburg,* 1916). In Blok's poem the "yellow peril" stands for all the tremendous, barbaric forces that threaten to destroy the achievements of European culture. Russia serves as both a dam and a conduit for its destructive power.

In *The Scythians,* which is full of high rhetoric and chauvinism, Blok warns the old European world that it must cease its stubborn pursuit of war and death and come to embrace the barbaric, vital, new world arising in Russia or else risk the fury of its Asiatic power. In spite of its highly topical nature, the poem's violent strength and high oratory make it a powerful statement of some political relevance even today.

Blok spent the terrible years of the Revolution in Petrograd. He continued to see Del'mas irregularly, and she remained a loyal and helpful friend until he died. Lyubov' Dmitrievna's practical skills and great strength helped Blok's mother and aunt get needed supplies of goods and food, and she also assisted Blok with his work on the Extraordinary Commission of Inquiry. She gave public readings of *The Twelve* and shared some of the public rejection and hostility that Blok met in certain quarters.

In response to the condemnation of his poem by some of his best friends and most respected colleagues, Blok wrote his essay *Katilina,* in which he compares Rome of the first century B.C. to his own revolutionary time. The essay is remarkable for several reasons, not the least of which is its style, which combines the directness of an eyewitness report with the allusive methods of Blok's other essays. In a typical juxtaposition of images and facts, Blok evokes the meaning of a historical moment by suggesting correspondences among disparate events rather than by devising academic schemes that isolate them and explain nothing. What emerges is an unmistakable and convincing analogy between the declining Roman republic and modern European civilization in its Russian variant. We have met the terms of the comparison before in Blok's earlier writings, and it is not difficult to see in Blok's presentation of the "Roman Bolshevik" Catiline the same destructive forces he embodies in his Red Guardsmen of *The Twelve.* Blok describes Catiline as "the son of a cruel and practical people," "a revolutionary in his whole spirit and body," to whom "any theoretical thought was alien." He suggests that Catiline's seizure of power in Rome against Cicero, whom he calls "a civilian intellectual in a time when it was more fashionable to be a soldier," was but a pale portent of the present days.

Significantly, Blok feels the rhythm of this epoch not in the historical accounts of Cicero, Plutarch, or Sallust, but in the poetry of the love poet Caius Valerius Catullus. Blok singles out Catullus' account of the self-emasculation of the Phrygian shepherd Attis as the true reflection not only of Catiline's wrath and revolutionary brutality but also of the tense, stormy atmosphere of a Rome torn apart by civil war. Blok writes: "Do you hear this uneven, hurried stride of the doomed, the stride of the revolutionary, the stride in which there resounds the storm of savage rage in the choppy musical sounds?"

What fascinates Blok is the poem's rare galliambic meter, which is associated with orgiastic dance and the gender transformation that Attis undergoes after he has "lightened himself" by castration. Driven by "a hatred of Venus," Attis' act is one of consecration to the primal forces of Cybele, the earth goddess. It is a renunciation of civilization and an acceptance of nature. Given Blok's obsessive striving to cast "servile sensuality" into the purifying fires of religious ecstasy, which structures every aspect of his poetic experience and political thought, Blok sees Attis' act as the result of insane devotion. His metamorphosis into a woman is reflected in the rhythm of the poem, which "becomes lighter, as if feminine." The poetic form itself undergoes a transformation into something that no longer resembles Latin poetry: "It is as if, in that place where Attis laments his country, himself, his friends, his parents, his school, his youth, and his manhood, the poem flows out in lyrical tears characteristic of the Christian spirit." As he does in the androgynous figure of Christ that appears out of the snowstorm in *The Twelve*, Blok "hears" the sound of the future in Catullus' poem but he cannot name it or describe it.

Blok's choice of a poem like this in the context of his essay on revolution may be further explained if we recall that "Nature and Culture" ends by linking an ecstatic religious poem with a song about the violence of an urban gang of thugs. Behind the religious poem is the background of Russian religious sectarianism, whose extreme form in the Khlysty fascinated intellectuals during the first decades of the twentieth century. These sectarians were reported to engage in wild, orgiastic rites as well as practicing mortification and chastity by castration. (Bely's novel *Serebrianyi golub'* [*The Silver Dove*, 1910] is about this group. Bely enthusiastically received Blok's essay *Katilina* and saw in it "a great dramatic poem.")

The essay ends with a discussion of the epilogue to Henrik Ibsen's drama *Catilina* (1850). In that play two women go with Cati-

line throughout his whole life. They are the antithetical symbols of the demonic or seductive woman who urges rebellion and destruction and the "morning star" or life figure who leads to peace. Catiline kills the latter, according to Blok, because "she wanted to condemn him to the horrors of only half a life." He is himself killed by the former as a result of his rebellion against the state. Although he believes that he will be condemned to hell after his death, his soul, together with the soul of the woman he has killed, falls to the right, into Elysium. Responding to Ibsen's critics as if to his own, Blok justifies Ibsen's "naive and somewhat clumsy ending":

> The crux of the matter is not democracy or aristocracy, but something totally different. It follows from this that the critics should not particularly rejoice that Catiline "goes to the right." . . . They should rather turn their attention to the fact that . . . Ibsen ended his drama in a way no one could consider liberal: he who is found worthy of Elysium and accepted in love is none other than the rebel, the murderer of the most sacred thing in his own life—Catiline.
>
> (6:91)

For Blok, Ibsen's Catiline "was the friend not of solid, positive 'liberties' that fell from the sky; he was the friend of a freedom flying ever farther away." Catiline wanted something unattainable, something that did not freeze into some boring, solemn, historical form. It was his struggle for freedom that staved off oppressive stagnation, as Blok suggests in quoting Ibsen's 1871 letter to the Danish literary critic Georg Brandes: "The very concept of freedom is distinguished by the fact that it continually expands in so far as we endeavor to draw it into ourselves. Consequently, he who in the struggle for freedom stops and says, 'I have it,' shows that he has forfeited it." Blok's essay is not only an argument for the elemental freedom expressed in the revolutionary violence of his poem *The Twelve*. It contains, as well, the prophetic glimmer of what the revolutionary storm actually turned into.

The last years of Blok's life were plagued by endless, overburdening committee meetings and by literary work to support himself and his family. Russia's withdrawal from the war did not result in peace, and 1918 saw the outbreak of civil war and the anti-Soviet intervention of Great Britain, the United States, and other countries. Conditions were appalling: food was scarce, prices were high, and there were epidemics of typhus in which Blok's half-sister, Angelina, died. House searches and arrests by the secret police began in 1919, and Blok himself was arrested for a few days on suspicion of taking part in a conspiracy to overthrow the government. His notebook speaks most poignantly of his experiences: "Life is becoming monstrous, ugly, senseless. . . . Troubles. Silence and murky darkness."

Blok's stepfather died in January 1920, and Blok, Lyubov' Dmitrievna, and Blok's mother moved into a small apartment together. In spite of their terrible hardships and the exhausting, routine work, Blok continued his literary work, preparing another new edition of his own poems. He also served as the editor of the fifth volume of the selected works of Heinrich Heine in Russian translation and edited a book of Mikhail Lermontov's poetry that was published in 1921. He continued to work on *Retribution* and gave many public readings of his poems.

In February 1921 Blok gathered his strength to produce his great speech in honor of Alexander Pushkin, "O naznachenii poeta" (On the Calling of the Poet). In it he appeals to the bureaucrats now coming into power to leave the poet that "secret freedom," that "peace and independence" of which Pushkin had written during another, earlier repressive regime that had contributed to his death. Blok attacks state censorship explicitly, and alludes to the destructive role of certain nineteenth-century precursors of official Soviet literary doctrine. In addition he harks back to his earlier theme concerning the creative potential of violence: "Chaos is primordial, elemental anarchy; cosmos is the establishment of harmony, culture.

Out of chaos is born cosmos; the elements hide within themselves the seeds of culture. Out of anarchy is created harmony." It is a fine piece of oratory, as much a visionary statement about the creative process as it is about the real world of Soviet literary politics.

After a short, debilitating poetry-reading tour in Moscow in May 1921 Blok returned home and thereafter was confined to bed. He spent May and June working on his archives and destroying some of his letters and diaries.

His last days were spent in great chest pain caused by a condition similar to that of his mother, and he was unable to breathe. He died on 7 August 1921 in the presence of his wife and mother.

CONCLUSION

In his contribution to an important collection of critical essays, *Ob Aleksandre Bloke* (About Alexander Blok, 1921), which appeared shortly after Blok's death, the critic Boris Eikhenbaum writes: "To imagine Blok as an old man is just as difficult as to imagine Tolstoy young." Indeed, Blok's image among his contemporaries was cast forever in the mold of the persona of his poetry, and it is for this reason, perhaps, that Blok so often appears in the works of his fellow poets.

Four writers in particular, Anna Akhmatova, Marina Tsvetaeva, Osip Mandelshtam, and Boris Pasternak, provide an entrance into their world and Blok's through their poetic encounters with him. All of them, as Pasternak wrote in his autobiographical sketch "Liudi i polozheniia" ("People and Situations," 1967), "went through the years of [their] youth with Blok as [their] guide," and all of them had to respond to and overcome his enormous influence in order to form their own unique poetic voices.

Akhmatova, to whom Blok dedicated his poem "Anne Akhmatovoi" ("To Anna Akhmatova," 1914), wrote several poems to him and re-created the literary atmosphere of 1913 Petersburg in her great *Poema bez geroia* (*Poem*

Without a Hero, 1960). Blok figures prominently in this poem both as a character and in references to his poetry and style. He is cast as "the rival" in a love triangle that ends in suicide. Akhmatova's portrait of Blok in this poem gives us an idea of the impression he made on his contemporaries:

> He's there alone. Sharp profile on the wall. Is he Gabriel or Mephistopheles . . . ? The Demon himself with Tamara's smile, but there are hidden such charms in that terrible smoky face: flesh, almost become spirit, and an antique lock of hair over his ear—all is mysterious in this visitor.

With characteristic vividness, Akhmatova's friend and fellow poet Mandelshtam provides an image in his essay "Barsuch'ia nora" ("The Badger's Den," 1922) that summarizes Blok's position within the history of Russian poetry:

> Blok was a man of the nineteenth century and he knew that its days were numbered. Greedily he widened and deepened his inner world in *time,* just as a badger, burrowing into the ground to make his den, builds two exits. The century during which one lives is one's "badger's den" and to each is apportioned a narrow, limited space in which to move about; in a frenzy each tries to expand his territory, valuing above all else the exits from his underground den. Driven by his badger's instinct, Blok deepened his poetic understanding of the nineteenth century.

Although she never actually met him, Tsvetaeva maintained a deep attraction to and reverence for Blok throughout her life. He is mentioned many times in her prose works, but it is in her intensely personal "Stikhi k Bloky" ("Poems to Blok," 1922), a cycle of eighteen often difficult poems, that she creates a poetic diary, recording her awe, her excitement, her love, and her grief after his death. A poem she wrote a week after he died "Vot on—gliadi—ustavshii ot chuzhbin" ("Here he is—look—exhausted from foreign lands," 15 August

1921), expresses some of the tragic isolation Blok felt during the last year of his life:

> Here he is—look—exhausted from foreign lands,
> A leader without an armed retinue.
>
> Behold—with a cupped hand he drinks from the mountain rapids—a prince without a country.
>
> There all is given him: a principality, an army, Bread and a mother.
>
> Beauty is your legacy—command, O friend without friends.

Perhaps more than in any other work, Blok plays a cardinal role in Pasternak's *Doctor Zhivago* (1957), where he appears not only as the leading poet about whom "young people in both capitals were mad," but more significantly as the incarnation of the spirit of an age approaching catastrophe. Pasternak makes this clear in a poem from a small cycle entitled "Veter (Chetyre otryvka o Bloke)" ("The Wind [Four Fragments About Blok]," 1959):

> Blok saw a pattern in the sky. The heavens foretold him that there would be a terrible thunderstorm, foul weather, a great storm, a cyclone.
>
> Blok awaited this storm and convulsion. Its fiery features etched by fear and craving for its outcome in his life and poetry.

In his novel Blok's influence is clearly felt in the central love story of Yuri Zhivago and Lara. Pasternak develops the *fin-de-siècle* opposition between the Madonna and the whore that is so central to Blok's poetic universe.

For his contemporaries who survived him Blok remained an eloquent symbol for their culture, whose sudden end they had all lived through. If his influence on Russian poetry has waned and if the meaning of his poems sometimes seems hopelessly obscure or his style excessively mannered, it is perhaps because time now passes more swiftly than it did for him and the rhythms and meters of our age are so vastly different.

Selected Bibliography

EDITIONS

INDIVIDUAL WORKS

POETRY

Stikhi o Prekrasnoi Dame: Pervyi sbornik stikhov. Moscow, 1905.

Nechaiannaia radost': Vtoroi sbornik stikhov. Moscow, 1907.

Snezhnaia maska: Poema. St. Petersburg, 1907.

Zemlia v snegu: Tretii sbornik stikhov. Moscow, 1908.

Nochnye chasy: Chetvertyi sbornik stikhov, 1908–1910. Moscow, 1911.

Kruglyi god: Stikhotvoreniia dlia detei. Moscow, 1913.

Skazki: Stikhi dlia detei. Moscow, 1913.

Stikhi o Rossii. Petrograd, 1916.

Dvenadtsat' (poema), Skify (stikhotvorenie). Petrograd, 1918.

Solov'inyi sad: Poema. Petrograd, 1918.

Iamby: Sovremennye stikhi (1907–1914). Petrograd, 1919.

Za gran'iu proshlykh dnei: Stikhotvoreniia. Petrograd, 1920.

Sedoe utro: Piatyi sbornik stikhov. Petrograd, 1920.

Stikhotvoreniia: Kniga tret'ia (1907–1916). Petrograd, 1921.

Vozmezdie: Poema. Petersburg, 1922.

THEATER

Liricheskie dramy (Balaganchik, Neznakomka, Korol' na ploshchadi). St. Petersburg, 1908.

Roza i krest. Moscow, 1916.

Pesnia sud'by: Dramatichiskaia poema. Petrograd, 1919.

O liubvi, poezii, i gosudarstvennoi sluzhbe: Dialog. Berlin, 1920.

Ramzes: Stseny iz zhizni drevnego Egipta. Petrograd, 1921.

ESSAYS AND HISTORICAL WORKS

Rossiia i intelligentsiia (1907–1918): Sem' statei. Moscow, 1918. Contains "Narod i intelligentsiia," "Stikhiia i kul'tura," "Intelligentsiia i revoliutsiia," etc.

Katilina: Stranitsa iz istorii mirovoi revoliutsii. Petrograd, 1919.

O simvolizme (O sovremennom sostoianii russkogo simvolizma). Petrograd, 1921.

Poslednie dni imperatorskoi vlasti: Po neizdannym dokumentam sostavil Aleksandr Blok. Petrograd, 1921.

COLLECTED WORKS

Sobranie stikhotvorenii v trekh knigakh. Moscow, 1911–1912.

Sobranie stikhotvorenii i teatr v chetyrekh knigakh. Moscow, 1916.

Sobranie stikhotvorenii i teatra. 4 vols. (incomplete). Petrograd, 1918.

Sobranie sochinenii Aleksandra Bloka. 7 vols. Petrograd and Berlin, 1922.

MODERN EDITIONS

Iskusstvo i revoliutsiia. Edited by L. Asanova and T. Ul'ina. Moscow, 1979.

Na dal'nem gorizonte: Stikhi i dramy zarubezhnykh poetov v perevode A. Bloka. Edited by N. Shupletsov. Moscow, 1970.

Neizdannye stikhotvoreniia 1897–1919. Edited by P. Medvedev. Leningrad, 1926.

Ob iskusstve. Edited by L. K. Dolgopolov. Moscow, 1980.

O naznachenii poeta. Edited by V. V. Dement'ev. Moscow, 1971.

Otrocheskie stikhi. Moscow, 1922.

Polnoe sobranie stikhotvorenii v dvukh tomakh. Edited by V. N. Orlov. Leningrad, 1946.

Sobranie sochinenii. Edited by V. V. Gol'tseva. Moscow and Leningrad, 1929.

Sobranie sochinenii v dvenadtsati tomakh. 12 vols. Edited by V. R. Ivanov-Razumnik (vols. 1–7) and V. N. Orlov (vols. 8–12). Leningrad, 1932–1936.

Sobranie sochinenii v shesti tomakh. 6 vols. Edited by V. N. Orlov and A. A. Surkova. Leningrad, 1980.

Sobranie sochinenii v vos'mi tomakh. 8 vols. Edited by V. N. Orlov et al. Moscow and Leningrad, 1960–1963.

Sochineniia v dvukh tomakh. 2 vols. Edited by V. N. Orlov. Moscow, 1955.

Sochineniia v odnom tome. Edited by V. N. Orlov. 2d ed., Moscow and Leningrad, 1946.

Stikhi ne voshedshie v sobranii sochinenii Aleksandra Bloka. Edited by L. Blok. Moscow and Leningrad, 1925.

Stikhotvoreniia. Edited by V. N. Orlov. Leningrad, 1955.

Stikhotvoreniia i poemy. Edited by V. N. Orlov. Leningrad, 1961; 2d ed., 1969.

Stikhotvoreniia, poemy, Roza i krest. Edited by A. Tarkhov. Moscow, 1974.

DIARIES AND NOTEBOOKS

Dnevnik A. Bloka 1911–1913. Edited by P. N. Medvedev. Leningrad, 1928.

Dnevnik A. Bloka 1917–1921. Edited by P. N. Medvedev. Leningrad, 1928.

Zapisnye knizhki A. Bloka. Edited by P. N. Medvedev. Leningrad, 1930.

"Iunosheskii dnevnik A. Bloka." Edited by V. N. Orlov. In *Literaturnoe nasledstvo.* Moscow, 1937.

Dnevniki 1901–1921. Edited by V. N. Orlov et al. In *Sobranie sochinenii,* vol. 7. Moscow and Leningrad, 1960–1963.

Zapisnye knizhki 1901–1920. Edited by V. N. Orlov et al. Moscow, 1965.

CORRESPONDENCE

Pis'ma Aleksandra Bloka. Leningrad, 1925.

Pis'ma Aleksandra Bloka k rodnym. 2 vols. Edited by M. A. Beketova. Leningrad, 1927, 1932.

Pis'ma A. Bloka k E. P. Ivanovu. Edited by C. Vol'pe. Moscow and Leningrad, 1936.

Aleksandr Blok i Andrei Belyi: Perepiska. Edited by V. N. Orlov. In *Letopisi.* Moscow, 1940. Reprinted in Munich, 1969.

Aleksandr Blok: Pis'ma k zhene. Edited by V. N. Orlov. In *Literaturnoe nasledstvo.* Moscow, 1978.

Pis'ma. Edited by V. N. Orlov et al. In *Sobranie sochinenii,* vol. 8. Moscow and Leningrad, 1960–1963.

TRANSLATIONS BY BLOK

Grillparzer Franz. *Pramater'.* St. Petersburg, 1908.

Rutebeuf. *Deistvo o Teofile.* Petrograd, 1915.

Grigor'ev, Apollon. *Stikhotvoreniia.* Moscow, 1916.

Heine, Heinrich. *Izbrannye sochineniia.* (Putevye kartiny i memuary.) Vol. 5. Petrograd, 1920.

Lermontov, Mikhail. *Izbrannye sochineniia v odnom tome.* Berlin and Petrograd, 1921.

WORKS EDITED BY BLOK

Flaubert, Gustave. *Perepiska: Chast' pervaia.* Translated by A. Kublikaia-Piottukh. Edited by A. Blok. Petrograd, 1914.

TRANSLATIONS

Alexander Blok: Selected Poems. Translated and edited by Avril Pyman. Oxford, 1972.

"Italian Poems." Translated by Lucy Vogel. In *Alexander Blok: The Journey to Italy.* Ithaca, N.Y., 1973.

The King in the Square. Translated by Oleta Joan O'Connor and George Rapall Noyes. *Slavonic Review* 12:489–512 (1934).

Love Poetry and the Civil Service. Translated by F. O'Dempsey. London, 1953.

"On the Present State of Russian Symbolism." In *The Russian Symbolists: An Anthology of Critical and Theoretical Writings.* Edited and translated by Ronald E. Peterson. Ann Arbor, Mich., 1986.

The Puppet Show. Translated by Mary Kriger and Gleb Struve. *Slavonic Review* 7:309–322 (April 1950).

———. Translated and edited by F. D. Reeve. In *Twentieth-Century Russian Plays.* New York, 1963.

———. Translated by Michael Green. In *The Russian Symbolist Theater: An Anthology of Plays and Critical Texts.* Ann Arbor, Mich., 1986.

Retribution. In *Selected Poems.* Translated by Alex Miller. Moscow, 1981.

The Rose and the Cross. Translated by Ingeborg E. Smith and George Rapall Noyes. *Slavonic Review* 14:497–549 (1936).

———. Translated by Michael Green. In *The Russian Symbolist Theater: An Anthology of Plays and Critical Texts.* Ann Arbor, Mich., 1986.

Selected Poems. Translated by Alex Miller. Moscow, 1981.

Selected Poems of Alexander Blok. Translated and edited by James B. Woodward. Oxford, 1968.

———. Translated by Jon Stallworthy and Peter France. New York, 1974.

"The Scythians." Translated by Babette Deutsch and Avrahm Yarmolinsky. *Nation* 111:271–272 (4 September 1920).

The Song of Fate. Translated by Oleta Joan O'Connor and George Rapall Noyes. *Poet Lore* 44:1–41 (1938).

The Spirit of Music: Essays. Translated by I. Freiman. London, 1946. Includes "The People and the Intelligentsia," "Nature and Culture," and "The Intelligentsia and the Revolution."

The Twelve. Translated by C. E. Bechofer. London, 1920.

———. Translated by Babette Deutsch and Avrahm Yarmolinsky. New York, 1920.

——————. Anonymous translation. *Living Age* 305: 419–425 (15 May 1920).

——————. Translated by Robin Fulton. Lancashire, England, 1968.

——————. Translated by Arthur Clifford. In *The Silver Age of Russian Culture,* edited by Carl and Ellendea Proffer. Ann Arbor, Mich., 1975.

The Twelve and Other Poems. Translated by Jon Stallworthy and Peter France. New York, 1970.

The Twelve and The Scythians. Translated by Jack Lindsay. London, 1982.

The Unknown Woman. Translated by Olive Frances Murphy. *Transition* 2, 3, 4 (May, June, July 1927).

ANTHOLOGIES

A Book of Russian Verse. Edited by C. M. Bowra. London, 1943.

Modern Russian Poetry: An Anthology. Edited by Vladimir Markov and Merrill Sparks. Indianapolis, Ind., 1967.

The Oxford Book of Russian Verse. Edited by Maurice Baring. London, 1925.

The Penguin Book of Russian Verse. Edited by Dimitri Obolensky. Baltimore, 1962.

Russian Poetry. Edited by Avrahm Yarmolinsky and Babette Deutsch. London, 1923.

Soviet Literature: An Anthology. Edited by Bernard Reavey and Marc Slonim. New York, 1934.

BIOGRAPHICAL AND CRITICAL STUDIES

Banianin, M. "The City Poetry of Baudelaire and Blok." Ph.D. dissertation. Washington University, 1970.

Beamish-Thiriet, F. "The Myth of Women in Baudelaire and Blok." Ph.D. dissertation. University of Washington, 1973.

Beketova, Mariia Andreevna. *Aleksandr Blok: Biograficheskii ocherk.* Petrograd, 1922. Reprinted in The Hague, 1969.

Bely, Andrey. *Vospominaniia o A. A. Bloke.* Published in four issues of the journal *Epopeia.* Berlin, 1922–1923.

Blok, Liubov' (Mendeleeva). *Byli i nebylitsy o Bloke i o sebe.* Edited by I. Paul'mann and L. S. Fleishman. Bremen, 1977.

——————. "Facts and Myths About Blok and Myself." In *Blok: An Anthology of Essays and Memoirs,* translated and edited by Lucy Vogel. Ann Arbor, Mich., 1982.

Blokovskii sbornik I: Trudy nauchnoi konferentsii, posviashchennoi izuchenniiu zhizni, i tvorchestva A. A. Bloka, mai 1962 goda. Edited by Y. M. Lotman et al. Tartu, Estonia, 1964.

Blokovskii sbornik II: Trudy vtoroi nauchnoi konferentsii, posviashchennoi izuchenniiu zhizni, i tvorchestva A. A. Bloka. Edited by Z. G. Mints et al. Tartu, Estonia, 1972.

Bowlt, John E. "Aleksandr Blok: The Poem 'The Unknown Lady.'" *Texas Studies in Literature and Language* 17:349–356 (1975).

Bowra, C. M. *The Heritage of Symbolism.* London, 1943.

——————. "The Position of Alexander Blok." *Criterion* 11:422–438 (1932).

Bugaev, Boris N. *Vospominaniia ob Aleksandre Aleksandroviche Bloke.* Letchworth, England, 1964.

Byrns, R. "Alexander Blok and *Hamlet.*" *Canadian Slavonic Papers* 18:58–65 (1976).

Chukovskii, K. I. *Kniga ob Aleksandre Bloke.* Berlin, 1922.

Donchin, Georgette. *The Influence of French Symbolism on Russian Poetry.* The Hague, 1958.

Ehrlich, Victor. *The Double Image: Concepts of the Poet in Slavic Literatures.* Baltimore, 1964.

Eikhenbaum, Boris. "Blok's Fate." In *Blok: An Anthology of Essays and Memoirs,* edited and translated by Lucy Vogel. Ann Arbor, Mich., 1982.

Eng, Jan van der. "Aspects of Poetic Communication: Time and Space in Four Poems by Aleksandr Blok." *Russian Literature* 8:377–402 (1982).

Feinberg, Lawrence. "The Poem as Such: Three Lyrics by Blok." *International Journal of Slavic Linguistics and Poetics* 22:117–130 (1976).

Forsyth, James. "Prophets and Supermen: 'German' Ideological Influences on Aleksandr Blok's Poetry." *Forum for Modern Language Studies* 13:33–46 (1977).

——————. *Listening to the Wind: An Introduction to Alexander Blok.* Oxford, 1977.

Gippius, Z. N. "Moi lunnyi drug: O Bloke." In *Zhivye litsa.* Prague, 1925.

Gordon, Andrew. "From Lyricism to History: The Longer Poetic Form in Blok and Pasternak." Ph.D. dissertation. Yale University, 1973.

Gorky, Maxim. *Reminiscences.* New York, 1946.

Hackel, Sergei. *The Poet and the Revolution: Aleksandr Blok's "The Twelve."* Oxford, 1975.

Kemball, Robin. *Alexander Blok: A Study in Rhythm and Metre.* The Hague, 1965.

Kisch, Sir Cecil. *Alexander Blok, Prophet of Revolu-*

tion: *A Study of His Life and Work.* London, 1960.

Mandel'shtam, Osip. "Barsuch'ia nora." In *Sobranie sochinenii v trekh knigakh.* 3 vols. Edited by Gleb Struve and Boris Filipoff. Washington, D.C., 1967.

————. "The Badger's Den." In *Blok: An Anthology of Essays and Memoirs,* translated and edited by Lucy Vogel. Ann Arbor, Mich., 1982.

Masing-Delic, Irene A. *A. Blok's "The Snow Mask": An Interpretation.* Stockholm, 1970.

————. "The Mask Motif in A. Blok's Poetry." *Russian Literature* 5:79–101 (1973).

Matlaw, Ralph E. "The Manifesto of Russian Symbolism." *Slavic and East European Journal* 3: 35–53 (1957).

Mirsky, D. S. *Contemporary Russian Literature, 1881–1925.* New York, 1926.

Mochulsky, Konstantin. *Aleksandr Blok.* Translated by Doris V. Johnson. Detroit, 1983.

Muchnic, Helen. *From Gorky to Pasternak: Six Writers in Soviet Russia.* Toronto, 1961.

Orlov, Vladimir. *Hamayun: The Life of Alexander Blok.* Moscow, 1980.

Pasternak, Boris. *I Remember.* Translated by David Magarshack. New York, 1959.

————. "Veter (Chetyre otryvka o Bloke)." In *Stixotvoreniia i poemy.* Moscow and Leningrad, 1965.

————. "Liudi i polozheniia." *Novyi Mir* 1 (1967).

————. *Selected Poems.* Translated by Jon Stallworthy and Peter France. New York, 1984.

Pirog, Gerald. *Aleksandr Blok's "Ital'ianskie stikhi": Confrontation and Disillusionment.* Columbus, Ohio, 1983.

————. "The Language of Love and the Limits of Language." In *Aleksandr Blok Centennial Conference,* edited by Walter Vickery. Columbus, Ohio, 1984.

Poggioli, Renato. *The Poets of Russia 1890–1930.* Cambridge, Mass., 1960.

Pyman, Avril. *The Life of Alexander Blok.* 2 vols. Oxford, 1979–1980.

Reeve, F. D. *Aleksandr Blok: Between Image and Idea.* New York, 1962.

Sloan, David. *Aleksandr Blok and the Dynamics of the Lyric Cycle.* Columbus, Ohio, 1986.

Taranovsky, Kiril. "Certain Aspects of Blok's Symbolism." In *Studies in Slavic Linguistics and Poetics in Honor of Boris O. Unbegaun,* edited by Robert Magidoff et al. New York, 1968.

Vickery, Walter N., and Bogdan B. Sagatov, eds. *Aleksandr Blok Centennial Conference.* Columbus, Ohio, 1984.

Vogel, Lucy. *Aleksandr Blok: The Journey to Italy.* Ithaca, N.Y., 1973.

————. *Blok: An Anthology of Essays and Memoirs.* Edited and translated by Lucy Vogel. Ann Arbor, Mich., 1982.

White, D. "The Figurative Language and the Fiction in the Poetry of Aleksandr Blok." Ph.D. dissertation. University of Michigan, 1971.

Zhirmunskii, V. M. *Drama Aleksandra Bloka "Roza i krest."* Leningrad, 1964.

————. "Two Tendencies of Contemporary Lyric Poetry: Blok and Akhmatova." *Russian Literature Triquarterly* 4:157–180 (1972).

————. "The Passion of A. Blok." In *Twentieth-Century Russian Literary Criticism,* edited by V. Ehrlich. New Haven, Conn., 1975.

————. *Poeziia Aleksandra Bloka.* Letchworth, England, 1975.

BIBLIOGRAPHIES

Ashukin, N. A. *A. Blok: Sinkhronisticheskie tablitsy zhizni i tvorchestva, 1880–1921.* Moscow, 1923.

Blium, E., and V. Gol'tsev. "Literatura o Bloke za gody revoliutsii: Bibliografiia." In *O Bloke,* edited by E. F. Nikitina. Moscow, 1923.

Kolpakova, E., et al. *Materialy k bibliografii A. Bloka za 1928–57 gody.* In *Vil'nusskii gosudarstvennyi universitet: Uchenye zapiski,* vol. 6 (1959).

Nikitina, E. F., and S. V. Shuvalov. *Poeticheskoe iskusstvo Bloka.* Moscow, 1926.

Pomirchii, P. E. "Materialy k bibliografii A. Bloka za 1958–1970 gody." In *Blokovskii sbornik II.* Tartu, Estonia, 1972.

Pymen, Avril. "Materialy k bibliografii zarubezhnoi literatury ob A. A. Bloke." In *Blokovskii sbornik I.* Tartu, Estonia, 1964.

Sendich, Munir. "Blok's *The Twelve:* Critical Interpretations of the Christ-Figure and Bibliography." *Russian Literature Triquarterly* 4:462–471 (1972).

GERALD PIROG

JUAN RAMÓN JIMÉNEZ
(1881–1958)

STROLLING UNDER THE Puerto Rican sun, his ascetic figure gently bowed, the eyes dark glowing sentinels over a trim white beard, Juan Ramón Jiménez would often in the final years of his life shake his head and sadly remark that he had written too much, and that he would never live to edit the ceaseless flow from his pen. More than thirty books, hundreds of aphorisms, vast quantities of unpublished material in the form of notes, editing projects, and revisions contained in archives in Madrid, Moguer, and the University of Puerto Rico testify to the assiduous labor of half a century. International recognition of such exemplary dedication came on 25 October 1956, when the Nobel Prize for Literature was bestowed on this Spanish poet.

Juan Ramón, as he is universally known in the Hispanic world, was born in Moguer in the region of Andalusia in southern Spain on 23 December 1881, into a well-to-do family that had made its money from wine. He attended a Jesuit academy in Cádiz from 1893 to 1896. A schoolboy copy of *The Imitation of Christ* by St. Thomas à Kempis, in which Jiménez underlined such passages as "Show not your heart to every man," foretells the poet's strong adult penchant for solitude. He began the study of law at the University of Seville in 1896, but since he preferred to paint or to read the poetry of the nineteenth-century Spanish poet Gustavo Bécquer and the French and Italian romantics far into the night, he soon withdrew.

During his student days in Seville he was primarily interested in painting and might have continued in that field had he had more respect for his teacher. But he also wrote poetry, learned much of Bécquer's work by heart, and eventually began to publish some of his verses in provincial reviews. His poems caught the attention of the leaders of the *modernista* (modernist) movement in Spanish poetry, who in 1900 invited him to Madrid. Two books redolent of *modernismo* were published almost at once, and in later years they were vigorously disowned by their author.

One summer night in 1900, shortly after Juan Ramón had returned home to Moguer after his brief sojourn in Madrid, his father suddenly died. The poet remembered the screams of women filling the house like the harsh, metallic cries of peacocks and his instant conviction that he himself was also about to die. He sank into a neurasthenic and incapacitating melancholy, in which state he was taken "half mad" to the sanatorium of Castel d'Andorte near Bordeaux. During the slow process of recovery he began to write again, and for the next year occupied himself with the task of ridding his lyrics of the more pompous trappings of *modernismo*. A pathological fear of death was to plague him for the rest of his life.

Moody, petulant, and restlessly experimenting with different poetical forms, Juan Ramón was already an established poet when he met

Zenobia Camprubí Aymar in 1912; after a long courtship in which the pert young lady gracefully dealt with doubts about her somber suitor, they were married in New York City in 1916. The influence upon Jiménez of this auspicious event can hardly be exaggerated. The voyage to New York brought him in direct contact with the sea, one of the most powerful symbols in his poetry; the English-speaking background of Zenobia, who had been partly educated in the United States, introduced him to William Blake, Percy Bysshe Shelley, William Butler Yeats, Emily Dickinson, and Robert Frost, an experience that caused him to qualify as "empty talk" much of the French and Spanish poetry he had heretofore cherished and that led him to redirect his energies into the most creative period of his life. Finally, the marriage gave him a commonsensical and cheerful partner, a foil for his often dolorous temperament who, in the varied roles of lover, secretary, nurse, chauffeur, and mother, set about protecting her hypersensitive husband from the nagging details of life and fame.

Jiménez's poetry acquired a new sense of direction and his importance in the Spanish-speaking world grew rapidly. Back in Madrid, he wrote incessantly, founded new reviews, encouraged young poets destined for greatness (Pedro Salinas, Rafael Alberti, Jorge Guillén), impatiently suffered fools, helped his wife translate Rabindranath Tagore, John Millington Synge, and William Butler Yeats, and acquired in the small intellectual circles of the Spanish capital a reputation for a thin skin and certain eccentricities. As rapidly as he befriended young poets, he abandoned them for real or imagined slights, sometimes it seemed merely because they wished to go their own way. And as the high priest of beauty writing daily in a cork-lined study, he was the butt of many a joke in Madrid cafés.

At the onslaught of the Spanish Civil War, Juan Ramón immediately aligned himself on the side of the Republicans, and with his wife he took an active interest in a relief program for children that was sponsored by the legiti-

mate government. But the intense hatred now loose in the land made it impossible for Juan Ramón to write. He and his wife, having long planned a return visit to America, where Zenobia had many relatives, decided to leave the Peninsula, which was engulfed in what the poet, with reference to the bitterness of Iberian character and history, called "the terrible Spanish war of three centuries." On 19 August 1936 Manuel Azaña, the president of the Republic, made him an honorary cultural attaché of the Spanish Embassy in Washington, D.C., and the couple left later that month, never to return to Spain again.

In America the poet and his wife set about arguing the Republican cause. They visited Malcolm Cowley in the offices of *The New Republic,* talked to influential people in Washington, and then went to Puerto Rico and Cuba, drawn by the lure of Hispanic lands. In 1939 the University of Miami invited him to give a series of lectures, and thus was inaugurated a long and fruitful relationship between Juan Ramón and American academic life. He taught and lectured at Duke, Vassar, and the University of Maryland, which in 1981 named its language building in his honor. While in Riverdale, Maryland, he made the acquaintance of his favorite American, Henry A. Wallace. Jiménez was impressed that a man of such high ideals was also in a position of considerable prominence. He recalled asking, "Are you really vice president of the United States?" To this Wallace replied, "Yes, Don Juan Ramón, I am. Why don't you take some of these tomatoes with you for lunch?" Finally, the couple returned to the Caribbean, attracted by the language and by the climate that Christopher Columbus in his journal had compared to Andalusia's in April. In between bouts of despondency he continued to read and write, and he delivered an important series of lectures on *modernismo* at the University of Puerto Rico. When on 25 October 1956 he received the news of the Nobel Prize, his wife was on her deathbed, suffering from cancer. She died at four o'clock in the afternoon three days later. Mortally stricken by this loss, he never wrote again and died on 29 May 1958.

As a good part of the civilized world heads swiftly into the arms of standardization, it may seem anachronistic to insist on the importance of a regional influence upon a writer (although Ireland and the American South underline the effect of ingrained traditional cultures on a literature). In considering a country like Spain, so late in acquiring the unifying benefits of technology, the critic cannot slight the formative factor of *la patria chica* (the little country). Andalusia, with its unruffled blue sky and perfumed air, the clear profile of objects in its environment, and its ready aesthetic response to the world, left a permanent stamp on Juan Ramón's mind. At a time when Arab-haunted Andalusia had given to Spain two poets of the quality of Antonio Machado and Federico García Lorca, it was Juan Ramón who had the audacity to invent for himself the epithet *el andaluz universal* (the universal Andalusian), and to wear it well.

Juan Ramón firmly believed in placing a limit on the number of themes he allowed to enter his poetry. The reaction of the sensitive poet-narrator to timeless objects such as the sea, flowers, sky, and landscape, and to the eternal human encounters of love, death, and god: these were the enduring topics of his verse. Two world wars, the Spanish Civil War, all traces of strife and grime, were judged by him to be nonpoetic.

In view of this conviction, to which he rigorously adhered throughout his life, it is easy to assume that Juan Ramón was apolitical, but such was not the case. He was one of the first poets to come out unequivocally for the Republican cause, and three days after the Japanese attack on Pearl Harbor, he wrote to Richard Pattee at the State Department offering the services of a fifty-nine-year-old poet to the United States, for, as he said in his letter, it was the duty of every free man to assist in the defense of ideals of the mind. In reply, the Voice of America invited him to prepare a series of lectures on Hispanic and North American poets for broadcast in Latin America.

For nearly four decades, Juan Ramón's star was in eclipse in his own country. Studied and admired abroad, especially in the United States and England, he was rejected by the young poets who began to write after the Spanish Civil War. They rejected "the aestheticism of the rose" in favor of social alignment, brotherhood, and poems about the unfortunate Spanish situation during the Francisco Franco dictatorship. In 1981, one hundred years after his birth, he had regained popularity and influence in his own country. The government sponsored several symposia and underwrote a centennial edition of his chief works. It is now generally recognized that, in his best moments, he represents one of the greatest lyric voices in the language.

"Are you a *modernista*," an admiring young lady of Moguer asked Juan Ramón in 1900, "and, if you are, what does it mean?" Juan Ramón was not sure, but he had read Rubén Darío, and when sometime later he received a postcard from Darío and Francisco Villaespesa inviting him to Madrid, he was filled, as he put it, with a mad, frenetic happiness.

Modernismo, in its broadest sense, was the Hispanic reaction in art and literature to the currents of change flowing through Europe at the turn of the century, currents best typified for the Iberian Peninsula by Charles Baudelaire and the French symbolist poets (especially Paul Verlaine and later Stéphane Mallarmé), by Edgar Allan Poe, and by English and French decadent writers like Oscar Wilde and Joris-Karl Huysmans. In its more narrow sense *modernismo* was the literary movement begun by the Nicaraguan poet Rubén Darío, who blended the rhetoric of Victor Hugo, the musicality of Verlaine, and the self-restraint of such Parnassian poets as Théophile Gautier and José María de Heredia into verse that, in content and technique, was decidedly new in the Hispanic world. Moody princesses, swans, Nordic myths, and eighteenth-century Versailles are the themes that circumscribe Darío's verse, but his poetic skill was superb, and his lines have an elegance and a sensual delight that stand in sharp contrast to the prevailing Spanish poetry at the turn of the century.

Juan Ramón's first two books, *Ninfeas* (Water Lilies) and *Almas de violeta* (Violet Souls), are strongly marked by *modernismo* and symbolism. Printed in 1900 in green and violet ink, respectively, they proclaim the expectedly high-flown summons to the banner of art and announce that beauty is the sole criterion of life. In their animosity toward prevailing taste and their desire for renovation, these two books are part of the beneficent influence of *modernismo* in Spain. Unfortunately, they are in themselves generally tasteless, tending to lack focus and to be overly sentimental. The sweet melancholy of such symbolist painters as Henri Le Sidaner and Pierre Puvis de Chavannes was still beyond Juan R. Jiménez, as he signed himself then, and the delicate soul portraits such as Sidaner's *Sunday* (1898) awaited a more mature writer. But Jiménez's greatest problem on the threshold of his career is a weakness for cloying morbidity. In the hundreds of tears and flowers rained down upon virgin cheeks resting against satiny coffin pillows, we can recognize two factors: the hypersensitivity characteristic of the early Jiménez style and the imposing fear of death that on occasion crippled his personality. Both problems continued to haunt him during his long career.

It was while recovering from his mental illness in Bordeaux that he first managed to set his poetry in the direction he wanted it to take. With the wings of madness often brushing his face, he began work on *Rimas* (Rhymes), published in 1902. This is the first of his books to display a highly endowed poetic talent in the making. To the Spanish critic Ricardo Gullón he remarked that a nostalgia for Spain was behind the composition of *Rimas,* and this is apparent in the echoes of the *romances* (Spanish ballads), of Andalu-

sian popular songs, and especially of Bécquer, whose chief collection of poetry was also called *Rimas* (1871).

Bécquer can be overly sentimental but never diffuse, sad but not complacently morbid, and these were qualities that Jiménez took to heart as he struggled in Bordeaux. Half a century later the Nobel Prize winner paid this simple tribute: "In Bécquer I discovered brevity and concision." He also felt drawn to Bécquer's lesson that poetry should concern itself with the ineffable, the light and airy, the perfect and therefore unattainable love, and that the poet must constantly wrestle with the clumsiness of words, those "undisciplined squads," as T. S. Eliot put it, with which one attempts a raid on the inarticulate.

In *Rimas* Juan Ramón still mourns the death of a sweetheart and gives way to melancholy: "I suffer forever a snowfall within." But there is a sensitivity toward landscape not formerly present, and above all there occasionally appears a simple, direct, clear, and delicate tone that gives us the first inkling of the talent to be developed: "El alegre mes de mayo / ha nacido esta mañana . . ." (The happy month of May / was born this morning. . .). These bell-like lines, with their unobtrusive consonance and their gentle suggestion of May songs, exemplify the *poesía desnuda* (unadorned poetry) that the mature poet will single-mindedly court.

Instant critical acclaim greeted the publication of *Arias tristes* (Sad Songs) in 1903, and today it is generally conceded that this book's successfully sustained tone and charm is the author's first noteworthy achievement. The work is a tuneful hymn to sadness, not the affected and mawkish *tristesse* of the earlier poetry but rather a gently irrepressible melancholy that views every afternoon as a quiet rehearsal for the close of life and assuages itself with sweet sounds and a preference for penumbra.

In addition to the title, a framework of printed scores from Franz Schubert stresses the musical nature of the book. Jiménez had read Verlaine in France, and from Verlaine's famous enjoinder about the importance of music in poetry he took to heart the idea of a weightless song: "Sans rien en lui qui pèse ou qui pose" (With nothing in it that is heavy or static). *Arias tristes* contains much melodious, nostalgic music, very little weighted by words (it is the sentiment that lies heaviest). But most important of all, in this book, Juan Ramón crystallizes the note of simplicity and delicacy in his diction to produce the tone and vocabulary that will gradually develop into the most winged and graceful verse in Spanish letters since the sixteenth century. Here is poem 1 of the opening section, "Arias otoñales" (Autumn Airs):

> *Entre el velo de la lluvia*
> *que pone gris el paisaje,*
> *pasan las vacas, volviendo*
> *de la dulzura del valle.*
> *Las tristes esquilas suenan*
> *alejadas, y la tarde*
> *va cayendo tristemente*
> *sin estrellas ni cantares.*
> *La campiña se ha quedado*
> *fría y sola con sus árboles;*
> *por las perdidas veredas*
> *hoy no volverá ya nadie.*
> *Voy a cerrar mi ventana*
> *porque si pierdo en el valle*
> *mi corazón, quizás quiera*
> *morirse con el paisaje.*

> Between the veils of rain
> that cover the fields with gray,
> the cattle are coming back
> from the sweetness of the valley.
> Their sad bells ring
> far off, and the afternoon
> falls dolefully down
> without a star or a song.
> The countryside is grown
> cold, alone with its trees;
> by these lost pathways
> none will return today.
> I shall close my window,
> for if my heart in the valley
> wanders, perchance it will
> die with the landscape.

When the poet moves from the countryside to an Andalusian patio, flowers become profuse, and in the center of the scene is a fountain, its diamondlike thread pulsing skyward. Jiménez's early description of a fountain suggests Georges Rodenbach as a source, but he goes on to develop the fountain as one of his basic symbols, representing the ascension through lyrical expression to higher levels of awareness. Among flowers, Juan Ramón eventually selected the rose as one of his preferred symbols of beauty and perfection, "a brief image of the world." When a poem is perfect, he later says in a celebrated verse ("El poema," a poem from *Piedra y cielo* [Stone and Sky, 1919]), it is like a rose and should not be changed in any way. These objects are present in the poetry of *Arias tristes,* but they do not yet function as fully developed symbols.

The horror of death never abandoned Juan Ramón, but in *Arias tristes* he was for the first time able to handle his preoccupation in a way that was fruitful for his poetry. In poem 17 of the section "Nocturnos" (Nocturnes), he describes a frightening encounter. One night in his garden he saw a man dressed in black smiling at him through the shrubbery and drawing close. He fled to his room only to find the man waiting for him, perched in a tree outside the window. In the image of the unknown man in black, Jiménez creates an authentic tingle of fear that is never elicited by his earlier scenes of lifeless virgins encased in coffins. Also, in the same section (poem 1) the author first asks a momentous question: what will the world be like without him? Common sense dictates the initial answer: the sounds of the piano wafting through his patio at night will continue even though he is not on hand to hear them. But, as we shall see, the mature poet tends to doubt, if not completely to reject, the commonsense notion of his relation to the world.

A stay in the Guadarrama Mountains north of Madrid accounts for *Pastorales,* written in large part in 1903 but not published until 1911. In these poems, Jiménez continues what has been called his simple confrontation with the countryside, an encounter free of the sermonizing of Horace and far from the bombastic rhetoric produced whenever the romantics viewed nature. Segments of this work must have been closely influenced by Francis Jammes's beatific nature poetry, which had made Yeats weep; and in Jammes at this time Jiménez may have read of "l'âne si doux" (the gentle donkey), possible forebear of Platero. *Jardines lejanos* (Faraway Gardens, 1904) is spiritually akin to *Arias tristes,* although more sorrowful. It is the last of the trilogy that gave new direction to poetry in Spain and prompted a letter from Antonio Machado: "A spirit as sensitive as yours does not exist among us; no one has such sweetness of rhythm, such delicacy for dampened harmonies."

Dispirited from the hypochondria that kept its dreary hand upon him, Juan Ramón left Madrid in 1905 for Moguer; he was, as he wrote the Spanish philosopher, poet, and novelist Miguel de Unamuno shortly after arriving, "devoured by a yearning for contemplation." During the next six years in the village where he was born, he wrote poetry that is generally a continuation of the work already begun, with no truly significant change. The favorite themes prevail: love lost or unattainable, sensual lassitude, beauty, solitude; the favorite objects of nature still provide background: flowers, water (fountain), birds, and moonlight. With an indifferent munificence he displays a complete mastery of technique; no device was unyielding to his craftsmanship. Skillful enjambment causes the heretofore sturdily monotonous ballad meter to flow like water, and his alexandrines, whether with full rhyme or assonance, are as supple as his shorter lines. There is ample proof that from a technical point of view Jiménez could do anything he liked with Spanish verse (only the sonnet remained to be assayed a few years later).

Las hojas verdes (Green Leaves), composed in 1906, registers the strong presence of Verlaine. *Baladas de primavera* (Spring Ballads),

composed in 1907 and published in 1910, offers a collection of the light songs he could always carry off so well; added to later editions is "Verde verderol" (Green Greenfinch), the lovely poem of the bird whose music in the dusky pine grove makes the wind stop and listen. Between 1907 and 1908 he composed a series of elegies (*Elegías puras* [1908], *Elegías intermedias* [1909], *Elegías lamentables* [1910]) that reveal a skillful use of synesthesia. *La soledad sonora,* composed in 1908 and published in 1911, its title taken from St. John of the Cross, finds Jiménez still proclaiming in the symbolist manner that the essence of poetry is "an indifferent vagueness of forms and tones." *Poemas mágicos y dolientes,* composed in 1909 and published in 1911, pleases by its use of color, and there are explicitly sexual memories of Francine, a servant girl at the sanatorium of Castel d'Andorte. *Melancolia,* composed in 1910–1911 and published in 1912, recalls his travels at the turn of the century, in particular a train trip through the Pyrenees punctuated by "momentary villages." *Laberinto,* composed in 1910–1911 and published in 1913, is gracefully dedicated to seven women in his past and contains images that tend to be slightly more provocative and varied than those of the previous books.

The total performance is impressive in terms of technical variety, and there are moments of genuine beauty, but the modern reader turns away, weary of such relentless, although strangely tepid, emotion. As for the names of women that sprinkle these books in the epigraphs, the titles, and, once or twice, the contents, recent biographical studies have shown that they indeed may have, on occasion, been lovers of the poet. Juan Ramón, like Shelley, was in love with love and was especially prone to eidetic affairs. His weakness was so well known that two Peruvian poets perpetrated a hoax that involved inventing a twenty-year-old reader of Juan Ramón's works who fell in love with him through his poetry. This is the infamous Georgina Hübner of *Laberinto,* who upon her "demise" inspired the lovely poem "Carta a

Georgina Hübner en el cielo de Lima" (Letter to Georgina Hübner in Lima's Heaven). In ironic contrast to this invented affair, Jeanne Roussie, to whom a section of *Laberinto* is dedicated, was in real life the wife of Juan Ramón's doctor at Castel d'Andorte and was briefly the poet's mistress.

The masterpiece of these years in Moguer is unquestionably *Platero y yo: Elegía andaluza* (*Platero and I: An Andalusian Elegy*), published first in 1914 and subsequently revised and enlarged in 1917. Prose poems of the first rank, the lovely vignettes of *Platero and I* were for a time one of the most widely read works of literature in the language. When the author visited Argentina in 1948, thousands of schoolchildren crowded around the creator of the little Andalusian donkey. Platero, with jet black eyes, gentle ways, and a brisk trot, carries the poet into the corners of Moguer and over the Andalusian landscape. Together they watch sunsets, ride through showers, pick wildflowers, and in general shun the company of their fellow men. While the entire village attends a bullfight, Platero and his master ride out of town, the shouts of the ring growing fainter as they approach the sea. In a note of pantheism that will increase in later years, Jiménez feels his spirit become ruler over Nature, who, in payment for his regard, offers the eternal spectacle of her submissive beauty.

The subtitle of *Platero and I* suggests that we consider the book in terms of polarities. In a prologue to the first full edition, Jiménez points out that happiness and grief, like Platero's ears, are twin aspects of this work. *Platero and I* is therefore more than just an exceptional example of a twentieth-century impressionist pastoral. The models that come to mind for a more satisfying reading are *Songs of Innocence* (1789) and *Songs of Experience* (1794) by William Blake, a poet whom Jiménez admired and translated. If Platero is innocence, his coat recalling the fleecy wool of Blake's lambs, much of the Andalusian environment signifies experience: fear, idiocy, sickness, rabid dogs, cockfights, and poverty

crowd around the many shimmering moments of beauty. Epiphany shares the stage with squalor, beauty with suffering.

Enrique Díez-Canedo, reviewing *Baladas de primavera,* remarked that these songs are merely the variations of a preoccupied man who in reality wanted to write about something else. That topic was his own engrossing sadness, which, as we have seen, he was rarely able to relegate to a minor role in his poetry. When he was sixty, Juan Ramón defined his sadness as "the anguish of the adolescent, the young man, and the mature person who feels himself unattached and alone in his vocation." The melancholia went hand in hand with his deeply inscribed fear of dying. Ever since his father's sudden death, Jiménez was convinced that the same unforeseen finale awaited him. From that time on, he arranged that his living quarters were never more than a few minutes away from a doctor, who could respond at once to a summons when his heart began to give out (in reality his heart was strong and healthy: he died of pneumonia). Neurasthenia, constant need for doctors, expectation of imminent death, a cork-lined study: these were the maladies of another famous twentieth-century writer, Marcel Proust.

In her youthful gaiety his future wife reacted at once to the cloud of gloom around her poet's brow. It was she whose teasing laughter made his spirit brighten in spite of itself and who thereby enabled his mind to exercise greater control of the expression of his emotions. The letters of their courtship are marked by pertinent advice from Zenobia: "You need to break out of that woebegone rut." And on another occasion: "To my illustrious friend Juan R. Jiménez, in deep gratitude, for having seen him smile on August 10, 1913." Shortly after he met Zenobia, a new note of assurance and a more searching quality appeared in his verse.

Except for one or two instances, Jiménez carefully avoided the sonnet form until 1914, when he began a series of fifty-two sonnets, published in 1917 as *Sonetos espirituales* (Sonnets of the Spirit). While adhering strictly

JUAN RAMÓN JIMÉNEZ

to the classical rhyme scheme and to the convention that the theme be presented in the quartets and resolved in the tercets, he subtly experimented with the internal accents of the hendecasyllable, giving his sonnets a tenuousness that belies their strict form. They do not suffer in comparison with the classical models of Garcilaso de la Vega or Fray Luis de León.

The fortunes of his love for Zenobia form one of the topics of this book, and several sonnets protest, in a Petrarchan manner, the neglected feelings of the lover. More than once he tries to arm himself against her influence. In "Guardia de amor" (Love's Guardian), sonnet 6, we read:

> Mas el dormir me ata con tus rosas,
> y tú te entras, cruel y desveladora,
> por la puerta vendida de mi sueño.

> But sleep binds me with your roses,
> and you break in, vigilant and cruel,
> through the door betrayed in dreams.

Sonnet 15, "Retorno fugaz" (Fleeting Return), muses upon memory, volatility, and actuality:

> Todo tu cambiar trocóse en nada
> —¡memoria, ciega abeja de amargura!—
> ¡No sé cómo eras, yo que sé que fuiste!

> All your volatility changed into nothingness
> —memory, a blind bee of bitterness!—
> I know not what you were like, I who know you existed!

Most interesting in these sonnets is a new note of enhanced self-awareness that became the characteristic mark of Jiménez. He began to realize that refinement of experience, simple everyday encounters with the objects of this world, could provide the material for great poetry and that for such refinement the spirit, the poetic awareness, was a priceless alembic:

> Signo indeleble pones en las cosas.
> Luego, tornada gloria de las cumbres,
> revivirás en todo lo que sellas.

> Tu rosa será norma de las rosas,
> tu óir de la armonía, de las lumbres
> tu pensar, tu velar de las estrellas.

> On objects you inscribe indelible signs;
> then glorified by light from peaks,
> you live again in everything you mark.
> Your rose will be the norm of every rose,
> your ear of harmony, your mind a pattern
> or all flames, your vigil goal of every star.

Estío (Summer, 1916), written in 1915 during the height of the courtship between Juan Ramón and Zenobia, is a lovers' book, a beguiling blend of actuality and idealization. The spirit of Shelley presides over the volume; Shelley's poem "Mutability" is its epigraph, and the couple was also translating other Shelley poems at the time, including "Love's Philosophy." Zenobia's changing moods, her indecision, which at times seemed pure fecklessness to the poet, provide the theme of many poems. At the same time, to offset the ups and downs of courtship, *Estío* proposes to place the lover on a pedestal, where she can symbolize beauty, poetry, and love itself, and the poet says in striking assonance: "Pasan todas, verdes, granas . . . / Tú estás allá arriba, blanca" (Gaudy and green they all go by . . . / You are white and over all). This love affair will now consume Juan Ramón's attention, and will be part of the inspiration for the theme of love as it appears in the rest of his poetry. In his romantic courtship, Juan Ramón longs as did Shelley for the perfect union of one spirit in two bodies. He proclaims in poem 2 of *Estío* that the lovers blend together as do sea and sky on the horizon. Long strides have been made away from the languid sensuality of *Elegías* and *Laberinto*, books predictably disliked by Zenobia.

When Jiménez boarded ship at Cádiz in January 1916 to sail for New York, he was keeping a multiple rendezvous with destiny. The ship carried him to the long-desired wedding with Zenobia and also, during the voyage, provided an intimate encounter with the great natural force that became one of his basic symbols. At the same time, through Zenobia's interests and her contacts in New York cultural circles, Juan Ramón became familiar with North American poetry and enhanced his knowledge of British poetry as well. The intimate exposure to Anglo-American verse led him to modify his Latin rhetoric and to move in the direction of a style that he baptized *poesía desnuda* (naked poetry).

The record of this voyage first appeared in 1917 as the *Diario de un poeta recién casado* (Diary of a Newlywed Poet), but in 1948 the title was changed to *Diario de poeta y mar* (Diary of Poet and Sea). The change of titles is significant, for although love plays an important part, it is the presence of the sea that dominates long sections of the book, even to the extent of influencing the meter. Jiménez later claimed that his use of free verse in this work was due to the waves, to his not feeling "firm and secure." He thought the *Diario* his best book, and both critics and peers agreed. It stands between the twin towers of Bécquer's *Rimas* and Lorca's *Romancero gitano* (*Gypsy Ballads*, 1928) as one of the indisputable landmarks in modern Spanish lyrics. It transformed the style and content of Spanish language poetry, and during a ten-year period fledgling poets had to assimilate Jiménez before struggling to find their own voices.

Jiménez found the very depths of his nature bestirred by this ocean voyage. Thrust upon him in all its force, literally clamoring for clarification, was the puzzle of the true nature of the relationship between man and the world, as signified by his being a small dot of consciousness on the implacable waves. How to incorporate such vastness into a mind that had been attuned to sweet chords from Andalusian landscapes or had dwelt for hours on the perfection of the rose was a riddle in creativity, and in the end he apprehended the image of his own mental process in the ocean's rapidly changing yet fixed nature.

The book begins in Madrid. Uprooted, in motion toward the port of embarkation, the poet is dwelling passionately on his love as the train wends its way to Moguer. At the scene of his childhood he is momentarily overcome by the reality of the past suddenly become here and now. Yet all is falling in the direction of the sea, which, while he is on the edge of it, he describes as being as indescribable as woman, one of his favorite similes.

He embarks, and the theme of love disappears almost at once, submerged for the time being in the depths of the imposing, gigantic body of water. Initially the ocean appears to him as the personification of solitude, so dear to his way of being. Its waves come and go, like his fluctuating thoughts, in eternal knowing and unknowing. Everything is in the sea, yet the sea seems to be without itself, lacking the identification possible through consciousness. The solitude has no inner warmth. Stupefied, Jiménez begins to rebel at the limitations of language. The sensation of something so imperative, incomprehensible, and separate from himself creates one of his new preoccupations: nomenclature—the art of choosing the exact word. Neither the sea, nor the sky, as characterized by the sea, has a name. Until he can learn the proper designation, he cannot make the sea his own; baptism is an act of identification and, thereby, possession. The early pages of the *Diario* make frequent recourse to the word *todo*, and that is the initial name of the sea: all, everything—strange, aloof, vast.

Accompanying the wonder elicited by this event of wind and wave is the opposite reaction of distress and revulsion before the enormous mindlessness of the sea. One day, during his protracted pondering upon the water, the word *nada* (nothingness) suddenly takes on perfect meaning, finding its exact site, says Jiménez, like a body in its grave. The state of fullness (*todo*) and its antonym (*nada*) appear more and more in his work, sometimes in opposition, sometimes in the kind of paradoxical relationship one finds among mystics.

Arriving in New York, he records penetrating prose observations about life in the United

States, overstuffed hotels, and Brahmin Boston, and he writes tender love poems to his bride. But when the couple embark in June upon the return voyage, their steamer trunk full of volumes of Anglo-American verse, the ocean once more becomes the chief protagonist. Now he can accept the sea; it stands before him naked, unadorned (*sin nada*), pure, as he will forever want his verse to be. And in an act of baptism he proclaims simply, "Today, sea, thy name is life."

In his record of the return voyage, he gives the first unmistakably clear expression of a mystical desire to transcend himself, an impulse that, as we shall see, gradually ruled him. Gazing at the roadway the moon lays down upon the sea, he suddenly feels seized by a *gana celestial* (celestial need) to leave himself and go to some undefined center. With *todo* and *nada, centro* (center) becomes part of the new vocabulary that stands alongside *rosa* (rose), *mujer* (woman), and *fuente* (fountain) as Jiménez enters the most productive and influential part of his career.

Underpinning the revolutionary *poesía desnuda* of the *Diario* are many prose vignettes that concentrate upon the North American context of the honeymoon. Allusions to Amy Lowell and Robert Frost, prove Jiménez's awareness of contemporary poetry on the Atlantic seaboard, and he and his wife make the obligatory pilgrimages to sites connected with Edgar Allan Poe and Walt Whitman. In addition, Juan Ramón does Emily Dickinson the honor of including three translated selections from *The Single Hound*, a selection of her poems that was published in 1914, in his own journal. Literary allusion as a technique is put to full use in an account of a train trip from Boston to New York. The landscape glimpsed from the window by the detached traveler provokes literary and artistic comparisons and foreshadows the device of free association, which Jiménez employed in an American setting several decades later in his prose poem "Espacio" (Space).

The cruel contrasts of New York City and its rich pockets of cultural oddities account for some of the most interesting pieces of prose in the *Diario*. Jiménez is the first in a line of famous Spanish poets to visit New York and respond to its overwhelming character; he precedes Lorca's encounter with the city in the late 1920's as well as that of Salinas in the 1940's. The large black population fascinated him, as it later did Lorca. In "La negra y la rosa" (The Black Woman and the Rose), a sleeping black woman clutching a white rose in her hand transforms the dirty, hot subway car into the setting for a moment of epiphany: the passengers look up from their newpapers and stop chewing gum as a sense of beauty emanates from the rose in the black woman's hand. Once late at night, walking alone on Fifth Avenue, he passes a lame black man who ceremoniously lifts a worn top hat in greeting, and the poet, with a reaction that his compatriot Lorca shared, turns to watch this "rey de la ciudad" (king of the city) disappear up Fifth Avenue. The profusion of neon lights on Broadway alternatively captivates and offends him, and as Salinas later does, he contrasts their garishness with the natural beauty of the sky. Coming from a conservative, staid country like Spain, he is amused to see a suffragette forcing an old man into a seat and is entertained by the baseball sermons ("The Sacrifice Hit") delivered by the enterprising A. Ray Petty, disciple of Billy Sunday, in a little Anabaptist Church near Macdougal Alley in Greenwich Village, with the doors open and the shouts of drunks mingling with the sweaty gestures of Reverend Petty.

Eternidades (Eternities, written in 1916–1917, published in 1918) contains two poetic statements of utmost importance. One is the famous metaphorical account of the evolution of his poetry, "Vino, primero, pura" (First she appeared pure). When a woman becomes the symbol for poetry (*la poesía* equals *la mujer,* an equation from Bécquer), she appears first in innocence, gradually dons colorful but specious clothing (the trappings of *modernismo*), and then discards superfluous raiment until she is once again cloaked in a tunic of innocence. Finally, she disrobes and stands naked before him. William Butler Yeats chose a similar metaphor to describe the evolution of his poetry and concluded that there is more enterprise in walking naked. Jiménez's *poesía pura* is the Spanish equivalent of Paul Valéry's *poésie pure,* a term that means nothing more complicated than poetry stripped of unpoetic or prosaic elements. As Valéry pointed out, the rudiments of pure poetry exist in every poet, but the idea of pure poetry, applied to an entire poem, signifies only an ideal: pure poetry must be looked upon as "almost impossible to attain in a poem consisting of more than one line." Jiménez went even further and said that the best poem was the unwritten one. Simplicity and spontaneity, the twin criteria of his verse, are, he explains, the result of long and careful preparation, after which the poem results from the effortless combination of the smallest number of elements: "Only the right word, the most direct and close, without effort, but apt."

This aphorism leads us into the second poem from *Eternidades.* It is cast in the imperative mood and begins: "Intelligence, give me the exact name of things!" While in New York, Jiménez probably saw Amy Lowell's imagist dictum counseling poets to use the language of common speech and always to find the *exact* word, and he adapted this to the needs of *poesía desnuda.* Instead of the vague sensorial images and the constantly shifting impressionism of the *modernistas,* the poet requests unadorned clarity. It is a petition that T. S. Eliot echoed a decade or so later when he voiced his approval of "the common word exact without vulgarity." The key role of Juan Ramón's poem in *Eternidades* can thus be appreciated in an historical context. But there is also an intensity at work that is unique to him: "Let my word become the thing itself, newly created by my spirit." Here is the role of the poet, as old as Plato and reaffirmed by Martin Heidegger: take words in their direct sense and reinterpret them in a special way.

There are three radii of meaning in the exact name: the label supplied by intelligence, the title provided by the things themselves, and the name bequeathed by the poet. These are the spokes of connotation that fan out from the exact, that is, pure, name.

By this time Jiménez had begun to look at what he was writing not in terms of a single poem nor even a book but instead as a unified whole. He became concerned with the sum of his work, which he called *la Obra.* Faced by the pressure of time and the rarity of the perfect phrase he constantly sought, he reminded himself that the task of developing *la Obra* should be deliberate and perforce ceaseless. He chose the following lines from Johann Wolfgang von Goethe as an epigraph that appears unfailingly in the rest of his books: "Like the stars, / Without haste, / But without rest."

In *Arias tristes* Jiménez had posed the question as to the continued existence of the world after his death, and as we have seen, he gave the logical reply that things would struggle on without him. In poem 122 of *Eternidades,* he changes his answer radically:

> Sé bien que soy tronco
> del árbol de lo eterno.
> Sé bien que las estrellas
> con mi sangre alimento.
> Que son pájaros míos
> todos los claros sueños. . . .
> Sé bien que cuando el hacha
> de la muerte me tale,
> se vendrá abajo el firmamento.

> Well I know I am the trunk
> of eternity's tree;
> well I know the stars
> feed on my blood;
> that every noble dream
> is a bird from my net. . . .
> Well I know that when
> death's ax cleaves me,
> the sky will come crashing down.

This spendid assurance is part of an ill-defined pantheism that may be detected in his work about this time, but it also reflects the growing sweep and increasing sense of grandeur of his own consciousness, the divine awareness that will live again in every "exact name" it renders.

The plenitude and air of satisfaction that characterize *Piedra y cielo,* composed in 1917, make it one of his most pleasing and unified works. Death, fear, and depression, usually expressed through the image of the black wind or the presence of *la nada,* seem temporarily banished. The poet imparts a gratified sense of poetic labor, of coming and going among the books of his library. He approaches his poetry with a permanent but controlled haste and likens his creative urge to a colt in May, "free slave of his intelligence." Ineffability, the theme he took from Bécquer, is given its most striking utterance: beauty is like a butterfly; we chase it here and there and close our hands on it, only to be left with nothing but "the form of its flight." A section called "Nostaljia del mar" (Sea Nostalgia) recalls the ocean voyage of three years before and contains the lovely sailor's epitaph: "Search the skies for his tomb, his death rains from a star."

Toward the end of this book an unusual desire becomes noticeable: the poet wants to be everywhere, to enjoy everything, to lose himself in his world. A tiny leaf glowing in the sun stands for his wish to be beside himself and to alter for a moment his private reality. To put it simply, contemplation of beauty is not enough; he must join it, flow into it, become one with it. These moments of epiphany represent for the critic Antonio Sánchez Barbudo an overwhelming need on the poet's part to conquer death through a realization of eternity. According to this interpretation, the record of Jiménez's poetry since 1916 is the search for these interludes of fullness.

One may also see in them a nascent mysticism. This is the natural progress that could be expected, given the exalted role in which Jiménez cast consciousness. That spirit, which was to seal everything with an indelible sign

and to become glorious among mountain peaks, quite easily began to develop into the enlarged sense of consciousness that pervades mystical practice and thought. Being, says the Hindu mystic Sri Aurobindo, is supreme consciousness. In all ages and in all climates, the first stage of the mystical experience is this heightened awareness; on the other side of this threshold is found the unifying vision that sees all things as one and swallows up the identity of the individual. Jiménez was clearly headed in this direction; just how far he would go remained to be seen.

The necrophobia that acutely afflicted him throughout his life appeared in various guises in his poetry, but none are so interesting as those in *Poesía* (Poetry) and *Belleza* (Beauty), both published in 1923 and containing work written since 1917. Instead of the array of coffins and withered flowers, we have the image of death as the great knowledge of shadow, the end of a beautiful book, a fruit plucked in season, or a dark subterranean summer.

But Jiménez was not satisfied with a series of pleasant images, for these books include a handful of poems that provide a taut and wholly engrossing dialectic between life and death. Poem 126 of *Poesía* may be paraphrased as follows: Cord, binding tightly my life to life, bind, as you must, without slackening, at once, my life with death; do not place emptiness and tedium between each knot; do not leave my life vacillating with death. Cord, life, death: taut until the end, taut from the beginning.

This extended conceit clearly states that life and death run along the same thread and that to think of one is to evoke the other. Rainer Maria Rilke said that whoever celebrates death, at the same time magnifies life; Jiménez would agree and point out that praise of life is also praise of death. The sets of contrary pairs reinforce the image of a rope being pulled at both ends: life-death, beginning-end, strong-hesitant.

Here is a literal prose translation of the well-known poem 42, also from *Poesía:*

JUAN RAMÓN JIMÉNEZ

How can I fear you, death? Do you not labor here with me? Do I not touch you in my eyes; do you not tell me that you know nothing, are hollow, unconscious, and peaceful? Do you not enjoy everything with me: glory, solitude, love, unto the marrow of your bones? Do you not endure erectly, death, life for me? Do I not lead you around in your blindness like a guide? Do you not repeat with your passive mouth what I wish you to say? Do you not support like a slave the kindness with which I oblige you? What could you see or say, where could you go without me? Might not I, death, be your death, whom you, O death, should indulge and love?

With its serenity and profound irony, this poem attempts to vanquish fear of death by establishing a physical and affective identification that translates death into human terms and assigns it the role established by John Donne as "slave to Fate, Chance, kings and desperate men." The vocabulary depicts humble tasks: the familiarity of laboring side by side, the paradoxical intimacy of serving as blind death's guide.

Finally, we have the poem "Cenit" (Zenith) from *Belleza:*

I shall not be I, death, until you join my life and thus make me complete; until my luminous half closes with my dark half and I become eternal equilibrium in the mind of the world; half of me radiant, half of me in oblivion. I shall not be, death, until you, in your turn, will clothe my soul in your pale bones.

The laconic title completes the irony of this cycle of poems, each one stressing the theme that life and death are inextricably bound together. The peculiar triumph of these poems is not the recognition that death is ubiquitous, a fact that was always painfully clear to Jiménez; rather, their accomplishment is the placement of death on an equal and friendly footing with life. Together the two bend over in the fields, while life teaches death what to say and guides it through eternity. However enervating Jiménez's morbidity was in daily living, in literature he was finally able to overcome his pusillanimity and to write about death in terms as courageous and noble as those to be read anywhere. The theme as such, along with its attendant images, will now gradually disappear from his work.

During these fruitful years in Madrid in the decades between the wars, while Juan Ramón's influence was at its peak, he and his wife enjoyed considerable success with their translations of works of the Bengali writer Rabindranath Tagore. Their common interest in Tagore dates from 1913, and it was one of their earliest bonds. When they first met, Zenobia had begun to translate the English version of Tagore's international success *The Crescent Moon* (1913) into Spanish; Juan Ramón immediately offered to help, and they began exchanging paragraphs. The instant success of *La luna nueva* in 1915 created a demand for the works of Tagore that, after their marriage, the couple worked hard to fill. The poet insisted that Zenobia receive all the credit, and her name appeared as the sole translator in the immensely popular editions that were published throughout the 1920's and 1930's in the Spanish-speaking world.

Between 1915 and 1922, they brought out twenty-one titles by Tagore. Zenobia prepared a literal Spanish version of the work they were translating, and at this point Juan Ramón entered the picture and began to make the obviously needed changes, selecting synonyms and finding poetic turns of phrase. The translation now entered its last stage. Banishing all thought of Tagore's own English translations from his mind, Juan Ramón took the emended literal version and rewrote it in a lovely limpid prose that made Tagore sound like the author of *Platero and I.* A phrase from the English version of *Gitanjali* (1912) that refers to a star and a planet becomes, in Spanish, "las estrellas infinitas" (the infinite stars); "sadness" becomes "no sé qué tristeza" (I know not what sadness). In both cases one hears the unmistakable accent of Juan Ramón Jiménez. *The Times Literary Supplement* remarked that whereas the Indian poet was not especially notable for his use of the English language, Juan Ramón always remained the master of the beautifully cadenced line.

Juan Ramón first began to take an interest in the art of translating at the turn of the century, and in 1912 he contributed some versions for an anthology of modern French poetry. These were followed by his translation of Romain Rolland's *Life of Beethoven* (1903) in 1915. That same year he published a translation of Shelley's "Hymn to Intellectual Beauty," a statement he found closely akin to his own ideas about the nature and theme of poetry. After returning from their honeymoon in the United States, Juan Ramón and Zenobia got busy translating plays and poems by William Butler Yeats. They had *The Countess Cathleen* (1899) completely rendered into Spanish and were planning to produce it in Madrid, but Yeats raised difficulties regarding translation rights, and the couple abandoned this project, which would have given Yeats one of his earliest and most complete exposures on the Continent. John Millington Synge's *Riders to the Sea* (1904) was translated and staged in Madrid in 1921. García Lorca was in the audience and took some ideas from it for his play *Bodas de sangre* (*Blood Wedding*, 1933). Translations of William Blake, Robert Frost, and T. S. Eliot, all signed by Juan Ramón but probably prepared with Zenobia's help, appeared in several reviews. The couple obviously enjoyed working together in the act of translation, for on their first lonely New Year's Eve away from Spain in 1937, Juan Ramón notes that they fended off utter gloom by reading and translating from *The Oxford Book of Modern Verse,* edited by Yeats.

It was sometime in 1916 that Jiménez cast a critical eye on all that he had done before and pronounced it to be nothing but a *borrador silveste* (an uncouth rough draft). He set about systematically trying to destroy all copies of *Ninfeas* and *Almas de violeta* he could get his hands on, and condemned nearly everything else he had written before meeting Zenobia. Out of this grew an unusual attitude toward the process of revision and the nature of the text. Poems, he insisted, were not rewritten: they were "relived." In returning to a poem composed two or even twenty years ago, the poet attempted to relive the experience that provoked the poem, in the process making changes dictated by the point of view imposed by the new time and circumstances prevailing during the "reliving." This notion raises interesting points about the relationship between a writer and his text, and especially about the function of a writer as a reader of his text. Clearly the "I" of a fifty-five-year-old poet rewriting a text is not the same "I" who first composed that text in 1900: time and circumstances modify whatever continuity may exist. Juan Ramón's position in this matter raises further questions about the supposedly fixed quality of the text. He avowed that any book he published was always provisional (a temporary solution arrived at in a moment of weakness) and that in the impossibly ideal situation he would rewrite his entire *Obra* the day before dying. "A poem is not finished, it is abandoned," Juan Ramón confided to his biographer Graciela Palau de Nemes. Underneath the quixotic desire to rewrite his entire *Obra* is the fascinating realization in this age of Jorge Luis Borges and computers that the text is only a momentary alignment in the flux of signs and symbols.

Rewriting, however, in most cases meant getting rid of dross, purifying the language. Out of this process was born the famous series of anthologies that readers so closely associated with Jiménez. The reader who comes to Jiménez through the *Segunda antolojía poética* (Second Poetic Anthology, 1922; composed in 1898–1918) will think that here is a poet who never made a mistake and never struck a false note. This deservedly popular book is the result of its author's rigorous self-criticism, the distillation of thousands of poems, but it provides a very limited idea of poetic development. Nevertheless, the vademecum for any

JUAN RAMÓN JIMÉNEZ

Jiménez enthusiast would have to be one of the anthologies, preferably the third (*Tercera antolojía poética,* 1957), put together by Zenobia and Eugenio Florit.

In his later life Jiménez began to believe that the notion of genre is somewhat arbitrary and that it confuses the clear thrust of voice that, pushing against the limits set by prose or poetry, seeks only to be supple and intense. To an audience in Buenos Aires he remarked that a blind man listening to reading could distinguish poetry from prose only if the former were marked by a pattern of rhyme; otherwise prose, just as much as poetry, depends upon rhythm and careful selection of words, although it could never, in his mind, be as intense or as compressed. To illustrate his point he read aloud the first sentence of *Don Quixote,* which breaks up naturally into octosyllabic units. He might have read with equal success passages from *Platero,* for it possesses a diaphanous musical prose that belies whatever visual pattern of arrangement it takes and exists as an orchestration of sounds that, except for their form on the printed page, could be either poetry or prose.

After *Platero,* Jiménez's greatest prose work, and indeed one of the most unusual books in twentieth-century Hispanic letters, is *Españoles de tres mundos* (*caricatura lírica*) (Spaniards of Three Worlds [Lyrical Caricatures]), published in Buenos Aires in 1942 and including pieces written between 1914 and 1940. The first of these lyric portraits came out in 1924, and thereafter with increasing regularity readers of Hispanic journals were treated to their acerbic yet tender style. The Spaniards of three worlds (Europe, America, and "the other world") number sixty-one, and they range from close friends to famous acquaintances to dead authors whose work had some special meaning for him. This form continued to hold Jiménez's attention until the close of his life, by which time he had prepared several more of these penetrating caricatures that he hoped to include in an enlarged edition.

The subtitle "Lyric Caricatures" points to the technique as well as the intent: he proposed to distort and exaggerate certain features and attributes of a subject in order to make its essential personality stand out. At the same time the satire is muted by a poetic tone and even at times by a loving touch. The work of Francisco de Quevedo, less its strong mordant touch, is an antecedent for these sketches, because in their intensity and involuted structure they unite two of the characteristics associated with the baroque style. In his prologue Jiménez says, "I think (and so did Quevedo) that in caricature the baroque is at its best."

With amazing regularity Jiménez usually manages to set the tone of his caricature in the opening sentence. The portrait of Unamuno begins: "Has Don Miguel come down out of his mountains?" Immediately one thinks of the geographic reference, the Gredos Mountains to the north of Madrid, and then the mind flies west to Unamuno's stronghold, the University of Salamanca. But there is also the suggestion of a prophet descending to the plains to enlighten the people, just as Unamuno periodically descended upon the Spanish capital to launch his diatribes against intellectuals, in the style of a "definitive pugilist." The sketch of José Ortega y Gassett opens with this phrase: "Distance defines him well." At once the reader recalls the air of Olympian withdrawal associated with the impressive Spanish thinker who wended his way through a "labyrinth of laurels." Caricatures, nevertheless, cannot wholly avoid traces of satire, and Juan Ramón's sharp eye spared no one a few ungentle jabs, least of all fellow poets like Jorge Guillén and Pedro Salinas. He was also very conscious of regional and national background, and when drawing his portraits of dead writers, he carefully weaves the features associated with the land of their birth into a kind of nimbus inseparable from their greatness: Cuba in the case of José Martí, Galicia in that of the poet Rosalía de Castro.

The quality of Jiménez's descriptions can perhaps be best glimpsed in this translation of the first few lines from the caricature of Francisco Giner de los Ríos, the widely respected educator whose life and intellect inspired a generation of writers:

> He came and went like a flame in the wind. He shot up, a whistling serpent, spread out and caught fire, a sparkling vine of hot coals. Like a lightning-maned lion he pounced; he channeled a stream of pure gold. Without visible union, he appeared everywhere: thin, airy, unattainable in the absolute elasticity of diabolical flame.

The reputation of Jiménez as a recluse is nourished by many anecdotes, none so typical as the one concerning Valéry's visit to Madrid in 1924. The great French poet was to lecture at the Residencia de Estudiantes, and Jiménez, certainly the most influential poet writing in the Spanish language at that time, admitted that the proximity of two such spirits deserved some kind of recognition. However, he abhorred all public acts, especially those in connection with poetry, and he neither attended nor gave any readings. True to his dislike, he accordingly wrote Valéry: "Before a poet as secret, exact, and unusual as you, my greatest homage will be to forgo the pleasure of your *persona;* words, phrases, gestures: what are they but the vicious rhetoric of the body?" In this apology there is at least tacit recognition of the Latin etymon of *persona,* the mask worn by players, which came to signify the public covering that conceals the essence of the individual. Valéry responded with a poem dedicated to his distinguished Spanish colleague, the last line of which reveals that Valéry was content to savor from a distance the essence of Jiménez without knowing his person: "J'y respire un autre poète" (I breathe another poet here).

Jiménez constantly refused to speak in public, but in the troubled summer of 1936 he was persuaded to lecture at the Residencia on the timely topic "Política poética" (Poetical Politics). At the last moment he was unable to be present for health reasons, and his lecture was read for him. In America, however, he came out of his shell and was transformed into—in Yeats's phrase—"a sixty-year-old smiling public man." He read the "Política poética" under the new title "El trabajo gustoso" (Enjoyable Work) at the University of Puerto Rico in October 1936, delivered a series of lectures in 1940 at the University of Miami, and in 1948 carried his Andalusian accent to Buenos Aires for talks before overflow crowds, which were enchanted to see the *persona* of the author of *Platero and I,* whose essence had already engaged their attention.

His collected lectures were published in 1961 under the title *El trabajo gustoso,* and they are undeniably important as a commentary on his poetry and an example of his uncompromising idealism in life and art. "El trabajo gustoso," the 1936 lecture, reads in some ways like an anchronism, and at that time it must have been greeted with cruel misunderstanding in Spain. Jiménez's basic thesis is that man naturally seeks a peaceful life and deviates from it only when his creative (or poetic) faculties are blocked. We are born, accommodate ourselves to our place, and in so doing experience the grace of existence, which is nothing more nor less than poetry. Man proceeds to build a house in nature made with love, each addition carefully attached as needed: "That which we ordinarily call social war, civil war, race or class war, is nothing but the lack of design and love in the elaboration of our house; the lack of pleasure in the establishing of our life, singly and together." The happy society is one in which we all work at what we like (Jiménez gives examples of a gardener, a mechanic, a coal dealer, and an irrigation worker, each one lovingly and creatively wrapped up in his labor); the origin of war is working at what we do not like.

The speech is remarkable for its refusal to come directly to grips with the political preoccupations common to the period, although the speaker is by no means ignorant of such themes. Instead, he prefers to abstract these topics and deal with them in his realm of poetic idealism. For example, throughout the lecture he pays no heed to Marxism or dialectical materialism (concepts that were tearing Europe apart in the 1930's) except to conclude that man's natural state was one of lyrical communism, lyrical because it was beautiful and communism because it was common to all.

The basic beauty of life, Jiménez insists, begins with the act of birth, when our senses are for the first time opened upon the world. In this assertion, he is as far removed from the modern existentialist view of man's entrance into life as a purely gratuitous act as he is from that of the Christian pessimism of his seventeenth-century compatriot Pedro Calderón de la Barca, who in *La vida es sueño* (*Life Is a Dream,* 1635) has his hero take it for granted that "the greatest crime of man is having been born."

Despite its simplified idealism and its strangely abstract tone, "El trabajo gustoso" should not be too promptly dismissed. It is, for its time and place, an impressive record of optimism. The avowal that life should be sensitive, loving, and creative because it starts out that way in the initial communion between our senses and the world is basically a Garden of Eden myth, cherished by poets from Plato to Shelley. Furthermore, it is pertinent to remark that laboring at what we like (*el trabajo gustoso*) is no more fanciful on one level than the nineteenth-century doctrine of utilitarianism, which proclaimed actions to be right in proportion to their usefulness or their tendency to promote happiness. John Stuart Mill's ultimate sanction was the "greatest happiness" principle. Jiménez's was essentially similar: the happiness of the man who loves his work, whatever it might be, provided he is prepared for it and is granted some freedom in selecting it. Jiménez does not explore these two vastly important qualifications, and he is, of course, talking about utopia. But those who bemoan his neglect of society and the great world might read with profit this lecture and its companion, "Aristocracia y democracia" (Aristocracy and Democracy, 1940), in which he defines aristocracy as a form of sensitivity and awareness for which democracy, far from being an end, is

merely a preparatory stage. Jiménez would have had differences of opinion with E. M. Forster about art, but he would have been immensely pleased with this quote from *Two Cheers for Democracy* (1951): "I believe in . . . an aristocracy of the sensitive, the considerate, and the plucky."

"Poesía y literatura" (Poetry and Literature), a lecture given at the University of Miami in 1940, provides a definition intended for a general audience of what he considered to be the qualities of great poetry, and it also offers a key to the verse that he later wrote in America. He declares at the outset that he wishes to establish a distinction between "written poetry" and "literature." The seemingly unnecessary adjective "written" comes as no surprise to his readers; it is his deference to the "daily weakness" that tempts a poet to try to set down in words the emanations of his feelings. Unfortunately, the only feelings worth writing about, according to Jiménez, are of such a remarkable degree of intensity that they cannot be adequately recorded. "Written poetry" thus embodies a paradox, for it is the expression of the ineffable, of the awesome, sacred feeling that defies utterance. All great poetry, states Jiménez with serene conviction, has its beginning in this emotion. Our courtship and cultivation of this feeling may take many forms (contemplation, mysticism, love), but the effort of expression always departs from visible reality and soars toward invisible reality. Poetry, he remarks in a most fortunate phrase, is fusion of evidence and imagination. One of the exciting aspects of Jiménez's late poetry is his insistence upon the evidence of that most pressing and visible reality, the human body. The resultant tension between flesh and spirit informs many of his best poems written in America. As he said at the beginning of the *Diario,* one must have "roots that fly."

In order to express the ineffable the poet must write in a state of ecstasy, or grace, from which flows his essential style. As Socrates tells Phaedrus, there is a possession and a madness inspired by the muses. To a certain extent, the poet is a medium, an outlet for the ascendant spirit. In the hands of a "possible god," he has no need for an absolute god, a concept invented by man in order to establish communication with the transcendental. Without reference to doctrine, in daily ecstasy, touched by grace, the poet soars on sacred wings, becomes for a moment the Platonic "soul" whose feathers have not yet fallen. "True poetry," Jiménez concludes, "is sustained by and rooted in reality; it desires by ascension to know invisible reality." By contrast, literature, instead of being a state of grace, is merely a form of culture; it is concerned with relative and not absolute beauty; it is Plato's poetry of sense. In a later lecture, Jiménez employed a different nomenclature in order to make the same distinction: "open poetry" ascends, "closed poetry" tells a story.

In Spanish letters the greatest poetry has been fatefully linked with mysticism; Jiménez himself insisted that the poet was a mystic *sin dios necessario* (without necessary recourse to a god). St. John of the Cross is the ultimate example of great poetry: his talent, notable for its concentration into only seven poems, produced the purest lyricism in the language. Its fusion of inspiration, sound, and sense is breathtaking. Brevity, Jiménez says, is one of the basic qualities of true poetry, for ecstasy is always short-lived, occurring rapidly although seeming to last for some time, just as dreams appear to endure for hours when in reality they last only for minutes. Bécquer, of course, is another example of true poetry, as are Gil Vicente and the early Machado. Poets of *gracia intermedia* (intermediate grace) are Gonzalo de Berceo, Lope de Vega, and Lorca; those who created only literature include Luis de Góngora, Quevedo, and Unamuno. Like all critics who write from a Platonic persuasion, Juan Ramón's task seems to be one of classification: the point is to determine which poets meet the demands of ideal poetry as they were long ago outlined by Plato. It is becoming increasingly clear that in theory and practice,

Juan Ramón Jiménez was one of the most sustained Platonists of the twentieth century.

From this lecture we can extract the guidelines for the kind of poetry that Jiménez wrote for the rest of his life. The preoccupation with purity and the need to transcend translate themselves into the spirit that seeks to dominate *La estación total con las canciones de la nueva luz* (The Total Season with the Songs of the New Light, 1946) and finally breaks through in triumph to inform *Animal de fondo* (Animal of Depths, 1949). It is a spirit enraptured, possessed by the gods of earth and air, a poetry of what Plato called "inspired madness."

The poems in *La estación total* were written between 1923 and 1936, and nearly half of them have as their subject moments of transcendent experience. Sánchez Barbudo's illuminating study takes great pains to distinguish between those poems that impart the excitement of immediacy and those that are merely a nostalgic re-creation of ecstasy, an intellectual realization of past emotion. Nearly all the lyrics in this volume that are concerned with transcendental feelings fall into this second category. Although pleasingly gongoristic and occasionally of special beauty, they are not swept up in rapturous transport as are the lyrics of *Animal de fondo*.

"Su sitio fiel" (Its Faithful Site) begins with a description of landscape in which clouds, trees, and sun "fuse" into a single deep harmony; on the edge of this fusion the sea, apparently in memory, rumbles and presses for admittance. There follows a recognition of what mystics call the undifferentiated reality of the world:

> *El cerco universal se va apretando,*
> *y ya en toda la hora azul no hay más*
> *que la nube, que el árbol, que la ola,*
> *síntesis de la gloria cenital.*
> *El fin está en el centro. Y se ha sentado*
> *aquí, su sitio fiel, la eternidad.*

The rim of the universe slowly enfolds
until everywhere in the blue hour

there is only the cloud, the tree, the wave
drawn together at the peak of splendor.
The end is in the center. Eternity
here, in its faithful site, is seated.

This stanza marshals many of the traditional elements of mysticism found in practitioners East and West. From the Hindu scriptures known as the Upanishads to St. Paul to the Hungarian-born English writer Arthur Koestler, one of the common characteristics of the mystical state of mind has been the unifying vision, the firm sense that objects lose their identity and flow together into what can be expressed abstractly by the formula "All is One." Thus the *Vishnupurana*, a collection of Hindu tales from the first century B.C., enjoins, "Let go the mirage of multiplicity." In Jiménez's poem, clouds, trees, and waves become cloud, tree, and wave, which are in turn drawn together in the synthesis of "la gloria cenital" (the peak of splendor). In the unifying vision it is usual for the ego of the beholder also to be dissolved, but in this poem there is no clear reference to Jiménez's ego disappearing into Oneness.

The concept of the center has also always contained mystical connotations: to go within, to leave the circumference for the center, is, in the words of the poet-critic Juan Eduardo Cirlot, to go from time to timelessness, from multiplicity to unity. The end of man is to discover the supreme purpose of the universe in its center.

There can be little doubt, then, that what had heretofore been moments of epiphany, radiant flashes of ecstasy permeated by a vague pantheism, have been converted into a concern that partakes of all the elements of formal mysticism. This transition began to occur gradually around 1930 and was coincidental with the general lessening of quantity in Jiménez's writing and with a return of his old despondency. *La estación total*, published in America in 1946, consists of poetry that was written in Spain, and although he may have "relived" (his euphemism for "corrected") some of these poems in the United States before their publication, they nonetheless represent his state of mind from 1930 to 1936. The transplantation from Europe to America undoubtedly hastened the process that had begun in Spain, but it must be emphasized that the mysticism of his American period represents the logical development of his work. The prologue to the *Diario* mentions the oneness of feeling and refers to this inner state as a "cluster of diversity" bound together in endless harmony.

One of the favorite symbols of myth, poetry, and folklore is the bird, long associated in nearly every culture with the soul. In Jiménez's heavily sentimental early period, birds and their songs provide sweet music in which the sad ego bathes, but in his purer style he looked more and more to the bird as contributing to his transcendent spells, as representing all that he desired to be: pure, self-sufficient song. The bird is truly, in his eyes, a "criatura afortunada" (fortunate creature), and in "El mirlo fiel" (The Faithful Blackbird) the *mirlo*, like the graceful greenfinch in *Baladas de primavera*, sings with such full-throated enchantment that its song transforms present reality and turns the detained hour into eternity.

The final poem of *La estación total* praises the messenger of grace who bears the gift of plenitude. It was published in the influential Madrid newpaper *El sol* one year before the outbreak of civil war, and its final stanza, composed in the environment of imminent social chaos, quietly exults: "Messenger, you did exist. And I knew it."

The long prose poem "Espacio" (Space), which was edited by Aurora de Albornoz and published in a separate volume in 1982, provides another example of his indecision about genre. The first two fragments were published in free verse form and bore the date 1941–1942. In 1954, when the third and final fragment was composed, all three parts appeared in prose, the form he finally chose for this particular work. Aside from an occasional comma there is no significant difference between the version in free verse and that in prose. The change confronts us once again with his preoccupation with form and his desire to discover how the visual arrangement of words relates to the total effect of poetry.

The dates of "Espacio" (1941, 1942, 1954) span almost the entire period of his creative activity in America, and therefore the work as a whole is a valuable register of his growth during the last decade of his life. The first two fragments clearly reflect his mental confusion resulting from the ordeal of transplantation from one culture to another. Exile made him more than ever aware of man's odd relationship to physical reality—of the contingency of being in this time and that place. Hence the flow of adverbs in "Espacio," the constant qualification of a toponym with "here" or "there." Fragments 1 and 2 are a struggle to reassert his identity in a strange environment. The third fragment, written after the metaphysical éclat of *Animal de fondo,* again reveals concern with death and the relationship between body and soul.

"Espacio" also merits attention because it is his first sustained attempt to write poetry in the New World. He informed the Spanish critic Enrique Díez-Canedo that "Espacio" was dictated by the smooth, open terrain of southern Florida, whence undoubtedly the title. "It was," he noted, "a fusion in memory of ideas and anecdotes, without chronological order, like a film unreeled backwards in my life." Although this description does suggest automatic writing, as Sánchez Barbudo observes, the element of control is plainly present, and to a far stronger degree than usually associated with surrealistic specimens of this nature. "Espacio" displays a succession of coherent unities, each one built around a single image or symbol. Since these are readily familiar to any reader who knows Jiménez's canon, the total experience of "Espacio" is like a loose, undulating review of his life and works. Although on occasion a scene is plainly labeled "here in Miami, Florida," most of the items in the poem have been released from the galleries of his memory to wander in free association in the present.

"The gods have no more substance than I," he begins in the first fragment, quoting a phrase he heard or wrote long ago. The assertion is unsurprising; on the one hand, the soul itself is godlike, as he has described it since the *Sonetos espirituales;* on the other hand, Jiménez's efforts were always directed toward elevating man's roots to the level of the temple: "I am a swordless god without anything men make from science, the product only of that which is alive." The man-god equation, with its many sources in the past from Empedocles to Ralph Waldo Emerson and Unamuno, clearly foreshadows *Animal de fondo.*

If there can be said to be a link in the first fragment, it is the theme of love, which runs like a golden thread though these loosely connected remembrances. Love, whether associated—as Yeats would have it—with "the place of excrement," a biting phrase that Juan Ramón included in fragment 1, or with the life-giving warmth of the sun, as the Spaniard preferred, is the single constant: "Love is one and only and returns each day." Love and light (or flame), which are traditional instruments of fusion in mystical testaments, play the same role for Jiménez, without, of course, any doctrinaire connotations. Another image of transcendent experience that predictably appears is the bird: "You and I, bird, are one; sing to me, for I hear you, my ear is perfect for your pitch." The first fragment finishes on a jubilant note that anticipates the strongly sustained optimism of *Animal de fondo:* "I with immensity. This is different; I never suspected it, and now I have it."

The second fragment is much shorter (only fifty-one lines), and begins with an evocation of the Hudson River that expands to include the sea in toto, and relates water to sun and love. New York's Morningside Heights and the Jiménez apartment in Madrid are the chief foci of memory, and there is a suggested confusion between the two points: "In the garden of St. John the Divine, the green poplars were of Madrid; I spoke Spanish to a cat and a dog; and the children of the choir, eternal language, were singing." Out of the confusion arises the simple but moving affirmation that time and space are "accidental frontiers," that the bearded, ascetic Spaniard is the same vessel of awareness whether buffeted by the wind in Madrid, wandering the streets of New York, or listening to a dog bark at midnight in Miami. The song alone is eternal and the language accessible to all.

The presence of a barking dog in all three fragments, as well as the foreseeable singing of birds, is clearly explained in the poet's own words. He kept a diary on the gloomy trip from Cherbourg to New York in 1936. The following passage was recorded shortly after his arrival:

> Yesterday in Woodmere, the swallows by day, the dogs and crickets at night, drew me close to Spain, Moguer, Madrid, so joined together from this vantage point. It seems that animals (large and small) express in the same way their existence in every country. They alone have a self-sufficient means of universal expression. Later this evening, Washington Square sounded, from a distance, with its cosmopolitan crowd, like any Spanish plaza at dusk. Perhaps it's the same with crickets, dogs, and birds. Maybe the nuances of any language are lost in the distance. Perhaps one day in the distance, all men will speak the same and understand each other.
>
> (*Estética y ética estética,* p. 175)

The third fragment, begun in Florida and rewritten in Puerto Rico in 1954, well after the transcendental experience of *Animal de fondo,* is in many ways the most interesting of the segments of "Espacio." It is also the most confusing. In the first pages, Jiménez seems to be remembering in Puerto Rico things that he had summoned in free association from the past during the genesis of his long prose poem in Coral Gables, Florida. The line between the physical "here" of the body and the mental "here" of memory is thoroughly confused. Nevertheless, the point remains clear that time and space are accidental boundaries, superseded by the mind's ability to create a continual present. Thus did Juan Ramón react to the emotion of homesickness, which is one of the chief motivations of "Espacio." There must have been special poignancy in the fact that Coral Gables was so much like the part of Andalusia where he grew up (his letters are full of this similarity), setting up the fusion of present and past that characterizes "Espacio."

This final fragment shows a preoccupation with destiny. Before he died, Juan Ramón had planned to edit all of his vast writings under the single title "Destiny." In the last portion of "Espacio," written after *Animal de fondo,* the word "Destiny" is capitalized, as the god of his sea mysticism never was, and is presented as a creative awareness of fate. Man should yield to destiny in the way that a ship yields to the sea, not to capsize but to glide upon the water. The journey ends in death at the moment destiny determines: "Destiny assumes many forms, death and life, taking and leaving; it is useless to flee it or seek it." It came to Shelley, he notes, in the Bay of Lerici, and to the criminal Barabbas, who was freed in exchange for Christ; it was present in the instrument of the donkey that carried St. Paul to Damascus and in the dray that killed Pierre Curie. A man, said Yeats in *Per Amica Silentia Lunae* (1917), must learn to love his destiny. Jiménez, who knew this essay, took it to heart. "Reality is nothingness," he wrote in "Espacio," "without the Destiny of a consciousness that realizes it."

For a poet who had wagered his all on the card of brevity, "Espacio" was an audacious experiment with the difficulties posed by the long poem. Perhaps inspired in part by Eliot's solution of similar problems in *The Four Quartets* (1935–1942), Juan Ramón abandoned his *verso desnudo* for the pell-mell openness of "Espacio." Octavio Paz's admiration for Juan Ramón's willingness to turn discourse into an examination of the possibilities of language may be excessive, but one cannot fail to recognize this poem's importance in the history of the long poem in Spanish, and in this sense, as Paz says, it belongs in the company of Pablo Neruda's *Las alturas de Macchu Picchu* (*The Heights of Macchu Picchu*, 1950).

Animal de fondo, a hymn of triumph celebrating the highest level yet reached by Jiménez's consciousness, was born during his third ocean voyage in 1948 to Buenos Aires. On the trip south he felt himself once more aroused by the vastness of water and sky, and he later confided to his Argentine audience: "Life without the sea cannot be understood. All my experiences of eternity I owe to it; I have always renewed my poetry on the high seas." The *gana celestial* (celestial need), which had made its presence felt in 1916 on the Atlantic between New York and Cádiz, burst forth anew in twenty-nine poems, samples of which he read aloud in Argentina. The poems are of such sustained inspiration that one might believe the entire book to have been written in a single stroke. Significantly, he chose free verse to represent this enraptured state. Although some lines scan at seven or eleven syllables and there is even an occasional couplet, the general effect is one of fluid movement to which stanzas of poetry or paragraphs of prose are incidental boundaries.

One of Carl Sandburg's definitions of poetry, published in *Good Morning, America* (1928), has been suggested as the source of Jiménez's title. It reads, "Poetry is the journal of a sea animal living on land, wanting to fly in air." What might have attracted Jiménez to this statement is the notion of man climbing out of the sea and wishing to continue his ascent, which reflects an idea close to the poet's heart. At the same time, a more likely source for the provocative title of his last book is the Platonic dialogue *Phaedrus*. Plato says that when the soul is perfect and fully feathered, like Juan Ramón's birds, it roams the upper air, but once it has lost its feathers it settles down to an earthly body and then takes on the name of "animal," which means a compound of soul and body. It is difficult to overlook this possible origin, especially since Jiménez remarked in 1953 that "certain critics,

who appear to be obtuse, might learn something from Plato." The closing poem of *Animal de fondo* has strong Platonic connotations:

> *Soy animal de fondo de aire*
> *con alas que no vuelan en el aire,*
> *que vuelan en la luz de la conciencia.*

> I am an animal of the depth of air,
> with wings that do not fly in the air,
> that fly in the light of awareness.

Mortal man, locked on earth yet possessing a soaring consciousness, is coveted and inspired by a curious dynamic god, whose discovery constitutes the motive for celebration in *Animal de fondo*. In no uncertain terms the first poem announces that this god is not a redeemer, brother, son, or father—in other words, not the Hebrew Christian God of Western religion. The god that appeared to Jiménez as the bow of his ship plunged through the sea on the way to Buenos Aires was consciousness itself, the familiar divine awareness that had been called upon more than thirty years ago to place its indelible sign on all things. *Animal de fondo* is a paean to this god, who stands for the vast capabilities and transcendentalizing urge of the human mind. All former symbols—rose, love, star, even the sea itself—were merely surrogates for this final divinity, the ultimate revelation to the devoted poet.

After being identified explicitly as consciousness (*la conciencia*), this god is given two permanent attributes that reveal its dynamic dual nature. It is a god desired and desiring (*dios deseado y deseante*). Desired by the poet as the ultimate level of existence, the *dios-conciencia*, by means of the active participle *deseante*, also proclaims itself as desirous of the poet. But it is at the same time desirous of the world. The images of *Animal de fondo* show that consciousness seeks to expand, that awareness desires its own extension into the world in order to feed upon outside objects. Consciousness is within and without, desired and desiring; it comes from another star to the sacred well (*pozo*) of the soul and flows back again in a constant giving and receiving. The *dios deseado y deseante* is an image of the poet's elated mind grappling with the world in a struggle of love that resembles the intense, rapid, yet tenuous relationship between flame and air.

One may be inclined to see the *dios-conciencia* as a mystical, somewhat more subjective presentation of William Wordsworth's sublime spirit "that impells / All thinking things, all objects of all thought, / And rolls through all things," with the reservation that Wordsworth's spirit would seem to originate from the outside and flow within while Jiménez takes the opposite course. Both poets emphasize the warm embrace between imagination and the world, and Wordsworth's classification of the mind and the universe as the one "insatiate" and the other "inexhaustible" comes close to Jiménez's view.

Animal de fondo may be allowed into the mystical canon, but only with several qualifications. In traditional Christian mysticism the body was considered an impediment, and before the beatific vision could occur the senses had to be stilled, the devil of the flesh made to descend into the waters, as in the final image of St. John's *Canticle.* By contrast, Jiménez clearly explains in his first poem, "I have nothing to purge. / All my impedimenta are but a foundation for this moment." He also exalts the body as part of the *dios deseado y deseante,* a sheath with a diamond in its center, and he coins the word *cuerpialma* (bodysoul) to describe the intimacy between flesh and spirit. Therefore, despite the vocabulary common to the classical Spanish mystics (fire, flame, torch, love), Jiménez's book does not accord in a doctrinaire sense with this tradition.

Furthermore, we have seen that in the mystical state of mind the one common experience is the so-called unifying vision in which all objects are synthesized into One. Examples of this particular phenomenon may be found from *Estío* onward. But a corollary of the mystical unification is the merging of the individual consciousness into a universal consciousness,

the single spark into the greater flame, until, in the words of the medieval German mystical theologian Meister Eckhart, "the knower and the known are one." In *Animal de fondo* this does not happen; the poet's consciousness flows out to the effulgent world and returns, ever more aware of itself and the body that houses it. Jiménez's mysticism does not negate the individual: "Your glory in me and my glory in you," he tells his *dios,* who "is great and small in a proportion that is mine."

In the third fragment of "Espacio" we hear the poignant cry of a man only too aware of the reality of his body:

> With great difficulty can flesh have loved its soul more than my body loved you [consciousness] . . . because you were for it the ideal sum, and it became through you, with you, what it is. . . . Tell me again: Do you not weep to leave me? Why must you leave me, spirit? Did you not like my life? I sought your essence. What substance can the gods give your essence that I could not give you? I have already told you: "The gods had no more substance than I."

Rarely has the quandary of mortality been rendered in such humanistic and poignant tones.

Readers continue to face certain obstacles in approaching the work of Juan Ramón Jiménez. One problem has to do with the texture of the poetry. Wallace Stevens has noted that imagination applied to the whole world is vapid in comparison to imagination that fastens on detail. The lucidity of the great poetry of Juan Ramón's middle period (from *Eternidades* to *Belleza*) is so attached to generic objects (tree, stone, flower) that a lack of detail may suggest, especially in translation, the quality Stevens deplores. However, if one follows the symbolist injunction and allows suggestion to fill in the empty spaces, the result is more than satisfying, and on occasion the balance between mind and the world is perfect and delicate.

The second difficulty likely to be encountered by a reader concerns the overwhelming quantity of the oeuvre. Aside from the inevitable unevenness and repetition, the sheer bulk can be discouraging; one finds it difficult to know the Juan Ramón canon the way one does that of Bécquer or Machado. Nevertheless, the enormous creative energy behind the prolixity is also responsible for a final sense of optimism that, despite neurasthenia and personal suffering, imbues much of the work. The commitment to the ongoing nature of life and, in this case, of poetry, is typified in the following aphorism: "There are those who are convinced that everything has already been done, that norms exist which we cannot avoid. I, on the contrary, believe that at every moment beauty waits to be born all over again."

Like all great poets, Jiménez deeply affected the language of his time. For two decades his style and tone dominated all other Spanish poets, making even the talented ones sound clumsy when compared to his pure lyric voice. After he jettisoned the excessive ornaments of his youthful verse, he was able to write a shimmering lyric that presented the most intense emotions in a deceptively simple way. His sensitivity permitted him to define ever more subtle nuances of experience. In the end, he discovered that the human mind, in the elation of poetic activity, was the most godlike thing he could ever know. Resisting all temptations, he espoused a secular religion in which poetry was the only rite, and its creation the only form of worship.

Selected Bibliography

EDITIONS

POETRY
Almas de violetas. Madrid, 1900.
Ninfeas. Madrid, 1900.
Rimas. Madrid, 1902.
Arias tristes. Madrid, 1903.
Jardines lejanos. Madrid, 1904.
Elejías puras. Madrid, 1908.

Elejías intermedias. Madrid, 1909.
Elejías lamentables. Madrid, 1910.
Baladas de primavera, 1907. Madrid, 1910.
La soledad sonora, 1908. Madrid, 1911.
Pastorales. Madrid, 1911.
Poemas mágicos y dolientes, 1909. Madrid, 1911.
Melancolía, 1910–1911. Madrid, 1912.
Laberinto, 1910–1911. Madrid, 1913.
Estío, 1915. Madrid, 1916.
Sonetos espirituales, 1914–1915. Madrid, 1917.
Diario de un poeta recién casado, 1916. Madrid, 1917. Later published as *Diario de poeta y mar.* Buenos Aires, 1948.
Poesías escojidas (1899–1917). New York, 1917.
Eternidades: Verso (1916–1917). Madrid, 1918.
Piedra y cielo: Verso (1917–1918). Madrid, 1919.
Segunda antolojía poética (1898–1918). Madrid, 1922.
Poesía (en verso) (1917–1923). Madrid, 1923. Coauthored with Zenobia C. de Jiménez.
Belleza (en verso) (1917–1923). Madrid, 1923. Coauthored with Zenobia C. de Jiménez.
Canción. Madrid, 1935.
Voces de mi copla. Mexico City, 1945.
La estación total con las canciones de la nueva luz (1923–1936). Buenos Aires, 1946.
Romances de Coral Gables (1939–1942). Mexico City, 1948.
Animal de fondo. With the French version of Lysandro Z. D. Galtier. Buenos Aires, 1949.
Tercera antolojía poética (1898–1953). Text arranged by Eugenio Florit. Madrid, 1957.
Libros de poesía. Edited by Agustín Caballero. Madrid, 1957. Contains all titles from *Sonetos espirituales* to *Animal de fondo.*
Primeros libros de poesía. Edited by Francisco Garfias. Madrid, 1959. Contains works from *Almas de violeta* to *Melancolía.*
Leyenda (1896–1956). Edited by Antonio Sánchez Romeralo. Madrid, 1978. This is the "relived" edition of his poetry, long planned by the poet.
Poesías últimas escojidas (1918–1958). Edited by Antonio Sánchez Romeralo. Madrid, 1982.
La realidad invisible (1971–1920). Unpublished text, critical and facsimile edition. Edited by Antonio Sánchez Romeralo. London, 1983.

PROSE
Platero y yo: Elegía andaluza. First published in Madrid, 1914. First complete edition, Madrid, 1917.

Españoles de tres mundos: Viejo mundo, Nuevo mundo, Otro mundo (1914–1940). Buenos Aires, 1942.

Cuadernos de Juan Ramón Jiménez. Edited by F. Garfias. Madrid, 1960.

La corriente infinita (1903–1954). Edited by F. Garfias. Madrid, 1961.

Por el cristal amarillo (1902–1954). Edited by F. Garfias. Madrid, 1961.

El trabajo gustoso (1948–1954). Edited by F. Garfias. Mexico City, 1961.

La colina de los chopos (Madrid posible e imposible) (1915–1924). Edited by F. Garfias. Barcelona, 1963.

Estética y ética estética (crítica y complemento). Edited by F. Garfias. Madrid, 1967.

Libros de prosa. 4 vols. Edited by F. Garfias. Madrid, 1969. Vol. 1, *Primeras prosas*; vol. 2, *Platero y yo*; vol. 3, *La colina de los chopos*; vol. 4, *Por el cristal amarillo*.

Historias y cuentos (1900–1952). Edited by Arturo del Villar. Barcelona, 1979.

Espacio. Edited by Aurora de Albornoz. Madrid, 1982.

Guerra en España. Edited by Angel Crespo. Barcelona, 1985.

CORRESPONDENCE

Cartas (1898–1958). Edited by F. Garfias. Madrid, 1961.

Cartas literarias (1937–1954). Edited by F. Garfias. Barcelona, 1977.

Selección de cartas (1899–1959). Edited by F. Garfias. Barcelona, 1973.

TRANSLATIONS

Fifty Spanish Poems. Translated by J. B. Trend. Oxford, 1950.

Forty Poems. Translated by Robert Bly. Madison, Wis., 1967.

God Desiring and Desired. Introduction by Louis Simpson. Translated by Antonio T. de Nicolás. New York, 1987.

Invisible Reality (1917–1920, 1924). Introduction by Louis Simpson. Translated by Antonio T. de Nicolás. New York, 1987.

Platero and I: An Andalusian Elegy. Translated by William and Mary Roberts. Oxford, 1956.

Platero and I: An Andalusian Elegy. Translated by Eloïse Roach. Austin, Tex. 1957.

Roots and Wings: Poetry from Spain, 1900–1975. Edited by Hardie St. Martin. New York, 1976.

The Selected Writings of Juan Ramón Jiménez. Translated by H. R. Hays. New York, 1957.

Stories of Life and Death. Translated by Antonio T. de Nicolás. New York, 1986.

Three Hundred Poems, 1903–1953. Selected by George Schade and Ricardo Gullón. Translated by Eloïse Roach. Austin, Tex., 1962.

BIOGRAPHICAL AND CRITICAL STUDIES

Actas del Congreso internacional commemorativo del centenario de Juan Ramón Jiménez. 2 vols. Huelva, 1983.

Allen, Rupert C. "What Is an 'Exact' Name? A Comment on Jiménez' '¡Intelijencia!'" *Bulletin of Hispanic Studies* 58:47–54 (1981).

Blasco Pascual, Francisco Javier. *La poética de Juan Ramón Jiménez: Desarrollo, contexto, y sistema*. Salamanca, 1981.

Campoamor González, Antonio. *Vida y poesía de Juan Ramón Jiménez*. Madrid, 1976.

―――. *Bibliografía general de Juan Ramón Jiménez*. Madrid, 1983.

Cardwell, Richard A. *Juan Ramón Jiménez: The Modernist Apprenticeship (1895–1900)*. Berlin, 1977.

Coke-Enguídanos, Mervyn. *Word and Work in the Poetry of Juan Ramón Jiménez*. London, 1982.

Cole, Leo R. *The Religious Instinct in the Poetry of Juan Ramón Jiménez*. Oxford, 1967.

Cuadernos hispanoamericanos 125, nos. 376–378 (October–December 1981). Issues dedicated to Jiménez.

Díez-Canedo, Enrique. *Juan Ramón Jiménez en su obra*. Mexico City, 1944.

Estudios sobre Juan Ramón Jiménez. Published in commemoration of the centennial of his birth. Mayagüez, P.R., 1981.

Fogelquist, Donald F. *Juan Ramón Jiménez*. Boston, 1976.

Font, María Teresa. *Espacio: Autobiografía lírica de Juan Ramón Jiménez*. Madrid, 1972.

Gicovate, Bernardo. *La poesía de Juan Ramón Jiménez*. Barcelona, 1973.

González, Ángel. *Juan Ramón Jiménez*. Madrid, 1974.

Guerrero Ruiz, Juan. *Juan Ramón de viva voz*. Madrid, 1961.

Gullón, Ricardo. *Conversaciones con Juan Ramón*. Madrid, 1958.

―――――. *El último Juan Ramón*. Madrid, 1968.

Olson, Paul R. *Circle of Paradox: Time and Essence in the Poetry of Juan Ramón Jiménez*. Baltimore, 1967.

Pablos, Basilio de. *El tiempo en la poesía de Juan Ramón Jiménez*. Madrid, 1965.

Palau de Nemes, Graciela. *Vida y obra de Juan Ramón Jiménez: La poesía desnuda*. 2 vols. Madrid, 1974.

―――――. *Inicios de Zenobia y Juan Ramón Jiménez en América*. Madrid, 1982.

Paraíso de Leal, Isabel. *Juan Ramón Jiménez: Vivencia y palabra*. Madrid, 1976.

Paz, Octavio. "Una de cal. . . ." *Papeles de Son Armadans* 47:175–197 (1967).

Poesía, nos. 13–14 (Winter 1981–1982). Issues dedicated to Jiménez.

Poetry 82 (July 1953). An issue dedicated to Jiménez.

Prat, Ignacio. "Juan Ramón Jiménez (1901–1902): Nuevos datos." *Insula* 33:1–12 (December 1978).

Predmore, Michael P. *La poesía hermética de Juan Ramón Jiménez*. Madrid, 1973.

Renaissance and Modern Studies 25 (1981). An issue dedicated to Jiménez.

Salgado, María A. *El arte polifacético de las "Caricaturas liricas" juanramonianas*. Madrid, 1968.

Sánchez Barbudo, Antonio. *La segunda época de Juan Ramón Jiménez (1916–1953)*. Madrid, 1962.

Sánchez Romeralo, Antonio. "Juan Ramón Jiménez en su fondo de aire." *Revista hispánica moderna* 27:299–319 (1961).

Santos Escudero, Ceferino. *Símbolos y Dios en el último Juan Ramón Jiménez*. Madrid, 1975.

Saz-Orozco, Carlos. *Desarrollo del concepto de Dios en el pensamiento religioso de Juan Ramón Jiménez*. Madrid, 1966.

Studies in Twentieth-Century Literature 7 (1983). An issue dedicated to Jiménez.

La torre 29, nos. 111–114 (January–December 1981). Issues dedicated to Jiménez.

Wilcox, John C. "'Naked' Versus 'Pure' Poetry in Juan Ramón Jiménez, with Remarks on the Impact of W. B. Yeats." *Hispania* 66:511–521 (1983).

―――――. *Self and Image in Juan Ramón Jiménez: Modern and Post-modern Readings*. Champaign, Ill., 1987.

―――――. *The Victorious Expression: A Study of Four Contemporary Spanish Poets*. Madison, Wis., 1964.

―――――. "Génesis y forma de 'Espacio' de Juan Ramón Jiménez." *Revista hispánica moderna* 34:462–470 (1968).

―――――. *The Line in the Margin: Juan Ramón Jiménez and His Readings in Blake, Shelley, and Yeats*. Madison, Wis., 1980.

Young, Howard T. "The Exact Names." *Modern Language Notes* 96:212–223 (1981).

HOWARD T. YOUNG

SIGRID UNDSET
(1882–1949)

SIGRID UNDSET WAS the third woman and the third Norwegian to receive the Nobel Prize for Literature. She was presented with the prestigious award in 1928, one year earlier than Thomas Mann. The Nobel Prize Committee cited Mann for *Buddenbrooks* (1901) and Undset primarily for her cyclical novels *Kristin Lavransdatter* (1920–1922) and *Olav Audunssön* (*The Master of Hestviken*, 1925). Mann's and Undset's novels are in the same mold; they are historical novels of a rich and varied texture. Undset's works are family novels set in medieval Norway. Mann's opus has a late-eighteenth- and nineteenth-century setting and chronicles the rise and demise of a merchant dynasty in Lübeck, Germany. Both wrote in the realistic mode of the great novelists of the nineteenth century, and both attained immediate international fame.

Coincidentally, their personal lives took a similar turn about a decade later: in the wake of the politically turbulent Nazi era, both spent the war years as honored and active emigrés in the United States, and both wrote passionately for the cause of freedom. Their careers as authors diverged, however. Mann wove his experiences into the complex philosophical novel *Doktor Faustus* (1947), in which he used the Faustian theme to explore the nature of civilization and the ever-present peril to its existence. Specifically, he attempted to reconcile the image of the Germany he had loved and revered with the reality of Nazi Germany; in a larger context he analyzed and represented the recurrent paroxysms of violence in the history of Western civilization, pathological social conditions that culminated in the collapse of humanism in the Nazi era. For Undset the war spelled the end of her career as a novelist. She declared that she no longer had the leisure to write fiction. Although this was an overstatement, she failed to achieve in her later writings the immediacy, balance, or verisimilitude she had always striven for. Simultaneously, the success that she had enjoyed during her long career waned.

BIOGRAPHICAL SOURCES

Undset's life is well known in its outlines, though intimate details of major aspects of her life are few. To date there are two important biographies. The first, by A. H. Winsnes, was published in 1949 and was reviewed by Undset herself. The second appeared two decades later. Written by Borghild Krane, it is considered the standard biography.

Both works were affected in varying degrees by the Undset family's respect for privacy. Winsnes had the advantage of Undset's advice and of consultation with her favorite sister and confidante, Signy Thomas. Nevertheless, as the work's subtitle, "A Study in Christian Realism," suggests, the biographical element is ancillary to a specific literary question. As a biography this study is useful but lacking in psychological interest.

In Krane's work biography also comprises less than half of the book. While biographical detail is prominent, the second and longer part of the study records Undset's stands on political and social issues, including the women's rights question. This disproportionate interest in her career as essayist and public commentator might be rationalized by the belief that Undset's true character is revealed in these writings rather than in her fiction.

Krane's biographical analysis is substantial, in part because it is based on previously inaccessible sources. As Nicole Deschamps lamented a few years prior to the publication of Krane's work, consultation of the family's holdings and of Undset memorabilia in the hands of friends had long been a problem. This particular obstacle was partially overcome by Krane, who was able to review unpublished correspondence to various friends: she analyzed the collected letters to and the extensive diaries of Undset's colleague and friend Nini Roll Anker, now held at the University Library of Oslo. The widow of Fredrik Paasche, an eminent Old Norse scholar and friend of Undset, also allowed Krane to utilize letters in her possession. More important, Undset's family generously permitted the study of the author's correspondence and of her impressive library.

In recent years the "savage discretion" of Undset's family and friends, which Deschamps noted plaintively, has been attenuated, though it still exists to some extent. Much of Undset's correspondence awaits publication, including the repository of letters at Rutgers University addressed to her American friend Hope Emily Allen, written between February 1941 and December 1948. The major collection of Undset's letters, those to her pen pal in Sweden, Dea Forsberg, was edited by Christiane Undset Svarstad in 1979. These afford insight into Undset's youthful ambition: she confides both her dislike for the secretarial work that was

her means of subsistence and her hopes and plans for a professional writing career. This edition was also reviewed by a family member, Undset's son, Hans Benedict Undset Svarstad, who exercised editorial control over the notes to the correspondence.

The lack of a comprehensive edition of Undset letters remains a serious lacuna. The memoirs that have been published are also wanting. In general they exhibit too great a restraint in providing significant detail. Anker's recollections of her friendship with Sigrid Undset are self-admittedly noncritical. The circumspection evident in her selection of topics manifests her respect for Undset's dislike of publicity. Somewhat more penetrating are the 1982 reminiscences of a niece, Charlotte Blindheim, collected in a handsomely illustrated tribute on the centennial of Undset's birth. Still, a deep-rooted desire to uphold the family tradition of privacy is apparent in these memoirs; for all its intrinsic interest, the book remains chatty. This is also true of Arne Skouen's memoirs of Undset's journalistic activity during the war years. Skouen incorporates only excerpts from letters written to her sister Ragnhild Wiberg in Stockholm and to her own son Hans. Characteristically, none of these letters is appended in full. In important biographical questions, the privacy that insulated Sigrid Undset's private life from her public career persists.

What is known about her feelings and thoughts during selected phases of her life derives to a large extent from these inhibited reminiscences and from a corpus of published and unpublished letters. These are augmented by three major autobiographical writings, two of them in fictional guise, and by numerous essays and journalistic pieces dealing with issues that animated her work and life, such as her conversion to Catholicism, and the women's rights movement. Her autobiographical works cover only her childhood (*Elleve aar* [*The Longest Years*, 1934]), a single year of her family life in Lillehammer (*Happy Times in Norway* [1942; published in Norwegian as *Lykkelige dager* in 1947]), and her flight to the

United States through Russia and Japan during World War II (*Return to the Future* [1942; published in Norwegian as *Tilbake til fremtiden* in 1945]).

The spottiness of her autobiographical works, the relative dearth of letters in the public domain, and the sparseness of personal papers relating to her career account for the lacunae that exist in the public record of her life and in our knowledge of her evolution as a writer.

EARLY YEARS

Undset was born in Kalundborg, Denmark, on 20 May 1882 at her mother's parental home. When she was two years old her parents, Ingvald and Anna Charlotte (neé Gyth), moved to Oslo, where she spent her formative years. The first eleven years of her life were in many ways privileged. She grew up in a cultured family in Oslo, and in her home and among her Danish relatives storytelling was a cultivated art. Both parents invented stories to amuse their children, and Undset emulated them: after she and her two younger sisters were bundled off to bed, she would spin tales long enough to entertain them for several nights. In Kalundborg, where Sigrid often spent the summer, her great aunt held Sigrid spellbound with the tales in her repertoire. While the tradition of storytelling developed Undset's imagination, it also gave her an understanding of the fundamentals of a storyteller's craft. The realism for which her works are noted is grounded in part in the depictive, down-to-earth style of folk tales. Her sense of realism was honed in stories she herself invented, in which she, her two sisters, and her playmates played central roles.

Both parents were highly educated, liberal, and exacting in their educational aims and standards. Accordingly, they were intent on providing Sigrid with an education that would both stimulate her imagination and develop her reasoning power. In pursuing his career as an archeologist, her father had traveled widely

with his wife. He had attained international recognition with a seminal book, *Fra Norges ældre jernalder* (The Beginnings of the Iron Age in Northern Europe, 1880). Even as a child Undset's father had been fascinated by the Middle Ages. With a friend he had explored the cathedral in Trondheim, the medieval capital of Norway, until he knew every stone and cranny. He also delighted in medieval historiography, particularly in the renowned history of Norway by Snorri Sturluson, a master of Old Norse prose.

Undset's passion for studying and writing about medieval Norway dated from her childhood. Her father had nurtured this love. He introduced her to the Icelandic sagas, specifically the medieval family sagas, which chronicle the lives of chieftains and their families or of heroes in the chieftain mold. Subsequently, on a trip to her paternal grandparents, she herself discovered a masterpiece of Old Norse prose, the thirteenth-century *Brennu-Njáls saga* (Njal's Saga). A complex and dramatic work, *Njal's Saga* made a profound impression on her. Her absorption in this admittedly difficult text illustrates that at a young age Undset was a sophisticated and discriminating reader in a discipline unfamiliar to many adults. During the last years of her father's life love of the sagas formed a bond between the two; she entertained him by reading favorite passages to him both in Norwegian and in the original Old Norse. One of these sessions stood out poignantly in her recollection: as she read to him one day from *Hávarðar saga Ísfirðings* (Saga of Howard the Halt; the dating of this work is much disputed, as is common with the sagas), she dimly apprehended the onset of his death, for when her father failed to ask for the Old Norse text, she sensed the gravity of his condition. A day later, he died.

Reading the sagas formed only part of the apprenticeship Undset served under her father's tutelage. He also trained her to observe and to appreciate the concrete details and objects that illuminate and enliven the study of the past. As a toddler she played with a small terra-cotta horse that Heinrich Schliemann had given her father from the excavation site at Troy. On their visits to her paternal grandparents in the Trondheim district, he taught Sigrid the sites and names of the great medieval manors. Thus she came to love the area that she depicted so fondly, realistically, and poetically in her historical novels. More important, he gave her the discipline to read works that in subject matter and in treatment were too difficult for a child her age. Once, when he saw her leafing through a six-volume history of the world, he promised the child two crowns if she managed to read the study from cover to cover. She did read it, though it took her two years. This dedicated application to intellectual tasks became part of her nature; if she found that a work was too complex for her to understand, she would study it until she was able to grasp more of the subject matter. Thus her intellectual training led to character formation. Perseverance and pertinacity were conspicuous character traits that she also embodied in the personalities of her strong-willed protagonists.

Since the Middle Ages were the inspirational source of Undset's best works, her father's direction of her intellectual training has been justly emphasized. In *The Longest Years* Undset herself seems to give greater weight to her father's role than to her mother's by concluding her thinly fictionalized childhood account with her father's death and with the family's changed circumstances thereafter. Still, her mother exerted equal influence on her development. She supervised the child's daily studies and nurtured by word and example the independence of spirit that characterized Undset as well as her best-known fictional heroine, Kristin Lavransdatter. She taught Sigrid the fundamentals of reading and writing, encouraged her in reading the classical works of Scandinavian fiction, and criticized the maudlin intellectual fare that the school at times dispensed to its students. Her father had taught Sigrid that intellectual judgments are never fixed and are constantly subject to revision. Her

mother imbued Sigrid with the notion that official pronouncements must be examined critically for their validity. In particular her mother turned passionate when it came to countering her children's faith in the judgment of their peers; she exhorted Undset not to be foolish and care what people think, saying that what most people think is nearly always fatuous.

This defiant attitude strengthened Sigrid's belief in her own ability and judgment, although her mother's notions probably made Sigrid's life as a schoolgirl uncomfortable. At a time when conservatives were appalled by coeducational schools, Mrs. Undset's ideas on girls' clothing, for instance, were considered radical. She believed that little girls would be more comfortable in slacks, and accordingly, her daughters wore both slacks and their traditional skirts in the cold Norwegian winters. This anecdote, trivial at first glance, suggests Mrs. Undset's rational bent, which Undset later characterized as a cast of mind typical of the eighteenth century.

Undset's mother was well educated, highly literate, and fluent in German and French. She as well as her husband formed Sigrid's literary taste. In leisure hours, the sharing of literary masterpieces was a traditional mode of family entertainment. In *The Longest Years* Sigrid recalls her mother reading to her father German classical works of the nineteenth century: Adelbert von Chamisso's *Peter Schlemihl* (1814) and Heinrich Heine's *Harzreise* (*The Journey to the Harz*, 1826). Mrs. Undset valued the classics above all, and she conveyed her appreciation and literary understanding to her daughters. Although Undset secretly indulged in reading dime novels, she learned to enjoy great literary works even if she was too young to understand them on an adult level. Her mother thus reinforced her father's endeavor to train her to accept intellectual challenges that seemed beyond the child's grasp.

Her mother also shaped Sigrid's passionate sense of family and her commitment to fostering cohesiveness through unstinting support to those in need. Throughout their marriage, Mrs. Undset was her husband's partner. As amanuensis and helpmate she shared in the achievements of her husband's career, and she enabled him to pursue his professional interests when his health deteriorated. In Undset's fictional writings the theme of marital support and dependency figures largely, in both its positive and negative manifestations. In her own life, however, marital happiness and mutual support eluded her.

In assessing her mother's role, critics have made much of Undset's closeness to her father, a judgment she herself encouraged. Her mother's influence is commonly regarded as less pervasive. This assessment appears skewed. Blindheim, Undset's niece, asserts categorically that Sigrid's mother was the dominant parental figure and points out that there was a character affinity between the two: those personality traits which people found difficult to cope with in Undset also characterized her mother. Blindheim's judgment must be taken seriously, for her mother was Undset's longtime confidante, and she herself knew her aunt well. Undset's last novel, *Madame Dorthea* (1939), also lends support to this view. It is a commonplace in Undset biographies that her mother's intellectual and emotional orientation had an affinity for the eighteenth century. *Madame Dorthea*, the first of a planned multivolume work set in the eighteenth century, takes place not in Norway but in Denmark, her mother's homeland, and features a widow with a rational outlook as the titular heroine.

Undset's first schooling took place at home. By the time she was registered in a school she had been taught not to mouth the opinions of others but to attempt to arrive at her own interpretation of facts. This was but one reason why Sigrid was unhappy at a distinguished private school run by Fru Ragna Nielsen, who was noted for the liberalism of her ideas. Although Sigrid's teachers reiterated the shibboleth on independent thinking, her answers were seldom taken seriously; her

views were considered those of a maverick. In truth the child's factual knowledge surpassed the standard fare of the textbooks, and her intellectual leanings, as she grew older, were out of tune with the liberal ideas promoted by the teaching staff. In particular she scoffed at the facile notion of progress in human affairs. Her formal schooling was apparently of little use in her intellectual development, except that it promoted in her a deep and abiding distrust of liberalism and its adherents.

Undset was only eleven years old at the time of her father's death. Since the family was in straitened circumstances the school awarded the sisters scholarships to complete their secondary education at Fru Nielsen's school. Undset, however, decided to terminate her formal education after graduation from the middle-school level. She felt stifled: even then she "wanted the right to be in opposition," as she puts it in *The Longest Years.*

At age fifteen she took a year's secretarial training at the Christiania Commercial College, a course of study that seems to have been at odds with her temperament, vivid imagination, and intellect. She did not do well, and had no affinity for office work. In her letters to her Swedish friend Forsberg, she repeatedly complains of boredom, of the tediousness of her secretarial work, and of her sense of intellectual alienation from her co-workers. Still, she held her first position, at the German Electric Company, for ten years, from 1899 to 1909.

She took her work seriously and came to be highly regarded, particularly for her prodigious memory. At the same time she tested her sense of independence, which she describes in her fiction as the will to accept and to mold life. Despite the long hours of drudgery, these were her apprentice years as an author. She read widely, immersing herself in the works of Norwegian writers, in William Shakespeare, in the classical British novels, in the poetry of Percy Bysshe Shelley and John Keats, in medieval poetry, legends, and sagas, and in historiography. She also honed her language and craftsmanship by listening to and observing people from all walks of life. Within less than a decade she began to write fictional works with contemporary settings. She depicted this fictional world with intimacy, particularly the conflicts and disillusionments women encountered in their tortuous search for fulfillment.

LIFE AS AN AUTHOR

Undset's first steps as an author were faltering. She tried her hand at a medieval theme, but the editor rejected the novel and advised her pointedly to work on a modern topic. This she did in *Fru Marta Oulie* (Mrs. Marta Oulie, 1907), but her attempt to persuade another major publishing house to accept this novel was also in vain. The reason given this time was that the theme of adultery had been overworked in modern fiction. Still, she persisted. Upon the suggestion of her sister Signy she sent the manuscript to Gunnar Heiberg, one of the era's foremost dramatists and an influential man of letters. Upon his recommendation *Fru Marta Oulie* was published in 1907. Her career as a writer was launched.

From 1909 to 1913 she undertook a series of travels that took her to Germany, Italy, France, Belgium, and England. These travels did not constitute a grand tour. She disliked Germany, and while in Rome she associated mainly with a small group of Scandinavian friends. In Antwerp in 1912 she married Anders Castus Svarstad, an artist she had met in Rome. They spent a few happy months in London and then returned to Rome, but Undset moved back to Oslo in 1913 because of the precarious health of her newborn son. Her husband followed only later.

With her marriage Undset assumed a burden that might have squelched the career of a woman with less fortitude and physical strength. Svarstad was a divorcé, and his three children lived with Undset intermittently. Moreover, she herself bore three children. The second child, a girl, brought her much heartache, for the baby was retarded and required her constant care. Undset took her motherly duties seriously and wrote only when the children were asleep, toiling until two or three o'clock in the morning. Her friend and colleague Anker recalled that Undset looked and felt exhausted during this period. In the months before Undset's third child was born the conflict between the demands of motherhood and her dedication to her career became crushing. She felt so taxed that she lost faith in her willpower. She wrote in a letter that this was unnerving: she had always relied on her will to infuse her with the energy to attain her goals.

Her marriage was apparently also difficult, although the reasons are not easily discernible. From Anker's recollections one deduces that in all major family and household decisions Undset stood alone: she was in charge of moving and relocating the family, and she undertook the renovation of their premises and homes. Anker rarely mentions Undset's husband, but she does note that Undset finally faced up to the fact that it was imperative for her to rethink and to reorder her life. Although the marriage lasted eleven years, the two lived apart for several years prior to the annulment of the marriage in 1924, when Undset converted to Catholicism.

At the time of her marriage Undset was an established writer. She had written a story imitative of the Old Norse sagas, *Fortællingen om Viga-Ljot og Vigdis* (*Gunnar's Daughter*, 1909). She had also published the successful and controversial novel *Jenny* (1911). Apparently the weight of her obligations and the periodic separations from her husband had no noticeable effect on her literary career. She continued writing short stories and a novel, *Vaaren* (Spring, 1914), on contemporary themes. Besides her success in modern fiction she also tried her hand at a popular medieval theme. This was a collection of tales on King Arthur and his Round Table, *Fortællinger om Kong Artur og ridderne av det runde bord* (Tales of King Arthur and the Knights of the Round Table, 1915).

SIGRID UNDSET

None of these works ranks among her best. These are apprenticeship pieces and precursors to her major medieval novels. The trilogy *Kristin Lavransdatter* and the tetralogy *The Master of Hestviken* stand by themselves. The Nobel Prize Committee was correct in singling out these novels as her finest works, for no subsequent novels exhibit the psychological breadth and penetration, the richness and appropriateness of detail, and the skilled evocation of an era that Undset wove into her historical fiction.

The historical writings in the mid 1920's and 1930's attest to her intense preoccupation with the medieval era. She composed essays on the lives of Norwegian saints, a series expanded and published as *Norske helgener* (*Saga of Saints*, 1937). The vita of Saint Olaf is acknowledged to be its centerpiece, a scholarly work of empathic insight into King Olaf's turbulent and controversial life. In the 1930's she also wrote three highly regarded chapters on religious and spiritual aspects of the Middle Ages for *Norsk kulturhistorie*, volume 2 (Norwegian Cultural History, 1939), edited by A. Bugge and Sverre Steen. Undset's chapters have been reprinted in *Kirke ag klosterliv: Tre essays fra norsk middelalder* (Church and Monastic Life: Three Essays On the Norwegian Middle Ages, 1963). In spite of her lack of university training she had established herself as an eminent medievalist.

A review of her life history indicates that her success was based on a long and rigorous, though informal, course of study, in which several stages of apprenticeship are discernible. First, in spite of the confirmed Protestantism of Norway and the secular humanism practiced in her own home, Undset developed an appreciation of medieval civilization. Her father introduced her, for instance, to the most powerful expression of Catholicism in medieval Norway, the cathedral of Trondheim (Nidaros in medieval Norwegian), the former capital of the kingdom. The cathedral, which is prominent in Undset's fiction, had been dedicated to Scandinavia's royal patron and mis-sionary saint, Saint Olaf (reigned 1015–1030). Since it was also the site of Saint Olaf's interment, it had been one of the wealthiest and most popular pilgrimage places in the North. The second phase of her studies was in her late teens. At age eighteen she was the first to borrow from the library a famous, if neglected, Old Norse edition of saints' lives, C. R. Unger's *Heilagra manna sögur* (1877). Two years later she was in the midst of writing a novel set in the thirteenth century (which was never published). More significantly, while working on *Kristin Lavransdatter* she developed a spiritual and intellectual appreciation of Catholic doctrine.

Her intense preoccupation with Catholicism enriched and deepened the historical novels of the 1920's. The contemporary novels she published in the late 1920's and 1930's lack the balance and complexity in character delineation that distinguish her historical fiction. At this time Undset was preoccupied with both religious experience and the agnostic, secular attitude that she felt divested modern life of meaning. Three novels of this period deal with this dichotomy, *Gymnadenia* (*The Wild Orchid*, 1929) and its sequel, *Den brændende busk* (*The Burning Bush*, 1930), as well as *Den trofaste hustru* (*The Faithful Wife*, 1936).

The Wild Orchid and its sequel are sometimes stigmatized as doctrinaire; these narratives depict the conflict engendered in family life as one or more members of a family indulge in liberalism as a substitute for religion, while another is drawn to a life enriched by religion. *The Faithful Wife* questions the concept of a secularized marriage in which only one partner, the husband, believes in God. The novel appears to reflect Undset's own uncertainty about the ability of modern women to invest a secularized marriage with meaning. Nathalie, the emancipated wife, ultimately finds happiness in her marriage, but her happiness is flimsy; marital bliss amounts to no more than sexual satisfaction.

The fourth novel of this period, *Ida-Elisabeth* (1932), is less obviously religious. Its

1023

main theme is a woman's tenacity and self-sacrifice in preserving her unhappy marriage. She forgoes a second marriage to a congenial partner in order to safeguard the well-being not only of her children but also of her inept husband and his relatives. The patience and forbearance of Ida-Elisabeth, her endurance of a marriage she has outgrown, suggests, as Winsnes puts it, that she personifies the essence of a Christian soul.

World War II brought a disruption to and a hiatus in Undset's literary composition. By 1939 she had completed *Madame Dorthea,* the first volume of a planned series of historical novels set in the eighteenth century. When Germany invaded Norway in 1940 she was working on the second volume, which she intended to be a panoramic, generational history that was to include the lives of Madame Dorthea's sons. This project was never completed. Although after 1940 she wrote three works noteworthy enough to appear in English—*Return to the Future, Happy Times in Norway,* and the posthumously published *Caterina av Siena* (*Catherine of Siena,* 1951)—she had passed her prime as an author.

She spent the war years in Brooklyn, New York. When the Germans invaded Norway she had become active in Norway's short-lived war effort. As the German army approached her hometown, Lillehammer, the Norwegian government counseled her and helped her to flee, fearing that she might be forced to broadcast Nazi propaganda. Undset wrote a detailed account of her life at the time of the invasion, including a report on the first leg of her flight, the arduous crossing of the sea and the mountains into Sweden. The account is published as the first essay in *Return to the Future,* "Norway, Spring 1940." The essay is unusual in that it is unabashedly autobiographical. Undset describes her activities in the days of turmoil, telling of her passionate hatred of the invaders and of anything German, a hatred that included even a German refugee whom she sheltered in her home, a priest who had helped Jews escape.

She also records her anxiety for her sons, who had joined the Norwegian volunteer army. She had cause for worry, since one of her two sons died in action early in the war. The other son, Hans, fled with her to the Soviet Union, to Japan, and ultimately to America, an odyssey described in other essays in the volume.

The war years in America were hectic. She made a living as a researcher for the United States government and as an essayist, writer, and editor. She was also honored for her past accomplishments. In 1942 and in 1943 she received honorary degrees from Rollins College and from Smith College. The government also commissioned her to compile a cultural index of Norway, which entailed laborious listing of her country's cultural and historical monuments and institutions.

Her sense of mission during the war years and her tentative resumption of writing in the postwar years contributed to the decline evident in the few works she wrote during this period. *Return to the Future* exemplifies her perennial interest in essays as a vehicle for expressing impressions and passionately espoused ideas on contemporary issues. The volume contains five essays. In addition to the autobiographical description of her flight from Norway to Sweden, there are four essays that are a mixture of travelogue and autobiography. The last and titular essay, "Return to the Future," is also ideological. The viewpoint is historical; Undset discusses both the past and the future. She introduces a non-Norwegian public to Norway, to its cherished institutions, to its national ideals of freedom and justice, and to the deep-rooted animosity toward Germany that hearkens back to the Middle Ages. She also deals with the physical and psychological difficulty of restoring European civilization after the devastation of the war. In fact Undset viewed the effort to rebuild a future as so formidable and overwhelming that the title of the collection, *Return to the Future,* is an oxymoron.

Happy Times in Norway was part of a cooperative venture by refugee authors. It belongs to

SIGRID UNDSET

a series that describes the prewar life of children in countries overrun by Hitler's armies. The idea for the project came from Eleanor Roosevelt, and it was congenial to Undset. She loved children and her home, Bjerkabæk, and at a time when she feared she might never see her home again, she broke through the veil of privacy and depicted a typical year in the life of her children.

The strain of her toil for the Norwegian cause was heavy, and so was her loneliness. In Norway her life had centered on her family, but in the United States she was alone. By this time her son Hans had left America, and her life was one of constant labor. In a letter to her friend and fellow medievalist Allen, she complained of the many demands made upon her: "The people in the Norwegian Embassy and Information Service and Norwegian Newspapers have come to regard me as a kind of encyclopedia." Later she characterized her life in those years as that of a conscript forced to serve his time before a typewriter. Still, she was gratified to serve her country. In a letter dated 18 March 1943, she told Allen, "I still get an opportunity to give at least some people some idea of what we really are like—not at all the simple and honest teddybears and national costume maidens of Mr. Steinbecks [sic]—and some dreadful moviemakers' concept." She was considered an authoritative representative of Norway, and she made it a point to be one.

It is surprising, however, how rarely Undset spoke of modern or classical literature in her correspondence with Allen; most of her literary comments are on the sagas. Half in jest, she warned her friend of her planned visit: "I shall talk saga until you get tired of me and my enthusiasm for the Old Icelanders." The love for the sagas that her father had nurtured in her early years thus seems to have been abiding.

Despite her activity as a political polemicist she still continued her research as a medieval historian. She also turned inward. Her publications reflect her homesickness for Norway and her strong, abiding love for children. She wrote the two volumes of recollections, edited a collection of Norwegian folk tales, and published in English a children's story set in medieval Scandinavia that, ironically, had appeared in German a decade earlier. She outlived the war by a mere four years.

At the end of the war she returned home. By then her status as a prominent writer had to some extent faded. She no longer held an office with the Norwegian Writers' Association. She still engaged in polemics on women's issues and wrote articles and contributions to newspapers. Fittingly, her posthumous work was historical, a biography of the Italian mystic Catherine of Siena.

In Catherine of Siena Undset turned again to the era that had brought her fame as an accomplished novelist and the reputation of a professional historian. Unfortunately, this is an uncritical work, loosely composed and devotional in tone. Some scenes bear the touch of a master craftsman, but these are too few to sustain interest. It appears that the inspiration for the project was not solely religious but also nostalgic. Undset dwells on Catherine's ability to sway statesmen to change their course of action in the name of God and for the sake of brotherly love and justice. In an age that was willing to heed spiritual imperatives, Catherine prevailed upon the pope to relocate the papacy from Avignon back to Rome. She also intervened in the government of Italian city-states when political policies endangered the commonweal. Behind Undset's admiration for this saintly woman seems to lie not only an appreciation of her strength of character but also Undset's experience of World War II, of the impotence of men of good will to combat Hitler's bloody attempt to rule Europe.

The biography brought her professional disappointment. Before her departure from America she had an agreement with Doubleday, Doran to write a saint's life, but when she submitted the manuscript it was refused by the editorial board. Thus, by an irony of fate, both her first and last works were rejected.

Nevertheless, the vita is a fitting monument to the intellectual and spiritual force that directed Undset's life and that impinged upon her work in her last two decades. Her conversion to Catholicism and her devotion to Catholic practice and thought changed the tone and by necessity also the texture of her writing. By her tendency to polemicize she compromised the realism that she aspired to and for which the best of her works are noted. She lost the power to hone her prose. Still, her past achievement was recognized when the Norwegian government, a month after her sixty-fifth birthday, conferred on her the Grand Cross of the Order of Saint Olaf. This was a treasured honor not only because it recognized her distinction as an author and patriot but also because she was the first woman recipient of non-royal descent.

She spent the postwar years in her beloved home in Lillehammer. For her age she was in reasonably good health until the last year of her life, when her physical condition deteriorated. On a trip to Denmark in May 1948 she suffered what may have been a slight brain hemorrhage. In June 1949 she was bedridden with the kidney inflammation that led to her death. Partly because of her stoic nature, the gravity of her condition was not recognized, and she was alone when she died on 10 June 1949.

Despite her physical ailments in the last year of her life she continued to work busily, reading for and composing a biography of Edmund Burke, conservative politician and advocate of individual freedom and national liberty. These were ideals she had always espoused. She had experienced both the threat to these ideals and their successful defense. In a sense, therefore, her immersion in Burke's life constituted her final endeavor to reflect on the political, social, and spiritual turmoil of World War II and of the reconstruction era. This project, although uncompleted, represents a tribute to the ideals she had passionately and consistently advocated throughout her career.

KRISTIN LAVRANSDATTER

Kristin Lavransdatter is rightly considered Undset's major work. Although she herself disputed this, citing her preference for *The Master of Hestviken,* no other novel has *Kristin Lavransdatter*'s narrative scope, richness in historic detail, spiritual depth, and psychological understanding. Because of its central position in the corpus of her writings *Kristin Lavransdatter* deserves extended discussion. A quick review of *The Master of Hestviken* follows this discussion, highlighting its position as a lesser companion piece to its distinguished predecessor.

The three volumes that comprise *Kristin Lavransdatter* appeared at the height of Undset's career and of her artistic power. She had long been interested in composing an epic novel on the Middle Ages. Her choice of the fourteenth century as the novel's historical setting gave her the freedom to depict an era for which she felt an affinity and which she knew well. The medieval background also gave her license to incorporate her strongly held beliefs on family issues without arousing offense. Undset held that she perceived no basic difference in writing modern or historical novels. To be sure, the settings of these two types of novels demand descriptions of different backgrounds, and historical circumstances do condition specific human responses, but she saw humanity's emotional and spiritual life as invariable. Accordingly, the material of *Kristin Lavransdatter,* the life cycle of an intelligent, passionate woman within a religious society, was congenial to her.

Undset had long been concerned about women's position. She had vigorously challenged the reasoning of feminists who crusaded for the idea of remaking women in the image of men. Still, she led the dual life of devoted mother and professional writer. In her writings as in her life she championed, therefore, in altered form, a cherished tenet of the feminist movement: the right of women to determine their destiny without, however, abrogating their responsibility toward others. Her female protagonists are predominantly strong-willed, as she was herself, and are driven to assess and to rethink their lives. Kristin is cast

SIGRID UNDSET

in this mold; she is rebellious when her desires cannot be fulfilled or when her will cannot loosen or unfetter the constraints of her life. In her marriage Kristin is forced to transcend the traditional role assigned to the lady of the manor. First, she takes charge of rebuilding the economic basis of her husband's neglected estates; later she is the administrator of her inherited manorial lands. She, not her husband, is in effect the provider and for many years the emotional center of her large family.

The fourteenth century was historically a hazier era than the thirteenth, the cultural and political high point of medieval Norway. For Undset the choice of this later period lifted the constraints of historical accuracy; she was able to place her protagonists in events that, though patently fictional, were possible and plausible. Indeed, one of the strengths of the novel is her mastery of historical verisimilitude. For this she drew on her intimate knowledge of medieval fiction, art, theology, and more prosaic forms of documentation, such as letters and charters. What also attracted her was the transitional character of the era. Politically, the Norwegian kingdom was inherited by an outsider, a Swede by birth and by upbringing, Magnus Eriksson, a man whose ways and inclinations were alien to Norwegians and to their traditional form of government. Economically, trade and a monetary economy came to coexist and transformed the self-sufficiency and self-containment of the manorial system. She was thus able to weave into the texture of the novel the conflicts that arise from a clash between the old and the new, between tested and alien values. The themes of historical flux and of people's adjustment to new circumstances both within and beyond their control serve to heighten the novel's power.

The tripartite stucture of the novel points to Undset's view of the cyclical nature of life and of the growth and psychological adjustment that accompany each stage of life. In *Kransen* (*The Bridal Veil*, 1920), the first part of the three-volume novel, we accompany Kristin from her childhood to her wedding, from the security of her pious home to the restless, turbulent, and morally ambiguous experiences of her youth. In *Husfru* (*The Mistress of Husaby*, 1921) Kristin struggles to establish her identity as an adult, as wife, mother, and lady of Husaby. Though she is successful in all three roles, her dream of happiness is elusive. She retains Erlend's love throughout his life despite a pronounced streak of unsteadiness in his character, she is the mother of seven sons, and she restores her husband's dilapidated manorial holdings. Still, her expectations of her husband and of her household, her rebellious nature, and her sense of sinfulness vitiate her accomplishments. Unrealistic demands undermine her sense of happiness and fulfillment. Fate also undercuts her longing for security, her desire for the unruffled security she had known as a child protected by her father's affection and constancy. Subsequent to an imprudent fling her husband is charged with treason and forfeits his estates, and as a result she loses all that she had physically and administratively toiled for; while she manages to keep her family and friendships intact, she now owns only her father's manor, Jörundgaard. In effect she has to reconstruct her life and that of her family in a district and in a community that are familiar only to herself.

Korset (*The Cross*, 1922) describes this period of her life, when she labors in vain for identity in her old community and for a sense of family cohesion. She experiences the de facto dissolution of her marriage and then the death of her husband. She suffers from her inability to bind her growing sons to her and to the traditional life of the estate; increasingly she finds herself excluded from sharing their thoughts or from knowing and influencing their actions. She perceives keenly and bitterly the superfluousness that the change of circumstances forces upon her: the onset of old age, her status as widow, the marriage of the son administering the farm and the concomitant transfer of the manor to the young couple.

When she fully realizes that life has stripped her of her accustomed functions she enters as a layperson a convent for aristocratic women, as her mother had also done at the death of her father. For Kristin, however, the religious life constitutes more than a pious living-out of her last years. It requires not only casting off her family and relinquishing the comfort that wealth once provided her but also the negation of her self.

On the final day of her life she risks her health as she ministers to those whom society has cast off. First she rescues a youngster from being interred in a pagan rite intended to counteract and to halt the Black Death. Then, in a passionate act intended to prove the existence of godliness, she ventures to carry singlehandedly the decaying corpse of the boy's mother from a hovel to hallowed ground. Kristin herself falls prey to the plague at the end of her mission. Still, by assuming in the dead of night a task everyone else shuns, by tending the poorest of the poor, she follows in Christ's footsteps: she bears the cross that brings her death and salvation.

The individual parts of the novel appear to have simple and factual titles referring to their dominant subject matter. From a retrospective view, however, the titles have an extended meaning and function; the deceptively simple names have psychological and religious significance that links their subject matter in the manner of a triptych. Each panel of a triptych stands by itself and points to the others by virtue of both the scenes depicted and the meaning conveyed. This stylistic device, also common in Old Norse sagas, is used to good effect in the trilogy. The device interlinks works that are crammed with dramatic incident, flashbacks, interior monologues, and lengthy descriptive passages.

The Bridal Wreath refers first of all to Kristin's wedding, the climax of the first part of the novel. On a psychological plane the title expresses Kristin's anguish that on her wedding day she not only is wearing the bridal wreath wrongfully but also is with child. Und-

set makes it very clear that Kristin's torment has little to do with her lost virginity or with the dissolution of her prior engagement to a man much like her father, Lavran. She loves her husband-to-be deeply, and her earlier surrender of herself was a passionate, amoral self-abandon. Up to the point of her betrothal, despite occasional pangs of guilt, love is not a sin for Kristin. The religious significance of the betrothal, however, changes this feeling of blissful surrender into a sense of compromised responsibility and a burden of sin. When after the betrothal she gives herself to her husband, Erlend, unwillingly, to be sure, she feels she has failed both Lavran and God. The religious implication of her betrayal is found in the importance attached by the medieval church to the act of betrothal. The required ceremony expressed in the eyes of God the partners' consent to form a family. To Kristin her ill-timed pregnancy is, consonant with medieval thought, the outward if concealed sign of her transgression.

The title is also invested with religious meaning. The metaphor of the wreath has a dual connotation. Its centrality is stressed by the twofold use of the image at the beginning of the work, when Kristin is a youngster. First the wreath appears as a fairy-tale symbol of the dangerous enchantment of life. She sees the wreath during her first stay away from home, at a *saeter* (summer dairy) high in the mountains; while exploring the surroundings on her own, gazing at her image in a brook, she catches sight of the dwarf maiden beckoning to her with a wreath of golden flowers. Terrified, as is her father's stallion, which has followed her, the child flees to Lavran. Apprehensively Lavran secures around Kristin's neck his golden chain with its relic-holding cross. For the rest of her childhood the cross and her parents' love shield Kristin from the temptations that lurk beyond the boundaries of Jörundgaard.

The image of the wreath is next alluded to in a scene at the cathedral of Hamar. In this religious setting the wreath is not explicitly mentioned, but can be inferred in a deliberate reference to the bride of Christ, a popular phrase signifying a true Christian. Brother Edvin, a Franciscan friar who acts as Kristin's spiritual father and guide, expresses in religious imagery his hope that she will assume the monastic life. He suggests that she might wish to offer her free-flowing hair, in medieval times a publicly displayed sign of maidenhood, in exchange for the religious bridal habit. Although Kristin rejects his suggestion for a pragmatic reason, her obligation to continue the family line, the conversation functions as a guidepost. It points to the extended and dual meaning of the title, to the conflict in Kristin's soul between her love for the world and her love for God, and to the final phase of her life, when she achieves redemption in the service of Christ.

The title *Mistress of Husaby* is of a different order, factual but ironic. This part of the trilogy begins with Kristin as Erlend's wife and as mistress of the Husaby estate, but it ends with the loss of the estate and of her position. For much of the narrative Kristin is in fact the mistress of Husaby. Similarly, she largely controls her destiny: she exerts her authority on her physical surroundings and to a degree on the attitudes of those around her; she runs and rebuilds the manor; she tends her seven sons and her two stepchildren; and she directs a staff of servants who grudgingly come to accept her rule of order and comfort. What eludes her control is the attainment of inner harmony and, ultimately, of the continued social and economic security she has toiled for.

Toward the end of *The Cross*, when Kristin is about to die, Ulf, her husband's former retainer and her close associate and friend, rebukes her gently for never having learned that others will act without her bidding or consent. While Ulf is referring to a specific situation, her dogged transfer of the pauper's corpse, the wording suggests that Kristin has always acted upon the belief that she is mistress of her life and destiny. In fact, as mistress of Husaby, she jeopardizes what she has striven for. Partly because of her personality

defects—her long, unforgiving memory and her lack of inner harmony—she drives Erlend into the arms of a vengeful woman. Of course, Kristin bears the brunt of Erlend's impulsive, heedless, and honest nature. Erlend, while taunting his mistress with his love for Kristin, unwittingly reveals the secret of a revolt that has been planned under his leadership, and is arrested. While Kristin ultimately gains his freedom through the good offices of her former fiancé, Erlend's trial ends in the forfeiture of his estates. Their loss is directly attributable to Erlend's imprudence, but the confiscation of the manor also points to Kristin's culpability in the calamitous events that cut short their tenure of Husaby.

The title *The Cross* refers foremost to the religious climax of the work, Kristin's death and redemption. Metaphorically, the title also denotes the religious aspect of the many secular trials that beset Kristin. The final segment of the trilogy stands under the sign of suffering, suffering she experiences because of circumstances beyond her control and suffering that results from misery of her own making. Jörundgaard is no longer morally and economically a self-sufficient, closed society with its dignity and honor intact. Her husband, an aristocrat and courtier-warrior, cannot adapt himself to the narrow, self-contained outlook of a farmer bound to the land; his disdain for farm labor is an extension of his disdain for the landed gentry and the independent peasantry. Kristin herself has lost the respect her community had freely given Lavran. In a sense she is also alone, for as her sons grow up they model themselves more and more on Erlend.

She also suffers calumny. The community cannot understand her long-standing separation from her husband. They look askance upon Kristin's pregnancy, the result of a single, rapturous meeting between Erlend and Kristin, and upon the subsequent birth of an ailing and dying child. She is accused of adultery with Ulf. No one stands by her, not even Lavran's former arms-bearer, who has known her from infancy. Her pride and self-sufficiency have isolated her from the community. Maliciously, if reluctantly, the community has for the moment cut her loose.

Again, her unforgiving will, her sovereign disregard for the sensibilities of others, causes the collapse of her social standing. If her separation from Erlend has given offense, even more so her defiance at the baptism. Flaunting established custom, she calls the child Erlend. Since in medieval Scandinavia a child was named not after the living but after the dead, this naming signals that for her Erlend is dead. Her corrosive bitterness has its roots in Erlend's rebellion against her lifelong demands and expectations of him: he had stubbornly refused to rejoin her at Jörundgaard, and he had not come to see her during the pregnancy or after the birth of his son. In a protracted battle of will he had insisted that she leave her manor and her grown-up sons and move to his inherited but dilapidated farmstead in the distant mountains. To Kristin Erlend is therefore dead. To the community only adultery can explain her outrageous presumption in naming the infant. The baby's premature death seems to confirm her culpability.

Erlend's violent end is ultimately attributable to Kristin. He attempts to stand by her in the turmoil that follows the accusation of her as an adulteress at an episcopal circuit court. Unforgiving as ever, she reviles him as he seeks both her forgiveness and her freedom. At that point his life loses its meaning. In a reckless challenge of the guard posted at Jörundgaard, Erlend is mortally wounded.

In large measure the religious significance of these secular trials is implicit. Still, there are some explicit religious references. The symbol of the cross, chosen as the title, confers religious meaning both upon her suffering and upon her struggle against her refractory will. That her will forms part of her blind search for redemption is intimated in one of Kristin's introspective musings on the dissension that has marred her marriage. She recognizes that for her love expresses itself in mean-

ingful activity; her restoration of Husaby has been inspired not simply by her love for order but also by her love for Erlend. Even in her daily activities Erlend is at the center of her success or failure. If the task she has undertaken is successful, her heart is full of love. If things go awry, she is filled with bitterness toward him. Her reflection leads her to acknowledge that Erlend's personality—his irresponsibility, as she calls it—has little to do with her feelings of happiness and distress. Still, she fails to realize that she is deifying Erlend, that she is seeking to establish by her will a universe ordered according to her ideals and desires. In effect she is experiencing the religious drama of every person, the prideful attempt to pit one's will against that of God. The conclusion of *The Cross* presents the end of this struggle. As layer after layer of authority is stripped from her, Kristin learns, imperceptibly at first, to deny her own will. She never renounces positive activity, the care of others; what she does relinquish is her expectation of material and emotional reward. Ultimately, she tames her will to the purpose of God.

The relationship of humanity to God is thus a central and multifaceted, if at times implicit, theme of *Kristin Lavransdatter*. Sin, at times clearly and at times only dimly perceived, is the pivot of Kristin's universe. The novel's conception of sin, if expressed in modern idiom and in psychological terms, is essentially that of the Middle Ages. In medieval times the most egregious sin was *superbia,* or pride, setting oneself up as the arbiter of things human and divine, or, to express it another way, loving oneself more than God. Also, in *Kristin Lavransdatter* alienation from God means cherishing one's will and desires more than the divine commandments. Thematically, however, sin has an extended and vital function. It serves as a device to illuminate character and, in Kristin's life, as a corollary to the formation and expression of a strong and passionate will.

Undset held that the home developed an individual's attitudes and typical behavior pat-

terns. Kristin's passionate nature and her longing for a life pleasing to God are her parents'
legacy to her. In the Jörundgaard of her childhood, a closed, interdependent community,
God is ever-present. This omnipresence assumes two forms: piety and a psychological
burden of personal guilt. Kristin's father is a
pious man: in a society that abhors excess he
melds his deep piety with the demands of his
chieftaincy. To the outside world, as to Kristin,
his ingrained sense of honor is as much a part
of his personality as is his humility toward
God and magnanimity toward servants and the
humble. Still, his piety is flawed; it is a refuge
from his inability to feel sexual passion. In a
rare expression of introspection Lavran singles
out the insufficiency and inadequacy of his religious observances as a substitute for passion: "Ragnfrid, you and I have kept every
single fast and have always endeavored to do
God's bidding. And now it almost seems to me
that we might have been happier if we had more
to repent." Years after his death Lavran's piety
is held up to ridicule: for a man who had led a
seemingly blameless life it is considered excess piety to have acted like an abject sinner.
He is thought to have demeaned himself for
having emerged from monthly confession pale
and with red eyes and for having scourged himself, if in secret, on Good Friday. Posthumously, Lavran loses respectability, as his ostensibly blameless life could not be reconciled with
his covert expression of deep guilt.

Kristin's mother, though overtly less pious,
shares Lavran's deep-seated feeling of guilt
and inadequacy, perhaps not in relationship to
God but to life in general. This feeling does
not manifest itself religiously, but rather as
deep-seated melancholia. Also, this private
burden of guilt determines the external circumstances of Kristin's upbringing and molds
Kristin's characteristic attitude to the particulars of her life. She is raised at Jörundgaard
and not at Lavran's ancestral estate near Oslo.
Lavran had hoped that the move to his wife's
distant district would alleviate her depression. Jörundgaard is described as a haven, a

manor in a valley encircled by mountains.
Life at Jörundgaard is comfortable. Kristin is
shielded not only from unpleasantness but
also from the new values challenging Jörundgaard's traditional way of life.

Kristin's infancy is untouched by regret; her
apperception of guilt develops only in adulthood. This begins when she meets Erlend
surreptitiously, in violation of the betrothal to
Simon that her father had arranged. She
senses that inevitable suffering will follow her
bliss. Perversely, this perception of guilt manifests itself in her remembrance of injury and
slights and in her habitual reproachfulness in
moments of marital crisis.

Her recognition of sinfulness is likewise
emotional, although early in life she does
receive an intellectual explanation of the nature of sin. Brother Edvin explains sinfulness
to her as the cause of man's unhappiness.
Mankind, he asserts, loves and fears God.
Mankind's unhappiness is rooted in the divisiveness of its nature, in its love of God and
fear of the devil and its simultaneous fondness for the world and the flesh. While Kristin
cannot at this point understand the wisdom of
his words, his definition of humanity's precarious condition informs her life. She herself
feels a spiritual rootlessness. Forlorn after a
domestic catastrophe she could not prevent,
she muses in chapel that surely, after death,
she will be condemned to exist as a restless
spirit haunting the living. In Ulf's secular
wording in *The Cross*, Kristin has grown old
but not wise. Still, the intensity of her feelings,
while often a burden to her and to those she
loves, is at the root of her salvation. In medieval
thought love of humanity leads to love of God.

In her choice of Erlend as lover and husband Kristin ventures onto a perilous road of
material and moral uncertainty. In medieval
terms she chooses the way of the world, the
allurements of life that conceal this deadly
danger to the soul. This spiritual risk is both
verbalized and metaphorically portrayed. First
she encounters the enchantment that life offers
in the fairy-tale image of the golden wreath,

and then, as Kristin approaches puberty, Lady Ashild, a woman reputed to be a sorceress, defines for her the beauty and peril of a secular life. Lady Ashild had lived a life apparently untouched by religion. She had ventured all—her high position at court, her wealth, her reputation, and her friends—for an illicit love. She now lives at a remote and small farm high in the northern mountains with her lover. She has salvaged her love, but none of her comforts. Reflecting on her life she tells Kristin that the price paid for the best days in life is steep, that regret of the purchase price is foolish, and that one acts immorally if one regards an act as immoral solely because of fear of its consequences. Although she hopes that Kristin will take after her father, she warns Kristin of the contented, lazy, unquestioning ways of the gentry around Jörundgaard. Lady Ashild, a descendant of a Norwegian queen and aunt to Erlend, introduces Kristin to a way of thought that is secular, venturesome, and alien to Lavran and to her community. Kristin herself believes that she recognizes in her older friend the features of the dwarf maiden.

In fact Kristin demonstrates her independence in her choice of a husband. Lavran had betrothed her to a young man of irreproachable family and character; Simon is a man in Lavran's mold. But from the beginning Kristin is not enamored of Simon. Ironically, Simon suggests that Kristin spend a year in a convent in Oslo to be educated in the manners and the ways of the world at large. During this stay she emancipates herself from the secure life she had led at Jörundgaard. Meeting Erlend, she embraces the golden garland proffered by the dwarf maiden. Enraptured, she casts aside the teachings and hopes of her parents, her religious compunctions, and her moral upbringing. That her religious environment is ineffectual in inhibiting her heedless love affair illustrates her fervent surrender to secular life; at this point her paramount concern is the indulgence of her will.

She rebels in silence when her father rules out her marriage to Erlend. Although Erlend is descended from one of Norway's most illustrious families, Lavran rightly feels that Erlend will not give Kristin the psychological security she craves and has known at home. For substantive reasons Lavran considers Erlend irresponsible. During a tour of duty at the bleak northern frontier, Erlend had abducted the wife of his host, had lived ten years with her, and had had two children by her. Moreover, he had been excommunicated on the charge of adultery. During his courtship with Kristin his mistress commits suicide. Kristin's silent struggle to obtain Lavran's consent to the marriage also marks her stubborn attempt to gain her independence from the closed circle of her family. With Erlend she has chosen a perilous life, one that is basically alien to her aspirations, but one that enhances her perceptions of herself and of the world at large. Metaphorically, this is indicated by her status as wife of a warrior-courtier, a member not of the countrified gentry but of the aristocracy, allied and related to members of the royal court.

Both parents transmit their capacity for love to Kristin. The depth of her caring affection is at first directed solely to Lavran, who envelops her with tender love. In turn Kristin lavishes on her children the constant affection and care that Lavran has showered on her. Toward Erlend her love is of a different kind. She is as passionate, as demanding, and as insistent on changing his personality as Ragnfrid was, in her own way, toward Lavran, but Kristin shares none of her mother's depressive moods, which resulted from unrequited passion. She views life positively. Her fervor in attempting to change the constraints of her life is solely an extension of her unswerving devotion to her family and friends. Within the novel Undset repeatedly symbolizes a woman's fulfillment or contentment in marriage by her success or failure in raising a healthy family. In this regard it is noteworthy that while Kristin has seven sons, Ragnfrid has none and despite many pregnancies manages to raise only two daughters to adulthood (the third daughter-succumbs at a young age to a crippling accident she suffered as an infant). By this measure Kristin's marriage, however flawed, is emotionally more fulfilling than that of her mother or that of any other major character in the novel.

Despite her self-centeredness, Kristin's ability to love and to inspire affection are her dominant character traits. This is both her strength and the weakness that is the wellspring of her disharmony. Kristin inspires love and affection. In the masculine-oriented world of the Middle Ages she moves, appropriately, in a sphere in which men predominate in her emotional and spiritual life. Accordingly, she assumes a significant role in the fate of the men who direct and determine aspects of her life or who give her assistance and spiritual guidance. Her former fiancé, Simon, cannot forget her in spite of two marriages. Ulf confesses after her death that he also had loved her in silence. To her father, Lavran, she means more than her mother or sisters, and for Erlend life without her is meaningless. Also, men at the periphery of her life are impressed by her, not simply on account of her beauty but also because of the strength and integrity of her character. Her capacity to love, to care for others, thus evokes and cements permanent bonds of friendship and love.

However, her love, as unselfish as it often is, manifests a generous dose of egocentricity. As she herself recognizes, her marital discord is largely founded on her incomprehension of Erlend's secular outlook and impulsive conduct. He never bears a burden of guilt. What particularly irks her is his inability to acknowledge personal failure or responsibility. On a religious level, confession rids Erlend of the feeling of sinfulness. Still, his secular outlook is part of his attractive personality. His memory for injuries dealt and injuries suffered is ephemeral. His impulsiveness arises from a quick and penetrating intelligence. In his own way Erlend is a moral man to his fellow men as well as to Kristin. Despite physical torture and the threat of death he refuses to reveal the names of his conspirators, and his love for his children and for Kristin is abiding. It survives Kristin's humiliation of him, her reproach that he is unworthy to occupy Lavran's high seat at Jörundgaard. He dies steadfast in his love for her. For Erlend love has no institutionalized religious dimension; trusting in the mercy of God, he dies rejecting extreme unction.

Woven into the dense texture of *Kristin Lavransdatter* is, of course, a sensitive and accurate evocation of the Middle Ages. Undset describes ably and at times dramatically the church's control over its members and the vehement force that the symbols of religious power exercised on the minds of medieval men. Nidaros (the cathedral of Trondheim) and the cult of Saint Olaf are central to her depiction of medieval spirituality. She endows Lavran, Kristin's beloved father, with a piety that he turns more toward Saint Olaf than to his own patron saint. She also uses Nidaros as the setting for the most intense spiritual illuminations in Kristin's life, illuminations that begin in Kristin's adult life and end in her redemption in a convent. Kristin's twenty-mile pilgrimage from Husaby to Saint Olaf's Cathedral ranks among the most impressive series of scenes in the novel. Its power rests to some degree on the historically accurate and evocative descriptions of the locale and customs. To a much larger extent, however, the interest springs from the protagonist's emotional reactions to spiritual experiences and or imperatives. These feelings range from sudden, violent despair, a sense of sinfulness, and humility to a modulated experience of gratitude and bliss.

Kristin's pilgrimage is as much a spiritual quest as it is a psychological attempt to come to terms with her feelings of disharmony and ambivalence toward Erlend. Thus the spiritual nature of her pilgrimage touches him also. Erlend's awareness of his wife's agony in having conceived her son during their betrothal has been limited. He is stunned when, two months after their marriage, he discovers by chance that she is pregnant. He is equally at a loss when confronted with her moods, which make his life miserable. He fails to comprehend the cause of her intense spiritual passion until he sees her with her son on her back, dressed as a penitent and carrying the golden bridal crown she is to offer at Saint Olaf's shrine. Only then does he feel despair at his culpability and sympathy for Kristin's wretchedness. Ironically, it is the symbolic expression of her spiritual state of mind, not the recurrent bitterness in her that wells up against him, that apprises him of the depth of her spiritual longing.

Erlend's reaction to the pilgrimage illustrates Undset's use of the medieval commonplace that the elements of our concrete experience, objects as well as events, are signs, however imperfect, of a higher reality. These signs deepen Kristin's understanding of the grace that God has bestowed upon her. Some of these signs appear in memories, others in actual experience. She realizes both on the pilgrimage and in the cathedral that she has been blessed: God has given her a healthy son born in the security of wedlock.

Others are less fortunate. For example, Kristin remembers her parents' arduous pilgrimage from Jörundgaard to the cathedral of Nidaros, when they had borne her sister Ulfhild on a litter to Saint Olaf in the vain hope that he would heal her broken back. In an unexpected meeting with her former fiancé, Simon, she hears of his sister's tragic fate, a fate that might have been her own. His sister's lover had died in an accident a few days before their betrothal. At the time she was carrying his child. As a result her social status was tenuous, and she was separated from her infant, who was raised by the father's kin, she herself remaining, a dependent, with her own family.

Thus the signs of God's love inform Kristin's experience of penitence and absolution even before she reaches the cathedral. As she gazes on the city from the summit of a surrounding hill, she is overcome with gratitude for God's mercy in helping mankind "on the journey through this beautiful, if perilous, world." Still, the stern splendor of the cathedral invokes in her an apprehension of the omnipotence of God, of mankind's insignificance, of her abject sinfulness, and of her dependence on Saint Olaf's intercession. As she catches sight of the withered limbs of a child crawling toward Saint Olaf's shrine she is again overwhelmed with humility and a profound sense of blessing. Her own son, conceived in sin, is healthy and sound. In a sense her memory of Brother Edvin, the wandering Franciscan friar, merges with her perception of her own pilgrimage. As Brother Edvin brought blessings to both the animals and the people he encountered, so she will receive God's blessing on her penitential quest.

Undset's description of medieval life encompasses myriad facets of experience, not solely the spiritual. She re-creates a spectrum of medieval life that ranges from the life of the gentry to that of the aristocracy, from the activities of servants to those of peasants, from the obligations and conduct of parish priests and friars to the functions of the higher clergy. Moreover, she shows us a society in flux. The transformation of Jörundgaard is but one example. During her childhood Jörundgaard is a self-sufficient manor with limited and sporadic ties to the world at large. As Kristin reaches old age life at the manor has changed. Produce is no longer consumed solely by the owners and inhabitants or by the poor in time of famine, but is exported to the cities. Her son and heir to the farm is a trader whose mode of life and values are perceptibly different from those of Lavran; he is stamped not with Lavran's traditionalism but with the freer spirit of enterprise and with the sense of economy exhibited by the tradesman. The magnanimity that pervaded Jörundgaard when Lavran presided has vanished. The variety and depth of Undset's medieval panorama thus add depth and interest to the novel. When the novel appeared not only did the general public respond with enthusiasm but eminent historians praised her scholarly precision and wide range of knowledge. This judgment has withstood the test of time. *Kristin Lavransdatter* is still considered Undset's most successful and skilled work.

THE MASTER OF HESTVIKEN

The Master of Hestviken, along with its companion volume, *Olav Audunssøn og hans börn* (*The Son Avenger*, 1927; hereafter both works are referred to under the title *The Master of Hestviken*), is the second of Sigrid Undset's monumental medieval novels.

Although she had conceived the work earlier than *Kristin Lavransdatter, The Master of Hestviken* bears signs of haste. In structure and in her use of standard stylistic devices it is a cumbersome work. Despite its inventive plot and its important secondary and many minor characters, *Kristin Lavransdatter* revolves uncrringly around the protagonists, Kristin and her husband. In *The Master of Hestviken,* this coherence is missing. The plot wanders from Olav to Ingunn, his beloved foster sister and later wife, and then to Ingunn's illegitimate son, Erik. Also, the standard devices that illuminate her characters' states of consciousness and connect the past with the present—flashbacks and inner monologues— are overused; the protagonists' spiritual and psychological traumas are overexposed; and the overwrought, discursive passages do little to inspire sympathy with the characters' psychological and spiritual dilemmas. Still, the novel has the makings of good fiction. The narrative includes moments of high drama, the psychological, social, and ethical problems raised are intrinsically of interest, and the depiction of medieval life is varied and striking.

In important aspects, in the unfolding of the illicit love affair and in the characterization of the protagonists, the work is a counterpoint to *Kristin Lavransdatter. The Master of Hestviken* explores a love story, but one that is ultimately burdensome to both partners. This time both protagonists, Olav and Ingunn, are introduced

as children who by the vagaries of fate are betrothed and are raised together, Olav, an orphan, being brought up by his father's erstwhile comrade-at-arms. Both youngsters grow up without much supervision from their elders. In effect Undset seems to explore the psychological consequences of a neglected childhood. Ingunn's parents are absorbed by a traumatic assault that keeps them apart from and unmindful of the children. When the husband finally avenges the affront to his honor death awaits both him and his wife. The children, now in their teens, seek in each other comfort, protection, and love. Of the two, Olav is strongminded and protective, whereas Ingunn, unlike Kristin, is weak-willed and egocentric.

For Ingunn orphanhood means dependence on relatives who are solely interested in the social advantage of marrying her off. For Olav it means that her kinsmen fraudulently conceal his childhood betrothal to her. Deeply in love, the two consider themselves married and act as if they were. At this point the novel's dominant themes are introduced: concealment and its possible or attendant consequences; fear of discovery or actual discovery; and desire to confess and to submit to the consequences of transgression. Spiritually, the impulse to acknowledge guilt leads to an ardent longing to confess, to do penance, and to receive absolution.

Their clandestine, unofficial marriage is the fateful cornerstone of their lives. In their anguish they appeal to the archbishop for help, and he supports them by prodding Ingunn's kinsmen to give their consent to her marriage with Olav. To the couple, however, he explicates the sinfulness and the consequences of the concealment and illegality of their union. Nevertheless, the hope of legitimizing their love comes to nought as Olav, in anger, kills one of Ingunn's kinsmen for slandering his only fatherly friend. While in earlier times slaying was legally an acceptable mode of avenging honor, the state with the aid of the church had by this time proscribed such acts of private feuds, and hence Olav is imprisoned.

SIGRID UNDSET

With the aid and connivance of his kinsman and of a priest who has befriended him, Olav escapes. The penalty, outlawry, is serious, and the consequences are long-standing. Olav assumes the life of a mercenary. In the ten years of his absence Ingunn leads a miserable existence, mostly caring for his senile grandmother, cut off by her own volition and by her kinsmen's unfeeling attitude toward her. Famished for laughter and cheerfulness, she falls prey to Teit, an itinerant, imaginative, and friendly Icelander, by whom she conceives a son, Erik. The weight of this transgression against Olav and her constant desire to atone blight both her future life and Olav's. Concomitantly, Olav's cold-blooded murder of Teit likewise casts a deep shadow on their happiness, as Olav wrestles with the burden of his unconfessed sin.

When they finally get married they move to Hestviken, Olav's inherited estate, where they hope to establish a new future unmarred by the traumatic events of the past. Olav even accepts Erik as his legitimate son after Ingunn gives birth to a series of stillborn children. They are finally blessed with the birth of a healthy daughter, Cecilia, but their hopes nonetheless turn to despair. Ingunn's self-centeredness and weak moral fiber, symbolized in her physical frailty and unending, debilitating ailments, preclude the possibility of marital happiness, as does Olav's spiritual despair at having murdered Ingunn's lover in cold blood.

In medieval Norway there was a legal distinction between murder and slaying. Murder was defined as a concealed slaying, that is, the slayer did not announce the killing at the next farm. Olav is clearly guilty of murder in the eyes of the state, as he is in the eyes of the church. Socially, the consequences of admitting to murder years after the fact are serious, and the social penalties for both Ingunn and Erik are equally grave, as his confession of murder would bare the fact of Erik's illegitimate birth. For Ingunn this would result in loss of social esteem; for Erik it would entail a change in social status: as an acknowledged illegitimate son he would have no right to his inheritance and no right to aspire to the priesthood.

Ingunn's insistence on Olav's concealment of his murder is therefore understandable, but the intensity of Olav's wretchedness is less fathomable. His misery is so pervasive that family life is usually cheerless. Father-son relations, which are often difficult, are even more so in Olav's family. Olav cannot warm up to Erik, although Erik attempts again and again to win his father's love and attention. The fact that Erik's personality clashes with Olav's exacerbates their relationship. Erik is cheerful and imaginative but given to fanciful tales and to idealization. Olav is morose, pragmatic, and faithful to fact and to purpose. Olav's failure as father is illustrated both in Erik's erratic life and in the murderous hatred his daughter conceives for him.

As Undset presents it Olav's faithfulness is his redemption. He stands by Ingunn and by his children, surrendering all claims to personal happiness in order to fulfill his obligations to them and to the management of his estate. His wretchedness is correspondingly the spiritual outgrowth of his dogged retrospection. His murder of Teit is ever-present to his inner mind, and he feels forever culpable in the sight of God, although his obsession is also paradoxical to him, for as a warrior he has killed and has seen men perform crimes more heinous than the murder of Teit. Clearly, Olav is singled out by God for the depth and longevity of his spiritual struggle. In order to come to terms with his sin and to fulfill the duties he had assumed with his marriage, he essentially lives as a penitent.

That Olav leads a redemptive life despite his grave failings is confirmed at the end of the novel. As Olav is dying, Erik, within earshot of Olav, sits in judgment over his father. In the end Erik accepts his adoptive father for his steadfastness and love. He recognizes that his father has shown his love in countless ways that at the time went unrecognized. As that of a man who has decided to give up his estate

1036

and his wife in order to enter the religious life, Erik's voice is that of a sympathetic but disinterested judge.

The novel's medieval panorama is again varied and often dramatic, but the importance of the setting recedes as the forlornness of the characters dominates the plot. In contrast to *Kristin Lavransdatter*, the interplay between character and setting is also sporadic. The novel's lasting impression is of the overwrought misery of the titular protagonist. Olav manifests a will as strong and an integrity as solid as Kristin's, but he lacks the spontaneity and charm that animate both her and Erlend.

SUMMARY

Undset is a traditional writer. She wrote in the idiom of Norwegian realism, a movement that stretched over several generations, from that of Camilla Collett (1838–1895), Bjørnstjerne Bjørnson (1832–1910), and Jonas Lie (1833–1908) to that of Knut Hamsun (1859–1952) and Hans Kinck (1865–1926) and finally to the writers of Sigrid Undset's age, in particular Johan Falkberget (1879–1967) and Olav Duun (1876–1939). The realistic mode of writing suited her rationalistic temperament and her receptivity to nature; for her, events and human conduct could be explained by or traced to political or social circumstances, to psychological and spiritual factors. She ably describes the process of change in a universe that *au fond* is stable. Her protagonists are firmly rooted in their geographical, historical, social, and moral environments. In her contemporary works her characters' spiritual quests are often directed toward love or God, while in her medieval novels God and his commandments stand in the center of their universe.

The literary devices she uses are few and are staples of realism. They are found in all her works but appear in harmonious balance above all in *Kristin Lavransdatter*. In this novel, for instance, she relies heavily on the characters' perceptions of their physical surroundings to create a historical verisimilitude that is dramatic and lyrical as well as empathic and scholarly. Nature, portrayed with geographical accuracy, functions as a barometer to the characters' states of mind and as a referent to their psychological awareness. Seasonal changes correspond to the flux of circumstances in the protagonists' lives and to the outbreak or cycle of their psychological, even physiological, reactions. Perhaps because of her adeptness in painting and in sketching, but also because of her conviction that man is only to be visualized in a concrete setting, descriptive passages are a hallmark of her writing. So are lengthy flashbacks and reflections.

Flashbacks and reflections have two functions. They interlink the narrative, clarifying and enriching a plot that bursts with dramatic incident. They also have a psychological purpose, facilitating penetration into the characters' personality and awareness of their psychological and spiritual growth. The musings and descriptive passages that spread over substantial sections of the medieval novels set these apart from the sagas that inspired her. In the sagas characters express themselves through their deeds. In Undset's novels, modern as well as medieval, personal musings are as essential as actions for perceiving and judging a character's personality and dilemma.

In *Kristin Lavransdatter* Undset exhibits control, restraining the complexity of the story line and the deployment of narrative devices the overuse of which flaws her lesser works. The novel also incorporates the elements that typify the best of her works: inventiveness and empathy, descriptions of lyrical beauty and dramatic intensity, structural balance, and psychological insight into man's struggle to attain both personal and spiritual fulfillment. Her success was based in part on her inventiveness and on her strict adherence to the compositional demands of realism. If Undset eschewed experimental forms of literary expression, so did her well-known colleagues

Duun and Falkberget. They all wrote for an audience that was comfortable with and partial to realism and that had little sympathy for a nontraditional mode of writing or a fractured representation of an irrational world.

Selected Bibliography

EDITIONS

INDIVIDUAL WORKS
Fru Marta Oulie. Kristiania, 1907.
Den lykkelige alder. Kristiania, 1908.
Fortællingen om Viga-Ljot og Vigdis. Kristiania, 1909.
Ungdom. Kristiania, 1910.
Jenny. Kristiania, 1911.
Fattige skjæbner. Kristiania, 1912.
Vaaren. Kristiania, 1914.
Fortællinger om Kong Artur og ridderne av det runde bord. Kristiania, 1915.
Splinten av troldspeilet. Kristiania, 1917.
De kloge jomfruer. Kristiania, 1918.
Et kvindesynspunkt. Kristiania, 1919.
Kristin Lavransdatter: Kransen. Kristiania, 1920.
Kristin Lavransdatter: Husfru. Kristiania, 1921.
Kristin Lavransdatter: Korset. Kristiania, 1922.
Fortællingen om Viga-Ljot og Vigdis og Sankt Halvards liv, død og jærtegn. Oslo, 1925.
Olav Audunssøn i Hestviken. Oslo, 1925.
Katolsk propaganda. Oslo, 1927.
Olav Audunssøn og hans børn. Oslo, 1927.
Etapper. Ny række. Oslo, 1929.
Gymnadenia. Oslo, 1929.
Den brændende busk. Oslo, 1930.
Hellig Olav, Norges Konge. Oslo, 1930.
Ida-Elisabeth. Oslo, 1932.
Elleve aar. Oslo, 1934.
Den trofaste hustru. Oslo, 1936.
Norske helgener. Oslo, 1937.
Selvportretter og landskapsbilleder. Oslo, 1938.
Madame Dorthea. Oslo, 1939.
Lykkelige dager. Oslo, 1947. First published in an English translation by J. Birkeland as *Happy Times in Norway.* New York, 1942.
Tilbake til fremtiden. Oslo, 1949. First published in an English translation by Henriette C. K. Naeseth as *Return to the Future.* New York, 1942.
Caterina av Siena. Oslo, 1951.

Sigurd og hans tapre venner. Oslo, 1955.
Kirke og Klosterliv: Tre essays fra norsk middelalder. Oslo, 1963. Contains three essays on the religious aspects of the Middle Ages.

COLLECTED WORKS
Samlede romaner og fortællinger fra nutiden. 5 vols. Oslo, 1921.
Middelalderromaner. 10 vols. Oslo, 1932.
Sigrid Undset: Artikler og taler fra krigstiden. Edited by A. H. Winsnes. Oslo, 1952. Contains articles and speeches written during the war years.
Romaner og fortællinger fra nutiden. 10 vols. Oslo, 1964.
Kritikk og tro. Tekster av Sigrid Undset. Edited by Liv Bliksrud. Stavanger, 1982.

CORRESPONDENCE

Furuland, L. "Ett brev från Sigrid Undset till Alfred Kämpe om Kristin Lavransdatter." *Studiekamraten* 51:85–86 (1969).
Paasche, Stina. "Fredrik Paasche, Sigrid Undset, och Kristin Lavransdatter." *Edda* 75:377–382 (1975).
Kjære Dea. Edited by C. Undset Svarstad. Oslo, 1979.

TRANSLATIONS

The Burning Bush. Translated by A. G. Chater. New York, 1932.
Catherine of Siena. Translated by K. Austin-Lund. New York, 1954.
The Faithful Wife. Translated by A. G. Chater. New York, 1937.
Four Stories. Translated by N. Walford. New York, 1959. Contains "Selma Brøter," "Miss Smith-Tellefsen," "Simonsen," and "Thjodolf."
Gunnar's Daughter. Translated by A. G. Chater. New York, 1936.
Happy Times in Norway. Translated by J. Birkeland. New York, 1942.
Ida Elisabeth. Translated by A. G. Chater. New York, 1933.
Images in a Mirror. Translated by A. G. Chater. New York, 1938.
Jenny. Translated by W. Emme. New York, 1921; repr., 1930 and 1975.

SIGRID UNDSET

————. Translated by A. Grippenwald and J. Alexander. New York, 1921; repr., 1925.

Kristin Lavransdatter: The Bridal Wreath. Translated by C. Archer and J. S. Scott. New York, 1923.

Kristin Lavransdatter: The Cross. Translated by C. Archer. New York, 1927.

Kristin Lavransdatter: The Mistress of Husaby. Translated by C. Archer. New York, 1925.

The Longest Years. Translated by A. G. Chater. New York, 1935.

Madame Dorthea. Translated by A. G. Chater. New York, 1940.

The Master of Hestviken, The Axe, The Snake Pit, In the Wilderness, The Son Avenger. Translated by A. G. Chater. New York, 1934.

Men, Women, and Places. Translated by A. G. Chater. New York, 1939. Contains "Blasphemy," "D. H. Lawrence," "Marie Bregendahl," "Margery Kempe of Lynn," "Cavalier," "The Strongest Power," "Leo Weismantel," "Summer in Gotland," and "Glastonbury."

Return to the Future. Translated by Henriette C. K. Naeseth. New York, 1942.

Saga of Saints. Translated by E. C. Ramsden. New York, 1934. Contains "The Coming of Christianity," "St. Sunniva and the Selje-Men," "St. Olav, Norway's King," "St. Hallvard," "St. Magnus, Earl of the Orkney Islands," "St. Eystein, Archbishop of Nidaros," "St. Thorfinn, Bishop of Hamar," and "Father Karl Schilling-Barnabite."

Stages on the Road. Translated by A. G. Chater. New York, 1934. Contains "Ramón Lull of Palma," "Saint Angela Merici," "Robert Southwell," "S. J. Margaret Clitherow," "To Saint James," and "Reply to a Parish Priest."

The Winding Road. Translated by A. G. Chater. New York, 1936. Contains *The Wild Orchid* and *The Burning Bush.*

BIOGRAPHICAL AND CRITICAL WORKS

Anker, N. Roll. *Min venn Sigrid Undset.* Oslo, 1946.

Bayerschmidt, C. F. *Sigrid Undset.* New York, 1970.

Bing, J. "Historisk kunst i Sigrid Undset: *Kristin Lavrandsdatter.*" *Kirke og kultur* 29:241–252 (1922).

Blindheim, C. *Moster Sigrid: Et familieportrett av Sigrid Undset.* Oslo, 1982.

Brady, C. A. "An Appendix to the Sigrids Saga." *Thought* 40:73–130 (1965). Includes Undset's comments on a master's thesis and related letters.

Brøgger, N. C. *Korset og rosen: En studie i Sigrid Undsets middelalder-diktning.* Oslo, 1952.

Brynhildsvoll, K. "Die verzögerte Rezeption der Moderne in Norwegen unter Berücksichtigung der Entwicklung in den nordischen Nachbarländern." *Skandinavistik* 15:93–106 (1985).

Bull, F. "Sigrid Undset: *Kristin Lavransdatter.*" *Samtiden* 31:601–607 (1920).

Ciklamini, M. "Sigrid Undset's Letters to Hope Emily Allen." *Journal of the Rutgers University Library* 33:20–27 (1969).

Dahl, W. "Sigrid Undsets trofaste hustru." *Edda* 65:48–64 (1965).

Deschamps, N. *Sigrid Undset, ou la morale de la passion.* Montreal, 1966.

Dunn, M. "*The Master of Hestviken*: A New Reading." *Scandinavian Studies* 38:281–294 and 40:210–224 (1966 and 1968).

Engelstad, C. F. *Mennesker og makter: Sigrid Undsets middelalderromaner.* Oslo, 1940.

Grøndahl, C. H. *Ormens bitt: Menneskets vilkår i Sigrid Undsets roman "Olav Audunssøn."* Oslo, 1982.

Gustafson, A. "Christian Ethics in a Pagan World: Sigrid Undset." In *Six Scandinavian Novelists.* Princeton, N.J., 1940.

Heltoft, B. "Sigrid Undset." In *Fremmede digtere i det 20. århundrede.* Vol. 1. Edited by Sven Møller Kristensen. Copenhagen, 1967.

Johansen, K. Gullerød. *Guds lys og mannens mørke: Realisme og symbolikk i Sigrid Undsets "Olav Audunssøn."* Oslo, 1982.

Johnson, Pål Espolin et al. *Sigrid Undset i dag.* Oslo, 1982.

Kielland, E. "Sigrid Undset: Historisk digtning." *Ord og bild* 35:748–756 (1926).

Krane, B. "Sigrid Undsets kvinnesynspunkt i essayistikk og diktning." *Edda* 65:36–47 (1965).

————. *Sigrid Undset: Liv og meninger.* Oslo, 1970.

Kvinge, A. B. *Sigrid Undsets "Jenny": En analyse.* Oslo, 1981.

Larsen, H. Astrup. "Sigrid Undset." *American-Scandinavian Review* 17:344–352 and 406–414 (1929).

Liestøl, K. "Norsk millomalder i moderne diktning: Sigrid Undset—*Kristin Lavransdatter.*" *Syn og segn* 28:385–400 (1922).

Lunde, J. "Sigrid Undsets trofaste hustru: Noen

betraktninger over inspirasjon og estetikk." *Edda* 65:251–255 (1965).

Lyttkens, A. *Leva om sitt liv: Fyrtiotalet-barbariets tid.* Stockholm, 1980.

McFarlane, J. W. "Sigrid Undset." In *Ibsen and the Temper of Norwegian Literature.* London, 1960.

Marble, A. Russell. "Sigrid Undset: Novelist of Medieval Norway and Ageless Humanity." In *The Nobel Prize Winners in Literature 1901–1931.* New York, 1932.

Moen, H. H. *Opplysninger til Sigrid Undsets middelalderromaner.* Oslo, 1950.

Monroe, N. E. "Art and Idea in Sigrid Undset." In *The Novel and Society.* Chapel Hill, N.C., 1941.

Paasche, F. "Sigrid Undset og norsk middelalder." *Samtiden* 40:1–12 (1929).

Paasche, S. "Sigrid Undset og Fredrik Paasche under krigen 1940." *Samtiden* 59:36–42 (1950).

Rogers, B. J. "The Divine Disappointment of Kristin Lavransdatter." *Cithara* 2:44–48. (1962).

Sæther, A. "Sigrid Undset: Revaluations and Recollections." *Scandinavica* 23:53–57 (1984).

Skouen, A. "Sigrid Undset i Amerika." *Samtiden* 56:323–332 (1947).

———. *Sigrid Undset skriver hjem: En vandring gjennom emigrantårene i Amerika.* Oslo, 1982.

Slochower, H. "Feudal Socialism: Sigrid Undset's *Kristin Lavransdatter.*" In *Three Ways of Modern Man.* New York, 1937.

Steen, E. *Kristin Lavransdatter.* Oslo, 1959.

Svarstad, C. Undset. "Disposisjonen til *Kristin Lavransdatter.*" *Edda* 55:349–351 (1955).

Vinde, V. *Sigrid Undset, a Nordic Moralist.* Translated from the French by B. and G. Hughes. Seattle, 1930.

Whitehouse, J. C. "Religion as Fulfillment in the Novels of Sigrid Undset." *Renascence* 38:2–12 (1985).

Winsnes, A. H. "Sigrid Undset and the Christian Renaissance in Modern Literature." *Norseman* 7:293–302 (1949).

———. *Sigrid Undset: En studie i kristen realisme.* Oslo, 1949. Translated as *Sigrid Undset: A Study in Christian Realism* by P. G. Foote. London and New York, 1953.

BIBLIOGRAPHY

Packness, I. *Sigrid Undset bibliografi.* Bergen, 1963.

MARLENE CIKLAMINI

JEAN GIRAUDOUX
(1882–1944)

I N FRANCE THE 1930's were, according to one critic, "the decade of Giraudoux." As early as 1909 the novelist, essayist, dramatist, and diplomat had begun publishing his writings professionally. Twenty years later he had secured some critical and public attention with several works of fiction, had adapted one novel for the stage, and had followed up on the popular acclaim for his drama, *Siegfried* (1928), with a glittering and successful comedy, *Amphitryon 38* (1929). But the 1930's saw Giraudoux come into his own. His plays, with their exquisitely imaginative dialogue, cascades of wit, and hard-edged romanticism, dominated French theater and letters. In *Judith* (1931), *Intermezzo* (*Intermezzo* or *The Enchanted*, 1933), *La guerre de Troie n'aura pas lieu* (*Tiger at the Gates*, 1935), *Electre* (*Electra*, 1937), *L'Impromptu de Paris* (*Paris Impromptu*, 1937), and *Ondine* (1939), the range of subject matter and the dramatic bounty have not been excelled by those of any French writer since.

Giraudoux saw his mission as being, in part, a sustaining of the neoclassical tradition. Launched by Pierre Corneille, Molière, and Jean Racine some three centuries before, the French rejuvenation of classical myths, disciplined forms, and understatement persisted with a wealth of variations in the plays, poetry, and prose of Voltaire, Anatole France, André Gide, Paul Valéry, and others. But Giraudoux also incurred stylistic debts, some

inadvertent, to far less restrained nineteenth-century romantics such as Victor Hugo, Alfred de Musset, Alfred de Vigny, and Edmond Rostand. The tricky business of tracing influences and obligations—never much of a science, even in accounts of the history of science—suggests that Giraudoux be viewed, in addition, as a bridge (some might say a chasm) between the wildly experimental poem-plays of the surrealists and Jean Cocteau in the 1920's and, in the 1940's, "the forgers of myths," a quartet of socially conscious artists who, according to Jean-Paul Sartre, were allies and comprised himself, Albert Camus, Simone de Beauvoir, and Jean Anouilh. In *their* successors, including Jean Genet, Boris Vian, Eugène Ionesco, and Samuel Beckett, we can still discern traces of Giraudoux's legacy to French drama.

Despite this family tree of imposing literary forebears, cousins, and descendants, Giraudoux's voice has a uniquely recognizable tone that floats up from the page and the stage alike, summed up by the adjective derived from his name, Giralducian. No one, not even Genet, that master of imagistic complexity, has managed (or, perhaps, attempted) to imitate his language, sometimes rococo in its texture, sometimes harshly realistic, and usually subtle, sonorous, and vivid with tropes.

His father, Léger Giraudoux, and his mother, Anne (née Lacoste), christened him Hippolyte-Jean. Although he soon discarded the Hippolyte, he later attached it, and the name Jean, to a number of his fictional characters. He was born on 29 October 1882 in Bellac, situated in the province of Limousin, between Poitiers and Limoges. Léger Giraudoux, a minor government employee, switched jobs several times and moved his family to neighboring small towns. Some of the place-names from his son's boyhood found their way into his writings.

Changing homes and schools apparently did not trouble Jean or his older brother, Alexandre. He proved to be an eager student with aptitudes for philosophy, Greek, Latin, and German literature, as well as soccer, track, and tennis. His provincial upbringing made him uncommonly sensitive to the plant, animal, and insect life of the countryside, as well as to its topography, to the superstitions, prejudices, ideals, and behavior patterns in isolated communities, and to the inconstancies of mood induced by the weather and the seasons.

At eighteen, graduating from high school in Châteauroux with a scholarship and his diploma, the *baccalauréat,* he left home for Paris to study for admission to the École Normale Supérieure, an institution with a rigorous academic program that enabled the privileged, and a few others like Giraudoux, to train for lofty positions in French society. After two years, two tries at the entrance examination, and a stint in the infantry reserves, he was admitted in his twenty-first year to the École Normale.

There, under the tutelage of the gifted teacher Charles Andler, he came to concentrate on German history and literature. After two years and the completion of his first phase of study, he traveled to southern Germany for the second phase, registering at the University of Munich. He planned to write a lengthy paper on the poet-playwright August von Platen, which later earned him the École's "superior diploma," and ultimately he hoped to teach.

Giraudoux's biographers agree that his one-year stay in Germany impressed him immeasurably and turned his ambitions away from teaching and toward imaginative writing. They stress the contrast between the logical methods of thinking taught in France, in which the young man had been steeped, and the more intuitive ways of thinking he encountered in Bavaria. From reason to inspiration and from classicism to romanticism—the jump implies a cleanly dramatic new direction for Giraudoux's life; indeed, the notion of such a jump comes originally from his own memoirs. But France has repeatedly been receptive to the romantic spirit, and it seems likely that his arrival in southern Germany represented not so much an awakening to something fresh as a reawakening to things once familiar. Bavaria and the parts of Limousin and Berry where he grew up both belonged at one time to the empire of Charlemagne. Obvious differences of geography, language, architecture, and culture notwithstanding, there were and still are noticeable parallels between these two separated regions. As evidence that his visit to Germany gave him a new slant on the scenes of his upbringing rather than turning him suddenly and mysteriously into a Germanophile, one may cite the subject matter of his first book, a collection of magazine pieces about his provincial background, written two to three years afterward and published in 1909 as *Provinciales* (From Provincial Places).

As for teaching, Giraudoux was not yet ready to give that up, since he needed to supplement his meager income in Germany with some tutoring. But on his leisurely return to France by way of Austria, Hungary, Switzerland, and Italy in the spring of 1906 he could not settle down to do the scholarly work required for the *agrégation,* the difficult examination that marked the end of the third phase at the École, and that he did not pass.

Far from being deterred by the setback, Giraudoux embarked the following year on another one-year trip, this time a transatlantic one, to Harvard, as part of a French-American exchange program. In America, apart from meeting the formal requirements of the program, he improved his conversational English, took side trips in New England and into Can-ada, dated a number of young women, and evidently could afford to spend more than before on clothes and social activities.

Back in Paris in mid 1908, he found a job on the daily newspaper *Le matin* as an assistant to the publisher, using the opportunity to contribute lighthearted stories to the literary pages. He did not release these for publication; they appeared eight years after his death in a book called *Les contes d'un matin* (Morning Stories, 1952). At this time he was placing in other journals the more serious and connected essays, portraits, and narratives that eventually became *Provinciales.*

By 1910 he had decided on a double career: he would persist with his writing but also move into diplomacy. He passed the lesser of two competitive examinations for the French Foreign Ministry and, doubtless because of his language skills, took up a post in which he reported on and analyzed the foreign press. He was also entrusted with delivering and returning the secret contents of diplomatic pouches to and from French embassies in Europe. By 1913 he had risen to the rank of vice-consul. Meanwhile, in 1911 he published another assortment of stories, *L'École des indifférents* (The School for the Uncommitted), a variation on Molière's play titles *L'École des maris* (*The School for Husbands,* 1661) and *L'École des femmes* (*The School for Wives,* 1662), in which his young male characters evade the difficulties of arriving at a set of firm convictions amid the pleasurable distractions of the time and circumstances, the years of calm before the 1914–1918 storm. The *indifférence* displayed by those characters was subsequently cited by politically and artistically committed critics as one of their author's own weaknesses.

Because he was a reserve infantry sergeant, Giraudoux went promptly into action in September 1914, soon after the declaration of World War I. He fought first in Belgium and later in the Dardanelles battle. He suffered several wounds in addition to an intestinal infection that plagued him on and off for the rest of his life and may have eventually been

a factor in his death. Promoted to lieutenant and decorated for courage with, among other awards, the cross of the Legion of Honor, he remained in the army until after the Armistice in November 1918. But by 1916 he had been retired from the fighting, after several stays in military hospitals, and had gone to Lisbon to train Portuguese soldiers.

The following April (1917) he returned to Harvard, this time as a military instructor, about one month after America entered the war. He recorded his experiences there in *Amica America* (Friendly America, 1919). In the late war years and shortly afterward he published two further books of nonfiction, war memoirs entitled *Lectures pour une ombre* (Readings for a Shadow, translated as *Campaigns and Intervals,* 1917) and *Adorable Clio* (1920), in which he regrets losing the companionship of wartime. His fiction composed in this period consisted of another batch of short stories about adolescence and youth, *Simon le pathétique* (Simon the Susceptible, 1918), the novella *Elpénor* (1919), named after an unknown soldier in the retinue of Odysseus—the story is a jocular updating of some chapters from *The Odyssey*—and a gently satirical desert-island tale in which Simon the susceptible briefly reappears, *Suzanne et le Pacifique* (*Suzanne and the Pacific,* 1921).

The heroine of this last book may well have been named after Suzanne Boland, whom Giraudoux had sporadically courted, without neglecting other women, since before the war. They married in 1918 (according to some biographers) or 1921 (according to others); in any case, their only son, Jean-Pierre, was born in 1919. From an earlier marriage Suzanne had two grown children. She and Giraudoux, both in their late thirties, had headstrong temperaments, and the marriage later deteriorated. Although they never divorced, during Giraudoux's last eight years, from 1936 on, he moved out and lived alone. Jean-Pierre ascribes most of the blame for the quarreling and separation to his mother's decline from her earlier charming self into a fractious middle age.

However, during the 1920's Giraudoux's two careers continued to thrive. By 1922 he had taken charge of a bureau for encouraging French culture overseas. In 1934 he became a liaison officer with French embassies and consulates abroad, traveling on many inspections and missions to near and remote parts of the world. When war broke out again in 1939 Giraudoux was appointed chief of the office of wartime propaganda; but he had been shunted aside by the time the Germans occupied France in 1940, when Marshal Pétain's government, operating out of Vichy, took over. Pétain gave him a minor and almost irrelevant position, the safeguarding of national monuments. But not long after, he retired from public life in order to write full-time.

Not that his writing had slackened off even during his busiest years in the diplomatic corps. Between 1922, when the novel came out from which he adapted *Siegfried,* and 1944, the year of his death, he published thirty-four books, and more than a dozen posthumous works have appeared since: prose fiction, plays, screenplays, and political, social, and literary essays, some based on his many public lectures. His reputation received its greatest boost in 1929 with Louis Jouvet's dazzling production of *Siegfried,* followed by publication of the text. From then on, thanks to the partnership between playwright and director, one of the most productive in the history of the theater, new plays came from Giraudoux's pen every year or two. It seems that his salaried employment stimulated his creative impulses rather than hampering them. Some of his colleagues said he often kept up his writing during office hours. Even toward the end, when he was beset by influenza and his recurrent intestinal condition, he wrote copiously and fluently.

His death on 31 January 1944 at the age of sixty-one has never been satisfactorily explained. He is believed to have been compiling a record of crimes committed by the German occupation forces against French citizens, and there is a theory that the Germans somehow poisoned him. Jean-Pierre Giraudoux dismissed this theory in favor of another: his father had eaten something toxic by accident. If any poisoning did take place, it very likely aggravated an undiagnosed illness that debilitated him in his final years, possibly an outcome of the early intestinal infection.

EARLY FICTION

Since his death critics have arrayed Giraudoux's varied output in a pattern of comparisons. As generally happens to the work of prolific artists, the popular material has been praised at the expense of the remainder. (Some of that remainder remains untranslated into English.) Most of the plays have come in for close and valuable critical attention; but as yet there are few critical discussions in English of his prose fiction, and hardly anybody but his biographers mentions his nonfiction. In the early 1920's his fiction received tributes from such luminaries as Marcel Proust, André Gide, and Benjamin Crémieux (as well as brickbats from people who found his style too ornate). As he turned more and more to the theater, his plays came to overshadow his other writings. But those other writings have much in common with the plays, which are principally a contest between characters who are realists and those who cling to ideals; or, to put it another way, between pragmatists and purists, the pragmatists insisting that one must take life as it comes in this (unfortunately) beastliest of worlds, while the purists haphazardly seek a world that cherishes all forms of life. According to this division of Giralducian humanity, the few purists lose every time. They are overwhelmed by the opposition and induced to conform to the ways of the solid, pragmatic majority.

In most of the novels the purist is a young woman. Suzanne of *Suzanne and the Pacific* personifies a reproach to Defoe's Robinson Crusoe, who despoiled his island's natural features for the sake of security and to allay his loneliness by chopping, building, rearranging. Suzanne, by contrast, lives for years in harmony with the Pacific isle on which she is shipwrecked.

Conflicts, which the marooned Suzanne is lucky enough to avoid for a time—until she is rescued—loom menacingly in *Siegfried et le Limousin* (*My Friend from Limousin,* 1922). A German, Zelten, who has spent many years in France and has become captivated by French culture and manners, opposes a Frenchman, Jacques Forestier, who was wounded during World War I on German soil, lost his uniform and his memory, and found himself virtually reborn as a German. Forestier now speaks the language fluently and has been given the name Siegfried von Kleist, after the Wagnerian hero and the extraordinary Prussian playwright. Because of his innate gifts and rational thinking, Siegfried has become a leading statesman in postwar Germany. Zelten discovers that Siegfried is French and tries to depose him by setting up a revolutionary government founded on older social ideals; he wants to counteract Germany's drift into industrialism, efficiency, and aggressive nationalism. Giraudoux thus pits a German Frenchman against a French German. He means to plead for a pact between the neighboring countries in order to break the cycle of rivalry and bloodshed that dates back to the unification of Germany and the Franco-Prussian War of 1871. If the two countries could only appreciate their reciprocal qualities, the work suggests, they might form a bastion of peace in the heart of Europe.

But what distinguishes this novel from others written in the same era, winning it the Balzac Prize and an expanded readership for the author, is its opulent language. The abundant metaphors, the melodic style, the ironic tone, the virtuoso descriptions, and the comic vision, all overlaying subject matter that seethes with political provocation, make it hard for us to understand today how, at the urging of his publisher, he dashed it off in under four weeks.

Another young purist lives at the center of Giraudoux's next novel, *Juliette au pays des hommes* (Juliette in Men's Country, 1924). She too leaves home, only not for the tropics or even a foreign country. In a small town in central France, not unlike Giraudoux's Bellac, Juliette is engaged to Gérard; but shortly before her marriage she abruptly lights out for Paris in search of some men she has known slightly in the past. She half expects that at least one of them will prove more enlivening than she has found Gérard to be. She has gone to look for the ideal soul mate. But these older men, when she catches up with them, all appear wrapped up in their professions and themselves. On her return she settles for Gérard. In much the same way Suzanne, after her exotic adventures, settles for a provincial controller of weights and measures.

With *Bella* (1926) Giraudoux takes a new tack. In his earlier writings he had played an occasional satirical hand: *Suzanne* mocks men's depredations of nature; *Siegfried* pokes fun at French rationalism and German nationalism, and does so as forcefully as—but more gracefully than—the expressionist playwrights who were Giraudoux's contemporaries; and episode by episode *Juliette* paints satirical portraits of Paris. But *Bella* deals in personal specifics; it is a political roman à clef in which the characters obviously represent French individuals. The good-natured Dubardeau has some of the characteristics of Philippe Berthelot, an older man who had befriended Giraudoux in the diplomatic service. Dubardeau's son Philippe (a transference of the first name) acts as the novel's narrator and bears some resemblances to the author. And Dubardeau's political enemy, the flinty Rebendart, corresponds to Raymond Poincaré, who became foreign minister and later premier of France. Real statesmen of the period—Georges Clemenceau, Woodrow Wilson, and others—are named in the text to enhance its sense of actuality.

The young woman Bella functions as would-be mediator. Another in Giraudoux's line of female purists, she is the widow of Rebendart's son, but she falls in love with Philippe Dubardeau. Like a twenty-five-year-old Juliet Capulet who would do the impossible by reconciling her clan with Romeo's Montagues, she tries to persuade her father-in-law to join hands with the father of her lover. Rebendart refuses and, almost miraculously, Bella dies of disappointment. Her smile rigidifies; Philippe sees her "suddenly turn pale, drop to her knees, a little unfamiliar as yet with the motions that are braking her fall"; and "she bursts an artery."

In diplomatic circles the book set off a typically French artistic-cum-political scandal. Although meant as a defense of Berthelot, it widened the gap between Berthelot's allies and Poincaré's. But Giraudoux was already at work on its successor. The last chapter of *Bella* brings to the fore the heroine's father, Baron de Fontranges, a sad figure who in the course of the story loses his son as well as his daughter. Fontranges reappears in later novels, starting the following year with *Eglantine* (1927), in which he woos his ward, Eglantine, a young woman he adopted and raised with his own children. His friend Moïse, a banker born in the Levant, competes with him for the love of Eglantine. That two widowers in their sixties should become smitten by a woman forty years younger is not surprising: the winter-spring affairs connote the men's yearning for their vanished youth. The surprise lies in Eglantine's feelings. She is drawn indecisively to them both, believing herself safe with either one of them. Eventually she realizes that she must turn away from them, that she has been taking refuge from the world and its risks. Critics have pointed out that in the loosely defined figures of Fontranges and Moïse one can read a symbolic rivalry between Western and Eastern cultures.

A friend of Fontranges's represents yet another seeker of freedom in *Aventures de Jérôme Bardini* (Adventures of Jérôme Bardini, 1930), but not the only one in the story. Abandoning his devoted wife, child, home,

and job as a high-ranking civil servant, Bardini sails off to the United States, where he meets two more wanderers: first a young woman, Stéphy, who has also fled from an unexciting life, and subsequently a twelve-year-old boy who has, like Jacques Forestier, lost his memory; he is known simply as the Kid, a sobriquet possibly borrowed from Charlie Chaplin's famous movie released nine years before (*The Kid,* 1921). Bardini, although not divorced, undergoes a mock marriage with Stéphy, but she grows disillusioned with him and gives him up. The joyously rambling day-by-day existence he shares with the Kid similarly comes to a halt when the authorities track down the boy and reclaim him. Bardini himself finally submits to Fontranges, who has followed him to America. The triple cycle of escape and recovery closes with hints from Fontranges (and probably from the author) that Bardini's and Stéphy's—and to a lesser extent, the Kid's—desire to free themselves from the monotony of everyday living would release them not only from routine but also from responsibilities to their fellow human beings.

La France sentimentale (Sentimental France, 1932) consists of a republication of some earlier short stories, with several new ones added. In most of them characters from the novels reappear—Bardini, Fontranges, Philippe Dubardeau, Bella, and her twin sister Bellita. Critical speculation has it that these tales are either rejected chapters from the novels—comparable to movie outtakes—or preliminary sketches for chapters or elaborations of characters, ideas, situations, and themes that Giraudoux did not feel he had quite come to grips with before. Certainly he was economical as a writer in squeezing his utmost out of material that he had already plumbed. The themes relate once again to his obsessive notion that his purists color their daydreams with a false allure that makes them unrealizable; sometimes the real world gives the impression of measuring up to their dreams, but when it does, it cheats.

LATER FICTION

Giraudoux, by now a national celebrity, had his next novel serialized in the prominent literary periodical *La nouvelle revue française* before it appeared in book form. In *Combat avec l'ange* (Combat with the Angel, 1934) the angel in question is a hallucination that attacks Maléna Paz while she is in a coma. A young woman born in Latin America and now living in France, Maléna has every apparent reason to be content but torments herself by imagining she is unworthy of her lover, Jacques, and that she does not deserve her financial security and comfort: she wants to suffer for people who are deprived, and she goes in search of them. Not quite as much the purist as Giraudoux's previous heroines, Maléna is, rather, a figuration of stricken conscience who, after her "combat" with the "angel," gains a feeling of inward peace (her Spanish surname's meaning) and transmits that feeling to the man for whom Jacques works as a secretary—no less than the premier of France. This character, Brossard, is modeled on the former premier, Aristide Briand.

Brossard is dying after spending his public life in the cause of trying to patch up relations between France and Germany. He takes the sight of Maléna at his bedside as a kind of final blessing on his efforts. Maléna, often viewed by critics as an implausible case of near-psychosis, can therefore be interpreted instead as a symbolic character. Indeed, in a play written at about the same time, *Tiger at the Gates,* Giraudoux does introduce a personification of Peace, much as Aristophanes did in his *Lysistrata*. A number of Giraudoux's works have been found wanting in qualities (psychological literalness is only one) that the author was not trying to achieve, while the poetic suggestiveness he did strive for tends to be overlooked or misconstrued.

In all these novels we notice the protagonist's dissatisfaction with the humdrum, a flight from it into the unexplored, and a series of picaresque travels that amount to a quest for what Carl Jung calls self. Do the characters find that will-o'-the-wisp self? As a rule, no; they return to a preordained marriage or a family, their elation evaporated, their mood one of acceptance, even defeat. Giraudoux's last novel is no exception. In *Choix des élues* (Choices of the Elite, 1938) a French housewife named Edmée, living in America with her engineer husband and two children, takes her daughter away with her to visit friends—and stays away. Her West Coast excursion lasts for years as she moves restlessly to Hollywood, San Francisco, and Santa Barbara. In the course of those years she works in a movie studio and as a housekeeper. For a time she has an affair with a man she does not love. Gradually she also loses touch with her daughter, Claudie, for whom she at first had a possessive, almost worshipful affection. She rather than Claudie is the dependent in a relationship reminiscent of Jérôme Bardini's with the Kid. And rather as Fontranges comes to summon Bardini back to his home, so Edmée's son, now an adult, reappears like destiny to break his mother's spell. In the closing scene Giraudoux tells us that Claudie, who has married, has already caught the unease from her mother, as though it were a hereditary ailment, and will go off on her own quest. What, then, are the "choices of the elite"? In the French title the word for "elite" or "privileged" (*élues*) is feminine plural and therefore refers to Edmée and her daughter, but it is also cognate with the English "elusive." The two women, blessed with most of the material goods they could want, lack adventure, which they see as a sort of asexual "romance." They choose to pursue this elusive ideal, but they are not sure what it is or how to recognize it. And they do not find it. But was it ever attainable in the first place?

There remains to be considered one novel, published posthumously. Giraudoux wrote *La menteuse* (*Lying Woman,* 1969) in the mid 1930's but held it back, possibly for revisions, although it has scenes unequaled in his other novels for their dramatic intensity. Its lying woman, Nelly, is the only Giraudoux heroine who does meet the man of her dreams. His name is Reginald, and for a time she enchants him. She does so by lying about her past and present, pretending to be what she is not: a member of a superior social class, the widow of an aristocrat. In fact, she has been previously involved with three men, and she again takes up with one of them, Gaston, after his return to Paris from a business trip. Yet she is still desperately in love with Reginald. She is also reluctant to hurt Gaston by breaking off with him. Juggling the two love affairs terrifies her; she grows incautious, lying more outrageously than before. Reginald comes to suspect her with one of those intuitive flashes that Giraudoux's characters are prone to and that make laborious plot maneuvers unnecessary. In a plane crash Gaston loses all memory of Nelly, and although this might seem like the sort of plottiness the author strove to avoid, he uses it ironically. Reginald proves to be a prig: even when Nelly is freed from her commitment to Gaston, he cannot forgive her lies.

Enter Baron de Fontranges again. He too falls in love with Nelly, having lost Eglantine. When Reginald continues to keep away from her, Nelly accepts the Baron's proposal. Then comes an amazing scene, worthy of one of the renunciations in Corneille's dramas. Fontranges, who has divined that Nelly loves Reginald, goes to see him and offers him the option of marrying her before he does. He promises that her marriage to Reginald will transform her, will make her everything that she purported to be in her lies, and therefore will cancel out the lies. Reginald responds politely, noncommittally. He has six days in which to intervene before the wedding. Fontranges expects him to attend the wedding, which he does, but in order to stop it, which he does not. He hides until the ceremony has finished, allowing Nelly to marry on the rebound this older, saintly man who will be good to her but whom she does not love. By virtue of the author's skill, Nelly, despite her lies, becomes a sympathetic figure whose

plight is almost tragic; she has walked into a trap of her own contriving from which Reginald could, and, morally speaking, should, have extricated her. Her fault, we perceive, consists not in lying but in being unable to lie convincingly or to cover up the lies—if she had been truthful, Reginald would not have loved her—or it consists in falling in love so helplessly with an "ideal" figure who is a defective person.

EARLY PLAYS

Giraudoux the twenty-six-year-old fiction writer had been lucky to excite the interest of Bernard Grasset, who published *Provinciales* and the bulk of his subsequent writings. Giraudoux the playwright in his mid forties was luckier still. In 1926 he was introduced to Jouvet—director, actor, designer, and one of the most daring French theater figures of the 1920's and 1930's, who made a policy of producing mostly new plays. Giraudoux had already attempted a dramatization of *My Friend from Limousin*. About a month later, poring over his first, lengthy draft of a full playscript with Jouvet, he cut it back drastically, reorganized scenes, rewrote and reordered lines, and halved the number of characters. Six versions went by before the theatrical compression called *Siegfried* was ready. It was first performed on 3 May 1928 at Jouvet's playhouse, the Comédie des Champs-Elysées.

As the four-act play opens, we learn that Siegfried (Forestier) has risen in less than seven years from being a naked, wounded amnesiac on the battlefield to becoming not merely an eminent German politician but the German chancellor. This ascent has happened largely because of the ministrations of a young woman named Eva, his nurse in the field hospital. She taught him the new language, steeped him in German history and culture, and is now his closest adviser.

His adversary, Baron von Zelten, the German who loves France, knows that Siegfried is

JEAN GIRAUDOUX

the "reborn" Frenchman and calls on Forestier's former lover Geneviève to come from Paris and identify him. Siegfried would like to learn French, he says, and Geneviève, whom he no longer recognizes, agrees to give him lessons. Zelten tries to supplant Siegfried as chancellor, but the Germans—the military, the public, and the politicians—want Siegfried. They treat him as a hero. In his tall, fair, striking presence they see the Siegfried of legend, the leader who can revive their country's fortunes. Here Giraudoux prophesies, unknowingly but with the prescience of a diplomat, historian, and artist, the welcome given a few years later to Adolf Hitler—an Austrian and therefore, like Siegfried, an *Ausländer*—by a Germany in political and financial turmoil in the aftermath of World War I. But Siegfried is no Hitlerian demagogue. Quite the opposite. Considerate and good-humored, he has in him something of the Giralducian purist's strain. Nevertheless, his belief in a Germany with a God-given destiny, inculcated by Eva and other associates, including the military, suggests the danger Germany faced from someone who promulgated similar doctrines and happened to be a power-grabber and a promoter of hatred.

Acts 1, 2, and 3 take place in the postwar capital of Gotha. Act 4 is set in a railroad station built squarely on the border between Germany and France. Geneviève waits there. Siegfried now knows who he was: a poet and political journalist who reported as a conservative for one journal, as a socialist for another. But he has not regained his memory. He must now pick up the pieces of his old life and relearn what he is. Torn between love for his recent nationality (represented by Eva) and love for his original one (Geneviève), he crosses the border at last and catches the train with Geneviève back to Paris.

The ending is not upbeat. There is poignancy in his plight, much as there is in many of the play's exchanges, especially those that take place between him and Geneviève before he has uncovered his origins. He has abdi-

cated, exchanged his power and fame for an unknown but certainly humble future. As Geneviève puts it, he chooses "between the magnificent life that does not belong to him and the emptiness that does." Yet he carries in his soul the German he has been, and he will not try to efface it, for "there are no experiences so opposed that they cannot be contained in the life of one human being." The German dramatist Bertolt Brecht makes a comparable assertion (with an entirely different purpose) in *Mann ist Mann* (*A Man's a Man*, 1926), written in the years between the appearance of Giraudoux's novel and its dramatization: Galy Gay, the mild-mannered porter, metamorphoses into Jeraiah Jip, a ferocious soldier, after he dons an army uniform.

Jouvet secured an unusually strong cast for his production: Pierre Renoir as Siegfried, Valentine Tessier as Geneviève, and Lucienne Bogaert as Eva, with Michel Simon and himself in cameo roles. Even so, neither the playwright nor the director expected the heartily positive notices, the public acclaim, and the substantial run. In 1952, seven years after the end of World War II, Paris saw a triumphant revival of *Siegfried*. Giraudoux and Jouvet were not alive to witness it.

In 1928 their partnership had just begun. Giraudoux eagerly set to work. If *Siegfried* had dealt tragicomically with a concealed identity, his next play took over a well-worn mythical plot about borrowed identities—so worn, in fact, that he claimed the Amphitryon tale had served thirty-seven previous playwrights. To date nobody has bothered to track down all thirty-seven, including the Greek original, but versions existed then by Plautus in Latin, Jean de Rotrou and Molière in French, John Dryden in English, and, in German, one by Kleist, whose surname Giraudoux had appropriated for his Siegfried.

Amphitryon 38 is not a farce, like Plautus' and Molière's, but a drawing-room comedy without the drawing room. The first and last of the three acts occupy a terrace near the palace of Amphitryon, king and commanding general of Thebes, that birthplace of doomed Oedipus, Antigone, her brothers, Creon, and the god of the drama, Dionysus, while act 2 lets us discreetly into the bedroom of Amphitryon's queen, Alcmene.

Giraudoux imparts several twists to the ancient story. His Jupiter arrives on earth in the likeness of her husband to make love to Alcmene, the most desirable and virtuous woman in the world, and to plant in her the seed of Hercules, the half-god who will become mankind's savior. As his first twist, Giraudoux has Jupiter plead with her for the assignation; she declines with a display of wit, charm, and courtesy, but she doesn't know that Jupiter took her the night before in the guise of Amphitryon and has already impregnated her. As a second twist, Alcmene, expecting him to visit her that night, arranges to have her bed taken over by Leda, who was Jupiter's partner once before when he glided down from Olympus as a swan. Leda longs to repeat the experience, but Alcmene mistakenly sends Amphitryon, not Jupiter, into the bedroom with Leda.

In his third twist, the playwright anticipates *Tiger at the Gates* in connecting Jupiter's love as an objective with warfare as the means to it: the god concocts a swift war between Thebes and Athens, two city-states that have no reason to quarrel, so that Amphitryon will be away fighting when Jupiter seduces his wife. Behind its bantering tone, act 1 dwells on war's horrors. Amphitryon's servant calls peace "the intermission between two wars" and exclaims in its praise: "How good it is to sleep in a land ungutted by trenches . . . among birds, dogs, cats, and rats that don't know the taste of human meat." In contrast, a warrior demands, "Who prefers peace to the glory of hunger and thirst, plunging through mud, and dying for his country?"

Jupiter offers Alcmene immortality if she will love him. But the faithful purist of a wife cleverly replies that immortality for her alone would betray the rest of humanity. For her counter-offer she invites the king of the gods to

be her friend! Seeing that he cannot snare her with words, he relents, accepts the friendship, and departs, letting it be known that he has annulled the adultery. Alcmene does suspect that he has had his way with her, but he denies it. She has been deceived twice, the second time by herself when she maneuvered another woman into her husband's bed.

Giraudoux shows no scenes of lovemaking in the action. Still, the audiences, evidently expecting a commercial sex-tease, gave it an eight-month run after its opening on 8 November 1929. It added luster not only to the playwright's reputation but also to those of Tessier (Alcmene), Renoir (Amphitryon), and Jouvet, who played Jupiter's companion, Mercury, and directed.

Love and war intertwine more tightly than before as twin motives for the action of *Judith.* The book in the Apocrypha, the story's source, and many subsequent retellings, including D. W. Griffith's film *Judith of Bethulia* (1913), take a young woman out of her besieged city during the invasion of Israel by the Assyrians to confront the enemy general Holofernes. Infatuated, he invites her into his tent for a feast. As soon as he falls asleep she takes out his sword, cuts off his head, and returns with it to Bethulia and its exultant, delivered Israelites.

Giraudoux, however, alters and modernizes many significant details. Judith is not the biblical widow but a spoiled young society lady, ripe for love. She ventures into the Assyrian camp only after the Bethulians call on her to save them. The Holofernes she encounters is no rude barbarian but a polished orator, a dignified charmer who rescues her from his subordinates' teasing and swears to liberate her from the power of Jehovah. Judith herself defies the Hebrew myth signally when she falls in love with Holofernes and blasphemes against God, who allowed her to go on this mission and has turned her into a "symbol of hate." She kills Holofernes by driving a knife into his heart, then longs to be reunited with him in death. She has killed him, she says, in order to kill herself.

With a climactic theatrical coup the playwright reveals an Assyrian guard to be an angel, one of the heavenly cohort who protected her and later bore down on her will and on the knife. God, the angel tells her, kept her sexually intact during her lovemaking. In the final scene Judith passively accepts the role decreed for her. She will live in seclusion, become the Israelites' judge who pronounces sentence on the wicked, and acquire the reputation of a saint.

Here Giraudoux observes the tradition of the Greek drama, according to which young virgins (Antigone, Iphigenia, Macaria, Polyxena, and others) serve as sacrificial steps in the gods' long-range plans. Jupiter's ravishing of Alcmene will result in Hercules' twelve labors, which free the earth of monsters. Judith's act of murder similarly arises from Jehovah's intention, defended by the angel, to convert sin into holiness. Her personal sufferings do not count; she has been used as a divine instrument.

After its opening on 4 November 1931 *Judith* did not sit well with the public. Then, as today, a heroic deed preferably proceeds from strictly heroic motives. In the biblical story Holofernes falls asleep after carousing; there is no suggestion that Judith gave herself to him. Giraudoux's Judith not only indulges in ecstatic lovemaking (unseen, between acts 2 and 3) but she also glories in having been "tainted" by him. She murders Holofernes to preserve the purity of their love and afterward voices no regrets. The reviews acknowledged the strength and verve of the dialogue but found the play depressing. Such is often the fate of tragedies in the twentieth century. Even when they hark back to ancient stories, they do not provide the conventional catharsis and uplift.

Some appraisers of Giraudoux link the alternation of serious and comic plays to different moods in his private life. After *Siegfried* he felt happy and successful: he wrote the effervescent *Amphitryon 38*. His marriage turned rocky and he turned sour: he gave us the

somber *Judith*. He got good notices for his snapping-up of mostly old trifles in *La France sentimentale:* he produced an entertaining and fantastical *Intermezzo.* Do such biographical guesses make sense? How long does a mood last? An hour? A day? Five days? Surely not for as long as it takes to complete a play. Besides, any play infects its author with its own moods while he struggles with it. And then, most of Giraudoux's writings are not consistent in their moods: his serious drama coruscates with wit, and his comedies have their moments of affecting melancholy, as happens in *Intermezzo.*

In that play's setting, a small town much like Bellac, everything is going right. Wives walk out on husbands who beat them. Children refuse to put up with mistreatment from parents. Lottery prizes go to people who need the winnings. Even the rare fatal accident takes the lives of old people, not young ones. Is there a spell on the town? If so, it has two likely causes. First, the ghost of a good-looking young man sidles around the desolate spots, generally at dusk; he may or may not be the shade of the fellow who once slew his wife and her lover and then chose or did not choose to drown himself. Second, the substitute teacher at the girls' school, delightful young Isabelle, has induced her pupils to love learning and all natural phenomena. To complicate matters, she has fallen in love with the Ghost, if he really is a ghost.

Local officials are not displeased with the recent turn of events, but a district inspector arrives to investigate the Ghost and the apparently enchanted town. A figure of fun to the audience but not to the characters onstage, he is a Giralducian pragmatist who abhors what he calls superstitions and irregularities. His men shoot the Ghost and kill it. But it reappears. Whether it was a ghost before is now immaterial, like its present form—in which it has more than one rendezvous with Isabelle.

The structural conflicts in the play thus consist of two triangles, one communal, one personal. The larger, communal triangle features a contest for the soul and control of the town between the Inspector, an outsider, and the imaginative supernatural, unnamed powers. In the personal triangle an agreeable Controller of Weights and Measures competes with the Ghost for Isabelle's affection. He wins her because he creates a wonderfully persuasive tissue of arguments in favor of marrying him and taking pleasure in the here and now instead of sighing for the ectoplasm that would be accessible to her (like Holofernes to Judith) only on the far side of dying. When she accepts the Controller, the Ghost vanishes, the Inspector triumphs, and everything in the town starts going wrong. As in several of Giraudoux's novels, the heroine settles for an ordinary life, the most attractive one sanctioned by fate under the circumstances, but a spiritual letdown nonetheless.

MIDDLE PLAYS

Jouvet had moved his company in early 1933 from the Comédie des Champs-Élysées to the Théâtre Pigalle and thence to a more capacious and convenient playhouse, the Athénée, which was renamed the Théâtre Louis Jouvet. He wanted a play from Giraudoux to inaugurate his new house; by the next season he had mounted four of them. He revived *Amphitryon 38,* a certified crowd-pleaser. Giraudoux meanwhile completed a translation, suggested by Jouvet, of *The Constant Nymph* (1924), dramatized in English by the theater and film director Basil Dean from Margaret Kennedy's best-selling novel. He worked from—but slightly *away* from—the Dean script and called his adaptation *Tessa* (1934).

Tessa belongs with Giraudoux's winsome and innocent young heroines, although she is rather more fragile than the others. She loves an older man, a composer. He marries a different woman but ultimately leaves her for Tessa. Not long after, Tessa dies. The play, a tear-jerker sharpened by Giraudoux's language and with some—but not enough—of its more maudlin effects suppressed, did well for Jouvet at the box office and won him applause for his performance as the lover. Madeleine Ozeray played a dainty Tessa.

A year later Jouvet put together two new Giraudoux plays, the one-act romp *Supplément au voyage de Cook* (*The Virtuous Island,* 1937) prefacing the more substantial *Tiger at the Gates.* He assumed leading roles in both. *The Virtuous Island* revisits the latitudes of *Suzanne and the Pacific,* only this time the island is populated Tahiti in the late eighteenth century. A middle-aged, missionary-minded British couple, Mr. and Mrs. Banks, disembark from the frigate of the explorer Captain Cook. Their plans to civilize the islanders by teaching them manners and monogamy go astray when a Tahitian maiden almost seduces Mr. Banks, and his wife is wooed by the island's crown prince. The Banks pair, magnificently unaware of how ridiculous they appear out of their element, commit comic arabesques in their speech and behavior, but Giraudoux does not altogether deny them sympathy. For them civilization means repression: Mrs. Banks desires the men who waft into her dreams, not the men she meets in the flesh. The lesson the Tahitians learn from their guests, veneration for the ways of more advanced societies, boils down to Pierre Proudhon's famous motto that property, the hallmark of civilized society, is theft.

The French title of *Tiger at the Gates* comes from the play's opening line, spoken by Andromache: "The Trojan War will not take place," a hopeful sentiment rather than a conviction, although it is shared by most of the other women of Troy. But what of Troy's men? Led by King Priam, they will not relinquish Helen, wife of King Menelaus of Sparta. She was abducted by Priam's son Paris, who is also Andromache's brother-in-law. The enormous Greek army has crossed the Mediterranean Sea to retake Helen. It waits at the gates of Troy. Its diplomats, Ulysses and Ajax, arrive to bargain with Andromache's husband, Hector, who commands the Trojan forces.

Hector, a great warrior, has just returned from a campaign in which he wiped out every enemy soldier. He knows the sufferings brought about by war and its meager gains, if any. He takes preparatory steps to return Helen to the Greeks. She admits that she does not love Paris, although she likes the way he makes love, and she expresses her willingness to return to Sparta. However, she thinks such an outcome unlikely. As the play's two acts surge forward, her intuition proves correct. Hector puts himself out to conciliate the Greek representatives, even tolerating abuse from Ajax, and he imposes his will ruthlessly on his Trojan followers to ensure that they go along with his peacemaking. But war fever has already heated them up.

The Trojans lust to conquer, and they lust to retain the beauteous Helen: the two lusts are made by the author to seem manifestations of the same urge. Hector negotiates skillfully with Ulysses, convincing him that a war will be fruitless for both sides, and he would succeed in averting the conflict but for that urge. As always, it is the older men, the men past fighting, as well as a rabble-rousing poet named Demokos, who cry out for war. Hector stabs Demokos to silence him, thinking that it would be better to have one Trojan dead than all Troy massacred and ruined. But before he expires Demokos blames Ajax for his death. Ajax is then set upon and slain by the Trojan mob, and the war is on with a vengeance, a double vengeance. The tiger of destiny, stalking outside Troy, enters with a roar as "the gates of war slowly open. They reveal Helen in an embrace"—not with Paris but with his and Hector's young brother Troilus. Helen has seized the hearts of the young Trojans as well as the old ones; but the irony of this final image hits the audience like a blow: the war will be fought to keep Helen for Paris, and here she is amusing herself with an adolescent.

Tiger predates by three years the frantic meetings and the "peace in our time" pact between the British, French, and Germans at Munich, and by four years the start of World War II. But its action does not really parallel the events that led up to that war nor, indeed, those that led to the outbreak of World War I in 1914. It does not have to in order to be prophetic. As a study of the relentless movement of nation-states into periodic collisions, it has much to say about the attitudes responsible for all wars. Giraudoux makes clear that national pride is as distinctive from personal pride as crowd psychology is from individual feelings, motives, and acts. Despite the best intentions in the world, Hector is as much to blame as anybody else. In killing Demokos he struck the first lethal blow.

With *Electra* Giraudoux illustrates once again his determination to mingle comic and serious elements in one play by adding to the grim main plot a subplot that reflects it in an amusing and anachronistic manner, rather as Shakespeare and his Jacobean contemporaries once did. He also intersperses among the scenes some ruminative and, at times, farcical choral interludes. The dark, sensual myths of the house of Atreus have fascinated playwrights from the three Greek tragedians to Eugene O'Neill in his *Mourning Becomes Electra* (1931). Agamemnon's murder at the hands of his queen Clytemnestra and her lover Aegisthus, who is Agamemnon's cousin, has terrible consequences. Electra the princess provokes her brother Orestes into killing their mother and Aegisthus. In Aeschylus' trilogy *The Oresteia,* Orestes, as punishment for his matricide, is haunted by the chorus of *Erinyes* or Furies. Electra's complex, as Freud dubbed it, commits her to retaliation at any cost for her beloved father's death, and Giraudoux's Electra is his most inflexibly purist heroine. She must have justice, even if it wrecks Argos. Out of the devastation, she believes, there will emerge a cleansed city-state.

When the play begins, Aegisthus, now governor of Argos, has achieved prosperity and a tranquil life for its citizens. He has also arranged to neutralize Electra, the one person who is discontented and an irritant to him, by marrying her off to a gardener and so separating her from the palace and from access to power. Orestes' return to his homeland as a grown man—his mother had sent him abroad when he was a child—puts a stop to the marriage. Aegisthus now pleads with Electra not to oppose him, to ratify his rule and publicly approve his marriage to her mother. It is her duty, he says, to do what she can to save Argos from an invasion by the neighboring Corinthians. He advances wise and persuasive arguments. Electra scorns them: the state is infected and, with its present leadership, not worth saving.

He and Clytemnestra go off to parley with the Corinthians, who are already murdering and plundering in the streets nearby. But Orestes catches up with them and kills them both. The play ends with a report of the chaotic offstage events and the thin promise of a dawn, a new day. But Electra's implacable justice, now realized, has unleashed the Furies.

The latter are represented not by hags but by small girls who have grown magically taller and older each time they appear. They gloat over the cruelties perpetrated in the palace and the ones still to come. To supplement the choral activities of this spiteful, sinister trio, Giraudoux provides some extraordinary narrative speeches for two characters on the fringes of the play—the Gardener, who was Electra's intended, and the Beggar, who seems to embody an unnamed god. The Beggar sees through the smooth rhetoric of Aegisthus though pretending he doesn't know what it means: "I don't understand men's words. . . . I understand men." It is the Beggar who, as if with second sight, describes the offstage deaths of Clytemnestra and Aegisthus, graphically, while they are happening.

The subplot presents a second unfaithful wife, young Agatha, who is married to a grandfatherly president of the Argive tribunal. Like Clytemnestra, she has a lover. Unlike Clytemnestra, who had reason to hate Agamemnon for sacrificing their daughter Iphigenia and for bringing home a Trojan mistress, Agatha holds no grudges against her husband other than that he bores her. She stands in contrast to the play's other beautiful young woman, Electra, for she imitates the adultery of the rulers. For Electra there will be no marriage and no deceptions—no lies of any kind. If she has justice, she says, she has everything.

Electra has sometimes been taken as a call to arms. When Giraudoux had proposed in *Siegfried* a friendly mutuality between France and Germany, he had not foreseen the triumph of Nazism in Europe. Now the French could no longer afford to dither in the face of Hitler's annexations in Central Europe. The war must be joined, if only to preserve some decency in the character of France. Did Giraudoux mean to go this far in recommending war rather than implying that it would come inevitably, as in *Tiger at the Gates*? He may simply have been making a drama out of an irresolvable clash between opponents both of whom insist they are in the right—G. W. F. Hegel's prescription for tragedy, deduced from the *Antigone* of Sophocles. And yet as a highly placed diplomatic official, he was certainly privy to the frenzied discussions among France's politicians over whether to intervene militarily, and if so, how soon.

While Giraudoux practiced diplomacy as a profession and also commented on it in his novels and plays, borrowing from its methods for his artistry—after all, every conflict in the drama consists of negotiations and strategic ploys—he went beyond writing *for* the theater to writing *about* theater, sometimes in the plays themselves. Nine crowded years after his debut as a playwright he crammed into a one-act comedy many observations on theater as literature and as a performance art and put them into the mouths of characters named after, and played by, Jouvet and his troupe. *Paris Impromptu* has a direct story line. In the play, Jouvet is working on Molière's comparable one-act comedy about the theater, *L'Impromptu de Versailles* (*The Rehearsal at Versailles*, 1663). He is interrupted by Robineau, "a former professor of grammar, member of the

1054

JEAN GIRAUDOUX

Chamber of Deputies, a party leader," who is a theater buff looking for a suitable receptacle for "a large sum" of public funds collected from increased taxes. (The name Robineau is a play on the French word for "faucet.")

At first Jouvet behaves coldly toward the intruder, as Molière does in his play when pestered by a tiresome marquis. But as soon as he learns Robineau's identity he and his actors talk volubly about the art of the theater, criticism of the theater, the economy of the theater, the state of the theater, perils in putting on theater, and the therapeutic effects of theater on its audiences. In the final scene, Jouvet advises Robineau to use his subsidy to chase the moneylenders out of the temple and so cleanse the theater of its rotten elements—in other words, to support the noncommercial theater so that it competes more effectively with commercial productions and defeats them. But just then Robineau starts to rise up and up on a "glory," a flying machine. As he "ascends majestically" out of sight, like a god at the end of a Greek drama, he blissfully intones the words, "This is really theater!" The play does not record that Jouvet received any government subsidy.

As a tribute to Molière, the play brought Giraudoux an honor. The Comédie-Française, France's oldest national theater, known as "the House of Molière," commissioned a work from him. His one-act *Cantique des cantiques* (*Song of Songs,* 1938), directed there by Jouvet, delicately evokes the end of a love affair.

The President of the Republic meets his young mistress, Florence, on a fine October day at an open-air cafe. She tells him she is marrying another man, Jérôme. She confesses that she still loves the President and finds him wise, kind, a joy to be with—in every way admirable—whereas Jérôme is a blunderer, constantly tripping, falling, wounding himself against inanimate objects. He is, she says, "the god of little accidents." She doesn't even remember what he looks like. And yet, while the cafe's waiter, cashier, and manager eavesdrop on the conversation, hoping the couple

will stay together, Florence bids good-bye to the man she still loves. Jérôme comes to claim her. She hands back the valuables the President has given her and takes a cheap ring from Jérôme. He behaves tactlessly, confirming Florence's description. But his lack of affectation, his naturalness, has somehow won her. Worst of all, he is young. The President ruefully and unprotestingly departs in a limousine for an appointment with the prime minister.

The President's hopelessness, Florence's candor, Jérôme's clumsy innocence, and the outdoor setting near the Bois de Boulogne confer on this brief, autumnal comedy a sense of the pangs caused by unspoken regrets.

LATER PLAYS

A different triangle, two women to one man, forms the underlying structure of *Ondine,* a medieval fantasy in which a German knight named Hans falls in love with a water sprite, an "undine" called simply Ondine. He finds her in a French peasant's hut. She has supernatural powers, but she will eagerly relinquish them and become a woman in order to marry Hans. After a feverish courtship Hans cannot wait to take her out of the forest with him to show the world her perfection. They go to the German palace from which Hans had set out. The king's adopted daughter, Bertha, had been Hans's fiancée and had sent him on his knightly quest to prove himself worthy of her before their marriage. The old attraction between Hans and Bertha rekindles itself, partly out of nostalgia, partly because Hans now feels he cannot measure up to Ondine's love. She "has nothing but me for thoughts, for food, for her god. . . . She pushes love as far as blasphemy."

Ondine, who has meanwhile become a human adolescent, not yet fifteen, finds herself out of tune with the hypocrisy and insincere chivalry she encounters among the courtiers. Seeing that Hans has grown disenchanted with her, she gives him up—another renunciation in the name of love—knowing that if Hans has broken his vows to her, the king of all the undines, "the Old One," will take Hans's life.

By act 3 she has reverted to her element, the water. But a fisherman catches her in a net—a mermaid without a tail!—and she goes on trial as a witch. The Old One rescues her from the trial's farcical proceedings. Although she insists that Hans did not deceive her and that she deceived him (another gesture of self-sacrifice), she is shown to be lying, like a human being, and Hans must undergo punishment. He gradually weakens as his life slips away from him. At the same time Ondine loses her human attributes, including her memory of having been a young woman. Noticing his body, she asks why "the beautiful young man" lies there inert. On being told he is dead and cannot be revived, she murmurs, "How sad! I could have loved him so much."

Ondine is packed with theatrical devices: a chorus of undines who, like the heroine, yearn for an all-consuming love; magic performed by the Old One and his conjuring-up of scenes that foretell the future; Giraudoux's hinting at a larger theme: another metaphorical union between France and Germany, but a union that, this time, is doomed (the play opened on 27 April 1939 and ran beyond the outbreak of World War II on 3 September); and a matching of opposites, Ondine and Bertha, reminiscent of Judith the virgin and the whore Suzanne who accompanies her to the tent of Holofernes.

In *Giraudoux: Three Faces of Destiny* Robert Cohen, referring to a line from the text to the effect that Ondine is a dream, comments: "Ondine exists because Hans dreams of her. Ondine is the fire in his blood and the carnal taste in his mouth." Hans's knightly quest is, then, a delusion that culminates not merely in self-discovery—he bitterly sums himself up as "a miserable, mediocre human being"—but also in his overreaching himself. His death and Ondine's bemused and final wish to see

him restored to life bring the play to a plaintive end.

By mid 1941 Jouvet could no longer put up with the restraints imposed on him by the German occupation forces in France, who would not let him stage two of his favorite authors, Jules Romains and Giraudoux, and he gladly accepted an invitation to tour some Latin American countries where he could revive *Tiger at the Gates, Electra,* and *Ondine,* as well as introduce, in 1942, a new one-act play mailed to him by Giraudoux, *L'Apollon de Bellac (The Apollo of Bellac,* 1946).

The Apollo in question is a nondescript-looking man who appears to a young woman named Agnes. She is looking for a job with a company that comes up with "inventions large and small" to order. But she cannot get past the reception clerk until the mysterious Apollo advises her to tell men that they are beautiful. She practices on a statue, which proudly twirls its mustache; on a fly, which sparkles in the sunlight; on a chandelier, which spontaneously lights up; on the recalcitrant clerk, who turns cooperative; and then on the president of the company—and beyond. Flattery gets her everywhere. She winds up standing hand in hand with the chairman of the board. In the meantime her miracle-working mentor has disappeared. Is Giraudoux serious about this facile optimism? Quite possibly. The Apollo of Bellac's advice, if taken to heart, might do wonders for the corporate world. And everywhere else.

During Jouvet's absence, Giraudoux's next play, *Sodome et Gomorrhe (Sodom and Gomorrah,* 1943), was performed at Jacques Hébertot's theater in Paris on 11 October 1943. It starkly contradicts the assumptions of *The Apollo of Bellac.* Men and women, it maintains, are irreconcilable.

God sends an archangel and an angel to earth to warn that he will spare humanity only on condition that at least one loving couple can be found in the apparently loveless, and therefore sinful, twin cities of biblical notoriety. In a prologue the Archangel looks down on Sodom and announces the divine ultimatum to a gardener. The play's viewpoint then swoops down, as if with the aid of a zoom lens, and focuses on a couple, Lia and Jean, in whom God discerns some hope of an example for other couples. Alas, God has erred. Lia and Jean's five-year marriage has foundered. Jean would preserve it anyway and keep a presentable face on it, but Lia's caustic, frequently savage cries of disappointment will not allow for any repairs, much less a new start.

Perhaps if they swapped partners with another couple, Ruth and Jacques, a decent marriage might be salvaged? But no. A brief crossover experiment fails. Even an ostensibly happy pair, Samson and Delilah, have based their marriage on a lie, an inequality, for Delilah bosses and deceives her husband under the guise of caring for him. Giraudoux does not allude directly to the story of Samson's betrayal by Delilah as told in the Book of Judges, but it is implicit in his drama.

The source of the discontent is woman. Lia wants not a man but an angel; she actually tries to seduce the Angel, who keeps watch over the city. Her lengthy harangues against life, men, her fate, and God's unfairness form the backbone of the play, repellent and at the same time fascinating in their severity and bleakness. These tirades, passionately delivered in that first production by the great actress Edwige Feuillère, mark the play as the nearest modern equivalent to a tragedy by Corneille or Racine, an interrupted monologue chastely freed of the encumbrances (and the relief) of stage activity. One French critic pronounced *Sodom and Gomorrah* "not a play but a dissertation." A condemnation is more like it: not of a woman's rage or all women's rage, but of the institution of marriage and the false glow of prospects it holds out. When he wrote it Giraudoux's own marriage had broken up, a probable reason why he names the principal male character after himself and why, feeling impotently that he would never emerge from a tangle of hatred, he has Lia declare that Jean "is weakness"—not just weak, but *all* weakness.

As Lia spurns the last chance for life to continue, the world crumbles. One horse survives and the Gardener has saved a single rose, but humanity is finished. Yet amid the destruction we hear Lia and Jean still squabbling in the void as the Angel remarks, "Death was not enough. The scene goes on"—a comic touch that reinforces the drama's harsh meanings.

Jouvet sailed back to France in early 1945 after adventures and misadventures: a theater fire in Buenos Aires, a truckful of scenery designed for five shows lost in the Andes, a flu epidemic, strikes, and two members of the company recalled to France for military service. The following December he opened *La folle de Chaillot* (*The Madwoman of Chaillot*, 1945), which Giraudoux had sent him several years before. The playwright had died before Jouvet's return, but his fantasy and its assortment of outrageous characters matched the exuberant spirit of the postwar months, and it ran longer than any of his previous plays. Jouvet had to close it to make way for an incoming show while it was still playing to full houses.

The madwoman of the title, who calls herself the Countess Aurélie, is a grotesquely garbed aristocratic bag lady who lives in a cavernous retreat belowground in the stylish sixteenth arrondissement of Paris. Overhearing talk by a group of loathsome speculators who scheme to wreck the neighborhood (and perhaps the whole metropolis) by digging oil wells there, she devises a counter-plan. With a band of helpers recruited from three other "madwomen," the "king" of the sewer men, a ragpicker, and other friends off the streets, she holds a mock trial of the oilmen. The "court" finds them guilty, and she asks all those people present for the right, which they grant her, to exterminate the absent defendants.

She then summons the oilmen to tell them she has located oil below her quarters. Arriving in limousines and cabs, the procession of prospecting engineers, power brokers, presidents of interlocking boards of directors, press agents, and other flunkies hand the Countess a gold brick as payment, get her to sign waivers to her share of the profits, steal back the gold brick, and troop eagerly into a hole in the wall "from which a circular staircase winds into the bowels of the earth." A huge stone closes the hold on them forever.

The Countess, who has carried around with her for thirty years the remembrance of a man she loved, urges a hesitant young couple who met each other during the escapade to kiss, now, or in an hour the girl will be another madwoman and the boy will have a white beard. They do kiss. And *voilà*—the world is saved, she cries, saved as it could not be in *Sodom and Gomorrah.* It is saved, one might add, not only from the brutalities of commerce but also from people's apathy toward the marvels of nature. The air clears, pigeons fly again, grass springs up, passersby on the sidewalks clasp one another in friendship.

From the heady atmosphere of this modern morality play, with its cartoon-like characters and rapid, wildly inventive dialogue, the conclusion seems simple-minded: steer the rats into the sewers, where they belong. And it hit home after the war years with their black-marketeering, collaboration with the Nazis, and other disgraces. Since Giraudoux wrote it during the war, it can equally be seen as a call to throw off all traces of the invaders and to rebuild the life of France spiritually instead of becoming fixated on technological advance, which brings in its wake destruction alongside construction. *The Madwoman* has been faulted for the all-out badness of its villains and the all-out goodness of the Countess and her allies. But there is another way of looking at the conflict. It has no pragmatists, no "realistic" compromisers. It consists of a struggle between one set of purists whose only motive is greed and another set of purists who, led by the Countess, mean to exterminate the other side. In this play Giraudoux abandoned his old formula for a new one.

In August 1951 Jouvet died. His contributions to Giraudoux's public reception can hardly be exaggerated. He meticulously staged all but two of the plays. He took on large and small roles and rewarded the author and his audiences by his performances in all of them, from Hector, Hans, and himself (in *Paris Impromptu*) to the godly Beggar in *Electra* and the lawyerly Ragpicker in *The Madwoman.* He solicited settings from Christian Bérard, Édouard Vuillard, Camille Cipra, Pavel Tchelichew, and other masters of theatrical design. And in enhancing Giraudoux's reputation as a dramatist, he helped enhance his standing as a novelist and diplomat. A man who had so much to say in the theater, and said it so well through so many distinctive voices, all of which were immediately identifiable as his, had to be taken with the utmost seriousness in his every endeavor.

Jouvet performed a final task for his friend in collating several drafts of a late play, but he never got to stage that work. Giraudoux's widow kept delaying permission for the first production. Then *Pour Lucrèce* (*Duel of Angels,* 1953) passed into the care of Jean-Louis Barrault, another supremely gifted director. Barrault's wife, Madeleine Renaud, had already played Florence in *Song of Songs* and now assumed the leading role in *Duel of Angels,* that of Lucile, the very soul of purity—and prudishness.

In Aix-en-Provence, the city in southern France notable for its remnants of Roman architecture, Lucile enacts a nineteenth-century version of the rape of the faithful Roman wife, Lucrezia. With a horror of carnality that exceeds Isabella's in William Shakespeare's *Measure for Measure* (1604), she believes she has the ability to detect adulterous persons merely by looking at them; she claims to see insects and reptiles crawling on their features. She is herself spotless, has never had sex with her impossibly puritanical husband, and dresses in virginal white. Her opposite, another married woman, named Paola, sustains something like twenty love affairs on the side, more than most people can manage in a lifetime. Lucile "reads" Paola's lasciviousness in her face and reports on it to Paola's incredibly trusting spouse. Incensed by this betrayal of one woman by another, Paola takes a cruel revenge, crueler than she intends. She arranges to have Lucile drugged and abducted for a night; then she pretends that Lucile was ravished by a local philanderer, one of Paola's own lovers. When Lucile reveals what she thinks happened, her husband, the local magistrate, berates and renounces her. Feeling shamed and sullied, Lucile shocks Paola and her accomplices by swallowing poison.

Giraudoux had earlier thought of writing two other plays on Roman themes. He announced in 1934 that he was working on a play called "Brutus," but no manuscript of it has been discovered. It would probably have interpreted "the noblest Roman" as a Giralducian purist. Another play, begun in 1936, *Les Gracques* (The Gracchi, 1958), was to deal with the Roman general Tiberius and his brother, Caius the revolutionary, but the manuscripts went no further than several versions of act 1. *Duel of Angels* is thus Giraudoux's closest approach to a Roman play, as well as being his last word in the theater. It takes the purist mentality to an extreme and makes us realize that under the skin of each one of his purists lurks a potential reformer who will be subdued or punished. Not content with setting an example by living up to their beliefs (which are more like morbid compulsions), Lucile and her husband try to foist them on the rest of the community, and they denounce those who will not or cannot subscribe to them. Lucile's despairing suicide, however, does not quite end the play. The final scene consists of an old bawd's rambling monologue. She argues for solidarity among women and rebukes men for their "stupidity and coarseness and wickedness," closing with the words, "And lead them all straight to eternal damnation. Amen." Meanwhile, she is robbing Lucile's corpse of its jewelry.

OTHER WRITINGS

If the monologue has an ironic cast, Giraudoux still feels sympathy for the plight of women in their differing societies. He gives us an assembly of female characters who, like Henrik Ibsen's and Racine's (Lucile's fixation on purity has much in common with that of Racine's Phaedra or Ibsen's Hedda and Irene), are stronger-minded and clearer-sighted than their men and yet, because of circumstances, remain incapable of effecting change. The women characters dominate, too, in the two screenplays Giraudoux composed. *La Duchesse de Langeais* (*The Duchess of Langeais*, 1942), adapted from a novella by Honoré de Balzac and directed by Jacques de Baroncelli, tells of the love, discord, and teasing between the Duchess and Montriveau, the man she wants but refuses to take. In *Les anges du péché* (*The Angels of Sin*, 1944), directed by Robert Bresson, who doubtless stripped down its dialogue to his spare requirements, we meet Anne-Marie, a young woman who strives for a purity and an absolute honesty that she cannot practice even in the convent where she had hoped to lead an immaculate life. By no coincidence this last screenplay, which ends in the heroine's death, occupied Giraudoux at the time when he was drafting *Duel of Angels*. His two principals, Anne-Marie and Lucile, become outsiders and victims of a world that cannot absorb them, but to which there is no alternative.

In his nonfiction Giraudoux had his say on a multitude of topics. The dozen books published during and after his lifetime contain literary and political essays; writings on the theater as art and as performance; essays on sports, town planning, women in society; travelogues; portraits; reprinted radio talks; and lectures given at universities and elsewhere. It is not possible to summarize their miscellaneous content in an essay of this length; readers are referred to the bibliography and advised that most of the nonfiction has not been translated into English. Giraudoux's discussions of other French writers—among them Jean de La Fontaine, Racine, Molière, Pierre Marivaux, Choderlos de Laclos, Gérard de Nerval, and Paul Claudel—are personal appreciations studded with astute snap judgments rather than systematic critical analyses, although he did use the centenary celebration in 1930 of Hugo's *Hernani* to find fault with Hugo and other early-nineteenth-century romantics such as Alfred de Musset, Alphonse Lamartine, and Alfred de Vigny for proving inferior to the classical authors against whom they rebelled. In these essays, as in his novels and plays, Giraudoux wields a powerful pen, charging his discourses with felicities of expression and startling opinions.

A CRITICAL OVERVIEW

What are the principal features of Giraudoux's art? In distinguishing them we will draw mostly for illustrations on his drama rather than his fiction, for he wrote more plays than novels, and the structures of both types of writing are broadly similar. The plays are more compact, but he clearly means his dramatic texts to be both performed and read as literature, and so a general analysis of the plays applies, for the most part, to the novels also. Besides, not all the novels are available in English. In this next section we will look briefly at the following features: structure, genre, character, argument, fantasy, theatricalism, language, and implications.

Structure

At the heart of nearly every work by Giraudoux lies a conflict for possession of a soul: in *Siegfried* for Siegfried-Forestier between Eva and Geneviève, that is, between Germany and France; in *Amphitryon 38* for Alcmene between her husband and Jupiter—earth against heaven; in *Intermezzo* for Isabelle between the Ghost and the Inspector—the spirit world against the material world; in *Judith* for the heroine between the Angel or heaven and Holofernes or godlessness; in *Tiger at the Gates* for Hector between Andromache or peace and the militant Trojan males; and in *Duel of Angels* for Lucile between her (and her husband's) impossibly chaste ideals and the indulgent sexuality of Paola and the other citizens of Aix. Thus, in each of these contests at least one figure of a tempter confronts the protagonist. This is a pattern that seems Faustian, but it goes back at least as far as one of the earliest recorded plays in history, Aeschylus' *Prometheus Bound* (ca. 454 B.C.). In *Ondine* and *Electra* there are two such contests: for Hans between Ondine (the supernatural) and Bertha (the earthbound), and for Ondine between Hans (human marriage) and the Old One (an incorporeal life); for Orestes between his sister and his mother and for Electra herself between retribution for her father's murder, which leads her to accept war and chaos, and the ability of Aegisthus to maintain peace. This last contest is something of a foregone conclusion: we do not expect Electra's resolve to weaken.

In much the same way, there is no doubt about which side the Countess in *The Madwoman* is on from the beginning to the end, but she does contend for the soul of a young man who was in the ranks of the profiteers; and thus a subplot echoes the conflict of the main plot—the struggle between avaricious progress and the will to preserve what is good.

The early works show us destiny, in one or another form or characterization, enticing the soul at issue away from a natural inclination, sometimes an affinity with nature itself (for example, Isabelle). Even Siegfried, who will revert to his native surroundings and existence, nevertheless abandons his role as a "natural" leader. Two particularly obstinate heroines, Lia in *Sodom and Gomorrah* and Lucile, opt for death—and in Lia's case the accompanying destruction of the world—rather than retreat from their entrenched moral positions.

From *Siegfried* to *Tessa* each play subdivides into three or four acts. But most of the later plays—five out of the six—have only one intermission, as though Giraudoux wished to simplify by reducing the visual requirements to two sets or only one and by splitting the action into two fundamental parts, exposition and outcome. He may have been trying to avoid giving the impression that he wrote lavish spectacles, but the division into two acts served two other purposes: it put more weight on the text, and it emphasized the tragic quality of the consequences in the second half by making the play flow into them unstoppably.

Genre

Critics disagree over which, if any, of Giraudoux's plays comply with a formal definition of tragedy. It can safely be said that none of them, perhaps no play ever written, satisfies every definition of tragedy, even every famous and authoritative one. That is a flaw in the definitions, not in the plays. All of Giraudoux's later plays except *The Madwoman of Chaillot* have a tragic initiative—the self-willed death or downfall of the protagonist. Those same plays, though, have their comic moments and some outcroppings of farce and melodrama. The question of which genre each play belongs to hardly seems a momentous one in any case. Since most of them are mixtures, each director or reader can interpret certain ambiguous scenes according to personal notions of what is suitable; directors may take into account the actors who have been cast and the potential audiences, and strive for the maximum in theatrical effectiveness. Such ambiguous scenes include the encounter between prudish Lucile and the prurient man she thinks seduced her, the trial sequence in *Ondine,* the debate between Hector and Ulysses, and the Gardener's monologue at the end of act 1 in *Electra,* when he bows out of the action.

Playing Giraudoux with old-fashioned tragic pomp dampens the impact of his wit, but letting the hilarity rip detracts from the dignity of his characters and the gravity of his themes. The secret seems to be to find the rhythm of his sentences without either rushing or laboring them. Most of the time Jouvet discovered the right line to take, the right balance to strike, the right tone to achieve, speech by speech. He studied the text without imposing preconceived ideas on it. He cast the play meticulously and rehearsed with Giraudoux sitting beside him as he listened to the actors with one ear and to the playwright's breathing with the other.

Character

Giraudoux had no use for psychological or environmental determinism, which, in the theater, generally results in characters who are called "naturalistic." In one of the stories collected in *La France sentimentale*, a painter who has tried to exorcise a painful memory of the town he lived in as a child goes back on a visit. As he sees it again, the ugly memory dissolves, and he feels healed and proclaims, "Shit on Freud Sigmund. . . . And shit on psychiatry." A Giraudoux character's background and upbringing, if he had supplied them, might have assisted the actor's understanding of the role. But the personality exists as the author's given portrait, usually without a history or further explanation. An actress must realize that a young woman who suspected that her father was murdered but was *not* Electra might never have developed Electra's thirst for justice. Such figures, which resist psychoanalysis, seem like artificial constructs, each impelled to a course of action he or she may not comprehend and sometimes will not question. What holds our attention is their energetic, clashing speeches and their tenacity in clinging to their principles.

In general, Giraudoux's women characters, especially the purists, will not be deterred, whereas the men, compromisers and often comic, bluster defensively. Lia repeatedly outpoints her husband, Jean. Isabelle confounds the Inspector. Alcmene keeps perplexing Jupiter. The men do not want to make trouble. They are easily placated—the women, never. In every man-woman skirmish the woman carries the argument. But women lose the contests because the men hold positions of power. (The Countess Aurélie is a striking exception. She wins the contest possibly because she doesn't engage in an argument with the oilmen.) Within these rough limits Giraudoux conceived an astonishing range of personalities of both sexes and of various ages, from different walks of life, and at different flights of abstraction, the roles inviting versatile explorations from actors and a never-quite-satisfied inquisitiveness from spectators.

Some of his most colorful, wise characters are poor people or servants: the Beggar, the Gardeners in both *Electra* and *Sodom and Gomorrah,* the Madwoman and the Ragpicker, the Second Fisherman in *Ondine* (who turns out to be the Old One), the French customs man in *Siegfried,* and Sosie, Amphitryon's batman. Giraudoux often liked to cloak his sages in humble garb.

Argument

The seventeenth-century plays of Corneille, Molière, and Racine raised argumentation as an art form to a standard that matches the oratory in the Greek drama and Plato. They have since served as models for ambitious playwrights of all nationalities. In the dialectic of each of those neoclassical plays the thesis and antithesis in the speeches of the contending characters find their synthesis only in the totality of the drama. Giraudoux's protagonists and antagonists make comparably powerful cases for themselves, putting forward their points of view in trains of thought that advance step by well-placed step, even when they interrupt themselves to allow for the refinement or expansion of a proposition. Much as with classical and neoclassical characters, in these arguments one party refers to the irresistibility of the forces of nature

and the supernatural, and the other party refers to the drives and deficiencies of humanity. Relayed with passion as well as internal logic, the speeches almost never convince the opponents. Isabelle and the Inspector, Hector and the poet Demokos, Electra and Aegisthus have no hope of reaching a meeting of minds or emotions. But—and this is the point of their speeches—they do alternately convince spectators, hauling them first to one side and then to the other side of the verbal tug of war. Giraudoux's plays consist of debates, and no matter how emphatic the other dramatic pressures, they rely on the characters' eloquence.

Fantasy

As used here the word "fantasy" means unreality. A fantasy may seem convincing (and a good one must), even though the audience tacitly accepts that it could not happen in real life. It will be entered by beings who are not human or mortal but who speak or behave as human beings: gods, ghosts, animals, mermaids, and other monsters.

Three of Giraudoux's most successful plays are outright fantasies: *Amphitryon 38, Intermezzo,* and *Ondine.* Three more have secondary characters who are not earthbound (*Judith, Tiger, Sodom*), and *The Apollo of Bellac* has its moments of fantasy, as when the statue and the chandelier react to Agnès' compliment. But the remaining plays and all his novels operate wholly in the realm of reality; they could happen. We can, if we wish, classify the unearthly apparitions as visions, daydreams, or delusions entertained by the more receptive (or less balanced) human characters, and Giraudoux sometimes gives us grounds for such a supposition. A little girl in *Lying Woman* plays with an imaginary dog while neglecting the actual pet dog she has been given, which is less real to her. In *Judith* the Angel appears only to the heroine while the external action and the other characters "freeze" onstage. Ondine has no tail, not even, to the surprise of the trial judges, the benefit of webbed feet,

JEAN GIRAUDOUX

only "an odor of algae, of pine," according to the fisherman who netted her: did Hans fall in love with a mere girl? The Ghost in *Intermezzo* is shot and falls, but a phantom shape arises from the corpse and drifts away; everyone sees it except the Inspector from out of town, as though to remind us that the citizens are under a collective spell that does not govern outsiders. As he is dying, Hans hears his servants begin to speak in verse, but the other witnesses hear prose.

In *Tiger at the Gates,* however, everyone on-stage perceives and hears Iris, the messenger of the gods, when she delivers contradictory instructions from Olympus. In this respect Giraudoux aligns his work with ancient Greek, biblical, medieval, and Elizabethan texts, which mention envoys from celestial and infernal regions or from other corners of the hereafter. At the same time he qualifies his period settings and sharpens the fantasy by introducing anachronisms: his characters speak in distinctly modern cadences and refer to twentieth-century tasks and tools. But a sense of near-fantasy—anything *can* happen—is never quite negated, even in his non-fantasies. The author toys zestfully with his themes so that his characters seem to hover above their situations rather than being rooted (or mired) in them, as happens in plays with "tape-recorder" dialogue. Giraudoux's fantasy permits the audience to keep its emotional distance from the stage, to remember continually that it is watching theater, not life.

Theatricalism

As if to jog spectators into this awareness that they only observe and do not participate in a play, Giraudoux makes use of what Luigi Pirandello called theater-in-the-theater (*teatro nel teatro*), that is, plays within the play. Jouvet's actors in *Paris Impromptu* enter reciting lines from Molière's *L'Impromptu des Versailles,* which they are rehearsing. The Old One in *Ondine,* disguised as a magician, stages scenes from the future between Bertha

and Hans to warn Ondine that Hans will be unfaithful to her. The Beggar in *Electra* describes Orestes' killing of his mother and Aegisthus while it is taking place elsewhere. The murder is not enacted, but the narration gives us more particulars than an audience could take in if it saw the slayings. The effect here is cinematic, like slow-motion camera work, but the results are theatricalist, as are the accounts of death in Greek tragedies, for the action departs or frees itself from the visible happenings onstage; it becomes two-fold and does so not by *showing* but by employing the theater's most potently suggestive instrument, the power of language.

Language

Giraudoux insisted that he wrote hastily during breaks from his official duties and that he improvised, discovering successive sentences as he went along, almost by free association. Whether or not he was being strictly accurate—his phrases and images seem too carefully selected, too sculptured, to have poured out without consideration and reconsideration, even if we make allowances for his rapidity of composition—they do give the impression of spontaneity that he evidently wanted. The plays' characters in their long speeches and the novels' narrators in their lyrical passages almost seem unprepared for what they say next. Yet the speeches and narratives have a satisfying final form. They may wind away from a topic sentence, but they return to the direction in which the scene is heading and gather force from their excursions and occasional verbal acrobatics.

At the École Normale Giraudoux had learned to shun adjectives and adverbs when nouns and active verbs would keep his writing more sinewy. Yet his style has often been censured as "precious," and one French critic has even defended his preciosity in a book-length study, tracing it back to the *précieuses* of the seventeenth century. These ladies (and a few men) tried for the most flowery and indirect ways of expressing themselves, writing and speaking to each other in what became virtually a private tongue. Giraudoux's language is not, in this sense, at all precious. The charge seems to have arisen not because his detractors (and defenders) believe he wished to communicate in an encoded manner but rather because some of his characters and narrators claim that they share some means of communication with other forms of life and with inanimate matter. Giraudoux's literary tic, related to the euphuism of John Lyly's sixteenth-century romances and to the figure of speech known as pathetic fallacy, implies that doors, chairs, and vases can speak; that animals, birds, fish, and trees think like people; that hills, rivers, and plains understand the destiny that rules human existence and may even act on its impersonal behalf.

Siegfried declares that snow and the stars and the river bisecting Gotha spoke to him about Germany the night before he left that country. Aegisthus, affirming his right to the throne of Argos, says: "Over my horse's hoof beats I heard trees, children, streams hail me as king. . . . A pair of magpies . . . gave me independence. An ant hill gave me generosity." Holofernes tells Judith he chose the site where he pitched his tents because it was not inhabited by gods; he recognized their absence "by chance and by the accent of the palm trees and the voice of the waters." Now and then the mannerism comes close to being whimsy, but when recited by capable actors the references to nonhuman powers have a rhetorical fervor that gives the speakers the mysterious air of those who have penetrated secrets kept intact from everyone else.

Implications

The nexus of ideas in Giraudoux's total writings defies a straightforward synopsis. Still, it is worth recapitulating some of the ideas that recur in the prose fiction, the drama, and the nonfiction. He would like France to set an example of amity, born of respect and even affection, for other peoples and, in the most magnanimous sense of the word, for their cultures (customs, arts, cumulative wisdom). When a nation distorts or abandons its cultural heritage, as Germany did grotesquely, his sympathy dries up—his sympathy not for the country but for the purposes of its leadership. If it attacks or threatens others, it has forfeited its right to further tolerance; it is inviting war as the only means of restoring international decency. But war exacts a grievous price, apart from the obvious futility risked in using destruction to fend off destruction. He knew from firsthand experience that public emotion could be whipped into a frenzy of hatred for an enemy and that the hatred can fester until it proves almost impossible to cure.

In a period when international understanding gave way to jingoism, new tides of hatred, and a renewal of war fever, Giraudoux did not stop at being a steadfast internationalist. He revered all forms of life. Around the turn of the century Anton Chekhov's *Uncle Vanya* (1897), its earlier version, called *The Wood Demon* (1889), and *The Cherry Orchard* (1904) anticipated warnings by the environmentalists of our own time that we blight and plunder our lives by thoughtless encroachment on natural preserves. Giraudoux echoed and re-echoed the warning that we are a species that endangers itself, and he did so with an unmatched grace and humor that dissipated any suggestion of preachiness. But how can men and women live in harmony with other nations and with their own environments when they cannot live with one another? As he grew older, he grew increasingly dispirited over their chances of living up to that primary pact, the marriage bond.

Giraudoux has often been accounted a political conservative, and it is true that he wanted to conserve—but only what is best in what man has done and the best of what he has left undone. Realizing that he was reaching for ideals that might never be attained but that must still be striven for despite the contradictions inherent in them, he would have liked to see a world that was genuinely a community, perhaps the fantasy of a world-sized Bellac.

Selected Bibliography

EDITIONS

INDIVIDUAL WORKS

NOVELS AND SHORT STORIES
Provinciales. Paris, 1909; enl. ed., 1922.
L'École des indifférents. Paris, 1911; rev. ed., 1934.
Simon le pathéthique. Paris, 1918; rev. ed., 1926.
Elpénor. Paris, 1919.
Suzanne et le Pacifique. Paris, 1921; illustrated edition, Lyons, 1928.
Siegfried et le Limousin. Paris, 1922.
Juliette au pays des hommes. Paris, 1924.
Bella. Paris, 1926.
La première disparition de Jérôme Bardini. Paris, 1927.
Eglantine. Paris, 1927.
Aventures de Jérôme Bardini. Paris, 1930.
La France sentimentale. Paris, 1932.
Combat avec l'ange. Paris, 1934.
Choix des élues. Paris, 1938.
Les contes d'un matin. Paris, 1952.
La menteuse. Partial text, Paris, 1958. Complete text, Paris, 1969.

PLAYS
Siegfried. Paris, 1928.
Fugues sur Siegfried. Paris, 1929.
Amphitryon 38. Paris, 1929.
Judith. Paris, 1931.
Intermezzo. Paris, 1933.
Tessa. Paris, 1934.
La guerre de Troie n'aura pas lieu. Paris, 1935.
Supplément au voyage de Cook. Paris, 1937.
Electre. Paris, 1937.
L'Impromptu de Paris. Paris, 1937.
Cantique des cantiques. Paris, 1938.
Ondine. Paris, 1939.
Sodome et Gomorrhe. Paris, 1943.
La folle de Chaillot. Neuchâtel and Paris, 1945.
L'Apollon de Bellac. Neuchâtel and Paris, 1946.
Pour Lucrèce. Neuchâtel and Paris, 1953.
Les Gracques. Paris, 1958.

SCREENPLAYS
La Duchesse de Langeais. Paris, 1942.
Béthanie [Les anges du péché]. Paris, 1944.

ESSAYS
Lectures pour une ombre. Paris, 1917.
Amica America. Paris, 1919.
Adorable Clio. Paris, 1920.
La prière sur la Tour Eiffel. Paris, 1923.
Le sport. Paris, 1928.
Racine. In *La nouvelle revue française* (December 1929). Republished in *Littérature,* Paris, 1941. Published separately, Paris, 1950.
Les cinq tentations de La Fontaine. Paris, 1938.
Plein pouvoirs. Paris, 1939.
Littérature. Paris, 1941.
Hommage à Marivaux. Paris, 1944.
Sans pouvoirs. Monaco, 1945.
Armistice à Bordeaux. Monaco, 1945.
Visitations. Neuchâtel and Paris, 1946.
Pour une politique urbaine. Paris, 1947.
La Française et la France. Paris, 1951.
Portugal: Combat avec l'image. Paris, 1958.
Or dans la nuit. Paris, 1969.
Carnet des Dardanelles. Paris, 1969.
Lettres. Paris, 1975.
Souvenir de deux existences. Paris, 1975.

COLLECTED WORKS
Théâtre complet. 16 vols. Neuchâtel and Paris, 1945–1953.
Oeuvre romanesque. 2 vols. Paris, 1955.
Oeuvres littéraires diverses. Paris, 1958.
Théâtre. 4 vols. Paris, 1958–1959.
Théâtre complet de Jean Giraudoux. Paris, 1982.

TRANSLATIONS AND ADAPTATIONS

Amphitryon 38. Adapted by S. N. Behrman. New York, 1938.
———. Translated by Phyllis La Farge with Peter H. Judd. New York, 1964.
———. Translated by Roger Gellert. London and New York, 1967.
The Apollo of Bellac. Adapted by Maurice Valency. New York, 1958.
Bella. Translated by J. F. Scanlan. New York, 1927.
Campaigns and Intervals. Translated by Elizabeth S. Sergeant. New York, 1918.
Duel of Angels. Translated by Christopher Fry. London and New York, 1963.

JEAN GIRAUDOUX

Electra. Translated by Winifred Smith. In *From the Modern Repertoire*, vol. 2, edited by Eric Bentley. Bloomington, Ind., 1952.
————. Translated by Phyllis La Farge with Peter H. Judd. New York, 1964.
Elpénor. Translated by Richard Howard with Renaud Bruce. New York, 1958.
Intermezzo. Adapted by Maurice Valency as *The Enchanted*. New York, 1958.
————. Translated by Roger Gellert as *Intermezzo*. New York and London, 1967.
Judith. Translated by John K. Savacool. In *The Modern Theatre,* vol. 3, edited by Eric Bentley. New York, 1955.
————. Translated by Christopher Fry. New York and London, 1963.
Lying Woman. Translated by Richard Howard. New York, 1972.
The Madwoman of Chaillot. Adapted by Maurice Valency. New York, 1958.
My Friend from Limousin. Translated by Louis Collier Willcox. New York, 1923.
Ondine. Adapted by Maurice Valency. New York, 1958.
————. Translated by Roger Gellert. New York and London, 1967.
Paris Impromptu. Translated by Rima Drell Reck. *Tulane Drama Review* 3:107–108 (Summer 1959).
Racine. Translated by Percy Mansell Jones. Cambridge, England, 1938.
Siegfried. Translated by Philip Carr. New York, 1930.
————. Translated by Phyllis La Farge with Peter H. Judd. New York, 1964.
Song of Songs. Translated by John Raikes. *Tulane Drama Review* 3:88–106 (Summer 1959). Reprinted in *The Genius of the French Theatre*, edited by Albert Bermel. New York, 1961.
Suzanne and the Pacific. Translated by Ben Ray Redman. New York, 1923.
Tiger at the Gates. Translated by Christopher Fry. New York and London, 1963.
The Virtuous Island. Adapted by Maurice Valency. New York, 1956.

BIOGRAPHICAL AND CRITICAL STUDIES

Albérès, René M. *Esthétique et morale chez Jean Giraudoux.* Paris, 1957.

Barrault, Jean-Louis. "A propos d'une reprise: *Intermezzo,* c'est Giraudoux lui-même." In *Cahiers Jean Giraudoux.* Paris, 1975.
Bermel, Albert. "The Warrior as Peacemaker." In *Contradictory Characters.* Lanham, Md., 1984.
Body, Jacques. *Giraudoux et l'Allemagne.* Paris, 1975.
Bourdet, Maurice. *Jean Giraudoux: Son oeuvre.* Paris, 1928.
Cocteau, Jean. *Souvenir de Jean Giraudoux.* Paris, 1946.
Cohen, Robert. *Giraudoux: Three Faces of Destiny.* Chicago, 1968.
Debidour, V. H. *Giraudoux.* Paris, 1955.
Giraudoux, Jean-Pierre. *Le fils.* Paris, 1967.
Houlet, Jacques. *Le théâtre de Jean Giraudoux.* Paris, 1945.
Inskip, Donald. *Jean Giraudoux: The Making of a Dramatist.* London and New York, 1958.
Lemaitre, Georges. *Jean Giraudoux: The Writer and His Work.* New York, 1971.
LeSage, Laurent. *Jean Giraudoux: His Life and Works.* University Park, Pa., 1959.
Magny, Claude-Edmonde. *Précieux Giraudoux.* Paris, 1945.
Mander, Gertrud. *Jean Giraudoux.* Munich, 1976.
Mankin, Paul A. *Precious Irony: The Theatre of Jean Giraudoux.* The Hague, 1971.
Mauron, Charles. *Le théâtre de Jean Giraudoux.* Paris, 1971.
May, Georges. "Jean Giraudoux: Diplomacy and Dramaturgy." *Yale French Studies* 5:88–94 (Spring 1950).
Mercier-Campiche, Marianne. *Le Théâtre de Jean Giraudoux et la condition humaine.* Paris, 1954.
Raymond, Agnes. *Jean Giraudoux: The Theatre of Victory and Defeat.* Amherst, Mass., 1966.
Reilly, John H. *Jean Giraudoux.* Boston, 1978.
Robichez, Jacques. *Le théâtre de Giraudoux.* Paris, 1976.
Sartre, Jean-Paul. "Monsieur Jean Giraudoux et la philosophie d'Aristote à propos des *Choix des élues.*" In *Situations,* vol. 1. Paris, 1947.
Tulane Drama Review 3 (Summer 1959). Special issue on Giraudoux.
Weil, Colette. Six essays analyzing *Intermezzo.* In *Cahiers Jean Giraudoux.* Paris, 1975.
Zenon, Renée. *Le traitement des mythes dans le théâtre de Jean Giraudoux.* Lanham, Md., 1981.

ALBERT BERMEL

1066

NIKOS KAZANTZAKIS

(1883–1957)

THE CAREER AND reputation of Nikos Kazantzakis are both very curious. After struggling for forty years, he suddenly became an international celebrity in the early 1950's. Since then, his books have continued to appeal to a large number of cultivated readers while being generally ignored in critical and academic circles. There is no agreement about his ultimate worth; it would seem impossible to predict at this stage whether he will be read fifty years after his death, like Constantine Cavafy, or will share the fate of his friend Panaït Istrati, who enjoyed a vogue in the 1920's and is now largely forgotten. Book reviewers and critics have tended toward polarized excesses of eulogy or vilification when writing about Kazantzakis. His novels have been called "among the most impressive of our time" and his *Odyssey* an "astonishing . . . creation," but he has also been dismissed as "an atrocious writer . . . whose faults are so glaring as to be dazzling." Many of his compatriots insist that he falsifies everything Hellenic, whereas some see in him the very epitome of their nation. The polarities have become so fixed that it would seem useless to argue any longer along such lines or even to worry about whether Kazantzakis is a great or an atrocious writer. Instead, let us start with the fact of his popularity. We may assume, since his books are intellectual and have no salacious interest, that his readership consists of discriminating people of superior educa-

tion. No one really knows why an author enjoys wide appeal. Perhaps it is because of his remoteness from both the banal and the eccentric, perhaps just because of an affinity between his concerns and those of his audience. In any case, the fact that Kazantzakis is interesting to many readers offers a place to begin. The most immediate critical questions then become: Why is he interesting? Why does he speak to our condition?

Kazantzakis' chief interest lies in his totality. This of course shines through individual works, yet it is difficult to detect until we know the career as a whole—not the succession of outward events that constitute Kazantzakis' "life" but the development of attitudes that constitute his artistic personality. The "life," he always insisted, was only an outer husk hiding the kernel within. It was nevertheless an immensely varied and fascinating one, beginning with childhood in Turkish-occupied Crete in an atmosphere of revolutionary ferment. Indeed during one of the insurrections Kazantzakis had to be evacuated for safety to the island of Naxos, where his father enrolled him in a school run by French monks. Here he gained his first glimpse of the broader world of European culture. Returning to Iraklion, he completed high school there and then went off the University of Athens to study law with the apparent aim of becoming a Greek politician, although his all-consuming interest was already literature. Graduate studies in Paris followed, again with law as the pretext. In 1909 he returned to a Greece that was beginning a decade of nationalistic expansion. He joined the movement in various ways, campaigning for the demotic language, serving as a volunteer in the Balkan Wars, and leading a mission to the Caucasus in 1919 to repatriate 150,000 Greeks who were being persecuted by the Bolsheviks. When Greece's expansion collapsed in 1922 owing to her disastrous defeat by the Turks in Asia Minor, a disillusioned Kazantzakis turned his sights toward international Communism. The 1920's and early 1930's were difficult times for him in which he struggled unsuccessfully to earn a living outside of Greece—in the Soviet Union, Germany, and Spain—but was forced to maintain himself by working as a foreign correspondent for Athenian newspapers. Although his extensive experience in the Soviet Union ended in disillusion, he refused to denounce Communism and therefore was generally branded a leftist (not to mention an anti-Christ) for the rest of his life. Back in Greece in the mid and late 1930's, he continued to eke out a living as a journalist while completing his massive sequel to Homer, the *Odíssia* (*The Odyssey: A Modern Sequel*, 1938). When the Axis powers occupied Greece during World War II, Kazantzakis was confined to the island of Aegina. In 1944, immediately after the war, he moved to Athens, witnessed the Civil War of December 1944–January 1945, and thereafter entered politics as the head of a small Socialist Party attempting to unify the non-Communist left. When the Civil War resumed in 1946 he commenced a final period of self-imposed exile in France. The decade 1947–1957 was one of increasing acclaim for Kazantzakis on a worldwide scale. He died in Germany and was given a Christian burial in Iraklion despite the opposition of the Greek Orthodox hierarchy in Athens.

We are mainly interested, however, not in these events that constitute the "life" but in the governing characteristics of Kazantzakis' overall artistic personality. This artistic totality is complicated: a visible exterior with an invisible bull inside butting against the walls. Outwardly, there is a particular voice, a professionalism, and an elaborate worldview. Inside this three-ply integument are strains and growths—toward rootedness, aestheticism, prose, and the prosaic—that threaten the outward aspect yet never quite crack it. But these too are part of the whole, and it is precisely the tension between the masks Kazantzakis laboriously carved and the strains that came largely in spite of himself that gives the totality so much interest and makes it so touchingly human. To discover this interest we must go the roundabout way of identifying the visible exterior and then attempting to see the fluctuations within.

How, then, can we characterize Kazantzakis' particular voice? Once we do this with reasonable accuracy for the career as a whole, we shall be less likely to expect the impossible from individual works. People complain, for example, that the novel *Víos ke politía tu Aléksi Zorbá* (Life and Times of Alexis Zorba, translated as *Zorba the Greek*, 1946) is not realistic. But Kazantzakis' artistic personality prevented him from writing in the realistic mode. The critic who harps on defective realism in Kazantzakis' novels prevents us from granting those novels their own premises. Similarly, it is easy to say that Kazantzakis' plays are not theatrical because they offer long intellectual declamations. But theatricality is larger than any one definition. John Milton's *Comus* (1634), with very little dramatic interest to be sure, was theatrical to its viewers; John Lyly wrote plays without plot, rounded characters, or dramatic tension, yet they were entertaining and theatrical for other reasons: pageant, language, even their "delicate evocations of profound ideas." We should try to discover the kind of writer Kazantzakis was instead of condemning him for not being what he wasn't. An anonymous reviewer once claimed that "in the state of Greek writing as it was in [Kazantzakis'] youth it was hardly possible for him to see the importance of Cavafy or later of Seferis, nor was he intelligent enough . . . to overcome the obstacles and make the same discoveries about poetry and style for himself as greater writers had made." This comment assumes that all significant literature in our age is terse, restrained, and ironic. But Kazantzakis could never have written poetry in the style of George Seferis or Seferis' model, T. S. Eliot, any more than he could have written Pinteresque plays or novels like Jane Austen's. In his plays he favored the declamatory mode and the elaborate *mise-en-scène* rather than wit or psychological subtlety. In his novels he was allegorical, rambling, polysemous, rhetorical. In everything he displayed romantic excess; he painted sprawling canvases rather than miniatures; he valued fervor over precision, sincerity over craftsmanship. These are constants in his career and should be accepted as such. They characterize certain artists in all ages and assuredly are among the multiform ways in which the human spirit may legitimately manifest itself.

But how can we sum him up? What single adjective is sufficiently flexible to define his particular voice? A workable one might be E. M. Forster's "prophetic," by which Forster describes discourse that stimulates us not so much by realism, plotting, characterization, or a web of causal relationships as by tone— specifically, a tone that displays the urgency found in the Old Testament prophets. In prophetic discourse, content and form are subordinate to élan.

Kazantzakis liked to think of himself as a Byzantine border guard stationed bravely and alone at the outer limits of light, apostrophizing the abyss. His circumstances, however, made him a workaday professional writer dependent on his pen for a livelihood. This professionalism is the second element of his totality that we must consider, for only by recognizing the attitudes and diversity it engendered can we avoid expecting from him what we expect from writers specializing in poetry, prose fiction, or drama. As a professional man of letters, he was eager to work in any

and all forms. With the exception of *The Odyssey: A Modern Sequel,* which occupied him on and off for more than a decade, he simply wrote what had to be written, quickly, and then turned with compulsive haste to the next project. Too busy to retreat into genre-specialization, he produced an oeuvre of astonishing variety. Besides novels, poems, and plays, he wrote travel books, children's stories, fictionalized biographies of historical figures, literary history, encyclopedia articles on diverse subjects, journalism, political and ethical polemics, translations in prose and verse of scientific, literary, and philosophical works, school textbooks, and even a dictionary. Given such prodigality, it is hardly surprising that he produced nothing that is fully satisfying technically. Some of his novels, plays, and poems are very bad, and the good ones are uneven. Furthermore, his best writing sometimes appears in nonliterary pieces that he himself considered secondary: lucid argumentation graces his political effusions, for example, and descriptive and narrative gems are scattered throughout the travel articles. In so many of his works where we may demur at the total effect we nevertheless find astonishing fragments: unexpected metaphors, vivid and moving descriptions, convincing wisdom. We should avoid belaboring the fact that Kazantzakis was not a deliberate craftsman pushing back the frontiers of a given genre and should accept him in his totality as the prodigal, professional, diverse man of letters that he was.

Kazantzakis' professionalism led him to subordinate letters in the narrow sense to something much more comprehensive. G. K. Chesterton once said, "I have never taken my books seriously; but I take my opinions quite seriously." Kazantzakis did take some of his books seriously, but this was chiefly because they promulgated his opinions. For him, being a man of letters meant being a controversialist promulgating and defending his ideas. This in turn meant being an intellectual. Kazantzakis' truest profession was that of thinking and articulating, of entering his extraordinary mind in the lists against obscurantism and outmoded thought. Writing was only one tool among many, but the one that he found served him best. (He gradually learned that as a speaker and political organizer he was less gifted.) To be a man of letters, furthermore, meant assuming a way of life consistent with one's opinions and remembering that a play or novel was just a single aspect of an overall response to experience.

The third and most important element of Kazantzakis' totality is his worldview. This determined his professionalism as a man of letters and his fervor as a prophet. Although severely cerebral, the ingredients of this worldview were not bloodless; they had for him the urgency and passion of emotions. Nor were they changeable. Despite Kazantzakis' growth in many areas during the five decades of his career, he adhered steadfastly to certain basic positions developed at the start. There is no mistaking what these positions were, for Kazantzakis continually supplemented his imaginative writings with didactic glosses lest his readers misunderstand.

He began with a theory of history and then expanded this into a theory of "metahistory." The keystone of his historical thinking is his doctrine of the transitional age. The trouble with our times, Kazantzakis argues, is that we are caught in the middle. On the one hand we have lost our spontaneous appreciation of this world's beauty; on the other we have lost our faith in the heavens above. We cannot be pagans because Christianity has poisoned our relationship to material things; we cannot be Christians because Darwinism has destroyed the perfect spiritual world that underlies Christian behavior. We are thus the melancholy victims of a transitional age. The novella *Ófis ke kríno* (*Snake and Lily*, 1906) treats in particular the impossibility of an idealized pagan devotion to earthly beauty. Things have come to such a pass that the heroine must choose suicide rather than existence in a contingent world. The novella's complement, a bleak one-act play sardonically entitled *Ko-*

modía (*Comedy*, 1909), focuses on the impossibility of Christian hope. Taken together, these two works show the deaths of both Apollo and Christ, deaths that proclaim "no exit" for those with spiritual aspiration. An early novel bearing the significant title *Spasménes psihés* (*Broken Souls*, 1909–1910) presents additional victims of the spiritual impasse.

As Kazantzakis advanced in his career and broadened his own experience, he merely poured old wine into new bottles: the doctrine of the transitional age remained while the historical details changed. But although his characters continued to be squashed between the jaws of conflicting impossibilities, he refused to let them remain totally broken souls. In the play *Ksimerónei* (Day Is Breaking, produced 1907) the theory is developed in a semi-optimistic fashion, and an exit of sorts is provided. Lalo, the tragic heroine, is trapped between Christ (duty) and Apollo (beauty and romantic love), but now a third god is introduced as well: Dionysus. His spokesman, a forceful polemicist resembling Kazantzakis himself, preaches a virile neo-paganism that will overthrow both Christian self-denial and romantic self-indulgence. Lalo knows that this third way is right yet lacks the strength to follow it because she is caught in a transitional age; hence she finds her "solution" only in suicide. Yet the play is partially optimistic in its implication that we are able to escape the trap imaginatively. The transitional age has advanced to the point at which we can envision and herald the succeeding age even if we cannot bring our outward lives into accord with our vision. Right thought is possible; right action is not. Moreover, the very proclamation of right thought—what Kazantzakis later termed the *kravyí* (cry)—brings action closer. If day is breaking, full daylight cannot be far behind.

The increasing optimism of these early works tempted Kazantzakis to advance a step further. In *O protomástoras* (*The Master Builder*, 1910), a play that reflects the political optimism that Kazantzakis shared with other Greeks at the start of the expansionist decade 1910–1920, the dauntless hero bludgeons his way to freedom in act as well as thought. But Kazantzakis did not continue in this direction, which contradicts his earlier equation of freedom with complete immateriality and thus with death, as well as his romantic sense that fulfillment involves the infinite. In addition, he had already given the doctrine of the transitional age a cosmological as well as a historical dimension, seeing the universe itself as a huge transition between two abysses. All his subsequent work is a struggle to devise some form of extrication from these metahistorical jaws without giving way either to the facile optimism of *The Master Builder* or to the resignation of *Snake and Lily* and *Comedy*.

The result is Kazantzakis' well-known "heroic pessimism." We find hero after hero caught in a transitional situation, able to envision the exit imaginatively and therefore to voice a cry, but confined to only two kinds of action. The first is suicide once more. Now, however, self-destruction is no longer necessarily a defect of will, a broken soul's capitulation to the superior forces of history and fate. On the contrary, it can be a supremely voluntaristic act, an ultimate affirmation that impels the universe forward both historically and cosmologically. Though formulaic, this solution allowed Kazantzakis sufficient scope because he could vary the historical circumstances and also the vibrancy with which his characters respond. In *Nikifóros Fokás* (1927) and *Iulianós o Paravatis* (Julian the Apostate, 1956), for example, the protagonists are still weak; in *O Hristós ksanastavroñetai* (*Christ Recrucified, 1954*, published as *The Greek Passion* in the U.S.), *O Kapetán Mihális* (*Freedom or Death*, 1953), *O teleftaíos pirasmós* (*The Last Temptation of Christ*, 1955), *O Kapodístrias* (1946), and *Mélissa* (1939), their strength is more assured. The artistic success of each work depends on the effective fusion of history with cosmology, the particular transition with the general, and the degree to which

the work allows us to forget the worldview that governs both plot and characterization.

The second "action" that Kazantzakis allowed was artistic creativity. In his search for an exit he came to insist that the *kravyí* itself could be affirmative. Some achieve freedom and cheat fate by heroic suicide, others by heroic assertions of the imagination. He tended not to broadcast the latter possibility in his works (perhaps because he favored it in his life); however, it is explicit enough in *Zorba the Greek, Vúdas* (*Buddha*, 1956), and parts of the *Odyssey*. This solution catered to Kazantzakis' inborn aestheticism, but it also emerged from the cosmological expansion he accorded his original ideas and in particular from his conviction that the universe per se is evolving toward self-consciousness.

To understand how Kazantzakis developed his earliest notions into formulaic solutions, we must consider his graduate studies in Paris from October 1907 to February 1909. Although he was ostensibly preparing to teach political philosophy in the law faculty of Athens University, his real purpose was to broaden his understanding of history and metahistory until he could discern his own role in the cosmic process. The deliberate self-consciousness of this endeavor is indicated in a letter he wrote to Dimitrios Kafoyerópoulos in January 1908: "At present I am studying philosophy and literature at the Sorbonne, the College de France, and the École des Hautes Études. I want to work out an individual, personal conception of life, a world-theory and a theory of man's destiny, and then, in accord with these, systematically and with a determined purpose and program, to write what I shall write." He consequently immersed himself in modern philosophical doctrines, especially epistemology and metaphysics, with emphasis on Immanuel Kant. This in turn led to two figures who had a lasting effect on his thought: Friedrich Nietzsche and Henri Bergson.

Much has been said, and rightly, about Kazantzakis' debt to Nietzsche, but very little about his debt to Bergson. Yet it is clear that Bergson played the greater role in Kazantzakis' intellectual life, enabling him to expand the doctrine of the transitional age into a complete cosmology and giving him a new vocabulary ("ascent," "transubstantiation," "*élan vital*") with which to articulate his system. Kazantzakis' attraction to Nietzsche was largely emotional. He advocated a way of life that Kazantzakis dreamed of emulating so that he too might be a prophetic tempest churning together philosophy, art, and moral fervor until ideas became incandescent. Kazantzakis liked the way Nietzsche's writings spilled out into ecstasy, and he did not care if the master's ideas lacked originality; his importance was his ability to convert ideas into passions.

Nietzsche's main contribution to Kazantzakis' worldview was his insistence that nihilism need not signify decadence, that it may be a positive force, a homeopathic medicine hastening the end of Europe's current impasse. His influence was thus largely negative. He taught Kazantzakis that to smash old values is a moral imperative if we wish new ones to emerge and daybreak to develop into full day. In particular he taught Kazantzakis to reject Christianity, since hopes and fears based on a false conception of the universe can only lead to decreased moral vitality. The entire value system resting on the mistaken notion of a rational universe had to be smashed. Nietzsche thus encouraged in Kazantzakis an antipathy toward everything bourgeois, which meant everything comfortable, inert, equable, and flabby. This hatred embraced democracy, cosmopolitanism, socialism, egalitarianism, pacifism, tolerance, women's rights, rationalism—everything liberal, everything that attempts to minimize pain, conflict, or other vital manifestations of the flux, unrest, contradiction, irrationality, and self-overcoming that Nietzsche posited as the true nature of reality. In sum, Nietzsche's negative teachings encouraged Kazantzakis to smash a false metaphysic and the false religion, morality, and social organization based on that metaphysic.

Perhaps Nietzsche's greatest effect was to prepare Kazantzakis for Bergson by insisting that our value system must agree with scientific knowledge. Ever since Kazantzakis had seen his allegiance to the Christian worldview destroyed by Darwin, he had nonetheless adhered to a belief in spirit, infinitude, and salvation while hoping that these could be redefined in scientific terms. Here now was Bergson with redefinitions ready to hand and with a "proof" that the driving force in the universe is an evolving vitality that transubstantiates flesh into spirit. Kazantzakis became an eager auditor of Bergson's lectures; he was anxious to use the latter's philosophy as an intellectual foundation for the spiritual yearnings he had developed earlier. Christ had murdered Apollo; Darwin had murdered Christ. Dionysus was unscientific and non-evolutionary. Bergson supplied Kazantzakis with a new god.

To discover the nature of this god we must first ask certain cosmological questions—precisely those that Kazantzakis asked and answered under Bergson's tutelage. They are the "where" questions: Where have we come from? Where are we going? The answers appear in the prologue to Kazantzakis' *Salvatores Dei: Askitikí* (*The Saviors of God: Spiritual Exercises*, 1927), the book in which he eventually expounded his Bergsonian ideas with Nietzschean passion: "We come from a dark abyss [and] we end in a dark abyss." Life thus becomes a luminous interval between two black voids. These formulations support Kazantzakis' earlier doctrine of the transitional age and indeed expand it into a cosmological principle. The whole of life, the whole of the cosmos, is now a transition from one void to another.

The next question involves the relation of the luminous interval to the abysses at either end. These might seem to annihilate life, rendering all evolution futile; however, Bergson taught Kazantzakis otherwise. The so-called voids are absolute freedom and spirituality; hence they paradoxically fulfill life's strivings rather than negate them.

Bergson's "proof" of these conclusions is complicated. He posits a preexistent life force (*élan vital*), a pure energy that wills to become alive. But to become alive it must collaborate with matter. Not that matter is anything separate; life, Bergson writes in *Évolution créatrice* (*Creative Evolution*, 1907), is the vital current "loaded with matter, that is, with congealed parts of its own substance." However, once the life force has created life, it tends to divest itself of its congealments and return to pure energy. Evolution shows us that life is a creative action that unmakes itself—change moves toward inertness, heterogeneity toward homogeneity. Our solar system, says Bergson, is "ever exhausting something of the mutability it contains." This means that death is not something that negates all the "desires" of the cosmos but rather something toward which life is moving. The black abyss at the end of life is not a sudden, arbitrary, "unjust" negation of life; it is the logical conclusion of the very process it seems to nullify. Death, in effect, is life burning itself out; both life and death are willed by the same "god." Furthermore, the sloughing-off of matter means a release of the primal force, a complete freeing and spiritualizing of what had previously been weighed down by its own congealments. Life evolves toward increasing spiritualization by means of transubstantiation. Rocks evolve into plants, thence into animals, thence into man; sensation develops into instinct, intelligence, and finally self-consciousness. But life's crown is death, in which all materiality is dissolved. Annihilation equals fulfillment.

Although Bergson strives for a monism, he actually speaks of spirit and matter as two distinct and antagonistic entities. Thus he pictures (a) the life force surging upward toward creativity, motion, heterogeneity, and consciousness, and (b) matter pressing downward toward stability and homogeneity. Life is the meeting of the two. Kazantzakis echoes this definition in the prologue to *The Saviors of God:* "In the temporary living organism, these two streams collide: (a) the ascent toward composition, toward life, toward immortality; (b) the descent toward decomposition, toward matter, toward death. Both streams well up from the depths of primordial essence." The prologue goes on to state that "it is our duty . . . to grasp that vision which can embrace and harmonize these two . . . indestructible forces."

Precisely here, in this synthesizing vision, Kazantzakis found his new god. Seen monistically, god is the entire evolutionary process; he is the primordial essence that first wills its own congealment into life and then wills the unmaking of this creative action. But the human mind can apprehend this synthesis only in rare intuitive flashes; thus it tends to fall into dualistic and analytical formulations. Just as Bergson speaks of matter and spirit as distinct, so Kazantzakis analyzes his god into distinct and indeed antagonistic "persons" (hypostases). One of these corresponds to Bergson's downward stream and another to Bergson's upward stream. The latter is further analyzed into sexual and mental aspects so that in sum we have one-in-three, a trihypostatic monad!

The descending god is everything that frustrates the life force's upward surge. It is *necessity*, the inexorable downward push of matter toward decomposition. In the *Odyssey* this god is called the "killer"; he is heroically but always unsuccessfully defied by man and in particular by man's sexual and mental powers. Indeed, man's purpose in life (seen narrowly in terms of this god only) is to kill the killer-god in all his manifestations—that is, to battle against all forms of stagnation, homogeneity, and inertness.

The god corresponding to Bergson's upward movement is much more complex. Seen in his totality, he is also a killer, but a killer with a difference. "What devours mankind, I call god," Kazantzakis once wrote in a letter, at the same time proclaiming his hope that he would never cease to be devoured by this god whom he loved. This, then, is not the downward-moving god, for our proper response to that god is defiance and hate. Here, Kazantzakis is invoking the primordial force that drives man to burn himself out in the interests of pushing life upward. This god is the cry rolling down from Sinai: "Reach what you cannot! Evolve!"

But the self-incineration needed if one is to respond fully to this cry can take both sexual and mental forms. Sexually, man burns himself out in order to evolve by means of progeny. The overall upward surge is accomplished only because each generation produces vibrant successors and then dies. If we truly understand this god who devours man, we will love him for furnishing us the opportunity to participate in universal processes that demand our own extinction. In *The Saviors of God* Kazantzakis speaks of this god as the husband. His wife is matter. He is the sperm inside all the eggs of the universe, the male propulsion of the upward stream working inside the female inertia of the downward stream. (This metaphysical or rather metabiological view of women is of course reflected in all of Kazantzakis' works.) He is the force that loves all things and sticks to none, loves all things *because* he sticks to none; for only through successive deaths can he jump from body to body and roll out the red line that is life. This god is the spark, the flame centered in man's loins.

The same god in his other aspect pushes man to burn himself out mentally. Here, too, the metaphor of flame is appropriate. In the *Odyssey* Kazantzakis speaks of the mind as a hearth containing a world-destroying, world-creating spark. Or we might say, as Kazantzakis liked to, that the sperm can also reside in the head. God in this aspect is the upward-surging force pushing all of created life toward self-consciousness. This recalls Bergson's view that consciousness is the opposite of materiality and inertness and hence by definition the acme of the ascending stream: "The destiny of consciousness is not bound up . . . with the destiny of cerebral matter. . . . Consciousness is essentially free; it is freedom itself." The course of evolution has been an attempt by the life force to create a "machine

which should triumph over mechanism" by means of self-consciousness. To accomplish this, evolution has spurred life to refine its materiality—to transubstantiate rocks into reflection—thereby burning itself out. Mankind's duty, aside from defying the killer-god and serving the philoprogenitive god, is to liberate the fire inside its head, thus liberating the god who has become entrapped in the mechanism he created for his own deliverance.

All this constitutes the worldview that Kazantzakis learned from Bergson in Paris and expressed in terms of a trihypostatic deity with the characteristics we have seen. It should be clear that this god, despite his several persons, is a true monad, a unified life force working in ways that appear disparate but are not. Kazantzakis struggled all his life to evoke this unity. Consistent with his profoundest vision of reality, he tried to show that the apparent antagonists are secret collaborators welling up from the depths of a unified primordial essence.

What implications did this worldview have for Kazantzakis? We should remember that his ideas stood behind his prophetic fervor and determined his way of life. He wished to answer the great questions not as an academic exercise but as a spur to personal responses. Having satisfied himself about whence we have come and whither we are going, having seen the relationship between the abysses and the luminous interval, having—finally—been able to formulate a new theology based on these "scientific" facts, Kazantzakis addressed himself to more practical questions. First he asked: If the universe is the way it is, why are we here? We are here, he answered audaciously, in order to save god. God has trapped himself in his own congealments and is now dependent on us, his material embodiments, if he is to be set free. As a sperm he can get nowhere without an egg. The only way he can evolve to the second abyss of purity is through the machine he created to triumph over mechanism. Life as a whole moves from rocks to reflection, and each individual life has the potential of traveling a similar arc in minia-ture, progressing from infantile corporeality to mature self-understanding. In doing this as both individuals and species, we gradually liberate god. At any given point the deity can be no further along in his evolution than we are in ours. "My god is not Almighty," Kazant-zakis writes in *The Saviors of God*. "He clings to warm bodies; he has no other bulwark. . . . He cannot be saved unless we save him with our struggles; nor can we be saved unless he is saved." What Kazantzakis accomplished here was to install humanity at the center of the universe once more, albeit in a way entirely different from the Christian anthropocentricity made unacceptable by Charles Darwin. He re-established humanity's significance by en-abling individualistic voluntarism to serve transindividualistic ends. By realizing our own potentialities, by overcoming sluggish-ness and exerting our vitality—whether sexu-ally, martially, or mentally—we save god and push evolution forward.

Having answered why we are here, Kazant-zakis proceeded to establish with increasing precision exactly what we should do to save god. His first prescription tells us that we must "adjust . . . the rhythm of our small and fleeting life to his." Christians had counseled the im-itation of Christ as a practical guide to behav-ior; Kazantzakis now counseled the imitation of the *élan vital*. We should act in ways favoring motion, sensation, creativity, heterogeneity, self-consciousness, and freedom. We should burn ourselves out in the service of something beyond ourselves, transubstantiating our flesh into spirit. According to this view, the greatest sin is satisfaction, an immobility that halts evolution's progress and smothers god. The greatest virtue is vitality, the life force strutting in full regalia. All actions arising sincerely and intensely from man's vital center are good, for such actions imitate the gushing *élan* of which we are part. On the contrary, all actions or thoughts that bring completion, that close off further development and therefore serve the forces of stagnation and inertia, are bad.

But these prescriptions were still too gen-eral, too abstract. Kazantzakis knew that he had to pursue the elusive problem of actual responses until he could determine our proper behavior in the here and now. Yet he also knew that to provide a precise formula for "vital, creative action" would be a contradic-tion in terms since such action by definition must be non-formulaic. To escape this di-lemma Kazantzakis had recourse to his old standby, the doctrine of the transitional age. The ways of saving god are many, he said. In various ages men and women as diverse as Jesus, Genghis Khan, William Shakespeare, Vladimir Lenin, El Greco, Yoryis Zorbas (the real-life model for Zorba the Greek), Buddha, Yannis Psycharis (the "Saint George" who killed the dragon of puristic Greek), Rosa Lux-emburg (the Communist revolutionary), Don Quixote, Nietzsche, and Dante Alighieri have been saviors of god, each in his or her own manner. But not all paths are applicable in any given era. For each transitional age there is a dominant way to fight stagnation and to liberate the flame. There is also a dominant group that follows this way. Kazantzakis' non-formulaic formula, therefore, is that we must seek out the group in our own age that seems to have the greatest vitality and sincerity, the group whose actions favor motion, creativity, and freedom, thereby tending to bring new possibilities rather than completion. In his own age, he concluded, the way chosen by the ascending spirit was war. The groups he ad-mired at various stages in his life were mili-tant ones like the Bolsheviks that did not shrink from violence as a means to express their vitality. Kazantzakis did not love violence for its own sake. What he loved was his god—the life force evolving toward spirituality by devouring man—and it is only because of his conviction that warfare was the twentieth cen-tury's strongest power for spiritual growth that he lent it his support.

To understand any individual work by Ka-zantzakis we must see it in light of what was constant in all the works, namely his worldview. This will save us from misinterpreting his enthusiasms and forcing upon him narrow allegiances that misrepresent the facts. If we forget the metaphysical constants we can easily err by calling him a Communist (he admired Lenin) or a Fascist (he admired Benito Mussolini). Conversely, when we read *The Last Temptation of Christ,* we might believe that in his dotage he renounced violence for Christian love. The truth is that he was not a Communist, not a Fascist, not a Christian; he was a Bergsonist. If at various stages in his life he admired Lenin, Mussolini, African blacks, Greek nationalists, and Mao Zedong, it was because these people had discerned, so he thought, the particular spiritual path appropriate for their age. If he presented Christ as a hero it was not because he had reverted to Christianity but because he admired Christ as a savior of god following a way appropriate to another transitional situation. Once he had discovered his Bergsonian god, he maintained his allegiance with unwavering constancy; indeed his sin (for those who need to accuse him of something) was not his Olympian heartlessness toward individual suffering, but—strangely—his uncompromising loyalty to the spirit. This inflexible virtue made his system such a neat response to the particular problems of our time that it cut him off from further progress and negated precisely what the system was meant to accomplish. But this very sin—the fact that the great fighter against orthodoxies allowed himself to be taken prisoner by his own orthodoxy—is what makes Kazantzakis interesting, and even human. Realizing the trap he had created, he struggled against his own orthodoxy. Although these struggles were largely fruitless, they give him stature.

All the major ideas in Kazantzakis' worldview were acquired by the time he left Paris at the age of twenty-six. In the dozen years intervening before he definitively formulated his position in *The Saviors of God,* there were reinforcements and shifts of emphasis, but nothing substantially new. When he returned to Greece in 1909 and attempted to act on his beliefs, he found encouragement in the nationalistic mystique of the Greek author, diplomat, and political activist Ion Dragoumis. Itself an amalgam of Nietzsche and Maurice Barrès, Dragoumis' program stressed Greece's vibrancy and its right to self-assertion. In 1922, when Greek vibrancy burned itself out in total defeat by the Turks in Asia Minor in a mockery of Dragoumis' vision, Kazantzakis became suddenly attracted to Oswald Spengler's declaration that Western civilization is in decline and to Gautama Buddha's insistence on the vanity of all human desire. Spengler was helpful because, arguing from historical "law," he predicted that the next phase would involve "a new element of inwardness." He called this a "second religiousness" and asserted that it would start "with rationalism's fading out into helplessness." Although Kazantzakis called it meta-Communism, he meant more or less the same thing: a culture "where the worship of the machine, of reason and of practical goals will be considered unworthy." Spengler reinforced Kazantzakis' metabiological belief in an evolutionary surge moving beyond practical reason toward inwardness and intuitive wisdom.

But of the various influences between the Paris years and *The Saviors of God,* Buddhism was the most important. Reading the Eastern scriptures in Vienna in 1922, Kazantzakis re-encountered in concentrated form certain Buddhistic elements that had entered his earlier thinking indirectly, via Arthur Schopenhauer. His distrust of the phenomenal world dates from *Snake and Lily;* from Bergson he learned "scientifically" that matter does not exist in its own right and that the abyss is ultimate reality. All this he found starkly expressed in the Buddhistic insistence that phenomena are a deceptive phantasmagoria of nothingness and that we should therefore purge ourselves of desire and embrace the void. It is important to note that he was attracted to this extreme and distorted form of his own ideas in a period of personal turmoil, a private transitional age

NIKOS KAZANTZAKIS

between an allegiance to Greek nationalism that had just died and an allegiance to Lenin that was struggling to be born. Thus he momentarily heeded the temptation to become a broken soul. But this path was so contrary to his Bergsonian belief that we reach the abyss by living vibrantly and burning ourselves out that he was able to resist. Ultimately, his flirtation with Buddhistic nihilism served merely to reinforce certain of his own ideas. For example, in determining how to save god in a particular transitional age, he could easily have forgotten that life itself is a colossal transitional age, a luminous interval situated between one abyss and another. Buddhism helped him retain this awareness.

With these adjustments behind him, Kazantzakis was ready to set down his definitive worldview. He called his *Saviors of God* a meta-Communistic credo, which means a theology of activism justifying the destruction of capitalism's decadent remains in the interests not so much of economic or social justice (i.e., materialistic progress) as of a vital inwardness higher in the spiritual scale than either capitalism or Communism—in the interests, more precisely, of an inwardness capable of discovering and honoring the Kazantzakian worldview! For Kazantzakis the aim of revolution was to raise men sufficiently in the evolutionary scale to make them understand what he himself had understood about ultimate reality. The book's ingredients are everything that we have been discussing: the two abysses, the luminous interval between, the relation of that interval to the abysses, god's trihypostatic nature, our duty to save him, and how to do this in our own transitional age. But Kazantzakis was not content simply to state the conclusions of his philosophical quest; true to his subtitle, "Askitikí" (ascetic discipline), he also offered a systematic manual of the steps leading to enlightenment. Like W. B. Yeats, he places gyres within gyres: while one set of steps leads in Bergsonian fashion from the widest circle of awareness to the precise point that is our person, another set begins with this personal center and leads outward to the whole. These steps in turn presuppose a theory of knowledge. Accordingly, Kazantzakis begins with an epistemological section.

Called "I proetimasía" ("The Preparation"), it offers a Kantian critique of pure reason. Dividing reality into the phenomenal and the noumenal (the unknown source or cause of phenomena), Kazantzakis insists that the mind can deal only with the former, although even here it simply squeezes phenomena into its own categories: "I impose order on disorder and give a face—my face—to chaos." Epistemologically, our first duty is to recognize these limitations of the human mind. As for the noumenal realm, with luck this can be known too—not by the mind, of course, but by the heart (Bergson's intuition). Our second duty is to attempt to pierce to this unified essence beyond appearances. Let us skip the crucial third duty for a moment, for in the psychology of spiritual questing this can only come after, not before, the next two exercises. In the first of these, "I poría" ("The March"), Kazantzakis describes the mind's attempt to understand phenomena; in the second, "To órama" ("The Vision"), he describes the heart's attempt to understand noumena. The march employs the method of expanding consciousness; it is a journey through phenomena beginning with the self-centeredness of the infant and ending with the universal awareness of the sage. Although this awareness can tell us only of the relationships among phenomena, it can provide an intimation of the unity underlying the visible world. Thus it prepares us for the heart's vision, which is the next step. Psychologically, this step involves an intuitive awareness that pierces through the divisiveness of clock time to the "succession without distinction" that characterizes Bergsonian duration—to a "momentary eternity that encloses everything, past and future." What is seen behind time and phenomena is of course the primordial spirit (Bergson's *élan vital*) struggling painfully upward via matter and transubstantiating that matter into spirit.

Now that the mind and heart have done their work, we come to the third duty. The mind, which hopes to impose order on the phenomenal realm, imposes on it nothing but relationships derived subjectively from its own categories; the heart, which hopes to apprehend the noumenal realm, apprehends merely a human meaning, a human myth, and imposes this on the unknowable. The third duty, therefore, is to conquer the mind's hope to understand phenomena and the heart's to understand noumena. We abolish these dualities in a joyously synthetic acceptance of the meaninglessness of our existence: "Where are we going? Do not ask! . . . Life is good and death is good. . . . I surrender myself to everything. . . . It is your duty . . . to say 'Nothing exists!'"

This would seem to nullify all that went before, but it does not. The final acceptance of meaninglessness, though surpassing the previous attempt to discover meaning, does not reject that attempt. Just as god in the Bergsonian system can achieve his goal of non-congealment only by the laborious process of evolution through congealment, so the acceptance of meaninglessness can be achieved only after a previous conviction that meaning can be found. Only when the mind and heart have labored futilely in pursuit of their respective chimeras do we have the right to proclaim universal futility. This proclamation cannot nullify the previous efforts since those are its own ineluctable precondition. We must remember that Kazantzakis was toiling to develop a rationale for action while remaining within a framework of philosophical pessimism. He tells us that the mind and heart must burn themselves out through aspiration if the freedom of non-aspiration is ever to be achieved. He tells us furthermore that this is also the "rhythm" of the universe. His message is not Communist doctrine. It is his own meta-Communist credo: a justification for trying to make the world a better place not in spite of the abyss but because of it.

Thus the spiritual exercises conclude (or all but conclude) with a section on practical behavior. The third duty must be held in abeyance until we have burned ourselves out. Kazantzakis passes directly from "The Vision" to "I práksi" ("The Action"), reminding us that once we have discovered "the rhythm of God's march," our responsibility is to adjust the rhythm of our small and fleeting lives to that larger rhythm. This section begins with a metaphysics of action describing the relationship between man and god; it proceeds to a morality of action describing the relationship between man and man and defining good and evil in ways we have seen, good being everything that enhances the life force's creativity, evil being everything that inhibits it. The final section insists that our actions should push nature forward in the evolutionary process and reminds us that each person must do this in his or her own way. In the original version Kazantzakis followed this section with a recapitulation of the third duty but then concluded positively with a call to everyone to shoulder the "supreme responsibility" of saving god in the here and now. This he modified in 1928 during another personal transition, brought on this time by his disillusion with the Soviet Union during an extended stay there. The epilogue called "I siyí" ("The Silence") that Kazantzakis appended to the second edition (1945) does not add anything new; it merely lets Buddha have the last word, reminding us that the evolutionary struggle so laboriously illumined for us does not really exist. (Cosmologically, this means that matter is just a deceptive form of energy; psychologically, it means that our sensual and intellectual conceptions of supposedly objective reality are projections of our mind's subjective categories.) In the revised version the luminous interval called life is accordingly framed between both a prologue ("We come from a dark abyss [and] we end in a dark abyss") and an epilogue proclaiming nonexistence. Without being thereby nullified, all the efforts of the human mind, heart, and body are encased in universal vanity.

NIKOS KAZANTZAKIS

This, then, is the doctrine that remained constant throughout Kazantzakis' career and that suffused his works, accounting for their prophetic urgency. This is the personal response that he felt must govern his life as well as his books. The fruit of his intellectual engagement with society's problems, it constituted his great hope for guiding humanity upwards toward a better future. But it was also an obstacle in his path toward artistic perfection.

We must see Kazantzakis in his totality; this means seeing how each work issues from an amalgam of his worldview, his prophetic zeal, and his professionalism. But once we look at the works in this way we may also become aware that the best of them strain to transcend the worldview, to undercut the prophetic voice to some degree, and to modify the professionalism. We begin to notice a certain flexibility in the areas that make up the outward integument of Kazantzakis' totality.

His artistic task in each work was to find a particular historical situation that could be fused successfully with the general cosmological situation as he saw it. He then had to show his hero burning himself out in this context that rendered all action futile but in which, paradoxically, a freely willed death, or a cry, is not futile at all, since either response imitates universal rhythms and pushes evolution forward, saving god. The artistic problem, however, was to trick the reader into forgetting the formulaic nature of all this—something that Kazantzakis could not do very well until he discovered how to transcend his own formulas. Although he never abandoned them, he did modify them in crucial ways, the most important of which involved the aestheticizing of his worldview.

We shall be able to follow this development if we look first at *The Odyssey*. A gargantuan retelling of *The Saviors of God* by means of picture, metaphor, character, and plot, this epic poem attempts to portray the entire cosmic situation as understood by Bergson. Thus it presents a luminous interval surrounded by two dark abysses, and it traces, within that

interval, the life force's journey through matter in a creative process that unmakes itself, transubstantiating matter into spirit. The prologue and epilogue call our attention to the dark silence at each end of existence. The sun rises at the beginning, inaugurating life, and sets at the end, extinguishing it. Multiple levels are established immediately, for the sun is also Odysseas' (i.e., humanity's) mind. Hence the luminous interval consists of unreal shadows produced by our subjective categories. When the entire universe disintegrates into nothingness at the conclusion, it is because Odysseas' mind has gone dark.

The epic proper is divided into twenty-four cantos that are the alpha to omega of existence. Integrated into this universal history are contemporary politics and personal vicissitudes. Politically, the epic cryptically employs our own transitional age as the setting for Odysseas' efforts to save god. This means that violence is the hero's initial way of transubstantiating matter into spirit; it means, furthermore, that Odysseas destroys decadent establishments (the bourgeois West) in the interests of blond barbarians (the Russians). But Odysseas is not a Communist, and although he cooperates with figures standing loosely for Lenin, Leon Trotsky, Joseph Stalin, and Luxemburg, he ultimately leaves them and their narrowness behind in order to pursue his meta-Communist quest for a new inwardness.

On the level of personal vicissitudes the epic reflects Kazantzakis' frustrations. He tried to convince the Russians to overcome their materialism, telling them that their ideals were just Americanism in disguise. His meta-Communism, too mystical for the Stalinists and too pessimistic for the Trotskyites, was ignored by everyone. All this is confessed in the autobiographical novel *Toda-Raba* (1934), written hastily in French in 1929 immediately after the frustration it records and immediately before *The Odyssey*'s crucial second draft. Kazantzakis' alter ego in the novel fails not only in politics but also in love and friendship. In the epic, by contrast, the hero is a

1079

great activist, a remarkable lover, and an irresistible friend. Seen on this (admittedly secondary) level, *The Odyssey* is a wish-fulfilling fantasy reflecting Kazantzakis' problems by means of inversion.

But the poem's most important level is the cosmic one. It is Bergsonian—that is to say, incomprehensible if we ignore Kazantzakis' metabiological beliefs. Proclaiming that both bodily and mental experiences are compassed by universal vanity, the epic explores this situation in an attempt to show that death is not life's negation but its fulfillment and that life on earth, despite its struggles that end in failure, is necessary and good. Why is it good? Because only through fleshly experience may we evolve to the understanding that all fleshly experience is futile. Why is it necessary? Because this is how the universe operates. Do not ask further!

The twenty-four cantos fill in the details. Odysseas, in whom all men and all history are represented, adjusts his life superbly to the universal rhythm; he imitates god, saving both god and himself in the process. This imitation naturally takes the form of an evolution from brutishness to refinement, sexuality to intellectuality, martial exploit to imaginative exploit. Progressing from instinctive responses to deliberative ones, Odysseas ends as an artist self-consciously playing with the shadows that we mistakenly think are real. In these and in the other ways in which he evolves, he of course defies satisfaction and stagnation in the interests of motion, freedom, and decongealment. In the largest sense he moves from an outwardness of destroying, copulating, and building to an inwardness in which all his outward actions are recapitulated mentally. Thus he burns himself out twice over, first outwardly, then inwardly, loves all things and sticks to none twice over, as though operating initially in the lower half and subsequently in the upper of a multilevel Byzantine icon. These two realms correspond roughly to the two halves of the epic, with the utopian city (in canto 15) acting as fulcrum. Odysseas first

evolves to the point where he knows what actions are demanded of him. After burning up the world, he rebuilds it. When the ideal society he has created is obliterated by a life force that loves all things yet sticks to none, he is able to evolve to the third duty, whereby he joyously accepts the futility of action and the meaninglessness of existence. On this upper level of the icon he learns to say "Nothing exists" in various ways and moves steadily toward the eternal silence that is his essence and fulfillment.

We must remember that Odysseas is not only imitating the universe; he is saving it, which means that he is enabling it to evolve. The life force can liberate itself only through the successively refined congealments of Odysseas' (humanity's) upward march. This universal evolution is indicated by the series of masks corresponding to Odysseas' expanding awareness as (negatively) he defies the killer-god by warring against all forms of stagnation, first with his martial and sexual lances, then with his mind, and as (positively) he serves the upward-moving god by burning himself out in the creation of progeny, of societies, and finally of complete self-consciousness, the most spiritual aspect of the trihypostatic monad. The masks become increasingly less bestial as the divine flame is gradually liberated from its prison of flesh, until the final face has no features at all—"for all its flesh had turned to soul, and soul to air!" Thus god himself is vaporized back into his initial purity. With Odysseas' death—the death of the mind that has enabled life's shadows to dance before us as though they were real—all that remains of the universe is a voiceless wail lingering like the incandescence from a disintegrated star, a nostalgia for the creative action that has unmade itself.

Unquestionably a feat of endurance, *The Odyssey* demonstrates Kazantzakis' ability to organize huge amounts of material on multiple levels of signification. None of Kazantzakis' books represents his total doctrine so completely, none is more filled with prophetic

NIKOS KAZANTZAKIS

urgency, none more devoted to the promulgation of his opinions. But is *The Odyssey* a successful work of art? That a poem issues from its author's total vision does not mean that it is genuinely true to that vision or able to evoke it for the reader. This is especially so in Kazantzakis' case, for his vision demanded its own annihilation. An absolutely conscious, willed fidelity, even to the third duty that systematizes the system's overthrow, is a denial of the creative evolution on which Kazantzakis based his life. This is why his total doctrine, albeit the crucial ingredient of everything he wrote, was also a hindrance to his artistry. To be genuinely true to himself, he had to develop a nonchalance and self-assurance enabling him to forget the system at least momentarily and to transubstantiate his urgent fidelity to it into a naive acceptance of life and death, a simpleminded awe.

The Odyssey fails artistically because it is too faithful doctrinally. We feel at every moment that the dynamo generating all 33,333 verses is the worldview and not an immediate feeling for human beings, human development, and human annihilation. It does not fail because it is doctrinal poetry; rather, it does not do what its own doctrine expects of it.

In this poem Kazantzakis was incorrigibly the man of letters driving home his opinions. Distrustful of art's subtleties, he committed the technical mistakes of embodying the entire evolutionary voyage in a single character and of being too relentlessly prophetic in his style. These problems relate directly to Kazantzakis' growth in the years following *The Odyssey*. In a letter written to Eleni Samiou in the autumn of 1924 while he was composing the epic, he claimed that he was "striving to experience the vanity of all endeavor and simultaneously the eternity of every moment." In Bergsonian language this means that he was attempting to evoke (a) the essential oneness underlying life's individuated shadows and simultaneously (b) the paradox that only by believing these shadows to be real can we mount to a vision of their unreality. But the poem works

against its own aims by placing the burden of both (a) and (b) on Odysseas. Although meant to interact with individual people and objects that are supposedly real, the over-universalized hero cannot do this convincingly because his own individuation is subordinated to his role as the life force's "succession without distinction" and also because he embodies Kazantzakis' solipsistic doctrine that the mind is the self-contained creative force out of which reality is spun. His object is to love all things and stick to none, but love presupposes a naive belief in the reality of everyday life so that the lover may both affect and be affected. Odysseas cannot have this belief because he is Kazantzakis' totality and as such cannot relate to people, history, or environment. He never allows himself to be touched by someone else. Instead, he is an impervious, autonomous wedge driving resolutely through experience.

In heaping every ingredient of universality upon Odysseas, Kazantzakis hoped to guide the reader beyond the individual to the all. What he accomplishes, however, is merely to present the grotesquely magnified agonizing of a single alienated soul, one who, because of his fabricated universality, never achieves the particularity that is the sine qua non of universal significance. Happily, Kazantzakis soon realized that one character cannot play scores of different roles convincingly, that it is the author who must synthesize the contradictions and supply the unity, doing so surreptitiously. But this, in turn, demanded an artistic self-assurance that he had not yet attained.

The goal of conveying both a vision of oneness and a sense of the eternity of every moment found further hindrance in Kazantzakis' style. As a poet he achieves some striking lines and metaphors but never enough suppleness to evoke varying moods. We should compare his single verbal texture with the diversity seen in *Paradise Lost* (1674), where the lushness of Eden, the undeniable grandeur of Satan, and the final serenity of our chastened first parents each dictates its appropriate rhythms and sonorities. Kazantzakis misses his goal of sublime urgency because his unvarying "high seriousness" weighs on the reader instead of uplifting him; conversely, he fails to convey an unmediated sense of everyday life because his language never descends to quotidian simplicity. He did much better when he turned to prose.

In certain of the later plays and novels the defects of *The Odyssey* are at least partially remedied. In these works we feel the bull butting against the outward parts of Kazantzakis' totality; in other words, we apprehend a tension between these outward parts and a straining toward prosaicness, rootedness, and faith in the eternal efficacy of art—a tension that provides artistic and human interest. Even if we decide ultimately that no one of the books can stand on its own as a masterpiece, we should recognize in the complete oeuvre a remarkable growth. Indeed, the only enduring masterpiece may be the entire career, with its attempt to create a worldview and then its increasing need to transcend, without rejecting, what it had created.

The questions to ask in assessing Kazantzakis' growth should now be evident. Does he fashion a system of thought and at the same time make us realize that absolute fidelity to that system is the system's denial? Does he truly fulfill his third duty—fulfill it naively, without allowing us to feel that it is consciously willed and thus still part of the intellectual system it is meant to transcend? Does he convey a genuine sense of the eternity of every moment despite the abyss that ends existence? Does he develop a style sufficiently flexible to express the varying and contradictory moods that constitute his total experience? Does he convince us that his characters achieve a true relatedness with people and things outside themselves? Does he discover more subtle methods of synthesizing contradictions and collecting life's variety into oneness? Does he achieve universality without sacrificing particularity? Does he fuse history

with cosmology and yet make us forget that his characters and incidents are formulaic?

Before attempting to see how these questions may be answered in relation to specific works written after *The Odyssey*, we should dwell on the three general factors that seem to account for Kazantzakis' growth. As noted above, these are his increasing reliance on prose, his increasing sense of rootedness in Greece, and his increasing acceptance of his own role as artist. By using prose, he liberated himself from the single texture to which verse restricted him. He was thus able to create linguistic embodiments for a much wider range of human moods and, if nothing else, to provide the variety that is the spice of art. By rooting himself once more in Greece (or rather, by relaxing sufficiently so that Greece's soil could embrace him, for rootedness demands passive acceptance), he was able to introduce into his works a natural, unforced, and therefore convincing particularity that they had previously lacked, a particularity that no amount of universalizing could then erase. Moreover, in helping him escape the tyranny of mind and self, this rootedness had the additional effect of allowing a true sense of community to enter an oeuvre that previously had tended toward individualism and indeed toward solipsism. Lastly, by accepting his role as artist, he was able to draw from his worldview in a way that transcended it and thus paradoxically fulfilled its own prescriptions.

Until this time he had ostentatiously shielded himself against aestheticism, perhaps because he knew in his heart that his doctrine of the "abiding spirit" was if anything an aesthetic truth rather than a scientific one. When Kazantzakis came to accept as his innermost drive the normal artistic desire to cheat time by means of beauty, he acquired a serenity that he had not enjoyed earlier. This reconciliation with his own inescapable aestheticism enabled him to pay more attention to the technical side of his craft and therefore to achieve an aloof distance from his characters—a distance arising not from indifference but from a calm engagement with figures whom he alone had the power to immortalize. It also enabled him to subdue the hysteria of earlier works that seem determined to reform the world instantaneously, as though doubting their own longevity. Instead, in many (not all) of the later books there is a controlled fervor that presents us with Kazantzakis' own obsessions, to be sure, but at the same time dissolves these into the artistic whole. Because these works emerge from the author's increased faith in art, they are more willing to let art accomplish whatever improvements in our lives it is destined to accomplish, and in its own good time, its own manner. In sum, by allowing his system to be aestheticized, Kazantzakis acquired the self-confidence and nonchalance he needed to escape the tyranny of mind and consequently to fulfill his third duty in a genuine way.

All this came in fits and starts. Some of the works written after the *Odyssey* merely continued the old modes; others fail to display the full range of growth. But scattered among certain of the novels and plays are unmistakable signs of change—all of which again makes it imperative for us to think of Kazantzakis' total career when we judge him.

A few examples will make this clearer. *Melissa,* although written shortly before the *Odyssey*'s final draft, may be placed with the later works. (The epic was by this time in its definitive form except for minute verbal changes.) This play shows considerable advance in artistic control. Autobiographical elements are subordinated to internal artistic needs; ideas arise from the personalities of the characters who express them. At the same time, the play possesses earthiness and immediacy. In other words, Kazantzakis found a mythos that could effectively transubstantiate his own experiences into art and he handled that mythos with the dignified calm of someone who had faith in art's ability to speak to us on its own terms. As a result, the play does not strive blatantly for sublimity by means of philological affec-

tation and didactic importunity, as does the *Odyssey.* Its linguistic vehicle, prose, gives it a natural quality, exploiting the speech rhythms and nonchalant fluency of demotic Greek. Yet this naturalness does not preclude an exalted and indeed epic flavor. What Kazantzakis began to do in this play was to achieve grandeur and prophetic urgency not by bulk or forced heightening, but by simplicity. The most exalted moments are those in which humble everyday emotions are allowed to speak for themselves. Although like all tragedy the play attempts to show the transitoriness of human life and to provide a vision of something constant behind this transitoriness, it does this solely by means of the particular. If the characters are phantoms, they nevertheless matter. We feel in *Melissa* the vanity of all endeavor and simultaneously the eternity of every moment.

The same elements of growth, as well as others, can be seen in the play *Buddha,* which dates from 1941. Kazantzakis intended this work to be a summa like the *Odyssey.* But it outdoes the epic in its technique of handling a large amount of complicated and contradictory material. All possible human reactions are no longer squeezed unconvincingly into a single character. Those who respond actively and believe in the reality of phenomena are accordingly unburdened of the subjectivism that constantly sabotages Odysseas' credibility as a man in significant relation to the outside world. Instead, subjectivism is concentrated in the Magician and Poet, who "invent" the proceedings. They stand outside the drama proper, framing it in a more artistically justifiable fashion than the rising and setting sun frame the epic. What Kazantzakis achieves here is a successful wedding of realism and vision, of action and the knowledge that all action is futile. Craftsmanship is responsible for this improvement, but not exclusively responsible. Another factor is the aestheticizing of the play's subjectivity. Bergsonian cosmology remains, of course; there is still some nonmaterial force in the universe that is the energizing reality behind all these phantoms. Yet for practical purposes this energizing force is now simply the artist. We are less aware that the characters are congealments of the life force and more aware of something we find easier to understand—that they are inventions of the artistic imagination. A wholly simple and familiar element of legitimate stylization is thus introduced into the play, for we grant the artist a right to make reality fit a schema of his choosing, provided that he tricks us into forgetting both the schema and the ultimate control he exercises until he wishes to remind us of them again. The excellence of the result then depends on this exciting coexistence of artificiality and realism in a way that enhances both. This is achieved in *Buddha* and also, supremely, in *Christ Recrucified* and *The Last Temptation*.

Zorba the Greek, written immediately after *Buddha,* provides a crucial transition to the later novels. In *Buddha* the aesthetic approach to life is thrust at us by means of the Poet and Magician, who stand as it were on a gangway between stage and audience. In *Zorba the Greek* this attitude is much less visible; it can be glimpsed only at the end, peeking out through the wings. In *Christ Recrucified* and *The Last Temptation* it is fully hidden. These stages reflect Kazantzakis' increasing acceptance of phenomenal reality, an acceptance made possible by his progressive reconciliation with both Greece and his own irrepressible aestheticism. *Zorba the Greek,* like everything Kazantzakis wrote, is a mythopoesis of Bergsonian doctrine, a parable showing the life force at work. Once more we see a creative action that unmakes itself. Human effort is presented as futile and yet radiant because people like Zorba, when they burn themselves out, imitate god and save him, pushing universal evolution toward the freedom of unencumbered spirituality. In this book, however, the cosmological element is subordinated to the artistic, indeed is framed within it. At the very end we find as the "abyss" of spirituality neither the silence of *The Saviors of God* nor the voiceless *kravyí* of the *Odyssey,* but art. The book ends with the Boss sitting down and writing the book. All the events have conspired to enable the artistic flame within the Boss to be freed. He will now congeal his imagination into a *lógos* and thereby save all the incidents and characters from oblivion.

This novel is an important fulcrum in Kazantzakis' career since it so openly records his passage from embroilment to serenity. Its events and people present the author's own agonized conflict between activism and Buddhistic withdrawal, his own journey by means of rationality, intuition, and action to the point where big ideas are transcended and he can truly say: "Where are we going? Do not ask!" This is the third duty, synthesizing life and death by means of the simpleminded, profound awe we see exemplified in that untutored yet quintessential artist, Alexis Zorba. In performing on the upper level of the icon what Zorba performs on the lower, the Boss accomplishes in action what his creator had envisioned in thought many years before. In his early career Kazantzakis had yearned for the freedom of impeccable spirituality conceived first aesthetically, then in terms of Dionysiac neo-paganism; this yearning was later "cosmologized" so that freedom became heroic cooperation with a universe that unmakes itself. The ideal figure was Odysseas, and Kazantzakis felt while writing the *Odyssey* that he himself had attained the "Cretan glance" exemplified in his hero. "My own guide," he writes in *Toda-Raba,* "is neither Faust nor Hamlet nor Don Quixote, but Don Odysseas." His meaning is glossed in a notebook: "Faust sought to find the essence behind appearances. Hamlet is entangled in appearances and writhes." Don Quixote gives way to a "ridiculous and sublime impetus." Odysseas "rejoices in appearances and, rejoicing, creates the essence." What Kazantzakis could not know at this time was that in defining Odysseas he had also perfectly defined the artist, and that he himself would not achieve identification with his hero until he had re-aestheticized his cosmological yearnings and had thus moved closer to his own impulses, bringing the Hamletian-Faustian-Quixotic transition more or less to an end. The novel *Zorba the Greek* records this transition and does so from the viewpoint of an author who had already achieved "Odyssean" freedom.

This is why the book succeeds. Because Kazantzakis himself had already completed the growth he depicts in the book, because he had attained a self-assurance enabling him to stand integrally in the wings viewing with equanimity his own agonized multiplicity, the book transcends its schematizations and dualities, embodying the synthesis it preaches. As in *Melissa,* a character is made to mouth the usual ideas about freedom. But in both works these ideas are felt to be more than hollow formulas since the works themselves exemplify Kazantzakis' own liberation from the embroilments of his past.

In addition, they convey his thankfulness for life's gifts. This loving and yet distanced relationship to his materials is carried forward in the final novels, especially in *Christ Recrucified* and *The Last Temptation.* (*Freedom or Death, I aderfofádes [The Fratricides,* 1963], and *O ftohúlis tu Theú [Saint Francis,* 1956] seem flawed by comparison.) In the more successful novels Kazantzakis' artistic self-assurance has reached the point where the energizing force can be kept entirely invisible; the director is so confident now that he allows his characters to perform largely on their own. Despite its autobiographical content, *Zorba the Greek* transcends Kazantzakis' personality by establishing its characters as independent beings. *Christ Recrucified,* which depicts an entire Greek village reliving the mission and passion of Jesus, carries this transcendence further, for it includes a vivid evocation of community. Without in the least diminishing the importance or grandeur of its individual saviors of god, the novel convincingly demonstrates the individual's unreality apart from the unity that is the group. This paradox is conveyed nonchalantly, without philosophical

strain. As the refugees pick up their meager belongings and set out once more despite the frustrations they have just endured, we feel that, like the *élan vital* itself, they will continue to ascend higher and higher along the track of earthly vicissitude, their collective impetus sweeping up individuals as they go. What could have been just rhetoric (and indeed may sound like rhetoric here) is transformed by the book's simplicity into a successful evocation of both particularized human aspiration and the force that drives men to subordinate their personal well-being to a collective surge that will survive them.

Technically, *Christ Recrucified* and *The Last Temptation* walk a tightrope between stylization and realism, the universal and the particular. Insofar as Kazantzakis achieves a compelling evocation of real life, we are tricked into forgetting the rigidity of his schema; insofar as the schema calls up in us a compelling response in its own right, we are tricked into forgetting the rigidity of plotting and characterization. Each element is a sponge absorbing the defects of the other. Kazantzakis' ultimate accomplishment as a craftsman may be the way he learned to exploit his limitations.

Is Kazantzakis an impressive, astonishing writer or an atrocious one? Will his books be read fifty years from now or will they be forgotten? We cannot know. Yet we do know that he is widely appreciated today and that presumably he speaks to the condition of many readers. He does this initially through individual works, but the reason that even a single, isolated book attracts us is the presence in it of his totality. When we dip more widely into his oeuvre we become initiated into the subtleties of his prophetic fervor, professionalism, and worldview as well as into the internal strains and tensions that mark his career.

Those who read only sparingly will most likely find Kazantzakis appealing because of the opinions he promulgates—or, more accurately, because of the way he makes these ideas incandescent. For some, the ideas themselves will seem less important than the sincerity and *élan* with which he voices them. Others will find that he speaks directly to their own needs. Like Kazantzakis, people today are all too conscious that they have been born into a transitional age; like him, they crave an exit and feel that the direction must be away from materialism and toward a new inwardness. Some are already convinced, as was Kazantzakis, that any such turn ought to be based on a scientifically defensible view of what life and death are all about; others are first awakened to this conviction by Kazantzakis. They share his strong determination to adjust the rhythm of individual behavior to a larger rhythm outside themselves. They also appreciate his insistence that action, not withdrawal, is the road to spirituality, his equal insistence that action may take many forms, and his strict abhorrence of a linear, laissez-faire activism based on the gospel of increased gross national product. Like Kazantzakis, they wish to make the world better in concrete ways, and they therefore value materiality; but at the same time their consciousness of nuclear weapons makes them recognize how fragile materialistic progress is and how justified Kazantzakis was to brood about the dark abyss. Caught in Kazantzakis' own dilemma, they feel that his attempt to combine Western practicality and utopianism with an Eastern vision of universal vanity may give direction to their own gropings. On the other hand, many are comforted by Kazantzakis' inability to exclude Christianity and Hellenism from his visions of future humanity. His mixture of traditionalism and iconoclasm soothes at the same time that it disturbs.

These are some of the reasons why Kazantzakis has appealed to a thoughtful and searching readership. But surely these are not enough to give him lasting value. Fifty years from now our present transitional age will presumably be over and our progeny will be caught in a different transition with different problems. If Kazantzakis is still read then, it will probably be because of the basically human, and thus abiding, interest we find in him only when we know his oeuvre more or less as a whole. It is doubtful whether future generations will suddenly consider him a superb thinker or craftsman; they may, however, consider him a superb human being. By this I do not mean a perfect or even a good human being but rather a superbly self-conscious one. Although Kazantzakis' great talent and drive perhaps never produced a work of the highest quality, they did produce a sprawling, undisciplined, impassioned oeuvre that gives us an intimate view of a straining totality and in particular of an outward integument that was increasingly challenged by factors enabling him to write better books than before but that by no means remade his entire being. It is the tension in this contradictory yet integral totality that transforms Kazantzakis from a pompous and stridently provincial rhetorician into a touchingly human figure worthy of respect.

His autobiography, *Anaforá ston Gréko* (*Report to Greco,* 1961), holds a particular interest because it anthologizes and epitomizes the oeuvre, giving us a sense of the artist in his wholeness. It shows us the busy man of letters promulgating his opinions while he races around the world and sends home dispatches to make a living; it allows the prophet to vent his sincerity; it offers partial summaries of the worldview. In addition, it witnesses to Kazantzakis' eventual rootedness in things Greek and his awe-filled gratitude for the wonders of everyday life. At the same time it aestheticizes all these elements by giving the entire life an outward coherence that it never possessed in reality. The book thus tugs in different directions yet coheres in spite of itself because of the huge personality—the huge attempt at self-consciousness—that suffuses it.

The testimonies Kazantzakis gives us in this work are touching because beneath their eclecticism lies a simple paradigm that has lasting worth. The first thing we see in him is the colossal intellectual arrogance of youth: the desire to control self and the world by understanding it. Next we see the clash in middle age between intellectual systems and a physical and psychological reality that refuses to be neatly contained within them. Finally, in old age the youthful arrogance is confessed, surpassed to great degree, and yet not regretted. Kazantzakis acquires a serenity distilled out of everything that has preceded. It is a completely shaped life, a rebuke to the desultory lives of so many others, yet a life whose validity comes only because the shaping forces were not wholly under Kazantzakis' control. If everything had arisen from his own volition and foreknowledge, we would consider him a monster. The testimonies are genuine only because so many of the forces stood outside his desires and indeed warred against them. He gained serenity, we might say, in spite of himself; he honored his basically aesthetic instincts in spite of himself, still brandishing his prophetic fist. And though the intellectual arrogance decreased, the curiosity and articulateness did not. From beginning to end Kazantzakis tried to express what was happening to him, to understand even his own failure to understand. The result is a touching witness for self-consciousness, one that transcends self and becomes meaningful to the rest of us. If we think of Kazantzakis in his totality and see his individual books each as a different entrance to that straining wholeness, we shall appreciate how fully, notwithstanding his imperfect artistry, he performed the artist's primal task of giving a face to chaos.

Selected Bibliography

EDITIONS

INDIVIDUAL WORKS

NOVELS
Ófis ke kríno. Athens, 1906.
Spasménes psihés. In the journal *O Numas* 7–8 (1909–1910). The serialization ran from 30 August 1909 until 7 February 1910.
Toda-Raba. Paris, 1934.

Le jardin des rochers. Amsterdam, 1939.
Víos ke politía tu Aléksi Zorbá. Athens, 1946.
O Kapetán Mihális. Athens, 1953.
O Hristós ksanastavrónetai. Athens, 1954.
O teleftaíos pirasmós. Athens, 1955.
O ftohúlis tu Theú. Athens, 1956.
I aderfofádes. Athens, 1963.

EPIC POETRY
Odíssia. Athens, 1938.

THEATER
Ksimerónei. Produced in 1907. Printed in *Nea Estia* 102:182–210 (special Christmas number, 1977).
Komodía. In *Kritiki Stoa.* Iraklion, 1909. Reprinted in *Nea Estia* 63:616–625 (15 April 1958).
O protomástoras. Athens, 1910.
Nikifóros Fokás. Athens, 1927; 2d ed., 1939.
Hristós. Athens, 1928.
Odisséas. Athens, 1928.
Mélissa. Athens, 1939.
Iulianós. Athens, 1945.
O Kapodístrias. Athens, 1946.
Theatro. Vol. 1. Athens, 1955. Includes *Promithéas Pirfóros, Promithéas Desmótis, Promithéas Liómenos, Kúros, Odisséas,* and *Mélissa.*
Theatro. Vol. 2. Athens, 1956. Includes *Hristós, Iulianós o Paravátis, Nikifóros Fokás,* and *Konstandínos o Palaiológos.*
Theatro. Vol. 3. Athens, 1956. Includes *Kapodístrias, Hristóforos Kolómvos, Sódoma ke Gómora,* and *Vúdas.*

ESSAYS
"I arróstia tu aiónos." *Pinakothiki* 6:8–11, 26–27, 46–47 (March–May 1906). Reprinted in *Nea Estia* 63:691–696 (1958).
O Frideríkos Nítse en ti filosofía tu dikaíu ke tis politías. Iraklion, 1909.
"I epistími ehreokópise?" *Panathinaia* 19:71–75 (15 November 1909). Reprinted in *Nea Estia* 64:1374–1378 (1958).
H. Bergson. Athens, 1912. Reprinted in *Kainuria Epohi* 3:12–30 (Autumn 1958).
Salvatores Dei: Askitikí. Athens, 1927. Second edition with revised ending, Athens, 1945, under the title *Askitikí Salvatores Dei.*
"Rosa Luxemburg." *Ilisia* (22 May 1927). Reprinted in *Kainuria Epohi* 3:171–175 (Winter 1958).
Istoria tis Rosikís logotehnias. 2 vols. Athens, 1930.

"To dráma ke o simerinós ánthropos." *Nea Estia* 56:1636–1638 (1954).

"I dío adelfí: Ta ogdónda hrónia tu Sweitzer." *Nea Estia* 57:214–215 (1955).

Simpósion. Athens, 1971.

To sosialistikó manifésto tu 1945. Nicosia and Lund, 1974.

AUTOBIOGRAPHICAL WORKS

Anaforá ston Gréko. Athens, 1961.

TRAVEL WRITING

Taksidévontas. Alexandria, 1927. Collects articles on Spain, Italy, Egypt, and Sinai.

Ti eída sti Rusía. 2 vols. Athens, 1928.

Ispanía. Athens, 1937.

"Ena taksídi eis tin Pelopónnison." *Kathimerini* (7 November–15 December 1937).

Iaponía-Kína. Athens, 1938.

Anglía. Athens, 1941.

Taksidévontas. Athens, 1961. Collects articles on Italy, Egypt, Jerusalem, Cyprus, and the Peloponnese.

CORRESPONDENCE

"Anékdota grámmata tu Níku Kazantzáki." *Kainuria Epohi* 4:30–38 (Autumn 1959).

Anékdotes epistolés Kazantzáki apó ta neaniká éos ta órima hrónia tu (1902–1956). Athens, 1979.

O asimvívastos. Edited by Eleni Kazantzakis. Athens, 1977.

Epistolés pros ti Galátea. Athens, 1958.

O Kazantzákis mileí ya Theó. Athens, 1972. Letters to Papastefanou.

"84 grámmata tu Kazantzaki ston Kakridí." *Nea Estia* 102:257–300 (special Christmas number, 1977).

Tetrakósia grámmata tu Kazantzáki ston Preveláki. Athens, 1965.

TRANSLATIONS BY KAZANTZAKIS

James, William. *I theoría tis sinkiníseos.* Athens, 1911.

Nietzsche, Friedrich. *I yénnisis tis tragodías.* Athens, 1912.

Nietzsche, Friedrich. *Táde éfi Zaratústras.* Athens, 1913.

Darwin, Charles. *Perí tis genéseos ton eidón.* Athens, 1913.

Bergson, Henri. *To yélio.* Athens, 1915.

Dante. *I theía komodía.* Athens, 1934.

Jørgensen, Johannes. *Áyios Frankískos tis Asízis.* Athens, 1951.

Homer. *Iliáda.* With I. T. Kakridis. Athens, 1955.

Homer. *Odíssia.* With I. T. Kakridis. Athens, 1965.

TRANSLATIONS

Buddha. Translated by Kimon Friar and Athena Dallas-Damis. San Diego, 1983.

"Drama and Contemporary Man." Translated by P. A. Bien. *Literary Review* 19:115–121 (1976).

England: A Travel Journal. Anonymous translation. New York, 1965.

The Fratricides. Translated by Athena Dallas. New York, 1964.

Freedom or Death. Translated by Jonathan Griffin. New York, 1956.

The Greek Passion. Translated by Jonathan Griffin. New York, 1953. Published as *Christ Recrucified* in England. London, 1960.

Japan/China. Translated by George C. Pappageotes. New York, 1963.

Journey to the Morea. Translated by F. A. Reed. New York, 1965.

Journeying. Translated by Themi Vasils and Theodora Vasils. Boston, 1975. Collects articles on Italy, Egypt, Sinai, Jerusalem, and Cyprus.

The Last Temptation of Christ. Translated by P. A. Bien. New York, 1960.

The Odyssey: A Modern Sequel. Translated and introduced by Kimon Friar. New York, 1958.

Report to Greco. Translated by P. A. Bien. New York, 1965.

The Rock Garden. Translated by Richard Howard. New York, 1963.

Saint Francis. Translated by P. A. Bien. New York, 1962.

The Saviors of God: Spiritual Exercises. Translated and introduced by Kimon Friar. New York, 1960.

Serpent and Lily. Translated by Theodora Vasils. Berkeley, Calif., 1980.

Spain. Translated by Amy Mims. New York, 1963.

The Suffering God: Selected Letters to Galatea and to Papastephanou. Translated by Philip Ramp and Katerina Anghelaki Rooke. New Rochelle, N.Y., 1979.

Symposium. Translated by Theodora Vasils and Themi Vasils. New York, 1974.

Three Plays. Translated by Athena Dallas. New

York, 1969. Contains *Christopher Columbus, Melissa,* and *Kouros.*

Toda-Raba. Translated by Amy Mims. New York, 1964.

Two Plays by Nikos Kazantzakis: Sodom and Gomorrah and Comedy. Translated by Kimon Friar. St. Paul, Minn. 1982.

Zorba the Greek. Translated by Carl Wildman. New York, 1953.

BIOGRAPHICAL AND CRITICAL STUDIES

Alexiou, Elli. *Yia na yinei megalos.* Athens, 1966.

Anapliotis, J. *The Real Zorba and Nikos Kazantzakis.* Chicago, 1968.

Anthonakes, Michael A. "Christ, Freedom, and Kazantzakis." Ph. D. dissertation. New York University, 1966.

Bidal-Baudier, Marie-Louise. *Nikos Kazantzaki: Comment l'homme devient immortel.* Paris, 1974.

Peter Bien. *Zorba the Greek,* Nietzsche, and the Perennial Greek Predicament." *Antioch Review* 25:147–163 (1965).

————. "Kazantzakis and Politics." In *The Politics of Twentieth-Century Novelists,* edited by George A. Panichas. New York, 1971.

————. "Kazantzakis' Nietzschianism." *Journal of Modern Literature* 2:245–266 (1971–1972).

————. *Kazantzakis and the Linguistic Revolution in Greek Literature.* Princeton, N.J., 1972.

————. "The Mellowed Nationalism of Kazantzakis' Zorba the Greek." *Review of National Literatures* 5:113–136 (1974).

————. "*Buddha,* Kazantzakis' Most Ambitious and Most Neglected Play." *Comparative Drama* 11:252–272 (1977).

————. *Tempted by Happiness: Kazantzakis' Post-Christian Christ.* Wallingford, Pa., 1984.

Dillistone, F. W. *The Novelist and the Passion Story.* London, 1960.

Doulis, Tom. "Kazantzakis and the Meaning of Suffering." *Northwest Review* 6:33–57 (1963).

Friar, Kimon. *The Spiritual Odyssey of Nikos Kazantzakis.* St. Paul, Minn., 1979.

Hoffman, Frederic J. *The Imagination's New Beginnings: Theology and Modern Literature.* Notre Dame, Ind., 1968.

Izzet, Aziz. *Nikos Kazantzaki: Biographie.* Paris, 1965.

Janiaud-Lust, Colette. *Nikos Kazantzaki: Sa vie, son oeuvre, 1883–1957.* Paris, 1970.

Kazantzakis, Helen. *Nikos Kazantzakis: A Biography Based on His Letters.* Translated by Amy Mims. New York, 1968.

Lea, James F. *Kazantzakis: The Politics of Salvation* University, Ala., 1979.

Levitt, Morton P. *The Cretan Glance: The World and Art of Nikos Kazantzakis.* Columbus, Ohio, 1980.

McDonough, B. T. *Nietzsche and Kazantzakis.* Washington, D.C., 1978.

————. "Níkos Kazantzákis: Symbolí sti hronografía tu bíu tu." *Nea Estia* (Christmas 1959). Article translated into French in Izzet's *Nikos Kazantzaki.*

————. *Nikos Kazantzakis and His Odyssey.* New York, 1961.

————. "Schedíasma esoterikís biographías." In *Tetrakósia grámmata tu Kazantzáki ston Prevelakí.* Athens, 1965.

Prevelakis, Pandelis. "Kazantzakis: Life and Works." *The Charioteer,* nos. 22 and 23:23–65 (1980–1981).

Stanford, W. B. *The Ulysses Theme.* Oxford, 1954.

Vrettakos, Nikiforos. *Nikos Kazantzakis: I agonía tu ke to érgo tu.* Athens, 1960.

Zografu, Lili. *N. Kazantzákis: Énas tragikós.* Athens, 1960.

BIBLIOGRAPHIES

Bien, Peter. "Nikos Kazantzakis: An Annotated Checklist of Primary and Secondary Works Supplementing the Katsimbalis Bibliography." *Mandatoforos* 5:7–53 (1974).

Katsimbalis, G. K. *Bibliografía N. Kazantzáki 1906–1948.* Athens, 1958.

Parker, Sandra A. "Kazantzakis in America: A Bibliography of Translations and Comment." *Bulletin of Bibliography* 25:166–170 (1968).

Rooke, Rodney J. "Nikos Kazantzakis: A Bibliography." Ph.D. dissertation. University of London, 1965.

Stavropoulou, Erasmia-Louiza. *Bibliografía metafráseon neoellinikís logotehnías.* Athens, 1986.

PETER BIEN

JAROSLAV HAŠEK
(1883–1923)

JAROSLAV HAŠEK WAS a prose writer from the periphery of Czech literature who created the Good Soldier Švejk, a figure who has amused and provoked readers over most of the world. As far as sheer skill of writing, style, and linguistic cultivation are concerned, the short stories and feuilletons he wrote before he went into Russian captivity in 1915 are of a higher standard than the incomplete novel that made his name: *Osudy dobrého vojáka Švejka za světové války* (*The Good Soldier Švejk and His Fortunes in the World War*, 1921–1923).

Hašek produced some fifteen hundred short stories and feuilletons and used more than a hundred pseudonyms. Usually stimulated by coffee and rum, he wrote easily, working only for money and paying little or no attention to the politics of the periodicals to which he sent his pieces, although he was probably more or less left-wing even before World War I. He was a sarcastic, impish, sometimes teasing, but often scurrilous writer. Few institutions of the Habsburg monarchy escaped his satire, as did few Czech politicians. Some of his prewar satirical attacks were not published until many years after his death because Hašek himself or a publisher feared court action. Nevertheless, Hašek never actually attacked individuals who could fight back, and only rarely did he attack Austrian institutions that might actually react, as he did in "Rozmluvas cenzorem" (A Conversation with the Censor, 1912), a story about the court of appeal against censorship. When he satirized individuals, they were either politicians, who expected such sallies from periodicals run by another party, or insignificant writers, who were easy targets anyway. Moreover, he so frequently published in such minor or ephemeral periodicals that it was unlikely that the objects of his gibes ever knew they had been attacked.

Hašek was on the periphery of literature throughout his career. He wrote in the tradition of disposable literature, consumer-friendly, popular, and humorous; his short stories were more likely to end up useful in a lavatory than useless in a library. The leading literary journals practically never reviewed his works. He was an uncultured man and, indeed, possibly of limited intelligence, although he was clever. His seeming lack of culture may have been a pose, but critics and biographers have been too quick to look for poses in Hašek. He did not read literature after leaving school, although he voraciously read encyclopedias, technical manuals, popular scientific books, almanacs, and works on the occult and on natural history, and these preferences reflected something of the dilettantism of the period. His tastes were those of an uneducated man, and he wrote primarily for the uneducated man. But there is no reason why an uncultured writer of limited intelligence should not be what the romantics called a genius. And in Hašek one might detect something of the savant.

Hašek was not seriously unstable mentally; he was just a petty vandal and drunkard, a defrauding, blaspheming, raucous, feckless, fickle, déclassé, chattering charmer. During his stay in Russia he underwent something of a change of character, for, when he came back to the new republic of Czechoslovakia, he seems to have become a more pleasant person. Throughout his life he retained his charm, a charm that issued from insolent indolence; he also retained his fascination for anything bizarre or ridiculous.

LIFE

Jaroslav Matěj František Hašek was born on 30 April 1883 in Prague, the capital of Bohemia and a provincial Austrian city that vied with Vienna as cultural center of the monarchy when Hašek was in his teens. Turn-of-the-century Prague did not, however, produce the same number of writers and artists of lasting renown as Vienna did. That may be because Viennese intellectuals used a language more accessible to the rest of the world than the non-Jewish intellectuals of Prague. It may be that Adolf Hitler helped cause the products of *fin-de-siècle* Vienna to be known by making it necessary for so many of their creators to emigrate to the United Kingdom and the United States. It may also be that more important ideas came out of Vienna than out of Prague. Some of the products of *fin-de-siècle* Vienna proffered solutions to the *maladie du siècle:* Freud attempted to make humanity at peace with itself; Hitler had his idea of a neo-Hellenic master race. But most intellectuals of Vienna and Prague, such as Arthur Schnitzler, Franz Kafka, and Hašek himself, at the time saw and sought no solutions.

During this period the social background of most Czech-speaking intellectuals of Prague was lower-middle-class urban with rural roots. Hašek's father, Josef, was a schoolmaster in Prague who taught at a private grammar school instead of one of the superior state schools because he had not completed his teaching qualifications. Hašek's mother, Kateřina, had the maiden name Jareš, and the Jareš family of water bailiffs and peasants appears off and on in Hašek's stories. Both the Hašek and the Jareš families came from South Bohemia. Some critics have made much of that, and, referring to the dissenter Hussite army strongholds of the early fifteenth century, they speak sentimentally of the rebellious blood of South Bohemia running in Hašek's veins. This conception of modern Czechs in the tradition of the Hussite revolutionary ideology is a product of romantic historiography, greatly fostered by the first president of Czechoslovakia, Thomas G. Masaryk, and the Communists after World War II.

Hašek's father was an alcoholic, as were his schoolmaster brother, Bohuslav, and Hašek himself. The father's drinking led to financial worries, and during the author's childhood the family was constantly moving from one faded, seedy flat to another. Marxist-Leninist critics and biographers, such as Radko Pytlík, see Hašek's none too comfortable childhood as resulting in a lifelong morbid fear of poverty, the bitterness that characterizes his humor, and, as Pytlík says, a "revulsion to Austrian schooling, bureaucracy and ecclesiastical obfuscation."

Like many boys of his background the young Hašek served at mass in local churches, and that stood him in good stead for his writing, in which he often uses and sometimes parodies the liturgy. In these and other parodies Hašek demonstrated that he had a quite extraordinary memory. In 1893 he went to grammar school, where he did well in the first and second forms, but then he began to have serious difficulties in the third form. His father, however, died in 1896, and that had a considerable emotional impact on him, which impaired his academic performance. He was kept in the fourth form, and in February 1898 he left school and worked for some months in chemists' shops. Then in 1899 he went to the Czecho-Slav Commercial Academy, where he did better than in his previous school, particularly in technical subjects. He was worst at French and German, which reveals not that he was a bad linguist, but that he was a somewhat sloppy linguist, something the reader notices in his works.

At the academy Hašek's gift as a storyteller was clearly evident; one of his masters said he would become the Czech Mark Twain. While still at school Hašek had started going in the summer on walks in Moravia and Upper Hungary (today's Slovakia) alone or with his brother, and the first story he published, notably in the most distinguished Czech newspaper, *Národní listy,* reflects those tours. That was in January 1901. The story itself, "Cikáni o 'hodech' " (Gypsies at the Fete), is dull, but it manifests the author's abiding interest in outsiders and the unusual. Gypsies were by that time quite common in Czech literature, appearing in the works of August Eugen Mužík, who later helped Hašek in placing his stories, Adolf Heyduk, and Ignát Hořica, a writer who possibly influenced Hašek, but still they were considered exotic subject matter for the Prague readership.

In 1902 he left the Commercial Academy and later on in the same year took a job as a clerk in the Slavie Bank. He lost that job in 1903 due to his unreliability, and by the following year he was an established member of Prague bohemian and anarchist circles and had published fifty pieces in various periodicals. In 1904 he began working for the anarchist press in Prague and North Bohemia. Critics such as Zdeněk Hoření, Cecil Parrott, and Pytlík argue that Hašek's anarchism evinces a more genuine negation of contemporary institutions and values than is the case with other writers. Nothing suggests that is true, but certainly Hašek was something of a frustrated sentimentalist, and that may have caused him to imagine that in anarchism he would find an adequate mask for his oversensitivity or, indeed, a way of getting rid of it.

In 1905 he first met his nouvelle riche future wife, Jarmila Mayerová, whose father forbade her seeing Hašek from time to time because of his dissolute living and his politics, for which Hašek was put under police surveillance in April 1907. On 1 May he received permission from her father to start seeing Jarmila again, if he quit anarchism—which he promised to do. But later in that same month he was arrested for inflicting bodily harm on a policeman and for inciting a crowd to similar violence; eventually he received a one-month prison sentence. Soon after being released, in the summer of 1907, he had his first contact with the theater, when he took a one-week director's course for amateurs at the Organization of Czech Actors in Prague. Hašek was a show-off, and, furthermore, theater and cabaret seemed to provide another possible mask for his sensitivity. He then spent months and months looking for a job and did work for a brief time as an agent for the National Socialist Party in 1908.

In 1909, however, with the help of a friend, Hašek got what looked like a permanent post as editor of the popular zoological magazine *Svět zvířat* (Animal World), so he was able to write to Jarmila's parents and ask for her hand. In 1910 they were married after Hašek had rejoined the Roman Catholic church, which he had left when he became an anarchist. Soon after their wedding Hašek lost his job because he began inventing animals and animal behavior, and not long after that his father-in-law retrieved Jarmila. In 1910 he also produced and acted in his first plays (not extant) at the Deklarace Theater in the Prague working-class area of Žižkov.

In 1911 Hašek spent over a fortnight in the Prague state mental hospital, Kateřinky, as the result of an attempted suicide. If it was not a hoax, as it is generally assumed, the suicide attempt probably derived from a depression occasioned by alcohol.

For the by-election in the Vinohrady suburb of Prague later in 1911 Hašek set himself up as candidate for a party he had invented with some bohemian friends, the Party of Moderate

JAROSLAV HAŠEK

Progress Within the Limits of the Law. In connection with this mock party's spoof campaign Hašek began to be involved for the first time with cabaret. His Vinohrady cabaret performances continued in various pubs and restaurants until 1912, when he started performing and acting as master of ceremonies in various nightclubs in central Prague. Also in 1912 Jarmila gave birth to their son, Richard, after which the marriage broke up forever, although Hašek never ceased to be fond of Jarmila.

In February 1915 Hašek was called up, and he joined the 91st Infantry in Budweis. Initially he was sent to short-service commission school, but after some malingering he ended up an ordinary ranker. In July 1915 he arrived on the Galician front, and after the week-long Battle of Sókal he was promoted to lance corporal, and his name was put forward for the Silver Medal for Gallantry. During a Russian counteroffensive, on 24 September, Hašek became a prisoner of war. Tradition has it that he deliberately let himself be captured, but there is no firm evidence to that effect. After an unpleasant march he arrived in a disease-infested prisoner of war camp, and some weeks later he had himself quickly recruited into the Czech section of the tsar's army. That meant that his living conditions improved immediately. He became a fervent Russophile Czech patriot, hoping for a Romanov on the Bohemian throne. He first published in the conservative Czech expatriate periodical in Kiev, *Čechoslovan*, on 10 July 1916, and he became a regular contributor.

The anti-Habsburg nationalism of his Kiev stories and articles is quite as vicious and one-sided as the anti-British and anti-French and anti-bourgeois propaganda he produced two years or so later. In Kiev he was not yet quite free of his prewar bohemian ways, and as a result he did have a spot of trouble with the tsarist military police. He fought with the Czechoslovak Legion at the Battle of Zborov (3 July 1917), and he was awarded the Order of Saint George Fourth Class for valor in that battle and in the retreat from Tarnopol. By then Hašek was becoming an ever more reliable man, so, in September, for the first time he found himself an agent rather than a victim of the law, when he was appointed assistant to the bench of the Czechoslovak regimental court. Indeed, by November he had become a member of the central brigade committee. But then, suddenly, after having been an ardent anti-Communist, Hašek joined the Bolsheviks.

One wonders whether the decision that the Czechoslovak Legion should march east across the Russian Empire and then sail via America to join the French on the western front had not put Hašek off. The very thought of the discomfort such a march would entail cannot have pleased Hašek. On the other hand, Hašek liked the unusual and was probably attracted also to the idealism of the Bolsheviks. Whatever his motives, Hašek certainly became an even harder worker for the Communist cause than he had been for the Czechoslovak. There is little reason for doubting that he believed in the cause during the two years he worked for it, although some members of the Czechoslovak section of the Russian Communist Party had profound doubts about his revolutionary convictions from the time he joined to the time he left. The punishments the Red Army administered for drunkenness led the alcoholic Hašek to become a teetotaler. In 1918 he joined the Russian Communist Party, and by April of that year he had put together his band of 120 Czechoslovak and Serbian Red Army volunteers in Samara (now Kuibyshev).

Samara fell in June 1918, and Hašek disappeared; if one is to believe Hašek himself, he spent three months wandering about pretending to be the congenital idiot son of a German colonist from Turkestan. In September he appeared in Simbirsk (now Ulyanovsk), and thence he was eventually sent to Bugulma, of which, in December, he was appointed deputy commandant. Hašek spent ten weeks in Bugulma and wrote a cycle of tales about that stay, which resulted in the Tatar town's later establishing a Hašek museum.

JAROSLAV HAŠEK

When the Red Army took Ufa and its printing works, Hašek was asked to start a new periodical. The first number of his *Nash put'* (Our Way) appeared at the beginning of 1919. Ufa soon fell, and when the Red Army retook it in June, Hašek took part in the avenging purge. Most of the Hašek hagiographers stress that he never indulged in any violence during his time in the Fifth Army, but critics note that he worked in league with the secret police, and one story telling of his rescue of a captured Czech from execution implies that all the other prisoners held in that barn had been shot in cold blood with Hašek's condonation. According to his second wife, Aleksandra Lvova, whom he picked up in Ufa, Hašek always felt sick when he heard a death sentence, but the physical violence encouraged, sometimes glorified, in some of Hašek's wartime journalism casts doubt on that assertion.

In January 1919 he became political commissar of the foreigners' section in the Fifth Army, and in that capacity he edited and wrote for periodicals such as the Hungarian-German *Roham/Sturm* (Charge), the German *Weltrevolution* (World Revolution), and the Russian *Krasnaya Evropa* (Red Europe). In the Soviet Union Hašek's propaganda writing from this period is considered part of the classical foundations of Soviet political journalism. To a non-Soviet reader it appears cumbersome, uninspired, and uninspiring. One is inclined to agree with Parrott's view that some of it might well have been lifted straight from standard propaganda brochures or manuals. This does not mean that Hašek was cynical; he may have believed that that was the most efficacious method.

Toward the end of 1919 Hašek set up a special political police section to deal with Czechoslovak legionary spies, and then in the spring of 1920 he was appointed secretary to the Fifth Army's party cell. By the summer of 1920 he was in Irkutsk, trying to learn Chinese and Mongolian and editing the Buryati periodical *Ör* (Dawn). *Ör* apparently had a circulation of 2,500—but not a single copy of any

issue has survived, although it is considered a cornerstone of Buryati socialist journalism. In October, apparently at the urging of Czech Communists who wanted Hašek to help with the Kladno soviet in Czechoslovakia, he went to Moscow; he handed in his party card when he left Moscow with Aleksandra Lvova in November, to arrive in Prague via quarantine camp in Pardubice on 19 December 1920.

The only documentation concerning Hašek's leaving Russia supports the idea that the Comintern sent him to Kladno. There is very little indeed to support Gustav Janouch's view that Hašek ran away from Russia—just one ambiguous word in a letter. Certainly, however, Hašek undertook practically nothing to gain entry into Czechoslovak Communist Party circles and thus engage in party work in his native country. No one will ever know exactly what the circumstances of his departure from the Soviet Union were. It is quite probable, however, that the sight of Prague attracted him back to a life more natural for him than political commissardom: drinking and smoking and chattering. Many of his former friends in Prague refused to have anything to do with him because they linked him with atrocities perpetrated by the Red Army. Most left-wing Social Democrats in Prague were not interested in him because they still could not take him seriously. The newspapers did report his return to Prague, partly because several obituaries had already been published announcing his death, partly because he was now a deserter from the Czechoslovak Legion and a bigamist, and partly because Hašek was still remembered as a prewar comic writer.

In 1921 Hašek again became involved with cabaret, albeit unwillingly. In March 1921, coincidentally perhaps, the day after publishing an article on Kronstadt in *Rudé právo* (Red Right), he was again considered politically unreliable and placed under police surveillance. Hašek clearly felt uncomfortable; he is said to have declared, "I shouldn't have come back. People hate me here." After having started writing the novel *The Good Soldier*

Švejk and having helped distribute the first fascicles (for the first part of his novel was published in cheaply produced brochure-like parts, or fascicles, for peddling), he was persuaded to leave Prague. He went to live in the little hillside town of Lipnice in the Bohemian-Moravian uplands, a town with nothing special about it except the dull ruins of a castle. After he had settled down he sent for Aleksandra, and there he remained, drinking, smoking, and writing or, later, dictating until the end of his life. He died of heart failure on 3 January 1923. Hašek, however, lives on in socialist Czechoslovakia. In 1967 the president awarded him the Order of the Red Banner for services rendered in the Russian Civil War, and in 1983 a Prague square was renamed after him. The greatest irony of all is that his grandson is a regular officer in the Czechoslovak People's Army.

HAŠEK AND THE CZECH LITERARY CONTEXT

Hašek's writing fits in with the contemporary and preceding Czech literary tradition far more closely than the secondary literature usually has us believe. Anticlericalism had been part of the norm in Czech political and satirical literature at least since 1848. Both his prewar and his postwar antimilitarism have their forerunners and contemporaries. Czech satire of the 1890's and 1900's is replete with attacks on Vienna, on the Czechs' kowtowing to Vienna, and on Czech patriotism. Writers such as J. S. Machar, Josef Šimánek, or Viktor Dyk published bolder satire before the war than Hašek. Something of the same storytelling technique is to be seen in the grand old man of the Czech comic tale, Ignát Herrmann. Hašek's Švejk has three more or less obvious predecessors. The figures and particularly the language of Josef Holeček's autobiographical sketches of army life, *Obšit* (Demob, 1887), might have provided models for Hašek. Furthermore, the monologues of the postwar ver-

sions of the Švejk characters are prefigured in the gypsy woman's address to the court in K. M. Čapek-Chod's skeptical experimental novel, *Kašpar Lén, mstitel* (Kašpar Lén, the Avenger, 1908). Most important, in his collection of military tales, *Z vln života* (From the Tide of Life, 1893), the army officer Ignát Hořica refers to homosexuality in the army and the fate of a Gypsy's soul once regimented and uses that most colloquial type of Czech, known as Common Czech, for dialogue—all of which Hašek does later. The story "Vítězství!" (Victory!) prefigures the postwar version of Švejk on two counts: the relationship between the batman (orderly) Blecha and his Lieutenant Kárný is similar to that of Švejk and Lieutenant Lukáš; the story itself—that of the batman being sent out to woo for his officer and some of the slapstick the situation involves—looks forward to an episode in Hašek's novel. Hořica's attitude to Magyars corresponds to Hašek's, not in *The Good Soldier Švejk,* but in the prewar short stories: he condemns the magnates, but likes the ordinary peasants.

However many kindred authors one might find for Hašek, he remains distinctly himself, even in his prewar tales. His narrative has a briskness and his punchlines a sure-fistedness that are generally lacking in his contemporaries. His subject matter has greater breadth, and he shows virtually no signs of any nationalist parochialism. He also has an unfailing bitterness, which is new to modern Czech literature, and the anti-authoritarian attitude he consistently expresses is more thoroughgoing than anything in Czech literature since the Middle Ages.

EARLY WORKS

Only the beginnings of that attitude are evident in his first book, *Májové výkřiky* (Shrieks of May, 1903), a collection of verse he wrote with his friend Ladislav Hájek-Domažlický. The title constitutes a sarcastic paradox.

JAROSLAV HAŠEK

The word *Máj* for May, as against the neutral *květen*, has suggested burgeoning love in Czech at least since the mid-fourteenth century; it has acquired a political connotation only since the 1890's, that is, since the Socialist International made 1 May a workers' holiday. The concept *výkřik*, the sort of "shriek" one might expect from a child or the victim of a crime, makes an uneasy partner to *máj*.

Hašek's and Hájek's poems appear on alternate pages. On the whole Hašek's poems are those of a hooligan, although sometimes unwanted sentimentality is evident. The desire to deflate, which became a hallmark of all his later works, comes through. Some of the themes he pursued until his death are also already present: a hypocritical priest cavorts in the bushes with the village schoolmistress; spring may be the time of love, but it is also the time conscription papers come and nature in romantic May actually whispers, "Long live the great army!"; the clichéd petit bourgeois erotic is mocked when a girl is moved by a boy's having plucked violets for her—he had actually bought them on the street corner.

Hašek's two-stanza introductory poem is a belated decadent work. The decadents had rejected spring and summer as bourgeois and vulgar, and in this poem Hašek rejects spring as bourgeois. The influence of mainstream Czech decadence, an elitist, anarchist trend, is strong throughout Hašek's works. It is clearest when Hašek is parodying features of decadent literature, like their lusciously mobid descriptions of autumn; in *The Good Soldier Švejk* he parodies decadent olfactory sensuality in an evocation of latrines. Contrary to what Czech critics say, Hašek never satirized the decadents proper; he satirized only their epigones. The decadents of the 1890's were far too close to Hašek in their anarchism. And yet they would have abhorred the sheer anti-aesthetic vulgarity of much of Hašek's writing. In *Májové výkřiky* we find also an un-decadent rejection of spring, a vulgar lout's rejection that signifies a more thorough condemnation of conventional Czech middle-class standards

than any of the decadents' rejections. This poem, "Etuda" (A Study), is an incipient bohemian manifesto. The most appropriate way of celebrating a beautiful spring evening is to play cards and get drunk in a pub. Its ending prefigures what Hašek allegedly said once back in Prague after his spell in the Russian civil war: "We look out from the pub into the night of vernal beauty / and probably no one likes us." Essentially, however, *Májové výkřiky* is unconcerned with psychology, just as his prewar prose is unconcerned with psychology. (In this essay "prewar" means published before Hašek arrived at the front in 1915; "postwar" means after his return to Prague in 1920.)

Hašek's prose bears the hallmark of naturalism, in which psychological motivation is not necessary and people behave in such and such a manner because of heredity and environment. Naturalism, like decadence, had little room for knockabout humor. Both, however, exploited irony, and Hašek's sarcasm could be linked with naturalist social irony. However, it is not derived from it; Hašek was too much of an autodidact. In his writing Hašek's view of human behavior is entirely materialist. The most frequent concerns of the prewar stories are clerics, the police, the army, the bureaucracy, Hungarians, Gypsies, and mass political parties. Topical events do also creep in, like the Austrian annexation of Bosnia and Herzegovina in 1908 or the killing by Hungarian gendarmes of Slovaks who were objecting to their local church's being consecrated by a Hungarian-speaking priest in Černová in 1907. In his prewar stories Hašek is particularly interested in fleas—creatures of which he no doubt had intimate experience—but life itself is clearly controlled not by fleas but by money. Hašek never laughs at money, although he could laugh at himself.

In his narration he frequently employs linguistic parody and even self-parody, which puts him in the mainstream of European modernism. That is by chance, however, for Hašek was not a conscious innovator. His prewar stories are essentially workmanlike, quick-money spinners, but, because he uses the humor and often the idiom of the uncultured classes, he appears to be a conscious modernist. That humor also approaches the cynicism that became fashionable among European intellectuals after World War II, although in Hašek's case it seems to flow from deep-seated misanthropy.

He had very little regard for anyone's sensitivities, and his writing is as amoral as the rest of his behavior was. Sentimentalization, an aspect of popular culture Hašek rejected, is rare, and when he finds he has become sentimental, deflation usually follows. Thus in the cycle of stories about his mother's family, "Historky z ražické bašty" (Tales from the Ražice Water-Bailiff's Cottage, 1908), he sentimentalizes the natural loyalty of manorial servants by making much ado about a bailiff's helping to carry the coffin of a steward he could not stand in life. The sentimentalization is at the very least toned down by the fact that the fat steward explodes in his coffin.

Sometimes he adapted popular tales. One of the best-beloved tales in European (and French Canadian) popular literature is the legend of Saint Eustace, who was led to conversion by a stag. In most versions of the legend his two sons were killed, one by a bear, the other by a stag, as the saint was taking his family away from Rome into exile. Hašek has a scurrilous, eccentric version in "Světci a zvířata" (Saints and Animals, 1912):

> This good man met a bear in the forest. The bear was so impudent that it made to devour the saint. Catholic newspapers would claim that that bear was a freethinker. Eustace, however, struck the bear with his staff and ordered it to carry him to Rome. The bear bent its head and back low; Saint Eustace sat on the bear, and thus he had an easy journey, bear-back, to Rome. The bear was soon given a special audience by the pope and after the audience it was stuffed. It is still today exhibited in the Vatican collections.
>
> (*První dekameron, Procházka přes hranice, Idylky z cest a jiné humoresky,* p. 363)

The humor here is more inventive though less sharp than is usually the case. When Hašek's humor is crass, it is intentionally so; that is part of his shock technique—and his self-parody.

Crassness also belongs to his antibourgeois sarcasm, part of which consists in the denial of anything metaphysical associated with the *Lumpenproletarier.* Conscience is the fear of being found out. Poor people threaten the affluence of the nation and therefore the stake of politicians. In "Zápas o duše" (Fighting for Souls, 1913) a forestry worker says to the priggish curate, "Being honorable's for the rich and no honorable person's ever been born hereabouts." Scholarship is equally only for the rich and for fools. In "Babámovy archeologické snahy" (Babám's Endeavors as an Archaeologist, 1914) the Gypsy Babám, when asked by an archaeologist to keep his eye open for fragments of Roman pots, sets about buying pots, smashing them, burying the shards at appropriate places, discovering them for the gullible scholar, and taking his reward. As in this example, Hašek's worldview almost always becomes apparent from the tale itself rather than from some express statement or judgment.

The most skillful example of this technique is his stream-of-consciousness tale "U holiče" (At the Barber's, 1911), which is probably Hašek's supreme artistic achievement. Indeed, "U holiče" is far from popular literature, and one could conceive of it as a monodrama. In this presentation of the narrator as victim the fundamental situation concerns a man being shaved. The garrulous barber turns out first to be clumsy and then to be interested in war and human bloodthirstiness. The pace of the narration increases as the barber inflicts more and more injuries on his customer-victim. The latter does not utter a word, although the author conveys the narrator's winces and gesticulations through the reactions of the barber. Essentially, then, the story consists in the barber's interminable blather, addressed to the customer and to the assistant, Josef, but at the same time it constitutes antimilitarist grotesquery and a satire on Czech petit bourgeois prejudices. The injuries begin close to home and end in blackest gloom. First, the barber says, "Things have come to the boil in the Balkans, don't worry, dear sir, that was a wart, nick them off with a razor and they never grow again." And finally:

" . . . Africa. Did you know, sir, I'll soon be finished with your neck, did you know that the savages there cut their prisoners' throats? They catch a prisoner; they get a long knife, they put it at his throat like this, don't worry, sir, you'll be ready in a moment, like this, sir, and, snick, off comes his head. Josef, pick up that head and put it away somewhere. . . ." After a moment's pause: "For Christ's sake, sir, what have you done?"

(*Druhý dekameron, Lidožroutská historie, Parodie, morytáty a banality*, pp. 24–25)

The barber is a type, the pub-politicking, sycophant shopkeeper. Hašek produces types because he has no time for psychology and because, in his misanthropy, he would render himself vulnerable if he considered human beings anything more complex than types. The describing of types notionally supports his inhumanity or insensitivity.

One of the most common of Hašek's types is the schlimazel, the hapless fellow for whom nothing ever goes right. In "Výprava zloděje Šejby" (Burglar Šejba's Expedition, 1913), the first day Šejba decides to do an attic in a "better-class" area, he succeeds only in being beaten by a series of irate wives who think he is their drunken husband and in losing his boots, his skeleton key, and his faithful rum bottle. In "Šťavnická Idyla" (Štiavnica Idyll, 1920) the police inspector László Halás arrests his father and then his landlord for breaking the peace; then he chops off a secret policeman's nose in a demonstration; finally, he catches his commissioner gambling. He serves two months in prison for catching him and is sent away from civilized Budapest into wild Upper Hungary. Similarly, all Lindiger's business ventures go wrong in "Obchod s rakvemi" (A Coffin Shop, 1914), and so he decides he will begin to trade in coffins, since everyone has to buy a coffin one day. He finds a little mountain town where there is no coffin maker and sets up shop. But everyone is so healthy there that no one dies for many years; thus, just after sending to Vienna for some phials of typhus germs, he hangs himself so that at least one of his coffins finds a customer. This is an example of Hašek's use of grotesque non sequiturs in his story line. "Fialový hrom" (Purple Thunderclap, 1913) concerns the purple, thunderbolt-like creature created by the College of Cardinals when they decreed in 1596 that all blasphemers should be struck down by lightning. He keeps on striking the wrong people, first the cardinals in Rome (for which he gets six weeks' house arrest), then a pedant who is trying to become a martyr, then a Jesuit, and finally a priest administering extreme unction to a blasphemous sinner—whom the purple creature cures by electrotherapy.

In this story, Hašek's schlimazel serves as a vehicle for satire on the church of Rome; a type is used as a lightning conductor for satire on an institution. Another example of this strategy appears in "Psychiatrická záhada" (A Psychiatric Enigma, 1911), in which the central character is a faddist. He is secretary of the Temperance League (actually he had been forbidden beer by his doctor) and a vegetarian and has learned Esperanto. One day he is walking across a bridge in Prague, hears a scream, looks over to see whether he can help someone, and is suddenly grabbed and "saved from suicide." He is then locked up in a lunatic asylum. Hašek has been compared with Franz Kafka too often and usually unhelpfully, but any reader will be reminded of Kafka and Joseph Heller in the ending of "Psychiatrická záhada": "He has been looked after in the asylum for eighteen months now, since the doctors have so far not ascertained an awareness of mental sickness, which, according to psychiatric theory, would be a sign of an improvement in the patient's mental state."

Hašek will have no truck with the then-fashionable psychiatry, but the story satirizes not only the practices of psychiatrists but also bureaucracy and the police-informer mentality of the do-gooder, the upright citizen of the type who saves suicides.

The ludicrous pettiness of the Austrian bureaucracy as a whole is satirized in another story, "Úřední horlivost pana Štěpána Brycha, výběrčího na pražském mostě" (The Professional Zeal of Mr. Štěpán Brych, Tollman on a Prague Bridge, 1911). It too centers on a type, the obsessive petty bureaucrat, a type without which Austria would fall. One day Brych has the police arrest his chief for not paying his one-kreutzer toll, but soon after that worse happens. Brych chases for miles after a man who has the temerity simply to run past his booth. Eventually Brych begins to foam at the mouth and acquire a maniacal look in his eye. The terrified prey jumps into the river to save his life, but Brych plunges after him. Shouting, "Hand over one kreutzer" all the time, he eventually catches the delinquent and holds him fast. A sudden wave sweeps both men into a whirlpool, but while they are being sucked down, Brych succeeds in fishing a kreutzer from the man's pocket. When his corpse is washed up, his hand is still victoriously clutching the coin. Since that day the bridge has been haunted; every day at midnight Brych's voice is to be heard shouting, "Hand over one kreutzer!" In another story, "Historie dačická" (A Dačice Tale, 1910), Hašek describes the way that petty officials are afraid of being made to look ridiculous. Here his political satire is directed mainly at small-town conservatism: he derides the unthinking conservatism that imagines all the poor are socialists, and simultaneously he mocks those socialists who imagine the *Lumpenproletariat* will support them; *Lumpenproletarier* tend to be conservative.

He also criticizes small-town egocentricity, but in "Sportovní fejeton" (Sports Column, 1911) he criticizes small-nation egocentricity and Czech officials' lack of fun. The piece centers on a soccer match between a Prague team, Slávie, and Aberdeen United. In the key passage he compares Czech official historicism and national mythology with the down-to-earth philistinism of the British. The Aberdonians are interested only in soccer and cannot understand why the deputy mayor goes on speaking to them about the Council of Constance (by whose order the Czech church reformer Jan Hus was burned at the stake in 1415), the execution of the rebellious Czech gentlemen (1621), and the Czech National Revival. In this sally against official Czech patriotism Hašek expresses an attitude shared by most original Czech writers of the time.

In many stories, he also attacks Czech politics and particularly political corruption. Hašek was amazed that the Aberdonians earned as much as £2 a day, and that same pecuniary obsession dominates the picture he gives of Czech politics. (Hašek was always short of money, and no doubt that explains why he wrote so much about it.) For example, in "Obecní býk v Jablečnu" (The Jablečno Parish Bull, 1913) the Christian Socialists use beer to sway voters, and in "Mladočeské volby na Malé straně" (The Young Czech Party's Election in the Lesser Town, 1909) the Young Czechs waste 35,000 crowns exploiting the new universal suffrage act by trying to bribe all manner of riffraff with alcohol. In another story he satirizes Austrian social democracy. He parodies would-be compassionate socialist sloganizing in "Osudy medvěda od Hamagbúha" (The Fortunes of the Bear from Hamagbúh, 1912), in which the bloated, disintegrating corpse of a bear is fished out of the river, given a postmortem, and eventually buried. The funeral orator declares, "This unfortunate man was the victim of class hatred." On the other hand, a clever, if schoolboyish, parody of uncompassionate journalese is combined with a satire on petit bourgeois hypocrisy in "Novoroční nadělení" (New Year Gift, 1912):

NEW YEAR GIFT. The typesetter is swearing that I am late, so in brief: Master-baker Karel J. from S.

Bohemia. Departure for Prague. Shopping for New Year presents. Meeting with belle by Powder Tower. Fusion of souls in certain hotel. Belle disappears. Money, watch, rings disappear. Baker cannot pay bill. Police called. Baker questioned. Faithless lover discovered to be "Lojzka." Hapless man's sad return to family.

(Quoted in Hoření, p. 55)

That is the complete story. "Novoroční nadělení" epitomizes Hašek's anti-lyricality. Hašek hates the lyrical, which is particularly significant for a writer who belongs to a nation that conventionally prides itself on its lyric verse.

When he uses his black humor to political or social critical ends, Hašek is also being anti-lyrical. Implicitly he is rejecting the patriotic tear-jerking used by Czech politicians and writers as well as the Czechs' false pride in their lyrical tradition. The satire of "Nešťastná historie s kocourem" (An Unfortunate Business with a Tomcat, 1911), which is leveled against the politicization of everyday life as well as the bureaucracy, is gentle, however black the humor. Křička tells his son to stamp on the tail of the cat of his acquaintance Hustoles, who has opposing political views. Soon the cat has its revenge by biting Křička's son. Křička complains to the authorities, who find Hustoles guilty of "failing to muzzle and chain a cat." The government vet examines the cat, finds it has periostitis and its bite is potentially dangerous, and recommends that the cat should be killed. The vet's report is sent to the police, and four constables are sent to Hustoles. They arrest him and inform him that he is to be put down. Hašek thus also implicitly satirizes police informers and bureaucratic incompetence as well as the ludicrousness of a certain law. The story constitutes a hyperbolic depiction of factional squabbling in Czech politics.

In contrast to that story the satire of "Loupežný vrah před soudem" (A Murderer and Robber in Court, 1907) is cynically grotesque. Powerful social criticism is rendered comic both by the main character's irrepressible humor and by the inane pomposity of the lawyers. Essentially the story depicts a *Lumpenproletarier* confronting petit bourgeois prejudices. A man is caught filching a loaf of bread by a shopkeeper, who shoots at and slightly wounds him. The thief begins to wrestle with the shopkeeper and eventually strangles him. In court he knows he will be sentenced to death and so decides to go down laughing. He proclaims that he will leave the rope that hangs him to the presiding judge so that he can use it to hold his trousers up. Defense counsel follows the murderer's comment by explaining that in introducing the judge's trousers the accused is attempting to arouse the sympathy of the jury. Now a lightly ironic scene (containing a degree of linguistic parody) develops into slapstick (with a strong attack on the judiciary as an instrument of the government):

> Then the defense was interrupted by the prosecution, who, pursuing the former's argumentation, stated that it was immoral to drag the presiding judge's trousers into the debate. To that the defense wittily retorted that he did not find the judge's trousers immoral, but him whom they clad, nay more, the whole judiciary system was immoral from the warder to the executioner. At that moment it was seen fit that the defense counsel be restrained and a spittoon be borne to the bench so that the learned judge might expectorate. There was great excitement in the courtroom after the judge's expectoration; several ladies swooned, and one member of the public put his hand by mistake into his neighbor's pocket and drew forth a piece of chocolate which he began nervously to eat before the eyes of the man from whom he had stolen it. A brief adjournment was announced, which the accused murderer and robber used for addressing obscene gestures to the prosecuting counsel.
>
> (*První dekameron*, pp. 287–288)

Although the murderer accepts the rules of society in that he acknowledges that his action will be punished by hanging, his behavior in court questions those rules. That behavior also serves to emphasize the fact that he is to be hanged for being too poor to buy a loaf of bread. In court the murderer plays a game that gives him pleasure, but also gives society pleasure. It pleases him because it is fun, especially since he has nothing to lose—if he had ever had anything to lose. It pleases society because it confirms its self-righteous opinion of the criminal mentality. Society's only defense against the pauper's mockery of its institutions is laughable spitting and swooning. The mercantile class's horror at the indigent is helpless. The content and the expression of his personal background the murderer gives the court serves to emphasize society's helplessness. He says that he does not believe in God, "that God can piss off," for God has never done anything for him. His grandfather had starved to death, and his grandmother had been raped by a captain of the gendarmerie. The ending of the story, when the judge reads the death sentence and the condemned man is led off farting, constitutes an example of Hašek's scatological humor and of social critical bathos. Hašek enjoys infringing taboos.

His satire occasionally touches on taboo subjects as well, subjects such as police brutality, which occurs in several stories. "Jak Tövöl vrátil zlatník" (How Tövöl Returned a Guilder, 1913) is particularly sophisticated and in attitude recalls "Loupežný vrah před soudem." Here a gendarme captain had had a Romanian Gypsy beaten over the belly with ropes until he died. When the matter is investigated, the captain reacts: "These Gypsies are so insolent. As soon as you catch one he dies on you at the station. That race can't take anything." The story satirizes police brutality and police prejudice against Gypsies but also the Czech readership's own prejudice against the Gypsies Hašek and some other Czech writers were so fond of. In cases like this despair flickers through a chink in Hašek's amoral cynicism.

Although he expresses hatred for the police, in the prewar tales he scarcely ever does more than laugh at the army. Usually it is seen sim-

ply as part of the clumsy state machine. "Čáka pěšáka Trunce" (Infantryman Trunec's Cap, 1909), the second half of which was confiscated and not printed until after the dissolution of Austria-Hungary, provides a grotesque testimony to the bureaucratization of the common army and a satire on bullying officers. In the uncensored part Trunec is called up and no cap can be found big enough for his head; the captain trounces him for his impertinence in having such a head. In the censored half Hašek has some perceptive parody of bureaucrats' letters. By the time the Vienna headquarters decides what should be done with the first hat Trunec had been given and with the new hat, Trunec has long been dead; presumably he has died of old age. One of Hašek's cleverest stories is a very brief satire on bureaucratic foolishness in the campaign against pacifism, "Obět antimilitarismu" (A Victim of Antimilitarism, 1910): "ANTIMILITARISM VICTIM. The pavement on Palacký Avenue in Vršovice is very antimilitaristic. František Kahl, a lieutenant serving in the 73rd Foot Regiment, slipped on it yesterday and sprained his ankle. A rigorous inquiry has been instigated into the pavement's activities." This also ridicules the officer concerned.

There is nothing new about ridiculing state institutions or their servants. Ordinary human weakness, also, forms the subject of classical comedy. The way Hašek ridicules infidelity, jealousy, disappointment, decency, honorable ambition, emotional pain, and joy is coarse and innovative. On the one hand, one might describe his attitude as that of an overgrown child; Pytlík frequently characterizes him like that. On the other hand, that attitude suggests a premeditated rejection of accepted social values. Again, Hašek the man could be hiding within Hašek the writer's attitudes; Hašek's life and his writing could be more intimately connected than is usual with mature writers. Hašek's attitude to human emotions produces something akin to catharsis. Scurrilous callousness has an effect similar to that of grand pathos.

JAROSLAV HAŠEK

The narrator of "Rodinná tragédie" (A Family Tragedy, 1912) is the child who stands to suffer most from the fact that his mother is having an affair. He appears to pretend he does not know what is going on, and his mother and her lover believe he does not know. The reader is left a little bemused; the reader is an emotional victim. Either the narrator is playing with the reader or the author is playing with the narrator and the reader. And the author is making fun of everyone in the story, including the boy. The fundamental situation is one of the oldest in comic writing: a man married to a woman twenty years his junior. The boy tries to support both his mother and his father and to show respect for his mother's lover, Fingulín. Fingulín is a repulsive drip of a miserly sponger; the father pays little attention to his wife, expects her simply to serve up food on time and to allow him the peace to visit regularly the local pub. Hašek introduces us to the state of affairs with effectively sparse irony: "Mummy is very nice to everyone. She gives a stroke and a kiss to everyone. She strokes me, Daddy, and Mr. Fingulín, and our dog and she has a cheerful smile for everyone, for me, for Daddy and for Mr. Fingulín, and for our dog, and she gives most kisses to me and Mr. Fingulín." When the mother and Fingulín go off for a weekend, they take the dog with them, and it makes two piles in the railway compartment and bites the chambermaid in the hotel. That results in a scene in which the cuckolded husband is comically humiliated by Fingulín's persuading him that the dog he so loves is an unnecessary burden. That is paralleled by the scene in which Fingulín begins to complain about the father's morals the evening the father has decided that he can endure it no longer and that he will stay out late and get drunk. As Hašek refuses to accept that emotional pain inherently demands respect or sympathy, so he shows no sign of compassion for physical affliction.

The same attitude shows up in a story that is mainly a sarcastic comment on religious institutions, "Smutný osud nádražní misie"

(The Sad Fate of the Railway Mission, 1911), in which he writes, "And if a girl is old, hunchbacked, and cross-eyed, she will not fall into the hands of the pimps, for faith in eternal happiness gives her strength and her religious conviction protects her from depravity and dens of iniquity." Even more glorious bad taste is evident in the scatologically macabre ending to a story about cheating in a Latin test, a story primarily concerned, once again, with authority, "Pan Florentin kontra Chocholka" (Mr. Florentin Versus Chocholka, 1912). The cheat Chocholka locks himself in the lavatory, which is then besieged by two teachers. When they break in, the boy has managed to flush himself down the lavatory and thus avoid both doing the composition and being caught alive. Shouting down the lavatory pan, the headmaster gives him six hours' detention. This situation recalls "Na opuštěné latríně" (On an Abandoned Latrine, 1910), in which a retired major gets such a shock at seeing a civilian, a tramp, sitting in a disused army latrine that he falls into an excrement-filled trench and drowns. Before he leaves, the tramp goes through the drowned man's pockets. *Lumpenproletarier* or bohemian practicality vanquishes authority.

The literary work that is most clearly a product of Hašek's own bohemianism, his pranks in the Vinohrady by-election of 1911, is *Politické a sociální dějiny Strany mírného pokroku v mezích zákona* (The Political and Social History of the Party of Moderate Progress Within the Limits of the Law). He had more or less completed this series of mock pamphlets, tall stories, diary tales, and literary critical feuilletons in 1912, when he handed it to a publisher who was frightened of publishing it. Some parts appeared between the two world wars, but it was not published in its entirety until 1963.

The party did exist; it was created by chance, as the result of a joke; Hašek's candidacy in the by-election was, however, never official. Some electors did apparently write his name on their ballots, but these counted as spoiled votes. The party program has 2,701 articles; we hear seven of them in the chapter entitled "Oprava podle paragrafu 19 tiskového zákona" (Correction in Accordance with Article 19 of the Press Law): (1) the re-introduction of slavery; (2) the nationalization of concierges (this point was at the time a satire on tsarist Russia's use of concierges as police informers; when the chapter dealing with this article was published in the Communist newspaper *Rudé právo* in 1937, the editor noted that satire; in 1963 the satire seemed topical); (3) the rehabilitation of animals; (4) the establishment of educational institutions for mentally retarded members of parliament; (5) the re-introduction of the Inquisition; (6) a law forbidding criticism of the clergy; and (7) the forced introduction of alcoholism. Other articles include stricter treatment of the poor, the nationalization of vergers, and the transferral of credit banks to the clergy.

Politické a sociální dějiny is primarily a satire of Czech political life. The characters who appear in the book are based on authentic personages and no doubt many of the stories told about them are authentic. One example, which is also an example of Hašek's anti-police satire, is his friend and fellow satirist and journalist, Karel Pelant, an atheist who, quips Hašek, has been given a bursary to go to the United States to convert the red Indians back to paganism. Pelant allegedly threw stinkbombs into the Týn church in Prague while the pious were at prayer. He is subsequently arrested for stinking, but it turns out he has aged Moravian cheeses in his pockets, not stinkbombs. Hašek also mocks Pelant, manifesting a superior bitterness incompatible with friendship:

Pelant, mystic, anti-alcohol campaigner, atheist, anti-spiritist, fighter against prostitution, revolutionary, leader of those thinking souls who argue in cafés, who debate at those little tables by café windows so that they are seen from the street, those proud, zealous men, permeated by the intoxication of their own glory, destroying

worlds and raising new flags while they drink black coffee.

(*Politické a sociální dějiny strany mírného pokroku v mezích zákona*, p. 372)

His satire on the trashy novelist Quido Maria Vyskočil, who did actually make a serious attempt at symbolist drama, is cheap; Vyskočil was not worth satirizing. Hašek's parody scheme for a trite, muddled Vyskočil novel is, however, valid as a typification:

Take a maiden; examine her to see if she is pretty and inform the readers in what luxury she lives; then catch a poor youth; examine him to see if he is noble-minded; now leave both of them, the rich maiden and the poor youth, on squares of paper for as long as you can before it is time to put a rich nobleman between them. Then take the maiden's father and mother and wrap up the whole story with them somehow; have the youth get in some sort of fix; for example, you could plunge him into water; then pull the maiden out of the stately home and hang her on a birch tree on the sunny side of the house.

(p. 337)

Although of value as a panoramic critique of Czech or Prague society before World War I, the humor in it has not survived as well as it has in the more original prewar stories.

EARLY VERSIONS OF THE GOOD SOLDIER SVĚJK

The first version of the character Švejk appeared in periodicals in 1911 in five stories that make a coherent cycle. These appeared in Hašek's first volume of prose, *Dobrý voják Švejk a jiné podivné historky* (The Good Soldier Švejk and Other Strange Tales), the following year. The Švejk of these stories is more consistent and, thus, less inscrutable than the Švejk of the postwar novel. Furthermore he is not a yarn spinner, and he speaks standard literary Czech. Socially he is also different. In the tales he has done an apprenticeship as a cabinetmaker; in the novel he is a well-read shoddy-dog dealer. He is as optimistic as he will always be, and in these tales the indestructibility of that optimism is expressly stated when he blows up an arsenal where he is on duty by smoking while working with guncotton at the same time. Several men are killed, and several buildings are razed. After three days' digging (the three days of the resurrection appear in popular literature since Greek times) the rescue party finds Švejk seated and smiling. His reaction is to demand compensatory rations for the meals he had lost while buried under the rubble.

In the hagiography this Švejk not only parodies military subordination but also prefigures the destruction of the Habsburg monarchy by the will of common optimism and the survival of the ordinary man afterward. If that were true, Hašek would have had to have been a far more political and less primitivist writer than he was, and Švejk would have hardly received the medal and the junket in the officers' mess after his survival. Certainly the medal and the junket are part of Hašek's derisive satire on establishment institutions, but he is not prophesying, even unconsciously, some Austrian state masochism.

The Švejk of the five stories was immediately popular, at least in bohemian and inchoate intellectual circles. He appeared as a figure on the cabaret stage almost immediately. That no doubt helped persuade Hašek that he was a character he could do more with—could earn more money from. However more tangible this Švejk is than the postwar version, the essentials of the last version are there. In the first of the five stories his indelible smile is already threatening authority:

> Švejk was always smiling and his manners were always winsome; it was because of that perhaps that he was always in the garrison prison. And when he left prison, he answered all questions with a smile, let himself be imprisoned again quite calmly, satisfied in himself that all the officers of the whole Trent garrison were afraid of him. Afraid, not of his coarseness, but of his respectful answers, his respectful behavior, and those nice, friendly smiles that made them feel uneasy.

> (*Druhy dekameron*, p. 103)

The entire story is dominated by his smile. Hašek's attitude to Švejk is not absolutely clear. When he gets lost in the woods and strays across the Italian frontier, Hašek adds, "as could be expected," which suggests either that Švejk is a schlimazel or that he really is a congenital idiot. But one could also interpret the "as could be expected" as a storyteller's intrusion, signifying "as you must be expecting the story to go on."

In the second story Švejk is batman to a padre (chaplain), as he is for a time in the postwar novel. Here we see a parody of military obedience: when the padre orders Švejk to buy some Vöslau communion wine, instead of going to an off-license (liquor store) he takes the long train journey to Vöslau itself. The literal carrying out of orders travesties military discipline and simultaneously suggests that Švejk is an idiot. This tale also satirizes the positions of the church and the army as the two chief arms of state power in the dual monarchy.

The third story sees Švejk called before the army medical board to ascertain whether he should be invalided out on the grounds of imbecility. The story satirizes board procedures and life in a military hospital; the procedure itself is so terrifying that soldiers do not dare feel ill. When Švejk is prescribed the clyster (enema), he says to the Ukrainian orderly in dignified tones, "Brother, don't spare me, I was not afraid of the Italians, and I shall not be afraid of your clyster either." When the Ukrainian calls him a malingerer, Švejk gives him a good punch in the jaw. This is the only example of Švejk's physical violence in the stories, and it stresses that he is no nambypamby. He is not, however, averse to physical violence in personal matters later on, in the postwar novel. While the hagiographers tend to argue that

Švejk is never violent to support the political views they attribute to Hašek, in the stories Švejk belongs to a class that, like the proletariat, does indulge in physical violence. At the end of the third story Švejk deserts so that he has to be punished and is thus able to continue to serve in His Imperial Majesty's armed forces.

The fourth story is the arsenal story; it contains more slapstick and inventive comic writing than the other four. At the junket we first meet Švejk as the heavy drinker he is in *The Good Soldier Švejk*. In the last story Švejk is in the flying corps; he smiles here as much as he does in the first story. And again he is the schlimazel: whenever an aircraft crashes, Švejk is the first thing to emerge from the shambles. As in *The Good Soldier Švejk,* he is incompetent here, as, for example, when he forgets to refuel an aircraft. Švejk's incompetence, however, results in major achievements. Once he breaks the world altitude record and once the distance record. In the latter case Švejk lands in Tripolitania; thus, as in the first story, Hašek has introduced a topical element, the uncomfortable political relations between Austria and Italy.

There is nothing bitter about the humor of the Švejk stories. In the next version of Švejk, which Hašek wrote and published while he was working as a journalist in Kiev, the humor is bitter, indeed, even sour. The somewhat amorphous brief novel *Dobrý voják Švejk v zajetí* (The Good Soldier Švejk in Captivity, 1917) lacks the good-natured fun of the stories and the wide-ranging rambunctiousness of *The Good Soldier Švejk*. Švejk's occupation has now changed; he has proceeded up the social scale: he is a shoemaker with a shop in Vinohrady, he has a room behind the shop, and he keeps guinea pigs under his bed. His character also has a new dimension, one that conforms with the mounting Czech nationalism of contemporary Kiev and is therefore absent from the postwar novel.

Švejk is something of a martyr; since Hašek is at this time an ardent supporter of Masaryk, whom, naturally, he had gently satirized in prewar stories, we may assume that Hašek is referring to Masaryk's criticism of the Czechs as too prone to martyring themselves. Švejk's constant smile has changed: "He was in something like an exalted state of martyrdom, kindhearted, contented martyrdom." He has the qualities of the holy fool that he has in *The Good Soldier Švejk*, but here they are more concrete: "the icy expression on Švejk's face, that divine calm, resignation, but at the same time an animation of the sort to be seen only in the pictures of martyrs in churches." One significant change is that Švejk's Austrophilia is more ambivalent here than it is in the stories. Nevertheless, he accepts just as willingly whatever happens to him. As in the postwar novel he has rheumatism (which Hašek himself had; Pytlík states he acquired his rheumatism and alcoholism on his summer hikes in Upper Hungary), and he is wheeled by a friend in a Bath chair to enlist; as he is wheeled he shouts, "To Belgrade! To Belgrade!" He spends some time as a malingerer in a hospital; the depiction of that is horrific. Švejk also spends time in prison, and the only thing that worries him there is his concern for his guinea pigs, which he imagines starving without him. So here Švejk is an animal lover, while in *The Good Soldier Švejk* he professes love of animals but demonstrates only cruelty.

In *Švejk v zajetí* the good soldier's prison spell is disturbed by a dream: he is ordered to shave Francis Joseph; while he is doing that, the judge advocate comes in, making Švejk jump and cut off the emperor's nose. This "caesarian section" mentally affects Švejk, and he ends up in a Vienna psychiatric clinic. Švejk is just as calm as he is in the postwar novel, although here that calm is more clearly contrasted with the behavior of officers. Two other important characters of the postwar novel appear briefly, Cadet Biegler and Lieutenant Lukáš. In the wartime novel, however, Švejk is first batman to a padre (as in the postwar work), but then to Dauerling, a Slav-hating, bullying coward. At the front Švejk banters the quivering Dauerling with cool, deferential reports on the state of battle such as, "They are going to smash us into little pieces, sir." In the end Dauerling asks Švejk to shoot him in the arm so that he will be sent behind the lines; Švejk kills him by mistake—and then wanders over to the Russian side.

In *Švejk v zajetí* Švejk himself takes up a smaller proportion of the action than in either the stories or *The Good Soldier Švejk*. In the latter the anecdotes are almost all recounted by Švejk, but in *Švejk v zajetí* that is not the case; in fact, *Švejk v zajetí* contains much anecdotal reportage that has nothing to do with Švejk. While the anecdotes in the postwar novel tend to remind the reader of normal, humdrum life back home, most of the anecdotes in *Švejk v zajetí* constitute simple anti-Austrian propaganda. In *The Good Soldier Švejk* the humor is of considerable variety, but in *Švejk v zajetí* most of it is so politically committed that it becomes heartless sarcasm. Sometimes that sarcasm exceeds the bounds of political or aesthetic effectiveness. For example, the reader is told that two Prague senior policemen live by a certain park, where there are two plane trees that would make fine gallows, and that officer Klíma wears a sixteen-inch collar and officer Slavíček a seventeen-inch collar. Sometimes the sarcasm is heavy-handedly aphoristic: "Austria's greatest desire was to become redundant." In his depiction of Austrian officers' cowardice Hašek overreacts to Central Powers propaganda:

> All the men were pale, the officers very pale. It was clear as anything now that the Austrians' stout hearts were in their boots. Pure crystal cowardice glistened in their every movement. None of them looked bellicose and not a moment went by but one or other officer, hearing an explosion in the distance, would shout out, "Cover! Take cover!"
>
> (*Dobrý voják Švejk v zajetí*, 1973, p. 70)

Švejk v zajetí speaks out more insistently against World War I than *The Good Soldier Švejk*. Švejk's neighbor Bílek represents Hašek's conception of the standard Czech view:

he sees no reason for fighting the Serbs, who have done nothing to him. War is also inglorious and inefficient: the German soldiers Švejk's company replaces at the front line have not eaten for two days and beg for bread. War also corrupts: the best quarters in Bruck an der Leitha are inhabited by senior officers and directors of war-supplies firms; officers steal other men's wives, but they also steal or have their batmen steal their own soldiers' rations. In *Švejk v zajetí* Hašek indulges in traditional Czech anti-German and anti-Hungarian virulence, something his bohemian indifference or tolerance would not allow at other periods of his life. Similarly he expresses sentimental Czech patriotism of the kind he jeered at before and after the war. Most telling of all is the anti-Semitism of *Švejk v zajetí*. Before the war Hašek felt the same sort of empathy with the Jews as he did with Gypsies. Like his fellow writer of grotesque fiction, Čapek-Chod, he utterly rejected the Czech anti-Semitic tradition. In this brief novel, however, Hašek has adopted that vicious anti-Jewish stance characteristic of Czech novels about the war, especially about the Czechoslovak Legion. He even spews out the idea that the insignia with F. J. I. (that is, Francis Joseph I) on Austro-Hungarian caps really signifies "For Jewish Interests." Czech World War I anti-Semitism was intimately linked with the fact that the Prague Jews generally spoke German rather than Czech. In other words, it could be partly explained by anti-German feeling. Hašek attacks the Jews for being German nationalists and for being police informers. The nationalism and racism comport with the way in which Hašek's views changed in accordance with who was paying him. On the other hand, in Kiev Hašek does seem to have been gripped by some idealist enthusiasm that was otherwise alien to him.

OTHER WRITINGS DURING THE WAR

Most of the articles and short stories he wrote while attached to the Czechs and Slovaks in Russia are all too serious. His political fickleness is evident here too. First he is pro-Romanov; indeed he even suspects Vladimir Ilyich Lenin. Once they are out of the way, he begins to attack Rasputin, tsardom, and the Russian court. Similarly, once in Kiev, he starts writing about the Austrian royal family as if they were degenerates. By the beginning of 1918 he is writing like a left-wing social democrat, as for example in his comments about class vision: "One group consists in the bourgeois capitalists, who in their selfish greed see in socialism an attack on the personal interests of their pockets; another group is formed by people who have no capital, are also proletarians, but who are afflicted by the bourgeois mentality." Some of his wartime anti-German satire is coarse, like the picture of soldiers as "haggard, hungry figures whom German pseudo-culture and Kaiser Wilhelm II's speeches had failed to fill." A year later he writes like a bloodthirsty lout, as he reminisces on the 1897 riots in Prague: "I joined in the pursuit of a German student who took refuge in a cellar, where he was eventually lynched. There was such a throng there that I was not able to take part in the lynching, which still irks me, but I hope I shall make up for it someday." This might sound ironic to a reader of today, but Hašek was in earnest. Here the misanthropic Hašek is just as fanatical as in an October 1917 article in which he describes a German officer who has his mistress embroider her garters with the slogan, "Gott strafe England" (God punish England). According to an article from April, that was the slogan used as a normal greeting by Prague Jews.

Hašek was truly disappointed when the Czechs had to stop fighting Germany on the eastern front; his frustrated nationalism together with the political power of the pen he had begun to enjoy in Kiev and his own impetuosity made him choose to join the Red Army rather than remain with the legion. It is also possible that he had marginally greater sympathy with the Bolshevik than the Czechoslo-vak cause. Hašek's writing for the Communist press was on the whole of even less literary interest than his propaganda-writing in Kiev. On the other hand, his imagination was certainly constrained by the fact that he was writing in foreign languages. A German poem he wrote for *Krasnaya Evropa* called "Spartaks Helden" (The Heroes of Spartak), a poem greatly praised by Marxist-Leninist critics, is interesting because it shows what platitudes Hašek was capable of and how he lacked any sensitivity to the German language. Hašek managed to toe the party line with enthusiasm; only occasionally did he transgress because of his residual bourgeois values. Thus to a Russian article, "Khristos i popy" (Christ and the Priests), published in *Nash put'*, the editorial board had to add a rider that stated that they did not entirely agree with Hašek's assessment of the meaning of Christ, whom Hašek views in the Christian socialist tradition as a revolutionary. Hašek's political fickleness is evident again in an article entitled "Chto budet c chekhoslovatskoy burzhuaznoy respublikoy?" (What Will Become of the Czechoslovak Bourgeois Republic?; Russian original lost; Hungarian translation printed in a Soviet periodical published in 1934), in which Hašek condemns Masaryk for leading an anti-Communist crusade.

HAŠEK'S POSTWAR WORKS ON RUSSIA

Hašek's semifictional accounts of his journey back from Russia and his experiences during the Civil War were not published in left-wing journals in Prague. Nevertheless his writing after the war, with the probable exception of *The Good Soldier Švejk*, often shows a clear political bias to the left, which was not generally evident before the war. Furthermore his writing has mellowed, occasionally to the point of clumsy tediousness. One sees something of his old sarcastic bitterness in the monologue he delivered at the Seven of Hearts cabaret in January 1921, "Jak jsem se setkal s autorem svého nekrologu" (How I Met the Author of My Obituary). This is a fictional account of his punishment of the poet Jaroslav Kolman Cassius, who really did write Hašek's obituary. The piece lacks comic sparkle and evinces guttersnipe vengefulness.

The semifictional "I vyklepal prach z obuvi své . . ." (And He Shook off the Dust from His Feet . . . , 1921) describes the narrator's arrival in Estonia and voyage from Reval (now Tallinn) to Stettin. Hašek presents a sardonic picture of what it felt like to be back in the West: American YMCA volunteers spend most of their time speculating with black-market money; the British are doing their capitalist best by supplying the starving citizens of the Baltic states with china dishes for chicken hutches, electric kettles, and sports goods. In this tale we see Hašek the hooligan again when he praises the refugees for beating up an official. We also see Hašek the creator of types. Here it is a Czech officer who behaves in accordance with the best tradition of unintelligent know-all bores, and the satire is well-nigh dadaist; Hašek may also be parodying his own inclination to be a walking encyclopedia: "The sea is rich in fish and fishing is the sole occupation of fishermen. Many fish eat each other; otherwise they would die of starvation. The shark is dangerous for people bathing in the sea. The sea has a tendency to be shallow and deep. Seawater is salty."

When in 1961 the cycle of stories set in and around Bugulma was first published in Russian in *Sovietskaya Tatariya* (Soviet Tartary) and *Vokrug sveta* (Round the World), correspondents to those periodicals accused Hašek of distorting facts and defaming the memory of revolutionary heroes. The editors persuaded all, however, that Hašek was a reliable socialist writer. In fact these stories glorify the Red Army and make it look as if the Civil War had been rather gentle and gentlemanly.

In one of the stories Hašek gives a mock account of his career in the Austrian army. He had, for example, been promoted to noncom-missioned officer for getting his commanding officer, Lieutenant Lukas, a pretty Polish girl, and had received a medal for gallantry for massaging him with mercury ointment. The binding theme in the story is the cool, generous, rational Gashek's relationship with the wild, violent, irrational Jerochymov; in the end it transpires that, though he may be wild and devious, he is not the cruel man Gashek imagined him to be. The first story, "Velitelem města Bugulmy" (Commandant of Bugulma, 1921), depicts Gashek's appointment, his introduction of a calm, nonviolent regime, and his usurpation by the ranting Jerochymov. In the subsequent stories we see Gashek as the competent, kind leader eventually asserting his authority over a dashing, drunken, plundering, incompetent one. The only time Gashek uses a pistol is to smash Jerochymov's vodka bottle.

Hašek is keen to absolve himself of any blame for his activities in Russia. He condemns nothing in the Red Army or its activities and so, at least implicitly, he denies all reports of Red Army barbarism. That does not mean he has to refrain from poking gentle fun at the new forms of authority in revolutionary Russia. Hašek cannot suddenly cease to be anti-authoritarian in his writing, however much he had bowed to circumstances while he had been in Russia.

The revolutionary tribunal Gashek finds himself before has three members, each a different type of political enthusiast. The liberal, sensitive, rational propagandist Sorokin wins the day, whereby Hašek suggests the Bolshevik leaders were sensible and well-intentioned—and educated. Sorokin had once published a collection of verse, but it "had been confiscated by the Commissariat for the Press. Today he does not regret that, since his poetry had been foolish." Sorokin had read modern languages at the university and was now party chairman for the eastern front. We hear little about the second member of the tribunal, Kalibanova, no doubt because she is a woman. She is an intellectual fanatic who has been a medical student and knows the whole of Karl Marx by heart. Her name suggests she is plain. Hašek spends most time on the third member whose name, Agapov, ironically suggests Christian love. A former clerk, he is the most radical member. He has a chip on his shoulder and a black mustache. At least to some extent he is a caricature of what the contemporary Czech would expect the member of a revolutionary tribunal to resemble:

> Everything about him declared that what had preceded the fall of tsardom had made him a hard, cruel, merciless, terrifying man who had long since settled his scores with those who had once paid him a miserable fifteen rubles a month. He clearly wrestles with these shades of the past wherever he goes; he transfers his suspicions to all that surrounds him and constantly imagines unknown traitors.
>
> (*Velitelem města Bugulmy: Z tajemství mého pobytu v Rusku*, p. 140)

There is far more psychological insight in that description of a lower-middle-class radical than in any other characterization in Hašek's works. Agapov belongs to the class that was slowly assuming power over much of Europe.

In a story that does not strictly belong to the Bugulma cycle, "Malé nedorozumění" (A Slight Misunderstanding, 1921), Gashek is a schlimazel who has much in common with the final version of Švejk. The formula of the story itself, however, suggests the guncotton tale. Gashek is sent by the Siberian revolutionary committee to Urga in Mongolia to meet and accompany back to Irkutsk a Chinese general for negotiations on the Russo-Chinese frontier. The mission goes spectacularly wrong. It results in a two-day battle in which twenty thousand Buryats, ten thousand Mongolians, and an unspecified number of Chinese and Japanese die. On top of that Urga is ceded to China. This story is simply a farce that satirizes nothing except, just possibly, the picture Hašek presents of himself in the Bugulma cycle.

THE GOOD SOLDIER SVĚJK

The Good Soldier Švejk and His Fortunes in the World War satirizes the past almost exclusively. It satirizes in particular the Austro-Hungarian army and the Austrian bureaucracy. There is nothing bold in that. It also satirizes less generally other institutions Hašek had frequently attacked in his prewar stories: the police, the church, particularly its money-mindedness and mock piety, the judiciary, psychiatrists, Czech flag-waving, and human sexual relationships. So there is nothing new in all that. What criticism he has for the new Czechoslovak republic generally consists in muted versions of what writers such as Machar or Dyk were saying more stridently. To be sure, there is one more or less personal attack, presumably on the nonentity J. S. Hevera, the editor of *Čzekoslovenská republica*, when the baroness von Botzenheim gives Švejk "a prettily bound book, 'Stories from the Life of Our Monarch,' which was written by the present, most reputable editor in chief of the official government newspaper, *Československá republika*."

In the next chapter Hašek satirizes the way former members of the Austrian police, military police, and prison service still hold high rank in the new republic. Even Klíma and Slavíček, who appear in *Švejk v zajetí*, have had their Austrian service counted toward their pensions in the special branch. One Austrian prison governor, Slavík, had, however, become a thief in the new republic and was now himself in prison: "Poor chap, he did not find a cosy niche for himself like other officers." Elsewhere he satirizes the batman type who has made himself into a retired Napoleon in the republic. As types these soldier-servants do not appear far removed from Agapov in the Bugulma cycle: "For the most part they were reactionaries and the other ranks loathed them. Some of them were informers and it gave them particular pleasure when they saw some soldier being tied up. . . . Their selfishness knew no bounds." And in the epilogue to part

JAROSLAV HAŠEK

1 Hašek writes that many former Austrian secret policemen are still "extraordinarily interested in what who is talking about." Hašek's attitude to Masaryk is more or less positive again. In part 4, chapter 1, he has a would-be private joke with him, when he intrudes to say that he just wanted the president to know that an arrest warrant was out for him even on the Galician front. All in all, *The Good Soldier Švejk* is of little relevance to the new republic except insofar as it gives the average Czech citizen who had once been an average Austrian soldier the chance to have a laugh.

The plot of this picaresque novel (Hašek calls it "an historical portrait of a definite time") is certainly not interesting enough to have made it the most widely read Czech work of the twentieth century. Švejk hears about the assassination of Franz Ferdinand in Sarajevo and goes to his usual pub, where, after he has told the secret policeman Bretschneider that there is bound to be a war, he is arrested. Thus begins what has been called, essentially at the suggestion of Hašek's title for chapter 6 of part 1, "Švejk opět doma, proraziv začarovaný kruh" (Švejk Back Home, Having Broken Out of a Vicious Circle"), Švejk's series of circular journeys to the Galician front. The first circle takes him from the pub to police cell to medical board and lunatic asylum to the police station and finally back home. Then he is called up while suffering from a bout of rheumatism, is wheeled by his servant, Müllerová, into military service, again lands in the hospital and then in prison. Now he is noticed by the Jewish convert army chaplain, Otto Katz, who takes him as his batman. (Katz both embodies a residue of stock Czech anti-Semitic attitudes, Jewish opportunism, and so on, and has the scurrilous, playful, disreputable, debauched behavior and attitudes both Hašek and Švejk find attractive.) Katz loses Švejk in cards to Lieutenant Lukáš, a Czech who usually speaks German and a noted batman-basher. In the course of the novel Švejk gradually deprives Lukáš of any power over him, although Švejk adores Lukáš with something like homosexual

love. That undermining of fearsomeness recalls Gashek's gradual assertion of his authority over Jerochymov in the Bugulma cycle. Gashek, however, has no homosexual feeling toward him, though he does toward the tribune Sorokin, whose blond beard he playfully tugs as they drink tea. On the other hand, Jerochymov does gaze at Gashek with eyes strikingly similar to Švejk's "childlike blue eyes." Švejk begins by being a successful protective batman to Lukáš, but gradually he gets his officer and himself into more and more trouble. Soon after an episode in which Švejk has a dog stolen from a colonel for Lukáš, they are sent to Budweis to prepare for the front. In the train on the way Švejk pulls the communication cord. He is brought before a station commandant and is eventually sent on foot to Budweis, but he goes terribly wrong and his determined march describes a large circle in the midst of South Bohemia. Eventually he does arrive in Budweis to the dismay of Lukáš and he is put in prison. Soon the regiment is sent to Királyhíd-Bruck an der Leitha, the border between Hungary and Austria. There is more trouble here when Švejk meets a friend from Prague while he is on the way to a certain married Hungarian woman with a delicate message; the Hungarian woman had been as disgusted and excited as Lukáš by the shaven genitalia of the dancing girls the night before. Unfortunately for Lukáš, Švejk's friend the degenerate lout Vodička is a maniacal Magyarophobe, and so Švejk gets involved in a Czech-Magyar riot, and Lukáš' name and his attraction to the "tasteful" Hungarian reach the press. The regiment is now hastily sent up into Galicia; Švejk is no longer batman, but a regimental factotum. Lukáš has a new batman, the massive Baloun, who is insatiable and steals most of Lukáš' rations. So Lukáš still depends on Švejk. While on a billeting mission for Lukáš, Švejk comes across a Russian uniform by a lake, tries it on, and is arrested. Eventually he is to be executed as a Czech traitor, but he is rescued by a telegram and despatched to rejoin his regiment. The novel breaks off as Švejk is listening to his regiment's officers upstairs becoming more and more drunk.

The novel is sloppily constructed and the narrative is in uninspired Czech; it contains Russianisms and inelegant archaisms, grammatical mistakes and non sequiturs. Hašek has lost the narrative gift he had before the war. On the other hand, the dialogue is lively, well observed, often witty. And many individual scenes constitute accomplished slapstick. One example occurs when the dotty major general walks by as the men are on the latrines and Švejk, trousers down, orders everyone to stand at attention with eyes right. The scene epitomizes life in the Austrian army; it takes place in three languages, Czech, German, and Polish, if one does not count the mongrel Germano-Czech of some of the major general's utterances as a fourth language.

Still, the key to the novel's success lies neither in the dialogue nor in the comic scenes, but in the figure of Švejk himself. Švejk in this third version is more inconsistent than complex. There are two ways of looking at him, both of which are rooted in the fact that Švejk is a popular hero. The first way is that of the ordinary Czech, the non-intellectual, for whom Švejk is a hero as the embodiment of the common man's rebellion against authority but also as a perfect dodger. The fact that Švejk does not dodge duties in the novel is irrelevant. Švejk the dodger is a synthetic impression, like the impression most middle-class Czechs had of him in the 1920's and 1930's: that he was a coarse coward interested only in saving his own skin. That is also true, although there is nothing in the novel to support it. Dodger and coward are the same thing to different people. The second way of looking at Švejk is the way of the literary critic, the close reader. Unless the critic either assumes a strong political stance or ignores inconsistencies for the sake of elegance, he or she will not be able to arrive at any firm conclusion about Švejk.

However one looks at Švejk, certain charac-

teristics will be agreed upon by every reader. He is a new type, a new mythic figure; it is only difficult to know exactly what common human experience or predicament he embodies. It does appear certain that this predicament is socially restricted, for he is not admirable by any normal post-medieval Christian European standards. Admirability seems nearly always to involve some sort of sacrifice. The Titan is admirable because he vies with authority and is punished for that by destruction. Švejk does not vie with authority; he renders authority irrelevant. His anti-authoritarianism is as absolute as the authority of the gods. Hence most readers will find Švejk repugnant as a human being. The ridiculous Second Lieutenant Dub is to Švejk what Phaëthon is to Zeus.

Hašek himself encouraged the idea of Švejk as a myth in his introduction to the novel, where he writes that Švejk "was during the monarchy on the lips of all citizens of the kingdom of Bohemia" and that "his fame will not die in the republic either." Like other mythic figures, Hašek's hero has accumulated features that do not exist in the original versions. One sentence attributed to Švejk ("Don't shoot, there are people there") is at least traceable to a particular dramatization by E. F. Burian. Another phrase, said to be Švejk's catchphrase, and one that has been quoted as deriving from Hašek by critics (including myself) is "To chce klid" (roughly translated: "No panic"); that results from folk interpretation of Švejk's character. This is also true of the notion that Švejk is a nice chap.

Although the third version of Švejk may appear actually baser than the previous two versions, he is higher on the social scale. He appears to own his own flat. He has enough money to keep a domestic servant and to spend a lot of time in pubs, though he does little but disfigure and sell dogs to the gullible. He is, then, a petty criminal or confidence trickster by occupation. He has a brother who is a master at a grammar school and who has passed his short-service commission examinations. He is fairly well traveled for the time, before the war has started. He has wandered about the Great Hungarian Plain and has been to Bremen, presumably as a journeyman, though the Czech words "Když jsem před léty vandroval" (Years ago, when I was a-wandering), which introduce that information, echo a popular song; thus the word *vandroval* may not mean, as it does literally, "traveled as a journeyman"; the sentence "When I was on my journeys years ago" may simply constitute an example of Hašek's copious use of intertextual allusion. Švejk spent some time working in Mährisch Ostrau in Austrian Silesia, but the reader never learns at what. He had done his compulsory military service and during it had taken part in maneuvers in South Bohemia. He had also been stationed in Trent as he was in the prewar version. His military service had been cut short: "I was invalided out for imbecility and pronounced official idiot by a special board."

His education is limited, or so it seems. He lets fall a malapropism "horizontální radost" for "hrozitánskou radost" ("horizontal pleasure" for "enormous pleasure"), but that may be intentional, since the preceding sentence contains parody and since Švejk's words often do contain seemingly innocuous parody or travesty, especially when he is speaking to Lieutenant Lukáš, as he is here. Furthermore, "horizontal pleasure" would make sense in the novel, given its scatological element and the frequent references to forms of bowel sickness, since the pleasure is to be provided by chicken soup. The horizontal pleasure will be lying in bed with diarrhea rather than performing military duties. Švejk is educated enough to recognize a scrap of paper in the latrines as part of a page from a schoolgirl novel by the writer Růžena Jesenská. Švejk also has a smattering of Hungarian. He reads German well since he can read the detailed description the colonel whose dog he purloined for Lukáš has put in the personal columns of *Bohemia*. He can also read the novel that has been chosen as a basis for the regiment's code at the front. When he speaks German (for example, to the Hungar-

ian woman's maid), he speaks a broken Viennese, although some clauses are perfect literary, even bureaucratic, German. When Švejk has been captured by the Austrians and is to be used as an interpreter for Russian prisoners of war, the reader learns that he spins one of his yarns in broken German; but clearly his German is not bad since the Austrian noncommissioned officer thoroughly enjoys the story.

Švejk is unremarkable to look at. One would not notice him in the street because, apart from anything else, he embodies the man-in-the-street myth. He is "of small, sturdy stature, symmetrical face and nose, blue eyes, no distinguishing marks." He has big ears, and he wears his army cap "rammed down" over his forehead. He seems to be attractive to women, if the reader goes by the reaction of Katy, who comes to stay with Lukáš. Katy is so impressed by Švejk's "sturdy stature and strong thighs," that she imperiously commands him to take off his trousers and come to bed. Their copulation is vigorous, and she falls sound asleep immediately afterward.

Švejk's attitude to female sexuality represents the notional *Lumpenproletarier* attitude that Hašek himself pretends to express in previous works and as narrator in *The Good Soldier Švejk*. It could be that Katy is not particularly attracted to Švejk except inasmuch as he is male and looks virile enough. She perhaps cannot wait for Lukáš' return in the evening, and her hop-dealer husband is boring and disagreeable and goes on too many business trips. We have, then, either a vulgar picture of sexual frustration or Hašek indulging in a conventional *fin-de-siècle* picture of female sexuality. Most heterosexuality described in the novel concerns either marital infidelity or brothels. Hašek or his persona's self-stylization as a Don Juan in the poem "Jste dcerou z lepší rodiny" (You Are a Young Lady From a Better-Class Family) from *Májové výkřiky* could indicate sexual insecurity. In the short story "Elindult az Ajgó Márton . . ." (Márton Ajgó Set Off . . . , 1905) Hašek describes how a perfectly happy rich farmer, contented with a life of eating and drinking, loses his life by setting off to woo a miller's daughter. The manner in which Hašek narrates the tale makes for a grotesque parody of decadent stories about men being destroyed by vamps. His feuilleton "Jak vypadají ženy" (What Women Are Like, 1911) may also satirize *fin-de-siècle* literary attitudes, but the result is a comic anti-feminism in which the writer is parodying himself. It opens: "I admit I have always had difficulties in the company of ladies. Substantial difficulties, for I was very afraid of women. I presumed by using their amiability and charming appearance that women were creatures who wished to live well and wanted to bewitch men into marrying them." Hašek himself once wrote to Jarmila about a venereal disease he had caught from a Slovak Gypsy; since they had a son, his disease had not made him impotent, or it had never existed. He did not, perhaps, derive pleasure from the sexuality of women.

It has been suggested he was homosexual. He certainly sometimes wore women's clothes. That could offer some explanation for his bohemian life and his treatment of his friends: the sexual outcast escapes by becoming or pretending to become a social outcast. His enthusiasm as a jingo legionary and then as a commissar and the radical change of life-style that entailed may also be connected with his own sexuality. Certainly the discipline and anonymity of life in the Red Army probably helped him mask his desires. In *The Good Soldier Švejk* he does mention homosexuality. The occultist cook, Jurajda, declares that "only aesthetes are homosexual; that derives from the very essence of aestheticism," an allusion to the homosexual occultist writer Jiří Karásek. When drunk, the chaplain Katz reminisces about some schoolboy homosexual romance. Švejk also remembers a homosexual colonel in Trent who was always nice to the soldiers and had attempted to blackmail a cadet into buggery. We also have the transvestite officers, one of whom vomits into the lap of a formerly lesbian noblewoman. That scene, like the description of the loud-mouthed, priggish Second Lieutenant Dub drunk in a brothel, forms part of Hašek's picture of Austro-Hungarian degeneracy.

Švejk makes no connection between sexuality and love. He enjoys a story he tells about a conservatory student who forces a bourgeois father to give him his daughter by taking her virginity, not because the student loves the girl (the student is a womanizer), but because he thus makes good use of sexual intercourse: he spites a bourgeois, who is a hypocrite anyway. There had been a time when Švejk had not known what one could do with girls, as he tells Lukáš, and now he regrets his missed opportunities. He has no idea of male shame, but he does have some idea of female shame; even that he turns into a slapstick anecdote:

> I understand, sir. If I suddenly came into the bedroom, it might actually be unpleasant for some woman. Once I brought a young lady home with me, and the maid brought us coffee just when we were having a whale of a time. She got a shock and poured hot coffee all over my back, and, to beat it all, she said, "The top of the morning to you." I know what's right and proper when a lady's in bed somewhere.
>
> (*Osudy dobrého vojáka Švejka*, 1:172)

Švejk is not homosexual, however loving the smile he directs at Lukáš, however much he misses Lukáš (his only straightforward emotions in the novel), and however much his soft blue eyes could suggest that Hašek has some sexual interest in Švejk.

Švejk's optimistic smile rules the novel. That smile signals an imperturbability that contrasts with and copes with the violently perturbed times. It lies at the very center of the myth. It represents the folk magic that can destroy all the grandiose, grandiloquent mythopoeia that attends institutionalized authority. Perhaps it is also the smile of a fool. Švejk is a schlimazel like so many of Hašek's earlier characters. The narrator himself tells the reader so, when Švejk innocently asks the plainclothes police superintendent whether he has permission to raid a certain pub. Usually, however, Švejk says so himself; indeed, words like "I've had bad luck ever since I was a kid" form something of a refrain in the first two parts of the novel. He is also constantly getting into scrapes, but it is not quite clear whether these might not represent some devious sort of insubordination. In the epilogue to part 1 Hašek tells us he does not know whether he will succeed in fulfilling his aim with his novel. He continues: "The very fact that I heard one man swearing at another, 'You're as big a fool as Švejk,' makes me think I shall not succeed." He informs us, then, that Švejk is not a fool, although he had been declared a fool by an army medical board. (We already know Hašek has no time for psychiatrists.)

Hašek displays his hero's ambivalence when Švejk is before another medical board: "Half the board said that Švejk was 'ein blöder Kerl' [an idiot] and the other half that he was a villain trying to make an ass of the army." Similarly, when Lukáš discovers his dog has been stolen from the colonel, he shouts, "Švejk, you vermin, for God's sake shut your mouth! You are either a master cad or a prize numbskull, a clumsy idiot." Then, right at the beginning of part 2, Lukáš says to Švejk, "I still don't know whether you were born an idiot or you just behave like one." The greatest definite idiot of the novel, the pompous Second Lieutenant Dub, is sure Švejk is a fraud. Dub tells the gouty Colonel Gerbich that Švejk "pretends to be an idiot, so that he can conceal his rascalry behind that idiocy." A few moments later he turns to Švejk and says, "You're sapping my patience, aren't you?" To that Švejk just replies, "Yes." In a brief on Švejk compiled by the judge advocate Bernis, which is mislaid and found again only after the war, the army legal service's charge against him is clear: "He intended casting off his mask and publicly declaring his opposition to the emperor and the state." If, however, Švejk were shamming idiocy the whole time, then he would not cause someone he is so fond of, Lukáš, so much trouble. There is no doubt that Švejk is playing a game, as critics such as Karel Kosík and

Radko Pytlík have said, and that some characters are on his side (most other ranks and Lukáš, Katz, Marek, and others) and some are his opponents (Dub, Biegler, Bretschneider). Švejk himself considers a good game of cards more important than the whole war.

Švejk can utter loyal slogans because they refer to abstract concepts, which mean nothing to him. He is a materialist. He can use clichés about serving Francis Joseph to the last drop of his blood and simultaneously reason that Francis Joseph must be an awful fool. That suggests that Švejk is a lover of his fellow human beings and a hater of institutions. But this is not true. He is a creature of little compassion. He is utterly dispassionate and cheerless when he has to guard two soldiers who had formed his escort and whose only crime was to have become very drunk. He is completely unmoved when a man falls off a troop train and impales himself on a pointslever. Švejk's fearlessness is inhuman—or that of a mentally retarded thug. He is the toughest man in the battalion, the only one not needing to put his pack on a wagon during the march to the front. He needs no possessions, as he himself states when he is arrested during his circular "anabasis" to Budweis. At the same time he is money-minded. He actually trembles uncontrollably when Lukáš sends the money Katy had left back to her husband. He is a thief: he steals a roadhouse doorbell for Katz to use at mass. He is physically violent, as is seen in the way he manhandles Katz's creditor, in the verve he exhibits as he lays into Hungarians with Vodička, or in his knocking the Polish pimp down the stairs during the disembrothelment of Dub. He is sarcastic, as when he tells Dub's batman how much he likes and admires Dub. He is impertinent, like an overgrown child. He is a liar and encourages the loutish Vodička to follow his example; one must never tell the truth at a courtmartial. He even lies to Lukáš, when the latter catches him with a disguised bundle of rations he has scrounged from the officers' mess. Švejk is also a bully, as we see in his ostentatiously merciless treatment of the frightened batman, Mikulášek, or in the way he drills the edacious Baloun just to make a laughingstock of him. Švejk himself is unbullyable. He usually disarms bullies with a smile or a show of zeal. He is a trickster; he tricks the gullible maid of the colonel into telling him how to lure away the colonel's dog; he gets rid of an informer who has been planted in his prison cell by calling the guard and telling him the man who has been put in his cell is mentally sick and suffering from hallucinations. But Švejk is also a keen observer and has a certain boyish quick-wittedness: a fellow prisoner in Prague tells the story of a mean peasant whose provisions his cellmates had been driven to stealing; one day another prisoner receives some cigarettes and the mean peasant asks for a puff, but no one gives him one; Švejk's comment is: "I was afraid you had given him a puff. That would have spoiled the whole story. Noble behavior is all very well in novels, but in a situation like that in the cooler it would be bloody ridiculous." When the chairman of the medical board asks him how much 12,897 times 13,863 is, he immediately answers, 729. For Švejk the war is a game. It is easy for a mythic figure to treat the war as a game, for he is indestructible. Any inconsistency in his behavior becomes unimportant, once we cease to expect him to act like a believable human being.

The Good Soldier Švejk was banned from Czechoslovak barracks in 1925; the first Hungarian translation was published in Paris and not allowed into Hungary; in 1928 the Polish translation was confiscated; on 10 May 1933 the German translation was burned in the famous Nazi bonfire; in Bulgaria a translation began to appear in fascicles, but after the fourth fascicle it was banned (1935). It has inspired continuations by other authors, notably Bertolt Brecht, but none of those continuations has been successful. Hašek has a special irreverence for authority, sometimes to language, often for human beings themselves, which is inimitable. Very few serious Czech critics took much notice of Hašek or *The Good Soldier Švejk* before the late 1940's. Gustav Pallas' standard *Slovníček literární* (Small Dictionary of Literature, 1923) does not even list him, although it lists his cousin, Roman Hašek. The only work it gives for the latter is Jaroslav Hašek's *Májové výkřiky*. In the standard illustrated history of Czech literature, by Pallas and Vojtěch Zelinka (1926), two lines are devoted to Hašek and *The Good Soldier Švejk*, but the authors have the title wrong, and what they say about the contents of the novel is misleading. Most respected Czech critics disliked *The Good Soldier Švejk*. As late as 1946 Karel Sezima labeled the novel simply "embarrassing." Before World War II *The Good Soldier Švejk* was best received in the two countries where a complete political system had been demolished, Germany and the Soviet Union. Since World War II the same is true; the novel has received most critical attention and has been most popular in the countries of the socialist bloc and West Germany. In Switzerland it is hardly read at all. To that the Czech would answer with words Švejk used of Hungarians in *The Good Soldier Švejk*: "It's not every Swiss what can help being a Swiss."

Hašek is a not very serious writer who is taken very seriously by critics of all political persuasions. He has little gift for psychology, linguistic adornments, or imagery. He has a gift of comedy that smells somewhat of beer halls and undergraduate lavatories, but which is inimitable. He is a genius of crassness.

Selected Bibliography

EDITIONS

INDIVIDUAL WORKS
Májové výkřiky a jiné verše. With Ladislav H. Domažlický. Prague, 1903.
Dobrý voják Švejk a jiné podivné historky. Prague, 1912.
Trampoty pana Tenkráta. Prague, 1912.

JAROSLAV HAŠEK

Kalamajka. Prague, [1913].

Průvodčí cizinců a jiné satiry z cest i z domova. Prague, [1913].

Můj obchod se psy a jiné humoresky. Prague, 1915.

Dobrý voják Švejk v zajetí. Kiev, 1917.

Dva tucty povídek. Prague, [1920].

Pepíček Nový a jiné povídky. Prague, 1921.

Tři muži se žralokem a jiné poučné historky. Prague, 1921.

Osudy dobrého vojáka Švejka za světové války. 4 vols. in 3. Prague, [1921–1923].

Mírová konference a jiné humoresky. Prague, 1922.

COLLECTED WORKS

Dílo Jaroslava Haška. 16 vols. Prague, 1955–1973. Contains works as follows (listed in order of publication):

Črty, povídky, a humoresky z cest (vol. 1, 1955).

Dobrý voják Švejk před válkou a jiné podivné historky (vol. 10, 1957).

Loupežný vrah před soudem (vol. 2, 1958).

Fialový hrom (vol. 5, 1958).

O dětech a zvířátkách (vol. 7, 1960).

Dědictví po panu Šafránkovi (vol. 3, 1961).

Utrpení pana Tenkráta (vol. 6, 1961).

Zrádce národa v Chotěboři (vol. 4, 1962).

Politické a sociální dějiny Strany mírného pokroku v mezích zákona (vol. 9, 1963).

Galerie karikatur (vol. 8, 1964).

Velitelem města Bugulmy: Z tajemství mého pobytu v Rusku (vol. 15, 1966).

Moje zpověď (vol. 16, 1968).

Májové výkřiky: Básně a prózy (vol. 11, 1972).

Dobrý voják Švejk v zajetí: Stati a humoresky z dob války (vols. 13–14, 1973).

Zábavný a poučný koutek Jaroslava Haška (vol. 12, 1973).

Osudy dobrého vojáka Švejka. 4 vols. in 3. Prague, 1967.

První dekameron, Procházka pres hranice, Idylky z cest a jiné humoresky. Prague, 1976.

Druhý dekameron, Lidožroutská historie, Parodie, morytáty a banality. Prague, 1979.

Politické a sociální dějiny strany mírného pokroku v mezích zákona. Prague, 1982.

TRANSLATIONS

The Good Soldier Schweik. Translated and abridged by Paul Selver. London, 1930.

The Good Soldier Švejk and His Fortunes in the World War. Translated by Cecil Parrott. New York and London, 1973.

The Red Commissar, Including Further Adventures of the Good Soldier Švejk and Other Stories. Translated by Cecil Parrott. London, 1981.

The Tourist Guide: Twenty-Six Stories. Translated by J. T. Havlů. Prague, 1961.

BIOGRAPHICAL AND CRITICAL STUDIES

Doležal, Bohumil, ed. *Podoby: Literární sborník.* Prague, 1967.

Frynta, Emanuel. *Hašek, the Creator of Schweik.* Translated by J. Layton and G. Theiner. Prague, 1965.

Hoření, Zdeněk. *Jaroslav Hašek novinář.* Prague, 1983.

Janouch, Gustav. *Jaroslav Hašek, der Vater des "Braven Soldaten Schwejk."* Berne and Munich, 1966.

Klusák, Milan, et al. *Mezinárodní konference: Dílo Jaroslava Haška v boji za mír a pokrok mezi národy.* Prague, 1983.

Kunstmann, Heinrich. "Hašek, Jaroslav." In *Encyclopedia of World Literature in the Twentieth Century.* New York, 1969.

——————. *Tschechische Erzählkunst im 20. Jahrhundert.* Cologne and Vienna, 1974.

Marlow, Frank J. *Rejstřík jmenný, místní, a věcný ke knize Jaroslava Haška "Osudy dobrého vojáka Švejka za světové války."* Toronto, 1985.

Matejka, Ladislav, and Benjamin Stolz, eds. *Cross Currents: A Yearbook of Central European Culture.* Ann Arbor, Mich., 1983. Includes criticism by Karel Kosík.

Parrott, Cecil. *The Bad Bohemian: The Life of Jaroslav Hašek, Creator of "The Good Soldier Švejk."* London, 1978.

——————. *Jaroslav Hašek: A Study of "Švejk" and the Short Stories.* New York, Cambridge, and London, 1982.

Pytlík, Radko. *Zpráva o Jaroslavu Haškovi (Toulavé house).* 2d rev. ed., Prague, 1982.

——————. *Jaroslav Hašek and "The Good Soldier Schweik."* Translated by D. Short. Prague, 1983.

——————. *Kniha o Švejkovi.* Prague, 1983.

Ripellino, Angelo Maria. *Praga magica.* Turin, 1973.

JAROSLAV HAŠEK

Sezima, Karel. *"Z mého života": Smetanovo smyčcové kvarteto E-moll*. Prague, 1946.

BIBLIOGRAPHIES

Mědílek, Boris. *Bibliografie Jaroslava Haška: Soupis jeho díla a literatury o něm*. Prague, 1983.

Pytlík, Radko, and Miroslav Laiske. *Bibliografie Jaroslava Haška: Soupis jeho díla a literatury o něm*. Prague, 1960.

ROBERT PYNSENT

1118

JOSÉ ORTEGA Y GASSET
(1883–1955)

IN A PROLOGUE to *El tema de nuestro tiempo* (*The Modern Theme*, 1923) written for German readers and published separately as *Prólogo para alemanes* (*Preface for Germans*, 1958), José Ortega y Gasset declares:

> I have to be a university professor, a journalist, a man of letters, a politician, a café conversationalist, a bullfighter, a "man of the world," something like a parish priest, and I don't know how many other things more. Whether this *polypragmosyne* [multiple practice] is good or bad is not so easy to decide.[1]

Ortega y Gasset was versatile, prolific, multiconversant. His highly public career was uncompromised by specialization, which he denounced as a modern form of barbarism in his most famous book, *La rebelión de las masas* (*The Revolt of the Masses*, 1930). His lucid and eloquent works, which overflow twelve volumes, make an immense range of modern culture understandable to the intelligent layman, as they were intended to, for the bulk of them appeared first in newspapers and periodicals of wide circulation. Ernst Curtius is justly comprehensive in his praise of Ortega, who, he says, is "perhaps the only man in contemporary Europe who can speak with equal assurance of judgment, with equal brilliance of expression, about Kant and Proust, prehistoric art and cubist painting, Scheler and Debussy."

Ortega was much more than a writer. The breadth of his achievements equaled the scope of his writings. He launched or participated in launching no fewer than six newspapers and journals, and he directed two publishing houses. His *Revista de Occidente* was undoubtedly one of the great journals of twentieth-century Europe. Together with its book-publishing arm, it brought renown to Federico García Lorca, Jorge Guillén, and other poets of the *vanguardia* (avant-garde), and it introduced foreign authors such as Albert Einstein, Carl Jung, Edmund Husserl, Joseph Conrad, William Faulkner, Franz Kafka, Luigi Pirandello, and Virginia Woolf to the Spanish public, sometimes when they were only beginning to be admired in their own countries. It was Ortega who in 1922 had Sigmund Freud's works translated into Spanish. His forty-eight years of university teaching and public lecturing and his relish for informal symposia, which the Spanish call *tertulias,* spawned a host of disciples in the Iberian Peninsula and in Latin America. Anyone who does intellectual work in Castilian is indebted to him for having enriched the language with a vocabulary that supports professional philosophy. Ortega was also active in Spanish politics during the momentous period from 1909 to 1932. After the fall of the monarchy, which he had criticized severely, he was elected deputy to the first Cortes

---

[1] *Obras completas,* vol. 8 (1946–1969), p. 16. Further quotations from *Obras completas* are also from this edition.

(parliament) of the Second Republic, whose constitution he helped to frame. All these activities did not leave him without time to correspond generously with personages as diverse as Miguel de Unamuno and Gary Cooper. Even his claiming to be a bullfighter in the *Preface for Germans* is not altogether facetious: there is at least one photograph of Ortega, author of an essay on tauromachy, passing a cape around a fighting bull, though a small one. Finally, among the "other things" that Ortega professes not to know must be counted his having been one of the great stylists in Spanish expository prose, as was apparent from the moment he began publishing, and having been one of the important figures in existentialist philosophy, as has been recognized with increasing frequency since his death in 1955. Ortega played a multifaceted and public role, but he far surpassed a merely peripatetic performance.

Ortega was a fountain of ideas. Fecundity was his virtue; but it was his weakness as well. To read his works is to reap a harvest of insights into virtually every topic now being discussed in the humanities. But the writings of this seminal thinker, this one-man university, are often unrevised or unfinished or both. In the torrent of his words there is much that is suppositious, undeveloped, contradictory, or materially wrong. Even the brilliance of his style is marred by infelicitous mannerisms (glaringly, overuse of "radical" and "precisely") that moderately careful second-drafting would have eliminated. He would not halt the flow of ideas: it was his strength and his weakness. Two generations of Ortega scholars, among whom Julián Marías, Ciriaco Morón Arroyo, Paulino Garagorri, Philip Silver, and Nelson Orringer stand out, have had to labor to establish his texts, identify his sources, develop his insights, scrutinize his many and frequently casual opinions, and systematize his dispersed wisdom. As Octavio Paz has said, "More than they are true or false, Ortega's ideas are fertile."

More than most authors, Ortega should be evaluated with reference to his historical situation. It is meaningful that in the *Preface for Germans* he writes that he "has to be" many things to many people. Although he was temperamentally equipped for the role of public figure, he regularly denigrated it, vowing repeatedly to write a proper academic book. Nor did he ever make a secret of his disdain for the masses and for politics. We can only speculate as to what psychological foundations this ambivalence might have had. (Notwithstanding the conversational tone of his works, Ortega is rarely confessional, and as yet no thorough biography has appeared.) But Ortega himself wrote that "man is a being condemned to translate necessity into freedom." His family, the political condition of his country, its harassed tradition of liberal dissent, and European philosophical currents all thrust upon Ortega an evangelical mission that he, on the whole, accepted. He was the last in a long line of writers and educators who dedicated themselves to rousing Spaniards to free thought.

HISTORICAL BACKGROUND

Jean-Paul Sartre maintained that the success of the revolutions of the eighteenth and nineteenth centuries left the bourgeois intelligentsia of Europe without a progressive role to play. But no such obsolescence overtook middle-class intellectuals south of the Pyrenees, where the failure of revolution prolonged the historical moment of the *philosophes.* There is a continuity between Ortega and eighteenth-century *ilustrados* (enlightened ones) such as Benito Feijóo y Montenegro, who as early as the 1720's was producing the sort of critical encyclopedia that later proved so influential in France. Protected by the enlightened despotism of the Spanish Bourbons, Feijóo set out to "impugn common errors without restriction of subject matter" in hopes of overcoming a national resistance "against all novelty" that appalled him.

The struggle of reformist dissidents against entrenched obscurantism continued into the nineteenth century. In 1873 the Spanish had their first republican experience. Offspring of a liberal *pronunciamiento* (coup d'état), the First Republic dissolved within the year. Liberalism in education was dramatically asserted in 1876, when a group of university professors, who had been dismissed for refusing to agree to teach nothing contrary to Catholic dogma or the monarchy, banded together under the leadership of Francisco Giner de los Ríos to form an independent multilevel school that they named the Institución Libre de Enseñanza (Free Institution of Learning). Politically off-center by Spanish standards and pedagogically innovative by any standards, the small school had an influence on modern Spain so great that it bears comparison with that of Marsilio Ficino's Platonic Academy on Renaissance Italy. Many if not most of the important writers, liberal politicians, and educators of the period that spans the founding of the school and its closing at the outbreak of the Civil War—including Lorca, Antonio and Manuel Machado, Miguel de Unamuno, and Ortega—had ties of one sort or another with the Institución. Giner and his rebellious colleagues defined an educational mission that, in its essential features, would be taken up by Ortega. The purpose of the Institución, according to Giner, was to join in "the common task of redeeming the fatherland." To this end the school would provide "total education," "forming," as Giner liked to say, and not merely instructing a vanguard of men and women (for the Institución soon became coeducational), who would "heal society and the state" and lead Spain out of its backwardness. In opposition to the professionalist orientation of the established universities, Giner argued for a curriculum with "a universality of interests that excludes none of the orders of contemporary knowledge." He urged the faculty of the Institución to work not only with students but also "widely and freely throughout society, directing the evolution of the national spirit."

As the nineteenth century drew to a close, a growing chorus of voices exhorted, sometimes hectored, the Spanish nation to break with the past. Among the most commanding were those of the essayists Joaquín Costa, Ángel Ganivet, and Giner. Gifted at coining slogans such as "school and pantry" and "double-lock the sepulcher of *El Cid,*" underscoring the necessity for both physical and intellectual sustenance and repudiating the romance of Spain's glorious past, Costa argued for Europeanization. Most of the members of the famous "Generation of '98"—including Unamuno, Azorín, Ramiro de Maeztu, Ramón Pérez de Ayala, and Pío Baroja—expended buckets of ink in explicit or fictionalized denunciation of Spanish life and institutions. Their work was pervaded by "an acrid spirit of social criticism," in the words of Azorín. The Generation of '98 received its name from the year when Spain lost the remains of its empire in the Western hemisphere, along with its navy, in the Spanish-American War. These disasters, as Costa pointed out at the time, had the effect of unmasking the fiction of enduring imperial glory that the conservatives and the monarchy were using to maintain public confidence.

"Regenerationism," as it was called, was also helped by a rapidly growing Spanish press. Though intermittently molested by censorship, it provided a forum for the reformers and gave them a degree of contact with the people that was unprecedented in the history of Spanish heterodoxy. The Generation of '98 largely owed its success to the press, particularly to *El imparcial* and to the fledgling journals *Vida nueva* and *España,* whose concerns are best conveyed by their titles. Ortega's first article was to appear in *Vida nueva,* and he would apply the name *España* to one of his own journalistic ventures. Lacking the resources to maintain extensive networks of correspondents, the Spanish press filled its pages with features, educational articles, and opinion columns. Thus by the time Ortega began his career, popular essay writing was a well-established practice. The conditions of the journalism of the day defined a genre that Ortega, whom Henri Bergson called "a journalist of genius," would perfect.

A long tradition of socially conscious writing, speaking, and teaching leads to Ortega, but his direct inheritance was the role of public philosopher created by Miguel de Unamuno. Among the writers of the Generation of '98, none was as sanguine as Unamuno about the propagation of culture through journalism, and only Azorín and Maeztu contributed as much to the daily press. Like Ortega, Unamuno repudiated both idealist philosophy and cloistered academicism, and saw Spain's political problem as a pedagogical problem. He too wrote extensively in support of reform from within the educational system while practicing an extramural and politically conscious form of pedagogy that he chose to call "demagogy." Not surprisingly, it was Unamuno, the *Excitator Hispaniae* (Arouser of Spain) as Curtius called him, who in a 1904 article in a popular journal first directed the attention of the Spanish public to the man who was to be given the titles *Praeceptor Hispaniae* (Preceptor of Spain) and *Magister Hispaniae* (Teacher of Spain).

EARLY YEARS

It was in that disastrous year of 1898 that José Ortega y Gasset entered the impassioned world of Spanish intellectuals, when he presented himself at Salamanca to take his first-year university examination before a panel that happened to include Miguel de Unamuno. Even then he must have seemed destined to appear at such a time before a figure already so influential, for the young Ortega was the flower of patrician liberalism. His father, José Ortega Munilla, was the editor of the literary supplement of Madrid's *El imparcial,* where the voices of '98 were being welcomed. The paper's founder was Ortega's maternal grandfather, Eduardo Gasset. "I was born on top of a printing press," Ortega once joked. Both the father and the grandfather had sat on the board of the Institución Libre de Enseñanza. The candidate was a dedicated student, and he was taking the examination at the precocious age of fifteen, which did not prevent him from earning high grades. Unamuno and the student were corresponding lengthily by 1904.

Born in Madrid on 9 May 1883, the second of four siblings, Ortega had been intellectually inclined since childhood, when he was already an avid reader of Miguel de Cervantes, Alexandre Dumas, Jules Verne, Honoré de Balzac, Benito Peréz Galdós, and even Ernest Renan. His generalist soul was perhaps first revealed in a strange, quixotic episode, reported by his brother, that followed his reading of Balzac's *Le comédie humaine* at the age of eleven or twelve. The doctor had to be called, for the boy was feverish, convinced that he had already lived dozens of lives. This scion of a liberal family was sent to a Jesuit middle school in Málaga—perhaps because of the influence of his mother, Dolores Gasset, who was devout. Ortega had no fond memories of the Jesuits. They had tried, he protested in 1910, to make him disdain the great secular thinkers from René Descartes to Charles Darwin. They had given the name of morality to "stupid rules and exercises," and about art, he added accusingly, they had said nothing. Ortega must have turned away from Catholicism at an early age. It is recorded that he was prefect of the school's Marian sodality when he was eleven, but there is no positive reference to religion in his early works, and at the age of twenty-five he already writes of religious belief as something lost long ago.

After his success at Salamanca—"at the time of the great fall of leaves from the patriotic legend," as he later wrote to Unamuno—Ortega enrolled at the University of Madrid, where he received the doctoral degree in philosophy and letters in 1904. His dissertation was on medieval millenarianism. During this period Friedrich Nietzsche and Renan were his favorite authors. He became friends with the '98 writer Ramiro de Maeztu, who interested him in philosophy, as well as with Unamuno. These were also Ortega's "sentimental years," as he called them, when he courted Rosa Spottorno, his future wife.

Before he completed his dissertation Ortega published his first article, "Glosas" (Glosses, 1902) in *Vida nueva,* at the age of nineteen. This first publication was a lyrically phrased attack on the purportedly impersonal literary criticism of Hippolyte Taine. Like most of Ortega's earliest writings, the article was consistent in tone and tendency with the emotionalism and anti-rationalism of the Generation of '98. It also introduced the elitist theme that appears throughout his work: "The multitude as crowd, as *foule,* is impersonal through a gathering of abdications, involuntary, clumsy as a primitive animal." Within three years of obtaining his doctorate, Ortega published another eight articles, mostly book reviews in the literary supplement edited by his father.

Ortega's attainment of more than reasonable success as a writer by his early twenties was no doubt largely due to the exaltation and vividness of his style. As he grew older, his writing became less poetic, more reliant on abstraction, but it never lost the qualities that are showcased in his earliest pieces: richness and audacity of imagery and interpenetration of image and concept, of the particular and the general. In the essay "Las Ermitas de Córdoba" (The Hermitages of Córdoba, 1904), Ortega connects the universe with monasteries nestled on a Córdoba hilltop:

> You sense the beneficent fine rain of silence falling all around and peace rising like smoke from among the trees. You breathe emanations of pure idealism, and upon plucking a wildflower, it seems to explicate words of St. John of the Cross or of Novalis, and I mix these two names because here one is so above it all that orthodoxy and heterodoxy are hardly distinguished, like two black mules that are moving across now, down there, on a road of silver. The spirit is projected toward ultimate questions: What is life? What is death? What is happiness?
>
> (*Obras completas,* 1:422)

The writer does not merely use images to illustrate and clarify; rather, the thought appears first incarnate and concrete, or the image is already invested with an abstract sense, which, once made explicit, easily returns the reader to the domain of the particular. In "Tres cuadros del vino" (Wine in Three Paintings, 1911), Ortega's commentary on Titian's *Bacchanal* (*ca.* 1519), a painting he renamed "The Triumph of the Moment," shifts nimbly between description and interpretation:

> The sun gilds the atmospheric dust and places blue shadows under luxuriant branches. Someone has brought amphoras, narrow pitchers, and small decanters of delicately wrought silver and gold. Within these vessels wine is shining. They drink. The hysterical tension between wills gives way: the pupils grow incandescent, fantasies awaken in the little cells of the brain. The truth is that life is not so adverse a condition, that human bodies are beautiful against the open-air background of gold and blue, that souls are noble, grateful, and apt for understanding and reply. They drink. It seems as if invisible fingers have woven our being with the earth, the sea, the air, the sky; as if the world were a tapestry and ourselves figures within that tapestry, and the threads that form our breast went on beyond it and were the same that compose the matter of that radiant cloud. They drink. How long have they been here?
>
> (*Obras completas,* 2:53)

"They drink," and the literal statement, strategically repeated, begins to convey transcendence of time. Ortega's prose manifests the "unified sensibility," the "direct sensuous apprehension of thought" that his contemporary T. S. Eliot found wanting in the literature of the time. Here is the man who can, in Eliot's words, "feel the thought as immediately as the odor of a rose."

What ought to be done about Spain is the major theme in the early correspondence between Ortega and Unamuno. The dean of the Generation of '98 proffers the office of politically engaged authorship to the youth, who joins him in criticizing the regenerationists. The older man was by then reacting against the ruthless Voltairean anti-traditionalism that had flourished around the time of the war with the United States, and he had taken to reaffirming values, like faith and idealism, that he considered authentically Spanish. But the disciple asserted himself and would have no part of Unamuno's *casticismo* (nativism), as it was being called. He too repudiated the majority of reformists, but not because they lacked respect for things Spanish. It was their lack of respect for systematic reason and disciplined learning that bothered Ortega. "I must confess to you," he wrote to the elder philosopher in 1904, "that this classic-Spanish mysticism that appears from time to time in your repertoire of ideas does not convince me." Ortega goes on to quote approvingly Ivan Turgenev's warning to another backward nation: "For God's sake do not extend through Russia the idea that things can be accomplished without learning." This conflict, with Oedipal overtones, that emerges in the letters was played out over years of growing acrimony until 1914, when the government dismissed Unamuno from his post as rector of the University of Salamanca and Ortega publicly came to his defense.

For Ortega the direction to take in pursuit of national redemption was not toward the soul of Spain, as his mentor would have it, but toward Europe. Between 1905 and 1907 he twice crossed the Pyrenees to study the great architectures of German thought at the universities of Leipzig, Berlin, and Marburg. During these pilgrimages, funded with postdoctoral grants from the Board for Extension of Study (an offshoot of the Institución), Ortega studied ravenously and demonstrated the "tremendous educability" that Robert McClintock has attributed to him. The stay at Marburg had an especially strong influence on his intellectual development, and he returned there in 1911 on what can only be called a working honeymoon. At Marburg he studied with the great neo-Kantians Paul Natorp and Hermann Cohen, becoming the personal friend of the latter. Neo-Kantian philosophy was just what Ortega had set out to find. The Marburg school was dedicated to bringing Kant up to date by elaborating a total philosophical system that would incorporate the scientific methodologies that had developed since Kant's time. Reacting against the excesses of romantic idealism—as was Ortega within the context of Spanish culture—the Marburg neo-Kantians took impersonal physico-mathematical thought as a model for the grand synthesis of reason and empiricism that they sought. In the first issue of the Marburg journal *Philosophische Arbeiten* Cohen and Natorp identified philosophy with the theoretical principles of science.

The influence of Marburg is evident in the positions taken by Ortega during the years following his return to Spain. Writing in *El imparcial* in 1908 he declares that "Spain must, above all, produce science." Like Cohen, Ortega uses the word "science" in a broad sense, to refer to logic, rigor, and systematic thought, and to signify opposition to mysticism, traditionalism, nationalism, and romanticism. From Marburg he had written to Unamuno urging that "we save ourselves from the energumens," and back in Spain he expressed abomination of "all faith in the spontaneous." These years when Ortega was the faithful disciple of the neo-Kantians were also his years of support for socialism, which had many partisans at Marburg and which Ortega regarded as "a scientific conception." Against hotheaded sectarianism and the politics of personality he advanced the principle, learned from Natorp, that only the socialized individual is fully human.

After his studies in Germany Ortega felt sure enough of himself to challenge some formidable conservative spokesmen. When Marcelino Menéndez y Pelayo, the most respected of traditionalist academics, wrote an open letter attacking a proposal for the establishment of a system of lay schools, Ortega replied that "the most wise and noble modern theodicies are theodicies without God, as the most certain psychologies are psychologies without the soul." When Unamuno publicly referred to the Europeanizers as "simpletons," Ortega declared himself personally insulted, and went on to tax his mentor with having belittled the value of foreign scholarship to Hispanic philology. Before long Ortega was recognized as a champion of the Europeanizing reformists, while his having dissociated himself from the nihilism of '98 disarmed the conservatives. His impressive education, his already voluminous writing, his political outspokenness, and his ambivalent but prestigious association with Unamuno all led to his being appointed in 1910—the year he married Rosa Spottorno—to the tenured chair in metaphysics at the University of Madrid, when he was still only twenty-seven.

Before ascending to the university chair, Ortega had been teaching for two years at Madrid's teachers' college, the Escuela Superior del Magisterio. María de Maeztu, Ramiro's sister and one of Ortega's first students, provides a glimpse of his teaching at the college:

> Beneath the appearance of a cold, serene, incorruptible objectivity, "beyond good and evil," there springs from the subsoil, as from a fountainhead, a warm emotion, a contained passion. He honestly tries to flee, to distance himself from all pathos; but Ortega is a man of the south, and the fire that lights his spirit remains there, betraying his best efforts.
>
> (*Antología del siglo XX: Prosistas españoles,* 2d ed. [Buenos Aires, 1945], p. 82)

This snapshot of Ortega at his nine A.M. class captures a tension that runs through his work and gives it much of its value. Ortega could have returned from Germany, with all that European intellectual prestige, and settled down to a purely academic progressivism of the sort that Cohen and Natorp practiced in the north. It could be argued, as Maeztu suggests, that the very doctrines of dispassionate scientific rationalism that he had accepted called for a purely cerebral dissemination from the lofty precincts of the university. And Ortega himself remarked that after receiving his tenured post "nothing would have been easier for me . . . than to imitate the existence of a German *Gelehrte* [man of learning]." But to do so would have been to deny too much, not only his own deep-seated extroversion, his passion, and his poetic gifts, but also Spain, the distinctive circumstance of Spain. Only a coterie of graduate students and intellectuals would have been able to assimilate neo-Kantianism in pristine form, and in the meantime in the rest of Spain the cacophony of progressive and conservative energumens would have clamored on. In 1910, addressing a liberal club in the Basque provinces, Ortega told the audience that a professor in a country such as Germany "can spend twenty years thinking only of infinitude," and he can "deposit his vote at election time and go back to his desk without fear of his will being falsified. . . . Among us the situation is quite different; . . . Spain is the primary, the plenary, and the peremptory problem."

Actually, Ortega's studies under Natorp in Germany had encouraged him to look beyond the confines of academia. He had taken the Marburg professor's course in *Sozialpedagogik,* a theory of education that posited criticism of society as the first obligation of schools. Natorp and like-minded thinkers hoped that pedagogy aimed at social transformation would eventually displace politics as the efficacious means of influencing history. In that 1910 address to the Basque club Ortega presented Natorp's ideas, maintaining that "the Spanish problem is a pedagogical problem." The neo-Kantian had provided him with an up-to-date, theoretical, European justification of the public role. It was a German blessing on the Spanish mantle worn by Feijóo, Costa, and Unamuno and now falling on Ortega's shoulders.

In the Iberian Peninsula social pedagogy would have to meet politics on the ground of politics. Ortega had to join the "open-air ministry" that Giner had spoken of. This meant accepting engagements at political clubs—descendants of the Masonic lodges and secret societies that had helped liberalism to survive during the past two centuries—and assuming the roles of itinerant toastmaster, raconteur, café intellectual, father confessor, and so on.

Most of all, he who would bring secular enlightenment to Spain in the early years of this century had to write for the newspapers. As Ortega explained in 1932, in the prologue to the first edition of his collected works:

> The varieties of detached aristocracy have always been sterile in this peninsula. He who wants to create—and all creators are aristocrats—must find a way to be an aristocrat in the public square. This is why, docile to circumstances, I have brought forth work in the intellectual marketplace of the daily press.
>
> (*Obras completas,* 6:353)

Sensitivity to circumstances, which led Ortega to become a professor of philosophy *"in partibus infidelium"* (partly unfaithful), as he styled himself, also left its stamp on his language. Ortega is one of the most *oral* of twentieth-century authors. Whether what we read of his was originally delivered live or intended for print, he always seems present to us, because he is himself perpetually conscious of circumstances as audience. Unabashedly using the first-person pronoun, he apostrophizes, exhorts, anticipates objections, lapses easily into colloquialism, scolds. Who but Ortega could have the mannerism of appending to statements he fears we shall find unpalatable the phrase *"¡Qué le vamos a hacer!"*—an idiom conventionally accompanied by, and roughly translatable as, a shrugging of the shoulders? As Ortega tell us in the *Preface for Germans,* "I have tried to return the book to its origins in dialogue."

The Spanish tradition of socially engaged intellectual labor that began with the *ilustración* came to an end with Ortega. He was a twentieth-century encyclopedist, in the general and the historical senses of the word, in producing a comprehensive body of work and in taking the socio-pedagogical attitude that originates with the encyclopedia writers of the eighteenth century. Perhaps more keenly than any of his precursors, Ortega felt the tensions inherent in being, as he once referred to himself, a propagandist for enlightenment. His mission, in the last analysis, was to resolve those tensions, those contraries, implicit in the phrase "public intellectual": cosmopolitanism and patriotism, elite and people, university and society, philosophy and journalism, reason and life.

PHILOSOPHY

Ortega's philosophy may be understood, at a first level of approximation, as an attempt to bring reason into concord with life. He spent much of his youth studying philosophy, and when he took up the public educational mission, one of his aspirations was, as he put it, "to get Madrid to philosophize." But to accomplish that he had to do more than recast German ideas into Spanish idioms, mixing the language of technical philosophy with the language of the marketplace. His discourse could not have been rhetorically and socially effective in Spain if it had not been based on a deeper awareness of the limitations of traditional European philosophy and of the just claims of the vital against the transcendental. Perhaps the one thing that those thinkers broadly referred to as "existentialists" have in common is an encounter with a reality that rationalist philosophy had failed to take into account—the incomprehensible deity of Søren Kierkegaard, the power of Dionysian impulse for Nietzsche, unjust and inescapable death for Unamuno, 'Being-in-the-world' as ground of all cognition for Martin Heidegger, the visceral epiphany of the absurd for Jean-Paul Sartre. In Ortega's case the intractable reality was his passionate and unruly country, which obliged him, if he was to communicate with its people, to recognize that beyond neo-Kantian physico-mathematical reason there lies "an infinite morphology of thought." But this recognition did not lead him into mysticism. Ortega "holds fast to reason," as Curtius writes. He made affirmation of reason "as a form and a function of life" his distinctive concern as a modern philosopher and as a proselytizer for philosophy in Spain. Though the world is not, as rationalists believe, rational in itself, we have to be. "Man has a mission of clarity," Ortega stated in 1914. And in a 1924 essay entitled "Ni vitalismo ni racionalismo" (Neither Vitalism Nor Rationalism), he made it clear that his philosophy "accepts no method toward theoretical knowledge other than the rational one, but finds it necessary to situate the problem of life at the center of the ideological system."

As soon as he returned from his German studies, Ortega had to face the conflict between commitment to totalizing systematic philosophy in the Kantian and neo-Kantian tradition and the necessity of writing brief, ad hoc pieces for the daily press, which his commitment to public education imposed on him. From Leipzig he had written to a Madrid professor that journalistic literature is fit for "the troubadour and the comedian." It merely amuses the public with "café paradoxes" and "amputated" ideas without philosophical basis. Shortly after his accession to the chair in metaphysics, Ortega worked out a resolution of the conflict in an essay entitled "Vejamen del orador" (Vexation of the Orator, 1911), in which he at first opposes "the serious man," the philosopher, and "the circumstantial man," the orator, who caters to audience, moment, and place and whom Plato likened to a bronze vase that emits sound when tapped. But "what are the circumstances?" Ortega asks. "Are they no more than these one hundred persons, these fifty minutes, this minor question?" In the end he endorses the writer or speaker who takes circumstances into account, "provided he forgets none of them." "And there are orators who know how to amplify upon the circumstantial until it becomes one with the human: their voices resonate with lasting timeliness."

In that essay Ortega articulates the attitude that is already implicit in his earliest writings, where he transforms the topic at hand into a crystal through which the reader glimpses the manifold. He followed the same procedure in his teaching. According to H. L. Nostrand, Ortega in class had an "ingenious way of starting from everyday experience . . . to arrive at some general idea." Metonymy—in the sense of discovering the general in the particular—is the underlying form of much of Ortega's discourse, and the formal reflection of the philosopher's docility to circumstances. His acceptance of the topical always kept him from producing complete, organized expositions of his philosophy that might be compared to the capital texts of Heidegger and Sartre, but it enabled him to reach a wide public and "get Madrid to philosophize."

Unamuno and phenomenology were the two circumstantial elements to which Ortega was reacting when he began to write philosophical works. Both were hostile to the systematic rationalism that Ortega had learned at Marburg. In the *Preface for Germans* he recalls that during his last study trip to the school of Cohen and Natorp in 1911, he had already begun to feel that neo-Kantian thought was somehow "contrived . . . profound, serious, acute, full of truth, and, *nevertheless, without veracity.*" At that time, the foundations of neo-Kantianism—and of rationalist thought since René Descartes—were being shaken by the phenomenology of Husserl and Max Scheler. The neo-Kantians, for whom a statement had philosophical value only if it could be fitted into a system of propositions, derided what they called "impressionistic" or "intuitive" knowledge. In contrast, the motto of the phenomenologists was "Back to the things themselves!"—to the thing as it shows itself, which is what the word "phenomenon" means.

Meanwhile, the most influential philosopher in Spain was Unamuno, an admirer of Kierkegaard and an eloquent opponent of rationalism. In *Del sentimiento trágico de la vida* (*The Tragic Sense of Life,* 1913), a work of philosophy that rivals those of Nietzsche in emotional force, Unamuno argues that if we take reason seriously it leads us to rational doubt, and thus, logically, to doubting reason as well. The intellect, devouring itself, leaves us free to hope and believe, without reason and yet rationally. The "rational absurd" is the only formula of conjunction between reason and life that Unamuno accepts, precisely because it is contradictory. He insists that "reason is not vital," that "any philosophy that pretends to undo the eternal and tragic contradiction must fail." In 1905 Unamuno had published a book on *Don Quixote* that foreshadows his thinking in *The Tragic Sense;* in *Vida de Don Quijote y Sancho* (*The Life of Don Quixote and Sancho,* 1905) Unamuno writes of Cervantes' characters as if they had been living persons, because scholarly reason cannot demonstrate otherwise, and, more importantly, because denying the fictionality of Cervantes' novel is the most fitting homage to the absurd idealism of the Knight of the Mournful Countenance.

"As if reason were not a vital and spontaneous function with the same lineage as seeing and touching!" Ortega replies in his first book, *Meditaciones del Quijote* (*Meditations on Quixote,* 1914), which appeared one year after *The Tragic Sense.* The book, like the exclamation, is at once a response to the elder philosopher, as the first word of the title suggests, and an attempt to adapt neo-Kantianism to phenomenology. Typically, Ortega completed only two of ten projected meditations. It is Ortega's inaugural philosophical statement and the key to much of what he wrote later in life.

Mindful of Unamuno's dissevering of reason from vitality and of the popular inclination to consider philosophy abstract and bloodless, Ortega tries to persuade his readers that the ordering and systematizing activity of the intellect is a natural, indeed an erotic, response to phenomenal realities. As ground for his argument, Ortega evokes an actual place, the forest of El Escorial, not far from Madrid. To a contemplator in its midst the forest is not immediate, not a phenomenon. It does not show itself, and the observer cannot see it, because of the trees. The commonplace adage tells Ortega that the forest is a depth we uncover through a spontaneous labor of connection, exploration, construction:

The forest is a possibility. It is a trail we could follow; it is a brook whose feeble rumor comes to us in the arms of silence and which we could discover after a few steps; it is the verses of songs chanted far away by birds on branches we might reach. . . . Only when we fully realize that the visible landscape is hiding other, invisible landscapes do we feel ourselves within the forest.

(*Obras completas,* 1:331)

And from where does it spring, this unfolding and weaving of the mosaic of phenomena? From love, Ortega answers, from Eros, "divine architect who comes to earth, according to Plato, 'so that all in the universe may live in connection.'" Philosophy is "the general science of love," of an "impetus toward all-encompassing connection." To find "the plenitude of significance in things . . . letting the sun bring out their innumerable reverberations" is an act of *amor intellectualis.* In Unamuno's writings this phrase, originally Baruch Spinoza's, refers to an ascetic turning-away from the world. For Ortega, the meaning of *amor intellectualis* is that thinking can be a way of loving the world. Ortega integrates phenomenological attention to surfaces with neo-Kantian system-building to arrive at what Antonio Machado called "gnostic-constructive erotism," the antithesis of the tragic sense of life.

In the *Meditations on Quixote* truth is neither an abstraction nor a felt reality. Our author has recourse to one of the ancient names of truth, retrieved from oblivion by his Marburg friend Nicolai Hartmann. The pre-Socratic term *aletheia* signifies truth as "unveiling," "uncovering"—the very process of moving from surface to depth, from the phenomenon to what lies beyond. For the man who is merely erudite, truth is a fixing and limiting of meaning, but Ortega says that the reality of truth in life is illumination, a sudden opening-up of possibilities of meaning. And if we would bring another human being to truth, our method should be a "pedagogy of allusion," which incites the learner to his own unveiling and discovery.

The ontological basis for *amor intellectualis* is "perspectivism":

When shall we open ourselves to the conviction that the definitive being of the world is neither matter nor soul, nor any determinate thing, but a perspective? God is the perspective and the hierarchy: the sin of Satan was an error of perspective.

And yet, perspective may be perfected by the multiplication of its terms and by the exactitude of our reactions before each of its ranks.

(*Obras completas*, 1:321–322)

Perspective is the human condition understood as a particular situation, characterized by outwardness, openness, and expansive connection between the immediate and the distant. Perspective appears as a philosophical concept in the writings of Gottfried Leibniz, Nietzsche, and others. But as Ortega's disciple Julian Marías has shown, for all those thinkers perspective carried the taint of error or contingency. For Ortega, it is "the definitive being of the world."

In the *Meditations* the thrust of perspectivism is not so much against pre-phenomenological philosophers who consider knowledge of the immediate irrelevant, but at thinkers with an Iberian turn of mind who, like Unamuno, believe in a quixotic sovereign self majestically disdainful of reality. Instead of "detaining ourselves in perpetual ecstasy over hieratic values," Ortega would have us "search for the meaning of what is around us," our circumstances. If perspective constitutes human reality, it can only be erroneous to postulate a despatialized and detemporalized transcendent self, or to offer as hero he who would detach himself from "specific contents of life." Ortega goes so far as to say that "circumstantial reality is the other half of my person," and a few lines afterward he writes a sentence that he later singled out as the keystone of all his philosophy: "Yo soy yo y mis circunstancias" (I am myself and my circumstances).

The Modern Theme is another essay in redefining reason so as to reconcile it to life. In the first part of the book Ortega argues against two positions he considers inimical to his philosophy of perspective: relativism and rationalism. Calling attention to the interminable rising and falling of claims to truth, the relativist asserts that there is no truth, that there are *only* points of view. If this is so, Ortega retorts, then it follows that what the relativist is saying is not true. Relativism is "a suicidal theory." The skeptic testifies to the human reality of what he denies. "Faith in truth is a radical fact of human life," Ortega concludes. He then turns to the two classic rationalists, Descartes and Spinoza, who think of reason as an "abstract subject," as "pure intellect" disenthralled from the vicissitudes of life and "functioning in a vacuum." Descartes amputates the will to truth from reason and then, moreover, charges it with responsibility for error, when he writes in the fourth meditation that the will extends him "to things I do not understand," while "all that reason conceives is conceived as it should be." Ortega responds that truth is not a mere articulation of what I already understand. On the contrary, understanding begins with "a desire, more or less confused, that things be a certain way," which leads us to find proof and which nevertheless does not invalidate the proof we find, Ortega says, any more than the postulation of four-dimensional physics, thirty years before Einstein, discredits Einstein's theories. Ortega's positioning of truth after the will that seeks it brings to mind the popular inversion of a shopworn formula: "If I hadn't believed it with my own mind, I wouldn't have seen it."

The alternative to relativism and rationalism, which share a utopian conception of truth, is reason in harmony with life, or "vital reason," as Ortega calls it in *The Modern Theme* and in numerous subsequent texts. Like many of Ortega's most important formulations, "vital reason" should be taken as an apothegm rather than as a term to be rigorously defined. In the first place, the expression "vital reason" indicates that all reason springs within and from life, whether this is admitted or not. "Vital reason" also identifies a form of reason that does not forget its origin and thus opposes all varieties of idealism. The first and second meanings lead to the third: vital reason is something that appears in history. It emerges, Ortega tells us, when a generation can no longer live by the truths of the fathers. In this sense, idealism too can be vital, as when Socrates set about "ironizing life," as Ortega puts it, from the standpoint of the idea, opposing *episteme* (knowledge) to *doxa* (received opinions). Because philosophies come from the living, they are fated to die. For Ortega every culture originates in a "lyrical hour" and proceeds inexorably to its "hieratic hour" (here the influence of Spengler is palpable), which comes when ideas are no longer recognized "as the opinions of determinate men, but as truth itself, having anonymously descended to earth." It then behooves generations that follow this deification to discover that their culture is (once again) an amalgam of *doxa* received from the dead.

Vital reason, in a fourth sense, is the awareness of vital reason that Ortega is attempting to bring to our epoch, or vital reason having become conscious of itself. "The theme of our time consists in submitting reason to vitality," he writes. In the culture that the nineteenth century has passed down to us, he finds the "ludicrous contradiction" that science, democracy, and rationalism have become religious beliefs. As life was once subjugated by Christian doctrine, it now lies prostrate before the *doxa* of modernity. In its recognition that secular culture has fallen into the dogmatism it once challenged, vital reason is "not at all modern, but very twentieth-century," to quote the title of one of Ortega's articles from this period ("Nada 'moderno' y 'muy siglo XX,'" 1916). Hence the inaccuracy of rendering *El tema de nuestro tiempo* as *The Modern Theme*. For Ortega modernity is our past.

In *¿Qué es filosofía?* (*What Is Philosophy?* 1957), an extramural lecture course given in 1929, Ortega attempts to explain, and justify, philosophy to the general public. Echoing the *Meditations,* he affirms that it is natural to philosophize:

From where—it will be asked—does this appetite for the Universe, for the integrity of the world, which is the root of philosophy, come from? In simple terms, this appetite that seems peculiar to philosophy is the native and spontaneous attitude of our mind in life. With confusion or clarity, we live toward a surrounding world that we sense or pre-sense as complete.

(*Obras completas,* 7:310)

It is the professional, the specialist, "who truncates that integrity of our vital world and turns an isolated portion of it into his subject." He must base his inquiries on knowledge from other fields and on assumptions about knowledge itself. The philosopher, on the other hand, pursues the "unknown as such." Philosophy, as Ortega understands it, is "absolute problematism."

In the latter part of *What Is Philosophy?* Ortega presents a critique of the Cartesian *cogito* that follows Heidegger's but avoids the abstruse language that makes *Being and Time* (1927) inaccessible to the layperson. The main thread of the critique is as follows: It is true that consciousness itself (the *cogito*) is indubitable because doubt cannot appear without consciousness. But *sum* (I am) does not follow from *cogito,* Ortega maintains. Self cannot be equated with consciousness, because in consciousness subject and object are always inseparable. There are no grounds for privileging the subject while making objects mere "contents of consciousness." Such a move only leads to the "crude" idealism of Arthur Schopenhauer, who goes to the extreme of saying that "the world is my representation." In consciousness things appear as evidentially as I do: "If there were nothing to see, think, or imagine, I would not see, think, or imagine— that is, I would not be."

Commenting on Ortega's critique, Arroyo points out that if the Cartesian and idealist privileging of the self is unwarranted, then the very term "consciousness" ought to be abandoned, since it implies a subject conscious *of* whatever is prepositionally attached to it. Better to drop all egocentric subordination, as

Heidegger does, and speak of what stands out, what is evident, existence, being-there. One might add that by locating both self and world within consciousness, Ortega seems to be restating the paralogism of 1914: "I am myself and my circumstances." But as he concludes his critique of Descartes, Ortega does begin to use another term in place of "consciousness." He speaks of *la vida* (life) as that which "includes both subject and world."

It is at this point, the end of the next-to-last lesson of *What Is Philosophy?*, that Ortega arrives at his mature philosophy, which he continued to explicate in *The Revolt of the Masses, En torno a Galileo (Man and Crisis,* lecture course 1933, first published 1933–1934), *Historia como sistema (History as a System,* 1935), and many other texts. Ortega's conception of *la vida* is succinctly conveyed at the beginning of *History as a System.* For Ortega, there is nothing beyond our insecure personal existence. "Life," he writes,

> is the radical reality, in the sense that we must refer to it all other realities, since these, whether effective or presumed, must in one way or another appear in it.
>
> The most trivial but at the same time most important note of human life is that man has no choice but to be doing something to sustain himself in existence. Life is given to us, since we do not bestow it on ourselves but rather find ourselves in it suddenly and without knowing how. But the life that is given to us is given unmade. We have to make it ourselves, each one his own. Life is to do [*quehacer*].
>
> (*Obras completas*, 6:13)

Like Husserl, Heidegger, Sartre, and other twentieth-century thinkers, Ortega expounds a philosophy that is not centered on the rationally indubitable, which he regards as "only the preliminary chapter of philosophy." The logos of premises and demonstration has yielded to the logos of the evident: description of life as lived, perpetual project, *quehacer*. Some pages farther into *History as a System,* Ortega expresses the existentialist sense of the instability of human being through another paralogism, one that he had introduced in *The Revolt of the Masses* and that Sartre would make famous years later: "I am forced to be free." "To be free," Ortega explains, "is to lack constitutive identity . . . to be able to be other than I was and to be unable to install myself once and for all in any determinate being." But what sets Ortega apart from the existentialist mainstream is that he manages to remain an apostle of reason. Heidegger was interested, as he said, in the antepredicative "commercium of the subject with a world," a form of understanding that is prior to all reasoning. Ortega—in the titles mentioned above, in shorter essays from the 1930's and 1940's, and in *Ideas y creencias* (Ideas and Beliefs, 1940)—reaffirms the value of thought, be it thought without knowledge, thought within the radical uncertainty of life.

A distinction between ideas and beliefs is the point of departure for Ortega's post-rationalist theory of reason. Beliefs are the numberless assumptions large and small on the basis of which we make decisions in life. To decide to cross the street, for example, I have to believe that there is an external world. What defines a belief for Ortega is that it is unexamined—indeed, the immense majority of beliefs, even those of a philosopher, are simply absorbed from cultural circumstances. But as we live, "fissures" constantly open up in the ground of belief. The "ceaseless discovery of ourselves and the world" is at the same time a ceaseless finding of ourselves in doubt. It is then that we turn to ideas. "We are in beliefs, but we have ideas," Ortega says. Beliefs are mute, but ideas are what we discuss, defend, deny, explain. We perform these operations, that is, we think, because we repeatedly find ourselves lost and "shipwrecked" and needing to "know what to hold on to" in order to decide what to do next. For Ortega ideas are not what Plato and many other Western philosophers have affirmed or assumed them to be: they are not "ideal." "No, Monsieur Descartes," he apostrophizes in "En el centenario de una universidad" (On the Centennial of a University, 1932),

> by thinking, your Worship has reached the conclusion: I exist because I think. But remember that your Worship set out to think, that you did not take notice of your thinking just like that, but because you felt lost in a strange, problematic, insecure, doubtful element. . . . You started to think, then, "because" you existed.
>
> (*Obras completas*, 5:472)

As this passage suggests, awareness of the "constitutive instability" of existence led Ortega to the recognition that vital reason must be "narrative reason," which he offers as the illuminating alternative to "pure physico-mathematical reason" in *History as a System.* "Man does not have a nature; he has a history," he writes. "To understand something human, personal or collective, it is necessary to tell a story. . . . Life becomes a little transparent only before *historical reason.*"

Ortega's major historical works can be thought of as extended glosses on the Cartesian principle turned upside down: *sum ergo cogito. Man and Crisis, Origen y epílogo de la filosofía (The Origin of Philosophy,* written in 1946, published in 1960), and *Una interpretación de la historia universal (An Interpretation of Universal History,* written in 1948, published in 1960) are dense, learned accounts of epoch-making attempts to find "something to hold on to." Riddled though they are with philosophical and sociological digressions, they focus on great historical "transits" from exhausted beliefs to new ideas that time weathers into mere beliefs again: from Homeric myth through redemptive cults to the philosophical logos; from Roman law through monarchic *imperium* to Christianity, which offers belief itself; from messianic faith through the theology of the medieval scholars to a new valuation of the power of the human mind unaided by revelation; from the Cartesian legitimization of doubt through rationalism to worship of the will.

Ortega applies historical reason to philosophy itself, laying waste the claims of philosophers to transhistorical truth. In *The Origin of Philosophy* he proposes that the very notion of "being"—as something metaphysical, independent of the mutability of life—is a hypothesis. "It is repeated with excessive facility that philosophy is inquiry into Being," Ortega writes, alluding to Heidegger. "Perhaps," he suggests, "Being was already an answer." Unlike Heidegger, for whom Being precedes existence, Ortega looks upon Being as an invention of particular men—Parmenides and the Eleatics—who had come to believe that the gods were capricious or illusory. In the midst of life's flux and shipwreck "Being is just what is missing, the gap that thought tries to fill." Under Ortega's historical gaze Being is revealed as the faithful lover imagined by men condemned to lie with sluttish time.

La idea de principio en Leibniz y la evolución de la teoría deductiva (The Idea of Principle in Leibniz and the Evolution of Deductive Theory, written in 1947, published in 1958), is the culminating achievement of Ortega's historical reason. It anticipates the ruthless undermining of philosophical tradition that has brought acclaim to French intellectuals of the last few decades and mesmerized American academics. Yet Ortega's book is read almost exclusively by *Orteguistas.* It is an extraordinarily difficult text, written feverishly in eighty days and, typically, left unrevised and unfinished by its author. He begins by stating that "formally or informally, knowledge is always contemplation of something through a principle"—the Kantian position in a nutshell. He proceeds to a history of attempts to justify deductive practice, from Aristotle, Euclid, and the Stoics to Thomas Aquinas, the early European scientists, Descartes, Leibniz, and others. And what emerges in this account, from underneath a luxuriant overgrowth of digression, is that no one has ever succeeded in establishing a principle.

Aristotle's reliance on *aisthesis,* the evidence of the senses, which was inherited by the Stoics and the medieval theologians, is founded on an uncritical assumption of "the principle of the presence of the real," Ortega tells us. When Aristotle attempted to ground the principle of identity, according to which no thing can be other than itself, he was doing no more than pleading that the principle is indispensable if there is to be any reasoning. The secular philosophy and new science of the late Renaissance developed modes of thought that do not depend on *aisthesis,* modes such as algebra, analytic geometry, and methodical doubt. For centuries "the principle of the intelligibility of the real" and with it the authority of rationalism were upheld by the success of science. But scientists themselves eventually admitted that science can be said to reveal reality only to the extent that reality is susceptible to measurement and mathematical manipulation. For Ortega, the modesty of contemporary science unmasks the "fantastical" character of all thought that aims at precision: "Because it is exact, it is not valid for the things that man is in the midst of. . . . Instead of seeking concepts that will work for things, it fatigues itself looking for things that will validate concepts." So it has been since Parmenides first "projected the features of logical thought onto the Real." Near the end of the book we find a tightly argued critique of Husserlian phenomenology's positing of "consciousness of" as the fundamental reality. Ortega's verdict is that consciousness too is "a hypothesis, the very one we have inherited from Descartes."

One might expect that such an assault without quarter on the tribe of philosophers would leave Ortega with no options save skepticism and despair. Yet, going further than Aristotle, he affirms principles "as a necessity and an aspiration," notwithstanding their "permanent revocability." He reserves his harshest denunciations for the pathos and negativism he sees in much of the philosophy of this century. He reiterates that the thoughtful life is "a finding oneself lost, drowning, falling," but he insists that "alongside the nothingness and the anguish there is an infinite sportive joy that leads

to, among other things, the great game of theorizing, and especially to its superlative, which is philosophy."

AESTHETICS AND LITERARY CRITICISM

In his most well-known writings on aesthetics, Ortega, the philosopher of *la vida,* finds value in art insofar as it is distinct from life. *La deshumanización del arte (The Dehumanization of Art,* 1925), often wrongly assumed to be a soulful Mediterranean's denunciation of cold modernist abstraction, is actually filled with disparagement of those who expect the artist to reach out toward common humanity—which is what Ortega himself attempted during most of his career. He offers a resolution of these paradoxes in the same essay: "What are we to make of this disgust for the human in art? Is it, indeed, a revulsion against the human, the real, the vital, or is it rather the opposite: respect for life, and repugnance at seeing it confused with art, with something as sublunary as art?"

At first, Ortega pleaded for "human art." In 1904 he criticized the modernist Ramón del Valle-Inclán for being "inhumanly dry, without tears." As late as 1914, in the *Meditations on Quixote,* he affirmed that "poetry and all art discourses on the human, and only on the human." A justification of art as something that answers a human need for knowledge is found in "Adán en el paraíso" (Adam in Paradise, 1910), where he proceeds logically from a neo-Kantian conception of reason to a conception of art. Reason is the discovery of relations between things, a systematization of experience. But Ortega points out that we shall never attain an understanding of the totality of relations. Hence the Faustian character of the enterprise of science—taking the word in the broad neo-Kantian sense: "From the tragedy of science, art is born." Instead of reducing particulars to cases or instances of general laws, as science does, art universalizes by disclosing the fullness of meaning, of relation, in particular things—though this exhaustive disclosure, says Ortega, turns out to be impossible.

From this position, which modernizes Aristotle's point that art instructs by example, Ortega proceeded to a critique of slice-of-life realism in an essay on the art of Ignacio Zuloaga (1870–1945), "La estética de 'Elenano Gregorio el Botero'" (Gregorio el Botero the Dwarf), where he writes that "anecdotal art is not art," and in "Tres cuadros del vino." In this latter essay the author contrasts the bacchic scenes of Titian and Nicolas Poussin with Diego Velázquez's realistic and demythifying *The Drunkards* (1629), and finds the Spanish master's canvas "limited" in its denial of the Dionysian aspects of intoxication and in its suggestion that things, being no more than they appear to be, "have no aroma and nimbus of ideal signification."

In "Arte de este mundo y del otro" (Art of this World and of the Other World, 1911), Ortega began to put forth the view that anchored his aesthetics until the 1930's: that art springs from a will to unreality that requires no justification. In this essay, a review of Wilhelm Worringer's *Form probleme der Gotik* (*Form Problems of the Gothic,* 1910), he claims that "the Renaissance assiduously investigates the forms of the real, not in order to copy them, but to glean from them the treasures of harmony that in its triumphant optimism it suspects are scattered throughout cosmic diversity." This search for universal harmonies in real things is none other than the function of all true art, according to the "Adán en el paraíso" essay, but here the belief in incarnated universals is treated as a peculiar tendency of the optimistic Renaissance. The author reserves his greatest admiration for the Gothic artist, who "lives in an imaginary atmosphere." "A man without imagination" would impute to the medieval artisan "a refusal to deal with the ineluctible conditions of the cosmos, a wanton fleeing from the laws that bind men to earth." But this waywardness, which is very much like what Ortega would later denounce as inauthenticity in *Man*

and Crisis, is legitimate in art: "Through the geometric design . . . I save myself from the interior shipwreck, forget myself in that regulated, clear, precise reality, removed from flux and confusion. In it I am saved from life, from my life." In "Del realismo en pintura" (On Realism in Painting, 1912) Ortega flatly rules that "art is not the copying of things but the creation of forms."

As he moved from a view of art as a species of cognition comparable to science to the doctrine of *ars gratia artis* (art for art's sake), Ortega must have felt some obligation to write a new philosophical essay on aesthetics, and this he did four years after "Adán en el paraíso." The idea of art in the "Ensayo de estética a manera de prólogo" ("Essay in Aesthetics by Way of a Preface," 1914) is essentially the same as the idea of art proposed in 1790 by Immanuel Kant in the *Kritik der Urteilskraft* (*Critique of Judgment*), where he argues that a contemplative stance, as opposed to a practical or interested attitude, is the necessary and sufficient condition of art. Suspension of concern with the reality or existence of an object, with what it may do, or impede, or be used for, is what turns it into an art object. As Ortega puts it apropos of the *Penseroso* statue in the Medici chapel: "Consciousness of the reality of that marble body does not intervene in our aesthetic fruition: the intuiting of a purely imaginary object that could be wholly transported into our fantasy."

"Art is essentially *derealization,*" Ortega goes on to say, echoing the Russian formalist concept of *ostranenie* (estrangement), which is also rooted in Kant. For Ortega the consequence of derealization is a special relation between contemplator and art object: a relation of "intimacy," a glimpse into "absolute presence," a vision of the object in its "executive reality." To see the object "executing itself" means that we see it as if it had a self and, moreover, as if we were that self and it were transparent to us, which, paradoxically, our own selves never are. Ortega cautions against assuming that the thing transformed into a self is "the secret of

JOSÉ ORTEGA Y GASSET

life and being." Rather, identity has been replaced by "activity," "executivity," a selfhood or life of the object's own, as a noun in a poem can cease to be the name of something and "begin to erupt, go into activity, and take on a verblike quality."

The longest section of the essay is a meditation on a single metaphor, from a line of verse by the Catalan poet López Picó that figures a cypress as "the specter of a dead flame." "Which is the metaphorical object here?" Ortega asks. "Neither the cypress nor the flame nor the specter: all these belong to the orb of images of reality." The metaphorical object is "a new object," "a cypress-specter of flame" that surges out of a context in which the representational function of the component images is discredited by the falseness of their being identified. Ortega acknowledges that all metaphor involves a degree of similarity, but the inadequacy of this similarity, he argues, has the effect of heightening awareness of dissimilarity. Once derealization has taken place, once we have been led to discount the referential value of the images, we enliven them, feel free with them, "we make of them a mere point of departure, a raw material, a sign beyond which we are to find identity in a new object, the cypress that can be regarded as a flame without absurdity." The value of derealization, and of art, is neither more nor less than that our world is "augmented," Ortega says, referring etymologically to the word "author." Each poet speaks "a new idiom that allows us to reach objects, like the cypress-flame, of which we had no inkling."

In the 1914 essay, and other essays on aesthetics from that period, Ortega rejects the popular notion that art's purpose is to "express real sentiment," or any prior interiority, for the new object "lives" in a world "distinct from the physical and psychological worlds." The state of mind of the viewer, listener, or reader is called into being, not brought out, by art, and the more authentic the work of art, the more extraordinary, even inhuman, the feelings it provokes. Ortega applies this principle in "Musicalia" (1921), where he extols Claude Debussy and denigrates Felix Mendelssohn. The latter, to Ortega's ears, does little more than stimulate commonplace emotions, while Debussy brings unheard-of feelings to life. Ortega is not against emotion in aesthetic experience; rather, as César Barja puts it, he is against vulgar emotion. He sees modern literature and music as a purification of romanticism. Artists like Ludwig van Beethoven and Johann Wolfgang von Goethe brought vital passions into art. Debussy, Paul Verlaine, Rubén Darío—they belong to a second romanticism, as Ortega calls it, that pursues "secondary sentiments felt not by a participant but by a contemplator."

The Dehumanization of Art, Ortega's most well-known and most frequently anthologized essay, has long been considered one of the defining statements of modernism. Taking the sociological fact of the new art's unpopularity as his starting point, Ortega notes that all young art is unpopular and that romanticism too was at first ostracized. But the young art of the twentieth century is rejected because it is not understood, and not because it is disliked, if dislike implies enough understanding to pass judgment. "The old wigs who attended performances of Hugo's *Ernani* disliked it precisely because they understood it very well," Ortega comments. Modernist art can be peremptorily rejected by the general public only because the recognizably human is absent from it. No longer do painters offer a Mona Lisa for Englishmen to fall in love with, Ortega quips. The composers write music to be heard "without effusion or weeping." The poets have effaced their own personality and turned their words into "a superior algebra of metaphors" (the phrase became famous). It is as if the public were expected to look at a glass and not through it, Ortega explains. That glass is art having turned inward and become "artistic art," dedicated to pure beauty with minimal extrinsic reference.

Ortega distinguishes seven tendencies in the new pure styles:

1135

First, toward the dehumanization of art; second, toward avoidance of living forms; third, toward making the work of art nothing but a work of art; fourth, toward considering art as a game, and nothing more; fifth, toward an essential irony; sixth, toward eluding all falseness, and therefore toward scrupulous execution. Finally—seventh—art, according to young artists, is entirely without transcendence.

(*Obras completas*, 3:360)

The unpopularity of the new art appeals to Ortega's lifelong detestation of the judgments of the ignorant, of the "good bourgeois" who "knows no other attitude toward objects than the practical one" and who condemns modern art because it leaves him "as if humiliated, with a dim consciousness of inferiority for which he needs to compensate." Contempt for vulgarity is a leitmotif in the culture of post-romanticism and modernism. Stéphane Mallarmé, the symbolist poet, reportedly declared that he found it distasteful if more than fifteen Parisians understood his latest poem. But Ortega was no aloof dandy. His position and mission as "aristocrat in the public square" obligated him to polemicize for the esoteric new styles. Modern art, as Ortega understands it, compels a choice between living and contemplating. Yet he knows his readers are more inclined to the former, so he insists that the choice is being offered not out of haughtiness but out of modesty, not out of revulsion but out of respect for life. In modern art's "clownishness" and persistently ironical tone, in its "conscious and elaborate negation of the traditional," Ortega discovers, much as the American critic Lionel Trilling did decades later, a distrust of culture itself, with its pretensions to being the salvation of humanity: "If it can be said that art saves mankind, it is only because it saves him from the seriousness of life and summons in him unexpected puberty. Pan's magic flute returns as the symbol of art."

Ortega's brief for the art of the first half of the twentieth century is compromised by his attempt to make it a paradigm of all art. For him any artist is or "ought to be an anti-Odysseus, who liberates himself from quotidian Penelope and navigates between rocks toward the witchcraft of Circe." Although he protests that it is not his intention to derogate the realist art of the nineteenth century, he affirms, as in "Musicalia," "a tendency toward purification," and in other places in the essay he leaves no doubt that he thinks purer is better: "Interest in what is human in a work of art is, in principle, incompatible with strict aesthetic fruition."

In his passion to counter popular fallacies—that art has to be useful, psychologically expressive, imitative of reality—Ortega lapses into a complementary and extravagant aestheticism. "All great epochs of art have avoided placing the human at the center of gravity of the work," he pronounces, thereby marginalizing all past and present claims that art is a source of truths about our existence. The narrowness of Ortega's position is evident in a section of the essay on Heinz Werner's theory linking the origin of metaphor with primitive taboos. Werner's point is that metaphor originates as euphemism for a tabooed referent, and Ortega takes this as evidence of the "elusive," "fleeing" character of metaphor and of its being rooted in "an instinct that induces mankind to avoid reality." But surely euphemism, if that is the primal function of metaphor, *circumvents* the taboo. It discloses the forbidden object as it turns away from it. An antirepresentational bias also informs the discussion of metaphor in the 1914 essay. It can just as well be argued that the "cypress-specter of flame" is pregnant with an unreal and impossible flame-cypress as that it re-presents the worldly cypress seen anew, defamiliarized and rediscovered, in the likeness of a flame standing still.

There are, however, other pages by Ortega where the cognitive value of metaphor is acknowledged. In "Las dos grandes metáforas" (The Two Great Metaphors, 1924), which appeared the same year as part one of *The Dehumanization of Art,* Ortega speaks of metaphor as "an intellectual procedure by means of which we apprehend what is beyond our conceptual powers." It captures "a slippery reality" outside the limits of ordinary literal discourse by yoking words together in ways that make no literal sense, as when we speak of "the bottom of the soul." "This implies that one of the dimensions of poetry is investigation." Still, for Ortega, metaphor as discovery is but a supplementary aspect of poetry. What gives a metaphor its aesthetic value, Ortega tells us, drawing from the 1914 essay, is its presentation of similitude as identity, that is, its falseness. "Metaphor begins to radiate beauty at the point where its truthfulness ends."

The novel was one of Ortega's main interests during the first half of his career. In addition to the second (and last) of the *Meditations on Quixote,* entitled "Breve tratado de la novela" ("Brief Treatise on the Novel"), and *Ideas sobre la novela (Notes on the Novel,* 1925), Ortega wrote a short essay on Proust and two longer ones on the Spanish novelist Baroja that are also concerned with the nature of the genre. In large measure this interest was yet another expression of Ortega's patriotic mission. He considered the novel characteristically Spanish, since it originated with Cervantes and his picaresque precursors, and the announced purpose of his first full-length book was to foster understanding of Spain through meditations on *Don Quixote.* But for a theorist whose sympathies are with pure art, the novel, which is usually a conscientiously realistic form of writing, is a problematic genre. "How is it possible," Ortega asks in the "Brief Treatise," "for the market and Sancho and the mule driver and that uncouth Master Peter to be poetic?" His answer is that reality can never be poetic

> in itself, directly regarded; that is the prerogative of the mythical. But we can take it obliquely as the destruction of myth, as critique of myth. In this form reality, which is by nature inert and insignificant, still and mute, acquires a movement, is converted into an active power of aggression against the crystalline orb of the ideal. . . . Speaking rigorously, reality does not become poetic nor does it enter into the work of art, but

only its gesture or movement of reabsorption of the ideal.

> (*Obras completas,* 1:384)

And a few pages farther on he writes: "Myth is always the point of departure for poetry, including the realistic kind. But in the latter we accompany the myth in its descent, its fall. The theme of realistic poetry is the collapse of the poetic" (1:387).

Ortega places Cervantes' invention of the genre in its historical context. The author of *Don Quixote* was too much a man of late-Renaissance Spain to have faith in the mythical, in the epic-chivalric tradition that he satirized. He had to accept the real "in its mute, terrible materiality." Ortega imagines him uttering his own favorite shoulder-shrugging phrase, "¡Qué le vamos a hacer!" But the prototypical novelist attempted to preserve or recover the poet by "enfolding" it within the real in the only form that the advanced thought of his time would admit: as a mental entity, a madness, "a humor," "a vapor of the brain" of a personage who is correspondingly marginalized by society. Unlike the epic protagonist, who is a champion of his people and moves about "in the same field as his desire," the hero in the novel must be himself ("I know who I am," says Don Quixote), for the ideal no longer has a dwelling outside of the self: "Achilles forges an epic, the [novelistic] hero desires one."

Ortega's theory of the novel in the *Meditations* looks back to the aesthetics of G. W. F. Hegel and Cohen, who had already identified criticism of the epic as the ground of novel writing, and forward to György Lukács' *Die Theorie des Romans (The Theory of the Novel,* 1920), first published in a journal two years after Ortega's treatise. Lukács thinks of the novelist in terms similar to Ortega's, as one who has understood that literature "is only a demand, not an effective reality." And for Lukács too the hero in the novel is "a soul that sets out to know itself."

Ortega returned to the problem of reconciling realism and art at the height of his period of advocacy of aesthetic purity. In *Notes on the Novel* he insists that the novel is a "hermetic" genre: the novel writer cultivates realism and strives for fullness and detail of presentation not because he wants to mirror reality, but the better to displace it. The novel, as Ortega thinks of it in this text, has much in common with those infinite objects in short stories by Jorge Luis Borges that make people forget the real world by offering an equally rich alternative. "When we finish reading a great novel," Ortega writes, "we feel that we are emerging from another existence, that we have exited from a world that does not communicate with our authentic one." It would seem that our author is again letting himself be carried away by his own quixotic love of pure art. If the novelist's purpose were no more than to bewitch the reader into believing that an elaborately fabricated world is real, then the last thing he would do is remind the reader, as Cervantes does, that books are not like life and that he will go mad if he submerges himself in them. The novelist would not pursue the theme of conflict between illusion and reality, which points to a genesis of the novel in that anguish, that longing for the ideal and resignation to the real, attributed to Cervantes by Ortega in the "Brief Treatise."

What is more convincing in *Notes on the Novel* and in a superb 1923 essay entitled "Tiempo, distancia, y forma en el arte de Proust" (Time, Distance, and Form in the Art of Proust) is Ortega's analysis of modern novelistic technique. Building upon the German scholar Käte Friedemann's observation that the modern novel stresses "presentation" at the expense of narration, Ortega maintains that Stendhal, Fyodor Dostoyevsky, and Marcel Proust have developed an increasingly meticulous, "morose," "microscopic" technique that expatiates each narrated incident and pushes its sequential aspect to the background. In the 1923 essay he writes that for Proust "remembrance is not, like reasoning, a traversing of mental space, but a spontaneous enlargement of that space." The arrival of Swann at the Combray garden in Proust's major work, for exam-

ple, frustrates the reader's expectation of narrative linkage. It is a moment that "dilates without progress, widens without changing into another . . . taking on new details and meanings, expanding like a bubble of soap and acquiring a bubble's iridescence and reflectivity."

Ortega never did admit the second term of the Horatian *dolce et utile* (sweet and useful) into his aesthetics, but his embrace of existential and historical reason in the early 1930's made him turn his attention to the question of how art and literature emerge in specific vital situations and how we are to respond to them in our own lives. In taking this approach, he became a proponent of one of the theses he had denied in 1914: that original works of art or utterances issue from the desire of individuals to express something that is within them.

Most readers, especially in America, still identify Ortega's aesthetics with the relatively immature and strident *Dehumanization of Art.* But in a series of writings that began in 1933 Ortega developed, in his dispersed and sporadic way, a hermeneutic, or methodology of interpretation, that was remarkably sophisticated and comprehensive for the time. The most important of these works are *Man and Crisis,* "Miseria y esplendor de la traducción" (Misery and Splendor of Translation, 1937), *The Origin of Philosophy,* "Qué es leer" (What Reading Is, written in 1946, published in 1962), *Velázquez* (written 1943–1954, published in 1959), *The Idea of Principle in Leibniz, Goya* (written 1949–1950, published in 1958), and *El hombre y la gente* (*Man and People,* written in 1949, published in 1957). During this period Ortega studied the work of Ferdinand de Saussure and the Prague linguistic circle as well as German philosophy of language, and his interpretive practice integrated ideas that operated or would eventually operate in the discourses of phenomenology, existentialism, structuralist linguistics, speech-act theory, Heideggerian-Gadamerian hermeneutics, and even deconstructionism.

What puts Ortega's late-period critical theory ahead of "the level of the times," to borrow his phrase, is his freedom from illusions about the intelligibility of texts. Already in 1933, in *Man and Crisis,* Ortega had recognized that meaning is marked by absence: "the sign is constitutively an enigma, in that it claims to be other than what it appears to be." And in the 1937 essay on translation he put forward the thesis that understanding one's native language is not essentially different from translating: both are "utopian exercises." Ortega goes farther: "To think is to speak to oneself and consequently to misunderstand oneself." Nor are there any natural concepts: "The world proposes innumerable classifications and imposes none." Granted that "Miseria y esplendor de la traducción" is an Ortegan exercise in audacity, in the form of a seriocomic imaginary colloquium between the author and several linguists; but there is no obliqueness in "Qué es leer" where Ortega asserts that polysemia (multiplicity of meaning) is a "constitutive characteristic" of all language, though linguists have treated the phenomenon "as if it were a mere accident that befalls words." In this essay, and in another from the same year, "La Reviviscencia de los cuadros" ("Reviving the Paintings"), which subsequently became the first chapter of *Velázquez,* Ortega formulates his "law" of deficiency and exuberance, applicable "to all semantic activity": "All utterance is deficient—it says less than is intended. All utterance is exuberant—it gives more to understand than is intended." In its exuberance, the utterance conveys meanings "that the author did not propose to communicate, or even sought to hide."

Withal, Ortega remained committed to interpretation. The hermeneutic and the skeptical stances coexist in his late critical writings—sometimes side by side, as in "Qué es leer"—because for him attempting to understand an author is, in the last analysis, an ethical obligation that overrules linguistic considerations. "The vital root of reading," he writes in *Man and Crisis,* is "the radical solitude" of life, which leads to "fervid essays in breaking

out" and gives rise to "the intention of coinciding." Ortega could not think of the author as many of today's theorists do, as a construct of the reader. In *Velázquez* he insists on history as "the technique of conversation and friendship with the dead." Nor does he regard texts as autonomous verbal structures that have severed all ties with their creators. In *The Idea of Principle in Leibniz* he writes: "Every utterance is a vital action of man; therefore, what is properly and ultimately real in a 'saying' is not what is 'said,' not the *dictum* . . . but the fact that someone says it, and in saying it acts, performs, commits himself."

Ortega is faithful to Wilhelm Dilthey, the patriarch of modern hermeneutics, in basing his interpretive strategy on historical reconstruction of original contexts. The "conventional situation" of the speaker or writer, as Ortega calls it, limits the exuberance of the utterance. In *Man and People* he gives the word *tinto* (red wine) as an example. By itself it can be associated with many things, but called out in a Castilian tavern it indicates a request for a specific beverage and even a size of glass and price.

But for Ortega the restricted range of meanings that we arrive at through recovery of contexts and conventions is not the terminal point of interpretation. In "Qué es leer," *Man and People,* and other writings from this period he explicates utterance as the product of conflict between a unique, personal "wanting to say" and socially established signifying systems that would distort and betray the antepredicative desire. Most utterances are little more than capitulations of individual vision to ready-made language, but "to write well," Ortega declares in *El libro de las misiones* (The Book of Missions, 1940), "is continually to bring about small erosions of grammar, of usage, of the ruling norms of language. It is an act of permanent revolt against the social surroundings, an act of subversion." We can say that "style is the man" precisely because "style is the deformation of language," Ortega writes two years later.

The same conflictive relationship obtains between what we sense we must do in life— our mission—and the roles made available to us by society. "Vocation clashes with circumstance," and is therefore distinct from profession, to which one ought to be, like Ortega, *in partibus infidelium* (partly unfaithful). First in the discussion of Cervantes in the "Brief Treatise," again in *Guillermo Dilthey y la idea de la vida* (Wilhelm Dilthey and the Idea of Life, 1933), and most explicitly in *Velázquez* and *Goya,* Ortega refines the inherited hermeneutic by showing how a great thinker or artist is not so much of his time but "against his time."

It follows that after closing the distance that separates the author's world of meanings from our own the interpreter must penetrate into that further distance between the author's world and what Ortega variously refers to as "the vocation," "the primary direction of his saying," "the lyrical need for confession," "the ferment of the soul behind and before [the work]," "the adjectives that appear before their nouns." He also cites as an antecedent Worringer's concept of *Kunstwollen* (will to art). Whatever the wording, Ortega now finds at the root of art interior urgencies that he had in no uncertain terms separated from art during his aestheticist period. The change is consistent with his turning to existentialism, because the nucleus of expressive intention, "anterior to speech," is nothing other than the authentic, futurizing self posited by Ortega in philosophical writings after 1929. It hardly needs saying that to understand this self, masked even by the language of its epoch and visible only in its subversions of that language, requires going beyond reconstructive scholarship to imaginative empathy: "We have to imagine Goya the man . . . facts are only points of reference." Thus in the last phase of his hermeneutic method Ortega places himself in the camp of the radical phenomenological critics who came after him and attempted to transport themselves into the very consciousness of authors, except that Ortega seeks the living, materially and socially engaged consciousness. In *Ve-*lázquez he speaks of the leap beyond texts and data as "a reviving." Ortega is satisfied only with the artist "living integrally in the instant when his fingers hover over the palette."

In *Velázquez* and *Goya* Ortega draws extensively from historical documents in order to place the two painters in their respective circumstances; then he attempts to resurrect them in their individuality and opposition to those circumstances. Though Ortega's characterizations may be judged suppositious by some, they have the virtue of disintegrating the great twin banalities of Spanish art appreciation: Velázquez the phlegmatic naturalist master and the populist, nationalized Goya dancing the fandango in taverns.

The complex Velázquez summoned by the necromancer-critic is, on one level, a realist—as Ortega had regarded him in 1911—but his realism came from the milieu of his early years, when Caravaggio presided over the conventional situation. Velázquez, whose art was "a ceaseless combat against his century," extinguished Caravaggio's dramatism through accretion of detail and went on to dissolve reality in pale light. His great innovation, according to Ortega, was to eliminate tactile values—the painting of bulk—from the canvas, leaving a pure visuality that is as much a derealization as mythology. Velázquez's idiom was realism, but he was a painter of specters. Ortega notes that he was probably the first to paint nonrepresentative backgrounds, which at the time would have been "read" as unfinished portions of canvas.

In that dedication to the visual as such, in that suffusing luminosity that the impressionists came to admire, though it bears none of their joie de vivre, in those recurring deformed personages who seem to stare back at the viewer, in the artist's punctilious manners and total avoidance of court rivalries, Ortega sees not serene realism but an icy contumely. He calls Velázquez "a genius of disdain" and his art "the art of distance." His profession was painting, but he practiced it sparingly, and when, as Ortega tells us, Innocent X sent him a gold chain as remuneration for a portrait, Velázquez's unheard-of gesture was to send it back to him. His vocation was to be an aristocrat in the Ortegan sense: "to be himself and obey only his own resolutions, which were most tenacious and indeformable."

POLITICS AND SOCIAL THOUGHT

Ortega's politics, like other aspects of his life, seem contradictory at first sight. One can argue, on the one hand, that he was a liberal democrat, citing his calls for an end to the Spanish monarchy, his criticisms of the church and the military, his advocacy of regional autonomy, his rejection of Unamuno's traditionalism, and his position of leadership in the Second Republic. But a case can also be made that Ortega was a conservative, even a reactionary. Did he not proselytize for order and unity in Spain? And were not his words repeated by dictators and right-wing extremists? Did he not oppose mass political movements, flee from the Republican zone during the Civil War, and fail to condemn the regime that followed it? Is he not "notorious," as he said himself, "for a radically aristocratic interpretation of history"?

Ortega's concrete political statements and acts may be seen as circumstantial expressions of an underlying and permanent preoccupation with the relation between the extraordinary individual—particularly the intellectual individual—and society. This primary concern leads him to three essential positions: public pedagogy, which casts the intellectual as bringer of enlightenment, and traditional institutions as his enemies; distrust of majorities, which entails critical examination of democracy and opposition to mass political movements; and radical individualism, according to which the authentic individual must distance himself from society and especially from politics. These three attitudes do not neatly succeed each other in the course of Or-

tega's career. Rather, they accumulate and turn his politics into a mosaic of partisanships that resists analysis by means of established ideological categories.

When Ortega returned from the German universities in 1907, he took up the politics of enlightenment. He attempted to carry out the mission of public education he had inherited from the tradition of the Spanish *ilustrados* and the German promulgators of "social pedagogy." Although Ortega never ceased to be an intellectual "in the marketplace," it was only during his early years that he played the role without reservations. In "Los problemas nacionales y la juventud" (National Problems and Youth, 1909), at the age of twenty-six, he said that "the popular mass . . . needs the few, the select, the moral aristocracies to shape and orient its will." Here is how the idealistic youth concluded the public lecture "La ciencia y la religión como problemas políticos" (Science and Religion as Political Problems) that same year: "We bring a scientific conception of nature and of politics. . . . We bring a new religion; we bring the sublime eucharist: we bring culture."

For Ortega, as for the propagandists of the Enlightenment, culture is something that the population must be led to ("to lead" is the etymological meaning of "educate"), and cultural leadership is what he has in mind when he begins, early in his career, to speak approvingly of "aristocracy," dissociating the term from its connotations of authoritarianism. "Aristocracy means a condition of society in which the best have decisive influence," he explains in "Socialismo y aristocracia" (Socialism and Aristocracy, 1913). "It does not matter to me," he adds, "if [aristocrats] do not govern. . . . What matters to me is that . . . the most sound, most noble, most just, most beautiful opinions acquire the dominance in the hearts of men that is rightfully theirs." To marshal the cultural aristocracy around him, in 1914 Ortega founded the League for Political Education, which addressed itself to those who were, as he put it, "more cultivated, more reflective, more responsible," asking that they transmit their virtues to "the great aggrieved multitudes."

During this first phase of his public life, Ortega aligned himself with the Europeanizers ("Europe is science") and with the socialists. It should be understood, however, that his socialism was not Marxist or revolutionary. He criticized Marxism as the reduction of history to economics, and he believed that the very purpose of socialist politics is to make revolution unnecessary. Ortega had learned his socialism at Marburg, so that for him the term signified the rational and systematic ordering of a nation, to be achieved through Natorp's "social pedagogy," which Ortega took as a kind of German imprimatur for practices originated by the *ilustrados* of Spain. He condemned capitalism, but not on the grounds that it is exploitative. Rather, acknowledging his debt to Marxist thought, he charged it with having imposed quantity, productivity, and accumulation as standards, at the expense of quality and excellence. Deploring the extinction of unmarketable ways of life, he defined capitalism as "the condition of society in which aristocracies are impossible."

The concrete political stances taken by Ortega during this period can be classified as "liberal." He denounced the repression (his word) of the workers' uprising in Barcelona in 1909 and the prosecution of the colonial war in Morocco. He supported plans for the establishment of lay schools, though he chafed at being labeled "anti-clerical" because, as he explained, it is the clergy who are "anti-masonic, anti-socialist, anti-science, anti-moral, anti-democratic, anti-us." Ortega did not, however, urge electoral or agrarian reform, nor did he call for an end to the monarchy at this time. Implicit in his culturalism is the faith of the eighteenth-century encyclopedist that if enlightenment is spread far and wide then justice and prosperity for all will surely follow.

That Ortega was more interested in elevating than in liberating the people is evident in "La fiesta del trabajo" (The Workers' Feast Day), an article he wrote for that occasion in 1915:

If the community of workers were beautiful and noble, gracious and delicate, democratic aspirations would make no sense. If hunger and anguish, humiliation and toil produced those delightful fruits, democracy would be a crime. Precisely because the plebeian mass is what it is, we ought to put an end to it and uplift it.

(*Obras completas*, 10:308)

But the article also betrays Ortega's fear of the proletariat, fear that they will take power without waiting to be illuminated. It begins with a description of workers marching through Madrid in tight ranks, "bronzed or atrociously pale," with "violent pupils that wound," singing "music charged with menace."

The threat posed by a militant proletariat is one of the factors that account for Ortega's growing pessimism and waning enthusiasm for political education as the decade of the 1910's drew to a close. The league he had formed in 1914 failed to attract more than ninety-eight members, though they were indeed the elite of Spanish intellectuals, and Ortega dissolved it in 1918. Oswald Spengler's *Der Untergang des Abendlandes* (*Decline of the West*) appeared that same year and made a strong impression on Ortega, as Arroyo has shown. Above all, neither his nor anyone else's efforts had put a stop to the discord, strikes, violent factional rebellions, and revolving-door succession of governments under the constitutional monarchy.

From about 1917 through the 1920's distrust of politics and an estimation of the peoples of Spain and of the modern West as resistant to, if not unredeemable by, the cultural elite predominated in Ortega's social thought. In "Democracia morbosa" (Morbid Democracy, 1917) he protests what to his eyes was a rising tide of "plebeianism, the most insufferable of tyrants." Here Ortega defines his attitude toward the "noble idea" of democracy. "Strictly and exclusively as a norm of political law," as a "means," he supports it, but not democracy as a religion, democracy "exasperated beyond itself" to every aspect of life. He adds: "Whoever is irritated when he sees equals treated unequally, but remains unperturbed by the equal treatment of those who are not equal, is not democratic. He is plebeian."

By the early 1920's Ortega was espousing a detached intellectualism that resembled Julien Benda's critique of politicized writers, as Victor Ouimette has pointed out. In 1922 he censured those who "deformed their intellectuality by placing it at the service of political purposes" during World War I. Three years later, in "Reforma de la inteligencia" ("The Reform of Intelligence"), he wrote that the exercise of the intellect should stop being "a public affair" and become a private pursuit of "spontaneously akin persons."

España invertebrada (*Invertebrate Spain,* 1921) is Ortega's diagnosis of Spain's malaise and his first extended argument for aristocratic culture. It borders on a denial of the educability of the Spanish people. Like the Russians, Ortega tells us, they are "a peasant race," hostile to ideas and to heroic enterprise because they lack experience in being led by the vital, creative minorities who generate them. Ortega does not believe that modern Spain is the product of imperial decadence. He argues that the trouble with Spain is that it has always lacked an aristocratic backbone, a leading minority of the best and the brightest capable of making the diverse factions and classes put aside "particularist" interests and accept a national purpose. If Spaniards were the first of European peoples to produce a strong national state, it was precisely because the feudal nobility, which frustrated the ambition of kings in other countries, was feeble in the Iberian Peninsula. The historical origin of Spain's weakness, according to Ortega, is that after the fall of Rome the country was settled by the Visigoths, a Germanic tribe that had exhausted its finest energies by the time it reached the southern terminus of Europe.

Ortega's retelling of Spain's history, and especially his characterization of the Visigoths, was deemed unempirical and amateurish by more scholarly authors. (A synthesis of their indignant refutations is found in Cesar Barja's pages on Ortega.) But no one could contest that Spain had been without effective leadership for centuries, and Ortega was by no means the only one who was taking a dim view of the country's past. In spite of the pessimistic tendency of *Invertebrate Spain,* at the end of the book and almost as an afterthought Ortega reaffirms the educational mission and the possibility of regeneration. "Political improvements are not enough," he writes. What is needed is a "more profound" labor toward "refinement of the race."

Ortega's aristocratic sociology is more fully articulated in *The Revolt of the Masses,* sections of which began to appear in the daily press in 1927. Ortega maintains that whether one likes it or not the natural tendency of human societies is to resolve themselves into select minorities and mediocre masses. The revolt of the masses occurs when they refuse to admire the select and reject their guidance, without ceasing to consist of essentially dependent individuals, whereupon by sheer weight of numbers they force base values on the whole of society. Ortega contends that this is what has happened—not for the first time in history—in the twentieth-century West, which has settled into "a strange duality of preponderance and insecurity" because "there are no protagonists anymore: there is only chorus." "The characteristic of our time," he writes, "is that the vulgar soul, knowing that it is vulgar, has the insolence to assert the rights of vulgarity and to impose them everywhere." The revolt of the masses is readily noticeable (as during the last centuries of ancient Rome) in the phenomenon of human "agglomeration" and in the proliferation of public buildings and facilities designed for crowds: movie houses, stadiums, department stores, vacation resorts. The political parties, the providers of goods and services, the cultural media—all seek the favor of crowds. Rights common to all men, which Ortega does not deny, are now thought to be the only human rights. He hears the masses echoing Louis XIV: "I am the state."

The revolt of the masses, Ortega explains, is not the inevitable result of democracy, but rather the morbid condition of democracy he had described in 1917, which he now calls "hyperdemocracy." In the nineteenth century European democracy was not, according to Ortega, an imposition of the vulgar will, but a true election of leaders from the select minority and with them of political programs formulated without subservience to the popular mind. In those days the common people did not presume to have "ideas": "They had beliefs, traditions, experiences, proverbs, mental habits."

The central chapters of Ortega's book are devoted to profiling the typical mass man and to differentiating him from the excellent man. For Ortega, aristocracy is not in the blood but in the spirit. In fact, as he had already contended in *Invertebrate Spain,* the automatic inheritance of nobility inevitably entails degeneration of aristocracy, which is the opposite of privilege. The mark of the select man "is not that he considers himself superior to others, but that he demands more of himself than others. . . . Nobility is defined by exertion, by obligations, not by rights. 'Noblesse oblige.'" Intellectually, the outstanding individual "has little regard for what he finds in his mind without previous effort." Everything that the masses now enjoy like "spoiled children" is the fruit of his creative efforts.

In contrast, the mass man is he "who does not value himself—rightly or wrongly—for special reasons; rather he feels that he is 'like everyone else,' and yet he is not in anguish. It pleases him to feel identical to others." He is comfortable in the state of agglomeration. But Ortega applies the word "mass" to this sort of man "not so much because he is multitudinous, but because he is inert." His only efforts are those that external necessities require of him; he does not perceive the nobility of human striving. He likes to think that "life is easy, munificent, without tragic limitations." He is content to answer questions with "what he effortlessly finds in his head," which is a collection of "clichés, prejudices, bits of ideas, or simply hollow phrases."

The mass man is not concerned with "being right," Ortega continues. If his revolt finds political expression, it is through the mindless politics of "direct action"—that is, he joins many others like him in movements that seek to impose their collective will without troubling to persuade. When *The Revolt of the Masses* began to appear, the phrase "direct action" had been in currency for some time as a slogan of Spanish and other European left-wing militants. In Ortega's view the politics of direct action and contempt for parliaments and debate characterize syndicalism and fascism as well as Bolshevism. Ortega jointly condemns them as exemplary mass movements, with ideologies that are no more than "appetites put into words."

One should guard against mechanically placing Ortega on the right of the political spectrum because of his unabashed elitism. After all, what could be more elitist than the Marxist-Leninist claim that the party can legitimately seize power because it possesses a superior understanding of history? It must also be stressed that Ortega takes pains to make it clear that when he speaks of the masses he is not referring "merely or principally to the working-class masses." He is dividing the polity not "into social classes, but into classes of men." In fact, the "prototypical" mass man for Ortega is the modern professional specialist. His social status encourages him to think that his one-dimensional knowledge is wisdom, but to Ortega he is "a learned ignoramus," "a modern barbarian." And even aristocrats, when the "tragedy" of hereditary power befalls them, will degrade into a subspecies of mass man.

There are numerous logical gaps in Ortega's polemics. For one thing, the very title *The Revolt of the Masses* seems oxymoronic. It is difficult to understand how beings distinguished by inertia and complacency can revolt and overturn what Ortega considers the natural tendency of human societies. On the other

JOSÉ ORTEGA Y GASSET

hand, if the masses consolidate into effective and threatening political movements, it would appear that they can do so only by accepting organization and leadership (even the Spanish anarchists had leaders), which means, by Ortega's logic, that they have accepted their appointed place and are no longer in revolt. Ortega tells us that parties such as the Fascists and the Bolsheviks are directed by "mediocrities," but he has insisted on a sharp dividing line between those who direct and those who are mediocre. Nor does the author explain how the revolt of the masses has come about. He concludes the book with a suggestion that he will take up the matter in future writings. Nor does he at any point seriously examine the mechanics of power within the complicated economic and political engines of contemporary Western society, thus making it easy for writers of Marxist orientation such as Michael Harrington to argue persuasively that the revolt of the masses never took place. If one leaves aside the philosophical exposition of *la vida* in *The Revolt,* the early and visionary call for a "United States of Europe" that appears toward the end of the book, and the many fine insights into specific historical events and issues scattered through its pages (admittedly, a prejudicial way of reading an author whose best quality is fertility and multiplicity of thought), then one is left with not much more than sustained pillorying of a type of person who is given no sociological coordinates other than that he constitutes a majority.

And yet, in spite of having discoursed brilliantly about so many things, Ortega remains identified with *The Revolt of the Masses* and "notorious," as he said, for his elitism. But this should cause no surprise. More than in any other of his works, in *The Revolt* Ortega is a writer "against his time." In an age that sounds fanfares for the common man and in which no political party, however tyrannical its designs, can hope to get anywhere if it speaks disrespectfully of "the people," Ortega offers a sharply heretical portrait of most of

mankind. He is certainly not the only modern thinker who denigrates the masses. Ortega aligns himself with a tradition that includes Nietzsche, Spengler, Vilfredo Pareto, Gaetano Mosca, and, to a certain extent, Unamuno. But Ortega's is the most uncompromising assault on what is surely the most pervasive mythology of modern times: the mythology that departs from Jean-Jacques Rousseau's dream of "the noble savage" and that, through countless images and slogans, propaganda and advertising, from left and right, East and West, has succeeded in planting the idol of the noble commoner in every corner of our world. The triumph of populist ideology in the twentieth century makes *The Revolt of the Masses* a necessary counter-discourse.

While Ortega was bringing out installments of his most famous book in the daily press, Spain was under military rule. In 1923 General Miguel Primo de Rivera had taken control of the government through yet another coup d'état, issuing an inaugural proclamation that borrowed ideas from *Invertebrate Spain.* Nonetheless, Ortega was not exempted from the censorship in force under Primo, and he ventured few topical political articles during the first years of the dictatorship. But in 1927 he began to write a series of essays proposing "vertebration" of Spain through decentralization of the government. These daring briefs for moderate regional autonomy appeared, after some official pruning, in *El sol,* another of the journals whose guiding spirit was Ortega. In 1929 he further dissociated himself from the dictatorship by joining Unamuno and other academics in resigning from teaching posts as a protest against the regime's educational policies. Ortega continued to give his philosophy course (published as *What Is Philosophy?*) in a Madrid theater, which proved too small for his audiences.

After long years of unrest and equally inept constitutional monarchy and military autocracy, there was growing clamor for a Second Republic. When the aging Primo retired in 1930, Ortega declared for the Republic in "El

1145

error Berenguer" (The Berenguer Error), an article whose ringing conclusion was "Delenda est Monarchia!" (The Monarchy must be destroyed!). That this paraphrase of Cato became a slogan repeated throughout the country indicates that many Spaniards were by then amenable—largely thanks to Ortega's pen and voice—to letting the intellectuals have a turn at saving Spain. But King Alfonso XIII, who had remained in the background during the dictatorship, forced *El sol* to stop publishing Ortega's pieces. Early in 1931, Ortega, with the essayist Gregorio Marañon and the novelist Ramón Pérez de Ayala, formed the Group at the Service of the Republic. Its manifesto censured the monarchy for having served special interests, but it also warned Spaniards not to enter the "blind alleys" of Bolshevism and Fascism.

The Republic became a reality when elections held in 1931 led to the abdication of the king. Ortega, now at the apogee of his political career, was elected a deputy to the constituent Cortes in June. The new constitution proclaimed that Spain was "a republic of workers"—Ortega's phrase—and it affirmed the principle of regional autonomy, which he had been upholding. In the parliamentary chamber and in articles and speeches that date from 1930 to 1933, Ortega argued for a centrally organized economy, separation of church and state, and limited regionalism, and he also supported programs for military and agrarian reform. Ortega's positions were not in any fundamental way discordant with those of the centrists, moderate leftists, and intellectuals who made up the majority of the constitutional assembly. Like them, he wanted to steer the new state between the twin rocks of the military-ecclesiastical alliance and the anarchist-socialist masses.

But "the professorial republic"—as that first Cortes has been called by the Hispanist Eléna de La Souchère—could hardly be the spinal column that Ortega had found wanting in 1921. By the early 1930's the perennial divisions between regions, classes, and interests were rapidly becoming fierce and flaunted hatreds, and in parliament the moderates gave way to increasingly fanatical left- and right-wing politicians. Ortega's early call for "rectification of the Republic" (in "Rectificación de la República," 1931) was widely discussed but had little effect on the ever-larger militant parties. Again disillusioned, Ortega permanently withdrew from politics in 1933, after publishing a final article with the title "¡Viva la República!" Like many perceptive Spaniards, Ortega could see what was coming. During a *tertulia* in the spring of 1936, he told the gathering that "atrocious things are going to happen in Spain, and they cannot be prevented."

When civil war finally erupted in July of that year, Ortega was in Madrid, where the Nationalist uprising had been crushed. The intellectuality and ambiguity of his politics endangered him at a time when uncompromising partisanship and "direct action" were the order of the day. Gravely ill when the war began, Ortega sought the relative sanctuary of the student residence of the Free Institution of Learning (which had suspended classes and never opened again). During the first outburst of revolutionary terror in Madrid men who identified themselves as "anti-Fascist writers" came to the residence demanding that Ortega sign a manifesto denouncing persons and groups as enemies of the Republic. Ortega refused. Within days an article appeared in one of the papers of the revolutionary left accusing him of "having nourished Fascist minds." The charge was not entirely unfounded. The chief of the Falange—one of the most extreme of the right-wing parties—was an avid reader, and quoter, of Ortega. But the appearance of such an article at such a time was tantamount to a death sentence. Ortega's family managed to spirit the ailing author out of the country. He was not to return to Spain until 1945, after having lived in exile, mostly in Argentina, for nine years.

Neither during his exile nor afterward did Ortega pass judgment on the Civil War or its outcome. Spain went through a "time of silence," as the writer Luis Martín Santos called it, and Ortega's political texts from the Republican years were kept out of print until long after his death. Outside of Spain Ortega continued to publish and lecture with his usual encyclopedic prolixity. After returning to the Peninsula, he founded the Institute for the Humanities, through which he attracted a following numerically comparable to the audiences he had gathered in the late 1920's, until the Institute was closed by the government in 1950.

Although Ortega abandoned politics in the strict sense in 1933, he did not give up writing about social and broadly political topics. In the mid 1930's and during the period after the civil war he produced a number of important texts whose common theme is the relation between social life and personal authenticity. In *Man and Crisis,* in articles such as "Ensimismamiento y alteración" ("The Self and the Other," 1939) and "El intelectual y el otro" (The Intellectual and the Other, 1940), in biographical studies of Vives, Velázquez, and Goya written during the 1940's, and in *Man and People,* Ortega proposes that man achieves full humanity only when he distances himself from the collectivity to think and create independently.

Man and People is an essay in philosophical sociology that Ortega first presented as a lecture course at the Humanities Institute in 1949–1950. In his first book Ortega invited the reader to meditate with an open and loving mind on the things that surround us. A measure of the evolution of Ortega's thought may be obtained by comparing that early vision of interpenetration between self and circumstance with the image he offers at the beginning of *Man and People:* monkeys in a cage at the Madrid zoo. What is it, Ortega asks, that distinguishes us from these creatures, in spite of the obvious resemblance of simian and human? He answers that the monkeys, like other animals, are constantly attentive to external stimuli. They can escape their condition of involvement in circumstances, in

otherness, only by going to sleep. Man, Ortega asserts, is the only creature that can separate itself from its environment without lapsing into stupor, the only creature that can reflect. He no longer conceives of thought as the making of connections, but as *ensimismamiento,* which can be translated literally as "in-selfing" or loosely as "introversion," a quintessentially human faculty through which we gain respite from the *alteración* (alteration or "otheration") that relentlessly grips the beast during its waking hours.

Social life is, to be sure, human, but it is inimical to *ensimismamiento.* "The collectivity," Ortega says, "is the human without man . . . the human dehumanized." It is the aggregate of things we do because they are expected of us, by "people," by "no one in particular." Ortega distinguishes properly social from "interindividual" relationships, which involve "reciprocity": understanding of the other as another individual, with motives that, for better or worse, I can relate to my own. *Nostrismo* (we-ness) is a cooperative introversion, "facing, *outside* of, and, in a certain way, *against* the others."

But social behavior, as Ortega defines it, is not reciprocal. When we do "what people do," "what one does," "what we are supposed to do," we behave as automatons: we do not have a reason for our conduct beyond a more or less vague fear of sanction. When we greet someone, for example, we do not know why we shake hands instead of rubbing noses—it is simply "what one does." Manners, dress, occupations, and, last but not least, language are all forms and means that we accept without reflection, without consciousness of a purpose that we could find in ourselves or ascribe to another. And yet all these automatisms have an existential origin. Shaking hands upon meeting someone was once a way of signifying willingness to place oneself in the hands of the other. Every word in every language was once invented by an individual who wanted to say something that had never before been spoken. "Only individuals create," Ortega says. But social life consists of deracinated "us-ages": conventional acts and utterances that have lost the meaning and purpose they once had for particular human beings: "All that is truly social is, for individuals, pressure, coercion, subjection." Ortega considers it no accident that the great founders of religions—Buddha, Muhammad, Jesus—prepared for their apostolates with "famous withdrawals."

In *Man and People* Ortega is not preoccupied, as in *The Revolt of the Masses,* with splitting up mankind into select, directive minorities and complacent but menacing masses. His message is that to be authentic we must in some way be antisocial. The conception of society as a field of meaninglessness in opposition to which the individual can define himself guides his biographical studies of Velázquez and Goya as men against their time, who did not do what "one is supposed to do" but what they had to do. That the distinction is significant for Ortega can be appreciated in an earlier biography, *Vives* (written in 1940, published in 1961), where the author who wrote in his first book that "I am myself and my circumstances" now tells us in lyrical tones that our identity is revealed in interior space:

> Intimate conscience constantly tells us who is the one we have to be, the person or personage that we have to struggle to make real, and it tells us with a mysterious interior voice that speaks and does not sound, a silent voice that needs no words, that, by rare condition, is monologue and dialogue, a voice that, like a thread of water, ascends within us from a deep fountainhead, and murmurs the commandment of Pindar: "Become whom thou art"; a voice that calls us to our most authentic destiny; in sum, the voice of vocation, of personal vocation.
>
> (*Obras completas,* 9:513–514)

Like the epical El Cid, whose dead body was mounted on a steed to captain a last charge against the Moors, Ortega became a political leader again after his death, from cancer, in October of 1955. General Francisco Franco's government organized a rapid and discreet funeral, while the controlled press claimed that he had undergone a religious conversion in his final days. But among his students and colleagues the rumor "He did not give in!" circulated, almost as a slogan. They organized a memorial of their own and distributed cards bearing the words, "Ortega, liberal philosopher." The unofficial ceremony triggered the first sizable demonstrations against the nationalist regime on the streets of Madrid. Less dramatically, Ortega's death intensified an ongoing debate between Catholic and secular intellectuals over the moral and political merits of his work. During that "time of silence," discussion of Ortega became one of the few avenues for expression of dissent. As Franz Niedermayer has remarked, what was really being debated was the future government of Spain. The events surrounding and following Ortega's death greatly helped to coalesce dissidents of varied persuasions into a movement for liberalization that in time was able to influence the regime and prepare for the advent of the Third Republic. As always, Ortega had provoked contention and ferment, and their net effect could only be to weaken a closed, dictatorial state.

Throughout his adult life, Ortega had promoted thought and its inseparable companion, dissent. A master of his circumstances, knowing how to take full advantage of the opportunities for public communication that this century offers, he reached and excited more Spanish minds than any of the secular preachers and extramural educators who preceded him. It does justice to the name of José Ortega y Gasset that his death caused so much controversy and that this controversy helped to set in motion forces that, at long last, brought about the fulfillment of those millennial hopes for a pluralistic and enlightened Spain.

Selected Bibliography

EDITIONS

INDIVIDUAL WORKS
Meditaciones del Quijote. Madrid, 1914.
Vieja y nueva política: Prospecto de la "Liga de Educación Política Española." Madrid, 1914.
El Espectador I. Madrid, 1916.

Personas, obras, cosas. Madrid, 1916.

El Espectador II. Madrid, 1917.

España invertebrada: Bosquejo de algunos pensamientos históricos. Madrid, 1921.

El Espectador III. Madrid, 1921.

El tema de nuestro tiempo. Madrid, 1923.

Las Atlántidas. Madrid, 1924.

La deshumanización del arte, Ideas sobre la novela. Madrid, 1925.

El Espectador IV. Madrid, 1925.

El Espectador V. Madrid, 1926.

El Espectador VI. Madrid, 1927.

Espíritu de la letra. Madrid, 1927.

Tríptico I: Mirabeau, o el político. Madrid, 1927.

Notas. Madrid, 1928.

El Espectador VII. Madrid, 1929.

Kant. Madrid, 1929.

Misión de la universidad. Madrid, 1930.

La rebelión de las masas. Madrid, 1930.

Rectificación de la República: Artículos y discursos. Madrid, 1931.

La redención de las provincias y la decencia nacional. Madrid, 1931.

La reforma agraria y el estatuto catalán. With Juan Díaz del Moral. Madrid, 1932.

Goethe desde dentro. Madrid, 1933.

Guillermo Dilthey y la idea de la vida. Madrid, 1933.

En torno a Galileo. Madrid, 1933–1934.

El Espectador VIII. Madrid, 1934.

Esquema de las crisis. Santiago, Chile, 1937.

Ensimismamiento y alteración: Meditación de la técnica. Buenos Aires, 1939.

Estudios sobre el amor. Buenos Aires, 1939. First published in a German translation by H. Weyl and F. Ernst as *Über die Liebe: Meditationen* (Stuttgart, 1933).

Ideas y creencias. Madrid, 1940.

El libro de las misiones. Buenos Aires, 1940.

Mocedades. Buenos Aires, 1941.

Historia como sistema: Del Imperio romano. Madrid, 1941. First published in an English translation by W. C. Atkinson as "History as a System," in *Philosophy and History* (Oxford, 1935).

Castilla y sus castillos. Madrid, 1942.

Teoría de Andalucía y otros ensayos. Madrid, 1942.

Dos prólogos: A un tratado de montenía, A un historia de la filosofía. Madrid, 1944.

De la aventura y la caza. Madrid, 1949.

Papeles sobre Velázquez y Goya. Madrid, 1950.

COLLECTED WORKS

Obras. Madrid, 1932.

Obras. 2 vols. Madrid, 1943.

El espectador. Madrid, 1950.

Selección de obras. 2 vols. Madrid, 1950.

Ensayos escogidos. Madrid, 1957.

Obras completas. 11 vols. Madrid, 1946–1969.

Obras completas. 12 vols. Madrid, 1983.

MODERN EDITIONS

Al pie de las letras. Madrid, 1956.

En torno a Galileo. Madrid, 1956.

Estética de la razón vital. Buenos Aires, 1956.

Caracteres y circunstancias. Madrid, 1957.

El hombre y la gente. Madrid, 1957.

Meditación de la técnica. Madrid, 1957.

¿Qué es filosofía? Madrid, 1957.

Viajes y países. Madrid, 1957.

Goya. Madrid, 1958.

La idea de principio en Leibniz y la evolución de la teoría deductiva. Buenos Aires and Madrid, 1958.

Idea del teatro: Una abreviatura. Madrid, 1958.

Kant, Hegel, Dilthey. Madrid, 1958.

Meditación del pueblo joven. Buenos Aires and Madrid, 1958.

Prólogo para alemanes. Madrid, 1958.

Apuntes sobre el pensamiento. Madrid, 1959.

Velázquez. Madrid, 1959.

Una interpretación de la historia universal: En torno a Toynbee. Madrid, 1960.

Meditación de Europa. Madrid, 1960.

Origen y epílogo de la filosofía. Mexico City, 1960.

Vives, Goethe. Madrid, 1961.

Misión del bibliotecario y otros ensayos afines. Madrid, 1962.

Pasado y porvenir para el hombre actual. Madrid, 1962.

Vieja y nueva política. Madrid, 1963.

Meditación de la técnica, Vicisitudes en las ciencias, Bronca en la física. Madrid, 1965.

Unas lecciones de metafísica. Madrid, 1966.

Discursos políticos. Madrid, 1974.

Epistolario. Madrid, 1974.

Sobre la razón histórica. Madrid, 1979.

Goethe, Dilthey. Madrid, 1982.

Investigaciones psicológicas. Madrid, 1983.

TRANSLATIONS

Concord and Liberty. Translated by Helene Weyl. New York, 1946.

The Dehumanization of Art. Translated by Willard R. Trask. New York, 1956.

The Dehumanization of Art and Notes on the Novel. Translated by Helene Weyl. Princeton, N.J., 1948.

The Dehumanization of Art and Other Writings on Art and Culture. Anonymous translation. Garden City, N.Y., 1948.

Historical Reason. Translated by Philip W. Silver. New York, 1948.

History as a System. Translated by W. C. Atkinson. In *Philosophy and History.* Edited by R. Kilbansky and H. J. Paton. Oxford, 1935.

History as a System and Other Essays Toward a Philosophy of History. Translated by Helene Weyl et al. New York, 1961.

The Idea of Principle in Leibniz and the Evolution of Deductive Theory. Translated by Mildred Adams. New York, 1971.

An Interpretation of Universal History. Translated by Mildred Adams. New York, 1973.

Invertebrate Spain. Translated by Mildred Adams. New York, 1937.

Man and Crisis. Translated by Mildred Adams. New York, 1957.

Man and People. Translated by Willard R. Trask. New York, 1957.

Meditations on Hunting. Translated by Howard B. Wescott. New York, 1972.

Meditations on Quixote. Translated by Evelyn Rugg and Diego Marin. New York, 1961.

Mirabeau: An Essay on the Nature of Statesmanship. Anonymous translation. Manila, 1975.

The Mission of the University. Translated by Howard Lee Nostrand. Princeton, N.J., 1944.

The Modern Theme. Translated by James Cleugh. London, 1931.

On Love: Aspects of a Single Theme. Translated by Tony Talbot. New York, 1957.

The Origin of Philosophy. Translated by Tony Talbot. New York, 1967.

The Revolt of the Masses. Anonymous translation. New York, 1932.

Some Lessons in Metaphysics. Translated by Mildred Adams. New York, 1969.

Velázquez. Translated by C. David Ley. New York, 1953.

Velázquez, Goya, and the Dehumanization of Art. Translated by Alexis Brown. New York, 1972.

What Is Philosophy? Translated by Mildred Adams. New York, 1960.

BIOGRAPHICAL AND CRITICAL WORKS

Arroyo, Ciriaco Morón. *El sistema de Ortega y Gasset.* Madrid, 1968.

Barja, César. *Libros y autores contemporáneos.* Madrid, 1935.

Borel, Jean-Paul. *Raison et vie chez Ortega y Gasset.* Neuchâtel, Switzerland, 1959.

Ceplecha, Christian. *The Historical Thought of José Ortega y Gasset.* Washington, D.C., 1958.

Curtius, Ernst Robert. "Ortega." Translated by Willard Trask. *Partisan Review* 17:259–271 (1950).

Díaz, Janet Winecoff. *The Major Themes of Existentialism in the Works of José Ortega y Gasset.* Studies in the Romance Languages and Literatures 94. Chapel Hill, N.C., 1970.

Ferrater Mora, José. *José Ortega y Gasset: An Outline of His Philosophy.* 2d. rev ed., New Haven, Conn., 1963.

Garagorri, Paulino. *Relecciones y disputaciones orteguianas.* Madrid, 1965.

Guy, Alain. *Ortega y Gasset ou la raison vitale et historique.* Paris, 1969.

McClintock, Robert. *Man and His Circumstances: Ortega as Educator.* New York, 1971.

Marías, Julian. *José Ortega y Gasset: Circumstance and Vocation.* Translated by Frances M. López-Morillas. Norman, Okla., 1970.

————. *Ortega: Las trayectorias.* Madrid, 1983.

Morón, Guillermo. *Historia política de José Ortega y Gasset.* Mexico City, 1956.

Niedermayer, Franz. *José Ortega y Gasset.* Translated by Peter Tirner. New York, 1973.

Orringer, Nelson R. *Ortega y sus fuentes germánicas.* Madrid, 1979.

Ouimette, Victor. *José Ortega y Gasset.* World Authors series 624. Boston, 1982.

Raley, Harold. *José Ortega y Gasset: Philosopher of European Unity.* University, Ala., 1971.

Rukser, Udo. *Bibliografía de Ortega.* Estudios Orteguianos 3. Madrid, 1971.

Silver, Philip. *Ortega as Phenomenologist: The Genesis of "Meditations on Quixote."* New York, 1978.

Weigert, Andrew J. *Life and Society: A Meditation on the Social Thought of José Ortega y Gasset.* New York, 1983.

ALBERT BADES FERNANDEZ

FRANZ KAFKA
(1883–1924)

FRANZ KAFKA WAS born into a German-speaking Jewish family in Prague, then capital of the Kingdom of Bohemia in the Austro-Hungarian Empire, on 3 July 1883. He was the eldest of six children, of whom two brothers died in infancy; Franz survived, along with three sisters. The father, Hermann Kafka, was a self-made man, born in bitter poverty in the South Bohemian town of Wossek, who had become the owner of a large dry-goods business in the center of the Old Town of Prague. Kafka's mother, Julie Kafka (née Löwy), was the daughter of a wealthy Prague brewer. Kafka later viewed the contrast between the paternal and maternal lines of his descent as a split within himself. While the Kafkas were robust, forceful, and self-assertive, his mother's ancestors, especially on the maternal side, tended to be reflective and introverted. They included rabbis, Talmudic scholars, pious sages, and eccentrics. His mother's grandmother, in a fit of depression, had taken her own life. Kafka later referred to himself as a Löwy with a certain Kafka-like foundation of tenacity and stubbornness. He felt that the powerful, self-righteous, and totally unselfconscious personality of his father had stamped him with an ineradicable conviction of his own inferiority and guilt. The many opportunities he found as a young boy to compare his own weak, skinny body with his father's gigantic frame and his own timidity and indecisiveness with his father's energy

and aggressive will led him to renounce, at an early age, all hope of ever attaining success in the two areas of life in which his father excelled: business and marriage. The only hope left to him was, as he put it, to find a spot on the world's map that his father's enormous shadow had not reached—and that spot was literature. At the same time, he internalized his father's perspective to such a degree that he would never be free of guilt feelings for not living up to his father's expectations.

Julie Kafka, helping her husband in the business, neglected the boy in his early years. Appearing to mediate between her husband and her son, she ultimately always sided with the former, so that Kafka felt deserted and betrayed. On the other hand, she later smothered him with solicitude, engendering and fostering in him extreme dependence. Extending this dependence from family to native city, Kafka said that "little mother Prague" had her claws in him and would never let go. Kafka lived with his parents until the age of thirty-one and even after that took his meals regularly at their house. He was unable to move away from Prague until the age of forty, less than one year before his death.

Kafka received a sound humanistic education at the Old Town *Gymnasium* and subsequently enrolled in the law faculty of the German-language Karl Ferdinand University, where he received his law degree in 1906. He eschewed the practice of law as an attorney,

1151

but his law degree procured him a career as a bureaucrat with legal expertise in the Workmen's Accident Insurance Administration of the Kingdom of Bohemia, where he worked from 1908 until his retirement in 1922. This post represented a compromise between Kafka's desire to devote himself entirely to writing and the need he perceived for a bourgeois occupation that would support him. His work schedule was relatively undemanding and left afternoons free. Nevertheless it gave rise to a severe inner conflict between vocation and avocation that, aggravated by his father's demand that he devote himself also to a newly founded family business venture, drove Kafka several times to thoughts of suicide.

Shy and lonely by disposition, Kafka yet had a profound need for friends. In his early school years he was close to Hugo Bergmann, later a leading Zionist thinker and one of the early Central European settlers in Jerusalem. In his adolescence and young adulthood, Oskar Pollak, who was to become a noted art historian before he was killed in World War I, exerted a powerful influence on Kafka, who called him his "window on the world." Through Pollak Kafka came under the spell of the romantic, Nietzschean, and German-nationalist ideology of Ferdinand Avenarius' journal, *Der Kunstwart.* Subsequently, however, Max Brod was to become of the greatest importance for Kafka. Kafka first met Brod in October 1902, in the German Students' Reading and Lecture Hall, the meeting place of a liberal student union, where Brod gave a lecture on Schopenhauer that Kafka attended. They became close friends for life.

Brod's significance for Kafka's literary development cannot be exaggerated. Hailing from a cultured family, and socially more advantaged than Kafka, Brod, who at a young age had already become a literary celebrity, provided the gateway for Kafka's entrance into the literary world. Well aware of Kafka's unique genius, Brod encouraged and prodded him to write. He urged him to show his writings to others, and by his own literary activity he pro-

vided a conscience for Kafka, goading him to produce more regularly and rousing him from frequent fits of lethargy and despondency. Brod also was instrumental in arranging Kafka's first publications. In 1912 he introduced him to the Leipzig publisher Ernst Rowohlt and his associate, Kurt Wolff. Wolff, who soon was to found his own publishing house, thought highly of Kafka's talent and became his publisher. Through Brod, Kafka also formed close friendships with the blind writer Oskar Baum and the philosopher Felix Weltsch. These four formed the nucleus of a coterie on Prague's cultural horizon. Together with Brod and other friends, Kafka made several extended trips from 1910 to 1912 that led him to Paris, Switzerland, the upper Italian lakes, Milan, and Weimar, the shrine of Germany's classical heritage. These journeys proved of importance to Kafka's development as a writer since they provided him with an impetus to keep journals. He joined Brod in beginning a novel about two friends whom they called Richard and Samuel; the first chapter of this common enterprise, "Die erste lange Eisenbahnfahrt" ("The First Long Railroad Ride"), was published in the Prague journal *Herderblätter* in May 1912. Sharing their admiration of Gustave Flaubert, the two friends read him together in the original French.

Before his so-called "breakthrough" in September 1912, Kafka had not yet found the manner of writing that was to make him the master we see in him today. Although he had been writing since childhood, his earliest extant work, "Beschreibung eines Kampfes" ("Description of a Struggle," 1936, written in 1904–1905, revised in 1909–1910), although an arresting example of modernism with striking passages, is disjointed and lacks coherence of focus. A novel, "Hochzeitsvorbereitungen auf dem Lande" ("Wedding Preparations in the Country," 1953), begun in 1907, was soon abandoned. For the rest, Kafka, before the age of twenty-nine, had written merely small vignettes, meditations or reflections and impressions, which appeared in book form under

FRANZ KAFKA

the collective title *Betrachtung* (Meditation) in 1913. He had also started the first version of his novel *Der Verschollene* (*Amerika,* 1927), which he later destroyed. The actual break-though to his inimitable literary style was preceded by three factors: the discipline afforded by his decision in late 1910 to keep a regular diary; his exposure to a Yiddish theater group from Lvov, in eastern Poland, which performed in Prague in late 1911 and early 1912; and his meeting Felice Bauer in August 1912.

In the guest performances of the Lvov Yiddish theater Kafka discovered his own Jewish roots—a discovery that gave his life a new direction. Hitherto, his attitude toward Judaism had been one of indifference. He found the conventionalized remnants of Jewish custom and religion in his family and social milieu pathetic and laughable. However, after exposure to East European Jewish culture, which the Yiddish theater and particularly his friendship with the Warsaw-born actor Yitzchak Löwy communicated to him, Kafka developed an intense interest in his Jewish heritage that—with a single brief exception, called by him his "anti-Zionist" phase—was never to wane; indeed, it deepened with time. He immersed himself in Jewish history; he underwent a period of socially oriented Zionist activism during World War I, when he followed with intense concern the educational work done with Jewish refugee children from Poland. The unbroken bond with one's religious and cultural past that distinguished East European Jews from their West European counterparts fascinated him. Eastern Jews provided his ideal of a true community. His friend Jiří (Georg) Langer, a convert to Hasidism, introduced him to the Hasidic world. In 1917, he took up the systematic study of Hebrew, a language in which he was able to attain a degree of fluency and reading comprehension. In 1917 and 1918 he occupied himself with the study of the Old Testament, with Jewish legends, folk tales, and mysticism, having received some knowledge about these areas from

Yitzchak Löwy and Jiří Langer as well as from the lectures and writings of Martin Buber, in whose journal *Der Jude* two of Kafka's stories appeared. Near the end of his life, Kafka even thought of immigrating to Palestine. Finally, it was on the grounds of their common Jewishness that Kafka had hoped to gain the longed-for rapproachment with his father.

Kafka met Felice Bauer, a young woman from a Berlin bourgeois family, when she visited Max Brod's family in August 1912. She was a highly successful employee in a dictaphone business, energetic, lively, and efficient, possessing those qualities Kafka felt sorely missing in himself. A correspondence of approximately five hundred letters and cards developed, extending over five years and two engagements during which time Kafka pursued a clearly discernible strategy. Initially, he would woo Felice assiduously. However, as soon as she showed signs of yielding to his courtship and was beginning to press for physical encounters, Kafka started to draw back. He warned Felice about himself, projected married life with him as one that would be beset by monstrous difficulties, and presented himself as fanatically dedicated to writing, which would condemn his spouse to monastic loneliness. He made every effort to discourage her hopes for a life together. Yet no sooner did she show signs of heeding his warnings than he returned to the role of ardent and insistent wooer. After a long pause, during which the relationship became dormant, Kafka resumed his advances, encouraged by Felice's friend Grete Bloch, who had come from Berlin to mediate between them. Kafka established a relationship with Grete that was freer and in some respects closer than the one he shared with Felice—so much so that many years later, Brod was led to believe, wrongly, that Grete had borne an illegitimate son by Kafka.

Kafka finally asked Felice whether she would marry him, and they were officially engaged in Berlin in June 1914. Immediately afterward, Kafka confided in his diary that he felt like a chained convict. One month later,

FRANZ KAFKA

the engagement was dissolved in a Berlin hotel room that Kafka called his "courtroom." A few weeks later, he began to write his novel of accusation and punishment, *Der Prozess* (*The Trial*, 1925).

Kafka's literary productivity was sporadic and closely connected with his relationships to women, first to Felice and then to Milena Jesenská-Polak. Brief and intense periods of creativity were interrupted by years of relative or near-total sterility. Two days after his first letter to Felice had gone out, Kafka wrote "Das Urteil" ("The Judgment," 1913) in a single night (September 22–23, 1912). He always considered it his best work, and it was the only one that always satisfied him. He saw in the uninterrupted inspirational flow with which this story had been committed to paper an ideal that he could never again attain. Immediately after finishing "The Judgment," he began with tremendous enthusiasm the second version of his novel *Amerika*. However, after an initial spurt Kafka's inspiration flagged. He started *Die Verwandlung* (*The Metamorphosis*, 1915) in November 1912, and finished it in December. Thereafter, his creativity seemed spent. He left the novel—as he would leave all his novels—in a fragmentary state and abandoned creative work for nearly two years. He started *The Trial* in August 1914, interrupted it to write "In der Strafkolonie" ("The Penal Colony," 1919) during a brief vacation that October, and continued to work on *The Trial* until the end of the year. Then his creativity flagged once more, and he dropped his work on the novel. After writing the fragment "Blumfeld, ein älterer Junggeselle" ("Blumfeld, an Elderly Bachelor," 1936) in early 1915, he again experienced two unproductive years.

Since 1915, a rapprochement with Felice had begun that culminated in a second engagement in July 1917. During the preceding winter and spring, Kafka had experienced a third period of intense creativity that resulted in numerous short narratives—parabolic or dreamlike vignettes—many of which he collected in the volume *Ein Landarzt* (*The Coun-*

try Doctor, 1919). With his renewed engagement to Felice and the purchase of furniture for their future household, Kafka again became oppressed by the actual prospect of marriage. As if in answer to his wish for a way out, he suffered a hemorrhage of the lungs in August 1917, which was diagnosed as tuberculosis. His illness serving as a reason, he suggested to Felice that they terminate their relationship, and the engagement was officially dissolved.

Having obtained an extended sick leave, Kafka moved to the village of Zürau in northwestern Bohemia, where his youngest sister, Ottla, lived at the time. Ottla was the only member of his family who was close to him; he had supported her in her struggle for independence against their father. He spent the winter of 1917–1918 in this rustic environment and perceived it as the happiest period of his life. It was then that he became deeply absorbed by metaphysical and religious problems and studied Arthur Schopenhauer, Leo Tolstoy, Søren Kierkegaard, and above all the Old Testament, Jewish legends, and Jewish mystical lore. Under those influences he wrote the largest number of his aphorisms. These meditations, written in octavo notebooks, contain the sole explicitly religious and metaphysical writings of Kafka. Even so, their content sharply diverges from any traditional and denominational elements of either Jewish or Christian faith.

After the aphorisms, a period of four relatively unproductive years followed. In 1919, Kafka became briefly engaged to Julie Wohryzek, a Jewish girl from a quasi-proletarian family. Kafka's father objected to the connection on social grounds, considering it a misalliance for his son. Kafka, now thirty-six, gave in and obediently broke off the engagement. However, in November of that year, he composed the long letter to his father that represents his autobiography and is conceived in terms of his father's fateful role in shaping his life. Kafka did not hand this letter to its addressee, but asked his mother to transmit it, a request that she understandably refused.

FRANZ KAFKA

Extensive sick leaves were granted to Kafka during this period, which he spent in various mountain resorts and sanatoriums. In the sanatorium in Matliary in the High Tatra Mountains in Slovakia, he met a young Hungarian medical student, Robert Klopstock, who became a good friend and later, toward the end of Kafka's life, would become his physician. While Kafka sojourned in Merano in South Tyrol in 1920, a correspondence began with Milena Jesenská-Polak, a beautiful young Czech intellectual who had translated several of Kafka's works into Czech. An emancipated woman, she had rebelled against her father's wishes by marrying Ernst Polak, a Jewish literatus of great personal magnetism whom she followed to Vienna. Polak "held court" in the Viennese café Herrenhof, probably the source for the name of the inn in Kafka's *Das Schloss* (*The Castle*, 1926) where the Castle officials lodge when they descend to the level of ordinary humanity. Polak's open unfaithfulness to Milena made her ready for the passionate affair that quickly developed between her and the author she admired. It culminated in a four-day visit from Kafka to Vienna in the early summer of 1920. Milena was the only non-Jewish woman with whom Kafka was seriously involved. Despite the happiness of those days together, and despite the beautiful intimacy that he achieved with Milena in his letters, Kafka, who referred to coitus as "the punishment for the happiness of being together," sought to avoid further physical contact with his beloved. Symptoms of anxiety tormented him at the prospect of an encounter, which Milena sought and Kafka tried to evade. At a final confrontation insisted upon by Milena in August 1920, she ended the affair.

Kafka's last great upsurge of creativity began soon after the termination of his intimacy with Milena. It resulted in "Ein Hungerkünstler" ("A Hunger Artist," 1924), "Forschungen eines Hundes" ("Investigations of a Dog," 1931), and above all, his most ambitious and longest work, *The Castle*, in which strong echoes of the Milena experience have been de-

tected. All these works were written in the first half or two-thirds of the year 1922. In the late summer of 1922, Kafka broke off all further work on his novel, and an extended period of sterility set in again. Ironically enough, his request for early retirement had been granted in midsummer, which meant that for the first time in his life Kafka would now be free to devote himself fully to his writing. During a stay on the Baltic coast of Germany in the summer of 1923, he met and fell in love with Dora Diamant, a Polish girl from an Orthodox Jewish family who was twenty years younger than himself. His affection was requited, and he moved to Berlin to live with Dora. He called himself "a repentant Jew" when he asked Dora's father for her hand in marriage, but the rabbi whom her father consulted counseled rejection of Kafka's plea. In this last six months of his life, Kafka's late-won contentment with Dora was marred by penury, since his Czech pension was utterly inadequate to the inflation raging in Germany, and by his rapidly advancing illness. In these winter months, Kafka wrote "Eine kleine Frau" ("A Little Woman") and his great last fragment, "Der Bau" ("The Burrow"). His worsening state of health forced him to move back to his parents' home in March 1924, which he felt as a final defeat. He still had the strength to write his last story, "Josefine, die Sängerin, oder Das Volk der Mäuse" ("Josephine the Singer, or the Mouse Folk," 1924). Because of excruciating pain in his throat, he was taken to Vienna for medical examinations. An advanced stage of tuberculosis of the throat was diagnosed. Kafka was admitted to a small sanatorium in Kierling, near Vienna, where he died on 3 June 1924. His last words, written to Dr. Klopstock, were: "Kill me, or you are a murderer." He was buried in Prague, where he rests next to his parents.

Few of Kafka's works were published in his lifetime. His first book was the collection of short pieces, *Betrachtung* (Meditation), published by Kurt Wolff in 1913. "Der Heizer" ("The Stoker"), the first chapter of *Amerika*, appeared in 1913, in Kurt Wolff's expression-

1155

ist series *Der jüngste Tag* (The Day of Judgment) with the subtitle "Ein Fragment" ("A Fragment"). In the same series, *The Metamorphosis* and "The Judgment" appeared as book publications in 1915 and 1916 respectively. In 1919, Wolff published "In the Penal Colony" and the collection of short pieces *The Country Doctor,* and in 1924, shortly after Kafka's death, his volume of four stories, *Ein Hungerkünstler,* was issued by the Berlin publishing house Die Schmiede. After Kafka's death, Max Brod brought out Kafka's three novels in quick succession—*The Trial* in 1925, *The Castle* in 1926, and *Amerika* in 1927. In 1931, a volume of unpublished stories and fragments appeared with the title *Beim Bau der chinesischen Mauer* (*The Great Wall of China*), and between 1935 and 1937 Brod published the first edition of Kafka's collected works. Diaries, letters, aphorisms, and further fragments were published in subsequent volumes in the 1940's, 1950's, 1960's, and 1970's.

Most of Kafka's posthumous publications were edited by Max Brod. To counter the changes in Kafka's texts made by Brod, a critical edition based on the original manuscripts—most of which are in the Bodleian Library at Oxford University—is being prepared under the general editorship of Jürgen Born. So far, two volumes—*The Castle* and *Amerika* (*Der Verschollene*)—have appeared.

It is difficult to place Kafka in a literary tradition. To be sure, there are influences on his writing, foremost among them Gustave Flaubert, Heinrich von Kleist, and Feodor Dostoevsky. Charles Dickens' *David Copperfield* played a decisive part in the inspiration of *Amerika.* Dostoevsky's "The Double" and *The Brothers Karamazov* left their traces on *The Metamorphosis* and *The Trial* respectively, while *Crime and Punishment* influenced both of Kafka's works. The nineteenth-century Czech novel *The Grandmother,* by Božena Nemcová, has been seen to have some bearing on *The Castle.* Kafka called Flaubert, Dostoevsky, August Strindberg, and the Austrian author Franz Grillparzer his "blood relatives."

He found himself confirmed by Kierkegaard "as by a friend," even though he subsequently developed a highly critical attitude toward the Dane. Most important, perhaps, is the influence of Jewish thought and literature, which is noticeable from "The Judgment" on, but most conspicuous in "Before the Law," in the aphorisms, and *The Castle.* Kafka's main interest in other writers, however, was not in their work or their art, but in their lives. Kafka was an avid reader of life documents—autobiographies, biographies, letters, diaries, and memoirs.

Kafka was not totally unknown in his lifetime. Apart from his circle of Prague friends and acquaintances, who formed an intellectual and cultural avant-garde in his native city, German literary circles became increasingly interested in him. Carl Sternheim's donation to him of the money he received from the prestigious Fontane Prize in 1915 symbolized the respect in which Kafka was held even then, despite the paucity of his publications. Still he remained during his life, and for the first two decades after his death, a special property of the cognoscenti and the avant-garde. Hitler's accession to power made any spread of Kafka's fame impossible in German-speaking lands. Meanwhile, however, the French existentialists had discovered him, and their frequent references to him began his worldwide reputation. Even though an English translation of *The Castle* had already appeared in 1930, Kafka's real entry into American letters came, on the one hand, by way of the French existentialists, and, on the other hand, by way of the Central European intellectual emigrés. The most exciting phase of Kafka's American reception occurred in the 1940's; by the fifties he was becoming the classical modernist we see in him today.

Kafka's work can be called a spiritual autobiography in metaphorical disguise. In a diary entry of 6 August 1914, Kafka noted that his sense for the presentation of his "dreamlike inner life" had stunted all his other interests and talents and had become the only quality that could afford him full satisfaction. Indeed, the oneiric character of Kafka's writings strikes every reader, for their enigmatic suggestiveness is their most pronounced feature. They are like dreams in that they compel interpretation but seem to withhold the key. Sometimes his stories did grow out of dreams, and the dreams Kafka frequently relates in his diaries show a striking resemblance to his stories. Yet his writings differ profoundly from those of the surrealists, who jotted down their dreams in automatic writing. Unlike theirs, Kafka's narratives are thoroughly disciplined. They are by no means simple copies of dreams; rather, they are structured analogously to dreams in some essential characteristics.

One of these characteristics is the peculiar relationship of Kafka's narratives to metaphor. His stories tend to present enactments of metaphors buried in language, not only in the German language in which he wrote but also in the universal symbolism of pre-rational thought. Basic metaphors by which pre-scientific language expresses experiences, attitudes, and relationships become events in Kafka's tales. He reinstates or re-creates the pictorial expressiveness that the original metaphor, now frozen in a cliché or idiom, once conveyed. Thus Kafka's writing conforms to or repeats the activity of the dreaming mind. As Sigmund Freud has shown in *The Interpretation of Dreams* (1900), a work with which Kafka was familiar, dreams speak in the pictorial language that speech once was. They take literally the metaphors hidden in speech and act them out as visualized events.

A few examples might help to clarify the preceding remarks. A decisive and profound experience is said to "leave a mark"; a lasting memory is "engraved" on one. Kafka's "The Penal Colony" depicts both metaphors as physical happenings. The penal machine slowly kills the condemned prisoner by literally engraving (*einkerben*) on his flesh the law he has transgressed. In fact, he dies remembering this legal lesson; "the mark left by the law" kills him. German usage applies the term *Ungeziefer* (vermin) to persons considered low and contemptible, even as our usage of "cockroach"

describes a person deemed a spineless and miserable character. In Kafka's *The Metamorphosis,* the traveling salesman Gregor Samsa is "like a cockroach" because of his spineless and abject behavior and parasitic wishes. However, Kafka drops the word "like" and the metaphor becomes reality when Gregor Samsa wakes up to find himself turned into a giant vermin. With this metamorphosis Kafka reverses the original act of metamorphosis carried out by thought when it forms metaphor; for metaphor is always "metamorphosis." Kafka transforms metaphor back into his fictional reality, and this counter-metamorphosis becomes the starting point of his tale. In a last example, German usage calls a sexually indecent and obscene character a "pig" or "swine" (*Schwein*). In Kafka's "A Country Doctor," the groom who assaults the doctor's maid walks out of the doctor's pigsty.

Kafka's narratives do not stop with reactivating single metaphors. They organically connect the enactment of one metaphor with the enactments of others, and together these metaphors establish a narrative development. "A Country Doctor" will serve as an example.

The swinish groom stands in a fateful relation to the protagonist of the story, the country doctor, through whose consciousness alone we witness the events. The doctor had lived next to his maid, Rose, without noticing her as a woman. As soon as she presents herself to him as desirable, the groom steps out of the doctor's "unused" pigsty and seeks to rape her. (The original text uses the German word for "unused"—*unbenützt*—which the English translation renders as "uninhabited.") The unused pigsty belongs to the doctor; in the words of the story, it is "his own." The groom is, then, literally a dweller in the doctor's forgotten lower depths. He embodies the doctor's unused sex drive in a strikingly literal way. The doctor's consciousness does not acknowledge his responsibility for the event he himself calls forth when he kicks the door of the pigsty open "absentmindedly" and thus releases the groom. The sudden emergence of the "filthy" contents of the doctor's depths—the unacknowledged component of his self—now overpowers his humanity and makes the girl a prey of bestial desire. In Kafka's stories acts and omissions reveal what consciousness hides from itself. It is not consciousness—the explicit comments of the story—but the narrated events that show the true meaning of Kafka's tale. "A Country Doctor" begins with a call of the night bell summoning the doctor to a patient. However, his horse has died from overexertion, and he cannot respond to the call. In his dilemma he calls "absentmindedly" on his forgotten pigsty. (The original text uses the German word for "absentmindedly"—*zerstreut*—which the English translation renders as "confused," but "absentmindedly" is critical in showing that this is an unconscious call on the doctor's part.) When he does so he releases the swinish groom and a team of "unearthly horses" and allows the groom to take the girl. Contrary to his verbal protestations, the doctor does in fact leave Rose behind with the groom. She is the price for the groom's aid.

The images and plot of this tale enable us to see Kafka's works as pieces of an autobiography in metaphorical disguise. The call of the night bell can be understood as a translation into sensory terms of Kafka's call to literature, which he understood as an art of healing and self-preservation, a "doctor's" art. For Kafka writing was night work for two reasons: literally, because he had no time for it during the day; figuratively, because to write he had to delve into the nocturnal regions of his mind, the representation of which he called his fatal talent. The death of the horse shows that no normal and natural way is available for transporting the self to its calling, and as the doctor finds his self in absentmindedness, so Kafka notes that he had done his best writing when all rational control was lifted. In one night, with "an outpouring of his soul," he wrote "The Judgment," which remained his favorite work and the model for all others.

"A Country Doctor" presents in the hieroglyphic language of dreams a clear and exact presentation of Kafka's inspirational process and the problems it posed for his life. In a revealing letter to Brod written in 1922, he calls his writing "a descent to the dark powers, an unchaining of spirits whose natural state it is to be bound servants." This description fits the groom of "A Country Doctor," who, instead of serving the self, expels it and takes over its vacated house. In that same letter to Brod Kafka says that in order to devote himself to literature the writer must sacrifice fulfillment in life, and "the unearthly horses" of inspiration, called forth from the unsavory depths, transport the doctor away from life, woman, and home. He is shown literally "carried away," "in the transport" of inspiration, since his unearthly team of horses proceeds without his conscious will and carries him off instantaneously and miraculously to his vocational destination. This destination is an existential encounter, symbolized by his being undressed and put in the same bed with his sick childhood self, the boy patient to whom he has been called.

The two houses pictorialize the two poles of the doctor's existence. In his own house, the house of the self, the doctor abandons the possibility of erotic fulfillment; in the other house, the house of the patient, he dedicates himself to his art, which is the confrontation with the congenital wound of mortality. The hero's ambivalence is such that he cannot be content at either pole. At home he sacrifices the girl to his mission, but at his destination he regrets the price he has paid and wants to return. His split existence, his inability to choose, becomes pure image in the doctor's final condition. He is shown riding aimlessly between the houses; the distance between them has become infinite, and he cannot stay at either place.

"A Country Doctor" became the title story of a volume of Kafka's short pieces published in 1919 and dedicated to his father, which makes quite evident the importance Kafka attached to this particular work. The detailed examination of its plot and images has enabled us to

FRANZ KAFKA

understand the allegorical principle informing Kafka's writings: his images are pictorial
translations of overriding personal concerns
in which personal meaning acquires universal
significance.

Any individual work by Kafka may baffle the
reader when considered in isolation. If examined within the context of Kafka's other works
and personal documents, however, the nature
and meaning of his images become clear, and
the individual work appears as a variation on
a single theme—the inner autobiography of the
author—and as a step in the development of
this theme. Each work is aesthetically self-
sufficient and, if written and published by
Kafka himself, a complete and satisfying statement of one approach to the master theme.

However, Kafka's images possess different
degrees of transparency in different works.
The central images of his long narratives—
Gregor Samsa's bug form, the court in *The
Trial*, the Castle in the late novel of that name—
are more opaque and denser than the symbols
of his shorter pieces. The reason is that the
central images of the long works have a variety of functions and meanings. Indeed, they
unite mutually contradictory meanings and
functions.

Gregor Samsa's metamorphosis, for instance, expresses a number of contradictory
tendencies in the single image of the giant bug.
Gregor's transformation gives shape to his
wish to abandon responsibility as breadwin-
ner and supporter of his family and thereby
returns Gregor's father to his former position
as head of the household. At the same time,
however, his metamorphosis embodies Gregor's opposite wish to avenge himself on his
family's parasitism by turning parasite himself. In the former case the metamorphosis
functions as submission, in the latter as ag-
gression and rebellion. The empirical impossibility of Gregor's form of existence serves as
objective correlative of his spiritual and psychic contradictoriness.

In addition to the actualizing of metaphors,
there are two further factors that make the

structure of Kafka's stories analogous to the
structure of dreams: unitary perspective and
tension between a manifest content and a
latent truth.

In fiction, ordinarily, the community of author and reader stands as an objective reality
outside and above the points of view of the
characters, forming a "true" frame of reference.
The traditional storyteller or novelist maintains this division by one or both of these
devices: he switches the point of view from one
character to another and thus enables us to
enjoy a relative omniscience since we can look
into all minds of the story, which none of the
characters can; or he keeps his own perspective separate, looks into his characters, and
comments as narrator upon their thoughts
and actions. These conventions are absent in
Kafka's fiction. His stories know only a single
point of view, that of the protagonist. Even in
his third-person narratives— and his major
works are all third-person narratives—we see
objects, scenes, and persons only through the
protagonist's eyes. An example from *The Trial*
may illustrate the means by which Kafka replaces independent authorial comment with
his protagonist's interpretation of the action.

The reaction of the Examining Magistrate to
a demagogic speech by the defendant Josef K.
is described as follows: "The Examining Magistrate kept fidgeting on his chair with embarrassment *or* impatience" [italics mine]. The
word "or" shows Kafka's radical deviation from
the conventional method of narration. Instead
of giving us a single authoritative explanation,
the author states his ignorance of his fictional
world. He blocks and prevents the traditional
communication of author to reader "over the
head of the character." In this way Kafka
achieves the most fundamental realism and removes the last vestiges of the author's presence
as an independent, visible personality, thereby
fulfilling Flaubert's ideal of an author who is as
invisible as God is in his creation. However, he
goes further than Flaubert by also taking away
the reader's superiority over the protagonist.
Together with the protagonist, the reader is

thrown into the basic condition of every individual man: he remains imprisoned in the solitary confinement of a limited and subjective consciousness that can only infer, but can never know, the external world. Normally we accept on trust the "truth" of our fellow man's feelings and motivations. The Kafka hero lacks this a priori trust; or if he does start out with it, events take it away from him, or at least from the reader. This loss of basic trust or faith in the interpretability of the world around the protagonist partially explains the peculiar effect of Kafka's fiction.

For reasons that we shall examine later, Kafka's hero must defend and assert himself or else be lost. Josef K.'s ambiguous interpretation, for instance, of the Examining Magistrate's fidgeting results from his need to calculate the effect of his speech. If it was embarrassment that made the Magistrate fidget, Josef K. has scored a victory. If, on the other hand, the Magistrate moved from impatience, K.'s speech has heightened the threat to himself. The fictional reality presented by Kafka is either threat or promise to the protagonist and is wholly determined by his fears, wishes, and hopes. Therefore there can be no presentation of facts in Kafka that is not, at the same time, interpretation. The situation of Kafka's protagonist reflects the fundamental insecurity of man's condition as prisoner of his own brain.

All aspects of Kafka's narrative form, from individual word and sentence to plot structure and thought, express this fundamental uncertainty of his protagonists, and it is this form that infects the reader and grips him with foreboding. Kafka's vocabulary is one of inference and conjecture. Favorite words are "apparently," "ostensibly," "maybe," and "actually." Kafka prefers "it seems" to "it is." His sentences often consist of two clauses: the first states a fact or a guess; the second qualifies, questions, negates it. The conjunction "but" is therefore most characteristic of Kafka's thought structure. The frequent use of "even if" clauses expresses the tendency to cancel expectations and refute inferences. Terminal

certainty there is in Kafka, but it is usually of a negative kind, identical with death or final despair. The fact that most of his works do not end with the protagonist's death attests to the inability to arrive at certainty.

As stated above, the tension between a manifest content and a latent "truth" also contributes to the dreamlike effect of Kafka's narratives. Although the protagonist's solipsistic perspective, through which we experience the narrative, does not allow us to speak of authorial truth in Kafka's work, there is nonetheless an objective and verifiable authorial point of view in most of his writings. It is obliquely smuggled in without the awareness of the protaganist. In the contradiction between the reader's perspective, as given him by the protagonist, and the hidden point of view or "truth" of the work lies the fundamental concern of Kafka's art, the basis of its structure, and the secret of its unsettling effect.

Those who think that the protagonist's perspective is the whole of Kafka are victims of the subtle deception that this perspective perpetrates. In fact, in the two novels about Joseph K. and in several of the longer narratives, the protagonist's motivation is precisely to hide the truth either from himself or from the world, including the reader. To be sure, the protagonist's perspective operates for the purpose of blocking access to and comprehension of the truth, but in most of Kafka's works the truth becomes known through the defeat of the protagonist's consciousness. In one of his aphorisms Kafka defines truth as the light reflected upon the retreating grimace (of falsehood) and art as the condition of being dazzled by that light. This aphorism supplies the key to Kafka's poetics, always implicit in his works. The annihilation or refutation suffered by Kafka's protagonist, bearer of the lie, becomes the negative revelation of truth.

This structural principle of Kafka's narratives explains the profound difference between Kafka's method and the stream-of-consciousness technique. The latter assumes the identity of consciousness and truth. Operating within the framework of psychology, it assumes that to reveal character is to reveal the truth of the narrative. In Kafka's narratives, on the contrary, consciousness hides truth. Therefore Kafka must transcend psychology. His concern is not the mechanism of self, but its moral and spiritual justification. In order to express this concern he must unmask the mechanism, and in doing that he reveals a great deal about it. Kafka is a master in uncovering the subtle workings of rationalization, subterfuge, and self-deception. But for Kafka this unmasking is not the end of his art. The end is always the revelation of the negative truth in the defeat of the self.

All of Kafka's works deal with this relationship in one of three ways, each of which corresponds to one of the three distinct phases of development in his mature writings. In the first phase of Kafka's maturity (1912–1914) the protagonist represses his inner truth, but his truth erupts in a catastrophe—it accuses, judges, and annihilates him. This is the phase of the punitive fantasies, the powerful tales of punishment and death that are Kafka's most dramatic and most popular—"The Judgment," *The Metamorphosis, The Trial,* with important modifications, and particularly "The Penal Colony." To all of these *Amerika* forms an "innocent" and "utopian" counterpart. The second phase (1914–1917) begins after "The Penal Colony" and continues with the short parabolic pieces of the *Country Doctor* volume, which includes "Before the Law" and "A Report to an Academy." In this phase a detached perspective views and contemplates a paradoxical discrepancy between self and truth.

The final phase (1920–1924) is Kafka's greatest and most profound. It encompasses the four stories included in *Ein Hungerkünstler,* the lengthy fragments "Investigations of a Dog" and "The Burrow," and the long fragmentary novel *The Castle.* In the three most important works of that phase—"A Hunger Artist," "Josephine the Singer, or the Mouse Folk," and *The Castle*—Kafka presents the protagonist's deception of the world, inspired by his desperate need to create and fulfill his existence.

The punitive fantasies form the foundation for all phases of Kafka's maturity. With "The Judgment," he said, he had achieved his "breakthrough" to his own proper form of expression. We shall therefore deal with the punitive fantasies in greater detail than with the two subsequent phases.

The alienation of the protagonist from his true self forms the structural basis of Kafka's punitive fantasies. These fantasies are adumbrated in the early fragment "Wedding Preparations in the Country." Here the hero—Raban, cryptographic forerunner of Samsa and disguise for Kafka—dreams of literally splitting his self in order to avoid visits to his fiancée in the country and other burdensome involvements. His true self, transformed into a giant beetle, would stay in bed, while the unreal image of his body, his facade, would go into the world to represent Raban in the performance of necessary duties. This facade would be a slave, utterly dependent upon the commands of the powerful dehumanized self at home. This buglike true self corresponds to the bachelor self of other early writings and diary entries of Kafka's. Raban's facade body, on the other hand, burdened with the task of conducting his engagement, corresponds to the engaged young men who appear in Kafka's juvenilia.

This split prefigures the structure of Kafka's punitive fantasies, with one essential qualification. What the early work presents as a conscious wish becomes in the punitive fantasies a strange destiny, seemingly imposed upon the protagonist from outside and eluding his conscious understanding. What in the early work is a split between facade body and true self reappears in Kafka's mature work as a contradiction between consciousness and truth.

Kafka's punitive fantasies—leaving "The Penal Colony" out of account for the present—are related to Raban's wish-dream in the following manner: The facade tries to make itself independent of the true self by seeking to repress it, but punishment acts as a recall to the self: having tried to emancipate itself, the facade is arrested, battered, and dissolved. Thus, what in Raban's wish-dream is an open horizontal coexistence of two halves now becomes a vertical division of two layers; a visible surface layer stands on top of a deeper, submerged layer that the surface tries to "cover up." And along with the element of repression, time is introduced into this split as a structural element. The protagonist's true self—essentially his childhood self—lies submerged but erupts one day in a strange guise, arrests him in his course of self-emancipation, involves him ever more deeply and catastrophically in his unacknowledged truth, and destroys him.

Arrest is central fact and symbol in *The Trial,* Kafka's longest and most ambitious tale of punishment. The German word for "arrest" (*Verhaftung*) carries the additional meaning of entanglement and fatal attachment, and in this basic meaning *Verhaftung* is the theme of all the punitive fantasies. The protagonist's condition of attachment to his childhood self has been repressed and put out of mind but never truly overcome. The act or happening of his being arrested (literally, stopped in his advance) by a catastrophic event actualizes the invisible condition of entanglement that had persisted in him all along. Estranged from his conscious intention, however, his true condition, when it does erupt, manifests itself in an unrecognizable disguise.

The turning point and "breakthrough" to his mature form, which Kafka considered "The Judgment" to be, lie in two factors: the introduction of the father figure as the authoritative and effective voice of truth; and the consistent shift of perspective to the facade layer of the split. Kafka's juvenilia is uncertain about perspective and is therefore hampered by a subjectivism unable to push through to an effective objectification of the themes and problems he sought to express. For example, in Raban's wish-dream the authentic consciousness of the story looks upon the facade, and

what the reader obtains is an unformed reverie. The revolution of "The Judgment" consists in the reversal of this perspective. Kafka made the facade the consciousness of the story, whereby he achieved the powerful alienation effect that we associate with his art. He was able to present consciousness estranged from itself in a way that involves the reader directly, from within the narration, instead of letting him look in from outside. Because of the thematic similarity, a comparison of Raban's wish-dream of transforming himself into a giant bug with Gregor Samsa's "involuntary" metamorphosis in the story of that name, written five years later, will highlight the difference between the juvenilia and Kafka's "breakthrough" to the first phase of his mature art.

In both stories the transformed self is the true self. However, whereas Raban's transformation occurs only in his dream, Samsa's transformation emerges from his night dreams and becomes reality. The text clearly refers to the subconscious origin of the metamorphosis by explicitly mentioning that Gregor finds himself changed into vermin upon awakening from "restless dreams." In the earlier story the transformation expresses what Raban wants to be; in the mature version truth is not what the self wants to be, but what it is. Also, in the perspective of the early version truth and consciousness are identical; in the mature version they are not. Furthermore, while both versions agree on the retrograde and inhuman nature of the true self, they differ as to the presentation of the facade. Whereas Raban's facade is a surrogate body, Samsa's facade is an evasive mind. It is consciousness finding itself imprisoned in a truth it cannot face. In the mature work the split between facade and true self is a discrepancy between a devious human mind and a non-human body.

Gregor pretends to himself, and tries to pretend to others, that his metamorphosis is a temporary inconvenience. At the same time he feels a vague uneasiness and sense of guilt for having reneged on his obligations toward his family. His stream of memories reveals that prior to his metamorphosis Gregor had indeed thought of giving up his distasteful job. However, for the sake of his family, who depended upon his income, he had to inhibit this wish and paid it no further attention. Viewed with this sequence in mind Gregor's metamorphosis appears and functions as the oblique fulfillment of a wish that had to be repressed. However, Gregor emphatically wards off such suspicions, claiming that he is "still around" and does not intend to abandon his responsibility. This is the manifest content of the story, which is identical with the protagonist's perspective. The reader tends to accept this content at face value, since he sees all happenings of the story through the protagonist's perspective and tends also to make that perspective his own.

However, Gregor's avowal to continue as his family's provider offers a glaring contradiction to his condition. The thought does indeed occur to Gregor that his situation must rule out his professed intention, and he allows himself the fleeting wish to be left in peace by his family. This wish accords perfectly with his new bodily state and resurrects his previously inhibited thought of abandoning his duties. At this point Gregor's physical change can be seen as a fulfillment of his wish for seclusion and irresponsibility; it is the abandonment of his family that he has indignantly denied in thought. When Gregor wishes to be left in peace his consciousness and condition meet harmoniously. They meet, however, only for a moment. Immediately thereafter Gregor's false consciousness—that is, thought inconsistent with condition—"covers up" and once more takes over the manifest content of the story.

In the punitive fantasies the repressed part of the self is identical with its childlike component. In a time now long past the protagonist enjoyed a harmonious relationship with his origins, his parents and family, and the loss of this harmonious past plays a very important part in bringing about the vengeance and punishment he suffers. This is

most obvious in "The Judgment," least so in *The Trial*. Yet even in *The Trial* the hero's attachment to his family functions importantly in his punishment. At one point in the novel Josef K. feels that only the pressures of his family have so desperately involved him in his strange trial. Josef K.'s mother in particular has a vital function in the structure of the novel. On his birthdays Josef K. had been in the habit of visiting his mother, whom he had left behind in the country. Being preoccupied with his strenuous career at the bank he had become estranged from her and had given up his visits. On the third birthday after he had stopped seeing her, the mysterious court visits him to arrest him for an unspecified guilt. His estrangement from his family—indicated also by his annoyance at his uncle, whom he calls "a revenant from the country," and by his neglect of his cousin—vaguely troubles him. However, like all protagonists of the punitive fantasies, Josef K. easily represses whatever makes him feel uneasy and pays little conscious attention to it.

In all his works Kafka equates truth or objective reality with the family, first in its basic meaning and later in a more and more extended meaning, in which family becomes identical with society, the stream of the generations, or the totality of living things—"the entire community of men and animals," as he once termed this total community from which he felt he had defected. It is against this family that he contrasts the self of his protagonists. The representative or spokesman of the family is the father figure.

A close study of the attributes of all representatives of authority in Kafka's entire opus, no matter how universalized and abstract, clearly reveals that these derive from the attributes of the fathers in "The Judgment" and *The Metamorphosis*. From "The Judgment" to Kafka's last work, "Josephine," this father figure possesses a power that, however unseen, mysterious, and generalized it becomes, retains a fundamental effectiveness that plays havoc with the assumptions, opinions, and claims of Kafka's protagonist. It is the father figure who proves the hero's consciousness to be illusion.

In Georg Bendemann and Gregor Samsa, heroes of the first two punitive fantasies, Kafka created characters who try to rival and succeed their fathers, fail in the attempt, and are horribly punished for it. Indeed, in *The Metamorphosis* Kafka places his protagonist in a condition in which he literally becomes incomparable to his father by ceasing to belong to the same species. The father is allied with the submerged pole of his son's divided self. He enforces those tendencies in his son that crave for regression to a childlike existence, one that finds its radical objectification in Gregor's vermin condition. This form of existence combines self-elimination as a possible rival and threat to the father with self-indulgence in a narcissistic freedom.

The composition of the story makes clear this alliance between the protagonist's father and the son's subconscious self. Each of the story's three parts shows an attempt on Gregor's part to break out into the world and reassert himself as a responsible adult human being. Each part ends with his being rebuffed and chased back into his prison room. It is Gregor's father who, as spokesman of the family, administers the first of these rebuffs. Thereby he enforces Gregor's own tendency toward withdrawal and seclusion, which Gregor had expressed by locking himself in his room and emerging from his dreams as a creature unable to communicate. The father accommodates Gregor's unacknowledged wish for isolation and irresponsibility. In "The Judgment" Georg Bendemann's father explicitly calls himself "the representative" of Georg's estranged childhood friend, who exerts upon Georg an effect analogous to the force that erupts in Gregor's metamorphosis.

"The Judgment" shows the son literally "covering up" his apparently senile father after having put him to bed like a child. On the manifest level he acts from filial solicitude, but on the latent level, which Georg's later reactions show to be the true one, he seeks to bury his father and establish his own position as new head of the household. Georg thinks of himself as a good and dutiful son, and seeing him through his perspective we are inclined to agree with him. Actually, however, by his deeds he has neglected his father, has allowed him to live in the gloomy back room of the apartment while he himself occupied the sunny front (literally the facade), and has not set foot in his father's room for a very long time. By comparing Georg's explicit thoughts with his behavior, the reader is able to get another perspective on Georg. Georg thinks he has taken his father's place in the family business and prides himself on having greatly improved and reformed it. With his impending marriage Georg consciously plans to move his father to his new apartment and there, reversing the role of child and parent, "take care of him." But Georg is only deceiving himself. He has not succeeded in keeping his father "covered." His father shouts, "No!" and throws off his covers, leaps up in bed, and reveals himself in his true stature as the giant and supreme judge in the heart of his son.

Truth is revealed to be the opposite of Georg's imaginings. His father is not senile, but is "still a giant" whose fingertips reach the ceiling, and Georg's fiancée, whom he had thought to be so important in his life, matters so little to Georg that she no longer enters his mind. What counts in his soul is not the girl he wanted to marry but the friend he thought he had long outgrown and whom he had patronized. This friend now grips and "touches his imagination as never before." Kafka, in his own analysis of "The Judgment," called the friend the only common bond between father and son. Important is not the question of the friend's existence as an independent character, but his function in Georg's relationship to his father. The friend represents an alternative way of life that, in the distant past, had been a possibility which Georg had rejected. He could have renounced his ambition to succeed his father. He could have refrained from trying to take over his father's business and found a household of his own in which the father would be reduced to a dependent role. Like the friend, he could have fled the scene of his father's activity, remained unmarried, and stayed clear of economic success. Given a father intent on maintaining his authority, Georg would then have been "a son after [his father's] heart." This alternative, which his friend embodies and which Georg has eschewed, is his true self. This can be seen in the "uncovering" scene, when the father proceeds to demolish Georg's facade. Even though his father threatens to rob him of fiancée, business, status, and power, the only loss that now matters to Georg is the loss of his friend. From the moment Georg feels that he has lost *him,* he is lost.

The father's accusations prove the entire content of Georg's consciousness to be error and self-deception. They shatter his false consciousness, his wrong self-estimation, and through this shattered facade they reach to and lay bare Georg's hidden, childlike self. By rushing to obey his father's death sentence and execute himself, he becomes again the loving, innocent, and obedient child he had once been. The inner division is gone; the facade is removed; harmony has returned. As Georg climbs over the railing to leap from the bridge his consciousness of loving his parents is his whole truth. It is the truth that his father demands of Georg at the beginning of his cross-examination, and Georg is unable to give it except by destroying the untruth that his life has become.

The guilt of the protagonists of "The Judgment" and *The Metamorphosis* is clearly established. In "The Judgment" Georg's guilt is his defection from father and childhood friend, and the "devilish" lechery with which he has utilized a woman as his instrument for the repression of his friend and childhood self. His father uses a drastic metaphor, accusing Georg of trying to subjugate him so that he could "set [his] bottom on him." Georg's guilt above all lies in the unconscious hypocrisy

with which he has attempted to displace his father while thinking himself a good son. Whether or not we accept the father's harsh judgment as justified is less relevant than the hero's active assent to his death sentence.

Less explicit than "The Judgment" on the verbal level, but equally lucid in poetic terms, *The Metamorphosis* supplies articulated reasons for accusing and condemning its protagonist. Gregor is clearly punished for trying to break out of the "otherness" that he has made his fate. Gregor's sister articulates what amounts to the family's death sentence over him. Her argument is clear and convinces Gregor. She says that if the insect were truly her brother, it would have left them of its own accord. His wish for isolation and absolute withdrawal would then have spared the family his presence. If he had acted according to the inner law that found its visible fulfillment in his ghastly change, he would have continued to withdraw not only from the human form but also from the human community represented by his family. If Gregor had followed his true self—withdrawal and isolation—he would have gone into ultimate loneliness, and death would have been self-fulfillment. Then his family could have honored his memory. The disgusting monster and parasite is a compromise between his true self (we remember that Raban appeared as a "beautiful" bug) and the facade self that prevents him from letting go of his family. This creature refuses to die. It makes forays outside Gregor's room; it has erotic daydreams about his sister; it seeks to cleave to and exploit his family, thereby threatening to ruin it. It is this parasitic self that Gregor's sister exposes, judges, and condemns, with uncompromising cruelty.

The sister's judgment in *The Metamorphosis* corresponds to the father's in the earlier story. More clearly than there, however, it is the judgment of the family and of life itself that speaks through her. Gregor had withdrawn from the possibility of procreating even before his metamorphosis; he had remained a bachelor who loved to lock himself in when he dreamed. Therefore the hope for a renewal of the family in the next generation comes to rest entirely with his sister. As the scene after Gregor's death shows, it is through her that the family will continue and the stream of the generations will flow. It is the authority of life itself that judges Gregor through his sister's cruelty. This clear judgment speaks to him with the voice of his own inner truth. As Georg rushes to execute his father's verdict on himself, Gregor is convinced, more firmly even than his sister, that he must go. Both stories end with statements of inner assent to death. Both protagonists become true sons and truly themselves by dying.

In "The Penal Colony" Kafka systematized the underlying idea of the two earlier punitive fantasies. In a six-hour process of physical torture and laceration, the penal machine produces the assent to death that the judgment of their families produced in Kafka's earlier protagonists. In this later work the father's judgment and the family consensus have evolved into the law of a penal system. The Old Commander, who invented and operated the penal machine, constitutes the obvious link between the concrete fathers of "The Judgment" and *The Metamorphosis* and the abstract law and collective, anonymous authorities of *The Trial* and all subsequent works. The colony is the first step in Kafka's extension of the empirical family to the societies, nations, and species with which his later work is concerned.

The Old Commander's verdict is inscribed into the flesh of the condemned prisoner, who deciphers the sentence through his wounds. As he recognizes the text of the law on his body, he experiences a union with the paternal will more intimate—because physical—than Georg Bendemann's merely symbolic reunion with his father's will in suicide. The penal machine does not restore but rather creates its victim's true self. Before his arrest the prisoner was not much more than an animal. He lived in an unconscious state, ignorant of the law he had violated. His dawning recognition of the sentence, as the machine inscribes it into his skin, creates a comprehensible continuity between act and atonement. In connecting his pain with the law he transgressed, he acquires a destiny that is uniquely his, and at the same time he acquires an inward relationship to a superior will.

The continuity of self produced on the penal rack parallels Kierkegaard's idea of the self. (At the time of the punitive fantasies Kafka called Kierkegaard a "friend." He first became acquainted with Kierkegaard through an anthology entitled *Book of the Judge* [1905], a title spelling out a significant affinity between the two authors.) The authentic self in Kierkegaard is identical not with the organism but rather with a moral continuity that we create by our choices and actions and through a special and unique personal relationship to the absolute. In Kafka's penal system suffering and dying give birth to the same kind of existential self.

Their dying not only restores Kafka's earlier protagonists to their true selves but also reconciles them to their families, and through their families to the world. The sacrifice of Georg's false self re-establishes the harmony of life not in actuality but in principle. Georg's drowning in the river symbolically reunites him with "the stream of life" that proceeds above him in "the unending traffic" over the bridge from which he has leaped to his death. When at the beginning of the story he had looked out upon the bridge, a quiet emptiness, a kind of frozen suspension of life prevailed. His dying re-animates life; although only a short time could have passed since the beginning of the action, a symbolic resurrection has taken place. The German word for "traffic" (*Verkehr*) also signifies "intercourse," alluding to the sexual and procreative aspect of the "unending" stream released by Georg's death. A remark made by Kafka to Brod corroborates this allusion: as he wrote the word *Verkehr*, which concluded the story, Kafka, according to Brod, had thought of an ejaculation.

The end of *The Metamorphosis* is more directly explicit about the sexual and procreative

FRANZ KAFKA

liberation achieved by the hero's voluntary death. Gregor's demise frees his family from the guilt and shame that had become embodied in him; it allows thoughts of the future, of youth, of marriage, and of a new bloom bursting forth. Fittingly, the day of his death is the first day of real spring. Gregor Samsa dies as a scapegoat for humanity as represented by his family, and in a letter to Brod Kafka designated the writer a scapegoat for mankind: by taking mankind's sins upon himself and suffering for them, the writer allows mankind to sin in freedom.

The idea of the scapegoat led Kafka to find analogous insights in the anthropological research of his time and in the proto-totalitarian tendencies then becoming noticeable in Central Europe. Both the anthropological and political implications of Kafka's work are most obvious in "The Penal Colony." In the officer's report of the penal colony's past, the victim's torture and gradual transfiguration through dying figure as the ritual of a communal cult. Undoubtedly with anthropological discoveries in mind, Kafka presented the human scapegoat sacrificed for the benefit and edification of the community. On the other hand, the "brainwashing" of the subject, who is made to assent joyously to his own destruction, creates obvious parallels to the political and cultural irrationality of World War I ("The Penal Colony" was written two months after its outbreak) and to the nascent totalitarianism that transformed most of Europe into a huge penal colony less than three decades after Kafka had called his story as embarrassing "as our whole age."

At the same time "The Penal Colony" illumines the autobiographical character of Kafka's whole work. No matter how interesting and fruitful the anthropological, sociological, and philosophical implications of Kafka's writings are—and they are considerable—the intimate autobiographical meaning must never be lost sight of, since it gives rise to and shapes all the rest. Kafka's greatness lay in his extraordinary ability to picture the universal in the intimate and the intimate in the universal; a multiplicity of referred meanings constitute the powerful allusiveness and suggestiveness of every image he created. The communal festiveness that surrounds the dying prisoner in the penal colony provides the external correlative to the inner illumination he experiences, and it also is an extension of the obviously personal conclusions of Georg Bendemann's and Gregor Samsa's lives. Georg Bendemann dies under a busy thoroughfare, in the center of city life, as it were. After his demise Gregor Samsa becomes, for a while, the center of his family's hushed attention, a scenic arrangement that anticipates the communal cult of death in "The Penal Colony" two years later.

In addition to systematizing in an image the whole first phase of Kafka's mature writing, the penal apparatus is also a metaphorical description of this writing itself. The machine transfigures and kills the prisoner literally by writing, by imprinting a sentence on the prisoner's flesh. The German word for "writing" (Schrift) that Kafka uses has the meaning of both "script" and "scripture," enabling Kafka to allude simultaneously to the literary and religious significance of his penal apparatus. Above all, the machine repeats Kafka's own activity as a writer of punitive fantasies who grants his characters illuminating insights as he kills them. In a diary entry of December 1914, Kafka indicates that the penal apparatus is like a pictorialized poetics of his writing. He confesses there that he savors his own dying in advance through the vicarious dying of his characters. Here Kafka attributes to himself the same attitude he depicts in the officer of the penal colony.

The officer exults in the executions he arranges and supervises; he envies the beatitude his victims seem to attain and craves to take their place. However, when he finally does so, the venerated machine merely "murders" him unceremoniously and instantly; he exhibits no sign of inner illumination. The whole penal system is reduced to the officer's subjective assertion about the effects of his machine—an effect that his own execution contradicts. The objective truth is withheld.

This withholding of the truth connects "The Penal Colony" with *The Trial,* which was begun a little over two months before the story and was left a fragment. Both Josef K., who in *The Trial* is accused and executed without specified charge, and the officer in "The Penal Colony," who executes himself to prove his claim for the penal machine and to savor the happiness he expects it to give, die meaningless deaths. Punishment there is; but it no longer shows the truth. Thereby the two punitive fantasies written in 1914 are profoundly different from those written two years before "The Judgment" and *The Metamorphosis.* This difference marks a turning point in Kafka's entire development. In "The Penal Colony" events are seen from the perspective of a detached observer, a traveler and explorer, who has included the penal colony in his study of penal systems. He listens to the officer with great interest but refuses to promote his cause. He will not lend his support to the officer's plea for the upkeep of the punitive machine, which has become neglected under the new commander of the colony. Its subsequent collapse comes as the objective correlative of his rejection.

The perspective of *The Trial* is still that of a facade personality. As in the earlier punitive fantasies, there is still a repressed past embodied in the protagonist's family, from which he has become estranged. However, the family is no longer central. An abstract authority, the Court, takes over the function of the accusing families of the earlier protagonists. It is no longer the intimate drama of father and son that shapes the narrative, but rather a conflict of principles.

Unlike the earlier punitive fantasies, *The Trial* does not specify the guilt for which its protagonist is arrested. The court that judges Josef K. withholds the clear message given by father and family in the earlier works. Indeed, the confrontation of the self with its judge fails to take place. Punishment and annihilation remain, but understanding and atonement are

gone. The physical circumstances of Josef K.'s death reflect its subjective meaninglessness. Whereas Georg Bendemann dies in broad daylight, in the center of life, and whereas Gregor Samsa departs with the first gleam of dawn, Josef K. is knifed in darkness and silence on the deserted periphery of his city. The external darkness surrounding him has its complement in the darkness within him. He does not understand his death. As he fails to see his judges, so he fails to recognize himself. He does not discern within himself a conviction certain and firm enough to be his truth. His inner self remains as unfathomable as the Court.

The Trial is the only truly opaque work among the major writings of Kafka. Its opaqueness results from two factors: the total ambiguity of the Court and the total ambivalence of its hero. To understand the ambiguity of *The Trial,* a look at the fundamental ambivalence of Kafka's religious attitude will be helpful.

If we understand that the Absolute had two distinct faces for Kafka, we shall do greater justice to his complexity than if we dismiss it as pure paradox. We might define these two aspects of the Absolute by attaching to one the name of Plato, a philosopher Kafka held in high esteem, and to the other the name of Jehovah. In its Platonic aspect, the Absolute is pure spirit, and the physical world is illusion; engagement in the latter is fatally wrong. In its other face—the face of Jehovah, in which the features of Kafka's robust and vital father lurked—the Absolute is energy and incessant will, a stream of generations and unending continuity of life. From this ambiguity within the Absolute it follows that the self would become guilty in two opposite directions. It would become guilty before the Platonic aspect by getting "engaged," not merely sexually but economically and socially as well—by "wanting to snatch at the world with twenty hands," as Josef K. says of himself. On the other hand, the self would become guilty before the creator and progenitor of life by refusing "engagement" in the fullest sense of the word, by keeping itself pure in sterile virginity.

In one case the self is the engaged and striving facade; in the other the celibate true self sins and must be sacrificed as a result of its engagement. The fate of Georg Bendemann shows the former, and the fate of the misogynist officer of "The Penal Colony" or of the chaste sister of Barnabas in *The Castle* shows the latter guilt. *The Trial,* however, begun under the immediate shattering impact of Kafka's first break with his fiancée Felice Bauer, illumines the double and consequently total guilt of the self. In Josef K.'s Court the two faces of the Absolute combine to form the enigmatic mask of total ambiguity.

There is a further reason for the novel's ambiguity—Josef K.'s inability to decide between the forces battling within him. In Josef K. an unacknowledged *homo religiosus* clashes with the consciousness of economic man. His official impulse toward self-preservation and self-assertion resists the upsurge of his unofficial religious impulse, the craving for self-surrender and self-transcendence that is objectified by his arrest. It is of highest significance that the Court comes closest to him and appeals to him most directly through a priest. The protagonists of "The Judgment" and *The Metamorphosis* are arrested by the submerged childhood self within them, but in Josef K. the submerged childhood of man, rather than that of the individual, arrests the apparently emancipated facade of modern rationality.

By naming his protagonist Josef and adding the name Josef to the initial K. of his own name, Kafka may have been hinting at this vertical split in himself and in modern man. The "Josefstown" district of Prague, on the edge of which Kafka had been born, had in his childhood still been the site of the ghetto and the center of criminal life. As he once remarked to Gustav Janouch, a young acquaintance who subsequently published Kafka's conversations with him, the new "Josefstown," with its broad streets and bright, airy buildings, presented only a "cover-up" surface beneath which the dark, filthy, and frightful alleys of the ghetto lay merely submerged.

The careful reader becomes aware of this division within Josef K. Verbally, he seems to fight for reason, for man, as defined by the rational legal system of the modern state, and he denies the possibility of any extra-legal guilt. By his acts, however, he seeks out and in the end submits to the Court. In his mind he never comes to a clear decision for either one or the other. Consequently, the inner truth can never come to light. His conflicting pulls toward surrender, which would give meaning to his death, and toward resistance, which denies meaning to it, tear the whole concept of a true self apart. To be sure, the pull toward surrender and death does prove stronger, for K. lets himself be executed. He even awaits his executioners and leads them toward his place of execution. To the last, however, his consciousness withholds definitive assent.

The total ambivalence of the hero becomes the total ambiguity of the story. To appreciate the full extent of this ambiguity we merely have to compare the last thoughts of Georg Bendemann and Gregor Samsa with the last thoughts of Josef K. The last thoughts of Georg and Gregor express not only assent to their deaths but also affirmation of and affection for life as embodied in their families. The last thought of *The Trial,* however, is "shame." Shame, it seems, will survive the protagonist. This final noun of the novel not only emphasizes a desperate negativity in contrast to the tragic affirmation with which the earlier punitive fantasies ended; it also expresses a total ambiguity that makes it impossible to decipher the final meaning of *The Trial.* For it is entirely uncertain to what the noun "shame" refers. It could refer to Josef K.'s failure to resist his execution or to the senselessness of his murder and the shamefulness of a court that orders such injustices. In either case "shame" would express Josef K.'s mental defiance coexisting with his physical submission. However, it could also refer to his refusal to kill himself or to understand what the Court expects of him. Then the novel would have the opposite meaning: Josef K. would be justly punished for his stubborn rejection of the possibility of his guilt. Both interpretations are equally justified, even though they are contrary to each other. Therefore the unrelieved ambiguity of *The Trial* dissolves not only the idea of a true self but also the possibility of discerning a truth altogether.

Kafka excised passages that would have shown Josef K.'s craving to be united with the Court or his longing to be transfigured in death—passages that would have made him resemble the officer of "The Penal Colony." Kafka crossed out a reverie of Josef K.'s that would have opposed the meaning of his death in the novel's final scene. In the excised passage Josef K. succeeds in entering the courthouse whence the warrant of his arrest had been issued, and he experiences a transfiguration, symbolized by a new garment of perfect fit. By eliminating this radiant vision from the novel, that is, from the consciousness of his protagonist, Kafka himself enacted the process of repression in which his hero is engaged. Josef K.'s tendencies toward surrender and suicide form the powerful subterranean drift that counteracts his ever-conscious intention and action and pulls him ever further along toward destruction. His impulses drive him to look for the Court and provoke its verdict. These persist subliminally in fleeting thoughts, gestures, and unreasoned acts, to which Josef K. seems to be compelled. Except for the initial arrest it is always Josef K. who either actively seeks or welcomes contact with the Court. Josef K.'s longing for contact with the Court emerges perhaps most clearly in the Titorelli chapter. Josef K. rejects the painter's suggestions for compromise solutions and insists on absolute acquittal by the highest judges. His insistence amounts to a full recognition of their supreme authority over him and, beyond that, implies his wish to be accepted and approved by them. This is the limit to which Kafka allows K.'s wish for acceptance by the Court to become conscious.

In his preceding works Kafka revealed the strategies of repression his heroes engaged in and let the truth be known. In writing *The Trial,* however, he imitated his character and deleted anything that might reveal him directly and unambiguously. Thus, in the process of creating his protagonist Kafka himself performed the very activity that constitutes his fictional character. He excised and refused to show the "whole truth," expunging dreams that would have betrayed Josef K. to himself and to the reader. In *The Castle,* where he deals with a hero much more conscious of his purposes, Kafka leaves K.'s dream in the text and also allows him a revealing childhood memory.

The reasons for Kafka's excisions in *The Trial* are twofold. First, they show that he desired to make the division between the conscious surface and the subterranean level in his protagonist's character so complete that Josef K. becomes utterly unaware of one level of himself and the reader becomes unaware of what impels Josef K. toward his destruction. Josef K. thus becomes the precise image of the modern Central European bourgeois who was later caught unaware by the eruption of destructive irrationality around him; yet the work also makes clear that the tendencies that made this possible were to be found within the bourgeois himself. In this respect Kafka's own art did what he ascribed to the art of Pablo Picasso: it portrayed the distortions of reality that had not yet entered consciousness. Second, at the stage when he wrote *The Trial* Kafka could no longer bring himself to condone his hero's conscious assent to the judgment that would destroy him.

In one part of the novel, however, Kafka openly reveals the other side of Josef K., which the author elsewhere excludes. This is the parable "Before the Law," which the prison chaplain tells to Josef K. in the cathedral chapter. Here the radiance that streams from the Court in Josef K.'s repressed dream is allowed to shine forth openly, and the man from the country, who seeks entrance into the Law, is allowed to express freely what Josef K., who thinks of himself as a modern, rational man, can never bring himself to acknowledge: that the desire for union with the mystic Law is the fundamental concern of his existence. This parable, or "legend," as Kafka himself called it, presents the split within Josef K. as an explicit coexistence between desire and fear. The man from the country comes to join the Law but is prevented by the doorkeeper, who tells him that he cannot let him enter now. He adds that the man might try to go in, but he frightens him with the prospect of more dreadful doorkeepers farther along.

The Law thus presents an ambiguity that the man had not expected. He had thought of the Law only as highly desirable and enticing, but now it also shows a threatening face. It seems that this ambiguity of the Law, its having two faces, offers the key to the parable—but only if we restrict ourselves to the perspective of the man. However, as we shall see, here, in the second phase of Kafka's maturity, the perspective of the protagonist is not the perspective of the narrative, for a narrator has been placed between reader and protagonist, that is, the man from the country. If we see the man from the perspective of the narrator, we find that the ambiguity of the Law is a tool and catalyst for making the man's ambivalence his destiny, since the ambiguity introduced by the doorkeeper merely brings out an ambivalence within the man: his desire for the Law is now complicated by his fear of it, and desire and fear begin to exist side by side within him.

What connects him with Josef K. and makes his destiny a perfect illustration of the novel is his inability to opt for either side of his ambivalence. He decides to yield to his fear without giving up his desire: he defers his entrance and begins to wait before the door to the Law, thus choosing a life of ambivalence. The consequences of his choice are degradation and lifelong frustration: he is literally lowered by having to spend his life crouching on a footstool at the feet of the forbidding sentry; he is morally degraded by resorting to bribery and cajolery; and he is intellectually reduced to

begging the fleas in the doorkeeper's collar to intercede for him. In the end he dies without having attained his goal.

The relationship of the parable to the novel illustrates very well the different narrative principle of the second phase of Kafka's maturity. The rest of the novel was composed before the parable and indeed before "The Penal Colony," and both of these later parabolic stories help Kafka to clarify the problem of his novel. What the parable "Before the Law" accomplishes is to illuminate the basic problem of Josef K., his paralyzing ambivalence. In the narrative form of Kafka's punitive fantasies, which employ the perspective of the facade, this ambivalence could not be clarified since it could not enter the conscious level of the narrative; Josef K.'s proud rationality, his facade, could not permit his longing for the Court to show itself openly at any time. In the parable, however, there is no facade, and the two conflicting forces within man are clearly presented as existing side by side. In place of the vertical division of layers in the punitive fantasies, here there is again the horizontal split that we found in Raban's wish-dream, but without the separation of facade and true self.

The man from the country is Josef K.'s repressed truth exposed to view. This emerges clearly from the fact that when he hears the parable Josef K. spontaneously identifies with the man from the country. Josef K. shares with the subject of the parable an ambivalence of desire and fear. Unlike Josef K., however, the man from the country does not repress his desire; he merely defers it. In contrast to the opaqueness of Josef K.'s fate the parable, therefore, makes transparent the fatal incompatibility of man's desire for union with the Absolute and his fear for life and safety, by showing us the man's refusal to risk entrance not authorized by the doorkeeper. By its transparency the parabolic form, which characterizes Kafka's second phase, goes even further in elucidating the problem it presents. The parable "Before the Law" implies quite clearly that the man from the country could find a "way out" of his

FRANZ KAFKA

impasse by abandoning his fear and entering the gate regardless of the risks awaiting him; if he were to choose to go forward despite the injunctions of the doorkeeper, he would attain true self-fulfillment. However, the man in the parable could also do the opposite: he could yield to his fear, abandon his desire, leave the gate, and turn his back forever on doorkeeper and Law. Such a retreat would amount to an abandonment of self, insofar as his self is identical with its dominant concern. By the same token it would ensure not only his physical survival—that he ensures anyway by choosing not to go into the Law—but also a survival in dignity and independence. He would gain a life emancipated from obsession.

The choice open to the man in the priest's parable defines the problem around which Kafka's subsequent work revolves. In his second and third phases Kafka no longer describes the catastrophic eruption of a hidden truth and the resultant destruction of his protagonist; instead he presents a dilemma attendant upon his protagonist's attempt to realize his true self, a realization that would at the same time be a union with or recognition by a higher power, authority, or collective. In Kafka's late work the self of his protagonist is undivided and is openly dedicated to its craving or quest; the conflict is not between a facade and a true self but rather between the true self and an external power that disavows the self's claims or frustrates its expectations. Like the Law in the "legend," the external power in Kafka's later works both beckons and forbids entrance to itself. Between the protagonist's imaginings and the behavior of external reality there exists a discrepancy that is the subject of the self's reflections and comments. The protagonist hopes that somehow the contradiction will be resolved. He hopes that reality will conform eventually to his expectations, and this hope constitutes his true self and is the mission to and for which he subordinates and utilizes everything. If he were to give up his hope he would have to renounce his self and nature, as the ape does in "A

Report to an Academy." All the characters of Kafka's later work cling to their missions yet are unable to change reality according to their desire. They spend their lives waiting in front of closed entrances, locked out from the goal they crave. Indeed, the title of Kafka's last and greatest novel, *Das Schloss* (*The Castle*), a marvelous elaboration and development of the theme of "Before the Law," carries in German the subsidiary meaning of "lock." For K. the Castle is literally a lock that locks him out. Unable to gain the entrance and likewise unable to resign and turn their backs on it, the protagonists of Kafka's late works stay doggedly loyal and true to their quest. But their loyalty or stubbornness immobilizes them. They waste their lives in visible or invisible cages, prisons of their own devising.

The cage, castle, lock, and underground fortress or burrow are dominant images of Kafka's last works. At the end of his second phase he presents the image of the cage in "A Report," which concludes the volume of parables that "Before the Law" initiated chronologically; and the cage appears again in "A Hunger Artist," title story of his last volume of narratives. The two stories are contrasting approaches to the theme of the cage. In the first, the captured ape who cannot stand life in the cage finds a "way out" by ceasing to be what he is, by becoming something else. The hunger artist takes the opposite course: he voluntarily enters and stays in the cage in order to express his true self.

The hunger artist does not achieve fulfillment of his wish to be recognized as the incomparable artist he is; the public first misunderstands, then neglects and ignores him. Looking at the narrative through the protagonist's perspective, we are inclined to accuse the public of callousness, vulgarity, and cruelty. Similarly, seeing through Josef K.'s perspective in *The Trial*, we are inclined to blame the Court for his fate. However, Kafka underwent a great change in the direction of analytic clarity and explicitness in the near-decade after he wrote *The Trial*. If we understand the story "A

Hunger Artist" as an indictment of the public, Kafka's text convicts us of being wrong, for at the end of his life the hunger artist explicitly informs the world that he deserves no admiration. He had been a sport of nature, a freak, unable to find food that satisfied him and therefore incapable of doing anything else but starving. If he had found food to his taste he would have eaten like everyone else and led a completely undistinguished life.

Like the punitive fantasies "A Hunger Artist" presents a discrepancy between the official perspective of the story—given by the protagonist—and the truth. The perspective of the punitive fantasies, which presents the protagonists as victims of external injustice and outrageous fortune, tends to prevent us from noting the submerged inner force that drives them to their catastrophes. Similarly, the hunger artist's perspective makes us sympathize with him as the victim of the public and encourages us to overlook the crucial fact that his exhibition is a fraud. He makes us accept as an admirable achievement something that, as he himself admits in the end, is nothing more than a necessity and, indeed, a debility, for which pity rather than admiration might be the proper response. Knowing his natural defect the hunger artist should not have expected admiring recognition; but he made us—the readers—believe that this was his due.

In Kafka's final phase we return to the deviousness and deceptiveness of a perspective that distorts and conceals the truth of the story and is defeated by it. Again the protagonist's claim and grievance against the world are unjustified; they are deceit. His frustration and final refutation or capitulation reveal the truth, and as in the punitive fantasies truth conquers and shines forth in the dying of the self: dying, the hunger artist unmasks the fraud his life had been. Like Gregor Samsa, with whom many analogies connect him, he finds in death the contentment that life had consistently denied him.

Yet there is an essential difference between the punitive fantasies and Kafka's final phase.

The punitive fantasies unveil a contrast between the facade and the truth of the self whereas the late works oppose a unified self to truth. The hunger artist's self is not divided between facade and true self. On the contrary, his mission, symbolized by the cage in which it takes place, is the uncompromising and absolute expression of his true and only self. His starving is the full revelation of his inner truth. However, this inner truth is in itself a deception, and herein lies the paradox of Kafka's last phase, in which the self is a pretense and presumption.

The hunger artist's complete "otherness," his inability to eat and therefore to be like other men, would in itself not be a fraud but rather a mere eccentricity that would exclude him from humanity. The hunger artist, however, refuses to stay outside humanity. This refusal drives him to proclaim as art the defect with which he was born and to exhibit this aberration for public acclaim. Art and fraud are inseparable in him: he is an artist only by virtue of committing his fraud; or, to put it differently, his decision to treat his natural want as though it were a skill makes him artist and fraud at the same time. It is this decision that makes him enter the cage. The cage exhibits both untruth and art, yet it also symbolizes absolute subjectivity and otherness. No one but he can fast indefinitely; no one resembles him. His isolated existence in the cage dooms any hope for true appreciation and understanding from the public beyond his bars, for he is on exhibit as a freak. His "art," or, more truly said, his nature, is unique—so subjective, so different from the interests and feelings of other men, that the hunger artist's monstrous spirituality cannot possibly be more than a short-lived sensation in the life of mankind.

Whereas the hunger artist makes his fraud explicit, the immense deception perpetrated by the Land Surveyor K. in *The Castle* is never stated explicitly, and K. has therefore fooled most readers, critics, and exegetes of the novel. K. claims to have been called to and appointed land surveyor by the castle that controls the village into which he has strayed one night. He makes us believe that the Castle authorities, by refusing to honor his claim, treat him unjustly and deprive him of what by right is his. He presses his claim with such urgency and consistency that the reader feels compelled to accept it at face value and to see in K. a victim of soulless bureaucracy or to construct elaborate schemes of interpretation based on the "injustice" done to K. Consequently *The Castle* has appeared in critical literature as a satire on bureaucracy, an adumbration of totalitarianism, and an allegory of social injustice or of the religious problem of man's insistence on justice and God's grace. All these interpretations are the result of the critics' being duped by K.'s colossal fraud. A close reading of the text reveals that K. has no legitimate claim on the Castle because he never was appointed land surveyor. This truth of the novel is revealed by inconsistencies in the plot and by a brief passage of K.'s inner monologue. These allow only one conclusion: K. was never called by the Castle.

K. has no document to prove his call, but he promises that his assistants will soon arrive with his apparatus. They never come. Instead K. is given two new "assistants" by the Castle. These assistants know nothing about land surveying and have no apparatus. K. has never seen them before. Thus the "proof" of K.'s appointment, which the promised arrival of his old assistants and apparatus was supposed to be, never materializes. The fact that K. accepts his new assistants without waiting for his old assistants or ever thinking of them indicates that in all likelihood they do not exist.

A telephone inquiry at the Castle produces the answer that nothing is known of K.'s appointment. Immediately thereafter, a call from the Castle reverses this first answer and confirms K.'s claim. K.'s mental reaction to this information unmasks him as an imposter. Instead of registering with simple satisfaction the news that the "misunderstanding" has been cleared up, K. considers the Castle's

recognition of his claim "unpropitious." He takes it to be a "smiling acceptance" of his "challenge," designed to "cow him" by "lofty superiority." The term "challenge," used by K. in this context, shows that he does not expect to step into a promised position but that he has come with the purpose of fighting the Castle and forcing it to yield something to him, either the coveted office or something else. It is clear that he was never appointed land surveyor and was never called to the Castle. He is a stranger who, for reasons that we shall examine, "challenges" the Castle to submit to his unfounded claim. The Castle seems to "accept" his "challenge" and plays a game with him that forms the plot of the novel.

This close reading of the text alters the whole basis of interpretation of Kafka's last and greatest novel. It can no longer be maintained that the conflict between justice and injustice, no matter on what level, is its theme. Rather, its theme is K.'s attempt to make everyone, including the reader, believe that justice is the problem and that the injustice inflicted upon him is his motive in struggling with the Castle. Kafka has K. conduct his campaign so skillfully and emphatically that he persuades most readers to believe him, contrary to the textual evidence he himself provides. In his richest and most profound work Kafka depicts the victory of fiction over reality. The deception perpetrated by his character triumphs not over the other characters—for no one in the novel really believes K.—but over the reader.

Kafka achieves this amazing triumph of art by the masterful application of a narrative perspective that misleads the reader into mistaking the protagonist's view for the truth. However, while creating this victory of fiction, Kafka at the same time exposes its falseness through his protagonist's own oblique self-revelations. Furthermore, the fact that the hero's claim never attains true recognition in the novel shows its vanity. In a letter to Brod written in 1922, at the time of *The Castle*'s composition, Kafka defined the writer's essence as "vanity." Kafka's late work, especially his artist stories, "A Hunger Artist" and "Josephine," depicts vanity both as narcissism and as futility. It shows that the attempt of subjectivity to impose its terms upon external reality must always fail.

The Castle answers K.'s attack with an ironically exact retribution: it meets his unreal claim with an equally unreal appointment. Klamm's letter appoints K. as land surveyor, and he is henceforth addressed as such; but he obtains no land to survey and is never established in an appropriate office. The title given him by the Castle is as gratuitous and empty as his pretended call. The Castle gives him assistants who are irrelevant to his professed profession, for they are no more capable of assisting him in his land surveying than the instruments he claims he has but is unable to produce. These assistants also cause him to do to them what he claims the Castle has done to him: just as the Castle locks him out and will not admit him, so he locks out his assistants and refuses to let them come to him. K. himself displays the cruelty and injustice he ascribes to the Castle. Moreover, even as he takes his mistress away from Klamm, his own chief, so he loses her again to one of his assistants. In this late work judgment appears not as destruction but as ironic retribution.

The Castle counters K.'s maneuver by presenting a universe in which there is no certainty and nothing is what it seems to be. This is the necessary consequence of the fact that the protagonist, too, is not what he seems to be. That is, K.'s self is not a fact but a pretense. His is a desperate experiment, an attempt to impose his fiction upon the reality that confronts and excludes him. He needs this fiction to break into and become part of the reality that he faces.

In *The Castle* Kafka describes the fundamental situation of modern man, for whom neither the world nor his own self is given and certain. Like every man, K., in order to be, must be recognized and must be related as an individual to the whole of society; he must have a specific calling. In order to get his call,

he must already be someone, an accredited and required expert. However, K. knows he has no call and is therefore nothing. He is a stranger, utterly unconnected and superfluous—locked out by the *Schloss,* here functioning according to the word's basic meaning of "lock." Since a human being cannot live permanently outside humanity, K. desperately needs to enter it, to become someone needed and recognized. In order to live he must "unlock" the lock with which humanity excludes him. As the dominant necessity of life and the essence of desirability, the *Schloss* presents to him its other meaning in the guise of the magically beckoning and unattainable castle. It is K.'s staggering and superhuman task to create the call he needs. He has to pretend that he already possesses what he has come to get—the necessary prerequisite for beginning an integrated and authentic existence. Therefore his battle with the Castle is not a whim but a desperate necessity. Precisely because he has no objectively valid claim for recognition, he must force the Castle to honor his subjective pretense—his fiction—as the truth. K. fights to become in truth what he pretends he is—the land surveyor called by the Castle.

K.'s quest is a metaphorical statement of the lifelong struggle that Kafka's entire writing sought to describe. (In this regard the title of his first work, "Beschreibung eines Kampfes" ["Description of a Struggle," 1936], is significant.) At the time he composed *The Castle* Kafka wrote to his woman friend and lover, Milena, that he had been given nothing, that he must create not only his present and his future but his past as well. His task is therefore infinitely more difficult than that of other men, for not only must he fight the battle for his future that everyone must wage, but while engaged in that battle, he must also be acquiring a past, a ground on which he can stand and that all others can take for granted as their birthright and inheritance.

Kafka related this peculiar predicament to the fate of the Westernized Jew in Europe, who, already uprooted and cut off from his ancestral traditions, is not yet permitted to enter fully and truly into the life of his hosts. Beyond this personal and ethnic meaning, however, Kafka presents in *The Castle* the task facing modern man in general. Unmoored from his spiritual and social anchorage, expelled from his once secure place in the cosmos, modern man, as the existentialists pointed out, must make his own identity and project his own existence instead of assuming it as given. Kafka's fragmentary novel depicts the tragic irony and ultimate impossibility of this enterprise.

Selected Bibliography

EDITIONS

INDIVIDUAL WORKS
Betrachtung. Leipzig, 1913.
Der Heizer: Ein Fragment. Leipzig, 1913.
Das Urteil: Eine Geschichte. Leipzig, 1913.
Die Verwandlung. Leipzig, 1915.
In der Strafkolonie. Leipzig, 1919.
Ein Landarzt: Kleine Erzählungen. Munich and Leipzig, 1919.
Ein Hungerkünstler: Vier Geschichten. Berlin, 1924.
Der Prozess. Edited by Max Brod. Berlin, 1925.
Das Schloss. Edited by Max Brod. Munich, 1926.
Amerika. Edited by Max Brod. Munich, 1927. This novel is also sometimes referred to as *Der Verschollene,* Kafka's original title for it.
Beim Bau der chinesischen Mauer. Edited by Max Brod. Berlin, 1931.
Beschreibung eines Kampfes: Novellen, Skizzen, Aphorismen aus dem Nachlass. Edited by Max Brod. Prague, 1936.
Beschreibung eines Kampfes. Edited by Ludwig Dietz. Frankfurt, 1969.

COLLECTED WORKS
Gesammelte Schriften. 6 vols. Edited by Max Brod with Heinz Politzer. Prague, 1935–1937.
————. 5 vols. Edited by Max Brod. New York, 1946.
Gesammelte Werke. 11 vols. Edited by Max Brod et al. New York and Frankfurt, 1950–1974.
Schriften, Tagebücher, Briefe: Kritische Ausgabe. Edited by Jürgen Born et al. Frankfurt, 1982— .

TRANSLATIONS
Amerika. Translated by Edwin Muir. New York, 1962.
The Castle. Translated by Willa and Edwin Muir. New York, 1954.
The Complete Stories. Edited by Nahum Glatzer. New York, 1946.
Dearest Father: Stories and Other Writings. Translated by Ernst Kaiser and Eithne Wilkins. New York, 1954.
Description of a Struggle. Translated by Tania and James Stern. New York, 1958.
The Diaries of Franz Kafka 1910–1923. Translated by Joseph Kresh. Edited by Max Brod. New York, 1948.
The Diaries of Franz Kafka 1914–1923. Translated by Martin Greenberg with Hannah Arendt. Edited by Max Brod. New York, 1949.
The Great Wall of China: Stories and Reflections. Translated by Willa and Edwin Muir. New York, 1970.
I Am a Memory Come Alive: Autobiographical Writings by Franz Kafka. Edited by Nahum Glatzer. New York, 1974.
"The Judgment." Translated by Malcolm Pasley. In *The Problem of the Judgment,* edited by Angel Flores. New York, 1977.
Letters to Felice. Translated by James Stern and Elisabeth Duckworth. Edited by Erich Heller and Jürgen Born. New York, 1973.
Letters to Friends, Family, and Editors. Translated by Richard and Clara Winston. Edited by Max Brod et al. New York, 1977.
Letters to Milena. Translated by Tania and James Stern. Edited by Willy Haas. New York and London, 1953.
Letters to Ottla and the Family. Translated by Richard and Clara Winston. Edited by Nahum Glazer. New York, 1981
Letter to His Father. Translated by Ernst Kaiser and Eithne Wilkins. New York, 1953. Bilingual edition.
The Metamorphosis. Translated and edited by Stanley Corngold. New York, Toronto, and London, 1972.
Parables and Paradoxes in German and English. Edited by Nahum Glazer. New York, 1958.
The Penal Colony: Stories and Short Pieces. Translated by Willa and Edwin Muir. New York, 1948.
Shorter Works. Translated and edited by Malcolm Pasley. London, 1973.

Stories 1904–1924. Translated by J. A. Underwood. London, 1981.

The Trial. Translated by Willa and Edwin Muir. Illustrated by George Salter. New York, 1957.

Wedding Preparations in the Country and Other Posthumous Prose Writings. Translated by Ernst Kaiser and Eithne Wilkins. London, 1954.

BIOGRAPHICAL AND CRITICAL STUDIES

BIOGRAPHICAL WORKS

Bauer, Johann. *Kafka and Prague.* Text by Johann Bauer. Photos by Isidor Pollak. Design by Jaroslav Schneider. Translated by P. S. Falla. New York, Washington, D.C., and London, 1971.

Binder, Hartmut. *Franz Kafka: Leben und Persönlichkeit.* Stuttgart, 1983.

Brod, Max. *Franz Kafka: A Biography.* Translated from the German by G. Humphreys Roberts and Richard Winston. Second, enlarged edition, New York, 1960.

Hayman, Ronald. *Kafka: A Biography.* New York, 1982.

Janouch, Gustav. *Conversations with Kafka: Notes and Reminiscences.* Translated by Goronwy Rees. Introduction by Max Brod. New York, 1953. (Original German edition: Frankfurt, 1951.)

Pawel, Ernst. *The Nightmare of Reason: A Life of Franz Kafka.* New York, 1984.

Unseld, Joachim. *Franz Kafka: Ein Schriftstellerleben—Die Geschichte seiner Veröffentlichungen, mit einer Bibliographie sämtlicher Drucke und Ausgaben der Dichtungen Kafkas 1908–1924.* Munich and Vienna, 1982.

Wagenbach, Klaus. *Franz Kafka: Eine Biographie seiner Jugend 1883–1912.* Berne, 1958.

————. *Franz Kafka: Pictures of a Life.* Translated by Arthur Wensinger. New York, 1984.

GENERAL CRITICAL STUDIES

Albright, Daniel. *Representation and the Imagination: Beckett, Kafka, Nabokov, and Schoenberg.* Chicago, 1981.

Anders, Günther. *Franz Kafka.* Translated by A. Steer and A. K. Thorlby. New York and London, 1960. (Original German edition: Munich, 1951.)

Barthes, Roland. "Kafka's Answer." In *Critical Essays,* translated by Richard Howard. Evanston, Ill., 1972. Pp. 133–137. (Original French edition: Paris, 1964.)

Beck, Evelyn Torton. *Kafka and the Yiddish Theater: Its Impact on His Work.* Madison, Wis., 1971.

Beicken, Peter U. *Franz Kafka: Eine kritische Einführung in die Forschung.* Frankfurt, 1974.

Beissner, Friedrich. *Der Erzähler Franz Kafka: Ein Vortrag.* Stuttgart, 1952.

Benjamin, Walter. "Franz Kafka: On the Tenth Anniversary of His Death" and "Some Reflections on Kafka." In *Illuminations,* edited and introduced by Hannah Arendt, translated by Harry Zohn. New York, 1969. Pp. 111–145. (Original German editions: Berlin, 1934, and Frankfurt, 1966.)

Bernheimer, Charles. *Flaubert and Kafka: Studies in Psychopoetic Structure.* New Haven, Conn., 1982.

Binder, Hartmut, ed. *Kafka-Handbuch.* 2 vols. Stuttgart, 1979.

Blanchot, Maurice. "Reading Kafka," "Kafka and Literature," "Kafka or the Demands of Literature." In *The Sirens' Song: Selected Essays,* edited by Gabriel Josipovici, translated by Sacha Rabinovitch. Bloomington, Ind., 1982. Pp. 21–42, 129–143. (Original French editions: Paris, 1949 and 1955.)

Bridgwater, Patrick. *Kafka and Nietzsche.* Bonn, 1974.

Camus, Albert. "Hope and the Absurd in the Work of Franz Kafka." In *The Myth of Sisyphus and Other Essays,* translated from the French by Justin O'Brien. New York, 1955. Pp. 124–138. (Original French edition: Paris, 1943.)

Deleuze, Gilles and Felix Guattari. *Kafka: Pour une littérature mineure.* Paris, 1975.

Dentan, Michel. *Humour et création littéraire dans l'oeuvre de Kafka.* Geneva, 1961.

Emrich, Wilhelm. *Franz Kafka: A Critical Study of His Writings.* Translated by Sheema Zeben Buehne. New York, 1968. (Original German edition: Bonn, 1958.)

Flores, Angel, ed. *Franz Kafka Today.* Madison, Wis., 1958.

————, ed. *The Kafka Debate: New Perspectives for Our Time.* New York, 1977.

Foulkes, Peter. *The Reluctant Pessimist: A Study of Franz Kafka.* The Hague, 1967.

Gray, Ronald, ed. *Kafka: A Collection of Critical Essays.* Englewood Cliffs, N.J., 1962.

Greenberg, Martin. *The Terror of Art: Kafka and Modern Literature.* New York, 1969.

Grundlehner, Philip, ed. *Kafka Centenary Essays.* *Literary Review* 26 (Summer 1983).

Heller, Erich. *Kafka.* New York, 1975.

Heller, Peter. *Dialectics and Nihilism: Essays on Lessing, Nietzsche, Mann, and Kafka.* Amherst, Mass., 1966.

———. "Kafka and Nietzsche." *Comparative Literature Studies* 8:71–95 (1971).

———. "On Not Understanding Kafka." *German Quarterly* 49:373–393 (1974).

Hughes, Kenneth, ed. *Franz Kafka: An Anthology of Marxist Criticism.* Hanover, N.H., and London, 1981.

Kuna, Franz. *Franz Kafka: Literature as Corrective Punishment.* London, 1974.

———, ed. *On Kafka: Semi-Centenary Perspectives.* London, 1976.

Pascal, Roy. *Kafka's Narrators.* Anglica Germanica series 2. Cambridge, England, 1982.

Politzer, Heinz. *Franz Kafka: Parable and Paradox.* Ithaca, N.Y., 1962.

Robert, Marthe. *As Lonely as Franz Kafka.* Translated by Ralph Manheim. New York, 1982.

Robertson, Ritchie. *Kafka: Judaism, Politics, and Literature.* Oxford, 1985.

Rolleston, James. *Kafka's Narrative Theater.* University Park, Pa., and London, 1974.

Sokel, Walter H. *Franz Kafka: Tragik und Ironie—Zur Struktur seiner Kunst.* Munich and Vienna, 1964.

———. "Kafka's Poetics of the Inner Self." *Modern Austrian Literature* 11:37–58 (1978).

———. "Language and Truth in the Two Worlds of Franz Kafka." *German Quarterly* 52:364–384 (1979).

Spann, Meno. *Franz Kafka.* Detroit, 1976.

Spilka, Mark. *Dickens and Kafka: A Mutual Interpretation.* Bloomington, Ind., 1963.

Stern, J. P., ed. *The World of Franz Kafka.* London and New York, 1980.

Sussman, Henry. *Franz Kafka: Geometrician of Metaphor.* Madison, Wis., 1979.

Szanto, George H. *Narrative Consciousness: Structure and Perception in the Fiction of Kafka, Beckett, and Robbe-Grillet.* Austin, Tex., 1972.

Thorlby, Anthony. *Franz Kafka: A Study.* London, 1972.

Tiefenbrun, Ruth. *Moment of Torment: An Interpretation of Franz Kafka's Short Stories.* Carbondale, Ill., 1973.

Udoff, Alan, ed. *Kafka's Contextuality.* New York and Baltimore, 1986.

Urzidil, Johannes. *There Goes Kafka.* Translated by Harold A. Basilius. Detroit, 1968.

Walser, Martin. *Beschreibung einer Form: Versuch über Franz Kafka.* Munich, 1961.

STUDIES ON INDIVIDUAL WORKS

ON *AMERIKA*

Nicolai, Ralph. *Kafkas Amerika-Roman "Der Verschollene": Motive und Gestalten.* Würzburg, 1981.

ON *THE CASTLE*

Cohn, Dorrit. "K. Enters the Castle: On the Change of Person in Kafka's Manuscript." *Euphorion* 62:28–45 (1968).

Gray, Ronald. *Kafka's Castle.* Cambridge, 1956.

Heller, Erich. "The World of Franz Kafka." In *The Disinherited Mind.* Cambridge, England, 1956. Pp. 155–181.

Neumeyer, Peter, ed. *Twentieth-Century Interpretations of "The Castle."* Englewood Cliffs, N.J., 1969.

Philippi, Klaus-Peter. *Reflexion und Wirklichkeit: Untersuchungen zu Kafkas Roman "Das Schloss."* Studien zur Deutschen Literatur, vol. 5. Tübingen, 1966.

Robert, Marthe. *The Old and the New: From Don Quixote to Kafka.* Translated by Carol Coseman. Foreword by Robert Alter. Berkeley, Calif., 1977.

Sheppard, Richard. *On Kafka's "Castle": A Study.* Worcester and London, 1973.

ON *THE TRIAL*

Jaffe, Adrian. *The Process of Kafka's "Trial."* East Lansing, Mich., 1967.

Marson, Eric. *Kafka's "Trial": The Case Against Josef K.* Brisbane, Queensland, 1975.

Rolleston, James, ed. *Twentieth-Century Interpretations of "The Trial": A Collection of Critical Essays.* Englewood Cliffs, N.J., 1976.

Ziolkowski, Theodore. "Franz Kafka: *The Trial.*" In *Dimensions of the Modern Novel: German Texts and European Contexts.* Princeton, N.J., 1969. Pp. 37–67.

ON "BEFORE THE LAW"

Derrida, Jacques. "Préjugés." In *Philosophy and Literature,* edited by Phillip Griffiths. Cambridge, England, 1984. Pp. 173–188.

FRANZ KAFKA

ON "THE BURROW"

Henel, Heinrich. "Kafka's *Der Bau,* or How to Escape from a Maze." In *The Discontinuous Tradition: Studies in German Literature in Honour of Ernst Ludwig Stahl,* edited by P. F. Ganz. Oxford, 1971. Pp. 224–246.

ON *THE COUNTRY DOCTOR*

Triffit, Gregory B. *Kafka's "Landarzt" Collection.* Berne and Frankfurt, 1985.

ON "A HUNGER ARTIST"

Spann, Meno. "Franz Kafka's Leopard." *Germanic Review,* 34:85–104 (1959).

ON "INVESTIGATIONS OF A DOG"

Ziolkowski, Theodore. *Varieties of Literary Thematics.* Princeton, N.J., 1983. Pp. 86–122, 240–245.

ON "THE JUDGMENT"

Ellis, John. *Narration in the German Novelle.* New York, 1974. Pp. 188–211, 218ff.

Flores, Angel, ed. *The Problem of "The Judgment."* New York, 1977.

Sokel, Walter H. "Frozen Sea and River of Narration: The Poetics behind Kafka's 'Breakthrough.'" *New Literary History: A Journal of Theory and Interpretation* 17:351–363 (1986).

ON *THE METAMORPHOSIS*

Beicken, Peter, ed. *Franz Kafka: "Die Verwandlung"—Erläutcrungen und Dokumente.* Stuttgart, 1974.

Corngold, Stanley. *The Commentator's Despair: The Interpretation of Kafka's "Metamorphosis."* Port Washington, N.Y., and London, 1973.

Nabokov, Vladimir. *Lectures on Literature.* Edited by Fredson Bowers. Introduction by John Updike. New York, 1980. Pp. 251–284.

Sokel, Walter H. "Kafka's *Metamorphosis:* Rebellion and Punishment." *Monatshefte* 48:203–214 (1956).

Todorov, Tzvetan. *The Fantastic: A Structural Approach to Literature.* Translated from the French by Richard Howard. With a new foreword by Robert Scholes. Ithaca, N.Y., 1975. Pp. 169–175. (Original French edition: Paris, 1970.)

ON *THE LETTERS TO FELICE*

Canetti, Elias. *Kafka's Other Trial: The Letters to Felice.* Translated by Christopher Middleton. New York, 1974. (Original German edition: Munich, 1969.)

BIBLIOGRAPHIES

Caputo-Mayr, Marie-Luise, and Julius M. Herz. *Franz Kafkas Werke: Eine Bibliographie der Primärliteratur (1908–1980).* Bern and Munich, 1980.

Flores, Angel. *A Kafka Bibliography, 1908–1976.* New York, 1976.

WALTER H. SOKEL